DICTIONARY OF CONTEMPORARY AMERICAN ARTISTS

FOURTH EDITION

PAUL CUMMINGS

St. Martin's Press New York

193 8661

Library of Congress Cataloging in Publication Data

Cummings, Paul.
  Dictionary of contemporary American artists.

  Bibliography: p.
  Includes index.
  1. Artists—United States—Biography.   2. Art,
Modern—20th century—United States.   I. Title.
N6536.C8   1982   709'.2'2 [B]   82-7337
ISBN 0-312-20097-8

Design by Tim McKeen

First Edition
10 9 8 7 6 5 4 3 2 1

DICTIONARY OF CONTEMPORARY AMERICAN ARTISTS

Contents

Acknowledgments

To all the artists who so graciously took time to complete the questionnaires I should again like to express my gratitude. Without their assistance this fourth revised edition could not have been completed.

In addition I wish to thank the many art dealers and their gallery staffs for always generously helping to provide information and photographs for this and so many other projects. The following people and institutions deserve a particular word of gratitude: May Fitzgerald, librarian, Whitney Museum of American Art; the librarians of the Museum of Modern Art, The Frick Art Reference Library and The Metropolitan Museum of Art Library. I should also like to acknowledge the special assistance of Anita Duquette of the Whitney Museum in securing photographs. A special note of thanks to Judith Sonntag for the vital editorial assistance she brought to the job of checking the manuscript in draft and in its proof-reading. To Carolyn Parqueth thanks for her accurate typing of the many hundreds of manuscript pages.

To the artists, collectors, museums and art dealers for permission to illustrate works of art in their possession, my sincere appreciation.

PC

May, 1981
New York City

How to Use This Book

This extensively revised edition of the Dictionary, first published in 1966, includes 71 new artists and deletes 19. The annotated bibliography serves as a ready reference for additional research and reading on these artists and on American art of the past half century. There is a new selection of illustrations.

Questionnaires, personal interviews, and intensive research have brought together significant data regarding the careers of these 923 artists, chosen essentially on the basis of the following criteria: representation in museum, public, and private collections; representation in major American and international exhibitions; influence as teachers; recognition received from fellow-artists, dealers, critics, and others with a professional interest in the fine arts. January 1981 was chosen as the terminal date for all data, except for obituary notices which are accurate through 1981.

The artists' entries are organized on the following plan: where they studied art, and with whom; teaching experience; participation in the Federal Art Project; commissions executed; scholarships and/or awards won (P.P. in this category denotes "purchase prize" or "purchase award"); spouse (if prominent in art); address and dealer(s) of record; important one-man retrospectives, and group exhibitions (circ. in this category indicates that the exhibition circulated among various institutions); and bibliography. Archives, appearing at the end of some of the entries, indicates that the artist's papers and/or taped, in-depth interviews with the artist are available at the Archives of American Art, Smithsonian Institution. The Archives maintains complete microfilm files in their Boston, New York, Washington, D.C., Detroit, and San Francisco offices.

Naturally many artists have won the same awards, been represented in the same exhibitions and collections, and are mentioned in the same books. Repetition of the complete data in each case would have made this volume far too large. Therefore the data have been compressed into a series of keys, found in the front of the book; the keyed, annotated bibliography is located at the back. Abbreviations used in the body of the book are explained in the keys. The often long and complex names of museums and public collections have generally been abbreviated and codified in the Key to Museums and Institutions. Commonsense methods have been used, most often acronyms (MOMA for The Museum of Modern Art) and reductions, either to the name of the city (Mons, for the Musée des Beaux-Arts, Mons, Belgium), to a combination of city and key word (Albany/Institute for the Albany Institute of History and Art), or to city and acronym (Akron/AI for the Akron Art Institute).

In the listing entitled Galleries, addresses are given for those dealers representing the artists listed in this volume; other galleries cited in the Exhibitions portions of the entries are identified therein by city.

The use of boldface type in the Bibliography sections of the entries distinguishes the writings of the artist himself, comprehensive exhibition catalogues, or monographs.

The Index of Artists in the front of this volume offers both a pronunciation guide and breakdown of the types of work for which each artist is best known.

Example:
. . . **One-man Exhibitions**: (first) The Babcock Gallery, 1946; Blank Gallery, Washington, D.C., 1949. **Group:** Toledo/MA; Corcoran, 1950; NAD, 1951; Venice Biennials. **Collections:** Springfield, Mass./MFA; Montclair/AM. **Bibliography:** Baur 1, 5, **6**, 7.

Explanation:
Because it functions as a dealer, the address of The Babcock Gallery is given in the Gallery list at the front of this book; the Blank Gallery was located in Washington, D.C., at the time of this exhibition and may still be there, but it does not represent any of the artists listed. Toledo/MA stands for the Toledo Museum of Art, and its full name may be found under T in the Key to Museums; the names of all coded institutions are listed alphabetically in the Key. The bibliographic notation indicates that this artist, among others, is referred to in the four similarly numbered books among the seven by Baur listed in the Bibliography, with boldface number 6 being a monograph.

Illustrations

inks on black paper
Collection of the Whitney Museum
of American Art: Gift of Mr. &
Mrs. Benjamin Weiss
Photograph by Geoffrey Clements

Christo
Running Fence, Project for Sonoma
County and Marin County,
State of California. 1976
22 × 28 in. collage, pastel, charcoal,
engineering data, cloth, and tape
Collection of the Whitney Museum
of American Art: Paul Rewald
Memorial Fund
Photograph by Geoffrey Clements

Bruce Conner
23 Kenwood Ave. 1963
26 × 20 in. ink on paper
Courtesy private collection

William N. Copley (CPLY)
Untitled. 1978
66 × 55 in. acrylic on canvas
Courtesy Brooks Jackson Iolas
Gallery
Photograph by Nathan Rabin

Joseph Cornell
Untitled (Celestial Set). c. 1952–54
13⅛ × 18⅛ × 5⅛ in. box
construction
Courtesy The Estate of Joseph
Cornell: Castelli Feigen Corcoran
Gallery

Robert Cottingham
Money. 1972
10½ × 10½ in. acrylic on paper
Promised gift of Norman Dubrow to
the Whitney Museum of
American Art
Photograph by Geoffrey Clements

Andrew Dasburg
Summer Meadows. 1952–53
13½ × 21½ in. watercolor on paper
Collection of the Whitney Museum
of American Art: Lawrence H.
Bloedel Bequest
Photograph by Geoffrey Clements

Stuart Davis
Schwitzki's Syntax. 1961–64
42 × 56 in. oil and wax casien
emulsion
Courtesy Borgenicht Gallery

Willem de Kooning
Untitled VI. 1979
80 × 70 in. oil on canvas
Courtesy Xavier Fourcade, Inc.
Photograph by Bruce C. Jones

Edwin Dickinson
Roses. 1939
10¾ × 12¾ in. pencil on paper
Promised 50th Anniversary Gift of
Mrs. Robert M. Benjamin to the
Whitney Museum of American
Art
Photograph by Geoffrey Clements

Jim Dine
Two Mighty Robes at Night in
Jerusalem. 1980
89½ × 106 in. (two panels) overall.
oil on canvas
Courtesy The Pace Gallery
Photograph by Al Mozell

Rackstraw Downes
Behind the Store at Prospect.
1979–80
18¾ × 46¾ in. oil on canvas
Courtesy The Kornblee Gallery
Photograph by eeva-inkeri

Phillip Evergood
Homage to Eve. n.d.
71¾ × 25 in. oil on canvas
Courtesy Kennedy Galleries, Inc.

Herbert Ferber
Baldwin Hill. 1979
87 × 38 × 45 in. steel
Courtesy M. Knoedler & Co., Inc.

Janet Fish
Goldfish and Autumn Leaves.
1979–80
42 × 92 in. oil on canvas
Courtesy Robert Miller Gallery, Inc.
Photograph by eeva-inkeri

Sondra Freckelton
Harvest. 1978
44¼ × 58 in. watercolor on paper
Courtesy Brooke Alexander, Inc.
Photograph by Eric Pollitzer

Gregory Gillespie
Still Life with Squash and
Rutabagas. 1975
50 × 41 in. oil and magna on wood
Hirshhorn Museum and Sculpture
Garden
Courtesy the Forum Gallery

Fritz Glarner
Tondo with Echo. 1955
20½ × 13⅝ in. charcoal
Courtesy private collection

Joseph Glasco
Untitled. 1978
90 × 66 in. acrylic on canvas
Courtesy Gimpel & Weitzenhoffer
Gallery

Robert Goodnough
Theme Variations (Blue). 1969–70
30 × 30 in. acrylic and oil on
canvas
Courtesy Andre Emmerich Gallery

Arshile Gorky
Drawing. 1931–32
31 × 34 in. ink on paper
50th Anniversary Gift of Mr. & Mrs.
Edwin Bergman to the Whitney
Museum of American Art

Robert Graham
Lise Dance Figure I. 1979
94 in. high cast bronze (painted)
Courtesy The Robert Miller Gallery,
Inc.

Morris Graves
Summer Fruit and Flowers. 1978
26 × 44½ in. tempera on paper
Courtesy The Willard Gallery
Photograph by Roy M. Elkind

Maurice Grosser
Still Life with Turk's Head Squash.
1980

25½ × 32 in. oil on canvas
Courtesy The Fischbach Gallery

Philip Guston
Untitled. 1980
20 × 30 in. ink on board.
Collection of the Whitney Museum
of American Art: Gift of Martin
and Agneta Gruss and Mr. and
Mrs. William A. Marsteller
Photograph by Bevan Davies

David Hare
Dog Elephant. 1979
68 × 82 in. acrylic on canvas
Courtesy The Hamilton Gallery of
Contemporary Art
Photograph by eeva-inkeri

Michael Heizer
Untitled. 1969
39 × 30 in. photograph, pencil, and
watercolor
Promised gift of Norman Dubrow to
the Whitney Museum of
American Art
Photograph by Geoffrey Clements

Al Held
Florentine II. 1980
7 × 7 ft. acrylic on canvas
Private Collection
Courtesy Andre Emmerich Gallery
Photograph by Steve Sloman

Charles Hinman
La Lande. 1980
64 × 89 × 6 in. acrylic on shaped
canvas
Courtesy the artist

Budd Hopkins
Ixion II. 1978
81½ × 37 in. acrylic on panel
Courtesy the artist

Bryan Hunt
Balearic Islands VI. 1979
22½ × 22½ in. graphite and linseed
oil on paper
Courtesy Blum Helman Gallery Inc.
Photograph by David Lubarsky

Robert Indiana
The Great American Dream: New
York. 1966
39½ × 26 in. colored crayon and
frottage on paper
Collection of the Whitney Museum
of American Art: Gift of Norman
Dubrow
Photograph by Geoffrey Clements

Angelo Ippolito
Summer Morning. 1979
48 × 54 in. oil on canvas
Courtesy Borgenicht Gallery

Miyoko Ito
Migraine. n.d.
31 × 23 in. oil on canvas
Courtesy Phyllis Kind Gallery

Yvonne Jacquette   •
Southview of New York Harbor.
1978
62 × 77 in. oil on canvas
Courtesy Brooke Alexander, Inc.
Photograph by Jacob Burckhandt

Valerie Jaudon
Carthage. 1980
100 × 168 in. oil on canvas
Courtesy Holly Solomon Gallery
Photograph by D. James Dee

Jess
Melpomene and Thalia. 1965
23 × 18 in. oil on canvas over wood
Courtesy Odyssia Gallery
Photograph by Geoffrey Clements

Lester Johnson
Street Scene. 1979
80 × 60 in. oil on canvas
Courtesy Gimpel & Weitzenhoffer
Gallery

Craig Kauffman
Tell Tale Heart, 3rd Version. 1980
84 × 58 in. paint stick, tempera,
acrylic on silk
Courtesy Blum Helman Gallery
Photograph by Roy M. Elkind

Franz Kline
Untitled. 1960
8½ × 10½ in. ink on paper
Collection of the Whitney Museum
of American Art: Gift of Mr. &
Mrs. Benjamin Weiss
Photograph by Geoffrey Clements

Lee Krasner
Gothic Landscape. 1961
64 × 58 in. oil on canvas
Courtesy The Pace Gallery
Photograph by Al Mozell

Nicholas Krushenick
Untitled collage. 1965
39½ × 37½ in. acrylic on paper
Collection of the Whitney Museum
of American Art: Gift of Marilyn
Cole Fischbach and A. Aladar
Marberger
Photograph by Geoffrey Clements

Robert Kulicke
Triptych: A Persimmon, a Dollar
Bill, and a Pear. 1981
7 × 5½; 7 × 8; 7 × 5½ in. oil on
gessoed wood
Courtesy Davis & Langdale Co.,
Inc.

Robert Kushner
Biarritz. 1975
74 × 85 in. acrylic on synthetic and
cotton lace and fringe
Courtesy Holly Solomon Gallery
Photograph by Harry Shunk

Gaston Lachaise
Equestrienne. 1918
10⅝ × 10 × 4⅝ in. bronze
The Lachaise Foundation
Courtesy Robert Schoelkopf Gallery
Photograph by John D. Schiff

Ellen Lanyon
The Pond. 1976
48 × 60 in. acrylic on canvas
Courtesy Odyssia Gallery

Barry Le Va
Installation Study for Any
Rectangular Space: Accumulated

Vision: Boundaries Designated
(Configurations Indicated). 1977
42 × 62½ in. ink and pencil on
construction and tracing papers
Collection of the Whitney Museum
of American Art, The List
Purchase Fund
Photograph by Geoffrey Clements

Les Levine
Billboard Project for Outside the
Department of Commerce,
"Steer." 1979
114" × 146" Paint stick on canvas
screen with Plexiglas frame
Courtesy Ronald Feldman Fine Art,
Inc.
Photograph by eeva-inkeri

Kim MacConnel
Jingle. 1980
103 × 108 in. acrylic on cotton
Courtesy Holly Solomon Gallery

Man Ray
Etude pour la Fortune. 1938
10¼ × 13¼ in. ink on paper
The Whitney Museum of American
Art: Gift of The Simon
Foundation
Photograph by Geoffrey Clements

Paul Manship
Atalanta. 1921
27 in. high bronze
Courtesy Robert Schoelkopf Gallery
Photograph by eeva-inkeri

Marcia Marcus
Double Self-Portrait III. 1979
23 × 34 in. oil on canvas
Courtesy the artist

Jan Matulka
Bohemian Landscape. 1920–21
17 × 23¼ in. watercolor on paper
The Whitney Museum of American
Art: Gift of Mrs. William A.
Marsteller
Photograph by Geoffrey Clements

Michael Mazur
In the Wood—Afterwards. 1980

41 × 40 in. pastel on paper
Courtesy The Robert Miller Gallery,
Inc.
Photograph by eeva-inkeri

James McGarrell
Double Double Portrait—Gail. 1968
78 × 59½ in. oil on canvas
Courtesy Allan Frumkin Gallery
Photograph by Eric Pollitzer

Joan Mitchell
No Daisies. 1980
102 × 87 in. oil on canvas
Courtesy Xavier Fourcade, Inc.
Photograph by Bruce C. Jones

John Moore
Downtown. 1980
8 × 3 ft. oil on canvas
Courtesy of Hirschl and Adler
Modern, New York

Robert Motherwell
Dublin Collage. 1975
72 × 36 in. collage and acrylic on
canvas
Courtesy M. Knoedler & Co., Inc.

Robert Natkin
Apollo Series. 1980
32 × 40 in. acrylic on paper
Courtesy Gimpel & Weitzenhoffer
Gallery
Photograph by Quesada/Burke

Bruce Nauman
Smoke Rings: 2 Concentric Tunnels
Skewed, Non Communicating.
1980
Courtesy Leo Castelli Gallery
Photograph by Bevan Davies

Isamu Noguchi
Noh Musicians. 1958–74
76 × 34 × 11⅝ in. stainless steel
Courtesy The Pace Gallery
Photograph by Al Mozell

David Novros
  Untitled. 1975
  30 × 41¾ in. charcoal and ink on
    paper
  Collection of the Whitney Museum
    of American Art: Lawrence H.
    Bloedel Bequest (by exchange)
  Photograph by Geoffrey Clements

Jim Nutt
  I Am Here to Show You. 1978–79
  21⅛ × 19⅛ in. oil on canvas
  Courtesy Phyllis Kind Gallery

Claes Oldenburg
  Batcolumn. 1977
  100′ high. welded steel bars painted
    gray
  Collection: US Social Security
    Admin., Chicago
  Courtesy Leo Castelli Gallery
  Photograph by Harry Shunk

Ray Parker
  Untitled #102. 1980
  78 × 174 in. acrylic on canvas
  Courtesy Susan Caldwell, Inc.

Ed Paschke
  Fumare Blanco. 1979
  42 × 60 in. oil on canvas
  Courtesy Phyllis Kind Gallery

Beverly Pepper
  Ternana Wedge. 1980
  89¾ × 47¼ in. cast iron and steel
  Courtesy Andre Emmerich Gallery
  Photograph by Grant Barker

Liliana Porter
  Still Life (detail). 1979
  42 × 52 in. acrylic, charcoal on
    canvas
  Courtesy Barbara Toll Fine Arts

Christina Ramberg
  Sedimentary Disturbance. 1980
  49¼ × 37¼ in. acrylic on canvas
  Courtesy Phyllis Kind Gallery

Abraham Rattner
  Portrait of Don Quixote. 1950

36 × 28 in. watercolor
Courtesy Kennedy Galleries, Inc.

Robert Rauschenberg
  Jackpot Derby (Spread). 1979
  85¼ × 73¼ × 11¾ in. combine,
    mixed mediums
  Collection: Torsten Lilja, Courtesy
    Leo Castelli Gallery
  Photograph by Bevan Davies

Ad Reinhardt
  Untitled (N.Y. World's Fair). 1939
  10 × 13¼ in. gouache on mat board
  50th Anniversary Gift from Rita
    Reinhardt to the Whitney
    Museum of American Art
  Photograph by Geoffrey Clements

James Rosenquist
  Untitled. 1980
  78 × 66 in. oil on canvas
  Courtesy Leo Castelli Gallery
  Photograph by Bevan Davies

Theodore Roszak
  Untitled. 1959
  10½ × 7¹⁵⁄₁₆ in. ink and wash on
    paper
  Collection of the Whitney Museum
    of American Art: Gift of Sara-
    Jane Roszak
  Photograph by Geoffrey Clements

Paul Rotterdam
  Substance #328. 1979
  42 × 37 in. acrylic, encaustic on
    canvas
  Courtesy Susan Caldwell Gallery
  Photograph by James Dee

Robert Ryman
  Sentinel. 1980
  75½ × 72 in. oil on canvas with
    metal fasteners
  Courtesy Sidney Janis Gallery
  Photograph by Otto E. Nelson

Lucas Samaras
  Reconstruction #71. 1980
  90½ × 91½ in. sewn fabrics
  Courtesy The Pace Gallery
  Photograph by Al Mozell

Ludwig Sander (est. 70—72)
Untitled. 1970
24¾ × 19 in. charcoal on paper
Courtesy M. Knoedler & Co., Inc.

Paul Sarkisian
Untitled #3. 1980
79 × 119½ in. acrylic on canvas
Courtesy Nancy Hoffman Gallery
Photograph by D. James Dee

George Segal
Three Bathers with Birch Tree. 1980
72 × 64 × 14 in. plaster and wood
Courtesy Sidney Janis Gallery
Photograph by Otto E. Nelson

Joel Shapiro
Untitled. 1980
52⅞ × 64 × 45½ in. wood
Courtesy Paula Cooper Gallery
Photograph by Geoffrey Clements

Alan Shields
Mt. Saint Helena. 1980
5' 11" × 8' 8". acrylic, thread,
canvas
Courtesy Paula Cooper Gallery
Photograph by eeva-inkeri

David Smith
Untitled. 1946
22 × 30¼ in. tempera on paper
The Whitney Museum of American
Art: Gift of the Lauder
Foundation–Drawing Fund
Photograph by Geoffrey Clements

Raphael Soyer
Paul Resika and Warren Brandt.
1977
49½ × 32 in. oil on canvas
Courtesy Forum Gallery

Joseph Stella
Boy with Bagpipe. 1910–12
21 × 16 in. charcoal and pencil on
paper
Promised 50th Anniversary Gift of
Lucille and Walter Fillin to the
Whitney Museum of American
Art
Photograph by Geoffrey Clements

Myron Stout
Untitled. c. 1957–63
25 × 18⅞ in. charcoal on paper
Collection of the Whitney Museum
of American Art: Gift of Martin
and Agneta Gruss and the
National Endowment for the
Arts
Photograph by Geoffrey Clements

George Sugarman
The Big Ride. 1979
68 × 47 in. relief collage
Courtesy Robert Miller Gallery
Photograph by eeva-inkeri

Paul Thek
Uncle Tom's Cabin. 1975
94 × 9 × 15 in. bronze
Courtesy Brooks Jackson Gallery
Iolas
Photograph by eeva-inkeri

Walasse Ting
Untitled. 1979
70 × 38 in. acrylic on rice paper
Courtesy the artist

Cy Twombly
Roma. 1963
48¾ × 39 in. oil on canvas
Courtesy Leo Castelli Gallery
Photograph by Eric Pollitzer

Charmion von Wiegand
107' 59. 1959
15 × 13⅝ in. gouache on bristol
board
Courtesy Marilyn Pearl Gallery
Collection of Dr. and Mrs. Leroy
Levine
Photograph by Eric Pollitzer

Andy Warhol
Marilyn. 1968
69 × 71 in. wool
Courtesy Leo Castelli Gallery
Photograph by Eric Pollitzer

Max Weber
Apollo in Matisse's Studio. 1908
23 × 18 in. oil on canvas
Courtesy The Forum Gallery

H. C. Westermann
  The Sweetest Flower. 1978
  22⅛ × 31 in. watercolor on "green"
    paper
  The Whitney Museum of American
    Art: Gift of the Lauder
    Foundation–Drawing Fund
  Photograph by Geoffrey Clements

William T. Wiley
  Vague-A-Bond. 1975
  106 × 96 in. charcoal and acrylic on
    canvas
  Courtesy Allan Frumkin Gallery
  Photograph by eeva-inkeri

Christopher Wilmarth
  Gnomon's Parade (Parting). 1980
  90 × 28 × 30 in. glass and steel
  Courtesy the artist: Collection
    Princeton University

Philip Wofford
  Dancer. 1980

60 × 60 in. acrylic on canvas
Courtesy Nancy Hoffman Gallery
Photograph by Bevan Davies

Jean Xceron
  U Form No. 553 A. 1962
  30 × 21⅜ in. watercolor on paper
  The Whitney Museum of American
    Art: Lawrence H. Bloedel
    Bequest
  Photograph by Geoffrey Clements

Jack Youngerman
  Tabriz. 1981
  74 × 124 in. painted aluminum
  Courtesy the artist
  Photograph by Al Mozell

Robert S. Zakanitch
  Savannah Nights. 1979
  7 × 12 feet. acrylic on canvas
  Courtesy Robert Miller Gallery
  Photograph by eeva-inkeri

Index of Artists and Pronunciation Guide

(A) Painter; (A¹) Watercolorist; (B) Sculptor; (C) Printmaker; (D) Assemblagist; (E) Teacher; (F) Happenings; (G) Mosaicist; (H) Draftsman; (I) Conceptualist

A

1. Aach, Herb (A)
2. Acconci, Vito (B)
   Ah con she
3. Acton, Arlo C. (B)
4. Adams, Clinton (A,C)
5. Adams, Pat (A)
6. Adler, Samuel M. (A)
7. Agostini, Peter (B)
8. Albers, Josef (A,C,E)
9. Albert, Calvin (B)
10. Albright, Ivan Le Lorraine (A)
11. Alcalay, Albert (A)
12. Allan, William B. (A)
13. Alston, Charles Henry (A)
14. Altman, Harold (C,A)
15. Altoon, John (A)
16. Amen, Irving (C)
17. Anderson, Guy Irving (A)
18. Anderson, Jeremy R. (B)
19. Anderson, John S. (B)
20. Anderson, Lennart (A)
21. Andre, Carl (B)
22. Andrejevic, Milet (A)
    An **dre** avic, Millet
23. Andrews, Oliver (B)
24. Antonakos, Stephen (B)
25. Antreasian, Garo (C)
    An **tray** sian
26. Anuszkiewicz, Richard (A)
    Anu **skay** vitch
27. Arakawa, Shusaku (A,C)
28. Archipenko, Alexander (B,E)
29. Arman (B,D)
30. Arneson, Robert (B)
31. Arnold, Anne (B)
32. Arnoldi, Charles (B)
33. Aronson, David (A)
34. Artschwager, Richard (A,B)
35. Atherton, John C. (A)
36. Ault, George, C. (A)
37. Austin, Darrel (A)
38. Avedisian, Edward (A)
39. Avery, Milton (A)
40. Azuma, Norio (C)

B

41. Baber, Alice (A)
42. Baer, Jo (A)
    Bear
43. Bailey, William (A,E)
44. Baizerman, Saul (B)
45. Baldessari, John (I)
46. Bang, Thomas (B)
47. Bannard, Darby (A)
48. Baringer, Richard E. (A)
49. Barnes, Robert (A)
50. Barnet, Will (A,C,E)
51. Barry, Robert (B,I)
52. Barth, Frances (A)
53. Bartlett, Jennifer (A)
54. Baskin, Leonard (B,C,E)
55. Bayer, Herbert (A)
56. Baylinson, A.S. (A)
57. Baynard, Edward (A,C)
58. Baziotes, William A. (A,E)
59. Beal, Gifford (A)
60. Beal, Jack (A)
61. Bearden, Romare (A)
    Roh **mayr**
62. Beasley, Bruce (B)
63. Beattie, George (A)
64. Beauchamp, Robert (A)
    Beechem
65. Bechtle, Robert (A)
    Beck tle
66. Beck, Rosemarie (A)
67. Behl, Wolfgang (B)
68. Bell, Larry (B)
69. Benglis, Lynda (B)

V

857. Valentine, De Wain (B)
858. Vander Sluis, George (B,E)
      Sluice
859. Vasilieff, Nicholas (A,E)
860. Venezia, Michael (A)
861. Vicente, Esteban (A)
862. Vollmer, Ruth (B)
863. Von Schlegell, David (B)
864. Von Weigand, Charmion (A)
      Wee Gand, Sharmion
865. von Wicht, John (A)
      Vicht
866. Voulkos, Peter (B,E)
      Vole kos
867. Vytlacil, Vaclav (A,E)
      Vitt la sill

W

868. Wald, Sylvia (A,C)
869. Waldman, Paul (A)
870. Walkowitz, Abraham (A)
871. Warhol, Andy (A)
872. Warshaw, Howard (A)
873. Washington, James W., Jr. (B)
874. Watkins, Franklin C. (A)
875. Watts, Robert M. (D,F)
876. Wayne, June (A,C)
877. Weber, Hugo (A)
878. Weber, Idelle (A)
879. Weber, Max (A)
880. Weeks, James (A)
881. Weinberg, Elbert (B)
882. Weinrib, David (B)
883. Welliver, Neil (A)
      Williver
884. Wells, Lynton (A)
885. Wesley, John (A,C)
886. Wesselmann, Tom (A)
887. Westermann, H.C. (B)
888. Whitman, Robert (A,F)
889. Wieghardt, Paul (A,E)
      Wig hart
890. Wilde, John (A,E)
      Will dee
891. Wiley, William T. (A)
892. Wilfred, Thomas
      (Richard Edgar Løvstrøm) (B)

893. Wilke, Ulfert S. (A)
      Will ka
894. Willenbecher, John (B)
      beck
895. Williams, Hiram (A)
896. Williams, Neil (A)
897. Wilmarth, Christopher (B)
898. Wilson, Jane (A)
899. Wines, James (B)
900. Wirsum, Karl (A)
901. Witkin, Isaac (A)
902. Woelffer, Emerson (A)
903. Wofford, Philip (A)
904. Wolff, Robert Jay (A,E)
905. Wolfson, Sidney (A)
906. Wonner, Paul John (A)
907. Wood, Grant (A)
908. Wyeth, Andrew (A)

X

909. Xceron, Jean (A)
      Zeron

Y

910. Yektai, Manoucher (A)
      Manu shay
911. Yoshida, Ray (A)
912. Youngerman, Jack (A)
913. Yrisarry, Mario (A)
      Year a sahri
914. Yunkers, Adja (A,C)
      Odd ya

Z

915. Zacharias, Athos (A)
      Zacka **rye** as
916. Zajac, Jack (A)
917. Zakanitch, Robert S. (A)
918. Zammitt, Norman (B)
919. Zerbe, Karl (A)
920. Zogbaum, Wilfrid (B)
921. Zorach, Marguerite (A)
922. Zorach, William (B)
923. Zox, Larry (A)

Key to Museums and Institutions and Their Schools

reflecting ownership of art collections in which are represented works of the artists in this book

A

AAAL. American Academy of Arts and Letters, NYC

A.F.A. American Federation of Arts, NYC

ASL. Art Students League, NYC

AT&T. American Telephone and Telegraph Co.

Aachen. Museen der Stadt Aachen, Germany

Aachen/Kunstverein. Kunstverein, Aachen, Germany

Aachen/NG. Neue Galerie in der Stadt Aachen, Aachen, Germany

Abbott Academy, Andover, Mass.

Abbott Laboratories

Abilene Christian College

Abraham Lincoln High School, Brooklyn, N.Y.

Academy of Fine Arts, Warsaw—*see* Warsaw

Academy of Natural Sciences, Philadelphia—*see* PMA

Achenbach Foundation for Graphic Arts, San Francisco, Calif.

Ackland. William Hays Ackland Memorial Art Center, Chapel Hill, N.C.

Addison Gallery of Art—*see* Andover/Phillips

Adelaide. The Art Gallery of South Australia, Adelaide, Australia

Adelphi U.

Aetna Oil Co.

Agricultural and Mechanical College of Texas

Ain Harod. Mishkan Le'omanuth Museum of Art, Ain Harod, Israel

Akademie der Kunste, Berlin, West Germany

Akron/AI. Akron Art Institute, Akron, Ohio

Alabama Institute of Technology

Alabama Polytechnic Institute, Auburn, N.Y.

U. of Alabama

Albany/Institute. Albany Institute of History and Art, Albany, N.Y.

Albany Mall—*see* South Mall, Albany

Albany/SUNY. State University of New York, at Albany

U. of Alberta, Edmonton (Alta.), Canada

Albertina (Vienna)—*see* Graphische Sammlung Albertina

Albion College

Albrecht Gallery Museum of Art—*see* St. Joseph/Albrecht

Albright-Knox Art Gallery—*see* Buffalo/Albright

Alcoa. Aluminum Company of America

Larry Aldrich Museum—*see* Ridgefield/Aldrich

Alfred/SUNY. State University of New York, at Alfred

Allegheny College

Allen-Bradley Co., Inc.

Allen Memorial Art Museum—*see* Oberlin College

Allentown/AM. Allentown Art Museum, Allentown, Pa.

Lyman Allyn Museum—*see* New London

Alverthorpe Gallery, Jenkintown, Pa.

Amarillo Art Center, Amarillo, Texas

Amerada Hess Corp., Inc.

American Academy, Rome

American Academy (and Institute) of Arts and Letters—*see* AAAL (AAIAL)

American Airlines

American Association of University Women

American Broadcasting Co.

American Can Corp.

American Car and Foundry Co.
American Export Isbrandtsen Lines, Inc.
American Federation of Arts—*see* A.F.A.
American Foundation for the Arts, Miami, Florida
American Life and Casualty Insurance Co.
American Locomotive Co.
American Museum of Immigration, NYC
American National Fire Insurance Co. Collection
American Republic Insurance Co.
American Swedish Historical Museum, Philadelphia, Pa.
American Swedish Institute, Minneapolis, Minn.
American Telephone & Telegraph Co.—*see* AT&T
American Tobacco Co.
American U.
Amherst College
Amsterdam/Stedelijk. Stedelijk Museum, Amsterdam, Holland
Amstar Corp.
Anchorage. Anchorage Historical and Fine Arts, Anchorage, Alaska
Arthur Anderson & Co.
Anderson Clayton Company
Andover/Phillips. Phillips Academy, Addison Gallery of American Art, Mass. Phillips Academy
The M. L. Annenberg Foundation, Philadelphia, Pa.
Anthology Film Archives
Antwerp. Musée Royal des Beaux-Arts, Antwerp, Belgium
Antwerp/Middelheim. Musée de Sculpture en pleine air, Middelheim, Antwerp, Belgium.
Argentina/Nacional. Museo Nacional de Bellas Artes, Buenos Aires, Argentina
Arizona State College
Arizona State U.
U. of Arizona
U. of Arkansas (incl. Arkansas Art Center)
Thurman Arnold Building, Washington, D.C.
Arnot Art Museum, Elmira, N.Y.
Art Academy of Cincinnati, Cincinnati, Ohio

Art Council of Pakistan—*see* Karachi
Art Gallery of New South Wales—*see* Sydney/AG
Art Gallery of South Australia, Adelaide—*see* Adelaide
Art Museum of South Texas, Corpus Christi, Texas
Art Students League—*see* ASL
Art of This Century (Peggy Guggenheim), Venice, Italy
Arts Club of Chicago, Illinois
Arts Council of Great Britain, London, England
Asheville Art Museum, Asheville, N.C.
Ashland Oil Inc., NYC
Aspen Institute for Humanistic Studies, Aspen, Colo.
Associated Coin Amusement Company
Astor Place, NYC
Atlanta/AA. Atlanta Art Association, Atlanta, Ga.
Atlanta Corp., Atlanta, Ga.
Atlanta U.
Atlantic Richfield Co.
Atwater Kent Museum, Philadelphia, Pa.
Auburn U.
Aubusson. College de la Manufacture d'Aubusson, Aubusson, France
Auckland. Auckland City Art Gallery, Auckland, New Zealand
Augusta, Me./State. Maine State Museum, Augusta, Me.
Austin. Texas Fine Arts Association, Austin, Tex.
Australian National Gallery, Canberra—*see* Canberra/National
Avco Corp
Avon Products, NYC
L. S. Ayres & Co.

B

Baker U.
Ball State U. (formerly Teachers College), Muncie, Ind.
Baltimore/MA. Baltimore Museum of Art, Baltimore, Md.
U. of Baltimore
Baltimore/Walters. Walters Art Gallery, Baltimore, Md.
Bangor Public Library, Bangor, Me.

Bank of America
Bank of California
The Bank of California N.A., Portland, Ore.
Bank of Chicago
The Bank of New York (NYC)
Bank of Omaha (Neb.)
Bankers Trust Company, NYC
Banque Lambert, Brussels, Belgium
Barat College of the Sacred Heart
Barcelona. Museo de Arte Moderno, Barcelona, Spain
Barnard College
Barnes Foundation, Merion, Pa.
Baseball Museum, Baltimore, Md.
Basel. Kunstmuseum Basel, Switzerland
Bat-Yam Museum—see Rybak
Baton-Rouge. State of Louisiana Art Commission, Baton Rouge, La.
Bauhaus-Archiv, Darmstadt, Germany
Beach Public School, Portland, Ore.
Belgian Ministry of National Education, Brussels, Belgium
Belgrade/National. Narodni Muzej (National Museum), Belgrade, Yugoslavia
Bellevue Hospital, NYC
Bellevue, Wash. Bellevue Arts & Crafts Association
Beloit College (incl. Wright Art Center)
Belvedere. Osterreichische Galerie im Belvedere in Wein, Vienna, Austria
Bennington College
Berea College
Bergen Community College, Paramus, N.J.
John Nelson Bergstrom Art Center and Museum—see Neenah/Bergstrom
Berkshire Atheneum—see Pittsfield/Berkshire
Berlin. Staatliche Museen, Berlin, West Germany
Berlin/National. Nationalgalerie, Berlin, West Germany
Berne. Kunsthalle Berne, Switzerland
Betcar Corp.
Bethlehem Steel Corp.
Bezalel Museum, Jerusalem, Israel. Bezalel Art School
Bibliotheque Royale de Belgique, Brussels, Belgium
Bielefeld. Stadtisches Kunsthaus, Bielefeld, Germany

Birla Academy of Art and Culture—see Calcutta
Birmingham, Ala./MA. Birmingham Museum of Art, Birmingham, Ala.
Black Mountain College, Beria, N.C.
Blanden Memorial Art Gallery—see Fort Dodge/Blanden
Block Drug Co., Jersey City, N.J.
Bochum. Museum Bochum, Bochum, Germany
Boise-Cascade Corp.
Bonn. Rheinisches Landesmuseum, Bonn, Germany
Bordighera. Galleria d'Arte Moderna, Bordighera, Italy
Borgon Associates
Borg-Warner International Corporation
Boston/MFA. Museum of Fine Arts, Boston, Mass. Boston Museum School
Boston Public Library, Boston, Mass.
Boston U.
Boulogne. Musée des Beaux-Arts, Boulogne, France
Bowdoin College
Bowling Green State U., Bowling Green, Ohio
Bradford Junior College, Bradford, Mass.
Bradley U.
Brandeis U. (incl. Rose Art Museum)
Archie Bray Foundation, Helena, Mont.
Bremen. Kunsthalle Bremen, Germany
Brenton Bank, Des Moines, Iowa
Bridgeport. Museum of Art, Science and Industry, Bridgeport, Conn.
Bridgestone Museum, Tokyo, Japan
Brigham Young U.
Bristol-Myers Co.
Britannica. Encyclopaedia Britannica
U. of British Columbia, Vancouver (B.C.), Canada
British Museum, London, England
Brockton/Fuller. Fuller Memorial Art Center, Brockton, Mass.
Brookgreen Gardens, Georgetown, S.C.
Brookings Institute, Washington, D.C.
Brooklyn College of the City University of New York
Brooklyn Museum, Brooklyn, N.Y. Brooklyn Museum School
Bobbie Brooks Inc.

Brooks Memorial Art Gallery—*see* Memphis/Brooks

Brown U.

Bruce Museum, Greenwich, Conn.

Brunswick. Stadtisches Museum, Braunschweig, Germany

Brunswick Corp.

Brussels/Beaux-Arts. Palais des Beaux-Arts, Brussels, Belgium

Brussels/Moderne. Musée d'Art Moderne, Brussels, Belgium

Brussels/Royaux. Musées Royaux des Beaux-Arts de Belgique.

Bryn Mawr College

Buckingham Palace, London, England

Budapest/National. Hungarian National Gallery, Budapest, Hungary

The Budd Co.

Buenos Aires-Moderno. Museo de Arte Moderno, Buenos Aires, Argentina

Buenos Aires/Municipal. Museo Municipal de Bellas Artes y Arte Nacional, Buenos Aires, Argentina

Buffalo/Albright. Albright-Knox Art Gallery, Buffalo, N.Y. **Albright Art School** (prior to 1962)

Buffalo/SUNY. State University of New York, at Buffalo

Bundy Art Gallery—*see* Waitsfield/Bundy

Burlington Industries

Burlington Mills Collection

Harry and Della Burpee Gallery—*see* Rockford/Burpee

Burroughs Wellcome Co., Raleigh, N.C.

Busch-Reisinger Museum, Cambridge, Mass.

Business Card, Inc.

The Butler Institute of American Art—*see* Youngstown/Butler

C

CIA. Central Intelligence Agency, Washington, D.C.

CIT Corporation

CNAC. Centre National d'Art Contemporain, Paris, France (*see also* Paris/Beaubourg)

CSCS. California State College System (when known, individual campuses are listed in the artists' entries)

CSFA (California School of Fine Arts)—*see* SFAI

Calcutta. Birla Academy of Art and Culture, Calcutta, India

U. of Calgary, Alberta, Canada

California Academy of Science, Museum and Library, San Francisco, Calif.

California College of Arts and Crafts

California Federal Savings and Loan Association, Los Angeles

California Palace of The Legion of Honor, San Francisco, Calif.

California School of Fine Arts—*see* SFAI

California State College System—*see* CSCS

California State Fair

California State Library

California State U.

California Watercolor Society

U. of California

The Cambridge School, Weston, Mass.

Cambridge, University of, Cambridge, England

The Canada Council, Ottawa (Ont.), Canada

Canadian Industries Ltd., Montreal (Que.), Canada

Canadian Society of Graphic Art

Canajoharie Library and Art Gallery, Canajoharie, N.Y.

Canberra/National. Australian National Gallery, Canberra, Australia

Canton Art Institute, Canton, Ohio

Capehart Corp.

Cape Town. South African National Gallery, Cape Town, Union of South Africa

Capitol Records, Inc.

Capitol Research Co., Los Angeles, Calif.

Caracas. Museo de Bellas Artes de Caracas, Venezuela

Caracas/Contemporaneo. Museo de Arte Contemporaneo, Caracas, Venezuela

Carborundum Company

Cardiff—*see* National Museum of Wales

Carleton College

Carnegie Institute of Technology, Pittsburgh, Pa.

Carolina Art Association—*see* Charleston/Carolina

Amon Carter Museum of Western Art,

Fort Worth, Tex.

La Casa del Libro, San Juan, Puerto Rico

Case Institute of Technology

The Catholic U. of America

Cedar Rapids/AA. Cedar Rapids Art Association, Cedar Rapids, Iowa

Cedars-Sinai Medical Center, Los Angeles, Calif.

Center for Inter-American Relations, New York City

Central Florida Museum—*see* Orlando

Centraal Museum, Utrecht—*see* Utrecht

Central Research Corp., NYC

Centre National d'Art Contemporain—*see* CNAC

Centro Artistico de Barranquilla, Barranquilla, Colombia

Centro Cultural de los Estados Unidos, Madrid, Spain

Century Association, NYC

Ceret. Musée d'Art Moderne, Ceret, France

Chaffey College

Charleston/Carolina. Carolina Art Association, Charleston, S.C.

Charleston, W. Va. Charleston Art Gallery, Charleston, W. Va.

Charlotte/Mint. Mint Museum of Art, Charlotte, N.C.

Chase Manhattan Bank

Chase Park Plaza Hotel, St. Louis, Mo.

Chateau de Rohan, Strasbourg, France

Chattanooga/AA. Chattanooga Art Association, Chattanooga, Tenn.

Chattanooga/Hunter. Hunter Museum of Art, Chattanooga, Tenn.

Chautauqua Institute, Chautauqua, N.Y.

Cheekwood. The Tennessee Botanical Gardens and Fine Arts Center, Nashville, Tenn.

Cheney Cowles Memorial Museum, Spokane, Wash.

Chicago/AI. The Art Institute of Chicago, Ill. **Chicago Art Institute School (and Junior School)**

Chicago Arts Club—*see* Arts Club of Chicago

Chicago/Contemporary. Museum of Contemporary Art, Chicago, Ill.

Chicago Public Schools, Chicago, Ill.

The U. of Chicago (incl. Renaissance Society)

Chico State College (incl. Chico Art Center)

Choate–Rosemary Hall School, Wallingford, Conn.

Chouinard Art Institute, Los Angeles, Calif.

Christian Theological Seminary, Indianapolis, Inc.

Chrysler Corp.

Walter P. Chrysler Museum of Art—*see* Norfolk/Chrysler

Ciba-Geigy Corp., Ardsley, N.Y.

Cincinnati/AM. The Cincinnati Art Museum, Cincinnati, Ohio. **Cincinnati Museum School**

Cincinnati/Contemporary. Contemporary Arts Center, Cincinnati, Ohio

U. of Cincinnati

Cinematheque de Belgique, Brussels, Belgium

Cinematheque Francaise, Paris, France

Citicorp, NYC

Citizens Fidelity Bank, Louisville, Ky.

City of Chalon-sur-Soane, France

City of Claremont, Calif.

City College of the City University of New York

City of Fresno, Calif.

City of Hamburg, Germany

City of Hannover, Germany

City Investing Corp., NYC

City of Mill Valley, Calif.

City of Oakland, Calif.

City of Portland, Ore.

City of San Francisco, Calif.

City of Tilburg, Holland

City of Toronto (Ont.), Canada

Civic Center Synagogue, NYC

Clairol Inc.

Claremont College

Clearwater/Gulf Coast. Florida Gulf Coast Art Center, Inc., Clearwater, Fla.

Cleveland/MA. The Cleveland Museum of Art, Cleveland, Ohio

Cleveland Trust Co.

The Coca-Cola Co.

Cochran Memorial Park, St. Paul, Minn.

Coe College

Colby College

Colgate U.

Collection de l'Etat, Paris, France

College des Musées Nationaux de

France, Paris, France

College of St. Benedict

Cologne. Wallraf-Richartz-Museum, Cologne, Germany

Cologne/Kunstverein. Kolnischer Kunstverein, Cologne, Germany

Cologne/NG. Neue Galerie im Alten Kurhaus, Cologne, Germany

Colonial Bank & Trust Co., Waterbury, Conn.

Colonial Williamsburg. Williamsburg, Va.

Colorado College

Colorado Springs/FA. Colorado Springs Fine Arts Center, Colorado Springs, Colo.

Colorado State U.

U. of Colorado

Columbia, Mo. State Historical Society of Missouri, Columbia, Mo.

Columbia, S.C./MA. Columbia Museum of Art, Columbia, S.C.

Columbia Banking, Savings and Loan Association, Rochester, N.Y.

Columbia Broadcasting System

Columbia U.

Columbus. Columbus Gallery of Fine Arts, Columbus, Ohio

Columbus, Ga. Columbus Museum of Arts and Crafts, Columbus, Ga.

Commerce Bank (or Bancshares) of Kansas City, Mo.

Commerce Bank of St. Louis

Commerce Trust Co., Kansas City, Mo.

Community Arts Foundation, Los Angeles, Calif.

Concordia Teachers College (Ill.)

Concordia Teachers College (Neb.)

Connecticut Community College

Connecticut Life Insurance Company

Connecticut College

U. of Connecticut

Conover-Mast Publications Inc.

Container Corp. of America

Continental Grain Company

Cooperative Insurance Society, Manchester, England

Cooper Union. The Cooper Union Museum, NYC

Coos Bay Art Museum, Ore.

Copenhagen. Statens Museum fur Kunst, Copenhagen, Denmark

Corcoran. The Corcoran Gallery of Art, Washington, D.C. The Corcoran

School of Art

Cordoba/Municipal. Museo Municipal de Cordoba, Argentina

Cordoba/Provincial. Museo Provincial de Bellas Artes, Cordoba, Argentina

Cornell College, Mt. Vernon, Iowa

Cornell U. (incl. Herbert F. Johnson Museum)

Cortland/SUNY. State University of New York, at Cortland

Corvallis (Ore.) First Federal Savings and Loan

Courtauld Institute, London, England

Craig Elwood Associates

Cranbrook. Cranbrook Academy of Art, Bloomfield Hills, Mich.

E. B. Crocker Art Gallery—see Sacramento/Crocker

Crown Zellerbach Foundation, San Francisco, Calif.

Cuenca. Museo Municipal de Arte, Cuenca, Spain

Cummer Gallery of Art—see Jacksonville/Cummer

Currier. Currier Gallery of Art, Manchester, N.H. Currier Gallery School

D

Dallas Museum for Contemporary Arts, Dallas, Tex.—see Dallas/MFA

Dallas/MFA. Dallas Museum of Fine Arts, Dallas, Tex. Dallas Museum School

Dallas Public Library, Dallas, Tex.

Dalton School, NYC

Darmstadt/Hessisches. Hessisches Landesmuseum, Darmstadt, Germany

Darmstadt/Kunsthalle. Kunsthalle, Darmstadt, Germany

Dartmouth College (incl. Hopkins Art Center)

Davenport/Municipal. Davenport Municipal Art Gallery, Davenport, Iowa

Davidson, N.C. Davidson Art Center, Davidson, N.C.

Davison Art Center—see Wesleyan U. (Conn.)

Dayton/AI. Dayton Art Institute, Dayton, Ohio. Dayton Art Institute School

De Beers Collection, Johannesburg, South Africa

Debevoise, Plimpton, Lyons and Gates, NYC

Decatur. Decatur Art Center, Decatur, Ill.

De Cordova and Dana Museum—*see* Lincoln, Mass./De Cordova

DeKalb. Northern Illinois U., DeKalb, Ill.

Delaware Art Center—*see* Wilmington

Delaware Art Museum, Wilmington, Del.

U. of Delaware.

Isaac Delgado Museum of Art—*see* New Orleans/Delgado

Denison U.

Denver/AM. Denver Art Museum, Denver, Colo.

De Pauw U.

Des Moines. The Des Moines Art Center, Des Moines, Iowa

Des Moines Register & Tribune, Des Moines, Iowa

Detroit/Institute. The Detroit Institute of Arts, Detroit, Mich.

de Young. M. H. de Young Memorial Museum, San Francisco, Calif.

Diablo Valley College

Didrichsen Foundation, Helsinki, Finland

Dillard U.

Djakarta Museum, Djakarta, Indonesia

Doane College

Donaldson, Lufkin & Jenrette, Inc.

Jay Dorf, Inc.

Downey Museum of Art, Downey, Calif.

Downtown Community School, NYC

Drake U.

Dresdener Bank, Los Angeles, Calif.

Dublin/Municipal. Municipal Gallery of Modern Art, Dublin, Ireland

U. of Dublin, Dublin, Ireland

Dubuque/AA. Dubuque Art Association, Dubuque, Iowa

Duisburg. Wilhelm-Lehmbruck-Museum der Stadt Duisburg, Germany

Duke U.

Dulin Gallery of Art, Knoxville, Tenn.

Dusseldorf. Kunstmuseum der Stadt Dusseldorf, Germany

Dusseldorf/KN-W. Kunstsammlung Nordrhein-Westfalen, Dusseldorf, Germany

Dusseldorf/Kunsthalle. Stadtische Kunsthalle, Dusseldorf, Germany

E

Earlham College

U. of East Anglia, Norwich, England

East Tennessee State College Museum of Art, Johnson City, Tenn.

Eastern Michigan U.

Eastern Oregon College

Eastland Shopping Center, Detroit, Mich.

Eaton Paper Corp.

Edinburgh/Modern. Scottish National Gallery of Modern Art, Edinburgh, Scotland

Edinburgh/National. National Gallery of Scotland, Edinburgh, Scotland

Eilat. Museum of Modern Art, Eilat, Israel

Eindhoven. Stedelijk van Abbe-Museum, Eindhoven, Holland

Ellerby Associates

Elmira College (N.Y.)

Emory U., Atlanta, Ga.

Equitable Life Assurance Society of the U.S.

Escuela Nacional de Artes Plasticas, Mexico City, Mexico

Essen. Museum Folkwang, Essen, Germany

Essen/NG. Neue Galerie, Essen, Germany

Esslingen. Stadtische Museum, Esslingen, Germany

Evansville. Evansville Museum of Arts and Sciences, Evansville, Ind.

Evansville Museum School

Everett Junior College, Everett, Wash.

Everhart Museum—*see* Scranton/Everhart

Everson Museum of Art—*see* Syracuse/Everson

Exchange National Bank, Chicago, Ill.

Exeter. Phillips Exeter Academy, The Lamont Art Gallery, Exeter, N.H.

F

F.T.D. Association (Florists Transworld Delivery Association)

Fabick Tractor Co.

Fairleigh Dickinson U.

Fairmont Park Association, Philadelphia, Pa.

Farmers Elevator Insurance Co.

William A. Farnsworth Library and Art Museum—*see* Rockland/Farnsworth

Father Judge Mission Seminary, Lynchburg, Va.

Fayetteville Museum of Art, Fayetteville, N.C.

Federal Deposit Insurance Corporation

Fidelity Bank, Philadelphia, Pa.

Hamilton Easter Field Foundation, Portland, Me.

57th Madison Corp., NYC

First City National Bank, Houston, Tex.

First National Bank of Boston

First National Bank of Chicago

First National Bank of Dallas

First National Bank, Iowa City, Iowa

First National Bank, Madison, Wisc.

First National Bank of Memphis, Tenn.

First National Bank, Minneapolis, Minn.

First National Bank of Nevada, Reno, Nev.

First National Bank of Ohio, Columbus, Ohio ·

First National Bank of Oregon

First National Bank of Seattle, Wash.

First National Bank, Tampa, Fla.

First National Bank of Tulsa, Tulsa, Okla.

First National City Bank

Fisk U.

Fitchburg/AM. Fitchburg Art Museum, Fitchburg, Mass.

525 William Penn Plaza, Philadelphia, Pa.

Robert Hull Fleming Museum—*see* U. of Vermont

Flint/Institute. Flint Institute of Arts, Flint, Mich.

Florence, Italy. Galleria dell'Accademia, Florence, Italy

Florence (Italy)/Modern. Galleria d'Arte Moderna, Florence, Italy

Florence, S.C. Museum. Florence Museum, Florence, S.C.

Florida Gulf Coast Art Center, Inc.—*see*

Clearwater/Gulf Coast

Florida Southern College

Florida State U.

U. of Florida

Florsheim Foundation, Chicago, Ill.

Fogg Art Museum—*see* Harvard U.

Fontana-Hollywood Corp.

Ford Foundation

Fordham U.

Ford Motor Company

Fort Dodge/Blanden. Blanden Memorial Art Gallery, Fort Dodge, Iowa

Fort Lauderdale. Fort Lauderdale Museum of Art, Fort Lauderdale, Fla.

Fort Wayne/AM. Fort Wayne Art Museum, Fort Wayne, Ind.

Fort Worth. Fort Worth Art Center, Fort Worth, Tex.

Fort Wright College, Spokane, Wash.

Foundation Maeght, St. Paul-de-Vence, France

405 Park Avenue, NYC

Four Seasons Restaurant, NYC

Fourth National Bank and Trust, Wichita, Kansas

France/National. Musée National d'Art Moderne, Paris, France (*see also* Paris/Moderne)

Franchard Corp.

Frank Construction Company

Frankfurt am Main. Stadelsches Kunstinstitut, Frankfurt am Main, Germany

Franklin Institute, Philadelphia, Pa.

Simon Frazer U.

Fredonia/SUNY. State University of New York, at Fredonia

Free Library of Philadelphia, Pa.

French Ministry of National Education, Paris, France

Fresno State College

Friends of Art, Uniontown, Pa.

Friuli, Italy/MOMA. Museum of Modern Art, Friuli, Italy

Fuller Memorial Art Center—*see* Brockton/Fuller

Fullerton Junior College (Calif.)

Fundacion Juan March, Madrid, Spain

G

Galerie des 20. Jahrhunderts, Berlin, Germany

Galleria Comunale d'Arte Contemporanea, Arezzo, Italy

Gallery of Modern Art, NYC—*see* New York Cultural Center

Gallery of Modern Art, Washington, D.C.—*see* WGMA

Galveston. Galveston Historical Foundation Inc., Galveston, Tex.

Garcia Corp.

Garnett Public Library, Garnett, Kans.

Geigy Chemical Corp.—*see* Ciba-Geigy Corp.

Gelsenkirchen. Stadtische Kunstsammlung, Gelsenkirchen, Germany

General Electric Corp.

General Mills Inc.

General Motors Corp.

General Reinsurance Corp.

Geneseo/SUNY. State University of New York, at Geneseo

George Washington U.

George Washington Carver Junior College, Rockville, Md.

Georgia Institute of Technology

Georgia State U.

U. of Georgia (incl. Georgia Museum of Art)

Gettysburg College

Ghent. Musée des Beaux-Arts, Ghent, Belgium

Ghent/Moderne. Musée d'Art Moderne, Ghent, Belgium

Gibraltar Savings & Loan Association

Gimbel Bros.

U. of Glasgow. Glasgow, Scotland

Glen Alden Corp.

Goddard Art Center, Ardmore, Okla.

Goddard College

Golden Gateway Center, San Francisco, Calif.

Golden State Mutual Life Insurance Co.

Goldring International

Gothenburg—*see* Sweden/Goteborgs

Goucher College

Govett-Brewster Art Gallery, New Plymouth, New Zealand

The Grace Line

Grand Palais, Paris, France

Grand Rapids. Grand Rapids Art Gallery, Grand Rapids, Mich.

Graphische Sammlung Albertina, Vienna, Austria

Graphische Sammlung der E. T. H. (Eidg. Technischen Hochschule), Zurich, Switzerland

Great Southwest Industrial Park, Atlanta, Ga.

Great Western Savings and Loan Association of South California, Los Angeles

Greece/National. National Picture Gallery, Athens, Greece

Greenville County Museum of Art, S.C.

Grenchen. Sammlungen der Museumgesellschaft, Grenchen, Switzerland

Grenoble. Musée des Beaux-Arts de Grenoble, France

Griffiths Art Center—*see* St. Lawrence U.

Grinnell College

Grolier Club, NYC

Grunewald Foundation for Graphic Arts, Los Angeles, Calif.

Guadalajara. Museo de Bellas Artes, Guadalajara, Mexico

The Solomon R. Guggenheim Museum—*see* SRGM

Guild Hall, East Hampton, N.Y.

Guild Plastics Co.

Gulf Coast Art Center—*see* Clearwater/ Gulf Coast

Gulf Life Insurance Co., Jacksonville, Fla.

Gulf Oil Corp.

Gulf and Western Industries Inc.

A. V. Gumuchian, Inc.

H

Hackley Art Center—*see* Muskegon/ Hackley

Hagen. Karl-Ernst-Osthaus-Museum, Hagen, Germany

Hagerstown/County MFA. Washington County Museum of Fine Arts, Hagerstown, Md.

The Hague. Haags Gemeentemuseum, The Hague, Holland

Haifa. Museum of Modern Art, Haifa, Israel

Haifa/National. National Maritime Museum, Haifa, Israel

Hall of Justice, San Francisco, Calif.

Hallmark Collection
Hamburg. Hamburger Kunsthalle, Hamburg, Germany
Hamburg/Kunstverein. Kunstverein in Hamburg, Hamburg, Germany
Hamilton College
Hamline U.
Hampton Institute
Hampton School, Townson, Md.
Hannover. Stadtische Galerie, Hannover, Germany
Hannover/K-G. Kestner-Gesellschaft, Hannover, Germany (*see also* Kestner-Museum, Hannover)
Hannover/Kunstverein. Kunstverein Hannover, Hannover, Germany
Harcourt Brace Jovanovich Inc.
Harlem Hospital, NYC
Harmon Foundation Inc., NYC
Harrisburg, Pa./State Museum. Pennsylvania State Museum, Harrisburg, Pa. (incl. William Penn Memorial Museum)
Hartford (Conn.) State Library
Hartford/Wadsworth. The Wadsworth Atheneum, Hartford, Conn.
U. of Hartford
Harvard U. (incl. Fogg Art Museum)
Havana/Nacional. Museo Nacional, Havana, Cuba
Hayden Stone Inc.
Le Havre/Municipal. Musée Municipal, Le Havre, France (*see also* Musée du Havre)
Hawaii State Foundation
U. of Hawaii
Health and Hospital Corp., NYC
Hebron Academy, Hebron, Me.
Heckscher Museum—*see* Huntington, N.Y./Heckscher
H.J. Heinz Co., Pittsburgh, Pa.
Hellerup Commune, Copenhagen, Denmark
Helsinki. Ateneumin Taidemuseo, Helsinki, Finland
Hemisphere Club, NYC
Hempstead Bank, Hempstead, N.Y.
Henies-Onstadts Stiftelser, Hovikodden, Norway
John Herron Art Institute—*see* Indianapolis/Herron
Hershey Foods Corp.
Christian Herter Center, Boston, Mass.

Hessisches Landesmuseum, Darmstadt—*see* Darmstadt/Hessisches
The Hertz Corp.
Hickory, N.C. Hickory Museum of Art, Hickory, N.C.
High Museum of Art, Atlanta, Ga.
Hiroshima State Museum of Art (Japan)
Hirshhorn. The Hirshhorn Museum and Sculpture Garden, Smithsonian Institution, Washington, D.C.
Historical Society of Montana, Helena, Mont.
Hoffmann-La Roche Inc.
Hofstra U.
Hollins College
Holyoke Public Library, Holyoke, Mass.
Home Savings and Loan Association, Los Angeles, Calif.
Honolulu Academy of Arts, Honolulu, Hawaii. **Honolulu Academy School**
Hope College, Holland, Mich.
Hopkins Art Center—*see* Dartmouth College
Hospital Corp. of America
Hotel Corp. of America, NYC
Housatonic Community College, Stratford, Conn.
Houston/Contemporary. Contemporary Arts Museum, Houston, Tex.
Houston/MFA. Museum of Fine Arts of Houston, Texas. **Houston Museum School**
U. of Houston
Howard College
Howard U.
J.L. Hudson Co.
Hudson River Museum, Yonkers, N.Y.
Humlebaek/Louisiana. Louisiana Museum of Art, Humlebaek, Denmark
Hunt Foods & Industries
Hunter College of the City University of New York
Hunter Museum of Art—*see* Chattanooga/Hunter
Huntington, N.Y./Heckscher. Heckscher Museum, Huntington, N.Y.
Huntington, W. Va. Huntington Galleries, Huntington, W. Va.
Huntsville Museum of Art, Huntsville, Ala.
Hyde Collection, Glens Falls, N.Y.

I

IBM. International Business Machines
ICA, Boston. Institute of Contemporary Art, Boston, Mass.
ICA, U. of Pennsylvania. Institute of Contemporary Art, U. of Pennsylvania
ICA, Washington, D.C. Institute of Contemporary Arts, Washington, D.C.
IIE. International Institute of Education
ILGWU. International Ladies' Garment Workers Union
Idaho, College of
Idemitsu Museum, Tokyo, Japan
Illinois Bell Telephone Company
Illinois State Museum of Natural History and Art—*see* Springfield, Ill./State
Illinois State Normal U.
U. of Illinois (incl. Krannert Art Museum)
Illinois Wesleyan U.
Immaculate Heart College, Los Angeles, Calif.
Imperial Household, Tokyo, Japan
Indian Head Mills, Inc.
Indiana National Bank, Indianapolis, Ind.
Indiana State U. (formerly **College),** Terre Haute, Ind.
Indiana (Pa.) State Teachers College
Indiana U.
Indianapolis/Herron. John Herron Art Institute, Indianapolis, Ind.
Indianapolis Museum of Art, Indianapolis, Ind.
Industrial Electronics Engineers, Inc.
Industrial Museum, Barcelona, Spain
Inland Steel Co.
Inmont Corporation
Institut fur Moderne Kunst Nurnberg (Germany)
Institute of Contemporary Art(s)—*see* ICA, various cities
Institute of International Education—*see* I I E
Institute for Policy Studies, Washington, D.C.
Interchemical Corporation
Interchurch Center, NYC
International Institute for Aesthetic Research, Turin, Italy

International Minerals & Chemicals Corp.
International Monetary Fund, Washington, D.C.
International Nickel Co.
International Museum of Photography at George Eastman House, Rochester, N.Y.
Iowa Arts Council, Des Moines, Iowa
Iowa State Education Association, Des Moines, Iowa
Iowa State Fair, Des Moines, Iowa
Iowa State Teachers College
Iowa State U. of Science and Technology
U. of Iowa
Iowa Wesleyan College
Ithaca College
Ivest-Wellington Corp.

J

Jacksonville/AM. Jacksonville Art Museum, Jacksonville, Fla.
Jacksonville/Cummer. Cummer Gallery of Art, Jacksonville, Fla.
Jacksonville U.
Jamestown/Prendergast. James Prendergast Free Library Art Gallery, Jamestown, N.Y.
Japanese Craft Museum, Tokyo, Japan
Jay Mfg. Co.
Jerusalem/National. National Museum, Jerusalem, Israel
Jesus College (Cambridge U.), Cambridge, England
Jewish Museum, NYC
Jewish Theological Seminary of America
Johannesburg/Municipal. Municipal Art Gallery, Johannesburg, South Africa
Johns Hopkins U.
Johnson College
Herbert F. Johnson Museum—*see* Cornell U.
Lyndon B. Johnson Library, Austin, Texas
Johnson Publishing Co., Chicago, Ill.
S. C. Johnson & Son. Inc.—*see* NCFA
Johnson Wax Co.
J. Turner Jones, Inc.

Jones & Laughlin Steel Corp.
Joslyn Art Museum—*see* Omaha/Joslyn
James Joyce Museum, Dublin, Ireland
Julliard School, The, NYC

K
Kaiserslautern Museum, Kaiserslautern, Germany
Kalamazoo College
Kalamazoo/Institute. The Kalamazoo Institute of Arts, Kalamazoo, Mich. (incl. Kalamazoo Art Center)
Kamakura. Modern Art Museum of Kanagawa Prefecture, Kamakura, Japan
Kansas City/AI. Kansas City Art Institute and School of Design, Kansas City, Mo.
Kansas City/Nelson. William Rockhill Nelson Gallery of Art, Kansas City, Mo.
U. of Kansas City
Kansas State College
U. of Kansas
Karachi. Art Council of Pakistan, Karachi, Pakistan
Karamu House, Cleveland, Ohio
Karlsruhe. Staatliche Kunsthalle, Karlsruhe, Germany
Kassel. Stadtische Kunstsammlungen, Kassel, Germany
Kemper Insurance Co.
Kennedy Library, Cambridge, Mass.
Kent State U.
Kentucky Southern College, Louisville, Ky.
U. of Kentucky
Kenyon College
Kestner-Museum, Hannover, Germany (*see also* Hannover/K-G.)
Kingsborough Community College
Kirkland College, Clinton, N.Y.
Knox College, Galesburg, Ill.
Kolnisher Kunstverein, Cologne—*see* Cologne/Kunstverein
Krakow/National. National Museum, Krakow, Poland
Krannert Art Museum—*see* U. of Illinois
Krefeld/Haus Lange. Museum Haus Lange Wilhelmshofallee, Krefeld, Germany

Krefeld/Kaiser Wilhelm. Kaiser Wilhelm Museum, Krefeld, Germany
Kresge Art Center—*see* Michigan State U.
Kultusministerium, Hannover, Germany
Kultusministerium Baden-Wurttemberg, Stuttgart, Germany
Kunsthalle, Basel, Basel, Switzerland
Kunstkredit, Basel, Switzerland
Kunstverein in Hamburg—*see* Hamburg/Kunstverein
Kunstverein Hannover—*see* Hannover/Kunstverein
Kupferstichkabinett, Berlin, Germany
Kutztown State College
Kyoto National Museum of Modern Art, Kyoto, Japan

L
La France Art Institute, Philadelphia, Pa.
Laguna Beach Museum of Art, Laguna Beach, Calif.
La Jolla. Museum of Art (formerly Art Center in La Jolla, La Jolla, Calif.)
Lakeview Center for Arts and Sciences, Peoria, Ill.
The Lamont Art Gallery—*see* Exeter
Lane Foundation, Leominster, Mass.
Lannan Foundation, NYC/Palm Beach, Fla./Chicago, Ill.
Lansing Sound Corp.
La Plata. Museo de La Plata, Argentina
H. E. Laufer Co.
Lawrence College
Layton School of Art, Milwaukee, Wisc.
League of Nations, Geneva, Switzerland
Lehigh U.
Lehman Bros, NYC
Leicester Education Committee, London, England
Leipzig, Museum der Bildenden Kunste, Leipzig, Germany
Lembke Construction Co.
Lenox School, Lenox, Mass.
Leverkusen. Stadtisches Museum, Leverkusen, Germany

Levin Townsend Computer Corp.
Lewiston (Me.) Public Library
Liaison Films, Inc.
Library of Congress, Washington, D.C.
Liege. Musée des Beaux-Arts, Liege, Belgium
Lille. Palais des Beaux-Arts, Lille, France
Eli Lilly & Co.
Lima, Peru. Instituto de Arte Contemporaneo, Lima, Peru
Lincoln, Mass./De Cordova. De Cordova and Dana Museum, Lincoln, Mass.
Lincoln Center for the Performing Arts, NYC
Lincoln Life Insurance Co.
Lindenwood College
Linz. Oberösterreichisches Landesmuseum, Linz, Austria
Lipschultz Foundation
Little Rock/MFA. Museum of Fine Arts, Little Rock, Ark.
Litton Industries
Liverpool/Walker. Walker Art Gallery, Liverpool, England
Loch Haven Art Center, Orlando, Fla. (see also Orlando)
Lodz. Muzeum Sztuki w Lodzi, Lodz, Poland
London Film Society
Long Beach/MA. Long Beach Museum of Art, Long Beach, Calif.
Long Beach State College
Long Island U.
Longview Foundation
Longwood College
Los Angeles County Fair Association, Los Angeles, Calif.
Los Angeles/County MA. Los Angeles County Museum of Art, Los Angeles, Calif.
Los Angeles Public Library, Los Angeles, Calif.
Los Angeles State College, Los Angeles, Calif.
Lotus Club, NYC
Louisiana Museum of Art, Denmark— see Hummlebaek/Louisiana
Louisiana State U. and Agricultural and Mechanical College
Louisville/Speed. J. B. Speed Art Museum, Louisville, Ky.

U. of Louisville
The Joe and Emily Lowe Art Gallery— see U. of Miami
The Joe and Emily Lowe Foundation, NYC
Lucerne. Kunstmuseum Luzern, Lucerne, Switzerland
Lugano. Museo Civico di Belle Arti, Lugano, Switzerland
Lummis Tower Building, Houston, Texas
Luther College
Lynchburg Art Gallery—see Randolph-Macon Woman's College
Lytton Savings and Loan Association

M

MIT. Massachusetts Institute of Technology, Cambridge, Mass.
MMA. The Metropolitan Museum of Art, NYC
MOMA. The Museum of Modern Art, NYC. MOMA School
Norman MacKenzie Art Gallery—see Regina/MacKenzie
MacMurray College
MacNider Museum, Mason City, Iowa
Macomb County Community College, Warren, Mich.
R. H. Macy & Co.
Madison Art Center, Madison, Wisc.
Madison College
Madison Square Garden, NYC
Madrid/Nacional. Museo Nacional de Arte Contemporaneo, Madrid, Spain
Maeght—see Foundation Maeght
Maine State Museum—see Augusta Me./State
U. of Maine
Malmo Museum, Malmo, Sweden
Manchester, England. City of Manchester Art Galleries, Manchester, England
Manila. Ateneo de Manila, P.I.
Mannheim. Stadtische Kunsthalle, Mannheim, Germany
Mansfield State College
Mansion House Project, St. Louis, Mo.
Manufacturers Hanover Trust Co.
Manufacturers and Traders Trust Co., Buffalo, N.Y.
Marbach Galerie, Berne, Switzerland

Marin Art and Garden Center, Ross, Calif.

Marine Midland Bank and Trust Co.

Marist College, Poughkeepsie, N.Y.

Mark Twain Bankshares, St. Louis, Mo.

Mark Twain South County Bank, St. Louis, Mo.

Marquette U.

Marshall Field & Co.

Marshall U.

Martha Washington U.

U. of Maryland

Maryhurst College

Mary Washington College of the U. of Virginia

U. of Massachusetts

Massillon Museum, Massillon, Ohio

McCormick Place-on-the-Lake, Chicago, Ill.

McCann-Erickson, Inc.

McCrory Corporation

McDonald & Company

McDonnell & Co., Inc.

Marion Koogler McNay Art Institute— *see* San Antonio/McNay

Mattatuck Historical Society Museum, Waterbury, Conn.

Mead Corporation

Mechanics National Bank, Worcester, Mass.

Melbourne/National. National Gallery of Victoria, Melbourne (Victoria), Australia

Memphis/Brooks. Brooks Memorial Art Gallery, Memphis, Tenn.

Memphis State U.

Mendoza. Museo de Historia Natural, Mendoza, Argentina

Mestrovic Gallery, Split, Yugoslavia

Mestrovic Museum, Zagreb, Yugoslavia

Metalcraft Corp.

Meta-Mold Aluminum Co.

The Metropolitan Museum of Art, NYC—*see* MMA

Mexico City/Nacional. Museo Nacional de Arte Moderno, Mexico City, Mexico

Miami-Dade Junior College

Miami/Modern. Miami Museum of Modern Art, Miami, Fla.

U. of Miami (incl. The Joe and Emily Lowe Art Gallery)

James A. Michener Foundation—*see* U. of Texas

Michigan Consolidated Gas. Co.

Michigan State U. (incl. Kresge Art Center)

U. of Michigan

Middlebury College, Middlebury, Vt.

Middle Tennessee State U.

Milan. Civica Galleria d'Arte Moderna, Milan, Italy

Miles College, Birmingham, Ala.

Miles Laboratories Inc.

Miles Metal Corp., NYC

The Miller Co.

Millikin U.

Mills College

Mills College of Education

Milton Academy, Milton, Mass.

Milwaukee. Milwaukee Art Center, Milwaukee, Wisc.

Milwaukee-Downer College

Milwaukee Journal

Minneapolis College of Art & Design

Minneapolis/Institute. Minneapolis Institute of Arts, Minneapolis, Minn.

Minneapolis Institute School

Minnesota/MA. Minnesota Museum of Art, St. Paul, Minn.

Minnesota State Historical Society, St. Paul, Minn.

U. of Minnesota (Duluth campus, incl. Tweed Gallery)

Mint Museum of Art—*see* Charlotte/Mint

U. of Missouri

Mitsui Bank of Japan

Mobil Oil Co.

Moderna Museet—*see* Stockholm/National

Monchengladbach. Stadtisches Museum, Monchengladbach, Germany

Mons. Musée des Beaux-Arts, Mons, Belgium

Montana State College

Montana State U.

U. of Montana

Montclair/AM. Montclair Art Museum, Montclair, N.J.

Montclair State College

Montevideo/Municipal. Museo Municipal de Bellas Artes, Montevideo, Uruguay

Montgomery Museum of Fine Art, Montgomery, Ala.
Montpelier/Wood. Thomas W. Wood Art Gallery, Montpelier, Vt.
Montreal/Contemporain. Musée d'Art Contemporain, Montreal (Que.), Canada
Montreal/MFA. Montreal Museum of Fine Arts, Montreal (Que.), Canada
Montreal Trust Co.
Moorpark College, Moorpark, Calif.
Moravian College, Bethlehem, Pa.
The Morgan Library, NYC
Morgan State College
Moriarty Brothers, Manchester, Conn.
Morristown/Junior. Morris Junior Museum, Morristown, N.J.
Moscow/Western. Museum of Western Art, Moscow, USSR
Mount Holyoke College
Mt. Vernon High School, Mt. Vernon, Wash.
Muckenthaler Cultural Center, Fullerton, Calif.
Muhlenberg College
Mulvane Art Museum—*see* Washburn U. of Topeka
Munich/Modern. Modern Art Museum, Munich, Germany
Munich/SG. Stadtische Galerie, Munich, Germany
Munich/State. Munchner Stadtmuseum, Munich, Germany
Municipal U. of Omaha
Munson-Williams-Proctor Institute—*see* Utica
Munster. Landesmuseum fur Kunst und Kulturgeschichte, Munster, Germany
Munster/WK. Westfalischer Kunstverein, Munster, Germany
Murray State U., Murray, Kentucky
Musée d'Art Contemporain, Montreal—*see* Montreal/Contemporain
Musée des Arts Decoratifs, Paris, France
Musée Cantonal des Beaux-Arts, Lausanne, Switzerland
Musée Guimet, Paris, France
Musée du Havre, Le Havre, France (*see* also Le Havre/Municipal)
Musée du Jeu de Paume, Paris, France
Musée Municipal, Brest, France

Musée de Quebec—*see* Quebec
Musée de Verviers, Verviers, Belgium
Musée du Vin, Pauillac (Gironde), France
Museo de Arte Contemporaneo, Caracas—*see* Caracas/Contemporaneo
Museo de Arte Contemporaneo "La Tertulia," Cali, Colombia
Museo de Arte Contemporaneo R. Tamayo, Mexico City, Mexico
Museo de Arte Moderno, Barcelona—*see* Barcelona
Museo de Arte Moderno, Bogota, Colombia
Museo de Arte Moderno, Buenos Aires—*see* Buenos Aires/Moderno
Museo Dr. Genaro Perez, Cordoba, Argentina
Museo Emilio A. Caraffa, Cordoba, Argentina
Museo Juan B. Castagnino, Rosario, Argentina
Museo Municipal de Bellas Artes, Montevideo—*see* Montevideo/Municipal
Museo Municipal de Bellas Artes y Arte Nacional, Buenos Aires—*see* Buenos Aires/Municipal
Museo Nacional de Bellas Artes, Buenos Aires—*see* Argentina/Nacional
Museo Nacional de Bellas Artes, Montevideo—*see* Uruguay/Nacional
Museo Nacional de Historia, Mexico City, Mexico
Museo Provincial de Bellas Artes, Bilbao, Spain
Museo Provincial de Bellas Artes, Vitoria, Spain
Museo Rosario, Santa Fe, Argentina
Museu de Arte Contemporanea, Sao Paulo—*see* Sao Paulo/Contemporanea
Museum der Stadt Leoben, Leoben, Austria
Museum of the City of New York
Museum of Contemporary Crafts, NYC
Museum of Living Art—*see* PMA
Museum of Military History, Washington, D.C.
Museum of Modern Art, Haifa—*see* Haifa
The Museum of Modern Art, NYC—*see* MOMA

Museum of Modern Art, Skopje—*see* Skopje/Modern

Museum of New Mexico Art Gallery— *see* Santa Fe, N.M.

Museum Schloss Marburg. Leverkusen, Germany

Museum of Science and Industry, Chicago, Ill.

Museum des 20. Jahrhunderts, Vienna, Austria

Muskegon/Hackley. Hackley Art Center, Muskegon, Mich.

Mutual Life Insurance Building, Chicago, Ill.

N

NAACP. National Association for the Advancement of Colored People

NAD. The National Academy of Design, NYC

NCFA. National Collection of Fine Arts, Washington, D.C.

NIAL. National Institute of Arts and Letters, NYC

NPG. National Portrait Gallery, Washington, D.C.

NYPL. The New York Public Library, NYC

NYU. New York University

Nagaoka City Hall, Nagaoka, Japan

Nagaoka, Japan. Museum of Contemporary Art, Nagaoka, Japan

Nantucket. Artists' Association of Nantucket, Nantucket, Mass.

The Naropa Institute, Boulder, Col.

Nashville. Tennessee Fine Arts Center, Nashville, Tenn.

Nassau County Museum, Syosset, N.Y.

The National Academy of Design—*see* NAD

National Academy of Sciences, Washington, D.C.

National Arts Foundation, NYC

National Bank of Des Moines

National Economics Research Association

National Gallery of Canada—*see* Ottawa/National

National Gallery, Reykjavik—*see* Reykjavik

National Gallery of Scotland—*see* Edinburgh/National

National Gallery, Washington, D.C. (incl. Rosenwald Collection)

National Institute of Arts and Letters— *see* NIAL

National Life Insurance Co

National Museum, Athens—*see* Greece/ National

National Museum, Jerusalem—*see* Jerusalem/National

National Museum, Sofia—*see* Sofia

National Museum of Wales, Cardiff, Wales

National Museum of Western Art, Tokyo, Japan

National Orange Show, San Bernadino, Calif.

National Portrait Gallery—*see* NPG

National U.—*see* George Washington U.

Nebraska State Teachers College

U. of Nebraska (incl. Sheldon Memorial Art Gallery)

Needham Harper & Steers Inc.

Neenah/Bergstrom. John Nelson Bergstrom Art Center and Museum, Neenah, Wisc.

Neiman-Marcus Co.

William Rockhill Nelson Gallery of Art—*see* Kansas City/Nelson

Netherlands Film Museum, Amsterdam, Holland

Neue Galerie, Essen—*see* Essen/NG

U. of Nevada

Newark Museum, Newark, N.J.

Newark Public Library, Newark, N.J.

Newberry Library, Chicago, Ill.

New Britain. Art Museum of the New Britain Institute, New Britain, Conn.

New Britain/American. New Britain Museum of American Art, New Britain, Conn.

New Brunswick Museum—*see* St. John, N.B.

New College, Sarasota, Fla.

New England Merchants National Bank, Boston

U. of New Hampshire (incl. Paul Creative Arts Center)

The New Harmony Gallery of Contemporary Art, New Harmony, Ind.

New Haven Public Library, New Haven, Conn.

New Jersey State Cultural Center, Trenton, N.J.

New Jersey State Museum—see Trenton/State

New London. Lyman Allyn Museum, New London, Conn.

New Mexico State U.

U. of New Mexico

New Orleans/Delgado. Isaac Delgado Museum of Art, New Orleans, La.

New Orleans Museum of Art, New Orleans, La.

New Paltz/SUNY. State University of New York, at New Paltz

Newport Harbor. Newport Harbor Art Museum, Newport Beach, Calif.

New School for Social Research, NYC

Newsweek Magazine

New Trier High School, Winnetka, Ill.

The New York Bank for Savings, NYC

New York Coliseum, NYC

New York Cultural Center (formerly Gallery of Modern Art, NYC)

New York Hilton Hotel

New York Hospital, NYC

The New York Public Library—see NYPL

New York School of Interior Design

New York State Art Commission, Albany, N.Y.

New York State Health and Hospitals Corp.

New York State Museum, Albany, N.Y.

New York, State University of—see under names of individual campuses

The New York Times

New York University—see NYU

Niigata Museum, Japan

Norfolk. Norfolk Museum of Arts and Sciences, Norfolk, Va.

Norfolk/Chrysler. Walter P. Chrysler Museum of Art, Norfolk, Va.

North Carolina Museum of Art—see Raleigh/NCMA

North Carolina National Bank

North Carolina/State. North Carolina State Museum, Raleigh, N.C. (see also Raleigh/NCMA)

North Carolina State U.

U. of North Carolina (incl. Weatherspoon Art Gallery of The Women's College at Greensboro)

North Central Bronx Hospital, Bronx, N.Y.

U. of North Dakota

Northeast Missouri State Teachers College

Northern Illinois U.—see DeKalb

U. of Northern Iowa

Northern Trust Co., Chicago, Ill.

Northland College

North Shore State Bank, Milwaukee, Wisc.

North Texas State U.

Northwest Missouri State College

Northwestern National Life Insurance Co.

Northwestern U.

Northwood Institute, Dallas, Tex.

Norton Gallery and School of Art—see West Palm Beach/Norton

U. of Notre Dame

Nurnberg. Stadtische Kunstsammlungen, Nurnberg, Germany

O

OBD/Basel. Offentliche Basler Denkmalpflege, Basel, Switzerland

Oak Cliff Savings and Loan, Dallas, Tex.

Oakland/AM. Oakland Art Museum, Oakland, Calif.

Oakland Public Library, Oakland, Calif.

Oberlin College (incl. Allen Memorial Art Museum)

Ogunquit. Museum of Art of Ogunquit, Me.

Ohara Art Museum, Kurashiki, Japan

The Ohio Company, Columbus, Ohio

The Ohio State U.

Ohio Wesleyan U.

Ohio U.

Oklahoma. Oklahoma Art Center, Oklahoma City, Okla.

Oklahoma City U.

Oklahoma State Art Collection

U. of Oklahoma

Oldenburg. Oldenburger Stadtmuseum, Oldenburg, Germany

Olivet College

The Olsen Foundation Inc., New Haven, Conn.

Olympia/Washington State Capital Museum, Olympia, Wash.

Omaha/Joslyn. Joslyn Art Museum, Omaha, Neb.

The 180 Beacon Collection of Contemporary Art, Boston, Mass.

The Art Gallery of Ontario, Toronto, Ontario, Canada

Oran. Musée Demaeght, Oran, Algeria

Orange Coast College, Costa Mesa, Calif.

Oregon State U.

U. of Oregon

Orlando. Central Florida Museum, Orlando, Fla. *(see also* Loch Haven Art Center)

Osaka/Municipal. Osaka Municipal Art Museum, Osaka, Japan

Oslo/National. Nasjonalgalleriet, Oslo, Norway

Oswego/SUNY. State University of New York, at Oswego

Otis Art Institute, Los Angeles, Calif.

Ottawa/National. National Gallery of Canada, Ottawa, Canada

Otterbein College

Outre-Mer—*see* Paris/Outre-Mer

Owens-Corning Fiberglas Corp.

Oxford, University of, Oxford, England

Oxford/MOMA. Museum of Modern Art, Oxford, England

P

PAFA. The Pennsylvania Academy of the Fine Arts, Philadelphia, Pa.

PCA. Print Council of America, NYC

PMA. The Philadelphia Museum of Art, Philadelphia, Pa. (incl. the Museum of Living Art, the Academy of Natural Sciences, and the Rodin Museum)

Philadelphia College of Art (formerly the **Philadelphia Museum School)**

P.S. 144, NYC

Pacific, University of the

Pacific Indemnity Co.

Palais des Beaux-Arts, Brussels—*see* Brussels/Beaux-Arts

Palm Beach—*see* Society of the Four Arts

Palm Beach Company, NYC

Palm Springs Desert Museum, Palm Springs, Calif.

Palomar College, San Marcos, Calif.

Palos Verdes. Palos Verdes Art Gallery, Palos Verdes, Calif. **Palos Verdes Community Arts Association**

Paris/Beaubourg. Centre National d'Art et de Culture Georges Pompidou (Centre Beaubourg), Paris, France

Paris/Moderne. Musée d'Art Moderne de la Ville de Paris, Paris, France (see also France/National)

Paris/Outre-Mer. Musée de la France d'Outre-Mer, Paris, France

Park College

Parkersburg Art Center, Parkersburg, W. Va.

The Parrish Museum—*see* Southampton/Parrish

Pasadena/AM. The Pasadena Art Museum, Pasadena, Calif. **Pasadena Museum School**

Paul Creative Arts Center—*see* U. of New Hampshire

Peabody College, Memphis, Tenn.

Peabody Institute of the City of Baltimore

Peabody Museum, Salem, Mass.

Pendleton High School, Pendleton, Ore.

William Penn Memorial Museum—*see* Harrisburg, Pa./State Museum

The Pennsylvania Academy of the Fine Arts—*see* PAFA

The Pennsylvania State U.

U. of Pennsylvania

J. C. Penney Corp.

Pensacola. Pensacola Art Center, Pensacola, Fla.

The Pentagon, Washington, D.C.

Pepsi-Cola Co.

Philadelphia Art Alliance, Philadelphia, Pa.

The Philadelphia Museum of Art—*see* PMA

Philadelphia Zoological Gardens

Philbrook Art Center—*see* Tulsa/Philbrook

Philip Morris Collection, NYC

Phillips. The Phillips Gallery, Washington, D.C. **The Phillips Gallery School**

Phillips Academy, Addison Gallery of American Art—*see* Andover/Phillips

Phillips Exeter Academy, The Lamont Art Gallery—*see* Exeter

Phoenix. Phoenix Art Museum, Phoenix, Ariz.

Pinacotheca Museum, Osaka, Japan

Pinacotheque National Museum, Athens, Greece

Pinakothiki. Athens, Greece

Pioneer Aerodynamic Systems

Pittsfield/Berkshire. Berkshire Atheneum, Pittsfield, Mass.

Pitzer College

Pomona College

Ponce. Ponce Museum of Art, Ponce, Puerto Rico

Poole Technical College, Dorset, England

Port Authority of New York & New Jersey

Port Washington, L.I., Library Gallery, Port Washington, L.I., N.Y.

Portland, Me./MA. Portland Museum of Art, Portland, Me.

Portland Ore./AM. Portland Art Museum, Portland, Ore. **Portland (Ore.) Museum School**

Portland State College (Ore.)

Potsdam/SUNY. State University of New York, at Potsdam

Power Gallery of Contemporary Art—*see* U. of Sydney

Prague/National. Norodni (National) Galerie, Prague, Czechoslovakia

Pratt Institute

Prendergast Free Library Art Gallery—*see* Jamestown/Prendergast

Prentice-Hall Inc.

Princeton Print Club, Princeton, N.J.

Princeton U.

The Print Club, Philadelphia, Pa.

Print Club of Rochester, Rochester, N.Y.

Print Council of America—*see* PCA

Pro-Civitate-Christiana, Assisi, Italy

Provincetown/Chrysler—*see* Norfolk/Chrysler

Prudential Insurance Co. of America, Newark, N.J.

Prudential Lines Inc.

Publishers Printing Co.

U. of Puerto Rico

Purchase/SUNY. State University of New York, at Purchase (incl. The Neuberger Museum)

Purdue U.

The Pure Oil Co.

Q

Quaker Oats Co.

Quaker Ridge School, Scarsdale, N.Y.

Quebec. Musée de Quebec (Que.), Canada

Queens College of the City University of New York

Queens U., Kingston (Ont.), Canada

Quimica Argentia, Buenos Aires, Argentina

R

RAC. Richmond Art Center, Richmond, Calif.

RISD. Rhode Island School of Design

Radcliffe College, Cambridge, Mass.

Radio Corporation of America

Raleigh/NCMA. North Carolina Museum of Art, Raleigh, N.C. (*see also* North Carolina/State)

Randolph-Macon College

Randolph-Macon Woman's College (incl. Lynchburg Art Gallery)

Ration Mfg. Co.

Raycom Industries

Reader's Digest

Reading/Public. Reading Public Museum and Art Gallery, Reading, Pa.

Recklinghausen. Stadtische Kunsthalle, Recklinghausen, Germany

U. of Redlands

Red Wing. Interstate Clinic, Red Wing, Minn.

Reed College

Regina/MacKenzie. Norman Mackenzie Art Gallery, Regina (Sask.), Canada

Remington-Rand Corp.

Renaissance Society—*see* The U. of Chicago

Renault & Cie, Paris, France

Rennes. Musée des Beaux-Arts (of the Musée de Rennes), Rennes, France

Rensselaer Polytechnic Institute

Revere Copper & Brass, Inc.

Revlon Inc.

Reykjavik. National Gallery, Reykjavik, Iceland

Reynolds Metals Co.

Rhode Island School of Design—*see* RISD

U. of Rhode Island

Rice U., Houston, Tex.

Rich-Lan Corp.

Richmond (Calif.) Art Center—*see* RAC

Ridgefield/Aldrich. Larry Aldrich Museum of Contemporary Art, Ridgefield, Conn.

Rijksmuseum Amsterdam, Amsterdam, Holland

Rijksmuseum Kroller-Muller, Otterlo, Holland

Ringling. John and Mable Ringling Museum of Art, Sarasota, Fla. **Ringling School of Art**

Rio Cuarto. Museo Municipal de Bellas Artes, Rio Cuarto, Argentina

Rio Hondo College, Whittier, Calif.

Rio de Janeiro. Museu de Arte Moderna, Rio de Janeiro, Brazil

Ripon College

Riverside Museum, NYC—*see* Brandeis U.

Roanoke Fine Arts Center, Roanoke, Va.

Sara Roby Foundation, NYC

Rochester Institute of Technology, Rochester, N.Y.

U. of Rochester (incl. Rochester Memorial Art Gallery)

Rockefeller Brothers Fund, NYC

Rockefeller Center, NYC

Rockefeller Institute—*see* Rockefeller U.

Rockefeller U., NYC

Rockford/Burpee. Harry and Della Burpee Gallery, Rockford, Ill.

Rockland/Farnsworth. William A. Farnsworth Library and Art Museum, Rockland, Me.

Rock River (Wyo.) High School

Rodin Museum, Philadelphia—*see* PMA

Nicholas Roerich Museum, NYC

Will Rogers Shrine, Colorado Springs, Colo.

Rohan, Chateau de—*see* Chateau de Rohan

Rome/Nazionale. Galleria Nazionale d'Arte Moderno, Rome, Italy

U. of Rome, Rome, Italy

Edward Root Collection—*see* Utica

Rose Art Museum—*see* Brandeis U.

Rosenthal China Co.

Rosenwald Collection—*see* National Gallery, Washington, D.C.

Roswell. Roswell Museum and Art Center, Roswell, N.M.

Rotterdam. Museum Boymans-van Beuningen, Rotterdam, Holland

Rouen. Musée des Beaux-Arts et de Ceramique, Rouen, France

Rumsey Hall School, Washington, Conn.

Russell Sage College

Rutgers U.

Rybak. Ryback Art Museum, Bat Yam, Israel

S

SAGA. The Society of American Graphic Artists, NYC

SFAI. San Francisco Art Institute, San Francisco, Calif.

SFMA. San Francisco Museum of Art, San Francisco, Calif.

SFPL. San Francisco Public Library, San Francisco, Calif.

SRGM. The Solomon R. Guggenheim Museum, NYC

Saarlandmuseum, Saarbrucken, Germany

Sacramento/Crocker. E.B. Crocker Art Gallery, Sacramento, Calif.

Sacramento State U. (formerly **College**)

Sacred Heart Seminary, Detroit, Mich.

Safad. Glicenstein Museum, Safad, Israel

Safeco Building

Saginaw Art Museum, Saginaw, Mich.

St. Albans School, Washington, D.C.

St. Anthony's College (Oxford U.), Oxford, England

St. Benedict, College of—*see* College of St. Benedict

St. Bernard's Church, Hazardville, Conn.

St. Cloud State College

St.-Etienne. Musée Municipal d'Art et d'Industrie, St.-Etienne, France

St. George's Episcopal Church, NYC

St. John, N.B. New Brunswick Museum, St. John (N.B.), Canada

St. John's Abbey, Collegeville, Minn.

St. Joseph/Albrecht. Albrecht Gallery Museum of Art, St. Joseph, Mo.

St. Lawrence U. (incl. Griffiths Art Center)

St. Louis/City. The City Art Museum of St. Louis, Mo.

St. Mary's College (Ind.)

St. Patrick's, Menasha, Wisc.

St. Paul Gallery and School of Art—*see* Minnesota/MA

St. Petersburg, Fla. Art Club of St. Petersburg, Fla.

U. of St. Thomas (Tex.)

Salk Institute, La Jolla, Calif.

Salt Lake City Public Library, Salt Lake City, Utah

Salzburg. Salzburger Museum Carolino Augusteum, Salzburg, Austria

San Antonio/McNay. Marion Koogler McNay Art Institute, San Antonio, Tex.

Carl Sandburg Memorial Library, S.C.

San Diego. The Fine Arts Gallery of San Diego, Calif. **San Diego Fine Arts School**

San Fernando Valley State U.

San Francisco Art Association—*see* SFAI

San Francisco Municipal Art Commission, San Francisco, Calif.

San Francisco Museum of Art—*see* SFMA

San Francisco Public Library—*see* SFPL

San Francisco State College

San Joaquin Pioneer Museum and Haggin Art Galleries—*see* Stockton

San Jose Library, San Jose, Calif.

San Jose Museum of Art, San Jose, Calif.

San Jose State College

San Salvador Museo Nacional, San Salvador, El Salvador

Santa Barbara/MA. Santa Barbara Museum of Art, Santa Barbara, Calif. **Santa Barbara Museum School**

Santa Fe, N.M. Museum of New Mexico Art Gallery, Santa Fe, N.M.

Santiago, Chile. Museo Nacional de Bellas Artes, Santiago, Chile

Sao Paulo. Museu de Arte Moderna, Sao Paulo, Brazil

Sao Paulo/Contemporanea. Museu de Arte Contemporanea, Sao Paulo, Brazil

Sarah Lawrence College

U. of Saskatchewan, Saskatoon (Sask.), Canada

City of Saskatoon (Sask.), Canada

Savannah/Telfair. Telfair Academy of Arts and Sciences, Inc., Savannah, Ga.

Savings Bank Association of New York State

Schaeffer School of Design, San Francisco, Calif.

The Schenectady Museum. Schenectady, N.Y.

Michael Schiavone & Sons Inc., North Haven, Conn.

Schiedam/Stedelijk. Stedelijk Museum, Schiedam, Holland

J. Henry Schroder Banking Corp.

Schwebber Electronics

Scientific American Inc.

Scottish National Gallery of Modern Art, Edinburgh—*see* Edinburgh/Modern

Scovill Mfg. Co.

Scranton/Everhart. Everhart Museum, Scranton, Pa.

Scripps College

Seagram Collection

Seaton Hall Inc., NYC

Seattle/AM. Seattle Art Museum, Seattle, Wash.

Seattle Civic Center, Seattle, Wash.

Seattle Public Library, Seattle, Wash.

Seattle U.

Security Pacific National Bank, Los Angeles, Calif.

Seibu Museum of Art, Tokyo, Japan

Shasta College, Redding, Calif.

Shelburne. Shelburne Museum Inc., Shelburne, Vt.

Sheldon Memorial Art Gallery—*see* U. of Nebraska

Shell Oil Co.

E. Sherry Truck Company

Shuttleworth Carton Co.

Silvermine Guild of Artists, New Canaan, Conn. **Silvermine Guild School of Art**

Simmons College
Norton Simon Museum, Pasadena, Calif.
The Singer Company Inc.
Sioux City Art Center, Sioux City, Iowa
Skidmore College
Skidmore, Owings & Merrill
Skopje/Modern. Museum of Modern Art, Skopje, Yugoslavia
Skowhegan School of Painting and Sculpture, Skowhegan, Me.
Slater Memorial Museum, Norwich, Conn.
W. & J. Sloane, Inc.
Smith College
Smithsonian Institution, Washington, D.C.
Societe National des Arts Contemporains, Paris, France
The Society of American Graphic Artists—*see* SAGA
Society of the Four Arts, Palm Beach, Fla.
Society of New York Hospitals
Sofia. National Museum, Sofia, Bulgaria
Sofu School of Flower Arrangement, Tokyo, Japan
Southampton/Parrish. The Parrish Museum, Southampton, N.Y.
South County Bank, St. Louis, Mo.
Southeast Banking Corp. Miami, Fla.
U. of Southern California
Southern Idaho College, Twin Falls, Idaho
Southern Illinois U.
Southern Methodist U.
Southern Oregon College
Southern Vermont Art Center, Manchester, Vt.
U. of South Florida
South Mall, Albany, Albany, N.Y.
Southwestern College, Chula Vista, Calif.
Southwestern (College) at Memphis
Southwest Missouri State College
J.B. Speed Art Museum—*see* Louisville/ Speed
Spelman College
Spokane Coliseum, Spokane, Wash.
Sports Museum, NYC
Springfield Art Center, Springfield, Ohio

Springfield College (Mass.)
Springfield, Ill./State. Illinois State Museum of Natural History and Art, Springfield, Ill.
Springfield, Mass./MFA. Museum of Fine Arts, Springfield, Mass.
Springfield, Mo./AM. Springfield Art Museum, Springfield, Mo.
Staatliche Graphische Sammlung Munchen, Munich, Germany
Stadtische Galerie im Lenbachhaus, Munich, Germany
Stadtische Galerie, Munich—*see* Munich/SG
Stadtische Kunsthalle, Dusseldorf—*see* Dusseldorf/Kunsthalle
Stamford Museum, Stamford, Conn.
Standard Oil Co. of California
Standard Oil Co. of New Jersey
Stanford U.
Starr King School for the Ministry, Berkeley, Calif.
State Art Collection, Oklahoma City
State of California
State College of Iowa
State College at Salem, Salem, Mass.
State of Hawaii
State Historical Society of Missouri—*see* Columbia, Mo.
State of Iowa
State U. of Iowa
State of Louisiana Art Commission—*see* Baton Rouge
Staten Island. Staten Island Institute of Arts and Sciences, St. George, S.I., N.Y.
State Street Bank and Trust Co., Boston, Mass.
Steel Service Institute, Cleveland, Ohio
Stephens College
Steuben Glass
Stockholm/National. Moderna Museet (Nationalmuseum), Stockholm, Sweden
Stockholm/SFK. Svenska-Franska Konstgalliert, Stockholm, Sweden
Stockton. San Joaquin Pioneer Museum and Haggin Art Galleries, Stockton, Calif.
Stony Brook/SUNY. State University of New York, at Stony Brook
Storm King Art Center, Mountainville,

N.Y.

Stratford College, Danville, Va.

Stuttgart. Staatsgalerie Stuttgart, Stuttgart, Germany

Stuttgart/WK. Wurttembergischer Kunstverein, Stuttgart, Germany

Peter Stuyvesant Collection, Amsterdam, Holland

Stuyvesant Foundation, Brussels, Belgium

Suffolk County National Bank, Riverhead, N.Y.

Sunflower Corp.

Svenska Handelsbanken, Stockholm, Sweden

Svenska-Franska Konstgalliert—*see* Stockholm/SFK

Svest, Germany

Swarthmore College (incl. Wilcox Gallery)

Sweden/Goteborgs. Goteborgs Konstmuseum, Gothenburg, Sweden

Sweet Briar College

Swiss Bank Corp.

Sheldon Swope Art Gallery—*see* Terre Haute/Swope

Sydney/AG. The Art Gallery of New South Wales, Sydney, Australia

U. of Sydney (incl. Power Gallery of Contemporary Art)

Syracuse/Everson. Everson Museum of Art, Syracuse, N.Y. **Syracuse Museum School**

Syracuse U.

T

Tacoma. Tacoma Art Museum, Tacoma, Wash.

Taconic Foundation, Inc., NYC

Taft Museum, Cincinnati, Ohio

Talavara. Museo Talavara, Ciudad Bolivar, Venezuela

Tampa/AI. Tampa Art Institute Gallery, Tampa, Fla.

Taos (N.M.) County Court House

Tate Gallery, London, England

Taubman Corp., Ann Arbor, Mich.

Tel Aviv. Tel Aviv Museum of Art, Tel Aviv, Israel

Telfair Academy of Arts and Sciences, Inc.—*see* Savannah/Telfair

Temple Beth El, Detroit, Mich.

Temple Israel, St. Louis, Mo.

Temple U.

Tennessee Fine Arts Center—*see* Nashville

Tennessee State Museum, Nashville, Tenn.

U. of Tennessee

Terre Haute/Swope. Sheldon Swope Art Gallery, Terre Haute, Ind.

Terry Art Institute, Miami, Fla.

Texas Fine Arts Association—*see* Austin

Texas Technological College, Lubbock, Tex.

Texas Tech U., Lubbock, Tex.

Texas Wesleyan College

Texas Western College

U. of Texas (incl. James A. Michener Foundation)

J. Walter Thompson., NYC

3M Company, St. Paul, Minn.

Louis Comfort Tiffany Foundation, NYC

Time Inc.

Tishman Realty & Construction Co., Inc.

Tokyo Folk Art Museum

Tokyo/Modern. National Museum of Modern Art, Tokyo, Japan (*see also* National Museum of Western Art, Tokyo)

Tokyo U. of Arts, Tokyo, Japan

Toledo/MA. Toledo Museum of Art, Toldeo, Ohio

Topeka Public Library, Topeka, Kans.

Topeka U.—*see* Washburn U. of Topeka

Toronto. Art Gallery of Toronto, Toronto (Ont.), Canada

Torrington Mfg. Corp.

Tougaloo College

Tourcoing. Musée Municipal, Tourcoing, France

Towner Art Gallery, Eastbourne, England

Towson State College, Baltimore, Md.

Trade Bank and Trust Company, NYC

Trade Building, Moscow, USSR

Traders National Bank, Kansas City, Mo.

Transamerica Corp.

Travenol Laboratories, Deerfield, Ill.

Treadwell Corp., NYC
Trenton/State. New Jersey State Museum, Trenton, N.J.
Tretyakov Art Gallery, Moscow, USSR
Trinity College, Dublin, Ireland
Harry S Truman Library, Independence, Mo.
Tucson Art Center, Tucson, Ariz.
U. of Tucson
Tufts Dental College, Boston, Mass.
Tulane U. of Louisiana
Tulsa/Philbrook. Philbrook Art Center, Tulsa, Okla.
Tupperware Museum, Orlando, Fla.
Turin/Civico. Museo Civico di Torino, Turin, Italy (incl. Galleria Civica d'Arte Moderna)
Turku Museum, Finland
Tusculum College, Greenville, Tenn.
Tweed Gallery—see U. of Minnesota
Twentieth Century–Fox Film Corp.
Two Trees, NYC

U

UCLA. U. of California, Los Angeles
USIA. United States Information Agency
US Coast Guard
US Department of the Interior
US Labor Department
US Maritime Commission
US Military Academy, West Point, N.Y.
US Navy
U.S. Rubber Co.
US State Department
U.S. Steel Corp.
US Treasury Department
Uffizi Gallery, Florence, Italy
Ulster Museum, Belfast, Northern Ireland
Underwood-Neuhaus Corp.
Union Camp Corp.
Union Carbide Corp.
Union College (N.Y.)
Union of Plastic Artists, Bucharest, Romania
Unitarian Church, Princeton, N.J.
United Aircraft Corp.
United Mutual Savings Bank
United Nations
United Tanker Ltd.

Upjohn Co.
Uris Buildings Corp.
Uris-Hilton Hotels
Uruguay/Nacional. Museo Nacional de Bellas Artes, Montevideo, Uruguay
Utah. Utah Museum of Fine Arts, Salt Lake City, Utah
Utah State U.
U. of Utah
Utica. Munson-Williams-Proctor Institute, Utica, N.Y. (incl. Edward Root Collection)
Utica Public Library, Utica, N.Y.
Utrecht. Centraal Museum, Utrecht, Holland

V

VMFA. Virginia Museum of Fine Arts, Richmond, Va.
Valley Bank of Springfield, Springfield, Mass.
Valparaiso U. (Ind.)
Vancouver. Vancouver Art Gallery, Vancouver (B.C.), Canada
Vanderbilt U.
Vassar College, Poughkeepsie, N.Y.
Venice/Contemporaneo. Museo dell' Arte Contemporaneo, Venice, Italy
U. of Vermont (incl. Robert Hull Fleming Museum)
Victoria (B.C.). Art Gallery of Greater Victoria, Victoria (B.C.), Canada
Victoria and Albert Museum, London, England
Vienna/Stadt. Museen der Stadt Wien, Vienna, Austria
Virginia Museum of Fine Arts—see VMFA
Virginia National Bank, Norfolk, Va.
Virginia State College
U. of Virginia

W

WDAY, Fargo, N.D.
WGMA. Washington Gallery of Modern Art, Washington, D.C.
WMAA. The Whitney Museum of American Art, NYC
The Wadsworth Atheneum—see Hartford/Wadsworth

Wagner College

Waitsfield/Bundy. Bundy Art Gallery, Waitsfield, Vt.

Wake Forest U. (formerly **College**)

Wales—*see* National Museum of Wales

Walker. The Walker Art Center, Minneapolis, Minn.

Walker Art Gallery, Liverpool, England—*see* Liverpool/Walker

Wallraf-Richartz-Museum—*see* Cologne

Walnut Creek Municipal Collection, Walnut Creek, Calif.

Walters Art Gallery—*see* Baltimore/Walters

Warner Bros.

Warsaw. Academy of Fine Arts, Warsaw, Poland

Warsaw/National. Muzeum Narodwe (National Museum), Warsaw, Poland

Washburn U. of Topeka (incl. Mulvane Art Museum)

Washington County Museum of Fine Arts—*see* Hagerstown/County MFA

Washington Federal Bank, Miami, Fla.

Washington Gallery of Modern Art—*see* WGMA

Washington Post

Washington State U. (incl. Spokane Art Center)

Washington U. (St. Louis)

U. of Washington

Wasserman Development Corp.

Waterloo. Waterloo Municipal Galleries, Waterloo, Iowa

Wayne State U., Detroit, Mich.

Weatherspoon Art Gallery—*see* U. of North Carolina

Wellesley College, Wellesley, Mass.

Wellington Management Co.

Wells College

Wells, Rich, Greene, Inc., NYC

Wesleyan College (Ga.)

Wesleyan U. (Conn.) (incl. Davison Art Center)

Western Art Museum, Tokyo—*see* National Museum of Western Art, Tokyo

Western Art Museum, USSR—*see* Moscow/Western

Western Michigan U.

Western New Mexico U.

Western Washington State College

Westfalischer Kunstverein, Munster—*see* Munster/WK

Westfield, Mass., State College at

Westinghouse Electric Corp.

Westminster Academy, Salisbury, Conn.

Westminster Foundation, Iowa City, Iowa

Westmoreland County/MA. Westmoreland County Museum of Art, Greensburg, Pa.

West Palm Beach/Norton. Norton Gallery and School of Art, West Palm Beach, Fla.

West Point—*see* US Military Academy

Westport Art Education Society, Westport, Conn.

Westport Savings Bank, Westport, Conn.

West Virginia State College

Whatcom Museum of History and Art, Bellingham, Wash.

Wheaton College

The White House, Washington, D.C.

Whitney Communications Corp., NYC

The Whitney Museum of American Art—*see* WMAA

Whitworth Art Gallery, U. of Manchester, Manchester, England

Wichita/AM. The Wichita Art Museum, Wichita, Kansas

Wichita State U.

Wiesbaden. Stadtisches Museum Wiesbaden, Wiesbaden, Germany

Wilberfeld. Stadtisches Museum, Wilberfeld, Germany

Wilcox Gallery—*see* Swarthmore College

College of William and Mary. Williamsburg, Va.

Williams College (incl. Williamstown Museum), Williamstown, Mass.

Williamstown/Clark. Sterling and Francine Clark Art Institute, Williamstown, Mass.

Willowbrook High School, Villa Park, Ill.

Wilmington. Delaware Art Center, Wilmington, Del.

Windsor. Windsor Art Museum, Windsor (Ont.), Canada

Winston-Salem Public Library, Winston-Salem, N.C.

Wisconsin State U.

U. of Wisconsin

Witte. Witte Memorial Museum, San Antonio, Tex.

Thomas W. Wood Art Gallery—*see* Montpelier/Wood

Woodward Foundation, Washington, D.C.

College of Wooster, Wooster, Ohio

Worcester/AM. The Worcester Art Museum, Worcester, Mass. **Worcester Museum School**

Wrexham Foundation, New Haven, Conn.

Wright Art Center—*see* Beloit College

Wright State U., Dayton, Ohio

Wuppertal. Stadtisches Museum, Wuppertal, Germany

Wuppertal/von der Heydt. Von der Heydt-Museum der Stadt Wuppertal, Wuppertal, Germany

Wurttembergischer Junstverein, Stuttgart—*see* Stuttgart/WK

Wylain Corp., Fort Worth, Texas

U. of Wyoming, Laramie, Wyo.

X

Xerox Corp.

Y

Yaddo. Saratoga Springs, N.Y.

Yale U., New Haven, Conn.

Yellowstone Art Center, Billings, Mont.

York U., Toronto (Ont.), Canada

Youngstown/Butler. The Butler Institute of American Art, Youngstown, Ohio

Youngstown U.

Z

Zanesville/AI. Art Institute of Zanesville, Zanesville, Ohio

Zurich. Kunsthaus Zurich, Zurich, Switzerland

Galleries Representing the Artists in This Book

A.A.A. Gallery
663 Fifth Avenue
New York, NY 10022

ACA Gallery
25 East 73 Street
New York, NY 10021

Acquavella Contemporary Art
18 East 79 Street
New York, NY 10021

Brooke Alexander
20 West 57 Street
New York, NY 10019

Allrich Gallery
251 Post Street
San Francisco, CA 94108

Alpha Gallery
12 Newbury Street
Boston, MA 02116

Jacqueline Anhalt Gallery
750 N. La Cienega Boulevard
Los Angeles, CA 90069

Ankrum Gallery
657 N. La Cienega Boulevard
Los Angeles, CA 90069

Arras Gallery
29 West 57 Street
New York, NY 10019

Art Asia Gallery
8 Newbury Street
Boston, MA 02116

The Babcock Gallery
20 East 67 Street
New York, NY 10021

Carl Battaglia Galleries Ltd.
11 East 57 Street
New York, NY 10022

Richard Bellamy
157 Chambers Street
New York, NY 10002

Gallerie Jacques Benador
7, rue de l'Hotel-de-Ville
Geneva, Switzerland

John Berggruen Gallery
228 Grant Avenue
San Francisco, CA 94108

Aaron Berman
50 West 57 Street
New York, NY 10019

Claude Bernard
5/7, rue des Beaux-Arts
75006 Paris, France

Jean & Karen Bernier
51 Marasli Street
Athens, Greece

Blum Helman Gallery
20 West 57 Street
New York, NY 10019

Blue Door
2223 S. Monaco Pkwy.
Denver, CO 80211

Bluestone Gallery
Woodstock, NY

Mary Boone
420 West Broadway
New York, NY 10012

Galerie Bonnier
Grand Rue 12
Geneva 1200, Switzerland

Grace Borgenicht Gallery
724 Fifth Avenue
New York, NY 10019

Bradley Galleries
2565 North Downes Avenue
Milwaukee, WI 53211

Braunstein-Quay Gallery
254 Sutton Street
San Francisco, CA 94108

Suzanne Brown Gallery
7156 Main Street
Scottsdale, AZ 85251

Galerie Farideh Cadot
11, rue du Jura
75013 Paris, France

Susan Caldwell, Inc.
383 W. Broadway
New York, NY 10012

Candy Store Gallery
605 Sutter
Folsom, CA 95630

Carone Gallery
600 S.E. Second Court
Ft. Lauderdale, FL 33301

Leo Castelli Inc.
420 West Broadway
New York, NY 10012

Shirley Cerf Gallery
173 Bluxome Street
San Francisco, CA 94107

Galerie Chalette
9 East 88 Street
New York, NY 10021

Merrill Chase Galleries
620 N. Michigan Avenue
Chicago, IL 60611

Cherry Stone Gallery
Wellfleet, MA 02667

Childs Gallery
169 Newbury Street
Boston, MA 02116

Clark Gallery
P.O. Box 339
Lincoln Station
Lincoln, MA 01773

Christopher Colt
6 Spring Street
New York, NY 10012

Comara Gallery
8475 Melrose Place
Los Angeles, CA 90069

Construet
233 East Ontario
Chicago, IL 60611

Paula Cooper Gallery
155 Wooster Street
New York, NY 10012

Rebecca Cooper Gallery
2130 P Street, N.W.
Washington, DC 20037

James Corcoran Galleries
82203 Santa Monica
Los Angeles, CA 90046

Cordier & Ekstrom, Inc.
417 East 75 Street
New York, NY 10022

Charles Cowles Gallery
420 West Broadway
New York, NY 10012

Andrew Crispo Gallery
41 East 57 Street
New York, NY 10022

Betty Cuningham Gallery
94 Prince Street
New York, NY 10012

Galerie Nina Dausset
16, rue de Lille
75007 Paris, France

Peter M. David Gallery
920 Nicollet Mall
Minneapolis, MN 55402

Davis & Langdale Co., Inc.
746 Madison Avenue
New York, NY 10022

La Demeure
128, avenue Emile Zola
75015 Paris, France

Dia Art Foundation
393 West Broadway
New York, NY 10012

Terry Dintenfass, Inc.
50 West 57 Street
New York, NY 10019

Robert Elkon Gallery
1063 Madison Avenue
New York, NY 10028

Andre Emmerich Gallery
41 East 57 Street
New York, NY 10022

Galerie Erval
16, rue de Seine
75006 Paris, France

Etchings International
200 East 58 Street
New York, NY 10022

Fairweather-Hardin Gallery
101 E. Ontario Street
Chicago, IL 60611

Il Fante di Spade
Via Ripetta 254/255
Rome, Italy

Feingarten Gallery
736 N. La Cienega Boulevard
Los Angeles, CA 90069

Ronald Feldman Fine Arts, Inc.
33 East 74 Street
New York, NY 10021

Barbara Fiedler
1621 21 Street, N.W.
Washington, D.C. 20009

Filmmakers Cooperative
175 Lexington Avenue
New York, NY 10016

Fischbach Gallery
29 West 57 Street
New York, NY 10019

Fountain Gallery
115 S.W. Fourth Avenue
Portland, OR 97200

Xavier Fourcade, Inc.
36 East 75 Street
New York, NY 10021

Nine Freudenheim
560 Franklin Street
Buffalo, NY 14202

Frumkin & Struve
620 N. Michigan Avenue
Chicago, IL 60611

Allan Frumkin Gallery
50 West 57 Street
New York, NY 10019

Galleria Il Gabbiano
via delle Frezza 51
Rome, Italy

Gimpel & Weitzenhoffer Ltd.
1040 Madison Avenue
New York, NY 10028

Barbara Gladstone
41 West 57 Street
New York, NY 10019

The Graham Gallery
1014 Madison Avenue
New York, NY 10021

Graphics Gallery
1 Embarcadero Center
San Francisco, CA 94111

Richard Gray Gallery
620 N. Michigan Avenue
Chicago, IL 60611

Greenberg Gallery
7526 Forsyth Boulevard
St. Louis, MO 63105

Green Mountain Gallery
17 Perry Street
New York, NY 10014

Grippi Gallery
315 East 62 Street
New York, NY 10021

Gump's Gallery
250 Post Street
San Francisco, CA 94108

E. P. Gurewitsch Gallery
55 East 74 Street
New York, NY 10021

Gruenebaum Gallery
38 East 57 Street
New York, NY 10022

Haber/Theodore Gallery
29 West 57 Street
New York, NY 10019

Juan Hamilton
20 West 57 Street
New York, NY 10019

Hansen Fuller Goldeen Gallery
228 Grant Avenue
San Francisco, CA 94108

Harmon Gallery
1258 Third Street South
Naples, FL 33940

Haslem Fine Arts, Inc.
2121 P. Street, N.W.
Washington, DC 20037

Hirschl & Adler Galleries
21 East 70 Street
New York, NY 10021

Nancy Hoffman Gallery
429 West Broadway
New York, NY 10012

Hokin Gallery
200 East Ontario Street
Chicago, IL 60611

Hooks Epstein
1200 Bissonnet
Houston, TX 97005

Hull Gallery
3301 New Mexico Avenue, N.W.
Washington, DC 20016

Max Hutchinson Gallery
138 Greene Street
New York, NY 10012

Impressions Workshop, Inc.
27 Stanhope Street
Boston, MA 02116

Ingber Art Gallery
3 East 78 Street
New York, NY 10021

Brooks Jackson Ioles Gallery
52 East 57 Street
New York, NY 10022

Sidney Janis Gallery
110 West 57 Street
New York, NY 10012

Janus Gallery
21 Market Street
Venice, CA 90291

The Jones Gallery
1264 Prospect Street
La Jolla, CA 92037

Marjorie Kauffman Gallery
5015 Westheimer
Houston, TX 77027

Kennedy Galleries, Inc.
40 West 57 Street
New York, NY 10019

Klonaridis, Inc.
144 Front Street West
Toronto, M5J 1G2, Canada

Kolbert Gallery
724 Fifth Avenue
New York, NY 10019

The Kornblee Gallery
20 West 57 Street
New York, NY 10019

Kraushaar Galleries
724 Fifth Avenue
New York, NY 10019

The Lanyon Gallery
700 Welch Road
Palo Alto, CA 94304

Roger Lapelle Gallery
2002 Rittenhouse Square
Philadelphia, PA 19103

Ledoux Gallery
Taos, NM 97571

Lerner-Heller Gallery
956 Madison Avenue
New York, NY 10021

Marion Lockes Gallery
1524 Walnut Street
Philadelphia, PA 19102

Elca London Gallery
970 Lucerne Road
Montreal H3R 2H6, Canada

Meredith Long Gallery
2323 San Felipe Road
Houston, TX 77019

Longpoint Gallery
Provincetown, MA 02659

Galleria Lorenzelli
Via San Michele 1a
Bergamo, Italy

Galerie Maeght
13, rue de Teheran
75008 Paris, France

Marlborough Gallery, Inc.
40 West 57 Street
New York, NY 10019

S.G. Mathews Gallery
1710 N. Main Avenue
San Antonio, TX 78212

Maxwell Galleries, Ltd.
551 Sutter Street
San Francisco, CA 94102

David McKee Gallery
41 East 57 Street
New York, NY 10022

Louis K. Meisel Gallery
141 Prince Street
New York, NY 10012

Mekler Gallery
651 N. La Cienega Boulevard
Los Angeles, CA 90069

The Midtown Galleries
11 East 57 Street
New York, NY 10022

Milch Gallery
1014 Madison Avenue
New York, NY 10028

Robert Miller Gallery, Inc.
724 Fifth Avenue
New York, NY 10019

Modernism Gallery
236 8th Street
San Francisco, CA 94103

Moody Gallery
2015-J West Gray
Houston, TX 79019

Morgan Gallery
5006 State Line
Shawnee Mission, KS 66205

Galeria Juana Mordo
Villaneuva 7
Madrid, Spain

Donald Morris Gallery
105 Townsend
Birmingham, MI 48011

Jerrold Morris
15 Prince Arthur Avenue
Toronto 5, Canada

Nardin Gallery, Inc.
25 East 73 Street
New York, NY 10021

North Star Gallery
Box 2
Grafton, VT 05146

Nielsen Gallery
179 Newbury Street
Boston, MA 02116

Odyssia Gallery
730 Fifth Avenue
New York, NY 10019

Frank Oehlschlager Gallery
107 East Oak
Chicago, IL 60611

Frank Oehlschlager Gallery
28 Boulevard of the Presidents
St. Armands Key
Sarasota, FL 33578

OK Harris Works of Art
383 West Broadway
New York, NY 10013

The Pace Gallery
32 East 57 Street
New York, NY 10022

Betty Parsons Gallery
24 West 57 Street
New York, NY 10019

Marilyn Pearl Gallery
29 West 57 Street
New York, NY 10019

The John Pence Gallery
550 Sutter
San Francisco, CA 94102

Peter Plone Associates
1108 North Tamarind Avenue
Los Angeles, CA 90038

Poindexter Gallery
1160 Fifth Avenue
New York, NY 10029

Galeria Ponce
Belgrado 5
Mexico City, DF6, Mexico

Princeton Gallery of Fine Art
9 Spring Street
Princeton, NJ 08540

Prints on Prince Street
410 West Broadway
New York, NY 10014

Pyramid Art Galleries Ltd.
2121 P Street, N.W.
Washington, DC 20037

Randall Galleries Ltd.
823 Madison Avenue
New York, NY 10021

Galerie Denise Rene
196, boulevard Saint-Germain
75017 Paris, France

Galerie Rolf Ricke
Lindenstrasse 22
Cologne 5, Germany

Robinson Galleries
1100 Bissonnet
Houston, TX 77005

Rosenfeld Gallery
113 Arch Street
Philadelphia, PA 19106

Jack Rutberg Fine Arts
1155 N. La Cienega Boulevard
Los Angeles, CA 90069

A.M. Sachs Gallery
29 West 57 Street
New York, NY 10019

Saidenberg Gallery
1018 Madison Avenue
New York, NY 10021

Salander-O'Reilly Galleries
22 East 80 Street
New York, NY 10021

Sunne Savage Gallery
398a Beacon Street
Boston, MA 02167

William Sawyer Gallery
3045 Clay Street
San Francisco, CA 94115

Ruth S. Schaffner Gallery
8406 Melrose Avenue
Los Angeles, CA 90069

Galerie Schreiner
115½ East 62 Street
New York, NY 10022

Robert Schoelkopf Gallery
825 Madison Avenue
New York, NY 10021

Galleria Arturo Schwarz
via Gesu 17
Milan, Italy

Jodi Scully Gallery
651 N. La Cienega Boulevard
Los Angeles, CA 90069

Francine Seders Gallery
6701 Greenwood Avenue North
Seattle, WA 98103

Serisawa Gallery
633 N. La Cienega Boulevard
Los Angeles, CA 90069

Silvan Simone Gallery
11579 Olympic Boulevard
Los Angeles, Ca 90031

Gallery 1640
1445 Crescent Street
Montreal (Quebec), Canada

Smith Andersen Gallery
200 Homer Street
Palo Alto, CA 94301

Sneed-Hillman Gallery
2024 Harlem Boulevard
Rockford, IL 61103

Ileana Sonnabend Gallery
420 West Broadway
New York, NY 10012

Sperone Westwater Fisher, Inc.
142 Greene Street
New York, NY 10012

Darthea Speyer Gallery
6, rue Jacques Callot
75006 Paris, France

Stables Gallery
Taos, NM 87571

Staempfli Gallery
47 East 77 Street
New York, NY 10021

Allan Stone Gallery
48 East 86 Street
New York, NY 10028

Galerie Tanit
Sternstrasse 17
Munich, Germany

Terrain Gallery
141 Greene Street
New York, NY 10012

Barbara Toll Fine Arts
146 Greene Street
New York, NY 10012

Tortue Gallery
2917 Santa Monica Boulevard
Los Angeles, CA 90404

Triangle Art Gallery
578 Sutter Street
San Francisco, CA 94102

Gallery 2
65 Central St.
Woodstock, VT 05091

Valley House Gallery
6616 Spring Valley Road
Dallas, TX 75240

Van Doren Gallery
1830 Union Street
San Francisco, CA 94123

Van Straaten Gallery
646 N. Michigan Avenue
Chicago, IL 60611

Washburn Gallery Inc.
42 East 57 Street
New York, NY 10022

John Weber Gallery
142 Greene Street
New York, NY 10012

Weinberg Gallery
560 Sutter
San Francisco, CA 94102

Elizabeth Weiner
21 East 73 Street
New York, NY 10021

Wellfleet Art Gallery
Route #6
Wellfleet, MA 02667

Weyhe Gallery
794 Lexington Avenue
New York, NY 10021

Nicholas Wilder Gallery
39 East 67 Street
New York, NY 10021

The Willard Gallery
29 East 72 Street
New York, NY 10021

Watson Willour & Co.
2000 Peden
Houston, TX 77019

Sandra Wilson Gallery
1756 Broadway
Denver, CO 80202

Gordon Woodside Gallery
803 East Union Street
Seattle, WA 98122

Worthington Gallery Inc.
233 East Ontario
Chicago, IL 60611

Yares Gallery
3625 Bishop Lane
Scottsdale, AZ 85251

The Zabriskie Gallery
29 West 57 Street
New York, NY 10019

AACH, HERB. b. March 24, 1923, Cologne, Germany. **Studied:** Stanford U.; Brooklyn Museum School; Pratt Institute; School of Fine Arts, Cologne; Escuela de Pintura y Escultura, Mexico City (with John Ferren, Rufino Tamayo, Max Beckmann, Edwin Dickinson, Arthur Osver, Xavier Gonzalez). Traveled Europe, USA, Central America, Middle East. **Taught:** Brooklyn Museum School,, 1947–51; Hazleton Art League; Kingsbridge Community Center, Bronx, N.Y.; Pratt Institute, 1966–69; Queens College, 1966–. **Member:** College Art Association; National Art Education Association. Technical consultant on colors. **Awards:** Hazleton Art League, First Prize, 1956, 63. **Address:** 523 East 14 Street, NYC 10009. **Dealer:** Aaron Berman, NYC. **One-man Exhibitions:** (first) Creative Gallery, NYC, 1952; Stroudsberg Gallery; Hazleton Art League; The Pennsylvania State U.; Scranton/Everhart; Albert Landry, NYC; J. Seligmann and Co., 1964; Martha Jackson Gallery, 1974; Buffalo/Albright, 1975. **Group:** WMAA; PAFA; U. of Illinois, 1961; ART: USA, NYC; Scranton/Everhart; Riverside Museum, NYC; Lehigh U., 1965, 67; Cranbrook, 5th Biennial; National Religious Art Exhibition, 1966; U. of Texas, Color Forum, 1972. **Collections:** Boston/MFA; Calcutta; Harrisburg, Pa./State Museum; Scranton/Everhart.

ACCONCI, VITO. b. January 24, 1940, Bronx, N.Y. **Studied:** College of the Holy Cross, Worcester, Mass., 1958–62, BA; U. of Iowa, Iowa City, 1962–64, MFA. Traveled Europe. **Taught:** School of Visual Arts, NYC, 1968–71. **Address:** 131 Chrystie Street, NYC 10002. **Dealer:** Ileana Sonnabend Gallery, NYC and Paris. **One-man Exhibitions:** John Gibson Gallery, 1971; Ileana Sonnabend Gallery, Paris, 1972, NYC, 1972, 73, 75, 76, 79; Galleria l'Attico, Rome, 1972; Modern Art Agency, Naples, Italy, 1973–77; Galerie D., Brussels, 1973–77; Galleria Schema, Florence, 1973; Galleria Forma, Genoa, 1974; Galleria A. Castelli, Milan, 1974, 75; Portland (Ore.) Center for the Visual Arts, 1975; Museum of Conceptual Art, San Francisco, 1975; James Mayor Gallery, London, 1975; The Kitchen, New York, 1976, 77; Anthology Film Archives, NYC, 1976; Minnesota College of Art, Minneapolis, 1978; Akron/AI, 1978; SFMA, 1978; Lucerne, 1978; Amsterdam/Stedelijk, 1978; Young-Hoffman Gallery, Chicago, 1979. **Retrospective:** Anthology Film Archives, 1977; Chicago/Contemporary, 1980. **Group:** Jewish Museum, Software, 1970; MOMA, Information, 1971; Dusseldorf/Kunsthalle, Prospect '71, 1971; VII Paris Biennial, 1971; Documenta V, Kassel, 1972; MOMA, Some Recent American Art, circ., 1973; Parcheggio di Villa Borghese, Rome, Contemporanea, 1974; MOMA, Eight Contemporary Artists, 1974; Cologne, Project '74, 1974; Chicago/AI, Idea and Image in Recent Art, 1974; MOMA, Video Art, 1975, Chicago/Contemporary, Body Art, 1975; Venice Biennale, 1976; ICA, U. of Pennsylvania, Improbable Furniture 1977; WMAA Biennial, 1977; Chicago/Contemporary, Art of the '70s, 1977. **Collections:** Los Angeles/County MA; MOMA. **Bibliography:** *Contemporanea; Drawings: The Pluralist Decade;* Hunter, ed.; Lippard 3; Lucie-Smith; Meyer; Pincus-Witten.

ACTON, ARLO. b. May 11, 1933, Knoxville, Iowa. **Studied:** Washington State U., 1958, BA; California Institute of Arts, 1959, MFA. US Army Medical Corps, 1955–57. Traveled France, Italy. **Taught:** U. of California, Berkeley, 1963, 67, 68. **Awards:** SFMA, Edgar Walter Memorial Prize, 1961; California State Fair, 1961; Richmond (Calif.) Art Association Annual, Second Prize, 1961; San Francisco Art Association, cash award, 1964. **Address:** 63 Bluxome Street, San Francisco, CA 94107. **One-man Exhibitions:** (first) Bolles Gallery, San Francisco, 1962; The Lanyon Gallery, 1965; Nicholas Wilder Gallery, 1965, 66; Esther Robles Gallery, 1969. **Group:** SFMA Annuals, 1960, 61, 62, 63, 64, 65; RAC, 1961, 62; Los Angeles/County MA, Cross-section LA-SF, 1961; Oakland/AM, 1960, 61; SFMA, Arts of San Francisco, 1962; Stanford U., Some Points of View for '62, 1962; Fort Worth, The Artist's Environment: The West Coast, 1962; WMAA, Fifty California Artists, 1962–63; Kaiser Center, Oakland, California Sculpture, 1963; III Paris Biennial, 1963; U. of Arkansas, Contemporary Americans, 1966; U. of California, Berkeley, Funk, 1967; Los Angeles/County MA, American Sculpture of the Sixties, circ., 1967; Portland, Ore./AM, The West Coast Now, 1968. **Collections:** U. of Nevada; Oakland/AM; SFMA; SFPL. **Bibliography:** Selz, P., 2; Tuchman 1.

ADAMS, CLINTON. b. December 11, 1918, Glendale, Calif. **Studied:** UCLA, 1940, BA, 1942, MFA. US Army, World War II. Traveled USA and Europe extensively. **Taught:** UCLA, 1946–54; U. of Kentucky, 1954–57; U. of Florida, 1957–60; U. of New Mexico, 1961. Associate Director, Tamarind Lithography Workshop, 1960–61; Director, Tamarind Institute, 1970–. Editor, *The Tamarind Papers*, 1974–. **Address:** 1917 Morningside Drive, N.E., Albuquerque, NM 87110. **One-man Exhibitions:** (first) UCLA, 1950; Felix Landau Gallery, 1952, 56, 58, 61, 63, 65; Pasadena/AM, 1954; Louisville/Speed, 1956; U. of Texas, 1957; U. of Florida, 1957; Galleria Mazzuchelli, Florence, Italy; Jonson Gallery, Albuquerque, N.M., 1961, 63, 68; Roswell, 1972. **Retrospective:** U. of New Mexico, 1973; U. of Iowa; U. of Georgia. **Group:** MOMA; MMA; Brooklyn Museum; Library of Congress; Carnegie; PAFA; Cincinnati/AM; Ringling; Oakland/AM; De Kalb, National Print and Drawing Exhibition, 1968; MOMA, Tamarind: Homage to Lithography, 1969; Honolulu Academy, First Hawaiian National Print Exhibition, 1971. **Collections:** Achenbach Foundation; Amon Carter Museum; Bibliotheque Nationale; Bradley U.; Brooklyn Museum; Chicago/AI; Dallas/MFA; De Kalb; De Pauw U.; Florida State U.; Grunwald Foundation; U. of Illinois; La Jolla; Los Angeles/County MA; MOMA; U. of New Mexico; NYPL; Otis Art Institute; Pasadena/AM; San Diego; Santa Fe, N.M.; Seattle/AM; UCLA; Victoria and Albert Museum. **Bibliography:** Archives.

ADAMS, PAT. b. July 8, 1928, Stockton, Calif. **Studied:** U. of California (with Glenn Wessels, John Haley, Margaret O'Hagan, Erle Loran), 1949, BA, PBK; Brooklyn Museum School (with Max Beckmann, Reuben Tam, John Ferren). Traveled Europe, Middle East. **Taught:** Bennington College, 1964–; Yale U., 1971–72, 76, 79; Queens College, 1972; U. of Iowa, 1976; U. of New Mexico, 1978. **Awards:** Yaddo Fellowship, 1954, 64, 69, 70; Fulbright Fellowship (France), 1956; National Council on the Arts, $5,000 Award, 1968; MacDowell Colony Fellowship, 1968, 72; National Endowment for the Arts. **Address:** 370 Elm Street, Bennington, VT 05201. **Dealer:** The Zabriskie Gallery. **One-man Exhibitions:** (first) Stockton, 1950; Korman Gallery, NYC, 1954; The Zabriskie Gallery, 1954, 56, 57, 60, 62, 64, 70, 72, 74, 76, 78, 79; Wheaton College, 1959; Bennett College, 1959; Green Mountain College, 1962; Arts and Crafts Gallery, Wellfleet, Mass.,

1963; Hotchkiss School, Lakeville, Conn., 1960; Windham College; Williams College, 1972; Yale in Norfolk, 1977. **Retrospective:** Cincinnati/Contemporary, 1979. **Group:** Bordighera, Americans in Europe, 1952; WMAA Annuals, 1956, 58, 61; A.F.A., Collage in America, circ., 1957–58; MOMA, 41 Watercolorists, circ., Europe, 1957; U. of Nebraska, 1958; A.F.A., The New Landscape in Art and Science, circ., 1958–59; WMAA, Fulbright Artists, 1958; Hirschl & Adler Galleries, Inc., NYC, Experiences in Art, I & II, 1959, 60; Tanager Gallery, NYC, The Private Myth, 1961; A.F.A., Lyricism in Abstract Art, circ., 1962–63; PAFA, Watercolor Annual, 1959; U. of Michigan, One Hundred Contemporary American Drawings, 1965; U. of Texas, Color Forum, 1972; GEDOK, Kunsthaus, Hamburg, American Women Artists, 1972; New York Cultural Center, Women Choose Women, 1973; Hirshhorn, Inaugural Exhibitions, 1974; IIE, 20 American Fulbright Artists, 1975; U. of Texas, Austin, New in the Seventies, 1977; Chicago/AI, 100 Artists, 100 Years, *Alumni of the SAIC*, 1979. **Collections:** Bordighera; Hirshhorn; U. of Michigan; U. of North Carolina; Williams College; WMAA. **Bibliography:** *Art: A Woman's Sensibility;* Chaet; *New in the Seventies.*

ADLER, SAMUEL M. b. July 30, 1898, NYC; **d.** November 12, 1979, NYC. **Studied:** NAD, 1911. Traveled North and Central America, Europe, Africa. A professional violinist through student years. **Taught:** Privately, 1934–48; NYU, 1948–72; U. of Illinois, 1959–60; Associate Member, Institute of Advanced Study, U. of Illinois, 1964; U. of Notre Dame, 1965; U. of Georgia, 1967–69. **Ex-member:** Artists Equity, formerly vice-president and president of the New York chapter. **Awards:** PAFA, J. Henry Schiedt Memorial Prize, 1951; U. of Illinois, **P.P.,** 1952; WMAA, **P.P.,** 1952, 63; Audubon Artists, 1956, First Hon. Men., 1957, 59,

Gold Medal of Honor, 1960; Staten Island, **P.P.,** 1962; Ford Foundation Artist-in-Residence, 1965; American Society of Contemporary Artists, Second Prize, 1967, First Prize, 1968. **One-man Exhibitions:** (first) Joseph Luyber Galleries, NYC, 1948; Indiana U., 1950; Louisville Art Center Association, 1950; Charlotte/Mint, 1951; Grace Borgenicht Gallery, Inc., 1952, 54; Philadelphia Art Alliance, 1954; U. of Illinois, 1959, 60, 64; Grand Central Moderns, NYC, 1960; The Babcock Gallery, 1962; U. of Notre Dame, 1965; Rose Fried Gallery, 1965 (2); U. of Iowa, 1966; U. of Georgia, 1967, 68; Ripon College, 1968; Rehn Galleries, 1971, 72, 76; Andover/Phillips, 1972; Wichita State U., 1976; **Group:** AAAL; Chicago/AI; ART: USA, NYC; Atlanta/AA; Audubon Artists; Birmingham, Ala./MA; Youngstown/Butler; California Palace; Cincinnati/AM; St. Louis/City; Columbia, S.C./MA; Columbus; Corcoran; Dallas/MFA; Dayton/AI; Lincoln, Mass./De Cordova; Denver/AM; Honolulu Academy; Howard U.; Jewish Museum; Omaha/Joslyn; Los Angeles/County MA; MMA; Milwaukee; Cranbrook; Boston/MFA; Santa Barbara/MA; NAD; PAFA; Stanford U.; WMAA; Royal Academy, London. **Collections:** Brooklyn Museum; Clearwater/Gulf Coast; Cornell U., Fourth National Bank and Trust, Wichita; U. of Georgia; Hirshhorn; Illinois Wesleyan U.; Michigan State U.; NCFA; NYU; U. of Nebraska; Norfolk; U. of Notre Dame; Safad; St. Lawrence U.; Slater; Staten Island; Utica; WMAA; Wichita State U.; Youngstown/Butler. **Bibliography:** Biddle 4; Nordness, ed.; Pearson 2; Pousette-Dart, ed.; Weller. Archives.

AGOSTINI, PETER. b. 1913, NYC. **Studied:** Leonardo da Vinci Art School, NYC. **Commissions:** New York World's Fair, 1964–65. **Awards:** Longview Foundation Grant, 1960, 61, 62; Brandeis U., Creative Arts Award, 1964. **Address:** 47 Grand Street, NYC 10012. **One-man Exhibitions:** Galerie

Grimaud, NYC, 1959; Stephen Radich Gallery, 1960, 62–65, 67, 68; Richard Gray Gallery, 1965; U. of North Carolina, 1969; The Zabriskie Gallery, NYC, 1971, 73, 76. **Group:** New School for Social Research; Jewish Museum, Recent American Sculpture, 1964; WMAA; MOMA; Claude Bernard, Paris, 1960; Chicago/AI, 1962; Hartford/Wadsworth, 1962; Battersea Park, London, International Sculpture Exhibition, 1963. **Collections:** Brandeis U.; Hartford/Wadsworth; ILGWU; Kalamazoo/Institute; MIT; MOMA; U. of Southern California; U. of Texas; Union Carbide Corp.; Walter. **Bibliography:** Hunter, ed.; Lippard 5; Read 3; Rose, B., 1. Archives.

ALBERS, JOSEF. b. March 19, 1888, Bottrop, Westphalia, Germany; **d. March 26, 1976, New Haven, Conn. Studied:** Royal Art School, Berlin, 1913–15; School of Applied Art, Essen, 1916–19; Academy of Fine Arts, Munich, 1919–20; Bauhaus, Weimar, 1920–23, where he became an instructor (Weimar-Dessau-Berlin), 1923–33. To USA, 1933, to teach and head art department at Black Mountain College, to 1949. US citizen, 1939. Headed Department of Design at Yale U., 1950–58; Visiting Critic, 1958–60. **Taught:** Design, drawing, color and painting. Presented courses, seminars, lecture series in many European and North and South American universities, until his retirement, 1960. **Member:** American Abstract Artists; PCA. **Commissions** (murals): Harvard U.; Corning Glass Building, NYC. **Awards:** German Federal Republic, Officers Cross First Class of the Order of Merit; Corcoran, William A. Clark Prize, 1954; Chicago/AI, Ada S. Garrett Prize, 1954; Hon. DFA, U. of Hartford, 1957; Ford Foundation Fellowship, 1959; PMA, Citation, 1962; Hon. DFA, Yale U., 1962; American Institute of Graphic Art, Medal of the Year, 1964; Carnegie, 1967; Hon. DFA, California College of Arts and Crafts, 1964; Bridgeport U., 1966; U. of North

Carolina, 1967; U. of Illinois, 1969; Kenyon College, 1969; Minnesota College of Art and Design, 1969. AAAL, Award, 1970; Royal Society, 1971; Maryland Institute, 1972; York U., 1973; Pratt Institute, 1975. **One-man Exhibitions:** (first) Goltz Gallery, Munich, 1919; Sidney Janis Gallery, NYC, 1949, 52, 55, 58, 59, 61, 64, 68, 70, 76; Cincinnati/AM, 1949; Yale U., 1956, 78; Galerie Denise Rene, Paris, 1957, 58; Kunstverein Freiburg im Breisgau, 1959; Zurich, 1960; Amsterdam/Stedelijk, 1961; Raleigh/NCMA, 1962; MOMA, Josef Albers, circ., Latin America, 1964; WGMA, 1965; Gimpel & Hanover Galerie, Zurich, 1965; Hannover/K-G, 1968; Landesmuseum fur Kunst und Kulturgeschichte, Munster, 1968; Bielefeld, 1968; Dusseldorf/Kunsthalle, 1970; MMA, 1971; Princeton U., 1971; Pollock Gallery, Toronto, 1972; Galerie Gmurzymska & Bargera, Cologne, 1973; Galerie Melki, Paris, 1973; and some 100 others. **Retrospective:** Yale U., 1956; WGMA, Josef Albers, The American Years, 1965; Josef Albers, circ., Germany and Switzerland. **Group:** American Abstract Artists, 1939; Herbert Hermann Gallery, Brooklyn, 1949; Galerie Stuttgart, 1948; U. of Illinois, 1951, 52, 53; Hartford/Wadsworth, Josef and Annie Albers, 1953; Zurich, 1956; WMAA, Geometric Abstraction in America, circ., 1962; SRGM, Cezanne and Structure in Modern Painting, 1963; SRGM, Abstract Expressionists and Imagists, 1961; Smithsonian, Paintings from the Museum of Modern Art, New York, 1963; MOMA, The Responsive Eye, 1965; MOMA, Two Decades of American Painting, circ., Japan, India, Australia, 1967; and some 500 others. **Collections:** Amsterdam/Stedelijk; Baltimore/MA; Basel; Bennington College; Berea College; Brown U.; Buffalo/Albright; Carnegie; Chicago/AI; Corcoran; Currier; Denver/AM; Detroit/Institute; Duke U.; Essen; Hagen; Hartford/Wadsworth; Harvard U.; Hollins College; Leverkusen; Los Angeles/County MA; U. of Louisville; MIT; MMA;

MOMA; Mills College; U. of Minnesota; Morgan State College; Muhlenberg College; Munster; New London; U. of New Mexico; North Texas State U.; Park College; Portland, Ore./AM; Rio de Janeiro; SFMA; SRGM; Smith College; Smithsonian; Springfield, Mass./MFA; Stockholm/National; Svest; Toronto; Utica; VMFA; WMAA; Wesleyan U.; U. of Wisconsin; Yale U.; Zurich. **Bibliography:** *Abstraction Creation 1931–1936;* Downes, ed.; *From Foreign Shores;* Gablik; Honisch and Jensen, eds.; Sandler; Tomkins 2; MOMA, The Albers Archive: 1. "Documentation in Manuscript" (photocopy, artist's personal record of his professional chronology); 2. Writings on art (photocopies of typescripts); 3. Scrapbooks, clippings, catalogues, photographs, etc. Additional and overlapping data may be found at the Bauhaus-Archiv, Darmstadt, Germany, the Busch-Reisinger Museum, Cambridge, Mass., and the Yale U. Library, New Haven, Conn. **Albers 1, 2, 3, 4, 5, 6, 7;** American Abstract Artists, ed.; Battcock, ed.; Baur 7; Bihalji-Merin; Blanchard; Blesh 1; Calas, N. and E.; Chaet; Cheney; Christensen; Coplans 3; Davis, D.; Dorner; Eliot; Frost; Gaunt; Gerstner; Gomringer; Goodrich and Baur 1; Haftman; **Hamilton, G.H.;** Henning; Hess, T.B., 1; Hunter, ed.; Janis and Blesh 1; Janis, S.; Kepes, ed.; Kuh 2; Lynton; MacAgy 2; McCurdy, ed.; Mendelowitz; *Metro;* Morris; Motherwell 1; Neumeyer; Nordness, ed.; Pearson 2; Ponente; Pousette-Dart, ed.; Read 2, 3; Rickey; Ritchie 1; Rodman 2, 3; Rose, B., 1, 4; Roters; Seuphor 1; Tomkins; Trier 1; Tyler, K. E.; Weller; Wingler, ed. Archives.

ALBERT, CALVIN. b. November 19, 1918, Grand Rapids, Mich. **Studied:** Institute of Design, Chicago, with Lazlo Moholy-Nagy, Gyorgy Kepes, Alexander Archipenko. Traveled Europe. **Taught:** Institute of Design, Chicago, 1941–1946; NYU, 1950; Brooklyn College, 1951–52; Pratt Institute, 1949–.

Federal A.P.; Painting, sculpture, design exhibitions. **Member:** College Art Association; AAUP (1969, president, Pratt chapter); Sculptors Guild. **Commissions:** St. Paul's Episcopal Church, Peoria, Ill.; Temple Israel, Bridgeport, Conn.; Temple Israel, Tulsa, Okla.; Park Avenue Synagogue, NYC; Temple Emmanuel, Grand Rapids, Mich., 1973, 74. **Awards:** Detroit/Institute, The Haass Prize, 1944; ICA, London/Tate, International Unknown Political Prisoner Competition, Hon. Men., 1953; Audubon Artists, First Prize, 1954; Fulbright Fellowship, 1961; L. C. Tiffany Grant, 1963, 65; Guggenheim Foundation Fellowship, 1966; NIAL, **P.P.,** 1975; NIAL, grant, 1975. **Address:** 325 West 16th Street, NYC. **One-man Exhibitions:** Paul Theobald Gallery, Chicago, 1941; Puma Gallery, NYC, 1944; Chicago/AI, 1945; California Palace, 1947; Grand Rapids, 1948; Laurel Gallery, NYC, 1950; Grace Borgenicht Gallery, Inc., 1952, 54, 56, 57; MMA, 1952; Walker, 1954; U. of Nebraska, 1955; The Stable Gallery, NYC, 1959, 64; U. of Georgia, 1970; Free Public Library, Fair Lawn, N.J., 1973; Landmark Gallery, Inc., NYC, 1974, 77; Benson Gallery, 1975; Guild Hall, East Hampton, N.Y., 1979. **Retrospective:** Jewish Museum, 1960. **Group:** Andover/Phillips, The American Line—100 Years of Drawing, 1959; Chicago/AI, Contemporary Drawings from 12 Countries, 1952; MMA, American Watercolors, Drawings, and Prints, 1952; A.F.A., The Embellished Surface, circ., 1953–54; Contemporary Drawing from the United States, circ. France, 1954; MOMA, Recent Drawings, USA, 1956; U. of Illinois, 1957, 65; WMAA Annuals, 1954, 55, 56, 58, 60, 62, 66, 68; A.F.A., God and Man in Art, circ., 1958–59; Brooklyn Museum, Golden Year of American Drawing, 1956, Chicago/AI, 1962; PAFA, 1949, 53, 64; Flint/Institute, American Sculpture, 1900–1965, 1965; PAFA Annual, 1967; U. of Nebraska, American Sculpture, 1970; AAL, 1975. **Collections:** Brooklyn Museum; Chicago/AI; Colby College;

Detroit/Institute; Guild Hall; Jewish Museum; Kansas City/Nelson; MMA; U. of Nebraska; Norfolk/Chrysler; U. of North Carolina. **Bibliography:** Weller. Archives.

ALBRIGHT, IVAN LE LORRAINE. b. February 20, 1897, North Harvey, Ill. **Studied:** Chicago Art Institute School, 1920–23; PAFA, 1923; NAD, 1924; Northwestern U., 1915–16; Illinois School of Architecture, 1916–17; Ecole Regionale des Beaux-Arts, Nantes, 1919. US Army, 1918–19. Traveled Venezuela, USA, Europe. **Member:** NAD; Chicago Society of Arts, Inc. **Commissions** (paintings): *The Portrait of Dorian Gray* for the film, 1943; *The Temptation of St. Anthony* for the film, 1943. **Awards:** Chicago/AI, Faculty Hon. Men., 1923; Chicago/AI, Hon. Men., 1926; Chicago/AI, John C. Shaffer Prize, 1928; Chicago/AI, Norman Wait Harris Medal, 1941, 43; Society for Contemporary American Art, Silver Medal, 1930, Gold Medal, 1931; Chicago/AI, First Prize, 1948; PAFA, Joseph E. Temple Gold Medal, 1942; MMA, Artists for Victory, First Prize, 1942; NAD, Benjamin Altman Prize, 1961; Corcoran, Silver Medal, 1955; Northwestern U., Centennial Award, 1951; Tate, $5,000 Dunn International Prize, 1963; NIAL, 1957. **Address:** 47 Elm Street, Woodstock, VT 05091. **Dealer:** Kennedy Gallery. **One-man Exhibitions:** Walden Book Shop, Chicago, 1930; Chicago/AI, 1931; A.A.A. Gallery, NYC (two-man), 1945, Chicago (two-man), 1946; Kennedy Gallery. **Retrospective:** Chicago/AI, 1964. **Group:** Chicago/AI, 1918, 23, 26, 28, 41, 43, 48; PAFA, 1924, 42; Brussels World's Fair, 1958; WMAA; Corcoran, 1955; NAD. **Collections:** Brooklyn Museum; Carnegie; Chicago/AI; Dallas/MFA; Hartford/Wadsworth; Library of Congress; MMA; MOMA; PMA; Phoenix; US Labor Department. **Bibliography:** Barker 1; Baur 7; Blesh 1; Canaday; Cheney; Cummings 1; Eliot; Flanagan; Flexner; Haftman; Hall; Jacobson, ed.; Kuh 1, 2, 3; McCurdy, ed.; Men-

delowitz; Newmeyer; Pearson 1, 2; Pousette-Dart, ed.; Reese; Richardson, E. P.; Rose, B., 1, 4; **Sweet;** Weller. Archives.

ALCALAY, ALBERT. b. 1917, Paris, France. To USA 1951. Traveled France, England, Italy, Yugoslavia, Israel, 1970–71. **Taught:** Harvard U., 1959–; U. of Maryland, 1971. **Awards:** Guggenheim Foundation Fellowship, 1959; Boston Arts Festival, First Prize, 1960. **Address:** 66 Powell Street, Brookline, MA 02146. **Dealers:** Clark Gallery, Lincoln, Mass.; Elca London Gallery, Montreal. **One-man Exhibitions:** Cortile Gallery, Rome, 1947; Gaetano Chiurazzi, Rome, 1950; Boston Museum School, 1951; Lincoln, Mass./De Cordova, 1954; Philadelphia Arts Club, 1951; The Krasner Gallery, 1959, 61, 62, 64, 66; The Swetzoff Gallery, Boston, 1952–54, 56, 58; Wittenborn Gallery, NYC, 1958; The Pace Gallery, Boston, 1961, 62; Mickelson's Gallery, Washington, D.C., 1964, 67; Ward-Nasse Gallery, Boston, 1965, 67; Pucker-Safrai Gallery, 1971, 73; Smith-Andersen Gallery, Palo Alto, 1973; Elca London Gallery, Montreal, 1975; Barbara Battin Fiedler, Washington, D.C., 1976. **Retrospective:** Lincoln, Mass./De Cordova, 1968. **Group:** Rome National Art Quadriennial, 1947; U. of Illinois, 1955, 57, 59; WMAA, 1956, 58, 60; ICA, Boston, View, 1960; PAFA, 1960; MOMA, 1955; AAAL. **Collections:** Andover/Phillips; Boston/MFA; Brandeis U.; Colby College; First National Bank of Boston; Harvard U.; Lincoln, Mass./ De Cordova; MOMA; Rome/Nazionale; U. of Rome; Simmons College; State Street Bank and Trust Co., Boston; Wellesley College. **Bibliography:** Archives.

ALLAN, WILLIAM. b. March 28, 1936, Everett, Washington. **Studied:** San Francisco Art Institute, BFA, 1958. **Taught:** U. of California, Davis, 1965–67; U. of California, Berkeley,

1969; San Francisco Art Institute, 1967–69; Sacramento State College, Sacramento, 1968–. Has made several 16mm films. **Awards:** National Endowment for the Arts, grant, 1972. **Address:** 327 Melrose Avenue, Mill Valley, CA 94941. **Dealer:** Odyssia Gallery, NYC; Hansen Gallery, San Francisco. **One-man Exhibitions:** Scott Galleries, Seattle, 1964, 65; Berkeley Gallery, San Francisco, 1968; SFMA, 1970; Reese Palley, San Francisco, 1971; Hansen-Fuller Gallery, San Francisco, 1973, 76; WMAA, 1973; Western Association of Art Museums, circ., 1974–75; Palace of the Legion of Honor, San Francisco, 1974; Nancy Hoffman Gallery, NYC, 1977; ICA, Boston, 1977; Odyssia Gallery, NYC, 1979. **Group:** Carnegie, 1957; PAFA Annual, 1957; Art USA, 1958; WMAA Annuals, 1969, 72, 73; La Jolla, Continuing Surrealism, 1972; Chicago/AI, 70th American Exhibition, 1972, 74; WMAA, American Drawings, 1973; U. of Illinois, Krannert, 1974; US Department of the Interior, America 1976, circ., 1976. **Collections:** Berkeley; U. of California; Charlotte/Mint; Chicago/AI; Dallas/MFA; Detroit/Institute; Fort Worth; Gulf Oil and Chemical Corp.; U. of Iowa; MOMA; PMA; RISD; Rutgers U.; Sacramento/Crocker; Santa Barbara/MA; SFMA; WMAA. **Bibliography:** *America 1976;* Arthur 2.

ALSTON, CHARLES HENRY. b. November 28, 1907, Charlotte, N.C.; **d.** April 27, 1977, NYC. **Studied:** Columbia U., BA; 1931, MA; Pratt Institute (with Alexander Kostellow). Traveled Europe, Caribbean. **Taught:** Joe and Emily Lowe Art School, NYC, 1949–57; ASL, 1950–77; City College; MOMA School; New School for Social Research. Federal A.P.: Mural and Lithography Supervisor; murals for Harlem Hospital, NYC; Golden State Mutual Life Insurance Co. **Commissions:** Murals, City College; American Museum of Natural History; P.S. 154, NYC; Harlem Hospital; Family Criminal Court Build-

ing, Bronx, N.Y. 1975. **Awards:** Columbia U., Dow Fellow, 1930; Lessing J. Rosenwald Fund Fellowship, 1939, 40; NIAL Grant, 1958; Atlanta U., First Prize, 1941; Dillard U., **P.P.,** 1942; Joe and Emily Lowe Foundation Award, 1960; National Council on the Arts, 1967. **One-man Exhibitions:** (first) Seymour Oppenheimer Gallery, Chicago, 1950; John Heller Gallery, NYC, 1953–57; Dunbarton Gallery, Boston, 1959; Feingarten Gallery, NYC, 1960. **Retrospective:** New York Cultural Center, Selective Retrospective, 1950–1969. **Group:** MMA, 1950; Boston/MFA; MOMA (several); Brussels World's Fair, 1958; Corcoran; WMAA; Detroit/Institute; Baltimore/MA; City College; U. of California, 1967; New York Cultural Center, 1969. **Collections:** Abraham Lincoln High School; Atlanta U.; City College; Detroit/Institute; Ford Motor Company; Golden State Mutual Life Insurance Co.; Harlem Hospital; Howard U.; IBM; U. of Illinois; MMA; NAACP; U. of Nebraska; WMAA; Youngstown/Butler. **Bibliography:** Dover. Archives.

ALTMAN, HAROLD. b. April 20, 1924, NYC. **Studied:** ASL (with George Bridgeman, Stefan Hirsch), 1941–42; Cooper Union (with Morris Kantor, Byron Thomas, Will Barnet), 1941–43, 1946–47; New School for Social Research (with Abraham Rattner), 1947–49; Black Mountain College (with Josef Albers), 1946; Academie de la Grande Chaumiere (with McAvoy), 1949–52; US Army, 1943–46. Traveled Europe, Mexico. **Taught:** N.Y. State College of Ceramics; U. of North Carolina; Indiana U.; U. of Wisconsin, 1956–62; The Pennsylvania State U., 1962–. **Member:** SAGA; California Society of Printmakers; PCA. **Commissions** (print editions): MOMA; Jewish Museum; New York Hilton Hotel; SAGA; Container Corp. of America, "Great Ideas of Western Man" advertising series. **Awards:** Guggenheim Foundation Fellowship, 1961, 63; NIAL

Grant, 1963; Chicago/AI, John Taylor Arms Medal; SAGA; PAFA; Tamarind Fellowship; Silvermine Guild; Fulbright-Hayes Research Scholar to France, 1964–65; The Pennsylvania State U., 1968, 69; Oklahoma, 1969; and some 200 others. **Address:** P.O. Box 57, Lemont, PA 16851. **Dealers:** A.A.A. Gallery; Impressions Workshop, Inc.; Haslem Fine Arts, Inc.; Marjorie Kauffman Gallery, Houston. **One-man Exhibitions:** (first) Galerie Huit, Paris, 1951; Martha Jackson Gallery, 1958; Philadelphia Art Alliance, 1959, 63; Peter H. Deitsch Gallery, 1960; Chicago/AI, 1961; SFMA, 1961; Santa Barbara/MA, 1961; Escuela Nacional de Artes Plasticas, Mexico City, 1961; The Goodman Gallery, Buffalo, 1961; Kasha Heman, Chicago, 1961, 63; Felix Landau Gallery, 1962; Gump's Gallery, 1962,64; Irving Galleries, Inc., Milwaukee, 1962, 64, 66; Kenmore Galleries, Inc., Philadelphia, 1963; The Pennsylvania State U., 1963; Kovler Gallery, 1963, 66; A. B. Closson Gallery, Cincinnati, 1965; Weyhe Gallery, 1966; Oklahoma, 1966; Ohio State U., 1966; Franklin Siden Gallery, Detroit, 1966; Sagot-Le Garrec Gallery, Paris, 1968, 74; Graphics Gallery, NYC, 1969, 71; Haslem Fine Arts, Inc., 1970, 71; David Barnett Gallery, Milwaukee, 1972; Gloria Luria Gallery, 1973; Gallery 1640, 1973; Marjorie Kauffman Gallery, Houston, 1973, 74; Wustum Museum of Art, 1974; Impressions Workshop, Inc., 1975. **Group:** WMAA Annuals; I Paris Biennial, 1959; PCA, American Prints Today, circ., 1959–62; SAGA, 1960–74; MOMA, Recent Painting USA: The Figure, circ., 1962–63; Festival of Two Worlds, Spoleto; St. Paul Gallery, Drawing USA, 1962, 64, 66, 71; PAFA Annuals, 1963, 66, 67, 69; MMA, Walter C. Baker Master Drawings Collection; Basel, Five American Printmakers, 1965; Santiago, Chile, II Interamerican Biennial of Printmaking, 1965; WMAA, A Decade of American Drawings, 1965. **Collections:** Achenbach Foundation; Amsterdam/Stedelijk; Auburn U.; Basel; Bibliotheque Nationale; Bibliotheque Royale de Belgique Nationale; Bibliotheque Royale de Belgique; Boston Public Library; Boston U.; Buffalo/Albright; Chicago/AI; Clairol, Inc.; Cleveland/MA; The Coca-Cola Co.; Container Corp. of America; Copenhagen; Detroit/Institute; Escuela Nacional de Artes Plasticas, Mexico City; First National Bank of Dallas; First National Bank, Minneapolis; U. of Georgia; U. of Glasgow; Grinnell College; Grunwald Foundation; Haifa; Hartford/Wadsworth; Hershey Foods Corp.; IBM; U. of Illinois; U. of Kentucky; Library of Congress; Lincoln Mass./De Cordova; Los Angeles/County MA; Lytton Savings and Loan Association; MMA; MOMA; Malmo; Milwaukee; Milwaukee Journal; NYPL; NYU; National Gallery; Newark Museum; New York Hilton Hotel; Norfolk; PAFA; PMA; The Pennsylvania State U.; Philip Morris Collection; Princeton U.; Raleigh/NCMA; SFAI; Smithsonian; Syracuse U.; Victoria (B.C.); WMAA; Walker; Woodward Foundation; Yale U.; Youngstown/Butler.

ALTOON, JOHN. b. 1925, Los Angeles, Calif.; **d.** February 8, 1969, Los Angeles, Calif. **Studied:** Otis Art Institute; Art Center School, Los Angeles; Chouinard Art Institute. US Navy, World War II. Traveled France, Spain. **Taught:** Otis Art Institute, 1951–62; Art Center School, Los Angeles, 1956–60; UCLA, 1962–63; Chouinard Art Institute, 1962–63; La Jolla, summer, 1962; Pasadena/AM, 1965–68. **Awards:** SFMA, Stacy Award, 1950; Joe and Emily Lowe Foundation Award, 1955; Pasadena/AM, **P.P.,** 1959; SFMA, James D. Phelan Award, 1961; Los Angeles/County MA, **P.P.,** 1962; William and Noma Copley Foundation Grant, 1964. **One-man Exhibitions:** (first) Santa Barbara/MA, 1951, also 1965; Artists' Gallery, NYC, 1953; Ganso Gallery, NYC, 1954; Ferus Gallery, Los Angeles, 1958–62; La Jolla, 1960; de Young, 1963; David Stuart Gallery, 1964, 65; Phoenix, Hack-Light, 1965; Quay Gallery, 1966,

68, 73; Fischbach Gallery, 1967; SFMA, 1967; Stanford U., 1967; Tibor de Nagy Gallery, NYC (three-man) 1970, 71, 73, 79; WMAA, 1971; Galerie Hans R. Neuendorf, Cologne, 1972; Felicity Samuel Gallery, London, 1973; Nicholas Wilder Gallery, 1973, 75; Seder/Creigh Gallery, Coronado, 1975; Braunstein/Quay Gallery, NYC, 1977; Tortue Gallery, Santa Monica, 1979; Edward Thorpe Gallery, NYC, 1979. **Group:** Carnegie, 1959; Santa Barbara Invitational, 1962; WMAA, Fifty California Artists, 1962–63; SRGM, American Drawings, 1964; SFMA, 1964, 65; U. of Texas, 1966; WMAA, 1967; NCFA, Eight from California, 1974. **Collections:** La Jolla; Los Angeles/County MA; MOMA; Pasadena/AM; SFMA; Stanford U.; WMAA. **Bibliography: John Altoon;** Lippard 5; *The State of California Painting.*

AMEN, IRVING. b. July 25, 1918, NYC. **Studied:** ASL with Vaclav Vytlacil, William Zorach, John Hovannes; Pratt Institute; Leonardo da Vinci Art School, NYC; Academie de la Grande Chaumiere, 1950; Florence and Rome, Italy. US Air Force, 1942–45. Traveled Europe extensively, Russia, Mexico. **Taught:** Pratt Institute, 1961; U. of Notre Dame, 1962. **Commissions:** A peace medal to commemorate the end of the Vietnam War. **Member:** Artists Equity; Audubon Artists; Boston Printmakers; SAGA; Fellow of the International Institute of Arts and Letters, 1960. **Address:** 45 West 27th Street, NYC 10001. **One-man Exhibitions:** (first) New School for Social Research, 1948; Smithsonian, 1949; The Krasner Gallery, 1948; Nebraska Wesleyan U., Lincoln, 1969. **Group:** USIA, Contemporary American Prints, circ. France, 1954; USIA, 20th Century American Graphics, circ., 1959–61; MOMA, Master Prints from the Museum Collection, 1949; MOMA, Young American Printmakers, 1953; MMA; Graphic Arts, 1955; U. of Illinois, 50 Contemporary American Printmakers, 1956; ART:

USA:59, NYC, 1959; Library of Congress; Brooklyn Museum; IV Bordighera Biennial, 1957; PAFA; NAD; Silvermine Guild; Audubon Artists; SAGA; American Color Print Society. **Collections:** Bezalel Museum; Bibliotheque Nationale; Bibliotheque Royale de Belgique; Boston/MFA; Cincinnati/AM; Graphische Sammlung Albertina; Harvard U.; Library of Congress; MMA; MOMA; NYPL; PMA; Smithsonian; Victoria and Albert Museum; Wilberfeld. **Bibliography:** Archives.

ANDERSON, GUY IRVING. b. November 20, 1906, Edmonds, Wash. Traveled USA, Mexico, Canada, Europe. Federal A.P.: Spokane (Wash.) Art Center, 1938–39; staff member, Seattle/AM, 1944; Helen Bush School, Seattle, 1954–55; Fidalgo Allied Arts, La Conner, Wash., 1957–59. **Commissions:** Tacoma Art League, 1960; murals for: Hilton Inn, Seattle-Tacoma International Airport; Seattle Opera House; Bank of California, Seattle, 1973; stone mosaic for First National Bank of Seattle; Seattle World's Fair, 1962; Washington Mutual Savings Bank, Seattle. **Awards:** L. C. Tiffany Grant, 1929; Seattle/AM, Art Award; Seattle/AM, Margaret E. Fuller, **P.P.;** State of Washington Governor's Award, Man of the Year, 1969; Guggenheim Foundation Fellowship, 1975. **Address:** Box 217, La Conner, WA 98257. **Dealer:** Francine Seders Gallery. **One-man Exhibitions:** (first) Seattle/AM, 1936, also 1945, 1953 (four-man), 1960; Zoe Dusanne Gallery, 1954, 59, 63, 65; College of Puget Sound, 1954; Tacoma, 1960; Smolin Gallery, NYC, 1962; Michel Thomas Gallery, Beverly Hills, Calif., 1962; Orris Gallery, San Diego, 1962; Kenmore Galleries, Inc., Philadelphia, 1963; Francine Seders Gallery, 1970, 73, 75, 77. **Retrospective:** Seattle/AM, 1977; Henry Art Gallery, U. of Washington, Seattle, 1977. **Group:** Seattle/AM, Northwest Annual, 1929–68, with four exceptions; MMA,

American Watercolors, Drawings and Prints, 1952; USIA, Eight American Artists, circ., Europe and Asia, 1957–58; Seattle World's Fair, 1962; Olympia, Wash., I Governor's Invitational, 1963; A.F.A., Drawing Society National Exhibition, 1970; NCFA, Art of the Pacific Northwest, 1974; Olympia, Two Centuries of Art in Washington, 1976; Seattle/AM, Northwest Traditions, 1977. **Collections:** Brooklyn Museum; Dublin/Municipal; Long Beach/MA; Melbourne/National; Mt. Vernon High School; NCFA; U. of Oregon; Santa Barbara/MA; Seattle/AM; Seattle Public Library; Tacoma; Utah; U. of Washington, Seattle; Utica; Victoria (B.C.); Washington State U.; Whatcom; Wichita/AM. **Bibliography:** *Art of the Pacific Northwest; Northwest Traditions.*

ANDERSON, JEREMY R. b. October 28, 1921, Palo Alto, Calif. **Studied:** San Francisco Art Institute (with David Park, Clyfford Still, Robert Howard, Mark Rothko, S. W. Hayter, Clay Spohn), 1946–50. US Navy, 1941–45. Traveled France. **Taught:** U. of California, Berkeley, 1955–56; SFAI, 1958–74; U. of California, Davis, 1974–75. **Awards:** SFAI, I. N. Walter Memorial Sculpture Prize, 1948; Abraham Rosenberg Foundation Traveling Fellowship, 1950; San Francisco Art Association, Sculpture Prize, 1959. **Address:** 534 Northern Avenue, Mill Valley, CA 94941. **Dealer:** Quay Gallery, San Francisco. **One-man Exhibitions:** (first) Metart Gallery, San Francisco, 1949; Allan Frumkin Gallery, Chicago, 1954; The Stable Gallery, 1954; Dilexi Gallery, San Francisco, 1960–62, 1964, 66; Dilexi Gallery, Los Angeles, 1962; SFMA, 1966; Quay Gallery, 1970, 75, 78. **Retrospectives:** SFMA and Pasadena/AM, 1966–67. **Group:** SFMA Annual, 1948, 49, 51–53, 58, 59, 63; U. of Illinois, 1955, 57; WMAA Annuals, 1956, 62, 64; Stanford U., Some Points of View for '62, 1962; WMAA, Fifty California Artists, 1962–63; Kaiser Center, Oakland, California Sculpture, 1963; Musée Cantonal

des Beaux-Arts, Lausanne, II Salon International de Galeries Pilotes, 1966; U. of California, Berkeley, Funk, 1967; Los Angeles/County MA, American Sculpture of the Sixties, 1967; Portland, Ore./AM, 1968; Expo '70, Osaka, 1970; Oakland/AM, 1973; Newport Harbor, drawing exhibition, 1975; JPL Fine Arts, London, Sculptors as Draughtsmen, 1975; SFMA, California Painting and Sculpture: The Modern Era, 1976. **Collections:** U. of California; MOMA; Oakland/AM; Pasadena/AM; SFMA; Dallas/MFA. **Bibliography: Jeremy Anderson;** McChesney; **Nordland 3;** Selz, P., 2; Seuphor 3; Tuchman 1.

ANDERSON, JOHN S. b. April 29, 1928, Seattle, Wash. **Studied:** Art Center School, Los Angeles, 1953–54; Pratt Institute, 1954–57, with Calvin Albert. US Army, 1951–53. Traveled Europe, Mexico, USA. **Taught:** Pratt Institute, 1959–62; School of Visual Arts, NYC, 1968–69; U. of New Mexico, 1969; Cooper Union, 1971–75. **Awards:** Guggenheim Foundation Fellowship, 1966, 67; New Jersey State Council on the Arts Grant, 1972. **Address:** Box 59, School Street, Asbury, NJ 08802. **Dealer:** Allan Stone Gallery. **One-man Exhibitions:** (first) Allan Stone Gallery, 1962, also 1964, 65, 67, 69, 71, 75, 77. **Group:** Waitsfield/Bundy, 1963; United States Plywood Corp., 1964; WMAA, 1964, Sculpture Annuals, 1965, 67, 69; World House Galleries, NYC, 1965. **Collections:** MOMA; WMAA. **Bibliography:** Atkinson.

ANDERSON, LENNART. b. August 22, 1928, Detroit, Mich. **Studied:** Chicago Art Institute School, 1946–50, BFA; Cranbrook Academy of Art, 1950–52, MFA; ASL, 1954, with Edwin Dickinson. Traveled Europe; resided Rome, 1958–61. **Taught:** Chatham College, 1961–62; Pratt Institute, 1962–64; Swain School, New Bedford, Mass., summers, 1963, 64; ASL; Yale U., 1967; Skowhegan School, 1968; Finch Col-

Lennart Anderson *Idyll I* 1980

lege, NYC; Brooklyn College. **Awards:** L. C. Tiffany Grant, 1957, 61; Prix de Rome, 1958–60; Silvermine Guild, Quinto Maganini Award, 1963; Ingram Merrill Foundation Grant, 1965; PAFA, Raymond A. Speiser Memorial Prize, 1966; National Council on the Arts, 1966. **Address:** 877 Union Street, Brooklyn, NY 11215. **Dealer:** Davis & Langdale Company. **One-man Exhibitions:** (first) Tanager Gallery, NYC, 1962; The Graham Gallery, 1963, 67; Kansas City/Nelson (two-man, with Edwin Dickinson), 1964; Davis & Long Co., NYC, 1976; Meredith Long and Co., Houston, 1974. **Group:** American Academy, Rome, 1958–60; Kansas City/Nelson, 1962, 64; IBM Gallery of Arts and Sciences, NYC; American Heritage, 1963; Silvermine Guild, 1963; WMAA Annuals, 1963, 64; Gallery of Modern Art, NYC, 1964; Boston U., 9 Realist Painters, 1964; Corcoran, 1964, and

Biennial, 1965; Carnegie, 1964, 67; Norfolk, Contemporary Art USA, 1966; Vassar College, 1968; Ravinia Festival, Highland Park, Ill., 1968. **Collections:** Bowdoin College; Brooklyn Museum; Hirshhorn; Minneapolis/Institute; U. of North Carolina; WMAA. **Bibliography:** *America 1976.*

ANDRE, CARL. b. September 16, 1935, Quincy, Mass. **Studied:** with Patrick Morgan, 1953, Frank Stella, 1958. US Army Intelligence Analyst. Employed by the Pennsylvania Railroad, 1960–64. Traveled England, France, Germany, Holland, Belgium. **Awards:** National Council on the Arts, 1968. **Address:** P.O. Box 1001 Cooper Station, NYC 10003. **Dealer:** Paula Cooper Gallery, NYC. **One-man Exhibitions:** (first) Tibor de Nagy Gallery, NYC, 1965, also 1966; Dwan Gallery, Los Angeles, 1967;

Dwan Gallery, NYC, 1967, 69, 71; Konrad Fischer Gallery, Dusseldorf, 1967,69,71,72,73,74,76; Monchengladbach, 1968; Galerie Heiner Friedrich, Munich, 1968, 71, Cologne, 73; Irving Blum Gallery, Los Angeles, 1969; Wide White Space Gallery, Antwerp, 1969, 71, 74; Galleria Sperone, Turin, 1969, 73; The Hague, 1969; ACE Gallery, Los Angeles, 1970, 76, 78; St. Louis/City, 1971; Yvon Lambert, Paris, 1971; Lisson Gallery, London, 1972; Janie C. Lee Gallery, Dallas, 1972; Galerie Annemarie Verna, Zurich, 1972; Max Protetch Gallery, Washington, D.C., 1973; Portland (Ore.) Center for the Visual Arts, 1973; Andover/Phillips, 1973; MOMA, 1973; Wide White Space Gallery, Brussels, 1974; John Weber Gallery, NYC, 1974, 75, 76; ACE Gallery, Vancouver, 1974, 75, 78; Cusack Gallery, Houston, 1975; Wesleyan U., Conn., 1976; The Clocktower, NYC, 1976; Kabinett fur Aktuelle Kunst, Bremerhaven, 1976; Minneapolis College of Art and Design, 1976; Otis Art Institute, 1977; Laguna Gloria Art Museum, Austin, 1978; Cincinnati/Contemporary, 1978; Buffalo/Albright, 1978; Chicago/AI, 1978; Newcastle Region Art Gallery, Australia, 1978; Art Gallery of South Australia, Adelaide, 1978; Van Abbemuseum, Eindhoven, 1978; Art Agency Co. Ltd., Tokyo, 1978; Pinacotheca, Melbourne, 1978; U. of California, Berkeley, 1979; Dallas/MFA, 1979; Musée d'Art Contemporain, Montreal, 1979; Palais des Beaux Arts, Brussels, 1979; Paris/Moderne, 1979; ICA, Boston, 1980; Lisson Gallery, London, 1975; Gran Enzo Sperone, Rome, 1975; Sperone Westwater Fischer, NYC, 1975, 77, 78; Weinberg Gallery, San Francisco, 1975; Cusack Gallery, Houston, 1976; ACE Gallery, Venice, 1976, 78; Galerie Lambert, Paris, 1976. **Retrospective:** SRGM, 1970. **Group:** Jewish Museum, Primary Structure Sculptures, 1966; Los Angeles/County MA, American Sculpture of the Sixties, 1967; Documenta IV, Kassel, 1968; The Hague, Minimal Art, 1968; MOMA, The Art of the Real, 1968;

Carl Andre *Triskaidek* 1979

Amsterdam/Stedelijk, Op Losse Schroeven, 1969; Berne, When Attitudes Become Form, 1969; WMAA, Anti-Illusion: Procedures/Materials, 1969; Chicago/AI, 69th American Exhibition, 1970; Tokyo Biennial, 1970; Foundation Maeght, 1970; SFMA, Unitary Forms: Minimal Sculptures, 1970; Seattle/AM, 557, 087, 1969; WMAA Sculpture Annuals, 1970, 73; MOMA, Information, 1970; SRGM, Guggenheim International, 1971; Arnhem, Sonsbeek '71, 1971; ICA, U. of Pennsylvania, Grids, 1972; New York Cultural Center, 3D into 2D, 1973; Basel Diagrams and Drawings, 1973; MOMA, Some Recent American Art, circ., 1973; Cologne/Kunstverein, Kunst uber Kunst, 1974; Indianapolis, 1974; Hayward Gallery, London, The Condition of Sculpture, 1975; NCFA, Sculpture: American Directions 1945–1975, 1975; Rijksmuseum Kroller-Muller, Functions of Drawing, 1975; MOMA, Drawing Now, 1976; WMAA, 200 Years of American Sculpture, 1976; Akademie der Kunst, Berlin,

SoHo, 1976; Corcoran, Andre, Long, Le Va, 1976; Paris/Moderne, Paris–New York, 1977; WMAA, 20th Century American Drawings, 1978; Venice Biennale; Lincoln, Mass./De Cordova, Born in Boston, 1979; Humlebaek/Louisiana, Andre, Dibbets, Long and Ryman, 1980. **Collections:** Basel; Brandeis U.; Buffalo/Albright; Chicago/Contemporary; Cologne; Columbus; Darmstadt/Hessisches; Dayton/AI; Krefeld/Haus Lange; La Jolla; MOMA; Milwaukee; Monchengladbach; Ottawa/National; Pasadena/AM; Ridgefield/Aldrich; Stuttgart; Tate; Toronto; Walker; WMAA. **Bibliography:** Alloway 4; *Art Now 74*; Battcock, ed.,; Calas, N. and E.; **Carl Andre Sculpture;** Celant; *Contemporanea*; Cummings 1; De Vries, ed.; Gablik; Goossen 1; Honnef; Honisch and Jensen, eds.; Johnson, Ellen H.; Krauss 2; Lippard 3; Lippard 4; Lippard ed.; Monte and Tucker; Muller; Tuchman 1; **Waldman 1;** *When Attitudes Become Form*. Archives.

ANDREJEVIC, MILET. b. September 25, 1925, Zrenjanin, Yugoslavia. **Studied:** School of Applied Arts, Belgrade, 1939–42; Academy of Fine Arts, Belgrade, 1942–47, BA. Traveled Europe; resided Paris, 1953–58. To USA, 1958. **Taught:** NYU, 1955–56; Brooklyn College, 1973–76. **Awards:** National Endowment for the Arts, grant. **Address:** 35 West 82nd Street, NYC 10025. **Dealer:** Robert Schoelkopf Gallery, NYC. **One-man Exhibitions:** (first) Belgrade/National, 1948; Green Gallery, NYC, 1961, 63; Noah Goldowsky, 1970, 72, 76. **Group:** Galerie Creuze, Paris, 1956–57; Dallas/MFA, 1962; Corcoran, 1963; WGMA, The Formalists, 1963; WMAA Annuals, 1963, 65; Chicago/AI, 1964; New York Cultural Center, Realism Now, 1972; Hofstra U., Green Gallery Revisited, 1972; MOMA, 76 Jefferson St, 1975. **Collections:** Allentown/AM; WMAA; Hirshhorn; U. of Texas, Austin; U. of Virginia; Charlottesville; RISD. **Bibliography:** Lippard 4.

ANDREWS, OLIVER. b. June 21, 1925, Berkeley, Calif. **Studied:** U. of Southern California, 1942; Stanford U., 1942–43, 1946–48, BA; U. of California, Santa Barbara, 1950–51; with Jean Helion, Paris, 1948–49. US Army, 1943–46. Traveled Europe, the Orient. Designed stage sets, 1951–52; began public events utilizing helium-filled balloons, 1969–. **Taught:** UCLA, 1957–; San Fernando Valley State College, 1962–63. **Commissions:** sculptural lighting fixtures for Yale U.; the David S. Ingalis Rink, 1958. Stiles and Morse Colleges, 1962; fountain for West Valley Professional Center, San Jose, Calif., 1963; I. Magnin Co., Los Angeles, 1965; UCLA, 1965; U. of California, Riverside, 1967; Metromedia Television Co., Los Angeles, 1969; Los Angeles Times-Mirror Co., 1970; Federal Reserve Bank of Cleveland, 1972. **Awards:** Los Angeles/County MA, Junior Art Council **P.P.,** for Sculpture, 1957, 61; U. of California Institute for Creative Work in the Arts, Travel Fellowship, 1963. **Address:** 408 Sycamore Rd., Santa Monica, CA 90402. **Dealer:** David Stuart Gallery. **One-man Exhibitions:** Santa Barbara/MA, 1950, 56, 63; Stanford U., 1952, 60 (three-man); The Alan Gallery, NYC, 1955, 59, 61, 66; Frank Perls Gallery, Beverly Hills, 1960, 61; Gallery Eight, Santa Barbara, 1961; Los Angeles Municipal Art Gallery (two-man), 1963; David Stuart Gallery, 1967, 70; Palomar College, 1967; UCLA, 1970; Nordness Galleries, 1971; A.B. Closson Co., Cincinnati, 1971; California State U., Fullerton, 1971; U. of Rochester, 1971; Northwest Craft Center, Seattle, 1974; Leslie Wenger Gallery, San Francisco, 1974. **Group:** Los Angeles/County MA, 1953, 56, 57, 59, 61; U. of Minnesota, Contemporary American Sculpture, 1955; WMAA Annual, 1956; Chicago/AI Annual, 1957; U. of California, Riverside, Four Sculptors, 1958; MOMA, Recent Sculpture USA, 1959; UCLA, 1959; Hartford/Wadsworth, Smallscale Sculpture, 1960; La Jolla, 1960, 61; SFMA Annual, 1960, 61, 63, 66; SRGM, The Joseph H. Hirshhorn Collection, 1962;

WMAA, Fifty California Artists, 1962–63; Long Beach State College, 1963; Buffalo/Albright, Contemporary Sculpture, 1963; Municipal Art Gallery, Los Angeles, 1965; U. of Hawaii, 1965; Southern Sculpture '67, circ., 1967; Century City Sculpture Park, Los Angeles, Sculpture in the City, 1968; UCLA, Electric Art, 1969; Columbus, Art in Public Places, 1973. **Collections:** U. of California, Riverside; Hirshhorn; Johnson Wax Co.; Los Angeles/County MA; SFMA; Santa Barbara/MA; Storm King Art Center; UCLA.

ANTONAKOS, STEPHEN. b. November 1, 1926, Greece. To USA, 1930. **Studied:** Brooklyn (N.Y.) Community College. Traveled Europe. **Taught:** Brooklyn Museum School; U. of North Carolina, Greensboro, 1967, 69; U. of Wisconsin, Madison, 1968; U. of California, Fresno, 1970. **Commissions:** Dayton, Ohio, Federal Building (GSA), 1978; Hampshire College, Amherst, Mass., 1978; Atlanta International Airport, 1980; Baltimore, Md., subway, 1983; Cambridge, Mass., subway line and commuter terminal, 1984; Seattle Center Resident Theatre, 1981. Made a film of "package" projects, 1970–75. **Awards:** CAPS, 1972; National Endowment for the Arts, 1973; DAAD, West Berlin, 1980. **Address:** 435 West Broadway, NYC 10012. **Dealers:** Young-Hoffman, Chicago; Bernier Gallery, Athens; Galerie Tanit, Munich; Galerie Bonnier, Geneva. **One-man Exhibitions:** Avant Garde Gallery, NYC, 1958; The Bryon Gallery, 1964; Miami Modern, 1964; Schramm Galleries, Fort Lauderdale, Fla., 1964; Fischbach Gallery, 1967–69, 1970, 71, 72; Madison Art Center, 1971; Wisconsin State U., Oshkosh, 1971; Houston/Contemporary, 1971; Fresno State College, 1972; CAPS, 1973; Rosa Esman Gallery, 1974; John Weber Gallery, 1974, 75, 76, 77; Buffalo/Albright, 1974; The Clocktower, NYC, 1974; Cusack Gallery, Houston, 1974; Fort Worth, 1974; Galleria Marilena Bonomo, Bari, Italy, 1975; Galerie 27, Paris, 1975; Wright State U., 1975; Art & Project, Amsterdam, 1976; Galerie Bonnier, 1976; Nancy Lurie Gallery, Chicago, 1976; Galerie Aronowitsch, Stockholm, 1977; Bernier Gallery, Athens, 1977; U. of Massachusetts, Amherst, 1978; Young-Hoffman, Chicago, 1978; Galerie Nancy Gillespie/Elizabeth de Laage, Paris, 1979; Galerie Tanit, Munich, 1980. **Group:** Martha Jackson Gallery, New Media—New Forms, I & II, 1960, 61; Van Bovenkamp Gallery, NYC, 1965; Eindhoven, Kunst-Licht-Kunst, 1966; Kansas City/Nelson, Sound, Light, Science, 1966; WMAA, 1966, 68–69; Carnegie, 1967; Worcester/AM, 1967; Los Angeles/County MA and PMA, American Sculpture of the Sixties, 1967; Trenton/State, Focus on Light, 1967; Milwaukee, Light Motion Space, 1967; A.F.A., 1968; Kansas City/Nelson, The Magic Theatre, 1968; WMAA, Light: Object and Image, 1968; UCLA, Electric Art, 1969; Newark Museum, Light in Contemporary Art, 1969; WMAA, Human Concern/Personal Torment, 1969, Annual, 1970; Jacksonville/Cummer, Light Art, 1970; Hayward Gallery, London, Kinetics, 1970; Portland, Me./MA, Light, 1971; U. of North Carolina, Works on Paper, 1971, 72; U. of Maryland, What's Happening in Soho, 1971; U. of Nebraska, Light and Motion, 1972; Katonah (N.Y.) Art Gallery, Drawing in Space, 1972; WMAA, American Drawings: 1963–1973, 1973; SFMA, Works in Spaces, 1973; Indianapolis, 1974; Webster College, Webster Groves, Mo., 4 Dimensions in 2, 1975; Ackland, Light/Sculpture, 1975; Leverkusen, USA Zeichnungen 3, 1975; Berlin/Akademie der Kunst, SoHo, 1976; Kassel, Documenta 6, 1977; SFMA, A Shade of Light, 1978; Ridgefield/Aldrich, The Minimal Tradition, 1979. **Collections:** Brandeis U.; Chase Manhattan Bank; Ciba-Geigy Corp.; Dayton, Ohio, Federal Building; SRGM; Hampshire College; Hartford/Wadsworth; La Jolla; MOMA; U. of Maine; Miami/Modern; Milwaukee; Newark Museum; U. of Massachusetts; U. of North Carolina;

Phoenix; Ridgefield/Aldrich; U. of Utah; WMAA. **Bibliography:** Battock, ed.; *Report*; Tuchman 1. Archives.

ANTREASIAN, GARO. b. February 16, 1922, Indianapolis, Ind. **Studied:** John Herron Art Institute, B.F.A. **Taught:** John Herron Art Institute, 1948–59, 1961–64; U. of New Mexico, 1964–. Technical director, Tamarind Lithography Workshop, 1960–61; Technical director, Tamarind Institute, 1970–72. **Commissions:** (murals) Butler U.; Indiana National Bank, Indianapolis; Indiana U., Bloomington. **Awards:** Hoosier Salon, 1944, 49; MOMA, 1953; The Print Club, Philadelphia, 1958, 61; Albion College, 1968; Northern Illinois U., 1968. **Awards:** Hon. DFA, Purdue U., 1972. **Address:** 1520 Los Alamos SW, Albuquerque, NM 87104. **Dealers:** Marjorie Kauffman Gallery; Blue Door, Denver; Etchings International, NYC; Alice Simsar, Inc., Ann Arbor; Heydt Blair Gallery, Santa Fe, N.M. **One-man Exhibitions:** Tulane U.; U. of Notre Dame; Stephens College; Wabash College; Kalamazoo/Institute; Martha Jackson Gallery, 1969; Maluina Miller Gallery, San Francisco; Marjorie Kauffman Gallery, Houston; Cottonwood Gallery, Albuquerque; Lantern Gallery, Ann Arbor; Marjorie Kauffman Gallery, Houston, 1979; Elaine Horwitch Gallery, Santa Fe, 1977–78; Alice Simsar, Inc., Ann Arbor, 1979. **Retrospective:** Ohio State U.; Washburn U.; U. of Nebraska; Miami U., Oxford, Ohio; Kansas State U.; U. of Georgia; U. of New Mexico. **Group:** SFMA, 1942; NAD, 1943; Library of Congress, 1949, 66, 68; MMA, 1950; Boston/MFA; PMA; NYPL; USIA; ART; USA:59, NYC, 1959; PCA, 1959; Brooklyn Museum Print Biennials; SAGA, 1964; Florida State U., 1965, 67, 69; Seattle/AM, 1966, 68; Smithsonian, 1968; Potsdam/SUNY, 1968; Albany/SUNY, 1968; Tokyo Print Biennial, 1972; U. of Kentucky, Graphics Now; USA, 1972; Bradford, England, III British Print Biennial, 1972; Honolulu

Academy Print Biennial, 1973; California State U., Sacramento, Print Invitational, 1974. **Collections:** Albion College; L. S. Ayres & Co.; Boston/MFA; Bradley U.; Brooklyn Museum; Chicago/AI; Cleveland/MA; Coos Bay; Dallas/MFA; Drake U.; Grand Rapids; Indiana National Bank; Indiana U.; Indianapolis; Los Angeles/County MA; MMA; MOMA; U. of Michigan; U. of Minnesota; NCFA; National Gallery; U. of Notre Dame, Olivet College; PMA; The Print Club, Philadelphia; Reed College; Roswell; SRGM; San Jose State College; Santa Fe, N.M.; Seattle/AM; Smith College; Southern Illinois U.; Stephens College; Terre Haute/Swope; USIA; US Coast Guard; U. of Wisconsin. **Bibliography:** Archives.

ANUSZKIEWICZ, RICHARD. b. May 23, 1930, Erie, Pa. **Studied:** Cleveland Institute of Art, 1948–53; Kent State U., 1955–56, BS.Ed.; Yale U., 1953–55, MFA. Traveled Western Europe, North Africa. **Taught:** Dartmouth College, Artist-in-Residence, 1967; U. of Wisconsin, 1968; Cornell U., 1968; Kent State U., 1968. **Awards:** Silvermine Guild, Philosophers Stone Prize, 1963, First Prize, 1964; Flint/Institute, **P.P.**, 1966. **Address:** 76 Chestnut Street, Englewood, NJ 07631. **Dealer:** Alex Rosenberg Gallery, NYC. **One-man Exhibitions:** Youngstown/Butler, 1955; The Contemporaries, NYC, 1960, 61, 63; Sidney Janis Gallery, 1965, 67, 69, 71, 73; Cleveland/MA, 1966; Dartmouth College, 1967; U. of Wisconsin, 1968; Kent State U., 1968; J.L. Hudson Art Gallery, Detroit, 1968; Free Public Library, Fair Lawn, N.J., 1969; Trenton/State (two-man), 1971; A.A.A. Gallery, 1973; Andrew Crispo Gallery, NYC, 1974, 75, 76; La Jolla, 1976; Pine Free Public Library, Fairlawn, N.J., 1976; U. of California, Berkeley, 1977; Columbus, 1977; Reed College, 1977; Graphics Gallery, Toronto, 1977; Montclair State College, 1977; Galerie 99, Bay Harbor Islands, 1978; Ringling, 1978; Allentown/AM, 1978; Terre Haute/Swope,

1978; Wichita/AM, 1978; Alex Rosenberg Gallery, NYC, 1979. **Retrospective:** Brooklyn Museum, 1980. **Group:** U. of Illinois, 1961, 63; NYU, 1961; PAFA, 1962, 67; WMAA, Geometric Abstraction in America, circ., 1962; U. of Minnesota, 1962; Silvermine Guild, 1962, 63; Allentown/AM, 1963; Lincoln, Mass./De Cordova, New Experiments in Art, 1963; MOMA, Americans 1963, circ., 1963–64; WGMA, The Formalists, 1963; WMAA Annual, 1963, 67; Chicago/AI, 1964; Tate, Painting and Sculpture of a Decade, 1954–64, 1964; Carnegie, 1964, 67; MOMA, The Responsive Eye, 1965; Corcoran Biennial, 1965; WMAA, A Decade of American Drawings, 1965; Buffalo/Albright, Plus by Minus, 1968; Flint/Institute, I Flint Invitational, 1966; WMAA, Art of the U.S. 1670–1966, 1966; Detroit/Institute, Color, Image and Form, 1967; Trenton/State, Focus on Light, 1967; Expo '67, Montreal, 1967; Documenta IV, Kassel, 1968; WMAA, Artists under 40, 1968; Corcoran Biennial, 1975. **Collections:** Akron/AI; Allentown/AM; Amherst College; Buffalo/Albright; Carnegie; Charlotte/Mint; Chicago/AI; Cleveland/MA; Corcoran; Dartmouth College; Detroit/Institute; Flint/Institute; Harvard U.; Hirshhorn; Honolulu/Academy; Milwaukee; MIT; Norfolk/Chrysler; MOMA; PMA; Princeton U.; Ridgefield/Aldrich; RISD; Rutgers U.; SFMA; U. of Texas; Trenton/State; VMFA; U. of Wisconsin; WMAA; Yale U.; Youngstown/Butler. **Bibliography:** Battcock, ed.; Hunter, ed.; MacAgy 2; Rickey; Weller. Archives.

ARAKAWA, SHUSAKU. b. 1936, Nagoya City, Japan. **Studied:** U. of Tokyo, 1954–58; Massachusetts College of Art, Boston. To USA, 1961. **Award:** DAAD Grant, 1972. **Address:** 124 West Houston Street, NYC 10012. **Dealer:** Ronald Feldman Fine Arts, Inc. **One-man Exhibitions:** Mudo Gallery, Tokyo, 1961; Galerie Schmela, 1963, 65, 66; Dwan Gallery, Los Angeles, 1964, 66; Brussels/Beaux Arts, 1964; Minami

Gallery, 1965; Galleria dell-Ariete, 1965; Dwan Gallery, NYC, 1966, 68, 69; Wide White Space Gallery, Antwerp, 1966; Stuttgart/WK, 1966; Eindhoven, 1966; Wuppertal/von der Heydt, 1967; Galeria Schwarz, 1967, 71; Yvon Lambert, Paris, 1969, 75; Paris/Moderne, 1970; Hannover/Kunsterverein, 1970; Badischer Kunstverein, Karlsruhe, 1970; Fendrick Gallery, 1971; Harcus-Krakow Gallery, 1971; Angela Flowers Gallery, London, 1971; Hamburg, circ., 1972; Galerie Art in Progress, Zurich, 1972; Galerie van der Loo, Munich, 1972; Ronald Feldman Fine Arts Inc., 1972, 74; Dayton's Gallery 12, Minneapolis, 1973; Galleria A. Castelli, Milan, 1974; MOMA, 1974; U. of Wisconsin, circ., 1974; Multiples Inc., NYC, 1974; Galerie Art in Progress, Munich, 1974; Humlebaek/Louisiana, 1974; Art in Progress, Dusseldorf, 1975; 77; Galerie Arnonowitsch, Stockholm, 1975; Isy Brachot, Brussels, 1975; Pasquale Trisorio, Naples, 1975; Henie Onstad Museum, Oslo, 1975; Berger Gallery, Pittsburgh, 1975; Carl Solway Gallery, Cincinnati, 1975; Ronald Feldman Fine Arts, NYC, 1976, 79; Multiples, NYC, 1976; Galeria 42, Barcelona, 1976; Toronto, 1976; Rubicon Gallery, Los Altos, 1976; Margo Leavin Gallery, Los Angeles, 1976, 78; Delahunty Gallery, Dallas, 1976; Grupo Quince, Madrid, 1976; I.C.C. Antwerp, 1976; U. of Wisconsin, Milwaukee, 1977; Kunsthalle, Dusseldorf, 1977; Galerie Maeght, Paris, 1977, 78; Museo de Arte Moderno, Bogota, 1977; Gallery Takagi, Nagoya, 1978; Berlin/National, 1978; Amsterdam/Stedelijk, 1978; Oesterreichisches Landesmuseum, Kunstsammlungen, Ludwigshafen, 1979; Seibu Museum, Tokyo, 1979; National Museum, Osaka, 1979. **Group:** U. of Illinois, 1965, 67; MOMA, New Japanese Paintings and Sculpture, 1966; Documenta IV, Kassel, 1968; XXXV Venice Biennial, 1970; Indianapolis, 1974; Cologne, Project '74, 1974; Brooklyn Museum Print Biennial, 1974; Cincinnati/MA, Japanese Prints of the 20th Century, 1975; Hirshhorn, The Golden

Door, 1876–1976, 1976; Milwaukee, From Foreign Shores, 1976; Chicago/ AI, Drawings of the 70's, 1976; Berlin/ National, SoHo, 1976; Documenta 6, Kassel, 1977; Chicago/Contemporary, Words at Liberty, 1977; WMAA, Art about Art, 1978; Cleveland/MA, 4 Contemporary Painters, 1978. **Collections:** Amsterdam/Stedelijk; Basel; Berlin; Brussels/Beaux Arts; Dayton/AI; Des Moines; Dusseldorf; Hirshhorn; MOMA; Paris/Moderne; Walker. **Bibliography:** Alloway 4; *From Foreign Shores;* Honisch and Jensen, eds.; *Art Now 74;* Calas, N. and E.; *Contemporanea; Kunst um 1970.*

ARCHIPENKO, ALEXANDER. b. May 30, 1887, Kiev, Ukraine; **d.** February 25, 1964, NYC. **Studied:** Kiev, an art school, 1902–05; Academie des Beaux-Arts, Paris, 1908. To USA, 1923; citizen, 1928. Traveled Europe and USA extensively. **Taught:** U. of Washington, 1935–36; U. of Kansas; Allegheny College; opened school in Paris, 1910; opened school in NYC, 1939. **One-man Exhibitions:** Hagen, 1910, 60; X Venice Biennial, 1920; Andover/Phillips, 1928; Karl Nierendorf Gallery, NYC, 1944; Dallas/MFA, 100th One-Man, 1952; A.A.A. Gallery, NYC, 110th One-Man, 1954; Darmstadt/Kunsthalle, circ. Germany, 1955; Perls Galleries, 1957, 59; Grosvenor (Gallery), London, 1961; Mannheim, 1962; Palazzo Barberini, Rome, 1963; Auckland, 1964; Finch College, NYC, 1967; UCLA, 1967; NCFA, 1968; Musée Rodin, Paris, 1969; Toronto, 1971; Paine Art Center and Arboretum, Oshkosh, 1971; The Pace Gallery, NYC, 1973; The Zabriskie Gallery, NYC, 1976, 79. **Retrospective:** Smithsonian, 1968. **Group:** Major international exhibitions. **Collections:** Amherst College; Andover/Phillips; Belvedere; Brandeis U.; Chicago/AI; Cleveland/MA; Cranbrook; Darmstadt/ Kunsthalle; U. of Delaware; Denver/ AM; Detroit/Institute; Dusseldorf; Essen; Hagen; Hanover; Honolulu Academy; U. of Kansas City; Leipzig;

MOMA; Mannheim; Miami/Modern; U. of Michigan; U. of Minnesota; Municipal U. of Omaha; Northwestern U.; Omaha/Joslyn; U. of Oregon; Osaka/ Municipal; Phillips; Phoenix; Rotterdam; SFMA; SRGM; San Antonio/ McNay; Seattle/AM; Tel Aviv; WMAA; Yale U. **Bibliography: Alexander Archipenko, A Memorial Exhibition; Archipenko 1, 2;** Barr 1; Baur 7; Biddle 4; Bihalji-Merin; Blesh 1; Brown; Brumme; Bulliet 1; Cassou; Cheney; Draven, W.; Christensen; **Daubler and Goll;** Dorner; Dreier 2; Gertz; Giedion-Welcker 1, 2; Goodrich and Baur 1; Guggenheim, ed.; Haftman; **Hildebrandt;** Huyghe; *Index of 20th Century Artists;* Janis and Blesh 1; Janis, S.; **Karshan;** Kuh 3; Langui; Lee and Burchwood; Licht, F.; Lynton; Masten; McCurdy, ed.; Mellquist; Mendelowitz; Neumeyer; Poore; Ramsden 2; **Raynal 1;** Read 3; Rickey; Ritchie 3; Rose, B. 1; Rosenblum 1; Salvini; Selz, J.; Seuphor 3; Trier 1, 2; Valentine 2; Verkauf; Wingler, ed.; *Woodstock;* Zaidenberg, ed.; Zervos. Archives.

ARMAN, PIERRE. b. November 17, 1928, Nice, France. **Studied:** Ecole du Louvre; Ecole Nationale des Arts Decoratifs. US citizen, 1972. Traveled Europe, Asia, Africa, North America. **Taught:** UCLA, 1967–68. Co-founder, Groupe des Nouveaux Réalistes, 1960, and L'Ecole de Nice, 1961. **Awards:** IV International Biennial Exhibition of Prints, Tokyo, 1964, Second Prize; Premio Marzotto, 1966; Order of Merit, for artistic achievement, Paris, 1972. **Address:** 380 West Broadway, NYC 10012. **Dealer:** Andre Emmerich Gallery. **One-man Exhibitions:** (first) Galerie du Haut Pave, Paris, 1956; Iris Clert Gallery, 1958, 60; Galleria Apollinaire, Milan, 1959; Galerie Schmela, Dusseldorf, 1960, 63; Galleria Schwarz, Milan, 1961, 63, 68; Cordier and Warren, NYC, 1961; Galerie Saqqarah, Gstaad, Switzerland, 1962, 66; Dwan Gallery, Los Angeles, 1962; Galerie Lawrence, Paris, 1962, 63, 65; Sidney Janis Gallery, 1963, 64, 68; Walker,

1964; Richard Feigen Gallery, Chicago, 1965; Galerie Bonnier, Lausanne, 1965, 66, 69; Galerie de Leone, Venice, 1965; Galerie Svensk-Franska, Stockholm, 1966, 69; Ileana Sonnabend Gallery, Paris, 1967, 69; Il Punto, Turin, 1967; Galerie Françoise Meyer, Brussels, 1967; Galerie Mathias Fels, Paris, 1969; Musée des Arts Decoratifs, 1969; Humlebaek/Louisiana, 1969; Kunsthalle, Berlin, 1969; Dusseldorf/Kunsthalle, 1969; Stockholm/National, 1970; Zurich, 1970; Ileana Sonnabend Gallery, Paris, 1970; ACE Gallery, Los Angeles, 1970; ACE Gallery, Vancouver, 1970; Galerie der Spiegel, Cologne, 1970; Galerie Lambert-Monet, Geneva, 1970; Galerie Bonnier, 1970, 71; Lawrence Rubin Gallery, NYC, 1970, 71; Galerie de la Salle, Vence, 1971; Galerie Bischofberger, Zurich, 1971; Galerie Michel Couturier & Cie., Paris, 1971; Galleria del Leone, Venice, 1972; Galeria Guillaume Campo, Antwerp, 1972; Galerie de l'Oeil, Paris, 1972; White Gallery, Lutry, 1973; John Gibson Gallery, 1973; Andrew Crispo Gallery, 1973, 74, 75; Musée d'Arles, 1974; Fort Worth, 1975; Paris/Moderne, 1975; Venice Biennial, 1976; Galerie Charles Kriwin, Brussels, 1976, 78; Wichita State U., 1977; Jollembeck Gmbh., Cologne, 1978; Andre Emmerich Gallery, NYC, 1979; Galleria Cavellini, Brescia, 1979; The Art Contact, Miami, 1979; Museo Civico da Portofino, 1980; Galerie Valeur, Nagoya, Japan, 1980. **Retrospectives:** Amsterdam/Stedelijk, 1964; Krefeld/Haus Lange, 1964; Brussels/Beaux-Arts, 1966; La Jolla, circ., 1974; Galerie de la Salle, St. Paul de Vence, 1976. **Group:** XXXIV Venice Biennial, 1968; Documenta IV, Kassel, 1968; Tokyo Biennial, 1969; Expo '70, Osaka, 1970. **Collections:** Amsterdam/Stedelijk; Antwerp; Brussels/Royaux; Buffalo/Albright; Chicago/Contemporary; Cologne; Dartmouth College; Eindhoven; France/National; Ghent/Moderne; Helsinki; Hirshhorn; Humlebaek/Louisiana; Krefeld/Haus Lange; MMA; MOMA; Munich/Modern; Musée des Arts Decoratifs, Paris;

PMA; Paris/Moderne; Renault & Cie., Paris; Rome/Nazionale; U. of St. Thomas (Tex.); Societe Nationale des Arts Contemporains; Stockholm/National; Stuyvesant Foundation; Sweden/Goteborgs; Talavera; Turin/Civico; Venice/Contemporaneo; Walker; Wells, Rich, Greene, Inc., NYC. **Bibliography: Arman;** *Contemporanea;* **Hahn;** *Happening & Fluxus;* **Martin, H.** Archives.

ARNESON, ROBERT. b. September 4, 1930, Benicia, Calif. **Studied:** College of Marin, Kentfield, Calif., 1949–51; California College of Arts and Crafts, BA, 1954; Mills College, MFA, 1958. **Taught:** Menlo-Atherton H.S., 1954–57; Santa Rosa Junior College, 1958–59; Fremont H.S., Oakland, Calif., 1960–62; Mills College, 1960–62; U. of California, Davis, 1962–. **Awards:** National Endowment for the Arts, grant, 1971, 78. **Address:** 110 East E Street, Benicia, CA 94510. **Dealer:** Allan Frumkin Gallery, NYC. **One-man Exhibitions:** Oakland/AM, 1960; de Young, 1962; Barios Gallery, Sacramento, 1962; Cellini Gallery, San Francisco, 1964; Allan Stone Gallery, NYC, 1964, 69; SFMA, 1967; Candy Store Gallery, Folsom, Calif., 1969, 70, 71; Hansen-Fuller Gallery, San Francisco, 1968, 69, 70, 71, 72, 73; Fresno State College, 1970; U. of Calgary, 1971; Manolides Gallery, Seattle (two-man), 1972; Miami Dade College, 1972; U. of Nevada, Reno, 1973; Deson-Zaks Gallery, Chicago, 1974; Allan Frumkin Gallery, NYC, 1975, 78, 79; Fendrick Gallery, Washington, D.C., 1976; Moore College of Art, Philadelphia, 1979. **Retrospective:** Chicago/Contemporary, 1974. **Group:** Oakland/AM, Sculpture, 1963; U. of California, Berkeley, Funk Art, 1967; MOMA, The Dada-Surrealist Heritage, 1968; NCFA, Objects USA, 1969; WMAA, Human Concern Personal Torment, 1969; Syracuse/Everson, Ceramics, 70, 1970; Museum of Contemporary Crafts, NYC, Clayworks: 20 Americans, 1971; SFMA, A Decade of Ceramic Art, 1962–72, 1973; U. of Illinois, 1974; WMAA Bien-

Robert Arneson *Santa Bob* 1975

nial, 1979; Syracuse/Everson, Nine West Coast Clay Sculptures, 1978. **Collections:** Amsterdam/Stedelijk; Canberra/National; Museum of Contemporary Crafts, NYC; Chicago/Contemporary; Des Moines; Hirshhorn; Mildura Art Center; PMA; Sacramento/Crocker; Santa Barbara/MA; SFMA; U. of Utah; WMAA.

ARNOLD, ANNE. b. May 2, 1925, Melrose, Mass. **Studied:** U. of New Hampshire, 1946, BA; The Ohio State U., 1947, MA; U. of Guadalajara, 1949; ASL, 1949–53. **Taught:** Geneseo/SUNY, 1947–49; Wagner College, 1951–52; Philadelphia College of Art, 1965–68; Brooklyn College, 1971,73–; Columbia

U. Graduate School, 1975–76. **Address:** c/o Dealer. **Dealer:** Fischbach Gallery. **One-man Exhibitions:** Tanager Gallery, NYC, 1960; Fischbach Gallery, 1964, 67, 69, 71, 74, 76, 79; Bard College, 1971; Galerie Dieter Brusberg, Hanover, 1972. **Retrospective:** Moore College of Art, Philadelphia, 1971. **Group:** Riverside Museum, NYC, Twelve Sculptors, 1962; Chicago/AI Annual, 1964; Milwaukee, Pop Art and the American Tradition, 1965; Sculptors Guild, 1967,68; PAFA Annual 1968; Finch College, NYC, The Dominant Woman, 1968; City Hall, Rockport, Me., Maine Coast Artists, 1969; Roko Gallery, Homage to Tanager: 1952–1962, 1971; U. of North Carolina, 1971, 72, 73; New York Cultural Center, Women Choose Women, 1973; Indianapolis, 1974; PMA/Museum of the Philadelphia Civic Center, Focus, 1974; Renwick Gallery, Washington, D.C., Object as Poet, 1977; Syracuse/Everson, The Animal Kingdom, 1978. **Collections:** Buffalo/Albright; Ciba-Geigy Corp.; Citibank, NYC; MMA; U. of North Carolina.

ARNOLDI, CHARLES. b. April 10, 1946, Dayton, Ohio. **Studied:** Chouinard Art School, 1968. **Awards:** Guggenheim Foundation Fellowship, 1975; National Endowment for the Arts, grant, 1974; Chicago/AI, Witkowsky Award, 1972. **Address:** 11 Brooks Avenue, Venice, CA 90291. **Dealer:** Robert Elkon Gallery, NYC. **One-man Exhibitions:** Riko Mizuno Gallery, Los Angeles, 1971; The Texas Gallery, Houston, 1972, 74, 75; Nicholas Wilder Gallery, Los Angeles 1975, 76, 78, 79; Robert Elkon Gallery, NYC, 1975, 76, 78, 79; Charles Cowles Gallery, 1980. **Group:** Chicago/Contemporary, Permutations: Light & Color, 1969; Pasadena/AM, Fifteen Los Angeles Artists, 1972; Chicago/AI, Seventieth American Exhibition, 1972; Documenta 5, Kassel, 1972; Indianapolis, 1978. **Collections:** Chicago/AI; Los Angeles/County MA; Pasadena/AM; Seattle/AM, SFMA.

ARONSON, DAVID. b. October 28, 1923, Shilova, Lithuania. To USA, 1929. **Studied:** Boston Museum School, with Karl Zerbe; Hebrew Teachers College, Boston. Traveled Europe, Near East. **Taught:** Boston U., 1954–; Boston Museum School, 1942–55. **Members:** NAD. **Commissions:** Container Corp. of America, 1962. **Awards:** ICA, Boston, First Prize, 1944; ICA, Boston, First Popular Prize, 1955; VMFA, 1946; Boston Museum School, Traveling Fellowship, 1946; Boston Arts Festival, Grand Prize, 1952, 54; Boston Arts Festival, Second Prize, 1953; Tupperware Annual, First Prize, 1954; NIAL Grant, 1958; J. S. Guggenheim Fellowship, 1960; NIAL, **P.P.,** 1961; NAD, Issac N. Maynard Prize, 1975; NAD, Joseph I. Isidor Gold Medal, 1976; NAD, Henry Ward Ranger Fund **P.P.** 1976. **Address:** 137 Brimstone Lane, Sudbury, MA 01776. **Dealer:** Pucker/Safrai Gallery, Boston. **One-man Exhibitions:** (first) Niveau Gallery, NYC, 1945, also 1956; Boris Mirski Gallery, Boston, 1951, 59, 64, 69; The Downtown Gallery, 1953; Lee Nordness Gallery, 1960, 61, 63, 69; Rex Evans Gallery, 1961; Westhampton Gallery, NYC, 1961; J. Thomas Gallery, Provincetown, Mass., 1964; Zora Gallery, Los Angeles, 1965; Hunter Gallery, Chattanooga, 1965; Kovler Gallery, 1965; Verle Gallery, Hartford, 1967; Dannenberg Gallery, 1969, 72; Pucker-Safrai Gallery, Boston, 1978, 79; Louis Newman Gallery, Los Angeles, 1977. **Retrospective:** Brandeis U., 1979. **Group:** MOMA, Fourteen Americans, circ., 1946; Chicago/AI; U. of Illinois; MMA; ICA, Boston; WMAA; Boston/MFA; Bridgestone Museum; Palazzo di Venezia, Rome. **Collections:** Atlanta/AA; Atlanta U.; Boston/MFA; Brandeis U.; Bryn Mawr College; Carnegie; Chicago/AI; Colby College; U. of Illinois; Lincoln, Mass./De Cordoba; MOMA; Milwaukee; NCFA; U. of Nebraska; U. of New Hampshire; PAFA; Portland, Me./MA; Tupperware Museum; VMFA; WMAA; Worcester/AM. **Bibliography:** Baur 7; Genauer; Miller, ed. 2; Nordness, ed.; Pearson 2; Soby 5; Weller. Archives.

Richard Artschwager   *Rocker II*   1965–79

ARTSCHWAGER, RICHARD. b. December 26, 1924, Washington, D.C. **Studied:** Privately with Amedee Ozenfant; Cornell U., BA. Traveled Mexico. **Address:** Box 23, Charlottesville, NY 12036. **Dealer:** Leo Castelli Inc., NYC. **One-man Exhibitions:** Leo Castelli Inc., NYC, 1965, 67, 72, 73, 75, 77, 79, 80; Galerie Rolf Ricke, 1969, 72; Eugenie Butler, 1970; Onasch Galerie, Berlin, 1970; LoGiudice, Chicago, 1970; Chicago/Contemporary, 1973; Dunkleman Gallery, Toronto, 1973; Weinberg Gallery, San Francisco, 1974; Jared Sable Gallery, Toronto, 1976; Neuendorf, Hamburg, 1976; Walter Kelly Gallery, Chicago, 77; Sable-Castelli Gallery, Toronto, 78; The Texas Gallery, Houston, 1978; The Clocktower, NYC, 1978; Hamburg/Kunstverein, 1978; Fisher-Faure, Los Angeles, 1980; Young-Hoffman Gallery, Chicago, 1980. **Retrospective:** Buffalo/Albright, circ., 1979. **Group:** Buffalo/Albright, 1964; Dwan Gallery, Boxes, 1964; SRGM, 1966; Jewish Museum, Primary Structures, 1966; WMAA, Contemporary American Sculpture, Selection I, 1966; Finch College, 1966; WMAA Sculpture Annuals, 1966, 68, 70, 72; MOMA, The 1960s, 1967; Ridgefield/Aldrich, 1968; Documenta IV, Kassel, 1968; Milwaukee, Directions I: Options, circ., 1968; Trenton/State, Soft Art, 1969; Berne, When Attitudes Become Form, 1969; U. of Notre Dame, 1969; Indianapolis/Herron, 1969; York U., Toronto, 1969; Hayward Gallery, London, 1969; Milwaukee, Aspects of a New Realism, 1969; Buffalo/Albright, Kid Stuff, 1971; MOMA, Information, 1971; Galerie des 4 Mouvements, Paris, Hyperrealistes americains, 1972; Documenta V, Kassel, 1972; Oakland U., American Realism—Post Pop, 1973; WMAA, American Pop Art, 1974; Leverkusen, Zeichnungen 3, USA, 1975; Musée d'Ixelles, Brussels, Je/Nous, 1975; WMAA, 200 Years of American Sculpture, 1976; Venice, Biennale, 1976; ICA, U. of Pennsylvania, Improbable Furniture, 1977; U. of Chicago, Ideas in Sculpture 1965–1977, 1977; Buffalo/Albright, American Painting in the 1970s, 1978. **Collections:** Aachen/NG; Basel; Basel/Kunstmuseum; Baxter Travenol Laboratories; Cologne; Estee Lauder Cosmetics, Inc., NYC; Kansas City/Nelson; La Jolla; Levi Strauss & Co.; MOMA; Milwaukee; NYU; Ridgefield/Aldrich; Rotterdam; R.S.M. Co., Cincinnati; Smith College; WMAA. **Bibliography:** Alloway 1, 4; Atkinson; Battcock, ed.; *Drawings: The Pluralist Decade;* Honisch and Jensen, eds.; *Kunst um 1970;* Lippard 5; Lippard, ed.; *New in the Seventies;* Sager; *When Attitudes Become Form.*

ATHERTON, JOHN C. b. June 7, 1900, Brainerd, Minn.; **d.** 1952, New Brunswick, Canada. **Studied:** College of the Pacific; California School of Fine Arts, 1922–25. US Navy, 1918–19. Painter, illustrator, and poster artist. **Awards:** MMA, Artists for Victory,

Fourth Prize, 1942; Bohemia Club, San Francisco, First Prize, 1928; Hartford/Wadsworth, First Prize, 1922. **One-man Exhibitions:** Julien Levy Galleries, NYC, 1938, 39, 42, 44, 46; A.A.A. Gallery, NYC, 1951. **Group:** U. of Illinois, 1950; MOMA; WMAA; PAFA; Chicago/AI. **Collections:** Buffalo/Albright; Chicago/AI; Hartford/Wadsworth; MMA; MOMA; PAFA; WMAA. **Bibliography:** Baur 7; Pousette-Dart, ed.

AULT, GEORGE C. b. October 11, 1891, Cleveland, Ohio; **d.** December 30, 1948, Woodstock, N.Y. **Studied:** U. of London, Slade School; St. John's Wood Art School. Resided Great Britain 1899–1911. **One-man Exhibitions:** Sea Chest Gallery, Provincetown, 1922; Whitney Studio Club, NYC; Bourgeois Gallery, NYC, 1923; The Downtown Gallery, 1926, 28; J. B. Neumann's New Art Circle, NYC, 1927; The Little Gallery, Woodstock, N.Y. 1943; Woodstock (N.Y.) Art Gallery, 1949; The Milch Gallery, 1950; Charlotte/Mint, 1951; WMAA, 1973; The Zabriskie Gallery, 1973, 74, 78. **Retrospective:** The Zabriskie Gallery, 1957, 63, 69. **Group:** Independents, NYC, 1920; WMAA. **Collections:** Albany/Institute; Andover/Phillips; Brooklyn Museum; California Palace; Columbus; Cleveland/MA; Dartmouth College; Los Angeles/County MA; MMA; MOMA; Montclair/AM; U. of Nebraska; Newark Museum; U. of New Mexico; Omaha/Joslyn; PAFA; PMA; Syracuse U.; WMAA; Walker; Worcester/AM; Yale U.; Youngstown/Butler. **Bibliography:** Ault; Baur 7; Brown 2; Bulliet 1; Cahill and Barr, eds.; *Woodstock.* Archives.

AUSTIN, DARREL. b. June 25, 1907, Raymond, Wash. **Studied:** U. of Oregon; U. of Notre Dame and Columbia U., 1926–29; and with Emile Jacques. **Commissions:** Medical College of the U. of Oregon, 1933 (mural). **Awards:** PAFA, Walter Lippincott Prize, 1950. **Address:** Saw Mill Hill Road, RFD #4, New Fairfield, CT

06810. **Dealers:** ACA Gallery; Harmon Gallery. **One-man Exhibitions:** (first) Howard Putzell Gallery, Los Angeles, 1938; MOMA, 1942; James Vigeveno Gallery, Los Angeles (two-man), 1949; Perls Galleries, NYC, 1940, 42, 43, 44, 45, 47, 48, 50, 55, 57, 59, 64, 78; Harmon Gallery, Naples, Fla., 1964, 67, 69, 70, 73, 74, 79; Harmon Gallery, Sarasota, Fla., 1980; ACA Gallery, 1970. **Group:** WMAA Annual, 1945; Carnegie, 1947, 48, 49, 50. **Collections:** Boston/MFA; Britannica; Detroit/Institute; U. of Georgia; Hartford/Wadsworth; IBM; Kansas City/Nelson; Los Angeles/County MA; MMA; MOMA; Montclair/AM; U. of Nebraska; PAFA; Phillips; Portland, Ore./AM; U. of Rochester; Smith College. **Bibliography:** Baur 7; Bazin; Flanagan; Frost; Miller, ed. 1; Newmeyer.

AVEDISIAN, EDWARD. b. 1936, Lowell, Mass. **Studied:** Boston Museum School. **Taught:** U. of Kansas, 1969; School of Visual Arts, NYC, 1970; U. of California, Irvine, 1972; U. of Louisiana, 1973. **Awards:** Guggenheim Foundation Fellowship, 1967; National Council on the Arts Award, 1968. **Address:** 26 Warren, Hudson, NY 12534. **Dealer:** Robert Elkon Gallery; Brooke Alexander, NYC. **One-man Exhibitions:** Boylston Print Center Gallery, Cambridge, Mass., 1957; Hansa Gallery, NYC, 1958; Tibor de Nagy Gallery, 1959, 60; Robert Elkon Gallery, 1962, 1964–68, 1970–74; Ziegler Gallery, 1964; Nicholas Wilder Gallery, 1966, 68, 69; Kasmin Ltd., 1966, 67; Bucknell U., 1970; Jack Glenn Gallery, Corona del Mar, 1971; Gallery Moos, Toronto, 1971; Janie C. Lee Gallery, Houston, 1974; The Carriage House Gallery, Buffalo, 1975; NYU (two-man) 1977; Nina Freudenheim Gallery, Buffalo, 1978. **Group:** WMAA Annuals, 1963, 65, 67; Dayton/AI, 1964; WMAA, Young America, 1965; MOMA, The Responsive Eye, 1965; Corcoran, 1966; SFMA,

1967; Expo '67, Montreal, 1967; Indianapolis, 1970; Buffalo/Albright, Six Painters, 1971. **Collections:** Hartford/Wadsworth; Los Angeles/County MA; MMA; Minneapolis/Institute; Norfolk/Chrysler; Pasadena/AM; Purchase/SUNY; Ridgefield/Aldrich; SRGM; WMAA. **Bibliography:** Wood.

AVERY, MILTON. b. March 7, 1893, Altmar, N.Y.; **d.** January 3, 1965, NYC. **Studied:** Connecticut League of Art Students, briefly 1913, with C. N. Flagg. Traveled Europe, USA. **Awards:** Chicago/AI, The Mr. & Mrs. Frank G. Logan Prize, 1929; Connecticut Academy of Fine Arts, Atheneum Prize, 1930; Baltimore Watercolor Club, First Prize, 1949; Boston Arts Festival, Second Prize, 1948; ART:USA:59, NYC, $1,000 Award, 1959. *A Painter's World*, a 14-min., 16mm color sound film, shows him at work. **One-man Exhibitions:** (first) Opportunity Gallery, NYC, 1928; Gallery 144, NYC, 1932; Curt Valentine Gallery, NYC, 1935, 36, 38, 41; Phillips, 1943, 44; P. Rosenberg and Co., 1943, 44, 45, 46, 47, 50; Arts Club of Chicago, 1944; The Bertha Schaefer Gallery, 1944; Durand-Ruel Gallery, NYC, 1945, 46, 47, 49; Colorado Springs/FA, 1946; Portland, Me./MA, 1946; Laurel Gallery, NYC, 1950; M. Knoedler & Co., NYC, 1950; Grace Borgenicht Gallery, Inc., 1951, 52, 54, 56, 57, 58, 68, 70, 74, 75, 76, 77, 78, 79, 80; Baltimore/MA, 1952; Boston/MFA, circ., 1956; U. of Nebraska, 1956, 66; Felix Landau Gallery, 1956; HCE Gallery, Provincetown, Mass., 1956, 58, 59; Otto Seligman Gallery, 1958; Philadelphia Art Alliance, 1959; Waddington Gallery, London, 1962, 66; MOMA, circ., 1965–66; Richard Gray Gallery, 1966, 70; Makler Gallery, Philadelphia, 1966; Esther Suttman Gallery, Washington, D.C., 1966; David Mirvish Gallery, 1966, 67, 69; Donald Morris Gallery, 1966, 67, 69; New Britain, 1968; Reese Palley Gallery, San Francisco, 1969; NCFA, circ., 1969;

Alpha Gallery, 1969, 70; Waddington Gallery, Montreal, 1970; Brooklyn Museum, 1970; U. of California, Irvine, 1971; Cynthia Comsky Gallery, 1972; A.A.A. Gallery, 1973; Andre Emmerich Gallery, NYC, 1973; Lunn Inc., Washington, D.C., 1973, 74; U. of Connecticut, 1976; U. of Texas, 1976; Yares Gallery, Scottsdale, 1980; Edmonton Art Gallery, 1978; Cleveland/MA (three-man), 1975. **Retrospective:** A.F.A./ Ford Foundation, circ., 1960. **Group:** Carnegie, 1944; PAFA, 1945; Chicago/ AI; Corcoran; WMAA; U. of Illinois; Buffalo/Albright. **Collections:** Andover/Phillips; Atlanta/AA; Baltimore/ MA; Barnes Foundation; Brandeis U.; Brooklyn Museum; Bryn Mawr College; Buffalo/Albright; Chase Manhattan Bank; Dayton/AI; Evansville; Exeter; Honolulu Academy; Houston/MFA; U. of Illinois; MMA; MOMA; U. of Minnesota; U. of Nebraska; Newark Museum; PAFA; PMA; Phillips; Santa Barbara/MA; Smith College; Tel Aviv; Utica; WMAA; Walker; West Palm Beach/Norton; Witte; Yale U. **Bibliography:** Bazin; Blesh 1; Eliot; Frost; Goodrich and Baur 1; Greenberg 1; Kootz 2; **Kramer 2;** Mellquist; Nordness, ed.; Pousette-Dart, ed.; Rose, B. 1; Sandler; **Wight 2, 3;** *Woodstock: An American Art Colony 1902–1977.*

AZUMA, NORIO. B. November 23, 1928, Japan. **Studied:** Kanazawa Art College, Kanazawa City, Japan; Chouinard Art Institute; ASL (with Will Barnet). **Commissions:** IBM. **Awards:** Seattle/AM; Boston Printmakers; American Color Print Society. **Address:** 142 Greene Street, NYC 10012. **Dealers:** A.A.A. Gallery; Weyhe Gallery; Fendrick Gallery. **One-man Exhibitions:** (first) A.A.A. Gallery, NYC, 1964, also 1969; The Print Club, Philadelphia, 1964; Tulsa/Philbrook, 1965; Benjamin Gallery, Chicago, 1965; International Monetary Fund, Washington, D.C., 1965; WGMA, 1967; Nashville, 1968; East Tennessee State U., 1969; Berman-Medalie Gallery, Massachusetts, 1969; Roanoke (Va.) Fine Arts Center, 1969. **Group:** American Color Print Society; Corcoran; Boston Printmakers; New York World's Fair, 1964–65; Brooklyn Museum Print Biennial; WMAA Sculpture Annual, 1966; SAGA. **Collections:** American Republic Insurance Co.; Boston Public Library; Brooklyn Museum; U. of California; Chase Manhattan Bank; Chicago/ AI; Chouinard Art Institute; Cleveland/ MA; Library of Congress; MIT; National Gallery; PAFA; PMA; Seattle/AM; Smithsonian; Trenton/State; USIA; The White House; Youngstown/Butler.

B

BABER, ALICE. b. August 22, 1928, Charleston, Ill. **Studied:** Lindenwood College; Indiana U., BA; Ecole des Beaux-Arts, Fontainebleau. Traveled Europe, Russia, Japan, Thailand, India, Middle East. **Taught:** Queens College; U. of Minnesota; Purchase/SUNY; C. W. Post College; U. of California, Santa Barbara; U. of California, Berkeley; School of Visual Arts, NYC, 1973–75; U. of New Mexico, 1979. **Member:** Women's InterArt Center. **Awards:** Yaddo Fellowship, 1958. Organized the exhibition Color Forum, U. of Texas, 1972. **Address:** 597 Broadway, NYC 10012. **Dealer:** A. M. Sachs Gallery. **One-man Exhibitions:** (first) March Gallery, NYC, 1958; Galerie de la Librairie Anglaise, Paris, 1963; New Vision Center, London, 1963; Pinacotheca Museum (two-man), 1964; A. M. Sachs Gallery, NYC, 1965, 66, 69, 71, 73, 75, 77, 78; Kölnischer Kunstverein, Cologne, 1966; Bernard Baruch College, NYC, 1968; Galerie Lambert, Paris, 1970; U. of Minnesota, 1971; Galerie fur Zeitgenossische Kunst, Hamburg, 1971; Tom Bortolazzo Gallery, Santa Barbara, 1972; Benson Gallery, 1973; Ingber Art Gallery, 1973; EuRo-Kunstgalerie, Saarbrucken, 1974; Chanakya Gallery, New Delhi, 1974; Iran-American Society, Teheran, 1974; Palm Beach Gallery, Palm Beach, 1975; American Library, Brussels, 1975; U. of Alabama, 1975; Arvil Gallery, Mexico City, 1976; Santa Barbara/MA, 1976; Kansas State U., 1976; Centro Colombo Americano, Bogota, Colombia, 1977; Centro de Arte Moderna, Guadalajara, Mexico, 1977; Henri Gallery, Washington, D.C., 1977; Allen House Galleries, Louisville, Ky., 1978; Frances Aronson Gallery, Atlanta, Ga., 1978; The Art Package, Chicago, Ill., 1979; Niagara U., 1979; Gallery West, Los Angeles, 1980; Galeria de l'Arte Nueva, Lima, Peru, 1980. **Group:** The Stable Gallery Annual, 1957; II Paris Biennial, 1961; Whitechapel Art Gallery, London, 1966; Maison de la Culture du Havre, 1966–67; Musee des Arts Decoratifs, 1966; U. of Texas, Color Forum, 1972; New York Cultural Center, Women Choose Women, 1973; Fordham U., IX Painters—IX Styles, 1973. **Collections:** Bezalel Museum; Brandeis U.; U. of California; Ciba-Geigy Corp.; Corcoran; Cornell U.; Fordham U.; MOMA; Manchester, England; Museo National, San Salvador; Newark Museum; NCFA; NYU; U. of Notre Dame; Purchase/SUNY; SRGM; Peter Stuyvesant Collection; Pinacotheca Museum; SFMA; Terre Haute/Swope; United Tanker Ltd.; Worcester/AM. **Bibliography:** *Art: A Woman's Sensibility.* Archives.

BAER, JO. b. August 7, 1929, Seattle, Wash. **Studied:** U. of Washington, 1946–49; New School for Social Research, 1952. **Taught:** School of Visual Arts, NYC, 1969–70. **Awards:** National Endowment for the Arts Grant, 1969. **Address:** Smarmore Castle, County Ardee, Louth, Ireland. **One-man Exhibitions:** Fischer Gallery, 1966; Galerie Rolf Ricke, 1969, 70, 73; Locksley-Shea Gallery, 1970; Noah Goldowsky, 1970; School of Visual Arts, NYC, 1970; Lo-Giudice Gallery, NYC, 1972; Nicholas Wilder Gallery, 1973; Galleria Toselli, Milan, 1974; Weinberg Gallery, San Francisco, 1974; MOMA, Oxford, England, circ., 1977. **Retrospective:**

WMAA, 1975. **Group:** SRGM, Systemic Painting, 1966; Finch College, NYC, Art in Series, 1967; WMAA Annuals, 1967, 69, 73; Documenta IV, Kassel, 1968; Cologne/Kunstverein, Eine Tendenz Zeitgenossischer Malerei, 1969; Detroit/ Institute, Other Ideas, 1969; Ars 69, Helsinki, 1969; Seattle/AM, Artists of the Sixties, 1969; Corcoran Biennial, 1969; Chicago/AI, Drawings, 1971; Yale U., Options and Alternatives, 1973; Chicago/Contemporary, Five Artists: A Logic of Vision, 1974; Baltimore/MA, 14 Artists, 1975. **Collections:** Aachen/NG; MOMA; SRGM. **Bibliography:** Arthur 1; Honisch and Jensen, eds.; *Kunst um 1970;* Lippard 3; Lucie-Smith; *Options and Alternatives.*

BAILEY, WILLIAM. b. November 17, 1930, Council Bluffs, Iowa. **Studied:** U. of Kansas, 1948–51; Yale U., 1955; BFA, 1957, MFA, with Josef Albers. US Army, 1951–53, Korea, Japan. Traveled Europe, Far East; resided Paris, Rome. **Taught:** Yale U., 1957–62, 69– ; Indiana U., 1962–69. **Awards:** Alice Kimball English Traveling Fellow, 1955; US State Department Grant, 1960; Guggenheim Foundation Fellowship, 1965; Ingram Merrill Foundation, grant, 1979–80. **Address:** 223 East 10th Street, NYC 10003. **Dealer:** Robert Schoelkopf Gallery; Galerie Claude Bernard, Paris; Galleria II Gabbiano, Rome. **One-man Exhibitions:** Kanegis Gallery, 1957, 58, 61; Indiana U., 1963; U. of Vermont, 1965; Kansas City/AI, 1967; Robert Schoelkopf Gallery, 1968, 71, 74, 75, 79; Galleria dei Lanzi, Milan, 1973; Galleria II Fante di Spade, Rome, 1973; La Parisina, Turin, 1974; Dart Gallery, Inc., Chicago, 1976; Galerie Claude Bernard, Paris, 1978; Fendrick Gallery, Washington, D.C., 1979. **Group:** U. of Illinois, 1961; Vassar College, Realism Now, 1968; Cincinnati/AM, American Paintings on the Market Today V, 1968; Swarthmore College, The Big Figure, 1969; WMAA, 22 Realists, 1970; Florida State U., Realist Painters, 1971; Cleveland/MA, 32 Realists, 1972; A.F.A., Realist Revival, 1972; Kansas City/AI, Five Figurative Artists, 1972; Yale U., Seven Realists, 1973; St. John's U., The Figure in Recent American Painting, 1975; New York Cultural Center, Three Centuries of the American Nude, 1975; Palazzo Strozzi, Florence, Biennale Internazionale della Grafica, 1977; Salon de Mai, Paris, 1978; William Patterson College, N.J., The Other Realism, 1978. **Collections:** Aachen/NG; Duke U.; Hirshhorn; Indiana U.; Kalamazoo Institute; Louisville/Speed; U. of Massachusetts; Michigan State U.; Minneapolis/Institute; U. of New Mexico; NCFA; U. of North Carolina; Ogunquit; PAFA; St. Louis City; WMAA; Yale U. **Bibliography:** Arthur 1,2; *Kunst um 1970;* Sager.

BAIZERMAN, SAUL. b. December 25, 1889, Vitebsk, Russia; **d.** August 30, 1957, NYC. **Studied:** Imperial Art School, Odessa; NAD; Beaux-Arts Institute of Design, NYC. To USA, 1910. Traveled England, Russia, Italy. Fire demolished New York studio, 1931, destroying almost all his work. **Taught:** American Artists School, NYC; U. of Southern California, summer, 1949; Baizerman Art School, 1934–40. **Awards:** PAFA, Hon. Men. 1949; AAAL Grant, 1951; Guggenheim Foundation Fellowship, 1952; PAFA, Alfred G. B. Steel Memorial Prize, 1952. **One-man Exhibitions:** (first) Dorien Leigh Galleries, London, 1924; Eighth Street Gallery, NYC, 1933; Artists' Gallery, NYC, 1938, 48, 57; Philadelphia Art Alliance, 1949; The New Gallery, NYC, 1952, 54; World House Galleries, NYC, 1963; The Zabriskie Gallery, 1967, 70, 72, 75, 80. **Retrospective:** Walker, circ., 1953; ICA, Boston, 1958; Huntington, N.Y./Heckscher, 1961. **Collections:** Andover/Phillips; Hirshhorn; U. of Minnesota; U. of Nebraska; U. of New Mexico; U. of North Carolina; PAFA; WMAA; Walker. **Bibliography:** Baur 7; Brumme; Chipp; Goodrich and Baur 1; Marter, Tarbell, and Wechsler; Pearson 2. Archives.

BALDESSARI, JOHN. b. June 17, 1931, National City, Calif. **Studied:** Otis Art Institute; Chouinard Art Institute; UCLA; U. of California, Berkeley; San Diego State College, 1953, BA, 1957, MA. Traveled Europe, Mexico, Canada, Middle East. **Taught:** San Diego Fine Arts School, 1953–54; San Diego city schools, 1956–57; San Diego State College, 1956, 59–61; Southwestern College, Chula Vista, 1962–68; U. of California, San Diego, 1962–70; La Jolla, 1966–70; California Institute of the Arts, Valencia, 1970– ; Hunter College, 1971. **Awards:** National Endowment for the Arts, 1973, 74–75. **Address:** c/o Dealer. **Dealer:** Ileana Sonnabend Gallery, NYC. **One-man Exhibitions:** La Jolla, 1960, 66, 68; Southwestern College, Chula Vista, 1962–64, 75; Molly Barnes Gallery, Los Angeles, 1968; Eugenia Butler, 1970; Richard Feigen Gallery, 1970; Nova Scotia College of Art and Design, Halifax, 1971, 72; Art & Project, Amsterdam, 1971, 72, 75; Galerie Konrad Fischer, Dusseldorf, 1971, 73; Jack Wendler Gallery, London, 1972, 74; Galleria Toselli, Milan, 1972, 74; Galerie MTL, Brussels, 1972, 74, 75; Ileana Sonnabend Gallery, NYC, 1973, 75, 78; Ileana Sonnabend Gallery, Paris, 1973, 75; Galleria Schema, Florence, 1973; Galerie Volker Skulima, Berlin, 1974; Felix Handschin Gallery, Basel, 1975; Galeria Saman, Genoa, 1975; Amsterdam/Stedelijk, 1975; Modern Art Agency, Naples, 1975; The Kitchen, NYC, 1975; U. of California, Irvine, 1976; Ewing and Paton Galleries, Victoria, Australia, 1976; Auckland, 1976; U. of Akron, 1976; Ohio State U., 1976; Cirrus Editions, Los Angeles, 1976; James Corcoran Gallery, Los Angeles, 1976; Massimo Valsecchi Gallery, Milan, 1977; Hartford/Wadsworth, 1977; Robert Self Gallery, London, 1977; Julian Pretto Gallery, NYC, 1977; Portland (Ore.) Center for the Visual Arts 1978; Theatre Vanguard, Los Angeles, 1978; Artists Space, NYC, 1978; Pacific Film Archives, Berkeley, 1978; WMAA (films), 1978. **Group:** La Jolla, The Un-common Denominator—13 San Diego Painters, circ., 1960; Long Beach/MA, Arts of Southern California VIII: Drawing, circ., 1960; SFMA Annuals, 1961, 62; San Diego State College, Seven-Man Show, 1962; Long Beach/MA, Arts of Southern California: Painting, circ., 1963; La Jolla, Some Aspects of California Painting and Sculpture, 1965; U. of California, San Diego, New Work, Southern California, 1968; Hayward Gallery, London, Pop Art, 1969; Leverkusen, Konzeption, 1969; Seattle/AM, 557, 087, 1969; California College of Arts and Crafts, Space, 1969; Chicago/Contemporary, Art by Telephone, 1969; WMAA Annuals 1969, 72; Jewish Museum, Software, 1970; Oberlin College, Art in the Mind, 1970; Turin/Civico, Conceptual Art, Arte Povera, Land Art, 1970; Kyoto Municipal Museum of Art, Nirvana, 1970; MOMA, Information, 1971; Buenos Aires/Moderno, Art Systems, 1971; Dusseldorf/Kunsthalle, Prospect '71, 1971; Festival of Two Worlds, Spoleto, 1972; Documenta V, Kassel, 1972; Basel, Twelve-Man Show, 1972; Venice Biennial, 1972; VI International Theater Festival: Aspects, Belgrade, 1972; Houston/Contemporary, Five-Man Show, 1972; Minnesota College of Art and Design, I National Videotape Festival, 1972; Houston/Contemporary, Videotapes, 1972; Basel, Konzept Kunst, 1972; Pasadena/AM, Southern California Attitudes, 1972; Syracuse/Everson, Circuit, circ., 1973; Musée Galliera, Paris, Festival d'Automne, 1973; Dusseldorf/Kunsthalle, Prospect '73, 1973; Parcheggio di Villa Borghese, Rome, Contemporanea, 1974; Cologne, Project '74, 1974; Eindhoven, Kunst Informatie Centrum, 1974; Malmo, New Media, 1975; Auckland; Pan Pacific Biennial, 1976; SFMA, Painting and Sculpture in California, 1976; Fort Worth, American Artists: A New Decade, 1977; WMAA Biennials, 1977, 79; Houston/Contemporary, American Narrative/Story Art: 1967–1977, 1978; WMAA, Art about Art, 1978; ICA, London, Wit and Wisdom, 1978; Chicago/AI, American Photography in the 70's, 1979. **Collections:** Basel; Cologne; Eindhoven; Institut fur Moderne Kunst; La Jolla; Los Angeles/ County MA; MOMA; Transamerica Corp. **Bibliography:** *Art Now 74; Contemporanea;* Meyer; *Report.*

BANG, THOMAS. b. 1938, Denmark. **Studied:** Cleveland Institute of Art, 1957–60; Yale U., 1962, BFA; U. of Southern California, Los Angeles, 1964, MFA. **Taught:** U. of California, Santa Barbara, 1967; Rice U., 1968; U. of Rochester. **Awards:** Fulbright Fellowship, 1964; La Jolla, **P.P.,** 1965; CSCS, **P.P.,** 1967. **Address:** 11 Menlo Place, Rochester, NY 14620. **Dealer:** OK Harris Works of Art. **One-man Exhibitions:** La Jolla, 1964; Santa Barbara/MA, 1965; Esther Baer Gallery, 1965; Esther Robles Gallery, 1966, 67, 69; Rice U., 1968; OK Harris Works of Art, 1970, 71, 72, 74, 78, 79; U. of Rochester, 1976; Punkt Gallery, Copenhagen, 1978; Skt. Agnes Gallery, Copenhagen, 1978; Adler Gallery, Los Angeles, 1979; Anna Leonowens Gallery, Halifax, N.S., 1980. **Group:** California State U., Long Beach, California Drawings, 1967; Western Michigan U., The Growing Edge, circ., 1967; Scripps College, The Mathematical Muse, 1967; U. of Colorado, New York—Los Angeles, Drawings of the 1960s, 1967; WMAA Annuals, 1967, 73; Tampa Bay Art Center, Forty California Sculptors, 1968; Trenton/State, Soft Art, 1969; ICA, U. of Pennsylvania, Between Object and Environment, 1969; Berne, When Attitudes Become Form, 1969; Vassar College, Twenty-six by Twenty-six, 1971; Duke U., Real Cool—Cool Real, 1973; WMAA Biennial, 1973; Potsdam/SUNY, Sculpture 77, 1977; U. of California, Santa Barbara, Sculptural Perspectives, 1979. **Collections:** La Jolla; Western Michigan U. **Bibliography:** *When Attitudes Become Form.*

BANNARD, DARBY. b. September 23, 1934, New Haven, Conn. **Studied:** Princeton U., BA. Contributing editor, *Artforum,* 1973–74; curator, Hans

Walter Darby Bannard *Faceoff* 1979

Hofmann, Hirshhorn, 1976; co-chairman, National Endowment for the Arts International Committee on the Visual Arts, 1979–. **Taught:** Columbia U., 1968; Princeton U., 1974; Brooklyn Museum, 1974; Kent State U., 1974; U. of Texas, 1975; Washington U., St. Louis, 1977; SFAI, 1979. **Awards:** Guggenheim Foundation Fellowship, 1968; National Council on the Arts, 1968. **Address:** P.O. Box 1157, Princeton, NJ

08540. **Dealer:** Knoedler Contemporary Art. **One-man Exhibitions:** (first) Tibor de Nagy Gallery, NYC, 1965, also 1966, 67, 68, 69; Kasmin Ltd., 1965, 68, 69, 70, 72; Richard Feigen Gallery, Chicago, 1966; Nicholas Wilder Gallery, 1967; Bennington College, 1969; David Mirvish Gallery, 1969; Lawrence Rubin Gallery, NYC, 1970, 73; Joseph Helman Gallery, St. Louis, 1970; Galerie Hans R. Neuendorf, Cologne, 1971; Newport Harbor, 1972; Pasadena/AM, 1973; Tibor de Nagy Gallery, Houston, 1973, 75; M. Knoedler & Co., Inc., NYC, 1974 (twice), 75, 77, 78, 79, 80; Laguna Gloria Art Museum, Austin, Tex., 1975; Ronald Greenberg Gallery, St. Louis, 1977; Exeter, 1977; David Mirvish Gallery, Toronto, 1978; Watson/De Nagy, Houston, 1979. **Retrospective:** Baltimore/MA, circ., 1973. **Group:** Los Angeles/County MA, Post Painterly Abstraction, 1964; MOMA, The Responsive Eye, 1965; Chicago/Contemporary, 1965; Smithsonian, 1966; U. of Pennsylvania, 1966; WMAA Annual, 1967; Detroit/Institute, Color, Image and Form, 1967; MOMA, The Art of the Real, 1968; New Delhi, First World Triennial, 1968; Dusseldorf/Kunsthalle, Prospect '68, 1968; Corcoran Biennial, 1969; XXXV Venice Biennial, 1970; Buffalo/Albright, Color and Field: 1890–1970, 1970; Toledo/MA, The Form of Color, 1970; WMAA, The Structure of Color, 1971; Illinois State U. Biennial, 1971; Buffalo/Albright, Six Painters, 1971; Houston/MFA, Toward Color and Field, 1971; WMAA Annual, 1972; Boston/MFA, Abstract Painting in the '70s, 1972; Winnipeg (Canada) Art Gallery, Masters of the Sixties, 1972; Montreal/Contemporarain, 11 Artistes Americans, 1973; Houston/MFA, The Great Decade of American Abstraction: Modernist Art 1960 to 1970, 1974; Cleveland/MA, Contemporary American Artists, 1974; WMAA (downtown), Continuing Abstraction in American Art, 1974; Indianapolis/Herron, 1978. **Collections:** Brandeis U.; Baltimore/MA; Boston/MFA; Buffalo/Albright; Cleveland/MA; Dayton/AI; Harvard U.; Honolulu Academy; Houston/MFA; MOMA; Melbourne/National; Newark Museum; Oberlin College; Princeton U.; Ridgefield/Aldrich; Storm King Art Center; Toledo/MA; Trenton/State; U. of Texas; SRGM. **Bibliography:** Battcock, ed.; **Cone 2;** *The Great Decade;* Goossen 1; Rose, B., 1; Wood.

BARINGER, RICHARD, E. b. December 3, 1921, Elkhart, Ind.; **d.** January 30, 1980, St. Croix, V.I. **Studied:** Southwestern U.; Institute of Design, Chicago, with Lazlo Moholy-Nagy, Emerson Woelffer. B. Arch., Harvard U. Graduate School with Walter Gropius, B. Arch., M. Arch. US Air Force, World War II. **Traveled** Europe, Russia, North Africa, Caribbean. **Taught:** Institute of Design, Chicago; Columbia U.; U. of Pennsylvania, 1965–66; Institute of Design, Chicago, Artist-in-Residence, 1966–67. **Member:** American Institute of Architects. **Awards:** Prix de Rome; Harvard U., Sheldon Traveling Fellowship; American Institute of Architects, 1958 (Residential Design); *Progressive Architecture* magazine, 1957; *Architectural Record* magazine, 1958. **One-man Exhibitions:** (first) Ovington Gallery, Los Angeles, 1945; South Bend (Ind.) Art Center, 1946; Margaret Brown Gallery, Boston, 1949; MIT, 1950; Cambridge (Mass.) School of Design, 1950; Segno Gallery, Chicago, 1956; Nelson Taylor Gallery, East Hampton, N.Y., 1962; The Bertha Schaefer Gallery, 1962, 63, 65; Columbia U., 1963; Dwan Gallery, 1967; U. of Notre Dame, 1967; Institute of Design, Chicago, 1967; 10 Downtown, NYC, 1968; Island Center, St. Croix. **Group:** Johns Hopkins U., 1941; California Palace, 1948; U. of Illinois, 1949, 62, 63; ICA, Boston, 5 Young Americans, 1950; Arts Club of Chicago, 1955–57, 1961; WGMA, The Formalists, 1963; U. of Massachusetts, 1967; Colgate U., 1968. **Collections:** Busch-Reisinger Museum; Choate–Rosemary Hall School; Cooperative Insurance Society; Farmers Elevator Insurance Co.; Fort Worth; MOMA; U. of Massachusetts; Pacific Indemnity Co.; Prudential Lines Inc.

BARNES, ROBERT. b. September 24, 1934, Washington, D.C. **Studied:** Chicago Art Institute School, 1952–56; The U. of Chicago, 1952–56, BFA; Columbia U., 1956; Hunter College, 1957–61; U. of London, Slade School, 1961–63. Traveled Great Britain, France, USA. **Taught:** Indiana U., summers, 1960, 61; Kansas City Art Institute and School of Design, 1963–64; Indiana U., 1964– . **Commissions:** New York Hilton Hotel, 1962 (edition of lithographs). **Awards:** William and Noma Copley Foundation Grant, 1961; Fulbright Fellowship, 1961, renewed 1962; Chicago/AI, 67th Annual; AAAL, **P.P.,** 1970. **Address:** c/o Dealer. **Dealer:** Allan Frumkin Gallery, NYC and Chicago. **One-man Exhibitions:** (first) Allan Frumkin Gallery, NYC, 1963, also 1968, 74, 77; Allan Frumkin Gallery, Chicago, 1964, 67, 75, 78; Galerie du Dragon, Paris, 1967; Coe College, 1967; Indianapolis/Herron, 1968; Quincy (Ill.) Art Club, 1971; Il Fante di Spade, Rome, 1973. **Group:** Chicago/AI, Exhibition Monumentum, 1952–55; Chicago/AI, Prints from the Graphic Workshop, 1955; Boston Arts Festival, 1958; Chicago/AI Annuals, 1958, 60, 61, 64; State U. of Iowa, Main Current of Contemporary American Painting, 1960; Ravinia Festival, Highland Park, Ill., 1961; WMAA Annual, 1962; Yale U., 1962; Kansas City/Nelson, 1962; SFMA, 1963; MOMA, 60 Modern Drawings, 1963; Chicago/AI, Drawings, 1963; WMAA, Young America, 1965; Salon des Jeunes Peintres, Paris, 1965; Museo Civico, Bologna, 1965; PAFA, 1966; RISD, Recent Still Life, 1966; U. of Illinois, 1967; VMFA, Works on Paper, 1970; Indianapolis, 1972; Chicago/Contemporary, Chicago Imagist Art, 1972; Galleria Comunale d'Arte Contemporanea, Una Tendenza Americana, 1973; Joslyn/Omaha, The Chosen Object, 1977. **Collections:** Chi-

cago/AI; **MOMA;** Pasadena/AM; St. Joseph/Albrecht; WMAA. **Bibliography:** Rose, B., 1.

BARNET, WILL. b. May 25, 1911, Beverly, Mass. **Studied:** Boston Museum School, with Phillip Hale; ASL, with Charles Locke. Traveled USA, Europe. **Taught:** ASL, 1936–; Cooper Union, 1945– ; U. of Washington, Summer, 1963; Boston Museum School, 1963; Famous Artists Schools, Inc., Guiding Faculty, 1954–64; PAFA, 1967– ; Cornell U., summers, 1968, 69. **Member:** American Abstract Artists; Federation of Modern Painters and Sculptors; Century Association; NAD. Federal A.P.: Technical advisor in lithography. **Member:** Fellow, Royal Society of Arts. **Awards:** Corcoran, William A. Clark Prize; Ford Foundation/A.F.A. Artist-in-Residence; PAFA, Walter Lippincott Prize, 1968; Library of Congress, **P.P.,** 1974; NAD, Benjamin Altman Prize, 1977. **Address:** 43 West 90th Street, NYC 10024. **Dealers:** Hirschl & Adler Galleries, A.A.A. Gallery. **One-man Exhibitions:** (first) Hudson D. Walker Gallery, NYC, 1939; Gallery St. Etienne, NYC, 1943; The Bertha Schaefer Gallery, 1947, 49, 51, 53, 55, 60, 62; Peter H. Deitsch Gallery, 1960, 63; Mary Harriman Gallery Inc., Boston, 1963; Galleria Trastevere di Topazia Alliata, Rome, 1960; Waddell Gallery, 1965, 66, 68; Fairweather-Hardin Gallery, 1971; David/David Inc., Philadelphia, 1972; Hirschl & Adler Galleries, NYC, 1973, 76; Century Association, 1974; Harmon Gallery, 1974; Meredith Long Gallery, 1974; Prince Arthur Galleries, Toronto, 1977; Haslem Fine Arts, Inc., Washington, D.C., 1977, 79; Alice Simsar Gallery, Inc., Ann Arbor, 1978; AAA Gallery, NYC, 1978; Charlottemont, 1979; Foster Harmon Galleries of American Art, Sarasota, 1980; Le Galerie Documents, Paris, 1980. **Retrospective:** U. of Minnesota, Duluth, 1958; ICA, Boston, 1961; Albany/Institute, 1962; PAFA, 1970; A.A.A. Gallery, 1972; Print Club of Philadelphia, 1977;

Purchase/SUNY, circ., 1979. **Group:** American Abstract Artists since the Mid-1940's; MMA, American Paintings Today, 1950; Yale U., 1955; Corcoran, 1960; International Biennial Exhibition of Prints, Tokyo, 1960; PAFA, 1962, 68, 69; WMAA, Geometric Abstraction in America, circ., 1962; Brooklyn Museum; Carnegie; ICA, Boston; MOMA; U. of California, 1968; U. of Illinois, 1969; Expo '74, Spokane, 1974; NAD, 1975; 100th Anniversary Exhibition of ASL, 1975. **Collections:** Boston/MFA; Brooklyn Museum; U. of California; Carnegie; Cincinnati/AM; Columbus; Corcoran; Harvard U.; Honolulu Academy; Library of Congress; MMA; MOMA; Montana State College; NYPL; NYU; PAFA; PMA; Phillips; SRGM; Seattle/AM; Sara Roby Foundation; U. of Texas; Utica; WMAA; Buffalo/Albright. **Bibliography:** American Artists Congress, Inc.; Farrell; Hayter 1; Janis and Blesh 1; Nordness, ed.; Reese; Smith, A. Archives.

BARRY, ROBERT. b. March 9, 1936, NYC. **Studied:** Hunter College, BFA, MA. **Awards:** National Endowment for the Arts, grant, 1976. **Address:** 1091 Emerson Avenue, Teaneck, NJ 10766. **Dealer:** Leo Castelli Inc., NYC. **One-man Exhibitions:** Westerly Gallery, NYC, 1964; Seth Siegelaub, Los Angeles, 1969; Art & Project, Amsterdam, 1969, 71, 72, 74; Gian Enzo Sperone, Turin, 1969, 70, 73, 74; Eugenia Butler, 1970, 71; Yvon Lambert, Paris, 1971, 73, 74, 77; Paul Maenz Gallery, Cologne, 1971, 72, 73, 74, 76, 77, 79; Leo Castelli Inc., NYC, 1971, 72, 74, 76, 78, 79; Galerie MTL, Brussels, 1972; Jack Wendler Gallery, London, 1972, 73, 74; Galleria Toselli, Milan, 1972, 73; Tate, 1972; Gian Enzo Sperone, Rome, 1973, 76; Galeria Foksal, Warsaw, 1973; Kabinett fur Aktuelle Kunst, Bremerhaven, 1973; Kunstmuseum, Lucerne, 1974; Rolf Preisig Gallery, Basel, 1974, 76, 79; Amsterdam/Stedelijk, 1974; Gian Enzo Sperone, NYC, 1975; Cusack Gallery, Houston, 1975; Julian

Pretto Gallery, NYC, 1976; P.S. 1, Long Island City, 1976; Robert Self Ltd., London, 1977; Eindhoven, 1977; Essen, 1978; Rudiger Schottle, Munich, 1977; U. of Colorado, 1978; Francoise Lambert Gallery, Milan, 1979. **Group:** Hudson River Museum, Eight Young Artists, 1964; SRGM, Systemic Painting, 1966; A.F.A., The Square in Painting, 1968; Berne, When Attitudes Become Form; Amsterdam/Stedelijk, Op Losse Schroeven, 1969; Seattle/AM, 557, 087, 1969; Dusseldorf/Kunsthalle, Prospect '69, 1969; Leverkusen, Konzeption, 1969; Oberlin College, Art in the Mind, 1970; La Jolla, Projections: Anti-Materialism, 1970; New York Cultural Center, Conceptual Art and Conceptual Aspects, 1970; MOMA, Information, 1971; Kyoto Municipal Museum of Fine Art, Nirvana, 1970; Jewish Museum, Software, 1970; Kunsthalle, Nurnberg, Artist, Theory and Work, 1971; Munster/WK, Concept Art, 1971; Paris Biennial, 1971; Mills College, Notes and Scores for Sound, 1972; Documenta V, Kassel, 1972; Venice Biennial, 1972; Amsterdam/Stedelijk, Kunst Als Boek, 1972; Munster/WK, Das Konzept ist die Form, 1972; Parcheggio di Villa Borghese, Rome, Contemporanea, 1974; Kunsthalle, Cologne, Kunst bleibt Kunst, 1974; Sarah Lawrence College, Word, Image, Number, 1975; U. of Chicago, Ideas on Paper 1970–1976, 1976; Chicago/Contemporary, Words at Liberty, 1977; Bochum, Words, Words, 1979; Chicago/AI, Annual, 1979. **Collections:** Amsterdam/Stedelijk; Basel; Cologne; Eindhoven. **Bibliography:** Art Now 74; Celant; Contemporanea; Honnef; Lippard, ed.; Meyer; When Attitudes Become Form.

BARTH, FRANCES. b. July 31, 1946, NYC. **Studied:** Hunter College, 1968, BFA, with Doug Ohlson, Ron Gorchov, Ralph Humphrey, Vincent Longo, George Sugarman; 1970, MA, with Tony Smith, Ray Parker. Traveled Europe, Russia, and USA; lived in Amsterdam, 1978. **Taught:** Bennington

College, 1975–76; Princeton U., 1976–79; Sarah Lawrence College, 1979–. **Awards:** CAPS, 1973; National Endowment for the Arts, 1974; Guggenheim Foundation Fellowship, 1977. **Address:** c/o Dealer. **Dealer:** Susan Caldwell, Inc., NYC. **One-man Exhibitions:** (first) Susan Caldwell Inc., 1974, 75, 76, 78, 79, 80. **Group:** WMAA Annuals, 1972, 73; Corcoran Annual, 1973; SFAI, S.F./L.A./NYC, 1978; ICA, U. of Pennsylvania, Eight Abstract Painters, 1978; Buffalo/Albright, American Paintings of the 1970s, circ., 1978; NYU, American Painting: The Eighties, 1979. **Collections:** Akron/AI; Buffalo/Albright; American Can Corp., Greenwich, Conn.; Amerada Hess Corp., NYC; Chase Manhattan Bank, NYC; Cornell U.; IBM Corp., NYC; Prudential Insurance Co. of America; WMAA; Lehman Brothers, NYC and Chicago; Swiss Bank Corp., NYC; MOMA.

BARTLETT, JENNIFER. b. 1941, Long Beach, Calif. **Studied:** Mills College, 1963, BA; Yale, 1964, BFA, 1965, MFA. **Awards:** CAPS, 1974; Chicago/AI, Harris Prize, 1976. **Taught:** School of Visual Arts, NYC. **Address:** c/o Dealer. **Dealer:** Paula Cooper Gallery, NYC. **One-man Exhibitions:** Mills College, Oakland, Calif., 1963; 119 Spring St., NYC, 1970; Reese Palley Gallery, NYC, 1972; Paula Cooper Gallery, NYC, 1974, 77, 79; Jacob's Ladder, Washington, D.C., 1973 (two-man); Galleria Saman, Genoa, 1974, 78; Garage Gallery, London, 1975 (two-man); John Doyle Gallery, Chicago, 1975; Dartmouth College, 1976; Cincinnati/Contemporary, 1976; Hartford/Wadsworth, 1977; SFMA, 1978; Hansen-Fuller Gallery, San Francisco, 1978; Baltimore/MA, 1978; Margo Leavin Gallery, Los Angeles, 1979; The Clocktower, NYC, 1979. **Group:** MOMA, Seven Walls, 1971; WMAA Annual, 1972, Biennials 1977, 79; Indianapolis, 1972; Walker, Painting: New Options, 1972; GEDOK, Hamburg, American Women Artists, 1972; WMAA, American Drawings:

1963–1973; Corcoran, 37th Biennial, 1975; Biennale de Paris, 1975; Chicago/AI, Annual, 1976; Akademie der Kunst, Berlin, SoHo, 1976; Dusseldorf, The Pure Form, 1976; Documenta 6, Kassel, 1977; Paris/Moderne, Historical Aspects of Constructivism and Concrete Art, 1977; WMAA, New Image Painting, 1978; U. of North Carolina, Drawings about Drawing Today, 1979; WMAA, Decade in Review, 1979. **Bibliography:** Drawings: The Pluralist Decade; Marshall.

BASKIN, LEONARD. b. August 15, 1922, New Brunswick, N.J. **Studied:** NYU, 1939–41; Yale U., 1941–43; New School for Social Research, MA, 1949; Academie de la Grande Chaumiere, 1950; Academy of Fine Arts, Florence, Italy, 1951; privately with Maurice Glickman. US Navy, 1943–46. **Taught:**

Leonard Baskin *Ruth and Naomi*

Worcester Museum School, 1952–53; Smith College, 1953–74. Operates the Gehenna Press. **Awards:** Prix de Rome, Hon. Men., 1940; L. C. Tiffany Grant, 1947; Library of Congress, Pennell **P.P.**, 1952; Guggenheim Foundation Fellowship, 1953; SAGA, Mrs. A. W. Erickson Prize, 1953; Tokyo/Modern, O'Hara Museum Prize, 1954; U. of Illinois, **P.P.**, 1954; Chicago/AI, Alonzo C. Mather Prize, 1961; VI Sao Paulo Biennial, 1961; American Institute of Graphic Art, Medal of Merit, 1965; PAFA, Gold Medal, 1965; NIAL, Gold Medal, 1969. **Address:** Lurley Manor, Lurley, nr. Tiverton, Devon, England. **Dealer:** Kennedy Gallery. **One-man Exhibitions:** Glickman Studio, 1939; Numero Galleria d'Arte, Florence, Italy, 1951; The Little Gallery, Provincetown, Mass., 1952; Mount Holyoke College, 1952; Fitchburg/AM, 1952; Boris Mirski Gallery, Boston, 1954, 55, 56, 64, 65; Grace Borgenicht Gallery, Inc., 1954, 60, 64, 66, 69; The Print Club, Philadelphia, 1956; Portland, Me./MA, 1956; Wesleyan U., 1956; U. of Minnesota, 1961; U. of Louisville, 1961; Rotterdam, 1961; Amerika Haus, Berlin, 1961; American Cultural Center, Paris, 1961; Royal Watercolor Society, London, 1962; Peale House, Philadelphia, 1966; FAR Gallery, 1970; NCFA, 1970; A. Lublin, Inc., NYC, 1970; Kennedy Gallery, NYC, 1971, 73, 74, 75, 76, 78; Amon Carter Museum, 1972; Jewish Museum, 1974; Summit (N.J.) Art Center, 1974; SFMA, 1976; Indianapolis, 1976; Towson State College, Baltimore, 1976; Port Washington (N.Y.) Public Library, 1977; Washington U., 1978. **Retrospective:** Bowdoin College, 1962; Rotterdam, 1961; Smith College, 1963; Worcester/AM, 1957. **Group:** MOMA; WMAA; Brooklyn Museum, 1949, 52, 53, 54, 55; Library of Congress; The Print Club, Philadelphia; SAGA, 1952, 53; Sao Paulo; Brandeis U.; Seattle/AM. **Collections:** Allegheny College; Auburn U.; Baltimore/MA; Bezalel Museum; Boston/MFA; Bowdoin College; Brandeis U.; Brooklyn Museum; Buffalo/Albright; Amon Carter Museum;

Chase Manhattan Bank; Chicago/AI; U. of Delaware; Detroit/Institute; Fitchburg/AM; Harvard U.; Hirshhorn; Holyoke Public Library; U. of Illinois; Library of Congress; MMA; MOMA; Mount Holyoke College; NYPL; National Academy of Sciences; National Gallery; U. of Nebraska; Newark Museum; New School for Social Research; Omaha/Joslyn; PAFA; PMA; Princeton U.; The Print Club, Philadelphia; Smithsonian; St. John's Abbey, Collegeville, Minn.; St. Louis/City; Seattle/AM; Skidmore College; Smith College; Trenton/State; Utica; WMAA; Wesleyan U.; Worcester/AM. **Bibliography: Baskin;** Chaet; Craven, W.; Downes, ed.; **Fern;** Geske; Goodrich and Baur 1; Honisch and Jensen, eds.; Peterdi; Read 3; Rodman 1, 3; Sachs; Soyer, R., 1; Strachan. Archives.

BAYER, HERBERT. b. April 5, 1900, Haag, Austria. **Studied:** Real-Gymnasium, Linz, Austria; architecture with Prof. Schmidthammer, Linz, 1919; Bauhaus, Weimar, 1921, with Vassily Kandinsky. Traveled Europe, Central America, Japan, North Africa. To USA, 1938. **Taught:** Bauhaus, Dessau, 1925–28; New York Advertising Guild, 1939–40. Designs and plans exhibitions for museums throughout the world. Typographer and designer of typefaces, packages, posters, books, and charts. Registered architect. **Member:** American Abstract Artists; Alliance Graphique Internationale; American Institute of Architects; Aspen Institute for Humanistic Studies; International Institute of Arts and Letters. **Commissions:** (architectural) Seminar Building, Aspen Institute for Humanistic Studies; factories, Container Corp. of America; private residences; (murals) Harvard U.; Seminar Building, Aspen Institute; Colonial Williamsburg; Elementary School, West Bridgewater, Mass.; Container Corp. of America; sculpture for Arco Plaza, Los Angeles, 1973. **Awards:** Poster competitions; art director awards and medals; Milan Triennial, 1930; Medal of the City of Salzburg; Oklahoma, First Prize; AIGA, Gold Medal for Excellence, 1970; Hon. DFA, Philadelphia College of Art, 1974; Austrian Honor Cross for Art and Science, 1978; Hon. DFA, Art Center College of Design, Pasadena, 1979; Fellow, American Academy of Arts and Sciences, 1979. **Address:** 184 Middle Road, Montecito, CA 93108. **Dealer:** Marlborough Gallery, Inc., NYC. **One-man Exhibitions:** (first) Galerie Povolotzki, Paris, 1929; Kunstverein, Linz, 1929; Bauhaus, Dessau, 1931; Kunstlerhaus, Salzburg, 1936; The London Gallery, London, 1937; PM Gallery, NYC, 1939; Black Mountain College, 1939; Yale U., 1940; The Willard Gallery, 1943; Art Headquarters Gallery, NYC, 1943; North Texas State Teachers College, 1943; Outline Gallery, Pittsburgh, 1944; Cleveland/MA, 1952; H. Schaeffer Galleries, Inc., NYC, 1953; Galleria II Milione, Milan, 1954; Kunst Kabinett Klihm, 1954, 57, 59, 62, 67, 78; Aspen Institute, 1955, 64; Fort Worth, 1958; Walker, 1958; Dusseldorf, 1960; Bauhaus-Archiv, 1961; Andrew-Morris Gallery, NYC, 1963; The Byron Gallery, 1965; Esther Robles Gallery, 1965; Boise (Idaho) Art Association, 1965; U. of New Hampshire, 1966; Conzen Gallery, Dusseldorf, 1967; Kunst-Amendt, Aachen, 1967; Marlborough Fine Art Ltd. 1968; Dunkelman Gallery, Toronto, 1970; Marlborough Gallery, Inc., NYC, 1971, 76, 79; Marlborough Godard Ltd., Montreal, 1972; Marlborough Galerie AG, Zurich, 1974; Arte/Contacto, Caracas, 1974; Marlborough Godard Ltd., Toronto, 1975; Die Neue Galerie der Stadt, Linz, Austria, 1976; Marion Locks Gallery, Philadelphia, 1977; A.F.A., Herbert Bayer: From Type to Landscape, circ., 1977–78; Museum Bochum, 1978; Galerie Breiting, Berlin, 1979. **Retrospectives:** Brown U., The Way Beyond Art, circ., USA, 1947–49; Germanisches National Museum, Nurnberg, 33 Years of Herbert Bayer's Work, circ. Germany and Austria, 1956–57; Denver/AM, 1973; Haus Deutscher Ring, Hamburg, circ., 1974.

Group: Julien Levy Galleries, NYC, 1931, 40; MOMA, Fantastic Art, DADA, Surrealism, 1936; MOMA, Bauhaus: 1919–28, 1938; MOMA, Art and Advertising Art, circ., 1943; ART: USA: 58, NYC, 1958; American Abstract Artists Annuals, 1959–64; Marlborough Fine Art Ltd., Bauhaus, 1962; Arts Club of Chicago, 1962; Musee des Arts Decoratifs, 1966; Kunstverein, Hannover, Germany, 1967; Bauhaus Exhibition, circ. Stuttgart, London, Amsterdam, Paris, 1967–71; Berlin/National, Trends of the Twenties, 1977; Paris/Beaubourg, Paris–Berlin, 1908–1933, 1978. **Collections:** Bauhaus-Archiv; Brandeis U.; Busch-Reisinger Museum; Cologne; Denver/AM; Duisburg; Dusseldorf; Essen; Evansville; Fort Worth; Graphische Sammlung Albertina; Hagen; Hannover; Harvard U.; Hudson River Museum; Kaiserslautern; Leverkusen; Linz; MOMA; U. of Michigan; Museum des 20 Jahrhunderts, Vienna; Nurnberg; Oklahoma; Oldenburg; Omaha/Joslyn; Roswell; Rome/Nazionale; SFMA; SRGM; Saarlandmuseum; Smith College; Stuttgart; Vassar College; Wiesbaden. **Bibliography:** Barr 1; Baur 7; **Bayer 1, 2;** Blanchard; Blesh 1; Dorner; Gaunt; Haftman; Janis; McCurdy, ed.; Rickey; Rotors; Wingler, ed.

BAYLINSON, A.S. b. 1882, Moscow, Russia; **d.** May, 1950, NYC. **Studied** with Lattard, and privately with Robert Henri, Homer Boss. **Taught:** ASL. Secretary of Society of Independent Artists, NYC, for 17 years. Fire destroyed studio, 1930. Federal A.P.: Supervisor of Painting, 1937–39. **One-man Exhibitions:** Kraushaar Galleries, 1931; Uptown Gallery, NYC, 1940; Laurel Gallery, NYC, 1946, 49; Mount Holyoke College, 1934; ASL, Memorial Exhibition, 1951; Joseph Brummer Gallery, NYC (two-man), 1929; Mortimer Brandt, NYC (four-man), 1944. **Group:** WMAA. **Collections:** Ain Harod; Boston/MFA; MMA; MOMA; Newark Museum; PMA. **Bibliography:** Baur 7;

Brown; Cheney; Dreier 2; Huyghe; *Index of 20th Century Artists;* Janis; Pach 3; Smith, S.C.K. Archives.

BAYNARD, EDWARD. b. September 5, 1940, Washington, D.C. **Address:** 212 East 14th Street, NYC 10003. **One-man Exhibitions:** Ivan Spence Gallery, Ibiza, 1970; The Willard Gallery, NYC, 1971 (2), 76; 98 Green Street Left, 1972; Paley & Lowe Inc., NYC, 1972; Betty Parsons Gallery, NYC, 1973; Vick Gallery, Philadelphia, 1974; Multiples, NYC, 1977; Aronson Gallery, Atlanta, 1978; Showcase Gallery, Southfield, Mich., 1978; Alexander F. Milliken Inc., NYC, 1978, 79. **Group:** Utica, New American Painters, 1971; MOMA, Landscape, 1972; WMAA, American Drawing 1963–1973, 1973; Cleveland/MA, Seven Contemporary Artists, 1978. **Collections:** Amerada, Hess, N.J.; Chase Manhattan Bank; Hartford/

Ed Baynard   *Composition with Tulips*   1979

Wadsworth; ICA; Lehman Brothers, Inc.; MMA; MOMA; U. of Philadelphia; PMA; Prudential Insurance Co. of America; Southeast Banking Corp.

BAZIOTES, WILLIAM A. b. June 11, 1912, Pittsburgh, Pa.; **d.** June 4, 1963, NYC. **Studied:** NAD, 1933–36, with Leon Kroll. Federal A.P.: Teacher, 1936–38; easel painting, 1938–41. **Taught:** NYU, 1949–53; Brooklyn Museum School, 1949–52; Peoples Art Center (MOMA), 1951–53; Hunter College, 1952–63. Cofounder of a school, "Subject of the Artist," with Robert Motherwell, Barnett Newman, and Mark Rothko, NYC, 1948. **Awards:** Chicago/AI, Abstract and Surrealist Art, First Prize, 1948; U. of Illinois, **P.P.,** 1951; Chicago/AI, The Mr. & Mrs. Frank G. Logan Medal, 1961. **One-man Exhibitions:** (first) Art of This Century, NYC, 1944; The Kootz Gallery, NYC, 1946–48, 1950–54, 1956, 58, 61; Galerie Maeght, 1947; Sidney Janis Gallery, 1961; Milwaukee, 1965; Marlborough Gallery, Inc., 1971; PAFA, 1971. **Retrospective:** SRGM, 1965; Newport Harbor Art Museum, circ., 1978. **Group:** California Palace, 1948; Chicago/AI, Abstract and Surrealist Art, 1948; WMAA Annuals, 1948, 50, 1952–57; U. of Illinois, 1949–51, 1953, 55, 61; Los Angeles/County MA, 1951; U. of Minnesota, 40 American Painters, 1940–50, 1951; I & II Sao Paulo Biennials, 1951, 53; MOMA, Fifteen Americans, circ., 1952; U. of Nebraska, 1952, 54; SRGM, Younger American Painters, 1954; WMAA, The New Decade, 1954–55; Brussels World's Fair, 1958; MOMA, The New American Painting, circ., Europe, 1958–59; Documenta II, Kassel, 1959; Walker, 60 American Painters, 1960; Galerie de France, Paris, 1961; MOMA, The New American Painting and Sculpture, 1969. **Collections:** Baltimore/MA; Brandeis U.; Buffalo/Albright; Chicago/AI; Detroit/Institute; Harvard U.; U. of Illinois; MMA; MOMA; Newark Museum; New Orleans/Delgado; U. of Rochester; SRGM; San Francisco Art Association;

Seattle/AM; Smith College; Tel Aviv; Vassar College; WMAA; Walker; Washington U. **Bibliography: Alloway 4;** Ashton 5; Baur 5, 7; Bazin; Biddle 4; Blesh 1; Dorner; Carleton, Hobbs, and Levin; Eliot; Finkelstein; Flanagan; Goodrich and Baur 1; Haftman; Hunter 6; Hunter, ed.; Janis and Blesh 1; Janis; McCurdy, ed.; Mendelowitz; *Metro;* Motherwell, ed.; Motherwell and Reinhardt, eds.; Neumeyer; Nordness, ed.; Paalen; Ponente; Pousette-Dart, ed.; Read 2; Richardson, E.P.; Ritchie 1; Rodman 2; Rose, B., 1, 4; Rubin 1; Sandler 1; Soby 5; Tuchman, ed.; Tomkins 2; Weller; William Baziotes; Archives.

BEAL, GIFFORD. b. January 24, 1879, NYC; **d.** February 5, 1956, NYC. **Studied:** Princeton U., 1900; privately with William M. Chase; ASL, with Frank V. DuMond. Traveled eastern USA. **Member:** NAD, 1914; President, ASL, 1914–29. **Commissions:** (murals) Interior Department Building, Washington, D.C.; U.S. Post Office, Allentown, Pa. **Awards:** Worcester/AM, Third Prize, 1903; St. Louis Exposition, 1904, Bronze Medal; NAD, Hallgarten Prize, 1910; NAD, The Thomas B. Clarke Prize, 1913; Chicago/AI, Hon. Men., 1913; Corcoran, Third Prize, 1914; Panama-Pacific Exposition, San Francisco, 1915, Gold Medal; PMA, 1917; National Arts Club, Gold Medal, 1918; NAD, Benjamin Altman Prize, 1919, 31; Chicago/AI, Watson F. Blair Prize, 1930; Corcoran Second William A. Clark Prize, 1930; NAD Annual, Andrew Carnegie Prize, 1932; Paris World's Fair, 1937, Silver Medal; NAD, Saltus Gold Medal for Merit, 1948; NAD, Samuel F.B. Morse Gold Medal, 1954; NAD, Edwin Palmer Memorial Prize, 1955. **One-man Exhibitions:** Kraushaar Galleries, 1920–23, 1925–27, 29, 31, 33, 34, 36, 38, 41, 45, 48, 50, 56, 65, 71, 75, 79; AAAL, Memorial Exhibition, 1957; Fitchburg/AM, 1960; Storm King Art Center, 1968, 71. **Retrospective:** Century Association, 1950; Cowie Galleries, Los An-

geles, circ., 1953; Phillips, 1971; Montclair/AM, 1972. **Group:** Chicago/AI, 1928, 34, 37, 40, 44; Whitney Studio Club, NYC, 1929; PAFA, 1929, 30, 39, 44, 47, 51; St. Louis/City, 1930, 32; MOMA, 1930; Carnegie, 1931, 36, 51; U. of Rochester, 1932, 62; Phillips, 1932, 40, 54; WMAA, 1935, 45; New York World's Fair, 1939; NAD, 1942, 49, 51, 55; MMA, 1943; California Palace, 1945, 59; Youngstown/Butler, 1953; Hartford/Wadsworth, 1955. **Collections:** ASL; Andover/Phillips; Arizona State College; Brooklyn Museum; Chicago/AI; Detroit/Institute; Indiana U.; Kansas City/Nelson; Lehigh U.; Los Angeles/County MA; MMA; NAD; Newark Museum; New Britain; Omaha/Joslyn; The Pennsylvania State U.; Phillips; Randolph-Macon Woman's College; Southampton/Parrish; Syracuse U.; Utica; WMAA; Washington State U. **Bibliography:** Baur 7; Bryant, L.; Cahill and Barr, eds.; Hall; Jackman; Kent, N.; Mather 1; McCurdy, ed.; Mellquist; Neuhaus; Pagano; Phillips 1; Reese. Archives.

BEAL, JACK. b. June 25, 1931, Richmond, Va. **Studied:** College of William and Mary; Virginia Polytechnic Institute; Chicago/AI School (with Kathleen Blackshear). **Taught:** U. of Indiana, 1966; Purdue U., 1967; U. of Wisconsin, 1967, 69; Cooper Union, 1968; Wagner College; Cornell U.; Skowhegan School; San Francisco Art Association; Stanford U.; Fort Worth College; Miami-Dade. **Commissions:** Washington and Lee U., 1975; US Department of the Interior, 1976; US Department of Labor, 1976. **Awards:** Chicago/AI, Emilie L. Wild Prize, 1972; National Endowment for the Arts Grant, 1972. **Address:** 67 Vestry Street, NYC 10013; 83A Delhi Stage, Oneonta, NY 13820. **Dealer:** Allan Frumkin Gallery, NYC and Chicago. **One-man Exhibitions:** (first) Allan Frumkin Gallery, NYC, 1965, also 1967, 68, 70, 72, 73, 75, 78, 80; Allan Frumkin Gallery, Chicago, 1966, 69, 74; Miami-Dade, 1972; Galerie

Claude Bernard, Paris, 1973, 75; Colorado State U., 1976; Fullerton College, 1977; Madison Art Center, circ., 1977–78; U. of Missouri, 1979. **Retrospective:** VMFA, circ., 1973. **Group:** Chicago/AI, 1965; WMAA, Young America, 1965; A.F.A., 1965; RISD, Recent Still Life, 1966; Bennington College, 1967; Vassar College, 1968; SFMA, 1968; WMAA Annuals, 1968, 69; Milwaukee, Aspects of a New Realism, 1969; WMAA, 22 Realists, 1970; Boston U., The American Landscape, 1972; A.F.A. Realist Revival, 1972; Chicago/AI, 70th American Exhibition, 1972; Cleveland/MA, Aspects of the Figure, 1974; US Department of the Interior, America 1976, circ., 1976; Brooklyn Museum, Print Biennial, 1976; U. of Virginia, American Tradition and the Image of Post Modern Man in Contemporary Painting, Drawing, and Sculpture, 1979; PAFA, Seven on the Figure, 1979. **Collections:** Auckland; Bruce Museum; Brunswick Corp.; Chicago/AI; Ciba-Geigy Corp.; Delaware Art Museum; Des Moines; MOMA; Minneapolis/Institute; U. of North Carolina; U. of Notre Dame; Purchase/SUNY; PMA; Philip Morris Collection; Ringling; Sara Roby Foundation; SFMA; Valparaiso U. (Ind.); U. of Vermont; WMAA; Walker. **Bibliography:** *America 1976*; Arthur; Lucie-Smith; Rose, B., 1; Sager. Archives.

BEARDEN, ROMARE. b. September 2, 1914, Charlotte, N.C. **Studied:** NYU, BA; ASL (with George Grosz), 1938. Traveled Europe, North Africa. US Army, 1942–45. **Taught:** Williams College, 1971; Yale College, 1980. **Member:** AAIAL; Board of New York State Council on the Arts. Designed environment for the Ed Bullins play *House Rent Party*, at The American Place Theater, NYC, 1973. **Commissions:** murals for the New Lincoln Hospital, NYC, and City Hall, Berkeley, Calif. **Awards:** AAAL, Painting Award, 1966; Guggenheim Foundation Fellowship, 1969; Ford Foundation Grant, 1973. **Address:** 357

Canal Street, NYC 10013. **Dealer:** Cordier & Ekstrom, Inc. **One-man Exhibitions:** (first) "G" Place Gallery, Washington, D.C., 1945; The Kootz Gallery, NYC, 1945, 46, 57; Duvuloy Gallery, Paris, 1945; Niveau Gallery, NYC, 1948; Barone Gallery, NYC, 1955; Michel Warren Gallery, NYC, 1960; Cordier & Ekstrom, Inc., 1961, 64, 67, 70, 73, 74, 75; Corcoran, 1966; Waitsfield/Bundy, 1966. **Retrospective:** Albany/SUNY, 1968; MOMA, circ., 1971; Charlotte Mint, circ., 1980. **Group:** Carnegie; WMAA; Galerie Maeght, 6 American Painters, 1948; MMA, Survey of American Art, 1951; Chicago/AI; Dallas/MFA; Boston/MFA; MOMA, The New American Painting and Sculpture, 1969. **Collections:** Akron/AI; Atlanta U.; Boston/MFA; Brooklyn Museum; Buffalo/Albright; Flint/Institute; Howard U.; MMA; MOMA; Madison Art Center; Newark Museum; PMA; Princeton U.; St. Louis/City; U. of Rochester; WMAA. **Bibliography:** Dover. Archives.

BEASLEY, BRUCE. b. May 20, 1939, Los Angeles, Calif. **Studied:** Dartmouth College, 1957–59; U. of California, 1959–62. Traveled Europe, Japan, South Pacific, Central America, Mexico. Resided in France, 1973. **Commissions:** State of California; Oakland/AM; Southland Center, Hayward, Calif.; City of San Francisco; GSA, Federal Office Building, San Diego, 1975; Taubman Co., Sterling Heights, Mich., 1976; San Francisco General Hospital, 1977; City of Salinas, California, 1977; Miami International Airport, 1977. **Awards:** Oakland/AM, Adele Morrison Memorial Medal, 1960; SFAI Annual, Hon. Men., 1961; Andre Malraux, **P.P.,** Paris Biennial, 1962; Marin, Frank Lloyd Wright Memorial, **P.P.,** 1965; San Francisco Arts Festival, **P.P.,** 1967. **Address:** 322 Lewis Street, Oakland, CA 94607. **Dealers:** Hansen-Fuller Gallery, San Francisco. **One-man Exhibitions:** RAC, 1961; Everett Ellin Gallery, Los Angeles, 1963; The Kornblee Gallery,

1964; Hansen-Fuller Gallery, 1965; David Stuart Gallery, 1966; Andre Emmerich Gallery, NYC, 1971; de Young, 1972; Santa Barbara/MA, 1973; San Diego, 1973. **Group:** RAC Annual, 1960; Oakland/AM Annual, 1960; MOMA, The Art of Assemblage, circ., 1961; III Paris Biennial, 1963; U. of California, Berkeley, Eleven American Sculptors, 1964; La Jolla, Some Aspects of California Painting and Sculpture, 1965; San Fernando Valley State College, Twenty-two Sculptors, 1966; U. of Illinois, 1969, 74; ICA, U. of Pennsylvania, Plastics and New Art, 1969; Jewish Museum, A Plastic Presence, 1969; Expo '70, Osaka, 1970; Stanford U., Sculpture Here and Now, 1970; Omaha/Joslyn, Looking West, 1970; Oakland/AM, Pierres de Fantaisie, 1970; U. of Nebraska, American Sculpture, 1970; Sacramento/ Crocker Biennial, 1970; Stanford U., Sculpture 72, 1972; Salon de Mai, Paris, 1973; Salon de la Jeune Sculpture, Paris/ Moderne, 1973; Oakland/AM, Public Sculpture, Urban Environment, 1974. **Collections:** U. of California, Berkeley; U. of Kansas; Los Angeles/County MA; MOMA; Marin; Oakland/AM; Paris/ Moderne; Santa Barbara/MA; SRGM; UCLA; Wichita/AM.

BEATTIE, GEORGE. b. August 2, 1919, Cleveland, Ohio. **Studied:** Cleveland Institute of Art. **Taught:** Georgia Institute of Technology, Architectural School; Atlanta Art Institute. **Member:** Audubon Artists. **Commissions:** State of Georgia Agricultural Building (mural). **Awards:** NIAL Grant, 1955; Fulbright Fellowship (Italy), 1956; Atlanta/AA, Southeastern Annual, 1949; Mead Painting of the Year, 1959; Audubon Artists, Minnie R. Stern Memorial Medal, 1955. **Address:** 857 Woodley Drive, N.W., Atlanta GA 30318. **One-man Exhibitions:** Grand Central Moderns, NYC, 1954; Hirschl & Adler Galleries, Inc., NYC, 1961; Atlanta/AA, 1950, 61; Georgia Institute of Technology, 1954; Columbus, 1956; U. of Virginia, 1956. **Group:** MMA, 1952; Utica, 1955; Uffizi Loggia, Florence, Italy, International Drawing Annual, 1957; Smithsonian, 1955, 1958–59, 61; ART:USA:59, NYC, 1959; Atlanta/AA, Southeastern Annual, 1949; Mead-Southeast Annual, 1955–61. **Collections:** Atlanta/AA; Atlanta U.; Columbus; Mead Corp.; Montclair/AM; WMAA. **Bibliography:** Pousette-Dart, ed.

BEAUCHAMP, ROBERT. b. November 19, 1923, Denver, Colo. **Studied:** U. of Denver; Cranbrook Academy of Art, BFA; Colorado Springs Fine Arts Center, with Boardman Robinson; Hofmann School. US Navy, 1943–46. Traveled Italy, 1973. **Taught:** U. of Wisconsin, 1968; Cooper Union, 1969–70; Louisiana State U., 1971; U. of Illinois, 1972; Brooklyn College, 1973; School of Visual Arts, NYC, 1974–75; U. of California, San Diego, 1977; U. of Ohio, 1978; Syracuse U., 1978; SUNY/ New Paltz, 1979; U. of Arizona, 1980. **Member:** Artists Equity. **Awards:** Fulbright Fellowship (Italy); Walter K. Gutman Foundation Grant; National Council on the Arts, 1966; Guggenheim Foundation Grant, 1974. **Address:** 463 West Street, NYC 10014. **Dealer:** Monique Knowlton Gallery, NYC. **One-man Exhibitions:** (first) Tanager Gallery, NYC, 1953; Great Jones Gallery, NYC, 1960, 61; Sun Gallery, Provincetown, 1961, 62, 63; Green Gallery, NYC, 1961, 63; Richard Gray Gallery, 1963; Felix Landau Gallery, 1963; East End Gallery, Provincetown, 1964, 65; The American Gallery, NYC, 1965; The Graham Gallery, 1965, 67, 69; Obelisk Gallery, 1966; U. of Utah, 1967; Tirca Karlis Gallery, 1967, 68, 71, 72; Louisiana State U., 1971; Galerie Simone Stern, New Orleans, 1971; French & Co. Inc., NYC, 1972; Robert Dain Gallery, NYC, 1972, 73; U. of Southern Florida, 1974; Terry Dintenfass, Inc. NYC, 1976; Monique Knowlton Gallery, NYC, 1978, 79, 80. **Group:** Bernault Commission, circ., Asia; Carnegie, 1958, 61; WMAA An-

Robert Beauchamp   Untitled   1978

nuals, 1961, 63, 65, 67, 69; Corcoran; Chicago/AI; MOMA, Recent American Painting and Sculpture, circ., USA and Canada, 1961–62; MOMA, Recent Painting USA: The Figure, circ., 1962–63; U. of Illinois, 1963; SRGM, 10 Independents, 1972. **Collections:** Brooklyn Museum; U. of California; Carnegie; Cornell U.; Denver/AM; Hartford/Wadsworth; MMA; MOMA; International Telephone and Telegraph Corp.; U. of Massachusetts; Norfolk/Chrysler; Ridgefield/Aldrich; U. of Texas; WMAA. **Bibliography:** Archives.

BECHTLE, ROBERT. b. May 14, 1932, San Francisco, Calif. **Studied:** California College of Arts and Crafts, 1954, BA, 1958, MFA; U. of California, Berkeley. Traveled Europe, Mexico. **Taught:** California College of Arts and Crafts, 1957– ; U. of California, Berkeley, 1965–66, Davis, 1967–68; San Francisco State College, 1968– ; SFAI, 1975. **Awards:** Oakland/AM, **P.P.,** 1957, 59; RAC, 1958, 61, 64; Bay Printmakers Society, Oakland, Adell Hyde Morrison Memorial Medal, 1959, 61;

SFMA, James D. Phelan Award, 1965; National Endowment for the Arts, grant, 1977. **Address:** 850 Mendocino Avenue, Berkeley, CA 94707. **Dealers:** OK Harris Works of Art; John Berggruen Gallery. **One-man Exhibitions:** (first) SFMA, 1959, also 1964, 67; Berkeley Gallery, Berkeley, 1965, San Francisco, 1967; RAC, 1965; Sacramento/Crolker, 1966; U. of California, Davis, 1967; Achenbach Foundation, 1969; OK Harris Works of Art, 1971, 74, 77; John Berggruen Gallery, San Francisco, 1973; Jack Glenn Gallery, San Diego, 1973. **Retrospective:** Sacramento/Crocker, 1973; San Diego, 1973. **Group:** Witte, 1965; USIA 1965–67; WMAA Annual, 1967; MOMA, The Artist as His Subject, 1967; California Palace, Painters behind Painters, 1967; U. of Illinois, 1967, 69; West Coast Now, 1968; Vassar College, 1968; Milwaukee, Aspects of a New Realism, 1969; WMAA, 22 Realists, 1970; Indianapolis, 1970; Omaha/Joslyn, Looking West, 1970; Syracuse/Everson, Cool Realism, 1970; Indiana U., American Scene: 1900–1970, 1970; Chicago/Contemporary, Radical Realism, 1971; Govett-Brewster, The State of California Painting, 1971; Documenta V, Kassel, 1972; Stuttgart/WK, Amerikanischer Fotorealismus, circ., 1972; WMAA Biennial, 1973; Hartford/Wadsworth, New/Photo Realism, 1974; Tokyo Biennial, 1974; Toledo/MA, Image, Color, and Form, 1975; Renwick Gallery, Washington, D.C., Signs of Life: Symbols in the City, 1975; Centennial Museum/Vancouver, Aspects of Realism, 1976; Baltimore, Super Realism, 1976; Canberra/National, Illusion and Reality, 1977–78; U. of Rochester, Perceiving Time & Space through Art, 1979; Albuquerque/MA, Reflections of Realism, 1979–80. **Collections:** Aachen/NG; Achenbach Foundation; U. of California, Berkeley; Chase Manhattan Bank; Concordia Teachers College (Ill.); Diablo Valley College; Doane College, Charleston/Carolina; U. of Miami; Govett-Brewster; Indiana National Bank; Library of Congress; U. of Miami;

Robert Bechtle *Mercury* 1974

MOMA; Mills College; NCFA; U. of Nebraska; Oakland/MA; SFMA; Sacramento/Crocker; San Francisco Municipal Art Commission; San Jose State College; Starr King School for the Ministry; USIA; Valparaiso U. (Ind.); WMAA. **Bibliography:** Alloway 4; *America 1976; Amerikanischer Fotorealismus;* Arthur 1, 2; Honisch and Jensen, eds.; *Kunst um 1970;* Lucie-Smith; Sager; *The State of California Painting.*

BECK, ROSEMARIE. b. July 8, 1923, NYC. **Studied:** Oberlin College, BA; Columbia U.; NYU. Traveled Europe. **Taught:** Vassar College, 1957–58, 61–62, 64–65; Middlebury College, 1958, 59, 63; Parsons School of Design, 1965–68; Queens College, 1968– . **Commissions:** Ration Mfg. Co., 1956. **Awards:** Ingram Merrill Foundation Grant, 1966, 79; Yaddo Fellowship; MacDowell Colony Fellowship. **Address:** 6 East 12th Street, NYC 10003. **Dealer:** Ingber Art Gallery, NYC. **One-**

man Exhibitions: (first) The Periodot Gallery, 1953, also 1955, 56, 59, 60, 63, 64, 66, 68, 70, 72; Oberlin College, 1957; Vassar College, 1957, 61; New Paltz/SUNY, 1962; Duke U., 1971; Kirkland College, 1971; Zachary Waller Gallery, Los Angeles, 1971; Poindexter Gallery, NYC, 1975, 79; Queens College, 1975; Ingber Art Gallery, NYC, 1979; Middlebury College, 1979. **Retrospective:** Wesleyan U., 1960. **Group:** PAFA, 1954; U. of Nottingham (England), 1954, 57; WMAA Annuals, 1955, 57; U. of Michigan, 1956; Chicago/AI; Brooklyn Museum; Tate; Youngstown/Butler; Arts Club of Chicago; NIAL, 1969, 70, 71, 72, 73; NAD, 1973. **Collections:** Fort Wright College; U. of Nebraska; New Paltz/SUNY; Ration Mfg. Co.; Vassar College; WMAA; Yaddo; Hirshhorn. **Bibliography:** Baur 5.

BEHL, WOLFGANG. b. April 13, 1918, Berlin, Germany. **Studied:** Academy of Fine Arts, Berlin, 1936–39; RISD,

1939–40. US citizen. Traveled Europe, Mexico, USA, Middle East. **Taught:** Perkiomen School, 1940–42; Lake Forest Academy, 1942–44; Layton School of Art, 1944–45; College of William and Mary, 1945–52; Silvermine Guild, 1955–57; U. of Hartford, 1955– . **Member:** Sculptors Guild. **Commissions:** Temple Beth El Sholom, Manchester, Conn.; St. Louis Priory, Creve Coeur, Miss.; Church of St. Timothy, West Hartford, Conn.; U. of Hartford; Willow Lawn Shopping Center, Richmond, Va.; St. Joseph's Cathedral, Hartford, Conn.; Church of the Resurrection, Wallingford, Conn.; Connecticut General Insurance Co. **Awards:** Chicago/AI, Joseph N. Eisendrath Prize, 1944; Milwaukee, Wisconsin Prize for Sculpture, 1945; Connecticut Academy of Fine Arts, First Prize for Sculpture, 1961; NIAL Grant, 1963; Ford Foundation, **P.P.,** 1964. **Address:** 179 Kenyon Street, Hartford, CT 06105. **Dealer:** Rosenfeld Gallery, Philadelphia; Texann Ivy Gallery, Orlando, Fla. **One-man Exhibitions:** Charlotte/ Mint, 1949, 50; The Bertha Schaefer Gallery, 1950, also 1955, 63, 65, 68; Hollins College, 1951; Randolph-Macon Woman's College, 1951; Sweet Briar College, 1951; Amerika Haus, Schweinfurt, Wurzberg, and Munich; Bucknell U., 1965; U. of Connecticut, 1965; New Britain/American, 1969; Bienville Gallery, 1974; U. of New Hampshire, 1974; Hampshire College, 1976; Texann Ivy Gallery, Orlando, Fla., 1979; Rosenfeld Gallery, Philadelphia, 1979. **Group:** Chicago/AI, 1943, 44; Milwaukee, 1945; Boston Arts Festival, 1946, 47; Silvermine Guild, 1946, 47; VMFA, 1946–49, 1951; U. of Illinois, 1957; Hartford/ Wadsworth, 1957; Carnegie, 1962, 64; PAFA, 1964; Harvard U., 1966; Cranbrook, 6th Biennial, National Religious Art Exhibition, 1968. **Collections:** Andover/Phillips; Cornell U.; U. of Hartford; U. of Massachusetts; U. of Miami; New Britain; New Britain/American; PAFA; Slater.

BELL, LARRY. b. 1939, Chicago, Ill. **Studied:** Chouinard Art Institute, 1957–59; with Robert Irwin, Emerson Woelfer. **Awards:** Guggenheim Foundation Fellowship, 1969. **Taught:** U. of California, Berkeley; U. of California, Irvine; California State at Hayward; U. of Southern Florida. **Address:** P.O. Box 1778, Taos, NM 87571. **Dealer:** Marion Goodman/Multiples; Janus Gallery, Venice, California. **One-man Exhibitions:** Ferus Gallery, Los Angeles, 1962, 63, 65; The Pace Gallery, 1965, 67, 70, 71, 72, 73; Ileana Sonnabend Gallery, Paris, 1967, 68; Amsterdam/ Stedelijk, 1967; Walker, 1968; Buffalo/ Albright, 1968; Mizuno Gallery, 1969, 71, 75; Galerie Rudolf Zwirner, 1970; Joseph Helman Gallery, St. Louis, 1971; ACE Gallery, Los Angeles, 1972; Felicity Samuel Gallery, London, 1972; Pasadena/AM, 1972; Wilmaro Gallery, Denver, 1972; Oakland/AM, 1973; Fort Worth, 1975; Galleria del Cavallino, Venice, 1975; Marlborough Galleria d'Arte, Rome, 1975; Marion Goodman/ Multiples, NYC, 1978; Talley Richards Gallery, Taos, 1975, 77, 78, 79; Texas Gallery, Houston, 1978; Delahunty Gallery, Dallas, 1978; Hansen Fuller Goldeen Gallery, San Francisco, 1979; U. of Massachusetts (two-man), 1977. **Group:** Pavillion Art Gallery, Balboa, Calif., 1964; MOMA, The Responsive Eye, 1965; VIII Sao Paulo Biennial, 1965; WMAA Sculpture Annual, 1966; WMAA, Contemporary American Sculpture, Selection I, 1966; U. of California, Irvine, 5 Los Angeles Sculptors, 1966; La Jolla, 1966; Seattle/AM, 1966; MOMA, The 1960s, 1967; WGMA, A New Aesthetic, 1967; Los Angeles/ County MA, American Sculpture of the Sixties, 1967; SRGM, Sculpture International, 1967; Documenta IV, Kassel, 1968; Vancouver, 1968; Eindhoven Kompas IV, 1969; Walker, 14 Sculptors: The Industrial Edge, 1969; Princeton U., American Art since 1960, 1970; MOMA, Spaces, 1969; Tate (three-man), 1970; Hayward Gallery, London,

11 Los Angeles Artists, 1971; Detroit/ Institute, Art in Space, 1973; Kennedy Center, Washington, D.C., Art Now '74, 1974. **Collections:** Buffalo/Albright; Chicago/AI; Denver/AM; Des Moines; Fort Worth; Hartford/ Wadsworth; Los Angeles/County MA; MOMA; Oakland/AM; Pasadena/AM; Sydney/AG; Tate; WMAA; Walker. **Bibliography:** *Art Now 74*; Calas, N. and E.; Coplans, 3; Davis, D.; Friedman, M., 2; Kozloff 3; Lucie-Smith; *Report*; Rose, B., 1; *Transparency*; Tuchman 1; *USA West Coast*.

BENGLIS, LYNDA. b. October 25, 1941, Lake Charles, La. **Studied:** Newcomb College, Tulane U., 1964, BFA, with Pat Trivigno, Ida Kohlmeyer, and Hal Carney; Brooklyn Museum Art School, 1964–65, with Rubin Tam. Traveled Greece, Great Britain, Italy, France, Indiana. **Taught:** U. of Rochester, 1970–72; Hunter College, 1972–73; Princeton U., 1975; California Institute of the Arts, 1976; Kent State U., 1977; Skowhegan School of Painting and Sculpture, 1979. **Commissions:** Atlanta Airport, 1979–80; Federal Building, Albany, N.Y., 1979–80. **Awards:** Guggenheim Foundation Fellowship, 1975; Artpark, Grant, 1976; Australian Art Council Award, 1976; National Endowment for the Arts, Grant, 1979. **Address:** 222 Bowery, NYC 10002. **Dealer:** Paula Cooper Gallery, NYC. **One-man Exhibitions:** U. of Rhode Island, 1969; Paula Cooper Gallery, NYC, 1970, 71, 74, 75, 76, 78; Janie C. Lee Gallery, Dallas, 1970; Galerie Hans Muller, Cologne, 1970; Kansas State U., 1971; MIT, 1971; Hansen Gallery, San Francisco, 1972, 73, 74, 77, 79; Portland (Ore.) Center for the Visual Arts, 1973; Jack Glenn Gallery, Corona del Mar, 1973; The Clocktower, NYC, 1973; The Texas Gallery, Houston, 1974, 75, 79; The Kitchen, NYC, 1975; Margo Leavin Gallery, Los Angeles, 1977, 80; Douglas Drake Gallery, Kansas City, 1977; Dart

Gallery, Chicago, 1979; Georgia State U., 1979; Albert Baronian, Brussels, 1979. **Retrospective:** U. of South Florida, 1980; U. of Miami, 1980. **Group:** Dusseldorf/Kunsthalle, Prospect 69, 1969; Finch College, Art in Process IV, 1969; Walker, Works for New Spaces, 1971; Milwaukee, Directions 3: Eight Artists, 1971; GEDOK, Kunsthaus, Hamburg, American Women Artists, 1972; Walker, Painting: New Options, 1972; Indianapolis, 1972; Chicago/AI, 32nd Annual, 1972; Detroit/Institute, 12 Statements, 1972; WMAA Biennial, 1973; Yale U., Options and Alternatives, 1973; New Orleans Museum, Five from Louisiana, 1977; Amsterdam/ Stedelijk, Made by Sculptors, 1978. **Collections:** Betcar Corp., Northfield, Ill.; Detroit/Institute; SRGM; MOMA; Canberra/National; National Gallery of Victoria, Melbourne; PMA; Storm King Art Center; Walker; SFMA. **Bibliography:** *Art: A Woman's Sensibility; Drawings: The Pluralist Decade*; Lucie-Smith.

BENGSTON, BILLY AL. b. June 7, 1934, Dodge City, Kans. **Studied:** Los Angeles City College; Los Angeles State College; California College of Arts and Crafts; Los Angeles County Art Institute. **Taught:** Chouinard Art Institute, 1961; UCLA, 1962–63; U. of Oklahoma, 1967; U. of Colorado, 1969; U. of California, Irvine, 1973. **Awards:** National Council on the Arts, 1967; Tamarind Fellowship, 1968; Guggenheim Foundation Fellowship, 1975. **Address:** 110 Mildred Avenue, Venice, CA 90291. **Dealer:** Acquavella Contemporary Art, Inc., NYC; James Corcoran Galleries, Los Angeles. **One-man Exhibitions:** (first) Ferus Gallery, Los Angeles, 1957, also 1958, 1960, 61, 62, 63; Martha Jackson Gallery, 1962; SFMA, 1968; Pasadena/AM, 1969; Utah, 1969; Santa Barbara/MA, 1970; Mizuno Gallery, 1970; Galerie Hans R. Neuendorf, Cologne, 1970, 71; Galerie Hans R. Neuendorf, Hamburg, 1970, 72; Margo

Leavin Gallery, 1971; La Jolla, 1971; Contract Graphics Associates, Houston, 1971; Felicity Samuel Gallery, London, 1972; Corcoran & Greenberg, Inc., Coral Gables, 1973; Nicholas Wilder Gallery, 1973 (2), 1974; Southern Methodist U., 1973; Houston/Contemporary, 1973; The Texas Gallery, 1974, 75, 76, 77, 78, 79; John Berggruen Gallery, 1974; Jared Sable Gallery, Toronto, 1974; Pyramid Art Galleries Ltd., Washington, D.C., 1975; Seder/Creigh Gallery, Coronado, 1975; Tortue Gallery, Santa Monica, 1975; Dootson Calderhead Gallery, Seattle, 1975; Dobrick Gallery, Chicago, 1976; Portland (Ore.) Center for the Visual Arts, 1976; U. of Montana, 1977; James Corcoran Galleries, Los Angeles, 1977, 78; Security Pacific National Bank, Los Angeles, 1978; John Berggruen Gallery, San Francisco, 1978; Mizuno Gallery, Los Angeles, 1978; Conejo Valley Art Museum, 1979; Acquavella Contemporary Art Gallery, NYC, 1979; Cantor/Lemberg Gallery, Birmingham, Mich., 1979. **Retrospective:** Los Angeles/County MA, circ., Vancouver, Corcoran, 1968. **Group:** Los Angeles/County MA Annual, 1957; Pasadena/AM, Pacific Profile of Young West Coast Artists, 1961; WMAA, Fifty California Artists, 1962–63; Oakland/AM, Pop Art USA, 1963; Milwaukee, Pop Art and the American Tradition, 1965; VIII Sao Paulo Biennial, 1965; Seattle/AM, Ten from Los Angeles, 1966; WMAA Annuals, 1967, 69; U. of California, San Diego, Los Angeles to New York, 1968; Palazzo Strozzi, Florence, Italy, 1 Biennale Internazionale della Grafica, 1968; MOMA, New Media: New Methods, circ., 1969; Jewish Museum, Superlimited: Books, Boxes, and Things, 1969; MOMA, Tamarind: Homage to Lithography, 1969; Eindhoven, Kompas IV, 1969–70; Pasadena/AM, West Coast: 1945–1969, 1969; Minnesota/MA, Drawings USA, 1971; Govett-Brewster, The State of California Painting, 1971; Kunstverein, Hamburg, USA: West Coast, circ., 1972; Akron/AI, Four Artists, 1972; Corcoran Biennial, 1973; Santa Barbara/MA, Fifteen Abstract Artists, 1974; WMAA, American Pop Art, 1974; Scripps College, Painting: Color, Form and Surface, 1974; U. of California, Santa Barbara, 4 from the West, 1975; Newport Harbor, The Last Time I Saw Ferus, 1976; SFMA, Painting and Sculpture in California: The Modern Era, 1976; California Institute of Technology, Pasadena, Watercolors and Related Media by Contemporary Californians, 1977; WMAA Biennial, 1979. **Collections:** A.F.A.; Amon Carter Museum; Chicago/AI; Community Arts Foundation; Fort Worth; Houston/MFA; La Jolla; Los Angeles/County MA; MOMA; Newport Harbor; Oakland/AM; Pasadena/AM; Ridgefield/Aldrich; SFMA; SRGM; UCLA; WMAA. **Bibliography:** Alloway 1; Kozloff 3; Lippard 5; *The State of California Painting; USA West Coast.*

BENJAMIN, KARL. b. December 29, 1925, Chicago, Ill. **Studied:** Northwestern U.; U. of Redlands, 1949, BA; Claremont Graduate School, with Jean Ames, 1960, M.A. US Navy, 1943–46. **Taught:** General elementary school, Southern California, 1949– ; Pomona College. **Address:** 675 West Eighth Street, Claremont, CA 91711. **Dealers:** Tortue Gallery, Santa Monica; Francine Seders Gallery, Seattle; Modernism, San Francisco. **One-man Exhibitions:** U. of Redlands, 1953, 56, 62, 72; Pasadena/AM, 1954; Jack Carr Gallery, Pasadena, 1955, 56; Occidental College, 1958; Long Beach/MA, 1958; Esther Robles Gallery, 1959, 60, 62, 64, 65; Scripps College, 1960; La Jolla, 1961, 70; Bolles Gallery, 1961; Santa Barbara/AM, 1962, 68; Hollis Gallery, San Francisco, 1964, 66; Jefferson Gallery, 1965; Henri Gallery, 1968; Utah, 1971; William Sawyer Gallery, 1972; Tortue Gallery, Santa Monica, 1975, 77, 78; Chafey College, 1975; Francine Seders Gallery, Seattle, 1978. **Group:** Los Angeles/County MA Annuals; A.F.A., New Talent, circ., 1959; UCLA, California Painters under 35, 1959; Los Angeles/County

MA, Four Abstract Classicists, circ., 1959–61; ICA, London, West Coast Hard Edge, 1960; Carnegie, California Artists, 1961; Pasadena/AM, Pacific Profile, 1961; WMAA, Geometric Abstraction in America, circ., 1962; Fort Worth, The Artist's Environment: The West Coast, 1962; Amon Carter Museum, circ., 1962–63; WMAA, Fifty California Artists, 1962–63; Colorado Springs/FA Annual, 1964; Denver/AM, 1965; MOMA, The Responsive Eye, 1965; SFMA, The Colonists, 1965; M. Knoedler & Co., Art Across America, circ., 1965–67; Corcoran Biennial, 1967. **Collections:** U. of California; City of Claremont; Haifa Museum of Modern Art, Israel; La Jolla; Long Beach/MA; Los Angeles/County MA; NCFA; Newport Harbor; Pasadena/AM; Pepsi-Cola Co.; J. Pitzer College; Pomona College; U. of Redlands; SFMA; Salk Institute; San Diego; Santa Barbara/MA; Scripps College; Seattle/AM; Utah; WMAA. **Bibliography:** Rickey; *Black and White Are Colors.*

BENTON, FLETCHER. b. February 23, 1931, Jackson, Ohio. **Studied:** Miami U., 1955, BFA. Traveled Northern Europe, Mediterranean, parts of Africa and Asia, 1963. US Navy, 1949–50. **Taught:** California College of Arts and Crafts, 1959; SFAI, 1964–67; California State U., San Jose, 1967– . **Commissions:** Atlantic Richfield Co. **Awards:** AAAL, Distinguished Service to American Art Award, 1979. **Member:** Artists Equity. There are three films on his work, 1969, 73, 75. **Address:** 2100 Pine Street, San Francisco, CA 94103. **Dealer:** John Berggruen Gallery, San Francisco. **One-man Exhibitions:** (first) Gump's Gallery, 1957; California Palace, 1964; SFMA, 1965; Hansen Gallery, San Francisco, 1965, 66; Esther Robles Gallery, 1966, 67; SFAI, 1967; Sonoma State College, 1967; Galeria Bonino Ltd., 1967, 69; Humboldt State College, 1968; Galerie Francoise Mayer, Brussels, 1969; SFMA, 1970; Buffalo/Albright, 1970; Chico State College, 1970; London Arts, Detroit, 1970;

Berkeley (Calif.) Art Center, 1970; Reed College, 1970; Galeria Bonino Ltd., Buenos Aires, 1970; Estudio Actual, Caracas, 1970; Stanford U., 1971; La Jolla, 1972; Esther Robles Gallery, 1971, 72; Danenberg Gallery, 1972; Landry-Bonino Gallery, NYC, 1972; Phoenix, 1973; U. of California, Davis, 1973; Galeria Bonino Ltd., Rio de Janeiro, 1973; Elaine Horwitch Gallery, Scottsdale, 1974; U. of Santa Clara, 1975; Smith-Andersen Gallery, San Francisco, 1975; Fresno State U., 1977; John Berggruen Gallery, San Francisco, 1977, 80; Tortue Gallery, Los Angeles, 1978; San Jose Museum of America 1978. **Retrospective:** Arts Club of Chicago, circ., 1979. **Group:** Santa Barbara/MA, 1962, 66; San Francisco Art Association, 1964; La Jolla, 1965; New York World's Fair, 1964–65; U. of California, Berkeley, Directions in Kinetic Sculpture, 1966; SFMA, 1966; U. of Illinois, 1967, 69; Los Angeles/County MA and PMA, American Sculpture of the Sixties, 1967; U. of Hawaii, 1967; Carnegie, 1967; Flint/Institute, 1967; HemisFair '68, San Antonio, Tex., 1968; Milwaukee, Directions I: Options, circ., 1968; WMAA Sculpture Annual, 1968; Lytton Art Center, Los Angeles, 1968; UCLA, Electric Art, 1969; U. of Illinois, 1969; Expo '70, Osaka, 1970; Kent State U. Annual, 1970; Indianapolis, 1970; Hayward Gallery, London, Kinetics, 1970; Omaha/Joslyn, Looking West, 1970; U. of California, Santa Barbara, Constructivist Tendencies, circ., 1970; Hudson River Museum, Kinetic Art, 1971; Stanford U., A Decade in the West, 1971; WMAA Annual, 1973; U. of Califonia, Berkeley, Kinetic Exhibition, 1973; Philadelphia Art Alliance, Sculpture of the Sixties, 1974; Hirshhorn, Inaugural Exhibition, 1974; Huntsville Museum of Art, Ala., The California Bay Area Painting and Sculpture Update, 1977; Sonoma State U., Northern California Artists, 1978. **Collections:** Atlantic Richfield Co.; Banque Lambert, Brussels; U. of California; Capital Research Co., Los Angeles; Denver/AM; First National City Bank of Dallas; First

National Bank of Ohio, Columbus; Hirshhorn; IBM; Interchemical Corporation; La Jolla; Milwaukee; Neiman-Marcus Co.; The New York Bank for Savings; Newport Harbor; Oakland/AM; Purchase/SUNY; Ridgefield/Aldrich; SFMA; Sacramento/Crocker; The Singer Company, Inc.; Stanford U.; Taubman Corp.; Thurman Arnold U. Building, Washington, D.C.; WMAA. **Bibliography:** Atkinson; Davis, D.; Rickey; Selz, P., 1; Tuchman 1.

BENTON, THOMAS HART. b. April 15, 1889, Neosho, Mo.; **d.** January 19, 1975, Kansas City, Mo. **Studied:** Western Military Academy, 1906–07; Chicago Art Institute School, 1907; Academie Julian, Paris, 1908–11. Gallery director and art teacher for Chelsea Neighborhood Association, NYC, 1917. US Navy, 1918–19. Traveled Europe, USA, Canada. **Taught:** ASL, 1926–36; Kansas City Art Institute and School of Design, 1935–40; lectured at many colleges and universities. **Commissions:** (murals) New School for Social Research, with Jose Clemente Orozco, 1928; WMAA, 1932; State of Indiana, 1933 (mural now located at U. of Indiana); Missouri State Capitol, 1935–36; "Achelous and Hercules" for Harzfeld Department Store, Kansas City, 1947 (Encyclopedia Britannica filmed his progress on this mural); Lincoln U., 1952–53; Kansas City River Club, 1947; New York State Power Authority, Massena, 1957–61; Truman Library, Independence, Mo., 1958–61. **Awards:** Architectural League of New York, Gold Medal, 1933; Academia Argentina de Bellas Artes, Buenos Aires, Hon. Men., 1945; Accademia Florentina dell'Arte del Disegno, Hon. Men., 1949; Accademia Senese degli Intronati, Siena, 1949; Hon. D. Litt., Lincoln U., 1957; Hon. DFA, U. of Missouri, 1948; Hon. PBK, 1948; Hon. DFA, New School for Social Research, 1968. **One-man Exhibitions:** Lakeside Press Gallery, Chicago, 1927; Ferargil Galleries, NYC, 1934, 35; Des Moines (two-man),

1939; A.A.A. Gallery, NYC, 1939, 41, 65; A.A.A. Gallery, Chicago, 1946; U. of Arizona, circ., 1962; The Graham Gallery, 1968, 70; Madison (Wisc.) Art Center, 1971; Kansas City/Nelson, 1974. **Retrospective:** Kansas City/Nelson, 1939; Omaha/Joslyn, 1951; New Britain, 1954; U. of Kansas, 1958; Cranbrook, 1966; A.A.A. Gallery, 1969; Rutgers U., 1972. **Group:** Anderson Galleries, NYC, Forum Exhibition, 1916; The Daniel Gallery, NYC, 1919; PMA, Modern Americans, 1922; Architectural League of New York, 1924; Delphic Studios, NYC, 1928, 29; WMAA, The 1930's; A.A.A. Gallery, NYC, 1939, 40, 42. **Collections:** Andover/Phillips; Brooklyn Museum; California Palace; Canajoharie; Columbia, Mo.; Kansas City/Nelson; U. of Kansas City; MMA; MOMA; U. of Nebraska; New Britain; Omaha/Joslyn; PAFA; St. Louis/City; Terre Haute/Swope. **Bibliography:** *Avant-Garde in America, 1910–1925;* **Baigell** 1, **2;** Baur 7; Bazin; **Benton 1, 2, 3, 4;** Biddle 4; Biederman 1; Blesh 1; Boswell 1; Brown 2; Bruce and Watson; Bryant, L.; Cahill and Barr, eds., Canaday; Cheney; Christensen; Cummings 1; **Craven, T.** 1, 2, **3;** *Cityscape 1919–39;* Downes, ed.; Eliot; **Fath, ed.;** Flanagan; Flexner; Goodrich and Baur 1; Haftman; Hall; Hunter 6; Huyghe; *Index of 20th Century Artists;* Kent, N.; Kootz 2; Lee and Burchwood; Levin 2; McCoubrey 1; McCurdy, ed.; Mellquist; Mendelowitz; Myers 2; Neuhaus; Newmeyer; Pagano; Pearson 1; Poore; Reese; Richardson, E.P.; Ringel, ed.; Rodman 2; Rose, B., 1, 4; Smith, S.C.K.; Soby 6; Tomkins and Time-Life Books; Wight 2; Wright 1; Zigrosser 1. Archives.

BEN-ZION. b. July 8, 1897, Old Constantin, Ukraine. Self-taught. Traveled Europe, Mexico, USA. To USA, 1920; citizen, 1936. **Taught:** Cooper Union, 1946–53; Ball State Teachers College, 1956; State U. of Iowa, 1959; Municipal U. of Omaha, 1959. Federal A.P.: Teacher. A co-founder of the Expressionist group The Ten, 1935. **Commis-**

sions: Drawings for Wisdom of the Fathers, Limited Editions Club (1960) and Heritage Press (1962). **Address:** 329 West 20th Street, NYC 10011. **One-man Exhibitions:** (first) Artists' Gallery, NYC, 1936; The Willard Gallery, 1937; Buchholz Gallery, NYC; The Bertha Schaefer Gallery; Jewish Museum, 1948, 52; Curt Valentine Gallery, NYC, 1952; A.F.A., circ., 1953–54; Duveen-Graham Gallery, NYC, 1955–56; Baltimore/MA; Taft Museum; SFMA; State U. of Iowa; St. Louis/City; Bezalel Museum; Brandeis U., 1969; National Maritime Museum, Haifa, 1975, 77, 78. **Retrospective:** Jewish Museum, circ., 1959. **Group:** PAFA; NYU; Carnegie, 1945; WMAA, 1946. **Collections:** Ball State U.; Bezalel Museum; Chicago/AI; Jewish Museum; Kansas City/Nelson; MMA; MOMA; NYPL; Newark Museum; Phillips; St. Louis/City; Tel Aviv; WMAA; U. of Washington. **Bibliography:** Baur 7; Pearson 2. Archives.

BERGER, JASON. b. January 22, 1924, Malden, Mass. **Studied:** Boston Museum School, 1942–43, 1946–49; U. of Alabama, 1943–44; Zadkine School of Sculpture, Paris, 1950–52. Traveled Europe, Mexico. **Taught:** Boston Museum School, 1955–69; Mount Holyoke College; Wellesley College; Buffalo/SUNY, 1969–70; Boston U., 1971–72; Art Institute of Boston, 1973–. **Aw·ds:** Boston/MFA, James William Paige Fellowship, 1957; Boston Arts Festival, Grand Prize, 1956; Boston Arts Festival, First Prize, 1961. **Address:** 40 University Road, Brookline, MA 02146. **One-man Exhibitions:** The Swetzoff Gallery, Boston, 1952, 56; Deerfield (Mass.) Academy, 1954; Fitchburg/AM, 1955; The Peridot Gallery, 1956, 57, 58, 61; Nova Gallery, Boston, 1960; The Pace Gallery, Boston, 1961; Joan Peterson Gallery, 1962–72; MacIvor Reddie Gallery, Boston, 1979; Christian Herter Center, Boston, 1979. **Group:** Institute of Modern Art, Boston, 1943; Chicago/AI, 1952, 54; Salon de la Jeune Sculpture, Paris, 1952; ICA, Boston, 1952, 56,

60, 61; Boston Arts Festival, 1952–57, 1961; Boston/MFA, 1953–57; MOMA, Young American Printmakers, 1953; Library of Congress, 1954; Carnegie, 1954, 55; MOMA, Recent Drawings USA, 1956; PAFA, 1962; Silvermine Guild; Providence (R.I.) Art Festival, 1969; The Direct Vision Exhibitions, Boston and elsewhere, 1971, 72, 73, 74, 75, 76, 77, 78, 79. **Collections:** Brandeis U.; Chase Manhattan Bank; MOMA; Rockefeller Institute; SRGM; Smith College.

BERMAN, EUGENE. b. November 4, 1889, St. Petersburg, Russia; **d.** December 15, 1972; Rome. Studied privately in St. Petersburg with P.S. Naumoff, S. Grusenberg, 1915–18; Academie Ranson, Paris, with Edouard Vuillard, Maurice Denis, Pierre Bonnard, Felix Vallaton, 1920–22; with the architect Emilio Terry, 1920. Traveled Europe. To USA, 1935; first citizenship papers, 1937. Became active in designing for ballet, opera, 1937. **Member:** AAAL. **Commissions:** (murals) Wright Ludington, 1938, John Yeon, 1951; (theatre) Hartford Music Festival, 1936; *L'Opera de Quatre Sous*, Paris, 1936; *Icare* (ballet), NYC, 1939; *Concerto Barocco* (ballet), by George Balanchine, NYC, 1951. **Awards:** Guggenheim Foundation Fellowship, 1947, 49. **One-man Exhibitions:** (first) Galerie Granoff, Paris, 1927; Galerie de l'Etoile, Paris, 1928; Galerie Bonjean, Paris, 1929; Balzac Gallery, NYC, 1929; Galerie des Quatre Chemins, Paris, 1929; Julien Levy Galleries, NYC, 1932, 33, 35, 36, 37, 39, 41, 43, 46, 47; Galerie Pierre Colle, Paris, 1933; Zwemmer Gallery, London, 1935; Renoir and Lolle, Paris, 1937; Galerie Montaigne, Paris, 1939; Courvoisier Gallery, San Francisco, 1941; Princeton U., 1947; Kraushaar Galleries, 1948, 49, 54, 50; MOMA, 1945; Hanover Gallery, 1949; M. Knoedler & Co., 1965; Richard Larcada Gallery, 1967, 70, 72, 73; Utah, 1969; Maxwell Galleries, Ltd., San Francisco, 1970; La Medusa Gallery. **Retrospective:** Institute of Modern Art, Boston, circ., 1941; U. of Texas, Austin, 1975. **Group:** Galerie Drouant, Paris, 1924; MOMA; Chicago/AI; WMAA; Hartford/Wadsworth, 1931; Musée du Petit Palais, Paris, 1934; American Center, Paris, Artistes en exil 1939–1946, 1968; New York Cultural Center, Leonid and His Friends, 1974. **Collections:** Baltimore/MA; Boston/MFA; Cincinnati/AM; Cleveland/MA; Denver/AM; Graphische Sammlung Albertina; Hartford/Wadsworth; Harvard U.; U. of Illinois; State U. of Iowa; Los Angeles/County MA; MMA; MOMA; PMA; Paris/Moderne; Phillips; St. Louis/City; Santa Barbara/MA; Smith College; Tate; Vassar College; Venice/Contemporaneo; Washington U. **Bibliography:** Bazin; **Berman;** Canaday; Flanagan; Frost; Genauer; Holme 1, 2; Hunter 6; Huyghe; Kent, N.; **Levy 2;** McCurdy, ed.; Mendelowitz; Myers 2; Pearson 1, 2; Phillips 1; Richardson, E. P.; Rubin 1; Soby 1; Waldberg 4; Wight. Archives.

BERTHOT, JAKE. b. March 30, 1939, Niagara Falls, N.Y. **Studied:** New School for Social Research, 1960–61; Pratt Institute, 1960–62. **Address:** 66 Grand Street, NYC 10013. **Dealer:** David McKee Gallery. **One-man Exhibitions:** OK Harris Works of Art, 1970, 72, 75; Michael Wells Gallery, 1971, 72; Portland (Ore.) Center for the Visual Arts, 1973; Galerie de Gestlo, 1973, 77; Cunningham-Ward Gallery, 1973; Locksley-Shea Gallery, 1974; Daniel Weinberg, San Francisco, 1975; David McKee Gallery, NYC, 1976, 78; Nigel Greenwood Gallery, London, 1979; Nina Nielsen Gallery, Boston, 1979. **Group:** WMAA Annuals, 1969, 73; Indianapolis, 1970; Jewish Museum, Beautiful Painting & Sculpture, 1970; Foundation Maeght, 1970; Akron/AI, Watercolors and Drawings by Young Americans, 1970; Chicago/AI, Contemporary Drawings, 1971; U. of Rochester, Aspects of Current Painting, 1971; U. of Utah, Drawings by New York Artists, 1972; U. of California, Berkeley, Eight New York Painters, 1972; Paris

Biennial, 1973; U. of Rhode Island, Drawings, 1974; Corcoran Biennial, 1975; Venice Biennial, 1976; ICA, U. of Pennsylvania, 8 Abstract Painters, 1978; Hayward Gallery, London, New Painting—New York, 1979; Grand Palais, Paris, L'Amerique aux Independents 1944–1980, 1980. **Collections:** Brandeis U.; Caracas; Carnegie; Harvard U.; High Museum; MOMA; Dallas/MFA; Prudential Insurance Co. of America, Newark; VMFA; WMAA; SRGM. **Bibliography:** *Fundamentele Schiderkunst.*

BERTOIA, HARRY. b. March 10, 1915, San Lorenzo, Italy. **d.** October, 1978, Bally, Pa. To USA, 1930; became a citizen, 1946. **Studied:** Society of Arts and Crafts, Detroit; Cranbrook, 1936–38. Traveled Norway. Designed chairs with Charles Eames; designed the Bertoia chair for Knoll Associates, 1952. **Commissions:** General Motors Technical Center, Detroit; MIT Chapel; Manufacturers Trust Co.; Dayton Co., Minneapolis; First National Bank of Miami; First National Bank of Tulsa; Dulles International Airport, Washington, D.C.; Northwestern National Life Insurance Bldg., Minneapolis, 1964; Kodak Pavilion, New York World's Fair, 1964–65; Philadelphia Civic Center, 1967; Marshall U., 1973; Woodward Price Park, Wichita, Kan., 1974; Standard Oil Plaza, Chicago, 1974. **Awards:** Architectural League of New York, Gold Medal; Graham Foundation Grant ($10,000), 1957; American Institute of Architects, Gold Medal, 1973; AAAL Award, 1975. **One-man Exhibitions:** (first) Karl Nierendorf Gallery, NYC, 1940; Staempfli Gallery, 1961, 63, 68, 70, 72, 76, 78; Fairweather-Hardin Gallery; Museum of Non-Objective Art, NYC; Smithsonian, circ.; Galerie K.B., Oslo, 1977; Gross-McLeaf Gallery, Philadelphia, 1977; Allentown/AM, 1976. **Group:** WMAA; MOMA; Battersea Park, London, International Sculpture Exhibition, 1963. **Collections:** Buffalo/Albright; Colorado Springs/FA; Dallas Public Library; Denver/AM; Des

Moines; MIT; MOMA; Omaha/Joslyn; SFMA; Utica; VMFA; WMAA. **Bibliography:** Atkinson; Baur 7; Blesh 1; Craven, W.; *From Foreign Shores;* Janis; *Metro;* **Nelson;** Ragon 2; Seuphor 3; Trier 1. Archives.

BESS, FOREST CLEMENGER. b. October 5, 1911, Bay City, Tex.; **d.** November 10, 1977, Bay City, Tex. **Studied:** Agricultural and Mechanical College of Texas, 1929–32; U. of Texas, 1932–33. Traveled Mexico, 1934–40, and USA. Corps of Army Engineers, 1940–45. **Awards:** Mark Rothko Foundation Grant, 1973. **One-man Exhibitions:** Houston/MFA, 1938; Witte, 1939; Texas Technological College, 1939; Betty Parsons Gallery, 1949, 54, 57, 59, 62, 67; Andre Emmerich Gallery, Houston, 1958; Syracuse/Everson, 1974; Agricultural and Mechanical College of Texas; New Arts Gallery, Houston. **Group:** Corcoran, 1938; Dallas/MFA; Tulsa/Philbrook; A.F.A., Wit and Whimsey in 20th Century Art, 1962; de Young; Stanford U. **Collections:** Boston/MFA; Brandeis U.; Houston/MFA; Witte. **Bibliography:** Archives.

BIDDLE, GEORGE. b. January 24, 1885, Philadelphia, Pa.; **d.** November 6, 1973, Croton-on-Hudson, N.Y. **Studied:** Groton School, 1904; Harvard U., 1908, BA with honors, 1911, LLB; Academie Julian, Paris, 1911. Traveled Europe, Asia, Africa, Latin America, USA. **Taught:** Columbia U.; U. of California; Colorado Springs Fine Arts Center; Artist-in-Residence, American Academy, Rome. **Member:** American Society of Painters, Sculptors and Graveurs; National Society of Mural Painters; NIAL. **Commissions** (murals): Justice Department, Washington, D.C.; Supreme Court Building, Mexico City; National Library, Rio de Janeiro. **Awards:** Yaddo, MacDowell Colony, and Huntington Hartford Foundation Fellowships. **One-man Exhibitions:** (first) The Milch Gallery, 1919; more than 100 in

USA, Europe, Japan, India. **Retrospective:** PAFA, 1947; USIA, Prints, circ., 1950. **Collections:** Berlin/National; Corcoran; MMA; Mexico City/Nacional; National Gallery; Norfolk/Chrysler; Tokyo/Modern; WMAA; Youngstown/Butler. **Bibliography:** American Artists Congress, Inc.; American Artists Group, Inc.; **Biddle 1, 2, 3, 4;** Birchman; Boswell 1; Brown; Bruce and Watson; Cheney; *Index of 20th Century Artists;* Mayerson, ed.; Nordmark; Pagano; Parkes; Pearson 2; Poore; Reese; Rose, B., 1; Sachs; Zigrosser 1. Archives.

BIEDERMAN, CHARLES (Karel) JOSEPH. b. August 23, 1906. Cleveland, Ohio. **Studied:** Chicago Art Institute School, 1926–29, with Henry Poole, Laura Papalandem, John W. Norton. Resided Prague, Paris, New York. Traveled England. **Awards:** Amsterdam/Stedelijk, Sikkens Award, 1962; Ford Foundation, **P.P.,** 1964; National Council on the Arts, 1966; Walker Biennial, Donors Award, 1966; Minnesota State Arts Council, 1969; Hon. DFA, Minneapolis College of Art and Design, 1973; National Endowment for the Arts, 1973. **Address:** Route 2, Red Wing, MN 55066. **Dealer:** Grace Borgenicht Gallery, NYC. **One-man Exhibitions:** (first) Chicago Art Institute School; a movie-theater lobby in Chicago, 1930; Pierre Matisse Gallery, 1936; Arts Club of Chicago, 1941; Katharine Kuh Gallery, Chicago, 1941; St. Paul Gallery, 1954; Columbia U. School of Architecture, 1962; Georgia Institute of Technology, 1962; Rochester (Minn.) Art Center, 1967; Dayton's Gallery 12, Minneapolis, 1971; Grace Borgenicht Gallery, 1980. **Retrospective:** Walker, 1965; Hayward Gallery, London, 1969; Minneapolis/Institute, 1976. **Group:** Buffalo/Albright, 1936; Reinhardt Galleries, NYC, 1936; Galerie Pierre, Paris, 1936; Amsterdam/Stedelijk, 1962; Kunstgewerbemuseum, Zurich, 1962; Marlborough-Gerson Gallery, Inc., 1964; Chicago/Contemporary, Relief/

Charles Biederman   *#3 Paris*   1937

Construction/Relief, 1968; Akron/AI, Celebrate Ohio, 1971; Dallas/MFA, Geometric Abstraction, 1926–1942, 1972; Annely Juda Fine Art, London, The Non-Objective World: 1914–1955, 1972. **Collections:** Buffalo/Albright; Chicago/AI; Chicago Public Schools; Dallas/MFA; Des Moines; U. of East Anglia; High Museum; MOMA; Mc-Crory Corp.; Minneapolis/Institute; PMA; Red Wing; Rijksmuseum Kroller-Muller; U. of Saskatchewan; Tate; Walker; WMAA. **Bibliography: Bieder-man 1, 2, 3;** *Celebrate Ohio;* **Charles Biederman;** Hill, ed.; Marter, Tarbell, and Wechsler; Rickey; Seuphor 3. Archives.

BIRELINE, GEORGE. b. August 12, 1923, Peoria, Ill. **Studied:** Bradley U., 1949, BFA; U. of North Carolina, 1963, MFA. **Taught:** North Carolina State College, 1957–75. **Awards:** Guggenheim Foundation Fellowship, 1967; National Council on the Arts Grant, 1968. US Army, 1942–46. **Address:** 228 East Park Drive, Raleigh, NC 27605. **One-man Exhibitions:** U. of North Carolina, 1959, 63; Winston-Salem (N.C.) Gallery of Fine Arts, 1960, 62; Andre

Emmerich Gallery, NYC, 1964, 65, 67; Gallery of Contemporary Art, Winston-Salem, 1969; Meredith College, 1973; Southeastern Center for Contemporary Art, Winston-Salem, 1979. **Retrospective:** Raleigh/NCMA, 1976. **Group:** PAFA Annual, 1950; Youngstown/Butler, 1958; Raleigh/NCMA, 1959, 61, 63; High Museum, 1960; Birmingham, Ala./MA, 1960; Columbia, S.C./MA, 1960; Los Angeles/County MA, Post Painterly Abstraction, 1964; Rockford/Burpee, 1965; U. of Illinois, 1965; Philadelphia Art Alliance, Optical Paintings, 1965; A.F.A., Fifty Artists from Fifty States, circ., 1966–68; North Carolina Annual Artists' Exhibition, 1965–67, 1969–74; Buffalo/Albright, Color and Field: 1890–1970; Mississippi Museum of Art, Jackson, Southern Realism, 1979–80. **Collections:** Charlotte/Mint; Drake U.; East Tennessee State; Fayetteville Museum of Art; Federal Reserve Bank of Richmond, Va.; Hunter Museum; North Carolina National Bank; North Carolina State U.; Prentice Hall Inc.; Raleigh/NCMA; Reynolds Metal Co. Syracuse/Everson.

BIRMELIN, A. ROBERT. b. November 7, 1933, Newark, N.J. **Studied:** Cooper Union, 1951–54; Yale U., 1954–56, BFA, 1959–60, MFA; U. of London, Slade School, 1960–61. US Army, 1957–59. Traveled Europe. **Taught:** Queens College, 1964–. **Commission:** US Dept. of the Interior, 1974. **Awards:** Fulbright Fellowship, 1960–61; American Academy, Rome, Fellowship, 1961–64; PAFA, J. Henry Schiedt Memorial Prize, 1962; NIAL Grant, 1968; L. C. Tiffany Grant, 1973; National Endowment for the Arts, grant, 1976; NIAL, Childe Hassam Fund **P.P.,** 1976. **Address:** 176 Highwood Ave., Leonia, NJ 07605. **Dealer:** Odyssia Gallery, Inc. **One-man Exhibitions:** Kanegis Gallery, 1960, 64, 66; Ross-Talalam Gallery, New Haven, 1960; The Stable Gallery, NYC, 1960, 64, 67; Esther Baer Gallery, 1962; USIS Gallery, Milan, 1962; Florida State U., 1965; Jason-Teff Gallery,

Montreal, 1965; Antioch College, 1965; Alpha Gallery, 1968; Terry Dintenfass, Inc., 1970, 71, 75; Queens College Art Library, N.Y., 1970; Kirkland College, 1971; Alpha Gallery, Boston, 1971, 73; Brandeis U., 1973; Cortland/SUNY, 1973; U. of California, Santa Barbara, 1976; Anapamu Gallery, Santa Barbara, 1976; Peter Rose Gallery, NYC, 1978; Capricorn Gallery, Bethesda, 1977, 79; Bowdoin College,' 1980; Galerie Claude Bernard, Paris, 1980. **Group:** Corcoran Biennial, 1965; XXXV Venice Biennial, 1970; Indianapolis/Herron, 1972; Omaha/Joslyn, A Sense of Place, 1973; Ball State U., XX Annual, 1974; Kalamazoo/Institute, Fifty Works, 1974; US Dept. of the Interior, America 1976, circ., 1976; MIT, The Narrative Impulse, 1979. **Collections:** Andover/Phillips; Brandeis U.; Brooklyn Museum; Chase Manhattan Bank; Denver/AM; First National Bank of Chicago; U. of Florida; Hirshhorn; Indiana U.; Indianapolis/ Herron; Kalamazoo/Institute; MOMA; U. of Massachusetts; Nagaoka, Japan; U. of Nebraska; Newark Museum; U. of North Carolina; Oklahoma; SFMA; Terre Haute/Swope; U. of Texas; Worcester/AM; WMAA. **Bibliography:** *America 1976.*

BISCHOFF, ELMER. b. July 9, 1916, Berkeley, Calif. **Studied:** U. of California, Berkeley, with Margaret Peterson, Erle Loran, John Haley, 1939, MA. US Air Force, 1942–46. Traveled Europe, Morocco, Great Britain, Mediterranean Basin. **Taught:** San Francisco Art Institute, 1946–52, 1956–63; Skowhegan School, 1961; U. of California, Berkeley, 1963–; Yuba College, 1964. **Awards:** RAC, First Prize, 1955; Oakland/AM, **P.P.,** 1957; Ford Foundation Grant, 1959; NIAL Grant, 1963; Chicago/AI, Norman Wait Harris Medal, 1964. **Address:** 109 Strathmoor Drive, Berkeley, CA 94705. **Dealer:** John Berggruen Gallery, San Francisco. **One-man Exhibitions:** (first) California Palace, 1947; King Ubu Gallery, San Francisco, 1953; Paul Kantor Gallery, Beverly Hills,

Calif., 1955; SFMA, 1956, 71; Staempfli Gallery, 1960, 62, 64, 69; de Young, 1961; Achenbach Foundation (three-man drawing show), 1963; Sacramento/ Crocker, 1964; U. of Washington, 1968; RAC, 1969; SFAI, 1975; U. of California, Berkeley, 1975; John Berggruen Gallery, 1979; San Jose Museum of Art, 1979; Arts Club of Chicago, 1980; Houston/ Contemporary, 1980. **Group:** San Francisco Art Association Annuals, 1942, 46, 52, 57, 59, 63; Chicago/AI, 1947, 59, 64; California Palace, 1948, 50, 1960–63; Los Angeles/County MA, 1951; RAC, 1955, 56; Oakland/AM, 1957; Minneapolis/Institute, American Painting, 1945–57, 1957; A.F.A., New Talent, circ., 1958; ART: USA:59, NYC, 1959; U. of Illinois, 1959, 61; WMAA, 1959, 61, 63; A.F.A., West Coast Artists, circ., 1959–60; Denver/AM, 1960; Youngstown/Butler, 1960; Auckland, Painting from the Pacific, 1961; PAFA, 1962; Fort Worth, The Artist's Environment: The West Coast, 1962; SFMA, Fifty California Artists, circ., 1962; MOMA, Recent Painting USA, The Figure, circ., 1962–63; Art: USA: Now, circ., 1962–67, NIAL, 1963; Corcoran, 1963; Carnegie, 1967; Expo '70, Osaka, 1970; U. of Nebraska, 1973; U. of Illinois, 1974; Buffalo/Albright, American Painting of the 1970s, circ., 1979. **Collections:** Chase Manhattan Bank; Chicago/AI; MOMA; NCFA; Oakland/AM; Rockefeller Institute; SFMA; Sacramento/Crocker; U. of Texas; VMFA; WMAA. **Bibliography:** Downes, ed.; Goodrich and Baur 1; Nordness, ed.; Rose, B.; 1. Archives.

BISHOP, ISABEL. b. March 3, 1902, Cincinnati, Ohio. **Studied:** New York School of Applied Design; ASL, with Kenneth Hayes Miller. **Taught:** ASL, 1937; Skowhegan School. **Member:** AAAL; NAD; NIAL; SAGA; Audubon Artists. Federal A.P.: US Post Office, New Lexington, Ohio (mural). **Awards:** NAD, Isaac N. Maynard Prize; NAD, The Adolph and Clara Obrig Prize, 1942; NAD Annual, Andrew Carnegie Prize, 1945; Corcoran, Second William

Isabel Bishop   *Variations on the Theme of Walking*   1979

A. Clark Prize, 1945; AAAL Grant, 1943; PAFA, Walter Lippincott Prize, 1953; NAD, Benjamin Altman Prize, 1955; Library of Congress, Pennell **P.P.**, 1946; NAD, Joseph S. Isidora Gold Medal, 1957; Hon. DFA, Moore Institute; Brandeis U., Creative Arts Award and $1,000, 1975; Women's Caucus For Art, Outstanding Achievement Award, 1979; Hon. DFA, Bates College; Mayor's Award for Art and Culture, NYC, 1979. New York Film Co. produced a documentary film on her. **Address:** c/o Dealer. **Dealer:** The Midtown Galleries. **One-man Exhibitions:** The Midtown Galleries, 1932, 35, 36, 39, 49, 55, 60, 67, 74; Pittsfield/Berkshire, 1957; VMFA (two-man), 1960; Middendorf-Lane Gallery, Washington, D.C., 1979. **Retrospective:** U. of Arizona, circ., 1974. **Group:** Carnegie; VMFA; Corcoran; PAFA; New York World's Fair, 1939; Chicago/AI; WMAA; MOMA; St. Louis/City; NAD; Los An-geles/County MA, Women Artists 1940–1950, 1976; Hayward Gallery, London, The Modern Spirit, 1977. **Collections:** Andover/Phillips; Atlanta U.; Baltimore/MA; Boston/MFA; British Museum; Brooklyn Museum; California Palace; Clearwater/Gulf Coast; Colorado Springs/FA; Columbus; Corcoran; Cranbrook; Dallas/MFA; Des Moines; Hartford/Wadsworth; Harvard U.; Indianapolis; Kansas City/Nelson; Library of Congress; Los Angeles/County MA; MMA; Memphis/Brooks; Morgan Library; NAD; NYPL; U. of Nebraska; Newark Museum; New Britain; PAFA; PMA; Phillips; St. Louis/City; Southampton/Parrish; Springfield, Mass./ MFA; Tel Aviv; Terre Haute/Swope; Utica; VMFA; WMAA; Washburn U. of Topeka; Youngstown/Butler. **Bibliography:** Baur 7; Boswell 1; Brown 2; *Celebrate Ohio;* Cheney; Diamonstein; Downes, ed.; Goodrich and Baur 1; **Isabel Bishop;** Johnson 2; Kent, N.;

Lunde; McCurdy, ed.; Mellquist; Mendelowitz; Nordness, ed.; Pagano; Richardson, E.P.; Rose, B., 1. Archives.

BISHOP, JAMES. b. October 7, 1927, Neosho, Mo. **Studied:** Syracuse U., 1950, BA; Washington U., 1951–54; Black Mountain College, 1953, with Esteban Vicente; Columbia U., 1955–56. Traveled France, 1957–66. **Taught:** Cooper Union, 1969–70; U. of California, Irvine, 1970; Carnegie-Mellon Institute, 1971; School of Visual Arts, NYC, 1972. **Awards:** Guggenheim Foundation Fellowship, 1970. Editorial associate, *Art News*, 1969–72. **Address:** 5 Lispenard Street, NYC 10013. **Dealer:** Frank Kolbert Gallery, NYC. **One-man Exhibitions:** (first) Galerie Lucien Durand, Paris, 1963; Galerie Smith, Brussels, 1963; Galerie Lawrence, Paris, 1964; Fischbach Gallery, 1966, 68, 70, 72; Galerie Fournier, Paris, 1966, 71, 73; The Clocktower, NYC, 1973; Rosa Esman Gallery, 1974; Alessandro Ferranti, Rome, 1975; Galerie Annemarie Verna, Zurich, 1976, 78; Galerie Jean Fournier, Paris, 1976; Francoise Lambert, Milan, 1977; Rudiger Schottle, Munich, 1977; Droll Kolbert Gallery, NYC, 1979. **Group:** Salon des Realites Nouvelles, Paris, 1962–65; Salon du Mai, Paris, 1964, 65; Musée Galliera, Paris, Promesses Tenues, 1965; Amerika Haus, Berlin, Ten Americans, 1966; WMAA, 1967; Corcoran, 1967; Expo '67, Montreal, 1967; Jewish Museum, Large Scale American Painting, 1967; Foundation Maeght, 1968, 70; U. of California, Riverside, Recent Direction, 1968; NIAL, 1971; U. of North Carolina, 1971; Yale U., Options and Alternatives, 1973; Indianapolis, 1974; Paris/Moderne, Tendences actuelles de la nouvelle peinture americaine, 1975; A.F.A., Recent Drawings, 1975; Musée de Grenoble, Art americain, 1976; Bonn, Bilder ohne Bilder, 1977; Paris, Grand Palais, L'Art moderne dans les musées francaises, 1978; Paris/Beaubourg, Dessin et couleur, 1979. **Collections:** SFMA. **Bibliography:** *Options and Alternatives.*

BISTTRAM, EMIL. b. April 7, 1895, Hungary; **d.** 1976, Taos, New Mexico. **Studied:** NAD; Cooper Union; New York School of Fine and Applied Art (with Ivan Olinsky, Leon Kroll, William Dodge, Jay Hambridge, Howard Giles). **Taught:** New York School of Fine and Applied Art; Master Institute of United Arts, Inc., NYC; Bisttram School, Taos, N.M. **Commissions** (murals): Justice Department, Washington, D.C.; US Post Office, Ranger, Tex. **Awards:** Philadelphia Watercolor Club, First Prize, Gold Medal, 1926; Guggenheim Foundation Fellowship, 1931; California Palace, Hon. Men., 1936. **One-man Exhibitions:** Philadelphia Watercolor Club; Delphic Gallery, NYC; Stendahl Gallery, Los Angeles, 1945. **Group:** PAFA: Chicago/AI; XV Venice Biennial, 1930; WMAA, 1933. **Collections:** Buffalo/Albright; Nicholas Roerich Museum; Taos (N.M.) County Court House. **Bibliography:** Allen, ed.; Bruce and Watson; Cheney; Coke 2; *Index of 20th Century Artists;* Pearson 1, 2. Archives.

BLACKBURN, MORRIS. b. October 13, 1902, Philadelphia, Pa.; **d.** 1979, Philadelphia. **Studied:** PAFA, with Arthur B. Carles, Jr., Henry McCarter, Daniel Garber. Traveled Europe, Canada, Ireland, Caribbean. **Taught:** Philadelphia College of Art, 1933–73; Bryn Mawr College, 1947–48; Stella Elkins Tyler School of Fine Arts, Temple U., 1945–79; PAFA, 1952–79. Federal A.P.: Mural and easel painting. **Member:** Philadelphia Watercolor Club; Audubon Artists; The Print Club, Philadelphia; American Watercolor Society. Subject of a 16 mm film, *Portrait of a Painter*, by Emilio Angelo. **Awards:** Guggenheim Foundation Fellowship, 1952; PAFA, Cresson Fellowship, 1928, 29; PAFA, Gold Medal, 1946; PAFA, H. S. Morris Prize, 1951; PAFA, Thornton Oakley Prize, 1955. **One-man Exhibitions:** (first) Warwick Gallery, Philadelphia, 1930; PAFA; The Print Club, Philadelphia; Woodmere Art Gallery,

Philadelphia; Philadelphia Art Alliance; Newman Gallery, Philadelphia; Joseph Luyber Galleries, NYC; National Serigraph Society, NYC; Pennsylvania Art Center; Rutgers U.; Peirce Junior College. **Retrospective:** Woodmere Art Gallery, Philadelphia, 1956; Provident National Bank, Philadelphia, 1969; PAFA. **Group:** PAFA Annuals since 1937; NAD; Audubon Artists; New York World's Fair, 1939; Chicago/AI; Carnegie; Brooklyn Museum; WMAA; Library of Congress; USIA traveling print exhibitions; Youngstown/Butler; Santa Fe, N.M.; New Orleans/Delgado; Santa Barbara/MA; US State Department, circ. **Collections:** Clearwater/ Gulf Coast; Delaware Art Museum; Free Library of Philadelphia; Library of Congress; Memphis/Brooks; Montana State U.; PAFA; PMA; The Pennsylvania State U.; Santa Fe, N.M.; Trenton/State; USIA; US State Department; Youngstown/Butler. **Bibliography:** Bethers.

BLADEN, RONALD. b. July 13, 1918, Vancouver, B.C., Canada. **Studied:** Vancouver School of Art; CSFA. **Awards:** SFAI, Rosenberg Fellowship; National Council on the Arts; Guggenheim Foundation Fellowship, 1970. **Address:** 5 West 21st Street, NYC 10010. **Dealer:** Max Hutchinson Gallery, NYC. **One-man Exhibitions:** Brata Gallery, NYC, 1953; U. of British Columbia (two-man), 1955; Six Gallery, San Francisco, 1956; Green Gallery, NYC, 1962; NYU (three-man), 1967; Fischbach Gallery, 1967, 70, 71, 72; Hofstra U., 1967; Vancouver (two-man), 1970; Pasadena/AM, 1972; Tyler School of Art, Philadelphia, 1972; U. of Wisconsin, Madison, 1972; Hudson River Museum, 1977. **Group:** NYU, Concrete Expressionism, 1965; WMAA Annuals, 1966, 68, 73; Chicago/AI Annual, 1966; Jewish Museum, Primary Structure Sculptures, 1966; Los Angeles/County MA, Sculpture of the Sixties, 1967; A.F.A., Rejective Art, 1967; Corcoran, Scale as Content, 1967; Docu-

menta IV, Kassel, 1968; Walker, 14 Sculptors: The Industrial Edge, 1969; U. of Nebraska, American Sculpture, 1970; Arnhem, Sonsbeek '71, 1971; SFMA, Works in Spaces, 1973; Detroit/Institute, Art in Space, 1973; U. of Miami, Less Is More: The Influence of the Bauhaus on American Art, 1974; William Patterson College, N.J., Contemporary Drawing, 1975; Houston/Contemporary; Monumentalists in Modern Sculpture, 1975; Hirshhorn, The Golden Door: Artist Immigrants of America 1876–1976, 1976; WMAA, 200 Years of American Sculpture, 1976; Akron/AI, Project: New Urban Monuments, 1977. **Collections:** Buffalo/Albright; La Jolla; MOMA; Marine Midland Bank and Trust Co.; South Albany Mall, N.Y. **Bibliography:** Calas, N. and E.; Friedman, M., 2; *Report*; Sandler.

BLAINE, NELL. b. July 10, 1922, Richmond, Va. **Studied:** Richmond (Va.) School of Art, 1939–43; Hofmann School, 1943–44; Atelier 17, NYC, with S. W. Hayter; New School for Social Research, 1952–53. Traveled Europe, Near East, West Indies, Mexico. **Taught:** Great Neck (N.Y.) Public Schools, 1943–1956, and privately. **Member:** American Abstract Artists, 1944–57; Jane Street Group, 1945–49; Artists Equity. **Commissions:** Revlon Inc. (murals); New York Hilton Hotel (lithographs). **Awards:** Norfolk, First Prize, Watercolor, 1945; MacDowell Colony Fellowship, 1957; Yaddo Fellowship, 1957, 58, 64; Ingram Merrill Grants, 1962, 64, 66; Longview Foundation Grant, 1964, 1970; CAPS, 1972; Mark Rothko Foundation Grant, 1972; Guggenheim Foundation Fellowship, 1974; Governor's award, Award for the Arts in Virginia, 1979; Honorary Degree, Moore College of Art, Philadelphia, 1980; National Endowment for the Arts, 1975. Designed original logo, column headings, and styling for the *Village Voice*, 1955. **Address:** 210 Riverside Drive, NYC 10025; Eudora Cottage, 3 Ledge Road, E. Gloucester, MA

01930. **Dealer:** Fischbach Gallery, NYC. **One-man Exhibitions:** (first) Jane Street Gallery, NYC, 1945, also 1948; VMFA, 1947, 54, 73; Southern Illinois U., 1949; Tibor de Nagy Gallery, 1953, 54; Poindexter Gallery, 1956, 58, 60, 66, 68, 70, 72, 76; New Paltz/SUNY, 1959; Stewart Richard Gallery, San Antonio, 1961; Philadelphia Art Alliance, 1961; Yaddo, 1961; Longwood College, 1962; U. of Connecticut, Storrs, 1973; Webb and Parsons, Bedford Village, N.Y., 1973; Watson/de Nagy Gallery, Houston, 1977; Fischbach Gallery, NYC, 1979, 81; VMFA, 1979; Hull Gallery, Washington, D.C., 1979. **Retrospective:** Southampton/Parrish, 1974. **Group:** Art of This Century, NYC, The Women, 1944; Salon des Realites Nouvelles, Paris, 1950; Chicago/AI; Baltimore/MA; WMAA; PAFA; Corcoran; VMFA; ART:USA:59, NYC, 1959; MOMA, Abstract Watercolors and Drawings, USA, circ., Latin America and Europe, 1961–62; Festival of Two Worlds, Spoleto; MOMA, Hans Hofmann and His Students, circ., 1963–64; Hartford/Wadsworth, Figures, 1964; MOMA, Contemporary Still Life, circ., 1967–68; New School for Social Research, Humanist Tradition, 1968; NIAL, 1970, 74, 75; A.F.A., Painterly Realism, 1970; WMAA, Frank O'Hara: A Poet Among Painters, 1974; NAD, Annual, 1978; MMA, Hans Hofmann as Teacher: Drawings by His Students, 1979; Westmoreland County/MA, The New American Still Life, 1978. **Collections:** Brandeis U.; Brooklyn Museum; U. of California; Chase Manhattan Bank; Ciba-Geigy Corp.; Colgate U.; First and Merchants National Bank, Richmond, Va.; U. of Georgia; Hallmark Collection; Hirshhorn; State U. of Iowa; Longwood College; MMA; MOMA; U. of Massachusetts; Michigan State U.; Newark Museum; New Paltz/SUNY; U. of North Carolina; Reader's Digest; Revlon Inc.; Southern Illinois U.; Taconic Foundation; Trade Building, Moscow; Union Carbide Corp.; VMFA; WMAA. **Bibliography:** *Art: A Woman's Sensibility;* **Bryant, E.;** Sandler 1. Archives.

BLANCH, ARNOLD. b. June 4, 1896, Mantorville, Minn.; **d.** October 23, 1968, Kingston, N.Y. **Studied:** Minneapolis Institute School; ASL, with Kenneth Hayes Miller, Boardman Robinson, John Sloan, 1916–17. Traveled USA. **Taught:** ASL, 1915–21, 1935–39, 1947–68; California School of Fine Arts, 1930–31; Colorado Springs Fine Arts Center, summers, 1939–41; U. of Minnesota, 1949, 52; Rollins College, 1950; Florida Gulf Coast Art Center, Inc., 1950–51; Woodstock, N.Y., 1950–61; Ohio U., summers, 1952, 56; Minneapolis Institute School, 1954; U. of Hawaii, 1955; Norton Gallery and School of Art, 1961–62; Michigan State U., 1964. **Commissions:** US Post Offices, Fredonia, N.Y., Norwalk, Conn., and Columbus, Wisc. (murals). **Awards:** Chicago/AI, Norman Wait Harris Prize, 1929; SFMA, **P.P.,** 1931; California Palace, 1931; Guggenheim Foundation Fellowship, 1933; PAFA, Medal, 1938; Carnegie Medal, 1938; Syracuse/Everson, National Ceramic Exhibition, 1949, 51; Silvermine Guild. **One-man Exhibitions:** Rehn Galleries, 1923, 25; Philadelphia Art Alliance; Dudensing Gallery, NYC, 1928, 30; Walden-Dudensing Gallery, Chicago, 1930; Ulrich Gallery, Minneapolis, 1930; Beaux Arts Gallery, San Francisco, 1930; A.A.A. Gallery, NYC, 1943, 55, 63; Des Moines, 1952; Walker, 1952; The Krasner Gallery, 1954, 58, 59, 61, 62, 69; West Palm Beach/Norton, 1961. **Retrospective:** U. of Minnesota, 1949; Woodstock Artists Association, 1970. **Group:** Chicago/AI, 1930–43; Corcoran, 1931–45; WMAA, 1931–46, 1948–52; PAFA, 1931–45, 1948–52; New York World's Fair, 1939; MOMA; Carnegie; VMFA; MMA; Library of Congress; ART:USA, NYC. **Collections:** Abbott Laboratories; U. of Arizona; Britannica; Brooklyn Museum; California Palace; Carnegie; Cincinnati/AM; Clearwater/Gulf Coast; Cleveland/MA; Colorado Springs/FA; Cranbrook; Denver/AM; Detroit/Institute; Library of Congress; MMA; U. of Minnesota, Duluth; U. of Nebraska; U. of Oklahoma; PAFA; St.

Louis/City; Utica; WMAA; Youngstown/Butler. **Bibliography:** American Artists Congress, Inc.; Baur 7; **Blanch 1, 2, 3;** Boswell 1; Cheney; *Index of 20th Century Artists;* Jewell 2; Pagano; Pearson 1; Reese; Richardson, E.P.; *Woodstock;* Zaidenberg, ed. Archives.

BLAUSTEIN, AL. b. January 23, 1924, NYC. **Studied:** Cooper Union, with Morris Kantor; Skowhegan School. US Air Force, 3 years. Traveled Mexico, Africa, the Orient; resided Rome, 1954–57. **Taught:** Pratt Institute, 1959–. Yale U. **Commissions:** Drawings for *Life* magazine and British Overseas Food Corporation, 1948–49; fresco mural for South Solon (Me.) Meeting House, 1953. **Awards:** Prix de Rome, 1954–57; Guggenheim Foundation Fellowship, 1958, 61; AAAL Grant, 1958; Childe Hassam Award, 1962–68, and **P.P.,** 1969; PAFA, Alice McFadden Eyre Medal, 1959; ART:USA:59, NYC, Graphic Prize, 1959; Youngstown/Butler, First Prize, 1961; SAGA, First Prize, 1962; Audubon Artists, Gold Medal of Honor, 1962. **Address:** 141 East 17th Street, NYC 10003. **Dealer:** Terry Dintenfass, Inc. **One-man Exhibitions:** (first) Lee Nordness Gallery, NYC, 1959, also 1961, 62; U. of Nevada, 1961; Philadelphia Art Alliance, 1962; Walter Laubli Gallery, Zurich, 1962; Philadelphia Print Club, 1964; Franklin Siden Gallery, Detroit, 1965, 66; Randolph-Macon College, 1967; C. Troup Gallery, Dallas, 1968; Terry Dintenfass, Inc., 1969, 72. **Group:** MMA, 1950; A.F.A., 1951; Buffalo/Albright, Expressionism in American Painting, 1952; Carnegie, 1952; WMAA Annuals, 1953, 57; The Downtown Gallery, 1958; SAGA, 1962. **Collections:** Albany/Institute; Boston/MFA; Brooklyn Museum; Chicago/AI; Hartford/Wadsworth; Library of Congress; MMA; U. of Nebraska; Norfolk; PAFA; Scranton/Everhart; Syracuse U.; WMAA; Washington U.; Youngstown/Butler. **Bibliography:** Chaet; Nordness, ed.

BLEIFELD, STANLEY. b. August 28, 1924, Brooklyn, N.Y. US Navy, 1944–46. **Studied:** Stella Elkins Tyler School of Fine Arts, Temple U., with Raphael Sabatini, 1949, BFA. Traveled Israel, Mexico, and extensively in Italy; resided Rome, 1962–63. **Taught:** Weston (Conn.) Public Schools, 1950–53; New Haven State Teachers College, 1953–55; Danbury State College, 1955–63; Silvermine Guild, 1963–66; Bleifeld Studio Group, 1966–. **Member:** National Sculpture Society; Artists Equity. **Commissions:** Vatican Pavilion, New York World's Fair, 1964–65; Kokomo (Ind.) Public Library, 1969. **Awards:** Tyler Annual, First Prize, 1951; National Sculpture Society, John Gregory Award, 1964, Bronze Medal, 1970; elected Tyler Fellow, 1964; L. C. Tiffany Grants, 1965, 67; NAD, Shikler Award, 1977. **Address:** 27 Spring Valley Road, Weston, CT 06880. **Dealers:** The Jones Gallery, La Jolla; New Directions, St. Louis; Sandra Wilson Galleries, Denver. **One-man Exhibitions:** The Peridot Gallery, 1963, 68; Hoffman Fuel Co., Danbury, Conn., 1962; Kenmore Galleries, Inc., Philadelphia, 1967; New Canaan (Conn.) Public Library, 1967; Fairfield U., 1967; I.F.A. Gallery, 1968, 71; FAR Gallery, 1971, 73, 77; New Britain/American, 1974. **Group:** Silvermine Guild; Stella Elkins Tyler School of Fine Arts, Temple U.; International Arts Festival, Chetwode, Newport, R.I., 1964; A.F.A., 1966–67; Temple Emanuel, Houston, Tex., 1964; Indiana U., 1966. **Collections:** U. of Edinburgh, Scotland; Lyndon B. Johnson Library, Austin, Texas; New Britain/American; The Pennsylvania State U.; Tampa/AI; Temple U.; Westmoreland County/MA.

BLOOM, HYMAN. b. April, 1913, near Riga, Latvia. To USA, 1920. **Studied:** West End Community Center, Boston, with Harold Zimmerman; Harvard U., with Denman W. Ross. **Taught:** Wellesley College, 1949–51; Harvard U., 1951–53. Federal A.P.: Easel Painting.

Address: 1426 Cambridge Street, Cambridge, MA 02139. **Dealer:** Terry Dintenfass, Inc. **One-man Exhibitions:** Stuart Gallery, Boston, 1945; Durlacher Brothers, NYC, 1946, 48, 54; ICA, Boston; Boris Mirski Gallery, Boston, 1949; The Swetzoff Gallery, Boston, 1957; WMAA, 1968; U. of Connecticut, 1969; Terry Dintenfass, Inc., 1972, 75, 79; UCLA (two-man). **Retrospective:** Buffalo/Albright, circ., 1954. **Group:** MOMA, Americans 1942, circ., 1942; Boston/MFA; WMAA. **Collections:** Amherst College; Andover/Phillips; First National Bank of Boston; Harvard U.; Hirshhorn; Kalamazoo/Institute; Minnesota/MA; MOMA; Purchase/SUNY; Rutgers U.; St. Louis/City; Smith College; WMAA. **Bibliography:** Barker 1; Baur 7; Biddle 4; Chaet; Eliot; *From Foreign Shores;* Goodrich 1; Hess, T.B., 1; Hunter 6; Kootz 2; Kuh 3; Miller, ed., 1; Newmeyer; Pousette-Dart, ed.; Richardson, E. P.; Rodman 2, 3; Rose, B., 1; Soby 5; Wight 2; **Wight and Goodrich.**

BLUEMNER, OSCAR. b. 1867, Hanover, Germany; **d.** 1938, South Braintree, Mass. **Studied:** Academy of Fine Arts, Berlin. To USA, 1892. Practicing architect, 1894–1912. **One-man Exhibitions:** Berlin, 1885, 1912; Stieglitz Gallery, NYC, 1915; Mrs. Liebman's Art Room, NYC, 1926; Stieglitz's Intimate Gallery, NYC, 1928; Whitney Studio Club, NYC, 1929; Marie Harriman Gallery, NYC, 1935; U. of Minnesota, 1939; Today's Gallery, Boston, 1945; The Graham Gallery, 1956, 60, 67, 72; Harvard U., 1967; New York Cultural Center, 1969; Davis Gallery, 1971; Danenberg Gallery, 1972; Hirshhorn, 1979. **Group:** Anderson Galleries, NYC, Forum Exhibition, 1916; Bourgeois Gallery, NYC, 1917–23; J. B. Neumann Gallery, NYC, 1924–36; WMAA, Pioneers of Modern Art in America, 1946; WMAA, Juliana Force Memorial Exhibition, 1949. **Collections:** Boston/MFA; MOMA; Phillips; WMAA. **Bibliography:** *Avant-Garde Painting and Sculpture;* Baur 7; Brown 2;

Cheney; Frank, ed.; *From Foreign Shores;* Goodrich and Baur 1; Hunter 6; Janis; Levin 2; Mellquist; **Oscar Bluemner: American Colorist;** Rose, B., 1, 4; Wright 1. Archives.

BLUHM, NORMAN. b. March 28, 1920; Chicago, Ill. **Studied:** Illinois Institute of Technology, 1936; 1945–47, with Mies van der Rohe. US Air Force, 1941–45. Resided Paris, 1947–56. **Address:** P.O. Box 729, Millbrook, NY 12545. **One-man Exhibitions:** (first) Leo Castelli Inc., 1957, also 1960; Galleria d'Arte del Naviglio, Milan, 1959; Notizie Gallery, Turin, 1961; David Anderson Gallery, NYC, 1962; Paris, 1965; Galerie Semiha Huber, Zurich, 1963; The American Gallery, NYC, 1963; Galerie Anderson-Mayer, Paris, 1963; Galerie Smith, Brussels, 1964; Galerie Stadler, Paris, 1968, 70, 72, 75; Corcoran, 1969, 77; Martha Jackson Gallery, 1970, 71, 74; J. L. Hudson Art Gallery, Detroit, 1971; Syracuse/Everson, 1973; Vassar College, 1974; Galleria Venezia, Venice, 1974; Carlo Rubboli, Milan, 1974; Houston/Contemporary, 1976; Robinson Galleries, Houston, 1976. **Group:** Carnegie, 1958; Documenta II, Kassel, 1959; ICA, Boston, 100 Works on Paper, circ., Europe, 1959; Walker, 60 American Painters, 1960; WMAA Annual, 1960; Chicago/AI Annual, 1961; SRGM, The G. David Thompson Collection; SRGM, Abstract Expressionists and Imagists, 1961; Salon du Mai, Paris, 1964; MOMA, Two Decades of American Painting, circ., 1966; Jewish Museum, Large Scale American Painting, 1967; MOMA, Dada, Surrealism, and Their Heritage, 1968; Galleria d'Arte, Cortina, Espaces Abstraits, 1969; WMAA Annual, 1972; MOMA, Color as Language, circ., 1975. **Collections:** Baltimore/MA; Buffalo/Albright; Corcoran; CNAC; Dallas/MFA; Dayton/AI; Kansas City/Nelson; MIT; MOMA; U. of Massachusetts; Melbourne/National; National Gallery; NYU; National Museum of Wales; Phillips; Reed College; Stony Brook/SUNY;

Syracuse/Everson; Vassar College; WMAA. **Bibliography:** Alloway 4; *Metro;* O'Hara 1; Rubin 1; Sandler 1. Archives.

BLUME, PETER. b. October 27, 1906, Russia. To USA, 1911. **Studied:** Educational Alliance, NYC; ASL; Beaux Arts Academy, NYC. **Commissions:** Federal A.P.: US Post Offices, Cannonsburg, Pa., Rome, Ga., and Geneva, N.Y. (murals). **Awards:** Guggenheim Foundation Fellowship, 1932, 36; Carnegie, First Prize, 1934; MMA, Artists for Victory, 1942; NIAL Grant, 1947. **Address:** Sherman, Conn. 06789 **Dealer:** Terry Dintenfass, Inc., NYC. **One-man Exhibitions:** (first) The Daniel Gallery, NYC, 1930; Julien Levy Galleries, NYC, 1937; The Downtown Gallery, 1941, 47; Durlacher Brothers, NYC, 1949, 54, 58; Kennedy Gallery, 1968; Danenberg Gallery, 1970; Coe Kerr Gallery, 1975; Terry Dintenfass, Inc., NYC, 1980. **Retrospective:** Chicago/Contemporary, 1976. **Collections:** Boston/MFA; Columbus; Hartford/Wadsworth; MMA; Newark Museum; Randolph-Macon College; Williams College. **Bibliography:** Barker 1; Barr 3; Baur 7; Boswell 1; Brown 2; Cahill and Barr, eds.; Canaday; Cheney; Eliot; Flanagan; *From Foreign Shores;* **Getlein 3;** Goodrich and Baur 1; Haftman; Hunter 6; *Index of 20th Century Artists;* Janis; Jewell 2; Kootz 1, 2; Kuh 1; McCurdy, ed.; Mellquist; Mendelowitz; Neumeyer; Nordness, ed.; Pearson 2; Poore; Pousette-Dart, ed.; Richardson, E.P.; Ringel, ed.; Rose, B., 1; Sachs; Smith, S.C.K.; Soby 5, 6; Wight 2. Archives.

BOARDMAN, SEYMOUR. b. December 29, 1921, Brooklyn, N.Y. **Studied:** City College of New York, 1942, BS; Academie des Beaux-Arts, Academie de la Grande Chaumiere, and Atelier Fernand Leger, Paris, 1946–52. US Army, 1942–46. **Taught:** Wagner College, 1957–58. **Awards:** Longview Foundation Grant, 1963. **Address:** 234 West 27th Street, NYC 10001. **One-man Exhibitions:** (first) Salon du Mai, Paris, 1951; Martha Jackson Gallery, 1955, 56; Dwan Gallery, NYC, 1960; Stephen Radich Gallery, NYC, 1960–62; Esther Robles Gallery, 1965; A. M. Sachs Gallery, 1965, 67, 68; Dorsky Gallery, 1972; Cornell U., 1971; Aaron Berman, NYC, 1978. **Group:** WMAA, 1955, 61, 67; Youngstown/Butler, 1955; SFMA, 1955; Carnegie, 1955; U. of Nebraska, 1956; Santa Barbara/MA, 1964; Kunsthalle, Basel, 1964. **Collections:** Brandeis U.; Cornell U.; Ciba-Geigy Chemical Corp.; NYU; Newark Museum; SRGM; Santa Barbara/MA; Union Carbide Corp.; WMAA; Wagner College; Walker.

BOCHNER, MEL. b. 1940, Pittsburgh, Pa. **Studied:** Carnegie, 1962, BFA. **Taught:** School of Visual Arts, NYC, 1965–. **Address:** c/o Dealer. **Dealer:** Ileana Sonnabend Gallery, NYC. **One-man Exhibitions:** Visual Arts Gallery, NYC, 1966; ACE Gallery, Los Angeles, 1969; Galerie Konrad Fischer, Dusseldorf, 1969; Galerie Heiner Friedrich, Munich, 1969; Galleria Toselli, Milan, 1969, 72; MOMA, 1971; 112 Greene Street Gallery, NYC, 1971; Galerie MTL, Brussels, 1972; Galleria Marilena Bonomo, Bari, Italy, 1972; Lisson Gallery, London, 1972; Ileana Sonnabend Gallery, NYC, 1972, 73, 74, 76, 78, 80; Ileana Sonnabend Gallery, Paris, 1972, 73, 74, 78; Galleria Schema, Florence, Italy, 1974, 78; Weinberg Gallery, San Francisco, 1974, 78; U. of California, Berkeley, 1975; Baltimore/MA, 1976; Bernier Gallery, Athens, 1977; Art in Progress, Dusseldorf, 1979. **Group:** Finch College, NYC, Art in Series, 1967; Art in Process, 1969; Leverkusen, Konzeption—Conception, 1969; Seattle/AM, 557, 087, 1969; Chicago/Contemporary, Art by Telephone, 1969; Turin/Civico, Conceptual Art, Arte Povera, Land Art, 1970; New York Cultural Center, Conceptual Art and Conceptual Aspects, 1970; Oberlin College, Art in the Mind, 1970; MOMA, Information, 1971; Chicago/Contemporary, White on

White, 1972; Documenta V, Kassel, 1972; Basel, Konzept Kunst, 1972; Musée Galliera, Paris, Festival d'Automne, 1973; Seattle/AM, American Art: Third Quarter Century, 1973; WMAA, American Drawings: 1963–1973, 1973; New York Cultural Center, 3D into 2D, 1973; Parcheggio di Villa Borghese, Rome, Contemporanea, 1974; Princeton U., Line as Language, 1974; Cologne, Project '74, 1974; Leverkusen, Drawings 3: American Drawings, 1975; MOMA, Drawing Now, 1976; Chicago/AI, Annual, 1976; Fort Worth, Fourteen Artists: The New Decade, 1976; WMAA, Biennial, 1977, 79; PMA, Eight Artists, 1978; Palazzo Reale, Milan, Pintura Ambiente, 1979. **Collections:** WMAA. **Bibliography:** *Contemporanea;* Johnson, Ellen H.; Gablik; Krauss 2; Lippard, ed.; Meyer; Pincus-Witten; *When Attitudes Become Form.*

BODIN, PAUL. b. October 30, 1910, NYC. **Studied:** NAD; ASL, with Boardman Robinson. Traveled USA extensively. Federal A.P.: Easel painting and art teacher. **Awards:** Longview Foundation Grant, 1959; ART: USA:58, NYC, Special Distinction Award, 1958. **Address:** 207 West 86th Street, NYC 10024. **One-man Exhibitions:** (first) Playhouse Gallery, NYC, 1936; Theodore A. Kohn Gallery, NYC, 1937; Artists' Gallery, NYC, 1942; Laurel Gallery, NYC 1948, 50; The New Gallery, NYC, 1952; Betty Parsons Gallery, 1959, 61. **Group:** New York World's Fair, 1939; American-British Art Center, NYC, 1943, 44, 45; Yale U., 1949; Santa Barbara/MA, 1949; Philadelphia Art Alliance, 1949; Brooklyn Museum, 1949, 59; MMA, American Watercolors, Drawings and Prints, 1952; NAD, 1954; ART: USA:58, NYC, 1958; ART:USA:59, NYC, 1959; Parsons School of Design, NYC, WPA, 1977. **Collections:** Buffalo/Albright; Dallas/MFA.

BOGHOSIAN, VARUJAN. b. June 26, 1926, New Britain, Conn. **Studied:** Yale U., 1956–59, BFA, MFA (with Josef Albers); Vesper George School of Art, 1946–48; US Navy, 1944–46. **Taught:** U. of Florida, 1958–59; Cooper Union, 1959–64; Pratt Institute, 1961; Yale U., 1962–64; Brown U., 1964–68; American Academy, Rome, 1967; Dartmouth College, 1968–. **Awards:** Fulbright Fellowship (Italy), 1953; Brown U., Howard Foundation Grant for Painting, 1966; New Haven Arts Festival, First Prize, 1958; Portland (Me.) Arts Festival, 1958; Boston Arts Festival, 1961; Providence Art Club, First Prize, 1967; Hon. MA, Brown U.; AAAL; NIAL. **Address:** 1 Read Road, Hanover, NH 03755. **Dealer:** Cordier & Ekstrom, Inc. **One-man Exhibitions:** (first) The Swetzoff Gallery, Boston, 1949, also 1950, 51, 53, 54, 55, 59, 63, 65; R. M. Light & Co., Boston, 1962; The Stable Gallery, 1963–66; ACE Gallery, Provincetown, Mass., 1966; U. of Massachusetts, 1968; Dartmouth College, 1968; Currier, 1968; Cordier & Ekstrom, Inc., 1969, 70, 71, 73, 75, 77, 78, 79, 80; Arts Club of Chicago, 1970; Alpha Gallery, 1972; U. of Connecticut, 1972; Keene (N.H.) State College, 1972. **Group:** MOMA, Young American Printmakers, 1953; MOMA, Recent Drawings USA, 1956; U. of Illinois, 1961; Chicago/AI Annual, 1961; WMAA Annuals, 1963, 64, 66, 68; Yale U., 1965; ICA, Boston, As Found, 1966; WMAA, Contemporary American Sculpture, Selection 1, 1966; Grand Rapids, Sculpture of the 60s, 1969. **Collections:** Andover/Phillips; Brandeis U.; U. of California; Dartmouth College; Indianapolis/Herron; MOMA; U. of Massachusetts; NYPL; New Britain/American; Phoenix; RISD; WMAA; Wesleyan U. (Conn.); Worcester/AM.

BOHROD, AARON. b. November 21, 1907, Chicago, Ill. **Studied:** Crane Junior College, 1925–26; Chicago Art Institute School, 1927–29; ASL, 1930–32, with Boardman Robinson, John Sloan, Richard Lahey. Traveled USA, Europe, South Pacific. **Taught:** Illinois State Normal U.; 1941–42; Ohio

U., summers, 1949, 54; U. of Wisconsin, 1948–73. **Member:** NAD, Academician, 1952. Federal A.P.: Easel painting. Artist War Correspondent for *Life* magazine, 1942–45. **Commissions:** Eli Lilly & Co. (7 paintings, Medical Disciplines); *Look* magazine (14 paintings, Great Religions of America). **Awards:** Corcoran, William A. Clark Prize and Corcoran Silver Medal ($1,500); MMA, Artists for Victory, $1,000 Prize; Guggenheim Foundation Fellowship, 1936, renewed, 1937; Chicago/AI, The Mr. & Mrs. Frank G. Logan Prize, 1937, 45; PAFA, First Watercolor Prize, 1942; Illinois State Fair, First Award, 1955; Carnegie; NAD, Saltus Gold Medal for Merit, 1961; AAAL, Childe Hassam Award, 1962; Hon. DFA, Ripon College, 1960. **Address:** 4811 Tonyawatha Trail, Madison, WI 53716. **Dealers:** ACA Gallery; Frank Oehlschlaeger Gallery, Chicago and Sarasota, Fla. **One-man Exhibitions:** (first) Rehn Galleries, ca. 1935; A.A.A. Gallery, NYC, 1939, 41, 43, 45, 46, 49, 52, 55; The Milch Gallery, 1957, 59, 61, 65; Agra Gallery, 1966; The Banfer Gallery, 1967; Irving Galleries, Inc., Milwaukee, 1968; Hammer Gallery, 1969; Dannenberg Gallery, 1971. Oehlschlaeger Gallery, Chicago, 1976; Milwaukee, 1979. **Retrospectives:** Madison Art Center, 1966; Memphis/Brooks, 1975. **Group:** WMAA; Milwaukee; MMA; Boston/MFA; PAFA; Chicago/AI; Corcoran; Brooklyn Museum. **Collections:** Abbott Laboratories; U. of Arizona; Beloit College; Boston/MFA; Britannica; Brooklyn Museum; Chicago/AI; Corcoran; Cranbrook; Davenport/Municipal; Detroit/Institute; New York Cultural Center; Lawrence College; MMA; MacNider Museum; Madison Art Center; Neenah/Bergstrom; New Britain; Ohio U.; PAFA; St. Lawrence U.; San Antonio/McNay; Savannah/Telfair; Springfield, Mass./MFA; Terre Haute/Swope; Syracuse U.; WMAA; Walker; West Palm Beach/Norton; U. of Wisconsin; U. of Wyoming; Youngstown/Butler. **Bibliography:** American Artists Group Inc. 2; Baur 7; Bethers; Bruce and Watson;

Cheney; Christensen; Flanagan; McCurdy, ed.; Mendelowitz; Pagano; Pearson 1; Reese; Richardson, E. P.; Rose, B., 1; Wight 2. Archives.

BOICE, BRUCE. b. December, 1941, Boundbrook, N.J. **Studied:** Colgate U. US Army, 1964–66. **Taught:** School of Visual Arts, NYC, 1973–. **Awards:** National Endowment for the Arts, Grant, 1976; CAPS, 1979. **Address:** 189 Bowery, NYC 10002. **Dealer:** Sonnabend Gallery, NYC. **One-man Exhibitions:** (first) Ileana Sonnabend Gallery, NYC, 1975, 76, 77, 79; Capricorno Galleries, Venice, Italy, 1975; Galleriaforma, Genoa, Italy, 1975; Ileana Sonnabend Gallery, Paris, 1976; Galerie Rolf Ricke, Cologne, 1975; H.M., Brussels, 1976; Dart Gallery, Inc., Chicago, 1976; Thomas Segal Gallery, Boston, 1978; RAW Gallery, Hartford, Conn., 1978; Tyler School of Art, Philadelphia, 1979. **Group:** ICA, U. of Pennsylvania, Eight Abstract Painters, 1978; Cleveland/MA, Four Contemporary Painters, 1978; The University of Chicago, Ideas on Paper, 1976. **Collections:** MMA; MOMA; WMAA.

BOLLINGER, WILLIAM. b. July 15, 1939, Brooklyn, N.Y. **Studied:** Brown U., 1961. **Address:** c/o Dealer. **Dealer:** OK Harris Works of Art, NYC. **One-man Exhibitions:** Paul Bianchini Gallery, NYC, 1966; Bykert Gallery, 1967, 69; Galerie Rolf Ricke, 1967, 69; Galerie Joachim Ernst, Hannover, 1969; Gian Enzo Sperone, Turin, 1969; Starrett Lehigh Building, NYC, 1970; OK Harris Works of Art, 1972, 73, 74; Bard College, 1973; U. of Rhode Island, 1976. **Retrospective:** Bennington College, 1973. **Group:** WMAA, Anti-Illusion: Procedures/Materials, 1969; WMAA Annuals, 1969, 73; MOMA, Information 1971; Storm King Art Center, Sculpture in the Fields, 1974; U. of Rhode Island, Drawings, 1974. **Collections:** Four Seasons Restaurant; Mark Twain Bankshares; Mark Twain South

County Bank; U. of Rhode Island; Skidmore College; SFAI. **Bibliography:** *When Attitudes Become Form.*

BOLOMEY, ROGER. b. October 19, 1918, Torrington, Conn. **Studied:** Vevey, Switzerland, 1934–38; U. of Lausanne, 1947; Academy of Fine Arts, Florence, Italy, 1948–50; privately with Alfredo Cini, Switzerland. **Taught:** San Mateo Arts and Crafts, 1954–55; Dutchess Community College, Poughkeepsie, N.Y., 1965–66; Barlow School, Amenia, N.Y., 1967; Hunter College, 1968; Herbert H. Lehman College, Bronx, N.Y., 1968–75; Chairman, Department of Art, 1974–; California State U., Fresno, 1975–. **Commissions:** San Jose State College Art Building; South Mall, Albany (sculptures), 1967; Southridge Shopping Center, Milwaukee, 1968; Lehman High School, Bronx, N.Y., 1969; Eastridge Mall, San Jose, Calif.; Hauppauge, 1973; Mt. Hood Community College, Gresham, Ore., 1974; North Park, Dallas, 1975. **Awards:** SFMA, **P.P.,** 1960, Sculpture Prize, 1965; Walnut Creek (Calif.) Pageant, First Prize, 1962; Waitsfield/Bundy, Bundy Sculpture Competition, First Prize, 1963. **Address:** 4014 N. Van Ness Blvd., Fresno, CA 93704. **Dealer:** Alexander Gallery, Los Angeles. **One-man Exhibitions:** (first) SFMA, 1950; Sacramento/Crocker, 1950; Passedoit Gallery, NYC, 1951; Santa Barbara/MA, 1953; de Young, 1954; California Palace, 1958; Royal Marks Gallery, 1964; Circle Gallery, New Orleans, 1976. **Group:** SFMA Annuals, 1950, 1960–63, 65; ICA, Boston, 100 Works on Paper, circ., Europe, 1959; Chicago/AI, 1963; Salon du Mai, Paris, 1964; Carnegie, 1964; WMAA Sculpture Annual, 1964, 66; New York World's Fair, 1964–65; WMAA, Contemporary American Sculpture, Selection I, 1966; Quatrieme Exposition Suisse de Sculpture, Bienne, Switzerland, 1966; U. of Illinois, 1967; Southern Illinois U., 1967; Ridgefield/Aldrich, 1968; HemisFair '68, San Antonio, Tex., 1968; U. of Nebraska,

American Sculpture, 1970; Storm King Art Center, Outdoor Sculpture Indoors, 1972; Society of the Four Arts, Contemporary American Sculpture, 1974; Van Saun Park, Paramus, N.J., Sculpture in the Park, 1974. **Collections:** U. of California; Chase Manhattan Bank; Corcoran; Fontana-Hollywood Corp.; Los Angeles/County MA; MOMA; Oakland/AM; Ridgefield/Aldrich; SFAI; San Francisco Art Association; San Jose State College; WMAA; Waitsfield/Bundy. **Bibliography:** Archives.

BOLOTOWSKY, ILYA. b. July 1, 1907, Petrograd, Russia. To USA, 1923; citizen, 1929. **Studied:** College of St. Joseph, Istanbul; NAD, with Ivan Olinsky, 1924–30. US Air Force, 1942. Traveled Russia, Europe, North America. **Taught:** Black Mountain College, 1946–48; U. of Wyoming, 1948–57; Brooklyn College, 1954–56; Hunter College, 1954–56, 1963–64; New Paltz/SUNY, 1957–65; Long Island U., 1965–71; Wisconsin State College, summer, 1968; U. of New Mexico, spring, 1969; Queens College, 1973. Federal A.P.: Master easel and mural artist, teacher. **Member:** Cofounder, charter member, and former president of American Abstract Artists; cofounder and charter member of Federation of Modern Painters and Sculptors; AAAL. Produced 16 mm experimental films. Began constructivist painted columns 1961. **Commissions:** (murals) Williamsburgh Housing Project, NYC, 1936 (one of the first abstract murals); New York World's Fair, 1939; Hospital for Chronic Diseases, NYC, 1941; Theodore Roosevelt High School, NYC, 1941; Cinema I, NYC, 1962; Southampton College, Long Island U., 1968; North Central Bronx Hospital, 1973; First National City Bank, NYC 1974; P.S. 72, Brooklyn, N.Y., 1974 (tile mosaic mural); NYC, Passenger Ship terminal mural, 1978. **Awards:** Sharon (Conn.) Art Foundation, First Prize for Painting, 1959; Guggenheim Foundation Fellowship, 1941, 73; Yaddo Fellowship, 1935;

L. C. Tiffany Grant, 1930, 31; NAD, Hallgarten Prize for Painting, 1929, 30; NAD, First Prize Medal for Drawing, 1924, 25; The U. of Chicago, Midwest Film Festival, First Prize (for Metanois); State U. of New York Grant, for film research, 1959, 60; NIAL, Grant, 1971. **Address:** 2 Spring Street, NYC 10012. **Dealer:** Grace Borgenicht Gallery, Inc.; Washburn Gallery, NYC. **One-man Exhibitions:** (first) G.R.D. Studios, NYC., 1930; J. B. Neumann's New Art Circle, NYC, 1946, 52; Rose Fried Gallery, 1947, 49; Pratt Institute, 1949; Grace Borgenicht Gallery Inc., 1954, 56, 58, 59, 61, 63, 66, 68, 70, 72, 74, 75, 76, 77, 78, 79, 80; New Paltz/SUNY, 1960; Dickinson College, 1960; Elmira College, 1962; Southampton/Parrish, 1965; Long Island U., 1965; East Hampton Gallery, East Hampton, N.Y., 1965; Buffalo/SUNY, 1965 (two-man), 1966; Gorham State College, 1967; Wisconsin State College, 1968; Stony Brook/SUNY, 1968; London Arts, London and Detroit, 1971; David Barnett Gallery, Milwaukee, 1972; Reed College, 1973; Hokin Gallery, Chicago, 1976; Washburn Gallery, NYC, 1980. **Retrospectives:** U. of New Mexico, circ., 1970; SRGM, 1974; NCFA, circ., 1975. **Group:** American Abstract Artists Annuals; Federation of Modern Painters and Sculptors Annuals; WMAA Annuals; New York World's Fairs, 1939 and 1964–65; Seattle World's Fair, 1962; WMAA, Geometric Abstraction in America, circ., 1962; Corcoran, 1963; SRGM; Buffalo/Albright, Plus by Minus, 1968; Dallas/MFA, Geometric Abstraction, 1926–42, 1972; Chicago/Contemporary, Post-Mondrian Abstraction in America, 1973; Milwaukee, From Foreign Shores, 1976; Indianapolis, 1976; Philadelphia College of Art, Seventies Painting, 1978. **Collections:** AAAL; American Republic Insurance Co.; Andover/Phillips; Atlantic Richfield Co.; Bezalel Museum; Brandeis U.; Brooklyn Museum; Buffalo/Albright; Burlington Industries; Calcutta; Ceret; Chase Manhattan Bank; Ciba-Geigy Corp.; Cleveland/MA; Continental Grain Company; Harcourt Brace Jovanovich Inc.; Hirshhorn; Housatonic Community College; Indianapolis; U. of Iowa; MMA; MOMA; Manufacturers Hanover Trust Co.; U. of Michigan; The Miller Co.; Montclair/AM; NCFA; NYU; U. of Nebraska; New London; U. of New Mexico; New Paltz/SUNY; Norfolk/Chrysler; U. of North Carolina; Oklahoma; PMA; Phillips; RISD; Raleigh/NCMA; Ridgefield/Aldrich; Rock River (Wyo.) High School; SFMA; SRGM; Slater; Sweden/Goteborgs; U. of Texas; Union Carbide Corp.; Utica; U. of Vermont; WMAA; Walker; U. of Wyoming; Yale U. **Bibliography:** *Black and White Are Colors;* Blanchard; **Breeskin 2;** Brown 2; *From Foreign Shores;* Goodrich and Baur 1; MacAgy 2; Marter, Tarbell, and Wechsler; Rickey; Rose, B., 1. Archives.

BONEVARDI, MARCELO. b. 1929, Buenos Aires, Argentina. **Studied:** U. of Cordoba, 1948–51. Traveled Italy, USA. To USA, 1958. **Taught:** National U. of Cordoba, 1956. **Awards:** Salon Annual de Santa Fe, **P.P.,** 1956; Premio de Honor J. Pellanda, Cordoba, 1957; XXXVI Salon Annual de Rosario, **P.P.,** 1957; Salon Ministerio de Obras Publicas de la Nacion, Buenos Aires, First Prize, 1957; Guggenheim Foundation Fellowship, 1958; New School for Social Research Fellowship, 1963, 64; X Sao Paulo Biennial, International Award, 1969. **Address:** 799 Greenwich Street, NYC 10014. **Dealer:** Galeria Bonino Ltd. **One-man Exhibitions:** Museo Dr. Genario Perez, Cordoba, 1956; Galeria O. Rosario, 1956; Galeria Antigona, Buenos Aires, 1957; Amigos del Arte, Rosario, 1958; Radio Nacional de Cordoba, 1958; Gallery 4, Detroit, 1959; Roland de Anelle, NYC, 1960; Latow Gallery, NYC, 1961; Galeria Bonino Ltd., NYC, 1965, 67, 69, 73, 78; J. L. Hudson Art Gallery, Detroit, 1966; Arts Club of Chicago, 1968; Galeria Bonino Ltd., Buenos Aires, 1969, 70, 76; Museo Emilio A. Caraffa, Cordoba, Argentina, 1969, 78; Quebec, 1974; Montreal/Contemporain, 1974; Galeria Pecanins, Mexico City, 1974; Galeria Ponce, Mexico, 1978; Galeria Sandiego, Bogota, Colombia, 1979; The Art Contact Gallery, 1979; Galeria del Retiro, Buenos Aires, 1979. **Retrospective:** Center for Inter-American Relations, NYC, 1980. **Group:** Birmingham,, Ala./MA, Pan American Art, 1960; Riverside Museum, NYC, 30 Latin American Artists, 1960; ICA, Washington, D.C., Latin American Painters, 1964; U. of Illinois, 1965; Indianapolis, 1966; SRGM, The Emergent Decade, 1966; Cornell U., Latin American Art—Eight Argentines, 1966; Finch College, NYC, Art in Progress, 1967. **Collections:** Atlantic Richfield Co.; Baltimore/MA; Brooklyn Museum; Buenos Aires/Moderno; Buffalo/Albright; Caracas; Centro Artistico de Barranquilla; Chase Manhattan Bank; Ciba-Geigy Corp.; MIT; MOMA; Montreal/Contemporain; Museo de Arte Contemporaneo R. Tamayo; Museo Dr. Genaro Perez; Museo Emilio A. Caraffa; Museo Juan B. Castagnino; NYU; Owens-Corning Fiberglas Corp.; PMA; Quimica Argentina; RISD; Ridgefield/Aldrich; Southern Illinois U.; Sao Paulo/Contemporary; St. Jose Minerals Corp., NYC; Tel Aviv; U. of Texas; J. Walter Thompson Co.

BONTECOU, LEE. b. January 15, 1931, Providence, R.I. **Studied:** Bradford Junior College, with Robert Wade; ASL, 1952–55, with William Zorach, John Hovannes. Traveled Europe. **Taught:** Brooklyn College, 1971–75. **Commissions:** New York State Theater, Lincoln Center for the Performing Arts, NYC. **Awards:** Fulbright Fellowship (Rome), 1957, 58; L. C. Tiffany Grant, 1959; Corcoran, 1963. **Address:** P. O. Box 1290, East Hampton, NY 11937. **Dealer:** Leo Castelli Inc. **One-man Exhibitions:** (first) "G" Gallery, NYC, 1959; Leo Castelli, Inc., 1960, 62, 66, 71; Ileana Sonnabend Gallery, Paris, 1965; Leverkusen, 1969; Rotterdam, 1968; Kunstverein, Berlin, 1968; Chicago/Contemporary, 1972; Wesleyan U., 1975;

Halper Gallery, Palm Beach, Fla., 1976; Skidmore College, 1977. **Retrospective:** Rotterdam, 1958. **Group:** Festival of Two Worlds, Spoleto, 1958; Martha Jackson Gallery, New Media—New Forms I & II, 1960, 61; WMAA Annuals, 1961, 63, 64, 66; Carnegie, 1961, 67; MOMA, The Art of Assemblage, circ., 1961; VI Sao Paulo Biennial, 1961; Seattle World's Fair, 1962; Chicago/AI, 1962, 63, Sculpture—A Generation of Innovation, 1967; Corcoran, 1963; MOMA, Americans 1963, circ., 1963–64; Buffalo/Albright, Mixed Media and Pop Art, 1963; Documenta III, Kassel, 1964; Brandeis U., Recent American Drawings, 1964; Jewish Museum, Recent American Sculpture, 1964; U. of Texas, Drawings and . . ., 1966; Flint/Institute, I Flint Invitational, 1966; MOMA, The 1960s, 1967; WMAA Sculpture Annual, 1968; Denver/AM, Report on the Sixties, 1969; Foundation Maeght, L'Art Vivant, 1970; Carnegie, 1970; U. of North Carolina, Works on Paper, 1971; Yale U., American Drawing: 1970–1973, 1973; San Antonio/McNay, American Artists, 76, 1976; MMA, Contemporary American Prints, 1976; Corcoran, The Liberation: 14 American Artists, 1977; Dayton/AI, Skin, 1977; Albright College, Perspective 78: Works by Women, 1978. **Collections:** Akron/AI; Amsterdam/Stedelijk; Basel; Buffalo/Albright; Carnegie; Chase Manhattan Bank; Chicago/AI; Cleveland/MA; Corcoran; Cornell U.; Dallas/MFA; Hirshhorn; Houston/MFA; MOMA; PAFA; The Sinver Company Inc.; Smith College; SRGM; Stockholm/National; VMFA; WGMA; WMAA; Walker; Yale U. **Bibliography:** Battcock, ed.; Hunter, ed.; Janis and Blesh 1; Licht, F.; *Metro;* Rose, B., 1; Seitz 3; Trier 1; Weller; Honisch and Jensen, eds.; Johnson, Ellen H.

BOOTH, CAMERON. b. March 11, 1892, Erie, Pa.; **d.** March 7, 1980, Minneapolis, Minn. **Studied:** Fargo College, 1912; Chicago Art Institute School, 1912–17; Hoffmann School, Munich and Capri, 1927–28; Academie Andre Lhote,

Paris, 1972. Traveled Europe extensively. **Taught:** Minneapolis School of Art, 1922–28; St. Paul School of Art, 1929–40; Chicago/AI School, 1940; ASL, 1944–48; Queens College, 1946–47; U. of Minnesota, 1948–60; U. of California, Berkeley, 1957–58. **Member:** Federation of Modern Painters and Sculptors. **Awards:** Chicago/AI, J. Q. Adams Traveling Scholarship, 1917; Guggenheim Foundation Fellowship, 1942; Hon. Ph.D., Hamline U. **One-man Exhibitions:** Paul Elder Gallery, San Francisco, 1935; Howard Putzell Gallery, San Francisco, 1946; Denver/AM, 1936; Chicago/AI, 1942; Mortimer Brandt, NYC, 1943; The Bertha Schaefer Gallery, 1950; The Howard Wise Gallery, NYC, 1962; Wisconsin State U., 1967; Paul Kramer Gallery, St. Paul, 1968. **Retrospective:** A.F.A./Ford Foundation, circ., USA, 1961–64. **Group:** Many in 1920's and 1930's; WMAA, 1958; Carnegie. **Collections:** U. of California; Denver/AM; MMA; MOMA; Minneapolis/Institute; Newark Museum; PAFA; Phillips; SFMA; SRGM; Walker; Youngstown/Butler. **Bibliography:** Cheney; Hall; Pousette-Dart, ed.

BOSA, LOUIS. b. April 2, 1905, Codroipo, Italy. To USA, 1923; citizen. **Studied:** Academy of Fine Arts, Venice, with Mazotti; ASL, with John Sloan. Traveled Europe extensively. **Taught:** ASL, 1942–53; Parsons School of Design, 1950–53; Syracuse U.; U. of Notre Dame, summer, 1960; Cleveland Institute of Art, 1954–69. **Member:** NAD; ASL; Audubon Artists, Federal A.P.: Easel painting. **Awards:** Portrait of America, NYC, $1,500 Prize, 1944; NAD, Hon. Men., 1944; Rockport (Mass.) Art Association, $100 Award, 1945; Mead Painting of the Year ($500), 1947; AAAL, $1,000 Award, 1948; Los Angeles County Fair, First Prize ($700), 1948; Pepsi-Cola $500 Award, 1948; U. of Illinois, **P.P.** ($900), 1949; Audubon Artists, Gold Medal of Honor, 1949; Hallmark International Competition, $750 Award, 1949; NAD, Gold Medal,

1957; Hallmark International Competition, $900 Award, 1958; New Hope, Pa., First Prize, 1959, 62; Legionnaires of Pennsylvania, First Prize and Gold Medal, 1959; Youngstown/Butler, First Prize ($1,000); NAD, $400 Prize, 1961. **Address:** Upper Black Eddy, Bucks County, PA 18972. **Dealers:** Frank Oehlschlaeger Gallery, Chicago and Saratoga; Harmon Gallery. **One-man Exhibitions:** (first) Contemporary Arts Gallery, NYC, 1930; Springfield, Mass./ MFA; Coy Gallery, Miami; Cleveland Institute of Art; Kleemann Gallery, NYC; Frank Oehlschlaeger Gallery, Chicago, 1954, 59, 65; The Milch Gallery, 1958, 60, 63, 65; Frank Oehlschlaeger Gallery, Saratoga, Fla., 1975. **Group:** MMA; MOMA; WMAA: Carnegie; Corcoran; PMA; Boston/MFA; Toledo/MA; Buffalo/Albright; New Orleans/Delgado; Worcester/AM; Montclair/AM; Wilmington; Audubon Artists; Atlanta/AA; Cleveland/MA; Chicago/AI; Kansas City/Nelson; Argentina/Nacional; PAFA; NAD. **Collections:** AAL; Atlanta/AA; Britannica; Clearwater/Gulf Coast; Columbus, Ga.; Hartford/Wadsworth; IBM; U. of Illinois; Indianapolis/Herron; MMA; Montclair/AM; New Orleans/Delgado; U. of Notre Dame; PMA; U. of Rochester; San Diego; Springfield, Mass./MFA; Syracuse U.; Toronto; VMFA; WMAA; Wilmington; Worcester/AM; Youngstown/Butler. **Bibliography:** Kent, N.; Pagano; Watson, E.W., 2. Archives.

BOTKIN, HENRY. b. April 5, 1896, Boston, Mass. **Studied:** Massachusetts School of Arts, 1915–19, with Joseph de Camp, Ernest Major; ASL, with George Bridgeman. Traveled Europe, USA; resided Paris, eight years. Taught privately. Active as a lecturer, writer, and organizer of exhibitions. **Member:** Artists Equity (president, 1951–52); American Abstract Artists (president, 1954–55); Federation of Modern Painters and Sculptors (president, 1957–61, 1968–69); Fellow of the International Institute of Arts and Letters; Audubon

Artists; International Association of Plastic Arts. **Awards:** Audubon Artists, First Prize (2); Mead Painting of the Year, $500 Prize; AAAL, **P.P.**, 1967, 74, 75. **Address:** 56 West 11th Street, NYC 10011. **Dealer:** Rehn Galleries. **One-man Exhibitions:** (first) Billiet Gallery, Paris, 1927; The Downtown Gallery; Marie Harriman Gallery, NYC; Carstairs Gallery, NYC; J. Seligmann & Co.; A.A.A. Gallery, NYC; Otto Gerson Gallery, NYC; Riverside Museum; Denver/AM; Phillips; Arts Club of Chicago; Tirca Karlis Gallery; Rehn Galleries, 1974, 77. **Retrospectives:** Riverside Museum, NYC, 1962; Syracuse U., 1971. **Group:** Tate; Cleveland/MA; de Young; Carnegie; Chicago/AI; SFMA; MMA; WMAA; Boston/MFA; Brooklyn Museum; NIAL; PAFA; Detroit/Institute; Corcoran; Stadtische Kunstsammlungen, Bonn; Munich/State. **Collections:** Abbott Laboratories; Ain Harod; Akron/AI; Bath-Yam Museum; Boston/MFA; Brandeis U.; Brooklyn Museum; Colby College; Dallas/MFA; Denver/AM; Hagerstown/County MFA; Hartford/Wadsworth; La Jolla; Library of Congress; MMA; MOMA; Mount Holyoke College; Munich/State; NIAL; NYU; U. of Nebraska; Newark Museum; Norfolk; Norfolk/Chrysler; U. of Oklahoma; Phillips; U. of Rochester; Smith College; Syracuse U.; Tel Aviv; WMAA; Walker; Washington State U.; West Palm Beach/Norton; Youngstown/Butler. **Bibliography:** Archives.

BOUCHE, LOUIS. b. March 18, 1896, NYC; **d.** August 7, 1969, Pittsfield, Mass. **Studied:** Academie Colarossi; Academie de la Grande Chaumiere; Academie des Beaux-Arts, Paris, 1910–15, with Jules Bernard, Frank V. DuMond, Bernard Naudin; ASL, 1915–16. **Taught:** ASL; NAD, 1951–69. **Commissions** (murals): New Interior Department Building, Washington, D.C.; Justice Department Building, Washington, D.C.; US Post Office, Ellenville, N.Y.; Radio City Music Hall, NYC; bar lounge cars, Pennsylvania

Railroad (4); Eisenhower Center, Abilene, Kans. **Awards:** NAD, Saltus Gold Medal for Merit, 1915; Guggenheim Foundation Fellowship, 1933; PAFA, Carol H. Beck Gold Medal, 1944; MMA, Artists for Victory, Third Prize, 1944; NAD, The Adolph and Clara Obrig Prize, 1951; NAD, Benjamin Altman Prize, 1955, 62. **One-man Exhibitions:** Kraushaar Galleries, 1936, 38, 40, 42, 44, 46, 49, 51, 54, 58, 62, 64, 70; Des Moines; St. Gaudens Museum, 1966. **Retrospective:** Temple U. **Group:** Independents, NYC, 1917; The Daniel Gallery, NYC, 1918–31; Carnegie, 1937, 39; NAD; PAFA, 1941, 42, 45; Cincinnati/AM, 1948; MMA, Two Hundred Years of American Painting, 1965; WMAA, Art of the U.S. 1670–1966, 1966. **Collections:** AAAL; ASL; Britannica; Cincinnati/AM; Colorado College; Columbus; Cranbrook; Des Moines; Fort Dodge/Blanden; U. of Kansas; Lehigh U.; Los Angeles/County MA; MMA; U. of Nebraska; New Britain; U. of Oklahoma; PAFA; PMA; Phillips; Southampton/Parrish; US State Department; WMAA; Walker; Wichita/AM; Worcester/AM; Youngstown/Butler. **Bibliography:** Bethers; Bruce and Watson; Goodrich and Baur 1; Kent, N.; Pousette-Dart, ed.; Richardson, E.P.; Watson, E.W., 2; *Woodstock.* Archives.

BOURGEOIS, LOUISE. b. December 25, 1911, Paris, France. **Studied:** Lycee Fenelon, 1932, baccalaureate; Sorbonne, 1932–35; Ecole du Louvre, 1936–37; Academie des Beaux-Arts, Paris, 1936–38; Atelier Bissiere, Paris, 1936–37; Academie de la Grande Chaumiere, 1937–38; Academie Julian, Paris, 1938; Atelier Fernand Leger, Paris, 1938. Traveled Europe extensively. To USA, 1938. **Taught:** Docent at the Louvre, 1937–38; Academie de la Grande Chaumiere, 1937, 38; Great Neck (N.Y.) Public Schools, 1960; Brooklyn College, 1963, 68; Pratt Institute, 1965–67. **Address:** 347 West 20th Street, NYC. **Dealer:** Robert Miller

Gallery, NYC. **One-man Exhibitions:** The Bertha Schaefer Gallery, 1945; Norlyst Gallery, NYC, 1947; The Peridot Gallery, 1949, 50, 53; Allan Frumkin Gallery, Chicago, 1953; Cornell U., 1959; The Stable Gallery, 1964; Rose Fried Gallery, 1964; 112 Greene Street, NYC, 1974; Xavier Fourcade, Inc., NYC, 1978, 79; Hamilton Gallery of Contemporary Art, NYC, 1978; U. of California, 1979. **Group:** MOMA, 1943, 49, 51, 62; MMA, 1943; SFMA, 1944; Los Angeles/County MA, 1945; U. of Rochester, 1945; Brooklyn Museum, 1945; WMAA, 1945, 46, 53, 55, 57, 60, 62, 63, 68; Walker, 1954; U. of Illinois, 1957; Dallas/MFA, 1960; Claude Bernard, Paris, 1960; Salon de la Jeune Sculpture, Paris, 1965, 69; RISD, 1966; International Sculpture Biennial, Carrara, Italy, 1969; Baltimore/MA, 1969; MOMA, The New American Painting and Sculpture, 1969; WMAA, 1970, 72; Foundation Maeght, 1970; Lakeview Center, American Women: 20th Century, 1972; Storm King Art Center, The Emerging Real, 1973; PMA/Museum of the Philadelphia Civic Center, Focus, 1974; WMAA, 200 Years of American Sculpture, 1976; New Orleans Museum Sculpture: American Directions, 1976; Brandeis U., From Women's Eyes, 1977; Albright College, Perspective '78, 1978; Purchase/SUNY, Hidden Desires, 1980. **Collections:** Calcutta; Ciba-Geigy Corp.; Detroit/Institute; MOMA; NYU; Paris/Moderne; RISD; Storm King Art Center; WMAA. **Bibliography:** Baur 5; Giedion-Welcker 1; Goodrich and Baur 1; Lippard 3; Motherwell and Reinhardt, eds.; Rosen 1; Seuphor 3; Trier 1. Archives.

BOWMAN, GEOFFREY. b. December 29, 1928, San Francisco, Calif. **Studied:** City College of San Francisco, 1951, AA; San Francisco State College, with John Ihle, Seymour Locks, Alexander Nepote, John Gutman, Waldemar Johanssen, 1945, BA, 1957, MA; San Francisco Art Institute, graduate study with Henry Takemoto, 1960. US Navy, 1946–48. **Taught:** California State Prison, San Quentin, 1957–. **Member:** California Society of Printmakers. **Address:** c/o Dealer. **Dealer:** The Lanyon Gallery. **One-man Exhibitions:** (first) The East-West Gallery, San Francisco, 1957; Yakima Valley Junior College, 1959; David Cole Gallery, San Francisco, 1962; The Lanyon Gallery, 1963; RAC, 1964. **Group:** California Palace, James D. Phelan Art Awards, 1959; California Society of Printmakers Annuals, 1960–64; California Palace Annuals, 1961, 62, 64; SFMA, 1961; Santa Barbara Invitational, 1962; SFMA, Small Format, 1963; U. of Illinois, 1963; Brooklyn Museum, Print Biennial; California Palace, 50th Anniversary of the California Society of Printmakers, 1964; Denver/AM Annual, 1964. **Collections:** Lannan Foundation; SFMA.

BOWMAN, RICHARD. b. March 15, 1918, Rockford, Ill. **Studied:** Chicago Art Institute School, 1938–42, BFA; State U. of Iowa, 1947–49, MFA. Traveled Mexico, USA. **Taught:** Chicago Art Institute School, 1944–47, including summer school, 1944, 45; North Park College, 1944–46; State U. of Iowa, 1947–49; Stanford U., 1949–50, 57, 58, 63; U. of Manitoba, 1950–54; Washburn-White Art Center, Palo Alto, Calif., 1954. **Awards:** Chicago/AI, Scholarship, 1939–41; Rockford/Burpee Annual, First Prize, 1940; Edward L. Reyerson Traveling Fellowship, 1942; Chicago/AI, William R. French Memorial Gold Medal, 1945; Iowa State Fair, Second Prize, 1948; Montreal/MFA Annual, 1952; Oakland/AM, Hon. Men., 1955. **Address:** 178 Springdale Way, Redwood City, CA 94062. **One-man Exhibitions:** Beloit College, 1941; Rockford/Burpee, 1941, 47; Ras-Martin Gallery, Mexico City, 1943; The Pinacotheca, NYC, 1945; Chicago/AI, 1945; Milwaukee, 1946; U. of Illinois, 1946 (two-man, with Joan Mitchell), 1947; The Swetzoff Gallery, Boston, 1949; Pen and Palette Gallery, St. Louis, 1949; Contemporary Gallery, Sausalito,

Calif., 1949, 50; Stanford U., 1950, 56; Bordelon Gallery, Chicago, 1950; Kelly Gallery, Vancouver, B.C., 1954; The Rose Rabow Gallery, San Francisco, 1959, 61, 64, 68, 70, 72, 74; SFMA, 1959 (two-man, with Gordon Onslow-Ford), 1951, 70. **Retrospectives:** Stanford U., 1956; Washington State U., circ., 1957; SFMA, 1961; Roswell, 1972. **Group:** Chicago/AI, 1940, 44, 45; SFMA, 1941, 49, 50, 55, 60; Cincinnati/AM, 1941; Art of this Century, NYC, 1945; Chicago/ AI, Abstract and Surrealist Art, 1948; Chicago/AI, Exhibition Momentum, 1948; Omaha/Joslyn, 1948, 49; Iowa State Fair, 1948; Philadelphia Print Club Annual, 1949; Walker, 1949; Brooklyn Museum, 1949; Canadian Society of Graphic Art Annual, Toronto, 1952; Ottawa/National, Canadian Painters 1953, 1953; II Sao Paulo Biennial, 1953; Royal Ontario Museum, 1954; Oakland/AM, 1955; Stanford U., 50 Contemporary American Painters, 1956; SFMA, After Surrealism, circ., 1959; USIA, Contemporary American Prints, circ., Latin America, 1959–60; California Palace, 1960, 61, 62, 63, 64; Carnegie, 1961, 64; WMAA, Fifty California Artists, 1962–63; Stanford U., Some Points of View for '62, 1962; A.F.A., circ., 1966–68. **Collections:** de Young; New Britain/American; Oakland/AM; SFMA; Santa Barbara/MA; U. of Texas.

BOXER, STANLEY. b. June 26, 1926, New York City. **Studied:** Brooklyn College; Art Students League. US Navy, 1943–46. Traveled England, Germany, Canada. Designed and built set for Eric Hawkins Dance Company, *Classic Kite Tails*, 1972. **Awards:** Guggenheim Foundation Fellowship, 1975. **Address:** 37 East 18th Street, NYC 10003. **Dealer:** Andre Emmerich Gallery, NYC. **One-man Exhibitions:** (first) Perdalma Gallery, NYC, 1953, 54, 55, 56; Grand Central Galleries, NYC, 1965, 66, 67; Fischbach Gallery, NYC, 1966; Rose Fried Gallery, NYC, 1967, 68, 69; U. of Manitoba, 1967; NYU, 1968; Tibor de Nagy, NYC, 1971, 72, 73, 74, 75, 77;

Santa Barbara/MA, 1972; San Antonio/ McNay, 1973; Watson/De Nagy Gallery, Houston, 1974, 76, 78; Galerie Andre Emmerich, Zurich, 1975; Syracuse/Everson, 1975; Andre Emmerich Gallery, NYC, 1975, 76, 77, 78, 79, 80; PAFA, 1976; Richard Gray, Chicago, 1977, 79; Boston/MFA, 1977; Max Protetch Gallery, Washington, D.C., 1977; Hokin Gallery, Palm Beach, Fla., 1978; Galerie Wentzel, Hamburg, 1975, 78, 80; Meredith Long Gallery, Houston, 1979, 80; Galerie Regards, Paris, 1979; Dorsky Gallery, NYC, 1980; Thomas Segal, Boston, 1980. **Retrospective:** U. of North Carolina, circ., 1978. **Group:** Syracuse/Everson, New Works in Clay, 1976; U. of Saskatchewan, Boxer, Natkin, Ferber, 1977; Indianapolis, 1978. **Collections:** Santa Barbara/MA; Ball State U.; Des Moines; Wichita/AM; Calcutta; Boston/MFA; Chase Manhattan Bank, NYC; IBM; Cornell U.; WMAA; Charlotte/Mint; Brandeis U.; U. of Mass.; Trenton/State; Prudential Insurance Co. of America; Buffalo/Albright; Charlotte/State; Vienna, Museum des 20. Jahrhunderts.

BOYCE, RICHARD. b. June 11, 1920, NYC. US Army, 1940–44. **Studied:** Boston Museum School, 1945–49, with Karl Zerbe (highest honors in painting); assistant to O. Kokoschka, summer, 1948, Pittsfield, Mass. Traveled Europe, southern Mexico. **Taught:** Boston Museum School, 1946–49; Wellesley College, 1953–62; Boston U., 1959–61; UCLA, 1963–. **Member:** Artists Equity. **Awards:** Boston/MFA, James William Paige Fellowship, 1949–51; Boston/ MFA, Bartlett Grant, 1959, 60. **Address:** 1419 W. Washington Boulevard, Venice, CA 90291. **Dealer:** Silvan Simone Gallery, Los Angeles. **One-man Exhibitions:** Boris Mirski Gallery, Boston, 1952; The Swetzoff Gallery, Boston, 1956, 59, 61, 62; Brattle Gallery, Cambridge, 1956; The Zabriskie Gallery, 1961; The Alan Gallery, NYC, 1963, 65; Felix Landau Gallery, 1966, 69; The Landau-Alan Gallery, NYC, 1968.

Group: Johns Hopkins U., Three Young Americans, 1948; ICA, Boston, 1948, 52, 56, 62, 64; U. of Illinois, 1947, 65; Worcester/AM, 1959; Chicago/AI Annual, 1960; WMAA, 1963; PAFA Annual, 1964. **Collections:** Andover/Phillips; Harvard U.; Lincoln, Mass./De Cordova; RISD; WMAA; Wellesley College; Worcester/AM.

BOYLE, KEITH. b. February 15, 1930, Defiance, Ohio. **Studied:** State U. of Iowa, with James Lechay, BFA; Ringling School of Art, with Fred Sweet, Andrew Sanders. Traveled Europe; resided Rome. **Taught:** Lake Forest College, 1956; Barat College, 1957, 59; Sacramento State College, 1960; Stanford U., 1962–. **Commissions:** St. Thomas Episcopal Church, Sunnyvale, Calif. **Awards:** State of Iowa, Department of Education, **P.P.,** 1952; Indiana (Pa.) State Teachers College, 1953; Springfield, O./AM, 1955; The Pennsylvania State U., 1955; Chicago/AI, The Mr. & Mrs. Frank G. Logan Medal ($1,500), 1958; California Palace, Patrons of Art and Music Award, 1964. **Address:** 515 Newell Road, Palo Alto, CA 94303. **Dealer:** John Berggruen Gallery, San Francisco. **One-man Exhibitions:** (first) Feingarten Gallery, Chicago, 1958, also 1959; Feingarten Gallery, San Francisco, 1960; Triangle Art Gallery, 1960; The Lanyon Gallery, 1963; de Young, 1964; SFMA, 1964; Stanford U., 1964, 67, 77; Hollis Gallery, San Francisco, 1967; Hansen-Fuller Gallery, 1968; Smith Andersen Gallery, Palo Alto, 1971, 72, 77; St. Mary's College, Moraga, Calif., 1972; Linda Farris Gallery, Seattle, 1973; Martha Jackson Gallery, 1974; San Jose Museum of Art, 1978; Smith Andersen Gallery, San Francisco, 1975. **Group:** Springfield, Mo./AM, 1952–55; Des Moines, 1953; Denver/AM, 1953; Walker, 1954; Washburn U. of Topeka, 1955; Youngstown/ Butler, 1955, 56, 58; Omaha/Joslyn, 1956; Chicago/AI, 1957–60; Ravinia Festival, Highland Park, Ill., 1957; Chicago/ AI, 53 Chicago Artists, circ., France and

Germany, 1957; PAFA, 1958, 60, 62; Buffalo/Albright, 1960; SFMA, 1960, 62, 64; California Palace, 1964, Painters behind Painters, 1967; U. of Michigan, 1965; SFMA, The Colorists, 1965; M. Kroedler & Co., Art Across America, circ., 1965–67; California Palace, A Century of California Painting, 1970; Omaha/Joslyn, Looking West, 1970; Smithsonian, New American Monotypes, circ., 1978–80. **Collections:** Barat College; Dartmouth College; Indiana (Pa.) State Teachers College; U. of Iowa; Mead Corporation; NCFA; Oakland/AM; The Pennsylvania State U.; Purchase/SUNY; SFMA; Springfield, Mo./AM; Stanford U.; State of Iowa.

BOYNTON, JAMES W. b. January 12, 1928, Fort Worth, Tex. **Studied:** Texas Christian U., BFA, MFA. **Taught:** U. of Houston, 1955–57; San Francisco Art Institute, 1960–62; U. of New Mexico, 1963; Houston Museum School, 1968–69; Northwood Institute, Dallas, 1968–69; U. of St. Thomas (Tex.), 1969–70. **Awards:** Fort Worth, **P.P.,** 1951, 52, 54, 55; Texas Watercolor Society, First **P.P.,** 1951, 1953–55; Denver/- AM, **P.P.,** 1952, 54, 58; Texas State Fair, **P.P.,** 1953; Houston/MFA, **P.P.,** 1955; Underwood-Neuhaus Corp., 1957; Youngstown/Butler, 1957; ART: USA: 59, NYC, Hon. Men., 1959; SFMA, First Prize, 1962; Longview Foundation Grant, 1966; Tamarind Fellowship, 1967; Beaumont (Tex.) Art Museum, Second Prize, 1968. **Address:** 3723 Albans, Houston, TX 77005. **Dealer:** Moody Gallery, Houston, Texas. **One-man Exhibitions:** Fort Worth, 1955; La Escondida, Taos, N.M., 1956; Andre Emmerich Gallery, Houston, 1957; New Arts Gallery, Houston, 1957; Fairweather-Hardin Gallery, 1958; Barone Gallery, NYC, 1958; Dord Fitz Gallery, Amarillo, 1959; Bolles Gallery, San Francisco, 1959–62; Dallas Museum for Contemporary Arts, 1959; Lynchburg Art Gallery, Lynchburg, Va., 1960; Downtown Gallery, New Orleans, 1960; Haydon Calhoun Gallery, Dallas,

1960–62; Staempfli Gallery, 1961; Louisiana Gallery, Houston, 1964; David Gallery, 1966; Louise Ferrari Gallery, 1967; Chapman Kelly Gallery, 1968; Beaumont (Tex.) Art Museum, 1969; Galerie Simone Stern, New Orleans, 1970; New Orleans/Delgado, 1970; U. of St. Thomas, Tex., 1971; Du Bose Gallery, 1975; Amarillo Art Center, 1975; Loyola U., New Orleans, 1977; Moody Gallery, Houston, 1976, 77, 79; U. of Houston, Clear Lake City, 1979. **Retrospective:** Amarillo Art Center, 1980. **Group:** Fort Worth, 1950–55; WMAA, Young America, and others; Denver/AM, 1952, 54, 56, 58; Yale U.; Corcoran; Colorado Springs/FA, 1953, 54, 57; SRGM, Younger American Painters, 1954; Carnegie, 1955; Houston/MFA, 1955, Art and the Alphabet, 1978; MOMA, Recent Drawings USA, 1956; Santa Fe, N.M., 1957; Youngstown/Butler, 1957; Chicago/AI, 1957, 58; Brussels World's Fair, 1958; SFMA, After Surrealism, circ., 1959; MOMA, 1962; SFMA, 1962, 69; HemisFair '68, San Antonio, Tex., 1968; WMAA Annual, 1967; MOMA, Tamarind: Homage to Lithography, 1969; SFMA, Tamarind, 1969; International Exhibitions Foundation, Washington, D.C., Tamarind: A Renaissance of Lithography, circ., 1971–72; Houston/MFA, Wood in Art, 1979. **Collections:** Austin; Brooklyn Museum; Amon Carter Museum; Dallas/MFA; Denver/AM; Fort Worth; Hartford/Wadsworth; Houston/Contemporary; Houston/MFA; Inland Steel Co.; La Jolla; Los Angeles/County MA; MOMA; New Orleans/Delgado; Oak Cliff Savings and Loan; PMA; Pasadena/AM; SRGM; U. of Texas; UCLA; Underwood-Neuhaus Corp; WMAA; Witte; Youngstown/Butler. **Bibliography:** MacAgy 1. Archives.

BRACH, PAUL. b. March 13, 1924, NYC. **Studied:** Fieldston School, NYC; State U. of Iowa (with Philip Guston, Mauricio Lasansky), 1941–42, 1945–48, BFA, 1967–69, MFA. US Army, 1942–45. Traveled Spain, France, Italy;

resided in California, 1967–75. **Taught:** U. of Missouri, 1949–51; New School for Social Research, 1952–55; Parsons School of Design, 1956–67; Cooper Union, 1960–62, 1978–80; U. of New Mexico, A.F.A. Visiting Artist, 1965; U. of California, San Diego, 1967–69; California Institute of the Arts, 1969–75; Fordham U., 1975–79; Lincoln Center Campus, 1975. **Awards:** Tamarind Fellowship, 1964. **m.** Miriam Schapiro. **Address:** 393 W. Broadway, NYC 10013; Montauk Highway, East Hampton, NY 11037. **Dealer:** Lerner-Heller Gallery, NYC; Janus Gallery, Venice, Calif. **One-man Exhibitions:** (first) Leo Castelli Inc., 1957, also 1959; Union College (N.Y.), 1958; Dwan Gallery, 1960; Cordier and Warren, NYC, 1962; Cordier & Ekstrom, Inc., 1964; U. of New Mexico, 1965; NYU, 1966; The Kornblee Gallery, 1968; Andre Emmerich Gallery, NYC, 1974; Cirrus Editions Ltd., 1975; Benson Gallery, 1975; Lerner-Heller Gallery, NYC, 1978, 80; Yares Gallery, Scottsdale, Ariz., 1979; Janus Gallery, Venice, Calif., 1980. **Retrospective:** Newport Harbor and La Jolla/MA, Paul Brach and Miriam Schapiro, 1969. **Group:** WMAA; Chicago/AI; Corcoran; Baltimore/MA; St. Louis/City; Jewish Museum; Brandeis U., 1964; MOMA, The Responsive Eye, 1965; SFMA, 1965; Los Angeles/County MA, 1970; MOMA, Tamarind: Homage to Lithography, 1969; Newport Harbor, 1974. **Collections:** Albion College; U. of Arizona; Avco Corp.; U. of California, San Diego; Los Angeles/County MA; Newport Harbor; NYU; U. of Nebraska; U. of New Mexico; St. Louis/City; Smith College; WMAA. **Bibliography:** Blesh 1; Sandler; Weller.

BRACKMAN, ROBERT. b. September 25, 1898, Odessa, Russia, **d.** July 16, 1980, New London, Conn. **Studied:** Ferrer School, San Francisco; NAD; and with George Bellows, Robert Henri. **Taught:** ASL, 1934–75; American Art School, NYC, 1951–80; Brooklyn Museum School, 1936–38. **Member:** Royal

Society of Arts. Consultant on the motion picture *A Portrait of Jennie*, 1950. **Awards:** Chicago/AI, 1929; NAD: The Thomas B. Clarke Prize, 1932; Saltus Gold Medal for Merit, 1941; Andrew Carnegie Prize, 1965; Gold Medal of Honor, 1966; Noel Flagg Prize, 1936; Connecticut Academy of Fine Arts, First Award, 1947; Carnegie, Hon. Men., 1949; PAFA, Carol H. Beck Gold Medal, 1958; Audubon Artists, **P.P.**, 1960; elected to Royal Society of Arts, London, 1962; Ford Foundation Grant, 1965. **One-man Exhibitions:** Macbeth Gallery, NYC, 1930, 31, 33, 34, 36, 40, 44; Grand Central, NYC, 1946. **Group:** NAD; Connecticut Academy of Fine Arts; PAFA; Audubon Artists; Montclair/AM. **Collections:** Atlanta/ AA; Britannica; Brooklyn Museum; Bryn Mawr College; Canajoharie; The U. of Chicago; Colonial Williamsburg; Connecticut Life Insurance Company; U. of Connecticut; Davenport/Municipal; U. of Georgia; Harvard U.; Honolulu Academy; Houston/MFA; IBM; MMA; Memphis/Brooks; Milton Academy; Minneapolis/Institute; Montclair/ AM; Newark Museum; New Britain; New Haven Public Library; Norfolk/ Chrysler; Pasadena/AM; The Pentagon; Princeton U.; RISD; Radio Corporation of America; U. of Rochester; Rockford/ Burpee; Toledo/MA; US Military Academy; US State Department; West Palm Beach/Norton; Wilmington; Yale U. **Bibliography:** Bates; Bazin; Boswell 1; Cheney; Hall; Jewell 2, 3; Watson, E. W., 1. Archives.

BRAINARD, JOE. b. March 11, 1942, Salem, Ark. A poet who has published many books. **Taught:** Cooper Union, 1967–68. **Awards:** Copley Foundation Grant. **Address:** 8 Green Street, NYC, 10013. **Dealer:** Fischbach Gallery, NYC. **One-man Exhibitions:** The Alan Gallery, NYC, 1965; The Landau-Alan Gallery, NYC, 1967, 69; Gotham Book Mart, NYC, 1968; Jerrold Morris Gallery, Toronto, 1968; Benson Gallery, 1970; Phyllis Kind Gallery, Chicago,

Joe Brainard   *Love*   1972

1970; Fischbach Gallery, NYC, 1971, 72, 74, 75; School of Visual Arts, NYC, 1972; New York Cultural Center, 1972; Utah, 1973; Vick Gallery, Philadelphia, 1976; EG Gallery, Kansas City, Mo., 1976; Suzette Schochett Gallery, Newport, R.I., 1976; Coventry Gallery, Paddington, N.S.W., 1976; Hamilton College, N.Y., 1977; Benson Gallery, Bridgehampton, N.Y., 1977; Art 3 Associates, Savannah, Ga., 1978. **Group:** U. of North Carolina, 1967; MOMA, In Memory of My Feelings: Frank O'Hara, 1967; U. of Illinois, 1969; VMFA, 1968; Chicago/Contemporary, White on White, 1972; Corcoran, Seven Young Artists, 1972; Moore College of Art, Philadelphia, Artists' Books, 1973; Harvard U., New American Graphic Art, 1973; Yale U., American Drawing: 1970–73, 1973; Tyler School of Art, Philadelphia, American Drawings, 1973; William Paterson College, N.J., Contemporary Drawing, 1975. **Collections:** Amerada-Hess Corp., Inc., NYC; Chase Manhattan Bank, NYC; Colorado Springs/FA; Harvard U.; U. of Kansas; Liaison Films, Inc.; McCrory Corp., NYC; MOMA; RISD; Time Inc.; Utah;

WMAA. **Bibliography:** *Poets & Painters;* Lucie-Smith.

BRANDT, WARREN. b. February 26, 1918, Greensboro, N.C. **Studied:** Pratt Institute, 1935–37; ASL, 1946, with Yasuo Kuniyoshi; Washington U., with Philip Guston, Max Beckmann, 1947–48, BFA with honors; U. of North Carolina, 1953, MFA. Traveled Mexico, Europe. **Taught:** Salem College, 1949–50; Pratt Institute, 1950–52; Guilford College, 1952–56; U. of Mississippi, 1957–59; Southern Illinois U., 1959–61; School of Visual Arts, NYC, 1962–63; Director, New York Studio School, 1967. **Awards:** John T. Milliken Traveling Fellowship. **m.** Grace Borgenicht. **Address:** 138 East 95th Street, NYC 10028. **Dealer:** Fischbach Gallery, NYC. **One-man Exhibitions:** (first) Sacramento State College, 1943; Nonagon Gallery, NYC, 1959; Memphis State U., 1960; New Gallery, Provincetown, 1960; Michigan State U., 1961; The American Gallery, NYC, 1961; Esther Stuttman Gallery, Provincetown, 1962; Grippi Gallery, NYC, 1963, 64; Obelisk Gallery, Washington, D.C., 1963; Grippi and Waddell Gallery, NYC, 1964; A. M. Sachs Gallery, 1966, 67, 68, 70, 72, 73, 74, 75; U. of North Carolina, 1967; Reed College, 1967; Benson Gallery, 1967; Eastern Illinois U., 1968; Salem College, 1968; Molly Barnes Gallery, Los Angeles, 1968; Cord Gallery, Southampton, N.Y., 1968; Allentown/AM, 1969; Grand Avenue Galleries, Milwaukee, 1969; Mercury Gallery, London, 1969, 72; David Barnett Gallery, Milwaukee, 1969, 71, 74; Allentown/MA, 1969; Agra Gallery, Washington, D.C., 1969, 70; Pratt Manhattan Center, NYC, 1970; Hooks Epstein Gallery, Houston, 1971, 73; Agra Gallery, Palm Beach, 1971; Guild Hall, East Hampton, N.Y., 1973, 74; Benson Gallery, Bridgehampton, N.Y., 1976; Vick Gallery, Philadelphia, 1976; Raleigh/NCMA, 1977; Fischbach Gallery, NYC, 1977; Allenhouse Gallery, Louisville, Ky., 1978. **Retrospective:** Allentown/AM, 1962–1968. **Group:** MMA, American Watercolors, Drawings, and Prints, 1952; WMAA; Brooklyn Museum, Print Biennials; VMFA, Virginia Artists Biennial; PAFA; A.F.A.; Syracuse/Everson, Provincetown Painters 1890s–1970s, 1977. **Collections:** Carnegie; Chase Manhattan Bank; Ciba-Geigy Corp.; Guild Hall; Hirshhorn; Michigan State U.; Milwaukee; NCFA; Norfolk/Chrysler; U. of North Carolina; New Mexico State U.; U. of Rochester; Southern Illinois U.; WGMA. **Bibliography:** Archives.

BRECHT, GEORGE. b. 1925, NYC. **Studied:** Philadelphia College of Pharmacy and Science, BSC; Rutgers U.; New School for Social Research, with John Cage, 1958–59; Samuel S. Fleischer Art Memorial, Philadelphia. Traveled Western Europe, Mexico. **Taught:** Leeds (England) College of Art, 1968–69. Founder, *Sight Unseen,* a journal on research science and speculative art, 1968–69. **Commissions:** Music and sets for James Waring Dance Company, NYC. **Address:** Wildenburgstrasse 9, 5 Cologne-Sulz, West Germany. **Dealer:** Arturo Schwarz, Milan. **One-man Exhibitions:** (first) Reuben Gallery, NYC, 1959; Fischbach Gallery, 1965; Galleria Schwarz, 1967, 69; Galerie Rudolf Zwirner, 1969; Mayer Gallery, Stuttgart, 1969; Los Angeles/County MA, 1969; Onnasch Gallery, 1973. **Group:** Martha Jackson Gallery, New Media— New Forms, I & II, 1960, 61; Stockholm/National, Art in Motion, 1961; MOMA, The Art of Assemblage, circ., 1961; Buffalo/Albright, Mixed Media and Pop Art, 1963; Oakland/AM, Pop Art USA, 1963; Hartford/Wadsworth, Black, White, and Gray, 1964; Smith College, Sight and Sound; Jewish Museum, Superlimited, 1969; Tate, Pop Art, 1969; SRGM, Eleven from the Reuben Gallery, 1965; Chicago/Contemporary, Art by Telephone, 1969; Berne, Art after Plans, 1969; Documenta V, Kassel, 1972; Rijksuniversiteit, Utrecht, Toeval,

1972. Theater Pieces: Fluxus International Festival, NYC, 1962–63; Smolin Gallery, NYC, Yam Festival: A Series of Events, 1963; Arman's Key Event, NYC, 1965. **Collections:** CNAC; MOMA; Monchengladbach. **Bibliography:** Alloway 5; Becker and Vostell; *Contemporanea;* Gerdts; Hansen; *Happening & Fluxus;* Hunter, ed.; Johnson, Ellen H.; Kaprow; Lippard, ed.; *Report;* Richie; Russell and Gablik; Sandler 1.

BREER, ROBERT C. b. September 20, 1926, Detroit, Mich. **Studied:** Stanford U., BA. Resided Paris, 1949–59. Traveled Japan, 1969, Europe. **Taught:** Cooper Union, 1972–; Film Study Center, Cambridge, Mass.; Hampshire College, Amherst, Mass., 1974–79; Hampshire College, 1974–79; NYU, 1977. **Commissions:** Expo 70, Osaka, Pepsi-Cola Pavilion, 1970. **Awards:** Stanford U., Annual Painting Award, 1949; Creative Film Foundation Awards, 1957–60; Bergamo, Diplome Speciale, 1962; Oberhausen Film Festival, Max Ernst Prize, 1969; Film Culture Award, 1973; CAPS, NYC, 1975; National Endowment for the Arts, grant, 1976; American Film Institute, grant, 1977; Guggenheim Foundation Fellowship, 1978–79. **Address:** 25 Shadyside, S. Nyack, NY 10960. **One-man Exhibitions:** (first) Palais des Beaux-Arts, Brussels, 1955; Galeria Bonino Ltd., NYC, 1965, 66, 67, 70; Galerie Rolf Ricke, 1968; J. L. Hudson Art Gallery, Detroit, 1972; Dag Hammarskjold Plaza, NYC, 1973; Michael Berger Gallery, Pittsburgh, 1974; IBM Plaza, Pittsburgh, 1974; MOMA (films); Buffalo/Albright, 1976; Collective for Living Cinema, NYC, 1977; Walker 1979; Millennium, NYC, 1979. **Retrospectives:** Montreux Film Festival, 1974; Film Forum, NYC, 1975; WMAA, 1977, 1980. **Group:** WGMA, The Popular Image, 1963; MOMA, 1963; ICA, Boston, 1965; Stockholm/National, 1965; U. of California, Berkeley, Directions in Kinetic Sculpture, 1966; Jewish Museum, 1967; VI International Art Biennial, San Marino (Europe), 1967; Experimental Film Festival, Brussels, 1967; A.F.A., 1968; MOMA, The Machine as Seen at the End of the Mechanical Age, 1968; UCLA, Electric Art, 1969; MOMA, New Media: New Methods, circ., 1969; Hayward Gallery, London, Kinetics, 1970; Buffalo/Albright, Kid Stuff, 1971; Yale U., Options and Alternatives, 1973; Cannes Film Festival, 1974; WMAA, 1977, 1980. Paris/Beaubourg, Paris–New York, 1977; Drawing Center, NYC, Drawings for Animated Film, 1978; Hayward Gallery, London, Film as Film, 1979; New York Film Festival, 1979; WMAA Biennial, 1979. **Collections:** Anthology Film Archives; CNAC; Cinematheque de Belgique; Cinematheque Francaise; Krefeld/Kaiser Wilhelm; MOMA; NYPL; Stockholm/National. **Bibliography:** *Art Now 74;* Battcock, ed.; Davis, D.; Hulten; *Options and Alternatives;* Rickey; Selz, P., 1; Tomkins. Archives.

BREININ, RAYMOND. b. November 30, 1910, Vitebsk, Russia. **Studied:** Chicago Academy of Fine Arts, with Uri Penn. **Taught:** Southern Illinois U.; U. of Minnesota; Breinin School of Art, Chicago; ASL. Costumes and settings for Ballet Theater's "Undertow." **Awards:** U. of Illinois; ART:USA:58, NYC, 1958; Chicago/AI, Watson F. Blair Prize, 1942; Chicago/AI, Norman Wait Harris Silver Medal, 1942; MMA, **P.P.,** 1942. **Address:** 121 Inwood Road, Scarsdale, NY 10583. **One-man Exhibitions:** (first) The Downtown Gallery, 1939, also 1943; Indiana U., 1942; Chicago/AI, 1942. **Group:** MOMA, Twelve Americans, circ., 1956; WMAA. **Collections:** AAAL; Boston/MFA; Britannica; Brooklyn Museum; Capehart Corp.; Chicago/AI; Cranbrook; Edinburgh/National; Harvard U.; U. of Illinois; Indianapolis/Herron; Eli Lilly & Co.; MMA; MOMA; Newark Museum; Phillips; SFMA; San Diego; Williams College;

Zanesville/AI. **Bibliography:** Baur 7; Frost; Genauer; Halpert; Miller, ed. 1. Archives.

BRICE, WILLIAM. b. April 23, 1921, NYC. **Studied:** ASL; Chouinard Art Institute, Los Angeles. Traveled England, Spain, Greece. **Taught:** Jepson Art Institute, Los Angeles; UCLA, 1953–. **Address:** 427 Beloit Street, Los Angeles, CA 90049. **Dealer:** Robert Miller Gallery, NYC. **One-man Exhibitions:** The Downtown Gallery, 1949; Frank Perls Gallery, 1952, 55, 56, 62; The Alan Gallery, NYC, 1955, 56, 64; Santa Barbara/MA, 1958; Felix Landau Gallery, 1966; U. of California, San Diego, 1967; Colorado Springs/FA, 1967; Dallas/MFA, 1967; SFMA, 1967; The Landau-Alan Gallery, NYC, 1968; Hancock College, Santa Maria, Calif., 1975; Orange Coast College, 1975; Charles Campbell Gallery, San Francisco, 1976; U. of Redlands, 1978; ICA, Los Angeles, 1978; Nicholas Wilder Gallery, Los Angeles, 1978; Robert Miller Gallery, NYC, 1980. **Group:** Santa Barbara/MA, 1945; WMAA, 1947, 50, 51; Los Angeles/County MA, 1947–50; Sao Paulo; Carnegie, 1948, 49, 54; U. of Illinois; MMA, 1952; MOMA, 1952, 56; Chicago/AI, 1952, 56; Paris/Moderne, 1954; California Palace, 1951, 52; SFMA; de Young; VMFA, 1966; Des Moines, 1967. **Collections:** AAAL; Andover/Phillips; Chicago/AI; U. of Illinois; Los Angeles/County MA; MMA; MOMA; U. of Nebraska; San Diego; Santa Barbara/MA; Stanford U.; Utica; WMAA; Wichita/AM. **Bibliography:** Pousette-Dart, ed. Archives.

BRIGGS, ERNEST. b. 1923, San Diego, Calif. **Studied:** California School of Fine Arts, with Clyfford Still, David Park, Mark Rothko. US Army, 1943–45. A cofounder of Metart Gallery, San Francisco, 1949. **Taught:** U. of Florida, 1958; Pratt Institute, 1961– ; Yale U., 1967–68. **Awards:** CSFA, Albert M. Bender Fellowship, 1951; SFMA, Anne Bremer Memorial Prize, 1953; CAPS, 1975. **Address:** 128 West 26th Street, NYC 10001. **Dealer:** Gruenebaum Gallery, NYC. **One-man Exhibitions:** (first) Metart Gallery, San Francisco, 1949; The Stable Gallery, NYC, 1954, 55; CSFA, 1956; The Howard Wise Gallery, NYC, 1960, 62, 63; Yale U., 1968; Alonzo Gallery, NYC, 1969; Green Mountain Gallery, 1973; Susan Caldwell, Inc., 1975; Aaron Berman Gallery, NYC, 1977; Cape Split Place, Addison, Me. **Group:** San Francisco Art Association Annuals, 1948, 49, 53; WMAA Annuals, 1955, 56, 61; California Palace, Five Bay Area Artists, 1953; MOMA, Twelve Americans, circ., 1956; Corcoran, 1961; Carnegie, 1961; Dallas/MFA, "1961," 1962; SFMA, 1962, 63; Jewish Museum, Large Scale American Painting, 1967; AAAL, 1969, 70; Oakland/AM, San Francisco, 1945–1950, 1973; SFMA, California Painting and Sculpture: The Modern Era, 1976; Huntsville, Bay Area Update, 1977. **Collections:** Brooklyn Museum; Carnegie; CIBA-Geigy Corp.; Housatonic Community College; Michigan State U.; Oakland/AM; Rockefeller Institute; SFMA; WMAA; Walker. **Bibliography:** McChesney; Sandler 1.

BRODERSON, MORRIS (Gaylord). b. November 4, 1928, Los Angeles, Calif. **Studied:** Pasadena Museum School; U. of Southern California, with Francis De Erdely; Jepson Art Institute, Los Angeles. Traveled Europe, Japan, India, Far East. **Awards:** Pasadena Museum School, Scholarship, 1943; Los Angeles/County MA, **P.P.,** *Art in America* (magazine), New Talent, 1959; Los Angeles Art Festival, 1961; Carnegie, 1961. **Address:** 1241 North Flores Street, #5, Los Angeles, CA 90069. **Dealers:** Ankrum Gallery; Staempfli Gallery. **One-man Exhibitions:** Dixi Hall Studio, Laguna Beach, Calif., 1954; Stanford U., 1958; Santa Barbara/MA, 1958; U. of California, Riverside, 1959; Bertha Lewinson Gallery, Los Angeles, 1959, 60; Ankrum Gallery, 1961, 62, 70, 79;

The Downtown Gallery, 1963, 66; Los Angeles/County MA, 1966, 68; San Diego, 1969; Staempfli Gallery, 1971. **Retrospective:** San Diego, 1969; U. of Arizona, 1975. **Group:** Santa Barbara/MA, 1958; Los Angeles/MA, 1958, 59; PAFA, 1959, 60; Ringling, 1960; WMAA, 1960; de Young, 1960; California Palace; San Diego, 1961; Carnegie, 1961, 62, 64, 67; U. of Illinois, 1963; NIAL, 1967; Hirshhorn, Inaugural Exhibition, 1974; AAAL, 1976; NAD, 1977; Springfield, Mass./MFA, Bicentennial, Watercolor, USA, 1976; Santa Barbara/MA, Images of the Mind, 1976; Minnesota/MA, Art and the Law, 1979. **Collections:** Boston/MFA; Container Corp. of America; de Young; Hirshhorn; Home Savings and Loan Association; Honolulu Academy; Kalamazoo/Institute; La Jolla; Los Angeles/County MA; NIAL; Palm Springs Desert Museum; The Pennsylvania State U.; Phoenix; SFMA; San Antonio/McNay; San Diego; Santa Barbara/MA; U. of South Florida; Stanford U.; U. of Texas; WMAA; Yale U. **Bibliography:** Weller.

BRODERSON, ROBERT M. b. July 6, 1920, West Haven, Conn. **Studied:** Duke U., 1947–50, AB; State U. of Iowa, 1952, MFA, with Mauricio Lasansky, James Lechay, Stuart Edie. US Air Force, 1941–45. Traveled Europe, USA. **Taught:** Duke U., 1957–64. **Awards:** AAAL, 1962, Childe Hassam Award, also **P.P.,** 1968; Ford Foundation, **P.P.,** 1962; Guggenheim Foundation Fellowship, 1964. **Address:** P.O. Box 190, Raleigh, NC 27602. **Dealer:** Terry Dintenfass, Inc. **One-man Exhibitions:** (first) Charlotte/Mint, 1951; Raleigh/NCMA, 1957, 60; Catherine Viviano Gallery, 1961, 1963–65; Terry Dintenfass, Inc., 1965–68; Harpur College, 1967, 68; Binghamton/SUNY, 1969. **Group:** Southwestern Annual, 1950, 54, 60; Corcoran Biennials, 1953, 57, 61; WMAA, 1961; U. of Illinois, 1963. **Collections:** Carnegie; Charlotte/Mint; Colorado Springs/FA; Des Moines; Hartford/Wadsworth; NIAL; Princeton U.; Raleigh/NCMA; WMAA.

BRODIE, GANDY. b. May 20, 1925, NYC; **d.** October 22, 1975, NYC. **Studied:** Art-history courses with Meyer Schapiro; self-taught as artist. Traveled Mexico, Europe. **Taught:** privately; Carnegie-Mellon U., 1969–70; U. of Pennsylvania, 1970–71; Elmira College. **Awards:** Mark Twain Contest ($1,000) 1959; Ingram Merrill Foundation Grant, 1961; Hollins College, Artist-in-Residence, 1968; State of Washington, Title III Cultural Enrichment Grant, 1969; National Council on the Arts; Guggenheim Foundation Fellowship, 1969. **One-man Exhibitions:** (first) Urban Gallery, NYC, 1954; Durlacher Brothers, NYC, 1955, 57, 59, 61, 63; Saidenberg Gallery, 1964; Obelisk Gallery, Boston, 1965; Richard Gray Gallery, 1966; The Zabriskie Gallery, 1967; Andover/Phillips; Windham College; Krasner Gallery, NYC, 1970; All Souls Church, Brattleboro, Vt., 1971; Williams College, 1972; Knoedler & Co., NYC, 1980. **Group:** WMAA, Recent Acquisitions, 1957; MOMA, 1957, 61; Phillips; Hirshhorn, Inaugural Exhibition, 1974. **Collections:** Andover/Phillips; Baltimore/MA; Charlotte/Mint; Hirshhorn; The Jewish Museum, NYC; MIT; MMA; MOMA; Norfolk/Chrysler; Phillips; Purchase/SUNY; Sarah Lawrence College; Syracuse/Everson; WMAA; Williams College.

BRONER, ROBERT. b. March 10, 1922, Detroit, Mich. **Studied:** Wayne State U., 1940–46, BFA, MA; UCLA, 1946–47; Society of Arts and Crafts, Detroit, 1942–45; Atelier 17, NYC, 1949–52, with S. W. Hayter; New School for Social Research, 1949–50, with Stuart Davis. **Taught:** City U. of New York, 1963–64; Society of Arts and Crafts, Detroit; Wayne State U., 1964–; Haystack Mountain School of Crafts, 1964, 66, 68, 70, 75, 80; U. of Haifa, 1975; Detroit Times, 1958–60 (art critic); *Art in America* magazine, 1958–63 (correspondent); *Craft Horizons* magazine, 1961–68 (correspondent); Birmingham *Eccentric,* 1962–63 (art critic); *Pictures on Exhibit* magazine, 1963–64 (reviewer); Manhattanville College, 1976–77; Parsons School of Design, NYC, 1977; Pratt Institute, 1978. **Member:** SAGA; Philadelphia Print Club; British Printmakers Council; President, The Print Council. **Awards:** Brooklyn Museum, Print Biennial, **P.P.**, 1964; Los Angeles Art Festival, Bronze Medal, 1948; Detroit/Institute, Michigan Artist, **P.P.**, 1961, 66; SAGA, 50th Annual Print Exhibition, $1,000 **P.P.**, 1969; Wayne State U., Faculty Research Fellowship, 1965, 69; Probus Club, Achievement Award ($500), 1969. **Address:** 5440 Cass Avenue, Detroit, MI 48202. **One-man Exhibitions:** (first) Anna Werbe Gallery, Detroit, 1953; Wellons Gallery, NYC, 1954; Philadelphia Art Alliance, 1956; Garelick's Gallery, Detroit, 1956, 61; Michigan State U., 1957; Drake Gallery, Carmel, Calif., 1960; Society of Arts and Crafts, Detroit, 1962; Feingarten Gallery, Los Angeles, 1961; Raven Gallery, Birmingham, Mich., 1963; The Ohio State U., 1969; J. L. Hudson Art Gallery, Detroit, 1971; Rina Gallery, NYC, 1973; Klein-Vogel Gallery, Royal Oak, Mich.; Delson-Richter Gallery, Tel Aviv, 1975; Troy Gallery, Mich., 1977; Manhattanville College, Purchase, N.Y., 1977. **Group:** MMA, American Watercolors, Drawings, and Prints, 1952; MOMA, Young American Printmakers, 1953; Brooklyn Museum, Print Biennials; USIA, circ., Europe, 1959–60 (prints); PCA, circ., Europe and France, 1959–60; PAFA, 1959, 60; Pasadena/AM, 1962; SAGA, 1962, 63; ICA, London; Salon du Mai, Paris, 1969; British International Print Biennials, 1968, 70, 72; MOMA, Pop Art Prints, Drawings, and Multiples, 1970; Paris/Moderne, La Jeune Gravure, 1970; Bibliotheque Nationale, L'Estampe Contemporaine, 1973; Walker, Printmakers, 1973. **Collections:** Bibliotheque Nationale; Boston Public Library; Brooklyn Museum; Chicago/AI; Cincinnati/AM; Detroit/Institute; Harvard U.; Jerusalem/National; Los Angeles/County MA; MMA; MOMA; NYPL; National Gallery; PAFA; PMA; SRGM; Smithsonian; Walker. **Bibliography:** Archives.

BROOK, ALEXANDER. b. July 14, 1898, Brooklyn, N.Y.; **d.** February 26, 1980, Sag Harbor, N.Y. **Studied:** ASL, 1913–17, with R. W. Johnson, Frank V. DuMont, George Bridgeman, Dimitri Romanovsky, Kenneth Hayes Miller. Assistant Director, Whitney Studio Club, NYC. **Commissions:** US Post Office, Washington, D.C. (mural). **Awards:** Chicago/AI, The Mr. & Mrs. Frank G. Logan Medal, 1929; Carnegie, Second Prize, 1930; PAFA, Joseph E. Temple Gold Medal, 1931; Guggenheim Foundation Fellowship, 1931; Carnegie, First Prize, 1939; Los Angeles/County MA, First Prize, 1934; Paris World's Fair, 1937, Gold Medal; SFMA, Medal of Award, 1938. **One-man Exhibitions:** ACA Gallery; Curt Valentine Gallery, NYC, 1930; The Downtown Gallery, 1934, 37; Dayton/AI, 1942; Rehn Galleries, 1947, 60; M. Knoedler & Co., NYC, 1952; Richard Larcada Gallery, 1969, 74. **Retrospective:** Chicago/AI, 1929. **Group:** U. of Rochester, 1937; Brooklyn Museum; Carnegie; MMA; Toledo/MA; Buffalo/Albright; Chicago/AI; Newark Museum. **Collections:** Boston/MFA; Britannica; Brooklyn Museum; Buffalo/Albright; California Palace; Carnegie; Chicago/AI; Columbus; Corcoran; Detroit/Institute; de Young; Hartford/Wadsworth; IBM; Kansas City/Nelson; MMA; MOMA; Michigan State U.; U. of Nebraska; Newark Museum; SFMA; St. Louis/City; Toledo/MA; WMAA. **Bibliography:** Baur 7; Bethers; Biddle 4; Boswell 1; **Brook;** Cahill and Barr, eds.; Cheney; Eliot; Flexner; Goodrich and Baur 1; Hall; *Index of 20th Century Artists;* **Jewell 1,** 2; Kent, N.; Mellquist; Mendelowitz; Pagano; Pearson 1; Pousette-Dart, ed.; Richardson, E.P.; *Woodstock.* Archives.

BROOKS, JAMES A. b. October 18, 1906, St. Louis, Mo. **Studied:** Southern Methodist U., 1923–25; Dallas Art Institute, 1925–26, with Martha Simkins; ASL, 1927–31, with Kimon Nicolaides, Boardman Robinson; privately with Wallace Harrison. Federal A.P.: 1937–42. US Army in Middle East,

1942–45. Traveled Italy. **Taught:** Columbia U., 1947–48; Pratt Institute, 1947–59; Yale U., 1955–60; American Academy, Rome, Artist-in-Residence, 1963; New College, Sarasota, Fla., 1965–67; Miami Beach (Fla.) Art Center, 1966; Queens College, 1966–67, 1968–69; U. of Pennsylvania, 1971, 72; Cooper Union, 1975. **Member:** Century Association; NIAL. **Commissions** (murals): Woodside, N.Y., Library; La Guardia Airport; US Post Office, Little Falls, N.Y. **Awards:** Carnegie, Fifth Prize, 1952; Chicago/AI, The Mr. & Mrs. Frank G. Logan Medal, 1957; Chicago/AI, Norman Wait Harris Silver Medal and Prize, 1961; Ford Foundation, **P.P.**, 1962; Guggenheim Foundation Fellowship, 1967–68. **Address:** 128 Neck Path, The Springs, East Hampton, NY 11937. **Dealer:** Gruenebaum Gallery, Ltd., NYC. **One-man Exhibitions:** The Peridot Gallery, 1950, also 1951–53; Grace Borgenicht Gallery, Inc., 1954; The Stable Gallery, 1957, 59; The Kootz Gallery, NYC, 1961, 62; Philadelphia Art Alliance, 1966; Martha Jackson Gallery, 1968, 71, 73, 75; The Berenson Gallery, 1969; Gruenebaum Gallery, Ltd., NYC 1979. **Retrospectives:** WMAA, circ., 1963–64; Dallas/MFA, 1972; Finch College, NYC, circ., 1975. **Group:** WMAA Annuals from the 1950s; Galerie de France, American Vanguard, 1952; Carnegie, 1952, 55, 58, 61; SRGM, Younger American Painters, 1954; WMAA, The New Decade, 1954–55; MOMA, Twelve Americans, circ., 1956; IV Sao Paulo Biennial, 1957; MOMA, The New American Painting, circ., Europe, 1958–59; Documenta II, Kassel, 1959; II Inter-American Paintings and Prints Biennial, Mexico City, 1960; SRGM, Abstract Expressionists and Imagists, 1961; Seattle World's Fair, 1962; Cleveland/MA, 1963; SFMA, 1963; Tate, Dunn International, 1964; MOMA, The New American Painting and Sculpture, 1969; WMAA Annuals, 1970, 72; U. of Illinois, 1971; Ball State U., Collages by American Artists, 1971; Cranbrook, Drawings by Contemporary American Artists, 1975; Corcoran Biennial, 1975. **Collections:** Boston/MFA; Brandeis U.; Brooklyn Museum; Buffalo/Albright; U. of California, Berkeley; Carnegie; Chase Manhattan Bank; Chicago/AI; Ciba-Geigy Corp.; The Coca-Cola Co.; Dallas/MFA; Detroit/Institute; Fordham U.; Hartford/Wadsworth; Houston/MFA; U. of Illinois; International Minerals & Chemicals Corp.; MMA; MOMA; U. of Michigan; Miles Metal Corp.; NYU; U. of Nebraska; Owens-Corning Fiberglas Corp.; PAFA; Pepsi-Cola Co.; Philip Morris; Rockefeller U.; SRGM; The Singer Company Inc.; Southern Methodist U.; Tate; U. of Texas; Toledo/MA; Tulsa/Philbrook; Union Carbide Corp.; Utica; VMFA; WMAA; Walker; Yale U. **Bibliography:** Chaet; Flanagan; Goodrich and Baur 1; Haftman; Hess, T. B., 1; **Hunter** 1, 3, 6; Hunter, ed.; McCurdy, ed.; *Metro;* Motherwell and Reinhardt, eds.; Ponente; Pousette-Dart, ed.; Ritchie 1; Rodman 2; Sandler. Archives.

BROWN, JOAN. b. 1938, San Francisco, Calif. **Studied:** California School of Fine Arts, 1955; With Elmer Bischoff, Frank Lobdell, Sonia Gechtoff, Richard Diebenkorn, Manual Neri, Robert Howard, 1957–62. **Taught:** Raymond Wilkins High School, San Francisco, 1959; SFAI, 1961–. **Awards:** SFAI, Adaline Kent Award, 1973; National Endowment for the Arts, Grant, 1976. **Address:** 37 Cameo Way, San Francisco, CA **Dealer:** Allan Frumkin Gallery. **One-man Exhibitions:** Spasta Gallery, San Francisco, 1958; Staempfli Gallery, 1960 (two-man), 1961, 64; Batman Gallery, San Francisco, 1961; Ferus Gallery, Los Angeles, 1962; Hanson-Fuller Gallery, 1968; Lawson Galleries, San Francisco, 1970; SFMA, 1971; SFAI, 1973; Charles Campbell Gallery, San Francisco, 1974, 75; U. of California, Berkeley, 1974; Allan Frumkin Gallery, NYC, 1974, 76, 79; Allan Frumkin Gallery, Chicago, 1975–77; Clarke-Benton Gallery, Santa Fe, 1977; Re: Vision Gallery, Santa Monica, 1976; Wadsworth/

Hartford, 1977; U. of Akron, 1977; San Jose/MA, 1979; Newport Harbor, 1978. **Retrospective:** U. of California, Berkeley, 1974. **Group:** Oakland/AM; RAC; SFMA; PAFA; SFAI; Drawing Invitational, 1969; WMAA, 1972; Mt. Holyoke College, Art as a Muscular Principle, 1975; WMAA Biennial, 1977; New Museum, NYC, Bad Painting Show, 1978; U. of North Carolina, Art on Paper, 1978; American Foundation for the Arts, Miami, Story-Telling Art, 1979; PAFA, Seven on the Figure, 1979. **Collections:** Buffalo/Albright; U. of California; U. of Colorado; Los Angeles/County MA; Miami-Dade College; MOMA; Oakland/AM; Sacramento/Crocker; SFMA; WMAA; Williams College. **Bibliography:** *Art as a Muscular Principle; Art: A Woman's Sensibility;* McChesney; Lucie-Smith; Richardson, B., 1; Selz, P., 2. Archives.

BROWN, ROGER. b. December 10, 1941, Hamilton, Alabama. **Studied:** American Academy of Art, Chicago, 1964; Chicago Art Institute School, BFA and MFA, 1970. **Awards:** Renaissance Prize, Chicago/AI, 1969; Walter Campana prize, 1971, Chicago/AI. **Address:** 1926 N. Halsted, Chicago, IL. **Dealer:** Phyllis Kind Gallery, NYC, Chicago. **One-man Exhibitions:** Phyllis Kind Gallery, Chicago, 1971, 73, 74, 76, 77, 80; Phyllis Kind Gallery, NYC, 1975, 77, 79; PAFA, 1974; Darthea Speyer Gallery, Paris, 1974. **Group:** Chicago/Contemporary, Don Baum Sez, "Chicago Needs Famous Artists," 1969; ICA, U. of Pennsylvania, Spirit of the Comics, 1969; Chicago/Contemporary, Chicago Imagist Art, 1972; WMAA Biennials, 1973, 79; Sao Paulo Biennial, 1974; Chicago Art Institute School, Former Famous Alumni, 1976; Sacramento/Crocker, The Chicago Connection, 1977; U. of Texas, Austin, New In the Seventies, 1977; Buffalo/Albright, American Painting in the 1970s, 1978; Tyler School of Art, Philadelphia, Intricate Structure/Repeated Image, 1979. **Collections:** Akron/AI; Atlantic Richfield Co.; AT&T; Blue Cross of Southern California; Chicago/AI; Chicago/Contemporary; Museum des 20. Jahrhunderts; MOMA; NCFA; Rotterdam; WMAA. **Bibliography:** *The Chicago Connection; New in the Seventies.*

Roger Brown   *Capitol City*   1978

BROWN, WILLIAM, THEO. b. April 7, 1919, Moline, Ill. **Studied:** Yale U., 1941, BA; U. of California, Berkeley, 1952, MA. Traveled Europe. **Taught:** U. of California, Berkeley and Davis; California School of Fine Arts. **Address:** 1151 Keeler, Berkeley, CA 94708. **One-man Exhibitions:** SFMA, 1957; Felix Landau Gallery, 1958, 60, 63, 65, 67, 71; Barone Gallery, NYC, 1961; The Kornblee Gallery, 1962; Esther Baer Gallery, 1964 (two-man, with Paul Wonner); Hollis Gallery, San Francisco, 1965; Sacramento/Crocker, 1965; The Landau/Alan Gallery, NYC, 1968. **Group:** Oakland/AM, Annuals, 1952–58; RAC Annuals, 1952–58; SFMA Annuals, 1952–58; Minneapolis/Institute, American Painting, 1945–57, 1957; Oakland/AM, Contemporary Bay Area Figurative Painting, 1957; Santa Barbara/MA, II & III Pacific Coast Biennials, 1957, 59; SFMA, West Coast Artists, circ., 1957, 59; California Palace, 1959; The Zabriskie Gallery, East–West, 1960; U. of New Mexico, circ., 1964–67; Louisville/Speed, 1965; VMFA, 1966; U. of Illinois, 1969. **Collections:** California Palace; Capitol Records, Inc.; Commerce Trust Co., Kansas City, Mo.; Davenport/Municipal; U. of Kansas; U. of Nebraska; Oakland/AM; Reader's Digest; SFMA. **Bibliography:** Archives.

BROWNE, BYRON. b. 1907, Yonkers, N.Y.; **d.** December 25, 1961. **Studied:** NAD, 1924–28, with C. W. Hawthorne, Ivan Olinsky. **Taught:** ASL, 1948–61. Charter Member, American Abstract Artists. **Awards:** U. of Illinois, **P.P.**; PAFA, **P.P.**; NAD, Hallgarten Prize, 1928; La Tausca Competition, Third Prize. **One-man Exhibitions:** (first) New School for Social Research, 1936, also 1937; Artists' Gallery, NYC, 1939; The Pinacotheca, NYC, 1943, 44; The Kootz Gallery, NYC, 1946–48; Grand Central, NYC, 1949, 50, 53; Grand Central Moderns, NYC, 1950, 51, 52, 54, 55, 57, 58, 61, 62; Syracuse U., 1952; Tirca

Karlis Gallery, 1960; ASL, Memorial Exhibition, 1962; Washburn Gallery, Inc., 1975, 77. **Group:** Chicago/AI; Carnegie; WMAA; Corcoran; MOMA; MMA; ART: USA, NYC; U. of Illinois; PAFA. **Collections:** Brown U.; Dallas/MFA; U. of Georgia; NIAL; U. of Nebraska; Newark Museum; U. of Oklahoma; PAFA; Rio de Janeiro; Roswell; San Antonio/McNay; Tel Aviv; VMFA; WMAA; Youngstown/Butler. **Bibliography:** Baur 7; Blesh 1; Cheney; Janis; Kootz 2; Marter; Pousette-Dart, ed.; Ritchie 1. Archives.

BROWNING, COLLEEN. b. May 18, 1929, Fermoy, County Cork, Ireland. **Studied:** Privately, and U. of London, Slade School. Traveled the world extensively. **Taught:** City College of New York, 1962–75; NAD, 1978–80. Illustrated many children's books. **Member:** NAD; Carnegie, Edwin Austin Abbey Fellowship; Tupperware National Competition; Yaddo Fellowship; Los Angeles County Fair, 1956; Columbia, S.C./MA, Biennial, 1957; MacDowell Colony Fellowship. **Address:** 100 La Salle Street, NYC 10027. **Dealer:** Kennedy Gallery. **One-man Exhibitions:** Robert Isaacson Gallery, NYC; Little Gallery, London, 1949; Hewitt Gallery, NYC, 1951, 52, 54; J. Seligmann and Co., 1965, 67; Lehigh U., 1966; Lane Gallery, Los Angeles, 1968; Kennedy Gallery, 1968–72, 76, 79; Columbia S.C./MA, 1972; S.C. Museum, 1972; Columbus, Ga., 1972; Towson State College, Md., 1978. **Group:** A.F.A., 20th Century Realists; WMAA Annual; Chicago/AI; PAFA; NAD; NIAL; ART: USA, NYC; Walker; Carnegie; Festival of Two Worlds, Spoleto; Youngstown/Butler; Brandeis U.; U. of Rochester; U. of Illinois. **Collections:** California Palace; Columbia, S.C./MA; Corcoran; Detroit/Institute; U. of Miami; Milwaukee; NAD; New York State Museum, Albany; Randolph-Macon Woman's College; U. of Rochester; St. Louis/City; Wichita/AM; Williams College; Youngstown/Butler.

BRUCE, PATRICK HENRY. b. April 2, 1880, Long Island, Va.; **d.** November 12, 1937, NYC. **Studied:** Richmond (Va.) Art School; New York School of Art, with Robert Henri, W.M. Chase, 1901–03; with Henri Matisse in Paris, 1909. Traveled Europe; resided Paris, 1904–36. **One-man Exhibitions:** Rose Fried Gallery (three-man), 1950; Coe Kerr Gallery, 1970; Washburn Gallery, Inc., NYC, 1980. **Retrospective:** MOMA, 1979. **Group:** Salon d'Automne, Paris, 1907–10; The Armory Show, 1913; Herbstsalon, 1913; Montross Gallery, NYC, 1916, 17; Societe Anonyme, 1920; Worcester, Mass., 1921; MacDowell Club, NYC, 1922; Vassar College, 1923; WMAA, The Decade of the Armory Show, 1963; U. of New Mexico, Cubism: Its Impact in the USA, 1967; Utica, Armory Show 50th Anniversary Exhibit, 1963; NAD; Hirshhorn, Inaugural Exhibition, 1974. **Collections:** U. of Nebraska; Yale U. **Bibliography:** *Avant-Garde Painting and Sculpture;* Baur 7; Brown 2; Dreier 2; Du Bois 1; Hunter 6; Levin 2; MacAgy 2; Ritchie 1; Rose, B., 1; Seuphor 1; Wright 2. Archives.

BULTMAN, FRITZ. b. April 4, 1919, New Orleans, La. **Studied:** Privately with Morris Graves, 1931; New Orleans Arts and Crafts School; Munich Preparatory School; New Bauhaus, Chicago, 1937–38; Hofmann School, NYC and Provincetown, 1938–41. **Taught:** Pratt Institute, 1958–63; Hunter College, 1959–64; Fine Arts Work Center, Provincetown, Mass., 1968–72. **Awards:** Italian Government Scholarship, 1950; Fulbright Fellowship, 1951, 1964–65 (Paris); Guggenheim Foundation Fellowship, 1975. **Address:** 176 East 95th Street, NYC 10028. **One-man Exhibitions:** (first) Hugo Gallery, NYC, 1947, also 1950; The Kootz Gallery, NYC, 1952; The Stable Gallery, NYC, 1958; Martha Jackson Gallery, 1959, 73, 74, 76; New Orleans/Delgado, 1959, 74; Galerie Stadler, Paris, 1960; Michel Warren Gallery, NYC, 1960; Gallery Mayer, NYC, 1960; Tibor de Nagy Gallery, 1963, 64; Oklahoma, 1974; Newport (R.I.) Art Association, 1974; Long Point Gallery, Provincetown, Mass., 1977, 78, 79. **Group:** WMAA, 1950, 53; Chicago/AI; MOMA, Hans Hofmann and His Students, circ., 1963–64; IIE, 20 American Fulbright Artists, 1975. **Collections:** Brandeis U.; Ciba-Geigy Corp.; Grinnell College; Gutai Museum, Osaka; McCrory Corp.; U. of Minnesota; U. of Nebraska; New Orleans/Delgado; Norfolk/Chrysler; Union Carbide; U. of Texas; Tougaloo College; WMAA; Williams College. **Bibliography:** Pousette-Dart, ed. Archives.

BUNCE, LOUIS. b. August 13, 1907, Lander, Wyo. **Studied:** Portland (Ore.) Museum School, 1925–26; ASL, 1927–30, with Boardman Robinson, William Von Schlegell. Traveled USA, Mexico, Europe extensively. **Taught:** Salem (Ore.) Art Museum, 1937–38; Portland (Ore.) Museum School; U. of California, Berkeley; U. of British Columbia; U. of Washington; U. of Illinois; U. of Oregon, Federal A.P.: Mural Division, NYC, 1940–41. **Commissions:** Federal Building, Grants Pass, Ore., 1936–37 (mural); Portland (Ore.) International Airport 1958 (mural); Portland (Ore.) Hilton Hotel, 1963 (637 serigraphs). **Awards:** Seattle/AM, **P.P.,** 1936, 62; Northwest Printmakers Annual, 1948; U. of Washington, **P.P.,** 1950; Portland, Ore./AM, **P.P.,** 1952; SFMA, Emanuel Walter Bequest and Purchase Award, 1961; Ford Foundation, **P.P.,** 1964; Tamarind Fellowship. **Address:** 1800 S.E. Harold Street, Portland, OR 97202. **Dealers:** Fountain Gallery; Gordon Woodside Gallery; Comara Gallery. **One-man Exhibitions:** Seattle/AM, 1936, 53; Washburn U. of Topeka, 1937; Hollins College, 1941, 58; Portland, Ore./AM, 1945, 47, 56; U. of Washington, 1947; Harvey Welch Gallery, Portland, Ore., 1947; National Serigraph Society, NYC, 1947; Reed College, 1947, 51; Wilmette U., 1948; Santa Barbara/MA, 1948; Kharouba Gallery, Portland, Ore., 1950, 52; Cincinnati/AM, 1952; John Heller Gallery, NYC, 1953; Grants Pass (Ore.) Art League, 1953, 54; Salem (Ore.) Art Association, 1955; Morrison Street Gallery, Portland, Ore., 1955; Doris Meltzer Gallery, NYC, 1956, 57, 59, 60; Artists Gallery, Seattle, 1958; U. of California, Berkeley, 1960; Fountain Gallery, 1962, 64, 66, 72; Comara Gallery, 1964; Gordon Woodside Gallery, 1964; U. of Illinois, 1967. **Retrospective:** Portland, Ore./AM, 1955. **Group:** Golden Gate International Exposition, San Francisco, 1939; New York World's Fair, 1939; Chicago/AI, Abstract and Surrealist Art, 1948; Worcester/AM, 1949; MMA, American Paintings Today, 1950; Colorado Springs/FA, Artists West of the Mississippi, 1951, 53, 56, 59; WMAA Annuals, 1951, 53, 54, 59, 60; Corcoran, 1953; U. of Colorado, 1953; Los Angeles/County MA, 1953; VMFA, 1954; Des Moines, 1954; U. of Nebraska, 1954, 57; Carnegie Annual, 1955; Sao Paulo, 1955, 56; Denver/AM Annuals, 1955, 56, 59, 62; Santa Barbara/MA, 1957; PAFA, 1958; Detroit/Institute, 1958; Stanford U., Fresh Point, 1958; Grand Rapids, 1961; Seattle World's Fair, 1962. **Collections:** AAAL; American Association of University Women; Auburn U.; Colorado Springs/FA; Hollins College; Library of Congress; MMA; U. of Michigan; National Gallery; PMA; Portland, Ore./AM; Reed College; SFMA; Seattle/AM; Springfield, Mo./AM; US State Department; Utica; WMAA; U. of Washington; Youngstown/Butler. **Bibliography:** Art of the Pacific Northwest; **Bunce.**

BURCHFIELD, CHARLES. b. April 9, 1893, Ashtabula Harbor, Ohio; **d.** January 10, 1967, West Seneca, N.Y. **Studied:** Cleveland Institute of Art, 1912, with Henry G. Keller, F. N. Wilcox, William J. Eastman; NAD. US Army, 1918–19. **Taught:** U. of Minnesota, Duluth, 1949; Art Institute of Buffalo, 1949–52; Ohio U., summer, 1950; U. of Buffalo, summers, 1950, 51; Buffalo Fine Arts School, 1951–52. **Member:** American Academy of Arts and Sciences: NIAL; NAD. **Commissions:** Fortune magazine, 1936, 37. **Awards:** Cleveland/MA, First Prize and Penton Medal, 1921; PAFA, Jennie Sesnan Gold Medal, 1929; Carnegie, Second Prize, 1935; International Arts Festival, Newport, R.I., First Prize, 1936; PAFA, Dana Watercolor Medal, 1940; Chicago/AI, Watson F. Blair Prize, 1941; NIAL, Award of Merit Medal, 1942; U. of Buffalo, Chancellor's Medal, 1944; Carnegie, Second Hon. Men., 1946; PAFA, Dawson Memorial Medal, 1947, Special Award, 1950; MMA, 1952 ($500); Buffalo/Albright, J. C. Evans Memorial Prize, 1952; Buffalo/Albright, Satter's Prize, 1955; Buffalo Historical Society, Red Jacket Medal, 1958; Hon. LHD, Kenyon College, 1944; Hon. DFA, Harvard U., 1948; Hon. DFA, Hamilton College, 1948; Hon. LLD, Valparaiso U., 1951. **One-man Exhibitions:** (first) Sunwise Turn Bookshop, NYC, 1916; Cleveland Institute of Art, 1916, 17, 21, 44; Laukhuff's Bookstore, Cleveland, 1918; Garrick Theater Library, NYC, 1919; Little Theatre, Cleveland, 1919; H. Kevorkian, NYC, 1920; Chicago/AI, 1921; Grosvenor (Gallery), London, 1923; Montross Gallery, NYC, 1924, 26, 28; Eastman-Bolton Co., Cleveland, 1928; Rehn Galleries, 1930, 31, 34–36, 39, 41, 43, 46, 47, 50, 52, 54–64, 66, 71, 73; U. of Rochester, 1932; Phillips, 1934; Philadelphia Art Alliance, 1937; Town and Country Gallery, Cleveland, 1948; MOMA, 1954; Buffalo/SUNY, 1963, 71; Cleveland/MA, 1966; Danenberg Gallery, NYC, 1972; Kennedy Gallery, NYC, 1974, 75, 76, 77, 78, 79; Smithsonian, circ., 1978; Valparaiso U., 1976. **Retrospectives:** Carnegie, 1938; Buffalo/Albright, 1944, 63; Cleveland/MA, 1953 (drawings); WMAA, 1956; AAAL, 1968. **Group:** WMAA Annuals; Chicago/AI; U. of Illinois; MOMA; MMA; Carnegie. **Collections:** Boston/MFA; Brooklyn Museum; Buffalo/Albright; Carnegie, Chase Manhattan Bank; Chicago/AI; Cleveland/MA; Detroit/Institute; Harvard U.; IBM; U. of Illinois;

Charles Burchfield *Cicada Woods*

Indianapolis/Herron; Kalamazoo/Institute; Kansas City/Nelson; MMA; MOMA; Muskegon/Hackley; Newark Museum; New Britain; PAFA; Phillips; RISD; St. Louis/City; San Diego; Santa Barbara/MA; Sweet Briar College; Syracuse/Everson; Terre Haute/Swope; Utica; VMFA; Valparaiso U.; WMAA; Wichita/AM; Wilmington; Youngstown/Butler. **Bibliography:** Barr 3; **Baur 1, 7;** Bazin; Beam; Blesh 1; Boswell 1; Brown; **Burchfield 1, 2, 3;** Chaill and Barr, eds.; Canaday; *Celebrate Ohio;* Cheney; Christensen; Craven 1, 2; **The Drawings of Charles E. Burchfield;** *8 American Masters of Watercolor;* Eliot; Flanagan; Flexner; Gallatin 1; Goodrich 1, Goodrich and Baur 1; Haftman; Hall; Hunter 6; *Index of 20th Century Artists;* Jewell 2; **Jones, ed.;** Lee and Burchwood; McCurdy, ed.; Mellquist; Mendelowitz; Newmeyer; Nordness, ed.; Pagano; Pearson 1; Phillips 1; Poore; Pousette-Dart, ed.; Richardson, E. P.; Ringel, ed.; Rose, B. 1, 4; Sachs; Soby 5; Sutton; Watson, E. W., 1; Weller; Wight 2. Archives

BURKHARDT, HANS GUSTAV. b. December 20, 1904, Basel, Switzerland. To USA, 1924. **Studied:** Cooper Union, 1924–25; Grand Central School, NYC, 1928–29, with Arshile Gorky, and privately with Gorky, 1930–35. Resided Mexico, 1950–52. Traveled Europe, Mexico, USA. **Taught:** Long Beach State College, summer, 1959; U. of Southern California, 1959–60; UCLA, 1962–63; California Institute of the Arts, 1962–64; Laguna Beach (Calif.) School of Art and Design, 1962–64; San Fernando Valley State College, 1963–73; Otis Art Institute, summer, 1963; California State U., Northridge, 1973. **Member:** Artists Equity. **Awards:** Los

Angeles/County MA, First **P.P.**, 1946; California State Fair, **P.P.**, 1954, Second Prize, 1962; Santa Barbara/MA, Ala Story Purchase Fund, 1957; Los Angeles All-City Show, **P.P.**, 1957, 60, 61; California Watercolor Society, **P.P.**, 1962. **Address:** 1914 Jewett Drive, Los Angeles, CA 90046. **Dealer:** Robert Schoelkopf Gallery, NYC; Jack Rutberg Fine Arts, L.A. **One-man Exhibitions:** (first) Stendahl Gallery, Los Angeles, 1939; Open Circle Gallery, 1943, 44; Chabot Gallery, Los Angeles, 1946, 47, 49; Los Angeles/County MA, 1946, 62; U. of Oregon, 1947; Hall of Art, Beverly Hills, 1948; Guadalajara, 1951; Fraymont Gallery, Los Angeles, 1951, 52; Paul Kantor Gallery, Beverly Hills, 1953; Escuela de Bellas Artes, San Miguel de Allende, Mexico, 1956, 61; Esther Robles Gallery, 1957–59; Comara Gallery, 1959; Long Beach State College, 1959; Glendale (Calif.) Public Gallery, 1960; Whittier (Calif.) Art Association, 1960; SFMA, 1961; Ankrum Gallery, 1961, 63; La Jolla, 1962; Fresno Art Center, 1962; Palm Springs Desert Museum, 1964, 79; Freie Schule, Basel, Switzerland, 1965; San Fernando Valley State College, 1965; Bay City Jewish Community Center, San Francisco, 1966; Laguna Beach (Calif.) Art Gallery, 1966; San Diego, 1968; Michael Smith Gallery, Los Angeles, 1972; Four Oaks Gallery, South Pasadena, 1972; Moorpark College, 1974; California State U., Northridge, 1975; Santa Barbara/MA, 1977; Laguna Beach Museum of Art, 1978; Cerro Coso Community College, 1978; San Fernando Mission College, 1978; Robert Schoelkopf Gallery, NYC, 1979. **Retrospective:** Falk-Raboff Gallery, Los Angeles, 1954; Pasadena/AM (10-year), 1957; Santa Barbara/MA (30-year), 1961; San Diego (40-year), 1966; Long Beach/MA, 1972; California State U., Northridge, 1973, 75; Pasquale Iannetti Assoc., San Francisco, 1977. **Group:** Los Angeles/County MA Annuals, 1940, 45, 46, 53, 54, 57, 59; Los Angeles Art Association Annuals, 1940–63; Corcoran, 1947, 51, 53; Denver/AM, 1949, 53, 54; U. of Illinois,

1951; MMA, 1951; PAFA, 1951–53; WMAA Annuals, 1951, 55, 58; III Sao Paulo Biennial, 1955; Long Beach/MA, 1958, 60, 64; Kunsthalle, Basel, 1966; Trinity U., San Antonio, Tex., 1967; ICA, Los Angeles, 1974; Los Angeles Municipal Art Gallery, 1975. **Collections:** Basel; California State U., Northridge; The Coca-Cola Co.; Columbia, S.C./MA; Corcoran; Downey Museum; Grunewald Foundation; Guadalajara; Hirshhorn; Home Savings and Loan Association; La Jolla; Long Beach/MA; Los Angeles/County MA; Lucerne; U. of Miami; Moorpark College; Norton Smith Museum (Pasadena); Omaha/Joslyn; Pasadena/AM; Portland, Ore./AM; San Diego; Santa Barbara/MA; SRGM; State of California; Stockholm/National. **Bibliography:** Archives.

BURLIN, PAUL. b. September 10, 1886, NYC; **d.** March 13, 1969, NYC. Self-taught in art. Traveled Europe, North Africa, USA; resided Paris, 1921–32. **Taught:** U. of Minnesota, 1949; Washington U., 1949–54; U. of Colorado, 1951; U. of Wyoming, 1952; UCLA, 1954; Union College (N.Y.), 1954–55; Chicago Art Institute School, 1960. Federal A.P.: Easel painting. **Awards:** Portrait of America, First Prize ($2,500), 1945; ART: USA:59, NYC, First Prize, 1959; Chicago/AI, Watson F. Blair Prize ($2,000), 1960; PAFA, J. Henry Schiedt Memorial Prize, 1963. **One-man Exhibitions:** (first) The Daniel Gallery, NYC, 1913, also 1914–20; Kraushaar Galleries, 1926, 27; Westheim Gallery, Berlin, 1927; de Hauke Gallery, NYC, 1942; Vincent Price Gallery, Los Angeles, 1944; The Downtown Gallery, 1946, 49, 52, 53; U. of Minnesota, 1949; Southern Illinois U., 1950, 60; U. of Wyoming, 1952; Washington U., circ., 1954; The Stable Gallery, 1954; Poindexter Gallery, 1958, 59; The Alan Gallery, NYC, 1959; Chicago/AI, 1960; Holland-Goldowsky Gallery, Chicago, 1960; Grace Borgenicht Gallery, Inc., 1963–66, 1970, 71, 73, 75; Boston U., 1964. **Retrospective:** A.F.A., circ.,

1962. **Group:** The Armory Show, 1913; WMAA Annuals; Carnegie; PAFA; WMAA, Pioneers of American Art, 1946; Walker; Corcoran; U. of Nebraska; nationally since 1913. **Collections:** Auburn U.; Britannica; Brooklyn Museum; Carleton College; Exeter; Hartford/Wadsworth; IBM; S. C. Johnson & Son, Inc.; MOMA; U. of Minnesota; Newark Museum; Southern Illinois U.; Tel Aviv; WMAA; Washington U.; Wichita/AM. **Bibliography:** Baur 7; Biddle 4; Cheney; Coke 2; Genauer; Goodrich and Baur 1; Kootz 2; Nordness, ed.; Pagano; Passloff; Pearson 1, 2; Pousette-Dart, ed.; Richardson, E. P.; Rose, B., 1; *Woodstock: An American Art Colony 1902–1977:* Zaidenberg, ed. Archives.

BURLIUK, DAVID. b. July 22, 1882, Kharkov, Ukraine; **d.** January 15, 1967, Southampton, N.Y. **Studied:** Art schools in Kazan, 1898–1902, Odessa, 1911, Munich, Moscow, 1914; Bayerische Akademie der Schonen Kunst, Munich; Academie des Beaux-Arts, Paris. To USA, 1922; citizen, 1930. Traveled Europe, the Orient, USA. **Taught:** Painting, art history. Federal A.P.: Easel painting. A founder (with W. Mayakovsky and W. Kamiensky) of Futurist art movement in Russia, 1911. A founder-member of Der Blaue Reiter and Der Sturm groups, 1910–14. Cofounder (1930) and publisher (with Marussia Burliuk) of art magazine *Color Rhyme.* Owned and operated Burliuk Gallery, Hampton Bays, N.Y. **Awards:** Pepsi-Cola, 1946. **One-man Exhibitions:** (first) Cherson, South Russia, 1904; galleries in Moscow and St. Petersburg, 1907; Societe Anonyme, NYC, 1924; J. B. Neumann Gallery, NYC, 1927; Morton Gallery, NYC, 1928; California Palace, 1931; Dorothy Paris Gallery, NYC, 1933–35; Boyer Gallery, NYC, 1935–39; Phillips, 1937; ACA Gallery, 1941–50, 1952–54, 1956, 58, 60, 63, 67, 69; Havana/Nacional, 1955; Galerie Maeght, Der Blaue Reiter, 1962; Galerie

Stangl, Munich, 1962; Leonard Hutton Gallery, NYC, Der Blaue Reiter, 1963; Parrish Museum, Southampton, N.Y., 1978. **Group:** Brooklyn Museum, 1923, 26; PMA, 1962. **Collections:** Boston/MFA; Brooklyn Museum; MMA; Phillips; WMAA; Yale U. **Bibliography:** Baur 7; **Dreier 1;** Richardson, E.P.; Selz, P., 3; Soyer, R., 1. Archives.

BURTON, SCOTT. b. June 23, 1939, Greensboro, Ala. **Studied:** Columbia U., 1962, BA magna cum laude, with Trilling, Dupee, Marcus; NYU, 1963, MA; private studies 1957–60 with Leon Berkowitz, Washington, D.C., and Hans Hofmann, Provincetown, Mass. **Taught:** School of Visual Art, NYC, 1967–72; U. of North Carolina, 1976. Performance Artist & Sculptor, 1970–80. **Awards:** PBK; Woodrow Wilson Fellowship; National Endowment for the Arts, grant, 1973, 75, 79; CAPS, 1975; L. C. Tiffany Grant, 1980. **Address:** 86 Thompson Street, NYC 10012. **Dealer:** Max Protetch Gallery, NYC and Washington, D.C.; Lisson Gallery, London. **One-man Exhibition:** (first) Artists Space, NYC, 1975; Finch College, NYC, 1971; WMAA, 1972; SRGM, 1976; Droll/Kolbert Gallery, NYC, 1977, 80; Brooks Jackson Gallery Iolas, NYC, 1978; Max Protetch Gallery, Washington, D.C., 1979; U. of California, 1980; Weinberg Gallery, San Francisco, 1980. **Group:** U. of Iowa, Two Evenings, 1970; Hartford/Wadsworth, Four Theater Pieces, 1970; Oberlin College, Festival of Contemporary Arts, 1973; Akademie der Kunst, Berlin, So Ho, 1976; Documenta 6, Kassel, 1977; Chicago/Contemporary, performance week, 1977; ICA, U. of Pennsylvania, Improbable Furniture, 1977; SRGM, Young American Artists, 1978; Purchase/SUNY, Ten Artists/Artists Space, 1979; Detroit/Institute, Image and Object in Contemporary Sculpture, 1979. **Collections:** U. of California; Detroit/Institute; La Jolla; SRGM. **Bibliography:** Pincus-Witten.

BUTTON, JOHN. b. 1929, San Francisco. **Studied:** U. of California, Berkeley, 1947–50; California School of Fine Arts, 1949–50; U. of Caifornia Medical Center, San Francisco; and with Altina Barrett and Willard Cummings. **Taught:** Skowhegan School, 1964, 65; School of Visual Arts, NYC, 1965–67, 70–73, 74; Cornell U., 1967–68; Swarthmore College, 1969–70; U. of Pennsylvania, 1975–77. **Awards:** Artists of Los Angeles County, prize, 1952; Silvermine Guild Prize, 1964; Ingram Merrill Foundation, Grant, 1961, 69, 74. **Address:** 139 Prince Street, NYC 10012. **Dealer:** Fischbach Gallery, NYC. **One-man Exhibitions:** Tibor de Nagy Gallery, NYC, 1956, 57; The Kornblee Gallery, 1963, 65, 67, 68, 70, 72, 73; Franklin Siden Gallery, Detroit, 1967; J. L. Hudson Gallery, Detroit, 1970; Gallery of July & August, Woodstock, N.Y., 1976; Fischbach Gallery, NYC, 1978, 79. **Group:** U. of North Carolina, 1966; Vassar College, Realism Now, 1968; A.F.A., Painterly Realism, 1970; MOMA, Eight Landscape Painters, circ., 1972; Boston U., The American Landscape, 1972; School of Visual Arts, NYC, The Male Nude, 1973; Omaha-Joslyn, A Sense of Place, 1973; Hofstra U., The Male Nude, 1973; Indiana U., Contemporary Pastels and Watercolors. **Collections:** Amerada Hess Corp.; AT&T; Chase Manhattan Bank; Chicago/AI; Columbia U.; Commerce Bankshares, Kansas City; Debevoise, Plimpton, Lyons and Gates; First National City Bank; Hirshhorn; MOMA; U. of North Carolina; Port Authority of New York; R.J. Reynolds Inc.; Utah. **Bibliography:** *America 1976*; Arthur 1, 2; Downes, ed.

C

CADMUS, PAUL. b. December 17, 1904, NYC. **Studied:** NAD, 1919–26; ASL, 1929–31, with Joseph Pennell, Charles Locke. Traveled Europe, the Mediterranean. Federal. A.P.: Easel painting, 1934. Designed sets and costumes for Ballet Caravan, 1938. **Member:** Artists Equity; NAD; NIAL; SAGA. **Commissions** (mural): US Post Office, Richmond, Va, 1938. **Awards:** NIAL Grant, 1961; Norfolk, **P.P.,** 1967. **Address:** P.O. Box 1255, Weston, CT 06883. **Dealer:** The Midtown Galleries.

One-man Exhibitions: Midtown Galleries, NYC, 1937, 49, 76 (2), 78, 79; Baltimore/MA (three-man), 1942; The Print Cabinet, Ridgefield, Conn., 1978; Robert Samuel Gallery, NYC, 1979. **Retrospective:** The Midtown Galleries 1968. **Group:** MOMA; MMA; WMAA, 1934, 36, 37, 38, 40, 41, 45; Chicago/AI, 1935; Hartford/Wadsworth; Williams College; Golden Gate International Exposition, San Francisco, 1939; PAFA, 1941; Carnegie, 1944, 45; Corcoran; NPG, American Self-Portraits: 1970–

Paul Cadmus *Summer* 1979

1973, 1974. **Collections:** Andover/Phillips; Baltimore/MA; Cranbrook; Hartford/Wadsworth; Library of Congress; MMA; MOMA; Milwaukee; NCFA; Sweet Briar College; WMAA; Williams College. **Bibliography:** American Artists Congress, Inc., 3; American Artists Group, Inc., 3; Baur 7; Bazin; Boswell 1; Brown 2; Goodrich and Baur 1; Hall; **Johnson 3;** Kent, N.; McCurdy, ed.; Nordness, ed.; Pagano; Reese; Rose, B., 1. Archives.

CAESAR, DORIS. b. November 8, 1892, NYC; **d.** September 8, 1971. **Studied:** ASL; Archipenko School of Art; privately with Rudolph Belling. **Member:** Federation of Modern Painters and Sculptors; Sculptors Guild; Architectural League of New York; New York Society of Women Artists; National Association of Women Artists; Audubon Artists. **One-man Exhibitions:** Weyhe Gallery, 1933, 35, 37, 47, 53, 57, 59, 61, 64, 67, 69; Gallery Fifteen, NYC, 1940; Curt Valentine Gallery, NYC, 1943; Argent Gallery, NYC, 1948; Musée du Petit Palais, Paris, 1950; Katonah (N.Y.) Art Gallery, 1955; Margaret Brown Gallery, Boston, 1956; WMAA, 1959; Hartford/Wadsworth, 1960. **Group:** City of Philadelphia, Sculpture International, 1940–50; A.F.A., circ., 1953–54; MMA, 1955; New Burlington Galleries, London, 1956; I International Religious Art Biennial, Salzburg, 1958; WMAA, circ., 1959; Memphis/Brooks, 1960. **Collections:** Albion College; Andover/Phillips; Atlanta/AA; Busch-Reisinger Museum; La Casa del Libro; Cleveland/MA; Colby College; Colorado Springs/FA; Connecticut College; Dayton/AI; U. of Delaware; Father Judge Mission Seminary; Fort Worth; Grand Rapids; Hartford/Wadsworth; Harvard U.; Howard U.; Indiana U.; State U. of Iowa; Kansas City/Nelson; Memphis/Brooks; Minneapolis/Institute; U. of Minnesota; NYU; Newark Museum; PAFA; Pasadena/AM; Phoenix; Portland, Me./MA; Rockland/Farnsworth; St. Bernard's Church, Hazardville,

Conn.; St. John's Abbey, Collegeville, Minn.; Syracuse U.; Utica Public Library; WMAA; Williams College. **Bibliography:** Brumme; Bush 2; Goodrich and Baur 2.

CAJORI, CHARLES. b. March 9, 1921, Palo Alto, Calif. **Studied:** Colorado College, 1939–40, with Boardman Robinson; Cleveland Institute of Art, 1940–42; Columbia U., 1946–48, with John Heliker, Henry Poor; Skowhegan School, summers, 1947, 48. US Air Force, 1942–46. A co-organizer of the Tanager Gallery, NYC, 1952. Traveled Europe. **Taught:** College of Notre Dame of Maryland, 1950–56; American U., 1955–56; Cooper Union, 1956–; Philadelphia Museum School, 1956–57; U. of California, Berkeley, 1959–60; Pratt Institute, 1961–62; Cornell U., summers, 1961, 63; Yale U., 1963–64; U. of Washington, 1964; New York Studio School, 1964–; Queens College, 1965–. **Awards:** Fulbright Fellowship (Italy), 1952; Yale U., Distinction of Arts Award, 1959; Longview Foundation Grant, 1962; Ford Foundation, **P.P.,** 1962; NIAL, 1970; Childe Hassam Fund **P.P.,** 1975; NIAL; L. C. Tiffany Grant, NIAL, 1979. **Address:** Litchfield Road, Watertown, CT 06795. **Dealer:** Ingber Art Gallery. **One-man Exhibitions:** (first) Tanager Gallery, NYC 1956, also 1961; Watkins Gallery, Washington, D.C., 1956; The Bertha Schaefer Gallery, 1958; Oakland/AM, 1959; Cornell U., 1961; The Howard Wise Gallery, NYC, 1963; U. of Washington, 1964; Bennington College, 1969; Kirkland College, 1972; Landmark Gallery, Inc., NYC, 1974; Ingber Art Gallery Ltd., NYC, 1976; U. of Texas, Austin, 1976; Art Academy of Cincinnati, 1976; American U., Washington, D.C. 1977. **Group:** Walker, Vanguard, 1955; WMAA Annuals, 1957, 62; U. of Kentucky, 1957, 61; U. of Nebraska, 1958; Festival of Two Worlds, Spoleto, 1958; Corcoran, 1959; Brooklyn Museum, 1959; ICA, Boston, 100 Works on Paper, circ., Europe, 1959; MOMA, Abstract Watercolors and Drawings: USA, circ., Latin America and Europe, 1961–62; Chicago/AI, 1964; Santa Barbara/MA, 1964; U. of Texas, 1966, 68; U. of Washington, 1967; New School for Social Research, Protest and Hope, 1967, Humanist Tradition, 1968; MMA, Recent Acquisitions, 1979. **Collections:** Ciba-Geigy Corp.; Honolulu Academy Mfg. Co.; Kalamazoo/Institute; U. of Kentucky; Miami Univ.; MMA; NYU; Scovill Mfg. Co.; U. of Texas; WMAA; Wake Forest College; Walker, Wilmington.

CALCAGNO, LAWRENCE. b. March 23, 1913, San Francisco, Calif. US Air Force, 1941–45. **Studied:** California School of Fine Arts, 1947–50. Traveled Mexico, 1945–47; Europe North Africa, 1950–55; Peru, Yucatan. **Taught:** U. of Alabama, 1955–56; Buffalo/SUNY, 1956–58; U. of Illinois, 1958–59; NYU, 1960; Carnegie-Mellon U., 1965–68; Honolulu Academy School, 1968. **Member:** Artists Equity. **Awards:** Yaddo Fellowship, 1961–64, 1965–68; Ford Foundation Grant, 1965–68; MacDowell Colony Fellowship, 1965–68, 70, 72, 74. **Address:** Taos, NM 87571. **Dealer:** Yares Gallery, Scottsdale, Ariz.; Stables Gallery, Taos. **One-man Exhibitions:** (first) The Little Gallery, New Orleans, 1945; College of the Pacific, 1948; Lucien Labaudt Gallery, San Francisco, 1948, 54; Numero Galleria d'Arte, Florence, Italy, 1951–52; Galeria Clan, Madrid, 1955; Studio Paul Facchetti, Paris, 1955; Martha Jackson Gallery, 1955, 58, 60, 62; U. of Alabama, 1956; Howard College, 1956; Macon (Ga.) Art Association, 1956; Buffalo/Albright, 1956; Lima, Peru, 1957; U. of Illinois, 1959; Fairweather-Hardin Gallery, 1959; Philadelphia Art Alliance, 1960; New Arts Gallery, Houston, 1960; Mexico City U., 1961; Tirca Karlis Gallery, 1961, 62, 64; McRoberts & Tunnard Gallery, London, 1961; Galerie Kobenhavn, Denmark, 1962; Gallery 31, Birmingham, Ala., 1964; The Osborne Gallery, NYC, 1964; Carnegie, 1965; Houston/MFA, 1965; Franklin Siden

Gallery, Detroit, 1965, 66; Esther Robles Gallery, 1966; Meredith Long Galleries, Houston, Tex., 1968, 70, 72; U. of New Mexico, 1973; Yares Gallery, Scottsdale, 1975; Contemporary Art Center of Hawaii, Honolulu, 1976; Yares Gallery, Scottsdale, Ariz., 1974, 75, 78; Stables Gallery, Taos, 1978. **Retrospective:** Westmoreland County/MA, 1967. **Group:** Art: USA; Now, circ., 1962–67; WMAA Annuals, 1963, 65, 67; Smithsonian, 1966; Flint/Institute, Flint Invitational, 1966. **Collections:** U. of Alabama; Allentown/AM; Baltimore/MA; Boston/MFA; Buffalo/Albright; California Palace; Carnegie; Chase Manhattan Bank; Dayton/AI; Denver/AM; Honolulu Academy; Houston/MFA; ICA, Boston; U. of Illinois; Lima, Peru; Los Angeles/County MA; MOMA; McCann-Erickson, Inc.; NCFA; NYU; U. of Nebraska; New York State Art Commission, Albany; Norfolk; Norfolk/Chrysler; Phoenix; RISD; Reynolds Metals Co.; U. of Rochester; SFMA; Santa Barbara/MA; Santa Fe, N.M.; Slater; Smithsonian; Union Carbide Corp.; WGMA; WMAA; Walker; Westmoreland County/MA. **Bibliography:** Baur 5; Blesh 1; McChesney; Nordness, ed. Archives.

CALDER, ALEXANDER. b. July 22, 1898, Philadelphia, Pa.; **d.** November 11, 1976, NYC. **Studied:** Stevens Institute of Technology, 1915–19; ASL, 1923–26, with George Luks, Guy Du Bois, Boardman Robinson, John Sloan. Traveled Europe, USA, Latin America, India. To Paris, 1928. The subject of three films: *Alexander Calder: Sculpture and Constructions* (MOMA, 1944): *Alexander Calder* (Burgess Meredith and Herbert Matter, 1951); *Calder's Circus* (Pathe, 1961). Two Calder sequences are in the film *Dreams That Money Can Buy* (Hans Richter, 1948). Designed sets for *Horizons* and *Four Movements* (by Martha Graham, NYC, 1936); *Socrates* (by Eric Satie, 1936); *Happy as Larry* (by Donagh MacDonagh, NYC, 1946); *Balloons* (by Padraic Colum, Boston,

1946); *Symphonic Variations* (by Tatiana Leskova, 1949). **Commissions:** Spanish Pavilion, Paris World's Fair, 1937; New York World's Fair, 1939; Hotel Avila, Caracas, 1940; Terrace Plaza Hotel, Cincinnati, 1945; Aula Magna, University City, Caracas, 1952; General Motors Corp., 1954; New York International Airport, 1958; UNESCO, Paris, 1958. **Awards:** MOMA, Plexiglas Sculpture Competition, First Prize, 1939; XXVI Venice Biennial, First Prize, 1952; Sao Paulo, 1953, City of Philadelphia, Outstanding Citizen Award, 1955; Stevens Institute of Technology, Medal, 1956; Carnegie First Prize, 1958; Architectural League of New York, Gold Medal, 1960; Brandeis U., Creative Arts Award, 1962. **One-man Exhibitions:** (first) Weyhe Gallery, 1928 (wire sculpture); Billiet Gallery, Paris, 1929; Neumann-Neirendorf Gallery, Berlin, 1929; 56th Street Gallery, NYC, 1930; Galerie Percier, Paris, 1931; Galerie Vignon, Paris, 1932 (first mobiles exhibited); Julien Levy Galleries, NYC, 1932; Galerie Pierre Colle, Paris, 1933; Pierre Matisse Gallery, 1934, 36, 37, 1939–43; The U. of Chicago, 1935; Arts Club of Chicago, 1935; Honolulu Academy, 1937; Mayor Gallery, London, 1937; The Willard Gallery, 1940 (first jewelry exhibited), 1941, 42; Arts and Crafts Club, New Orleans, 1941; SFMA, 1942; Andover/Phillips, 1943; Buchholz Gallery, NYC, 1944, 45, 47, 49; The Kootz Gallery, NYC, 1945; Galerie Louis Carre, Paris, 1946; Cincinnati/AM, 1946; Berne, 1947 (two-man); Amsterdam/Stedelijk, 1947 (two-man), 1950, 59, 69; Brazilian Ministry of Education, Rio de Janeiro, 1948; Sao Paulo, 1948; Margaret Brown Gallery, Boston, 1949; Galerie Maeght, 1949, 64, 66, 71, 73, 75; Galerie Blanche, Stockholm, 1950; MIT, 1950; Lefevre Gallery, London, 1951; Gallery R. Hoffman, Hamburg, 1954; Palais des Beaux-Arts, Brussels, 1960; Kunstgewerbemuseum, Zurich, 1960; Galerie d'Art Moderne, Basel, 1962; Galleria d'Arte del Naviglio, Milan, 1964; Perls Galleries, 1966–68; Obelisk Gallery, 1967; Kiko Gallery, Houston, 1968; Wittenborn

Gallery, NYC, 1968; Dayton's Gallery 12, Minneapolis, 1968; Perls Galleries, 1968, 69, 72, 73, 74, 76; Gimpel Fils, 1969, 71; Grand Rapids, 1969; Musée d'Art Moderne, Geneva, 1969; Fundacion Eugenio Mendoza, Caracas, 1969; Leonard Hutton Gallery, NYC, 1972; Corcoran, 1972; Parker Street 470 Gallery, Boston, 1972; Sala Pelaires, Palma, Majorca, 1972; Source Gallery, San Francisco, 1974; Deson-Zaks Gallery, Chicago, 1975; Haus der Kunst, Munich, 1975; AAAL, 1976; M. Knoedler & Co., NYC, 1978, 79, 80; Rolly-Michaux, Gallery, NYC, 1979; Marisa del Re Gallery, NYC, 1979; Brewster Gallery, NYC, 1976, 77; **Retrospectives:** Springfield, Mass./MFA, 1938; MOMA, 1943; Tate, 1962; SRGM, 1964; Akademie der Kunst, Berlin, 1967; Foundation Maeght, 1969; Long Beach/MA, 1970; Chicago/Contemporary, 1974, WMAA, 1976. **Group:** Artists' Gallery, NYC, 1926 (first paintings exhibited); Salon des Humoristes, Paris, 1927; Salon des Artistes Independents, Paris, 1929, 30; MOMA, Painting and Sculpture, 1930; Salon des Surindependents, Paris, 1930; WMAA; Chicago/AI; SFMA; Cincinnati/AM, 1942; Berne, 1947; Yale U., 1950; Hannover/K-G, 1954; Documenta III, Kassel, 1964. **Collections:** Amsterdam/Stedelijk; Andover/Phillips; U. of Arkansas; Arts Club of Chicago; Basel; Chicago/AI; Dallas/MFA; Frankfurt am Main; Hartford/Wadsworth; Honolulu Academy; Lodz; MMA; MOMA; Mannheim; Marshall Field & Co.; Montreal/MFA; Moscow/Western; Museum of Science and Industry, Chicago; PAFA: Phillips; Pittsfield/Berkshire; SRGM; St. Louis/City; U. of St. Thomas (Tex.); Sao Paulo; Smith College; Stockholm/National; Toronto; VMFA; WMAA; Washington U.: Yale U. **Bibliography:** *Abstraction creation, 1931-1936;* **Alexander Calder,** 1967; **Alexander Calder,** 1971; Baldinger; Barr 1; Battcock, ed.; Baur 5, 7; Beam; Biederman 1; Bihalji-Merin; Blesh 1; Breton 3; Brion 1; Brumme; Calas, N. and E.; **Calder 1, 2; Calder and Liedl;** Canaday; Cheney;

Christensen; Craven, W.; Davis, D.; Evans, ed.; Flanagan; Gaunt; Gertz; Giedion-Welcker 1, 2; Goodrich and Baur 1; Guggenheim, ed.; Haftman; Hayter 2; Henning; Hess, T. B., 1; Honisch and Jensen, eds.; Hulten; Hunter 6; Hunter, ed.; Jakovski; Janis and Blesh 1; Janis, S.; Kozloff 3; Krauss 2; Kuh 1, 2, 3; Langui; Licht, F.; Lipman; Lowry; Lynton; McCurdy, ed.; Marter, Tarbell, and Wechsler; Mellquist; Mendelowitz; **Metro; Monumenta;** Moser 1; **Mulas and Arnason;** Myers 2; Neumeyer; Paalen; Pearson 2; Ragon 1, 2; Ramsden 1, 2; Read, 1, 3, 5, 6; Rickey; Ritchie 1, 3; Rodman 1, 3; Rose, B., 1, 4; Rubin 1; Sachs; Selz, J.; Seuphor 2, 3; Soby 1, 5; Sutton; Strachan; **Sweeny 1;** Tomkins; Tomkins and Time-Life Books; Trier 1, 2; Tuchman 1; Valentine 2; Waldberg 4; "What Abstract Art Means to Me"; Weller; Wilenski. Archives.

CALLAHAN, KENNETH. b. October 30, 1907, Spokane, Wash. Self-taught in art. Traveled USA, Europe, Central America, Mexico, Southeast Asia, South Pacific. **Taught:** Privately and as visiting artist in various parts of the USA; Boston U., 1954–66; Skowhegan School, 1958, 63, 66; Port Townsend Summer School, 1974. Curator, Seattle/ Am, 1933–53. Subject of *Callahan the Artist,* a 30-minute color film, 1973; overall design for *Macbeth,* Seattle Repertory Theater, 1973. **Member:** Washington State Arts Commission, 1970–74; NAD, 1975. **Commissions** (murals): Maine Hospital, Seattle; US Post Offices, Centralia and Anacostes, Wash., and Rugby, N.D.; Washington State Library, Olympia, Wash.; Syracuse U., 1964; Seattle Civic Center, 1966. **Awards:** Guggenheim Foundation Fellowship, 1954; AAAL, Arts and Letters Grant, 1968; State of Washington Governor's Award, 1968; AAAL, **P.P.,** 1972. **Address:** P.O. Box 493, Long Beach, WA 98631; 1221 Minor Ave., Seattle, WA 98101. **Dealer:** Kraushaar Galleries, NYC; Foster-White Gallery, Seattle.

One-man Exhibitions: (first) American-British Art Center, NYC, 1944; Maynard Walker Gallery, NYC, 11 exhibitions, 1946–64; SFMA; Santa Barbara/ MA; La Jolla; Colorado Springs/FA; Phoenix; Roswell; Williams College; Columbia, S.C./MA; U. of Arkansas; U. of Rochester; Detroit/Institute; Renaissance Society, Chicago; Seattle/AM; Portland, Ore./AM; Spokane Art Center of Washington State U.; Tacoma; Galerie George Giraux, Brussels, 1947; Boston U., 1966; Kraushaar Gallery, 1967, 69, 71, 74, 76, 80; Foster-White Gallery, Seattle, 1975, 79; Fountain Gallery, Portland, Oregon. 1980. **Retrospectives:** Emily Winthrop Miles Collection, circ., 1961–64; Syracuse/Everson; Henry Art Gallery, Seattle, circ., 1973. **Group:** Japan; Formosa; Korea; Philippines; Australia; New Zealand; Brazil; USA; Great Britain; France; Italy; Sweden; Denmark; Yugoslavia; Germany; Indianapolis, 1977; Seattle/AM, 1979; AAAL, 1980. **Collections:** Andover/Phillips; Beloit College; Brooklyn Museum; Chase Manhattan Bank; Chicago/AI; The U. of Chicago; Colby College; Columbus; Corcoran; Des Moines; Detroit/Institute; Fort Worth; Garnett Public Library; La Jolla; MMA; MOMA; Memphis/Brooks; U. of Michigan; Minneapolis/Institute; NCFA; U. of Nebraska; Norfolk/Chrysler; PAFA; PMA; Phillips; Phoenix; Portland, Ore./AM; U. of Rochester; SFMA; SRGM; St. Louis/City; Santa Barbara/MA; Seattle/ AM; Spellman College; Springfield, Mo./AM; Syracuse U.; Tacoma; Utica; WMAA; Walker; Washington State U.; U. of Washington; Wichita/AM. **Bibliography:** *Art of the Pacific Northwest;* Baur 7; Bruce and Watson; Cheney; Eliot; Nordness, ed.; *Northwest Traditions;* Pousette-Dart, ed.; Richardson, E.P.; Ritchie 1; Archives.

CALLERY, MARY. b. June 19, 1903, NYC; **d.** February 12, 1977, Paris. **Studied:** ASL, with Edward McCarten; privately in Paris with Jacques Loutchansky. Resided in Paris. **Taught:**

Black Mountain College. **Commissions:** Aluminum Co. of America, 1953; P.S. 34, NYC, 1954; Gen. George W. Wingate High School, Brooklyn, N.Y., 1955; Lincoln Center; Exxon Building, NYC; Brooklyn Court House, N.Y. **One-man-Exhibitions:** (first) Buchholz Gallery, NYC, 1944; Arts Club of Chicago, 1946; Curt Valentine Gallery, NYC, 1947, 49, 50–52, 55; Salon du Mai, Paris, 1949; Margaret Brown Gallery, Boston, 1951; Galerie des Cahiers d'Art, 1954; M. Knoedler & Co., NYC, 1957, 61, 65, Paris, 1962; B. C. Holland Gallery, 1968; Washburn Gallery, Inc., NYC, 1978. **Group:** Salon des Tuileries, Paris; MOMA; WMAA; Chicago/AI; Houston/MFA, 1939; St. Louis/City, 1946; PMA, 1949; Utica, 1956; Dallas/MFA, 1958; Brussels World's Fair, 1958. **Collections:** Alcoa; Andover/Phillips; CIT Corporation; Cincinnati/AM; Detroit/Institute; Eastland Shopping Center, Detroit; 525 William Penn Plaza; Hartford/Wadsworth; MOMA; NYU; Publishers Printing Co.; SFMA; Toledo/MA; WMAA. **Bibliography:** Baur 7; Gertz; Giedion-Welcker 1; Licht, F.; Ramsden 2; Read 3; Ritchie 3; Seuphor 3; Trier 1; Valentine 2; Zervos and Adams. Archives.

CAMPOLI, COSMO. b. 1922, South Bend, Ind. **Studied:** Chicago Art Institute School, 1950–52; Academie de la Grande Chaumiere. Traveled France, Spain, Italy, England. **Taught:** Hull House, Chicago, 1947, 48, 49; Contemporary Art Workshop, Chicago, 1952–69; Institute of Design, Chicago, 1953–69; The U. of Chicago, summers, 1963–66. **Member:** President, Active Arts Collaborative, Chicago, 1974. **Awards:** Chicago/AI, James Nelson Raymond Traveling Fellowship, 1950; Ford Foundation Grant, 1960; Chicago/AI, Sixteen Sculptors, First Prize. **Address:** 1150 East 54th Street, Chicago, IL 60615. **One-man Exhibitions:** Allan Frumkin Gallery, NYC and Chicago; Contemporary Art Workshop, Chicago; Institute of Design, Chicago; Illinois

State Council on the Arts, circ., 1971–73. **Retrospective:** Chicago/Contemporary, 1971. **Group:** Beloit College, 1958; MOMA, New Images of Man, 1959; Michigan State U.; Lake Forest College, 1960; Galerie du Dragon, Paris, Eight Chicago Artists, 1962; U. of Colorado, 1962; Silvermine Guild, 1962; Chicago/AI, Exhibition Momentum; Madrid/Nacional, II Biennial, 1969; Festival of Two Worlds, Spoleto, 1972; The U. of Chicago, Chicago-Style Sculpture, 1974. **Collections:** Exchange National Bank; MOMA; RAC; U. of Southern Illinois; VMFA; Willowbrook High School. **Bibliography:** Schulze.

CANDELL, VICTOR. b. May 11, 1903, Budapest, Hungary; **d.** February 15, 1977, NYC. To USA, 1921; citizen, 1927. Self-taught. Traveled Europe, resided Paris, 1928–31. Federal A.P.; Easel painting. **Taught:** Brooklyn Museum School, 1946–54; Columbia U., 1952–56; Cooper Union, 1954–68; Provincetown Workshop, summers, 1958–76; NYU, 1968–76; and privately since 1940. **Member:** International Institute of Arts and Letters; American Association of University Professors; Audubon Artists; Artists Equity. **Awards:** Audubon Artists, 1952, Emily Lowe Prize, 1956, The Lamont Award, 1961; AAAL, Childe Hassam Award; MacDowell Colony Fellowship; Silvermine Guild Prize for Painting ($500); Audubon Artists, Silver Medal, 1973. **One-man Exhibitions:** Grand Central Moderns, NYC, 1954–1964; Philadelphia Art Alliance, 1958; Hofstra College, 1959; Silvermine Guild, 1962; Scranton/Everhart; Mortimer Brandt, NYC. **Retrospective:** Molloy College, Rockville Centre, N.Y. 1974. Roko Gallery, NYC, 1978. **Group:** WMAA Annuals, 1951–61; Carnegie, 1952, 55; Brooklyn Museum, Watercolor Biennials; U. of Illinois, 1952, 55, 57; Corcoran, UNESCO Exhibition; Audubon Artists; U. of Nebraska; MOMA, American Painting, circ., Europe, 1956–57;

PAFA, 1964. **Collections:** Brandeis U.; Carnegie; Corcoran; U. of Illinois; MMA; Montclair/AM; Mount Holyoke College; NIAL; NYU; U. of Nebraska; Newark Museum; U. of Notre Dame; Slater; Syracuse U.; U. of Texas; US Treasury Department; Utica; WMAA. **Bibliography:** American Artists Congress Inc. Archives.

CAPARN, RHYS. b. July 28, 1909, Oneonta Park, N.Y. **Studied:** Bryn Mawr College; privately in Paris with Edouard Navellier; privately in New York with Alexander Archipenko. Traveled Europe; resided France. **Taught:** Dalton School, NYC, 1946–55, 1960–72. Master Institute of United Arts, Inc., NYC, 1963– . **Member:** Federation of Modern Painters and Sculptors; Sculptors Guild; American Abstract Artists; International Institute of Arts and Letters. **Commissions:** Brooklyn Botanic Garden; Wollman Library, Barnard College; National Furniture Mart, NYC; private portrait commissions. **Awards:** MMA, American Sculpture, Second Prize, 1951; New York State Fair, First Prize for Sculpture, 1958; National Association of Women Artists, Medal of Honor for Sculpture, 1960, 61. **Address:** Taunton Hill Road, Newtown, CT 06470. **One-man Exhibitions:** (first) Delphic Studios, NYC, 1933, also 1935; Architectural League of New York, 1941; New York Zoological Park (Bronx), 1942; Wildenstein & Co., NYC, 1944, 47; Dartmouth College, 1949, 55; John Heller Gallery, NYC, 1953; Doris Meltzer Gallery, NYC, 1956, 59, 60; La Boetie, NYC, 1970; The New Bertha Schaefer Gallery, 1973. **Retrospective:** Riverside Museum, NYC, 1961. **Group:** MOMA, Fifteen Sculptors, circ., 1941; WMAA Annuals, 1941, 53, 54, 56, 60; Musée du Petit Palais, Paris, 1950; PAFA, 1951–53, 60, 64; ICA, London/Tate, International Unknown Political Prisoner Competition, 1953; Silvermine Guild, 1956; USIA, American Drawings, Prints, and Watercolors, circ., Europe, 1957; VMFA, American Sculpture

Today, 1958; NIAL, 1968; PMA/Museum of the Philadelphia Civic Center, Focus, 1974. **Collections:** Barnard College; Brandeis U.; Bryn Mawr College; Colorado Springs/FA; Corcoran; Dartmouth College; Harvard U.; La Jolla; Museum of the City of New York; Norfolk-Chrysler; Raleigh/NCMA; St. Louis/City; WMAA; Youngstown/Butler. **Bibliography:** *Art: A Woman's Sensibility;* Seuphor 3. Archives.

CAREWE, SYLVIA. b. February 22, 1914, NYC. **Studied:** Columbia U.; Atelier 17, NYC; New School for Social Research, with Yasuo Kuniyoshi; Hofmann School. Traveled Europe extensively; Mexico; St. Thomas. **Commissions:** First American artist to be commissioned by the College de la Manufacture d'Aubusson, 1957; several portrait commissions. Lectures. **Address:** 500 East 83rd Street, NYC 10028. **One-man Exhibitions:** Three Arts Gallery, Poughkeepsie, 1947, 52, 54; ACA Gallery, 1948, 51, 53, 54, 56, 58, 61; Barnett Aden Gallery, Washington, D.C., 1950; Indiana U., circ., 1955; Galerie Granoff, Paris, 1957; Condon Riley Gallery, NYC, 1959; Youngstown/Butler, 1960; French & Co. Inc., NYC, 1962; Fordham U., 1970. **Group:** MOMA; WMAA; Brooklyn Museum; Boston/MFA; Bruges, Belgium; Smith College; Silvermine Guild; The Print Club, Philadelphia. **Collections:** Brandeis U.; Djakarta Museum; Howard U.; Paris/Moderne; Tel Aviv; WMAA; Youngstown/Butler. Archives.

CARLES, ARTHUR B. b. 1882, Philadelphia, Pa.; **d.** June 18, 1952, Chestnut Hill, Pa. **Studied:** PAFA. Traveled Spain, France, Italy. **Taught:** PAFA, 1917–25. **Awards:** PAFA: Cresson Fellowship; Walter Lippincott Prize, 1917; Stotesbury Prize, 1919; J. Henry Schiedt Memorial Prize, 1929; Joseph E. Temple Gold Medal, 1930; Chicago/AI, The Mr. & Mrs. Frank G. Logan Prize. **One-man Exhibitions:** Montross Gallery,

NYC, 1922; Gimbel Gallery, Philadelphia, 1935; Marie Harriman Gallery, NYC, 1936; PAFA, 1941, 53; Philadelphia Art Alliance, 1944; Karl Nierendorf Gallery, NYC, 1944 (two-man), 1946, 70; Dubin Gallery, Philadelphia, 1953; Oberlin College (two-man), 1955; The Graham Gallery, 1959; Peal Gallery, Philadelphia, 1967. **Retrospective:** PAFA, 1953. **Group:** The Armory Show, 1913; WMAA, 1963; PAFA. **Collections:** Chicago/AI; MOMA; U. of Nebraska; PAFA; PMA; SFMA; Syracuse U. **Bibliography:** *Avant-Garde Painting and Sculpture in America 1910–25*; Baur 7; Brown 2; Levin 2; Richardson, E. P.; Rose, B., 1, 4. Archives.

CASARELLA, EDMOND. b. September 3, 1920, Newark, N.J. **Studied:** Cooper Union, 1938–42; Brooklyn Museum School, 1949–51, with Gabor Peterdi. US Army, 1944–46. Traveled Italy and Greece, 1951–52, 1960–61, France. **Taught:** Brooklyn Museum School, 1956–60; Yale-Norfolk Summer Art School, 1958; NYU, 1962; Cooper Union; ASL; Hunter College, 1963– ; Columbia U., summers, 1963, 64; Pratt Graphic Art Center, 1964; Yale U., 1964– , Rutgers U., 1964– ; Pratt Institute, 1964– ; Finch College, NYC, 1969–74; Manhattanville College of the Sacred Heart, 1973, 74; Queens College, 1980. **Member:** SAGA; Sculptors Guild, National Youth Administration: Designed posters. **Awards:** Fulbright Fellowship (Italy), 1951; U. of Illinois, Graphic Art exhibitions, **P.P.,** 1954, 56; L. C. Tiffany Grant, 1955; Bay Printmakers Society, Oakland, 1955, 57; Library of Congress, 1955, 56, 58; The Print Club, Philadelphia, 1956; Northwest Printmakers Annual, 1956; Boston Printmakers, 1957; New York State Fair, 1958; PCA, 1959; Brooklyn Museum, Print and Watercolor Biennials; Guggenheim Foundation Fellowship, 1960; SAGA, 100 Prints of the Year, 1962, 63. **Address:** 83 East Linden Avenue, Englewood, NJ 07631. **Dealer:** Landmark

Gallery, NYC. **One-man Exhibitions:** Brooklyn Museum, 1952 (two man); The Zabriskie Gallery, 1953, 56; Obelisk Gallery, Washington, D.C., 1956, 61; Louisiana State U., 1957; U. of Mississippi, 1957; U. of Kentucky, 1964; Rutgers U., 1964; Hudson River Museum, Yonkers, N.Y., 1965; Montclair State College, 1966; Trenton State College, 1967; Merida Gallery, Inc., 1967, 68; Louisville/Speed, 1968–69; Naroden Muzejna Bitolkiot Kraj, Bitola, Yugoslavia; Free Public Library, Fair Lawn, N.J., 1970; Cramer Gallery, 1972, 73; Landmark Gallery, NYC, 1977, 80; Sculpture Center, NYC, 1977. **Retrospectives:** Naroden Muzej na Grad Skopje, Skopje, Yugoslavia, 1967; YMHA, Hackensack, N.J., 1969; Edward Williams College, 1979; Allegheny College, 1978. **Group:** Brooklyn Museum, Print and Watercolor Biennials; International Print Exhibition, Salzburg, 1952, 58; PAFA, 1953, 59, 63; Bay Printmakers Society, Oakland, 1955–57; Library of Congress, 1955, 56, 58; Corcoran, 1955, 56, 58, 59, 63; The Print Club, Philadelphia, 1956; U. of Illinois, 50 Contemporary American Printmakers, 1956; Boston/MFA, 1957; Grenchen, Graphics International, 1958; I Inter-American Paintings and Prints Biennial, Mexico City, 1958; The Pennsylvania State U., 10 American Printmakers, 1959; Trenton/State, Contemporary Printmakers, 1959; Victoria and Albert Museum, 1959; Gallery of Modern Art, Ljubljana, Jugoslavia, III & IV International Exhibitions of Prints, 1959, 61; WMAA, American Prints Today, 1959, 62; Yale U., 1960; Cincinnati/AM, 1960; Philadelphia Art Alliance, 1960; American Academy, Rome, 1960, 61; Memphis/Brooks, 1960–62; WMAA, American Painting, 1961; A.A.A. Gallery, NYC, 100 Prints of the Year, 1962; New York Foundation/USIA, American Prints Around the World, circ., 1963; Los Angeles/County MA, 1963; Riverside Museum, 1963; WMAA, New York Hilton Hotel Collection, 1963; USIA, Graphic Arts—USA, circ., USSR, 1963; Jewish Museum, 100 Contemporary

Prints, 1964; St. Louis/City, 1964; New York World's Fair, 1964–65; I Triennale Internazionale della Zilografia Contemporanea, Capri, 1969; Mostra Internazionale della Zilografia Contemporanea, Bologna, 1971; Madrid/Nacional, Exposicion Internacional de la Zilografia Contemporanea, 1972; Landmark Gallery, NYC, 1973, 74; Bergen Community College, Outdoor Sculpture, 1974. Terrain Gallery, 25th Anniversary, NYC, 1980. **Collections:** Bibliotheque National; Brooklyn Museum; U. of Illinois; Library of Congress; Louisville/Speed; Trenton/State; Victoria and Albert Museum; Cooper Hewitt Museum, NYC. **Bibliography:** Chaet; Peterdi.

CASTELLON, FEDERICO. b. September 14, 1914, Almeria, Spain; d. December 27, 1971, NYC. Self-taught in art.

Traveled Europe and Latin America extensively, resided Spain, 1914–21, 1961–62; France, 1934–36, 1962–63. US citizen, 1943. **Taught:** Columbia U., 1948–61; Pratt Institute, 1951–61, 1964–1971; Queens College, 1964; NAD, 1964–71. **Member:** SAGA; NAD; NIAL. **Commissions:** Illustrations for numerous books and magazines; two prints for International Graphic Arts Society. **Awards:** Four-year fellowship from the Spanish Republic, 1933; Chicago/AI, The Mr. & Mrs. Frank G. Logan Prize, ca. 1940; PAFA, Alice McFadden Eyre Medal, 1940; A.A.A. Gallery, NYC, National Print Competition, First Prize, 1948; Library of Congress, First Pennell **P.P.**, 1949; Guggenheim Foundation Fellowship, 1940, 50; NIAL Grant, 1950; SAGA, 1963. **One-man Exhibitions:** (first) Raymond and Raymond, Inc., NYC; Weyhe Gallery, 1934–41; A.A.A., Gallery, NYC,

Federico Castellon   Untitled #1   1936

1947–52, 78; Bucknell U.; Philadelphia Art Alliance; Albany/Institute; Bennington College; Swarthmore College; Princeton U.; Columbia U.; California Palace; Madrid/Nacional; Caracas; La Paz, Bolivia; Argentina/Nacional; Asuncion, Paraguay; Montevideo/Municipal; a gallery in Paris; Bombay; Los Angeles/County MA; Slater, 1969; Martin Summers Gallery, NYC, 1978. **Retrospective:** Syracuse U., 1978. **Group:** College d'Espagne, Paris, 1934; Corcoran; Chicago/AI; Brooklyn Museum; PAFA; WMAA; SAGA. **Collections:** Brooklyn Museum; Chicago/AI; Dartmouth College; U. of Georgia; Kalamazoo/Institute; Library of Congress; MMA; U. of Minnesota; Montclair/AM; NYPL; PAFA; PMA; Princeton U.; Syracuse U.; Utica; WMAA; Yale U. **Bibliography:** American Artists Group Inc. 3; Baur 7; Front; Goodrich and Baur 1; Mendelowitz; Pearson 1; Reese; Zigrosser 1. Archives.

CAVALLON, GIORGIO. b. March 2, 1904, Sorio, Vicenza, Italy. To USA, 1920. **Studied:** NAD, 1925–30; with C. W. Hawthorne, ca. 1929; Hofmann School, 1935–36. Resided Italy, 1930–33. **Taught:** Pratt Institute, 1952, 54 (woodworking); U. of North Carolina, 1964; Yale U., 1964; Columbia U., summer, 1969. **Member:** American Abstract Artists, 1936–57. Federal A.P.: Mural project assistant to Arshile Gorky, and easel painting. **Awards:** L. C. Tiffany Grant, 1929; Guggenheim Foundation Fellowship, 1966–67. **Address:** 178 East 95th Street, NYC 10028. **Dealer:** Gruenebaum Gallery, NYC. **One-man Exhibitions:** (first) Bottege d'Arte, Vicenza, Italy, 1932; ACA Gallery, 1934; Eighth Street Playhouse, NYC, 1940; Charles Egan Gallery, 1946, 48, 51, 54; The Stable Gallery, 1957, 59; The Kootz Gallery, NYC, 1961, 63; U. of North Carolina, 1964; A.M. Sachs Gallery, 1969, 71, 72, 74, 76; Gruenebaum Gallery, NYC, 1979. **Retrospective:** Purchase/SUNY, 1976. **Group:** WMAA, 1947, 48, 59, 61; Salon des Realites

Nouvelles, Paris, 1950; MOMA, Abstract Painting and Sculpture in America, 1951; MMA, American Watercolors, Drawings and Prints, 1952; U. of Nebraska, 1955; Documenta II Kassel, 1959; Chicago/AI, 1959; Carnegie, 1959, 61; Walker, 1960; SRGM, Abstract Expressionists and Imagists, 1961; U. of Illinois, 1963; MOMA, 60 Modern Drawings, 1963; PAFA Annual, 1966; WMAA, The 1930s, 1968; A.F.A., 1968–69; MOMA, The New American Painting and Sculpture, 1969; A.F.A., Geometric Abstraction of the 1930s, 1972, Hirshhorn, Bicentennial Exhibition, 1976. **Collections:** American Republic Insurance Co.; Avco Corp.; Avon Products; Buffalo/Albright; U. of California; Chase Manhattan Bank; Ciba-Geigy Corp.; Continental Grain Company; MOMA; Marine Midland Bank and Trust Co.; NYU; U. of North Carolina; Prudential Insurance Co. of America; SRGM; The Singer Company, Inc.; U. of Texas; Tishman Realty & Construction Co. Inc.; Union Carbide Corp.; WMAA. **Bibliography:** Blesh 1; Hess, T. B., 1; McCurdy, ed.; O'Hara 1; Pousette-Dart, ed.; Ritchie 1; Rose, B., 1. Archives.

CELMINS, VIJA. b. 1939, Riga, Latvia. To USA, 1949. **Studied:** John Herron Art Institute, Indianapolis, 1958–62, BFA; Yale U., 1961; UCLA, 1962–65, MFA. **Taught:** California State College, Los Angeles, 1965–66; U. of California, Irvine, 1967–72; California Institute of the Arts, Valencia, 1976. **Awards:** Cassandra Foundation, Award, 1968; National Endowment for the Arts, Grant, 1971; US Department of the Interior, 1975. **Address:** c/o Dealer. **Dealer:** Margo Leavin Gallery, Los Angeles. **One-man Exhibitions:** (first) David Stuart Galleries, Los Angeles, 1966; Riko Mizuno Gallery, Los Angeles, 1969, 73; WMAA, 1973; Felicity Samuel Gallery, London, 1975; Broxton Gallery, Los Angeles, 1975; Security Pacific National Bank, Los Angeles, 1978. **Retrospective:** Newport Harbor Art Museum, circ., 1979. **Group:** California State college, Hayward, Four Painters, 1966; U. of Colorado, Boulder, NYC–L.A. Drawings of the 60s, 1967; Fort Worth, Contemporary American Drawings, 1969; WMAA Annuals, 1970, 77; La Jolla, Continuing Surrealism, 1971; Los Angeles/County MA, 24 Young Los Angeles Artists, 1971; La Jolla, Earth, Animal, Vegetable, and Mineral, 1971; MOMA, California, Prints, 1972; Brooklyn Museum, national print exhibition, 1972; WMAA, American Drawings, 1963–1973, 1973; U. of Illinois, 1974; Chicago/AI, 71st American Exhibition, 1974; US Department of the Interior, America 1976, circ., 1976; Detroit/Institute, American Artists; A New Decade, 1976; SFMA, Painting and Sculpture in California; The Modern Era, 1976; Brooklyn Museum, 30 Years of American Printmaking, 1976. **Collections:** WMAA; Newport Harbor; MOMA; AT&T; Los Angeles/County MA; Fort Worth; Levi Strauss & Co., San Francisco; Paine Webber, Jackson and Curtis, Inc., NYC. **Bibliography:** Lippard 6; *New in the Seventies; America 1976*.

CHAET, BERNARD. b. March 7, 1924, Boston, Mass. **Studied:** Tufts U., B.S. Ed.; Boston Museum School, with Karl Zerbe. Traveled Europe; resided Paris, 1949. **Taught:** Yale U., 1951– ; American Academy, Rome. Contributing editor, *Arts* magazine, 1956–59. **Awards:** Silvermine Guild Award, 1955; Yale U., Senior Faculty Fellowship, 1962; St. Paul Art Center, Drawing USA, Merit Award, 1963; National Council on the Arts, Grant, 1966–67. **Address:** 141 Cold Spring Street, New Haven, CT 06511. **Dealer:** Alpha Gallery; Marilyn Pearl Gallery, NYC. **One-man Exhibitions:** (first) Boris Mirski Gallery, Boston, 1946, also 1951, 54, 57, 59, 61, 65; The Bertha Schaefer Gallery, 1954; The Stable Gallery, 1959, 61, 67; Cornell U., 1961; Alpha Gallery, 1967, 68, 69, 71; Swarthmore College, 1971; Haslem Fine Arts, Inc., 1973; The Forum Gallery, 1975; Alpha Gallery, Boston, 1975, 77; Marilyn Pearl Gallery, NYC, 1976, 78, 79; Trinity College, 1979. **Retrospective:** Brockton/Fuller, 1970. **Group:** U. of Illinois, 1951, 53, 61; PAFA; Los Angeles/County MA; Phillips; Chicago/AI; U. of Nebraska; ICA, Boston, 6 New England Painters, 1954; Corcoran; Contemporary American Drawings, circ., France, 1957–58; Hartford/Wadsworth, 8 From Connecticut, 1961; Detroit/Institute; MOMA; Brooklyn Museum; U. of North Carolina, 1977. **Collections:** Andover/Phillips; Boston/MFA; Brandeis U.; Brooklyn Museum; Brown U.; U. of Connecticut; Cortland/SUNY; Dartmouth College; Harvard U.; Indiana U.; Lincoln, Mass./De Cordova; U. of Massachusetts; RISD; UCLA; Worcester/AM; Yale U.; U. of North Carolina. **Bibliography: Chaet.**

CHAMBERLAIN, JOHN. b. 1927, Rochester, Ind. **Studied:** Chicago/AI School, 1950–52; Black Mountain College, 1955–56. US Navy, 1943–46. **Address:** 222 Bowery, NYC 10012. **Dealer:** Leo Castelli Inc. **One-man Exhibitions:** (first) Wells Street Gallery, Chicago, 1957; Davida Gallery, Chicago, 1958; Martha Jackson Gallery, 1960; Dilexi Gallery, Los Angeles, 1962; Dilexi Gallery, San Francisco, 1962; Leo Castelli Inc., 1962 (two-man), 1964, 65, 68, 69, 71, 73, 76; Leo Castelli Warehouse, 1969; The Pace Gallery, Boston, 1963; Robert Fraser Gallery, 1963 (two-man); Dwan Gallery, Los Angeles, 1965; Cleveland/MA, 1967; Contemporary Arts Center, Cincinnati, 1968; Mizuno Gallery, 1969; LoGiudice Gallery, Chicago, 1970; Taft Museum (two-man), 1972; Dag Hammarskjold Plaza, NYC, 1973; Walter Kelly Gallery, Chicago, 1974; Houston/Contemporary, 1975; Ronald Greenberg Gallery, St. Louis, 1975; Locksley-Shea Gallery, Minneapolis (two-man), 1975; Margo Leavin Gallery, Los Angeles, 1977; Dia Art Foundation, NYC, 1977; Heiner Friedrich, Inc., 1977; Berne, 1979;

Galerie Heiner Friedrich, Cologne, 1979. **Retrospective:** SRGM, 1971. **Group:** MOMA, Recent Sculpture USA, 1959; Buenos Aires Museum of Modern Art, International Sculpture Exhibition, 1960; Martha Jackson Gallery, New Media—New Forms, I & II, 1960, 61; WMAA Annuals, 1960, 62, 65; Sculpture Annuals, 1966, 68; Galerie Rive Droite, Paris, Le Nouveau Realisme, 1961; VI Sao Paulo Biennial, 1961; MOMA, The Art of Assemblage, circ., 1961; Chicago/AI, 1961, 67; Carnegie, 1961, 67; Seattle World's Fair, 1962; SRGM, The Joseph H. Hirshhorn Collection, 1962; Battersea Park, London International Sculpture Exhibition, 1963; Musée Cantonal des Beaux-Arts, Lausanne, I Salon International de Galeries Pilotes, 1963; Pasadena/AM, New American Sculpture, 1964; New York World's Fair, 1964–65; Tate, Painting and Sculpture of a Decade, 1954–64, 1964; XXXII Venice Biennial, 1964; Jewish Museum, 1964; ICA, U. of Pennsylvania, The Atmosphere of '64, 1964, also 1965; Flint/Institute, 1965; ICA, Boston, Painting without a brush, 1965; Indianapolis/Herron, 1965, 69; WMAA, Contemporary American Sculpture, Selection I, 1966; MOMA, The 1960's, 1967; HemisFair '68, San Antonio, Tex., 1968; Swarthmore College, 1969; Trenton/State, Soft Art, 1969; York U., Toronto, 1969; ICA, U. of Pennsylvania, Highway, 1970; Indianapolis, 1970, 72; Cincinnati/Contemporary, Monumental Art, 1970; WMAA Sculpture Annual, 1970; MOMA, Younger Abstract Expressionists of the Fifties, 1971; Hofstra U., Art around the Automobile, 1971; Dusseldorf/Kunsthalle, Prospect '71, 1971; NCFA, Sculpture, American Directions, 1945–75, 1975; WMAA, 200 Years of American Sculpture, 1976; Akademie der Kunste, Berlin, SoHo, 1976; Cambridge U., Jubilation, 1977; Flint/Institute, Art and the Automobile, 1978; WMAA, Art about Art, 1978. **Collections:** Buffalo/Albright; Dallas/MFA; Fort Worth; Hirshhorn; Los Angeles/County MA; MOMA; U. of North Carolina; Oberlin College; Pasadena/AM; Rome/Nazionale; SRGM; VMFA; WMAA. **Bibliography:** Battcock, ed.; Craven, W.; Honisch and Jensen, eds.; Hunter, ed.; Janis and Blesh 1; Kozloff 3; Kuh 3; Licht, F.; Lippard 5; *Metro; Monumenta;* Read 3; *Report:* Rose, B., 1; Sandler 1; Seitz 3; Seuphor 3; Tuchman 1; Warhol and Hackett.

CHESNEY, LEE R., JR. b. June 1, 1920, Washington, D. C. **Studied:** U. of Colorado with James Boyle, BFA; State U. of Iowa, with Mauricio Lasansky, James Lechay, MFA; Universidad Michoacana, Morelia, Mexico, with Alfredo Zalce. **Taught:** U. of Illinois, 1950–67; U. of Southern California, 1967–72; U. of Hawaii, 1972– . **Awards:** PMA, 1953; Bradley U., **P.P.,** 1953; U. of Southern California, **P.P.,** 1953, 54; Dallas/MFA, **P.P.,** 1953, 54; Brooklyn Museum, **P.P.,** 1953, 56; Library of Congress, 1954, 58; Denver/AM, **P.P.,** 1954, 59, 60, 61; Chicago/AI, John Taylor Arms Medal, 1955; Washington U., **P.P.,** 1955; Texas Wesleyan College, **P.P.,** 1955; Michigan State U., **P.P.,** 1956; Fulbright Fellowship, 1956–57; Oakland/AM, **P.P.,** 1957; Silvermine Guild, 1959; Youngstown/Butler, 1959; Seattle/AM, 1959, 61; Pasadena/AM, 1960; Oklahoma, 1960; SAGA, 1961. **Address:** c/o Dealer. **Dealer:** Downtown Gallery, Honolulu. **Group:** Des Moines, 1947–50; The Print Club, Philadelphia, 1947, 49, 50, 53, 55, 58; Seattle/AM, 1947–51, 1953–56; Brooklyn Museum, 1948, 50, 52, 54, 56, 58; SFMA, 1949, 50, 53, 54; Denver/AM, 1949, 52, 55, 56; Bradley U., 1950, 52–55; Library of Congress, 1950, 54, 56, 58; International Biennial Exhibitions of Paintings, Tokyo; U. of Illinois; IV Bordighera Biennial, 1957. **Collections:** Albion College; Bibliotheque Nationale; Bradley U.; Brooklyn Museum; Dallas/MFA; Denver/AM; Illinois Wesleyan U.; Library of Congress; MOMA; Michigan State U.; Milwaukee-Downer College; National Gallery; Oakland/AM; The Ohio State U.; PMA; Seattle/AM; Stockholm/National; Tate; Texas

Wesleyan College; Tokyo/Modern, Tokyo U. of Arts; Victoria and Albert Museum.

CHINNI, PETER. b. March 21, 1928, Mt. Kisco, N.Y. **Studied:** ASL, 1947, with Edwin Dickinson, Kenneth Hayes Miller, Julian Levi; Academy of Fine Arts, Rome, 1949–50, with Emilio Sorrini. Traveled Puerto Rico, Mexico, Europe; resided in Italy 19 years. **Member:** Sculptors Guild. **Commissions:** Denver/AM (bronze mural); City of Columbia, Mo., 1979. **Awards:** ASL, Daniel Schnackenberg Scholarship, 1948; Silvermine Guild, First Prize, 1958, 60, 61; Denver/AM, Second Prize, 1960. **Address:** RFD 2, Pines Bridge Rd., Katonah, NY 10536. **Dealer:** Valley House Gallery, Dallas. **One-man Exhibitions:** (first) Fairleigh Dickinson U., 1951; Galleria San Marco, Rome, 1955; Il Torcoliere, Rome, 1956; Kipnis Gallery, Westport, Conn., 1956; R. R. Gallery, Denver, 1957; Galleria Schneider, Rome, 1957; Janet Nessler Gallery, NYC, 1957; 61; Royal Marks Gallery, 1964; Albert Loeb Gallery, NYC, 1966; Loeb & Krugier Gallery, 1969; Tyler School of Art, Rome, 1979; Harcus Krakow Rosen Sonnabend Gallery, Boston, 1976; Galerie Alexandra Monett, Brussels, 1976; Galerie Bouma, Amsterdam, 1976; Musée d'Ixelles, Brussels, 1976; Beeckestijn Museum, Velsen, Holland, 1976; Hooks-Epstein Gallery, Houston, 1978. **Group:** Audobon Artists Annuals, 1958, 59, 61, 62; Festival of Two Worlds, Spoleto, 1960; Boston Arts Festival, 1960, 62; Connecticut Academy of Fine Arts, 1960, 62; WMAA Annuals, 1960, 62, 64, 65; Corcoran, 1962; Galleria Pagani del Grattacielo, Milan, 1962; Waitsfield/Bundy, 1963; Sculptors Guild, 1963, 64, 66, 68; Carnegie, 1964; Heseler Gallery, Munich, 1968; Rome/Nazionale, 1968; Utica, American Prints Today, 1970; WMAA, Art of the Sixties, 1975. **Collections:** Denver/AM; Fontana-Hollywood Corp.; St. Louis/City; WMAA; Beeckestijn Museum, Velsen, Holland; New School for Social Research; Louisville/Speed; National Gallery; MIT; Chase Manhattan Bank, Rome; Bank of New York, NYC; First National Bank, Chicago; Denver; Pace College, NYC; Middlebury College.

CHRISTENSEN, DAN. b. 1942, Lexington, Neb. **Studied:** Kansas City/AI, BFA. **Address:** 16 Waverly Place, NYC 10003. **Dealer:** Salander-O'Reilly Gallery, NYC. **One-man Exhibitions:** Noah Goldowsky, 1967, 68; Galerie Rudolf Zwirner, 1967; Galerie Rolf Ricke, Cologne, 1968, 71; Andre Emmerich Gallery, NYC, 1969, 71, 72, 74, 75, 76; Nicholas Wilder Gallery, 1970, 72; Edmonton Art Gallery, Alberta, 1973; Ronald Greenberg Gallery, St. Louis, 1974; Watson/De Nagy Gallery, Houston, 1977; B. R. Kornblatt Gallery, Baltimore, 1977; Douglas Drake Gallery, Kansas City, 1978, 79; Gloria Luria Gallery, Miami, 1978; Meredith Long Gallery, Houston, 1978; Meredith Long Contemporary, NYC, 1978, 79. **Group:** WMAA, 1967, 69, 72, 73; Washington U., Here and Now, 1979; Corcoran, 1969; Buffalo/Albright, Color and Field: 1890–1970, 1970; WMAA, The Structure of Color, 1971; WMAA, Lyrical Abstraction, 1971; Buffalo/Albright, Six Painters, 1971; Boston/MFA, Abstract Painting in the '70s, 1972; WMAA Biennial, 1973; Lehigh U., Freedom in Art, 1976; U. of Nebraska, Expressionism in the '70s, 1978. **Collections:** Boston/MFA; Buffalo/Albright; Denver/AM; Edmonton; High Museum; Houston/MFA; MMA; Mutual Benefit Life Insurance Co., Kansas City; U. of Nebraska; SRGM; Toledo/MA; WMAA. **Bibliography:** *Kunst um 1970;* Wood; *New in the Seventies.*

CHRISTO (Javacheff). b. June 13, 1935, Gabrovo, Bulgaria. **Studied:** Academy of Fine Arts, Sofia, 1951–56; theater design at Burian Theater, Prague, 1956; Academy of Fine Arts, Vienna, 1957. To Geneva, 1957, Paris, 1958, NYC, 1964.

Christo   *Running Fence, Project for Sonoma County and Marin County, State of California*   1976

Films of Projects: *Wrapped Coast*, 1969; *Christ's Valley Curtain*, 1972; *Running Fence*, 1973–76; *Wrapped Walk Ways*, 1978. **Address:** 48 Howard Street, NYC 10013. **One-man Exhibitions:** Galerie Haro Lauhus, Cologne, 1961; Galerie J. Paris, 1962; Galerie Schmela, 1963, 64; Galleria Apollinaire, Milan, 1963; Galleria del Leone, Venice, 1963, 68; Galleria la Salita, Rome, 1963; Galerie Ad Libitum, Antwerp, 1964; Gian Enzo Sperone, Turin, 1964; Eindhoven, 1966; Leo Castelli Inc., NYC, 1966; Walker, 1966; Wide White Space Gallery, Antwerp, 1967, 69; Galerie der Spiegel, Cologne, 1967, 69; John Gibson Gallery, 1968, 69; MOMA, 1968; ICA, U. of Pennsylvania, 1968; Chicago/Contemporary, 1969; Little Bay, Australia, Wrapped Coast, 1969; Central Street Gallery, Sydney, 1969; Melbourne/National, 1969; New Gallery, Cleveland, 1970; Francoise Lambert, Milan, 1970; Annely Juda Fine Art, London, 1971, 77, 79; Zurich, 1973; Allan Frumkin Gallery, Chicago, 1973; La Jolla, 1975; White Gallery, Lutry, 1975; Edificio Galipan, Caracas, 1975; Museo de Bellas Artes, Caracas, 1975; ICA, Boston, 1975; Galerie J. Benador, Geneva, 1975; Fabian Fine Arts, Cape Town, 1975; Galerie der Spiegel, Cologne, 1975; Museum des 20. Jahrhunderts, Vienna, 1976; SFMA, 1976; Pasadena/AM, 1976; Galerie Juan Prats, 1977; Rotterdam, 1977; Bonn, 1977; Hannover/K-G, 1977; Miami Gallery, Tokyo, 1977; Humlebaek/Louisiana, 1978; Kunstgewerbe, Zurich, 1978; Brussels/Beaux-Arts, 1978; American Foundation for the Arts, Miami, 1978; Kansas City/Nelson, 1978; Hartford/Wadsworth, 1978; Wiener Secession, Vienna, 1979; ICA, London, 1979; ICA, Boston, 1979; Corcoran, 1979. **Group:** Andover/Phillips; Harvard U.; Sorbonne; WMAA; Smithsonian; Brooklyn Museum; Boston/MFA; A.F.A., circ.; Boston Arts Festival; ICA, Boston, 1959–67, incl. View, 1960, 1960; Corcoran, 1961, 64, 65; Lincoln, Mass./De Cordova, 1966; Norfolk, 1967; AAAL, 1968; PAFA, 1969; NIAL, 1969. **Collections:** Andover/Phillips; Boston/MFA; Boston U.; Dartmouth College; Lincoln, Mass./De Cordova; U. of Massachusetts; Seattle/AM; U. of Tennessee; WMAA; Wichita/AM. **Bibliography:** Diamonstein; *Drawings: the Pluralist Decade;* Honisch and Jensen, eds.; Hunter, ed.; Strachan. Archives.

CHRISTOPHER, WILLIAM. b. March 4, 1924, Columbus, Ga.; **d.** December 5, 1973, Malaga, Spain. **Studied:** Sorbonne, 1946–47; Academie Julian, Paris, 1946–48, with Ossip Zadkine, Paris, 1974; Ecole des Beaux-Arts, Fontainebleau, 1947; with Amedee Ozenfant, NYC, 1948–50; with Hans Hofmann, NYC, 1950. Traveled Europe, Latin America. Changed from sculpture to painting in Paris, 1948. **Taught:** Polytechnic Preparatory School, Brooklyn (woodworking) 1956–60; Dartmouth College, 1966. **Awards:** Brooklyn Museum, Shiva Award, 1956; Silvermine Guild, Painting Award, 1962; Boston Arts Festival, Gold Medal of Merit, 1964; U. of Tennessee, First **P.P.;** AAAL, Childe Hassam Award, 1968; NAD, Frank C. Kirk Memorial Prize, 1968; NIAL Grant, 1969. **One-man Exhibitions:** (first) Roko Gallery, NYC, 1952; Nexus Gallery, Boston, 1957; 59, 60; Harvard U., 1959; The Amel Gallery, NYC, 1961; Joan Peterson Gallery, 1961, 62, 65, 66, 70, 72; Boston Architectural Center, 1963; Dartmouth College, 1964–66; Andover/Phillips, 1966; Richard Larcada Gallery, 1968; Drew U., 1968. **Group:** Andover/Phillips; Harvard U.; Brooklyn Museum; Boston/MFA; A.F.A., circ.; Boston Arts Festival; ICA, Boston, 1959–67, incl. View, 1960, 1960; Corcoran, 1961, 64, 65; Lincoln, Mass./De Cordova, 1966; Norfolk, 1967; AAAL,

1968; PAFA, 1969; NIAL, 1969. **Collections:** Andover/Phillips; Boston/MFA; Boston U.; Dartmouth College; Lincoln, Mass./De Cordova; U. of Massachusetts; Seattle/AM; U. of Tennessee; WMAA; Wichita/AM. **Bibliography:** Archives.

CHRYSSA. b. 1933, Athens, Greece. **Studied:** Academie de la Grande Chaumiere, 1953–54; California School of Fine Arts, 1954–55. US citizen, 1955. Traveled Europe, USA. **Awards:** Guggenheim Foundation Fellowship, 1973; MIT, grant, 1979–80. **Address:** 15 East 88th Street, NYC 10028. **Dealer:** Galerie Denise Rene, Paris. **One-man Exhibitions:** (first) Betty Parsons Gallery, 1961; SRGM, 1961; Cordier & Ekstrom, Inc., 1962; Robert Fraser Gallery, 1962; The Pace Gallery, 1966, 67, 68; The Graphic Gallery, San Francisco, 1968; Galerie der Spiegel, Cologne, 1968; Harvard U., 1968; Obelisk Gallery, 1969; Galerie Rive Droite, Paris, 1969; WMAA, 1972; Galerie Denise Rene, NYC, 1973, 76; Galerie Denise Rene, Paris, 1974; Galerie Andre Emmerich, Zurich, 1974, 75; Paris/Moderne, 1979. **Group:** MOMA, Americans 1963, circ., 1963–64; Sao Paulo Biennials, 1963, 69; WMAA Annuals; Carnegie; Martha Jackson Gallery, New Media—New Forms, I, 1960; Boston Arts Festival, 1960; Seattle World's Fair, 1962; Jewish Museum; Documenta IV, Kassel, 1968; Venice Biennial, 1972. **Collections:** Buffalo/Albright; Chase Manhattan Bank; MOMA; SRGM; WMAA. **Bibliography:** Battcock, ed.; Calas, N. and E.; Honisch; Hunter, ed.; Lippard 5; Strachan. Tuchman 1; **Waldman 2.**

CICERO, CARMEN LOUIS. b. August 14, 1926, Newark, N. J. US Army, World War II, Philippines. **Studied:** Newark State Teachers College, BA, 1947–51; Hunter College (with Robert Motherwell), 1953–55; Hofmann School, NYC. Traveled Europe. **Taught:** Sarah Lawrence College,

1959–68; School of Visual Arts, NYC, 1965–67; New School for Social Research, 1967–70; Newark State College, 1969–70; Montclair (N.J.) State College, 1969– . **Awards:** Guggenheim Foundation Fellowship, 1957, 63, 64; Ford Foundation, **P.P.,** 1961, 65. **Address:** 278 Bowery, NYC 10012. **One-man Exhibitions:** The Peridot Gallery, NYC, 1956, 57, 59, 61, 62, 64, 66, 68, 69; Arts Club of Chicago, 1958; Galerie Simone Stern, New Orleans; Kendall Gallery, Wellfleet, Mass., and Palm Beach; Rankow Gallery, 1971; Montclair College, 1975. **Group:** Corcoran, 1953; MOMA, 1953, 55; WMAA, 1955, 57, Annuals, 1960–63, 1965; U. of Nebraska, 1957; Chicago/AI, 1957; Worcester/AM, 1958; PAFA: Brooklyn Museum; Museum des 20. Jahrhunderts, 1963. **Collections:** Albion College; Amsterdam/Stedelijk; Brooklyn Museum; Cornell U.; Hirschhorn; MOMA; U. of Michigan; NYU; U. of Nebraska; Newark Museum; Ridgefield/Aldrich; Rotterdam; SRGM; Schiedam/Stedelijk; Southern Illinois U.; Toronto; Trenton/State; WMAA; Worcester/AM. **Bibliography:** Gerdts.

CIKOVSKY, NICOLAI. b. December 10, 1894, Pinsk, Russia. **Studied:** Royal Art School, Vilna; Technical Institute of Arts, Moscow. To USA, 1923. **Taught:** Ekaterinenburg Higher Technical Art Institute, Russia; Columbus, Ga., Museum of Arts and Crafts; St. Paul School of Art; Art Academy of Cincinnati; The Corcoran School of Art; Chicago Art Institute School; ASL. **Member:** NAD. **Commissions** (murals): Interior Department, Washington, D. C.; US Post Offices, Towson and Silver Spring, Md. **Awards:** Chicago/AI, Norman Wait Harris Bronze Medal, 1932; Chicago/AI, The Mr. & Mrs. Frank G. Logan Medal, 1933; Worcester/AM, First Prize, 1933; PAFA, Lambert **P.P.,** 1937; NIAL Grant, 1962; NAD, Isaac N. Maynard Prize, 1964; Southampton/Parrish, First Prize, 1968. **Address:** 500 West 58th Street, NYC. **One-man Exhibitions:**

The Downtown Gallery, 1933, 38; Whyte Gallery, Washington, D. C., 1939; A.A.A. Gallery, NYC, 1944, 46, 49, 52, 56; ACA Gallery, 1959, 63, 67. **Group:** Brooklyn Museum, 1927; Chicago/AI, 1932, 33, 60, 61; A Century of Progress, Chicago, 1933–34; New York World's Fair, 1939; NAD, 1959; Toledo/MA; MOMA; Newark Museum; U. of Glasgow; Walker; Carnegie; Corcoran; Boston/MFA; Worcester/AM; Cleveland/MA; Los Angeles/County MA. **Collections:** Brooklyn Museum; Chicago/AI; Cleveland/MA; Kansas City/Nelson; Los Angeles/County MA; MOMA; PAFA; Phillips; WMAA; Worcester/AM. **Bibliography:** American Artists Group Inc. 2, 3; Bethers; Cheney; Gerdts; Hall; Mellquist; Pagano. Archives.

CLARKE, JOHN CLEM. b. June 6, 1937, Bend, Ore. **Studied:** Oregon State U.; Mexico City College; U. of Oregon, BFA, 1960. Traveled Mexico, Europe, USA. **Address:** 465 W. Broadway, NYC 10012. **Dealer:** OK Harris Works of Art. **One-man Exhibitions:** The Kornblee Gallery, 1968, 69, 71; Franklin Siden Gallery, Detroit, 1969; OK Harris Works of Art, 1970, 72, 75, 77; Michael Walls Gallery, 1970; Galerie M. E. Thelen, Essen, 1970; Phyllis Kind Gallery, Chicago, 1971; Pyramid Art Galleries, Ltd., 1971; Galerie de Gestlo, 1971; Jack Glenn Gallery, Corona del Mar, 1972; Carl Solway Gallery, Cincinnati, 1972; D.M. Gallery, London, 1974; Morgan Gallery, Kansas City, 1977; Deson-Zaks Gallery, Chicago, 1977. **Group:** WMAA, 1967, 69, 72, 75; U. of Illinois, 1969; Milwaukee, Aspects of a New Realism, 1969; WMAA, 22 Realists, 1970; Chicago/AI, 1970; Potsdam/SUNY, New Realism, 1971; Chicago/Contemporary, Radical Realism, 1971; Santa Barbara/MA, Spray, 1971; U. of Miami, Phases of New Realism, 1972; New York Cultural Center, Realism Now, 1972; Indianapolis, 1974; Hartford/Wadsworth, New/Photo Realism, 1974; Tokyo Biennial, 1974; Cleveland/

MA, Aspects of the Figure, 1974; Skidmore College, New Realism, 1974; Potsdam/SUNY, The Presence and Absence of Realism, 1976; Stratford, Ontario, Aspects of Realism, circ., 1976; Indianapolis, 1976, 78; US Department of the Interior, America 1976, 1976; Fort Wayne, Hue and Far Cry of Color, 1976; Taft Museum, Look Again, 1976; Rice U., Abstract Illusionism, 1977; U. of Texas, Austin, New in the Seventies, 1977; Canberra/National, Illusion and Reality, 1977; St. Petersburg, Fla., Photo Realism, 1977; U. of Rochester, Perceiving Time and Space through Art, 1979; Aspen Center for the Visual Arts, Portraits of the Sixties/Seventies, 1979. **Collections:** Akron/AI; Baltimore/MA; U. of California, Berkeley; Chase Manhattan Bank; Cleveland/MA; Dallas/MFA; Flint/Institute; Kansas City/Nelson; Milwaukee; Security Pacific National Bank; Syracuse U.; VMFA; WMAA. **Bibliography:** *Amerikanischer Fotorealismus; America 1976; Arthur 1; Kunst um 1970; New in the Seventies;* Sager. Archives.

CLERK, PIERRE. b. March 26, 1928, Atlanta, Ga. **Studied:** McGill U., Montreal; Loyola College; Montreal/MFA; Academie Julian, Paris; Academy of Fine Arts, Florence, Italy. Resided seven years in Europe. **Commissions:** (tapestries) Skidmore, Owings & Merrill; Commerce Trust Co., Kansas City. **Awards:** Canada Council Award, 1971, 72; Tamarind Fellowship, 1972. **Address:** 66 Grand Street, NYC 10013. **One-man Exhibitions:** Numero Gallery, Florence, Italy; Galleria Totti, Milan; Cittadella Gallery, Ascona, Switzerland; Beno Gallery, Zurich; Montreal/MFA; New Gallery, NYC; Galleria del Cavallino, Venice; Siegelaub Gallery, NYC, 1965, 67; Gimpel Fils, 1971; Gimpel & Hanover, 1971; Gimpel & Weitzenhoffer Ltd., 1971; Tirca Karlis Gallery, 1971; Gallery Moos, Montreal, 1972; Syracuse/Everson, 1977; Manila, 1978. **Group:** XXVIII & XXIX Venice Biennials, 1956, 1958;

Carnegie, 1959; Expo '67, Montreal 1967; Dublin/Municipal, International Quadriennial (ROSC), 1971; Indianapolis, 1972; Bradford, England, III British Print Biennial, 1972. **Collections:** American National Fire Insurance Co.; Atlantic Richfield Co.; Avon Corp.; The Bank of New York; Brandeis U.; Buffalo/Albright; Burlington Mills; Chase Manhattan Bank; First National City Bank; U. of Glasgow; Gulf Oil Corp.; Gulf and Western Industries, Inc.; IBM; MOMA; McCrory Corporation; Mobil Oil Corp.; Montreal/Contemporain; Montreal/MFA; Ottawa/National; Philip Morris; Purchase/SUNY; Quebec; Queens College; Radio Corporation of America; SRGM; The Singer Company, Inc.; U.S. Steel Corp.; WMAA.

CLOAR, CARROLL. b. January 18, 1913, Earle, Ark. **Studied:** Memphis Academy of Arts; ASL, with William C. McNulty, Harry Sternberg; Southwestern College, BA. US Air Force, World War II, three years. Traveled Central and South America, Europe. **Taught:** Memphis Academy of Arts, 1956. **Member:** Artists Equity. **Awards:** MacDowell Traveling Fellowship, 1940; Guggenheim Foundation Fellowship, 1946; Youngstown/Butler, **P.P.;** Brooklyn Museum, **P.P.;** Library of Congress, **P.P.;** Mead Painting of the Year; Hon. PBK; Hon. Ph.D., Southwestern College. **Address:** 235 S. Greer, Memphis, TN 38111. **Dealer:** The Forum Gallery, NYC; **One-man Exhibitions:** (first) Memphis/Brooks, 1955, also 1957; The Alan Gallery, NYC, 1956, 58, 60, 62, 64, 65, 68; U. of Arkansas, 1956, 61; Fort Worth, 1963; Charleston Art Gallery, Charleston, W. Va.; U. of Georgia; Montgomery (Ala.) Museum of Fine Arts; Utah State Institute of Fine Arts, Salt Lake City; Columbia, S.C./MA; Dulin Gallery; Memphis/Brooks, 1957, 62, 72; Kennedy Gallery, NYC, 1973; Forum Gallery, NYC, 1979. **Retrospective:** Albany/SUNY, 1968; Memphis/Brooks,

1960, 76. **Group:** PAFA; MMA; Carnegie; MOMA; WMAA; Brooklyn Museum; Dallas/MFA; U. of Nebraska. **Collections:** Abbott Laboratories; Albany/SUNY; Atlanta/AA; Brandeis U.; Bridgeport; Brooklyn Museum; Chase Manhattan Bank; Corcoran; First National Bank of Memphis; Friends of Art; Hartford/Wadsworth; Library of Congress; MMA; MOMA; Mead Corporation; Memphis/Brooks; Newark Museum; St. Petersburg, Fla.; Southwestern (College) at Memphis; WMAA; Youngstown/Butler. **Bibliography:** Archives.

CLOSE, CHUCK (Charles). b. July 5, 1940, Monroe, Wash. **Studied:** U. of Washington, 1958–62, BA; Yale U. Summer School, Norfolk, Conn., 1961; Yale U., 1962–64; BFA, 1963, MFA, 1964; Akademie der Bildenden Kunste, Vienna, 1964–65. Traveled Europe. **Taught:** U. of Massachusetts, 1965–67; School of Visual Arts, NYC, 1967–71; NYU, 1970– ; U. of Washington, 1970; Yale U. Summer School, Norfolk, Conn., 1971, 72. **Awards:** National Endowment for the Arts, grant ($7,500), 1973. **Address:** 101 Prince Street, NYC 10012; Studio: 89 West 3rd Street, NYC 10012. **Dealer:** The Pace Gallery. **One-man Exhibitions:** U. of Massachusetts, 1967; Bykert Gallery, 1970, 71, 73, 75; Los Angeles/County MA, 1971; Chicago/Contemporary, 1972; MOMA, 1973; Akron/AI, 1973; Austin, 1975; Art Museum of South Texas, Corpus Christi, 1975; The Texas Gallery, Houston, 1975; Portland (Ore.) Center for the Visual Arts, 1975; Cincinnati/Contemporary, 1976; Baltimore/MA, 1976; The Pace Gallery, NYC, 1977, 79; Hartford/Wadsworth, 1977; Paris/Beaubourg, 1979. **Group:** WMAA Annuals, 1969, 72; WMAA, 22 Realists, 1970; Oberlin College, Three Young Americans (with Ron Cooper and Neil Jenny), 1970; Dusseldorf/Kunsthalle, Prospect 72, 1971; Documenta V, Kassel, 1972; Galerie des 4 Mouvements, Paris, Hyperrealistes Americains, 1972;

Stuttgart/WK, Amerikanischer Fotorealismus, circ., 1972; WMAA, American Drawings: 1963–1973, 1973; Ars 74, Helsinki, 1974; Worcester/AM, Three Realists, 1974; XI Tokyo Biennial, 1974; Corcoran, Biennial, 1975; Fort Worth, American Artists: A New Decade, 1976; Stratford, Ont., Aspects of Realism, 1976; MOMA, Drawing Now, 1976; Chicago/AI, 1976; A.F.A., American Master Drawings and Watercolors, 1976; Daniel Weinberg, San Francisco (three-man), 1976; Akademie der Kunst, Berlin, SoHo, 1976; WMAA Biennials, 1977, 79; Documenta 6, Kassel, 1977; Canberra/National, Illusion and Reality, 1977; Minnesota/MA, American Drawings, 1927–1977, 1977; Paris/Beaubourg, Paris–New York, 1977; U. of California, Santa Barbara, Contemporary Drawing/NY, 1978; Buffalo/Albright, American Painting of the 1970's, 1978. **Collections:** Aachen/NG; Berlin; Canberra/National; Chicago/Contemporary; U. of Georgia; Helsinki; Indiana U.; LIC; Milwaukee/MA; MMA; MOMA; Minneapolis/Institute; U. of North Carolina; Oberlin College; Ottawa; PMA; Toronto; Utrecht; WMAA; Walker; Worcester/AM. **Bibliography:** *Amerikanischer Fotorealismus; Kunst um 1970; Sager; Three Realists;* Arthur 2; Diamonstein, Honisch and Jensen, eds.

CLUTZ, WILLIAM. b. March 19, 1933, Gettysburg, Pa. **Studied:** Mercersburg Academy, 1948–51; State U. of Iowa, with James Lechay, Stuart Edie, 1951–55, BA; ASL, 1956, with Robert Brackman. **Taught:** Artist-in-Residence, Bucknell U., 1957; Philadelphia College of Art, 1967; U. of Minnesota, 1967–68; Parsons School of Design, NYC, 1969– . **Address:** 370 Riverside Drive, NYC 10025. **Dealer:** Brooke Alexander. **One-man Exhibitions:** (first) Penn Hall Junior College and Preparatory School, Chambersburg, Pa., 1954; Bucknell U., 1957; Mercersburg Academy, 1958, 59; Condon Riley Gallery, NYC, 1959; David Herbert Gallery,

NYC, 1962; The Bertha Schaefer Gallery, 1963, 64, 66, 69; Triangle Art Gallery, 1967; The Graham Gallery, 1972; Brooke Alexander, 1973; Exeter, 1973; Alonzo Gallery, NYC, 1977, 78, 79; Moravian College, Bethlehem, Pa., 1977; Walther-Rathenau-Saal, Rathaus, Wedding, West Berlin, 1978; Choate–Rosemary Hall School, 1979; **Retrospectives:** Brookyn College, 1969; Andover/Phillips, 1973. **Group:** MOMA, Recent Drawings USA, 1956; A.F.A., The Figure, circ., 1960; Houston/MFA, The Emerging Figure, 1961; MOMA, Recent Painting USA; The Figure, circ., 1962–63; PAFA Annuals, 1964–66; MOMA, Art in Embassies, circ.; U. of Nebraska, 1965; Norfolk/Chrysler, 1966; Purdue U., 1968; Ringling, 1969; Columbus, 1970; Smithsonian, American Drawings 1976–79; Westmoreland County/AM, The New American Still Life, 1978. **Collections:** Andover/Phillips; AT&T, Ashland Oil Inc.; Ball State U.; Brooklyn College; Chase Manhattan Bank; Exeter; Hagerstown/County MFA; Harvard U.; Hirshhorn; MOMA; Mills College; Milwaukee; Minnesota/MA, U. of Minnesota; NYU; U. of Nebraska; Newark Museum; New York School of Interior Design; J. Henry Schroder Banking Corp.; SRGM.

COATES, ROSS. b. November 1, 1932, Hamilton (Ont.), Canada. **Studied:** U. of Michigan, 1951–53; Chicago Art Institute School, 1956, BFA; NYU, 1960, MA; NYU, 1972, Ph.D., Traveled Canada, USA, Europe, resided Africa, 1968–70. **Taught:** New York Community College, 1963; Kansas City Art Institute and School of Design, 1963–64; Montclair State College, 1965–68; Canon Lawrence T.T.C., Lira, Uganda, 1968–70; Russell Sage College, 1971–76; Washington State U., 1976– . **Address:** S.W. 420 State Street, Pullman, WA 99163. **One-man Exhibitions:** (first) Isaacs Gallery, 1957, also 1961; Camino Gallery, NYC, 1961; Louis Alexander Gallery, NYC, 1963; Galerie Niepel,

Dusseldorf, 1966; Springfield College, 1966; Jerrold Morris Gallery, Toronto, 1967; Galerie Seyfried, Munich, 1967; Kansas City Jewish Community Center, 1968; Russell Sage College, 1972; Schenectady Museum, 1974; U. of Rochester, 1974; Washington State U., 1978; Spokane Falls Community College, 1979; Gordon Woodside Gallery, Seattle, 1979; Eastern Washington U., 1979. **Collections:** U. of Alberta; Brandeis U.; Chase Manhattan Bank; U. of California; NYU; Springfield College; Stony Brook/SUNY; Russell Sage College.

CONGDON, WILLIAM. b. April 15, 1912, Providence, R.I. **Studied:** Yale U., BA; Cape School of Art, with Henry Hensche; PAFA; Folly Cove School of Art, with George Demetrios. American Field Service, World War II. Active in postwar Italy with American Friends Service Committee. Traveled Mexico, North Africa, India, Cambodia, Central America, Europe. **Awards:** RISD, 1949, 50; PAFA, Joseph E. Temple Gold Medal, 1951; U. of Illinois, **P.P.,** 1951; Corcoran, William A. Clark Prize, 1952; International Novara, Trieste, Gold Medal, 1961; Hon. DFA, U. of Portland, 1969. **Address:** Monastery S.S. Peter-Paul, 20094 Buccinasco, Milan, Italy. **One-man Exhibitions:** (first) Betty Parsons Gallery, 1949, also 1950, 52, 53, 54, 56, 59, 62, 67; ICA, Boston, 1951; Margaret Brown Gallery, Boston, 1951, 56; Phillips, 1952; L'Obelisco, Rome, 1953, 58; Providence (R.I.) Art Club, 1953; Santa Barbara/MA, 1954; UCLA, 1954; Arts Club of Chicago, 1954; Art of This Century (Peggy Guggenheim), 1957; Denver/AM, 1957; MIT, 1958; Arthur Jeffress Gallery, London, 1958; Michigan State U., 1959; Pro-Civitate-Christiana, 1961; Palazzo Reale, Milan, 1962; U. of Notre Dame, circ., 1964–65; New York World's Fair, Vatican Pavilion, 1964–65; Cambridge U., 1968; Galleria Cadario, Milan, 1969–70. **Retrospectives:** RISD, 1965; Galleria Cadario, 1969. **Group:** PAFA, 1936–38, 1951–53, 1956, 58, 60; NAD, 1939; Carnegie,

1940–52, 58; Andover/Phillips, 1941; MMA, American Painters under 35, 1950; WMAA, 1950, 51, 53, 56, 58; Buffalo/Albright, 1952; California Palace, 1952; U. of Illinois, 1952, 53, 55, 57, 59; Chicago/AI, 1952, 54, 57; XXVI & XXIX Venice Biennials, 1952, 58; WMAA, The New Decade, 1954–55; Walker, Expressionism, 1900–1955, 1956; International Novara, Trieste, 1961, 66; Musée Cantonal des Beaux-Arts, Lausanne, II Salon de Galeries Pilotes, 1966; Hartford/Wadsworth; Cincinnati/AM; Lincoln, Mass./De Cordova. **Collections:** Andover/Phillips; Boston/MFA; Carnegie; Cleveland/MA; Detroit/Institute; Hartford/Wadsworth; Houston/MFA; U. of Illinois; MMA; MOMA; Phillips; Pro-Civitate-Christiana; RISD; U. of Rochester; St. Louis/City; Santa Barbara/MA; Smithsonian; Toledo/MA; Venice/Contemporaneo; WMAA. **Bibliography:** McCurdy, ed.; Nordness, ed.; Pousette-Dart, ed.; Rodman 2.

CONNER, BRUCE. b. November 18, 1933, McPherson, Kans. **Studied:** U. of Nebraska, BFA; U. of Wichita; Brooklyn Museum School, with Reuben Tam; Kansas City Art Institute and School of Design; U. of Colorado. **Taught:** California College of Arts and Crafts, 1965–66; SFAI, 1966, 67, 72; UCLA, summer, 1973; San Jose State U., 1974; San Francisco State U., 1976. Produced the light show for the Avalon Ballroom; filmmaker. **Awards:** IV International Art Biennial, San Marino (Europe), Gold Medal, 1963; The U. of Chicago, Midwest Film Festival, First Prize; SFMA, Nealie Sullivan Award, 1963; Ford Foundation Grant, 1964; Tamarind Fellowship, 1965; Copley Foundation Award, 1965; National Endowment for the Arts, grant, 1973; American Film Institute, grant, 1974; Francis Scott Key Award, 1975; Guggenheim Foundation Fellowship, 1975; Brandeis U. Creative Art Award for Film, 1979. **Address:** 45 Sussex Street, San Francisco, CA 94131. **One-man Exhibitions:** Rienzi Gallery,

Bruce Conner   23 *Kenwood Ave.*   1963

NYC, 1956; East West Gallery, San Francisco, 1958; Designers Gallery, San Francisco, 1958; Spatsa Gallery, San Francisco, 1959; The Alan Gallery, NYC, 1960, 61, 63, 64, 65, 66; Batman Gallery, San Francisco, 1960, 62; Glantz Gallery, Mexico City, 1962; Antonio Suza Gallery, Mexico City; Ferus Gallery, Los Angeles, 1963; Wichita/AM, 1963; The Swetzoff Gallery, Boston, 1963; George Lester Gallery, Rome, 1964; Robert Fraser Gallery, London, 1964, 66; Brandeis U., 1965; Western Association of Art Museums, circ., 1965–66; U. of British Columbia, 1965; Galerie J, Paris, 1965; Quay Gallery, 1966, 72, 74; ICA, U. of Pennsylvania, 1967; SFAI, 1967, 71; Molly Barnes Gallery, Los Angeles, 1971; Reese Palley Gallery, San Francisco, 1971, 72; Martha Jackson Gallery, 1972; The Texas Gallery, 1972, 73; Nicholas Wilder Gallery, 1972; Jacqueline Anhalt Gallery, 1973; Tyler (Tex.) Museum of Art, 1974; Smith Andersen Gallery, Palo Alto, 1974; de Young, 1974; Braunstein/Quay Gallery, San Francisco, 1975, 76. **Retrospective:** ICA, U. of Pennsylvania, 1967; de Young, circ., 1974–75. **Group:**

SFAI Annuals, 1958, 63; San Francisco Episcopal Diocese, Church Art Today, 1960; U. of Illinois, 1961; MOMA, The Art of Assemblage, circ., 1961; WMAA, Fifty California Artists, 1962–63; IV International Art Biennial, San Marino, 1963; Chicago/AI, 66th Annual, 1963; Brandeis U., Recent American Drawings, 1964; ICA, Boston, Selection 1964, 1964; U. of California, Berkeley, Funk, 1967; Omaha/Joslyn, Nebraska Art Today, 1967; Los Angeles/County MA, American Sculpture of the Sixties, circ., 1967; WMAA, Human Concern/Personal Torment, 1969; Dallas/MFA, Poets of the Cities, 1974; Newport Harbor, A Drawing Show, 1975; Dallas/MFA, Poets of the Cities, circ., 1974. **Collections:** U. of California, Berkeley; Brandeis U.; Chicago/AI; Indiana U.; Kansas City/Nelson; Los Angeles/County MA; MOMA; U. of Missouri; U. of Nebraska; Netherlands Film Museum; Oakland/AM; Pasadena/AM; SFMA; WMAA; Wichita/AM; Worcester/AM. **Bibliography:** *Art as a Muscular Principle;* **Bruce Conner Drawings;** Janis and Blesh 1; Lippard 5; Rose, B., 1; Selz, P., 2; Siegfried; Tuchman 1. Archives.

CONOVER, ROBERT. b. July 3, 1920, Trenton, N.J. **Studied:** Philadelphia Museum School, 1938–42; ASL, with Morris Kantor, Cameron Booth, Will Barnet; Brooklyn Museum School, with Max Beckermann, John Ferren, Reuben Tam, William Kienbusch, William Baziotes. Corps of Army Engineers, World War II. Traveled Europe, Canada. **Taught:** New School for Social Research, 1957– ; Brooklyn Museum School, 1961– ; Newark (N.J.) School of Fine and Industrial Art 1967– . **Member:** American Abstract Artists; SAGA; Federal A.P.: National Youth Act, Philadelphia, 1939–41. **Commissions:** International Graphic Arts Society, 1957, 62 (woodcuts); New York Hilton Hotel, 1963; *Business Week* magazine, 1963. **Awards:** MacDowell Colony Fellowship; Brooklyn Museum, **P.P.,** 1951, 56; The Print Club, Philadelphia, **P.P.;**

PAFA, Samuel S. Fleisher Memorial **P.P.;** SAGA, **P.P.,** 1976 ($1,000), 1969; Trenton/State, **P.P.,** 1969; SAGA, Vera List Award, 1979; CAPS, 1976. **Address:** 162 East 33 Street, NYC 10016. **Dealer:** A.A.A. Gallery. **One-man Exhibitions:** (first) Laurel Gallery, NYC, 1949; The New Gallery, NYC, 1951, 53, 55; The Zabriskie Gallery, 1957, 59, 61; New School for Social Research, 1968, 74; New School for Social Research, NYC, 1977. **Group:** WMAA Annuals, 1950, 51, 53, 54, 55, 61; PAFA, 1951–53; Chicago/AI; Cincinnati/AM; MOMA, Abstract Painting and Sculpture in America, 1951; Brooklyn Museum, 1952, 54, 56, 58, 60, 62, 64, 66, 68; Newark Museum; Los Angeles/County MA; Memphis/Brooks; Walker, The Classic Tradition, 1953; MOMA, Young American Printmakers, 1953; WMAA, American Prints Today, 1958; ART: USA: 59, NYC, 1959; New York World's Fair, 1964–65; SAGA, 1965–69; American Abstract Artists, 1966–69; International Graphic Arts Exhibition, Zagreb; WMAA, Landscape in American Art; Pratt Institute, circ., Japan, 1967; Newark Museum, 1968; Trenton/State, 1968, 69; Library of Congress, 1969. **Collections:** Baltimore/MA; Brooklyn Museum; Ciba-Geigy Corp.; Cincinnati/AM; Cooper Hewitt Museum, NYC; Detroit/Institute; U. of Illinois; Library of Congress; MMA: MOMA: NCFA; NYPL; National Gallery; PAFA; PMA; Syracuse/Everson; Tokyo/Modern; Trenton/State; VMFA; WMAA. **Bibliography:** Baur 5; Ritchie 1. Archives.

CONSTANT, GEORGE. b. April 2, 1892, Greece; **d.** 1978, NYC. **Studied:** Washington U., 1912; Chicago Art Institute School, 1914–18; and with George Bellows, C. W. Hawthorne. Traveled Europe, USA. **Taught:** Dayton Art Institute School, 1920–22. **Member:** Federation of Modern Painters and Sculptors; Audubon Artists; Federal A.P.: Easel painting and graphic art. **Awards:** MMA, Alexander Shilling Prize, 1939, 45, 56; Chicago/AI, The Mr.

& Mrs. Frank G. Logan Prize, 1943; Audubon Artists, 1946, Emily Lowe Prize, 1968; Library of Congress, Pennell **P.P.**, 1947; Southampton/Parrish, 1950, 51, First Prize, 1966; Greek Government, Cross of the Phoenix Brigade, 1963; Guild Hall, The Carolyn Tyson Award for Best Abstract Painting, 1966; Mark Rothko Foundation Grant, 1970. **One-man Exhibitions:** (first) Arts Club of Chicago, 1929; Albert Roullier Gallery, Chicago; J. B. Neumann Gallery, NYC; Contemporary Arts Gallery, NYC; College Art Association Exhibit, circ., 1932–35; Boyer Gallery, Philadelphia, 1937, NYC, 1939; Marquie, NYC; Dikram Kelekian Gallery, NYC; Weyhe Gallery; Ferargil Galleries, NYC, 1944–48, 1950, 51; Grace Borgenicht Gallery Inc., 1952, 55; Philadelphia Art Alliance; Valentine-Dudensing Gallery, NYC; A. Oliva Gallery, Southampton, N.Y., 1965; Southampton/Parrish, 1965; The Harbor Gallery, Cold Spring Harbor, N.Y., 1966; Tirca Karlis Gallery, 1968; and some 30 others. **Retrospectives:** Southampton/Parrish, 1971; June 1 Gallery, Washington, D.C., 1972. **Group:** Victoria and Albert Museum; Brooklyn Museum; WMAA; Chicago/AI; MMA; PAFA; Carnegie; Amsterdam/Stedelijk; Minneapolis/Institute; Paris/Moderne; Corcoran; Library of Congress; State U. of Iowa; Golden Gate International Exposition, San Francisco, 1939; New York World's Fair, 1939, 1964–65; Walker, 1944, 48; Brooklyn Museum, 10 Years of American Prints—1947–56, 1956; USIA, 1956–57, 1960–61; USIA, 20th Century Highlights, circ., 1957–58; ART:USA:59, NYC, 1959; New School for Social Research, Humanists of the 60's, 1963, also 1965. **Collections:** Amsterdam/Stedelijk; Andover/Phillips; Auburn U.; Ball State U.; Baltimore/MA; Brandeis U.; Brooklyn Museum; Dayton/AI; Detroit/Institute; Guild Hall; Hirshhorn; Library of Congress; MMA; Michigan State U.; NPG; NYU; U. of Nebraska; New Orleans/Delgado; Norfolk; PAFA; PMA; Pinacotheque National Museum; Purchase/SUNY; SFMA; St. Lawrence U.; Smithsonian; Tel Aviv; US State Department; WMAA; Walker; Wichita State U.; Youngstown/Butler. **Bibliography:** Archives.

COOK, HOWARD. b. July 16, 1901, Springfield, Mass., **d.** June 24, 1980, Santa Fe, New Mexico. **Studied:** ASL, 1919–21, with George Bridgeman, Wallace Morgan, Joseph Pennell, Andrew Dasburg, Maurice Sterne. Artist War Correspondent, South Pacific, World War II. Traveled extensively, USA, North Africa, the Orient, Europe. **Taught:** U. of Texas, 1942–43; Minneapolis Institute School, 1945–50; U. of New Mexico, 1947; U. of California, Berkeley, 1948; Colorado Springs Fine Arts Center, 1949; Scripps College, 1951; Washington U., 1954; New Mexico Highlands U., 1957. **Member:** NAD; SAGA. Federal A.P.: Mural painting. **Commissions** (murals): Hotel Tasqueno, Taco, Mexico; Law Library, Springfield, Mass.; Federal Court House, Pittsburgh, Pa.; US Post Offices, Alamo Plaza (San Antonio) and Corpus Christi; Mayo Clinic, Rochester, Minn. **Awards:** Two Guggenheim Foundation Fellowships; Architectural League of New York, Gold Medal; NAD, Samuel F.B. Morse Gold Medal; MMA, **P.P.**, 1942; PMA, **P.P.**; Denver/AM, **P.P.**; Tupperware National Competition, **P.P.**, 1956; Orlando, **P.P.**; Oklahoma, First Painting Award; Tucson Fine Arts Association, Art Prize. **One-man Exhibitions:** (first) Denver/AM, 1928; Weyhe Gallery, 1929, 31, 34, 37, 41; Springfield, Mass./MFA, 1936; The Print Club, Philadelphia, 1937; Kennedy Gallery, 1942, 44; National Gallery, 1944; Rehn Galleries, 1945, 50; Dallas/MFA, 1945, 53; Minneapolis/Institute, 1950; Grand Central Moderns, NYC, 1951, 53, 56, 60, 64; San Diego, 1952, Santa Barbara, MA, 1952; de Young, 1952; Kansas City/Nelson, 1953; Omaha/Joslyn, 1953; G.W.V. Smith Art Museum, Springfield, Mass., 1954; Houston/MFA, 1954; Dartmouth College, 1954; Montclair/AM, 1954; Carnegie, 1958; Raymond Burr Gallery, Los Angeles, 1962, 63. **Retrospective:** Roswell, 1975. **Group:** WMAA, 20th-Century Drawings from the Permanent Collection, 1975. **Collections:** Baltimore/MA; Chicago/AI; Denver/MFA; Dartmouth College; Denver/AM; de Young; Harvard U.; MMA; MOMA; Minneapolis/Institute; Oklahoma; Omaha/Joslyn; Orlando; PMA; U. of Rochester; Santa Barbara/MA; Santa Fe, N.M.; WMAA. **Bibliography:** American Artists Congress, Inc.; American Artists Group Inc. 1, 3; Bethers; Bruce and Watson; Cheney; Coke 2; Hall; Kent, N.; Mellquist; Pearson 1; Pousette-Dart, ed.; Reese; Wheeler; Zigrosser 1. Archives.

CPLY (William N. Copley)   Untitled   1978

COPLEY, WILLIAM N. (CPLY) b. January 24, 1919, NYC. **Studied:** Andover; Yale U. Self-taught artist. Proprietor of the Copley Gallerie in Beverly Hills, 1947–48. Designed sets and costumes for *Crosswalk*, by George Skibine, for the Harkness Ballet Co., 1965. Publisher of the S.M.S. Press. Address: 1 Frisbie Road, Roxbury, CT 06783. **Dealer:** Brooks Jackson Gallery Iolas, NYC. **One-man Exhibition:** (first) Royer's Bookstore, Los Angeles, 1947; Galerie Nina Dauset, Paris, 1953; Galerie Monte Napoleone, Milan, 1954; Galerie du Dragon, 1956; Iolas Gallery, NYC, 1956, 58, 60, 63, 65, 66, 67, 70, 71, 72, 76, 78; Brooks Jackson Gallery Iolas, NYC, 1979, 80; Galerie Furstenburg, Paris, 1959; Galleria Naviglio, Milan, 1960; Galleria Cavalino, Venice, 1960; ICA, London, 1960; Galerie Schwarz, Milan, 1961; Galerie Iris Clert, Paris, 1961, 62; Hanover Gallery, London, 1962; David Stuart Gallery, Los Angeles, 1964, 70, 72; Hanover Gallery, London, 1962; Louisiana Gallery, Houston, 1965; Southwestern College, Chula Vista, 1965; Allan Frumkin Gallery, Chicago, 1965; Galerie Iolas, Paris, 1966, 72; Bodley Gallery, NYC, 1968; Galerie Neuendorf, Hamburg, 1968; Galerie Springer, Berlin 1968, 70, 72, 78; Merida Gallery, Louisville, 1969; Galerie Aspects, Brussels, 1972; Galerie Iolas, Milan, 1972; Gallery Saxe, San Francisco, 1972; Galeria Il Fauno, Torino, 1973; Moore College of Art, Philadelphia, 1974; Onnasch Gallery, NYC, 1974; Gallerie Onnasch, Cologne, 1974; Erik Nord Gallery, Nantucket, 1975; Galerie Renate Fassbender, Munich, 1978; Galerie Zwirner, Cologne, 1978; Rice U., 1979. **Retrospective:** Amsterdam/Stedelijk, 1966; Berne, circ., 1980. **Group:** Nagaoka, Exposition International de l'art actuel, 1956; Salon de Mai, Paris, 1957, 58, 59, 61; Stockholm/National, Objects in Motion, 1961; Pasadena/AM, Collage out of California, 1962; Paris/Decoratifs, L'Antagonisme de l'objet, 1962; Oakland, Pop Art, 1963; Brandeis U., New Directions in American Painting, 1964; Huntington, N.Y./Heckscher, Whence Pop, 1965; U. of California, Santa Barbara, Surrealism, 1966; New School for Social Research, NYC, Erotic Art, 1971; New York Cultural Center, Three Generations of the American Nude, 1975; The New Museum, NYC, Bad Painting Show, 1977; Los Angeles/County MA; Cooper-Hewitt Museum, NYC, Box Museum, 1978. **Collections:** Amsterdam/Stedelijk; Chicago/AI; MOMA; Oberlin College; Paris/Beaubourg; Paris/Moderne; Pasadena/AM; PMA; Princeton U.; U. of Sydney; Tate; WMAA. **Bibliography:** Hunter, ed. Archives.

CORBETT, EDWARD. b. August 22, 1919, Chicago, Ill; **d.** June 6, 1971, Provincetown, Mass. **Studied:** California School of Fine Arts, two years. Traveled Mexico, USA, Philippines. US Army, US Navy, Merchant Marine, 1941–44. **Taught:** San Francisco State Teachers College, 1947; California School of Fine Arts, 1947–50; U. of California, Berkeley, 1950; Mount Holyoke College, 1953–62; U. of New Mexico, 1955; U. of Minnesota, 1960–61; Santa Barbara, 1967–68. **Awards:** Abraham Rosenberg Foundation Fellowship, 1951. **One-man Exhibitions:** Grace Borgenicht Gallery, Inc., 1956, 59, 61, 64, 70, 73, 81; Quay Gallery, 1967. **Retrospective:** MIT, 1959; Walker, 1961; SFMA, 1969. **Group:** California Palace, 1957, 50; Riverside Museum, 1948; Chicago/AI, American Abstract Artists, 1948; de Young, 1951; MOMA, Fifteen Americans, circ., 1952; WMAA Annuals, 1953, 55, 58, 61, 63, 65–68; U. of Illinois, 1954; U. of Nebraska, 1955; Carnegie, 1955; Corcoran, 1956, 1966–68; Walker, 1961; Sao Paulo, 1962; NCFA, 1966; WMAA, Art of the U.S. 1670–1966, 1966. **Collections:** Andover/Phillips; Bankers Trust Company; Buffalo/Albright; Burlington Mills Collection; Carnegie; Chase Manhattan Bank; Chicago/AI; Corcoran; Harcourt, Brace & World, Inc.; MOMA; Mount Holyoke College; National Gallery; Newark Museum; Phillips, SFMA; SRGM; Tate; WMAA; Walker. **Bibliography:** McChesney.

CORBINO, JON. b. April 3, 1905, Vittoria, Sicily; **d.** July 10, 1964, Sarasota, Fla. To USA, 1913. **Studied:** PAFA, with Daniel Barber; ASL, with George Luks, Frank V. DuMond, William Von

Schlegell. **Taught:** ASL, 1938–56; NAD, 1945. **Member:** NAD; ASL; Lotus Club; PAFA; Philadelphia Watercolor Club; Audubon Artists Federal A.P.: US Post Office, Long Beach, N.Y. (mural). **Awards:** Chicago/AI, The M.V. Kohnstamm Prize, 1937; PAFA, Walter Lippincott Prize and Purchase, 1938; NAD, The Adolph and Clara Obrig Prize, 1938; Lotus Club, Drawing Award, 1938; New Rochelle Art Association, Silver Medal, 1940; NIAL, Painting Award, 1941; Leonardo da Vinci Art School, NYC, Da Vinci Silver Medal, 1942; Chicago/AI, Watson F. Blair Prize, 1944; NAD, Saltus Gold Medal for Merit, 1944; Audubon Artists, Gold Medal of Honor, 1945; Salmagundi Club, NYC, **P.P.**, 1945; Pepsi-Cola, 1945; La Tausca Competition, 1946; Rockport (Mass.) Art Association, Hayward Neidringhause Memorial Prize, 1950; National Arts Club, Gold Medal, 1950; NAD, Ellen P. Speyer Prize, 1961. **One-man Exhibitions:** (first) Oberlin College 1927, also 1939; Contemporary Arts Gallery, NYC, 1934; Goodman Walker, Inc., Boston, 1935; Macbeth Gallery, NYC, 1937, 38, 40; A.A.A. Gallery, NYC, 1937; Corcoran, 1938; Warner Gallery, Los Angeles, 1939; Carnegie, 1939; Grace Horne Galleries, Boston, 1939; J. Seligmann and Co., 1942; Kleemann Gallery, NYC, 1944, 45; Marshall Field & Co., Chicago, 1948; Rehn Galleries, 1948; 51, 55, 59; Boris Mirski Gallery, Boston, 1950; The Manor Club, Pelham, N.Y., 1952; Frank Oehlschlaeger Gallery, Chicago, 1953, 56, 60; Cowie Galleries, Los Angeles, 1959; O'Brien's Art Emporium, Scottsdale, Ariz., 1960; Art Center, Bradenton, Fla., 1961; Ringling, 1963; Harmon Gallery, Naples, Fla., 1964. **Group:** Chicago/AI, 1926, 36, 43, 44; Brooklyn Museum, 1931, 39, 43; Andover/Phillips, 1936; Carnegie, 1936, 37, 38, 40, 42, 50; U. of Minnesota, 1936; WMAA, 1937, 38, 40, 49, 52; PAFA, 1937, 50; Detroit/Institute, 1937; Worcester/AM, 1938, 42; St. Louis/City, 1938; NAD, 1938, 39, 44, 47; VMFA, 1938, 44; Toledo/MA, 1938, 40, 41;

Golden Gate International Exposition, San Francisco, 1939; New York World's Fair, 1939; Cranbrook, 1940; MMA, 1941, 42, 50; Audubon Artists, 1945; Los Angeles/County MA, 1945; U. of Illinois, 1948; Sao Paulo, 1960; U. of South Florida, 1962. **Collections:** ASL; Amherst College; Andover/Phillips; Ball State U.; Brigham Young U.; Britannica; Brooklyn Museum; Canajoharie; Carnegie; Chicago/AI; Clearwater/Gulf Coast; Davenport/Municipal; Downtown Community School; Hebron Academy; Hickory, N.C.; Howard U.; IBM; Indianapolis/Herron; Kalamazoo/Institute; Kansas City/Nelson; Lotus Club; MMA; Memphis/Brooks; Montclair/AM; Mount Holyoke College; Municipal U. of Omaha; NAD; New Britain; Northwest Missouri State College; PAFA; Pasadena/AM; Portland, Me./MA; Quaker Ridge School; Ripon College; San Diego; Society of the Four Arts; Southampton/Parrish; Sweet Briar College; Toledo/MA; WMAA; Walker; Worcester/AM; Youngstown/Butler. **Bibliography:** Baur 7; Boswell 1; Cheney; Flexner; Genauer; Hall; Kent, N.; Pagano. Archives.

CORNELL, JOSEPH. b. December 24, 1903, Nyack, N.Y.; **d. December 29, 1972, NYC. Awards:** Copley Foundation Grant, 1954; Chicago/AI, Ada S. Garrett Prize, 1959; AAAL, Award of Merit, 1968. **One-man Exhibitions:** (first) Julien Levy Galleries, NYC, 1932, also 1933, 39; 40; Hugo Gallery, NYC, 1946; Copley Gallery, Hollywood, 1948; Charles Egan Gallery, 1949, 50; Allan Gallery, Chicago, 1953; Walker, 1953; The Stable Gallery, 1957; Bennington College, 1959; Richard Feigen Gallery, Chicago, 1960 (three-man); Ferus Gallery, Los Angeles, 1962; Robert Schoelkopf Gallery, NYC, 1966; J. L. Hudson Art Gallery, Detroit, 1966; Brandeis U., 1968; Allan Stone Gallery, 1972; Buffalo/Albright, 1972; Chicago/

Joseph Cornell *Untitled, Celestial Set* c. 1952–54

Contemporary, 1973; Castelli, Feigen, Corcoran Gallery, NYC, 1978, 79, 80; ACA Gallery, NYC, 1975, 77; Wichita State U., 1980; Greenberg Gallery, Clayton, Mo., 1976; Rice U., 1977; Baudoin Lebon, Paris, 1977. **Retrospectives:** Pasadena/AM, 1966; SRGM, 1967; MOMA, 1980. **Group:** MOMA, Fantastic Art, Dada, Surrealism, 1936; Galerie des Beaux Arts, Paris, Exposition Internationale du Surrealisme, 1938; Art of This Century, NYC, 1942; Carnegie, 1958; MOMA, The Art of Assemblage, 1961; Seattle World's Fair, 1962; WMAA Annuals, 1962, 66; NYU, Boxes and Collages, 1963; Chicago/AI, 1964; Musée Rodin, Paris, Sculpture of the 20th Century, 1965; U. of Illinois, 1967. **Collections:** Boston/MFA; MOMA; Pasadena/AM; WMAA. **Bibliography: Ashton, ed.**; Baur 7; Blesh 1; Breton 2; Calas, N. and E.; Downes, ed.; Finch; Flanagan; Guggenheim, ed.; Hunter 6; Hunter, ed.; Janis and Blesh 1; Janis, S.; Johnson, Ellen H.; Kozloff 3; Licht, F.; Marter, Tarbell, and Wechsler; McShine, ed.; *Metro*; O'Doherty; Read 3; Rickey; Rose, B., 1; Rubin 1; Steitz 3; Seuphor 3; *7 Decades*; Tuchman 1; **Waldman 3.** Archives.

CORNELL, THOMAS. b. March 1, 1937, Cleveland, Ohio. **Studied:** Amherst College, 1959, BA, with Leonard Baskin; Yale U., 1960–61, with N. Welliver, Wm. Bailey, B. Chaet. US Marine Corps, 1956–63. Traveled Europe and U.S. **Taught:** U. of California, Santa Barbara, 1960–62; Princeton U., 1969–71; Bowdoin College, Maine, 1963– . **Member:** CAA; Alliance of Figurative Artists. **Commissions:** IGAS, print edition, 1966; many portrait commissions. **Awards:** I. C. Tiffany Grant, 1961; National Endowment for the Arts, grant, 1966; Ford Foundation, grant, 1969. **Address:** 237 Lafayette Street, NYC 10012. **Dealer:** A.M. Sachs Gallery, NYC; **One-man Exhibitions:** (first) Esther Baer Gallery, Santa Barbara, 1961, 63; Rex Evans Gallery, Los Angeles, 1962; Sabarsky Gallery, Los

Angeles, 1965; Yale U., 1965; Princeton U., 1971; Dartmouth College, 1966; Tragos Gallery, Boston, 1966; Block Gallery, St. Louis, 1968; Bowdoin College, 1971; A.A.A. Gallery, NYC, 1972; Optik Gallery, Amherst, 1972; Frishman Gallery, Boston, 1974; Muhlenberg College, 1976; Barridoff Galleries, Portland, Me., 1977; A. M. Sachs Gallery, NYC, 1979; U. of Redlands, Calif., 1979. **Group:** MOMA, Contemporary Painters and Sculptors as Printmakers, 1964; Brooklyn Museum, Print Biennial, 1960; Grolier Club, 1966; Ringling, Young New England Painters, 1969; The Pennsylvania State U., Contemporary Artists and the Figure, 1974; Southern Connecticut State College, In Their Own Image, 1976; Brooklyn Museum, Thirty Years of American Printmaking, 1976. **Collections:** Amherst College; Bowdoin College; U. of California, Berkeley and Los Angeles; Cleveland/MA; Harvard U.; MIT, MOMA; NCFA; U. of North Carolina; NYPG; Princeton U. Library; Smith College; Yale U.

COTTINGHAM, ROBERT. b. September 26, 1935, Brooklyn, N.Y. **Studied:** Pratt Institute, 1959–64, Associate Degree in Advertising Art. US Army, 1955–58. At one time art director for Young and Rubicam, New York and Los Angeles. **Taught:** Art Center College of Design, Los Angeles, 1969–70. **Awards:** National Endowment for the Arts, 1974. **Address:** Blackman Road, Newtown, CT 06470. **One-man Exhibitions:** Molly Barnes Gallery, Los Angeles, 1968, 69, 70; OK Harris Works of Art, 1971, 74, 76, 78; D.M. Gallery, London, 1975; Galerie de Gestlo, Hamburg, 1975, Cologne, 79; John Berggruen Gallery, San Francisco, 1976; Morgan Gallery, Kansas City, 1978; Bethel Art Gallery, Bethel, Conn., 1978; Ridgefield/Aldrich, 1979; Beaver College, 1979; Landfall Press Gallery, Chicago, 1977, 79; Delta Gallery, Rotterdam, 1979. **Group:** Fresno State College, The Persistent Image, 1970; ICA, U. of Pennsylvania, Highway,

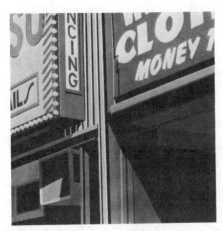

Robert Cottingham   *Money*   1972

1970; Chicago/Contemporary, Radical Realism, 1971; Potsdam/SUNY, New Realism, 1971; Documenta V. Kassel, 1972; Stuttgart/WK, Amerikanischer Fotorealismus, circ., 1972; New York Cultural Center, Realism Now, 1972; Lincoln, Mass./De Cordova, The Super-Realist Vision, 1973; Los Angeles Municipal Art Gallery, Separate Realities, 1973; Cincinnati/Contemporary, Options, 73/30, 1973; CNAC, Hyperrealistes Americains/Realistes Europeens, 1974; Hartford/Wadsworth, New Photo Realism, 1974; Tokyo Biennial, 1974; Toledo/MA, Image, Color and Form—Recent Paintings by Eleven Americans 1975; Wichita State U., The New Realism: Rip-Off or Reality? 1975; Nordjyllands Kunstmuseum, Aalborg, Tendenser i Modern Kunst, 1975; Renwick Gallery, Washington, D.C., Signs of Life: Symbols in the City, 1975; NCFA, Recent American Etchings, circ., 1975; Baltimore/MA, Super Realism, 1975; Brooklyn Museum, Thirty Years of American Printmaking, 1976; NCFA, America as Art, 1976; Canberra/National, Illusion and Reality, circ., 1977; U. of Texas, Austin, New in the '70's, 1977. **Collections:** Ackland; Arts Council of Great Britain; Baltimore/MA; Carnegie; Cincinnati/AM, Cleveland/MA; Currier; Dartmouth College; Detroit/Institute; Harvard U.; High Museum; Hirshhorn; Honolulu Academy; Indianapolis; U. of Iowa; U. of Kansas; Long Beach/MA; New Orleans Museum; NCFA; Notre Dame U.; PMA; RISD; Rotterdam; Rutgers U.; Springfield, Mass./MFA; Syracuse U.; U. of Utah; U. of Virginia; Wesleyan U. (Conn.); Williams College; WMAA; Yale U. **Bibliography:** *Amerikanischer Fotorealismus;* Sager; *The State of California Painting.*

COVERT, JOHN. b. 1882, Pittsburgh, Pa.; **d.** December 24, 1960, NYC. **Studied:** Pittsburgh School of Design, 1902–08; in Munich, 1908–12, on a German government scholarship. Traveled France, Germany, England. A founder and director of the Society of Independent Artists, 1916. The collection of the Societé Anonyme was started with a gift of six of his paintings in 1923. Stopped painting between 1923 and 1949. **Group:** Paris Salon, 1914; Independent Artists, NYC, 1917; PAFA, 1921; Societé Anonyme, 1921; Vassar College, 1923; Detroit/Institute, 1923; Brooklyn Museum, 1926; Delphic Studios, NYC, 1936; Dallas Museum for Contemporary Arts, 1961; WMAA, 1963; Hirshhorn, 1976. **Collections:** MOMA; PMA; Seattle/AM; Yale U. **Bibliography:** *Avante-Garde Painting and Sculpture; Avante-Garde Painting and Sculpture in America, 1910–1925;* Baur 7; Brown 2; Hunter 6; Rose, B., 1; Tashjian.

COWLES, RUSSELL. b. October 7, 1887, Alogna, Iowa; **d.** February 22, 1979, NYC. **Studied:** Dartmouth College; ASL; American Academy, Rome; NAD (assistant to Douglas Volk and Barry Faulkner in mural painting). Traveled Europe and Asia extensively. US Army Intelligence, 1917. **Awards:** Prix de Rome, 1915; Chicago/AI, Norman Wait Harris Silver Medal, 1926; Denver/AM, Yetter Prize, 1936; Hon. DFA, Grinnell College, 1945; Hon. DFA, Dartmouth College, 1951; Hon,

DFA, Cornell U., 1958. **One-man Exhibitions:** Ferargil Galleries, NYC, 1935; Los Angeles/County MA, 1937; Dalzell Hatfield Gallery, 1939, 43; Kraushaar Galleries, 1939, 41, 44, 46, 48, 50, 54, 59, 73; Dayton/AI, 1942 (three-man); Dartmouth College, 1948, 63; Des Moines, 1955. **Group:** Carnegie; PAFA; WMAA; Los Angeles/County MA; Des Moines; Architectural League of New York; Chicago/AI; California Palace; Wichita/AM; Corcoran. **Collections:** Andover/Phillips; Britannica; Dartmouth College; Denver/AM; Des Moines; Fort Dodge/Blanden; Los Angeles/County MA; Minneapolis/Institute; New Britain; PAFA; Santa Barbara/MA; Terre Haute/Swope; Wichita/AM. **Bibliography:** Baer; Bethers; Cheney; Hall; Kent, N.; Pearson 2; Watson, E. W., 2; Wheeler. Archives.

CRAMER, KONRAD. b. November 9, 1888, Wurzburg, Germany; **d.** January, 1965, Woodstock, N.Y. **Studied:** Academy of Fine Arts, Karlsruhe, Germany. **Taught:** Bard College, 1940. Founder, Woodstock (N.Y.) School of Photography, 1936. **One-man Exhibitions:** Woodstock (N.Y.) Art Gallery, 1952; New Paltz/SUNY, 1952; Long Island U., 1958; Rochester Institute of Technology, 1966; The Zabriskie Gallery, 1963, 73, 80. **Group:** MacDowell Club, NYC, 1912; Whitney Studio Club, NYC, 1924; WMAA, Abstract Painting in America, 1935; PAFA, 1936; Carnegie, 1937, 38; Corcoran, 1938, 39; WMAA, Pioneers of Modern Art in America, 1946; Woodstock (N.Y.) Art Gallery; WMAA, The Decade of the Armory Show, 1963; U. of New Mexico, Cubism, Its Impact in the U.S.A., 1910–1930, 1967; Delaware Art Museum, Avant-Garde Painting and Sculpture in America, 1910–1925, 1975; WMAA, Synchronism and American Color Abstraction: 1910–1925, 1978. **Collections:** International Museum of Photography; MMA; MOMA; NCFA; U. of North Carolina; PMA; San Diego; U. of Texas; WMAA. **Bibliography:** *Avant-Garde Painting and Sculpture;*

Bauer 7; Brown 2; Janis, S.; Levin 2; Rose, B., 1; Woodstock. Archives.

CRAMPTON, ROLLIN McNEILL. b. March 9, 1886, New Haven, Conn; **d.** January 17, 1970, Woodstock N.Y. **Studied:** Yale U., with Lanzetell, Thompson; ASL, with Thomas Fogarty, Renterdahl. Federal A.P.: Mural Supervisor. **Awards:** AAAL Grant; Longview Foundation Grant; Louisiana State U., **P.P. One-man Exhibitions:** (first) Woodstock (N.Y.) Art Gallery; The Peridot Gallery, 1958; The Krasner Gallery, 1960, 71; The Stable Gallery, NYC, 1961, 64, 68, 69. **Collections:** Buffalo/Albright; Hartford/Wadsworth; Kalamazoo/Institute; Louisiana State U.; MIT; MMA; New Paltz/SUNY; U. of Texas; WMAA; Walker. **Bibliography:** Read 4; *Woodstock: An American Art Colony, 1902–1977;* Zaidenberg, ed. Archives.

CRAWFORD, RALSTON. b. September 5, 1906, St. Catharines (Ont.), Canada; **d.** April 27, 1978, Houston, Texas. **Studied:** Otis Art Institute, Los Angeles, 1926–27; PAFA, 1927–30, with Henry Breckenridge, Henry McCarter; Barnes Foundation, 1927–30; Academie Colarossi and Academie Scandinave, Paris, 1932–33; Columbia U., 1933. Traveled Europe, Canada, South Pacific, North Africa, USA, Mediterranean. **Taught:** Art Academy of Cincinnati, 1940–41, 1949; Buffalo Fine Arts Academy, 1942; Honolulu Academy School, summer, 1947; Brooklyn Museum School, 1948–49; U. of Minnesota; Louisiana State U., 1949–50; New School for Social Research, 1952–57; U. of Colorado, summer, 1953; U. of Michigan, summer, 1953; lecture tour of U.S.A. for American Association of Colleges, 1956; Hofstra College, 1960–62; U. of Southern California, summer, 1961; U. of Nebraska, 1965; U. of Illinois, 1966. **Awards:** L. C. Tiffany Grant, 1931; Wilmington, 1933; Mary Curtis Bok Foundation Fellowship,

1937; MMA, **P.P.**, 1942; Tamarind Fellowship, 1966. **One-man Exhibitions:** (first) Maryland Institute, 1934; Boyer Gallery, Philadelphia, 1937, NYC, 1939; Philadelphia Art Alliance, 1938; Cincinnati/AM, 1941; Flint/Institute, 1942; Artists' Gallery, Philadelphia, 1943; The Downtown Gallery, 1943, 44, 46, 50; Arts Club of Chicago, 1945 (three-man); Portland, Ore./AM, 1946; Santa Barbara/MA, 1946; Howard U., 1947; MacMurray College, 1949; Hofstra College, 1952; U. of Alabama, 1953; Grace Borgenicht Gallery, Inc., 1954, 56, 58; Louisiana State U., 1956; Milwaukee, 1958; Lee Nordness Gallery, NYC, 1961, 63; U. of Nebraska, 1965; U. of Illinois, 1966; The Zabriskie Gallery, 1973, 76; Ronald Greenberg Gallery, St. Louis, 1974; Corcoran & Greenberg Gallery, Inc., Coral Gables; Middendorf-Lane Gallery, Washington, D.C., 1977; Century Association, NYC, 1978. **Retrospectives:** U. of Alabama, 1953; Milwaukee, 1958; U. of Kentucky, 1961; U. of Minnesota, 1961; Creighton U., 1968; U. of Nebraska (photographs); Utica; Montgomery Museum. **Group:** PAFA; WMAA; MOMA; MMA; Corcoran; Phillips; Chicago/AI. **Collections:** American Export Isbrandtsen Lines, Inc.; Auburn U.; Baton Rouge; Buffalo/Albright; Cincinnati/AM; Flint/Institute; U. of Georgia; Hamline U.; Hofstra U.; Honolulu Academy; Houston/MFA; Howard College; Illinois Wesleyan U.; Library of Congress; MMA; MOMA; MacMurray College; Michigan State U.; The Miller Co.; U. of Minnesota; Newark Museum; U. of Oklahoma; Phillips; SFMA; Toledo/MA; Vassar College; WMAA; Walker, Wesleyan U.; Youngstown/Butler. **Bibliography:** *America 1976*; Baur 7; Boswell 1; *From Foreign Shores*; Frost; Halpert, Janis, S.; Kootz 2; McCurdy, ed.; Nordness, ed.; Pagano; Reese; Ritchie 1; Rodman 2; Rose, B., 1. Archives.

CREMEAN, ROBERT. b. September 28, 1932, Toledo, Ohio. **Studied:** Alfred U., 1950–52; Cranbrook Academy of Art, 1954, BA, 1956, MFA. **Taught:** The Detroit Institute of Arts; UCLA, 1956–57; Art Center in La Jolla, 1957–58. **Awards:** Fulbright Fellowship (Italy), 1954; Tamarind Fellowship, 1966. **Address:** % Dealer. **Dealer:** Braunstein-Quay Gallery, San Francisco. **One-man Exhibitions:** Esther Robles Gallery, 1960–66, 73; The Landau-Alan Gallery, NYC, 1968; Wisconsin State U., 1969; Melbourne/National, 1970; Archer Gallery, London, 1972; Santa Barbara/MA, 1975; de Young, 1976; Braunstein-Quay Gallery, San Francisco, 1977. **Group:** Detroit/Institute, 1956; Houston/MFA, 1957; Santa Barbara/MA, 1957; U. of Nebraska, 1958; Chicago/AI, 1960, 61; Los Angeles/County MA, The Image Retained, 1961; SFMA, Bay Area Artists, 1961; California Palace, 1961; WMAA Annuals, 1961, 62; U. of Illinois, 1961, 63; Western Association of Art Museum Directors, Light, Space, Mass, circ., 1962; WMAA, Fifty California Artists, 1962–63; XXXIV Venice Biennial, 1968. **Collections:** Cleveland/MA; Detroit/Institute; Los Angeles/County MA; U. of Miami; U. of Michigan; U. of Nebraska; St. Louis/City; Santa Barbara/MA; Toledo/MA; UCLA. **Bibliography:** Geske.

CRISS, FRANCIS H. b. April 26, 1901, London, England; **d.** November 27, 1973, NYC. **Studied:** PAFA; ASL, with Jan Matulka. **Taught:** Brooklyn Museum School; Albright Art School; ASL; Graphic Sketch Club, Philadelphia. **Awards:** PAFA, Cresson Fellowship; Guggenheim Foundation Fellowship, 1934. **One-man Exhibitions:** (first) Contemporary Arts Gallery, NYC; Mellon Galleries, Philadelphia, 1933, 34; Philadelphia Art Alliance, 1953; School of Visual Arts, NYC. **Retrospective:** School of Visual Arts, NYC, 1967. **Group:** WMAA, 1936, 37, 38, 40, 42, 51; Corcoran, 1939; PAFA, 1939, 41, 43, 45; MMA, 1941; Chicago/AI, 1942, 43; Carnegie, 1944, 45. **Collections:** Kansas City/Nelson; La France Art Institute; National Gallery; PMA; WMAA. **Bibliography:** Baur 7; Pagano. Archives.

CRONBACH, ROBERT M. b. February 10, 1908, St. Louis, Mo. **Studied:** Washington School of Fine Arts, 1926, with Victor Holm; PAFA, 1927–30, with Charles Grafly, Albert Laesslie; assistant in Paul Manship Studio, NYC and Paris, 1930. Traveled Europe extensively. **Taught:** Adelphi College, 1947–62; North Shore Community Art Center, 1949–54; Skowhegan School, summers, 1959, 60, 64. **Member:** Sculptors Guild; Architectural League of New York; Artists Equity. Federal A.P.: Willerts Park Housing Project, Buffalo, N.Y., 1939 (sculpture). **Commissions** (architectural): St. Louis (Mo.) Municipal Auditorium, 1933, Social Security Building, Washington, D.C., 1940; Cafe Society Uptown, NYC, 1940; Hotel Hollenden, Cleveland, 1946; Hopping Phillips Motor Agency, Newark, N.J., 1948; 240 Central Park South, NYC, 1954; Dorr-Oliver Building, Stamford, Conn., 1957; Adelphi College, 1958; Ward School, New Rochelle, N.Y., 1959; National Council for U.S. Art, 1960 (a gift to the United Nations); Temple Chizuk Amuno, Baltimore, 1962, 68; Federal Building, St. Louis 1964; Temple Israel, St. Louis, 1964; Charleston (W. Va.) Public Library, 1965. **Awards:** PAFA, Stewardson Prize, 1938; PAFA, Cresson Fellowship, 1929, 30; National Sculpture Competition for Social Security Building, Washington, D.C., First Award, 1939. **Address:** 170 Henry Street, Westbury, NY 11590. **One-man Exhibitions:** (first) Hudson D. Walker Gallery, NYC, 1939; The Bertha Schaefer Gallery, 1951 (two-man), 1952, 1960 (two-man), 1967, 71; The New Bertha Schaefer Gallery, 1974. **Group:** New York World's Fairs, 1939, 1964–65; Sculptors Guild, 1939–42, 1945–62, 1967; City of Philadelphia Sculpture International, 1940, 49; MMA, 1943; Denver/AM, The Modern Artist and His World, 1947; WMAA Annuals, 1948,

1956–59; Riverside Museum, 1947; Silvermine Guild, 1947, 58, 60; Brussels World's Fair, 1958; ART: USA: 59, NYC, 1959; HemisFair '68, San Antonio, Tex., 1968; PAFA Architectural League of New York; Brooklyn Museum; St. Louis/City; Houston/MFA; MOMA. **Collections:** U. of Minnesota; Rosenthal China Co.; St. Louis/City; Springfield, Mo./AM; Walker. **Bibliography:** Baur 7; Archives.

CURRY, JOHN STEUART. b. November 14, 1897, Dunavant, Kans.; **d.** 1946, Madison, Wisc. **Studied:** Kansas City Art Institute and School of Design, 1916; Chicago Art Institute School, 1916–18, with E. J. Timmons, John W. Norton; Geneva College, 1918–19; Studio of B. Schoukhaieff, Paris, 1926–27. Traveled France. **Taught:** Cooper Union, 1932–34; ASL, 1932–36; U. of Wisconsin, 1936. **Commissions** (murals): Justice Department, Washington, D.C., 1936–37; Kansas State Capitol, 1938–40; U. of Wisconsin, 1940–42. **Awards:** Carnegie, 1933; PAFA, Gold Medal, 1941; MMA, Artists for Victory, Second Prize, 1942. **One-man Exhibitions:** (first) Whitney Studio Club, NYC, 1930; Feragil Galleries, NYC, 1933, 35; U. of Wisconsin, 1937; Hudson D. Walker Gallery, NYC, 1938; Milwaukee, 1946; A.A.A. Gallery, NYC, 1947; Syracuse U., 1956; U. of Kansas, 1957; NCFA, 1971. **Group:** WMAA; Chicago/AI; Wichita/AM; Milwaukee. **Collections:** Andover/Phillips, Britannica; Chicago/AI; First National Bank, Madison; Kansas State College; MMA; Muskegon/Hackley; U. of Nebraska; St. Louis/City; WMAA; Wichita/AM. **Bibliography:** American Artists Group, Inc., 1; Baigell 1; Baur 7; Bazin; Benton 1; Biddle 4; Blesh 1; Boswell 1; Brown 2; Bruce and Watson; Cahill and Barr, eds.; Canaday; Cheney; Christensen; Crayen, T., 1; **Curry 1, 2, 3;** Flanagan; Flexner; Goodrich and Baur 1; Hall; Hunter 6; *Index of 20th Century Artists;* Jewell 2; McCurdy, ed.; Mellquist; Mendelowitz; Newmeyer;

Pagano; Pearson 1; Reese; Richardson, E.P.; Rose, B., 1; **Schmeckebier 2;** Wight 2. Archives.

CUSUMANO, STEFANO. b. February 5, 1912, Tampa, Fla.; **d.** November 18, 1975, Eurica, Calif. **Studied:** Metropolitan Art School, with Arthur Schiewder; Cooper Union. Traveled Europe. **Taught:** Leonardo da Vinci Art School, NYC, 1932–40; Art Career School, 1945–54; NYU, 1954–74; Cooper Union, 1956–74; U. of Minnesota, 1971, 72; Cornell U., 1973; Paula Cooper Gallery, to 1974. **Awards:** Ford Foundation, **P.P.**, 1963; AAAL, Childe Hassam Award, 1968, 71. **One-man Exhibitions:** (first) Montross Gallery, NYC, 1942; G. Binet Gallery, NYC, 1946, 47, 48, 50; Philadelphia Art Alliance, 1948; Tampa/AI, 1949; Woodmere Art Gallery, Philadelphia, 1950; Oregon State College, 1951; Washington State U., 1951; Passedoit Gallery, NYC, 1953, 56, 57, 59; Mari Gallery, Woodstock, N.Y. 1962; Gallery 63, Inc., NYC, 1963, 64, Rome, 1964; Terry Dintenfass, Inc., 1967; U. of Minnesota, 1971, 72. **Group:** WMAA, 1947; Carnegie, 1949; U. of Illinois, 1950; Corcoran, 1951; PAFA, 1951, 52, 67; NIAL, 1952, 61; Youngstown/Butler, 1968; St. Paul Gallery, 1968; Indianapolis/Herron, 1968; AAAL, 1968, 71; Randolph-Macon Woman's College, 1968. **Collections:** Brooklyn Museum; Florida State U.; U. of Illinois; Johns Hopkins U.; MMA; U. of Minnesota; National Gallery; Newark Museum; U. of North Carolina; Omaha/Joslyn; PMA; Pensacola; WMAA; Wesleyan U.. **Bibliography:** Archives.

D

DAPHNIS, NASSOS. b. July 23, 1914, Krockeai, Greece. To USA, 1930. Self-taught. Traveled USA, Greece, Italy, France. **Taught:** Horace Mann School, Riverdale, N.Y., 1953–58. Leading tree-peony hybridizer. **Member:** American Abstract Artists. **Awards:** Ford Foundation, 1962; National Council on the Arts, 1966; National Endowment for the Arts, 1971; New England 350th Celebration Exhibition, 1972; A. P. Saunders Medal, Tree Peony Award, 1973; National Endowment for the Arts, 1971; Guggenheim Foundation Fellowship, 1977. **Address:** 362 West Broadway, NYC 10012. **One-man Exhibitions:** (first) Contemporary Arts Gallery, NYC, 1938, also 1947, 49; Charlotte/ Mint, 1949; Galerie Colette Allendy, Paris, 1950; Leo Castelli Inc., 1959–61, 1963, 65, 68, 71, 73, 75, 80; Galleria Toninelli, Milan, 1961; Iris Clert Gallery, 1962; Franklin Siden Gallery, Detroit, 1967; Syracuse/Everson, 1969; Brockton/Fuller, 1970; Andre Zarre Gallery, NYC, 1974, 76; Kingpitcher Gallery, Pittsburgh, 1976; Muhlenberg College, 1980. **Retrospective:** Buffalo/ Albright, 1969; Syracuse/Everson, 1969. **Group:** Carnegie, 1955, 58, 61, 70; Corcoran Biennial, 1959, 63, 69; WMAA Annuals, 1960–65, 1967; Walker, Purist Painting, 1961; American Abstract Artists Annual, 1961; SRGM, Abstract Expressionists and Imagists, 1961; Seattle World's Fair, 1961; WMAA, Geometric Abstraction in America, circ., 1962; Musée Cantonal des Beaux-Arts, Lausanne, I Salon International de Galeries Pilotes, 1963; Lincoln, Mass./De Cordova, 1965; U. of Illinois, 1969; Carnegie, International, 1970; Syracuse/ Everson, Provincetown Painters, 1890s–1970s, 1977; Brooklyn Museum, Noemata, 1977; **Collections:** Akron/AI; Baltimore/MA; Buffalo/Albright; Carnegie, Hirshhorn; MOMA; U. of Michigan; Norfolk; Norfolk/Chrysler; RISD; Reading/Public; Ridgefield/Aldrich; SRGM; South Mall, Albany; Syracuse/ Everson; Tel Aviv; Union Carbide Corp.; Utica; WMAA. **Bibliography: Murdock 2.** Archives.

D'ARCANGELO, ALLAN. b. June 16, 1930, Buffalo, N.Y. **Studied:** U. of Buffalo, 1948–52, BA (history and government); City College of New York; New School for Social Research, 1953–54; Mexico City College, 1957–59, with Dr. John Golding, Fernando Belain; studio work with Boris Lurie, NYC, 1956–66. Traveled Mexico, USA, Japan, Far East, North Africa. **Taught:** NYC public schools, 1956–62; School of Visual Arts, NYC, 1963–68; Cornell U., 1968; Syracuse U., 1971; U. of Wisconsin, 1972; St. Cloud State College, 1972; Memphis Academy of Arts, 1975; Brooklyn College, 1973– . **Member:** SAGA. **Commissions:** Transportation and Travel Pavilion, New York World's Fair, 1964–65 (mural). **Awards:** Municipal U. of Omaha, First **P.P.**, 1966; NIAL, 1970. **Address:** Kenoza Lake, NY 12750. **Dealer:** Marlborough Gallery, Inc., NYC. **One-man Exhibitions:** Galeria Genova, Mexico City, 1958 (two-man); Long Island U., 1961; Fishbach Gallery, 1964, 65, 67, 69; Ileana Sonnabend Gallery, Paris, 1965; Galerie Rudolf Zwirner, 1965; Galerie Hans R. Neuendorf, Hamburg, 1965; Galerie Muller, 1965; Dwan Gallery, Los Angeles, 1966; Wurttembergischer Kunstverein, Stuttgart, 1967; Galerie Rolf Ricke, Kassel,

1967; Minami Gallery, 1967; Obelisk Gallery, 1967 (two-man), 1970; Franklin Siden Gallery, Detroit, 1968, 72; Lambert Gallery, Paris, 1968; Wisconsin State U., Eau Claire, 1970; Marlborough Gallery, Inc., NYC, 1971, 75; U. of Wisconsin, Madison, 1972; Hokin Gallery, Chicago, 1974; Patricia Moore Inc., Aspen, 1974; Russell Sage College, 1974; Kingpitcher Gallery, Pittsburgh, 1975; Buffalo/SUNY, 1979. **Retrospective:** ICA, U. of Pennsylvania, 1971. **Group:** Sarah Lawrence College, Popular Imagery, 1963; ICA, London, 1963; Oakland/AM, Pop Art USA 1963; Buffalo/Albright, Mixed Media and Pop Art, 1963; Salon du Mai, Paris, 1964; The Hague, New Realism, 1964; Salon des Comparaisons, Paris, 1964; Dwan Gallery, Los Angeles, Boxes, 1964, also 1965; Milwaukee, 1965; Galerie Hans R. Neuendorf, Hamburg, 1965, 66; Galerie Friedrich & Dahlem, Munich, 1966; V. International Biennial Exhibition of Prints, Tokyo, 1966; Amsterdam/Stedelijk, New Shapes of Color, 1966; Expo '67, Montreal, 1967; Detroit/Institute, Color, Image and Form, 1967; Torcuato di Tella, Buenos Aires, 1967; WMAA Annual, 1967; Brandeis U., 1968; Foundation Maeght, 1968; MOMA, Social Comment in America, circ., 1968; ICA, U. of Pennsylvania, Highway, 1970; Utica, American Prints Today, 1973; WMAA, American Pop Art, 1974. **Collections:** Atlantic Richfield Co.; Brandeis U.; Brooklyn Museum; Buffalo/Albright; Chase Manhattan Bank; Cleveland/MA; Detroit/Institute; Gelsenkirchen; The Hague; Hannover/Kunstverein; The Hertz Corp.; Hirshhorn; MIT; MOMA; Munster/WK; NYU; Nagaoka, Japan; New Orleans/Delgado; Ridgefield/Aldrich; Skopje/Modern; WMAA; Walker; U. of Wisconsin. **Bibliography:** Alloway 4; Battcock, ed.; Calas, N. and E.; Honisch and Jensen, eds.; Hunter, ed.; *Kunst um 1970;* Lippard 5.

D'ARISTA, ROBERT. b. July 2, 1929, Pelham, N.Y. **Studied:** NYU, with Philip Guston; Columbia U., with John Heliker; American Art School, NYC; Academie de la Grande Chaumiere. Traveled France, Italy. **Taught:** American U., 1961– ; Artist-in-Residence, Boston U., spring, 1973. **Awards:** Fulbright Fellowship, 1956; NIAL. **Address:** 3125 Quebec Place, N.W., Washington, DC 20008. **One-man Exhibitions:** (first) The Alan Gallery, NYC, 1955, also 1956, 60; Grippi Gallery, NYC, 1962; Jefferson Place Gallery, 1962; Lee Nordness Gallery, 1964, 67, 69; Boston U., 1973. **Group:** PAFA, 1954, 60; Brooklyn Museum; U. of Illinois, 1955; U. of Nebraska, 1955, 56, 57; Columbia, S.C./MA Annual; Bogota, Colombia; SRGM; Detroit/Institute, 1955, 58; Chicago/AI; Carnegie, 1956, 59; WMAA Annuals, 1956, 57, 59. **Collections:** American U.; NCFA; Smith College; Toledo/MA; Yale U. **Bibliography:** Nordness, ed.

DARROW, PAUL GARDNER. b. October 31, 1921, Pasadena, Calif. **Studied:** Art Center School, Los Angeles; Colorado Springs Fine Arts Center, with Boardman Robinson; Claremont Graduate School, with Millard Sheets, Sueo Serisawa, Henry McFee, Howard Cook. **Taught:** Coronado School of Fine Arts, summers, 1953, 55; Brigham Young U., 1954; Otis Art Institute, 1955–69; Claremont Graduate School, 1955–69, 1970– ; Laguna Beach (Calif.) School of Art and Design, 1960–69. **Commissions** (murals): Richmond (Calif.) Youth Center, 1952; Convair Aircraft Corp., San Diego, 1953; National American Insurance Co., Los Angeles, 1954; Kaiser Aluminum Corp.; Disneyland, Calif., 1955; Broadway Dept. Stores, Anaheim and Van Nuys, Calif., 1955; Gourmet Shop, Hollywood, 1955; Air France, International Airport, Los Angeles, 1960–61; Home Insurance Co., Los Angeles. Traveled Japan, Taiwan, Philippines, Okinawa. US Navy artist correspondent, Vietnam. **Awards:** California State Fair, 1950; Los Angeles/County MA, First Prize Watercolor, 1954; Pasadena/AM,

Andrew Dasbury *Summer Meadows* 1952–53

P.P., 1954, 58; NEH, grant, 1973. **Address:** 690 Cuprien Way, Laguna Beach, CA 92651. **One-man Exhibitions:** Philadelphia Art Alliance, 1948; Mezzanine Gallery, Oakland, Calif., 1953; Gump's Gallery, 1954; RAC, 1954; Pasadena/AM, 1955; Scripps College, 1958; Drake Gallery, Carmel, Calif., 1960; Comara Gallery, 1961, 64, 68; San Joaquin Pioneer Museum and Haggin Art Galleries, Stockton, Calif., 1963; Sacramento State College, ˙1966; Hartnell College, 1968; California Institute of Technology, Pasadena, 1970; Muckenthaler Cultural Center, Fullerton, Calif., 1971; Newport Harbor, 1972; Galleria Forma, El Salvador, 1975. **Retrospective:** Scripps College, 1973. **Group:** U. of Vienna, 1951; Los Angeles/County MA, 1951–54; Santa Barbara/MA, 1952–55; SFMA, 1952, 53; Seattle/AM, 153; Youngstown/Butler, 1953, 54; PAFA, 1954; Denver/AM, 1954; Corcoran, 1954; Sao Paulo, 1955; Smithsonian, circ., 1955–56, Long Beach/MA, 1958–61; Oakland/AM; Newport Harbor Art Museum, Balboa,

Calif., 1964; Laguna Beach/MA, Southern California 100, 1977; Claremont Galleries, California Photographers, 1978. **Collections:** Long Beach/MA; Los Angeles Times; U. of Michigan; Newport Harbor; Palos Verdes; Pasadena/AM; Scripps College.

DASBURG, ANDREW. b. May 4, 1887, Paris, France. To USA, 1892. **d.** August 13, 1979, Ranchos de Taos. **Studied:** ASL, with Kenyon Cox, Frank V. DuMond; privately with Birge Harrison; also with Robert Henri. **Awards:** Pan-American Exhibition, Los Angeles, 1925; Carnegie, 1927, 31; Guggenheim Foundation Fellowship, 1932; Ford Foundation Grant; Arizona Governor's Art Award, 1976. **One-man Exhibitions:** Dallas/MFA, 1957; Rehn Galleries, 1958; U. of New Mexico, 1966; Governor's Gallery, Santa Fe, 1975, 76; Mission Gallery, Taos, 1978. **Retrospective:** A.F.A./Ford Foundation, circ., 1959; U. of New Mexico, Albuquerque, circ., 1979. **Group:**

WMAA; SFMA; MMA; Denver/AM; Santa Fe, N.M. **Collections:** Barnes Foundation; California Palace; Cincinnati/AM; Colorado Springs/FA; Dallas/MFA; Denver/AM; Fort Worth; Hirshhorn; U. of Kansas; Kansas City/Nelson; Los Angeles/County MA; MMA; U. of Nebraska/Sheldon; U. of Nebraska; U. of New Mexico; San Antonio/McNay; SFMA; Santa Barbara/MA; Santa Fe, N.M.; WMAA. **Bibliography:** *Avant-Garde Painting and Sculpture;* Baur 7; Brown, 1, 2; **Bywaters 1, 2;** Cahill and Barr, eds.; Cheney; Coke 2; Goodrich and Baur 1, Hunter 6; *Index of 20th Century Artists;* Janis, S.; Levin 2; McCurdy, ed.; Neuhaus; Richardson, E.P.; Rose, B., 1, 4; *Woodstock;* Wright 1. Archives.

DASH, ROBERT. b. June 8, 1934, NYC. **Studied:** U. of New Mexico, BA (anthropology and English). Traveled Italy, Mexico, USA, Ireland, West Germany. **Taught:** Southampton College, 1976; Dodfitz School, Amarillo, 1977; Long Island U., 1972. **Member:** Fellow, Royal Horticultural Society. **Awards:** New York State Board of Regents Scholarship. **Address:** Sagaponack, NY 11962. **Dealer:** Hirschl & Adler Galleries, NYC. **One-man Exhibitions:** (first) The Kornblee Gallery, 1961, also 1962, 63; The Osborne Gallery, NYC, 1964, 65, 66; The Graham Gallery, 1964, 68, 69, 70; Crane-Kalman Gallery, London, 1966; Munich/Modern, 1969; FAR Gallery, 1972, 73; Vick Gallery, Philadelphia, 1974; Fischbach Gallery, NYC, 1975, 77; Hirschl & Adler Gallerie, NYC, 1978. **Retrospective:** Southampton/Parrish, 1969; Allentown/AM, 1971. **Group:** Yale U., The New York Season, 1961; MOMA, Eight American Painters of the Landscape, circ., 1964; Corcoran; U. of Colorado; Norfolk, Contemporary Art USA, 1966; AAAL; Childe Hassam Fund Exhibition, 1973; Omaha/Joslyn, A Sense of Place, 1973; Lincoln, Mass./De Cordova, Candid Painting, 1975; U. of North Carolina, Art on Paper, 1976; U.

of Missouri, American Painterly Realists, 1977. **Collections:** Allentown/AM; AT&T; The Bank of New York; Bristol-Meyers Co.; Brooklyn Museum; U. of California; Chase Manhattan Bank; Brooklyn Museum; Commerce Bank, Kansas City; Continental Grain Corp.; Federal Deposit Insurance Corporation; First National Bank of Memphis; The Grace Line: NYU; NATO Headquarters, Brussels; U. of North Carolina; PMA; Southampton/Parrish; Suffolk County National Bank; Xerox Corp.; Youngstown/Butler. **Bibliography:** Downes, ed. Archives.

DAVEY, RANDALL. b. May 24, 1887, East Orange, N.J.; **d.** November 7, 1964, Santa Fe, N.M. **Studied:** Cornell U., 1905–07, in Europe with Robert Henri, 1908–09. Traveled USA. Europe. **Taught:** Chicago Art Institute School, 1920; Kansas City Art Institute and School of Design, 1921–24; Broadmoor Art Academy, Colorado Springs, 1924–31; U. of New Mexico, 1945–46. **Commissions:** (murals) US Post Offices, Vinita and Claremore, Okla., 1939. **Awards:** NAD, Hallgarten Prize, 1915; SFMA, Hon. Men., 1915; NAD, The Thomas B. Clarke Prize, 1938; NAD, 1939. **One-man Exhibitions:** California Palace; San Diego; U. of New Mexico; Vassar College; Vose Gallery, Boston; Whitney Studio Club, NYC; Macbeth Gallery, NYC, 1916; Montross Gallery, NYC, 1922; Rehn Galleries, 1930; Ferargil Galleries, NYC, 1933, 34; Kraushaar Galleries, 1938; Grand Central, NYC, 1941; Santa Fe, N.M., 1946; Buffalo/Albright; Chicago/AI; Symphony Hall, Boston; Broadmoor Art Academy, Colorado Springs; Carnegie; Carroll Gallery, NYC; Kleemann Gallery, NYC; Findlay Gallery, NYC, 1967. **Retrospective:** Santa Fe, N.M., 1957. **Group:** Corcoran; Chicago/AI; WMAA; Kansas City/Nelson; Santa Fe, N.M.; Taos, N.M. **Collections:** Britannica; Chicago/AI; Cleveland/MA; Corcoran; Detroit/Institute; Kansas City/Nelson;

Montclair/AM; U. of New Mexico; Will Rogers Shrine; Santa Fe, N.M.; US NAVY; WMAA. **Bibliography:** Bryant, L.; Cheney; Coke 2; **Davey;** Hall; Jewell 2; Neuhaus. Archives.

DAVIS, GENE. b. August 22, 1920, Washington, D.C. **Studied:** U. of Maryland; Wilson Teachers College. **Taught:** The Corcoran School of Art, 1967–68, 1970– ; American University, 1968–70; Skidmore College, 1969; U. of Virginia, 1972. **Member:** Washington Project for the Arts, vice-president, 1980. **Commissions:** South Mall, Albany, 1969 (mural); Neiman-Marcus Co., Bal Harbour, Fla., 1970 (mural). **Awards:** Corcoran, Bronze Medal for Painting and $1,000 Award, 1965; National Council on the Arts, $5,000 Grant, 1967; Guggenheim Foundation Fellowship, 1974. **Address:** 4120 Harrison Street, NW, Washington, DC 20015. **Dealer:** Kolbert Gallery, Inc., NYC. **One-man Exhibitions:** (first) The Catholic U. of America, 1953; American U., 1955; Bader Gallery, Washington, D.C., 1956; Jefferson Place Gallery, 1959, 61, 63, 67; Poindexter Gallery, 1963, 65–67; Corcoran, 1964, 68, 70, 77, 78; Hofstra U., 1966; MIT, 1967; Des Moines, 1967; Galerie Rolf Ricke, 1967; Fischbach Gallery, 1967–69, 1970, 71, 72, 73, 75, 77, 78; SFMA, 1968; WGMA, 1968; Jewish Museum, 1968; Henri Gallery, 1968–70; Chapman Kelly Gallery, 1969; Axiom Gallery, London, 1969; Nova Scotia College of Art and Design, 1970; Galerie Annemarie Verna, Zurich, 1971; Dunkelman Gallery, Toronto, 1971–73; J. L. Hudson Art Gallery, Detroit, 1972; U. of Utah, 1972; Omaha/Joslyn, 1972; Max Protetch Gallery, Washington, D.C., 1972, 77; Michael Berger Gallery, Pittsburgh, 1973; Quay Gallery, 1973; New Gallery, Cleveland, 1974; Tibor de Nagy, Houston, 1974; Reed College, 1975; Harcus Krakow Rosen Sonnabend, Boston, 1976; Walker, 1978; Dayton/AI, 1978; Protetch-McIntosh Gallery, Washington, D.C., 1978, 80; Droll/Kolbert Gallery, Inc., NYC, 1979, 80.

Group: WGMA, The Formalists 1963; Brandeis U., New Directions in American Painting, 1963; Los Angeles/County MA, Post Painterly Abstraction, 1964; MOMA, The Responsive Eye, 1965; WGMA, circ., 1965; MOMA, Two Decades of American Painting, circ., Japan, India, Australia, 1967; Corcoran Biennial, 1967, 75; Detroit/Institute, Color, Image and Form, 1967; WMAA Annuals, 1968, 71, 73; Milwaukee, Directions I, circ., 1968; Art Fair, Cologne, 1968; Edmonton Art Gallery, Alberta, Ten Washington Artists: 1950–1970, 1970; Baltimore/MA, Washington Art: 1950–1970, 1970; ICA, U. of Pennsylvania, Two Generations of Color Painting, 1970; WMAA, The Structure of Color, 1971; U. of Texas, Color Forum, 1972; West Palm Beach/Norton, The Vincent Melzac Collection—Part One: The Washington Color Painters, 1974; SRGM, Within the Decade, 1974; Indianapolis, 1978; U. of Southern Florida, Miami, Two Decades of Abstraction, 1979. **Collections:** Akron/AI; AT&T; Bank of America; Brandeis U.; Buffalo/Albright; Chicago/AI; Chase Manhattan Bank, NYC; Corcoran; Dayton/AI; Des Moines; Federal Reserve Bank of Boston; Federal Reserve Bank of Richmond, Virginia; Florsheim Foundation; Hirshhorn; High Museum; Indianapolis/Herron; Jacksonville/AM; Louisville/Speed; MIT; MMA; MOMA; Milwaukee; NCFA; National Gallery; Oklahoma; Omaha/Joslyn; Phillips; PMA; Princeton U.; Ringling; SFMA; SRGM; Tate; Walker; WMAA; Wellesley College; Woodward Foundation; Xerox; Yale U. **Bibliography:** *Art Now 74*; Atkinson; Davis, D.; **Gene Davis.**

DAVIS, JERROLD. b. November 2, 1926, Chico, Calif. **Studied:** U. of California, Berkeley, BA, 1953, MA. Traveled Latin America, Europe. **Taught:** U. of California, summer, 1967. **Awards:** Sigmund Martin Heller Traveling Fellowship, 1953; Guggenheim Foundation Fellowship, 1958; Ford Foundation Artist-in-Residence, 1964. **Address:** 66

Twain Avenue, Berkeley, CA 94708. **Dealer:** Jacqueline Anhalt Gallery. **One-man Exhibitions:** Instituto Brasil-Estados-Unidos, Rio de Janeiro, 1951; California Palace, 1957; Everett Ellin Gallery, Los Angeles, 1958; The Rose Rabow Gallery, San Francisco, 1963, 74; Esther Robles Gallery, 1964; Flint/Institute, 1964; Gallery of Modern Art, 1965; Quay Gallery, 1967, 68; Fleischer Anhalt Gallery; 1968; Jacqueline Anhalt Gallery, 1970; Newport Harbor, 1973. **Retrospective:** Richmond Art Center, Calif., 1980. **Group:** Sao Paulo Biennial, 1951; Oberlin College, 3 Young Painters, 1958; Carnegie, 1958; U. of Illinois, 1959, 61, 63; California Palace, 1960–64; Flint/Institute, 1964; Phoenix, 1964; Los Angeles/County MA, 1965; U. of Arizona, 1967; Omaha/Joslyn, A Sense of Place, 1973. **Collections:** Bank of America; Carnegie; Flint/Institute; Los Angeles/County MA; Oakland/AM; SFMA; Santa Barbara/MA.

DAVIS, RONALD. b. June 29, 1937, Santa Monica, Calif. **Studied:** U. of Wyoming; San Francisco Art Institute (with Jack Jefferson, Frank Lobdell), 1960–64; Yale-Norfolk Summer Art School (with Philip Guston), 1962. **Taught:** U. of California, 1967. **Awards:** National Council on the Arts Grant, 1968. **Address:** 6950 Grasswood Avenue, Malibu, CA 90265. **Dealers:** Blum-Helman Gallery, NYC. **One-man Exhibitions:** (first) Nicholas Wilder Gallery, 1965, also 1967, 69, 73, 77; Tibor de Nagy Gallery, 1966; Leo Castelli Inc., 1968, 74, 75; Kasmin Ltd., 1968, 71; David Mirvish Gallery, 1970, 75; Pasadena/AM, 1971; Galleria dell-Ariete, Milan, 1972; Joseph Hellman Gallery, St. Louis, 1972; John Berggruen Gallery, San Francisco, 1973, 78; Corcoran & Greenberg, Coral Gables, 1974; Gemini G.E.L., Los Angeles, 1974; Western Galleries, Cheyenne, 1974; Boise State U., 1975; Greenberg Gallery, St. Louis, 1975; Aspen Gallery of Art, 1976; Seder/Creigh Gallery, Coronado, Calif., 1976; U. of Nevada, 1977; Pep-

perdine U., 1979; Blum-Helman Gallery, New York, 1979. **Group:** San Francisco Art Festival, 1961–63; SFMA, Arts of San Francisco, 1964; RAC, 1964; U. of Illinois, 1965; WGMA, A New Aesthetic, 1967; WMAA Annual, 1967; Documenta IV, Kassel, 1968; Corcoran Biennial, 1967; Venice Biennial, 1972; Montreal/Contemporain, II Artistes Americains, 1973. **Retrospective:** Oakland, 1976. **Group:** Indianapolis, 1974; Corcoran Biennial, 1975; Leverkusen, Zeichnungen 3, USA, 1975; Cleveland/MA, Four Contemporary Painters, 1978. **Collections:** Baltimore/MA; MOMA; Tate. **Bibliography:** Davis, D.; *New in the Seventies; Report: The State of California Painting; USA West Coast; Wood.*

DAVIS, STUART. b. December 7, 1894, Philadelphia, Pa.; **d.** June 24, 1964, NYC. Studied with Robert Henri, 1910–13, US Army Intelligence, World War I. Traveled Europe, Cuba, USA. **Taught:** ASL, 1931–32; New School for Social Research, 1940–50; lectured at museums and universities. Federal A.P.: 1933–39. Editor: *Art Front* magazine. **Commissions** (murals): Radio City Music Hall, NYC, 1932; Indiana U., 1938; New York World's Fair, 1939; Municipal Broadcasting Co., NYC, 1939; Drake U., 1955; Heinz Research Center, Pittsburgh, 1957. **Awards:** Pepsi-Cola, 1944; Carnegie, Hon. Men. 1944; PAFA, J. Henry Schiedt Memorial Prize, 1945; Chicago/AI; Norman Wait Harris Silver Medal, 1948; La Tausca Competition, **P.P.,** 1948; VMFA, John Barton Payne Medal, 1950; Chicago/AI, Ada S. Garrett Prize, 1951; Guggenheim Foundation Fellowship, 1952; Hallmark International Competition, 1956; PAFA, Hon. Men., 1956; Brandeis U., Creative Arts Award, 1957; Guggenheim International, 1958, 60; Chicago/AI, Floral Mayer Witkowsky Prize, 1961; PAFA, Joseph E. Temple Gold Medal, 1964; Chicago/AI, The Mr. & Mrs. Frank G. Logan Medal and Prize. **One-man Exhibitions:** Sheridan Square Gallery,

Stuart Davis   *Schwitzki's Syntax*   1961–64

NYC, 1917; Ardsley Gallery, 1918; Newark Museum, 1925; Whitney Studio Club, NYC, 1926–29; The Downtown Gallery, 1927, 30, 31, 32, 34, 43, 46, 52, 54, 56, 60, 62; Curt Valentine Gallery, NYC, 1928; Crillon Galleries, Philadelphia, 1931; Katherine Kuh Gallery, Chicago, 1939; Modern Art Society, Cincinnati, 1941 (two-man); Arts Club of Chicago, 1945; MOMA, 1945; Baltimore/MA, 1946; Santa Barbara/MA, 1949 (three-man); XXVI Venice Biennial, 1952; Contemporary Arts Gallery, NYC, 1955, 59; Brandeis U., 1957; Peale House, Philadelphia, 1964; Lawrence Rubin Gallery, NYC, 1971; The Zabriskie Gallery, NYC, 1976; Grace Borgenicht Gallery, NYC, 1979, 80; Hirschl & Adler Gallery, NYC, 1978; Esther Robles Gallery, Los Angeles, 1979. **Retrospectives:** Walker, 1947; NCFA, 1965; Brooklyn Museum, 1978. **Group:** The Armory Show, 1913; Independents, NYC, 1916; Golden Gate International Exposition, San Francisco, 1939; Tate, American Painting, 1946; I Sao Paulo Biennial, 1951; MOMA, 12 Modern American Painters and Sculptors, circ., Europe, 1953–55; MOMA, Modern Art in the United States, circ., Europe, 1955–56; I Inter-American Paintings and Prints Biennial, Mexico City, 1958; American Painting and Sculpture, Moscow, 1959; WMAA, The 1930's, 1968; Brown U., Graham, Gorky, Smith & Davis, 1977. **Collections:** AAAL; Andover/Phillips; Arizona State College; U. of Arizona State College; U. of Arizona; Baltimore/MA; Bezalel Museum; Brandeis U.; Britannica; Brooklyn Museum; Buffalo/Albright; Carnegie; Chicago/AI; Cincinnati/AM; Cranbrook; Dartmouth College; U. of Georgia; Hartford/Wadsworth; Harvard U.; Honolulu Academy; IBM; U. of Illinois; State U. of Iowa; U. of Kentucky; Library of Congress; Los Angeles/County MA;

MMA; MOMA; Milwaukee; Minneapolis/Institute; U. of Nebraska; Newark Museum; New Trier High School; Ogunquit; U. of Oklahoma; PAFA; PMA; The Pennsylvania State U.; Phillips; Randolph-Macon Woman's College; Sara Roby Foundation; U. of Rochester; Roswell; SFMA; SRGM; St. Louis/City; San Diego; Seattle/AM; Utica; VMFA; Vassar College; WMAA; Walker; Washington U.; Wellesley College; Wichita/AM; Yale U. **Bibliography: Arnason 3, 4;** *Avant-Garde Painting and Sculpture in America, 1910–25;* Baigell 1; Barker 1; Barr 3; Battcock, ed.; Baur 5, 7; Bazin; Beekman; Biddle 4; Biederman 1; **Blesh 1, 2;** Brown 2; Cahill and Barr, eds.; Cheney; Chipp; Christensen; *Cityscape 1919–39;* Coke 2; **Davis S.;** Eliot; **Elliott;** Flanagan; Flexner; Frost; Genauer; Gerdts; Goodrich and Baur 1; **Goossen 4;** Greengood; Haftman, Graham, Gorky, *Smith & Davis in the Thirties;* Halpert; Hess, T.B., 1; Honisch and Jensen, eds.; Hunter 1, 6; Hunter, ed.; Huyghe; Janis, S.; Johnson, Ellen H.; **Kelder;** Kepes 2; Kootz 2; Kozloff 3; Kuh 2, 3; Lee and Burchwood; Lippard, 5; Levin 2; McCurdy, ed.; Mendelowitz; Munsterberg; Newmeyer; Nordness, ed.; O'Doherty; Pagano; Pearson 1; Phillips 1; Pousette-Dart, ed.; Read 2; Richardson E.P.; Rickey; Ringel, ed.; Ritchie 1; Rodman 2; Rose, B., 1, 4; Rosenblum, 1; Sachs; Sandler; Seuphor 1; Sutton; **Sweeney 4;** Tashjian; Weller; "What Abstract Art Means to Me"; Wheeler; Wight 2. Archives.

DAY, WORDEN. b. June 11, 1916, Columbus, Ohio. **Studied:** Randolph-Macon Woman's College, BA; NYU, MA; with Maurice Sterne, Jean Charlot, Vaclav Vytlacil, Hans Hofmann, S.W. Hayter, in NYC. Traveled USA, North Africa, Europe, Greece. **Taught:** Virginia Commonwealth U. 1940–41; U. of Louisville, Ky., 1945–46; U. of Wyoming, 1949–51; Pratt Institute; State U. of Iowa; New School for Social Research, NYC, 1961–66; Art Students League,

NYC, 1967–70. **Member:** Federation of Modern Painters and Sculptors; Sculptors Guild. Included in USIA film *Printmaking, USA.* **Commissions:** International Graphic Arts Society, 1964. **Awards:** VMFA Fellowship, 1940; Lessing J. Rosenwald Fund Fellowship, 1942–44; Guggenheim Foundation Fellowship, 1951, 52, 61, 62; Brooklyn Museum **P.P.**; Library of Congress, Pennell **P.P.**; New Jersey State Council on the Arts Grant, 1980. **Address:** R.D. 2, Newtown-Richboro Road, Newtown, PA 18940. **Studio:** Studios 21, 28, 427 Bloomfield Avenue, Montclair, NJ 07042. **One-man Exhibitions:** Perls Galleries, 1940; VMFA, 1940; The Bertha Schaefer Gallery, 1948, 51; Cincinnati/AM, 1948–58; Norfolk; Baltimore/MA, 1948–58; The Krasner Gallery, 1959; Grand Central Moderns, NYC, 1961; Mills College; U. of Minnesota. **Group:** U. of Illinois, 1950; WMAA; MOMA; Chicago/AI; Brooklyn Museum; MMA; USIA, 10 American Artists of Woodcut, circ.; Montclair/AM (two-man), 1970; Sculpture Center, 1972. **Collections:** Bradley U.; Brooklyn Museum; Carnegie; Detroit/Institute; Hartford/Wadsworth; U. of Illinois; Kalamazoo/Institute; Library of Congress; U. of Louisville; MMA; MOMA; Mills College; U. of Minnesota; Montclair/AM; NYPL; National Gallery; U. of Nebraska; Newark Museum; Norfolk; PMA; Rutgers U.; St. Louis/City; Seagram Collection; The Singer Company, Inc.; Trenton/State; Utica; VMFA; WMAA; Walker; U. of Wyoming; Yale U. **Bibliography:** Haser 1, Ritchie 1. Archives.

DE ANDREA, JOHN. b. December 24, 1941, Denver, Colo. **Studied:** U. of Colorado, 1964, BFA. Traveled Europe, Mexico, USA. **Taught:** U. of New Mexico, 1965. **Awards:** National Endowment for the Arts, 1974. **Address:** 1235 Pierce Street, Lakewood, CO 80214. **Dealer:** OK Harris Works of Art. **One-man Exhibitions:** OK Harris Works of Art, 1970, 71, 73, 76, 78. **Group:** Chicago/Contemporary, Radical Realism, 1971; VII Paris Biennial, 1971; Documenta V. Kassel, 1972; Galerie des 4 Mouvements, Paris, Hyperrealistes Americains, 1972; Harvard U., Recent Figure Sculpture, 1972; New York Cultural Center, Realism Now, 1972; Lunds Konsthall, Sweden, Amerikansk Realism, 1973; Lincoln, Mass./De Cordova, The Super-Realist Vision, 1973; Hofstra U., The Male Nude, 1973; CNAC, Hyperrealistes Americains/Realistes Europeens, 1974; Hartford/Wadsworth, New/Photo Realism, 1974; Wichita State U., Photo-Realism, 1975; Baltimore/MA, Super Realism, 1975; Vancouver, Aspects of Realism, 1976; Stamford Museum, American Salon des Refuses, 1976; Canberra/National, Illusion and Reality, 1977; Venice Biennial, 1978; PAFA, Seven on the Figure, 1979; Paris/Beaubourg, Copie Conforme, 1979. **Collections:** Aachen/NG; Belger Cartage Service, Kansas City, Mo.; Syracuse/Everson; U. of Virginia. **Bibliography:** *Kunst um 1970;* Lucie-Smith; *Recent Figure Sculpture;* Sager.

DE CREEFT, JOSE. b. November 27, 1884, Guadalajara, Spain. **Studied:** Atelier of Don Augustin Querol, Barcelona, 1906; apprenticed to Idalgo de Caviedas; Academie Julian, Paris, 1906; Maison Greber, Paris, 1910–14. To USA, 1929; citizen, 1940. **Taught:** New School for Social Research, 1932–48 1957–62; ASL, 1934–62. **Member:** Artists Equity (founding member); Audubon Artists; National Sculpture Society; Federation of Modern Painters and Sculptors (president, 1943); NIAL, 1955; NAD, 1964; AAAL; Sculptors Guild. **Commissions:** Saugues (Puy de Dome), France, 1918 (World War I Memorial); Fortress of Ramonje, Mallorca, 1932 (200 pieces of sculpture); Fairmount Park, Philadelphia, 1950; Central Park, NYC, 1959 (Alice in Wonderland group); Bronx (N.Y.) Municipal Hospital, 1962 (mosaic for nurses' residence); New Public Health Laboratory, NYC, 1966. **Awards:** Officier de l'Instruction

Publique, France; MMA, Artists for Victory, First Prize, 1942; PAFA, George D. Widener Memorial Gold Medal, 1945; Audubon Artists, Gold Medal of Honor, 1954, 57; Ford Foundation Traveling Retrospective, 1960; National Sculpture Society, Therese and Edwin Richard Prize for Portrait Sculpture, 1969; Comendador de la Orden de Isabel la Catolica, 1973; National Arts Club, Gold Medal, 1975. **m.** Lorrie Goulet. **Address:** 241 West 20 Street, NYC 10011. **Dealer:** Kennedy Gallery, Inc., NYC. **One-man Exhibitions:** (first) El Circulo de Bellas Artes, Madrid, 1903; Seattle/AM, 1929; Ferargil Galleries, NYC, 1929; Arts Club of Chicago, 1930; Philadelphia Art Alliance, 1933; Passedoit Gallery, NYC, 1936, 1938–49; Santa Barbara/MA, 1937; St. Paul Gallery, 1943; College of William and Mary, 1944; West Palm Beach/Norton, 1949, 50; The Contemporaries, NYC, 1956, 58, 60, 64, 65; Kennedy Gallery, 1970, 71, 72, 75, 79. **Retrospectives:** A.F.A./Ford Foundation, circ., 1960; New School for Social Research, 1974. **Group:** Salon d'Automne, Paris, 1910–29; Chicago/AI Annuals, 1939–51; MMA, National Sculpture Exhibition, 1942, 51; WMAA Annuals, 1942–57; PAFA Annuals, 1944–62; Carnegie; MOMA, Sculpture of the XXth Century, 1953; Worcester/AM; Brooklyn Museum; Sculptors Guild Annuals; Audubon Artists Annuals; Federation of Modern Painters and Sculptors; Artistes Francais; Societe Nationale des Beaux Arts, Paris; Salon des Artistes Independents, Paris. **Collections:** Bezalel Museum; Brooklyn Museum; Columbia U.; Hirshhorn; IBM; MMA; MOMA; Museum of the City of New York; U. of Nebraska; New Paltz/SUNY; PAFA; U. of Puerto Rico; SFMA; Seattle/AM; Trenton/State; U. of Tucson; Utica; WMAA; West Palm Beach/Norton; Wichita/AM. **Bibliography:** Baur 7; Brumme; **Campos;** Cheney; Craven, W.; **de Creeft; Devree;** Goodrich and Baur 1; McCurdy, ed.; Marter, Tarbell, and Wechsler; Pearson 2; Ritchie 3; Selz, J.; Seuphor 3. Archives.

DEEM, GEORGE. b. August 18, 1932, Vincennes, Ind. **Studied:** Vincennes U.; The U. of Chicago; Chicago Art Institute School, with Paul Wieghardt, Boris Margo, 1958, BFA. Traveled Europe; resided in England, 1966–67, Italy, 1970–77. US Army, 1951–53. **Taught:** School of Visual Arts, NYC, 1965–66; Leicester Polytechnic, England, 1966–67; U. of Pennsylvania, 1968–69. **Awards:** MacDowell Colony Fellowship, 1977, 79. **Address:** 10 West 18th Street, NYC 10011. **Dealer:** Allan Stone Gallery; Morgan Gallery, Shawnee Mission, Kans.; The Greenberg Gallery, St. Louis, Mo. **One-man Exhibitions:** (first) Allan Stone Gallery, 1962, also 1963–66, 68, 69, 75, 77; Merida Gallery, Inc., 1964, 68, 69, 78; James Goodman Gallery, Buffalo, 1965; Ferrier Gallery, Houston, 1969; Sneed-Hillman Gallery, Rockford, Ill., 1968, 69, 72, 76; M. E. Thelen Gallery, Essen, 1970; Indianapolis, 1975; Evansville, 1979; Ronald Greenberg Gallery, St. Louis, 1979. **Group:** Corcoran; Baltimore/MA, 1962; Buffalo/Albright, 1962; Chicago/AI, 1963, 65; MOMA; Barnard College; Silvermine Guild; The Hague, New Realism, 1964; Brandeis U., 1964; Cornell U., 1965; ICA, U. of Pennsylvania, 1965; U. of Illinois, 1965, 74; Indianapolis, Biennial, 1972, 76, 78; WMAA, Art about Art, 1978; Duisburg, Mona Lisa in the 20th Century, circ., 1978. **Collections:** Houston/MFA; Aachen/NG; Evansville; Indianapolis; Louisville/Speed; U. of Nebraska; Oberlin College; U. of Rochester, SFMA; The Singer Company, Inc. **Bibliography:** *Kunst um 1970*; Sager; Weller.

DE ERDELY, FRANCIS. b. 1904, Budapest, Hungary; **d.** 1959, Los Angeles, Calif. **Studied:** Academy of Fine Arts, Budapest; Real Academia de Bellas Artes de San Fernando, Madrid; Sorbonne; Ecole du Louvre. **Taught:** Royal Netherlands Art Academy, The Hague; Pasadena Museum School, 1944–46; U. of Southern California, 1945–59. **One-man Exhibitions:** Hun-garian Relief Library, NYC, 1939; Bonestell Gallery, NYC, 1940; de Young; Santa Barbara/MA; Pasadena/AM, 1950, 60; Laguna Beach (Calif.) Art Gallery; Sacramento/Crocker; San Joaquin Pioneer Museum and Haggin Art Galleries, Stockton, Calif.; La Jolla; Oakland/AM, 1950; Seattle/AM; Kansas City/Nelson; Lane Gallery, 1960; Los Angeles/County MA, Memorial Exhibition, 1960; Mills College, 1962. **Collections:** Antwerp; Brussels/Moderne; Carnegie; Chicago/AI; Colorado Springs/FA; Corcoran; Denver/AM; Detroit/Institute; Ghent; The Hague; Los Angeles/County MA; MMA; Melbourne/National; Mons; Oakland/AM; PAFA; Pasadena/AM; San Diego; Youngstown/Butler. **Bibliography:** Watson, E.W., 2.

DE FOREST, ROY DEAN. b. February 11, 1930, North Platte, Neb. **Studied:** Yakima Valley Junior College; California School of Fine Arts, with Edward Corbett, Hassel Smith, David Park; San Francisco State College, with Seymour Locks, Alexander Nepote (AA, BA, MA). Traveled Paris, London, 1971. **Taught:** California College of Arts and Crafts; Bayview High School (San Quentin Prison); San Francisco State College; Contra Costa College; Yakima Valley Junior College; U. of California, Davis, 1955– . **Awards:** Bay Printmakers Society, Oakland, **P.P.**, 1956; San Francisco Art Association, 1956; SFMA, Nealie Sullivan Award, 1962; National Endowment for the Arts, 1972. **Address:** P.O. Box 47, Port Costa, CA 94569. **Dealers:** Hansen-Fuller Gallery; Allan Frumkin Gallery, NYC; Darthea Speyer Gallery. **One-man Exhibitions:** (first) The East-West Gallery, San Francisco, 1955, also 1958; Stonecourt Gallery, Yakima, Wash., 1960; Dilexi Gallery, San Francisco, 1960, 63; Dilexi Gallery, Los Angeles, 1962; San Francisco Art Association, 1962, 65; Allan Frumkin Gallery, NYC, 1966, 73, 75; Peninsula Gallery, Menlo Park, Calif., 1966; Sacramento City College Art Gallery, 1967; Allan Frumkin Gallery, Chicago, 1966; Candy Store Art Gallery, Folsom, Calif., 1969; Mabikudes Gallery, Seattle, 1971; California Palace, 1971; Hansen-Fuller Gallery, 1971, 73, 73, 75, 78; Glenbow Alberta Institute, Calgary, 1974; Darthea Speyer Gallery, 1974, 77; Gallery Allen, 1974; Clark/Benton Gallery, Santa Fe, 1977. **Retrospective:** SFMA, circ., 1974. **Group:** Cincinnati/AM, 1952; SFMA, 1952, 63, 64; Sao Paulo, 1955; Reed College, 1957; California Palace, 1960, 63; WMAA, 1962; Pasadena/AM, 1962; Buffalo/Albright, 1963; Walker, 1963; U. of Illinois, 1964, 69; U. of California, Berkeley, Funk 1967; Portland, Ore./AM, The West Coast Now, 1968; WMAA, Extraordinary Realities, 1973; Sacramento Sampler 2, 1973; SFMA, Painting and Sculpture in California: The Modern Era, 1976; Washington State U., 6 from California, 1976; Halifax, 3 from California, 1976; U. of Texas, Austin, New in the Seventies, 1977; SFMA, Downtown Center, Dog Images through the Century, 1978; ICA, Boston, Roy de Forest, Robert Hudson, 1977. **Collections:** Arizona State U.; U. of California, Berkeley; California College of Arts and Crafts; Chicago/AI; U. of Kansas; U. of North Carolina; Oakland/AM; Omaha/Joslyn; PMA; SFMA; Sacramento/Crocker; Stanford U.; U. of Utah; WMAA. **Bibliography:** *Drawings: The Pluralist Decade;* Humphrey; Janis and Blesh 1; *New in the Seventies;* Selz, P., 2; The State of California Painting.

DEHN, ADOLF ARTHUR. b. November 22, 1895, Waterville, Minn.; **d.** May 19, 1968, NYC. **Studied:** Minneapolis Institute School; ASL. **Taught:** Famous Artists Schools, Inc. **Member:** NAD. **Awards:** Philadelphia Art Alliance, 1936; The Print Club, Philadelphia, 1939; Guggenheim Foundation Fellowship, 1939, 51; Chicago/AI, 1943; Library of Congress, Pennell **P.P.**, 1946. **One-man Exhibitions:** Macbeth Gallery, NYC, 1933; A.A.A. Gallery, NYC,

1941, 51; Brooklyn Public Library, 1944; Dayton/AI, 1946; The Milch Gallery, 1957, 60, 68; FAR Gallery, 1964, 65; Studio North, Towson, Md., 1969; Kennedy Gallery, 1971; Hirschl & Adler Galleries, Inc., NYC, 1976. **Retrospective:** Amon Carter Museum. **Group:** MMA; MOMA; NYPL; Brooklyn Museum; Chicago/AI; Boston/MFA; WMAA. **Collections:** Boston/MFA; Brooklyn Museum; Chicago/AI; Cincinnati/AM; Cleveland/MA; Indianapolis/Herron; Lehigh U.; MMA; MOMA; Minneapolis/Institute; NYPL; Newark Museum; Standard Oil Co.; US Navy; Utica; WMAA. **Bibliography:** American Artists Group Inc. 1, 2, 3; Brown; Dehn; Goodrich 1; Goodrich and Baur 1; *Index of 20th Century Artists;* Mellquist; Mendelowitz; Pagano; Pearson 1, 2; Pousette-Dart, ed.; Reese; Zigrosser 1. Archives.

DEHNER, DOROTHY. b. December 23, 1908, Cleveland, Ohio. **Studied:** UCLA; Skidmore College, BS (Art); Pasadena Playhouse, with Gilmor Brown; ASL, with Kimon Nicolaides, Boardman Robinson, Jan Matulka, Kenneth Kayes Miller. Traveled Europe, USSR, Mexico, USA. Began as a painter, became a sculptor in 1955. **Taught:** New York State Extension Program, 1952–54; Barnard School, NYC, 1954–56; Parsons School of Design, NYC, 1950– ; Boas Dance Studio, Bolton Landing, N.Y.; and privately. **Member:** Sculptors Guild; Federation of Modern Painters and Sculptors. **Commissions:** Great Southwest Industrial Park (outdoor relief), 1969; Union Camp Corp., Wayne, N.J., 1971; Rockefeller Center, 1972. **Awards:** Audubon Artists, First Prize, 1949; ART: USA: 59, NYC, Second Prize for Sculpture, 1959; Tamarind Fellowship, 1965; Kane Memorial Exhibition, Providence, R.I., First Prize for Sculpture, 1962; Yaddo Fellowship, 1971. **Address:** 33 Fifth Avenue, NYC 10003. **Dealer:** Barbara Fiedler, Washington, D.C. **One-man Exhibitions:** Albany/Institute, ca. 1944 (two-man, with

David Smith), also 1954; Skidmore College, 1948, 53, 59; Rose Fried Gallery, 1952; Howard U., 1954; U. of Virginia, 1954; Chicago/AI, 1955; The Willard Gallery, 1955, 57, 59, 61, 63, 66, 70, 73; Wittenborn Gallery, NYC, 1956; Gres Gallery, Washington, D.C., 1959; Columbia U., 1961; Philadelphia Art Alliance, 1962; U. of Michigan, 1963; Cornell U., 1964; Fort Wayne/AM, 1975; Benson Gallery, Bridgehampton, 1975; Jane Weis Gallery, Cleveland, 1974; Parsons-Dreyfus Gallery, NYC, 1978; Barbara Fiedler Gallery, Washington, D.C., 1980. **Retrospective:** Jewish Museum, 1965; Hyde Collection, 1967; Jacksonville/Cummer; Fort Wayne/AM; Design Corner, Cleveland; Storm King Art Center, 1978. **Group:** Brooklyn Museum; Sculptors Guild Annuals; Baltimore/MA; Los Angeles/County MA; Utica; PAFA; Walker; Hartford/ Wadsworth; New Sculpture Group, NYC; Rome/Nazionale; SFMA, 1944; WMAA Annuals, 1950, 51, 54, 60, 63; MMA, 1953; Carnegie, 1961; MOMA, 1962, 64. **Collections:** AT&T; Bankers Trust Company; Calcutta; Chase Manhattan Bank; Cleveland/MA; Columbia U.; Columbus; First National Bank of Chicago; Free Library of Philadelphia; Great Southwest Industrial Park; Hemisphere Club; Hyde Collection; Jacksonville/Cummer; MMA; MOMA; Minnesota/MA; NYPL; U. of New Mexico; The New York Bank for Savings; U. of North Carolina; St. Lawrence U; Seattle/AM; Skidmore College; US State Department; Utica; Wellesley College; Wichita State U.; U. of Wisconsin. **Bibliography:** Bihalji-Merin; Moser 1. Archives.

DE KNIGHT, AVEL. b. 1933, NYC. **Studied:** Ecole des Beaux-Arts, Paris, 1955–56; Academie de la Grande Chaumiere, Paris, 1956–57; Academie Julien, Paris, 1957–58. Art critic for *France-Amérique*, 1958–68. **Taught:** New School for Social Research, 1967; Brooklyn Museum School, 1969–70. **Member:** NAD; American Watercolor Society. **Awards:**

NAD, Palmer Memorial Prize, 1958, Ranger Fund, **P.P.**, 1958, 64, 66; AAAL, Childe Hassam Fund **D.P.**, 1960, 70; US State Department Exchange Grant to travel USSR, 1961; NAD, Grumbacher Award, 1962, 64, Samuel F. B. Morse Medal, 1966, William A. Paton Prize, 1967, 71; American Watercolor Society, Grand Prize and Gold Medal, 1967; Audubon Artists Medal of Honor, 1969. **Address:** 81 Perry Street, NYC 10014. **Dealer:** The Babcock Gallery. **One-man Exhibitions:** Richard Larcada Gallery, 1968, 71; The Babcock Gallery, 1973. **Group:** Youngstown/Butler, 1958–73; PAFA, 1965; Boston/MFA, Black Artists; New York and Boston, 1970; WMAA, Contemporary Black Artists in America, 1971; Finch College, NYC, Projected Art, 1971; Jacksonville/Cummer, Remnants of Things Past, 1971. **Collections:** Chase Manhattan Bank; Denison U.; Lehigh U.; MMA; Massilon Museum; Miles College; NAD; Norfolk; Southern Vermont Art Center; Springfield, Mo./AM; Walker.

DE KOONING, ELAINE. b. March 20, 1920, NYC. **Studied:** Leonardo da Vinci Art School, NYC, 1937; American Artists School, NYC, 1938, with Conrad Marca-Relli; privately with Willem de Kooning, 1938–43. Traveled France, Belgium, Spain. **Taught:** U. of New Mexico, 1959; The Pennsylvania State U., 1960; U. of California, Davis, 1963–64; Yale U., 1967; Pratt Institute, 1968; Carnegie-Mellon U., 1968–70; U. of Pennsylvania, 1971–72; Wagner College, 1971; New York Studio School, Paris, 1974; Parsons School of Design, NYC, 1974–75; U. of Georgia, 1976–79; Skowhegan School, 1979. **Member:** Artists Equity. Commissioned by President Harry S Truman to paint portrait of John F. Kennedy, 1963. **Awards:** Hon. DFA, Webster College, 1964; Moore College of Art, Philadelphia, 1972. **Address:** P.O. Box 1437, East Hampton, L.I., NY 11937. **Dealer:** The Graham Gallery. **One-man Exhibitions:** The Stable Gallery, NYC, 1954, 56; Tibor de

Nagy Gallery, NYC, 1957; U. of New Mexico, 1958; Santa Fe, N.M., 1959; Gump's Gallery, 1959; Dord Fitz Gallery, Amarillo, 1959; Holland-Goldowsky Gallery, Chicago, 1960; The Howard Wise Gallery, Cleveland, 1960; Ellison Gallery, Fort Worth, 1960; Tanager Gallery, NYC, 1960; The Graham Gallery, 1960, 61, 64, 75, 81; De Aenlle Gallery, NYC, 1961; Drew U., 1966; Montclair/AM, 1973; Benson Gallery, 1973; Illinois Wesleyan U., 1975; St. Catherine's College, St. Paul, 1975. **Retrospective:** New London, 1959. **Group:** The Kootz Gallery, NYC, New Talent, 1950; International Biennial Exhibition of Paintings, Tokyo; Walker, Expressionism, 1900–1955, 1956; Carnegie, 1956; A.F.A., Sports in Art, 1957; Jewish Museum, The New York School, Second Generation, 1957; MOMA, Younger American Painters, circ., 1957, 59; Houston/MFA, Action Painting, 1958; Walker, 60 American Painters, 1960; Hallmark Art Award, 1960; WMAA Annuals 1963, 74; Carnegie, 1964; PMA/Museum of the Philadelphia Civic Center, Focus, 1974; NPG, American Self-Portraits: 1670–1973; 1974. **Collections:** U. of Arkansas; Ciba-Geigy Corp.; Elmira College; Kennedy Library; MOMA; Montclair/AM; NYU; Purchase/SUNY; Harry S Truman Library. **Bibliography:** Blesh 1; Chipp; Downes, ed.; Hunter 6; Janis and Blesh 1; O'Hara 1.

DE KOONING, WILLEM. b. April 24, 1904, Rotterdam, Holland. **Studied:** Academie voor Beeldende Kunsten ed Technische Wetenschappen, Amsterdam, 1916–24. To USA, 1926. Federal A.P.; Mural painting, 1935–39. **Taught:** Black Mountain College, 1948; Yale U., 1950–51. **Member:** NIAL. **Commissions** (murals): New York World's Fair, 1939; French Line Pier, NYC (with Fernand Leger); Williamsburg Housing Project, NYC. **Awards:** State Academy Medal, Rotterdam; Academy of Plastic Arts, Rotterdam, Silver Medal; Chicago/AI, The Mr. & Mrs. Frank G.

Willem de Kooning   Untitled VI   1979

Logan Medal, 1951; The President's Medal, 1963. **Address:** Woodbine Drive, East Hampton, NY 11973. **Dealer:** Xavier Fourcade Inc. **One-man Exhibitions:** (first) Charles Egan Gallery, 1948, also 1951; Arts Club of Chicago, 1951; Sidney Janis Gallery, 1953, 56, 59, 62, 72; Boston Museum School, 1953; Workshop Art Center, Washington, D.C., 1953; Martha Jackson Gallery, 1955; Paul Kantor Gallery, Beverly Hills, Calif., 1961, 65; Allan Stone Gallery, 1962 (two-man), 1964, 65, 71, 72; The Goodman Gallery, Buffalo, 1964; Smith College, 1965; M. Knoedler & Co., NYC, 1967, 69, 71, Paris, 1968, 71; Betty Gold, Los Angeles, 1971; Fourcade, Droll, Inc., NYC, 1972, 75; Richard Gray Gallery, 1974; Walker, 1974; Galerie Biedermann, Munich, 1974; West Palm Beach/Norton, 1975; Seattle/AM, 1976; Amsterdam/Stedelijk, 1976; Musée de Grenoble, 1977; Corcoran Gallery, Los Angeles, 1976, 77; Gimpel Fils, London, 1976; Gimpel Fils, Zurich, 1976; Xavier Fourcade, Inc., NYC, 1976, 77, 78, 79; Galerie Daniel Templon, Paris, 1977; U. of Houston, 1976; Belgrade, 1977–78; Duisburg, 1977; SRGM, 1978; U. of Northern Iowa, 1978; Carnegie, 1979; Richard Gray Gallery, Chicago, 1980; Richard

Hines Gallery, Seattle, 1980. **Retrospective:** Amsterdam/Stedelijk, 1968; MOMA, 1968. **Group:** MOMA, New Horizons in American Art, 1936; WMAA Annuals, 1948, 50, 51; VMFA, American Painting, 1950; California Palace, 1950; XXV, XXVI, & XXVIII Venice Biennials, 1950, 52, 56; MOMA, Abstract Painting and Sculpture in America, 1951; Sao Paulo, 1951, 53; Chicago/AI, 1951, 54; Buffalo/Albright, Expressionism in American Painting, 1952; Carnegie, 1952; 55; Baltimore/MA, 1953; WMAA, The New Decade, 1954–55; WMAA, Nature in Abstraction, 1958; Brussels World's Fair, 1958; MOMA, The New American Painting, circ., Europe 1958–59; Hartford/Wadsworth, Continuity and Change, 1962; Seattle World's Fair, 1962; Art: USA: Now, circ., 1962–67; SRGM, Guggenheim International, 1964; Tate, Painting and Sculpture of a Decade, 1954–64, 1964; SRGM, American Drawings, 1964; Los Angeles/County MA, New York School, 1965; U. of Illinois, 1967; Melbourne/National, Two Decades of American Painting, 1967; Frankfurter Kunstverein, Kompass New York, 1968; ICA, London, The Obsessive Image, 1968; MOMA, The New American Painting and Sculpture, 1969; Corcoran Biennial, 1979; U. of California, Berkeley, Matrix, 1978; National Gallery, American Art Mid-Century, 1978; PAFA, Seven on the Figure, 1979. **Collections:** Baltimore/MA; Brooklyn Museum; Buffalo/Albright; Carnegie; Chicago/AI; Container Corp. of America; Inland Steel Co.; Kansas City/Nelson; MMA; MOMA; U. of Nebraska; U. of North Carolina; Phillips; SRGM; Vassar College; WMAA; Walker; Washington U. **Bibliography:** Alloway 4; Ashton 5; Barr 3; Battcock, ed.; Baur 5, 7; Becker and Vostell; Biddle 4; Bihalji-Merin; Blesh 1; Brion 1; Brown 2; Calas, N. and E.; Canaday; Carmean and Rathbone; Chipp; **de Kooning;** Downes, ed.; Eliot; Elsen 1; Finch; Flanagan; *From Foreign Shores;* Goodrich and Baur 1; Greenberg 1; Haftman; Henning; **Hess, T.B., 1, 4, 5;** Hobbs and Levin; Hunter 1, 6; Hunter, ed.; **Janis and Blesh 1, 2;** Janis, S.; Johnson, Ellen H.; Kozloff 3; Kuh 3; Langui; **Larson and Schjeldahl;** Lippard 5; Lynton; McCoubrey 1; McCurdy, ed.; Mendelowitz; **Metro; Monumenta;** Motherwell and Reinhardt, eds.; Neumeyer; Nordness, ed.; O'Doherty; Plous; *Poets & Painters;* Ponente; Pousette-Dart, ed.; Ragon 1; Read 2; Richardson, E.P.; Rickey; Ritchie 1; Rodman 1, 2, 3; Rose, B., 1, 4; **Rosenberg;** Rothschild; Sandler; Seitz 1, 3; Seuphor 1; Soby 6; Tomkins 1, 2; Tomkins and Time-Life Books; Tuchman, ed.; Weller; "What Abstract Art Means to Me".

DE LAP, TONY. b. November 4, 1927, Oakland, Calif. **Studied:** California College of Arts and Crafts; Menlo Junior College; Academy of Art, San Francisco; Claremont Graduate School, AA. Traveled in Europe for 3 months, 1954. **Taught:** Academy of Art, San Francisco, 1957–59; California College of Arts and Crafts, 1961–63; U. of Wisconsin, summer 1963; Scripps College, U. of California, Davis, 1964–65; Claremont Colleges, 1964; San Francisco Art Institute, 1964–67; U. of California, Irvine, 1965– . Art Commissioner, San Francisco Municipal Art Commission. **Commissions:** Brooks Hall, San Francisco; Carborundum Co., 1969; C.C.H. Building, San Rafael, Calif., 1972; City of Inglewood, Calif., 1973. **Awards:** San Francisco Art Festival, First Prize, Mural Competition, 1957; SFMA, Nealie Sullivan Award, 1964; Ford Foundation/A.F.A. Artist-in-Residence, 1966; Long Beach/MA., **P.P.,** 1969; 1st Prize, Los Angeles Department of Airports, sculpture competition, 1976. **Address:** 225 Jasmine Street, Corona del Mar, CA 92625. **Dealers:** Robert Elkon Gallery; Janus Gallery, Venice, Calif. **One-man Exhibitions:** (first) Gump's Gallery; SFMA; RAC, 1954; Oakland/AM, 1960; Dilexi Gallery, San Francisco, 1963, 67; Robert Elkon Gallery, 1965, 66, 68, 70, 73, 75, 77, 79; Felix Landau Gallery,

1966, 69; Mt. San Antonio College, 1969 (two-man); Nicholas Wilder Gallery, 1972, 74, 76; California State U., Long Beach, 1974; John Berggruen Gallery, 1974, 76; California Institute of Technology, Pasadena, 1975; Newport Harbor, 1977; Jack Glenn Gallery, Newport Beach, 1976; Casat Gallery, La Jolla, 1977; California State College, Chico, 1979; Janus Gallery, Venice City, 1979. **Retrospective:** U. of California, Irvine, Tony De Lap: The Last Five Years: 1963–68, 1969. **Group:** Stanford U., 1961; Kaiser Center, Oakland, Sculpture Today, 1964; Carnegie, 1964; WMAA, 1964; Chicago/AI; MOMA, 1964, The Responsive Eye, 1965, The 1960's, 1967; La Jolla, 1965, 66; Jewish Museum, Primary Structures, 1966; WMAA, Contemporary American Sculpture, Selection 1, 1966; Musée Cantonal des Beaux-Arts, Lausanne, II Salon de Galeries Pilotes, 1966; Seattle/ AM, 1966; Los Angeles/County MA, American Sculpture of the Sixties, 1967; Scripps College, 1967; San Marino (Europe), Nuove Tecniche dell'immagine, 1967; Portland, Ore./AM, 1968; U. of California, Irvine, A Los Angeles Esthetic, 1969; Pasadena/AM, West Coast; 1945–1969, 1969; La Jolla, The Wall Object, 1973; Newport Harbor, Modern and Contemporary Sculpture, 1974; Corcoran, Biennial, 1978; SFMA, California Painting and Sculpture: The Modern Era, 1976. **Collections:** Arizona State U.; Atlantic Richfield Co.; Claremont College; Hartford/ Wadsworth; Hirshhorn; Los Angeles/ County MA; MOMA; Oakland/AM; Ridgefield/Aldrich; SFMA; San Francisco Municipal Art Commission; Santa Barbara/MA; State of California; Tate; WMAA; Walker. **Bibliography:** Tuchman 1.

DELLA-VOLPE, RALPH. b. May 10, 1923, New Jersey. **Studied:** NAD; ASL (with Edwin Dickinson, Will Barnet, Harry Sternberg). Traveled USA, Mexico. US Army, 1942–45. **Taught:** Bennett College, Millbrook, N.Y., 1949–77;

Marist College, Poughkeepsie, 1977–79. **Member:** College Art Association; Association of American University Professors. **Awards:** MacDowell Colony Fellowship, 1963; Library of Congress, Pennell **P.P.**; NIAL, Drawing Prize, 1963, 64. **Address:** Altamont Road, RD #2, Box 295, Millbrook, NY 12545. **Dealer:** Munson Gallery, New Haven, CT. **One-man Exhibitions:** Bennett College, 1949–63; Three Arts Gallery, Poughkeepsie, N.Y., 1951; Artists' Gallery, NYC, 1959; The Babcock Gallery, 1960, 62, 63; Lehigh U., 1963; Mansfield State College, 1964; Pittsfield/Berkshire, 1964; Cobleskill/SUNY, 1968; Dutchess Community College, Poughkeepsie, N.Y.; Centenary College, Hackettstown, N.J.; The Hotchkiss School, Lakeville, Conn.; Wolfe Street Gallery, Washington, D.C., 1974, 77; Talking of Michelangelo Gallery, Washington, D.C., 1974. **Retrospectives:** The Gallery, West Cornwall, Conn., 1974; Columbia, S.C./MA, 1975. **Group:** PAFA; Library of Congress; NIAL; American Color Print Society; Youngstown/ Butler; Bradley U.; Brooklyn Museum; Hartford/Wadsworth; San Antonio/ McNay; Vassar College; Newport (R.I.) Art Association; Audubon Artists, NYC. **Collections:** ASL; Chase Manhattan Bank; Library of Congress; Mansfield State College; Slater; Wichita/ AM.

DE MARIA, WALTER. b. 1935, Albany, Calif. **Studied:** U. of California, BA, MA (with David Park). Traveled Europe, 1968. **Awards:** Guggenheim Foundation Fellowship, 1969; Mather Sculpture Prize, Chicago/AI, 1976. **Address:** 27 Howard Street, NYC 10013. **One-man Exhibitions:** (first) Nine Great Jones Street, NYC (two-man, with Robert Whitman), 1963; Paula Cooper Gallery, 1965; Cordier & Ekstrom, Inc., 1966; Nicholas Wilder Gallery, 1968; Galerie Heiner Friedrich, Munich, 1968; Dwan Gallery, 1969, 70; Cinema Odeon, Turin, 1969; Iris Clert Gallery, 1969; Gian Enzo Sperone,

Turin, 1969, 70; Basel, 1972; Darmstadt/ Hessisches, 1974; Heiner Friedrich, NYC, 1977; Dia Art Foundation, NYC, 1979, 80. **Group:** Jack London Outdoor Art Annual, Oakland, Calif., 1959; Douglass College, 1964; Jewish Museum, Primary Structures, 1966; WMAA Sculpture Annual, 1967, 68; Museum of Contemporary Crafts, 1967; Los Angeles/County MA, American Sculpture of the Sixties, 1967; A.F.A., circ., 1967; Milwaukee, Directions I: Options, circ., 1968; Documenta IV, Kassel, 1968; Prospect '68, Dusseldorf, 1968; Berne, When Attitudes Become Form, 1969; Amsterdam/Stedelijk, 1969; MOMA, circ., 1969; MOMA, Information, 1970; Dusseldorf/Kunsthalle, Prospect 71, 1971; SRGM, Guggenheim International, 1971; Philadelphia College of Art, Line, 1976; WMAA, 200 Years of American Sculpture, 1976; Chicago/AI, 1976; Hayward Gallery, London, Pier and Ocean, 1980; Venice Biennial, 1980; ROSC, Dublin, 1980. **Collections:** MOMA; WMAA. **Bibliography:** Atkinson; Battcock, ed.; Calas, N. and E.; Celanti; *Contemporanea; Davis, D.; Happening & Fluxus; Kunst um 1970;* Lippard, ed.; Muller; *Report;* Ruhe; Tuchman 1; *When Attitudes Become Form.* Archives.

DE MARTINI, JOSEPH. b. July 20, 1896, Mobile, Ala. **Studied:** NAD, with Leon Kroll, Ivan Olinsky. **Taught:** U. of Georgia, 1952–53. Federal A.P.: Easel painting. **Awards:** Pepsi-Cola, 1944; U. of Illinois, **P.P.,** 1948; NAD, 1950; Guggenheim Foundation Fellowship, 1951; PAFA, Gold Medal, 1952. **Address:** 103 West 27th Street, NYC 10001. **One-man Exhibitions:** (first) Dorothy Paris Gallery, NYC, 1932; Eighth Street Gallery, NYC, 1935; Macbeth Gallery, NYC, 1941, 43, 47; Hudson D. Walker Gallery, NYC, 1942. **Group:** WMAA, 1934, 42–45; St. Louis/City, 1938, 41, 42, 46; New York World's Fair, 1939; PAFA, 1940, 42–45; Chicago/AI, 1941, 42; de Young, 1941, 43; MOMA, 1941–43; Carnegie, 1941, 43, 44, 46; Corcoran 1941,

43, 45; Colorado Springs/FA, 1942; VMFA, 1942, 44, 46; Brooklyn Museum, 1943; Indianapolis/Herron, 1945; Worcester/AM, 1945; U. of Nebraska, 1945, 46. **Collections:** Andover/Phillips; U. of Arizona; Boston/MFA; Britannica; Canajoharie; U. of Georgia; IBM; Iowa State U.; MMA; MOMA; Memphis/Brooks; U. of Nebraska; New Britain; Pepsi-Cola Co.; Phillips; U. of Rochester; Rockland/Farnsworth; St. Louis/City; San Diego; U. of Texas; US State Department; WMAA; Walker; Washington State U.; Wichita/AM. **Bibliography:** Baur 7; Cheney; Frost; Genauer.

DEMUTH, CHARLES. b. November 8, 1883, Lancaster, Pa.; **d.** October 23, 1935. **Studied:** Franklin and Marshall College; Drexel Institute of Technology, 1901; Pennsylvania School of Industrial Art, Philadelphia; PAFA, 1905–08, with Thomas Anshutz, Henry McCarter; Academie Colarossi, Academie Moderne, and Academie Julian, Paris, 1912–14. Traveled Europe, eastern USA. **One-man Exhibitions:** (first) The Daniel Gallery, NYC, 1915, also 1916, 17, 18, 20, 22, 23, 24, 25; Stieglitz's Intimate Gallery, NYC, 1926, 29; An American Place (Gallery), NYC, 1931; The Downtown Gallery, 1931, 50, 54, 58; Smith College, 1934; WMAA, 1935; WMAA Memorial Exhibition, 1937; U. of Minnesota, 1937; Franklin and Marshall College, 1941, 48; Cincinnati/AM, 1941; Phillips, 1942; PMA, 1944; The U. of Chicago, 1946; Graphische Sammlung Albertina, 1949; Ogunquit, 1959; U. of California, Santa Barbara, 1971; Kennedy Gallery, 1971. **Retrospective:** MOMA, 1949; Harrisburg, Pa./State Museum, 1966. **Group:** MOMA; WMAA; MMA; PAFA; Phillips; Pomona College, Stieglitz Circle, 1958. **Collections:** Amherst College; Andover/Phillips; Arizona State College; Baltimore/MA; Barnes Foundation; Boston/MFA; Brooklyn Museum; Buffalo/Albright; Chicago/AI; Cleveland/ MA; Columbus; Detroit/Institute; Fisk

U.; Hartford/Wadsworth; Harvard U.; Honolulu Academy; MMA; MOMA; Milwaukee; National Gallery; U. of Nebraska; Newark Museum; New Britain; Ogunquit; PMA; Phillips; Princeton U.; RISD; San Antonio/McNay; Santa Barbara/MA; Toledo/MA; Utica; WMAA; Walker; Wellesley College; West Palm Beach/Norton; Wichita/AM; Worcester/AM; Yale U. **Bibliography:** *Avant-Garde Painting and Sculpture in America, 1910–25;* Barnes; Baur 7; Bazin; Biddle 4; Blesh 1; Born; Brown; Brown 2; Cahill and Barr. eds.; **Charles Demuth**; Cheney; Christensen; *8 American Masters of Watercolor;* Eliot; **Farnham;** *Forerunners; Frost; Gallatin 1; Goodrich and Baur 1; Haftman; Hall; Hunter 6; Huyghe;* **Index of 20th Century Artists;** *Janis, S.; Jewell 2; Kootz 1, 2; Lane; Mather 1; McCoubrey 1; McCurdy, ed.; Murrell 1; Neuhaus; Phillips 2; Poore; Richardson, E.P.; Rigel, ed.;* **Ritchie 2;** Rose, B., 1; Rosenblum 1; Sachs; Sager; Soby 5; Sutton; Tashjian; Tomkins and Time-Life Books; Wight 2. Archives.

DE NIRO, ROBERT. b. May 3, 1922, Syracuse, N.Y. **Studied:** Syracuse Museum School, 1935–39; Hofmann School, Provincetown, summers, 1939, 40; Black Mountain College, with Josef Albers. Traveled France; resided Paris. **Taught:** New School for Social Research, 1966– ; School of Visual Arts, NYC, 1966–70; Buffalo/SUNY, summers, 1969, 70, 71; Wagner College, 1970, 71; Cooper Union, 1971– ; The Pennsylvania State U., 1973; Fine Arts Work Center, Provincetown, Mass., 1973; Michigan State U., 1974; New York Studio School, Paris, 1974. U. of California, Santa Cruz, 1979. **Awards:** V Hallmark International Competition; Longview Foundation Grant; Guggenheim Foundation Fellowship, 1968; Tamarind Institute Grant, 1974. **Address:** 465 West Broadway, NYC 10012. **Dealer:** The Graham Gallery, NYC. **One-man Exhibitions:** (first) Art of This Century, NYC, 1946; Charles Egan Gallery, 1950, 52, 54; Poindexter Gallery, 1955, 56, 76; The Zabriskie Gallery, 1958, 60 (2), 62, 65, 70; (2), 67, 68, 70; Ellison Gallery, Fort Worth (two-man), 1959; Buffalo/SUNY, 1967; Galleries Reese Palley, Atlantic City and San Francisco, 1968, 69; Bard College, 1969; Brenner Gallery, Provincetown, 1971; The Pennsylvania State U., 1973; Kansas City/AI, 1974; The Graham Gallery, NYC, 1979; Swain School of Design, New Bedford, Mass., 1979; Charles Campbell Gallery, San Francisco, 1978, 79; David Stuart Gallery, Los Angeles, 1978. **Group:** WMAA Annuals; Jewish Museum, The New York School, Second Generation, 1957; ICA, Boston, 100 Works on Paper, circ., Europe, 1959; U. of Nebraska, 1960; A.F.A., The Figure, circ., 1960; Felix Landau Gallery, Los Angeles–New York, 1960; Colorado Springs/FA Annual, 1961; MOMA, Recent Painting USA; The Figure, circ., 1962–63; Illinois Wesleyan U. Annual, 1962; New School for Social Research, Portraits from the American Art World, 1965. **Collections:** Brandeis U.; Houston/MFA; Longview Foundation; U. of North Carolina. **Bibliography:** Sandler 1.

DE RIVERA, JOSE. b. September 18, 1904, West Baton Rouge, La. **Studied:** Studio School, Chicago, with John W. Norton, 1928–30. Traveled USA, Europe, Mediterranean, North Africa. Federal A.P.: Mural painting, 1937–38. US Army Air Corps, 1942–43. **Taught:** Brooklyn College, 1953; Yale U., 1954–55; North Carolina School of Design, Raleigh, 1957–60. **Member:** NIAL. **Commissions:** Cavalry Monument, El Paso, 1938–40; Newark Airport, 1938; Soviet Pavilion, New York World's Fair, 1939; Wm. Kaufman Inc., NYC, 1955; Hotel Statler-Hilton, Dallas, 1956; Moore-McCormack Lines Inc., SS *Argentina,* 1958; Reynolds Metals Co., 1958, City of Lansing, Mich. **Awards:** Chicago/AI, Watson F. Blair Prize, 1957; NIAL Grant, 1959; Hon. Ph.D., Washington U. **Address:** 435 East 57 Street, NYC 10022. **Dealer:** Grace Borgenicht

Gallery, Inc. **One-man Exhibitions:** Harvard U. (two-man, with Burgoyne Diller), 1945; Mortimer Levit Gallery, NYC, 1946; Grace Borgenicht Gallery Inc., 1952, 56, 57, 58, 59, 60, 72, 78; Walker, 1957. **Retrospective:** A.F.A./ Ford Foundation, circ., 1961; La Jolla, 1972. **Group:** Chicago/AI, 1934; Brooklyn Museum, 1938; WMAA Annuals, 1938– ; MOMA, Twelve Americans, circ., 1956; Brussels World's Fair, 1958; American Painting and Sculpture, Moscow, 1959; MOMA, Recent Sculpture USA, 1959; Public Education Association, NYC, 1966; U. of New Mexico, 1966, Los Angeles/County MA, Sculpture of the Sixties, circ., 1967. **Collections:** The M. L. Annenberg Foundation; Brooklyn Museum; Chicago/AI; Des Moines; Fort Dodge/Blandend; Hirshhorn; La Jolla; Lembke Construction Co.; MMA; MOMA; Newark Museum; U. of New Mexico; U. of Pennsylvania; Purchase/SUNY; Ridgefield/Aldrich; U. of Rochester; SFMA; St. Louis/City; Smithsonian; Tate; Toronto; Utica; VMFA; WMAA. **Bibliography:** Baur 7; Brumme; Craven, W.; Flanagan; Gerdts; Gertz; Goodrich and Baur 1; **Jose de Rivera**; Licht, F.; Marter, Tarbell, and Wechsler; McCurdy, ed.; Mendelowitz; Read, 3; Rickey; Ritchie 1, 3; Rodman 3; Seuphor 3; Trier 1. Archives.

DESHAIES, ARTHUR. b. July 6, 1920, Providence, R.I. **Studied:** Cooper Union, 1939–42; RISD, 1947–48, BFA; Indiana U., 1948–50, MFA; self-taught as a printmaker. Traveled Mexico, USA, Europe. **Taught:** RISD, 1947–48; Indiana U., 1949–56; Pratt Institute, 1956–57; Pratt Graphic Art Center, 1962; Florida State U., 1963–75; lectures and writes extensively on art and printmaking. **Awards:** Indiana U., Faculty Research Grant for Painting, 1950; Fulbright Fellowship, 1952; MacDowell Colony Fellowship, winters, 1959, 60, 61, 62; Yaddo Fellowship, 1960; L. C. Tiffany Grant, 1960; Guggenheim Foundation Fellowship, 1961; Brooklyn

Museum; Bradley U.; Oklahoma Print Society; Indianapolis/Herron; U. of Kentucky, **P.P.**; Otis Art Institute, Los Angeles; Memphis/Brooks, **P.P. Address:** 1314 Dillard Street, Tallahassee, FL 32303. **One-man Exhibitions:** (first) Weyhe Gallery, 1940; Philadelphia Art Alliance; Galerie Paul Fachetti, 1954; Coker College, Hartsville, S.C., 1957; The Little Gallery, Tallahassee, 1964. **Group:** PCA, American Prints Today, circ., 1959–62; Brooklyn Museum; III International Biennial Exhibition of Prints, Tokyo, 1962; Otis Art Institute; WMAA. **Collections:** Bibliotheque Nationale; Bradley U.; British Museum; Brooklyn Museum; MMA; MOMA; RISD. **Bibliography:** Hayter 1; Peterdi.

DICKINSON, EDWIN. b. October 11, 1891, Seneca Falls, N.Y.; **d.** December 2, 1978, Orleans, Mass. **Studied:** Pratt Institute, 1910–11; ASL, 1911–12, with William M. Chase; Provincetown, summers, 1912, 13, 14, with C. W. Hawthorne. US Navy, 1917–19. Traveled Europe, Near East, North Africa, Greece. **Taught:** Buffalo Fine Arts Academy, 1916, 39; ASL, 1922–23, 1944–66; Provincetown Art Association, 1929–30; Stuart School, Boston, 1940–41; Association of Art and Music, Cape Cod, 1941; Cooper Union, 1945–49; Midtown School, NYC, 1946–47; Brooklyn Museum School, 1946–47; Pratt Institute, 1950–58; Dennis Foundation, Dennis, Mass., 1951; Skowhegan School, 1956, 58; Cornell U., 1957; Boston U., 1961. **Member:** NAD, 1948; NIAL; AAAL; Audubon Artists; The Patteran Society. Federal A.P.: Easel painting, 1934. **Awards:** NAD, Benjamin Altman Prize, 1929, 58; Benjamin West Medal; NAD, First Prize, 1949; Century Association, Medal; NIAL Grant, 1954; Brandeis U., Creative Arts Medal, 1959; Ford Foundation Grant, 1959. **One-man Exhibitions:** (first) Buffalo-Albright, 1927, 77; Worcester/AM, Boston/MFA; Houston/ MFA; U. of Rochester; Cornell U.; Provincetown/Chrysler; Passedoit Gallery,

Edwin Dickinson *Roses* 1939

NYC, 1939; Wood Memorial Gallery, Provincetown, 1939; Wellesley College, 1940; Nantucket Museum, 1943; Cushman Gallery, Houston, 1958; MOMA (circ. only), 1961; The Graham Gallery, 1961, 65, 68; Kansas City/Nelson, 1964 (two-man, with Lennart Anderson); Peale House, Philadelphia, 1966; Katonah (N.Y.) Art Gallery, 1966; Gilman Galleries, Chicago, 1966; Provincetown Art Association, 1967; XXXIV Venice Biennial, 1968. **Retrospective:** Boston U., 1958; WMAA, 1965. **Group:** MOMA, Fifteen Americans, circ., 1952; WMAA; Brooklyn Museum; Boston/ MFA; PMA; PAFA; Carnegie; U. of Rochester. **Collections:** Atlanta/AA; Bowdoin College; Brooklyn Museum; Buffalo/Albright; Chicago/AI; Cornell U.; Hirshhorn; MMA; MOMA; Montpelier/Wood; NAD; U. of Nebraska; Sara Roby Foundation; Springfield, Mass./MFA; Syracuse U.; Yale U. **Bibliography:** *America 1976;* Goodrich, 2, 5; Goodrich and Baur 1; Haftman; Kuh 2; McCurdy, ed.; Mellquist; Nordness, ed.; Pousette-Dart, ed.; Rose B., 1; Soyer, R. 1. Archives.

DIEBENKORN, RICHARD. b. April 22, 1922, Portland, Ore. **Studied:** Stanford U., 1940–43; U. of California, Berkeley, 1943–44; CSFA, 1946; Stanford U., 1949, BA; U. of New Mexico, 1952, MA. US Marines, 1943–45. Traveled USSR. **Taught:** U. of Illinois, 1952–53; California College of Arts and Crafts, 1955–57; SFAI, 1959–63; Stanford U., 1963–64; UCLA, 1966–73; U. of

Colorado; U. of California at Los Angeles, 1966–73. **Member:** National Council on the Arts, 1966–69. **Awards:** CSFA, Albert M. Bender Fellowship, 1946; Rosenberg Traveling Fellowship, 1959; Olivet College, **P.P.**; NIAL, 1962; PAFA, Gold Medal, 1968; Skowhegan School, Medal for Painting, 1979; MacDowell Colony Medal, 1978. **Address:** 334 Amalfi Drive, Santa Monica, CA 90402. **Dealer:** M. Knoedler & Co., Inc. **One-man Exhibitions:** (first) California Palace, 1948, also 60; U. of New Mexico, 1951; Paul Kantor Gallery, 1952, 54; SFMA, 1954, 73; Allan Frumkin Gallery, Chicago, 1954; Poindexter Gallery, 1955, 58, 61, 63, 66, 68; Phillips, 1958, 61; de Young, 1963; Stanford U., 1964; Pavilion Art Gallery, Newport Beach, Calif., 1965; Waddington Galleries, London, 1965, 67; U. of Washington, 1967; Kansas City/Nelson, 1968; RAC, 1968; Los Angeles/County MA, 1969; Irving Blum Gallery, Los Angeles, 1971; Marlborough Gallery, Inc., NYC, 1971, 74; James Corcoran Galleries, Los Angeles, 1975; John Berggruen Gallery, San Francisco, 1975; UCLA, 1976; M. Knoedler & Co. Inc., NYC, 1977, 79. **Retrospectives:** Pasadena/AM, 1960; WGMA, 1964; Jewish Museum, 1964; UCLA, circ., 1976. **Group:** SRGM, Younger American Painters, 1954; WMAA Annuals, 1955, 58, 61; Carnegie, 1955, 58, 61, 70; IV Sao Paulo Biennial, 1957; Brussels World's Fair, 1958; MOMA, New Images of Man, 1959; Tate, Paintings and Sculpture of a Decade, 1964; Edinburgh/National, Two American Painters: Sam Francis Richard Diebenkorn, 1965; WMAA, Art of the United States: 1670–1966, 1966; XXIV Venice Biennial, 1968, 78; SFMA, Untitled 1968, 1968; Eindhoven, Kompas IV, 1969–70; Omaha/Joslyn, Looking West, 1970; Boston U., Drawings: Elmer Bischoff and Richard Diebenkorn, 1974; Oakland/AM, California Landscape, 1975; Corcoran Biennial, 1975; PAFA, Young American, 1975; Newport Harbor, The Last Time I Saw Ferus, 1976; Buffalo/Albright, American Paintings of the 1970's, 1978. **Collec-**

tions: U. of Arkansas; Baltimore/MA; Brooklyn Museum; Buffalo/Albright; California Palace; U. of California, Berkeley; Carnegie; Chicago/AI; Cincinnati/AM; Cleveland/MA; Corcoran; Grand Rapids; Hirshhorn; Kansas City/Nelson; Los Angeles/County MA; U. of Michigan; MMA; MOMA; U. of New Mexico; Norfolk/Chrysler; Oklahoma; Oakland/AM; Oberlin College; Olivet College; PAFA; Pasadena/AM; Phillips; Phoenix; Raleigh/NCMA; Readers Digest; SFMA; Santa Barbara/MA; Skidmore College; Stanford U.; Toronto; WMAA; Washington U. **Bibliography:** Arthur 2; Blesh 1; Geske; Johnson; Mendelowitz; Neumeyer; Nordness, ed.; Read 2; Rose, B., 1; *Richard Diebenkorn;* Sandler 1.

DILL, LADDIE JOHN. b. September 14, 1943, Long Beach, Calif. **Studied:** Chouinard Art Institute, Los Angeles, 1968, BA; with M. Kanamitsu, E. Woelffer, R. Irwin. Traveled Europe, South Seas, Mexico, and Central America. **Taught:** U. of California, Irvine; UCLA. **Awards:** National Endowment for the Arts, grant, 1975; Guggenheim Foundation Fellowship, 1979. **Address:** 638 Ashland Avenue, Santa Monica, CA 90415. **Dealer:** James Corcoran, Los Angeles; Charles Cowles, NYC. **One-man Exhibitions:** (first) Ileana Sonnabend Gallery, NYC, 1971, 72; Pasadena/AM, 1971; Portland State U., 1971; The Morgan Gallery, Shawnee Mission, Kans., 1972; Mizuno Gallery, Los Angeles, 1973; James Corcoran Gallery, Los Angeles, 1974, 75, 77, 78, 79; Douglas Drake Gallery, Kansas City, 1975, 78; Kansas State U., 1976; Dootson Calderhead Gallery, Seattle, 1976; Seder/Creigh Gallery, Coronado, 1976; Dobrick Gallery, Chicago, 1976, 78; Grapestake Gallery, San Francisco, 1977; Landfall Press, Chicago, 1978; California Institute of Technology, Pasadena, 1978; Linda Farris Gallery, Seattle, 1980; Osuna Gallery, Washington, D.C., 1980. **Group:** California State U., Los Angeles, Venice, California, 70,

1970; Los Angeles/County MA, 24 Young Los Angeles Artists 1971; Walker, Works for New Spaces, 1971; Govett-Brewster Art Gallery, New Plymouth, N.Z., The State of California Painting, 1972; California State U., Fullerton, Guy Dill/Laddie John Dill, 1972; Webster College, St. Louis, Some California Artists, 1973; Santa Barbara/MA, 15 Abstract Artists, 1974; Scripps College, Claremont, Light, 1974; Newport Harbor/Art Museum, Modern and Contemporary Sculptures, 1975; Brandeis U., Three California Painters, 1975; SFMA, Painting and Sculpture in California; The Modern Era, 1976; Kansas City/AI, Spectrum 77, 1977; Indianapolis, 1978; Buffalo/Albright, Painting of the Seventies, 1979; Sacramento/Crocker, Aspects of Abstraction, 1979; AAAL, 1979; Municipal Art Gallery, Los Angeles, It's All Called Painting, 1980. **Collections:** Los Angeles/County MA; Newport Harbor; Oakland/AM; Seattle/AM; SFMA.

DILLER, BURGOYNE. b. 1906, NYC; **d.** January 30, 1964, NYC. **Studied:** Michigan State College; ASL. US Navy, World War II. **Taught:** Brooklyn College, 1945–64; Pratt Institute, 1945–64. **Member:** American Abstract Artists. Federal A.P.: Head, Mural Division, 1935–40; Assistant Technical Director, New York Art Project, 1940–41; Director, New York Art Project, 1940–41; Director, New York City Art Section, 1939–42. **Awards:** Ford Foundation, **P.P.**, 1963. **One-man Exhibitions:** Harvard U., 1945 (two-man, with Jose de Rivera); The Pinacotheca, NYC, 1946; Galerie Chalette, 1961, 64; Goldowsky Gallery, 1968, 72; Los Angeles/County MA, 1968; Washburn Gallery, Inc., NYC, 1978; Meredith Long Gallery, Houston, 1979; Meredith Long Contemporary, NYC, 1979. **Retrospective:** Trenton/State, 1966; Walker, circ., 1971. **Group:** American Abstract Artists Annuals to 1940; WMAA; Geometric Abstraction in America, circ., 1962; VII Sao Paulo Biennial, 1963; Corcoran, 1963; WMAA, 1964; SFMA, Colorists 1950–1965, 1965; SRGM, Guggenheim International, 1967; WMAA, The 1930s, 1968; MMA, New York Painting and Sculpture: 1940–1970, 1969–70; U. of New Mexico, American Abstract Artists, 1977; Yale U. Mondrian and Neo-plasticism in America, 1979. **Collections:** Buffalo/Albright; Chicago/AI; Corcoran; Hirshhorn; MMA; MOMA; Milwaukee; NYU; Springfield, Mass./MFA; Trenton/State; WMAA; Yale U. **Bibliography:** Blesh 1; Brown 2; Gerdts; Hess, T.B., 1; Janis and Blesh, 1; Janis, S.; **Larson**; MacAgy 2; McCurdy, ed.; Marter, Tarbell, and Wechsler; Rickey; Ritchie 1; Rose, B., 1, 4; Seuphor 1, 3. Archives.

DINE, JIM. b. June 16, 1935, Cincinnati, Ohio. **Studied:** U. of Cincinnati; Boston Museum School; Ohio U., 1957; BFA, and 1958. An early creator of Happenings and Environments. Subject of a 16mm. sound film, *Jim Dine*, directed by Lane Slate, produced by National Educational Television. **Address:** Putney, VT 05346. **Dealer:** The Pace Gallery, NYC. **One-man Exhibitions:** Judson Gallery, NYC, 1959 (two-man, with Claes Oldenburg); Reuben Gallery, NYC, 1959 (two-man, with Oldenburg); Reuben Gallery, NYC, 1960; Martha Jackson Gallery, 1952; Galleria dell'Ariete, 1962; Ileana Sonnabend Gallery, Paris, 1963, 69, 72, 75, NYC, 71, 73, 74; Brussels/Beaux-Arts, 1963, 70; Sidney Janis Gallery, 1963, 64; Galleria Sperone, Turin, 1965; Oberlin College, 1965; Robert Fraser Gallery, London, 1965, 66, 69; Galerie Rolf Ricke, Kassel, 1967; Galerie Rudolf Zwirner, 1967; The Gallery Upstairs, Buffalo, 1967; Harcus-Krakow Gallery, 1967; Toronto, circ., 1967 (three-man, with Oldenburg, George Segal); MOMA, Jim Dine Designs for "A Midsummer Night's Dream," 1967; Sidney Janis Gallery, 1967; Amsterdam/Stedelijk, 1967; Cornell U., 1967; MOMA, 1969; Dunkelman Gallery, Toronto, 1970; Turin/Civico, 1970; Dus-

Jim Dine   *Two Mighty Robes at Night in Jerusalem*   1980

seldorf/Kunsthalle, 1970; Hannover/K-G, 1970; Rotterdam, 1970; Berlin Festival, 1970; Gimpel & Hanover, Gallery, 1972; Aronson Gallery, Atlanta, Ga., 1972; Modern Art Agency, Naples, 1972; Gimpel Fils, 1973; D. M. Gallery, London, 1973; Felicity Samuel Gallery, London, 1973; Galerie Sonnabend, Geneva, 1974; La Jolla, 1974; Dartmouth College, 1974; Petersburg Press, NYC, 1974; Centre d'Arts Plastiques Contemporains, Bordeaux, 1975; Gian Enzo Sperone, Rome, 1975; Williams College, 1976; The Pace Gallery, NYC, 1977, 78, 80; Waddington, Tooth Galleries II, London, 1977; Makler Gallery, Philadelphia, 1978; The Pace Gallery, Columbus, 1978; MOMA, 1978; Katonah Gallery, Katonah, 1979; Galerie Claude Bernard, Paris, 1979; California State U., Long Beach, circ., 1979; Galerie Alice Pauli, Lausanne, 1980; Janie C. Lee Gallery, Houston, 1980; Harcus-Krakow Gallery, Boston, 1980. **Retrospective:** WMAA, 1970. **Happenings:** Judson Gallery, NYC, The Smiling Workman, 1959; Reuben Gallery, NYC, Car Crash, 1960, Jim Dine's Vaudeville, 1960, The Shining Bed, 1960; First New York Theatre Rally, NYC, Natural History (The Dreams), 1965. **Group:** Cornell U., Young Americans, 1960; Martha Jackson Gallery, New Media—New Forms, I, 1960; USIA Gallery, London, Modern American Painting, 1961; Dallas/MFA, "1961," 1961; Sidney Janis Gallery, The New Realists, 1962; Philadelphia YM-YWHA Arts Council, Art, A New Vocabulary, 1962; Pasadena/AM, New Paintings of Common Objects, 1962; International Biennial Exhibition of Paintings, Tokyo; SRGM, Six

Painters and the Object, circ., 1963; Houston/MFA, Pop Goes the Easel, 1963; WGMA, The Popular Image, 1963; ICA, London, The Popular Image, 1963; Buffalo/Albright, 1963; Cincinnati/AM, An American Viewpoint, 1963; Jewish Museum, Black and White, 1963; Hartford/Wadsworth, Black, White and Gray, 1964; Tate, Gulbenkian International, 1964; Chicago/AI, 1964, 69; Milwaukee, Popular Art and the American Tradition, 1965; Worcester/AM, New American Realism, 1965; WMAA, A Decade of American Drawings, 1965; WMAA, Art of the U.S. 1670–1966, 1966; Dublin/Municipal, I International Quadrennial (ROSC), 1967; Expo '67, Montreal, U.S. Pavilion, 1967; Honolulu Academy, Signals of the 60's, 1967; Corcoran Annual, 1967; Documenta IV, Kassel, 1968; Hayward Gallery, London, 1969; Cincinnati/AM, 1973; WMAA, American Drawings: 1963–1973, 1973; Musée Galliera, Paris, Festival d'Automne, 1973; Parcheggio di Villa Borghese, Contemporanea, 1974; Dallas/MFA, Poets of the Cities, 1974; Moore College of Art, Philadelphia, 1975; Hayward Gallery, London, The Human Clay, 1976; Documenta 6, Kassel, 1977; Chicago/AI, Drawings of the 70's, 1977; U. of North Carolina, Drawings about Drawing, 1979. **Collections:** Amsterdam/Stedelijk; Ball State U.; Baltimore/MA; Boston/MFA; Brandeis U.; Brooklyn Museum; Buffalo/Albright; Carnegie; Chicago/AI; Chicago/Contemporary; Cincinnati/AM; Cleveland/MA; Dallas/MFA; Dayton/AI; Detroit/Institute; Eindhoven; Harvard U.; High/Atlanta; Hirshhorn; Indiana U.; Indianapolis; Jewish Museum; Los Angeles/County MA; La Jolla; MMA; MOMA; NCFA; New Orleans Museum; NYU; Oberlin College; Ohio U.; Paris-Beaubourg; Princeton U.; RISD; SRGM; Stockholm/National; St. Louis/City; Tate; Toronto; VMFA; WGMA; WMAA; Walker; Western Australia Art Gallery, Perth; Williams College; Worcester; Woodward Foundation; Yale U. **Bibliography:** Allen, V.; Alloway 1, 4; Battcock,

ed.; Becker and Vostell; Bihalji-Merin; Calas, N. and E.; *Celebrate Ohio; Contemporanea;* Diamonstein; Dienst 1; Finch; Hansen; *Happening & Fluxus;* Honisch and Jensen, eds.; Hunter, ed.; Janis and Blesh 1; Johnson, Ellen H.; Kaprow; Kirby; Kozloff 3; Lippard 5; *Metro;* Rose, B. 1; Rubin 1; *Poets & Painters;* Russell and Gablik; Sager; Sandler 1; Sontag; Tomkins 2; Tomkins and Time-Life Books.

DI SUVERO, MARK. b. September 18, 1933, Shanghai, China. To USA, 1941. **Studied:** U. of California, BA. Traveled USA, Mexico. **Awards:** Longview Foundation Grant; Walter K. Gutman Foundation Grant; Chicago/AI, 1963; National Endowment for the Arts, grant; Brandeis U., Creative Arts Award; Skowhegan School Award For Sculpture. **Address:** 195 Front Street, NYC 10038; 75 Holly Heights, Petaluma, CA 94952. **Dealer:** Richard Bellamy. **One-man Exhibitions:** (first) Green Gallery, NYC, 1960; Dwan Gallery, Los Angeles, 1965; Park Place Gallery, NYC, 1966; Goldowsky Gallery, 1968; LoGiudice Gallery, Chicago, 1968; Eindhoven, 1972; Duisburg, 1972; City of Chalon-sur-Saone, 1973; Le Jardin des Tuileries, Paris, 1975; Janie C. Lee Gallery, Houston, 1978. **Retrospective:** WMAA, 1975. **Group:** Green Gallery, NYC, 1961, 62, 63; Hartford/Wadsworth, Continuity and Change, 1962; March Gallery, NYC (three-man); Chicago/AI, 1963; 79 Park Place Gallery, NYC, 1963, 64; Peace Tower, Los Angeles, 1966; Los Angeles/County MA, American Sculpture of the Sixties, 1967; WMAA, 1966, 67, 68, 70; SFMA, 1969; MMA, New York Painting and Sculpture: 1940–1970, 1969–1970; Cincinnati/Contemporary, Monumental Art, 1970; Walker, Works for New Spaces, 1971; WMAA, American Drawings: 1963–1973, 1973; Seattle/AM, American Art—Third Quarter Century, 1973; Vassar College, Contemporary College, 1974; Venice Biennial, 1975. **Collections:** Chicago/AI; City of Chalon-sur-

Saone; City of Toronto; Dallas/MFA; Hartford/Wadsworth; Hirshhorn; U. of Iowa; MIT; NYU; Otterlo; RISD; St. Louis/City; Storm King Art Center; WMAA; Walker, Western Washington State College. **Bibliography:** Battcock, ed.; Hunter, ed.; Krauss 2; Sandler 1; MacAgy 2; *Report*; Rose, B., 1; Tuchman 1.

DOBKIN, ALEXANDER. b. May 1, 1908, Genoa, Italy; **d.** March 21, 1975, Saint-Martin, West Indies. **Studied:** City College of New York, BS; Columbia U., MA; ASL, with George Bridgeman, Dimitri Romanovsky, Jose Clemente Orozco. Traveled Europe, Scandinavia, Israel; resided Paris. **Taught:** Lecturer, A Century of Progress, Chicago, 1933–34; New Art School, NYC, 1937–41; City College of New York; Educational Alliance, NYC, Art Director, 1934–55, Director, 1955–75. **Member:** Artists Equity. Federal A.P.: Easel painting for public buildings. **Awards:** Augustus Saint-Gaudens Medal from Cooper Union, 1930; Roosevelt Memorial Award, 1936; AAAL, Childe Hassam Award, 1947; Library of Congress, Pennell **P.P.**, 1949, 55; AAAL, **P.P.**, 1956. **One-man Exhibitions:** (first) ACA Gallery, 1935, also 1938, 47, 51, 58; Philadelphia Art Alliance, 1957; Garelick's Gallery, Detroit, 1957; Michel Galerie, Paris, 1959; A.A.A. Gallery, NYC, 1960, 69; The Forum Gallery, 1962, 68. **Retrospective:** A.A.A. Gallery, NYC, 1969. **Group:** A Century of Progress, Chicago, 1933–34; ART:USA: 58, NYC, 1958; Brooklyn Museum; Chicago/AI; MOMA; PMA; PAFA; Carnegie; Corcoran; Festival of Two Worlds, Spoleto; Library of Congress; New York World's Fair, 1964–65. **Collections:** Harvard U.; Library of Congress; MOMA; Newark Museum; PMA; Phoenix; Tel Aviv; WMAA; Youngstown/Butler. **Bibliography:** Archives.

DODD, LAMAR. b. September 22, 1909, Fairburn, Ga. **Studied:** Georgia Institute of Technology, 1926–27; ASL,

1929–33, with George Luks, Boardman Robinson, John Steuart Curry, Jean Charlot, George Bridgeman. Traveled USA. Europe. **Taught:** Five Points, Ala., 1927–28; U. of Georgia, 1937–76; emeritus, 1976– . **Member:** NAD; Audubon Artists. Federal A.P.; Easel painting. **Awards:** Chicago/AI, 1936; Pepsi-Cola, 1947, 48; LHD, LaGrange College, 1947; VMFA, Virginia Artists Biennial, **P.P.**, 1948; NIAL Grant, 1950; NAD, Edwin Palmer Memorial Prize, 1953; PAFA, **P.P.**, 1958; WMAA, **P.P.**, 1958; DFA, U. of Chattanooga, 1959; DFA, Florida State U., 1968. **Address:** 590 Springdale, Athens, GA 30606. **One-man Exhibitions:** (first) Ferargil Galleries, NYC, 1933; Columbia, S.C./MA, 1961; LaGrange College, Ga., 1964, 78; College of St. Catherine, 1964; Grand Central Moderns, NYC, 1948, 52, 55, 57, 61, 64, 65, 67, 68; U. of Georgia, 1969; Clemson U. 1972; Georgia Southern College, 1977. **Retrospective:** High Museum, 1970; U. of Georgia, circ., 1971; Columbia, S.C., 1954. **Group:** U. of Nebraska; PAFA; NIAL; Audubon Artists; Chicago/AI; Corcoran; Boston/MFA; NAD; U. of Illinois; Santa Barbara/MA; Carnegie, 1936; WMAA Annuals, 1937–57; Golden Gate International Exposition, San Francisco, 1939; New York World's Fair, 1939. **Collections:** Andover/Phillips; Atlanta/AA; Chicago/AI; CIT Corporation; Cranbrook; High Museum; U. of Georgia; IBM; MMA; Montclair/AM; Montgomery Museum; PAFA; Pepsi-Cola Co.; U. of Rochester; Savannah/Telfair; VMFA; WMAA; Wilmington. **Bibliography:** Baur 7; Bethers; Cheney; Wheeler.

DODD, LOIS. b. April 22, 1927, Montclair, N.J. **Studied:** Cooper Union, with Byron Thomas, Peter Busa. Traveled Italy, France, Switzerland. **Taught:** Philadelphia College of Art, 1963, 65; Wagner College, 1963–64; Brooklyn College, 1965–69, 1971– . A co-founder of the Tanager Gallery, NYC. **Commissions:** New York Hilton

Hotel (lithographs). **Awards:** Italian Government Scholarship, 1959–60; Longview Foundation Grant, 1962; Ingram Merrill Foundation Grant, 1971. **Address:** 30 East Second Street, NYC 10003. **Dealer:** Fischbach Gallery, NYC. **One-man Exhibitions:** (first) Tanager Gallery, NYC, 1954, also 1957, 58, 61, 62; Purdue U., 1965; Ithaca College, 1966; Wilmington, 1967; Green Mountain Gallery, 1969, 70, 71, 74, 76; Colby College, Waterville, Me., 1977; Washington (Conn.) Art Association, 1977; Cape Split Place, Addison, Me., 1977; Fischbach Gallery, NYC, 1978. **Retrospective:** Cape Split Place, circ., 1979. **Group:** The Stable Gallery Annuals, 1956, 58; USIA, Americans in Rome, Rome, 1960; U. of Kentucky, Drawings, 1961; Yale U., Drawings and Watercolors, 1964; A.F.A., Painterly Realism, 1970; U. of Vermont, New England Landscapes, 1971; New York Cultural Center, Women Choose Women, 1973; Omaha/Joslyn, A Sense of Place, 1973; Queens Museum, New Images, 1974; Brooklyn College, Brooklyn College Art Department: Past and Present 1942–1977, 1977; Queens Museum, Flushing, N.Y., New Images, 1974. **Collections:** AT&T; Brooklyn Museum; Chase Manhattan Bank; Ciba-Geigy Corp; Colby College; Commerce Bank of Kansas City; Cooper Union; First National City Bank; Hartford/Wadsworth; Kalamazoo/Institute; Reynolds Metals Co.; New York Hilton Hotel; WMAA. **Bibliography:** Archives.

DOLE, WILLIAM. b. September 2, 1917, Angola, Ind. **Studied:** Olivet College (with George Rickey, Harris King Prior), 1937, BA; Mills College, 1940, 49; U. of California, Berkeley, 1947, MA. Traveled Mexico, Europe; resided Florence, Rome. **Taught:** U. of California, Berkeley, 1947–49, Santa Barbara, 1949– . **Member:** Trustee, Santa Barbara/MA. **Awards:** DFA, Olivet College, 1978; AAIAL, 1978. **Address:** 340 East Los Olivos, Santa Barbara, CA 93105. **Dealers:** William Sawyer Gallery, San Francisco; Mekler Gallery, Los Angeles; Staempfli Gallery. **One-man Exhibitions:** (first) Santa Barbara/MA, 1951, also 1954, 58, 62, 68; de Young, 1951; Mills College, 1951; Geddis-Martin Studios, Santa Barbara, 1952; Rotunda Gallery, San Francisco, 1954; La Jolla, 1954, 64; Bertha Lewinson Gallery, Los Angeles, 1955; Eric Locke Gallery, San Francisco, 1956; Galerie Springer, Berlin, 1956, 64; Galleria Sagittarius, Rome, 1957; U. of California, Santa Barbara, 1958; Duveen-Graham Gallery, NYC, 1958, 60; Esther Baer Gallery, 1960, 61, 63, 65, 67, 70, 71, 73; Galeria Antonio Souza, Mexico City, 1961; The Thatcher School, Ojai, Calif., 1961; Rex Evans Gallery, 1961, 63, 64, 65, 67, 68, 69; California Palace, 1962; McRoberts & Tunnard Gallery, London, 1966; San Antonio/McNay, 1969; U. of California, Santa Cruz, 1969; Mary Moore Gallery, 1971; Jodi Scully Gallery, 1971, 74; 77; Graphics Gallery, 1972; Mount Holyoke College, 1974; Staempfli Gallery, 1974, 76, 78; William Sawyer Gallery, San Francisco, 1977. **Retrospective:** U. of California, Santa Barbara, 1965; Los Angeles Municipal Art Gallery, circ., 1976. **Group:** California Palace, 1947, 52; Denver/AM, 1948; SFMA, 1948–51; California State Fair, 1950, 51; PAFA, 1950, 60, 65, 68; Los Angeles County Fair, 1951; Hallmark Art Award, 1958; Long Beach/MA, 1953, 60, 63, 69; Santa Barbara/MA, 1955, 57; Los Angeles/County MA, 1958; AAIAL, NYC, 1978. **Collections:** Allentown/AM; Amherst College; Atlantic Richfield Co.; Brooklyn Museum; U. of California; Chase Manhattan Bank; Fort Worth; Harvard U.; Hirshhorn; Honolulu Academy; Long Beach/MA; Mills College; Minnesota/MA; Mount Holyoke College; Newark Museum; Olivet College; Phillips; Phoenix; Rockefeller Institute; Santa Barbara/MA; Storm King Art Center; Walker.

DONATI, ENRICO. b. February 19, 1909, Milan, Italy. To USA, 1934; citizen, 1945. **Studied:** U. of Pavia, Italy;

New School for Social Research; ASL. Traveled Europe, India, USA. **Taught:** Yale U., 1960–62. **Member:** Advisory Board of Brandeis U., 1956– ; Jury of Fulbright Program, 1954–56, 1963–64; Yale U. Council for Arts and Architecture, 1962–72; belonged to the Surrealist group of Andre Breton, to 1950. **Address:** 222 Central Park South, NYC 10019. **Dealer:** Staempfli Gallery. **One-man Exhibitions:** New School for Social Research, 1942; Passedoit Gallery, NYC, 1942, 44; Arts Club of Chicago, 1944, 59; Durand-Ruel Gallery, NYC, 1945, 56, 47, 49; Galerie Drouant, Paris, 1947; P. Rosenberg and Co., 1950; L'Obelisco, Rome, 1950; Galleria II Milione, Milan, 1950; Alexander Iolas Gallery, 1952; Galleria del Cavallino, Venice, 1952; Galleria d'Arte del Naviglio, Milan, 1953; Betty Parsons Gallery, 1954, 55, 57, 59, 60; Syracuse U., 1958; Neue Galerie, Munich, 1962; Staempfli Gallery, 1962, 64, 66, 68, 70, 72, 74, 76, 80; MIT, 1964; J. L. Hudson Art Gallery, Detroit, 1964, 66, 69; Obelisk Gallery, 1965; Minnesota/MA, 1977; Ankrum Gallery, Los Angeles, 1977, 79; Norfolk/ Chrysler, 1977; Phillips, Washington, D.C., 1979; Grand Palais, Paris, 1980. **Retrospective:** Palais des Beaux-Arts, Brussels, 1961. **Group:** Carnegie, 1950, 52, 54, 56, 58, 61; Venice Biennial; Sao Paulo, 1953; International Biennial Exhibition of Paintings, Tokyo; A.F.A., The Embellished Surface, circ., 1953–54; Chicago/AI, 1954, 57; WMAA Annuals, 1954, 56, 58, 59, 61, 62, 64, 70; Santa Barbara/MA, 1954; SRGM, Younger American Painters, 1954; Utica, 1955; SFMA, 1955; Indiana U., 1957, 59; PAFA, 1957; VMFA, American Painting, 1958; Inter-American Paintings and Prints Biennial, Mexico City, 1958; U. of Illinois, 1959; Lincoln, Mass./De Cordova, Decade in Review, 1959; A.F.A., V International Exhibition, 1959; Corcoran, 1960; St. Paul Gallery, 1960; Walker, 60 American Painters, 1960; SRGM, Abstract Expressionists and Imagists, 1961; New York World's Fair, 1964–65. **Collections:** American Republic Insurance Co.; Arthur Anderson & Co.; Anderson Clayton Company; Atlantic Richfield Co.; Avon Products; Baltimore/MA; Bezalel Museum; Brussels/Moderne; Buffalo/Albright; U. of California; Chase Manhattan Bank; Detroit/Institute; Doane College; Ford Motor Company; High Museum; Houston-MFA; J. L. Hudson Co.; IBM; Indian Head Mills, Inc.; International Institute for Aesthetic Research; Johns Hopkins U.; MIT; MOMA; Michigan Consolidated Gas Co.; U. of Michigan; Milan; Minnesota/MA; Needham, Harper & Steers, Inc.; Newark Museum; Northwestern National Life Insurance Co.; Oslo/National; Owen-Corning Fiberglass Corp.; Palm Beach Company; Prudential Life Insurance Co.; St. Louis/City; The Singer Company, Inc.; Temple Beth El; U. of Texas; Tougaloo College; Turin/Civico; U.S. Steel Corp.; WGMA; WMAA; Washington U.; Yale U. **Bibliography:** Breton 2, 3; Goodrich and Baur 1; Read 2; Rubin 1.

DOVE, ARTHUR G. b. August 2, 1880, Canandaigua, N.Y.; **d.** November 1946, Centerport, N.Y. **Studied:** Cornell U., 1903. Commercial illustrator, 1903–07. Traveled Europe, 1907–9, with Alfred Maurer and Arthur B. Carles, Jr. Met Alfred Stieglitz, 1910. **One-man Exhibitions:** (first) Photo-Secession, NYC, 1912; Scott Thurber Gallery, Chicago, 1912; Stieglitz's Intimate Gallery, NYC, 1926, 27, 29; An American Place (Gallery), NYC, annually, 1930–46; Springfield, Mass./MFA, 1933; Phillips, 1937; Vanbark Studios, Studio City, Calif., 1947; Utica, 1947; The Downtown Gallery, 1949, 52, 54, 55, 56, 67; Houston/ MFA, 1951; Walker, 1954; Deerfield (Mass.) Academy, 1956; Paul Kantor Gallery, Beverly Hills, Calif., 1956; U. of Maryland, 1967; Terry Dintenfass, Inc., 1970, 71, 77, 78, 79, 80. **Retrospective:** The Downtown Gallery, 1947; Cornell U., 1954; UCLA, circ., 1958–59; SFMA, circ., 1974. **Group:** Salon d-Automne, Paris, 1908, 09; National Arts Club Annual, NYC, 1914;

Anderson Galleries, NYC, Forum Exhibition, 1916; Society of Independent Artists, NYC, 1917; PAFA, 1921; Wildenstein & Co., NYC, Tri-National Art, 1926; Brooklyn Museum, International Exhibition of Modern Art (assembled by Societe Anonyme), 1926; Salons of America, NYC, 1929; MOMA, Paintings by 19 Living Americans, 1929; Cleveland/MA Annuals, 1931, 32, 35; WMAA Annuals, 1932, 34; A.F.A., Abstraction, 1932; A Century of Progress, Chicago, 1933–34; WMAA, Abstract Painting in America, 1935; Buffalo/Albright, 1935; U. of Minnesota, 1937; Cleveland/MA, American Painting from 1860 until Today, 1937; Worcester/AM, 1938; Musée du Jeu de Paume, Trois Siecles d'Art aux Etats-Unis, 1938; MOMA, Art in Our Time; 10th Anniversary Exhibition, 1939; Boston/MFA, 10 American Watercolor Painters, 1939; Golden Gate International Exposition, San Francisco, 1939; Cornell U., 1940; MOMA, Cubist and Abstract Art, 1942; PMA, History of an American, Alfred Stieglitz: "291" and After, 1944. **Collections:** American U.; Andover/Phillips; Arizona State College; Baltimore/MA; Boston U.; Brittania; Brooklyn Museum; Buffalo/Albright; Carnegie; Chicago/AI; Colorado Springs/FA; Columbus; Cornell U.; Des Moines; Detroit/Institute; Fisk U.; Fort Worth; Hartford/Wadsworth; Honolulu Academy; IBM; Inland Steel Co.; MMA; MOMA; Milwaukee; U. of Minnesota; National Gallery; U. of Nebraska; Omaha/Joslyn; PMA; Phillips; Phoenix; Randolph-Macon Woman's College; U. of Rochester; SFMA; Smith College; Springfield, Mass./MFA; Utica; WMAA; Washington U.; Wellesley College; West Palm Beach/Norton; Wichita/AM; Wilmington; Yale U. **Bibliography:** **Arthur Dove: The Years of Collage;** Ashton 5; *Avant-Garde Painting and Sculpture in America, 1920–25;* Barr 3; Baur 5, 7; Blanchard; Blesh 1; Brown 2; Cahill and Barr, eds.; Cheney; Downes, ed.; *8 American Masters of Watercolor;* Eliot; *Forerunners;* Frank, ed.; Frost; Gerdts; Goodrich and Baur 1; Haftman; **Haskell 1;** Hess, T. B., 1; Hunter 6;

Janis and Blesh 1; Janis, S.; Kootz 1; Kozloff 3; Mather 1; McCurdy, ed.; Mellquist; Mendelowitz; Neuhaus; Newmeyer; Phillips 1, 2; Poore; Read 2; Richardson, E.P.; Ringel, ed.; Ritchie 1; Rodman 2; Rose, B., 1, 4; Rosenblum 2; Rubin 1; Seitz 3; Sutton; Tashijan; Wight 2; Wright 1. Archives.

DOWNES, RACKSTRAW. b. November 8, 1939, England. **Studied:** Cambridge U., BA, with Donald Davie; Yale U. MFA, with N. Welliver, Alex Katz, Al Held. **Taught:** Parsons School of Design, 1964–67; U. of Pennsylvania, 1967–79; Skowhegan School, 1975; Yale U., 1979–80. Art critic and writer. **Awards:** Yaddo Fellowship, 1970; Ingram Merrill Foundation Grant, 1974; CAPS, 1978. **Address:** 536 West 111th Street, NYC 10025. **Dealer:** The Kornblee Gallery, NYC. **One-man Exhibitions:** (first) Swarthmore College, 1969; The Kornblee Gallery, NYC, 1972, 74, 75, 78, 80; McLeaf Gallery, Philadelphia, 1969; Swain School of Design, New Bedford, Mass., 1978. **Group:** A.F.A., Painterly Realism, 1970–72; Colgate U., Painters of the Land and Sky, 1972; Omaha/Joslyn, A Sense of Place, 1973; Queens County Art and Cultural Center, New Images in American Painting, 1974; US Department of the Interior, America 1976, 1976; Los Angeles/County MA, Eighteen Artists, 1976; AAAL, 1977. **Collections:** Chase Manhattan Bank, NYC; U. of North Carolina. **Bibliography:** *America 1976.*

DOYLE, TOM. b. May 23, 1928, Jerry City, Ohio. **Studied:** Miami U.; The Ohio State U. (with Roy Lichtenstein, Stanley Twardowicz), BFA, MA. Traveled Europe. **Taught:** Brooklyn Museum School, 1961–68; New School for Social Research, 1961–68; School of Visual Arts, NYC, 1969; Queens College, CUNY, 1970– . **Commissions:** GSA, for Fairbanks, Alaska, 1980. **Awards:** Ohio State Fair, two First and two Second Prizes. **Address:** 130 West 18th

Rackstraw Downes *Behind the Store at Prospect* 1979–80

Street, NYC 10011. **Dealer:** Max Hutchinson Gallery, NYC. **One-man Exhibitions:** (first) The Ohio State U., 1956; Allan Stone Gallery, 1961, 62; Dwan Gallery, 1966, 67, 72; Brata Gallery, NYC, 1972; 55 Mercer Street, NYC, 1974, 76; Colgate U., 1976; Sculpture Now, Inc., 1978. **Group:** Cornell U., 1960; Martha Jackson Gallery, New Media—New Forms, I & II, 1960, 61; Oberlin College, 1961; Carnegie, 1961; Seattle World's Fair, 1962; Berne, 1964; WMAA Annual, 1966, 67; Los Angeles/County MA, American Sculpture of the Sixties, 1967; Jewish Museum, Primary Structures, 1967; Los Angeles/County MA, American Sculpture of the Sixties, 1967; Documenta, Kassel, 1972; Taft Museum, Painting and Sculpture Today, 1974; Indianapolis, 1974; Pratt Institute, Sitesights, 1980. **Collections:** Bard College; Brooklyn Museum; Carnegie; Manhattanville College; Nassau County Museum; Ohio State U.; Purchase, N.Y.; Wright State U. **Bibliography:** Atkinson; Tuchman 1.

DREWES, WERNER. b. July 27, 1899, Canig, Germany. **Studied:** Gymnasium, Brandenburg/Havel, 1909–17; Charlottenburg Technische Hochschule, Berlin, 1919; Stuttgart School of Architecture, 1920; Stuttgart School of Arts and Crafts, 1921; Bauhaus, Weimar, 1921–22, with Josef Itten, Paul Klee; Bauhaus, Dessau, 1927–28, with Vassily Kandinsky, Lyonel Feininger. To USA, 1930; citizen, 1936. Traveled Europe, South and Central America, Asia, USA. **Taught:** Columbia U., 1937–40; Master Institute of United Arts, Inc., NYC, 1940; Brooklyn College, 1944; Institute of Design, Chicago, 1945; Washington U., 1946–65. Federal A.P.: Instructor, Brooklyn Museum, 1934–36; Technical Supervisor, Graphic Art Project, 1940–41. **Member:** American Artists Congress; co-founder, American Abstract Artists, 1936. **Commissions:** International Graphic Arts Society, 1954, 57. **Awards:** 50 Best Prints of the Year, 1932, 44; PAFA, **P.P.**, 1933; MOMA; Plexiglas Sculpture Competition, Third Prize, 1939; MOMA, Textile Design Competition, First and Second Prizes, 1941; The Print Club, Philadelphia, Hon. Men., 1946; A.A.A. Gallery, NYC, **P.P.**, 1959; St. Louis Artists' Guild, Bader Art Prize, 1960. **Address:** 11526 Links Drive, Reston, VA 22090. **Dealer:** Princeton Gallery of Fine Art, Princeton. **One-man Exhibitions:** Madrid/Nacional, 1923; Montevideo/Municipal, 1924; St. Louis Public Library, 1924; Gump's Gallery, 1926; Flechtheim and Kahnweiler, Frankfurt, 1928; Galerie del Vecchio, Leipzig, 1929; Morton Gallery, NYC, 1932, 33; New School for Social Research, 1935; Artists' Gallery, NYC, 1939, 41; Lilienfeld Gallery, NYC, 1945;

Indiana U., 1945; Kleemann Gallery, NYC, 1945, 56, 47, 49; Princeton U., 1946 (four-man); Smithsonian, 1948; Pen and Palette Gallery, St. Louis, 1949; Lutz and Meyer Gallery, Stuttgart, 1951; Argent Gallery, NYC, 1951; Neue Gallerie Gurlitt, 1952; St. Louis Artists' Guild, 1953; Beloit College, 1954, 77; Schermahorn Gallery, Beloit, 1955, 56; Los Angeles/County MA, 1956; Memphis/Brooks, 1957; Springfield, Mo./AM, 1958; Oregon State College, circ., 1959; Cleveland/MA, 1961; Washington U., 1962; Hom Gallery, Washington, D.C., 1971; Princeton Gallery of Fine Art, 1972, 76; Haslem Fine Arts, Washington, D.C., 1978. **Retrospective:** California Palace, 1962; Washington U., 1965; Smithsonian, 1969; US Embassy Program, Turkey, 1974; St. Olaf College, circ., 1978. **Group:** Carnegie; Brooklyn Museum; Chicago/AI; MMA; USIA; WMAA; U. of Illinois; PAFA; SRGM; Bennington College. **Collections:** U. of Alabama; Andover/Phillips; Bibliotheque Nationale; Boston/MFA; Boston Public Library; Brooklyn Museum; Chicago/AI; Cleveland/MA; Cologne; Frankfurt am Main; Hartford/Wadsworth; Harvard U.; Honolulu Academy; U. of Illinois; Kansas City/Nelson; Karsruhe; Library of Congress; Los Angeles/County MA; MOMA; Memphis/Brooks; Mills College; NCFA; NYPL; National Gallery; Newark Public Library; PAFA; RISD; SFMA; SRGM St. Louis/City; Seattle/AM; Springfield, Ill./State; Springfield, Mo./AM; Trenton/State; Victoria and Albert Museum; Washington U.; Wells College; Wichita/AM; Worcester/AM; Yale U. **Bibliography:** American Artists Congress, Inc.; Baur 7; Bazin; Cheney. Archives.

DRUMMOND, SALLY HAZELET. b. June 4, 1924, Evanston, Ill. **Studied:** Rollins College, 1942–44; Columbia U., with John Heliker, Peppino Mangravite, 1946–48, BA; Institute of Design, Chicago, 1949–50, with Hugo Weber, Emerson Woelffer; U. of

Louisville, with Ulfert Wilke, 1950–52, MA. Traveled Italy, France, England. A co-organizer of the Tanager Gallery, NYC. **Taught:** Skowhegan School, 1973. **Awards:** Fulbright Fellowship (Italy), 1952; Guggenheim Foundation Fellowship, 1967–68. **Address:** 371 Wilton Road East, Ridgefield, CT 06877. **One-man Exhibitions:** (first) Hadley Gallery, Louisville, 1952, also 1961; Art Center Association, Louisville, 1955; Tanager Gallery, NYC, 1955, 57, 60; Green Gallery, NYC, 1962; Louisville/Speed, 1967 (two-man); Fischbach Gallery, 1968, 72, 78. **Retrospective:** Corcoran, 1972. **Group:** American Embassy, Rome, 1953; Bordighera, 1953; A.F.A., Fulbright Artists, circ., 1958; Houston/MFA, 1959; WMAA Annual, 1960; A.F.A., Lyricism in Abstract Art, circ., 1962–63; MOMA; Americans, 1963, circ., 1963–64; Trenton/State, Focus on Light, 1967; Silvermine Guild, 1970; PMA, FOCUS, 1974. **Collections:** Avco Corp.; Chase Manhattan Bank; Ciba-Geigy Corp.; Corcoran; Hirshhorn; Interchemical Corporation; U. of Iowa; Louisville/Speed; MOMA; MMA; U. of North Carolina; Union Carbide Corp.; WMAA.

DU BOIS, GUY PENE. b. January 4, 1884, Brooklyn, N.Y.; **d.** July 18, 1958, Boston, Mass. **Studied:** W. M. Chase School, NYC, 1899–1905, with J. C. Beckwith, Frank V. DuMond, Robert Henri, Kenneth Hayes Miller; Academie de la Grande Chaumiere, with Theophile A. Steinlen. Traveled USA, Europe. Reporter and critic for *New York American, New York Tribune, New York Evening Post;* editor of *Arts and Decoration* magazine for seven years. **Awards:** Pan-American Exhibition, Los Angeles, 1925, Third Prize; Chicago/AI Norman Wait Harris Silver Medal, 1930; NAD, Benjamin Altman Prize, 1936; Corcoran Second William A. Clark Prize, 1937. **One-man Exhibitions:** Kraushaar Galleries, 1922, 24, 30, 32, 35, 36, 38, 42, 43; 46; Staten Island, 1954; The Graham Gallery, 1961, 63, 79.

Retrosepctive: Hagerstown/County MFA, 1940. **Group:** Salon des Beaux-Arts, Paris, 1906; Corcoran; Chicago/AI; PAFA; WMAA. **Collections:** Amherst College; Andover/Phillips; Baltimore/MA; Barnes Foundation; Brooklyn Museum; Chicago/AI; Cleveland/MA; Detroit/Institute; Los Angeles/County MA; MOMA; Milwaukee; Newark Museum; New Britain; PAFA; PMA; Phillips; San Diego; Toledo/MA; WMAA. **Bibliography:** Baur 7; Bazin; Brown 2; Bruce and Watson; Cahill and Barr, eds.; Cheney; **Cortissoz 2; Du Bois 1, 2, 3, 4, 5, 6;** Ely; Gerdts; Glackens; *Cityscape 1919–39;* Goodrich and Baur 1; Hall; Hunter 6; *Index of 20th Century Artists;* Jewell 2; Kent, N.; Mather 1; McCoubrey 1; **Medford;** Mellquist; Neuhaus; Pagano; Pearson 1; Phillips 2; Poore; Richardson, E.P.; Ringel, ed.; Rose, B., 1, 4; Smith, S.C.K. Archives.

DUCHAMP, MARCEL. b. July 28, 1887, Blainville, near Rouen, France; **d.** October 1, 1968, Neuilly, France. **Studied:** Academie Julian, Paris, 1904. To USA, 1915; citizen, 1955. Traveled Europe, Argentina, USA. Founding member, Society of Independent Artists, 1916. Cofounder (with Man Ray and Francis Picabia) of DADA group, NYC, 1917. Co-organizer (with Katherine S. Dreier and Man Ray) of Societe Anonyme (Museum of Modern Art), 1920. Published one issue of *New York DADA* with Man Ray, 1921. Produced a film, *Anemic Cinema,* 1925. **One-man Exhibitions:** Montross Gallery, NYC, 1916 (four-man); Arts Club of Chicago, 1937; Rose Fried Gallery, 1952 (three-man); SRGM, 1957 (three-man); Galerie de l'Institut, Paris, 1957; Sidney Janis Gallery, 1958, 59; La Hune, Paris, 1959; Pasadena/AM, 1963; Eva de Buren Gallery, Stockholm, 1963; Walker, 1965; Milwaukee, 1965; Cordier & Ekstrom, Inc., 1965, 67, 68; Tate, 1966; Fourcade, Droll, Inc.; Galerie Rene Block, Berlin, 1971; Galleria Civica d'Arte Moderna, Ferrara, 1971; Galleria Schwarz, 1972; Jerusalem/ Jational, 1972; L'Uomo e

l'Arte, Milan, 1973; Dayton's Gallery 12, Minneapolis, 1973, 74; Holly Solomon Gallery, 1977. **Retrospective:** Gimpel Fils Ltd., 1964; Galleria Solaria, Milan, 1967; Paris/Moderne, 1967; Cologne, 1968; PMA, 1969, 73. **Group:** Salon des Artistes Independents, Paris, 1909–12; Salon d'Automne, Paris, 1909–12; Salon de la Section d'Or, 1912, The Armory Show, 1913; Societe Anonyme, NYC, 1920; Salon DADA, Paris, 1920; A Century of Progress, Chicago, 1933–34; MOMA, Cubism and Abstract Art, 1936; MOMA, Fantastic Art, DADA, Surrealism, 1936; WMAA, European Artists in America, 1945; MOMA, Eleven Europeans, 1946; XXIV Venice Biennial, 1948; California Palace, 1948; Chicago/AI, 1949; MOMA, The Machine, 1968; Haus der Kunst, Munich, Der Surrealismus, 1922–1942, 1972. **Collections:** MOMA; Ottawa/National; PMA; SRGM; Yale U. **Bibliography:** Alloway 4; Barr 1, 3; Battcock, ed.; Baur 7; Becker and Vostell; Biddle 4; Biederman 1; Bihalji-Merin; Blesh 1; Breton 2; Brion 2; Brown; Bulliet 1, 2; **Cabanne;** Calas, N. and E.; Canaday; Cassou; Chipp; Christensen; Coplans 3; Davidson 1; Davis, D.; De Vries; **D'Harnoncourt and McShine, eds.;** Dorival; Dorner; Dreier 2; **Duchamp 1, 2;** Elsen 1; Finch; Flanagan; Frost; Gablik; Gascoyne; Gaunt; Gerdts; Giedion-Welcker 1, 2; Guggenheim, ed.; Haftman; **Hamilton, R.;** Honnef; Hulten; Hunter 6; Hunter, ed.; Huyghe; Janis and Blesh 1; Johnson, Ellen H.; Kepes 2; Kozloff 3; Krauss 2; Kuh 1, 2, 3; Kyrou; Langui; Lippard 3; **Lebel;** Lee and Burchwood; Licht, F.; Lippard 5; Lippard, ed.; Lowry; Lynton; McCurdy, ed.; Marter, Tarbell, and Wechsler; Mellquist; Metro; Motherwell 1; Neumeyer; Newmeyer; Pach 2, 3; Ramsden 1; **Raymond Duchamp-Villon/Marcel Duchamp;** Raynal 3, 4; Read 2, 3; Richardson, E. P.; Richter; Rickey; Rose, B., 1, 4; Rosenblum 1; Rubin 1; Sager; **Schwarz 1, 2;** Sandler 1; Seitz 3; Selz, J.; Seuphor 1, 3; Soby 1, 5, 6; **Sweeney 2;** Tashijian; Tomkins; Tomkins and Time-Life

Books; Tomkins 2; Trier 1, 2; Valentine 2; Verkauf; Waldberg 2, 3, 4; Weller.

DUGMORE, EDWARD. b. February 20, 1915, Hartford, Conn. **Studied:** Hartford Art School, 1934–38; California School of Fine Arts (with Clyfford Still), 1948–50; U. of Guadalajara, 1951–52, MA. US Marine Corps, 1943–44. Traveled Mexico, USA extensively, Europe, 1966–67. **Taught:** St. Joseph College, 1946–49; Southern Illinois U.; Pratt Institute, 1964–72; U. of Minnesota, 1970; Des Moines, 1972; Maryland Institute, 1973, 74. A cofounder of Metart Gallery, San Francisco. **Awards:** Chicago/AI, The M.V. Kohnstamm Prize, 1962; Guggenheim Foundation Fellowship, 1966–67; National Endowment for the Arts, grant, 1976; AAAL Award, 1980. **Address:** 118 West 27th Street, NYC 10001. **One-man Exhibitions:** (first) Metart Gallery, San Francisco, 1949; The Stable Gallery, 1953, 54, 56; Holland-Goldowsky Gallery, Chicago, 1959; The Howard Wise Gallery, Cleveland, 1960; The Howard Wise Gallery, NYC, 1960, 61, 63; Green Mountain Gallery, 1971, 73; Des Moines, 1972. **Group:** Carnegie, 1955; Walker, Vanguard, 1955; WMAA Annual, 1959; SRGM, Abstract Expressionists and Imagists, 1961; Chicago/AI Annual, 1962; SFMA, Directions—Painting U.S.A., 1963; U. of Texas, Recent American Painting, 1964, also 1968; Green Mountain Gallery, 1971; Buffalo/Albright, Abstract Expressionism: First and Second Generations, 1972; Oakland/AM, A Period of Exploration, 1973; SFMA, California Painting and Sculpture: The Modern Era, 1976; NCFA, 1977; AAAL, 1980. **Collections:** Buffalo/Albright; Ciba-Geigy Corp.; Des Moines; Housatonic Community College; Michigan State U.; Minneapolis/Institute; U. of North Carolina; Southern Illinois U.; Walker. **Bibliography:** McChesney; Sandler.

DURAN, ROBERT. b. 1938, Salinas, Calif. **Studied:** Richard Stockton State College, 1958–60; San Francisco School of Fine Arts, 1960–61. Traveled Mexico, USA, Morocco, Europe, India. **Address:** 431 Broome Street, NYC 10013. **Dealer:** Susan Caldwell, Inc., NYC. **One-man Exhibitions:** Bykert Gallery, 1968 (two-man), 1970 (two-man), 1971, 72, 73; The Texas Gallery, 1973; Susan Caldwell Gallery, NYC, 1975, 77. **Group:** Park Place Gallery, NYC, 1966; Ithaca College, Drawings, 1967, 1967; A.F.A., Rejective Art, 1967; ICA, U. of Pennsylvania, Between Object and Environment, 1969; WMAA, 1969, 73; Columbus, Beaux-Arts, Twenty-Fifth Anniversary Exhibition, 1971; Corcoran Biennial, 1971; Indianapolis, 1972; Storm King Art Center, 1972; WMAA Biennial, 1973; Vassar College, New American Abstract Painting, 1973; Akron/AI, Contemporary Images in Watercolor, 1976; Georgia State U., Ten Painters, 1976. **Collections:** Amerada Hess Corp., N.J.; Amstar Corp.; Betcar Corp.; Business Card, Inc.; Columbus; General Reinsurance Corp.; Lehman Brothers, NYC; MOMA; National Gallery; Port Authority of New York & New Jersey; Prudential Insurance Co. of America, N.J.; J. Henry Schroeder Banking Corp.; Two Trees; United Mutual Savings; WMAA.

DZUBAS, FRIEDEL. b. April 20, 1915, Berlin, Germany. To USA, 1939. Traveled Europe extensively. **Taught:** U. of South Florida, 1962; Artist-in-Residence, Dartmouth College, 1962, Aspen Institute, 1965, 66; Cornell U., 1967, 1969–74; U. of Pennsylvania, 1968. **Commissions:** National Shawmut Bank of Boston (mural). **Awards:** Guggenheim Foundation Fellowship, 1966; J. S. Guggenheim Fellowship, 1968; National Council on the Arts, 1968. **Address:** Lakeville, CT 06039. **Dealers:** Knoedler Contemporary Art; David Mirvish Gallery; Watson/De Nagy. **One-man Exhibitions:** Tibor de Nagy Gallery, 1952, 76; Leo Castelli Inc., 1958; French & Co., Inc., NYC, 1959; Dwan Gallery, 1960; Robert Elkon Gallery, 1961–65; Kasmin Ltd., 1964, 65;

Nicholas Wilder Gallery, 1966; Andre Emmerich Gallery, 1966, 67, 68; Jack Glenn Gallery, Corona del Mar, 1971; Lawrence Rubin Gallery, NYC, 1971, 72, 73; Gallerie Hans Strelow, Cologne, 1971, 72; David Mirvish Gallery, 1973, 74, 75, 76; Knoedler Contemporary Art, 1974, 75, 76; Watson/De Nagy Gallery, Houston, 1976; Margo Leavin Gallery, Los Angeles, 1976; John Berggruen Gallery, San Francisco, 1977, 79; M. Knoedler & Co., NYC, 1977, 78, 79, 80; Kunsthalle, Bielefeld, 1977; Dart Gallery, Chicago, 1978. **Retrospective:** Houston/MFA, 1974; Boston/MFA, 1975. **Group:** Chicago/AI Annuals, 1942, 43, 44; MMA, American Painters under 35, 1950; Ninth Street Exhibition, NYC, 1951; WMAA Annuals, 1958, 59, 64; Corcoran, 1959, 63, Biennial, 1967; The Kootz Gallery, NYC, New Talent, 1960; Carnegie, 1961; SRGM, Abstract Expressionists and Imagists, 1961; Dayton/AI, 1963; Jewish Museum, Black and White, 1963; Los Angeles/County MA, Post Painterly Abstraction, 1964; Detroit/Institute, Color and Image and Form, 1967; U. of Illinois, 1967; Expo '67, Montreal, 1967; Buffalo/Albright, Color and Field, 1890–1970, 1970; Boston/MFA, Abstract Painting in the '70s, 1972; Houston/MFA, The Great Decade of American Abstraction: Modernist Art 1960 to 1970, 1974; Corcoran Biennial, 1975; Syracuse/Everson, New Works in Clay, 1976; US Embassy, Ottawa, Eighteen Contemporary Masters, 1977. **Collections:** Baltimore/MA; Boston/MFA; Brandeis U.; Buffalo/Albright; Chase Manhattan Bank; Cornell U.; Dayton/AI; Dartmouth College; Hirshhorn; Houston/MFA; MMA; Manufacturers Hanover Trust; Memphis/Brooks; NYU; Oberlin College; Phillips; Ridgefield/Aldrich; Rutgers U.; SFMA; SRGM; St. Louis/City; Syracuse/Everson; Tufts Dental College; Utica; WMAA; Wellesley College; Yale U. **Bibliography:** *The Great Decade*; Rose, B., 1; Sandler 1.

EDDY, DON. b. November 4, 1944, Long Beach, Calif. **Studied:** Fullerton Junior College; U. of Hawaii, 1967, BFA, 1969, MFA; U. of California, Santa Barbara, 1969–70. US Navy, 1967–68. **Taught:** U. of Hawaii, 1967–69; NYU, 1973–78; School of Visual Arts, NYC, 1977– . **Address:** 30 Christopher Street, NYC 10014. **Dealer:** Nancy Hoffman Gallery. **One-man Exhibitions:** Ewing Krainin Gallery, Honolulu, 1968; Molly Barnes Gallery, Los Angeles, 1970, 71; Esther Baer Gallery, 1970; Galerie M. E. Thelen, Essen and Cologne, 1970; Galerie de Gestlo, 1971; French & Co. Inc., NYC, 1971; Aktionsgalerie, Bern (two-man), 1971; Nancy Hoffman Gallery, 1973, 74, 76, 79; Galerie Petit, Paris, 1973; Williams College, Williamstown, Mass., 1975; Miami-Dade Community College, 1976. **Group:** Stockton, Beyond the Actual, 1970; Sacramento/ Crocker, West Coast '70, 1970; Munster/ WK, Verkehrskultur, 1971; Santa Barbara/MA, Spray, 1971; VII Paris Biennial, 1971; Potsdam/SUNY, New Realism, 1971; Documenta V, Kassel, 1972; Cleveland/MA, 32 Realists, 1972; Stuttgart/WK, Amerikanischer Fotorealismus, circ., 1972; Kunsthalle und Spritzpistole, 1973; Los Angeles Municipal Art Gallery, Separate Realities, 1973; U. of Illinois, 1974; Hartford/ Wadsworth, New/Photo Realism, 1974; Toledo, Image, Color and Form, 1975; Baltimore/MA, Super Realism, 1976; Canberra/National, Illusion and Reality, circ., 1977; Dayton/AI, Photo Images, 1977; U. of Texas, New in the 70's, 1977; Kansas City/Sheldon, Things Seen, 1978. **Collections:** Aachen/NG; American Republic Insurance Co.; Akron/AI; Claremont College; Cleveland/MA; Des Moines; Harvard U.; U. of Massachusetts; Museo de Arte Moderno, Bogota; U. of Nebraska; Oklahoma; RISD; St.-Etienne; Santa Barbara/MA; Storm King Art Center; Toledo/MA; Warner Bros., Los Angeles; Williams College; WMAA. **Bibliography:** Alloway 4; *Amerikanischer Fotorealismus;* Arthur; Honisch and Jensen, eds.; *Kunst um 1970; New in the Seventies;* Sager.

EDIE, STUART. b. November 10, 1908, Wichita Falls, Tex.; **d.** March 17, 1974, Guanajuato, Mexico. **Studied:** Kansas City Art Institute and School of Design; ASL, with Thomas Hart Benton, Boardman Robinson, John Sloan. Traveled Europe, Mexico, North Africa, Canada, West Indies. **Taught:** State U. of Iowa, 1944–71; Federal A.P.: Easel painting; mural for US Post Office, Honeoye Falls, N.Y. **Awards:** L. C. Tiffany Grant; Missouri Valley Annual. **One-man Exhibitions:** (first) An American Group (Gallery), NYC, 1932; galleries in Des Moines, Kansas City, Iowa City. **Retrospective:** U. of Iowa, 1979. **Group:** PAFA; Corcoran; NAD; WMAA; Chicago/AI; Brooklyn Museum; MMA; MOMA. **Collections:** ASL; U. of Arizona; Des Moines; First National Bank, Iowa City; U. of Georgia; Grinnell College; Iowa Arts Council, Des Moines; State College of Iowa; State U. of Iowa; Kansas City/ Nelson; MMA; NCFA; Newark Museum; Omaha/Joslyn; Syracuse U.; Toledo/MA; WMAA; Washburn U. of Topeka. **Bibliography:** *Stuart Edie Woodstock;* Zaidenberg, ed.

EDMONDSON, LEONARD. b. June 21, 1916, Sacramento, Calif. **Studied:** Los Angeles City College, 1934–37; U.

of California, Berkeley, 1937–42, BA (1940), MA (1942). US Army Intelligence, 1942–46. Traveled Europe, 1978. **Taught:** Los Angeles County Art Institute, 1954–56; Pasadena City College, 1947–54, 1956–64; U. of California, Berkeley, summers, 1960, 64; Pratt Institute, summer, 1961; Los Angeles State College, 1964–74; Otis Art Institute, 1974–76; California State U., Los Angeles, 1976– . **Member:** Board of Directors, Pasadena/AM, 1957–63; Los Angeles, Printmaking Society, president, 1966; Pasadena Society of Artists, president, 1967; AAAL, Hassam and Speicher Fund **P.P.**, 1977. **Commissions (prints):** International Graphic Arts Society, 1960; New York Hilton Hotel, 1962. **Awards:** SFMA, First **P.P.**, 1946, Second Prize, 1951, 52, James D. Phelan Award, 1951, 53, **P.P.**, 1957; California State Fair, First Prize for Etching, 1951, Second **P.P.**, 1952, 56; Brooklyn Museum, 1951, 56; Oakland/AM, First Prize, Etching, 1952; Seattle/AM, **P.P.**, 1952, 53, 54, 59; Pasadena/AM, **P.P.**, 1952, 54, 57, 58, 59, 62; L. C. Tiffany Grant, 1952, 55; U. of Illinois, **P.P.**, 1954, 55; MMA, $500; American Color Print Society, Prize for Etching, 1954, 55; Los Angeles/County MA, Patronnaires Prize, 1957; Library of Congress, Pennell **P.P.**, 1957, 63; J. S. Guggenheim Fellowship, 1960; Los Angeles State College, Foundation Grants, 1965, 67; U. of North Carolina, **P.P.**, 1966; Los Angeles Printmaking Society, **P.P.**, 1968; and many others; AAAL/Hassam and Speicher Fund **P.P.**, 1977. **One-man Exhibitions:** (first) Felix Landau Gallery, 1950, also 1953, 55, 58, 60; de Young, 1952; Pasadena/AM, 1953; Santa Barbara/MA, 1953, 66; SFMA, 1956, 67; The Gallery, Denver, 1963; Comara Gallery, 1963; Laguna Beach (Calif.) Art Gallery, 1964; Oklahoma City U., 1964; Adele Bednarz Gallery, 1965, 68; Lincoln, Mass./De Cordova, 1967; Ventura College, 1969; Heath Gallery, Atlanta, 1969; Louisiana State U., 1969; California State College, Dominguez Hills, 1969; California Institute of the Arts, Valencia, 1970; U. of

Colorado, 1972; Mount St. Mary's College, Los Angeles, 1979. **Group:** MMA, 1952; WMAA, 1952, 53, 55, 56, 58; U. of Illinois, 1953, 55, 58, 59, Fifty Contemporary American Printmakers, 1956; SRGM, Younger American Painters, 1954; Carnegie, 1955; Sao Paulo, 1955; SFMA, Art in the Twentieth Century, 1955; Corcoran, 1957, 59; Chicago/AI, 1957; VMFA, 1958; PCA, American Prints Today, circ., 1959–62; USIA, 30 Contemporary American Prints, circ., 1964; Taiheiyo Art Association, Tokyo, I International, LX Annual, 1964; California Society of Printmakers, 50th Anniversary Exhibition, 1964; New York World's Fair, 1964–65; Temple U., Rome, 1967; Brooklyn Museum, Print Biennial, 1968; Santa Barbara/MA, Artist-Teachers in Southern California, 1975; SFMA, Painting and Sculpture in California: The Modern Era, 1976; Laguna Beach Art Museum, Southern California 100, 1977; The College of St. Rose, Albany, N.Y., Draw 80, 1980. **Collections:** Bibliotheque Nationale; Brooklyn Museum; California State U., Los Angeles; Cornell U.; Cranbrook; Detroit/Institute; U. of California; U. of Colorado; Dallas/MFA; U. of Delaware; Grunwald Foundation; U. of Illinois; Ithaca College; Karachi; Library of Congress; Lincoln, Mass./De Cordova; Lindenwood College; Los Angeles/County MA; MMA; Montana State U.; NYPL; National Gallery; U. of North Carolina; U. of North Dakota; Oakland/AM; Olivet College; Orange Coast College; Otis Art Institute; PMA; Pasadena/AM; Potsdam/SUNY; SFMA; St. Lawrence U.; Seattle/AM; Southern Illinois U.; State of California; USIA; Utica; VMFA; Victoria and Albert Museum; Western Michigan U.; Western New Mexico U.; U. of Wisconsin; College of Wooster.

ELLIOTT, RONNIE. b. December 16, 1916, NYC. **Studied:** Hunter College; NYU; ASL. Traveled Europe, Mexico, Puerto Rico, Canada; resided continental USA, Honolulu, Paris. **Taught:** Fine Arts Work Center, Provincetown,

Mass., 1973. Federal A.P.: Easel and mural painting; also mosaic and stained-glass windows. **Member:** Artists Equity. **Awards:** New Orleans Arts and Crafts Society, First Prize for Sculpture, 1935. **Address:** 68 East Seventh Street, NYC 10003. **One-man Exhibitions:** (first) Delphic Gallery, NYC, 1937; Marquie, NYC, 1942, 43, 44; Norlyst Gallery, NYC, 1947; Carlebach Gallery, NYC, 1948; Galerie Creuze, Paris, 1948; Galerie Colette Allendy, Paris, 1952; Rose Fried Gallery, 1957, 58, 67; Granville Gallery, NYC, 1964; Brooklyn College, 1968; Andre Zarre Gallery, NYC, 1975, 77; St. Peter's College, 1976; Polo Gallery, Washington, D.C., 1976; Nardin Gallery, Inc., NYC, 1979. **Retrospective:** Grand Central Moderns, NYC, 1963. **Group:** PAFA, 1933, 34, 39; Golden Gate International Exposition, San Francisco, 1939; Corcoran, 1939, 41; NAD, 1941; MMA, Contemporary American Art, 1942; Museum of Non-Objective Art, NYC, 1946; MOMA, Collage, 1948; Salon des Realities Nouvelles, Paris, 1948, 49, 51; A.F.A., Cross-Currents, circ., 1958; Houston/MFA, 1958; A.F.A., Collage in America, circ., 1957–58; WMAA Annual, 1964; U. of Nebraska; Musée des Arts Decoratifs, 1964; St. Etienne, 1964; A.F.A., 1968; Annely Juda Fine Art, London, The Non-Objective World: 1914–1955, 1972; PMA/Museum of the Philadelphia Civic Center, Focus, 1974; Andre Zarre Gallery, NYC, 1977, 77; St. Peter's College, 1976; Polo Gallery, Washington, D.C., 1976. **Collections:** Baltimore/MA; Boston/MFA; Calcutta; Carnegie; Chase Manhattan Bank; Ciba-Geigy Corp.; Corcoran; Cornell U.; MOMA; NYU; New York Hospital; Purchase/SUNY; Rockland/Farnsworth; St.-Etienne; J. Walter Thompson, NYC; WMAA; Wellesley College. **Bibliography:** Janis and Blesh 1.

ENGMAN, ROBERT. b. 1927, Belmont, Mass. **Studied:** RISD, 1948–52, BFA; Yale U. (with Josef Albers, Jose de Rivera), 1952–54, MFA. US Navy, 1944–46. **Taught:** Yale U., 1954–64; U. of Pennsylvania, 1963– ; RISD, 1951–52. **Awards:** NAD, Samuel F. B. Morse Fellowship, 1963–64. **Commissions:** MIT, Independence Park, Jerusalem; City of New York; Girard Bank, Philadelphia; U. of Pennsylvania. **Address:** 37 Maple Dr., Haverford, PA 19041. **Dealer:** Fischbach Gallery, NYC. **One-man Exhibitions:** (first) The Stable Gallery, 1960, also 1962; Kanegis Gallery, 1967; John Bernard Myers Gallery, NYC, 1972; Fischbach Gallery, NYC, 1978. **Retrospective:** MIT, 1966. **Group:** ICA, Boston, 1959; MOMA, Recent Sculpture USA, 1959; Sao Paulo, 1961; SRGM, 1962; WMAA, 1965; Los Angeles/County MA, American Sculpture of the Sixties, 1967. **Collections:** Franchard Corp.; Container Corp. of America, NYC; MOMA; Revere; WMAA; MIT; Wellesley College; Yale U. **Bibliography:** Downes, ed.

ERNST, JIMMY. b. June 24, 1920, Cologne, Germany. **Studied:** Cologne-Lindenthal Real-Gymnasium; Altona Arts and Crafts School. To USA, 1938. **Taught:** U. of Colorado, summers, 1954, 56; Museum of Fine Arts of Houston, 1956; Brooklyn College, 1951–; Pratt Institute; lectures extensively. Sent by US State Department to USSR, 1961. **Commissions:** General Motors Technical Center, Detroit (10-ft. mural); NBC–TV, "Producers' Showcase," 1954 (plastic sculpture signature); Abbott Laboratories, 1955; *Fortune* magazine, 1955, 61 (paintings); NBC–TV, "Playwrights '56" (welded steel sculpture signature, with Albert Terris); American resident Lines, USS *President Adams*, 1956 (mural); Continental National Bank, Lincoln, Neb., 1956 (96-ft. mural); Envoy Towers, 300 East 46th Street, NYC, 1960 (relief mural). **Awards:** Pasadena/AM, Hattie Brooks Stevens Memorial **P.P.**, 1946; WMAA, Juliana Force Memorial **P.P.**, 1951; Chicago/AI, Norman Wait Harris Bronze Medal, 1954; Brandeis U., Creative Arts Award, 1957; Guggenheim

Foundation Fellowship, 1961. **Address:** Lee Avenue, East Hampton, NY 11937. **Dealer:** Grace Borgenicht Gallery, Inc. **One-man Exhibitions:** (first) Norlyst Gallery, NYC, 1941; Philadelphia Art Alliance, 1948; Grace Borgenicht Gallery, Inc., 1951–55, 1957, 61, 62, 68, 71, 72, 76; Walker, 1954; Silvermine Guild, 1955; Houston/MFA, 1956; Brandeis U., 1957; Detroit/Institute, 1963; PAFA, 1965; West Palm Beach/Norton, 1965; Des Moines, 1966; Arts Club of Chicago, 1968. **Group:** Pasadena/AM, 1946; Brooklyn Museum, Watercolor Biennial; California Palace, 1952; U. of Colorado, 1953, 54, 56; Detroit/Institute, 1953, 59; *Life* magazine, Painters under 35, NYC, 1954; MMA, 100 Years of American Painting, 1954; SRGM, Younger American Painters, 1954; American Embassy, Paris, American Drawing, 1954; Toronto, 1954; Toledo/MA, 1954, 55; Carnegie, 1955; WMAA, Young America, 1955; XXVIII Venice Biennial, 1956; U. of Nebraska, 1956; U. of Illinois, 1957; Brooklyn Museum, Golden Years of American Drawing, 1957; Brussels World's Fair, 1958; NIAL, 1958, 60, 65; PAFA, 1959, 65; Chicago/AI, Directions in American Painting, 1960; WMAA Annual, 1966; Washburn U. of Topeka, 1966; WMAA, Art of the U.S. 1670–1966, 1966; Honolulu Academy, 1967. **Collections:** Allentown/AM; Bielefeld; Brandeis U.; Brooklyn Museum; Buffalo/Albright; Chicago/AI; Clearwater/Gulf Coast; Cologne; U. of Colorado; U. of Connecticut; Corcoran; Cranbrook; Detroit/Institute; Hartford/Wadsworth; Houston-MFA; Lehigh U.; MMA; MOMA; Michigan State U.; U. of Michigan; NCFA; NYU; U. of Nebraska; PAFA; Pasadena/AM; SFMA; SRGM; Southern Illinois U.; Toledo/MA; Toronto; Tulsa-Philbrook; Utica; VMFA; WMAA; Walker; West Palm Beach/Norton. **Bibliography:** Baur 7; Beekman; Blesh 1; Goodrich and Baur 1; Guggenheim, ed.; McCurdy, ed.; Janis and Blesh 1; Janis, S.; Mendelowitz; Motherwell and Reinhardt, eds.; Nordness, ed.; Pousette-Dart, ed.; Read 2; Ritchie 1; Archives.

ESTES, RICHARD. b. May 14, 1936, Evanston, Ill. **Studied:** Chicago/AI School, 1952–56. **Address:** 300 Central Park West, NYC 10024. **Dealer:** Allan Stone Gallery. **One-man Exhibitions:** Allan Stone Gallery, 1968, 69, 70, 72, 74; Hudson River Museum, 1968; Chicago/Contemporary, 1974; New Gallery of Contemporary Art, Cleveland (three-man), 1979; Boston/MFA, 1978. **Group:** Milwaukee, Aspects of a New Realism, 1969; U. of Illinois, 1969; Newport Harbor, Directly Seen: New Realism in California, 1970; WMAA, 22 Realists, 1970; Syracuse/Everson, Cool Realism, 1970; Chicago/Contemporary, Radical Realism, 1971; Documenta V, Kassel, 1972; Stuttgart/WK, Amerikanischer Fotorealismus, circ., 1972; California State U., San Jose, East Coast/West Coast/New Realism, 1973; Serpentine Gallery, London, Photo Realism, 1973; Seattle, American Art: Third Quarter Century, 1973; Worcester/AM, Three Realists, 1974; VMFA, Twelve American Painters, 1974; US Department of the Interior, America 1976, 1976; NCFA, America as Art, 1976; Australian Council, Illusion and Reality, 1976; A.F.A., American Master Drawings and Watercolors, 1977; WMAA Annual, 1977. **Collections:** American Broadcasting Co.; Ivest-Wellington Corp. **Bibliography:** *America 1976; Amerikanischer Fotorealismus;* Arthur 1, 2; Honish and Jensen, eds.; Hunter, ed.; Sager; *Three Realists.*

ETTING, EMLEN. b. 1905, Philadelphia, Pa. **Studied:** Harvard U., 1928; Academie de la Grande Chaumiere; with Andre Lhote in Paris. **Taught:** Philadelphia Museum School; Stella Elkins Tyler School of Fine Arts, Temple U.; Philadelphia College of Art. Hon. President, Artists Equity. **Member:** Century Association. **Commissions** (murals): Market Street National Bank, Philadelphia; Italian Consulate, Philadelphia. **Awards:** Italian Star of Solidarity; Chevalier de la Legion d'Honneur. **Address:** 1927 Panama

Street, Philadelphia, PA 19103. **Dealer:** The Midtown Galleries. **One-man Exhibitions:** The Midtown Galleries, NYC, 1940, 43, 44, 46, 48, 50, 51, 57, 66, 71, 75, 80; ICA, Boston; Cleveland/MA; Warwick Gallery, Philadelphia; Philadelphia Art Alliance, 1946; Phoenix, 1965; Allentown/AM, 1974. **Group:** WMAA; Corcoran; PAFA; Florida Southern College; VMFA; NAD; Audubon Artists; St. Louis/City; Philadelphia Art Alliance; Youngstown/Butler; Dayton/AI; Indiana U.; Illinois Wesleyan U.; West Palm Beach/Norton. **Collections:** Andover/Phillips; Atwater Kent Museum, La France Institute; PAFA; WMAA. **Bibliography: Etting; Frost; Hall.** Archives.

EVERGOOD, PHILIP HOWARD FRANCIS DIXON. b. October 26, 1901, NYC; **d.** March 11, 1973, Bridgewater, Conn. **Studied:** Eton College, England, 1914–18; Trinity Hall, Cambridge, 1918–20; U. of London, Slade School, 1920–23, with Henry Tonks; ASL, 1923–25, with George Luks, William Von Schlegell; Academie Julian, Paris, 1925, with Jean Paul Laurens, Andre Lhote. Traveled North Africa, USA and Europe, extensively. **Taught:** The Kalamazoo Institute of Arts; American Artists School, NYC; Contemporary School of Art, NYC; Iowa State College, 1952–58; U. of Minnesota, Duluth, 1955; Muhlenberg College; Settlement Music School, Philadelphia; extensive lecturing. Wrote for *Art Front* and *Direction* magazines. **Member:** NIAL; Artists Equity. Federal A.P.: Mural painting; Managing Supervisor, Easel Painting Division; mural for Richmond Hill (N.Y.) Public Library. **Commissions** (murals): Kalamazoo College; US Post Office, Jackson, Ga. **Awards:** Chicago/AI, The M.V. Kohnstamm Prize, 1935; MMA, **P.P.,** 1942; Carnegie, Hon. Men., 1945; Chicago/AI, W.H. Tuthill **P.P.,** 1946; Carnegie, Second Prize, 1949; PAFA, Carol H. Beck Gold Medal, 1949, Joseph E. Temple Gold Medal, 1958; Corcoran, Second Prize, 1951;

Phillip Evergood *Homage to Eve*

AAAL Grant, 1956; Ford Foundation, **P.P.,** 1962. **One-man Exhibitions:** (first) Dudensing Gallery, NYC, 1927;

Montross Gallery, NYC, 1929, 33, 35; Balzac Gallery, NYC, 1931; Denver/AM, 1936; Atheneum Gallery, Melbourne, 1937; ACA Gallery, 1938, 40, 42, 44, 46, 48, 51, 53, 1955–62; Kalamazoo/Institute, 1941; Norlyst Gallery, NYC, 1948; State U. of Iowa; Utica; Hartford/Wadsworth; Halkins College, 1953; Garelick's Gallery, Detroit, 1953, 55; Tulane U., 1957; Gallery 63, Inc., Rome, 1963, NYC, 1964; Hammer Gallery, 1967; Kennedy Gallery, 1972; Terry Dintenfass, Inc., 1974. **Retrospective:** U. of Minnesota, Duluth, 1955; WMAA, 1960. **Group:** An American Group (Gallery), NYC; American Society of Painters, Sculptors and Graveurs; Salon d'Automne, Paris, 1924; NAD; Independent Artists, NYC; WMAA Annuals since 1934; PAFA; Chicago/AI; Brooklyn Museum; Corcoran; Carnegie; Venice Biennial. **Collections:** Arizona State College; Atlanta/AA; Baltimore/MA; Boston/MFA; Britannica; Brooklyn Museum; Carnegie; Chicago/AI; Corcoran; Cornell U.; Dallas/MFA; Denver/AM; Free Library of Philadelphia; Grolier Club; Hartford/Wadsworth; Harvard U.; IBM; U. of Illinois; Kalamazoo/Institute; Lehigh U.; Library of Congress; Los Angeles/County MA; U. of Louisville; MMA; MOMA; Melbourne/National; Muhlenberg College; PAFA; Pepsi-Cola Co.; Santa Fe, N.M.; Smith College; Syracuse U.; WMAA; Youngstown/Butler. **Bibliography:** American Artists Congress, Inc.; **Baur 6,** 7; Biddle 4; Cheney; Eliot; Finkelstein; Genauer; Goodrich and Baur 1; Haftman; Kootz 2; **Lippard 3,** 5; McCurdy, ed.; Mendelowitz; Nordness, ed.; Pagano; Pousette-Dart, ed.; Reese; Richardson, E.P.; Rose, B., 1; Shapiro, ed. Archives.

FAHLSTROM, OYVIND. b. 1928, Sao Paulo, Brazil; **d.** November 9, 1976, Paris. To Sweden, 1939; to USA, 1961. Wrote plays, poetry, journalism, criticism, 1950–55; manifesto for concrete poetry (Stockholm), 1953; produced happenings, 1966–68. **Awards:** Sao Paulo Biennial, Hon. Men., 1959; Guggenheim Foundation Fellowship, 1964. **One-man Exhibitions:** (first) Numero Gallery, Florence, Italy, 1952; Daniel Cordier, Paris, 1959, 62; Galerie Blanche, Stockholm, 1959; Cordier & Ekstrom, Inc., 1964; Sidney Janis Gallery, 1967, 69, 71, 73; MOMA, circ., 1969; Galerie Rudolf Zwirner, 1969; U. of Minnesota, 1969; Baudoin Lebon Gallery, Paris, 1977; Redbird Galleries, Brooklyn, 1978. **Group:** Exposition Phases, Paris, 1956; V Sao Paulo Biennial, 1959; Carnegie, 1960, 67; Venice Biennials, 1964, 1966; EAT, NYC, 1966; Chicago/Contemporary, Pictures to Be Read/Poetry to Be Seen, 1967; Musée des Arts Decoratifs, 1967; Documenta IV, Kassel, 1968; ICA, U. of Pennsylvania, The Spirit of the Comics, 1969; Hayward Gallery, London, Pop Art, 1969; Los Angeles/County MA, Art & Technology, 1971; Tokyo/Modern, Swedish Art 1972, 1972. **Collections:** Cologne; Los Angeles/County MA; Stockholm/National; Stuttgart.

FARR, FRED W. b. August 9, 1914, St. Petersburg, Fla.; **d.** June 16, 1973, NYC. **Studied:** U. of Oregon; ASL; American Artists School, NYC. Traveled Mexico. **Taught:** Brooklyn Museum School, 1950–73; MOMA School, 1947; Hunter College, 1954; Dalton Schools, NYC, 1950; U. of Colorado; Dayton Art Institute School; U. of Oregon, 1948. **Member:** Artists Equity. Federal A.P.: Social Security Building, Washington, D.C. (mural). **Commissions:** Moore-McCormack Lines Inc., SS *Argentina* (mural). **Awards:** Port-au-Prince Bicentennial Exposition, 1950, Haiti Silver Medal. **One-man Exhibitions:** (first) The Bertha Schaefer Gallery; P. Rosenberg and Co., 1957, 58, 61, 64, 69. **Group:** MOMA, 1946; Springfield, Mass./MFA, 1947; Walker, 1948; Utica; U. of Michigan; Ohio U.; The Ohio State U.; U. of Delaware, 1948; RISD, 1949; WMAA; U. of New Hampshire; Northwestern U.; U. of Tennessee; U. of Wisconsin; Port-au-Prince (Haiti) Bicentennial Exposition, 1950; Walters Art Gallery, Baltimore, 1953; ART:USA: 59, NYC, 1959; U. of Illinois, 1961. **Collections:** Ball State U.; Detroit/Institute; U. of Illinois; Phillips; Portland, Me./MA.

FAULKNER, FRANK. b. July 24, 1946, Sumter, South Carolina. **Studied:** U. of North Carolina, BFA, 1968, MFA, 1972. **Awards:** National Endowment for the Arts, 1974; SECCA 1976; American Institute of Architects, Collaborating Artist Award, 1976. **Address:** 150 West 26th Street, NYC 10010. **Dealer:** Monique Knowlton Gallery, NYC. **One-man Exhibitions:** North Carolina Central U., 1968; The Other Ear Gallery, Chapel Hill, N.C., 1968; Art Gallery of Chapel Hill (two-man), 1971; Southeastern Center for Contemporary Art, 1974, 77; Monique Knowlton Gallery, NYC, 1976, 77, 79, 80; East Tennessee

State U., 1977; Alexandra Monett Gallery, Brussels, 1978; Roy Boyd Gallery, Chicago, 1979; Davidson College, 1979; Galerie Haberman, Cologne, 1980. **Group:** WMAA Biennial, 1975; The Pennsylvania State U., The Material Dominant, 1977; High Museum, Southwestern Painters and Sculptors, 1977; Phoenix, New York Now, 1979; Buffalo/Albright, Patterns, 1979; Wesleyan U., Bloomington, Pattern Painters, 1980. **Collections:** Becton Dickinson, & Co., Paramus N.J.; Buffalo/Albright; Chase Manhattan Bank; Delaware Art Museum; The Hanes Corp.; Harris Bank, Chicago; Henkel Co., GMBH; Hirshhorn; Hollywood (Fla.) Federal Savings and Loan Assn.; NCFA; North Carolina State U.; U. of North Carolina; Owens-Corning Fiberglas Corp; The Pennsylvania State U.; Raleigh/NCMA; R.J. Reynolds Corp.; Smith College; Southeastern Baking Corp., Miami; Springfield, Mo./AM; Toledo/MA.

FEELEY, PAUL. b. July 27, 1913, Des Moines, Iowa; **d.** June 10, 1966, NYC. **Studied:** Menlo Junior College; privately with Hobart Jacobs, in California, and Cecilia Beaux, in NYC; ASL, with Thomas Hart Benton, George Bridgeman; Beaux-Arts Institute of Design, NYC. Traveled Spain, Morocco, Greece, USA. **Taught:** Cooper Union, 1936–39; Bennington College, 1940–66. US Marine Corps, 1943–46. **Member:** National Society of Mural Painters. **One-man Exhibitions:** (first) Palo Alto (Calif.) Public Library, 1929; New School for Social Research, 1948; Santa Barbara/MA, 1950; The Rose Rabow Gallery, San Francisco, 1951; Stanford U., 1951; Mills College, 1951; SFMA, 1951; Tibor de Nagy Gallery, 1955, 57, 58; Betty Parsons Gallery, 1960, 1962–66, 1970, 71; Kasmin Ltd., 1964, 65, 67; Nicholas Wilder Gallery, 1966; Smithsonian, 1970; Andre Emmerich Gallery, NYC, 1976. **Retrospective:** SRGM, 1968. **Group:** Walker, 1950; ICA, Boston, 1952; PAFA; The Kootz Gallery, NYC, New Talent, 1954; Chi-cago/AI; Lincoln, Mass./De Cordova, New Experiments in Art, 1963; Los Angeles/County MA, Post Painterly Abstraction, 1964; SRGM, American Drawings, 1964, also 1965, Systemic Painting, 1966; SFMA, The Colorists, 1965; MOMA, The Responsive Eye, 1965; Amsterdam/Stedelijk, New Shapes of Color, 1966; Mexico City/Nacional, 19th Olympiad, 1968. **Bibliography:** Alloway 3, 4; **Baro;** Battcock, ed.; Goossen 1. Archives.

FEININGER, LYONEL. b. July 17, 1871, NYC; **d.** January 13, 1956. Studied the violin with his father and played in concerts from the age of 12; went to Germany in 1880 to study music, but changed to painting. **Studied:** Kunstgewerbeschule, Hamburg; Academy of Fine Arts, Berlin, with Ernst Hancke, Woldemar Friedrich; Jesuit College, Liege, Belgium, 1887–91; Academie Colarossi, Paris, 1892–93. Traveled Europe, USA. **Taught:** Bauhaus, Weimar, 1919–24; Bauhaus, Dessau, 1925–33; Mills College, summers, 1936, 37. Cartoonist and illustrator for *Ulk* and *Lustige Blätter*, Berlin, 1893–1906; *Le Temoin*, Paris, 1906–07; and Chicago *Sunday Tribune*. A member of the Blue Four, 1924 (with Vassily Kandinsky, Paul Klee, and Alexej von Jawlensky). **Commissions:** New York World's Fair, 1939 (murals for Marine Transport Building and Masterpieces of Art Building). **One-man Exhibitions:** Emil Richter Gallery, Dresden, 1919; Anger-Museum, Erfurt, Germany, 1920, 27, 29, 30; Kunst und Bucherstube, Erfurt, 1921; Goldschmidt-Wallerstein, Berlin, 1922, 25; Anderson Galleries, NYC, 1923; Wiesbaden, 1925; Neue Kunstfides, Dresden, 1925, 26, 31; Brunswick, 1926; Kassel, 1927; Staatliche Galerie Moritzburg, Halle, Germany, 1928; Anhalt Gallery, Dessau, 1929; Kunstverein, Prague, 1930; Mills College, 1936, 37; SFMA, 1937; Los Angeles/County MA, 1937; Seattle/AM, circ., 1937; Andover/Phillips, 1938; Curt Valentine Gallery,

NYC, 1941, 44, 46, 48, 50, 52, 54; Buchholz Gallery, NYC, 1941, 43, 44; Karl Nierendorf Gallery, NYC, 1943; The Willard Gallery, 1943, 44; Dalzell Hatfield Gallery, 1944; Fort Worth, 1956; Harvard U., 1958; Detroit/Institute, 1964; R. N. Ketterer, Campione, Switzerland, 1965; Pasadena/AM, 1966; LaBoetie Gallery, NYC, 1966; MOMA, 1967; Marlborough-Gerson Gallery, Inc., 1969; A.A.A. Gallery, 1972; Serge Sabarsky Gallery, NYC, 1972, 74, 79; Haus der Kunst, Munich, 1973; Marlborough Gallery, Inc., NYC, 1974; Society of the Four Arts, 1976; AAA, NYC, 1974. **Retrospective:** Berlin, 1931, MOMA, 1944 (two-man); ICA, Boston, 1949; Jeanne Bucher, Paris, circ., Europe, 1950–51; Print Club of Cleveland, 1951; Hannover, circ., Europe, 1954–55; SFMA, circ., 1959–61. **Group:** Salon des Artistes Independants, Paris, 1911; Der Sturm, Berlin, 1917; Documenta I, Kassel, 1955; WMAA; Tate; Mannheim; Allentown/AM, The Blue Four and German Expressionism, 1974. **Collections:** Baltimore/MA; Buffalo/Albright; Chicago/AI; Cranbrook; U. of Houston; Kansas City/Nelson; Lehigh U.; MMA; MOMA; U. of Michigan; Milwaukee; Minneapolis/Institute; PMA; Phillips; RISD; Raleigh/NCMA; SRGM; San Antonio/McNay; Seattle/AM; Toledo/MA; Utica; WMAA; Walker; Washington U. **Bibliography:** Barr 1; Baur 5, 7; Bazin; Beekman; Biddle 4; Blanchard; Blesh 1; Born; Brion 2; Brown; Bulliet 1; Cassou; Cheney; *Cityscape 1919–39*; Eliot; Feininger, T.L.; Flanagan; Frost; Goodrich and Baur 1; Haftman; Hess, H.; Hess, T.B., 1; Hulten; Hunter 6; Huyghe; Janis S.; Kouvenhoven; Kuh 1; Langui; Lee and Burchwood; MacAgy 2; McCurdy, ed.; Mendelowitz; Munsterberg; **Ness, ed.;** Neumeyer; Newmeyer; Pousette-Dart, ed.; Raynal 3, 4; Read 2; Richardson, E.P.; Rickey; Ritchie 1; Rose, B., 1; Rosenblum 1, 2; Roters; Sachs; Scheyer; Selz, P., 3; Sutton; Valentine 2; Verkauf; Wight 2; Wingler, ed. Archives.

FEITELSON, LORSER. b. 1898, Savannah, Ga.; **d.** May 24, 1978, Los An-

geles, Calif. **Taught:** Art Center School, Los Angeles. **One-man Exhibitions:** The Daniel Gallery, NYC, 1924; San Diego, 1928; California Palace, 1928, 32; Los Angeles/County MA, 1929, 44; SFMA, 1944; Lucien Labaudt Gallery, San Francisco, 1949; San Antonio/McNay, 1955; Paul Rivas Gallery, Los Angeles, 1959 (two-man); Ankrum Gallery, 1964; Art Center School, Los Angeles (two-man); Scripps College, 1958, 61; Long Beach/MA, 1962; Chapman College, Los Angeles, 1963; Occidental College, Los Angeles, 1965; Los Angeles, Art Association Galleries, 1968, 79; David Stuart Gallery, Los Angeles, 1977; WMAA, 1978. **Retrospectives:** Pasadena/AM, 1952; Los Angeles Municipal Art Gallery, 1972. **Group:** Brooklyn Museum, 1936; SFMA, 1936; MOMA, Fantastic Art, DADA, Surrealism, 1936; Chicago/AI, Abstract and Surrealist Art, 1948; U. of Illinois, 1950, 51, 53, 65; Sao Paulo, 1955; WMAA, 1955, Annuals, 1965, 67; MOMA, The Responsive Eye, 1965; Sacramento/Crocker, 1967, 68; Pasadena/AM, West Coast: 1945–1969, 1969; Museum of Fine Arts, St. Petersburg, Color in Control, 1969; Sacramento/Crocker, Century of California Painting, 1970; VMFA, American Painting, 1970; Painting and Sculpture in California: The Modern Era, 1976; Rutgers U.; Surrealism and American Art: 1931–47, 1977. **Collections:** Atlantic-Richfield Co.; Bank of Omaha; Brooklyn Museum; Craig Elwood Associates; Great Western Savings and Loan Association; Hirshhorn; Industrial Electronics Engineers, Inc.; Lansing Sound Corp.; Long Beach/MA; Los Angeles/County MA; MOMA; SFMA; Xerox Corp. **Bibliography:** *Avant-Garde Painting and Sculpture;* Baur 7; *Black and White Are Colors;* Flanagan; Rickey. Archives.

FENTON, ALAN. b. July 29, 1927, Cleveland, Ohio. **Studied:** Pratt Institute, with Jack Tworkov, Adolph Gottlieb, BFA; ASL, with Richard Bove. US Merchant Marine, World War II. Traveled Europe, Mexico, Canada, USA. **Taught:** Housatonic State College, Stratford, Conn., 1968–69; Pratt Institute, 1968– ; Cleveland Institute of Art, 1977–78. **Awards:** City Center Gallery, NYC, Hon. Men., 1958; Cleveland/MA, First Prize, 1960, 61. **Address:** 333 Park Avenue South, NYC 10010. **One-man Exhibitions:** (first) The Pace Gallery, 1963; Alhar, Stratford, Conn., 1968; Bridgeport, 1973; New York Cultural Center, 1974; Isetan Galleries, Tokyo, 1976; Barbara Fiedler, Washington, D.C., 1977; Phillips, circ., 1977. **Group:** ART:USA:58, NYC, 1958; Cleveland/MA, 1959, 60, 61; Artists of the Western Reserve, circ., 1961; SFMA, 1963; New York World's Fair, 1964–65; Corcoran, 1970; Houston/Contemporary, 1977. **Collections:** Baltimore/MA; Bobbie Brooks, Inc.; CIA; Cleveland/MA; Corcoran; Cornell U.; H. E. Laufer Co.; U. of Iowa; NCFA; New College (Sarasota, Fla.); Phillips; Pratt Institute; Rich-Lan Corp.; Stony Brook/SUNY; West Palm Beach/Norton; Westport Savings Bank.

FERBER, HERBERT. b. April 30, 1906, NYC. **Studied:** City College of New York, 1923–26; Columbia U. School of Dental and Oral Surgery, 1927, BS, 1930, DDS; Beaux-Arts Institute of Design, NYC, 1927–30; NAD, 1930. Associate Fellow, Morse College, Yale U., 1967– . **Taught:** U. of Pennsylvania, 1963–64; Columbia U. School of Dental and Oral Surgery; Rutgers U., 1965–67. **Commissions:** B'nai Israel Synagogue, Millburn, N.J., 1950; Brandeis U., Jewish Chapel, 1955; Temple Anshe Chesed, Cleveland, 1955; Temple of Aaron, St. Paul, 1955; WMAA, Sculpture as Environment, 1961; Rutgers U., 1968; John F. Kennedy Federal Office Building, Boston, 1969; American Dental Association Building, Chicago, 1974. **Awards:** Beaux-Arts Institute of Design, NYC, Paris Prize, 1929; L. C. Tiffany Grant, 1930; MMA, Artists for Victory, $1,000 Prize, 1942; ICA, London/Tate, International Unknown Political Prisoner Competition, 1953; Guggenheim Foundation Fellowship, 1969. **Address:** 44 MacDougal Street,

Herbert Ferber *Baldwin Hill* 1979

NYC 10012. **Dealer:** M. Knoedler & Co. Inc., NYC. **One-man Exhibitions:** (first) The Midtown Galleries, 1937, also 1943; Betty Parsons Gallery, 1947, 50, 53; The Kootz Gallery, NYC, 1955, 57; Columbia U., 1960; Andre Emmerich Gallery, 1960, 62, 67, 69, 70, 71, 72, 73, 75, 76, 77; U. of Vermont, 1964; Rutgers U., 1968; M. Knoedler & Co., Inc., NYC, 1978, 79; Roy Boyd Gallery, Chicago, 1978. **Retrospectives:** Bennington College, 1958; WMAA, 1961; SFMA, 1962; Walker, circ., 1962–63. **Group:** NAD, 1930; Brooklyn Museum; PAFA, 1931, 42, 43, 45, 46, 54, 58; Corcoran, 1932; Philadelphia Art Alliance, 1933; American Artists Congress, 1936, 40; Musée du Jeu de Paume, 1938; Sculptors Guild, 1938–42, 1944, 48, 64; Golden Gate International Exposition, San Francisco/AI, 1940, 41,

45; WMAA Annuals, 1940, 42, 1945– ; Federation of Modern Painters and Sculptors, 1941–49; A.F.A., Sculpture in Wood, 1941; MMA, 1942; Sao Paulo, 1951; MOMA, Abstract Painting and Sculpture in America, 1951; MOMA, Fifteen Americans, circ., 1952; Tate, 1953; WMAA, The New Decade, 1954–55; Brussels World's Fair, 1958; Carnegie, 1958; A.F.A., God and Man in Art, circ., 1958–59; Documenta II, Kassel, 1959; St. Paul Gallery, Drawings, USA, 1961; Baltimore/MA; Cranbrook; Battersea Park, London, International Sculpture Exhibition, 1963; Musée Rodin, Paris, 1965; MOMA, The New American Painting and Sculpture, 1969; Newport, R.I., Monumenta, 1974; NCFA; Sculpture, American Directions, 1945–1975, 1975; Indianapolis, 1978. **Collections:** Bennington College; Brandeis U.; Buffalo/Albright; Cranbrook; Detroit/Institute; Grand Rapids; Indiana U.; MMA; MOMA; National Gallery; Paris-Beaubourg; NYU; Newark Museum; U. of Vermont; WMAA; Walker; Williams College; Yale U. **Bibliography:** Baur 5, 7; Blesh 1; Brumme; Chipp; Craven, W.; Flanagan; Giedion-Welcker 1; Goodrich and Baur 1; **Goosen 5;** Henning; Hunter 6; Hunter, ed.; Krauss 2; McCurdy, ed.; Marter, Tarbell, and Wechsler; *Monumenta;* Motherwell and Reinhardt, eds.; Read 3; Ritchie, 3; Rose, B., 1; Rubin 1; Seuphor 3; Strachan; Trier 1. Archives.

FERREN, JOHN. b. October 17, 1905, Pendleton, Ore.; **d.** July 24, 1970, Southampton, N.Y. **Studied:** Academie de la Grande Chaumiere; Sorbonne; U. of Florence; U. of Salamanca; Academie Ranson, Paris; Academie Colarossi, Paris. Traveled Europe, USA, Middle East; resided, worked in Paris, 1931–38. Civilian employee of War Department and OWI, 1941–45; Psychological Warfare Division, SHAEF (Propaganda Chief, Italian Radio Section); Algiers headquarters (Chief of Publications for France); received Bronze Star. **Taught:**

Brooklyn Museum School, 1946–50; Cooper Union, 1947–54; Art Center School, Los Angeles, summer, 1948; Queens College, 1952–70; UCLA, summer, 1953; privately in New York; U. of Saskatchewan, summer, 1960; Yale U., summer, 1962; lectured extensively and published essays. Advisory work on *The Trouble with Harry* (1955) and *Vertigo* (1958), films directed by Alfred Hitchcock. **Member:** Advisory Council to the School of Art and Architecture, Yale U., 1959–62. **One-man Exhibitions:** Art Center, San Francisco, 1930; Galerie Zak, Paris, 1932; Gallerie Pierre, Paris, 1936; Pierre Matisse Gallery, 1936, 37, 38; Minneapolis/Institute, 1936; Howard Putzell Gallery, Hollywood, 1936; SFMA, 1936, 52; Arts Club of Chicago, 1937; Galerie Beaune, Paris, 1938; The Willard Gallery, 1942; Art Project Gallery, Hollywood, 1942; Kleemann Gallery, NYC, 1947, 49; Santa Barbara/MA, 1952; Tacoma, 1952; Portland (Ore.) Arts Club, 1952; Alexander Iolas Gallery, 1953; UCLA, 1953; U. of Washington, 1953; The Stable Gallery, 1954, 55, 56, 57, 58; Phillips, 1958; U. of Wisconsin, 1959; Glassboro State College, 1959; Trenton State College, 1959; Rose Fried Gallery, 1962, 1965–68; Queens College, 1963; Centre d'Art Gallery, Beirut, Lebanon, 1964; American Embassy, London, 1965; Pageant Gallery, Florida, 1968; Southampton College, 1968 (two-man); A.M. Sachs Gallery, 1969, 72, 74, 75, 77; Southampton/Parrish, 1969; The Century Assn., NYC, 1971. **Group:** Los Angeles/County MA Annuals, 1925–29; SFMA Annuals, 1925–29; California Palace, 1931; American Abstract Artists 1934, 35, 37; Musée de l'Orangerie, Paris, 1937; Salon des Surindependants, Paris, 1937; Royal Institute of the Arts, Copenhagen, 1937; Corcoran, 1940; Chicago/AI, 1947; Brooklyn Museum, 1949; U. of Minnesota, Pioneers in American Abstract Art, 1951; Ninth Street Exhibition, NYC, 1951; MOMA, Abstract Painting and Sculpture in America, 1951; WMAA Annuals, 1952, 55, 56, 58, The 1930's, 1968; Carnegie

1955; MOMA, 7 American Watercolorists, circ., Europe, 1956; Chicago/AI, 1956; U. of Illinois, 1957; WMAA, Nature in Abstraction, 1958; U. of Kentucky, Graphics, 1958, 59; Pasadena/AM, A Decade in the Contemporary Gallery, 1959; ART:USA:59, NYC, 1959; Walker, 60 American Painters, 1960; SRGM, Abstract Expressionists and Imagists, 1961; A.F.A., Affinities, circ., 1962; PAFA, 1964, 66; Gallery of Modern Art, NYC, 1965. **Collections:** Allentown/AM; Art of This Century (Peggy Guggenheim); Arts Club of Chicago; Birmingham, Ala./MA; Brandeis U.; Buffalo/Albright; California Palace; U. of California; Cedar Rapids/AA; Cleveland/MA; Detroit/Institute; Hartford/Wadsworth; High Museum; Hirshhorn; Los Angeles/County MA; MOMA; NYU; U. of Nebraska; Norfolk/Chrysler; Oklahoma; PMA; Phillips; SFMA; SRGM; Sacramento/Crocker; Santa Barbara/MA; Scripps College; Tel Aviv; U. of Texas; Tougaloo College; WGMA; WMAA; Washington U.; Yale U. **Bibliography:** Baur 5, 7; Chipp; Downes, ed.; Eliot; Frost; Goodrich and Baur 1; Guggenheim, ed.; Hayter 2; Janis, S.; Passloff; Ritchie 1; Rose, B., 1, 4; Sandler 1; Archives.

FIENE, ERNEST. b. November 2, 1894, Eberfeld, Germany; **d.** August 10, 1965, Paris, France. To USA, 1912; citizen 1928. **Studied:** NAD, 1914–18; Beaux-Arts Institute of Design, NYC, 1916–18; ASL, 1923; Academie de la Grande Chaumiere, 1929; Florence, Italy (fresco painting), 1932. Traveled Europe, Mexico, USA. **Taught:** Westchester County Center, 1930–31; Colorado Springs Fine Arts Center, 1935; Cooper Union, 1938–39; ASL, 1938–65; Ogunquit School of Painting, 1950–51; Famous Artists Schools, Inc,. 1956–65; NAD, 1960–65. **Member:** Artists Equity (Hon. President); NAD; Century Association; ASL. **Commissions** (portraits): Columbia U.; New York Hospital; Ohio U.; Abbott Laboratories; (series of paint-

ings); Scruggs, Vandervoort, and Barney; Gimbel's, Philadelphia; Central Needle Trades High School of New York; (murals): International Ladies' Garment Workers Union, NYC; Abraham Lincoln High School, Brooklyn (2); US Post Office, Canton, Mass.; New Interior Building, Washington, D.C. **Awards:** Guggenheim Foundation Fellowship, 1932; Chicago/AI, Norman Wait Harris Prize, 1937; Corcoran, William A. Clark Prize, 1938; Carnegie, Hon. Men., 1938; Chicago/AI, Ada S. Garrett Prize, 1940; Library of Congress, Pennell **P.P.**, 1940; Library of Congress, First Pennell **P.P.**, 1944; NAD, Edwin Palmer Memorial Prize, 1961. **One-man Exhibitions:** (first) Whitney Studio Club, NYC, 1923; The New Gallery, NYC, 1924; Kraushaar Galleries, 1927; The Downtown Gallery, 1928, 33, 36; Rehn Galleries, 1930–32; Western Association of Art Museum Directors, circ., 1938; A.A.A. Gallery, NYC, 1938–41, 1945; M. Knoedler & Co., 1949–51; The Midtown Galleries, 1959; Stonington Gallery, Conn., 1963; Bay Head Art Center, 1964; Washington Irving Gallery, NYC, 1969. **Group:** WMAA, 1930–45; Carnegie, 1930–45; PAFA, 1930–45; NAD; MOMA; Youngstown/Butler; Chicago/AI, 1930–33, 1936–45; Corcoran, 1931–45; MMA; Boston/MFA. **Collections:** ASL; Abbott Laboratories; Boston/MFA; Bowdoin College; Britannica; Brooklyn Museum; California Palace; Chicago/AI; Cleveland/MA; Columbia U.; Dartmouth College; Denver/AM; Detroit/Institute; Drake U.; Library of Congress; Los Angeles/County MA; MIT; MMA; MOMA; NAD, NYPL; U. of Nebraska; Newark Museum; Ogunquit; Ohio U.; PAFA; Phillips; SFMA; Syracuse U.; Tel Aviv; Terre Haute/Swope; Tulsa/Philbrook; WMAA; Yale U. **Bibliography:** American Artists Congress, Inc.; American Artists Group Inc. 1, 2, 3; Cahill and Barr, eds.; Goodrich and Baur 1; Hall; Pearson 1; Phillips 1; Reese; Richardson, E.P.; *Woodstock: An American Art Colony, 1902–1977.* Archives.

Janet Fish *Goldfish and Autumn Leaves* 1979–80

FISH, JANET. b. May 18, 1938, Boston, Mass. **Studied:** Smith College, BA; Yale U., MFA. **Awards:** Chicago/AI; MacDowell Colony Fellowship, 1968, 69, 72; Norman Wait Harris Award, 1974; Australia Council for the Arts, Grant, 1975. **Taught:** Skowhegan School, 1973, 74; School of Visual Arts, NYC, 1968–69; U. of Bridgeport, 1971; Parsons School of Design, NYC, 1974; Syracuse U., 1974; U. of Chicago, 1976. **Address:** 101 Prince Street, NYC 10012. **Dealer:** Robert Miller Gallery, Inc., NYC. **One-man Exhibition:** (first) Fairleigh Dickinson U., 1967; Stony Brook/SUNY, 1967, 78; Ours Gallery, NYC, 1968; Mercer Street, NYC, 1969; The Kornblee Gallery, NYC, 1971, 72, 73, 74, 75, 76; Pace College, NYC, 1972; Russell Sage College, 1972; Galerie Alexandra Monett, Brussels, 1974; Galerie Kostiner-Silvers, Montreal, 1974; Hogarth Gallery, Paddington, Sydney, Australia, 1975; Tolarno Gallery, Stokitha, Victoria, 1975, 77; Phyllis Kind Gallery, Chicago 1976; Robert Miller Gallery, Inc., NYC, 1978, 79. **Group:** A.F.A., Still Life Today, 1970–71; NIAL, 1972; Chicago/AI, 1972, 74; Indianapolis, 1972; Lakeview Center, American Women; 20th Century, 1972; Randolph-Macon College, Paintings by Some Contemporary American Women, 1972; Cleveland/MA, 32 Realists, 1972; A.F.A., The Realist Revival, 1972; WMAA, American Drawings: 1963–1973, 1973; Yale U., 7 Realists, 1973; PMA/Museum of the Philadelphia Civic Center, Focus, 1974; Tokyo Biennial, 1974; Queens Museum, New Images, 1974; U. of North Carolina, 1975, 78; Ohio State U., Concept of Reality: Recent Art, 1975; Minnesota/MA, Drawings USA/75, 1975; Baltimore/MA, Super Realism, 1975; US Department of the Interior, America 1976, circ., 1976; PAFA, 8 Contemporary American Realists, 1977, Centro Colombo Americano, Bogota, 16 Realists, 1979; Lincoln, Mass./De Cordova, Born in Boston, 1979. **Collections:** A.F.A.; Art Museum of South Texas; AT&T; American Airlines, Amstar Corp.; Chase Manhattan Bank; Chicago/AI; Cleveland/MA; Colby College; Commerce Bank of Kansas City; Dallas/MFA; Heublein Inc.; Minneapolis/Institute; IBM; Minnesota/MA; National Gallery; Newark Museum; New York State Health and Hospitals Corp.; Oberlin College; PAFA; Port Authority of New York & New Jersey; RISD; Union Camp Corp.; U. of Sydney; WMAA; Wellington Management Corp; Westmoreland County/MA; Yale U. **Bibliography:** *America 1976*; Arthur 1; Arthur 2; Goodyear; *New in the Seventies.*

FLACK, AUDREY. b. May 30, 1931, NYC. **Studied:** Cooper Union, 1951;

Yale U., 1952 with J. Albers; NYU; Institute of Fine Arts, 1953. Traveled USA, Europe, India. **Taught:** Pratt Institute, 1960–68; NYU, 1960–68; Riverside Museum Master Institute, 1966–67; School of Visual Arts, NYC, 1970–74. **Awards:** Hon. Ph.D., Cooper Union, 1977. **Commissions:** Time Magazine, Man of the Year cover, Anwar Sadat, 1979. **Address:** 110 Riverside Drive, NYC 10024. **Dealer:** Louis K. Meisel Gallery, NYC. **One-man Exhibitions:** Roko Gallery, NYC, 1959, 63; French & Co., Inc., NYC, 1972; Louis K. Meisel Gallery, NYC, 1974, 76, 78; U. of Hartford, 1974; U. of Bridgeport, 1975. **Group:** NAD, 1948; The Stable Gallery, Annual, NYC, 1960; School of Visual Arts, NYC, 65 Self-Portraits, 1965; WMAA, 22 Realists, 1970; WMAA, Annual, 1972; Indianapolis, 1972; Cleveland/MA, 32 Realists, 1972; WMAA, American Drawings, 1963–73, 74; Serpentine Gallery, London, Photo Realism, 1973; U. of Illinois, 1974; Tokyo Metropolitan Art Gallery, 11th Tokyo Biennale, 1974; PMA/Museum of the Philadelphia Civic Center, Women's Work: American Art 1974, 1974; California Institute of the Arts, Art: A Woman's Sensibility, 1975; Toledo/MA: Image, Color and Form, 1975; Wichita State U., The New Realism, 1975; Baltimore/MA, Super Realism, 1975; Stratford, Ont., Aspects of Realism, circ., 1976–78; WMAA, Art about Art, circ., 1978. **Collections:** MOMA, WMAA; SRGM; MMA; Oberlin College; Canberra/National. **Bibliography:** *Art: A Woman's Sensibility; New in the Seventies.*

FLANNAGAN, JOHN. b. April 7, 1895, Fargo, N.D.; **d.** January 6, 1942, NYC. **Studied:** Minneapolis Institute School, 1914–17, with R. Koehler. US Merchant Marine, 1914–17. Traveled Ireland, USA, France. **Awards:** Guggenheim Foundation Fellowship, 1932; MMA, Alexander Shilling Prize, 1940. **One-man Exhibitions:** Whitney Studio Club, NYC, 1925; Weyhe Gallery, 1927, 28, 30, 31, 34, 36, 38, 73, 78; Arts Club of Chicago, 1934; Vassar College, 1936;

Bard College, 1937; Buchholz Gallery, NYC, 1942 (2); VMFA, 1946; A.F.A., circ., 1959; International Exhibitions Foundation, Washington, D.C., 1965–76. **Group:** WMAA; MOMA; MMA; Brooklyn Museum; Carnegie, Forerunners of American Abstraction, 1971. **Collections:** Andover/Phillips; Cincinnati/AM; Cleveland/MA; Detroit/Institute; Dublin/Municipal; Harvard U.; Honolulu Academy; MMA; U. of Nebraska; Oberlin College; Vassar College; WMAA; Wichita/AM. **Bibliography:** *Avant-Garde Painting and Sculpture;* Baur 7; Brumme; Cheney; Craven, W.; Fierens; *Forerunners;* Goodrich and Baur 1; Hunter 6; Jackman; Licht, F.; Marter, Tarbell, and Wechsler; McCurdy, ed.; Mellquist; Mendelowitz; **Miller, ed., 3;** Ritchie, 3; Rose, B., 1, 4; Selz J.; Seuphor 3; Seymour; **Valentine 1,** 2; Wheeler.

FLAVIN, DAN. b. 1933, NYC. **Studied:** Cathedral College of the Immaculate Conception, 1947–52; US Air Force Meteorological Technician Training School, 1953; U. of Maryland (Extension, Korea), 1954–55; New School for Social Research, 1956; Columbia U., 1957–59. **Address:** Garrison, NY 10524. **Dealers:** Leo Castelli Inc., NYC; John Weber Gallery. **One-man Exhibitions:** Judson Gallery, NYC, 1961; Kaymar Gallery, NYC, 1964; Green Gallery, NYC, 1964; Ohio State U., 1965; Galerie Rudolf Zwirner, 1966; Nicholas Wilder Gallery, 1966; The Kornblee Gallery, 1967; Chicago/Contemporary, 1968; Galleria Sperone, Turin, 1968; Galerie Heiner Friedrich, Munich, 1968; Konrad Fischer Gallery, Dusseldorf, 1969; Irving Blum Gallery, Los Angeles, 1969; Galerie Bischofberger, Zurich, 1969; Ottawa/National, 1969; Vancouver, 1970; Jewish Museum, 1970; Dwan Gallery, NYC, 1970; Leo Castelli Inc., NYC, 1970, 71, 72, 73, 74, 75, 76, 78, 79; Los Angeles/County MA, 1970; Galerie Heiner Friedrich, Munich, 1970; ACE Gallery, Los Angeles, 1971, 77; John Weber Gallery, 1971, 73; Galerie Heiner Friedrich, Cologne, 1971, 73; Janie C.

Lee Gallery, Dallas, 1971; Rice U., 1972; St. Louis/City, 1973; U. of Bridgeport, 1973; Locksley-Shea Gallery, 1973; Lisson Gallery, London, 1973; Ronald Greenberg Gallery, St. Louis, 1974; Jared Sable Gallery, Toronto, 1974; Pasquale Trisorio Naples, 1974; Weinberg Gallery, San Francisco, 1974; Rotterdam, 1975; Basel, 1975; Charlotte Square Gallery, Edinburgh, 1976; Portland (Ore.) Center for the Visual Arts, 1976; Heiner Friedrich, Inc., NYC, 1976, 77, 78 (two-man); Otis Art Institute, 1977; Chicago/AI, 1977; ACE Canada, Vancouver, 1977; Cincinnati/Contemporary, 1977; Austin, 1979; Ottawa/National, 1979. **Retrospective:** Fort Worth, 1976; Southampton/Parrish, circ., 1978. **Group:** Hartford/Wadsworth, Black, White and Gray, 1964; ICA, Boston, 1966; U. of California, Irvine, 5 Los Angeles Sculptors, 1966; Jewish Museum, Primary Structures, 1966; Finch College, 1966; Eindhoven, Kunst-Licht-Kunst, 1966; Los Angeles/County MA, PMA, American Sculpture of the Sixties, 1967; Trenton/State, Focus on Light, 1967; Goethe U., Frankfurt, Germany, 1967; WGMA, A New Aesthetic, 1967; VI International Art Biennial, San Marino (Europe), 1967; Buffalo/Albright, Plus by Minus, 1968; The Hague, Minimal Art, 1968; Documenta IV, Kassel, 1968; WMAA, Light: Object and Image, 1968; UCLA, Electric Art, 1969; MMA, New York Painting and Sculpture, 1940–1970, 1969–70; Fort Worth, Drawings, 1969; U. of California, Irvine, Five Sculptors, 1969; MOMA, Spaces, 1969; WMAA Annual, 1970; SRGM, Guggenheim International, 1971; Buffalo/Albright, Kid Stuff, 1971; Walker, Works for New Spaces, 1971; Los Angeles/County MA, Art & Technology, 1971; High Museum, The Modern Image, 1972; Detroit/Institute, Art in Space, 1973; MOMA, Some Recent American Art, circ., 1973; Musée Galliera, Paris, Festival d'Automne, 1973; Parcheggio di Villa Borghese, Rome, Contemporanea, 1974; Indianapolis, 1974; U. of North Carolina, Light/Sculpture, 1975; NCFA, Sculpture; American Directions 1945–1975, 1975; MOMA, Drawing Now, 1976; WMAA, 200 Years of American Sculpture, 1976; Chicago/AI, 1976; U. of Chicago, Ideas in Sculpture 1965–1977, 1977; ICA, Boston, The Reductive Object, 1979. **Collections:** Amsterdam/Stedelijk; Basel; Cologne; Eindhoven; Harvard U.; Krefeld/Kaiser Wilhelm; Los Angeles/County MA; MOMA; Ottawa/National; Pasadena/AM; RISD; SRGM; Tate; WMAA; Walker. **Bibliography:** *Art Now 74*; Battcock, ed.; Calas, N. and E.; *Contemporanea*; **Dan Flavin;** Davis, D.; De Vries; Gablik; Honisch and Jensen, eds.; Johnson, Ellen, H.; Krauss 2; Lippard 4, 5; MacAgy 2; Muller; *Report*, Tuchman 1.

FLEISCHMANN, ADOLF R. b. March 18, 1892, Esslingen, Germany; **d.** January 28, 1968, Stuttgart, Germany. **Studied:** Academy of Fine Arts, Stuttgart; Academy of Fine Arts, Munich, with Carl Caspar. Traveled Europe extensively. **Taught:** Palma de Mallorca, 1933–36; and privately. To USA, 1952. **Member:** American Abstract Artists; Groupe Espace, Paris; Salon des Realites Nouvelles, Paris. **One-man Exhibitions:** (first) Kunsthaus Schaller, Stuttgart; Galerie Creuze, Paris, 1948; Galerie Colette Allendy, Paris, 1950, 51; Lutz and Meyer Gallery, Stuttgart, 1952, 60, 62; Johannesburg/Municipal, 1953; Rose Fried Gallery, 1955, 57; Galerie Weiss, Kassel, 1959; Parma Gallery, NYC, 1961; Apiaw (Gallery), Liege, 1962; Kunstverein Freiburg im Breisgau, 1962; The Stable Gallery, 1963; Hessisches Landesmuseum, Kassel, circ., 1964. **Group:** Neue Sezession, Munich; Salon des Realites Nouvelles, Paris, 1946; Groupe Espace, Paris, 1946; American Abstract Artists Annuals; WMAA, Geometric Abstraction in America, circ., 1962; SFMA; Yale U.; Chicago/AI. **Collections:** Boulogne; Busch-Reisinger Museum; Ceret; Esslingen; Grenoble; Harvard U.; Kassel; New London; Stuttgart; Union Carbide

Corp.; WMAA; Wellesley College. **Bibliography:** Read 2; Seuphor 1.

FLOCH, JOSEPH. b. November 5, 1895, Vienna, Austria; **d.** October 27, 1977, NYC. **Studied:** Academy of Fine Arts, Vienna, MA. Traveled Europe; resided Paris, twenty years. To USA, 1941. **Taught:** New School for Social Research. **Member:** Federation of Modern Painters and Sculptors; NAD; Salon d'Automne, Paris; Salon des Tuileries, Paris. **Commissions:** French Government, 1939 (murals); costumes and stage sets (with Louis Jouvet) for the Jean Giraudoux play *Judith*. **Awards:** Chevalier of the Order of Arts and Letters (France); Paris World's Fair, 1937, Gold Medal; William Palmer Memorial Prize; PAFA, Walter Lippincott Prize; Eastern States exhibit, Springfield, Mass., 1966; NAD, Saltus Gold Medal for Merit, 1967. **One-man Exhibitions:** (first) a gallery in Vienna, 1917; Galerie Berthe Weill, Paris; A.A.A. Gallery, NYC; Toledo/MA; de Young; Syracuse U., 1965; The Forum Gallery (three-man), 1975. **Retrospective:** Belvedere, 1972. **Group:** MMA; WMAA; New York World's Fair, 1939; Paris World's Fair, 1937. **Collections:** Belvedere; Bezalel Museum; de Young; Graphische Sammlung Albertina; Grenoble; Kansas City/Nelson; Lille; MMA; MOMA; Montclair/AM; Musée du Jeu de Paume; Paris/Moderne; Smithsonian; Southampton/Parrish; Springfield, Mass./MFA; Tel Aviv; Toledo/MA; Vienna/Stadt; WMAA. **Bibliography: Held;** Huyghe; Pagano; Soyer, R. 1. Archives.

FOLLETT, JEAN F. b. June 5, 1917, St. Paul, Minn. **Studied:** U. of Minnesota; St. Paul School of Art, with Cameron Booth; Hofmann School; Atelier Fernand Leger, Paris. US Army, 1943–46. **Taught:** St. Paul School of Art, 1942–43. **Awards:** Longview Foundation Grant, 1961; Marie Hofmann Grant, 1963; National Council on the Arts, $5,000, 1967.

Address: 1510 English Street, St. Paul, MI 55106. **One-man Exhibitions:** (first) Hansa Gallery, NYC, 1952, also 1953, 56, 57; Leo Castelli Inc., NYC, 1960. **Group:** The Stable Gallery Annual, NYC, 1957; Houston/MFA, 1957; Cornell U., 1958; Carnegie, 1958; MOMA, Recent Sculpture USA, 1959; Claude Bernard, Paris, 1960; Martha Jackson Gallery, New Media—New Forms, 1, 1960; WMAA Annual, 1961. **Collections:** Houston/MFA; MIT; MOMA; WMAA. **Bibliography:** Kaprow; Rose B., 1; Sandler; Seitz 3.

FORAKIS, PETER. b. October 2, 1927, Hanna, Wyo. **Studied:** San Francisco Art Institute, with Bud Dixon, Thomas Hardy, Nathan Oliveira, 1954–57, BA. US Army, 1951–53. Traveled Japan, Philippines, and Pacific Islands. **Taught:** San Francisco Art Institute, 1958; Brooklyn Museum School, 1961–63; The Pennsylvania State U., 1965; Carnegie, 1965; U. of Rhode Island, 1966; Windham College, 1968–74. **Commissions:** Mural for a motion-picture theater, San Francisco, 1956; North Jersey Culture Council, Paramus; Great Southwest Industrial Park. **Awards:** National Endowment for the Arts, 1972. Editor, publisher, *Grope* magazine, 1964–66. **Address:** RFD 1, Box 5, Putney, VT 09346. **Dealer:** Paula Cooper Gallery. **One-man Exhibitions:** (first) Gallery Six, San Francisco, 1955, also 1956, 58; Spasta Gallery, San Francisco, 1959; David Anderson Gallery, NYC, 1961 (two-man); Tibor de Nagy Gallery, 1962, 64; Park Place Gallery, NYC, 1966; Windham College, 1967; Paula Cooper Gallery, 1968, 70; Sunne Savage Gallery, Boston, 1977; Sculpture Now, Inc., NYC, 1978. **Group:** Uiano Museum, Tokyo, 1952, 53; SFMA, 1955–58; Oakland/AM, 1957; Martha Jackson Gallery, New Media—New Forms, 1, 1960; SRGM, Drawings and Prints, 1964; Jewish Museum, Primary Structure Sculptures, 1966; Los Angeles/County MA, American Sculpture of the Sixties, circ., 1967; Milwaukee,

Directions I:Options, circ., 1968; Indianapolis, 1970; Storm King Art Center, Sculpture 1973, 1973; U. of Vermont, Vermont '73, 1973; Hirshhorn, Inaugural Exhibition, 1974. **Collections:** Bergen Community College; Buffalo/SUNY; Hirshhorn; U. of Houston; Northwood Institute; Ridgefield/Aldrich.

FORST, MILES. b. August 18, 1923, Brooklyn, N.Y. **Studied:** New School for Social Research; Veterans Art Center, MOMA, with Mervin Jules; ASL, with Morris Kantor; Hofmann School, NYC. Traveled Europe, Mexico, Nova Scotia. **Taught:** Assistant to Hans Hofmann at his school, 1952–53; Great Neck (N.Y.) Adult Education Program, 1958–60; School of Visual Arts, NYC, 1964–71; U. of California, Davis, 1965–66; Brooklyn Museum School, 1966–69; U. of California, San Francisco, 1971–72; Otis Art Institute, 1971–75. **Awards:** Laurian Fund Award, 1954; Walter K. Gutman Foundation Grant, 1960, 62, 65; Longview Foundation Grant, 1961, 62; Ford Foundation Fellowship, 1965; MacDowell Colony Fellowship, 1965, 67. **Address:** 14 Westminster Avenue, Venice, CA 90291. **One-man Exhibitions:** (first) Hansa Gallery, NYC, 1953, also 1954, 55, 58; Wittenborn Gallery, NYC, 1955; The Drawing Shop, NYC, 1964; Goldowsky Gallery, 1964. **Group:** Chicago/AI, 1953; SRGM, 1954; A.F.A., Collage in America, circ., 1957–58; Cornell U., 1958; Carnegie, 1959; A.F.A., The Figure, circ., 1960; Green Gallery, NYC, 1961, 62; MOMA, Hans Hofmann and His Students, circ., 1963–64; Hartford/Wadsworth, 1964; U. of Illinois; Gallery of Modern Art, NYC, 1965; 112 Greene Street, NYC, 1974; Otis Art Institute, 1975. **Collections:** Allentown/AM; Bowdoin College; Charlotte/Mint; Dillard U.; Hartford/Wadsworth; MIT; Newark Museum; Newport/Chrysler; Tulane U. **Bibliography:** Sandler 1.

FORTRESS, KARL E. b. October 13, 1907, Antwerp, Belgium. **Studied:** Chicago Art Institute School; ASL; Woodstock School of Painting, with Yasuo Kuniyoshi. US citizen, 1923. Traveled Europe. **Taught:** ASL; Brooklyn Museum School; Louisiana State U.; American Art School, NYC; Boston U. Federal A.P.: Artists Equity; SAGA. **Awards:** Woodstock Artists Association, E. Keith Memorial Award, 1935; Carnegie, First Hon. Men., 1941; Guggenheim Foundation Fellowship, 1946; AAAL, Childe Hassam Award, 1952; NAD, Salmagundi Club Prize, 1973; NAD, Obrig Award, 1978. **Address:** 311 Plochmann Lane, Woodstock, NY 12498. **Dealer:** A.A.A. Gallery, NYC; Bluestone Gallery, Woodstock, N.Y. **One-man Exhibitions:** Boris Mirski Gallery, Boston; A.A.A. Gallery, NYC, 1948, 51; Ganso Gallery, NYC; Vose Gallery, Boston; Sawkill Gallery, Woodstock, N.Y.; Bucknell U.; Louisiana State U.; U. of Georgia; The Krasner Gallery. **Retrospective:** A.A.A. Gallery, NYC, 1973. **Group:** NIAL; Chicago/AI; Carnegie; U. of Illinois; Boston Arts Festival; Corcoran; MOMA; NAD; PAFA; WMAA. **Collections:** U. of Arizona; Brandeis U.; Brooklyn Museum; Colby College; Cornell U.; Lincoln, Mass./De Cordova; MOMA; U. of Massachusetts; U. of Miami; Montpelier/Wood; New Britain/American; Newark Museum; U. of North Carolina; The Ohio State U.; Roanoke; U. of Rochester; St. Joseph/Albright; Smith College; Syracuse U.; Utica; U. of Washington; Youngstown/Butler. **Bibliography:** Cheney; Pearson 2; *Woodstock*; Zaidenberg, ed.

FOULKES, LLYN. b. November 17, 1934, Yakima, Wash. **Studied:** Central Washington College, 1953; U. of Washington, 1952–54; Chouinard Art Institute, 1957–59, with Richards Ruben, Emerson Woelffer, Don Graham. US Army, Germany, 1955–56. Traveled Europe, North Africa, USA. **Taught:** UCLA, 1965–71; Art Center School, Los Angeles, 1971–74. **Awards:** Chouinard Art Institute, First Prize, 1959; SFMA, First Prize, 1963; V Paris Biennial, First

Prize, 1967. **Address:** 6010 Eucalyptus Lane, Los Angeles, CA 90042. **Dealers:** David Stuart Gallery; Gruenebaum Gallery; Darthea Speyer Gallery. **One-man Exhibitions:** (first) Ferus Gallery, Los Angeles, 1961; Pasadena/AM, 1962, 67 (four-man); Rolf Nelson Gallery, Los Angeles, 1963–65; Oakland/AM, 1964; Robert Fraser Gallery, 1966 (four-man); David Stuart Gallery, 1969, 74; Darthea Speyer Gallery, 1970, 75; The Willard Gallery, 1975; Gruenebaum Gallery, NYC, 1977; Chicago/Contemporary, 1978. **Retrospective:** Newport Harbor, 1974. **Group:** Los Angeles/County MA Annuals, 1960, 61, 63; Pomona College, Object Makers, 1961; SFMA, West Coast Artists, circ., 1961; SFMA, Directions—Painting U.S.A., 1963; Pasadena/AM, Directors Choice, 1964; Sao Paulo, 1964; New York World's Fair, 1964–65; SRGM, 1966; V Paris Biennial, 1967; WMAA Annuals, 1967, 69, 71, 74; IX Sao Paulo Biennial, 1967; Brandeis U., 1968; Foundation Maeght, 1968; Los Angeles/County MA, 5 Los Angeles Artists, 1968; VMFA, American Painting, 1970; ICA, U. of Pennsylvania, The Topography of Nature: The Microcosm and Macrocosm, 1972; Los Angeles Municipal Art Gallery, Separate Realities, 1973; Chicago/AI, 71st American Exhibition, 1974; Corcoran Biennial, 1975. **Collections:** Chicago/AI; La Jolla; Los Angeles/County MA; MOMA; Museum des 20. Jahrhunderts; Oakland/AM; Pasadena/MA; Rotterdam; Stanford U.; UCLA; WMAA. **Bibliography:** *New in the Seventies*; Weller.

FRANCIS, SAM. b. June 25, 1923, San Mateo, Calif. **Studied:** U. of California, Berkeley, 1941–43; 1949, BA; 1950, MA; Atelier Fernand Leger, Paris. US Air Force, 1943–45. Began painting under the encouragement of David Park while hospitalized in 1945. Traveled Europe, Japan, USA; resided and worked in Paris, 1950–57. **Commissions** (murals): Kunsthalle, Berne, 1957; Sofu School of Flower Arrangement, Tokyo, 1957; Chase Manhattan Bank, NYC, 1959. **Awards:** III International Biennial Exhibition of Prints, Tokyo, First Prize, 1963; Hon. DFA, U. of California, 1969. **Address:** 345 West Channel Road, Santa Monica, Calif. **Dealers:** Pierre Matisse Gallery; Minami Gallery; Andre Emmerich Gallery, NYC; Brooke Alexander, NYC. **One-man Exhibitions:** (first) Galerie Nina Dausset, Paris, 1952; Galerie du Dragon, 1952; Galerie Rive Droite, Paris, 1955, 56; Martha Jackson Gallery, 1956, 58, 63, 64, 68, 70; Gimpel Fils Ltd., 1957; Klipstein & Kornfeld, Berne, 1957, 61, 66, 68, 73, 76; Zoe Dusanne Gallery, Seattle, 1957; Tokyo Department Store Gallery, 1957; Kintetsu Department Store Gallery, Osaka, 1957; Phillips, 1958; Seattle/AM, 1959; SFMA, 1959, 67; Esther Baer Gallery, 1962, 63; Galerie Engelberts, Geneva, 1962; Galerie Pauli, Lausanne, 1962; A. Tooth & Sons, London, 1965; Pierre Matisse Gallery, 1967; Houston/MFA, 1967; U. of California, 1967; Kunstverein, Basel, 1968; Galerie Gunther Franke, Munich, 1968; CNAC, 1968; Shasta College, 1969; Minami Gallery, 1969, 74; Andre Emmerich Gallery, 1969, 70, 71, 72, 73, 74, 75, 76, 78; Felix Landau Gallery, 1970; Los Angeles/County MA, 1970; Nicholas Wilder Gallery, 1970, 71, 73, 75, 78; Pace Editions, NYC, 1973; Galerie Fournier, Paris, 1973–75, 76, 78; Margo Leavin Gallery, 1974; Jack Glenn Gallery, San Diego, 1975; Minami Gallery, Tokyo, 1961, 64, 66, 68, 70, 74, 77, 78; Smith-Anderson Gallery, Palo Alto, 1972, 73, 76, 78; Smith-Anderson Gallery, San Francisco, 1975; Richard Gray Gallery, Chicago, 1975; Kornfeld and Klipstein, Zurich, 1975; Humlebaek/Louisiana, 1977; Otis Art Institute, 1978; Paris/Beaubourg, 1978; Honolulu, 1977. **Retrospectives:** Berne, 1960; Hannover/K-G, 1963; Amsterdam/Stedelijk, 1968; CNAC, 1969; Buffalo/Albright, circ., 1972. **Group:** Salon du Mai, Paris, 1950; Studio Paul Facchetti, Signifiants de l'Informal, 1952; Studio Paul Facchetti, Un Art Autre, 1953; ICA, London, Opposing Forces, 1953; Berne, Tendances Actuelles, 1955; Carnegie, 1955; MOMA, Twelve Americans, circ., 1956; International Biennial Exhibition of Paintings, Tokyo; Arts Council Gallery, London, New Trends in Painting, 1957; Brussels World's Fair, 1958; MOMA, The New American Painting, circ., Europe, 1958–59; American Cultural Center, Paris, 3 Americans, 1958; Brooklyn Museum, 1959; Sao Paulo, 1959; III International Biennial Exhibition of Prints, Tokyo, 1962; Chicago/AI, 1962; Musée Cantonal des Beaux-Arts, Lausanne, I Salon International de Galeries Pilotes, 1963; Tate, Dunn International, 1964; Gulbenkian International, 1964; Flint/Institute, The Coming of Color, 1964; WMAA Annuals, 1964, 65; Toronto, 1964; SRGM, American Drawings, 1964; Los Angeles/County MA, Post Painterly Abstraction, 1964; U. of Arkansas, 1965; Dayton/AI, 1966; Tokyo/Modern, 1966; II Internationale der Zeichnung, Darmstadt, 1967; Kunsthalle, Cologne, 1968; Carnegie, 1970; Buffalo/Albright, Color and Field, 1890–1970, 1970; Foundation Maeght, L'Art Vivant, 1970; VMFA, American Painting, 1970; Indianapolis, 1970; Chicago/AI Annual, 1970; Wilmington, 1970; Corcoran Biennial, 1971; Chicago/Contemporary, White on White, 1971–72; Toledo/MA, The Fresh Air School, 1973; Buffalo/Albright, Abstract Expressionism: The First and Second Generations, 1972; U. of Illinois, Contemporary American Painting and Sculpture, 1974; Santa Barbara/MA; 15 Abstract Artists, 1974; U. of California, Riverside, A View of Lithography in Los Angeles, 1975; SFMA, Painting and Sculpture in California: The Modern Era, 1977. **Collections:** Amsterdam/Stedelijk; Berlin/National; Berne; Buffalo/Albright; U. of California; Carnegie; Dallas/MFA; Dayton/AI; Dusseldorf/KN-W; Eindhoven; Essen; Fort Worth; Hamburg; Hannover/K-G; Hirshhorn; Humlebaek/Louisiana; Idemitsu Museum; Los Angeles/County MA; MOMA; Montreal/MFA; NCFA; National Gallery; National Museum of Western Art, Tokyo; OBD/Basel; Ohara Art Museum; Paris/Beaubourg; Paris/Moderne; Pasadena/AM; Phillips; SFMA; SRGM; St. Louis; Seat-tle/AM; Sofu School of Flower Arrangement; Stockholm/National; Stuttgart; Tate; Toronto; WMAA; Washington U.; Yale U.; Zurich. **Bibliography:** Blesh 1; Haftman; Honisch and Jensen, eds.; Hunter 1; Hunter, ed.; Langui; Lippard 5; Lynton; McCurdy, ed.; *Metro*; Nordness, ed.; Ponente; Read 2; *Report*; Restany 2; Rickey; Rose, B., 1; **Sam Francis**; Sandler 1; Schneider; Seuphor 1; *The State of California Painting*; **Sweeney 3**; Tapie 1; Weller. Archives.

FRANK, MARY. b. February 4, 1933, London, England. **Studied:** NYC, with Max Beckmann, 1950; Hans Hofmann, 1951. Traveled Spain, France, England. **Taught:** New School for Social Research, 1970–75; Queens College, 1970–75; Skowhegan School, 1976. **Awards:** Ingram Merrill Foundation Grant, 1962; Longview Foundation Grant, 1964–66; National Council on the Arts, 1969; Guggenheim Foundation Fellowship, 1973; CAPS, 1973. **Address:** 139 West 19th Street, NYC 10003. **Dealers:** The Zabriskie Gallery; Donald Morris Gallery; Richard Gray Gallery. **One-man Exhibitions:** (first) Stephen Radich Gallery, 1961, also 1963, 66; Boris Mirski Gallery, Boston, 1964, 66; The Drawing Shop, NYC; Bennett College, 1966; The Zabriskie Gallery, 1968, 70, 71, 73, 75, 77, 78, 79; Donald Morris Gallery, 1968; Richard Gray Gallery, 1969; U. of Connecticut, 1975; Harcus Krakow Gallery, Boston, 1976; Connecticut College, 1976; Arts Club, Chicago, 1976; Hobart College 1976; Alice Simsar Gallery, Ann Arbor, 1976; U. of Bridgeport, 1976. **Retrospectives:** Purchase/SUNY, 1978. **Group:** MIT; Yale U.; Brandeis U.; MOMA, Hans Hofmann and His Students, circ., 1963–64; SRGM, 10 Independents, 1972; GEDOK, Hamburg, American Woman Artist Show, 1972; WMAA Annuals, 1972, 73; PMA/Museum of the Philadelphia Civic Center, Focus, 1974. New York Cultural Center, Three Centuries of the American Nude, 1975; Philadelphia College of Art, Private Notation; Artists' Sketchbooks, 1976; Brooklyn Museum, Contemporary Women, 1977; Chicago/AI, 1977; PMA, Eight Artists, 1978; Albright College, Perspective 78, 1978; WMAA Biennial, 1979. **Collections:** Akron/AI; Brandeis U.; Brown U.; Chicago/AI; Bank of Chicago; Hirshhorn; Kalamazoo/Institute; MOMA; U. of Massachusetts; U. of New Mexico; U. of North Carolina; Southern Illinois U.; WMAA; Wichita/AM; Worcester/AM; Yale U. **Bibliography:** *Woodstock: An American Art Colony, 1902–1977.*

FRANKENTHALER, HELEN. b. December 12, 1928, NYC. **Studied:** Dalton School, NYC, with Rufino Tamayo; Bennington College; with Paul Feeley, 1945–49, BA; ASL; with Vaclav Vytlacil, 1946; with Wallace Harrison, NYC, 1948; with Hans Hofmann, 1950. Traveled Europe extensively. **Taught:** NYU, 1958; U. of Pennsylvania, 1958; Yale U., 1967, 70; School of Visual Arts, NYC, 1967; Hunter College, 1970; U. of Rochester, 1971; Bennington College, 1972; Brooklyn Museum School, 1973; Swarthmore College, 1974; Drew U., 1975. **Member:** NIAL, 1974. Trustee, Bennington College, 1967– ; Fellow, Calhoun College, Yale U., 1968. Member of the Corporation of Yaddo, 1974. Designed and executed set for *Of Love* for Erick Hawkins Dance Company, 1971. **Commissions:** Temple of Aaron, St. Paul (ark curtain tapestry); First Wisconsin National Bank, Milwaukee, 1973; North Central Bronx Hospital (mural), 1973–74; The Fourth National Bank, Wichita (tapestry), 1974. **Awards:** I Paris Biennial, First Prize, 1959; PAFA; Joseph E. Temple Gold Medal, 1968; Honorary Doctor of Humane Letters, Skidmore College, 1969; Albert Einstein College, Spirit of Achievement Award, 1970; Chicago/AI, Ada S. Garrett Prize, 1972; III Biennale della Grafica d'Arte, Florence, Italy, Gold Medal, 1972; Hon. DFA, Smith College, 1973; Hon. DFA, Moore College of Art, Philadelphia, 1974; Creative

Arts Award, American Jewish Congress, National Women's Division, 1974; Hon. DFA, Bard College, 1976; Hon. Ph.D., Radcliffe College 1978; Hon. Ph.D., Amherst College, 1979; Hon. DFA, NYU, 1979. Subject of the film *Frankenthaler: Toward a New Climate,* 1978, produced and directed by Perry Miller Adato. **Address:** 173 East 94th Street, NYC 10028. **Dealer:** Andre Emmerich Gallery, NYC. **One-man Exhibitions:** (first) Tibor de Nagy Gallery, 1951, also 1952–58; Andre Emmerich Gallery, NYC, 1959–63, 1965, 66, 68, 69, 71, 72, 73, 77, 78, 79; Jewish Museum, 1960; Everett Ellin Gallery, Los Angeles, 1961; Bennington College, 1962, 78; Galerie Lawrence, Paris, 1961, 63; Galleria dell'Ariete, 1962; Kasmin, Ltd., 1964; David Mirvish Gallery, 1965, 71, 73, 75; St. John, N.B., 1966 (three-man, with Kenneth Noland, Jules Olitski); Gertrude Kasle Gallery, 1967; Nicholas Wilder Gallery, 1967; Heath Gallery, Atlanta, 1971; Fendrick Gallery 1972, 74; Portland, Ore./AM, 1972; Waddington Galleries, London, 1973, 74; Janie C. Lee Gallery, Dallas, 1973; MMA, 1973; Swarthmore College, 1974; Corcoran, 1975; SRGM, 1975; John Berggruen Gallery, San Francisco, 1976, 79; Fendrick Gallery, Washington, D.C., 1974, 79; Janie C. Lee Gallery, Houston, 1975, 76, 78; SRGM, 1975; ACE Gallery, Vancouver, 1975; Rosa Esman Gallery, NYC, 1975; Diane Gilson Gallery, Seattle, 1976; Greenberg Gallery, St. Louis, 1977; Galerie Wentzel, Hamburg, 1977; Knoedler Gallery, London, 1978; Jacksonville, Fla., 1978; Kansas City/Nelson, 1978. **Retrospective:** WMAA, 1969; John Berggruen Gallery (prints) 1972; Corcoran, circ., 1975; International Communications Agency (World Tour), 1978. **Group:** The Kootz Gallery, NYC, New Talent, 1951; Ninth Street Exhibition, NYC, 1951; WMAA Annuals, 1955, 58, 61, 63, 67, 69, 70, 71, 72, 73, Young America, 1957, Nature in Abstraction, 1958, The Structure of Color, 1971; Carnegie, 1955, 58, 61; Sao Paulo, 1958; International Biennial Exhibition of Paintings, Tokyo; Documenta II, Kassel, 1959; U. of Illinois, 1959, 63, 65, 67; SRGM, Abstract Expressionists and Imagists, 1961; Chicago/AI, 1961, 63; Seattle World's Fair, 1962; PAFA Annuals, 1963, 66, 68; Los Angeles/County MA, Post Painterly Abstraction, 1964; New York World's Fair, 1964–65; U. of Michigan, 1965; Detroit/Institute, 1965, Color, Image and Form, 1967; ICA, Boston, Painting without a Brush, 1965; XXXIII Venice Biennial, 1966; Public Education Association, NYC, 1966; Expo '67, Montreal, 1967; Corcoran Biennial, 1967; MOMA, Two Decades of American Painting, circ., Japan, India, Australia, 1967; U. of Oklahoma, East Coast—West Coast Paintings, 1968; SFMA, Untitled 1968, 1968; Washington U., The Development of Modernist Painting, 1969; MMA, New York Painting and Sculpture, 1940–1970, 1969–70, Prints by Four New York Painters, 1969; Baltimore/MA, Washington Art: 1950–1970, 1970; Boston U., American Artists of the Nineteen Sixties, 1970; Foundation Maeght, L'Art Vivant, 1970; Buffalo/Albright, Color and Field: 1890–1970, 1970; ICA, U. of Pennsylvania, Two Generations of Color Painting, 1970; Boston/MFA, Abstract Painting in the '70s, 1972; Lakeview Center, American Women: 20th Century, 1972; Museum of Fine Arts, St. Petersburg, Flowing Form, 1973; Houston/MFA, The Great Decade of American Abstraction: Modernist Art 1960–1970, 1974; A.A.A. Gallery, One Hundred Prints, 1975; Wesleyan U., Middletown, Recent American Etching, 1975; Syracuse/Everson, New Work in Clay, 1976; PAFA, In This Academy, 1805–1976, 1976; Baltimore/MA, 200 Years of American Painting, 1976; Brooklyn Museum, 30 Years of American Printmaking, 1977; Syracuse/Everson, New Works in Clay, 1976; Chicago/AI, Drawings of the 70's, 1977; Syracuse/Everson, Provincetown Painters, 1977; Perth, Contemporary Drawing, 1977; Grand Rapids, Two Centuries of American Art, 1977; Buffalo/Albright, American Painting of the 70s,

1978; U. of Tampa, Two Decades of American Abstraction, 1979; MMA, Hans Hofmann as Teacher, 1979; Montgomery/Museum, Art, Inc., 1979; Syracuse/Everson, A Century of Ceramics in the U.S., 1979. **Collections:** Auckland; Baltimore/MA; Belfast/Ulster; Bennington College; Boston/MFA; Brooklyn Museum; Buffalo/Albright; U. of California, Carnegie; Canberra/National; Chicago/AI; Cincinnati/AM; Cleveland/MA; Cologne; Columbia U.; Columbus; Corcoran; Detroit/Institute; Fort Worth; Hartford/Wadsworth; Harvard U.; High Museum; Hirshhorn; Honolulu Academy; Houston/Contemporary; Houston/MFA; Jerusalem/National; Johannesburg/Municipal; Kansas City/Nelson; Louisville/Speed; MMA; MOMA; Mexico City/Nacional; Melbourne/National; Milwaukee; NCFA; NYU; Nagaoka, Tokyo; U. of Nebraska; Newark Museum; Omaha/Joslyn; Paris/Beaubourg; Pasadena/MA; Phoenix; PMA; Purchase/SUNY; RISD; San Antonio/McNay; Seattle/AM; SFMA; SRGM; St. Louis/City; Smithsonian; U. of Sydney; Syracuse/Everson; U. of Texas; Ulster Museum; Victoria and Albert Museum; Vienna/Stadt; WGMA; WMAA; Walker; Wichita/AM; U. of Wisconsin; Yale U. **Bibliography:** Alloway 4; Battcock, ed.; Baur 5; Friedman, ed.; Goodrich and Baur 1; Goossen 3; *The Great Decade;* Hunter 1, 6; Honisch and Jensen, eds.; Hunter, ed.; Janis and Blesh 1; Kozloff 3; *Metro;* O'Hara 1; **Rose, B.,** 1, 3; Sandler 1; Archives.

FRASCONI, ANTONIO. b. April 28, 1919, Montevideo, Uruguay. **Studied:** Circulo de Bellas Artes, Montevideo; ASL, 1946 with Yasuo Kuniyoshi; New School for Social Research, 1947, with Camilio Egas. To USA, 1945. **Taught:** New School for Social Research, 1951–52; Brooklyn Museum School; Pratt Institute; Vassar College; Atlanta Art Institute; Purchase/SUNY, 1973– . **Member:** SAGA; Educational Film Library. **Awards:** Guggenheim Foundation Fellowship, 1952; NIAL Grant, 1954; Venice International Film Festival, 1960, Grand Prix for *The Neighboring Shore* (15 minutes, more than 300 woodcuts); US Post Office Department, Design Competition, 1963; Connecticut State Commission on the Arts, 1974; IX International Biennial Exhibition of Prints, Tokyo; NAD, Cannon Prize, 1979. **Address:** 26 Dock Road, South Norwalk, CT 06854. **Dealers:** Terry Dintenfass, Inc.; Weyhe Gallery. **One-man Exhibitions:** Ateneo Gallery, Montevideo, 1939; Montevideo YMCA, 1940; Agrupacion Intelectual, Montevideo, 1944; Brooklyn Museum, 1946; San Jose State College, 1946; Pasadena/AM, 1946; Santa Barbara/MA, 1946, 50, 51, 55, 77; New School for Social Research, 1947; Philadelphia Art Alliance, 1948; Weyhe Gallery, 1948–54, 1956, 60; Pan-American Union, Washington, D.C., 1949; Utica, 1949; San Diego, 1950; SFMA, 1950, 75; Princeton Print Club, 1950, 52; Art Association, Madison, Wisc., 1951; Prang Institute, NYC, 1951; U. of Delaware, 1951; Bennington College, 1952; Louisville/Speed, 1953; Detroit/Institute, 1953; Los Angeles/County MA, 1953; Currier, 1955; Chattanooga/AA, 1955; Fort Worth, 1955; Wesleyan U., 1956; U. of Maine, 1956; Scripps College, 1958; Berea College, 1958; Collectors Art Center, Tallahassee, 1958; Atlanta/AA, 1959; Carnegie, 1959; San Antonio/McNay, 1959; Terry Dintenfass, Inc., 1962, 63, 64, 66, 69, 71, 76, 79; The Print Club, Philadelphia, 1963; The Pennsylvania State U., 1963; Ankrum Gallery, 1963; Esther Baer Gallery, 1967, 75; Bridgeport, 1967; Lincoln, Mass./De Cordova, 1967; Haslem Fine Arts, Washington, D.C., 1976. **Retrospective:** Cleveland/MA, 1952; Smithsonian, circ., 1953–55; Montevideo/Municipal, 1961; Baltimore/MA, 1963; Brooklyn Museum, 1964; Missouri State Council of the Arts, circ., 1976; Musedel Grabado, San Juan, Obra Grafica 1943–1975, 1976. **Group:** Brooklyn Museum; Corcoran; Boston/MFA; Detroit/Institute; Hartford/Wadsworth; PAFA; Newark Museum; MOMA; Carnegie; St. Louis/City; San Diego; Baltimore/MA; New School for Social Research, Protest and Hope, 1967; XXXIV Venice Biennial, 1968; Intergraphic 76, Berlin, 1976; Smithsonian, American Prints from Wood, circ., 1976; York U., Toronto, Spain 1936–1976, 1976; Purchase/SUNY, Americans, 1977. **Collections:** Akron/AI; Albion College; Allegheny College; Alverthorpe Gallery, U. of Arizona; Arts Council of Great Britain; Atlanta/AA; Baltimore/MA; Boston/MFA; Boston Public Library; Brandeis U.; Brooklyn Museum; U. of California, Berkeley; Carnegie; La Casa del Libro; Chicago/AI; Cincinnati/AM, Cleveland/MA; Dartmouth College; U. of Delaware; Des Moines; Detroit/Institute; Fort Worth; Genesco/SUNY; Georgia State U.; Grand Rapids; Hamilton College; Hartford/Wadsworth; Harvard U.; Honolulu Academy; Hunter College; State College of Iowa; Kalamazoo/Institute; U. of Kentucky; Lawrence College; Library of Congress; Louisville/Speed; MMA; MOMA; U. of Maine; Memphis/Brooks; U. of Michigan; U. of Minnesota; Minnesota/MA; Montclair/AM; Montevideo/Municipal; NYPL; Newark Museum; New Britain; New Paltz/SUNY; U. of Notre Dame; Omaha/Joslyn; PAFA; PMA; The Pennsylvania State U.; Princeton U.; RISD; U. of Rochester; Rutgers U.; St. Louis/City; San Diego; Santa Barbara/MA; Seattle/AM; Smith College; Smithsonian; Springfield, Mo./AM; Uruguay/Nacional; Utica; Wake Forest U.; Washington U.; Wesleyan U.; College of William and Mary; Williams College; U. of Wisconsin. **Bibliography: Frasconi; Sachs. Archives.**

FRECKELTON, SONDRA. b. June 23, 1936, Dearborn, Mich. **Studied:** U. of Chicago; School of the Art Institute of Chicago. **Taught:** Downtown Community School, NYC, 1960–63; Cooper Union, 1966. **Awards:** Ingram Merrill Foundation Grant, 1960; Michigan Artists Show, Prize, 1965; 6th British Inter-

Sondra Freckleton *Harvest* 1978

action Print Biennial, prize, 1979. **m.** Jack Beal. **Address:** 83A Delhi Stage, Oneonta, NY 13820; and 67 Vestry Street, NYC 10013. **Dealer:** Brooke Alexander, Inc., NYC. **One-man Exhibitions:** (first) Tibor de Nagy, NYC, 1960, 61, 63; B.C. Holland Gallery, Chicago, 1965; LoGuidice Gallery, Chicago, 1970; Brooke Alexander, Inc., NYC, 1976, 79, 80; Allan Frumkin Gallery, Chicago, 1978; Fendrick Gallery, Washington, D.C., 1980. **Group:** MOMA, Recent Sculpture USA, 1959; Chicago/AI, American Exhibition, 1962, 65; WMAA, Annual, 1964; A.F.A., Colored Sculpture, circ., 1965; Chicago/AI, 100 Artists—100 Years, 1976; Brooklyn Museum, Print Exhibition, 1978; Bradford Art Gallery, England, print biennial, 1979. **Collections:** Amerada Hess Corp., Inc.; Best Products Co.; Madison Art Center; Prudential Insurance Co. of America; Reader's Digest; Sara Roby Foundation; Southeast Banking Corp.; Springfield Mo./AM. **Bibliography:** Arthur 2.

FREILICHER, JANE. b. November 19, 1924, NYC. **Studied:** Brooklyn College, BA; Columbia U., MA; Hofmann School. Traveled Europe, Morocco. **Taught:** Great Neck (N.Y.) Adult Education Program; New Jersey public schools; U. of Pennsylvania, 1968; Skowhegan School, 1968; Boston U., 1968; Swarthmore College, 1969; Carnegie-Mellon Institute, 1971; Cooper Union, 1972; Louisiana State U., 1973; Galveston Arts Center, 1973; Maryland Institute, 1973. Brandeis U., 1979; American U., 1979. Designed set for *Red Robins,* by Kenneth Koch. **Awards:** Hallmark International Competition, 1960; *Art News* magazine, 10 Best Shows of 1962; National Endowment for the Arts, 1976. **Address:** 51 Fifth Avenue, NYC 10003. **Dealer:** Fischbach

Gallery. **One-man Exhibitions:** (first) Tibor de Nagy Gallery, 1952, also 1953–64, 70; John Bernard Myers Gallery, NYC, 1971; Benson Gallery, 1972, 74; Fischbach Gallery, 1975, 77, 79; Hartford/Wadsworth, 1976; Utah, 1979. **Group:** RISD, Four Young Americans, 1955; MOMA, Recent Drawings, USA, 1956; WMAA Annual, 1958; PAFA, 1961; U. of Nebraska, 1963; MOMA, Hans Hofmann and His Students, circ., 1963–64; Chicago/AI; Brooklyn Museum; Yale U.; Corcoran; A.F.A., 1965; MOMA, 1966; A.F.A., Painterly Realism, 1970; Omaha/Joslyn, A Sense of Place, 1973; PMA/Museum of the Philadelphia Civic Center, Focus, 1974; AAAL, 1975; US Department of the Interior, America 1976, 1976; U. of Missouri, American Painterly Realists, 1977; Westmoreland County/MA, The New American Still Life, 1979; Denver/AM, Poets and Painters, 1979. **Collections:** AT&T; Brandeis U.; Brooklyn Museum; Chase Manhattan Bank; Commerce Bank of Kansas City; Greenville; Hampton Institute; Lehman Brothers; MOMA; NYU; U. of North Carolina; Prudential Insurance Co. of America; RISD; Southampton/Parrish; Stratford College; Union Carbide Corp.; Utah; U. of Utah; WMAA. **Bibliography:** *America 1976; Art: A Woman's Sensibility;* Arthur 1; Arthur 2; Downes, ed.; *Poets & Painters;* Sandler 1.

FRENCH, JARED. b. February 4, 1905, Ossining, N.Y. **Studied:** ASL, with Thomas Hart Benton, Boardman Robinson, Kimon Nicolaides; Amherst College, 1925, BA, with Robert Frost. Traveled Europe, 1927–28, 31–33; northern USA. Federal A.P.: US Post Offices, Richmond, Va., and Plymouth, Pa., 1935–39 (murals). Designed costumes and sets for the ballet *Billy the Kid.* **Awards:** NIAL Grant, 1967. **Address:** Hartland, VT 05048. **One-man Exhibitions:** (first) Julien Levy Galleries, NYC, 1939; Hewitt Gallery, NYC, 1950; Robert Isaacson Gallery, NYC; The Banfer Gallery, 1967. **Retrospective:**

The Banfer Gallery, 1969. **Group:** Arts Club of Chicago; PAFA; WMAA; Chicago/AI; Carnegie; NAD; Walker; U. of Rochester, 1964–65; Youngstown/Butler, 1967. **Collections:** Baltimore/MA; Baseball Museum; Dartmouth College; WMAA. **Bibliography:** Baur 7; Goodrich and Baur 1.

FRIEDENSOHN, ELIAS. b. December 12, 1924, NYC. **Studied:** Stella Elkins Tyler School of Fine Arts, Temple U., 1942–43, with Rafael Sabatini; Queens College, with Cameron Booth, 1946–48, AB; NYU, Institute of Fine Arts, 1949–50; privately with Gabriel Zendel in Paris. Traveled Europe and Tunisia. **Taught:** Queens College, 1959– ; Kirkland College, 1970–71. **Member:** College Art Association. **Awards:** Joe and Emily Lowe Foundation Award, 1951; Fulbright Fellowship (Italy), 1957; U. of Illinois, **P.P.,** 1957; National Arts Club Annual, NYC, Stephens Award, 1958; Guggenheim Foundation Fellowship, 1960; MacDowell Colony Fellowship, 1969, 70; AAAL, **P.P.** 1972. **Address:** 209 Hillcrest Avenue, Leonia, NJ 07605. **Dealer:** Terry Dintenfass, Inc. **One-man Exhibitions:** (first) Roko Gallery, NYC, 1951; Hewitt Gallery, NYC, 1955, 57, 59; Vassar College, 1958; Robert Isaacson Gallery, NYC, 1960; Feingarten Gallery, NYC, San Francisco, Los Angeles and Chicago, 1961, 62; Feingarten Gallery, Los Angeles, 1964; The Contemporaries, NYC, 1964; Terry Dintenfass, Inc., 1967, 70, 74, 76, 80; Kirkland College, 1972; Moravian College, 1977; Jersey City State College, 1978. **Group:** Audubon Artists Annual 1957; WMAA, Young America, 1957, Fulbright Artists, 1958, Annuals, 1958, 59, 60, 62; Chicago/AI Annuals, 1957, 59; U. of Illinois, 1957, 59, 61, 63; National Arts Club Annual, NYC, 1958; Galleria Schneider, Rome, Fulbright Artists, 1958; Festival of Two Worlds, Spoleto, 1958; Corcoran Annuals, 1960, 62; Denver/AM, 1962; Smithsonian; Buffalo/Albright; Philadelphia Art Alliance; Syracuse U.; U. of Wisconsin;

PAFA Annual, 1967; New School for Social Research, 1969; Minnesota/MA, Drawings USA, 1971, 73; NAD, 1971; VMFA, Works on Paper, 1974. **Collections:** Chicago/AI; Hampton Institute; U. of Illinois; Huntington, N.Y./Heckscher; Indianapolis; Kalamazoo/Institute; Kirkland College; Little Rock/MFA; The Joe and Emily Lowe Foundation; U. of Massachusetts; U. of Oklahoma; Queens College; St. Mary's College, Md.; Sara Roby Foundation; WMAA; Walker. **Bibliography:** Weller.

FULLER, SUE. b. August 11, 1914, Pittsburgh, Pa. **Studied:** with Hans Hofmann, 1934; with S. W. Hayter, 1943–44; privately with Josef Albers, T. Tokuno; Carnegie Institute of Technology, 1936, BA; Teachers College, Columbia U., 1939, MA. Traveled Europe, Africa, Japan. **Taught:** U. of Minnesota, 1950; Stourbridge (England) School of Arts and Crafts, 1951; U. of Georgia, 1951, 52; Teachers College, Columbia U., 1958; Pratt Institute, 1964–65. **Commission:** All Souls Unitarian Church, NYC, 1980. **Awards:** Charles M. Rosenbloom Prize, 1942; The Print Club, Philadelphia, 1944, 1945, Charles M. Lea Prize, 1949; Northwest Printmakers Annual, **P.P.**, 1945; Society of American Etchers and Engravers, NYC, 1947; L. C. Tiffany Grant, 1948; Guggenheim Foundation Fellowship, 1949; NIAL Grant, 1950; Eliot D. Pratt Foundation Fellowship, 1966, 67, 68; Carnegie-Mellon U., Alumni Merit Award, 1974. **Address:** P.O. Box 1580, Southampton, NY 11968. **Dealer:** Galerie Chalette. **One-man Exhibitions:** Village Art Center, NYC, 1947; Corcoran, 1951; U. of Georgia, 1951; The Bertha Schaefer Gallery, 1952, 55, 56, 61, 65, 67, 69; Nishi Machi School, Tokyo, 1954; Fort Worth, 1956; Currier, 1956; San Antonio/McNay, 1956, 66; Grand Rapids, 1957; Charlotte/Mint, 1957; Grinnell College, 1960; Chatham College, 1960; Eleanor Rigelhaupt Gallery, Boston, 1965; Storm King Art Center, 1966; Norfolk, 1967; McNay Art Institute, 1967; Southern Vermont Art Center, 1968; Chat-

tanooga/AA, 1969; Port Washington Public Library, 1978; Benson Gallery, Bridgehampton, 1978; Plum Gallery, Kensington, Md., 1978. **Group:** MOMA, Master Prints from the Museum Collection, 1949, Abstract Painting and Sculpture in America, 1951, The Responsive Eye, 1965; SAGA, 1951; Sao Paulo Biennial, 1951; WMAA Annuals, 1951, 53, 54, 56, The New Decade, 1954–55, Geometric Abstraction in America, circ., 1962; Salon du Mai, Paris, 1952; PMA, A Decade of American Printmaking, 1952, also 1964; III Biennial of Spanish-American Art, Barcelona, 1955; Brooklyn Museum, 14 Painter-Printmakers, 1955; Chicago/AI Annual, 1957; A.F.A., 14 Painter-Printmakers, circ., 1957, Collage in America, circ., 1957–58, The New Landscape in Art and Science, circ., 1958–59, Explorers of Space, circ., 1961–62, Hayter and Atelier 17, circ., 1961–62; USIA, American Prints, circ., Middle East, 1957–59, Plastics—USA, circ. USSR, 1961; Corcoran Biennials, 1963, 65; Buffalo/Albright, Box Show, 1966; Cornell U., Small Sculpture, 1967; Flint/Institute, Made of Plastic, 1968; Denver/AM, Report on the Sixties, 1969; Colgate U., Viewpoints 3, 1969; Skidmore College, Contemporary Women Artists, 1970; U. of Nebraska, American Sculpture, 1970; Finch College, NYC, Projected Art, 1971; Potsdam/SUNY, Women in Art, 1971; PMA/Musuem of the Philadelphia Civic Center, Focus, 1974. **Collections:** Albion College; American Republic Insurance Co.; Amherst College; Andover/Phillips; Baltimore/MA; Boston/MFA; Brooklyn Museum; CIT Corporation; Carnegie; Chase Manhattan Bank; Chicago/AI; Des Moines; Ford Foundation; Hartford/Wadsworth; Harvard U.; Honolulu Academy; NYPL; National Gallery; Norfolk; PMA; Peabody Institute; Ridgefield/Aldrich; St. Louis/City; San Antonio/McNay; Seaton Hall, Inc.; Storm King Art Center; Tate; Union Carbide Corp.; WMAA. **Bibliography:** Hayter 2; Janis and Blesh 1; Moser; Newmeyer; Reese; Ritchie 1. Archives.

G

GABLIK, SUZI. b. September 26, 1934, NYC. **Studied:** Black Mountain College, 1951; Hunter College, NYC, BA, 1955, with Robert Motherwell. Author, critic, and lecturer. **Address:** 5 Westmoreland Street, London W1, England. **Dealer:** Terry Dintenfass, Inc., NYC. **One-man Exhibitions:** Alan Gallery, NYC, 1963, 66; Landau-Alan Gallery, NYC, 1967; Henri Gallery, Washington, D.C., 1971; Terry Dintenfass, Inc., 1972, 78; Hester van Royen Gallery, London, 1978. **Group:** SRGM, The Photographic Image, 1966; ICA, London, Young and Fantastic, 1969; New York Cultural Center, Women Choose Women, 1973. **Collections:** Sara Roby Foundation; Hirshhorn.

GABO, NAUM NEEMIA PEVSNER. b. August 5, 1890, Briansk, Russia; **d.** August 23, 1977, Waterbury, Conn. **Studied:** U. of Munich, medical faculty, 1910, natural science, 1911; Polytechnic Engineering School, Munich, 1912. Traveled Italy, Scandinavia, Great Britain, USA, Russia. To USA, 1946; citizen, 1952. **Taught:** Harvard U., 1953–54. Designed set for *La Chatte* (Ballet Russe, 1926). Edited *Circle* (with Leslie Martin and Ben Nicholson), 1937. **Member:** AAAL, 1965. **Commissions:** Bijenkorf Building, Rotterdam, 1955; U.S. Rubber Co. Building, NYC, 1956. **Awards:** ICA, London/Tate, International Unknown Political Prisoner Competition, Second Prize, 1953; Guggenheim Foundation Fellowship, 1954; Chicago/AI, The Mr. & Mrs. Frank G. Logan Medal, 1954; Hon. DFA, Royal College of Art, London, 1967; NIAL. **One-man Exhibitions:** Gallery Percier, Paris, 1924; Little Review Gallery, NYC,

1926; Hannover/K-G, 1930; Arts Club of Chicago, 1934, 1952 (two-man); Lefevre Gallery, London, 1936; Musée du Jeu de Paume, 1937; The London Gallery, London, 1937; Julien Levy Galleries, NYC, 1938; Hartford/Wadsworth, 1938, 53; Museum of the City of London, 1942; MOMA, 1948; Baltimore/MA, 1950; MIT, 1952; Pierre Matisse Gallery, 1953; France/National, Paris, 1971; Berlin/National, 1971. **Retrospectives:** Amsterdam/Stedelijk, circ., 1965–66; Buffalo/Albright, 1968. **Group:** Golden Gate International Exposition, San Francisco, 1939; MOMA; WMAA; Chicago/AI; Paris/Moderne. **Collections:** Buffalo/Albright; Hartford/Wadsworth; MOMA; Princeton U.; Tate; U.S. Rubber Co.; WMAA; Yale U. **Bibliography:** *Abstraction creation 1931–36*; Baldinger; Barr 1; Battcock, ed.; Baur 7; Biederman 1; Bihalji-Merin; Blanchard; Blesh 1; Calas, N. and E.; Canaday; Cassou; Chipp; Craven, W.; Davis, D.; Flanagan; **Gabo**; Gaunt; Gertz; Giedion-Welcker 1, 2; Goodrich and Baur 1; Guggenheim, ed.; Henning; Hess, T.B., 1; Hulten; Hunter, ed.; Janis and Blesh 1; Janis, S.; Kepes 2; Kepes, ed.; Krauss 2; Kuh 1, 2, 3; Langui; Licht, F.; Lowry; Lynton; MacAgy 2; McCurdy, ed.; **Martin, Nicholson, and Gabo, eds.**; Mendelowitz; *Metro*; Myers 2; Neumeyer; Newmeyer; Newton 2; **Olson and Chanin**; Ramsden 1, 2; Read 1, 3, 6; **Read and Martin**; Rickey; Ritchie 3; Rose, B., 1; Selz, J.; Pela, P. 3; Seuphor 3; Seymour; Trier 1, 2; Valentine 2; Zervos. Archives.

GALLATIN, ALBERT E. b. 1882, Villanova, Pa.; **d.** June 17, 1952. **Studied:** Cutler School, Vermont; New York Law

School. Traveled Europe, USA. Founder of Museum of Living Art, now housed at the Philadelphia Museum of Art. **One-man Exhibitions:** (first) Galerie Pierre, Paris, 1938; Passedoit Gallery, NYC, 1938, 42; Pittsfield/Berkshire, 1939; J. Seligmann and Co., 1939 (three-man); The Willard Gallery, 1941; Mortimer Brandt, NYC, 1945; Durand-Ruel Gallery, NYC, 1947, 48; The Pinacotheca, NYC, 1950; The Zabriskie Gallery, 1972. **Retrospective:** Rose Fried Gallery. **Group:** Salon des Surindependants, Paris, 1938; American Abstract Artists Annuals, 1938–48; New York World's Fair, 1939; Arts Club of Chicago, 1940; MOMA, 1942; Federation of Modern Painters and Sculptors, 1943; PMA, 1945; Corcoran, 1947. **Collections:** Black Mountain College; MMA; MOMA; PMA; Phillips; Pittsfield/Berkshire; SFMA; SRGM. **Bibliography:** American Abstract Artists, ed.; Baur 7; Bazin; Blesh 1; Frost; **Gallatin 1, 2, 3, 4, 5, 6, 7, 8**; McCurdy, ed.; Morris; Ritchie 1; Rose, B., 1. Archives.

GALLO, FRANK. b. 1933, Toledo, Ohio. **Studied:** Toledo/MA, 1954, BFA; Cranbrook, 1955; U. of Iowa, 1959, MFA. **Taught:** U. of Illinois, 1960– . **Awards:** Des Moines, First Prize, 1958, 59; Guggenheim Foundation Fellowship, 1966. **Address:** % Department of Art, U. of Illinois, Urbana, IL 61801. **One-man Exhibitions:** Toledo/MA, 1955; Gilman Galleries, Chicago, 1963–66; Sherry-Netherland Hotel, NYC, 1964; The Graham Gallery, 1965, 67; Felix Landau Gallery, 1966; Time, Inc., 1966; Danenberg Gallery, 1972; Puck Gallery, NYC, 1974; Jack Gallery, NYC. **Group:** Des Moines, 1958, 59; U. of Illinois, 1963–65; Chicago/AI, 1964; WMAA Annual, 1964–67; Youngstown/Butler, 1965; WMAA, Young America, 1965; Toronto International Sculpture Symposium, 1967; XXXIV Venice Biennial, 1968; Owens-Corning Fiberglas Corp., Corning, N.Y., 1970. **Collections:** Baltimore/MA; Caracas; Chicago/AI; Cleveland/MA; Colorado State U.;

U. of Illinois; Los Angeles/County MA; MOMA; Melbourne/National; U. of Nebraska; Princeton U.; WMAA; U. of Wisconsin. **Bibliography:** Geske; *Recent Figure Sculpture.*

GANSO, EMIL. b. April 14, 1895, Halberstadt, Germany; **d.** April 18, 1941, Iowa City, Iowa. To USA, 1912. **Studied:** NAD. **Taught:** Lawrence College, 1940; State U. of Iowa, 1941. **Awards:** Guggenheim Foundation Fellowship, 1933. **One-man Exhibitions:** Weyhe Gallery, 1926–28, 1930–36, 1944, 46; Washington Irving Gallery, NYC, 1960; Kenan Center, Lockport, N.Y., 1969; U. of Connecticut, 1976; Martin Sumers Gallery, 1978. **Retrospectives:** WMAA, 1941; Brooklyn Museum, 1944; U. of Iowa, 1979. **Group:** WMAA; Salons of America, NYC; Brooklyn Museum; Chicago/AI; Cleveland/MA; PAFA; Corcoran; NAD. **Collections:** Boston/MFA; Dartmouth College; Denver/AM; MMA; U. of Rochester; WMAA. **Bibliography:** American Artists Group, Inc. 1, 3; Cahill and Barr, eds.; Cheney; Hall; *Index of 20th Century Artists;* Jewell 3; Mellquist; Moser 2; Pearson 1; Reese; Ringel, ed.; *Woodstock: An American Art Colony, 1902–1977;* Zigrosser 1. Archives.

GATCH, LEE. b. September 10, 1902, Baltimore, Md.; **d.** November 10, 1968, Trenton, N.J. **Studied:** Maryland Institute, 1924; Academie Moderne, Paris, 1924, with Andre Lhote, Moise Kisling. Traveled France, Italy. **Member:** NIAL, 1966. **Commissions:** (murals) US Post Offices, Mullins, S.C., and Elizabethtown, Pa. **Awards:** Chicago/AI, Watson F. Blair Prize, 1957; Corcoran, 1960. **One-man Exhibitions:** (first) J. B. Neumann's New Art Circle, NYC, 1927, also 1932, 37, 46, 49; The Willard Gallery, 1943; Grace Borgenicht Gallery, Inc., 1954; Phillips, 1954, 56, 60; World House Galleries, NYC, 1958; Staempfli Gallery, 1963, 67, 72, 74; NCFA, 1971. **Retrospectives:** WMAA, 1960. **Group:**

XXV & XXVIII Venice Biennials, 1950, 56; Santa Barbara/MA, 1952; Detroit/ Institute, 1959; U. of Illinois, 1961. **Collections:** Andover/Phillips; Atlanta U.; Baltimore/MA; Boston/MFA; Detroit/Institute; Hartford/Wadsworth; U. of Illinois; Los Angeles/County MA; MMA; MOMA; U. of Nebraska; PAFA; PMA; Phillips; St. Louis/City; Utica; WMAA; Washington U. **Bibliography:** Baur 5; Blesh 1; *Cityscape 1919–37;* Eliot; Frost; Gerdts; Goodrich and Baur 1; Hess, T.B., 1; Janis and Blesh 1; Janis, S.; McCurdy, ed.; Nordness, ed.; Pousette-Dart, ed.; Richardson, E.P. Archives.

GECHTOFF, SONIA. b. September 25, 1926, Philadelphia, Pa. **Studied:** Philadelphia Museum School, BFA. Traveled Europe. **Taught:** California School of Fine Arts, 1957–58; NYU, 1961–70; Queens College, 1970–74; U. of New Mexico, 1974–75. **Member:** National Advisory Board, Tamarind Institute; Artists Equity. Awards: SFMA, **P.P.**, Santa Barbara/MA, **P.P.**; Tamarind Fellowship, 1963. Phoenix Art Museum, drawing award, 1975. **Address:** 130 Jane Street, NYC 10014. **Dealer:** Gruenebaum Gallery, Ltd., NYC. **One-man Exhibitions:** (first) Dubin Gallery, Philadelphia, 1949, Lucien Labaudt Gallery, San Francisco, 1952, 53; Gallery Six, San Francisco, 1955; de Young, 1957; Ferus Gallery, San Francisco, 1957, 59; Poindexter Gallery, 1959, 60; East Hampton Gallery, 1963, 67, 68; Montclair State College, 1974; Cortella Gallery, NYC, 1976, 78; Gruenebaum Gallery, Ltd., NYC, 1979. **Group:** SFMA Annuals, 1952–58; SRGM, Younger American Painters, 1954; Brussels World's Fair, 1958; Carnegie, 1958; I Paris Biennial, 1959; WMAA Annual, 1959; WMAA, Young America, 1960; Walker, 60 American Painters, 1960; VI Sao Paulo Biennial, 1961; MOMA, Abstract American Drawings and Watercolors, circ., Latin America, 1961–63; U. of Texas, 1966; Florida State U., 1967; Los Angeles/County MA; 1968; New York Cultural Center,

Women Choose Women, 1973; SFMA, California Painting and Sculpture: The Modern Era, 1976; MOMA, Extraordinary Women, 1977; MOMA, American Drawn and Matched, 1977. **Collections:** Achenbach Foundation; AT&T; U. of California; Amon Carter Museum; Baltimore/MA; Chase Manhattan Bank; U. of Iowa; La Jolla; Los Angeles/ County MA; MOMA; U. of Massachusetts; Oakland/AM; Pasadena/ AM; SFAI; SFMA; SRGM; The Singer Company, Inc.; Woodward Foundation. **Bibliography:** *Art: A Woman's Sensibility.*

GELB, JAN. b. July 18, 1906, NYC; **d.** 1978, NYC. **Studied:** Yale U., 1928; Atelier Sigrid Skou, NYC and Brittany, 1928–29; ASL, occasionally, 1930–34; NAD, 1924–27, 1928. Traveled Europe, Near East, Japan. **Taught:** Elementary Schools, 1928–early 1960s; Truro (Mass.) Center for the Fine Arts, 1973–75. **Member:** SAGA (vice-president); MacDowell Colony; Artists Equity. **Awards:** The Print Club, Philadelphia, **P.P.**, 1958; Boston Arts Festival, Second Prize; Potsdam/SUNY, **P.P.**, 1966, 67; Dulin Gallery, Knoxville, Tenn., **P.P.**, 1968; Vera List **P.P.**, 1968; SAGA, 1968. **m.** Boris Margo. **One-man Exhibitions:** (first) West Haven (Conn.) Public Library 1929 or 1930; Delphic Studios, NYC, 1940; Weyhe Gallery, 1948, 50; Research Studio, Maitland, Fla., 1948, 50; Ganso Gallery, NYC, 1954; Artists' Gallery, Provincetown, 1955, 56; New Brunswick (N.J.) Art Center, 1957; Ruth White Gallery, 1957, 59, 61, 62, 64; Esther Robles Gallery, 1958; Galerie A. G., Paris, 1960; Piccadilly Gallery, London, 1970; Shore Galleries, Provincetown, 1961; Marberg Inc., El Paso, 1965; Wichita State U., 1971; U. of Louisville, 1971; Charles W. Bowers Memorial Museum, Santa Ana, 1971; Michigan State U., 1972; The Ohio State U., 1972. **Retrospective:** Smithsonian, 1963. **Group:** WMAA Annuals; PAFA; Brooklyn Museum, Print Biennials; MMA, American Watercolors,

Drawings and Prints, 1952; Boston Arts Festival; NAD; Oakland/AM; SAGA; Brooklyn Museum, 14 Painter Printmakers, 1955; A.F.A. and USIA, circ., exhibitions; WMAA, Nature in Abstraction, 1958. **Collections:** Abbott Academy; Baltimore/MA; Brooklyn Museum; U. of Connecticut; U. of Delaware; Howard U.; Library of Congress; Los Angeles/County MA; MMA; MOMA; U. of Minnesota; NYPL; National Gallery; Norfolk; PMA; Phoenix; Potsdam/SUNY; St. Lawrence U.; Syracuse/Everson; Syracuse U.; WMAA. **Bibliography:** Baur 5. Archives.

GEORGE, THOMAS. b. July 1, 1918, NYC. **Studied:** Dartmouth College, 1940, BA; ASL; Academie de la Grande Chaumiere; Academy of Fine Arts, Florence, Italy. US Navy, 1942–46. Traveled Europe, Far East, North Africa, China. **Taught:** Dartmouth College, 1979. **Member:** MacDowell Colony. **Awards:** Brooklyn Museum, **P.P.**, 1955; Rockefeller Foundation Grant, 1957; Ford Foundation, **P.P.**, 1962, 63. **Address:** 20 Greenhouse Drive, Princeton, NJ 08540. **Dealer:** Betty Parsons Gallery, NYC. **One-man Exhibitions:** Ferargil Galleries, NYC, 1951, 53; Korman Gallery, NYC, 1954; Dartmouth College, 1956, 79; The Contemporaries, NYC, 1956; Bridgestone Museum, 1957; Diamaru, Osaka, 1957; Betty Parsons Gallery, NYC, 1959, 70, 72, 74, 76, 78; The Reid Gallery, London; Bennington College, 1967; U. of California, Santa Cruz, 1967; Axiom Gallery, London, 1968; Esther Baer Gallery, 1969; Delaware Art Museum, 1971; Henies-Onstadts Stiftelser, 1971; Tranegarden Gallery, Hellerup, Copenhagen, 1971; Princeton Gallery of Fine Art, 1972, 74; Oslo Kunstforening, 1973; Jefferson Place Gallery, Washington, D.C., 1974; Princeton U., 1975; NCFA, 1977; Artes Galleri, Oslo, 1979. **Retrospective:** Dartmouth College, 1965. **Group:** MOMA, Recent Drawings, USA, 1956; Carnegie, 1958, 61; WMAA Annuals, 1960–62, 1965; PAFA, 1962; Corcoran,

1963; International Biennial Exhibition of Paintings, Tokyo; Lincoln, Mass./De Cordova, 1963; San Antonio/McNay, 1964; SFMA, 1965; Musée Cantonal des Beaux-Arts, Lausanne, II Salon International de Galeries Pilotes, 1966; NCFA, 1968; US Mission to the United Nations; New School for Social Research, NYC, American Drawings of the Sixties, 1970; Trenton/State, New Jersey 6, 1971. **Collections:** Brandeis U.; Bridgestone Museum; Brooklyn Museum; Buffalo/Albright; U. of California, Santa Cruz; Chase Manhattan Bank; Colby College; Dartmouth College; Delaware Art Museum; Flint/Institute; Ford Motor Company; Henie-Onstadts Stiftelser; Library of Congress; MOMA; Musée Cantonal des Beaux-Arts; NCFA; Oklahoma; Princeton U.; U. of Rochester; SFMA; SRGM; Tate; Trenton/State; WGMA; WMAA; Yale U.

GEORGES, PAUL. b. 1923, Portland, Ore. **Studied:** U. of Oregon; Hofmann School; Atelier Fernand Leger in Paris, 1949–52. Traveled France, USA. **Taught:** U. of Colorado, 1960; Dartmouth College, 1961; Yale U. 1964– . **Awards:** Longview Foundation Grant; Hallmark International Competition, **P.P.**, 1961; PAFA, Carol H. Beck Gold Medal, 1964. **Address:** Sagaponack, NY 11962. **Dealers:** Fischbach Gallery; Green Mountain Gallery. **One-man Exhibitions:** Reed College, 1948, 56, 61; Tibor de Nagy Gallery, 1955, 57; The Zabriskie Gallery, 1959; Great Jones Gallery, NYC, 1960, 61; Allan Frumkin Gallery, NYC and Chicago, 1962, 64, 66, 67, 68; Dorsky Gallery, 1968; Fischbach Gallery, 1974, 76; Green Mountain Gallery, 1975. **Group:** Salon du Mai, Paris, 1949; The Kootz Gallery, NYC, New Talent, 1952; PAFA, 1952, 64; Corcoran, 1962; Chicago/AI, 1962; WMAA, 1962, 63; MOMA; U. of Colorado; U. of Kentucky, Drawings, 1963; MOMA, Hans Hofmann and His Students, circ., 1963–64; Boston U., 1964; Silvermine Guild, 1964; Youngstown/Butler, 1964. **Collections:** 57th Madison Corp.; Hallmark Collection; Hirshhorn; MIT; MOMA; U. of Massachusetts; NYU; Newark Museum; U. of North Carolina; Reed College; WMAA. **Bibliography:** Downes, ed. Archives.

GIAMBRUNI, TIO. b. August 30, 1925, San Francisco, Calif.; **d.** May 17, 1971, Davis, Calif. **Studied:** U. of California, Berkeley, with Glenn Wessels, John Haley, Jacques Schnier, Richard O'Hanlon, BA, MA. US Army. **Taught:** Modesto (Calif.) High School, 1951–52; Liberty High School, 1953–56; Miramonte (Calif.) High School, 1956–59; California College of Arts and Crafts, 1959–60; U. of California, 1960–71. **Commissions:** Golden Gateway Redevelopment Project, San Francisco. **Awards:** SFMA, Patrons of Music and Art Award, 1959. **One-man Exhibitions:** (first) Nevada Art Gallery, Reno, 1958; RAC, 1960; Barrios Art Gallery, Sacramento, 1963; Mills College, 1963; Berkeley Gallery, 1963, 64, 66. **Group:** SFMA Annuals, 1951–70; Santa Barbara/MA, 1959; SFMA, Tradition and Invention, 1962; SFMA, Molten Image—Seven Sculptors, 1962; Stanford U., Some Points of View for '62, 1962; Museum of Contemporary Crafts, Creative Casting, 1963; New Orleans/Delgado, Bay Area Artists, 1963; New School for Social Research, The Artist's Reality, 1964.

GIBRAN, KAHLIL. b. November 29, 1922, Boston, Mass. **Studied:** Boston Museum School, 1940–43, with Karl Zerbe. Changed from painting to sculpture, 1953–54. **Taught:** Wellesley College, 1958; Boston U. **Member:** National Sculpture Society; New England Sculptors Association. **Awards:** PAFA, George D. Widener Memorial Gold Medal, 1958; Guggenheim Foundation Fellowship, 1959, 60; NIAL Award, 1961; Boston Arts Festival Grand Prize, 1964. **Address:** 160 West Canton Street, Boston, MA 02118. **One-man Exhibi-**

tions: (first) Stuart Gallery, Boston, 1944; Mortimer Levitt Gallery, NYC; Margaret Brown Gallery, Boston; U. of Kansas; Lee Nordness Gallery, NYC, 1962 (sculpture); Cambridge (Mass.) Art Association, 1969, 1977. **Group:** WMAA Annual, 1960; Boston Arts Festival; Carnegie; Dallas/MFA; NAD; Chicago/AI; ICA, Boston. **Collections:** Brockton/Fuller; Kansas City/Nelson; Nashville; Norfolk; Norfolk/Chrysler; PAFA; Terre Haute/Swope. **Bibliography:** Pousette-Dart, ed. Archives.

GIKOW, RUTH. b. January 6, 1915, Russia. **Studied:** Cooper Union, 1932–35, with John Steuart Curry, Austin Purvis; American Art School, NYC, with Raphael Soyer. Traveled Europe, Mexico, Asia, USSR. **Taught:** New School for Social Research, ca. 1961–71. Illustrated *Crime and Punishment* (World Publishing Co.) and *History of the Jews in America* (Jewish Theological Seminary). Subject of a film demonstrating the cutting and printing of linoleum blocks, produced by Walter O. Gutjohn, 1943. **Member:** Artists Equity. Federal A.P.; Mural painter and graphic artist; mural for Bronx County Hospital, 1940. **Commissions:** (murals): New York World's Fair, 1939; Rockefeller Center, NYC, 1943. **Awards:** NIAL Grant, 1961. **m.** Jack Levine. **Address:** 68 Morton Street, NYC 10014. **Dealer:** Kennedy Gallery. **One-man Exhibitions:** (first) National Serigraph Society, 1943, also 1947; Weyhe Gallery, 1946; Grand Central Moderns, NYC, 1948, 50; Philadelphia Art Alliance, 1949; Ganso Gallery, NYC, 1952, 53, 54; Rehn Galleries, 1956, 57, 59; Lee Nordness Gallery, NYC, 1961, 63; The Forum Gallery, 1970; Kennedy Gallery, 1972, 76; The Margo Feiden Galleries, NYC, 1974. **Group:** Carnegie; Corcoran; Utica; Youngstown/Butler; MMA; MOMA; U. of Nebraska; PAFA; Springfield, Mass./MFA; WMAA; State U. of Iowa; SFMA; Toledo/MA; San Diego. **Collections:** Brandeis U.; Colby College; MMA; MOMA; NCFA; NIAL;

NYU: PMA; Portland, Me./MA; Smithsonian; Springfield, Mass./MFA; Syracuse/Everson; Terre Haute/Swope; WMAA. **Bibliography:** Bethers; Nordness, ed. Archives.

GILL, JAMES. b. December 10, 1934, Tahoka, Tex. **Studied:** U. of Texas. Traveled USA; Mexico, Europe. **Taught:** U. of Idaho, 1968. **Awards:** U. of Texas, painting fellowship, 1960; Chicago/AI, **P.P.**, 1964. **Address:** Whale Gulch, Whitehorn, CA 95489. **One-man Exhibitions:** (first) The Alan Gallery, NYC, 1962, also 1964; Felix Landau Gallery, 1963, 65, 68; Galleria George Lester, Rome, 1964; Sacramento/Crocker, 1966; The Landau-Alan Gallery, NYC, 1966, 69. **Group:** Chicago/AI Annual, 1964; Brandeis U., circ., 1964–65; San Francisco Art Institute Annual, 1965; WMAA Annual, 1966–68; IX Sao Paulo Biennial, 1967; NCFA, circ., 1968–69. **Collections:** U. of California; Chicago/AI; Container Corp. of America; MOMA; Mead Corporation; Time, Inc.; WMAA.

GILLESPIE, GREGORY. b. November 29, 1936, Roselle Park, New Jersey. **Studied:** Cooper Union, 1945–60; SFAI, BA, MFA, 1960–62. **Awards:** Fulbright Fellowship, 1962, 65; Chester Dale Fellowship, 1964, 65; L. C. Tiffany Grant, 1960; NAD, Childe Hassam Fund **P.P.**, 1965. Resided Italy, 1962–70. **Address:** % Dealer. **Dealer:** Forum Gallery. **One-man Exhibitions:** Forum Gallery, NYC, 1966, 68, 70, 73, 76, 79; American Academy, Rome, 1969; U. of Georgia, 1970; Alpha Gallery, Boston, 1971, 74; Smith College, 1971; Galleria il Fante de Spade, Rome, 1974. **Retrospective:** Hirshhorn, 1977. **Group:** AAAL, 1961, 64, 69; WMAA Annuals, 1965, 68; NAD, 1971, 72, 79; MOMA, 1975; U. of Bridgeport, 1980; New York Cultural Center, Realism Now, 1972; Ringling, After Surrealism, 1977. **Collections:** U. of Georgia; Hirshhorn; Lincoln/Woods; U. of Nebraska; The Pennsylvania State U.; U. of Virginia; WMAA. **Bibliography:** Lucie-Smith.

GILLIAM, SAM. b. 1933, Tupelo, Mississippi. **Studied:** U. of Louisville, 1952–56, BA; 1958–61, MA, with Mary Spencer Nay, Charles Crodel, Eugene Leake, Ulfert Wilke. **Awards:** National Endowment for the Arts, grant, 1967, 73, 74; Chicago/AI, Norman B. Harris Prize, 1969; Longview Grant, 1970; Guggenheim Foundation Fellowship, 1971. **Address:** 1752 Lamont Street, N.W., Washington, DC 20010. **Dealer:** Middendorf/Lane, Washington, D.C.; Hamilton Gallery of Contemporary Art, NYC. **One-man Exhibitions:** U. of Louisville, 1956; Frame House Gallery, Louisville, 1963; Alan Morgan Gallery, Washington, D.C., 1963, 64; Jefferson Place Gallery, Washington, 1965, 66, 67, 68, 70, 71; Phillips Gallery, 1967; Byron Gallery, NYC, 1968; Galerie Darthea Speyer, Paris, 1970, 73; MOMA, 1971; New Gallery, Cleveland, 1973; Greenberg Gallery, St. Louis, 1973; U. of California, Irvine, 1973; Maison de la Culture, Rennes, 1973; Linda Farris Gallery, Seattle, 1974, 75; Phoenix Gallery, Seattle, 1974; Solway Gallery, Cincinnati, 1974; Fendrick Gallery, Washington, D.C., 1975, 76, 78;

Gregory Gillespie *Still Life with Squash and Rutabagas* 1975

PMA, 1975; Collectors Gallery, Baltimore, 1975; Louisville/Speed, 1976; U. of Kentucky, 1978; Virginia Commonwealth U., 1978; Solway Gallery, NYC, 1978; Nina/Freudenheim Gallery, Buffalo, 1979; Middendorf/Lane Gallery, Washington, D.C., 1979, 80; Hamilton Gallery of Contemporary Art, NYC, 1979, 80. **Group:** ICA, Washington, D.C., Artists in Washington, 1966; UCLA, The Negro in American Art, 1966; First World Festival of Negro Arts, Dacca, 1966; Minneapolis/MA, Thirty Contemporary Black Artists, 1968; Corcoran, three-man, 1969; MOMA, Works on Paper, 1970; U. of Texas, Color Forum, 1972; Venice Biennial, 1972; Corcoran Biennial, 1975; Brooklyn Museum, 30 Years of American Printmaking, 1976; NAD, 1979; Trenton/State, 6 Black Americans, 1980. **Collections:** Chicago/AI; Baltimore/MA; Carnegie; Corcoran; Howard U.; Madison/Art Center; Phillips; U. of Iowa; MOMA; Smithsonian; Oberlin College; Oklahoma; Walker; MMA; Rotterdam; Tate; Princeton U.; Museum of African Art, Washington, D.C.; NCFA.

GINNEVER, CHARLES. b. August 28, 1931, San Mateo, Calif. Studied with Ossip Zadkine, William Stanley Hayter, Paris, 1953–55; SFAI, 1955–57, BFA; Cornell U., 1957–59, MFA. Traveled Europe, USA. USAF, 1951–52. **Taught:** Cornell U., 1957–59; Pratt Institute, 1963; New School for Social Research, NYC, 1964; Brooklyn Museum School, 1964–65; Newark School of Fine and Industrial Art, 1965; Dayton/AI, 1966; Aspen (Colo.) School of Contemporary Art, 1966; Orange County Community College, Middletown, N.J., 1966; Windham College, 1967–75. **Commissions:** GSA, St. Paul Courthouse, 1974; Walker, 1976; City of Houston, 1977; U. of Michigan, National Endowment for the Arts, 1977; Albany/SUNY, 1978; U. of Houston, 1979; K & B Plaza, New Orleans, 1979. **Awards:** Vermont State Council on the Arts, 1971; Guggenheim

Foundation Fellowship, 1974; National Endowment for the Arts, 1975. **Address:** P.O. Box 411, Putney, VT 05346. **Dealer:** Max Hutchinson Gallery; Construct, Chicago. **One-man Exhibitions:** (first) Allan Stone Gallery, 1961; Bennington College, 1965; Washington Square Park, 1968; Battery Park, NYC, 1969–74; Paula Cooper Gallery, 1970–72; Dag Hammarskjold Plaza, NYC, 1973; Sculpture Now, NYC, 1978, 79; Max Hutchinson Gallery, Houston, 1978; Max Hutchinson Gallery, NYC, 1978; Smith-Anderson Gallery, Palo Alto, 1978, Long Beach/AM, 1978; Galerie Simone Stern, New Orleans, 1978; Construct, Chicago, 1979. **Retrospective:** Sculpture Now, Inc., NYC, 1975. **Group:** SFMA Annuals, 1955, 56; SFMA, Bay Area Sculpture, 1956; Cornell U., New York Artists, 1961; Martha Jackson Gallery, NYC, New Forms— New Media, 1960; Riverside Museum, NYC, 10 New York Sculptors, 1963; Walker, Sculpture Made in Place, 1976; A.F.A., Color Sculpture, 1965; Greenwich, Conn., Sculpture '76, 1976; Washington State U., Two Decades 1957–77, 1977. **Collections:** Chicago; Cornell U.; Hartford/Wadsworth; Hirshhorn; U. of Houston; U. of Michigan; Norfolk/Chrysler; Park 470 Corp.; Storm King Art Center; Walker.

GIOBBI, EDWARD. b. July 18, 1926, Waterbury, Conn. US Army, 1944–46. **Studied:** Whitney School of Art, 1946, 47; Vesper George School of Art, 1947–50; ASL, 1950–51; Academy of Fine Arts, Florence, Italy, 1951–54, 1955–56. Traveled Europe. **Taught:** Memphis Academy of Arts, 1960, 61 (Artist-in-Residence). **Awards:** Joe and Emily Lowe Foundation Award, 1951, and Special Grant, 1952; Yaddo Fellowship, 1957; Ford Foundation, 1966; Guggenheim Foundation Fellowship, 1971. **Address:** 161 Croton Lake Road, Katonah, NY 10536. **Dealer:** Gruenebaum Gallery, NYC. **One-man Exhibitions:** (first) Ward Eggleston Gallery, NYC, 1950, also 1952; Galerie An der Reuss, Lucerne, 1953 (two-man); Nexus Gallery, Boston, 1956 (two-man); Artists' Gallery, NYC, 1956; John Heller Gallery, NYC, 1957, 58; The Contemporaries, NYC, 1960, 61, 63; Memphis/Brooks, 1961, 70; Memphis Academy, 1962; Katonah (N.Y.) Art Gallery, 1963, 69, 75; The New Art Centre, 1964, 67, 70; The Bear Lane Gallery, Oxford, 1964; The Queen Square Gallery, Leeds, 1964; Tirca Karlis Gallery, 1965–66; Mickelson's Gallery, Washington, D.C., 1966; The Alan Gallery, NYC, 1966; Waddell Gallery, 1967, 69; Obelisk Gallery, 1968; Gertrude Kasle Gallery, 1968, 70; Galleria Obelisco, Rome, 1974; Crane Kalman Gallery, London, 1975; Galleria del Naviglio, Milan, 1976; Purchase/SUNY, 1977; Gruenebaum Gallery, NYC, 1978, 79; Lee Hoffman Gallery, Detroit, 1978; Mattatuck Museum, Waterbury, Conn., 1978; Irving Gallery, Palm Beach, 1978. **Group:** WMAA Annuals, 1957, 61, 66, Young America, 1961, Forty Artists under Forty, circ., 1962; MOMA, Recent Drawings USA, 1956, Recent Painting USA: The Figure, circ., 1962–63; PAFA, 1961; U. of Arkansas, 1966; Finch College, 1967. **Collections:** Allentown/AM; Baltimore/MA; Boston/MFA; Brandeis U.; Brooklyn Museum; Cambridge; Chicago/AI; Dartmouth College; Detroit/Institute; Florence, Italy; Mattatuck Museum, Waterbury, Conn.; Memphis/Brooks; U. of Michigan; Oxford; Poole Technical College; San Antonio/McNay; Spelman College; Syracuse U.; Tate; WMAA; Wesleyan College; Williams College; U. of Wisconsin.

GIRONA, JULIO. b. December 29, 1914, Manzanillo, Cuba. **Studied:** Escuela San Alejandro, Havana, 1930–34; Academie Ranson, Paris, 1935–36; ASL, 1950–56, with Morris Kantor. Traveled Europe extensively, Mexico, Cuba. To USA, 1941. **Taught:** Werkkunstschule, Krefeld, Germany, 1963–64; Escuela Superior de Artes de Cubanacan, Havana, 1978. **Commissions:** Colegio Medicos, Havana (5 murals). **Awards:** Newark Museum, First Prize; Havana/Nacional. **Address:** 53 Genesee Avenue, Teaneck, NJ 07666. **One-man Exhibitions:** (first) Colegio de Arquitectos, Havana, 1934; Havana/Nacional, 1947, 54; Artists' Gallery, NYC, 1953; The Bertha Schaefer Gallery, 1956, 59, 61, 63; Galerie Gunar, Dusseldorf, 1958; Recklinghausen, 1959; Galerie Seide, Hanover, 1960; Werkkunstschule, Krefeld, Germany, 1963; Galeria de la Habana, Havana, 1979; Casa de la Cultura, Havana, 1979. **Retrospective:** Galeria de la Habana, Havana, 1975, 77. **Group:** Venice Biennial; Baltimore/MA, 1956, 59, 60; Chicago/AI, 1957; Minneapolis/Institute, American Painting, 1945–57, 1957; Ball State Teachers College, 1958, 60; MOMA, 1958, 60; Brooklyn Museum, 1959; U. of Nebraska, 1958, 59; Buffalo/Albright, 1959, 60; Argentina/Nacional; MMA; Houston/MFA; SFMA; Newark Museum; Denver/AM. **Collections:** Argentina/Nacional; Dortmund U., Germany; Havana/Nacional; Museo Municipal de Belles Artes, Buenos Aires; Newark Museum; Recklinghausen; Trenton/State; Union Carbide Corp. **Bibliography:** Janis and Blesh 1.

GLACKENS, WILLIAM. b. March 13, 1870, Philadelphia, Pa.; **d.** May 22, 1938, Westport, Conn. **Studied:** Central High School, Philadelphia, BA; PAFA. Traveled France, Spain, Canada. Newspaper illustrator for many years. **Member:** Society of Independent Artists, NYC (first president, 1916–17); The Eight; NAD, 1937 (Associate, 1896); NIAL. **Awards:** Buffalo/Albright, Gold Medal, 1901; St. Louis Exposition, 1904, Silver and Bronze Medals; Carnegie, Hon. Men., 1905; Panama-Pacific Exposition, San Francisco, 1915, Bronze Medal; PAFA, Joseph E. Temple Gold Medal, 1924; Carnegie, Second Prize, 1929; PAFA, Carol H. Beck Gold Medal, 1933; PAFA, Jennie Sesnan Gold Medal, 1936; Paris World's Fair, 1937, Grand Prix; PAFA, J. Henry Schiedt

Memorial Prize, 1938. **One-man Exhibitions:** (first) New Arts Club, NYC; Academy of Fine Arts, Berlin, 1910; Kraushaar Galleries, 1925, 28, 35, 42, 57; Andover/Phillips, 1936; Louisville/Speed, 1939; 10 West Ninth Street, NYC, Memorial Exhibition, annually, 1939–49; NCFA, 1972. **Retrospective:** WMAA, 1938, 67; Carnegie, 1939; Kraushaar Galleries, 1949; Dartmouth College, 1960; St. Louis/City, 1966; NCFA, 1967. **Group:** Paris Salon, 1895, 1900; Macbeth Gallery, NYC, The Eight, 1908; Independents, NYC, 1910; The Armory Show, 1913; WMAA, New York Realists, 1937; Brooklyn Museum, The Eight, 1943; PMA, Artists of the Philadelphia Press, 1945; Renaissance Society, Chicago, 1955; Syracuse/Everson, The Eight, 1958. **Collections:** Andover/Phillips; Barnes Foundation; Boston/MFA; Buffalo/Albright; Chicago/AI; Columbus; Detroit/Institute; MMA; U. of Nebraska; Newark Museum; PMA; Sweet Briar College; WMAA. **Bibliography:** Barnes; Bazin; Biddle 4; Born; Bulliet 1; Canaday; Cheney; **Du Bois 5, 6**; Gallatin 2; **Glackens**; Hall; Hartmann; Huyghe; *Index of 20th Century Artists;* Jackman; **Katz**; Kent, N.; McCoubrey 1; McCurdy, ed.; Neuhaus; Pach 1; Perlman; Phillips 2; Poore; Ringel, ed.; Rose, B., 1, 4; Sachs; **Watson, F.** Archives.

GLARNER, FRITZ. b. July 20, 1899, Zurich, Switzerland; **d.** September 18, 1972, Locarno, Switzerland. **Studied:** Academy of Fine Arts, Naples. To USA, 1936. **Commissions:** Time & Life Building, lobby, NYC, 1960 (mural); Dag Hammarskjold Library, United Nations, NYC. **Awards:** Corcoran, 1957. **One-man Exhibitions:** Galerie Povolotzki, Paris, 1930; Civic Club, NYC, 1931; The Kootz Gallery, NYC, 1945; Rose Fried Gallery, 1949, 51; Galerie Louis Carre, Paris, 1952, 55; ICA, U. of Pennsylvania, 1971; SFMA, 1971; Gimpel & Hanover Gallery, 1972; Gimpel Fils, 1972; Graham Gallery, NYC (three-man), 1980. **Retrospective:**

Fritz Glarner   *Tondo with Echo* 1955

Berne, 1972. **Group:** Buffalo/Albright, 1931; American Abstract Artists, 1938–44; Chicago/AI, 1947, 58, 64; Toronto, 1949; California Palace, 1950; WMAA, 1950, 51, 53, 54, 55; VMFA, 1950, 58; Sao Paulo, 1951; Brooklyn Museum, 1951; U. of Minnesota, 1951; MOMA, 1951, 52, 54, 55; U. of Illinois, 1952, 65; Carnegie, 1952, 58, 61; Tokyo/Modern, 1953; SRGM, 1954; U. of Nebraska, 1955; Documenta I, Kassel, 1955; Corcoran, 1955, 57, 60; Zurich, 1956; Musée Neuchatel, 1957; Kunstverein, Winterthur, 1958; Kongresshalle, Berlin, 1958; XXIX & XXXII Venice Biennials, 1958, 64; Heimathaus, Zurich, 1960; Seattle World's Fair, 1962; WMAA, Geometric Abstraction in America, circ., 1962; WGMA, The Formalists, 1963; St. Paul Gallery, Drawing USA 1963; Tate, Dunn International, 1964; Musée Cantonal des Beaux-Arts, Lausanne, 1964; MOMA, Contemporary Painters and Sculptors as Printmakers, 1964; Indiana U., 1965; PAFA,

1965. **Collections:** Baltimore/MA; Boston/MFA; Brandeis U.; Brooklyn Museum; Buffalo/Albright; Chase Manhattan Bank; Florida State U.; Karachi; MOMA; Minnesota/MA; NYU; National Gallery; U. of Nebraska; PMA; Phillips; Rockefeller Institute; Smithsonian; WMAA; Walker; Yale U.; Zurich. **Bibliography:** *Abstraction Creation 1931–1936;* Baur 7; Biddle 4; Blesh 1; **Fritz Glarner;** Haftman; Hess, T.B., 1; Janis, S.; MacAgy 2; McCurdy, ed.; Neumeyer; Pousette-Dart, ed.; Read 2; Rickey; Ritchie 1; Rose, B., 1; Seuphor 1; Staber; "What Abstract Art Means to Me."

GLASCO, JOSEPH. b. January 19, 1925, Paul's Valley, Okla. **Studied:** U. of Texas, 1941–43; Jepson Art Institute, Los Angeles; Art Center School, Los Angeles, 1946–48; privately with Rico Lebrun, 1946–48; Escuela de Bellas Artes, San Miguel de Allende, Mexico, 1948; ASL, 1949. US Army Air Force,

Joseph Glasco Untitled 1978

1943–45, Infantry, 1945–56. Traveled Mexico, Europe, Africa. **Member:** National Society of Literature and the Arts. **Commissions:** Amarillo (Tex.) Air Field (mural). **Address:** 100 Greene Street, NYC 10012. **Dealer:** Gimpel & Weitzenhoffer, Ltd. **One-man Exhibitions:** (first) Perls Galleries, 1950; Caterine Viviano Gallery, 1951, 52, 53, 54, 56, 58, 61, 63, 70; Arts Club of Chicago, 1954, 57; U. of Oklahoma, 1965 (three-man); Rizzoli Gallery, NYC, 1967; Kiko Gallery, Houston, 1968, 69, 70; Louisiana Gallery, Houston, 1973, 75; Gimpel & Weitzenhoffer, NYC, 1979. **Group:** MOMA, New Talent; MMA; WMAA; Corcoran; SRGM; Brooklyn Museum; Chicago/AI; Dallas/MFA; Detroit/Institute; Los Angeles/County MA; U. of Illinois; U. of Nebraska; Carnegie, 1958; PAFA; WMAA Forty Artists under Forty, 1963. **Collections:** Brooklyn Museum; Buffalo/Albright; Corcoran; High Museum; Hirshhorn; MMA; MOMA; Newark Museum; Princeton U.; WMAA; Yale U. **Bibliography:** Goodrich and Baur 1; Mendelowitz; Rodman 1; Tapie 1.

GOINGS, RALPH. b. May 9, 1928, Corning, Calif. **Studied:** California College of Arts and Crafts, 1953, BFA; Sacramento State U., 1966, MA. US Army, 1946–48. Traveled England, Europe. **Taught:** La Sierra High School, 1969; U. of California, Davis, 1971. **Address:** Charlotteville, NY 12036. **Dealer:** OK Harris Works of Art, NYC. **One-man Exhibitions:** Artists Cooperative Gallery, Sacramento, 1960, 62, 68; OK Harris Works of Art, 1970, 73, 77, 80; MOMA, 1977. **Group:** SFMA Annual, 1961; Milwaukee, Aspects of a New Realism, 1969; Newport Harbor, Directly Seen: New Realism in California, 1970; Potsdam/SUNY, New Realism, 1971; Hamburg/Kunstverein, USA; West Coast, circ., 1972; Documenta V, Kassel, 1972; Stuttgart/WK, Amerikanischer Fotorealismus, circ., 1972; Cincinnati/Contemporary, Options, 73/30, 1973; Randers Kunstmuseum,

Denmark, Amerikanske Realister, 1973; Tokyo Biennial, 1974; CNAC, Hyperrealistes Americains/Realistes Europeens, 1974; Akron/AI, Selections in Contemporary Realism, 1974; Hamilton College, California Climate, 1974. **Group:** Queens Museum, Urban Aesthetics, 1976; Akron/AI, Contemporary Images in Watercolor, 1976; Albright College, Buffalo, Perspective 1976, 1976; Canberra/National, Illusion and Reality, circ., 1977. **Collections:** Borgon Associates; Chicago/Contemporary; Essen/NG; F.T.D. Association; Hamburg/Kunstverein; ICA, U. of Pennsylvania; U. of Miami; U. of Nebraska. **Bibliography:** Alloway 4; *Amerikanischer Fotorealismus;* Arthur 1; Arthur 2; Honisch and Jensen, eds.; *Kunst um 1970;* Sager; *The State of California Painting; USA West Coast.*

GOLDBERG, MICHAEL. b. 1924, NYC. **Studied:** ASL, 1938–42, 1946, with Jose de Creeft; City College of New York, 1940–42, 1946–47; Hofmann School, 1941–42, 1948–50. US Army, 1942–46. **Taught:** U. of California, 1961–62. **Address:** 222 Bowery, NYC 10012. **Dealer:** Ileana Sonnabend Gallery, NYC. **One-man Exhibitions:** (first) Tibor de Nagy Gallery, 1953; Poindexter Gallery, 1956, 58; Martha Jackson Gallery, 1960, 64, 66; Paul Kantor Gallery, Beverly Hills, Calif., 1960; Holland-Goldowsky Gallery, Chicago, 1960 (two-man); B.C. Holland Gallery, 1961; Galerie Anderson-Mayer, Paris, 1963; Bob Keene, Southampton, N.Y., 1963; Paley & Lowe Inc., NYC, 1971 (two-man), 1972, 73; Vancouver, 1971 (two-man); Cunningham-Ward Gallery, NYC, 1975, 76; Ghent Gallery, Norfolk, Va., 1973; Galerie Hecate, Paris, 1975; Galerie Denise Rene, NYC, 1977; Galerie Sonnabend, Paris, 1978; Galerie December, Dusseldorf, 1978; Young-Hoffman Gallery, Chicago, 1978; Loyse van Oppenheim Gallery, Geneva, 1978; Daniel Weinberg Gallery, San Francisco, 1978; Sonnabend Gallery, NYC, 1979; Thomas Segal Gallery, Boston,

1979. **Group:** Ninth Street Exhibition, NYC, 1951; The Stable Gallery Annuals, 1952–57; Sidney Jarvis Gallery, Four Younger Americans, 1956; Carnegie, 1958; WMAA Annuals, 1958, 67; Gutai 9, Osaka, 1958; Turin Art Festival, 1959; Documenta II, Kassel, 1959; Walker, 60 American Painters, 1960; Columbus, Contemporary American Painting, 1960; MOMA, Hans Hofmann and His Students, circ., 1963–64; Musée Cantonal des Beaux-Arts, Lausanne, I Salon International de Galeries Pilotes, 1963; Lehigh U., 1966; Smithsonian, 66; Star Turtle Gallery, NYC, The Tenants of Sam Wapnowitz, 1969; Corcoran, 1969; Salon de Mai, Paris, 1969; WMAA Annual, 1973. **Collections:** Baltimore/MA; Buffalo/Albright; Cornell U.; Lincoln, Mass./De Cordova; Norfolk/Chrysler; Walker. **Bibliography:** Downes, ed.; Janis and Blesh 1; O-Hara; Sandler 1. Archives.

GOLDIN, LEON. b. January 16, 1923, Chicago, Ill. **Studied:** State U. of Iowa, with Mauricio Lasansky, 1948, BFA, 1950, MFA; Chicago Art Institute School, with Robert Von Neuman. Traveled Europe extensively; resided Paris, 1952–53, Rome, 1955–58. **Taught:** California College of Arts and Crafts, 1950–52, 1954–55; Philadelphia Museum School, 1960–62; Queens College, 1960–62; Cooper Union, 1961–64; Columbia, U., 1962– . **Awards:** L. C. Tiffany Grant, 1951; Fulbright Fellowship (France), 1952; SFMA, H.S. Crocker Co. Award, 1952; Prix de Rome, 1955, renewed 1956–57; Guggenheim Foundation Fellowship, 1959; Ford Foundation, **P.P.,** 1960; PAFA, Jennie Sesnan Gold Medal, 1965; National Endowment for the Arts Grant, 1966; NIAl Grant, 1968; and many print awards. **Address:** 438 West 116th Street, NYC 10027. **Dealer:** Kraushaar Galleries. **One-man Exhibitions:** (first) Oakland/AM, 1955; Felix Landau Gallery, 1956, 57, 59; Galleria L'Attico, Rome, 1958; Kraushaar Galleries, 1960, 64, 68, 72. **Group:** Chicago/AI Annuals,

1946, 48; SFMA Annuals, 1948, 51–54; Los Angeles/County MA, 1949, 50; MMA, American Paintings Today, 1950; PAFA, 1951, 1960–64; MOMA, Contemporary American Painting, 1953; Santa Barbara/MA, 1955; MOMA, Recent Drawings, USA, 1956; Corcoran, 1963; Carnegie, 1964. **Collections:** Andover/Phillips; Arts Council of Great Britain; Brooklyn Museum; Cincinnati/AM; Los Angeles/County MA; Morgan State College; NCFA; U. of Nebraska; Oakland/AM; PAFA; RAC; St. Louis/City; Santa Barbara/MA; U. of Southern California; Utica; Worcester/AM. **Bibliography:** Nordness, ed.

GOLUB, LEON. b. January 23, 1922, Chicago, Ill. **Studied:** The U. of Chicago, 1942, BA; Chicago Art Institute School, with Paul Wieghardt, Kathleen Blackshear, Robert Lifuendahl, 1949, BFA, 1950, MFA. US Army, 1942–46. Traveled Europe; resided Italy, 1956–57, Paris, 1959–64. **Taught:** Illinois Institute of Technology, 1955–56; Indiana U., 1957–59; Wright Junior College; Northwestern U.; Stella Elkins Tyler School of Fine Arts, Temple U., 1965–66; School of Visual Arts, NYC, 1966–69; Fairleigh Dickinson U., 1969; Rutgers U., 1970–. **Awards:** Chicago/AI, Florsheim Memorial Prize, 1954; Ford Foundation Grant, 1960; Chicago/AI, Watson F. Blair Prize; II Inter-American Paintings and Prints Biennial, Mexico City, Hon. Men., 1960; Cassandra Foundation Grant, 1967; Guggenheim Foundation Fellowship, 1968; AAAL; NIAL, 1973. **Address:** 530 LaGuardia Place, NYC 10012. **Dealer:** Olympia Galleries, Glenside, Pa. **One-man Exhibitions:** (first) Contemporary Gallery, Chicago, 1950; Purdue U., 1951; Wittenborn Gallery, NYC, 1952, 57; Kerrigan-Hendricks Gallery, Chicago, 1954; Artists' Gallery, NYC, 1954; Allan Frumkin Gallery, Chicago, 1955, 60, 64, NYC, 1959, 61, 63; Feigl Gallery, NYC, 1955, 56; Chicago Public Library, 1956; Pomona College, 1956; Pasadena/AM, 1956; ICA, London, 1957; Indiana U., 1958; American

Cultural Center, Paris, 1960; Iris Clert Gallery, 1962; Hanover Gallery, 1962; Gallery A. Melbourne, 1963, The U. of Chicago, 1966; Pro Graphica Arte, 1968; MIT, 1970; Melbourne/Nacional, 1970; Darthea Speyer Gallery, 1971; Herbert H. Lehman College, Bronx, N.Y., 1972; Bienville Gallery, 1972; Stony Brook/SUNY, 1975; Trenton/State, 1975; Haverford College, 1976; SFAI, 1976; Olympia Galleries, Glen Cove, Pa., 1977; Walter Kelly Gallery, Chicago, 1977; Colgate U., 1978; School of Visual Arts, NYC, 1979; Protetch-McIntosh Gallery, Washington, D.C., 1980. **Retrospectives:** Temple U., 1964; Chicago/Contemporary, 1974; New York Cultural Center, 1975. **Group:** Chicago/AI, Exhibition Momentum, 1948–58; SRGM, Younger American Painters, 1954; Chicago/AI, 1954, 62; Carnegie, 1955, 64, 67; Premio Marzotto; U. of Illinois, 1957, 61, 63; MOMA, New Images of Man, 1959; Documenta II & III, Kassel, 1959, 64; Sao Paulo, 1962; Corcoran, 1962; Salon des Realites Nouvelles, Paris, 1962; MOMA, Recent Painting USA: The Figure, circ., 1962–63; Art: USA: Now, circ., 1962–67; SFMA, Directions—Painting U.S.A., 1963; Smithsonian, Graphics, circ., USA, 1963; Ghent, Figuration d'Aujourd'hui, 1964; Paris/Moderne, Mythologiques Quotidiennes, 1964; PAFA Annuals, 1964, 65; New York World's Fair, 1964–65; VMFA, American Painting, 1966, 70; II Internationale der Zeichnung, Darmstadt, 1967; Paris/Moderne, Le Monde en Question, 1967; ICA, London, The Obsessive Image, 1968; Madrid/Nacional, II Biennial, 1969; Chicago/Contemporary, Chicago Imagist Art, 1972; Chicago Art Institute School, Visions, 1976; Paris/Beaubourg, Paris–New York, 1977; U. of Michigan, Chicago: The City and its Artists, 1945–1978, 1977; Chicago/AI, Centennial Exhibition, 1979; Brandeis U., Aspects of the 70's—Mavericks, 1980. **Collections:** Allentown/AM; Amon Carter Museum; U. of California; Chicago/AI; Grunwald Foundation; Hampton Institute; Hirshhorn; Indiana U.;

Kansas City/Nelson; Kent State U.; La Jolla; Los Angeles; MOMA; Melbourne/National; NCFA; Nashville; Nashville/State; U. of North Carolina; Pasadena/AM; Southern Illinois U.; Tel Aviv; U. of Texas. **Bibliography:** Nordness, ed.; Sandler 1; Schulze. Archives.

GONZALEZ, XAVIER. b. February 15, 1898, Almeria, Spain. US citizen, 1930. **Studied:** Chicago/AI. Traveled Greece, Crete, USA; resided Paris, 1930–40; Orient. **Taught:** H. Sophie Newcomb Memorial College; Brooklyn Museum School; Western Reserve U., 1953–54; Summer School of Art, Wellfleet, Mass. President, National Society of Mural Painters. **Member:** NAD; Century Association; Trustee, Lewis Comfort Tiffany Foundation. **Awards:** AAAL Grant; PAFA, Dawson Memorial Medal, 1946; Guggenheim Foundation Fellowship, 1947; Audubon Artists, Gold Medal of Honor; National Arts Club, Gold Medal, 1978. **Address:** 222 Central Park South, NYC 10019. **Dealers:** Oehlschlaeger Gallery, Sarasota, Fla; The Milch Gallery, NYC; Wellfleet Art Gallery, Wellfleet, Mass. **One-man Exhibitions:** Joseph Luyber Galleries, NYC, 1946, 47; Arts and Crafts Club, New Orleans, 1948; Philadelphia Art Alliance, 1949; Norlyst Gallery, NYC; Shore Studio, Boston; Grand Central Moderns, NYC, 1951, 52, 53; The Howard Wise Gallery, Cleveland, 1958; Widdifield Gallery, NYC, 1958; The Milch Gallery, 1960, 63; Richard Larcada Gallery, 1974. **Group:** PAFA; Corcoran; U. of Nebraska; Carnegie; Brooklyn Museum; WMAA; Indianapolis/Herron. **Collections:** Wellesley College. **Bibliography:** Biddle 4; Cheney; Pearson 2; Pousette-Dart, ed. Archives.

GOODE, JOE. b. March 23, 1937, Oklahoma City, Okla. **Studied:** Chouinard Art Institute. Traveled Mexico, England, Europe, South America, India, Iceland. **Awards:** Cassandra

Foundation Grant. **Address:** 1159 S. Hayworth, Los Angeles, CA 90035. **Dealer:** Charles Cowles Gallery, NYC. **One-man Exhibitions:** Nicholas Wilder Gallery, 1966, 69, 70, 72, 74, 75, 78, 79; Rowan Gallery, London, 1967; Gallery Hans R. Neuendorf, Hamburg, 1970, 72, 73, 75; Galleria Milano, Milan, 1971; La Jolla, 1971; Mueller Gallery, 1971; Felicity Samuel Gallery, London, 1972, 73; Fort Worth, 1973; Houston/Contemporary, 1973; Contract Graphics, Houston, 1972, 75; Cirrus Gallery, Los Angeles, 1974; California State College, Northridge, 1974; Seder/Creigh Gallery, Coronado, 1975; James Corcoran Gallery, Los Angeles, 1976; Washington U., 1976; St. Mary's College, L.A., 1977; Texas Gallery, Houston, 1979; Charles Cowles Gallery, NYC, 1980. **Group:** WMAA Annuals, 1966, 67, 69; Carnegie, 1967; Portland, Ore./AM, The West Coast Now, 1968; WMAA, American Pop Art, 1974; Chicago/AI, 1974; School of Visual Arts, NYC, 4 Los Angeles Artists, 1975; LAICA, Current Concerns, Part I, 1975; SFMA, California Painting and Sculpture: The Modern Era, 1976; Austin (two-man), 1976; Scripps College, Claremont, Black and White Are Colors, 1978; Buffalo/Albright, American Painting in the Seventies, 1978; Sacramento/Crocker, Aspects of Abstract, 1978. **Collections:** Fort Worth; Los Angeles/County MA; MOMA; Oklahoma; Pasadena/AM. **Bibliography:** Alloway 1; *Black and White Are Colors; New in the Seventies; The State of California Painting; USA West Coast.*

GOODMAN, SIDNEY. b. January 19, 1936, Philadelphia, Pa. **Studied:** Philadelphia Museum School, 1958, with Jacob Landau, Larry Day, Morris Berd. US Army, 1958–59. Traveled Europe. **Taught:** Philadelphia College of Art, 1960–78; Tyler School, Philadelphia, 1977; PAFA, 1978– . **Awards:** PAFA, First Watercolor Prize, 1961; Guggenheim Foundation Fellowship, 1963; Ford Foundation Fellowship, 1963; Ford

Foundation, **P.P.**, Yale-Norfolk Summer School Fellowship; National Endowment for the Arts, 1974; PAFA, Fellowship Prize, 1974. **Address:** 1730 Delancey Place, Philadelphia, PA 19103. **Dealer:** Terry Dintenfass, Inc. **One-man Exhibitions:** (first) The Print Club, Philadelphia, 1958, also 1963; Terry Dintenfass, Inc., 1961, 1963–1966, 68, 75, 77, 78; Bard College, 1968; George Washington U., 1969; PAFA, Peale House, 1969 (two-man), 1975 (two-man); U. of Rhode Island, 1974; Moravian College, 1974; The Schenectady Museum, 1977; Rhode Island College, 1979; College of William and Mary, 1979. **Retrospective:** Queens Museum, circ., 1980. **Group:** PAFA, 1960–64, 67, 68; MOMA, 1962; NAD, 1962, 77, 78; WMAA, Forty Artists under Forty, circ., 1962; MOMA, Recent Painting USA: The Figure, circ., 1962–63; WMAA Annuals, 1962–64, 1967–68; 73; Corcoran, 1963; Brooklyn Museum, 1963, 1968–69; Newark Museum, 1967; New School for Social Research, Protest and Hope, 1967; Vassar College, 1968; U. of Miami, 1968; U. of Kentucky, 1968; Indianapolis/Herron, 1969; U. of Illinois, 1969; Southern Methodist U., 1969; Tulsa/Philbrook, 1969; Iowa State U., American Drawing, 1971; Boston U., The American Landscape, 1972; Cleveland/MA, 32 Realists, 1972; Sweden/Gotenborgs, Warmwind: American Realists, 1972; Omaha/Joslyn, A Sense of Place, 1973; VMFA, Works on Paper, 1974; AAAL, 1974; Harrisburg, Pa./State Museum, The Figure in American Art, 1975; PMA, Three Centuries of American Art, 1976; Queens Museum, Urban Aesthetics, 1976; US Department of the Interior, America, 1976, 1976; U. of North Carolina, Art on Paper, 1977; PMA, Contemporary Drawing; Philadelphia II, 1979; WMAA, 20th Century Drawings from the Whitney Museum of American Art, circ., 1979–81. **Collections:** U. of Arkansas; Brandeis U.; Brooklyn Museum; Chicago/AI; Delaware Art Museum; Hirshhorn; Kalamazoo/Institute; Library of Congress; MOMA; U. of Maine; Miami-Dade; Minnesota/MA; Moravian College; NAAL; U. of Nebraska; U. of North Carolina; PAFA; PMA; The Pennsylvania State U.; Syracuse U.; WMAA; Wake Forest U. **Bibliography:** *America 1976*; Goodyear; Arthur 2.

GOODNOUGH, ROBERT. b. October 23, 1917, Cortland, N.Y. **Studied:** Syracuse U., BFA; NYU, MA; New School for Social Research; Hofmann School; Ozenfant School of Art, NYC. **Taught:** Cornell U.; NYU; Fieldston School, NYC. Critic for *Art News* magazine, 1950–57. Secretary, Documents of Modern Art (edited by Robert Motherwell), 1951. **Commissions:** Manufacturers Hanover Trust Co. **Awards:** Syracuse U., Hiram Gee Fellowship; Chicago/AI, Ada S. Garrett Prize, 1962; Ford Foundation, **P.P.**, 1962. **Address:** 15 Barrow Street, NYC 10014. **Dealer:** Andre Emmerich Gallery, NYC. **One-man Exhibitions:** (first) Tibor de Nagy Gallery, 1952, also 1953–70; RISD, 1956; Dwan Gallery, 1959–62; Jefferson Place Gallery, 1960; Ellison Gallery, Fort Worth, 1960; Nova Gallery, Boston, 1961; U. of Minnesota; U. of Notre Dame, 1964; Arts Club of Chicago, 1964; New Vision Center, London, 1964; USIS Gallery, London, 1964; Gertrude Kasle Gallery, 1966, 69, 72, 74; Reed College, 1967;

Robert Goodnough   *Theme Variations (Blue)* 1969–70

Buffalo/Albright, 1969; Axiom Gallery, London, 1969; Cayuga Museum of History and Art, Auburn, N.Y., 1969; Galerie Simone Stern, New Orleans, 1969, 70; Kasmin Ltd., 1970; Harcus-Krakow Gallery, 1972; Nicholas Wilder Gallery, 1972; Syracuse U., 1972; Andre Emmerich Gallery, NYC, 1972, 73; David Mirvish Gallery, 1973, 75; Waddington, Tooth Galleries II, London, 1975; M. Knoedler & Co., NYC, 1977; Hokin Gallery, Chicago, 1978; Nina Freudenheim Gallery, Buffalo, 1978; Watson/De Nagy, Houston, 1979; Wichita State U., 1978. **Group:** The Kootz Gallery, NYC, New Talent, 1950; Sidney Janis Gallery, Four Younger Americans, 1956; WMAA; Yale U.; Carnegie; Chicago/AI; NIAL, 1964; MOMA, The New American Painting and Sculpture, 1969; U. of Illinois, 1969; Indianapolis, 1969; XXV Venice Biennial, 1970; AAAL, 1971. **Collections:** Baltimore/MA; Birmingham, Ala./MA; Boston/MFA; Buffalo/Albright; Chase Manhattan Bank; Chicago/AI; Hartford/Wadsworth; MMA; MOMA; Manufacturers Hanover Trust Co.; Michigan State U.; NYU; Newark Museum; U. of Notre Dame; RISD; Raleigh/NCMA; SRGM; Syracuse U.; WMAA. **Bibliography:** Baur 5; Blesh 1; **Bush and Moffett**; Downes, ed.; Friedman, ed.; Goodrich and Baur 1; Guest and Friedman; Janis and Blesh 1; Nordness, ed.; Rose, B., 1; Sandler 1; Seitz 3.

GOODYEAR, JOHN. b. October 22, 1930, Los Angeles, Calif. **Studied:** U. of Michigan (with Richard Wilt, Chet LaMore, Gerome Kamrowski), B. Design, 1952, M. Design, 1954. Traveled Mexico, Western Europe; resided USA, Japan. **Taught:** U. of Michigan; U. of Massachusetts, Douglass College 1964–. **Awards:** Graham Foundation Fellowship, 1962, 70; Trenton/State, Gov. Hughes P.P., 1967; MIT, Center for Advanced Visual Studies Grant, 1970–71. **Address:** R.D. #2, Lambertville, NJ 08530. **One-man Exhibitions:** The Amel Gallery, NYC,

1964–66; ICA, Boston, 1971; Musée de Quebec, 1971; Electric Gallery, Toronto, 1971; Cornell U., 1972; Syracuse U., 1972; Allegheny College, 1972; Inhibodress Gallery, Sydney, 1972; New Jersey State Cultural Center, 1975. **Group:** MOMA, The Responsive Eye, 1965; Buffalo/Albright, 1965; ICA, Boston, 1965; Harvard U., 1965; WMAA, Art of the U.S. 1670–1966, 1966; Walker and Milwaukee, Light Motion Space, 1967; Buffalo/Albright, Plus by Minus, 1968; Milwaukee, Directions I: Options, circ., 1968; WMAA Sculpture Annual, 1968; Newark Museum, 1969; Jewish Museum, Software, 1970; Boston/MFA, Elements of Art, 1971; Centro de Arte y Communicacion, Buenos Aires, Arte de Sistemas, II, 1972; MIT, Interaction, 1973; New Jersey Cultural Central, Constructivist Art, 1975. **Collections:** Corcoran; Cornell U.; MOMA; U. of Massachusetts; Mills College; Milwaukee; Muskegon/Hackley; NYU; Newark Museum; New Jersey Cultural Center; Norfolk/Chrysler; U. of North Carolina; Purchase/SUNY; Quebec; Smith College; Spelman College; SRGM; U. of Texas; Trenton/State; WMAA. **Bibliography:** Atkinson; MacAgy 2; Rickey.

GORCHOV, RON. b. April 5, 1930, Chicago, Ill. **Studied:** U. of Mississippi, 1947–48; Roosevelt College; Chicago/AI School, 1948–50; U. of Illinois, 1950–51. Traveled USA, Europe. **Taught:** Hunter College, 1962– . Designed Stage sets for Theater Club of New York production of Lorca's *Shoemaker's Prodigious Wife*, 1957. **Awards:** Ingram Merrill Foundation Grant, 1959; National Arts Club Annual, NYC, Hon. Men., 1959. **Address:** P. O. Box 337, Canal Street Station, NYC 10013. **Dealer:** Hamilton Gallery of Contemporary Art, NYC. **One-man Exhibitions:** Tibor de Nagy Gallery, NYC, 1960, 63, 66; Syracuse/Everson, 1972; The Texas Gallery, 1974; Fischbach Gallery, 1975; Henri 2, Washington, D.C. (two-man), 1975; Texas Gallery, Houston, 1976; Suzanne Hilberry Gallery, Birmingham, Mich., 1977, 79; Galerie M, Bochum, Germany (two-man), 1978; U. of California, Berkeley, 1978; Palazzo Reale, Milan, 1979; P.S.7, Long Island City, 1979; Young-Hoffman Gallery, Chicago, 1979; Hamilton Gallery of Contemporary Art, NYC, 1979. **Group:** The Stable Gallery, NYC, Invitational, 1958; National Arts Club Annual, NYC, 1959; WMAA, Young America, 1960; VMFA, 1964; Syracuse/Everson, 1971; Akademie der Kunst, Berlin, SoHo, 1976; Brockport/SUNY, Recent Abstract Painting, 1976; California State U., Los Angeles, New Work/New York, 1976; New Museum, NYC, Early Work by Five Contemporary Artists, 1977; WMAA Biennial, 1977; NYU, American Painting of the 1980s, 1979. **Collections:** Glen Alden Corp.; Hartford/ Wadsworth; MOMA; MMA; SRGM; Syracuse/Everson; WMAA.

GORDIN, SIDNEY. b. October 24, 1918, Cheliabinsk, Russia. **Studied:** Cooper Union, 1937–41, with Morris Kantor, Carol Harrison, Leo Katz. **Taught:** Pratt Institute, 1953–58; Brooklyn College, 1955–58; New School for Social Research, 1956–58; Sarah Lawrence College, 1957–58; U. of California, Berkeley, 1958– . **Commissions:** (sculpture): Temple Israel, Tulsa, Okla., 1959; Envoy Towers, 300 East 46th Street, NYC, 1960. **Address:** 903 Camilia Street, Berkeley, Calif. **One-man Exhibitions:** Bennington College, 1951; Peter Cooper Gallery, NYC, 1951; Grace Borgenicht Gallery, Inc., 1953, 55, 58, 60, 61; New School for Social Research, 1957; Dilexi Gallery, San Francisco, 1959, 63, 65; de Young, 1962; Los Angeles/County MA, 1963; Zabriskie Gallery, NYC, 1979; Sid Deutsch Gallery, NYC, 1980. **Group:** MMA, 1951; WMAA Annuals, 1952–57; MOMA; Chicago/AI; PAFA, 1954, 55; Brooklyn Museum; Newark Museum; SFMA; Oakland/AM; Tulsa/Philbrook, 1960. **Collections:** Chicago/AI; Newark Museum; Norfolk/Chrysler; Southern Illinois U.; WMAA. **Bibliography:** Goodrich and Baur 1; Mendelowitz; Seuphor 3.

GORDY, ROBERT. b. October 14, 1933, Jefferson Island, Louisiana. **Studied:** Louisiana State U., Baton Rouge, BA, MA; Yale U., 1953, and with Hans Hofmann. **Awards:** National Council of the Arts, grant, 1967; National Endowment for the Arts, 1978. **Address:** 2630 Bell Street, New Orleans, LA 70119. **Dealer:** Phyllis Kind Gallery, Chicago and NYC. **One-man Exhibitions:** Emily Lowes Gallery, New Orleans, 1965; Glade Gallery, New Orleans, 1967, 68; Tampa Bay Art Center, 1969; Hank Baum Gallery, San Francisco, 1969, 71, 73; Cranfill Gallery, Dallas, 1971; Glasgow College of Arts, Scotland, 1972; Galerie Simone Stern, New Orleans, 1968, 70, 71, 72, 73; Mills College, 1973; Long Beach/MA, 1975; Phyllis Kind Gallery, Chicago, 1976; Delahunty, Inc., Dallas, 1977; Phyllis Kind Gallery, NYC, 1979. **Retrospective:** New Orleans Museum, 1981. **Group:** ICA, U. of Pennsylvania, The Spirit of the Comics, 1969; Fort Worth, Contemporary Drawings, 1969; WMAA Biennials, 1967, 73; Memphis/Brooks, American Painting and Sculpture, 1973; NCFA, Divergent Representation, 1973; WMAA, Extraordinary Realists, 1973; Moore College of Art, Philadelphia, North, East, South, West, and Middle, 1975; Brooklyn Museum, 21st National Print Exhibition, 1978. **Collections:** Corcoran; Dallas/MFA; Fort Worth; New Orleans Museum; Oklahoma; Tampa Bay Art Center; Wichita/AM; WMAA.

GORKY, ARSHILE (Vosdanig Manoog Adoian). b. 1905. Khorkom Vari Haiyotz Dzor, Armenia; **d.** July 21, 1948, Sherman, Conn. To USA, 1920. **Studied:** Polytechnic Institute, Tiflis, 1916–18; RISD; Providence (R.I.) Technical High School; New School of Design, Boston, 1923; NAD, 1925. **Taught:**

Arshile Gorky *Drawing* 1931–32

New School of Design, Boston, 1924; Grand Central School, NYC, 1925–31. **Commissions:** Federal A.P.: Newark (N.J.) Airport 1935–38 (mural). Aviation Building, New York World's Fair, 1939 (mural). Fire destroyed 27 paintings in his studio, January 1946. **One-man Exhibitions:** (first) Guild Art Gallery, NYC, 1932, also 1935, 36; Mellon Galleries, Philadelphia, 1934; Boyer Gallery, Philadelphia, 1935; Boyer Gallery, NYC, 1938; The Kootz Gallery, NYC, 1942, 50, 51; Julien Levy Galleries, NYC, 1945, 46, 47, 1948 (two-man, with Howard Warshaw); WMAA, Memorial Exhibition, 1951; Princeton U., 1952; Paul Kantor Gallery, Beverly Hills, Calif., 1952; Sidney Price Gallery, NYC, 1952, 55, 57; U. of Maryland, 1969; M. Knoedler & Co., 1969, 70, 73, 75; Dunkelman Gallery, Toronto, 1972; Galatea Galleria d'Arte, Turin, 1972; Allan Stone Gallery, 1973; Richard Feigen Gallery, NYC, 1973; U. of Texas, Austin, 1975; Oxford/MOMA, 1975; Washburn Gallery, NYC, 1978; Newark Museum, 1978; Xavier Fourcade, Inc., NYC, 1979, Hirshhorn, 1979. **Retrospective:** SFMA, 1941; MOMA, 1963; SRGM, 1981. **Group:** WMAA Annuals; MOMA, 46 Painters and Sculptors under 35 Years of Age, 1930; WMAA, Abstract Painting in America, 1935; MOMA, Fourteen Americans, circ., 1946; Galerie Maeght, 6 Surrealists in 1947, 1947; XXIV & XXV Venice Biennials, 1948, 50; Galerie de France, Paris, 1952; MOMA, The New American Painting, circ. Europe, 1958–59; MOMA, The New American Painting and Sculpture, 1969; 20th Century American Drawing; Three Avant-Garde Generations, 1976; Hirshhorn, The Golden Door, 1976; MOMA, The Natural Paradise; Painting in America 1800–1950, 1976; Milwaukee, From Foreign Shores, 1976; Oswego/SUNY, The New Deal for Art, 1977; Brown U., Graham, Gorky, Smith and Davis in the Thirties, 1977; Paris/Beaubourg, Paris–New York, 1977; Houston/MFA, American Paintings, 1910–1949, 1977;

Royal Scottish Academy, Edinburgh, Modern Spirit in American Painting, 1908–1935, 1977; Cornell U., Abstract Expressionism: The Formative Years, 1978; National Gallery, Washington, D.C., American Art at Mid-Century, 1978; Cleveland/MA, The Spirit of Surrealism, 1979. **Collections:** U. of Arizona; Baltimore/MA; Brooklyn Museum; Buffalo/Albright; Canberra/National; Chicago/AI; Cleveland/MA; High Museum; Hirshhorn; Indiana U.; Kansas City/Nelson; Los Angeles/County MA; MMA; MOMA; NYU; National Gallery; Oberlin College; Art Gallery of Ontario, Toronto; SFMA; SRGM; Seattle; Tate; U. of Texas, Austin; Utica; WMAA; Washington U.; Yale U. **Bibliography:** Ashton 5; Barr 3; Baur 5, 7; Blesh 1; Breton 2, 3; Calas; Cheney; Chipp; Eliot; Flanagan; Gerdts; Goodrich and Baur 1; Greenberg 1; Haftman; Hess, T.B., 1; Hunter 1, 6; Hunter, ed.; Janis, S.; **Joyner**; Kozloff 3; Langui; **Levy 1**; Lynton; McCoubrey 1; McCurdy, ed.; Miller, ed. 2; Myers 2; Neumeyer; Newmeyer; Passloff; Ponente; Pousette-Dart, ed.; Ragon 1; Read 2; Richardson, E.P.; Ritchie 1; Rodman 2; Rose, B., 1, 4; **Rosenberg 1**; Rubin 1; Sandler; **Schwabacher; Seitz 1, 2**; Seuphor 1; Soby 6; Tomkins and Time-Life Books; Tuchman, ed.; Waldbert 3, 4; Weller.

GOTO, JOSEPH. b. January 7, 1920, Hilo, Hawaii. **Studied:** Chicago/AI School; Roosevelt U. **Taught:** College of William and Mary, 1958–59; U. of Michigan, 1959–63; RISD, 1963–65; U. of Illinois, 1965, Carnegie, 1958; Brandeis U., 1970. **Awards:** Chicago/AI, **P.P.**, 1957; Graham Foundation Fellowship, 1957; John Hay Whitney Fellowship; Chicago/AI, Watson F. Blair Prize; Chicago/AI, The Mr. & Mrs. Frank G. Logan Prize; Chicago/AI, Pauline Palmer Prize; J.S. Guggenheim Fellowship, 1969; Rhode Island, Governor's Arts Award, 1972. **Address:** 17 Sixth Street, Providence, R.I. **One-man Exhibitions:** Allan Frumkin Gallery, NYC

and Chicago, 1962; Stephen Radich Gallery, NYC, 1964, 65, 67; Honolulu Academy, 1973; Contemporary Arts Center of Hawaii, Honolulu, 1973; The Zabriskie Gallery, 1973. **Retrospective:** RISD, 1972. **Group:** Chicago/AI; Carnegie; U. of Illinois; Louisville/Speed, WMAA; Chicago/AI, Exhibition Momentum; Denver/AM; Houston/MFA, 1957; VMFA, 1958; Carnegie, 1970. **Collections:** Chicago/AI; Indiana U.; MOMA; U. of Michigan; Union Carbide Corp. **Bibliography: Joseph Goto**; Rubin 1.

GOTTLIEB, ADOLPH. b. March 14, 1903, NYC; **d.** March 4, 1974, NYC. **Studied:** ASL, 1919, with John Sloan, Robert Henri; Academie de la Grande Chaumiere, 1921; Parsons School of Design, 1923. Exhibited with The Ten, NYC, 1935–40. President, Federation of Modern Painters, 1944–45. **Taught:** Pratt Institute, 1958; UCLA, 1958. **Awards:** Winner of Dudensing National Competition, 1929; US Treasury Department, Mural Competition, 1939; Brooklyn Museum, First Prize, 1944; U. of Illinois, **P.P.**, 1951; Carnegie, Third Prize, 1961; VII Sao Paulo Biennial, First Prize, 1963; American Academy of Achievement, 1965; Flint/Institute **P.P.**, 1966. **One-man Exhibitions:** (first) Dudensing Gallery, NYC, 1930; Uptown Gallery, NYC, 1934; Theodore A. Kohn Gallery, NYC, 1934; Artists' Gallery, NYC, 1942, 43; Wakefield Gallery, NYC, 1944; "67" Gallery, NYC, 1945; Karl Nierendorf Gallery, NYC, 1945; The Kootz Gallery, NYC, 1947, 1950–54; J. Seligmann and Co., 1949; Area Arts Gallery, San Francisco, 1953; Williams College, 1954; The Kootz Gallery, Provincetown, Mass., 1954; Martha Jackson Gallery, 1957; HCE Gallery, Provincetown, Mass., 1957; Andre Emmerich Gallery, 1958, 59, 77, 78, 79; Galerie Rive Droite, Paris, 1959; Paul Kantor Gallery, Beverly Hills, Calif., 1959; ICA London, 1959; French & Co. Inc., NYC, 1960; Sidney Janis Gallery, 1960, 62; Galleria dell' Ariete, 1961; Galerie

Handschin, Basel, 1961; Walker, 1963; Marlborough-Gerson Gallery, Inc., 1964–66, 71, 72, 73, 74; MIT, 1966; Arts Club of Chicago, 1967; U. of Maryland, 1970; Galleria Lorenzelli, Bergamo, 1970; Gertrude Kasle Gallery, 1970, 74; Marlborough Fine Art Ltd., London, 1972; MOMA, 1974; Edmonton Art Gallery, Alberta, circ., 1977–78; Thomas Segal Gallery, Boston, 1978; Klonaridis Inc., Toronto, 1979. **Retrospectives:** Bennington College, 1954; Jewish Museum, 1957; WMAA and SRGM, 1968. **Group:** WMAA Annuals, 1944, 45, 46, 48, 51, 53, 55, 61; PAFA; Walker; Chicago/AI, Abstract and Surrealist Art, 1948; Carnegie, 1952, 55, 58, 61; SRGM, Younger American Painters, 1954; WMAA, The New Decade, 1954–55; MOMA, The New American Painting, circ., Europe, 1958–59; Documenta II, Kassel, 1959; Seattle World's Fair, 1962; VII Sao Paulo Biennial, 1963; Tate, Gulbenkian International 1964, Dunn International, 1964; Chicago/AI Annual, 1966; Flint/Institute, Flint Invitational, 1966; Corcoran, 1966, Biennial, 1967; Winnipeg Art Gallery, 1967; MOMA, The New American Painting and Sculpture, 1969; Boston/MFA, Abstract Painting in the 70's, 1972; WMAA Biennial, 73; Cornell U., Abstract Expressionists: The Formative Years, 1978; Sao Paulo, Biennial, circ., 1979. **Collections:** Andover/Phillips; Atlanta/AA; Ball State U.; Bezalel Museum; Brandeis U.; Brooklyn Museum; Buffalo/Albright; Carnegie; Chicago/AI; Columbia U.; Corcoran; Cornell U.; Dallas/MFA; Des Moines; Detroit/Institute; Flint/Institute; Hartford/Wadsworth; U. of Illinois; Jewish Museum; Los Angeles/County MA; MMA; MOMA; U. of Miami; NYU; U. of Nebraska; U. of Nevada; Newark Museum; New Orleans/Delgado; Pasadena/AM; Phillips; SRGM; San Jose Library; Santa Barbara/MA; Seagram Collection; Smith College; Society of the Four Arts; Tel Aviv; Utica; VMFA; WMAA; Walker; Yale U.; Youngstown/Butler; **Bibliography:** Alloway 4; Ashton 5; Barr 3; Baur 5, 7; Blesh 1; Chipp; Eliot; **Friedman, M.,** 1;

Goodrich and Baur 1; *The Great Decade;* Greenberg 1; Haftman; Hess, T.B., 1; Hobbs and Levin; Hunter 1, 6; Hunter, ed.; Janis, S.; Kootz 2; Mendelowitz; *Metro:* Motherwell and Reinhardt, eds.; Myers 2; Neumeyer; Nordness, ed.; Pousette-Dart, ed.; Read 2; Richardson, E.P.; Rodman 1, 2, 3; Rose, B., 1, 4; Rosenblum 2; Rubin 1; Sandler; Seuphor 1; Soby 5; Tomkins 2; Tuchman, ed.; Weller; Wight 2. Archives.

GOULET, LORRIE. b. August 17, 1925, Riverdale, N.Y. **Studied:** Black Mountain College, 1943–45, with Josef Albers, Jose de Creeft. Traveled USA, Europe. **Taught:** Scarsdale Art Workshop, and privately, 1957–61; MOMA School, 1957–64; New School for Social Research, 1961–75. **Member:** Sculptors Guild; Artists Equity; Audubon Artists. **Commissions:** Grand Concourse (Bronx) Public Library, 1958 (ceramic relief); Nurses Residence and School, Bronx Municipal Hospital Center, 1961 (relief); 48th Precinct Police and Fire Station, Bronx, 1971. CBS–TV, lecture-demonstrations on sculpture for children's series "Around the Corner," 1964, 66, 67, 68. **Awards:** West Palm Beach/Norton, First Prize, 1949, 50; Westchester (N.Y.) Art Society, First Prize, 1964; Audubon Artists, Solten Engel Memorial Award, 1966. **m.** Jose de Creeft. **Address:** 241 West 20th Street, NYC 10011. **Dealer:** Kennedy Gallery. **One-man Exhibitions:** (first) Clay Club, NYC, 1948; Sculpture Center, 1955; The Contemporaries, NYC, 1959, 62, 66, 68; New School for Social Research, 1968; Temple Emeth, N.J., 1969; Kennedy Gallery, 1971, 72, 75, 78. **Group:** PAFA, annually since 1948; Audubon Artists, annually since 1948; WMAA Annuals 1948, 49, 50, 53, 55; Philadelphia Art Alliance, 1950; MMA, 1951; Sculptors Guild, annually since 1960; AAAL, 1961; A.F.A., Mother and Child in Modern Art, circ., 1963; Carroll Reece Memorial Museum, Johnson City, Tenn.; Black Mountain College, 1964; New York World's Fair, 1964–65;

NAD, 1966; New School for Social Research, Erotic Art, 1973; National Arts Club, NYC, 1978. **Collections:** Hirshhorn; Trenton/State; WMAA; Wichita/AM. **Bibliography:** Archives.

GRAHAM, JOHN D. b. 1881, Kiev, Russia; **d.** 1961, London, England. **Studied:** U. of Kiev, degree in law, 1911; ASL, 1921, with John Sloan. To USA, 1920; became a citizen. Traveled Europe, Asia, Africa, USA. **One-man Exhibitions:** (first) Baltimore/MA, 1926; Galerie Zborowski, Paris, 1929; Societe Anonyme, NYC, 1931; Eighth Street Gallery, NYC, 1933; Artists' Gallery, NYC, 1941; The Pinacotheca, NYC, 1946; Dudensing Gallery, NYC; The Stable Gallery, 1954; Gallery Mayer, NYC, 1960; Arts Club of Chicago, 1963; U. of Minnesota, 1964; Andre Emmerich Gallery, 1966; MOMA, 1968; Phyllis Kind Gallery, Chicago, 1970; Donald Morris Gallery, 1972; Allan Stone Gallery, 1973; The Zabriskie Gallery, 1973; Andre Emmerich Gallery, NYC. **Group:** MOMA; WMAA; U. of Minnesota; Societe Anonyme, NYC; Brown U., Graham, Smith, Gorky, & Davis in the Thirties, 1977. **Collections:** Carnegie; MOMA; Nashville; Phillips; WMAA. **Bibliography:** Baur 7; Brown 2; Downes, ed.; *From Foreign Shores;* **George 2; Graham;** *Graham, Gorky, Smith & Davis in the Thirties;* Hunter 6; Janis, S.; Kootz 2; Passloff; Phillips 1; Rose, B., 1, 4; Sandler. Archives.

GRAHAM, ROBERT. b. August 19, 1938, Mexico, D.F. **Studied:** San Jose State College; SFAI, MFA. Traveled Germany, Switzerland, England. US Citizen. **Address:** 69 Windward Avenue, Venice, CA 90291. **Dealer:** Robert Miller Gallery, Inc., NYC. **One-man Exhibitions:** The Lanyon Gallery, 1964; Nicholas Wilder Gallery, 1966, 67, 69, 74, 75, 77; M.E. Thelen Gallery, Essen, 1967; The Kornblee Gallery, 1968, 69; Galerie Hans R. Neuendorf, Hamburg, 1968, 70, 74, 76, Cologne, 1968, 70;

Robert Graham   *Lise Dance Figure I*   1979

Galerie Rudolf Zwirner, 1970; Galerie Rene Block, Berlin, 1970; Whitechapel Art Gallery, London, 1970; Ileana Sonnabend Gallery, NYC, 1971; Hamburg/Kunstverein, 1971; Galerie Herbert Meyer-Ellingen, Frankfurt, 1972; Dallas/MFA, 1972; Felicity Samuel Gallery, London, 1974; Gimpel & Hanover, 1975; Greenberg Gallery, St. Louis, 1975; Texas Gallery, Houston, 1975; Rosenthal Gallery, Chicago, 1975; Galerie Neuendorf, Hamburg, 1976; Gimpel Fils, London, 1976; John Stoller Gallery, Minneapolis, 1977; Robert Miller Gallery, NYC, 1977, 79. **Group:** WMAA Sculpture Annuals, 1966, 69, 71; Washington U. (St. Louis), Here and Now, 1969; Victoria and Albert Museum, Three Americans, 1971; Hamburg/Kunstverein, USA: West Coast, circ., 1972; NCFA, Sculpture: American Directions 1945–1975, 1975; Los Angeles/County MA, Los Angeles—Eight Artists, 1975; SFMA, Painting and Sculpture in California: The Modern Era, 1976; Rutgers U., Contemporary Artists Series Number 1, 1978; WMAA Biennial, 1979. **Collections:** Aachen; Cologne; Dallas/MFA; Des Moines; Hamburg/Kunstmuseum; Hirshhorn; MOMA; Paris/Moderne; Pasadena/AM; Rotterdam; Smith College; Victoria and Albert, London; WMAA. **Bibliography:** *Kunst um 1970;* Sager; *USA West Coast.*

GRANLUND, PAUL. b. October 6, 1925, Minneapolis, Minn. **Studied:** Gustavus Adolphus College, 1952, BA; U. of Minnesota; Cranbrook Academy of Art, 1954, MFA. **Taught:** Cranbrook Academy of Art, 1954; Minneapolis Institute School, 1955–68; U. of California, summer, 1959; Gustavus Adolphus College, 1968– . **Awards:** Cranbrook, George A. Booth Scholarship, 1953; Fulbright Fellowship, 1954; Guggenheim Foundation Fellowship, 1957, 58. **Address:** % Art Department, Gustavus Adolphus College, St. Peter, MI 56082. **One-man Exhibitions:** Minnesota State Fair, 1957; Minneapolis/Institute, 1959; Walker, 1965; Gustavus Adolphus College, 1956, 60; Allan Frumkin Gallery, Chicago, 1959, 66, 68, NYC, 1960, 63; Esther Robles Gallery, 1962; California Palace, 1962; Gethsemane Lutheran Church, Seattle, 1962; U. of Nebraska, 1964; Washington U., 1965. **Group:** American Academy, Rome, 1959; U. of Illinois, 1961; Cincinnati/AM, 1961; Corcoran, 1961; U. of Colorado, 1962; Buffalo/Albright, 1962; VMFA, 1962; Louisiana State U., 1964; Minneapolis School of Art, Art of Two Cities, 1965. **Collections:** A.F.A.; American Swed-

ish Institute; Cranbrook; Minneapolis/Institute; VMFA; Walker.

GRANT, JAMES. b. 1924, Los Angeles, Calif. **Studied:** U. of Southern California, B.Ed., 1945, MFA, 1950; Jepson Art Institute, Los Angeles, 1947–49. **Taught:** Pomona College, 1950–59. **Address:** % Dealer. **Dealer:** Hansen-Fuller Gallery. **One-man Exhibitions:** Pasadena/AM, 1952; U. of California, 1958; Humboldt State College, 1959; Pomona College, 1959; Grand Central Moderns, NYC, 1961, 63; Pogliani Gallery, Rome, 1962; de Young, 1963; Hansen Gallery, San Francisco, 1964–66. **Retrospective:** Mills College, 1970. **Group:** U. of Nebraska, 1962; U. of Virginia, 1963; M. Knoedler & Co., Art Across America, 1965–67; Sacramento/Crocker, 1966; San Francisco Art Association, 1966; U. of Illinois, 1967, 69; La Jolla; Cornell U.; Los Angeles/County MA; MOMA. **Collections:** Bank of America; Bank of California; Mary Washington College; Mead Corporation; U. of the Pacific; Pasadena/AM; Pomona College; SFMA.

GRAVES, MORRIS COLE. b. August 28, 1910, Fox Valley, Ore. Studied with Mark Tobey. Traveled Europe, the Orient, USA. Federal A.P.: Easel painting, 1936–39. US Army, 1943. **Awards:** Seattle/AM, Northwest Annual, $100 Award, 1933; Guggenheim Foundation Fellowship, 1946; Chicago/AI, Norman Wait Harris Medal, 1947; Chicago/AI, Watson F. Blair Prize, 1949; U. of Illinois, **P.P.,** 1955; NIAL Grant, 1956; Windsor Award, 1957. **Address:** Box 90, Loleta, CA 95551. **Dealer:** The Willard Gallery. **One-man Exhibitions:** (first) Seattle/AM, 1936, also 1956; The Willard Gallery, 1942, 44, 45, 48, 53, 54, 55, 59, 71, 73, 81; Arts Club of Chicago, 1943; U. of Minnesota, 1943; Detroit/Institute, 1943; Phillips, 1943, 54; Philadelphia Art Alliance, 1946; Santa Barbara/MA, 1948; Los Angeles/County

Morris Graves *Summer Fruit and Flowers* 1978

MA, 1948; Chicago/AI, 1948; Margaret Brown Gallery, Boston, 1950; Beaumont (Tex.) Art Museum, 1952; Kunstnernes hus Oslo, 1955; La Jolla, 1957; Bridgestone Museum, 1957; Phoenix, 1960; Roswell, 1961; Kalamazoo/Institute, 1961; Richard White Gallery, Seattle, 1969; Foster/White Gallery, Seattle, 1980; Charles Campbell Gallery, San Francisco, 1979. **Retrospective:** California Palace, 1948; WMAA, circ., 1956; Pavilion Gallery, Balboa, Calif., 1963; U. of Oregon, 1966; Tacoma, 1971. **Group:** Seattle/AM; WMAA; U. of Illinois; Chicago/AI; Phillips; MOMA, Americans 1942, circ., 1942; Houston/MFA, 1956; ICA, London, 1957; Brussels World's Fair, 1958; Seattle World's Fair, 1962; ICA, Boston, American Art since 1950, 1962; Amon Carter Museum, The Artist's Environment, West Coast, 1962; PAFA, 1963; Columbia, S.C./MA, Ascendency of American Painting, 1963; Tate, American Painting, 1963; St. Louis/City, 200 Years of American Painting, 1964; U. of Michigan, One Hundred Contemporary American Drawings, 1965; MOMA, The Object Transformed, 1966; U. of Illinois, 1969; Minnesota/MA, Drawings USA, 1971; St. Joseph/Albrecht, Drawing—America: 1973, 1973; NAD, 1974. **Collections:** Baltimore/MA; Boston/MFA; Buffalo/Albright; U. of California; Chicago/AI; Cincinnati/AM; Cleveland/MA; Denver/AM; Detroit/Institute; Fort Wayne/AM; Hartford/Wadsworth; Harvard U.; Hirshhorn; U. of Illinois; MMA; MOMA; Milwaukee; NIAL; U. of Nebraska; Ogunquit; Pasadena/AM; Phillips; Portland, Ore./AM; Purchase/SUNY; SFMA; SRGM; Santa Barbara/MA; Seattle/AM; Tacoma; U. of Texas; Toronto; Upjohn Co.; Utica; WMAA; U. of Washington; Wilmington; Worcester/AM. **Bibliography:** *Art of the Pacific Northwest;* Baldinger; Barker 1; Barr 3; Baur 7; Bazin; Beekman; Blesh 1; **Cage;** Canaday; Flanagan; Flexner; Frost; Goodrich and Baur 1; Haftman; Honisch and Jensen, eds.; Hunter 6; Janis, S.; Kootz 2; Kuh 1, 2; Langui; McCurdy, ed.; Mendelowitz; Miller, ed., 1; Munsterberg; Neumeyer; Nordness, ed.; *Northwest Traditions;* Pousette-Dart, ed.; Ragon 1; Read 2, 3; Richardson, E.P.; Rodman 1, 2; Rose, B., 1; Sachs; Soby 5; Sutton; Valentine 2; Weller; Wight 2; **Wight, Baur, and Phillips.**

GRAVES, NANCY STEVENSON. b. December 23, 1940, Pittsfield, Mass. **Studied:** Vassar College, 1961, BA; Yale U., 1962, BFA, 1964, MFA. **Awards:** Fulbright Fellowship, 1965; Vassar College Grant, 1971; Paris Biennial Grant, 1971; National Endowment for the Arts, 1972; CAPS, 1973; American Academy, Rome, Fellowship, 1979. Also produces films. **Address:** 69 Wooster Street, NYC 10012. **Dealer:** M. Knoedler & Co., Inc. **One-man Exhibitions:** The Graham Gallery, 1968; WMAA, 1969; Ottawa/National, 1970, 71, 73; Reese Palley Gallery, NYC, 1971, Reese Palley Gallery, San Francisco, 1971; Aachen/NG, 1971; Vassar College, 1971; MOMA, 1971; New Gallery, Cleveland, 1972; Janie C. Lee Gallery, Dallas, 1972, 73, 75; ICA, U. of Pennsylvania, 1972; Janie C. Lee Gallery, Houston, 1974, 75, 76, 77, 78; Pittsfield/Berkshire, 1973; Art Museum of South Texas, Corpus Christi, 1973; Andre Emmerich Gallery, NYC, 1974, 77; Buffalo/Albright, 1974, 80; Galerie Andre Emmerich, Zurich, 1977; Galerie im Schloss, Munich, 1977; M. Knoedler & Co., Inc., NYC, 1978, 79, 80; Diane Gilson Gallery, Seattle, 1978. **Group:** WMAA Annuals, 1970, 71, 73; MOMA, Information, 1971; Corcoran, Depth and Presence, 1971; Dusseldorf/Kunsthalle, Prospect '71, 1971; Chicago/Contemporary, Six Sculptors, 1971; VII Paris Biennial, 1971; Kunsthaus, Hamburg, American Women Artists, 1972; Documenta V, Kassel, 1972; New York Cultural Center, 3D into 2D, 1973; WMAA, American Drawings; 1963–1973, 1973; Cologne, Project 74, 1974; Sarah Lawrence College, Drawings by Women, 1975; Leverkusen, American Drawings, 1975; Corcoran, The Liberation, 1976; US Department of the Interior, America 1976, circ., 1976; WMAA, 200 Years of American Sculpture, 1976; Kassel, Documenta VI, 1977; U. of Texas, Austin, New in the Seventies, 1977; U. of California, Santa Barbara, Contemporary Drawing/New York, 1977; Albright College, Perspective 78, 1978; Buffalo/Albright, American Painting of the 1970s, circ., 1978;

Zurich/Kunsthaus, Weich und Plastisch—Soft Art, 1979; ICA, U. of Pennsylvania, Masks, Tents, Vessels, Talismans, 1979. **Collections:** Aachen/NG; Art Museum of South Texas; Buffalo/Albright; CNAC; U. of California, Berkeley; Chicago/AI; Cologne; Des Moines; Houston/MFA; La Jolla; Memphis/Brooks; MMA; MOMA; Ottawa/National; Vienna/Stadt; WMAA. **Bibliography:** *America 1976; Art: A Woman's Sensibility; Art Now 74; Drawings: The Pluralist Decade; Kunst um 1970;* Lippard 3; Lucie-Smith; *New in the Seventies;* **Nancy Graves,** 1973; **Nancy Graves,** 1971; Sager. Archives.

GRAY, CLEVE. b. September 22, 1918, NYC. **Studied:** Princeton U., 1940, BA summa cum laude, PBK; Academie Andre Lhote; privately with Jacques Villon in Paris. US Army, 1943–46. Traveled in Europe, USA. **Taught:** Honolulu Academy, 1970–71. Trustee, New York Studio School, 1970– . **Member:** Century Association. **Awards:** U. of Illinois, **P.P.**; Ford Foundation, **P.P. Address:** Cornwall Bridge, Cornwall, CT 06754. **Dealers:** Betty Parsons Gallery; Sneed-Hillman Gallery. **One-man Exhibitions:** (first) J. Seligmann and Co., 1947, also 1948, 49, 50, 52, 54, 57, 59; Staempfli Gallery, 1960, 62, 64; Galleria Pagani del Grattacielo, Milan, 1963; Jerrold Morris Gallery, Toronto, 1963; Oklahoma, 1963; Saidenberg Gallery, 1965, 67; Hargate Art Center, Concord, Mass., 1969; Betty Parsons Gallery, 1970, 72, 74, 76, 80; Sneed-Hillman Gallery, 1970, 73, 74; Honolulu Academy, 1970, 71; Princeton U., 1970. **Group:** WMAA Annuals; Chicago/AI; SRGM, Abstract Expressionists and Imagists, 1961; Hartford/Wadsworth; PAFA; El Retiro Parquet, Arte de America y Espana, 1963; Andover/Phillips, Decades, 1969; Minnesota/MA, Drawings USA, 1973. **Collections:** Andover/Phillips; Brandeis U.; U. of California; Corcoran; Columbia U.; Columbus; Hartford/Wadsworth; Honolulu Academy; U. of Illinois; MMA; Minnesota/

MA; NCFA; NYU; Nashville; U. of Nebraska; New School for Social Research; U. of Notre Dame; Oklahoma; Purchase/SUNY; RISD; SRGM; Vanderbilt U.; WMAA; Williams College. **Bibliography:** Goodrich and Baur 1; *7 Decades*. Archives.

GREENE, BALCOMB. b. May 22, 1904, Shelby, N.Y. **Studied:** Syracuse U., 1922–26, AB; Columbia U., 1927; U. of Vienna, 1926–27; NYU, 1943, MA; self-taught in art. Traveled Europe extensively. **Taught:** Dartmouth College (English), 1928–31; Carnegie, 1942–59. Editor, *Art Front* magazine, 1935–36. Fire in New York studio, 1941, destroyed many early paintings. **Member:** American Abstract Artists (first chairman, 1936–37, 1938–39, 1940–41); International Institute of Arts and Letters; Cosmopolitan Club, NYC. Federal A.P. Mural Division: New York World's Fair, 1939, Federal Hall of Medicine (mural); Bronx (N.Y.) High School of Science (stained-glass window); Williamsburg Housing Project, Brooklyn, 1939 (mural); NIAL. **Awards:** *Art News* (magazine) Critics Choice, 1950, 53, 55, 56; PAFA, Carol H. Beck Gold Medal, 1961; NAD, Benjamin Altman Prize for Figure Painting, 1976. **Address:** 2 Sutton Place South, NYC 10022; Montauk Point, N.Y. **Dealer:** ACA Gallery, NYC. **One-man Exhibitions:** (first) a gallery in Paris, 1932; J. B. Neumann's New Art Circle, NYC, 1947; The Bertha Schaefer Gallery, 1952, 54, 55, 56, 58, 59, 61; Arts and Crafts Center, Pittsburgh, 1953, 66; American U., 1957; Brookhaven National Laboratory, 1959; American Cultural Center, Paris, 1960; Saidenberg Gallery, 1962, 63, 65, 67, 68; Feingarten Gallery; Los Angeles, 1963, 64; La Jolla, 1965; U. of Florida, 1965; Tampa/AI, 1965; James David Gallery, Miami, 1965, 66; Main Street Gallery, Chicago, 1966; Santa Barbara/MA, 1966; Phoenix, 1966; Adele Bednarz Gallery, 1966–69; Occidental College, 1967; The Berenson Gallery, 1967, 68, 69; Makler Gallery,

Philadelphia, 1968; The Forum Gallery, 1970, 73, 74, 75; Fairweather-Hardin Gallery, Chicago, 1972, 73; Harmon Gallery, Naples, Florida, 1974, 75, 76, 77; International Oceanographic Institute, Key Biscayne, Fla., 1976; ACA Gallery, NYC, 1977, 79. **Retrospective:** WMAA/A.F.A., circ., 1961; Guild Hall, East Hampton, 1978. **Group:** American Abstract Artists Annuals; WMAA Annuals; U. of Illinois; Chicago/AI; Walker; SRGM; Brooklyn Museum; Carnegie. **Collections:** Ball State U.; Baltimore/MA; Brooklyn Museum; Carnegie; Chicago/AI; Corcoran; Guild Hall; Hartford/Wadsworth; Houston/MFA; Indianapolis/Herron; U. of North Carolina; MIT; MMA; MOMA; U. of Miami; NCFA; U. of Nebraska; U. of North Carolina; Omaha/Joslyn; PAFA; Pasadena/AM; Portland, Ore./AM; Purchase/SUNY; SRGM; U. of Texas; Vassar College; U. of Virginia; WMAA; Walker; Youngstown/Butler. **Bibliography:** Baur 5, 7; Flanagan; Frost; Goodrich and Baur 1; Hess, T.B., 1; Janis, S.; Kootz 2; Newmeyer; Nordness, ed.; Pousette-Dart, ed.; Read 2; Richardson, E.P.; Ritchie 1; Rodman 3; Rose, B., 4; Archives.

GREENE, STEPHEN. b. September 19, 1918, NYC. **Studied:** ASL, with Morris Kantor, 1937; State U. of Iowa, with Philip Guston, 1939–42, 1944–45, BFA, MA. Traveled Europe, North Africa. **Taught:** Indiana U., 1945–56; Washington U., 1946–47; Pratt Institute, 1959–64; Parsons School of Design; NYU; Princeton U., Artist-in-Residence, 1956–59; ASL, 1959–65; Columbia U., 1961–68; Stella Elkins Tyler School of Fine Arts, Temple U., 1968– . **Member:** Trustee, Louis Comfort Tiffany Foundation. **Awards:** Prix de Rome, 1949; Corcoran, William A. Clark Prize and Corcoran Medal, 1966; National Council on the Arts, $5,000, 1966; NIAL, $2,500, 1967; NAD, Andrew Carnegie Prize, 1970 **Address:** 408A Storms Road, Valley College, NY

10989. **Dealer:** Marilyn Pearl Gallery, NYC; Galeria Ponce, Mexico City. **One-man Exhibitions:** (first) Durlacher Brothers, 1947, also 1949, 52; Grace Borgenicht Gallery Inc., 1955, 57, 58; Staempfli Gallery, 1961 (circ., 1964), 64, 66, 69; William Zierler, Inc., 1971, 72, 73; U. of Wisconsin, 1972; U. of Alberta, circ., 1972; Galleria d'Arte l'Obelisco, 1975; College of William and Mary, 1977; U. of Connecticut, 1977; Marilyn Pearl Gallery, NYC, 1978, 80, Galeria Ponce, Mexico City, 1977, 79. **Retrospectives:** Corcoran, 1963; Lincoln, Mass./De Cordova, 1953; Akron/AI, circ., 1978. **Group:** MMA, American Paintings Today, 1950; Chicago/AI, Contemporary Drawings from 12 Countries, 1952; Walker, Reality and Fantasy, 1954; Paris/Moderne, American Drawings, 1954; WMAA, The New Decade, 1954-55; MOMA, Recent Drawings USA, 1956; I International Religious Art Biennial, Salzburg, 1958; VI Sao Paulo Biennial, 1961; WMAA Annuals; SRGM, Abstract Expressionists and Imagists, 1961; Corcoran; Carnegie; Chicago/AI; El Retiro Parquet, Madrid, Arte de America y Espana, 1963; Internationale der Zeichnung, Darmstadt, 1964; MMA, American Paintings, Drawings and Watercolors from the Museum's Collections, 1969; WMAA, Human Concern/Personal Torment, 1969; Foundation Maeght, L'Art Vivant, 1970; Museo Comunale, Prato, Italy, American Painters in Europe, 1973; SRGM, American Painters through Two Decades, 1973; Rome Quadriennial, 1977. **Collections:** American Republic Insurance Co.; Andover/Phillips; Atlantic Richfield Co.; Brandeis U.; Chase Manhattan Bank; Chicago/AI; Corcoran; Dayton/AI; Detroit/Institute; Hamline U.; Hartford; U. of Illinois; Indiana U.; Indianapolis/Herron; Kalamazoo/Institute; Kansas City/Nelson; U. of Kentucky; MMA; MOMA; Minnesota/MA; NYU; Nashville; New Orleans/Delgado; Owens-Corning Fiberglas Corp.; Pasadena/AM; Princeton U.; SFMA; SRGM; St. Louis/City; Santa Barbara/MA; Tate; Trenton/

State; Utica; VMFA; WMAA. **Bibliography:** Baur 7; Bazin; Genauer; Mendelowitz; Sachs; Soby 5. Archives.

GREENLY, COLIN. b. January 21, 1928, London, England. **Studied:** Harvard U., 1948, AB; American U. (with Robert Gates); Columbia U. (with Oronzio Maldarelli, Peppino Mangravite). Traveled western USA, France, Italy, England. **Taught:** Established art programs for employee groups at Standard Oil, Metropolitan Life Insurance Co., Union Carbide Corp., New York Life Insurance, all NYC, 1951-53; US Dept. of Agriculture, Graduate School, 1954-56; Madeira School, Greenway, Va., 1955-68; Colgate U., 1972-73; Central Michigan U., 1972; Finch College, NYC, 1974; Windham College, 1976. **Commissions:** New York State Office Building, Utica (twelve color panels), 1973. **Awards:** Corcoran, **P.P.**, 1956; The Corcoran School of Art, National Playground Sculpture Competition, First Prize, 1967; National Council on the Arts, Grant, 1967; CAPS, 1972, 77; Committee for the Visual Arts Grant, NYC, 1974. **Address:** RD1, Box 118, Campbell Hall, NY 15916. **One-man Exhibitions:** (first) Jefferson Place Gallery, 1958, also 1960, 63, 65; The Bertha Schaefer Gallery, 1964, 66, 68; Corcoran, 1968; Royal Marks Gallery, 1968, 70; Syracuse/Everson, 1971; Cornell U., 1972; Fredonia/SUNY, 1973; Colgate U., 1973; The Schenectady (N.Y.) Museum, 1973; Alfred/SUNY, 1974, 75; Nassau Community College, Garden City, N.Y., 1974; Finch College, NYC, 1974; Creative Arts Workshop, New Haven, 1975; 112 Greene Street, NYC, 1976. **Retrospective:** Corcoran, 1968. **Group:** MOMA, Young American Printmakers, 1953; Corcoran, 1955-57; Lincoln, Mass./De Cordova, 1965; Flint/Institute, Made of Plastic, 1968; Grand Rapids, Sculpture of the 60s, 1969; Baltimore/MA, Washington; Twenty Years, 1970; New York State Fair, Enviro-Vision, circ., 1972; U. of Illinois, 1974. **Collec-**

tions: Buffalo/Albright; Corcoran; Cornell U.; Des Moines; High Museum; MOMA; Manufacturers and Traders Trust Co., Buffalo, N.Y.; NCFA; National Gallery; PMA; Virginia National Bank.

GRIEFEN, JOHN ADAMS. November 24, 1942, Worcester, Mass. **Studied:** Williams College, 1966 BA; Bennington College, 1965–66, with Jules Olitski; Hunter College, 1966–68; Chicago/AI, 1964–65. Traveled Europe. **Taught:** Bennington College, 1968. **Address:** 57 Laight Street, NYC 10013. **One-man Exhibitions:** (first) The Kornblee Gallery, NYC 1969, 70, 73; Harcus/Krakow Gallery, Boston, 1972; Phyllis Kind Gallery, Chicago, 1973; Frank Watters Gallery, Sydney, Australia, 1975; Deitcher/ O'Reilly Gallery, NYC, 1976; William Edward O'Reilly Inc., NYC, 1978; B.R. Kornblatt Gallery, Baltimore, Md., 1978; Diane Brown Gallery, Washington, D.C., 1978; Martha Jackson Gallery, NYC, 1979; Sunne Savage Gallery, Boston, 1979; Galerie Wentzel, Hamburg, 1980; Williams College, 1980. **Group:** Ridgefield/Aldrich, Lyrical Abstraction, 1970; Akron/AI, Watercolors and Drawings by Young Americans, 1970; Indianapolis, 1970, 72; WMAA, Lyrical Abstraction, 1971; **Collections:** Boston/MFA; Brooklyn Museum; Chase Manhattan Bank; Hirshhorn; U. of Massachusetts; Mechanics National Bank, Worcester; MOMA; Newark Museum; Oberlin College; Ridgefield/Aldrich; Sydney/AG; St. Lawrence U.; U. of Texas; Utica; WMAA; Worcester/AM.

GRILLO, JOHN. b. July 4, 1917, Lawrence, Mass **Studied:** Hartford Art School, 1935–38; California School of Fine Arts, 1946; Hofmann School, NYC, 1949–50. US armed forces, 1944–46. **Taught:** Southern Illinois U., 1960; School of Visual Arts, NYC, 1961; U. of California, Berkeley, 1962–63; New School for Social Research, 1964–66; Pratt Institute, 1965–66; State U. of Iowa, 1967– ; U. of Massachusetts, Artist-in-Residence, 1968–69. **Awards:** CSFA, Albert M. Bender Fellowship, 1947; Ford Foundation Fellowship (Tamarind Lithography Workshop and Youngstown/Butler), 1964. **Address:** 19 Page Street, Amherst, MA 01002. **Dealer:** Grace Borgenicht Gallery, Inc., NYC. **One-man Exhibitions:** Daliel Gallery, Berkeley, 1947; Artists' Gallery, NYC, 1948; Tanager Gallery, NYC, 1952, 60; Tibor de Nagy Gallery, NYC, 1953, 70; The Bertha Schaefer Gallery, 1955, 57, 59; HCE Gallery, Provincetown, Mass., 1959, 62; The Howard Wise Gallery, NYC, 1961, 62, 63; Ankrum Gallery, 1962; U. of California, Berkeley, 1962; East End Gallery, Provincetown, 1963; Youngstown/Butler, 1964; Waitsfield/Bundy, 1966; New School for Social Research, 1967; State U. of Iowa, 1967; Simmons College, 1968; Eleanor Rigelhaupt Gallery, Boston, 1968; Benedict Art Center, St. Joseph, Minn. 1969; Horizon Gallery, NYC, 1969; Robert Dain Gallery, NYC, 1970; Landmark Gallery Inc., NYC, 1973; Borgenicht Gallery, Inc., NYC, 1975, 77, 78; Pisces Gallery, Wellfleet, Mass., 1977; Union College, Cranford, N.J., 1977; Art Association of Newport, R.I., 1979. **Retrospective:** The Olsen Foundation, Inc., circ., USA, 1956–60. **Group:** The Kootz Gallery, NYC, Fifteen Unknowns, 1950; Walker, Vanguard, 1955; WMAA Annual, 1959; Walker, 60 American Painters, 1960; SRGM, Abstract Expressionists and Imagists, 1961; Yale U., Contemporary Painting, 1961; Dallas/MFA, 1961, 62; Seattle World's Fair, 1962; MOMA, Hans Hofmann and His Students, circ., 1963–64; SFMA, Directions—Painting U.S.A., 1963, Buffalo/Albright, 1964; Brooklyn Museum Print Biennial, 1970; Oakland/AM, California Artists, 1944–1952, 1973; SRGM, 40 Modern Masters, 1977; Syracuse/Emerson, Provincetown Painters, 1890's—1970's, 1977; MMA, Hans Hofmann as Teacher: Drawings by His Students, 1979. **Collections:** Baton Rouge; Bennington College, Brooklyn Museum; Ciba-Geigy

Corp.; Dartmouth College; Hartford/ Wadsworth; Hayden, Shearson, Inc., NYC; Los Angeles/County MA; MMA; Newark Museum; Norfolk/Chrysler; The Olsen Foundation, Inc.; Pittsburgh; Portland, Me./MA; SRGM; Smith College; Southern Illinois U.; U. of Texas; Union Carbide Corp.; WMAA; Waitsfield/Bundy; Walker; Westinghouse; Youngstown/Butler. **Bibliography:** Blesh 1; McChesney; Sandler 1.

GRIPPE, PETER. b. August 8, 1912, Buffalo, N.Y. **Studied:** Albright Art School; Buffalo Fine Arts Academy, with E. Wilcox, Edwin Dickinson, William Ehrich; Atelier 17, NYC. Traveled Europe. **Taught:** Black Mountain College, 1948; Pratt Institute, 1949–50; Smith College, 1951–52; Atelier 17, NYC, 1951–52; Brandeis U., 1953– . Federal A.P.: Taught sculpture and drawing, 1939–42. **Commissions:** Creative Arts Award Medallion design for Brandeis U., 1954; Puerto Rican Information Center, NYC, 1958 (two sculpture murals); Theo Shapiro Forum, Brandeis U., 1963 (sculpture). **Awards:** Brooklyn Museum, **P.P.**, 1947; MMA, $500 First Prize, 1952; The Print Club, Philadelphia, Charles M. Lea Prize, 1953; National Council for United States Art, $1,000 Sculpture Award, 1955; Boston Arts Festival, First Prize for Sculpture, 1955; Rhode Island Arts Festival, Sculpture Award, 1961; Guggenheim Foundation Fellowship, 1964, 70. **Address:** 1190 Boylston St., Newton, MA 02164. **One-man Exhibitions:** (first) Orrefors Galleries, NYC, 1942; The Willard Gallery, 1944, 45, 46, 48; Brandeis U., 1957; The Peridot Gallery, 1957, 59; Lee Nordness Gallery, NYC, 1960, 63. **Group:** MMA, Contemporary American Art, 1942; WMAA Annuals, 1944, 45, 47, 48, 50, 51, 52, 54, 56, 57, 60, 62; Federation of Modern Painters and Sculptors, 1944, 45, 52; American Abstract Artists Annuals, 1946, 47, 49; Carnegie, 1946, 48; Brooklyn Museum, 1947, 48, 49, 53, 56, 58; Detroit/Institute, Origins of Modern Sculpture, 1948; Chicago/AI, Abstract and Surrealist Art, 1948; A.F.A., Tradition and Experiment in Modern Sculpture, circ., 1950–51; MMA, National Sculpture Exhibition, 1951; MOMA, Abstract Painting and Sculpture in America, 1951; Ninth Street Exhibition, NYC, 1951; MOMA, From Sketch to Sculpture, 1952; PAFA, 1952, 59; U. of Illinois, 50 Contemporary American Printmakers, 1956; ART:USA:59, NYC, 1959; PCA, American Prints Today, circ., 1959–62; ICA, Boston, View, 1960; U. of Illinois, 1961; Chicago/AI, 1961; Smithsonian, Drawings by Sculptors, circ., USA, 1961–63; A.F.A., Hayter and Atelier 17, circ., 1961–62; Hartford/Wadsworth, Eleven New England Sculptors, 1963; MOMA, The New American Painting and Sculpture, 1969; Brandeis U., 1973. **Collections:** Andover/Phillips; Brandeis U.; Brooklyn Museum; Buffalo/ Albright; Fort Dodge/Blanden; U. of Georgia; Library of Congress; MMA; MOMA; U. of Michigan; Milwaukee-Downer College; NYPL; National Gallery; Newark Museum; Norfolk/ Chrysler; PCA; PMA; The Print Club, Philadelphia; Raleigh/NCMA; Simmons College; Tel Aviv; Toledo/MA; USIA; WMAA; Walker; Washington U. **Bibliography:** Baur 7; Blesh 1; Brumme; Flanagan; Hayter 1; Mendelowitz; Moser 1; Motherwell and Reinhardt, eds.; Ritchie 1; Seuphor 3; Trier.

GROOMS, RED. b. June 1, 1937, Nashville, Tenn. **Studied:** Peabody College; privately with J. Van Sickle; New School for Social Research; Chicago Art Institute School; Hofmann School, Provincetown. Traveled Europe, Near East. Sets and costumes for *Guinevere*, a play by Kenneth Koch, 1964. **Commissions:** Center for Modern Culture, Florence, Italy (mural, with Mimi Gross); Hudson River Museum, Bookstore, 1978; Northern Kentucky U., 1978. **Awards:** Ingram Merrill Foundation Grant, 1968; AAAL Grant, 1969; CAPS, 1970. **Address:** 161 Mulberry Street, NYC. **Dealer:** Marlborough Gallery, Inc., NYC. **One-man Exhibitions:** (first) Sun Gallery, Provincetown, 1958; City Gallery, NYC, 1958–59; Reuben Gallery, NYC, 1960; Tibor de Nagy Gallery, NYC, 1963, 65, 66, 67, 69, 70; Artists Guild, Nashville, 1962; Walker, 1970; John Bernard Myers Gallery, 1971, 74; Allan Frumkin Gallery, Chicago, 1972; Fendrick Gallery, 1972; Graphics 1 & Graphics 2, Boston, 1972; Nashville, 1972; Rutgers U., 1973; Brooks Alexander Gallery, NYC, 1975; Marlborough Gallery, NYC, 1976, 77; Galerie Roger d'Amecourt, Paris, 1977; Van Straaten, Gallery, Chicago, 1976; Benjamin Mangel Gallery, Bala Cynwyd, 1977; Santa Barbara 1977; New Gallery, Cleveland, 1977; Showcase Galleries, Southfield, Mich., 1977; Martin Wiley Gallery, Nashville, 1978; Purchase/SUNY, 1978. **Happenings:** Fire, Sun Gallery, Provincetown, 1958; Walking Man, Sun Gallery, Provincetown, 1959; Burning Building, Delancey Street Museum, NYC, 1959; Magic Train Ride, Reuben Gallery, NYC, 1960. **Movies:** *Unwelcome Guests*, 1961; *Shoot the Moon*, 1962; *Miracle on the BMT*, 1963; *Lurk*, 1964; *Spaghetti Trouble*, 1964; *Man or Mouse*, 1964; *Umbrellas, Bah!* 1965; *Big Sneeze*, 1965; *Secret of Wendel Sampson*, 1965–66; *Before 'n' After*, 1966; *Washington's Wig Whammed!* 1966; *Fat Feet*, 1966; *Meow, Meow!* 1967; *Tappy Toes*, 1969–70; *Hippodome Hardware*, 1972–73; *The Conquest of Libya by Italia*, 1913–1912.1972–73; *Ruckus Manhattan*, 1975–76; *Little Red Riding Hood*, 1978. **Group:** Delancey Street Museum, NYC, 1959, 60; Chicago/AI, 1964; Provincetown/Chrysler; SRGM, 1965; Southampton/Parrish, 1965; Worcester/AM, 1965; A.F.A., 1965–66; Chicago/AI, Twenty Americans, 1966; MOMA, 1966; XXXIV Venice Biennial, 1968; Cologne/Kunstverein, Happening & Fluxus, circ., 1970; ICA, U. of Pennsylvania, The Spirit of the Comics, 1969; SRGM, 10 Independents, 1972; Harvard U., Recent Figure Sculpture, 1972; WMAA, Extraordinary Realities, 1973; Hirshhorn Inaugural Exhibition, 1974; Dallas/MFA, Poets of the Cities, 1974; Fort Worth, The Great American Rodeo, 1975; Stamford, Conn., American Salon des Refuses, 1976; Potsdam/SUNY, Off the Beaten Path, 1977; WMAA, Art about Art, 1978. **Collections:** Brooklyn/Musum; Caracas/Contemporaneo; Charlotte/Mint; Chicago/AI; Delaware Art Museum; Fort Worth; Hirshhorn; MOMA; Nashville/Cheekwood; New School for Social Research; Norfolk/Chrysler; Northern Kentucky U.; Raleigh/NCMA; Stockholm/National. **Bibliography::** Arthur 2; Becker and Vostell; Drawings, The Pluralist Decade; *Figures/Environments*; Geske; *Happening & Fluxus*; Honisch and Jensen, eds.; Janis and Blesh 1; Kaprow; Kirby; Lippard 5; *Poets & Painters; Recent Figure Sculpture*; Sandler 1; Sontag. Archives.

GROPPER, WILLIAM. b. December 3, 1897, NYC; **d.** January 4, 1977, Manhasset, N.Y. **Studied:** Ferrar School, San Francisco, with Robert Henri, George Bellows, 1912–13; NAD, 1913–14; New York School of Fine and Applied Art, with Howard Giles, Jay Hambridge, 1915–18. Traveled Europe, USA, USSR. Staff Artist, *New York Tribune*, 1919–21; *New York World*, 1925–27. **Taught:** American Art School, NYC, 1946–48. **Member:** Artists Equity; NIAL, 1968; NAD. **Commissions:** New Interior Building, Washington, D.C.; Northwestern Postal Station, Detroit; US Post Office, Freeport, N.Y.; Schenley Industries, Inc., NYC. **Awards:** Young Israel Prize; Los Angeles/County MA. **P.P.;** Indianapolis/Herron, Prize for Lithography; *Collier's* (magazine) Prize for Illustration, 1920; Harmon Foundation Award, 1930; J. S. Guggenheim Fellowship, 1937; Carnegie, Third Prize; MMA, Artists for Victory, Lithography Prize, 1942; Tamarind Fellowship, 1967; NAD, Thomas B. Clarke Prize, 1973; Andrew Carnegie Prize, 1975. **Retrospectives:** Phoenix; Evansville; Palm Springs Desert Museum; Syracuse U.; U. of Miami, 50 Years of Drawing and

Cartoons, circ., 1968. **Group:** MMA; WMAA; Chicago/AI; MOMA; Los Angeles/County MA. **Collections:** Abbott Laboratories; U. of Arizona; Brandeis U.; Britannica; Canton Art Institute; Chicago/AI; Cornell U.; Evansville; Hartford/Wadsworth; Harvard U.; Hirshhorn; Library of Congress; Los Angeles/County MA; MMA; MOMA; Montclair/AM; Moscow/Western; NYPL; Newark Museum; PAFA; Phillips; St. Louis/City; Sofia; Storm King Art Center; Syracuse U.; Tate; U. of Tucson; WMAA; Walker; Youngstown/Butler. **Bibliography:** American Artists Congress, Inc.; Barr 3; Baur 7; Bazin; Boswell 1; Brown; Brown 2; Canaday; Cheney; Christensen; **Freundlich**; Goodrich and Baur 1; Hall; Kootz 2; McCurdy, ed.; Mellquist; Mendelowitz; Pagano; Pearson 1; Reese; Richardson, E.P.; Rose, B., 1; Shapiro, ed.; Wight. 2.

GROSS, CHAIM. b. March 17, 1904, Kolomea, East Austria. To USA, 1921. **Studied:** Kunstgewerbe Schule; Educational Alliance, NYC; Beaux-Arts Institute of Design, with Elie Nadelman; ASL, with Robert Laurent. Traveled Europe, Israel, Turkey. **Taught:** Educational Alliance, NYC; New School for Social Research. **Member:** Sculptors Guild (President); Artists Equity; Federation of Modern Painters and Sculptors; NIAL. Federal A.P.: Teacher, supervisor, sculptor. **Commissions:** Main Post Office, Washington, D.C. 1936; Federal Trade Commission Building, Washington, D.C., 1938; France Overseas Building, New York World's Fair, 1939; US Post Office, Irwin, Pa., 1940; Reiss-Davis Child Guidance Clinic, Beverly Hills, 1961; Hadassah Hospital, Jerusalem, 1964; Temple Shaaray Tefila, NYC, 1964; U. of Rhode Island, 1972; International Synagogue, Kennedy International Airport, 1972. **Awards:** L. C. Tiffany Grant, 1933; Paris World's Fair, 1937, Silver Medal; MMA, Artists for Victory, $3,000 Second Prize, 1942; Boston Arts Festival, Third Prize for Sculpture, 1954; PAFA,

Hon. Men., 1954; Audubon Artists, Prize for Sculpture, 1955; NIAL Grant, 1956; Boston Arts Festival, First Prize, 1963; NIAL, Award of Merit Medal, 1963; Hon. DFA, Adelphi U., 1980; Hon. DHL, Yeshiva U., 1978. **Address:** 526 West Broadway, NYC. **Dealer:** The Forum Gallery. **One-man Exhibitions:** (first) Gallery 144, NYC, 1932; Boyer Gallery, Philadelphia, 1935; Boyer Gallery, NYC, 1937; A.A.A. Gallery, NYC, 1942, 69; Massilon Museum, Akron/AI, 1946; Youngstown/Butler, 1946; New Paltz/SUNY, 1952; Jewish Museum, 1953; Shore Studio, Boston, 1954; Muriel Latow Gallery, Springfield, Mass., 1956; Duveen-Graham Gallery, NYC, 1957; WMAA, circ., 1959; The Marble Arch Gallery, Miami Beach, 1961; Anna Werbe Gallery, Detroit, 1962; The Forum Gallery, 1962, 64, 67, 72, 73, 74, 77, 80; Irving Galleries, Inc., Milwaukee, 1963; New School for Social Research, 1971; NCFA, 1974; Leonard Hutton Gallery, NYC, 1974; U. of Miami, Fla., 1977; Montclair/AM, 1977; Jewish Museum, NYC, 1977; Prince Arthur Galleries, Toronto, 1977. **Group:** WMAA Sculpture Annuals; Sculptors Guild Annuals; PAFA; A.F.A., Sculpture in Wood, circ., 1941–42; American Painting and Sculpture, Moscow, 1959; MOMA, The Making of Sculpture, circ., 1961–62; Smithsonian, Drawings by Sculptors, circ., USA, 1961–63; New York World's Fair, 1964–65. **Collections:** Ain Harod; Andover/Phillips; Atlanta/AA; Baltimore/MA; Brandeis U.; Boston/MFA; Brandeis U.; Brooklyn Museum; Bryn Mawr College; Chicago/AI; Colby College; Dayton/AI; Des Moines; Fairleigh Dickinson U.; U. of Georgia; Haifa; Jewish Museum; Kalamazoo/Institute; Kansas City/Nelson; U. of Kansas; La Jolla; MMA; MOMA; Massillon Museum; Milwaukee; U. of Minnesota; Newark Museum; Ogunquit; PAFA; PMA; Phoenix; Queens College; Reading/Public; Reed College; Rutgers U.; Scranton/Everhart; Scripps College; Smith College; Tel Aviv; WMAA; Walker; West Palm Beach/Norton; Worcester/AM; Youngstown/

Butler. **Bibliography:** Baur 7; Brumme; Cheney; Craven, W.; Flanagan; **Getlein 1; Goodrich and Baur, 1, 2; Gross**; Lombardo; Martin; McCurdy, ed.; Marter, Tarbell, and Wechsler; Mendelowitz; Sutton; Wheeler. Archives.

GROSSER, MAURICE. b. October 23, 1903, Huntsville, Ala. **Studied:** Harvard U., 1920–24, with M. Mower. Traveled Europe, USA, Latin America, Africa. Art Critic for *The Nation*, 1961–67. **Member:** The Travelers, London, Librettist of the Gertrude Stein–Virgil Thomson Operas *Four Saints in Three Acts* and *The Mother of Us All.* **Address:** 219 West 14th Street, NYC 10011; Inmeuble Itese, Calle Campoamor, Tangier. **Dealer:** Fischbach Gallery. **One-man Exhibitions:** Grace

Horne Galleries, Boston, 1925; Grand Central Palace, NYC, 1928; Galerie Vignon, Paris, 1931; Galerie des Quatre Chemins, Paris, 1933, 39; Hendrix, Inc. (Gallery), NYC, 1935; Arts Club of Chicago, 1939; Julien Levy Galleries, NYC, 1940, 41, 42, 44, 46; High Museum, 1941; Houston/MFA, 1942; M. Knoedler & Co., 1948, 50; Hugo Gallery, NYC, 1954; Alexander Iolas Gallery, 1955; Carstairs Gallery, NYC, 1957, 60, 62; Garlen Gallery, Philadelphia, 1958; The Banfer Gallery, 1963, 65; U. of Ife, 1970; Hirschl & Adler Galleries, 1971; Capricorn Gallery, Washington, D.C., 74; Boston Atheneum, 1975; Richard Larcada Gallery, NYC, 1975, 77; Fischbach Gallery, NYC, 1979. **Group:** U. of Minnesota; MOMA; WMAA; Cleveland/MA; VMFA. **Collections:** The Bank of New York; Brooklyn Museum; Cleveland/MA; Columbus; MOMA; U. of

Maurice Grosser   *Still Life with Turk's Head Squash*   1980

Minnesota; Rockland/Farnsworth; Springfield Art Center; VMFA; U. of Vermont. **Bibliography: Grosser, 1, 2.** Archives.

GROSSMAN, NANCY. b. April 28, 1940, NYC. **Studied:** Pratt Institute, BFA. **Member:** Sculptors Guild; Foundation for the Community of Artists. **Awards:** Ida C. Haskell Scholarship for Foreign Travel, 1962; Guggenheim Foundation Fellowship, 1965; Pratt Institute, Inaugural Contemporary Achievement Award, 1966; AAAL, 1974. **Address:** 105 Eldridge Street, NYC 10002. **Dealer:** Barbara Gladstone. **One-man Exhibitions:** The Krasner Gallery, 1964, 65, (2), 67; Cordier & Ekstrom, Inc., 1969, 76 (two-man), 1971, 73, 75. **Retrospective:** U. of Nevada, Reno. **Group:** PAFA, 1963; Corcoran, 1963; WMAA Annuals, 1968, 73, Contemporary American Sculpture, 1968–69, Human Concern/Personal Torment, 1969; Museum of Contemporary Crafts, Face Coverings, 1970–71; Harvard U., Recent Figure Sculpture, 1972; PMA/Museum of the Philadelphia Civic Center, Focus, 1974; Soho Center for Visual Artists, Drawing Now: Ten Artists, 1976; Brooklyn Museum, Works on Paper—Women Artists, 1977; Kohler Art Center, Sheboygan, Wis., Unpainted Portrait, 1979; Dade Community College, Miami, Fla., The Figure of 5, circ., 1979, 80. **Collections:** Alcoa; Baltimore/MA; U. of California, Berkeley; Columbia Broadcasting System; Cornell U.; Dallas/MFA; Hamline U.; Kutztown State College; Minneapolis/MA; Pratt Institute; Princeton U.; Ridgefield/Aldrich; Rotterdam; U. of Utah; WMAA. **Bibliography:** Lucie-Smith; Nemser; *Recent Figure Sculpture.*

GROSVENOR, ROBERT. b. 1937, NYC. **Studied:** Ecole des Beaux-Arts, Dijon, 1956; Ecole Nationale des Arts Decoratifs, 1957–59; Universita di Perugia, 1958. Traveled France, England, Italy, Germany, USA, Mexico. **Taught:** School of Visual Arts, NYC. **Awards:** National Council on the Arts, 1969. **Address:** 543 Broadway, NYC 10013. **Dealer:** Paula Cooper Gallery. **One-man Exhibitions:** Park Place Gallery, NYC, 1962–66; Dwan Gallery, Los Angeles, 1966; NYU, 1967; Galerie Rolf Ricke, 1970; Fischbach Gallery, 1970; Paula Cooper Gallery, NYC, 1970, 71, 74, 75, 78, 79; La Jolla, 1971; City U. of New York Graduate Center, NYC, 1973; Francoise Lambert, Milan, 1974; Galerie Stampa, Basel, 1975; Galerie Eric Fabre, Paris. 1975, 77; Pasquale Trisorio, Naples, 1975; The Clocktower, NYC, 1976. **Group:** New York World's Fair, 1964–65; Jewish Museum, Primary Structures, 1966; ICA, U. of Pennsylvania, 1967; Buffalo/Albright, Plus by Minus, 1968; The Hague, Minimal Art, 1968; WMAA Sculpture Annual, 1968–69; U. of Minnesota, 1969; Walker, 1969; Chicago/Contemporary, 1969; ICA, Boston, Art on Paper, 1970; Cincinnati/Contemporary, Monumental Art, 1970; Arnhem, Sonsbeek '71, 1971; Middelheim Park, Antwerp, XI Sculpture Biennial, 1971; Houston/Contemporary, Eight, 1972; WMAA, 1973; Newport, R.I., Monumenta, 1974; Leverkusen, Zeichnungen III, 1975; Paris/Moderne, Tendances actuelles de la peinture americaine, 1975; WMAA, 200 Years of American Sculpture, 1976; Sydney/AG, Biennale, 1976; Documenta 6, Kassel, 1977; Minnesota/MA, American Drawings, 1927–1977, 1977; U. of Rochester, Drawings and Prints—New York, 1977. **Collections:** Lannan Foundation; Lipschultz Foundation; MIT; MOMA; NYU; Ridgefield/Aldrich; WMAA; Walker. **Bibliography:** Battcock, ed.; Friedman, M. 2; *Monumenta;* Lippard 4; MacAgy 2; Tuchman 1. Archives.

GROSZ, GEORGE. b. July 26, 1893, Berlin, Germany; **d.** July 6, 1959, Berlin, Germany. **Studied:** Royal Saxon Academy of Fine Art, Dresden, 1909–11, R. Muller. O. Schindler, R. Sterl. R. Wehle; School of Fine and

Applied Arts, Berlin, 1911, with E. Orlik; Academie Colarossi, Paris, 1913. German Army, 1914–16, 1917–18. Traveled Russia, Europe, USA. To USA, 1932; citizen, 1938. **Taught:** Maurice Sterne School, NYC, 1933; ASL, 1933–36, 1940–42, 1943–44, 1950–53; Columbia U., 1941–42. Designed sets for Max Reinhardt Theatre, 1920–30. **Commissions:** A. Harris & Co., Dallas (portfolio of drawings entitled *Impressions of the City*). **Awards:** Chicago/AI, Watson F. Blair Prize, 1931, 40; Guggenheim Foundation Fellowship, 1937; PAFA, Carol H. Beck Gold Medal, 1940; Carnegie, Second Prize, 1945. **One-man Exhibitions:** (first) Goltz Gallery, Berlin, 1918; Gallery A. Flechtheim, Berlin, 1926; M. Wasservogel, Berlin, 1926; A.A.A. Gallery, NYC, 1926, 41, 43, 46, 48, 54; Club of Chicago, 1933; Crillon Galleries, Philadelphia, 1933; Milwaukee, 1933; Mayor Gallery, London, 1934; An American Place (Gallery), NYC, 1935; Contemporary Arts Gallery, NYC, 1935; Harvard U., 1935, 49, 73; Municipal U. of Omaha, 1936; Smith College, 1936 (three-man); Chicago/AI, 1938; Currier, 1939; Hudson D. Walker Gallery, NYC, 1938 (2), 1941; MOMA, 1941, 69; Denver/AM, 1943; Baltimore/MA, 1944; Leicester Gallery, London, 1946; Print Club of Cleveland, 1949; The Swetzoff Gallery, Boston, 1950; Dallas/MFA, 1952; Vera Lazuk, Cold Spring Harbor, N.Y., 1959; The Forum Gallery, 1963; E. V. Thaw, NYC, 1963; Arts Council of Great Britain, circ., 1963; Paul Kantor Gallery, Beverly Hills, Calif., 1964; Graphische Sammlung Albertina, 1965; Claude Bernard, Paris, 1966; Ira Spanierman Gallery, NYC, 1967, 69; Donald Morris Gallery, 1968; Peter H. Deitsch Gallery, 1968, 69; LoGiudice Gallery, Chicago, 1969; Stuttgart/WK, 1969; La Medusa Gallery, 1970; Richard Feigen Gallery, NYC, 1971; Harvard U., 1973; Lunn Inc., Washington, D.C., 1974; Serge Sabarsky Gallery, NYC, 1975; Weintraub Gallery, NYC, 1978; Huntington/Hecksher, 1977; Hirshhorn, 1978. **Retrospective:** WMAA, 1954.

Group: WMAA Annuals; MOMA; Chicago/AI; Los Angeles/County MA; SFMA; Newark Museum; St. Louis/City; Dallas/MFA. **Collections:** Berlin/National; Boston/MFA; Chicago/AI; Cleveland/MA; Detroit/Institute; Essen; Galerie des 20. Jahrhunderts; Harvard U.; Huntington, N.Y./Heckscher; MOMA; Newark Museum; Stuttgart; WMAA. **Bibliography: Ballo, ed.; Baur 2, 7; Bazalgette**; Bazin; Biddle 4; Bihalji-Merin; **Bittner**; Blesh 1; Bulliet 1, 2; Canaday; Cassou; Cheney; Christensen; *Cityscape 1919–39*; Craven, T., 1, 2; Davidson 2; *Dessins et Aquarelles*; Flanagan; Frost; Genauer; *George Grosz*; Goodrich and Baur 1; **Grosz 1, 2, 3, 4, 5**; Haftman; Hess, T. B., 1; Hulten; Hunter, ed.; Huyghe; Janis, S.; Kent, N.; Kouvenhoven; Kuh 1, 3; Langui; Lynton; McCurdy, ed.; **Mehring**; Mendelowitz; Newmeyer; Pagano; Pearson 1, 2; Pousette-Dart, ed.; Read 2; Richardson, E.P.; Richter; Rodman 3; Rose, B., 7; Rubin 1; Sachs; Salvini; Sietz 3; Selz, P. 3; **Tavolato**; Verkauf; Wingler, ed. Archives.

GUERRERO, JOSE. b. October 29, 1914, Granada, Spain. **Studied:** Escuela de Artes y Oficios Artisticos, Granada, 1930–34; Real Academia de Bellas Artes de San Fernando, Madrid, 1940–44; Academie des Beaux-Arts, Paris, 1945–46. Traveled Europe, 1947–49; resided Spain, 1965–68. To USA, 1949; citizen, 1952. **Taught:** New School for Social Research, 1962– ; Cleveland Institute of Art, 1974; Atlanta College of Art, 1975; Iowa State U., 1978. **Awards:** *Art in America* magazine, New Talent, 1958; Graham Foundation Grant, 1958–59; Chevalier of the Order of Arts and Letters (France), 1959; Society for Contemporary American Art annual prize donation to The Art Institute of Chicago, 1959; Officer Order of Arts and Letters, 1979. **Address:** 406 West 20th Street, NYC 10011; and Cuenca, Spain. **Dealers:** Gruenebaum Gallery, Ltd., NYC; Galleria Juana Mordo, Madrid. **One-man Exhibitions:** Galerie Altarriba, Paris, 1946 (two-man); Galleria Secolo, Rome, 1948; Lou Cosyn Gallery, Brussels, 1948; St. George's Gallery, London, 1949 (two-man); Buchholz Gallery, Madrid, 1950; Arts Club of Chicago, 1954 (two-man); Betty Parsons Gallery, 1954, 57, 58, 60, 63; Rose Fried Gallery, 1964; Galeria Juana Mordo, 1964, 67, 71, 75, 76; Buchholz Gallery, Lisbon, 1967; French & Co. Inc., 1967, 70; Galleri Ostermalm, Stockholm, 1970; The Graham Gallery, 1970; Vali 30 Gallery, Valencia, 1972; Mikelki Gallery, Bilbao, 1972; A. M. Sachs Gallery, 1974; Galerie Wolfgang Ketterer, Munich, 1975; Juana de Azipuru Gallery, Seville, 1976; Hoover Gallery, San Francisco, 1976, 78; Museo Provincial de Bellas Artes, Victoria, Spain, 1977; Museo Provincial de Bellas Artes, Bilbao, Spain, 1976; Galeria Luzaro, Bilbao, 1978, Gruenebaum Gallery, Ltd., NYC, 1978, 80; Galeria Fucares, Almagro, Spain, 1979; Galerie Ditesheim, Neuchatel, Switzerland, 1979. **Group:** SRGM, Younger American Painters, 1954; Galerie de France, 10 Jeune Peintres de l'Ecole de Paris, 1956; Salon des Realites Nouvelles, Paris, 1957; Worcester/AM, 1958; Dallas/MFA, 1958; Rome–New York Foundation, Rome, 1958; Buffalo/Albright, 1958; I Inter-American Paintings and Prints Biennial, Mexico City, 1958; WMAA Annuals, 1958, 59, 62; American Abstract Artists, 1958, 61, 62; Carnegie, 1958, 61, 63; Corcoran, 1959; Spanish Art Today, circ., Germany, Holland, Denmark, 1967–68; Spanish Culture Institute, Munich, 1968; Sweden/Goteborgs, Spanish Painters, 1970; Dublin/Municipal, International Quadriennial (ROSC), 1971; Madrid, March Foundation Collection, circ., 1973–74; Mexico City/Nacional, Masters of Spanish Contemporary Art, 1974. **Collections:** Belgian Ministry of National Education; Beloit College; Brooklyn Museum; Buffalo/Albright; California Palace; Carnegie; Chase Manhattan Bank; Chicago/AI; Cornell U.; Cuenca; Dartmouth College; French Ministry of National Education; Fundacion Juan March, Madrid;

Harvard U.; Houston/MFA; Humlebaek/Louisiana; Indianapolis; Madrid/Nacional; Mobil Oil Co.; NYU; New School for Social Research; PAFA; Prudential Insurance Co. of America, Newark; Purchase/SUNY; RISD; SRGM; Sweden/Goteborgs; Toronto; WMAA; Westinghouse Electric Corp.; Yale U. **Bibliography:** Moser 1. Archives.

GUGLIELMI, O. LOUIS. b. April 9, 1906, Cairo, Egypt; **d.** September 3, 1956, Amagansett, N.Y. To USA, 1914. **Studied:** NAD, 1920–25. Corps of Army Engineers, 1943–45. **Taught:** Louisiana State U., 1952–53; New School for Social Research, 1953. Federal A.P.: Easel painting. **Awards:** L.C. Tiffany Grant, Yaddo Fellowship, and MacDowell Colony Fellowship, 1925–32; Chicago/AI, Ada S. Garrett Prize, 1943; Pepsi-Cola, Hon. Men., 1944; Carnegie, Hon. Men., 1944; AAAL Grant, 1946; PAFA, Joseph E. Temple Gold Medal, 1952. **One-man Exhibitions:** (first) The Downtown Gallery, 1938, also 1942, 46, 47, 51, 67; New Art Center, NYC; J. Seligmann and Co.; Julien Levy Galleries, NYC; Lee Nordness Gallery, NYC, 1958, 61, 62. **Retrospective:** Rutgers U., 1980. **Group:** Musée du Jeu de Paume; New York World's Fair, 1939; MOMA, Americans 1943; Realists and Magic-Realists, circ., 1943; Chicago/AI, 1943; WMAA, The Precisionists, 1961; PAFA; Pepsi-Cola Co.; Newark Museum; U. of Minnesota; Denver/AM; PMA. **Collections:** Auburn U.; Britannica; Chicago/AI; Cornell U.; Cranbrook; U. of Georgia; MMA; MOMA; Newark Museum; SFMA; Tel Aviv; WMAA; Walker. **Bibliography:** Baur 7; Bethers; Blesh 1; *From Foreign Shores*; Genauer; Goodrich and Baur 1; Haftman; Hall; Halpert; Janis, S.; McCurdy, ed.; Pagano. Archives.

GUSSOW, ALAN. b. May 8, 1931, NYC. **Studied:** Middlebury College, 1952, AB; Cooper Union, 1952–53, with

Morris Kantor; Atelier 17, NYC. Traveled Europe, USA; resided Rome, two years. **Taught:** Parsons School of Design, 1956–68, Chairman, Department of Fashion Illustration, 1959–68; Sarah Lawrence College, 1958–59; U. of Massachusetts, 1968–69; Rockland Community College, Suffern, N.Y., 1974; Pace U. 1977; Bard College, 1978. **Film:** *A Sense of Place, The Artist and the American Land,* 1973. **Commissions:** Skidmore, Owings and Merrill, Architects (mural). **Awards:** Prix de Rome, 1953–54, renewed 1954–55; Artist-in-Residence, Cape Cod National Seashore, 1968; CAPS, 1971; AFE Grant, Artist-in-Residence, Delaware Water Gap, 1974–75. US Department of the Interior, National Parks Service, Environmental Consultant, 1968– ; AAIAL, 1977. **Address:** 121 New York Avenue, Congers, NY 10920. **Dealers:** Washburn Gallery, Inc.; Joe deMers Gallery, Hilton Head Island S.C.; Hull Gallery, Washington, D.C. **One-man Exhibitions:** (first) Hagerstown/County MFA, 1961; Middlebury College, 1961, 77; The Peridot Gallery, 1962, 63, 66, 67, 69, 70; Kendall Gallery, Wellfleet, Mass., 1971; The Joe and Emily Lowe Art Gallery, Syracuse, 1972; Washburn Gallery Inc., 1972, 73, 77, 80; Jacobs Ladder Gallery, Washington, D.C., 1974; Joe deMers Gallery, Hilton Head Island, S.C., 1978; VMFA, 1979; St. Paul's School, Concord, N.H., 1979; Hull Gallery, Washington, D.C., 1980; William Sawyer Gallery, San Francisco, 1980. **Retrospectives:** Portland, Me./ MA, 1971; Arnot, 1975; Rockland Center for the Arts, West Nyack, N.Y., 1978. **Group:** III Mostra di Pittura Americana, Bordighera, 1955; Maine State Art Festival, 1961; Youngstown/ Butler, 1963; U. of Nebraska; PAFA Annual, 1966; A.F.A., Maine—50 Artists of the 20th Century, circ., 1966; AAAL, 1966; Colgate U., Viewpoints 7, 1972; Omaha/Joslyn, A Sense of Place, 1973; Queens Museum, New Images, 1974. **Collections:** Arnot; Guild Hall; Middlebury College; Montgomery Museum; U. of Nebraska; Portland, Me./ MA; VMFA; Wichita/AM.

GUSSOW, ROY. b. November 12, 1918, Brooklyn, N.Y. **Studied:** New York State Institute of Applied Agriculture (Farmingdale), 1938; Institute of Design, Chicago, 1945, with Lazlo Moholy-Nagy, and 1946, with Alexander Archipenko, 1948, BS. Traveled Europe and USA extensively. **Taught:** Bradley U., 1948; Colorado Springs Fine Arts Center, 1949–51; North Carolina State College, 1951–62; Pratt Institute, 1962–68. **Member:** Sculptors Guild, President, 1976– ; Artists Equity Association of New York. **Commissions:** US Commerce Department Trade Fair, circ., Bangkok and Tokyo, 1956 (American Pavilion); Lenoir-Rhyne College, 1957; Cooperative Savings & Loan Association, Wilmington, N.C., 1959; North Carolina State College, 1961; North Carolina State College Faculty Club, 1962; San Francisco Museum of Science and Industry, 1962; Phoenix-Mutual Building, Hartford, Conn., 1963 (8-ft. stainless-steel structure commissioned by Max Abramovitz); Reynolds Metal Co., 1967; Tulsa Civic Center, 1968; Xerox Corp., 1968; Creedmore State Hospital, Queens, N.Y., 1970; Heublein Inc., Farmington Conn., 1974; Family Court Building, NYC, 1975; Combustion Engineering Corp., Stamford, Conn., 1976; City of Reading, Pa., 1979. **Awards:** Raleigh/NCMA, **P.P.**, 1957, 61; PAFA, Hon. Men., 1958; Ford Foundation, **P.P.**, 1960, 62; National Gold Medal Exhibition for the Building Arts, NYC, NYC, 1962. **Address:** 4040 24th Street, Long Island City, NY 11101. **Dealer:** Grace Borgenicht Gallery, Inc., **One-man Exhibitions:** (first) Design Associates Gallery, Greensboro, N.C., 1952; The Pennsylvania State U., 1959; Grace Borgenicht Gallery, Inc., 1964, 71, 73, 77, 80; Chicago/AI, 1947, 48, 49; U. of Arkansas, 1948; Omaha/ Joslyn, 1949, 50; Denver/AM, 1949–51; SFMA, 1951; MMA, 1951; PAFA, annually 1951–59; Raleigh/NCMA, annually 1952–61; WMAA, 1956; Oakland/ AM, 1959; WMAA, Sculpture Annual, 1964, 66, 68; WMAA, Contemporary American Sculpture, Selection II, 1969; Albright College, 1979. **Collections:**

Philip Guston   Untitled   1980

American Tobacco Co.; Atlanta/AA; Brooklyn Museum; California Academy of Science; Equitable Life Assurance Society; MOMA; Newark Museum; U. of North Carolina; Radcliffe College; Raleigh/NCMA; Tulsa/Philbrook; WMAA. **Bibliography:** Craven, W. Archives.

GUSTON, PHILIP. b. June 27, 1913, Montreal, Canada; **d.** June 9, 1980, Woodstock, N.Y. To USA, 1916. **Studied:** Otis Art Institute, Los Angeles, for 3 months, 1930. Traveled Spain, Italy, France, USA. **Taught:** State U. of Iowa, 1941–45; Washington U., 1945–47; U. of Minnesota, 1950; NYU, 1951–59; Pratt Institute, 1953–57; Yale U., 1963; Brandeis U., 1966; Columbia U., 1969, 70, 74; New York Studio School; Skidmore College, 1968; Boston U., 1973–80. **Commission** Federal A.P., 1935–40, murals: WPA Building, New York World's Fair, 1939 (facade); Queensbridge Housing Project, 1940; Forestry Building, Laconia, N.H., 1941. Section of Fine Arts (murals), Social Security Building, Washington, D.C., 1942; US Post Office, Commerce, Ga., 1938. Trustee, American Academy, Rome. **Member:** NIAL. **Awards:** Carnegie, First Prize, 1945; Guggenheim Foundation Fellowship, 1947, renewed 1968; Prix de Rome, 1948; AAAL Grant, 1948; Ford Foundation Grant, 1948, $10,000, 1959; Hon. DFA, Boston U., 1970; College Art Association, Distinguished Teaching of Art Award, 1975; Brandeis U., Creative Arts Award, 1980. **One-man Exhibitions:** (first) The Midtown Galleries, 1945; Boston Museum School, 1947; Utica, 1947; U. of Minnesota, 1950; The Peridot Gallery, 1952; Charles Egan Gallery, 1953; Sidney Janis Gallery, 1956, 58, 60, 61; Dwan Gallery, Los Angeles (two-man, with Franz Kline), 1962; Jewish Museum, 1966; Santa Barbara/MA, 1966, 67; Gertrude Kasle Gallery, 1969, 73, 74; Marlborough Gallery Inc., NYC, 1970; Boston U., 1970, 74; La Jolla, 1971; MOMA, 1973; David McKee Gallery, 1974, 76, 77, 78, 79; Allan Frumkin Gallery, Chicago, 1978. **Retrospec-**

tives: V Sao Paulo Biennial, 1950; XXX Venice Biennial, 1960; SRGM, 1962; Amsterdam/Stedelijk, 1962; Los Angeles/County MA, 1963; Brandeis U., 1966; SFMA, circ., 1980–81. **Group:** U. of Illinois, 1944, 67; Walker, Contemporary American Painting, 1950; U. of Minnesota, 40 American Painters, 1940–50, 1951; MOMA, Abstract Painting and Sculpture in America, 1951; Baltimore/MA, Abstract Expressionists, 1953; MOMA, Twelve Americans, circ., 1956; Sao Paulo, 1957; WMAA, Nature in Abstraction, 1958; I Inter-American Paintings and Prints Biennial, Mexico City, 1958; MOMA, The New American Painting, circ., Europe, 1958–59; St. Louis/City, Modern American Painting, 1959; WMAA, 18 Living American Artists, 1959, also Annuals; Documenta II, Kassel, 1959; Ringling, 1961; SRGM/USIA, American Vanguard, circ., Europe, 1961–62; PAFA; SFMA; Chicago/AI; Corcoran; SRGM, circ., 1963; Tate, Painting and Sculpture of a Decade, 1954–64, 1964; Carnegie, 1964; Los Angeles/County MA, New York School: The First Generation, 1965; U. of St. Thomas (Tex.), 1967; ASL, 1967–68; MOMA, The New American Painting and Sculpture: The First Generation, 1969; MMA, New York Painting and Sculpture: 1940–1970, 1969–70; Ente Manifestazioni Genovesi, Immagine per la Citta, Genoa, 1972; National Gallery, American Art at Mid-Century, 1973; MIT, Drawings by Five Abstract Expressionist Painters, 1975; Buffalo/Albright, American Painting in the 1970s, 1978; Hayward Gallery, London, New Painting—New York, 1979; WMAA Biennial, 1979; Denver/AM, Poets-Painters, 1979; Akron/AI, Dialogue, 1980; Brandeis U., Mavericks, 1980. **Collections:** Allentown/AM; Baltimore/MA; Bezalel National Museum, Jerusalem; Brandeis U.; Buffalo/Albright; Chicago/AI; Cleveland/MA; Denver/AM; Detroit/Institute; Harvard U.; High Museum; Hirshhorn; IBM; U. of Illinois; State U. of Iowa; Los Angeles/County MA; MMA; MOMA; Minneapolis/Institute; NCFA; Phillips; Pur-

chase/SUNY; SFMA; SRGM; St. Louis/City; Seagram Collection; Tate; U. of Texas; Utica; VMFA; WMAA; Washington U.; Worcester/AM; Yale U. **Bibliography:** Arnason 2; Ashton 2, 3, 5, 6; Baur 5; Bazin; Biddle 4; Blesh 1; Canaday; *From Foreign Shores;* Genauer; Goodrich and Baur 1; Haftman; Henning; **Hunter** 1, 6, **7**; Hunter, ed.; Kozloff 3; Lucie-Smith; McCoubrey 1; McCurdy, ed.; Nordness, ed.; *Poets and Painters;* O'Hara 1; Ponente; Read 2; Ritchie 1; Rose, B., 1; Sandler 1; Seuphor 1; Tuchman, ed.; Tuchman, ed.; Weller; *Woodstock: An American Art Colony, 1902–1977.*

GUY, JAMES. b. 1910, Middletown, Conn. **Studied:** Hartford Art School, with Albertus Jones, Kimon Nicolaides. Traveled Mexico, Europe, USA. **Taught:** Bennington College, 1945–46; MacMurray College, Jacksonville, Ill., 1946–54; Wesleyan U., 1963–75. Filmmaker during the 1930s with the Film and Photo League. Articles on fishing for leading outdoor publications. Federal A.P.: Easel painting; mural for Hartford (Conn.) High School. **Address:** 82 Neptune Avenue, Moodus, CT 06469. **One-man Exhibitions:** (first) Boyer Gallery, NYC, 1939, also 1940; Ferargil Galleries, NYC, 1941, 42, 44; a gallery in Hollywood, Calif., 1945; Lehigh U., 1945; Bennington College, 1947; Carlebach Gallery, NYC, 1949, 50; MacMurray College, 1949; St. Louis/City, 1952; Hartford College for Women, 1960; Wesleyan U., 1961; Rose Fried Gallery; Charles Egan Gallery, 1969. **One-man Exhibitions:** Mattatuck Historical Society Museum. **Retrospective:** Hartford College for Women, 1970; Wesleyan U., 1976. **Group:** Paris World's Fair, 1937; New York World's Fair, 1939; Golden Gate International Exposition, San Francisco, 1939; WMAA Annuals, MOMA; MMA; Chicago/AI; Rutgers U., Surrealist & American Art: 1931–1947, 1977. **Collections:** Hartford/Wadsworth, The Miller Co.; Mattatuck Historical Society Museum;

MIT; The Olsen Foundation Inc.; SRGM; Society of the Four Arts. **Bibliography:** Hall.

GWATHMEY, ROBERT. b. January 24, 1903, Richmond, Va. **Studied:** North Carolina State College, 1924–25; Maryland Institute, 1925–26; PAFA, 1926–30, with George Harding, Daniel Garber. Traveled Europe, Caribbean, Mexico, Egypt. **Taught:** Beaver College, 1930–37; Carnegie Institute of Technology, 1938–42; Cooper Union, 1942–68; Boston U., 1968–69; Syracuse U., 1970. **Member:** Artists Equity; NIAL; NAD. **Commissions:** US Post Office, Eutaw, Ala. **Awards:** PAFA, Cresson Fellowship, 1929, 30; US Government 48-State Mural Competition winner, 1939; San Diego, First Prize, Watercolors, 1940; Carnegie, Second Prize, 1943; Lessing J. Rosenwald Fund Fellowship, 1944; AAAL Grant, 1946; Corcoran, Fourth Prize, 1957; NAD, Joseph Isidor Gold Medal, 1971; NAD, Saltus Gold Medal, 1977; Adolph and Clara Obrig Prize, 1978, Benjamin Altman Prize (figure) 1979. **Address:** Bluff Road, Amagansett, NY 11930. **Dealer:** Terry Dintenfass, Inc. **One-man Exhibitions:** (first) ACA Gallery, 1940, also 1946, 49; VMFA; Terry Dintenfass, Inc., 1961, 64, 68, 71, 74, 76. **Retrospective:** Randolph/Macon Woman's College, 1967; Boston U., 1969; St. Mary's College of Maryland, 1976. **Group:** WMAA Annuals; Corcoran; PAFA; MMA; Boston/MFA; Carnegie, 1964, 65; U. of Illinois, 1965; NAD, 1973; St. Joseph/Albrecht, Drawing—America: 1973, 1973; Ball State U. Annual, 1974; Skidmore College, An Exhibition of Twentieth-Century Drawings, 1975. **Collections:** Alabama Institute; Auburn U.; Birmingham, Ala./MA; Boston/MFA; Brandeis U.; Brooklyn Museum; California Palace; Carnegie; U. of Georgia; Guild Hall; Hirshhorn; IBM; U. of Illinois; Los Angeles/County MA; U. of Nebraska; U. of Oklahoma; PAFA; PMA; Randolph-Macon Woman's College; U. of Rochester; St. Joseph/Albrecht; San Diego; Sao Paulo; Savannah/Telfair; Springfield, Mass./MFA; U. of Texas; VMFA; WMAA; Youngstown/Butler. **Bibliography:** Baldinger; Baur 7; Bazin; Goodrich and Baur 1; McCurdy, ed.; Mendelowitz; Nordness, ed.; Pousette-Dart, ed.; Reese. Archives.

H

HAAS, RICHARD. b. August 29, 1936, Spring Green, Wisc. **Studied:** U. of Wisconsin, Milwaukee 1954–58, BS; U. of Wisconsin, with Joseph Friebert, Robert von Neuman, Harold Altman; U. of Minnesota, 1961–64, MFA, with Jack Tworkov, Peter Busa, Malcolm Myers. Traveled Mexico, Europe, Morocco. US Army, 1959. **Taught:** Lincoln High School, Milwaukee, 1959–61; School of Visual Arts, NYC, 1966–80; U. of Minnesota, 1963–64; Michigan State U., 1964–68; Bennington College, 1968–80; School of Visual Arts, NYC, 1976–80. **Member:** Art Commission of the City of New York, 1978–80; Architectural League of New York, vice-president, 1978–80. **Commissions:** Numerous wall murals indoors-outdoors nationwide. **Awards:** Taliesen Fellowship, 1955, 56; Ford Foundation **P.P.**, 1964; CAPS, 1972; National Endowment for the Arts grant, 1978; AIA, Medal of Honor, 1978; Municipal Art Society, NYC, award, 1979. **Address:** 81 Greene Street, NYC 10012. **Dealers:** Brooke Alexander, Inc., NYC; Young-Hoffman Gallery, Chicago. **One-man Exhibitions:** Bennington College, 1968, 71, 74; Hundred Acres Gallery, Ltd., 1971, 73, 74; Brooke Alexander, 1972, 75; Contract Graphics Associates, Houston, 1973; Boston U., 1973; WMAA, 1974; Harcus-Krakow Gallery, Boston, 1975; Delahunty Gallery, Dallas, 1976; Marion Locks Gallery, Philadelphia, 1976; Tyler School of Art, Philadelphia, 1977; The Art Center, Waco, 1977; Quincy College, 1978; Young-Hoffman Gallery, Chicago, 1978; Galerie Biedermann, Munich, 1978; Swain's Art Store, Plainfield, N.J., 1979; Brooke Alexander, Inc., NYC. **Retrospective:** West Palm Beach/Norton, 1977. **Group:** Walker, Five Young Minnesota Artists, 1963; Indianapolis, 1972; Yale U., American Drawing: 1969–1973, 1973; Brooklyn Museum Print Biennial, 1974; Akron/AI, Contemporary Images in Watercolor, 1976; Davidson, N.C., Art on Paper, 1976; U. of North Carolina, Art on Paper, 1976; A.F.A., American Master Drawings and Watercolors, 1976; Brooklyn Museum, Thirty Years of American Printmaking, 1976; US Department of the Interior, America, 1976, 1976; Library of Congress and NCFA, 25th National Exhibition of Prints, 1977. **Collection:** Allentown/AM; Boston/MFA, Boston Public Library; Chicago/AI; Detroit/Institute; Fort Worth; Free Library of Philadelphia; Hartford/Wadsworth; Harvard U.; High Museum; Houston/MFA; Library of Congress; MOMA; MMA; Minneapolis/Institute; NCFA; Newark Museum; NYPL; San Antonio/McNay; Walker; West Palm Beach/Norton; WMAA; Yale U. **Bibliography:** *America 1976;* Arthur 1, 2.

HADZI, DIMITRI. b. March 21, 1921, NYC. **Studied:** Brooklyn Polytechnic Institute, 1940–43; Cooper Union, NYC, 1946–50; Brooklyn Museum School, 1948–50; Polytechnion, Athens, 1950–51, Museo Artistico Industriale, Rome, 1952–53. US Air Force, 1943. Traveled Europe, USA. **Taught:** Dartmouth College, 1969; Fullerton Junior College, 1973; U. of Oregon, summer, 1974; Harvard U., 1975, 77–. **Commissions:** MIT; Philharmonic Hall, Lincoln Center for the Performing Arts, NYC; sculpture for the Reynolds Metal Co.

Memorial Award; Sun Life Insurance Co., Baltimore; John F. Kennedy Federal Office Building, Boston; Federal Reserve Bank, Minneapolis, 1971; St. Paul's Church, Rome; Lane County's Public Service Building; Federal Office Building, Portland, Ore., 1976; Johnson Wax Co., Racine, Wis., 1978–79; Dallas Center, Dallas, 1978–79. **Awards:** Fulbright Fellowship (Greece), 1950; L. C. Tiffany Grant, 1955; Guggenheim Foundation Fellowship, 1957; NIAL, 1962; American Academy, Rome, 1973–74; Hon. MA, Harvard U., 1977; American Academy of Arts and Sciences, fellow, 1978; Art Directors Club, Gold Medal Awards, 1978. **Address:** 7 Ellery Square, Cambridge, MA 02138. **Dealers:** Gruenebaum Gallery, Ltd., NYC; Richard Gray Gallery, Chicago; Mekler Gallery, Los Angeles. **One-man Exhibitions:** Galleria Schneider, Rome, 1958, 60; Seiferheld Gallery, NYC, 1959; Galerie Van der Loo, Munich, 1961; Stephen Radich Gallery, 1961; Gallery Hella Nebelung, Dusseldorf, 1962; MIT, 1963; Temple U., Rome, Temple Abroad, 1968; Felix Landau Gallery, 1969; Dartmouth College, 1969; Alpha Gallery, 1971, 77; Richard Gray Gallery, 1972; Jodi Scully Gallery, 1973; Galleria d'Arte l'Obelisco, 1974; Harvard U., 1975, 76; Mekler Gallery, Los Angeles, 1978; Gruenebaum Gallery, Ltd., NYC, 1978. **Retrospective:** MIT, 1963; Tyler School, Temple U., Rome, 1968. **Group:** MOMA, New Talent, 1956; Middelhelm Park, Antwerp, Outdoor Sculpture, 1957, 59, 71; Carnegie, 1958, 61; MOMA, Recent Sculpture, USA, 1959; Smith College, New Sculpture Now, 1960; WMAA, Business Buys American Art, 1960; RISD, Bronze Figure Sculpture Today, 1960; U. of Nebraska, 1960; Claude Bernard, Paris, Aspects of American Sculpture, 1960; WMAA Annuals, 1960, 63; Boston Arts Festival, 1961; XXXI Venice Biennial, 1962; Seattle World's Fair, 1962; Battersea Park, London, International Sculpture Exhibition, 1963; New York World's Fair, 1964–65; Hannover/Kunstverein, 1965; The White House,

Washington, D.C., 1965; Musée Rodin, Paris, 1966; Rome/Nazionale, 1970; Athens Panhellenic Exhibitions, 1973; Quadriennale, Rome, 1977; AAAL, 1978. **Collections:** Andover/Phillips; Buffalo/Albright; Chase Manhattan Bank; U. of Chicago; Ciba-Geigy Corp.; City of Tilburg; Cleveland/MA; Currier; Dallas/MFA; Fullerton Junior College; Harvard U.; Hirshhorn; U. of Massachusetts; MIT; MOMA; Montreal/MFA; New School for Social Research; NYU; PMA; Princeton U.; UCLA; RISD; U. of Chicago; SRGM; Smith College; U. of Southern California, Los Angeles; Sweet Briar College; Union Carbide Corp.; U. of Vermont; WMAA; Yale U. **Bibliography:** Craven, W.

HAINES, RICHARD. b. December 29, 1906, Marion, Iowa. **Studied:** Minneapolis Institute School, 1932–34; Ecole des Beaux-Arts, Fountainebleau. Traveled around the world, 1966. US Navy, combat artist, South Vietnam, 1967. **Taught:** Minneapolis Institute School, 1941; Chouinard Art Institute, 1945–54; Otis Art Institute, 1954–74. **Member:** President, California Watercolor Society, 1948, 50; American Association of University Professors. Federal A.P.: 1937–41, murals; Fort Snelling, Minn.; Sebeka (Minn.) High School; City Armory, Willmar, Minn.; US Post Offices in Wichita, Neb.; Cresco, Iowa; Hastings, Minn.; Clinton, Mo.; Berwyn, Ill.; Shelton, Wash. **Commissions:** Mayo Clinic, Rochester, Minn., 1952; UCLA, 1954, 63; Welton Beckett Building, Century City, Calif., 1958; U. of Kentucky, 1962; Federal Building, Los Angeles, 1965; library, Montebello, Calif., 1966–72; Temple Beth Hillel, North Hollywood, Calif., 1966. **Awards:** Vanderlip Traveling Scholarship, 1933; Los Angeles/County MA, First Award, 1944, Third Award, 1945; Oakland/AM, 1947; Denver/AM, Hon. Men., 1947; California State Fair, First **P.P.**, 1948; California Watercolor Society, First **P.P.**, 1948; SFMA, Artists Council Prize, 1948; Society of Etchers,

Engravers and Lithographers, NYC, First Prize, Lithography, 1948; California State Fair, Second Award, 1949; Los Angeles Centennial, Second **P.P.**, 1949; SFMA, Art Association Prize, 1949; Corcoran, Third Award, 1951; Los Angeles County Fair, First **P.P.**, 1951; Tupperware National Competition, 600 **P.P.**, 1957. **Address:** 247 Amalfi Drive, Santa Monica, CA 90406. **Dealer:** Abraxas Gallery, Newport Beach, California. **One-man Exhibitions:** (first) Dalzell Hatfield Gallery, 1948, also 1958, 62, 64; Rutherford Gallery, San Francisco, 1957; Santa Barbara/MA, 1959; Pasadena/AM, 1960; Santa Monica College Art Gallery, 1961; Roberts Art Gallery, Santa Monica, 1963; Laguna Beach Museum of Art, 1964; Adele Bednarz Gallery, Los Angeles, 1967, 69, 70, 73, 75; Palos Verdes Art Center, 1968; Abraxas Gallery, Laguna Beach, 1978, 79. **Group:** SFMA; Oakland/AM; Los Angeles/County MA; MMA; Dallas/MFA; Corcoran; San Diego; Kansas City/Nelson; California State Fair; U. of Illinois; Sao Paulo Biennial. **Collections:** Arizona State College; Britannica; California State Fair; California Watercolor Society; Corcoran; Dallas/MFA; Kansas City/Nelson; Library of Congress; Los Angeles/County MA; Los Angeles County Fair; MMA; Portland, Ore./AM; San Diego; Santa Barbara/MA; Seattle/AM; U. of Utah. **Bibliography:** Pousette-Dart, ed.

HALE, NATHAN CABOT. b. July 5, 1925, Los Angeles, Calif. **Studied:** Chouinard Art Institute, Los Angeles, 1945; ASL, 1945–50; Santa Monica City College, 1952. Traveled Mexico, Europe, South Pacific, USA, Greece, Israel. **Taught:** Los Angeles City Art Education and Recreation Program, 1956–57; Pratt Institute, 1963–64; ASL, 1966–72. Designed sets for off-Broadway production of *The Affairs of Anatole*, 1958. **Member:** Architectural League of New York; Municipal Art Society of New York. **Commissions:** Architectural and portrait; sculpture for St. Anthony of Padua, East Northport, N.Y. **Awards:** Los Angeles/County MA, **P.P.** for Sculpture, 1953; Audubon Artists, 1974. **Address:** Sheffield Road, Amenia, NY 12501. **Dealer:** The Midtown Galleries. **One-man Exhibitions:** (first) Felix Landau Gallery, 1957; Washington Irving Gallery, NYC, 1960; Feingarten Gallery, NYC and Chicago, 1961; The Midtown Galleries, NYC, 1964, 68, 74; Hazleton Art League, 1966; Fort Wayne/AM, 1966; Queens College, 1966; Franklin and Marshall College, 1967; NYU, 1967; Quinata Gallery, Nantucket, 1968. **Group:** J. Seligmann and Co., 1947–49; Roko Gallery, NYC, 1948–50; Los Angeles/County MA, 1953–55; Colorado Springs/FA, 1961; Hirschl & Adler Galleries, Inc., NYC, Continuing Traditions of Realism in American Art, 1962; Lehigh U., 1963; Corcoran, 1963, 64; Buffalo/Albright, 1963, 68; Wayne State U., 1964; United States Government, Art in the Embassies, 1964–66; National Art Museum of Sport, NYC, 1969. **Collections:** Indianapolis/Herron; Los Angeles/County MA; Sara Roby Foundation; Wake Forest U.

HALE, ROBERT BEVERLY. b. January 29, 1901, Boston, Mass. **Studied:** Columbia U. School of Architecture, 1923, AB; Sorbonne; with Jean Despujol, Fountainebleau and Paris; ASL, with George Bridgeman, William C. McNulty. Traveled Europe. **Taught:** ASL, 1942– ; Columbia U., 1946–67; PAFA, 1968; Cooper Union, 1973–79; Fellow of the Royal Society of Arts, London; Curator Emeritus, MMA. Associate Editor, *Art News* magazine, 1941–49. **Awards:** Hon. memb., ASL, 1975; Hon. life member of ASL (first); Benjamin Franklin Fellow; Royal Society, New York City Mayor Award of Honor for Arts and Culture, 1977; MMA, Tribute to a Curator: Robert Beverly Hale, 1978–79. **Address:** 2 West 67th Street, NYC 10023. **Dealer:** Staempfli Gallery. **One-man Exhibitions:** (first) Stamford (Conn.) Museum and Nature Center,

1959; Staempfli Gallery, 1960. **Collections:** U. of Arizona; Chase Manhattan Bank; MMA; Norfolk; WMAA. **Bibliography:** Biddle 4; **Hale.** Archives.

HALEY, JOHN CHARLES. b. September 21, 1905, Minneapolis, Minn. **Studied:** Minneapolis Institute School, with Cameron Booth; Hofmann School, Munich and Capri; Scuola Mosaico, Ravenna, Italy. US Navy, World War II. Traveled Europe, USA. **Taught:** U. of California, Berkeley. Federal A.P.; Fresco painter, briefly. **Commissions:** Stained glass in churches in St. Paul, Duluth, Rochester, and Benson, Minn.; a fresco at Government Island. **Awards:** San Francisco Art Association, 1936, 39, 44, 51, 53, 56; California State Fair, 1950, 51; RAC, 1956, 58. **Address:** Point Station, P.O. Box 31, Richmond, CA 94807. **One-man Exhibitions:** (first) SFMA, mid 1930; Mortimer Levitt Gallery, NYC, 1949, 52; U. of California, Worth Ryder Gallery, 1962; de Young, 1962; Chico State College, 1963; Four Winds Gallery, Kalamazoo, 1974. **Group:** SFMA Annuals, 1932– ; California Palace Annuals; U. of Illinois Annuals, 1948–51; III & VI Sao Paulo Biennials, 1955, 61; Chicago/AI; MMA; PAFA; Dallas/MFA; Denver/AM; RAC; Pasadena/AM; Colorado Springs/FA; Santa Barbara/MA; St. Louis/City; MOMA, circ. **Collections:** U. of California, Berkeley; Chico State College; First National Bank of Nevada; IBM; Mills College; MMA; Oakland/MA; Phillips; SFMA.

HAMMERSLEY, FREDERICK. b. January 5, 1919, Salt Lake City, Utah. **Studied:** U. of Idaho, 1936–38; San Francisco Junior College, 1938–39; Academy of Advertising Art, San Francisco, 1939–40; Chouinard Art Institute, Los Angeles, 1940–42; 1946–47, with Henry McFee; Jepson Art Institute, Los Angeles, 1947–49, with Rico Lebrun; Academie des Beaux-Arts, Paris, 1945. US Army, 1942–46. **Taught:** Jepson Art Institute, Los Angeles, 1949–51;

Pomona College, 1953–62; Pasadena Museum School, 1956–61 (children's painting class), 1963– (adult classes); occasional private lessons; Chouinard Art Institute, 1964–68; U. of New Mexico, 1968–71. **Awards:** Laguna Beach Art Gallery, First Prize, 1949; City of Claremont, First Prize, 1960; Youngstown/Butler, **P.P.**, 1961; Guggenheim Foundation Fellowship, 1973; National Endowment for the Arts, Grant, 1975, 77. **Address:** 608 Carlisle S.E., Albuquerque, NM 87106. **Dealer:** L.A. Louver Gallery, Venice, Calif. **One-man Exhibitions:** (first) Fullerton (Calif.) Art Museum, 1959; Pasadena/AM, 1961; Heritage Gallery, Los Angeles, 1961, 63; Occidental College, 1962; California Palace, 1962; La Jolla, 1963; Santa Barbara/MA; Hollis Gallery, San Francisco; Whittier College; U. of New Mexico; U. of New Mexico, 1969–75; L. A. Louvre Gallery, Venice, Calif., 1978; Middendorf Lane Gallery, Washington, D.C. (two-man), 1977. **Retrospective:** U. of New Mexico, 1975. **Group:** SFMA, Abstract Classicists, circ., Los Angeles/County MA; ICA, London; USIA, Drawings from California, circ., Europe, 1958–59; Queens U., Belfast, 1959–60; Western Association of Art Museum Directors, circ., 1960–61; A.F.A., Purist Painting, circ., 1960–61; WMAA, Geometric Abstraction in America, circ., 1962; WMAA, Fifty California Artists, 1962–63; MOMA, The Responsive Eye, 1965; M. Knoedler & Co., Art Across America, circ., 1965–67; U. of Nebraska, Geometric Abstraction, 1974; Los Angeles/County MA, California, 5 Footnotes to Modern Art History, 1977; Corcoran Biennial, 1977; Denver/AM Biennial, 1979. **Collections:** U. of California; Berkeley; City of Claremont; Foote, Cone & Belding Communications, Inc., Los Angeles; U. of New Mexico; Oakland/AM; Santa Barbara/MA; US Navy. **Bibliography:** Archives.

HANSEN, JAMES LEE. b. June 13, 1925, Tacoma, Wash. **Studied:** Portland (Ore.) Museum School. **Taught:** Oregon State U., 1957–58; U. of California, Berkeley, 1958; Portland (Ore.) State College, 1964–69. Founder of The Fine Arts Collaborative, 1959. **Commissions:** Vancouver (Wash.) Federal Savings and Loan Building; Land Title Building, Vancouver, Wash.; Sacred Heart Nurses Dormitory, Eugene, Ore.; Corvallis (Ore.) First Federal Savings and Loan; Alder Way Building, Portland, Ore.; St. Louis Church, Bellevue, Wash.; Providence Heights College, Pine Lake, Wash.; St. Mary's Mission, Pioneer, Wash.; Fresno (Calif.) Civic Mall; St. Ann's Church, Butte, Mont., 1966; Holy Trinity Parish, Bremerton, Wash., 1967; Graphic Arts Center, Portland, Ore., 1968; Harrison Square, Portland (Ore.) Civic Center; State Capitol Campus, Olympia, Wash.; U. of Oregon. **Awards:** SFMA, First **P.P.**, 1952, 60; Seattle/AM, First **P.P.**, 1952; SFMA, American Trust Co. Award, 1956; Seattle/AM, Norman Davis **P.P.**, 1958, Fellow of the International Institute of Arts and Letters. **Address:** 4115 Q Street, Vancouver, WA 98663. **Dealers:** Fountain Gallery; Polly Friedlander Gallery, Seattle. **One-man Exhibitions:** Kraushaar Galleries, 1952; Dilexi Gallery, San Francisco; The Morris Gallery, NYC, 1951; Fountain Gallery, 1966, 69; U. of Oregon, 1969; Cheney Cowles Memorial Museum, Spokane, 1972; Polly Friedlander Gallery, 1973, 78. **Retrospective:** Portland, Ore./AM, 1971. **Group:** Portland, Ore./ AM, 1951–60; Santa Barbara/MA; U. of Oregon; Fort Worth; U. of Washington; SFMA, 1952, 56, 60; Seattle/AM, 1952–57, 1959, 60, Northwest Annual, 1967; Denver/AM, 1952, 61; WMAA, 1953; San Diego; The Morris Gallery, NYC, 1961; State of Washington Governor's Invitational, circ., 1964–75. **Collections:** The Bank of California, N.A., Portland, Ore.; First Federal Savings and Loan Association of Corvallis; First National Bank of Oregon; First National Bank of Seattle; U. of Oregon; Portland, Ore./AM; SFMA; Seattle/AM. **Bibliography:** *Art of the Pacific Northwest; Recent Figure Sculpture.*

HANSEN, ROBERT. b. January 1, 1924, Osceola, Neb. **Studied:** U. of Nebraska, with Kady Faulkner, Dwight Kirsch, 1948, AB, BFA; Escuela de Bellas Artes, San Miguel de Allende, Mexico, with Alfredo Zalce. US Army, 1943–46. Resided Mexico, Hawaii, India, Spain. **Taught:** Bradley U., 1949–55; Occidental College, 1956– . **Commissions** (murals): Public School and State Library, Morelia, Mexico. **Awards:** Fulbright Fellowship (India), 1961; Guggenheim Foundation Fellowship, 1961; Tamarind Fellowship, 1965. **Address:** 1974 Addison Way, Los Angeles, CA 90041. **Dealer:** Comara Gallery. **One-man Exhibitions:** (first) Peoria (Ill.) Art Center, 1951; Occidental College, 1957; Ferus Gallery, Los Angeles, 1958; Bertha Lewinson Gallery, Los Angeles, 1959; Huysman Gallery, Los Angeles, 1961; Comara Gallery, 1963, 64, 66, 68, 70, 72, 75. **Retrospective:** Long Beach/MA, 1967; Los Angeles Municipal Art Gallery, 1973. **Group:** SFMA Annuals, 1957–59; Ball State Teachers College Annuals, 1957, 58, 60; U. of Nebraska, 1958; Oakland/ AM Annuals, 1958, 60; UCLA, California Painters under 35, 1959; Pasadena/ AM, Pacific Profile, 1960; Carnegie, 1961, 1964; WMAA, Fifty California Artists, 1962–63; MOMA, Recent Painting USA, 1963; Pasadena/AM, Ten Californians, 1964; WMAA Annual, 1965; US State Department, circ., 1968–70; MOMA, 1969. **Collections:** Long Beach/MA; Los Angeles/County MA; MOMA; U. of Nebraska; Princeton U.; San Diego; WMAA.

HANSON, DUANE. b. January 17, 1925, Alexandria, Minn. **Studied:** Luther College, 1943–44; U. of Washington, 1944–45; Macalester College, 1945–56, BA; Cranbrook, 1950–51, MFA. Traveled Western Europe, Egypt, USSR, Mexico, Canada, West Indies; resided seven years in Germany. **Taught:** public High Schools, 1946–47, 49–50, 52–53, 60–62; US Army schools, Germany, 1953–60; private school,

Greenwich, Conn., 1951–52; Ogle-
thorpe U., 1963–65; Miami-Dade Junior
College, 1965–69; U. of Miami, 1979.
Commissions: Chase Manhattan Bank,
1975; Kansas City/Nelson, 1975.
Awards: Harvard U., Ella Ayman
Cabot Trust, 1963; Chicago/AI, Blair
Award, 1974; DAAD Grant (Berlin),
1974; Hon. DHL, Nova U., Ft. Lauder-
dale. **Address:** 6109 Southwest 55
Court, Davie, FL 33314. **Dealer:** OK
Harris Works of Art. **One-man Exhibi-
tions:** Cranbrook, 1951; Wilton (Conn.)
Gallery, 1952; Galerie Netzel, Bremen,
1958; U. of South Florida, 1968; West
Palm Beach/Norton, 1968; Ringling,
1968; OK Harris Works of Art, 1970, 72,
74, 76; Onnasch Galerie, Berlin, 1972;
Berlin/Adademie der Kunst, 1975;
Humlebaek/Louisiana, 1975; U. of
Nebraska, 1976; Des Moines, 1977; U.
of California, Berkeley, 1977; Portland,
Ore./AM, 1977; Kansas City/Nelson,
1977; Colorado Springs/FA, 1977;
VMFA, 1977; Corcoran, 1977; WMAA,
1978. **Retrospective:** Stuttgart/WK,
circ., 1974; Wichita State U., 1976.
Group: WMAA, Human Concern/Per-
sonal Torment, 1969; WMAA Annuals,
1970, 73; Walker, Figures/Environ-
ments, circ., 1970–71; Aachen/NG,
Klischee und Antiklischee, 1970; Cor-
coran, Depth and Presence, 1971; Chi-
cago/Contemporary, Radical Realism,
1971; Documenta V, Kassel, 1972;
Galerie des 4 Mouvements, Paris, Hy-
perrealistes Americains, 1972; Harvard
U., Recent Figure Sculpture, 1972;
Lunds Konsthall, Sweden, Amerikansk
Realism, 1973; Lincoln, Mass./De Cor-
dova, The Super-Realist Vision, 1973;
Randers Kunstmuseum, Denmark,
Amerikanske Realister, 1973; Hartford/
Wadsworth, New/Photo Realism, 1974;
Chicago/AI, 1974; CNAC, Hyper-
realistes Americains/Realistes Euro-
peens, 1974; Baltimore/MA, Super
Realism, 1975; PAFA, 8 Contemporary
American Realists, 1977; Yale U., Seven
Realists, 1976; Berlin/National, Aspekts
der 60er Jahre, 1978. **Collections:**
Aachen/NG; Adelaide; Caracas; Co-
logne; Duisburg; Hannover/K-G; Mil-

waukee; RAC; Rotterdam; Hartford/
Wadsworth; Kansas City/AI; Kansas
City/Nelson; Utrecht; West Palm Beach/
Norton; WMAA. **Bibliography:** *Figures/
Environments;* Goodyear; *Kunst um 1970;*
Sager.

HARE, DAVID. b. March 10, 1917,
NYC. Studied in New York, Arizona,
Colorado (majored in experimental
color photography). Researched and
published a portfolio of color photographs on the American Indian, in collaboration with Dr. Clark Whissler of
the American Museum of Natural History, 1940. Editor, *VVV* (surrealist mag-
azine), 1942–44. Lectured extensively.
Taught: Philadelphia College of Art,
1964–65; U. of Oregon. **Commissions**
(sculpture): NYC; Massachusetts;
Rhode Island; Illinois. **Awards:** Hon.
DFA, Maryland Institute of Arts. **Ad-
dress:** 34 Leroy Street, NYC 10014.
One-man Exhibitions: (first) Hudson
D. Walker Gallery, NYC, 1939; Julien
Levy Galleries, NYC, 1946; Art of This
Century, 1946, 47; The Kootz Gallery,
NYC, 1946, 48, 51, 52, 55, 56, 58, 59;
SFMA, 1947; Galerie Maeght, 1948;
Saidenberg Gallery, 1960–63; Staempfli
Gallery, 1969; Tibor de Nagy, Houston,
1974; Alessandra Collection, NYC,
1976; SRGM, 1977; Hamilton Gallery of
Contemporary Art, NYC, 1978; Zolla-
Lieberman, Chicago, 1978. **Retrospec-
tive:** PMA, 1969. **Group:** MOMA, Four-
teen Americans, circ., 1946; I & IV Sao
Paulo Biennials, 1951, 57; WMAA, The
New Decade, 1954–55; MOMA, Mod-
ern Art in the United States, circ.,
Europe, 1955–56; Musée Rodin, Paris,
International Sculpture, 1956; Seattle/
AM, circ., Far East and Europe, 1958;
Brussels World's Fair, 1958; Chicago/
AI, 1961; Seattle World's Fair, 1962;
Pittsburgh Bicentennial, 1962; WMAA,
1962; MOMA, Dada, Surrealism and
Their Heritage, 1968; MOMA, The New
American Painting and Sculpture, 1969;
Foundation Maeght, L'Art Vivant,
1970; Baltimore/MA, The Partial Figure
in Modern Sculpture, 1970; WMAA,

David Hare   *Dog Elephant*   1979

200 Years of American Sculpture, 1976; Washington, D.C./Renwick Gallery, Object as Poet, 1977; Arts Council of Great Britain, Dada and Surrealism Revisited, 1978; Buffalo/Albright, American Painting in the 1970s, circ., 1978. **Collections:** Akron/AI; Brandeis U.; Brooklyn Museum; Buffalo/Albright; Carnegie; Hartford/Wadsworth; MMA; MOMA; New Orleans/Delgado; SFMA; SRGM; WMAA; Washington U.; Yale U. **Bibliography:** Baur 5; Biddle 4; Blesh 1; Breton 3; Brumme; Calas; Craven, W.; Giedion Welcker 1; Goodrich and Baur 1; **Goossen 5**; Hess, T.B., 1; Hunter 6; Janis and Blesh 1; Janis, S.; Muane 2; McCurdy, ed.; Mendelowitz; Miller, ed. 2; Motherwell and Reinhardt, eds.; Paalan; Read 3; Ritchie 3; Rodman 1; Rose, B., 1; Rubin 1; Seuphor 3; Trier 1; Waldbert 4. Archives.

HARRIS, PAUL. b. November 5, 1925, Orlando, Fla. **Studied:** with Jay Karen Winslow, Orlando, Fla.; Chouinard Art Institute; New School for Social Research (with Johannes Molzahn); U. of New Mexico; Hans Hofmann School. US Navy, W.W. II. **Taught:** U. of New Mexico; Knox College, Jamaica, W. I.; New Paltz State College; Montclair State College; California Institute of the Arts, Valencia; Universidad Catolica, Santiago; California College of Arts and Crafts. Editorial Associate, *Art News* magazine, 1955–56; U. of California, Berkeley. **Commissions:** U. of New Mexico. **Awards:** Fulbright Fellowship (Chile), 1962–63; Tamarind Fellowship, 1969–70; Guggenheim Foundation Fellowship, 1979; MacDowell Colony Fellowship, 1977; Longview Foundation Grant, 1978. **Address:** Box 1, Grove Road, Bolinas, CA 94924. **One-man Ex-**

hibitions: Poindexter Gallery, 1961, 63, 67, 70, 72; The Lanyon Gallery, 1965; Berkeley Gallery, San Francisco, 1965, Candy Store Art Gallery, Folsom, Calif., 1967; William Sawyer Gallery, 1969, 71; M. E. Thelen Gallery, Essen, 1970; SFMA, 1972; U. of California, Santa Barbara, 1972; U. of New Mexico, 1973; Arkansas Art Center, Little Rock, 1974. **Group:** New School for Social Research; U. of New Mexico; MOMA, Recent Sculpture USA, 1959; Hans Hofmann and His Students, circ., 1963; Chicago/AI, 1965; New York World's Fair, 1964–65; IX Sao Paulo Biennial, 1967; Los Angeles/County MA, American Sculpture of the Sixties, circ., 1967; Dusseldorf/Kunsthalle, Prospect '68, 1968; NCFA, New American Figurative, 1968; Trenton/State, Soft Art, 1969; International Exhibitions Foundation, Washington, D.C., Tamarind: A Renaissance of Lithography, circ., 1971–72. **Collections:** Aachen/NG; Los Angeles/County MA; MOMA; U. of New Mexico; Yale U. **Bibliography:** Tuchman 1.

HARTELL, JOHN. b. January 30, 1902, Brooklyn, N.Y. **Studied:** Cornell U. (Architecture), 1925; Royal Academy of Fine Arts, Stockholm. Traveled Europe, Puerto Rico, England. **Taught:** Clemson College (Architecture), 1927–28; U. of Illinois, 1928–30; Cornell U., now Prof. Emeritus after teaching since 1930. **Awards:** Utica, 1948, 52; Illinois Wesleyan U., 1950; New York State Fair, 1951; U. of Rochester, 1953; Fellow of the American Scandinavian Foundation. **Address:** 319 The Parkway, Ithaca, NY 14850. **Dealer:** Kraushaar Galleries. **One-man Exhibitions:** Kleemann Gallery, NYC, 1937; Kraushaar Galleries, 1943, 45, 49, 53, 57, 63, 66, 69, 72, 75, 77, 80; Cornell U., 1943, 46, 53, 57, 62, 66; Wells College, 1945, 49, 55; Utica, 1952; U. of Rochester, 1954; Upstairs Gallery, Ithaca, N.Y., 1968, 73, 80; Lehigh U., 1971. **Group:** Architectural League of New York, 1932; U. of Rochester, 1943, 53, 54; ICA, Boston; Cincinnati/AM, 1945; St. Louis/City, 1945; Carnegie, 1945–47; WMAA, 1946,

50, 53; Utica, 1948, 51, 52, 54; Illinois Wesleyan U., 1950, 57; U. of Illinois, 1951; PAFA, 1953; US State Department, Traveling Show to Australia, 1967–68; Indianapolis/Herron, 1970. **Collections:** Atlanta U.; Cornell U.; Illinois Wesleyan U.; U. of Nebraska; Northern Trust Co., Chicago, Ill.; Utica; Wake Forest U.

HARTIGAN, GRACE. b. March 28, 1922, Newark, N.J. Studied with Isaac Lane Muse, NYC, mid 1940s. Traveled Europe; resided Mexico, 1949. Designed set for *Red Riding Hood*, by Kenneth Koch, for the Artists Theater, NYC, 1953. **Taught:** Maryland Institute, Artist-in-Residence, 1967–1980. **Awards:** Moore Institute of Art, Science and Industry, Hon. DFA, 1969; AAAL, Childe Hassam Fund **P.P.**, 1975. **Address:** 1710 ½ Eastern Avenue, Baltimore, MD 21231. **Dealer:** Hamilton Gallery of Contemporary Art. **One-man Exhibitions:** (first) Tibor de Nagy Gallery, 1951, also 1952–55, 1957, 59; Vassar College, 1954; Gres Gallery, Washington, D.C., 1960; Chatham College, 1960; Carnegie, 1961; Martha Jackson Gallery, 1962, 64, 67, 70; U. of Minnesota, 1963; Franklin Siden Gallery, Detroit, 1964; Kent State U., 1966; The U. of Chicago, 1967; Maryland Institute, 1967; Gertrude Kasle Gallery, 1968, 70, 72, 74, 76; Grand Rapids, 1968 (two-man); William Zierler Inc., 1975; American University, Washington, D.C., 1975; Genesis Galleries, NYC, 1977, 78; U. of Maryland, 1979; Grimaldis Gallery, Baltimore, 1979; Plattsburg/SUNY, 1980; Hamilton Gallery of Contemporary Art, NYC, 1981. **Retrospective:** Fort Wayne, 1981. **Group:** Ninth Street Exhibition, NYC, 1951; U. of Minnesota, Rising Talent, 1955; MOMA, Modern Art in the United States, circ., Europe, 1955–56; MOMA, Twelve Americans, circ., 1956; Jewish Museum, The New York School, Second Generation, 1957; International Biennial, Exhibition of Paintings, Tokyo; IV Sao Paulo Biennial, 1957; MOMA, The New American Painting, circ., Europe, 1958–59; Brussels World's Fair, 1958; ART:USA:59, NYC, 1959; Documenta II, Kassel, 1959; Walker, 60 American Painters, 1960; SRGM, Abstract Expressionists and Imagists, 1961; SRGM/USIA, American Vanguard, circ., Europe, 1961–62; WMAA Annual, 1963; PAFA, 1963, 68; Ghent, The Human Figure since Picasso, 1964; White House Festival of the Arts, Washington, D.C., 1965; Drexel Institute of Technology, 1966; Flint/Institute, 1966; U. of Illinois, 1967, 69; Ball State U., Collages by American Artists, 1971; Delaware Art Museum, American Painting since World War II, 1971; WMAA, Frank O'Hara; A Poet Among Painters, 1974; Corcoran Biennial, 1975; NCFA, Poets & Painters, 1976; Syracuse/Everson, Critics Choice, 1977; Hirshhorn, Art of the Fifties, 1980. **Collections:** American Republic Insurance Co.; American U.; Baltimore/MA; Bezelel Museum; Brandeis U.; Brooklyn Museum; Buffalo/Albright; Carnegie; Chicago/AI; The U. of Chicago; Flint/Institute; Grand Rapids; Hartford/Wadsworth; Kansas City/Nelson; MMA; MOMA; Minneapolis/Institute; NCFA; New Paltz/SUNY; New School for Social Research; Oklahoma; PAFA; PMA; Princeton U.; RISD; Raleigh/NCMA; Ringling; Vassar College; WGMA; WMAA; Walker; Washington U.; Woodward Foundation. **Bibliography:** *Art: A Woman's Sensibility*; Downes, ed.; Friedman, ed.; Goodrich and Baur 1; Haftman; Hunter 1, 6; Hunter, ed.; McCurdy, ed.; *Metro*; Nemser; Nordness, ed.; Read 2; Sandler 1.

HARTL, LEON. b. January, 31, 1889, Paris, France; **d.** December 1973, Schenectady, N.Y. To USA, 1912; citizen, 1922. Self-taught. Expert on aniline dyes. **Taught:** Brooklyn Museum School. **Member:** Artists Equity. Federal A.P.: Easel painting. **Awards:** NIAL, Marjorie Peabody Waite Award, 1959; Youngstown/Butler, Hon. Men., 1960; MacDowell Colony Fellowship, 1959–61; Yaddo Fellowship, 1960, 61, 63; Ingram Merrill Foundation Grant, 1968. **One-man Exhibitions:** (first) Whitney Studio Club, NYC, 1925, also 1926; Curt Valentine Gallery, NYC, 1927, 30, 36; Joseph Brummer Gallery, NYC, 1934, 38; The Peridot Gallery, 1954, 55, 58, 60, 62, 64, 66; The Zabriskie Gallery, 1967; Ingber Art Gallery, 1971, 76. **Group:** Youngstown/Butler; Carnegie; Chicago/AI; Corcoran; Independent Artists, NYC, 1917, 18, 19; NIAL; Palazzo del Parco, Bordighera; PAFA; U. of Nebraska. **Collections:** Corcoran; Hallmark Collection; Hartford/Wadsworth; U. of Nebraska; Phillips; Society of New York Hospitals; Syracuse U.; WMAA. **Bibliography:** Downes, ed. Archives.

HARTLEY, MARSDEN. b. January 4, 1877, Lewiston, Me.; **d.** September 2, 1943, Ellsworth, Me. **Studied:** Cleveland Institute of Art, 1892, with C. Yates, N. Waldeck, C. Sowers; privately with John Semon; W. M. Chase School, NYC, 1898–99, with Frank V. DuMond, William M. Chase, F. L. Mora; NAD, 1900, with F. C. Jones, E. M. Ward, G. W. Maynard, E. H. Glashfield, F. J. Dillman, F. S. Hartley. Traveled USA extensively; Germany, France, Mexico. Federal A.P.: Easel painting. **Awards:** Guggenheim Foundation Fellowship, 1931. **One-man Exhibitions:** (first) Photo-Secession, NYC, 1909, also 1912, 14; The Daniel Gallery, NYC, 1915; Montross Gallery, NYC, 1920; Anderson Galleries, NYC, 1921; Stieglitz's Intimate Gallery, NYC, 1926–29; Arts Club of Chicago, 1928, 45; An American Place (Gallery), NYC, 1930, 36, 37; The Downtown Gallery, 1932; Galeria de la Escuela Nacional de Artes Plasticas, Mexico City, 1933; Hudson D. Walker Gallery, NYC, 1938, 39, 40; Carlen Gallery, Philadelphia, 1938; Symphony Hall, Boston, 1939; Portland, Ore./AM, 1940; California Palace, 1940; Walker, 1940; M. Knoedler & Co., 1942, 44, 68; Phillips, 1943; P. Rosenberg and Co., 1944, 47, 48, 50, 55;

Macbeth Gallery, NYC, 1945; Indianapolis/Herron, 1946; The Bertha Schaefer Gallery, 1948, 56; U. of Minnesota, 1952, Minneapolis, 1952, 79; Santa Fe, N.M., 1958; The Babcock Gallery, 1959–61, 75; Shore Studio, Boston, 1962; Alfredo Valente Gallery, NYC, 1966; La Jolla, 1966; Colby College, 1967; U. of Southern California, 1968; Tucson Art Center, 1969; U. of Texas, 1969; Danenberg Gallery, 1969; U. of Kansas, 1972; C. W. Post College, 1977; Bates College, 1978; Washburn Gallery, NYC, 1978. **Retrospectives:** Cincinnati/AM, 1941; MOMA, 1944; A.F.A., circ., 1960; Danenberg Gallery, 1969; WMAA, 1980. **Group:** The Armory Show, 1913; The Forum Gallery, 1916; Brooklyn Museum, 1926; WMAA, 1935, 38; U. of Minnesota, 1937; Baltimore/MA, 1942; Delaware Art Museum, Avant-Garde Painting and Sculpture in America, 1910–1925, 1975; U. of California, Santa Barbara, O'Keefe, Hartley and Marin in the Southwest, 1975; SRGM, 20th Century American Drawings, 1976; MOMA, The Natural Paradise, 1976; Royal Scottish Academy, Edinburgh, The Modern Spirit: American Painting 1908–1935, 1977; WMAA, William Carlos Williams and the American Scene, 1978; WMAA, Synchronism and American Color Abstraction, 1978; Dusseldorf, Two Decades of American Painting, 1929–1940, 1979. **Collections:** Andover/Phillips; Barnes Foundation; Boston/MFA; Bowdoin College; Brooklyn Museum; Buffalo/Albright; Carnegie; Amon Carter Museum; Cleveland/MA; Colorado Springs/FA; Columbus; Cornell U.; Denver/AM; Des Moines; Detroit/Institute; U. of Georgia; Hartford/Wadsworth; Indiana U.; Kalamazoo/Institute; Lewiston (Me.) Public Library; Los Angeles/County MA; Louisville/Speed; MMA; MOMA; U. of Michigan; Milwaukee; U. of Minnesota; U. of Nebraska; Newark Museum; Omaha/Joslyn; PMA; Pasadena/AM; Phillips, Phoenix; Portland, Ore./AM; SFMA; St. Louis/City; San Antonio/McNay; Santa Barbara/MA; Santa Fe, N.M.; Smith College; U. of Texas;

Utica; VMFA; Vassar College; WMAA; Walker; Wichita/AM; Williams College; Worcester/AM; Yale U.; Youngstown/Butler. **Bibliography:** *Avant-Garde Painting and Sculpture in America, 1910–25;* Barker 1; Baur 7; Bazin ; Biddle 4; Blesh 1; Born; Brown; Brown 2; Cahill and Barr, eds.; Canaday; Chipp; Coke 2; Eliot; Flexner; Frank, ed.; Frost; Goldwater and Treves, eds.; Goodrich and Baur 1; Haftman; **Hartley**; Haskell 4; Hunter 6; *Index of 20th Century Artists;* Janis, S.; Kootz 1, 2; Levin 2; **McCausland**; McCoubrey 1; McCurdy, ed.; Mellquist; Mendelowtiz; Phillips 2; Read 2; Richardson, E.P.; Ritchie 1; Rodman 2; Rose, B., 1, 4; Soby 6; Sutton; Tashjian; **Well, ed.**; Wight 2; Wright 1. Archives.

HARTMAN, ROBERT. b. December 17, 1926, Sharon, Pa. **Studied:** U. of Arizona, BFA, MA; Colorado Springs/FA, with Peppino Mangravite, 1947, with Vaclav Vytlacil, Ludwig Sander, Emerson Woelffer, 1951; Brooklyn Museum School, with William King, Hui Ka Swong, 1953–54. **Taught:** U. of Arizona, 1952–53; Texas Technological College, 1955–58; U. of Nevada, 1958–61; U. of California, 1961– . **Awards:** Youngstown/Butler, **P.P.,** 1955; La Jolla, 1962; SFMA, Emanuel Walter Bequest and Purchase Award, 1966; IV International Young Artists Exhibit, America-Japan, Tokyo, Hon. Men., 1967. **Address:** 1265 Mountain Boulevard, Oakland, CA 94611. **Dealer:** Shirley Cerf Gallery, San Francisco, Calif. **One-man Exhibitions:** (first) Kipnis Gallery, Westport, Conn., 1954; Roswell, 1957; U. of Nevada, 1958; U. of California, 1961; RAC, 1963; Comara Gallery, 1963, 65; Berkeley Gallery, 1965, 67, 68; The Bertha Schaefer Gallery, 1966, 69, 74; Santa Barbara/MA, 1973; Hank Baum Gallery, San Francisco, 1973, 78; Shirley Cerf Gallery, San Francisco, 1980. **Group:** New York World's Fair, 1964–65; U. of Illinois, 1965; M. Knoedler & Co., Art Across America, 1965–67; San Francisco Art

Association, 1966; VMFA, American Painting, 1966; U. of Washington, 1967; Colorado Springs/FA, 1967; IV International Young Artists Exhibit, America-Japan, Tokyo, 1967. **Collections:** Achenbach Foundation; Colorado Springs/-FA; Dublin/Municipal; Kaiser Industries, Oakland, Calif.; Long Beach/MA; Mead Corporation; NCFA; Oakland/AM; Roswell; SFAI; U. of Washington; Youngstown/Butler; Zischke Organization, San Francisco, Calif.

HARVARD, JAMES P. b. June 29, 1937, Galveston, Texas. **Awards:** Cresson scholar, 1964; PAFA, J. Henry Schiedt Memorial Prize, 1965; PAFA, Mabel Wilson Woodrow Award, 1962. **Studied:** Sam Houston State College, 1959, BS; Atelier Chapman Kelley, Dallas, 1960; PAFA, 1965. **Address:** 20 North Moore Street, NYC 10013. **Dealer:** Louis K. Meisel Gallery, NYC. **One-man Exhibitions:** Chapman Kelley Gallery, Dallas, 1965, 70; Temple U. 1967; Vanderlip Gallery, Philadelphia, 1969; Marian Locks Gallery, Philadelphia, 1970, 73, 74, 77; Henri Gallery, Washington, D.C., 1970; OK Harris Works of Art, NYC, 1971; Galerie Reckermann, Cologne, 1973; Gimpel & Weitzenhoffer, Ltd., NYC, 1973; Galerie Arnesen, Copenhagen, 1974; Galleriet Lunda, Sweden, 1974; Gallerie Fabian Carlsson, Goteborg, 1974; Galerie Ahlner, Stockholm, 1974; Deson-Zaks Gallery, Chicago, 1975; Louis K. Meisel Gallery, NYC, 1975, 77, 79, Galerie Krakeslatt, Bromolla, Sweden, 1975; Delahunty Gallery, Dallas, 1976; Morgan Gallery, Shawnee Mission, Kansas, 1976; Galerie le Portail, Heidelberg, 1977; Hanson-Cowles Gallery, Minneapolis, 1977; Irving Galleries, Palm Beach, 1978; Janus Gallery, Venice, Calif., 1978. **Group:** PAFA, Annuals 1962–67; A.F.A., Recent Drawing, 1967; Silvermine, Annual, 1969; PAFA, Sculpture: New Forms, New Materials, 1970; U. of North Carolina, Art on Paper, 1975; PAFA, Three Centuries of American Art, 1976; SRGM,

1977; Springfield, Mass./MFA, Abstract Illusionism, circ., 1979. **Collections:** Atlantic Richfield Co.; AT&T; First Pennsylvania Banking & Trust Co., Philadelphia; Kemper Insurance Co., Chicago, Ill.; NCFA; NYU; PAFA; PMA; Prudential Insurance Co. of America, N.J.; SRGM; Stockholm/National; Temple U.; Westinghouse Corp., NYC; Witte. **Bibliography:** Lucie-Smith.

HARVEY, JAMES. b. March 9, 1929, Toronto (Ont.), Canada; **d.** July 15, 1965, NYC. **Studied:** Chicago Art Institute School, with Paul Wieghardt, BFA. Traveled Middle East, Europe, Russia. **Awards:** Fulbright Fellowship (Egypt), 1953; Yaddo Fellowship, 1960. **One-man Exhibitions:** (first) Roko Gallery, NYC, 1953; Cairo Egypt, 1954; Parma Gallery, NYC, 1956, 58; The Graham Gallery, 1959, 60, 61, 63; Gertrude Kasle Gallery, 1968. **Group:** MMA, American Paintings Today, 1950; WMAA Annual, 1952; WMAA Fulbright Artists, 1958; Baltimore/MA, 1958; WMAA, Young America, 1960; Corcoran, 1960; Yale U., 1961. **Collections:** Toronto. **Bibliography:** Archives.

HARVEY, ROBERT. b. September 16, 1924, Lexington, N.C. **Studied:** Ringling School of Art, with Elmer Harmes, Georgia Warren; San Francisco Art Institute with Nathan Oliveira, Sonia Gechtoff. Traveled Great Britain, France, North Africa, Italy; Resided Spain, 1966–68. **Awards:** Corcoran, Hon. Men. and Ford Foundation Purchase 1963; San Francisco Art Festival, Award of Merit, 1963; Western Washington State College, **P.P.,** 1965; Mead Painting of the year, 1967. **Address:** La Huerta del Angel, Macharaviaya, Malaga, Spain. **Dealer:** Gump's Gallery, San Francisco. **One-man Exhibitions:** (first) Saidenberg Gallery, 1954; Gump's Gallery, 1959, 61, 63, 64; La Escondida, Taos, N.M., 1962; Bedell

Gallery, Santa Fe, N.M., 1962; Terry Dintenfass, Inc., 1963; Phoenix, 1964; Jefferson Gallery, 1964; David Stuart Gallery, 1964, 65, 67, 69; 75; Wichita/AM, 1965; Sacramento/Crocker, 1965; The Krasner Gallery, 1967–74, 78; San Diego, 1968; Richard White Gallery, Seattle, 1969; Owen Gallery, Denver, 1970–74; Charles Campbell Gallery, 1972, 74, 77; Parlade, Marbella, 1972; Galeria Diaz Lario, Malaga, 1975; Gallery Malacke, 1975; Centro Cultural de los Estados Unidos, Madrid, 1977; David Marshall Gallery, Puerto Banus, Spain, 1979. **Retrospective:** Ringling, 1970; Sacred Heart College, Atherton, Calif., 1974. **Group:** Corcoran, 1963; Biennial, 1967; deYoung, New Images of San Francisco; Oakland/AM; California Palace; Kansas City/Nelson; Denver/AM; Santa Barbara/MA; Phoenix; Santa Fe, N.M.; Raleigh/NCMA, 1965; VMFA, American Painting, 1966; Youngstown/Butler, 1966; U. of Illinois, 1967, 69; San Diego, Invitational American Drawing Exhibition, 1977; Oakland/AM, Bay Area Artist, 1977. **Collections:** City of San Francisco; Corcoran; Crown Zellerbach Foundation; The Fine Arts Museum of the South, Mobile, Ala.; Hirshhorn; Mead Corporation; Stanford U.; Storm King Art Center; Western Washington State College; Wichita/AM.

HATCHETT, DUAYNE. b. May 12, 1925, Shawnee, Okla. **Studied:** U. of Oklahoma (with John O'Neill), 1950, BFA, 1952, MFA; US Army Air Corps, 1943–46. **Taught:** U. of Oklahoma, 1949–50; Oklahoma City U., 1951–54; U. of Tulsa, 1954–64; The Ohio State U., 1964–65; Buffalo/SUNY, 1968–80. **Commissions:** First National Bank of Tulsa; Boston Avenue Methodist Church, Tulsa; Trader's National Bank, Kansas City, Mo.; Northeastern State College; Tulsa Fire Department. **Address:** 347 Starin Avenue, Buffalo, NY 14216. **Dealer:** Nina Freudenheim Gallery, Buffalo, N.Y. **One-man Exhibitions:** Haydon Calhoun Gallery, Dallas; U. of

Oklahoma; Oklahoma State U.; Oklahoma; Bryson Gallery, Columbus, Ohio; Royal Marks Gallery, 1966, 68, 69, 70; Tulsa/Philbrook (three-man), 1973; Rochester Institute of Technology, 1973; Buffalo/Albright, 1974; Nine Freudenheim Gallery, Buffalo, N.Y., 1976, 77. **Group:** New York World's Fair, 1964–65; WMAA Sculpture Annual, 1966, 68; U. of Illinois, 1967; Los Angeles/County MA, American Sculpture of the Sixties, 1967; Carnegie, 1967; HemisFair '68, San Antonio, 1968; U. of Minnesota, 1969; U. of Nebraska, American Sculpture, 1970; Carnegie, 1970. **Retrospective:** Buffalo/Albright, 1974. **Collections:** Alcoa; Andover/Phillips; Atlanta Corp.; Carnegie; Columbus; Dallas/MFA; First National Bank of Tulsa; Fort Worth; State U. of Iowa; Milwaukee; U. of Minnesota; The Ohio State U.; Oklahoma; U. of Oklahoma; Ridgefield/Aldrich; San Antonio/McNay; Traders National Bank, Kansas City, Mo.; WMAA. **Bibliography:** Tuchman 1.

HAYES, DAVID V. b. March 15, 1931, Hartford, Conn. **Studied:** U. of Notre Dame, with Antony Lauck, 1949–53, AB; Indiana U., with Robert Laurent, David Smith, 1955, MFA; Ogunquit School of Painting; Atelier 17, Paris, with Stanley Hayter. Traveled, resided Paris, 1961–68. US Navy, 1955–57; Traveled USA, Europe. **Taught:** Harvard U., 1972–73. **Awards:** Hamilton Easter Field Foundation Scholarship, 1953; Silvermine Guild, Sculpture Award, 1958; Fulbright Fellowship, 1961; Guggenheim Foundation Fellowship, 1961; Chicago/AI, The Mr. & Mrs. Frank G. Logan Medal, 1951; NIAL, 1965. **Address:** P.O. Box 109, Coventry, CT 06238. **Dealer:** Christopher Colt, NYC. **One-man Exhibitions:** (first) Indiana U., 1955; Wesleyan U., 1958; New London, 1959; The Willard Gallery, 1961, 63, 64, 66, 69, 71; David Anderson Gallery, Paris, 1966; Galerie de Haas, Rotterdam, 1968; Bard College, 1969; U. of Arizona, 1969; U. of Connecticut,

1970; Manchester Community College, 1970; St. Joseph College, West Hartford, Conn., 1970; Connecticut College, 1971; Agra Gallery, Washington, D.C., 1971, 72; Gallery 5 East, East Hartford, Conn., 1971, 73; Harvard U., 1972; New Britain, 1972; Munson Gallery, 1973; Sunne Savage Gallery, 1973, 74; Albany/Institute, 1973; Copley Square, Boston, 1974; Martha Jackson Gallery, 1974; Columbus, 1974; Syracuse/Everson, 1975; Brockton Art Center, 1975; Bader Gallery, Washington, D.C., 1977; George Washington U., Washington, D.C., 1977; Lincoln, Mass./De Cordova, 1977; Springfield, Mass/MFA, 1978; Albany/SUNY, 1978; Dartmouth College, 1978; Amherst College, 1979; Nassau County Museum, 1979. **Retrospectives:** U. of Notre Dame, 1962; Utica, 1963; New London, 1966. **Group:** MOMA, New Talent; SRGM, 1958; MOMA, Recent Sculpture USA, 1959; Boston Arts Festival, 1960; Claude Bernard, Paris, 1960; Chicago/AI, 1961; Forma Viva sculpture symposium, Portoroz, Yugoslavia, 1963; Salon du Mai, Paris, 1966, Musée Rodin, International Sculpture, 1966; Houston Festival of Arts, 1966; Carnegie, 1967; Paris/Moderne, 1968; Galerie D'Eendt NV, Amsterdam, Three Americans, 1970; Lincoln, Mass./De Cordova, Sculpture in the Park, 1972; Corcoran, 1973. **Collections:** Andover/Phillips; Albany/SUNY; Arizona State U.; Boston Public Library; Brooklyn Museum; Carnegie; U. of Connecticut; Columbus; Currier; Dallas/MFA; Dartmouth College; Detroit/Institute; Elmira College; First National Bank of Chicago; Great Southwest Industrial Park; Hartford/Wadsworth; Harvard U.; Hirshhorn; Houston/MFA; Indiana U.; Lincoln, Mass./De Cordova; Lydall Inc.; MOMA; U. of Michigan; Moriarty Brothers; Musée des Arts Decoratifs; The Norton Co., Worcester, Mass; NCFA; U. of Notre Dame; Price, Waterhouse, Inc., Hartford, Conn; Ringling; SRGM; Michael Schiavone & Sons Inc.; Syracuse/Emerson; U. of Vermont; Williams College.

HEBALD, MILTON. b. May 24, 1917, NYC. **Studied:** ASL, with Ann Goldwaithe, 1927–28; NAD, with Gordon Samstag, 1931–32; Roerich Master Institute of Arts, Inc., NYC, 1931–34; Beaux-Arts Institute of Design, NYC, 1932–35. US Army, 1944–46. Traveled Europe, Near East, North Africa, USSR; resided Italy, 1955– . **Taught:** Brooklyn Museum School, 1946–51; Cooper Union, 1946–53; U. of Minnesota, 1949; Skowhegan School, summers, 1950–52; Long Beach State College, summer, 1968. Federal A.P.: Taught sculpture and worked on sculpture project, three years. **Commissions:** Ecuador Pavilion, New York World's Fair, 1939 (façade); US Post Office, Toms River, N.J., 1940 (relief); Republic Aviation Trophy, 1942; Isla Verde Aeroport, San Juan, P.R., 1954; East Bronx (N.Y.) TB Hospital, 1954; AAAL, 1957 (portrait bust of Archibald MacLeish); Pan American Airways Terminal, NYC, 1957–58 (110-ft. bronze relief, *Zodiac*); 333 East 79th Street Building, NYC, 1962 (bronze fountain); U. of North Carolina, 1962; James Joyce Monument, Zurich, 1966; Central Park, NYC, 1973; C.V. Starr Memorial, Tokyo, 1974; Augenhaug Press, Oslo, 1975. **Awards:** ACA Gallery Competition, Exhibition Prize, 1937; Brooklyn Museum, First Prize, 1950; Prix de Rome, 1955–59. **Address:** Via Santo Celso 22, 00062 Bracciano, Italy. **Dealers:** Randall Galleries, NYC; Harmon Gallery, Naples and Sarasota, Fla. **One-man Exhibitions:** ACA Gallery (prize show), 1937, also 1940; Grand Central Moderns, NYC, 1949, 52; Galleria Schneider, Rome, 1957, 63; Lee Nordness Gallery, NYC, 1959–61, 1963, 66; Michelson's Gallery, Washington, D.C., 1963, 67, 79; Cheekwood, 1966; Penthouse Gallery, San Francisco, 1966; Gallery of Modern Art, 1966, 68; VMFA, 1967; Kovler Gallery, 1967–70; London Arts; Cincinnati/AM; West Palm Beach/Norton, 1969; Mickelson Gallery, Washington, D.C., 67, 79; Kovler Gallery, Chicago, 1968–70; Heritage Galleries, Los Angeles, 1978; Yares Gallery, Scottsdale, 1976–78; Harmon Gallery, Naples, Fla., 1978; Randall Galleries, NYC, 1978; Byck Gallery, Louisville, Ky., 1978; Cheekwood, Nashville, 1978; Sestiero Galleria, Rome, 1975; Ostaehag Gallery, Oslo, 1975. **Group:** Sculptors Guild, 1937–46; WMAA Annuals, 1937–63; PAFA, 1938–64; Arte Figurativo, Rome, 1964, 67; Carnegie, 1965. **Collections:** AAAL; U. of Arizona; Bezalel Museum; Calcutta; Cheekwood; James Joyce Museum; Little Rock/MFA; MOMA; Museum of the City of New York; U. of North Carolina; U. of Notre Dame; Oslo U.; PAFA; PMA; Pan American Airways, NYC; Tel Aviv; VMFA; WMAA; Yale U. **Bibliography:** Brumme; Cheney.

HEIZER, MICHAEL. b. 1944, Berkeley, Calif. **Studied:** SFAI, 1963–64. **Address:** % Dealer. **Dealer:** Fourcade, Droll Inc. **One-man Exhibitions:** Galerie Heiner Friedrich, Munich, 1969; Dwan Gallery, NYC, 1970; Detroit/Institute, 1971; ACE Gallery, Los Angeles, 1974, 77; Fourcade, Droll Inc., 1974; Xavier Fourcade, Inc., 1976, 77, 79; ACE Gallery, Venice, Calif., 1977; Galerie am Promenadenplatz, Heizer und Kinnius, Munich, 1977; Richard Hines Gallery, Seattle, 1979. **Retrospective:** Essen, 1979. **Group:** WMAA, 1968, 70; Amsterdam/Stedelijk, Op Losse Schroeven, 1969; Detroit/Institute, Other Ideas, 1969; Berne, When Attitudes Become Form, 1969; Dusseldorf/Kunsthalle, Prospect '70, 1970; XXXV Venice Biennial, 1970; Cornell U., Earth Art, 1970; SRGM, Guggenheim International, 1971; Durer Centennial, Nurnberg, 1971; Rijksmuseum Kroller-Muller, Diagrams and Drawings, 1972; WMAA, American Drawings: 1963–1973, 1973; New York Cultural Center, 3D into 2D, 1973; MIT, Interventions in Landscape, 1974; Chicago/AI, 71st American Exhibition, 1974; MOMA, Drawing Now, 1975; Chicago/AI, 1976, 79; WMAA, 200 Years of American Sculpture, 1976; Documenta 6, Kassel, 1977; U. of Texas, New in the Seventies, 1977; Hirshhorn,

Michael Heizer Untitled 1969

Probing the Earth, 1977; Indianapolis, 1978; Purchase/SUNY, Hidden Desires, 1980. **Collections:** MMA; MOMA; WMAA. **Bibliography:** Alloway 4; *Art Now 74*; Calas, N. and E.; Celant; *Contemporanea*; Honisch and Jensen, eds.; *Kunst um 1970*; Lippard, ed.; Lucie-Smith; Muller; *New in the Seventies*; *When Attitudes Become Form*.

HELD, AL. b. October 12, 1928, Brooklyn, N.Y. **Studied:** ASL, with Kimon Nicolaides, Robert B. Hale, Harry Sternberg; Academie de la Grande Chaumiere; Siquieros in Mexico, 1949. US Navy, 1945–47. Traveled France, USA. **Taught:** Yale U., 1962–. **Awards:** Chicago/AI, The Mr. and Mrs. Frank G. Logan Medal, 1964; Guggenheim Foundation Fellowship, 1966. **Address:** 435 West Broadway, NYC 10012. **Dealer:** Andre Emmerich Gallery, NYC. **One-man Exhibitions:** (first) Galerie Huit, Paris, 1952; Poindexter Gallery, 1958 (two-man), 1959, 61, 62; Galeria Bo-

Al Held   *Florentine II*   1980

nino, Buenos Aires, 1961; Ziegler Gallery, 1964, 70; Galerie Gunar, Dusseldorf, 1964; Andre Emmerich Gallery, NYC, 1965, 67, 68, 70, 72, 73, 75, 76, 78, 79; Amsterdam/Stedelijk, 1966; Galerie Muller, 1966; SFMA, 1968; Corcoran, 1968; ICA, U. of Pennsylvania, 1968; Houston/Contemporary, 1969; Current Editions, Seattle; Donald Morris Gallery, 1971, 74; Andre Emmerich Gallery, Zurich, 1974, 77; Jared Sable Gallery, Toronto, 1975; Adler Castillo Gallery, Caracas, 1975; Galerie Rene Ziegler, Zurich, 1977; Galerie Roger d'Amecourt, Paris, 1977; Annely Juda Fine Art, London, 1977, 80; Donald Morris Gallery, Birmingham, Mich., 1977; ICA, Boston, 1978; Friedland Gallery, Toronto, 1978; Janus Gallery, Venice, Calif., 1979. **Retrospective:** WMAA, 1974. **Group:** SRGM, Abstract Expressionists and Imagists, 1961; Marlborough Fine Art, Ltd., 1961; ICA, Boston, 1961; Carnegie, 1961; Dallas/MFA, 1961, 62; MOMA, Abstract American Drawings and Watercolors, circ., Latin America, 1961–63; WMAA, Geometric Abstraction in America, circ., 1962; Yale U., 1962; Corcoran, 1962; Jewish Museum, Toward a New Abstraction, 1963; Chicago/AI, 1963, 64; Los Angeles/County MA, Post Painterly Abstraction, 1964; WMAA Annuals, 1964, 65, 67, 69, 72, 73; Kunst-

halle, Basel, Signale, 1965; U. of Michigan, 1965; NYU, 1965; Amsterdam/Stedelijk, New Shapes of Color, 1966; WMAA, Art of the U.S. 1670–1966, 1966; SRGM, Systematic Painting, 1966; Flint/Institute, I Flint Invitational, 1966; Jewish Museum, 1967; Documenta IV, Kassel, 1968; Chicago/AI, 1969; Fort Worth Art Museum, Drawings, 1969; VMFA, 1970; Dublin/Municipal, International Quadriennial (ROSC), 1971; Indianapolis/Herron, 1974; Corcoran Biennial, 1975; Tulane U., Drawing Today in New York, 1977, 1976–77; Chicago/AI, Drawings of the 70's, 1976; Documenta, Kassel, 1977; U. of Texas, New in the Seventies, 1977; Minnesota/MA, American Drawing 1927–1977, 1977; Philadelphia College of Art, Point, 1978; Pomona College, Black and White Are Colors, 1979. **Collections:** Akron/AI; Brandeis U.; Buffalo/Albright; Ciba-Geigy Corp.; Cleveland Trust Co.; Dartmouth College; Delaware Art Museum; Dayton/AI; First National Bank of Seattle; Greenville; Harvard U.; High Museum; Hirshhorn; Kunsthalle, Basel; MMA; MOMA; U. of North Carolina; SFMA; Stuttgart; Syracuse/Everson; Treadwell Corp.; WMAA; Yale U.; Zurich. **Bibliography:** **Al Held**; Alloway 3; Battcock, ed.; *Black and White Are Colors*; Calas, N. and E.; Honisch and Jensen, eds.; Hunter, ed.; Lucie-Smith; *New in the Seventies*; Rose, B., 1; Sandler 1; Tucker. Archives.

HELIKER, JOHN EDWARD. b. January 16, 1909, Yonkers, N.Y. **Studied:** ASL, 1927–29, with Kimon Nicolaides, Thomas Hart Benton, Kenneth Hayes Miller, Boardman Robinson. Traveled Europe; resided Italy, two years. **Taught:** Colorado Springs Fine Arts Center; Columbia U. Federal A.P.: Easel painting. **Membership:** NIAL, 1969, vice-president, 1971–74. **Awards:** Corcoran, First Prize, 1941; Pepsi-Cola, 1946; Prix de Rome, 1948; NAD, The Adolph and Clara Obrig Prize, 1948; Guggenheim Foundation Fellowship 1952; NIAL Award, 1957; Ford Foundation, **P.P.,** 1960, 61; AAAL, Award of

Merit Medal and $1,000, 1967; NAD; Benjamin Altman Prize for Landscape, Benjamin Altman Prize for Figure, 1977. **Address:** 865 West End Avenue, NYC. **Dealer:** Kraushaar Galleries. **One-man Exhibitions:** (first) Maynard Walker Gallery, NYC, 1936, also 1938, 41; Kraushaar Galleries, 1945, 51, 54, 68, 71, 74, 77; Lehigh U., 1970; Drew U., Madison, N.J., 1971; Saint-Gaudens National Historical Site, Cornish, N.H., 1972; Edmonton Art Gallery, Alberta, 1974. **Retrospective:** WMAA, 1968. **Group:** MOMA; MMA; Corcoran; VMFA; WMAA, 1941–46, 1955–57; Chicago/AI, 1942, 43, 45; Toledo/MA, 1942, 43, 45; Carnegie, 1943–45; PAFA, 1944, 46; WMAA, The New Decade, 1954–55; Brussels World's Fair, 1958; U. of Illinois, 1961; New York World's Fair, 1964–65; Expo '70, Osaka, 1970; Huntington, N.Y./Heckscher, Windows and Doors, 1972; ASL Centennial, 1975; US Department of the Interior, America 1976, circ., 1976. **Collections:** Arizona State College; Atlanta U.; Atlantic Richfield Co.; Ball State U.; Britannica; Brooklyn Museum; Chicago/AI; Clearwater/Gulf Coast; Cleveland/MA; Colby College; Colorado Springs/FA; Columbia U.; Commerce Trust Co., Kansas City, Mo.; Corcoran; Currier; Denver/AM; Des Moines; Hartford/Wadsworth; Harvard U.; Hirshhorn; Illinois Wesleyan U.; U. of Illinois; Kansas City/Nelson; Lehigh U.; Louisville/Speed; MMA; U. of Miami; NCFA; U. of Nebraska; New Britain/American; U. of Notre Dame; Ogunquit; PAFA; PMA; The Pennsylvania State U.; RISD; U. of Rochester; SFMA; Savannah/Telfair; Storm King Art Center; U. of Texas; Utica; WMAA; Walker; Washington U.; Whitney Communications Corp.; Wichita/AM. **Bibliography:** *America 1976;* Baur 5, 7; Goodrich and Baur 1; **Goodrich and Mandel;** Kent, N.; Nordness, ed.; Pagano; Pousette-Dart, ed.; Ritchie 1. Archives.

HENDLER, RAYMOND. b. February 22, 1923, Philadelphia, Pa. **Studied:** Academie de la Grande Chaumiere; Contemporary School of Art, NYC; Temple U.; PAFA; Philadelphia Museum School; Graphic Sketch Club, Philadelphia, intermittently 1938–51. US Army in Europe, 1942–45. Traveled Europe extensively; resided Paris. **Taught:** Assistant to Moses Soyer in NYC, adult classes; Philadephia public school system; Contemporary School of Art, Brooklyn, N.Y., 1948–49; Fleicher Art Memorial, Philadelphia, 1953–55; Moore College of Art, Philadelphia, 1955–56; Minneapolis College of Art, 1958–62; Parsons School of Design, NYC, 1962–65; Pratt Institute, 1964–66; School of Visual Arts, NYC, 1966–68; Long Island U., 1968; U. of Minnesota, 1968– . A co-organizer of Galerie Huit, Paris, 1949. Director of the Hendler Gallery, Philadelphia, 1952–54. **Awards:** Longview Foundation Grant, 1963. **Address:** 2212 Seabury Avenue South, Minneapolis, MI 55406. **One-man Exhibitions:** (first) Galerie Huit, Paris, 1951; Dubin Gallery, Philadelphia, 1952; Hendler Gallery, Philadelphia, 1953; Minneapolis/Institute, 1959; Rose Fried Gallery, 1962, 64, 67. **Group:** Newark Museum; Paris/Moderne; Salon d'Art Libre, Paris; U. of Pennsylvania; U. of South Carolina; Montreal/MFA; Stanford U.; U. of Manitoba; Massillon Museum; Houston/MFA; Minneapolis/Institute; Walker; NYU. **Collections:** Calcutta; Ciba-Geigy Corp.; Minneapolis College of Art; NYU; U. of Notre Dame; PAFA; PMA; J. Walter Thompson Co.; Walker.

HESSE, EVA. b. January 11, 1936, Hamburg, Germany; **d.** May 29, 1970, NYC. **Studied:** Cooper Union, 1954–57; Yale U. Summer School, Norfolk, Conn., 1957; Yale U., 1969, BFA. **Taught:** School of Visual Arts, NYC, 1968; Oberlin College, 1968. **One-man Exhibitions:** Allan Stone Gallery, 1963; Dusseldorf/Kunsthalle; 1965; Fischbach Gallery, 1968, 70; School of Visual Arts, NYC, 1971; Droll/Kolbert Gallery, NYC, 1977. **Retrospective:** SRGM, circ., 1972. **Group:** Brooklyn Museum, Watercolor Biennial, 1961; Riverside Museum, NYC, American Abstract Artists, 1966; Ithaca College, Drawings, 1967, 1967; U. of North Carolina, 1967; New York State Fair, Art Today: 1967, 1967; Finch College, NYC, Art in Process, 1967, 69; Moore College of Art, Philadelphia, American Drawings, 1968; Milwaukee, Directions I: Options, circ., 1968; A.F.A., Soft Sculpture, 1968; WMAA, 1968; Fort Worth Art Museum, Drawings, 1969; Trenton/State, Soft Art, 1969; ICA, U. of Pennsylvania, Plastics and New Art, 1969; Seattle/AM, 557, 087, 1969; Milwaukee, A Plastic Presence, circ., 1969; Berne, When Attitudes Become Form; 1969; WMAA, Anti-Illusion: Procedures/Materials, 1969; Princeton U., American Art since 1960, 1970; Foundation Maeght, 1970; ICA, U. of Pennsylvania, Projected Art, 1970; New York Cultural Center, 3D into 2D, 1973; WMAA (downtown), Sculpture of the Sixties, 1975. **Collections:** Cologne; Dusseldorf/Kunsthalle; MOMA; Milwaukee; U. of North Carolina; Oberlin College; Ridgefield/Aldrich; WMAA. **Bibliography:** Celant; **Eva Hesse: A Memorial Exhibition**; Nemser; *When Attitudes Become Form.*

HIGGINS, EDWARD. b. 1930, Gaffney, S.C. **Studied:** U. of North Carolina, 1954, BA. **Taught:** Parsons School of Design, 1962–63; Philadelphia Museum School, 1963; Cornell U.; U. of Wisconsin; U. of Kentucky; School of Visual Arts, NYC. **Commissions** (sculpture); Cameron Building, NYC, 1962; New York State Theater, Lincoln Center, NYC, 1964. **Awards:** L.C. Tiffany Grant, 1962; Flint/Institute, I Flint Invitational, **P.P.,** 1966. **Address:** RFD #4, Box 345, Easton, PA 18042. **One-man Exhibitions:** (first) Leo Castelli Inc., 1960, also 1963, 66; Richard Feigen Gallery, NYC, 1964; Minneapolis/Institute, 1964. **Group:** MOMA, Recent Sculpture USA, 1959; Cornell U., 1959; Claude Bernard, Paris, 1960; WMAA, 1960, 62, Annual, 1965, Sculpture Annual, 1966; Houston/

MFA, 1961; Chicago/AI, 1961; Carnegie, 1961; Seattle World's Fair, 1962; SRGM, The Joseph H. Hirshhorn Collection, 1962; MOMA, Americans 1963, circ., 1963–64; Pasadena/AM, New American Sculpture, 1964; A.F.A., Decade of New Talent, circ., 1964; Tate, Gulbenkian International, 1964; New York World's Fair, 1964–65; WMAA, Contemporary American Sculpture, Selection I, 1966; Flint/Institute, I Flint Invitational, 1966; Documenta IV, Kassel, 1968; Duke U., 1969. **Collections:** Buffalo/Albright; Chase Manhattan Bank; Chicago/AI; Dallas/MFA; MOMA; SRGM; WMAA. **Bibliography:** Baur 7; Brown; Hunter, ed.; Janis and Blesh 1; *Metro;* Trier 1.

HILLSMITH, FANNIE. b. March 13, 1911, Boston, Mass. **Studied:** Boston Museum School, with Burns, Guthrie; U. of London, Slade School, 1930–34; ASL, 1934–35, with Alexander Brook, Yasuo Kuniyoshi, William Zorach, John Sloan; Atelier 17, NYC, 1946–50, with S. W. Hayter. **Taught:** Black Mountain College, 1945; Cornell U., 1963. **Awards:** Boston Arts Festival, First Prize, 1957, 63; Boston Museum School, Traveling Scholarship, 1958; Portland, Me./MA, First Prize, 1958. **Address:** % Wedgewood, Jaffrey, NH 03452. **One-man Exhibitions:** Norlyst Gallery, NYC, 1943; Charles Egan Gallery, 1949, 54; The Swetzoff Gallery, Boston, 1949, 50, 54, 57, 63; Colby College, 1950; Santa Barbara/MA, 1950; Milton Academy, 1952; Currier, 1954; Dayton/AI, 1954; ICA, Boston, 1954; Lincoln, Mass./De Cordova, 1954, 58; The Peridot Gallery, 1957, 58, 62, 65; Cornell U., 1963; Green Mountain College, 1965; Weeden Gallery, Boston, 1967; Fitchburg/AM, 1969; Jaffrey Civic Center, 1970; Brockton/Fuller, 1971; Thorne Gallery, Keene, N.H., 1972; Brattleboro (Vt.) Museum and Art Center, 1974. **Group:** Art of This Century, NYC; Corcoran; Phillips; A.F.A.; MOMA; Boston/MFA; Brooklyn Museum; The Print Club, Philadelphia; American Abstract Artists, 1946–58; Chicago/AI, 1947, 48, 54; WMAA, 1949, 51, 55; Walker, 1953, 54; SRGM, 1954; Carnegie, 1955; U. of Illinois, 1955, 57, 59; Federation of Modern Painters and Sculptors, 1956–58; AAAL, 1964; Hartford/Wadsworth, 1966. **Collections:** Andover/Phillips; Boston/MFA; Currier; Harvard U.; MOMA; NYPL; PMA. **Bibliography:** Janis, S.

HINMAN, CHARLES. b. December 29, 1932, Syracuse, N.Y. **Studied:** Syracuse U., BFA, 1955; ASL (with Morris Kantor), 1955–56. Played professional baseball, Milwaukee Braves, 1954–55. US Army, 1956–58. Traveled Japan, India, Europe, and around the world. **Taught:** Staten Island Academy, 1960–62; Woodmere Academy, 1962–64; Aspen Institute, Artist-in-Residence;

Cornell U., 1968–69; Syracuse U., 1971; Pratt Institute, 1975; School of Visual Arts, NYC, 1976; Cooper Union, NYC, 1977. **Commissions:** Neiman-Marcus Co., Atlanta (sculpture). **Awards:** Syracuse U., Augusta Hazard Fellowship, 1955–56; Nagaoka, Japan, First Prize, 1965; Flint/Institute, First Prize, 1966; Torcuato di Tella, Buenos Aires, Special Mention, 1967. **Address:** 231 Bowery, NYC 10002. **Dealers:** Donald Morris Gallery, Birmingham, Mich.; Hokin Gallery, Chicago and Palm Beach, Fla. **One-man Exhibitions:** (first) Richard Feigen Gallery, NYC, 1964, also 1966, 67; Feigen-Palmer Gallery, Los Angeles, 1964; Oberlin College (three-man), 1965; Richard Feigen Gallery, Chicago, 1965, 66; Tokyo Gallery, 1966; Galerie Denise Rene/Hans Mayer, Krefeld, W. Germany, 1970; Galerie Denise Rene, Paris, 1971, NYC, 1972, 73,

Charles Hinman *La Lande* 1980

75; Hokin Gallery, Chicago, 1976, 79; Hokin Gallery, Palm Beach Fla., 1977; Irving Galleries, Milwaukee, 1976; Donald Morris Gallery, Birmingham, Mich., 1979. **Retrospective:** Lincoln Center, 1969. **Group:** Riverside Museum, 1965; WMAA, Young America, 1965; Chicago/AI, 1965, 66, 69; SFMA, The Colorists, 1965; Nagaoka, Japan, 1975; U. of Notre Dame, 1965; Finch College, 1966; WMAA, Art of the U.S. 1670–1966; U. of Illinois, 1967; VI International Art Biennial, San Marino (Europe), 1967; Carnegie, 1967; WMAA Annual, 1967; Carnegie, 1967; WMAA Annual, 1967; Honolulu Academy, 1968; Jewish Museum, Superlimited, 1969; A.F.A., 1969; Indianapolis/Herron, 1969; Princeton U., American Art since 1960, 1970; NCFA, Disappearance and Reappearance of the Image, circ., 1969; U. of Illinois, 1971; Indianapolis, 1976. **Collections:** American Republic Insurance Co.; Aspen Institute; Boise-Cascade Corp.; Buffalo/Albright; Chase Manhattan Bank; Continental Grain Corp.; Delaware Art Museum; Detroit/Institute; U. of Illinois; Lehigh U.; Los Angeles/County MA; Milwaukee; MOMA; McCrory Corp.; Nagaoka, Japan; U. of North Carolina; Oberlin College; The 180 Beacon Collection: The Pennsylvania State U.; Ridgefield/Aldrich; WMAA. **Bibliography:** Battcock, ed.; Hunter, ed.; Johnson, Ellen H.

HIRSCH, JOSEPH. b. April 25, 1920, Philadelphia, Pa. **d.** Sept. 25, 1981, NYC. **Studied:** Philadelphia Museum School, 1927–31; privately with Henry Hensche in Provincetown; with George Luks in NYC. Traveled Europe, the Orient, USA; resided France, five years. **Taught:** Chicago Art Institute School; American Art School, NYC; U. of Utah; ASL, 1959– ; Dartmouth College, 1966; Utah State U. 1967; Brigham Young U., 1971; NAD. Artist war correspondent, 1943–44. **Member:** Artists Equity (founder and first treasurer); NAD; Philadelphia Watercolor Club; NIAL, 1967. Federal A.P.: Easel painting; first

WPA murals in Philadelphia, for Amalgamated Clothing Workers Building and Municipal Court. **Awards:** Scholarship from the City of Philadelphia; PAFA, Walter Lippincott Prize; American Academy, Rome; International Institute of Education Fellowship, 1935–36; New York World's Fair, 1939, First Prize; Guggenheim Foundation Fellowship, 1942–43; Library of Congress, Pennell **P.P.**, 1944, 45; NIAL Grant, 1947; Carnegie, Second Prize, 1947; Chicago/AI, Watson F. Blair Prize; Fulbright Fellowship, 1949; MMA, 1950; NAD, Benjamin Altman Prize, 1959, 66; NAD Annual Andrew Carnegie Prize, 1968; Davidson College, **P.P.**, 1972, 73; Oklahoma, **P.P.**, 1974; NAD, Altman Prize for Figure Painting, 1978. **One-man Exhibitions:** ACA Gallery, Philadelphia; A.A.A. Gallery, NYC, 1946, 48, 54; The Forum Gallery, 1965, 69, 74; Oklahoma, 1974; Century Association, NYC, 1980; Kennedy Gallery, NYC, 1975, 76, 78, 80. **Group:** WMAA; Newark Museum; Walker; MMA; Kansas City/Nelson; PAFA. **Collections:** AAAL; Andover/Phillips; U. of Arizona; Boston/MFA; Dartmouth College; U. of Georgia; IBM; Kansas City/Nelson; Library of Congress; MMA; MOMA; Museum of Military History; NAD; U. of Oklahoma; PMA; Southampton/Parrish; Springfield, Mass./MFA; Harry S. Truman Library; WMAA; Walker; College of Wooster. **Bibliography:** Baur 7; Cheney; Genauer; **Joseph Hirsch**; Miller, ed. 1; Nordness, ed.; Pagano; Phillips 2; Reese; Richardson, E.P.; Wight 2. Archives.

HOFMANN, HANS. b. March 21, 1880, Weissenberg, Bavaria, Germany; **d.** February 17, 1966, NYC. **Studied:** Gymnasium, Munich; Academie de la Grande Chaumiere, 1904. Resided Paris, 1904–14, with the patronage of Phillip Freudenberg, department-store owner and art collector. US citizen, 1941. **Taught:** Opened first art school, 1915, in Munich; held summer sessions at Ragusa, 1924, Capri, 1925–27, Saint-Tropez, 1928, 29; Chouinard Art Institute, Los Angeles, 1930; U. of California, Berkeley, summer, 1930; ASL, 1932–33; Thurn School, Provincetown, summers, 1923, 33; opened own school in NYC, 1933, own summer school in Provincetown, 1934. Stopped teaching 1958, to devote full time to painting. **Awards:** U. of Illinois, **P.P.**, 1950; Society for Contemporary American Art, Chicago, **P.P.**, 1952; PAFA, J. Henry Schiedt Memorial Prize, 1952; Chicago/AI, The Mr. & Mrs. Frank G. Logan Medal, 1953; Chicago/AI, Flora Mayer Witkowsky Prize, 1959; II Inter-American Paintings and Prints Biennial, Mexico City, 1960, Hon. Men.; Chicago/AI, Ada S. Garrett Prize, 1961; hon. degree, Dartmouth College, 1962; hon. degree, U. of California, 1964; elected to the NIAL, 1964. **One-man Exhibitions:** (first) Paul Cassirer Gallery, Berlin, 1910; California Palace, 1931; New Orleans/Delgado, 1940; Art of This Century, NYC, 1944; "67" Gallery, NYC, 1944, 45; Betty Parsons Gallery, 1946, 47; The Kootz Gallery, NYC, 1947, 49, 1950–55, 1957, 58, 1960–64, 1966; Galerie Maeght, 1949; Boris Mirski Gallery, Boston, 1954; Baltimore/MA, 1954; Rutgers U., 1956; Dartmouth College, 1962; Stamford U., 1966; Andre Emmerich Gallery, NYC, 1967–69, 1972, 73, 74, 75, 76, 77, 78, 79, 80; Richard Gary Gallery, 1968, 72; Obelisk Gallery, 1969; David Mirvish Gallery, 1969, 73, 74; MMA, 72; John Berggruen Gallery, 1973; Buffalo/Albright, 1973; Art Museum of South Texas, Corpus Christi, 1974; Santa Ana/Bowers, 1975; MMA, 1974; Waddington Galleries, Montreal, 1975; Garage Gallery, Birmingham, Ala., 1975; Fendrick Gallery, Washington, D.C., 1975; Deutsch Gallery, NYC, 1976; Schaffner Gallery, Los Angeles, 1976; Janie C. Lee Gallery, Houston, 1977; B. R. Kornblatt Gallery, 1977; David Mirvish Gallery, Toronto, 1977; Hokin Gallery, Chicago, 1977; Freudenheim Gallery, Buffalo, 1978; Thomas Segal Gallery, Boston, 1978; Richard Gray Gallery, Chicago, 1978; Hokin

Gallery, Palm Beach, 1978; MMA, Hans Hofmann as Teacher, 1979. **Retrospectives:** Arts Club of Chicago, 1944; Andover/Phillips, 1948; Bennington College, 1955; Philadelphia Art Alliance, 1956; WMAA, circ., 1957; The Kootz Gallery, NYC, 1959; Germanisches National Museum, Nurnberg, circ., Germany, 1962; MOMA, circ., USA, Latin America, and Europe, 1963. **Group:** Chicago/AI; U. of Illinois; Carnegie; Documenta II, Kassel, 1959; XXX & XXXIV Venice Biennials, 1960, 68; WMAA Annual, 1965; Corcoran Biennial, 1965; Marlborough-Gerson Gallery, Inc., 1967; MOMA, The New American Painting and Sculpture, 1969; Albright/Buffalo, Color and Field 1890–1970, 1970; WMAA, The Structure of Color, 1971; Birmingham, Alabama, American Watercolors 1850–1972, 1972; National Gallery, American Art at Mid Century, 1973; Houston/MFA, The Great Decade of American Abstraction, 1974; Kennedy Gallery, NYC, The Art Students League, 1875–1975, 1975; Harvard U., The New York School: From the First Generation, 1975; SRGM, Twentieth Century Drawings, 1976; A.F.A., American Master Drawings and Watercolors, 1976; Bonn, 200 Years of American Painting, 1976; Baltimore/MA, 200 Years of American Painting, 1977; Syracuse/Everson, Provincetown Painters, 1977; Cornell U., Abstract Expressionism, The Formative Years, 1978; Flint/Institute, Art and the Automobile, 1978. **Collections:** Abbott Laboratories; Andover/Phillips; Art of This Century (Peggy Guggenheim); Baltimore/MA; Buffalo/Albright; U. of California (Museum Hofmann); Chicago/AI; Cleveland/MA; Columbia Broadcasting System; Dallas/MFA; Dayton/AI; Fort Dodge/Blanden; Grenoble; U. of Illinois; Indianapolis/Herron; International Minerals & Chemicals Corp.; MMA; MOMA; Montreal/MFA; U. of Nebraska; Newark Museum; PMA; U. of Rochester; SRGM; Santa Barbara/MA; Toronto; WMAA; Walker; Washington U.; Yale U. **Bibliography:** Alloway 4; Ashton 5; Barker 1; Baur 5, 7;

Biddle 4; Blesh 1; Brion 1; Cheney; Chipp; Eliot; Goodrich and Baur 1; *From Foreign Shores; The Great Decade;* **Greenberg** 1, **2**; Haftman; Henning; Hess, T. B., 1; Hobbs and Levin; **Hofmann; Hunter 1**, 2, 6; Hunter, ed., Janis and Blesh 1; Janis, S.; Kozloff 3; Kuh 2; **Loran 2**; McCurdy, ed.; Mendelowitz; *Metro;* Motherwell and Reinhardt, eds.; Newmeyer; Nordness, ed.; Ponente; Pousette-Dart, ed.; Read 2; Richardson, E.P.; Ritchie 1; Rose, B., 1, 4; Rothschild; Sandler 1; **Seitz** 1, **4**; Tapie 1; Tomkins 2; Tuchman, ed.; Weller; **Wight 1**. Archives.

HOLLAND, TOM. b. June 15, 1936, Seattle, Wash. **Studied:** Wilamette U., 1954–56; U. of California, Santa Barbara and Berkeley, 1957–59. Traveled Chile. **Awards:** Fulbright Fellowship, 1960. **Taught:** SFAI, 1962–67, U. of California, Berkeley; San Francisco Art Institute, 1961–68, 72–80; U. of California, Los Angeles, 1968–70; U. of California, Berkeley, 1978–79; Cornish Institute, Seattle, 1978. **Awards:** National Endowment for the Arts, grant, 1976; Guggenheim Foundation Fellowship, 1980–81. **Address:** 28 Roble Road, Berkeley, CA 94705. **Dealers:** Blum Helman Gallery, Inc., NYC; Hansen Fuller Goldeen Gallery, San Francisco; Watson-Willour & Co., Houston, Texas. **One-man Exhibitions:** Universidad Catolica, Santiago, 1961; RAC, 1962; New Mission Gallery, San Francisco, 1962; Hansen-Fuller Gallery, 1962–66, 68, 70, 72, 73, 74, 76, 77, 80; The Lanyon Gallery, 1963–65; Nicholas Wilder Gallery, 1965, 68, 72, 73, 75, 76, 77, 79; Robert Elkon Gallery, 1970; Galerie Hans R. Neuendorf, Cologne, 1971; Lawrence Rubin Gallery, NYC, 1972; Ronald Greenberg Gallery, St. Louis, 1972, 75; Corcoran and Greenberg, Inc., Miami, 1972; Multiples, Los Angeles, 1972; Felicity Samuel Gallery, London, 1973; Knoedler Contemporary Art, NYC, 1973, 75; Current Editions, Seattle, 1973; Dootson Calderhead Gallery, Seattle, 1975; Seder/Creigh Gallery, Coronado, Calif., 1975; Watson/DeNagy Gallery, Houston, 1977; Smith Andersen Gallery, Palo Alto, 1978; Charles Casat Gallery, La Jolla, 1978; Droll-Kolbert Gallery, NYC, 1978; SFAI, 1979; Linda Farris Gallery, Seattle, 1979; Blum Helman, NYC, 1979; Watson-Willour & Co., Houston, 1979. **Retrospective:** RAC, 1975. **Group:** SFMA, Bay Area Artists, 1964; Stanford U., Current Painting and Sculpture of the Bay Area, 1964; La Jolla, 1965; PAFA, 1968; Ringling, California Painters, 1968; U. of Illinois, 1969; Corcoran, 1969; WMAA Annual, 1969; Pasadena/AM, West Coast: 1945–69, 1969; SFAI Centennial Exhibition, 1971; Hamburg/Kunstverein, USA: West Coast, circ., 1972; U. of Illinois Biennial, 1974; SFMA, California Painting and Sculpture: The Modern Era, 1976; Invitational American Drawing Exhibition, San Diego, 1977; U. of Texas, New in the Seventies, 1977. **Collections:** U. of California, Berkeley; Chicago/AI; Hirshhorn; MOMA; Oakland/AM; Ridgefield/Aldrich; RISD; St. Louis/City; Seattle AM; SFMA; SRGM; Stanford U., Walker; WMAA. **Bibliography:** *New in the Seventies; The State of California Painting; USA West Coast.*

HOLTY, CARL ROBERT. b. June 21, 1900, Freiburg, Germany; **d.** March 23, 1973, NYC. To USA, 1900; citizen, 1906. US Army, 1917–18. **Studied:** Marquette U., 1918–19; NAD, 1920–22; Academy of Fine Arts, Munich, 1925–26; Hofmann School, Munich. Traveled Europe. **Taught:** ASL, 1939–40, 1950–51; U. of Georgia, 1948–50; U. of California, Berkeley, summer, 1951; U. of Florida, 1952–53; Brooklyn College, 1955–60, 1964–73; U. of Wisconsin, 1961; U. of Louisville, 1962–63; lectured extensively. **Member:** Abstraction-Creation, Paris, 1931–32; American Abstract Artists, 1936–43. **Awards:** U. of Illinois, **P.P.**, 1948; Ford Foundation, 1963. **One-man Exhibitions:** J. B. Neumann Gallery, NYC, 1936–44; Karl Nierendorf Gallery, NYC, 1938; The Kootz Gallery,

NYC, 1946, 48; J.B. Neumann's New Art Circle, 1951, 52; Duveen-Graham Gallery, NYC, 1956; The Graham Gallery, 1959–62, 64, 67; Poindexter Gallery, 1972; City U. of New York Graduate Center, 1972; Andrew Crispo Gallery, 1974. **Group:** WMAA; PAFA; Corcoran; Chicago/AI; MMA; St. Louis/City; Los Angeles/County MA; Cincinnati/AM; Columbus. **Collections:** U. of Arkansas; U. of California; Chattanooga/AA; Exeter; U. of Georgia; U. of Illinois; Louisville/Speed; Milwaukee; NYU; U. of Nebraska; SRGM; St. Louis/City; Seattle/AM; U. of Tennessee; U. of Texas; WMAA; U. of Wisconsin; Youngstown/Butler. **Bibliography:** Baur 7; Blesh 1; **Carl Holty Memorial Exhibition**; Hess, T. B., 1; Janis, S.; Kootz 2; McCurdy, ed.; Passloff; Ritchie 1; Seuphor 1. Archives.

HOOD, DOROTHY. b. August 22, 1919, Bryan, Texas. **Studied:** RISD; ASL, NYC. Traveled Mexico, South and Central America, Europe, extensively. **Taught:** Museum School of Fine Arts, Houston, 1963–77; Colorado State U., 1976. **Commissions:** Mural, St. Worth National Bank, 1972; mural, Lumm's Tower Building, Houston, 1980; sets for several ballet companies. **Awards:** National Scholastic Scholar, 1937–41; NAAL Childe Hassam **P.P.**, 1973; Brown Foundation, travel grant, 1973. **Address:** 1408 Missouri, Houston, TX 77006. **Dealer:** Meredith Long Gallery, Houston. **One-man Exhibitions:** (first) The Willard Gallery, NYC, 1950; Proteo Gallery, Mexico City, 1955; Duveen-Graham Gallery, NYC, 1958; Galerie Genova, Mexico City, 1955; Philadelphia Art Alliance, 1958; Atelier Chapman Kelley, Dallas, 1961; Witte, 1965; Houston/Contemporary, 1970; Syracuse/Everson, 1972; Rice U., 1971; Houston Art Museum of South Texas, Corpus Christi, 1975; Houston/MFA, 1974; Tibor deNagy, NYC, 1974; Potsdam/SUNY, 1974; Davis & Long Company, NYC, 1975; U. of Texas, 1975; Meredith Long Gallery, Houston, 1962,

64, 66, 68, 70, 72, 74, 76; Marianne Friedland Gallery, Toronto, 1976; Meredith Long Contemporary, NYC, 1978, 80. **Retrospective:** San Antonio/McNay, 1978. **Group:** Brooklyn Museum, Golden Years of American Drawing, 1905–56, 1956; RISD, Four Young Americans, 1959; MOMA, Young American Printmakers, 1953; Potsdam/SUNY, Women in Art, 1972; Syracuse/Everson, New Works in Clay by Contemporary Painters and Sculptors, 1976. **Collections:** Boston/MFA; Brooklyn Museum; California State College, Long Beach; Fort Worth; U. of Houston; Houston/Contemporary; Jolla; Mexico City Nacional; MOMA; Montreal Contemporary; National Gallery; The New Harmony Gallery of Contemporary Art; PMA; Potsdam/SUNY; Rice U.; RISD; San Antonio/McNay; Santa Barbara/MA; SFMA; Syracuse/Everson; U. of Texas; Texas A & M; Worcester/AM.

HOPKINS, BUDD. b. June 15, 1931, Wheeling, W. Va. **Studied:** Oberlin College, 1949–53, BA. Traveled Europe. **Taught:** Wagner College, 1955; MOMA, summers, 1955, 56; WMAA, 1957–60; Pratt Institute, 1959, Provincetown, summer, 1974; RISD, 1967, 68, 69, 76, 77; U. of Minnesota, 1975. **Commissions:** Provincetown/Chrysler, 1958 (large painting). **Awards:** West Virginia Arts and Humanities Council; Guggenheim Foundation Fellowship, 1976; National Endowment for the Arts, grant, 1979. **Member:** American Abstract Artists; Provincetown Art Assn. **Address:** 246 West 16th Street, NYC 10011. **Dealer:** Lerner-Heller, NYC; Longpoint Gallery, Provincetown, Mass. **One-man Exhibitions:** (first) Poindexter Gallery, 1956, also 1962, 63, 66, 67, 69, 71; Tirca Karlis Gallery, 1958, 60, 1962–69, 73, 75; The Zabriskie Gallery, 1959; Kasha Heman, Chicago, 1962, 63; Art Galleries Ltd., Washington, D.C., 1963; Athena Gallery, New Haven, 1964; Bradford Junior College, 1965; Obelisk Gallery, 1966; Reed College, 1967; Exeter, 1968; William Zierler

Budd Hopkins *Ixion #2* 1978

Inc., 1972, 73, 74, 76; Galerie Lia-towitsch, Basel, 1974; Landmark Gallery, NYC, 1975; Pelham-von Stoffler Gallery, Houston, 1977; Andre Zarre Gallery, NYC, 1978; Middlebury College, Vt., 1978; Lerner-Heller Gallery, NYC, 1977, 78; Cultural Activities Center, Temple, Texas, 1979. **Retrospectives:** Huntington, W. Va., 1973; U. of North Carolina, 1974; Michigan State U., 1974. **Group:** Wagner College, 1957; Oberlin College, 3 Young Painters, 1957; Festival of Two Worlds, Spoleto, 1958; WMAA, 1958, 63, Annuals, 1965, 67, 72; WMAA, Young America, 1960; Charlotte/Mint, 1960; PAFA, 1964; Cincinnati/AM, 1968; WMAA, Free Form Abstraction, 1972; SRGM, American

Painters through Two Decades, 1973; New School for Social Research, Erotic Art, 1973. **Collections:** Ashland Oil Co.; Auckland; Block Drug Co.; Bradford Junior College; Brooklyn Museum; Ciba-Geigy Corp.; Conesta International Hotels; Corcoran; Delaware Art Museum; Hirshhorn; Historical Society of Montana; Hotel Corp. of America; Huntington, W. Va.; International Minerals and Chemicals Corp.; Litton Industries; U. of Massachusetts; MIT; Michigan State U.; Montana Historical Society; Norfolk; Norfolk/Chrysler; U. of North Carolina; Oberlin College; Oklahoma State Art Collection; Pepsi-Cola Co.; Pet Milk Co.; Pioneer Aerodynamic Systems; Reading/Public; Reed College; SRGM; SFMA; Simmons College; United Aircraft Corp.; United Grain Co.; WMAA; Westinghouse; Williams College.

HOPPER, EDWARD. b. July 22, 1882, Nyack, N.Y.; **d.** May 15, 1967, NYC. **Studied:** New York School of Art, 1900–06, with Kenneth Hayes Miller, Robert Henri, George Luks, A.B. Davies; a commercial art school, NYC, 1899–1900; Paris, 1906–07, 1909–10. Traveled USA, France. **Awards:** US Shipping Board, Poster Prize, 1918; Los Angeles/County MA, W. A. Bryan Prize, 1923; Chicago Society of Etchers, The Mr. & Mrs. Frank G. Logan Medal, 1923; NIAL, Gold Medal; Baltimore/MA, Hon. Men., 1931; Brooklyn Museum, 1931; PAFA, Joseph E. Temple Gold Medal, 1935; Worcester/AM, First **P.P.**, 1935; Corcoran, William A. Clark Prize, 1937; Chicago/AI, The Mr. & Mrs. Frank G. Logan Medal, 1945; Chicago/AI, Hon. Men. 1946; Chicago/AI, Hon. DFA, 1950; Hon. Litt. D., Rutgers U., 1953; Hallmark International Competition, 1957; Edward MacDowell Medal, 1966. **One-man Exhibitions:** (first) Whitney Studio Club, NYC, 1919, also 1922; Rehn Galleries, 1924, 27, 29, 46, 48, 65; PAFA, 1925, 71; Arts Club of Chicago, 1934; Carnegie, 1937; Currier, 1959; U. of Arizona, 1963; WMAA,

1971. **Retrospective:** MOMA, 1933; WMAA, 1960, 64, 80. **Group:** WMAA; Chicago/AI; Boston/MFA; PAFA; Corcoran; The Armory Show, 1913; Smith College, Five Americans, 1934; Cincinnati/AM, 1948; IX Sao Paulo Biennial, 1967. **Collections:** Andover/Phillips; U. of Arizona; Boston/MFA; Brooklyn Museum; California State Library; Carnegie; Chicago/AI; Cleveland/MA; Corcoran; Hartford/Wadsworth; Harvard U.; IBM; Indianapolis/Herron; Kansas City/Nelson; Library of Congress; MMA; MOMA; Montclair/AM; Muskegon/Hackley; NYPL; U. of Nebraska; Newark Museum; New Orleans/Delgado; PAFA; Phillips; Randolph-Macon College; Terre Haute/Swope; Toledo/MA; Victoria and Albert Museum; WMAA; Walker; West Palm Beach/Norton; Wichita/AM; Worcester/AM; Yale U.; Youngstown/Butler. **Bibliography:** Alloway 4; Barker 1; **Barr 2, 3**; Baur 7; Bazin; Blesh 1; Boswell 1; Brown 2; Canaday; Cheney; Christensen; *Cityscape 1919–39*; **Du Bois 2**; Eliot; Flexner; Goldwater and Treves, eds.; **Goodrich** 1, **3, 4**; Goodrich and Baur 1; Haftman; Hall; **Hopper**; Hunter 6; *Index of 20th Century Artists*; Jewell 2; Kozloff 3; Kuh 1, 2; Langui; Levin 1; McCoubrey 1; McCurdy, ed.; Mellquist; Mendelowitz; Neuhaus; Newmeyer; Nordness, ed.; O'Doherty; Pagano; Pearson 1; Phillips 1, 2; Poore; Pousette-Dart, ed.; Print Council of America; Reese; Richardson, E.P.; Ringel, ed.; Rodman 1; Rose, B., 1, 4; Sachs; Sager; Soby 5, 6; Soyer, R. 1; Sutton; Tomkins and Time-Life Books; Weller; Wight 2. Archives.

HORIUCHI, PAUL. b. April 12, 1906, Yamanashiken, Japan. Self-taught. **Commissions:** Seattle World's Fair, 1962 (free-standing mural). Awards: Ford Foundation, **P.P.**; Tupperware National Competition; Rockford/Burpee, 1966; U. of Puget Sound, Hon. H.H.D.; Hon. DFA, St. Martin College, 1979; and some 30 other awards. **Address:** 9773 Arrowsmith Avenue So.,

Seattle, WA 98118. **Dealer:** Gordon Woodside Gallery, Seattle. **One-man Exhibitions:** (first) Seattle/AM, 1954, also 1958; Little Rock/MFA; 1958; Zoe Dusanne Gallery, Seattle, 1959, 63; Everett Junior College, 1960; U. of Arizona, 1962; Lee Nordness Gallery, NYC, 1963, 65; Felix Landau Gallery, 1963; 66; Reed College, 1964; Spelman College, 1965; Utica 1965; Gordon Woodside Gallery, Seattle, 1965, 67, 72, 74, 76, 78; San Francisco, 1966, 68; Tacoma, 1967; Fountain Gallery, Portland, Ore. **Retrospective:** U. of Oregon, 1969; Seattle/AM, 1969. **Group:** Rome–New York Foundation, Rome, 1959; ART: USA:59, NYC, 1959; SFMA Annuals; Denver/AM; Seattle/AM; Carnegie, 1961; Seattle World's Fair, 1962; Rikkikai (Group), Tokyo, 1963; M. Knoedler & Co., Art across America, circ., 1965–67; VMFA, American Painting, 1966; Expo '74, Spokane, 1974; NCFA, Art of the Pacific Northwest, 1974. **Collections:** U. of Arizona; Chase Manhattan Bank; Colorado Springs/FA; Denver/AM; Everett Junior College; First National Bank of Seattle; Fort Worth; Hartford/Wadsworth; Harvard U.; Imperial Household, Tokyo; Little Rock/MFA; Lytton Savings and Loan Association; Marylhurst College; Mead Corporation; National Economics Research Association; U. of Oregon; Reed College; SFMA; Safeco Building; Santa Barbara/MA; Seattle/AM; Seattle Civic Center; Seattle Public Library; Seattle U.; Spelman College; Spokane Coliseum; Tacoma; Tokyo/Modern; Tupperware Museum; U.S. Steel Corp; Utica; Vancouver; Victoria (B.C.); U. of Washington. **Bibliography:** *Art of the Pacific Northwest; Northwest Traditions.*

HORNAK, IAN. b. January, 1944, Philadelphia, Pa. **Studied:** U. of Michigan, Wayne State U., BFA, MFA. **Taught:** Wayne State U., 1965–67; Henry Ford College, Dearborn, 1966–67. **Address:** 116 East 73rd Street, NYC 10021. **Dealer:** Fischbach Gallery, NYC. **One-man Exhibitions:** (first) Tibor de Nagy

Gallery, NYC, 1971, 72, 73, 74, 75, 76; Fischbach Gallery, NYC, 1977, 79; Wood Gallery, Philadelphia, 1979; Gertrude Kasle Gallery, Detroit, 1974; Jacob's Ladder Gallery, Washington, D.C., 1971, 72; Sneed Gallery, Rockford, Ill., 1976; Selby Museum, Sarasota, 1980. **Group:** Moore College of Art, Philadelphia, The New Landscape, 1971; Indianapolis, 1972, A.F.A., The Realist Revival, 1972; Oklahoma Art Center, Contemporary Landscape, 1975; Potsdam/SUNY, Landscape/Cityscape, 1978; Guild Hall, East Hampton, N.Y., Artists and East Hampton, 1976. **Collections:** AT&T; Canton Art Institute; Chase Manhattan Bank; Citibank Corp.; Dartmouth College; Commerce Bank, Kansas City; Corcoran; Detroit/Institute; Indianapolis; IT&T; U. of Maryland; Owens-Corning Fiberglas Corp.; St. Joseph/Albrecht; Toledo/MA; Xerox Corp., NYC.

HORWITT, WILL. b. January 8, 1934, NYC. **Studied:** Chicago/AI, 1952–54. **Awards:** Guggenheim Foundation Fellowship, 1965; L. C. Tiffany Foundation Grant, 1968; Hereward Lester Cooke Foundation, grant, 1979. **Address:** 60 Beach Street, NYC 10013. **Exhibitions:** Stephen Radich Gallery, NYC, 1963, 65, 67; Lee Ault & Co., 1972, 74, 77, 79; Tanglewood, Lenox, Mass., 1974. **Group:** MIT, Seven Sculptors, 1964; WMAA, 1964, 66, 68, 73; Flint/Institute, American Sculpture: 1900–1965, 1965; Chicago/AI, 1965; WMAA, Young America, 1965; Stephens College, 1966; Lincoln, Mass./De Cordova, Outdoor Sculpture, 1966; Hofstra U., Seven Sculptors, 1968, Middelheim Park, Antwerp, XI Sculpture Biennial, 1971; WMAA Biennial, 1973; Indianapolis, 1976. **Collections:** Amherst College; Boston/MFA; Buffalo/Albright; Chase Manhattan Bank; Cornell; Hartford/Wadsworth; Purchase/SUNY; SRGM; Smith College; South Mall, Albany; Stephens College; Yale U.

HOVANNES, JOHN. b. December 31, 1900, Smyrna, Turkey; **d.** April 2, 1973, NYC. **Studied:** RISD. **Taught:** Cooper Union, 1945–65; ASL, 1945–46. **Awards:** Guggenheim Foundation Fellowship, 1940; Eugene Meyer Award, 1941; MMA, Artists for Victory, 1942. **One-man Exhibitions:** Robinson Galleries, NYC, 1941; AGBU, NYC, 1967. **Group:** New York World's Fair, 1939; Chicago/AI, 1942, 43; PAFA, 1942, 43, 45, 46; WMAA, 1942–46; MMA, 1942, 51; NAD, 1943; Riverside Museum, 1943; U. of Nebraska, 1945. **Collections:** Newark Museum; Society of the Four Arts; Tel Aviv. **Bibliography:** Baur 7; Brumme. Archives.

HOWARD, CHARLES. b. January 2, 1899, Montclair, N.J.; **d.** 1978, Ponte, Italy. **Studied:** U. of California, Berkeley, 1921; Harvard U.; Columbia U. Traveled USA. Europe. **Taught:** Camberwell School, London, 1959. Federal A.P.: Design Supervisor, mural at US Naval Air Station, Alameda, Calif. **Awards:** SFMA, **P.P.,** 1940; SFMA, 1942; MMA, Artists for Victory, 1942; Pasadena/AM, Third Prize, 1946; California Palace, First Prize; La Tausca Competition, **P.P.,** 1947. **One-man Exhibitions:** (first) Whitney Studio Club, NYC, 1926; Julien Levy Galleries, NYC, 1933; Bloomsbury Gallery, London, 1935; Guggenheim Jeune (Gallery), London, 1939; Courvoisier Gallery, San Francisco, 1941; U. of California, Berkeley, 1941; SFMA, 1942; Karl Nierendorf Gallery, NYC, 1946; Hanover Gallery, 1949; Heller Gallery, Cambridge, England, 1951; Santa Barbara/MA, 1953; St. George's Gallery, London, 1958; The Howard Wise Gallery, 1965. **Retrospective:** California Palace, 1946; Whitechapel Art Gallery, London, 1956. **Group:** Salons of America, NYC, 1933; New Burlington Galleries, London, International Surrealist Exhibition, 1936; Sao Paulo, 1938; SFMA, 1940–46; Carnegie, 1941, 46; MOMA, Americans 1942, circ., 1942;

Chicago/AI, 1942, 46, 48; MMA, 1942, 52; WMAA, 1943–46; Corcoran, 1943–47; California Palace, 1945–59; Tate, American Painting, 1946; Salon des Realites Nouvelles, Paris, 1949. **Collections:** Chicago/AI; Container Corp. of America; Dallas/MFA; Jesus College; MMA; Pasadena/AM; SFMA; SRGM. **Bibliography:** Baur 7; Blesh 1; Frost; Genauer; Guggenheim, ed.; **Howard**; Janiz, S.; McCurdy, ed.; Miller, ed. 1; Ragon 2; Read 2; Richardson, E.P.; Ritchie 1; **Robertson 1.**

HOWARD, ROBERT A. b. April 5, 1922, Sapulpa, Okla. **Studied:** Phillips U.; U. of Tulsa, BA, 1949, MA; privately with Ossip Zadkine, Paris. US Army, 1943–46. Traveled Mexico and Western Europe. **Taught:** U. of North Carolina, 1951–72, 73– ; U. of Southern California, 1972–73. **Awards:** National Endowment for the Arts, grant, 1972. **Address:** 1201 Hillview Rd., Chapel Hill, NC 17514. **One-man Exhibitions:** (first) Person Hall Art Gallery, Chapel Hill, N.C., 1951; Charlotte/Mint, 1954; Greenville (N.C.) Library, 1959; Royal Marks Gallery, 1967, 68; St. Andrews College, 1969; Virginia Polytechnic Institute, 1969; The Southeastern Center for Contemporary Art, Winston-Salem, 1977. **Group:** Syracuse, National Ceramic Exhibition, 1949; PAFA Annual, 1958; Detroit/Institute, 1958; WMAA Sculpture Annual, 1964–68; New York World's Fair, 1964–65; Los Angeles/County MA, American Sculpture of the Sixties, 1967; U. of Illinois, 1969; WMAA Annual, 1970. **Collections:** Ackland; Duke U.; U. of North Carolina; Raleigh/NCMA. **Bibliography:** Tuchman 1.

HUDSON, ROBERT H. b. September 8, 1938, Salt Lake City, Utah. **Studied:** San Francisco Art Institute, BFA, MFA. **Taught:** U. of California, Berkeley, 1966–73; Davis; SFAI, 1976– . **Awards:** RAC, 1959; San Francisco Art Festival,

P.P., 1961; SFMA, 1963; San Jose State College, **P.P.**, 1964; SFMA, Nealie Sullivan Award, 1965; Guggenheim Foundation Fellowship, 1976. **Address:** 392 Eucalyptus Avenue, Cotati, CA 94928. **Dealer:** Allan Frumkin Gallery, NYC; Hansen-Fuller Gallery, San Francisco. **One-man Exhibitions:** RAC, 1961; Batman Gallery, San Francisco, 1961; Bolles Gallery, San Francisco, 1962; The Lanyon Gallery, 1964; San Francisco Art Institute, 1965; Allan Frumkin Gallery, Chicago, 1964, 68, 72; NYC, 1965, 71, 76, 78, 80; Nicholas Wilder Gallery, 1967; Michael Walls Gallery, 1970; U. of California, Berkeley, 1971, 72; Hansen-Fuller Gallery, San Francisco, 1973, 75, 77. **Retrospective:** Moore College of Art, Philadelphia, 1977. **Group:** RAC, 1959–61; La Jolla, 1961; Oakland/AM, 1961, 63; Stanford U., Some Points of View for '62, 1962; SFMA, 1962, 64; WMAA Sculpture Annual, 1964, 67, 68; WMAA, Young America, 1965; Westmoreland County/MA, 1966; U. of California, Berkeley, Funk, 1967; Los Angeles/County MA, American Sculpture of the Sixties, 1967; Chicago/AI, 1967; Walker, 1969; ICA, U. of Pennsylvania, The Spirit of the Comics, 1969; Walker, 14 Sculptors: The Industrial Age, 1969; U. of California, Berkeley, Impossible Dreams (two-man), 1970; U. of California, Santa Barbara, Six Californians, 1971; Corcoran Biennial, 1975; Hayward Gallery, London, The Condition of Sculpture, 1975; ICA, Boston, Hudson and De Forest, 1977; U. of Texas, New in the Seventies, 1977. **Collections:** American Republic Insurance Co.; Amsterdam/Stedelijk; Los Angeles/County MA; Oakland/AM; SFMA. **Bibliography:** Friedman, M. 2; *New in the Seventies;* Selz, P., 2; Tuchman 1.

HUETER, JAMES W. b. May 15, 1925, San Francisco, Calif. **Studied:** Pomona College, BA, MFA; Claremont Graduate School, 1963, with Henry McFee, Sueo Serisawa, Millard Sheets, Albert Stewart; Pitzer College, 1972. **Taught:**

Mount San Antonio College, 1952– ; Pomona College, 1959–60. **Awards:** Los Angeles County Fair, 1951; Pasadena/ AM, 1953; Los Angeles/County MA, 1955; California State Fair **P.P.**, 1957; Long Beach State College, 1960, 61. **Address:** 190 E. Radcliffe Drive, Claremont, CA 91711. **One-man Exhibitions:** Mount San Antonio College, 1952, 77; First National Bank, Ontario, Calif., 1954; Pasadena/AM, 1955; Long Beach State College, 1957; Whittier (Calif.) Art Association, 1959; Monrovia (Calif.) Public Library, 1961; Heritage Gallery, Los Angeles, 1964, 67; Mt. San Antonio College, 1977. **Group:** Los Angeles County Fair, 1949, 51, 52; Pasadena/AM, 1950–54; Newport Harbor, 1950, 54, 55; California State Fair, 1950–55, 1958; Chaffey College, 1951, 55, 59, 60; Los Angeles/County MA, 1952, 54, 55, 57, 58, 61; Palos Verdes, 1953, 55; Denver/AM; 1954; Youngstown/Butler, 1955, 58, 59; Long Beach/ MA, 1960; RAC, 1960; California Palace, 1960; Long Beach State College, 1960, 61; Pomona College, 1961; Mount San Antonio College, 1961; Laguna Beach Museum of Art, Southern California 100, 1977. **Collections:** California State Fair; Long Beach State College; Los Angeles County Fair Association; National Orange Show; Pasadena/AM; Scripps College.

HULTBERG, JOHN. b. February 8, 1922, Berkeley, Calif. **Studied:** Fresno State College, 1939–43, BA; ASL, 1941–51, with Morris Kantor, California School of Fine Arts, with Clay Spohn, Richard Diebenkorn, David Park, Clyfford Still, Mark Rothko. US Navy, 1943–46. **Taught:** Boston Museum School, 1958; ASL, summer 1960; Portland, Ore./AM, Artist-in-Residence, 1964. **Commissions:** *Fortune* magazine (portfolio of drawings of Newport News Shipbuilding Co.). **Awards:** CSFA, Albert M. Bender Fellowship, 1949; Corcoran, First Prize, 1955; Congress for Cultural Freedom, First Prize, 1955; Carnegie, Hon. Men., 1955; Gug-

genheim Foundation Fellowship; 1956; Hallmark International Competition, 1957; Chicago/AI, Norman Wait Harris Medal, 1962; Ford Foundation/A.F.A. Artist-in-Residence, 1964; NAD, Benjamin Altman Prize, 1972. **Address:** 495 Broome Street, NYC 10013. **One-man Exhibitions:** (first) Contemporary Gallery, Sausalito, Calif., 1949; Korman Gallery, NYC, 1953; Martha Jackson Gallery, 1955, 58, 59, 61, 63, 66, 67, 69, 79; ICA, London, 1956; Galerie Rive Droite, Paris, 1957; The Swetzoff Gallery, Boston, 1957; Phoenix, 1957; Galerie du Dragon, Paris, 1957, 59; Numero Galleria d'Arte, Florence, Italy, 1958; Main Street Gallery, NYC, 1961; Piccadilly Gallery, 1961, 65; Museum of Malmo, Sweden, 1962; Esther Baer Gallery, 1962, 64; Roswell, 1963; Galerie Pauli, Lausanne, 1965; Galerie Anderson-Mayer, Paris, 1966; Museum of Contemporary Crafts Council, 1966; Honolulu Academy, 1967; Gallery of Modern Art, 1967; Apiaw (Gallery), Paris, 1968; Long Island U., 1968; American Cultural Center, Paris, 1968. **Group:** California Palace, 1947; MOMA, New Talent; Corcoran, 1955; WMAA Annuals, 1955, 64, 68; XXVIII Venice Biennial, 1956; Gutai 9, Osaka, 1958; Carnegie, 1958; ART:USA:59, NYC, 1959; Chicago/AI, 1962; Brooklyn Museum, 1964; Salon du Mai, Paris, 1964; Ghent, 1964; VIII Sao Paulo Biennial, 1965; Museo Civico, Bologna, 1965; U. of Kentucky, 1968; PAFA, 1968; AAAL, 1969. **Collections:** U. of Arizona; Atlanta/AA; Baltimore/MA; Boston U.; U. of California; Carnegie; Chase Manhattan Bank; Dallas/MFA; Davenport/Municipal; Dayton/AI; Eindhoven; Honolulu Academy; U. of Illinois; Indianapolis/Herron; MIT; MMA; MOMA; U. of Michigan; Musée Cantonal des Beaux-Arts; NYU; U. of Nebraska; New School for Social Research; Philadelphia Art Alliance; Phoenix; Quaker Ridge School; RISD; Roswell; St. Louis/City; Santa Barbara/ MA; The Singer Company Inc.; Stamford Museum; Stockholm/National; WMAA; Walker. **Bibliography:** Blesh 1;

Janis and Blesh 1; Hunter, ed.; Mc-Chesney; Nordness, ed. Archives.

HUMPHREY, RALPH. b. 1932, Youngstown, Ohio. **Studied:** Youngstown U., 1951–52, 1954–56. **Taught:** ASL; Harley House, NYC, 1959–60; Bennington College, 1961–63; New School for Social Research; Hunter College. **Address:** % Dealer. **Dealer:** Willard Gallery, Inc., NYC. **One-man Exhibitions:** Tibor de Nagy Gallery, 1959, 60; Gallery Mayer, NYC, 1961; Green Gallery, NYC, 1965; Bykert Gallery, 1967, 68, 69, 70, 72, 73, 74, 75; Dunkleman Gallery, Toronto, 1970; Andre Emmerich Gallery, NYC, 1971; The Texas Gallery, 1973; Daniel Weinberg Gallery, San Francisco, 1975; John Weber Gallery, NYC, 1976, 77. **Group:** SRGM, Abstract Expressionists and Imagists, 1961; SRGM, Systemic Painting, 1966; Ithaca College, 1967; Trenton/State, Focus on Light, 1967; ICA, U. of Pennsylvania, A Romantic Minimalism, 1967; MOMA, The Art of the Real, 1968; WMAA, 1969; Buffalo/Albright, Color and Field; 1890–1970, 1970; WMAA, The Structure of Color, 1971; Indianapolis, 1972; Chicago/AI, 1974; UCLA, Fourteen Abstract Painter, 1975; Baltimore/MA, Fourteen Artists, 1975; U. of Chicago, Ideas on Paper, 1970–1976, 1976; WMAA Biennial, 1979; ICA, Boston, The Reductive Object, 1979. **Collections:** Bennington College; Brandeis U.; Canberra/National; Dayton/AI; Hartford/Wadsworth; MOMA; U. of North Carolina; SFMA; VMFA; WMAA. **Bibliography:** Alloway 3; Battcock, ed.; Goossen 1; *New in the Seventies.*

HUNT, BRYAN. b. June 7, 1947, Terre Haute, Indiana. **Studied:** U. of South Florida, Tampa, 1966–68; Otis Art Institute, Los Angeles, 1969–70; BFA; WMAA, Independent Study Program, 1972. Traveled Europe 1969, around the world 1979–80. **Taught:** School of Visual Arts, NYC, 1978. **Commissions:**

Bryan Hunt   *Balearic Islands VI*   1979

Edgar Kaufman, *Falling Water*, sculpture for Frank Lloyd Wright, 1979. **Address:** 31 Great Jones Street, NYC 10012. **Dealer:** Blum Helman Gallery, NYC. **One-man Exhibitions:** The Clocktower, NYC, 1974; Jack Glenn Gallery, Corona del Mar, 1974; Brussels Beaux-Arts, 1976; Weinberg Gallery, San Francisco, 1976, 78; Blum Helman Gallery, NYC, 1977, 78, 79; Greenberg Gallery, St. Louis, 1978; Bernard Jacobson Gallery, London, 1979; Galerie Bischofberger, Zurich, 1979; Margo Leavin Gallery, Los Angeles, 1980. **Group:** Portland Oregon, Center for the Visual Arts, Via Los Angeles, 1976; SRGM, Young American Artists, 1978; Amsterdam/Stedelijk, Made by Sculptors, 1978; WMAA Biennial, 1979; Venice Biennial, 1980. **Collections:** Amsterdam/Stedelijk; Burroughs Wellcom Co.; Des Moines; MOMA; SRGM; Vassar College; WMAA; Yale U.

HUNT, RICHARD. b. September 12, 1935, Chicago, Ill. **Studied:** U. of Illinois; The U. of Chicago; Chicago Art Institute School, 1959, BA. Ed. US Army, 1958–60. Traveled Europe. **Taught:** U. of Illinois, 1960–62; Chicago Art Institute School, 1960–61; Yale U., 1964; Chouinard Art Institute, Los Angeles, 1964–65; Purdue U., 1965; Northern Illinois U., 1968; Northwestern U., 1968–69; Wisconsin State U., Oshkosh, 1969; Southern Illinois U., 1969; Western Illinois U., 1970; U. of Indiana, 1975; U. of Georgia, 1977; Washington U., 1977–78. **Commissions:** Louisiana State U., 1960; Johnson Publishing Co., Chicago, 1972; Johnson Products Co., Chicago, 1974; U. of Chicago, 1975; U. of California, Los Angeles, 1975; U. of Illinois, Chicago Campus, 1975; Martin Luther King Community Service Center, Chicago, 1975; U. of Michigan, 1975; Social Security Center, Richmond, Calif., 1976; Roosevelt Square, NYC, 1976; Justice Center, Cleveland, 1977; Cartwright Park, Evanston, Ill., 1977; Martin Luther King Memorial, Memphis, Tenn., 1977; Carter Woodson Library, Chicago, 1977; Prairie View A. & M. U., 1978; Howard U., 1978; Greenville, 1978; Cultural Activities Center, Temple, Tex., 1979; Northwestern U., 1979. **Awards:** Chicago/AI, James Nelson Raymond Traveling Fellowship, 1957; Guggenheim Foundation Fellowship, 1962; Chicago/AI, The Mr. & Mrs. Frank G. Logan Prize; Cassandra Foundation Fellowship, 1970. **Member:** National Council on the Arts, 1968–74; Illinois Arts Council, 1970–75; Board of Trustees, Chicago/Contemporary, 1975–79; Board of Trustees, American Academy in Rome, 1980– . **Address:** 1035 West Lill Avenue, Chicago, IL 60614. **Dealer:** B.C. Holland Gallery, Chicago. **One-man Exhibitions:** (first) The Alan Gallery, NYC, 1958, also 1960, 63; Stewart Rickard Gallery, San Antonio, 1960, 64; B. C. Holland Gallery, 1961, 63, 70, 76; U. of Tulsa, 1964; Wesleyan College, 1964; Felix Landau Gallery; Cleveland/MA; Milwaukee; U. of Illinois; U. of Notre Dame; The Ohio State U.; Dorsky Gallery, 1968, 69, 71, 73, 75, 76, 77, 79; Wisconsin State U.,

Oshkosh, 1969; Southern Illinois U., 1970; MOMA, 1971; Indianapolis, 1973; U. of Iowa, 1975; Sears Bank and Trust Co., Chicago, 1976; Greenville, 1978. **Retrospective:** MOMA, 1971; Chicago/AI, 1971. **Group:** New Sculpture Group, NYC, 1960, 61; U. of Illinois; MOMA; WMAA; Michigan State U.; Smith College; Yale U.; Newark Museum; Carnegie; Seattle World's Fair, 1962; HemisFair '68, San Antonio, Tex., 1968. **Collections:** Bezalel Museum; Buffalo/Albright; Chicago/AI; Cleveland/MA; Cincinnati/AM; Hirshhorn; Kansas City/Nelson; Los Angeles/County MA; MMA; MOMA; Milwaukee; Trenton/State; Vienna, Museum des 20. Jahrhunderts, **Bibliography:** *The Chicago Connection;* Dover.

HUOT, ROBERT. b. September 16, 1935, Staten Island, N.Y. **Studied:** Wagner College, BS; Hunter College. Traveled Europe, Africa, Greenland, Iceland, California. **Taught:** Hunter College, 1963– . **Awards:** National Council on the Arts. **Address:** RD 1, New Berlin, NY 13411. **Dealer:** Filmmakers Coop, 175 Lexington Avenue, NYC. **One-man Exhibitions:** (first) Stephen Radich Gallery, 1964, also 1965–67; Galerie Muller, 1967; Ziegler Gallery, 1968, 70; Galerie Schmela, 1968; Paula Cooper Gallery, 1969, 73; Colgate U., 1975; Paula Cooper Gallery, 1974. **Group:** Hudson River Museum, Yonkers, N.Y., 1964; Vassar College, 1964; SRGM; Systemic Painting, 1966; IV International Young Artists Exhibit, American-Japan, Tokyo, 1967; A.F.A., 1967; MOMA, The Art of the Real, 1968. **Collections:** Torrington Mfg. Corp. **Bibliography:** Alloway 3; Battcock, ed.; Goosen 1; Lippard, ed.; Murdock 1.

I

INDIANA, ROBERT. b. September 13, 1928, New Castle, Ind. **Studied:** John Herron Art Institute, 1945–46; Munson-Williams-Proctor Institute, Utica, N.Y., 1947–48; Chicago Art Institute School, 1949–53, BFA; Skowhegan School, summer, 1953; U. of Edinburgh, Edinburgh College of Art, 1953–54; Aspen Institute, Artist-in-Residence, summer, 1968. Traveled USA, Mexico, Europe. **Commissions:** New York State Pavilion, New York World's Fair, 1964–65 (mural); New York State Theater, Lincoln Center for the Performing Arts, NYC (poster); costumes, sets, and poster for the Walker Art Center Opera Company's production of the Virgil Thomson-Gertrude Stein opera *The Mother of Us All*, Tyrone Guthrie Theater, Minneapolis, 1967; 8¢ US postage stamp (400,000,000 printed), 1973; Numerous Posters, banners, and several volumes of poetry with Robert Creely. **Awards:** Chicago/AI, Traveling Fellowship, 1953; Hon. DFA, Franklin and Marshall College, 1970; Indiana State Commission on the Arts Award, 1973; Hon. DFA, U. of Indiana, 1977. **Address:** Vinalhaven, ME 04863. **One-man Exhibitions:** (first) The Stable Gallery, 1962, also 1964, 66; ICA, Boston, 1963; Walker, 1963 (two-man, with Richard Stankiewicz); Rolf Nelson Gallery, Los Angeles, 1965; Dayton's Gallery 12, Minneapolis, 1966; Galerie Schmela, 1966; Eindhoven, 1966; Krefeld/Haus Lange, 1966; Wurttembergischer Kunstverein, Stuttgart, 1966; ICA, U. of Pennsylvania, 1968; San Antonio/McNay, 1968; Indianapolis/Herron, 1968; Toledo/MA, 1968; Hunter Gallery, Aspen, Colo., 1968; Creighton U., 1969; St. Mary's College (Ind.), 1969; Colby College, 1969; Dartmouth College, 1970; Bowdoin College, 1970; Brandeis U., 1970; Badischer Kunstverein, Karlsruhe, 1971; Humlebaek/Louisiana, 1972; Galerie Denise Rene, NYC, 1972, 75, 76; Didrichsenin Konsmuseum, Helsinki, 1972; Santa Fe, N.M., 1976; U. of Texas, Austin, 1977; Norfolk/Chrysler, 1977; Indianapolis, 1978; Purchase/SUNY, 1978; Art Center, South Bend, 1978. **Group:** MOMA, The Art of Assemblage, circ., 1961; Chicago/AI Annual, 1963; WMAA, New Directions in American Painting, 1963; ICA, London, The Popular Image, 1963; Bertrand Russell Peace Foundation, Woburn Abbey, England, 1963; MOMA, Americans 1963, circ., 1963–64; Tate, Dunn International, 1964; Tate, Painting and Sculpture of a Decade, 1954–64, 1964; Museum des 20. Jahrhunderts, 1964; New York World's Fair, 1964–65; WMAA Annuals, 1964, 65, 67, Sculpture Annual, 1966; Corcoran Biennial, 1965; Palais des Beaux-Arts, Brussels, 1965; WMAA, A Decade of American Drawings, 1965; SRGM, 1965; Milwaukee, 1965; U. of Illinois, 1965, 67; PAFA, 1966; ICA, Boston, 1966; Eindhoven, Kunst-Licht-Kunst, 1966; Expo '67, Montreal 1967; VI International Art Biennial, San Marino (Europe), 1967; IX Sao Paulo Biennial, 1967; Carnegie, 1967; Dublin/Municipal, I International Quadrennial (ROSC), 1967; Documenta IV, Kassel, 1968; Chicago/Contemporary, 1968; WMAA, Contemporary American Sculpture, Selection II, 1969; Cologne, 1969; Fine Arts Academy of Finland, Helsinki, 1969; Jewish Museum, Superlimited, 1969; WMAA, Seventy Years of American Art, 1969; Hayward Gallery, London, Pop Art,

Robert Indiana   *The Great American Dream: New York* 1966

1969; ICA, U. of Pennsylvania, Highway, 1970; Cincinnati/Contemporary, Monumental Art, 1970; Foundation Maeght, L'Art Vivant, 1970; Museo de Arte Contemporaneo, Cali, Colombia, S.A., I Bienal Graficas, 1971; Dusseldorf, Zero Raum, 1973; WMAA (downtown), Nine Artists/Coenties Slip, 1974; WMAA, American Pop Art, 1974; Newport, R.I., Monumenta, 1974; Hirshhorn, Inaugural Exhibition, 1974; Corcoran, 1975; MOMA, American Art since 1945, 1975; Philadelphia College of Art, Artists' Sets and Costumes, 1977; Indianapolis, Perceptions of the Spirit in 20th Century American Art, 1977. **Collections:** Aachen/NG; Allentown/AM; Amsterdam/Stedelijk; Baltimore/MA; Brandeis U.; Brigham Young U.; Buffalo/Albright; Carnegie; Cologne; Detroit/Institute; Delaware Art Museum; U. of Dublin; Eindhoven; Honolulu Academy; Humlebaek/Louisiana; ICA, U. of Pennsylvania; U. of Illinois; Indianapolis; Indianapolis/Her-ron; Krefeld/Kaiser Wilhelm; Los Angeles/County MA; MMA; MOMA; U. of Michigan; U. of Nebraska; Oklahoma; Purchase/SUNY; Ridgefield/Aldrich; SFMA; Spelman College; Stanford U.; U. of Texas; Toronto; VMFA; WGMA; WMAA; Walker; Wuppertal/von der Heydt. **Bibliography:** Alloway 1; Calas, N. and E.; Dienst 1; Diamonstein; Honisch and Jensen, eds.; Hunter, ed.; *Kunst um 1970;* Lippard 5; **McCoubrey 2;** *Monumenta;* Russell and Gablik; Seitz 3; Weller. Archives.

INSLEY, WILL. b. October 15, 1929, Indianapolis, Ind. **Studied:** Amherst College, BA, 1951; Harvard U., B. Arch., 1955. Traveled USA, Europe. US Army, 1955–57. **Taught:** Oberlin College, Artist-in-Residence, 1966; U. of North Carolina, 1967–68; Cornell U., 1969; School of Visual Arts, NYC, 1969; Cooper Union, 1972. **Commissions:** Great Southwest Industrial Park, 1968; Cmabridge Arts Council, 1978. **Awards:** National Council on the Arts, 1966; Guggenheim Foundation Fellowship, 1969–70. **Address:** 231 Bowery, NYC 10002. **Dealers:** Max Protetch, NYC; Galerie Annemarie Verna, Zurich; Paul Maenz, Cologne. **One-man Exhibitions:** (first) Amherst College, 1951; The Stable Gallery, NYC, 1965–68; Oberlin College, 1967; U. of North Carolina, 1967; Walker, 1968; Buffalo/Albright, 1968; Cornell U. (three-man), 1969; ICA, U. of Pennsylvania, 1969; John Gibson Gallery, 1969; MOMA, 1971; School of Visual Arts, NYC, 1972; Paul Maenz Gallery, Cologne, 1972; Krefeld/Haus Lange, 1973; Fischbach Gallery, NYC, 1973, 74, 76; Galerie Annemarie Verna, Zurich, 1974; Stuttgart/WK, 1974; Wisconsin State U., Max Protetch, NYC, 1977, 80; Protetch/McIntosh, Washington, D.C., 1977; Galerie Orny, Munich 1978. **Group:** WMAA Annuals, 1965, 67; Riverside Museum, 1966; SRGM, Systemic Painting, 1966; U. of Illinois, 1967; VI International Art Biennial, San Marino (Europe), 1967; U. of North Carolina,

1967; Ridgefield/Aldrich, 1968; J. L. Hudson Art Gallery, Detroit, 1968; New Delhi, First World Triennial, 1968; ICA, U. of Pennsylvania, 1969; Fort Worth, Drawings, 1969; Foundation Maeght, L'Art Vivant, 1970; Finch College, NYC, Projected Art, 1971; Arnhem, Sonsbeek '71, 1971; U. of Washington, Drawing from New York, 1972; ICA, U. of Pennsylvania, Grids, 1972; Documenta V, Kassel, 1972; WMAA, American Drawings: 1963–1973, 1973; Tyler School of Art, Philadelphia, American Drawings, 1973; Kennedy Center, Art Now '74, 1974; Minnesota/MA, Drawings USA '75, 1975; Stamford (Conn.)/ Museum, American Salon des Refuses, 1976; Rice U., Drawing Today in New York, 1976; Documenta VI, Kassel, 1977; ICA, U. of Pennsylvania, Dwell-ings, 1978; U. of North Carolina, Drawings about Drawings, 1979; Hayward Gallery, London,·Pier and Ocean, 1980. **Collections:** Brandeis U.; Colby College; U. of North Carolina. **Bibliography:** Alloway 3; *Art Now 74*; Battcock, ed.; Lucie-Smith.

IPPOLITO, ANGELO. b. November 9, 1922, St. Arsenio, Italy. **Studied:** Ozenfant School of Art, NYC, 1946–47; Brooklyn Museum School, 1948; Instituto Meschini, Rome, 1949–50. Traveled Europe. **Taught:** Cooper Union, 1956–59, 1962–64; Sarah Lawrence College, 1957; Yale U., Visiting Critic, 1961; U. of California, Berkeley, 1961–62; Queens College, 1963–64; Michigan State U., Artist-in-Residence, 1966–67;

Angelo Ippolito *Summer Morning* 1979

Binghamton/SUNY, 1971– . A co-founder of the Tanager Gallery, NYC. **Commissions:** New York Hilton Hotel, 1963. **Awards:** Fulbright Fellowship (Italy), 1959. **Address:** Friendsville Stage, Binghamton, NY 13903. **Dealer:** Grace Borgenicht Gallery Inc. **One-man Exhibitions:** (first) Galleria della Rotondo, Bergamo, 1950; Tanager Gallery, NYC, 1954, 62; The Bertha Schaefer Gallery, 1956, 58; HCE Gallery, Provincetown, Mass., 1957, 61; Massillon Museum; Canton (Ohio) Museum; Cleveland Institute of Art, 1960; U. of California, 1961; Michigan State U., 1962; Bolles Gallery, 1962 (two-man, with Harold P. Paris); Grace Borgenicht Gallery Inc., NYC, 1962, 64, 67, 72, 75, 77; Jesse Besser Museum, Alpena, Mich., 1968; Albion College, 1969; Western Michigan U., 1969; Grand Valley State College, Allandale, Mich., 1970. **Retrospective:** Binghamton/SUNY, 1975. **Group:** Arts Club of Chicago, 1953; Walker, Vanguard, 1955; Utica, 1955, 57; SMAA Annuals, 1955, 57, 59, 62; USIA, 20th Century Graphics, circ., 1956–58; WMAA, Young America, 1957; A.F.A., College in America, circ., 1957–58; WMAA, Nature in Abstraction, 1958; VI Sao Paulo Biennial, 1961; Silvermine Guild, 1963; IIE, 1975. **Collections:** Chase Manhattan Bank; CIT Corporation; General Electric Corp.; Hirshhorn; IIE; MMA; Massillon Museum; Michigan State U.; U. of Michigan; Milwaukee; Montreal Trust Co.; Norfolk/Chrysler; Phillips; Purchase/SUNY; Sarah Lawrence College; Utica; WMAA. **Bibliography:** Baur 5; Goodrich and Baur 1; Janis and Blesh 1; Sandler 1.

IRWIN, ROBERT. b. 1928, Long Beach, Calif. **Studied:** Otis Art Institute, 1938–50; Jepson Art Institute, Los Angeles, 1951. **Taught:** Chouinard Art Institute, 1957–58; UCLA, 1962; U. of California, Irvine, 1968–69. **Address:** 11044½ Strathmore Drive, Los Angeles, CA 90024. **Dealer:** The Pace Gallery. **One-man Exhibitions:** Felix Landau

Gallery, 1975; Ferus Gallery, Los Angeles, 1959, 60, 62, 64; Pasadena/AM, 1960, 68; The Pace Gallery, 1966, 68, 69, 71, 73, 74; Los Angeles/County MA (two-man), 1966; Jewish Museum, 1968; Fort Worth (two-man), 1969; MOMA, 1970; Walker, 1971, 76; ACE GAllery, Los Angeles, 1972; Harvard U., 1972; Ileana Sonnabend Gallery, Paris, 1972; Wright State U., 1974; U. of California, Santa Barbara, 1974; Mizuno Gallery, Los Angeles, 1972, 74, 76; Fort Worth, 1975; Chicago/Contemporary, 1975; Palomar College, San Marcos, Calif., 1975. **Retrospective:** WMAA, 1977. **Group:** Los Angeles/County MA, Annual, 1952–53, 1956–60; WMAA Annual, 1957; UCLA, 1960; SFMA, Fifty California Artists, circ., 1962; MOMA, The Responsive Eye, 1965; VIII Sao Paulo Biennial, 1965; Vancouver, 1968; Documenta IV, Kassel, 1968; Walker, 1968; Eindhoven, Kompas, 1970; U. of Washington, 1971; Corcoran, 1971; Hayward Gallery, London, 11 Los Angeles Artists, 1971; SMFA, Works in Spaces, 1973; Kennedy Center, Art Now '74, 1974; Long Beach State U., Transparencies, 1975; WMAA, 200 Years of American Sculpture, 1976; Philadelphia College of Art, Projects for PCA, 1976. **Collections:** Art Gallery of New South Wales; Buffalo/Albright; U. of California, Berkeley; Boston/MFA; Chicago/AI; Cleveland/MA; Des Moines; Fort Worth; Harvard U.; La Jolla; Los Angeles/County MA; MOMA; Melbourne/National; Omaha/Joslyn; Pasadena/AM; RISD; SFMA; Sydney/AG; Tate; Vancouver; WMAA; Walker. **Bibliography:** Art Now 74; Davis, D.; Drawings of the Pluralist Decade; Robert Irwin; Report; The State of California Painting; Transparency; USA West Coast.

ITO, MIYOKO. b. 1918, Berkeley, Calif. **Studied:** U. of Calif., Berkeley, BA, 1942; Smith College; School of the Art Institute of Chicago. **Awards:** MacDowell Colony Fellowship, 1970–77; Guggenheim Foundation Fellowship,

Miyoko Ito   *Migraine*

1977. **Address:** 1300 E. Madison Park, Chicago, IL 60615. **Dealer:** Phyllis Kind Gallery, Chicago, and NYC. **One-man Exhibitions:** Hyde Park Art Center, Chicago, 1971; Phyllis Kind Gallery, Chicago, 1973; Kornblee Gallery, NYC, 1976; Phyllis Kind Gallery, NYC, 1978. **Retrospective:** U. of Chicago, 1980. **Group:** WMAA Biennial, 1975; School of the Art Institute of Chicago, Former Famous Alumni, 1976; U. of Illinois, 1976; Sacramento/Crocker, The Chicago Connection, 1977; Chicago Public Library Cultural Center, Masterpieces of Chicago Art, 1977. **Collections:** AT&T, NYC; Atlantic Richfield, Co., San Francisco; Chicago/AI; Illinois State U.; U. of Illinois; Kemper Insurance Co.; McDermott, Will and Emery, Chicago; PAFA; SFMA; Vulcan Materials Co., New Orleans. **Bibliography:** *Chicago Connection.*

J

JACOBS, DAVID. b. March 1, 1932, Niagara Falls, N.Y. **Studied:** Orange Coast College, 1951–53; Los Angeles State College of Applied Arts and Sciences, 1953–57. Traveled Europe, Greece. **Taught:** The Ohio State U., 1957–62; Hofstra U., 1962–; Huntington Township Art League, Huntington, N.Y., 1963–64; Baruch College, 1976–78. **Commissions:** Valley Mall, Hagerstown, Md. **Awards:** CAPS, 1974, 76; National Endowment for the Arts and New York Foundation for the Arts, 1979. **Address:** 51 Eighth Avenue, Sea Cliff, NY 11579. **One-man Exhibitions:** Barone Gallery, NYC, 1961; The Kornblee Gallery, 1963–65; Emily Lowe Gallery, Hempstead, N.Y., 1964; D'Arcangelo Studio, NYC, 1967; Hofstra U., 1967, 73; Colgate U., 1970; San Jose State College, 1970; Albion College, 1970; Cornell U., 1971; Wesleyan U., 1971; Kenyon College, 1971; 152 Wooster Street Gallery, NYC, 1971; Colby College, 1973; Edinboro (Pa.) State College, 1973; Port Washington (L.I.) Library Gallery, 1979. **Group:** MOMA, 1961; SRGM; SFMA; Dayton/AI; Vassar College, Indianapolis/Herron; Akron/AI, 1964; Chicago/AI, 1966; Kansas City/Nelson, Sound, Light, Silence, 1966; Milwaukee, Directions I: Options, circ., 1968; Finch College, NYC, Documentation, 1968; Jewish Museum, Inflatable Sculpture, 1969; Vancouver, Sound Sculpture, 1973; P.S.I, NYC, Sound at P.S.I, 1979. **Collections:** Frank Construction Company; Hofstra U.; The Ohio State U.; Otterbein College; Raycom Industries; SRGM; E. Sherry Truck Company; VMFA. **Bibliography:** Atkinson.

JACQUETTE, YVONNE. b. December 15, 1934, Pittsburgh, Pa. **Studied:** RISD, 1952–56, with John Frazier; privately with Herman Cherry. **Taught:** U. of Pennsylvania, 1972–75, 1980; Parsons School of Design, NYC, 1977–79. **Member:** Artists Equity. **Commissions:** North Central Bronx Hospital, N.Y.; GSA, federal building and post office, Bangor, Maine. **Awards:** Ingram Merrill Foundation grant, 1975; CAPS, grant, 1979. **m.** Rudolph Burckhardt. **Address:** 50 West 29th Street, NYC 10001. **Dealer:** Brooke Alexander, Inc. **One-man Exhibitions:** (first) Swarthmore College, 1965; Fischbach Gallery, NYC, 1971, 74; Tyler School of Art, Philadelphia, 1972; Brooke Alexander, Inc., NYC, 1974, 76, 79, 81. **Group:** Vassar College, Realism Now, 1968; U. of North Carolina, Art on Paper, 1969; Buffalo/Albright, Cool Realism, 1970; WMAA Annual, 1972; New York Cultural Center, Women Choose Women, 1972; WMAA, Drawings 1963–1973; 1973; Chicago/AI, Small Scale in Contemporary Art, 1975; Minnesota/MA, Drawings USA, 1975; San Antonio/McNay, American Artists '76, 1976; P.S. 1, Long Island City, Couples, 1979. **Collections:** Akron/AI; Colby College; Corcoran; Minnesota/MA; MMA; U. of North Carolina; Pomona College; RISD; Yale U. **Bibliography:** Arthur 2; Lippard 3; *Poets & Painters*.

JARVAISE, JAMES. b. February 16, 1932, Indianapolis, Ind. **Studied:** U. of Southern California, 1950, BFA, 1953, MFA, 1955. Traveled Europe, resided Spain, France. **Taught:** U. of Southern

California, 1955–62, 1966, summer, 1967; The Pennsylvania State U., 1963; Occidental College, 1965–67; California Institute of the Arts, Valencia, 1964–68. **Address:** 726 Benson Way, Thousand Oaks, CA 19360. **Dealers:** Ruth S. Schaffner Gallery, Los Angeles. **One-man Exhibitions:** (first) Felix Landau Gallery, 1952, also 1955, 58, 60, 61, 62, 64; Thibaut Gallery, NYC, 1961; Gump's Gallery, 1961 (two-man); The Alan Gallery, NYC, 1967. **Group:** Seattle/AM, 1951; Santa Barbara/MA, 1951, 57; Oakland/AM, 1951, 57; MMA, 1953; Denver/AM, 1953, 54, 58; U. of Illinois, 1953, 57, 66; Long Beach/MA, Fifteen Americans, circ., 1956; Corcoran, 1958; U. of Nebraska, 1958; Carnegie, 1959; MOMA, Sixteen Americans, circ., 1959; El Retiro Parquet, Madrid, Arte de America y Espana, 1963; VMFA, American Painting and Sculpture, 1966. **Collections:** Andover/Phillips; Buffalo/Albright; Carnegie; The Coca-Cola Co.; Los Angeles/County MA; MOMA; Ridgefield/Aldrich; Youngstown/Butler.

JAUDON, VALERIE. b. August 6, 1945, Mississippi. **Studied:** Mississippi U. for Women, 1963–65; U. of the Americas, Mexico City, 1966–67; St. Martin's School of Art, London, 1968–69; Memphis Academy of Arts, 1965. Traveled Mexico, Europe. **Commission:** ceiling mural, Insurance Co. of North America, Philadelphia, 1977. **Address:** 139 Bowery, NYC 10002. **Dealer:** Holly Solomon Gallery, Inc., NYC. **One-man Exhibitions:** (first) Holly Solomon Gallery, Inc., 1977, 78, 79; PAFA, 1977; Galerie Bischofberger,

Yvonne Jacquette *Southview of New York Harbor* 1978

Valerie Jaudon *Carthage* 1980

Zurich, 1979; Galerie Hans Strelow, Dusseldorf, 1980. **Group:** Sarah Lawrence College, Painting 1975–77, 1977; P.S. 1, Queens, Pattern Painting at P.S. 1, 1977; Utica, Critic's Choice, 1976–77, 1977; Rice U., Pattern and Decoration, 1978; Rutgers U., Decorative Art: Recent Work, 1978; Claremont College, Black and White Are Colors, 1979; Dayton/AI, Patterns Plus, 1979; Brussels/Beaux-Arts, Patterning Painting, 1979; Mannheimer Kunstverein, Mannheim, Dekor, 1980, Aachen, Les Nouveau Fauves/Die Neuen Wilden, 1980. **Collections:** Hirshhorn; Humlebaek/Louisiana; Ridgefield/Aldrich. **Bibliography:** *Black and White Are Colors.*

JENKINS, PAUL. b. 1923, Kansas City, Mo. **Studied:** Kansas City Art Institute and School of Design, 1938–41; US Naval Air Corps, 1943–45; ASL, 1948–51. Resided Paris. **Awards:** Corcoran Biennial, Silver Medal, 1966; Golden Eagle Award for a film, *The Ivory Knife,* of which he is the subject, 1966; Honorary Doctor of Humanities, Linwood College, 1973. Officier des Arts et Lettres, 1980. **Address:** 169 East 94th Street, NYC 10028; studio: 831 Broadway, NYC 10003. **Dealers:** Gimpel & Weitzenhoffer Ltd., NYC, Elaine Horwisch Gallery, Scottsdale, Ariz.; Irving Gallery, Milwaukee; Galerie Karl Flinker, Paris. **One-man Exhibitions:** (first) Studio Paul Facchetti, Paris, 1954; Zimmergaleries Franck, Frankfurt am Main, 1954; Zoe Dusanne Gallery, Seattle, 1955; Martha Jackson Gallery, 1956, 58, 60, 61, 64, 66, 68, 69, 70, 71; Galerie Stadler, Paris, 1957, 59; A. Tooth & Sons, London, 1960, 63; Galerie Karl Flinker, 1960, 61, 63, 65, 73, 76; Galleria Toninelli, Milan, 1962; Galerie Charles Leinhard, Zurich, 1962; Galleria Odyssia, Rome, 1962; Cologne/Kunstverein, 1962; Esther Robles Gallery, 1963; Eva de Buren Gallery, Stockholm, 1963; Hannover/K-G, 1964; Tokyo Gallery, 1964; Court Gallery, Copenhagen, 1964; Gutai Museum, Osaka, 1964; Gertrude Kasle Gallery, 1965, 71; Gallery of Modern Art, 1965, 66; Makler Gallery, Philadelphia, 1966; SRGM, 1966; Moss Gallery Ltd., Toronto, 1968; Daniel Gervis Gallery, Paris, 1968; Bernard Raeder Gallery, Lausanne, 1968: Richard Gray Gallery, 1971; Suzanne Saxe Gallery, San Francisco, 1971; SFMA, 1972; Images Gallery, Toledo, 1972; Gimpel Fils, 1972, 80; Corcoran, 1972; Baukunst Galerie, Cologne, 1974; Gimpel & Weitzenhoffer Ltd., 1974, 76, 78, 79; Galerie Ulysses, Vienna, 1974; Galerie Tanit, Munich, 1975; Galerie Farber, Brussels, 1975; Ohio U., 1975; Miami U., Oxford, 1975; Ft. Lauderdale, 1975; Carone Gallery, Ft. Lauderdale, 1975; A.B. Classon Co., Cincinnati, 1975, 77; Tampa Bay Art Center, 1975; Montgomery Museum, 1975; Columbus, 1975; Haslem Fine Arts, Inc., Washington, D.C., 1976; Gimpel & Hanover, Zurich, 1977; La Galerie Cour St.-Pierre, Geneva, 1977; Contemporary Gallery, Dallas, 1977; Tulsa/Philbrook, 1977; Diane Gilson Gallery, Seattle, 1977; Galleria d'Arte Narciso, Turin, 1978; Balcon des Arts, Paris, 1978; Elaine Horwisch, Scottsdale, Ariz., 1980. **Retrospective:** Palm Springs Desert Museum, 1980. **Group:** Musée du Petit Palais, Paris, 1955; MOMA, Recent Drawings USA, 1956; Arts Council Gallery, London, New Trends in Painting, 1957; WMAA, Young America, 1957; WMAA, Nature in Abstraction, 1958; Carnegie, 1958, 61; Corcoran, 1958, 66; SRGM, Abstract Expressionists and Imagists, 1961; Salon du Mai, Paris, 1962; Seattle World's Fair, 1962; WMAA Annuals, 1962, 65; Art:USA:Now, circ., 1962-67; Salon des Realites Nouvelles, Paris, 1963; Tate, Painting and Sculpture of a Decade, 1954-64, 1964; PAFA, 1965; ICA, Boston, Painting without a Brush, 1965; M. Knoedler & Co., Art Across America, circ., 1965-67; Smithsonian, 1966; U. of Illinois, 1967, 68; U. of Oklahoma, 1968; Indianapolis, 1969; U. of California, Santa Barbara, 1970; VMFA, American Painting 1970, 1970; Brooklyn Museum, Annual, 1970; Musée des Beaux Arts de Caen, Peinture Contemporaine, 1970; U. of Illinois, 1971; Indianapolis, 1974, 76; Springfield, Mass./ MFA, Watercolor USA, 1977. **Collections:** Amsterdam/Stedelijk; Baltimore/ MA; Bezalel Museum; Brooklyn Museum; Buffalo/Albright; Busch-Reisinger Museum; U. of California,

Berkeley; Cologne/Kunstverein; Columbus; Corcoran; Dallas/MFA; Des Moines; Detroit; France/National; Hannover/K-G; Hirshhorn; U. of Illinois; Indianapolis; Jewish Museum; Liverpool/Walker; Los Angeles/County MA; Louisville State; MIT; Milwaukee; MOMA; Musée Guimet; NCFA; National Museum of Western Art, Tokyo; Niigata Museum; Norfolk/Chrysler; Paris/Beaubourg; PMA; Seattle/AM; SRGM; Stanford U.; Stuttgart; Tate; U. of Texas; Toronto; Victoria and Albert Museum; U. of Virginia; Walker; WMAA; Worcester/AM. **Bibliography: Elsen 1; Nordland 4**; Sandler 1. Archives.

JENSEN, ALFRED. b. December 11, 1903, Guatemala City, Guatemala; **d.** April 4, 1981, Livingston, N.J. **Studied:** San Diego Fine Arts School, 1925; Hofmann School, Munich, 1927-28; Academie Scandinave, Paris, with Charles Despiau, Charles Dufresne, Othon Friesz, Marcel Gromaire, Andre Masson. Traveled USA, Europe. **Taught:** Maryland Institute, 1958. **Commissions:** Time Inc. (mural). **Awards:** Tamarind Fellowship, 1965. **One-man Exhibitions:** (first) John Heller Gallery, NYC, 1952; Tanager Gallery, NYC, 1955; The Bertha Schaefer Gallery, 1957; Martha Jackson Gallery, 1957, 59, 61, 67; SRGM, 1961; Fairleigh Dickinson U., 1963; The Graham Gallery, 1963-65; Klipstein & Kornfeld, Berne, 1964; Rolf Nelson Gallery, Los Angeles, 1964; Kunsthalle, Basel, 1964 (two-man, with Franz Kline); Amsterdam/Stedelijk, 1964; Ziegler Gallery, 1966; Cordier & Ekstrom, Inc., 1967, 68, 70; The Pace Gallery, NYC, 1972, 73, 76; Hannover/ K-G, 1973; Humlebaek/Louisiana, 1973; Kunsthalle, Baden-Baden, 1973; Dusseldorf/Kunsthalle, 1973; Berne, 1973. **Retrospective:** Buffalo/Albright, circ., 1977. **Group:** San Diego; Baltimore/MA; MOMA; The Stable Gallery, 1954-57; II Inter-American Paintings and Prints Biennial, Mexico City, 1960; ICA, Boston, 1960; Chicago/AI, 1961; Corcoran Biennial, 1962; WMAA, Geometric Abstraction in America, circ., 1962; WMAA Annual, 1963; Los Angeles/County MA, Post Painterly Abstraction, 1964; XXXII Venice Biennial, 1964; International Biennial Exhibition of Paintings, Tokyo; Buffalo/Albright, Plus by Minus, 1968; Documenta IV, Kassel, 1968; Lafayette College, Black-White, 1969; Indianapolis, 1970; VMFA, 1970; WMAA, The Structure of Color, 1971; ICA, U. of Pennsylvania, Grids, 1972; Documenta V, Kassel, 1972; WMAA, 1973. **Collections:** American Republic Insurance Co.; Baltimore/MA; Brandeis U.; Chase Manhattan Bank; Dayton/AI; Health and Hospital Corp.; MOMA; SRGM; San Diego; Time Inc.; WMAA. **Bibliography: Alfred Jensen**; Calas, N. and E.; *From Foreign Shores*; Honisch and Jensen, eds.; *Kunst um 1970*; MacAgy 2; Sandler 1.

JESS (COLLINS). b. 1923, Long Beach, Calif. **Studied:** California Institute of Technology, BS, 1948; California School of Fine Arts, 1949–51, with Clyfford Still, Edward Corbett, Elmer Bischoff, David Park, and Hassel Smith. Opened the King Ubu Gallery, San Francisco, in 1953, with Harry Jacobus and Robert Duncan. Traveled Europe. **Address:** 3267 20th Street, San Francisco, CA 94110. **Dealer:** Odyssia Gallery, NYC. **One-man Exhibitions:** The Place (a bar), San Francisco, 1954; Gump's Art Gallery, San Francisco, 1959; City Lights Book Shop, San Francisco, 1959; Dilexi Gally, San Francisco, 1960; Borregaard's Museum, San Francisco, 1961; Rolf Nelson Gallery, Los Angeles, 1965; Cheney Cowles Museum, Spokane, 1967; SFMA, 1968; Odyssia Gallery, NYC, 1971, 78; Chicago/Contemporary, 1972; MOMA, 1974; Hartford/Wads-

Jess *Melpomene and Thalia, Translation #8* 1965

worth, 1975; Galleria Odyssia, Rome, 1975; Dallas/MFA, circ., 1977. **Group:** King Ubu Gallery, San Francisco, 1953; MOMA, The Art of Assemblage, 1961; Oakland/AM, Pop Art USA, 1963; U. of New Mexico, The Painter and the Photograph, 1964; SFMA, Looking Back, 1968; ICA, U. of Pennsylvania, The Spirit of the Comics, 1969; Hayward Gallery, London, Pop Art Redefined, 1969; Chicago/AI, 70th American Exhibition, 1972; WMAA, Extraordinary Realities, 1973; U. of Illinois, 1974; Dallas/MFA, Poets of the Cities, 1974; SFMA, California Painting and Sculpture: The Modern Era, 1976; Indianapolis, Perceptions of the Spirit in 20th Century American Art, 1977; ICA, Boston, Narration, 1978. **Collections:** Chicago/AI;   Dallas/MFA;   MMA; MOMA; PMA.

JOHNS, JASPER. b. May, 1930, Augusta, Ga. **Studied:** U. of South Carolina. Artistic adviser to Merce Cunningham Dance Company. A director of the Foundation for Contemporary Performance Arts since 1963. **Member:** NIAL, 1973. **Awards:** Gallery of Modern Art, Ljubljana, Yugoslavia, VII International Exhibition of Prints, First Prize, 1967; IX Sao Paulo Biennial, 1967; Skowhegan School, Award for Graphics, 1977; New York City Mayor's Award of Honor for Arts and Culture, 1978. **Address:** 225 East Houston Street, NYC 10002; St. Martin, French West Indies. **Dealer:** Leo Castelli Inc. **One-man Exhibitions:** Leo Castelli Inc., 1958, 60, 61, 63, 66, 68, 70, 71, 76, 77, 79; Galleria d'Arte del Naviglio, Milan, 1959; Galerie Rive Droite, Paris, 1959, 61; Columbia, S.C./MA, 1960; U. of Minnesota, 1960; Ferus Gallery, Los Angeles, 1960 (two-man); Ileana Sonnabend Gallery, Paris, 1962; Everett Ellin Gallery, Los Angeles, 1962; Whitechapel Art Gallery, London, 1964; Pasadena/AM, 1965; Ashmolean Museum, Oxford, England, 1965; American Embassy, London, 1965; Minami Gallery, 1965; NCFA, 1966; MOMA, circ., 1968;

Eva de Buren Gallery, Stockholm; Castelli-Whitney, NYC, 1969; PMA, 1970; U. of Iowa, 1970; MOMA, 1970; Minneapolis/Institute, 1971; Dayton's Gallery 12, Minneapolis, 1971; Chicago/Contemporary, 1971; MOMA, Thirty Lithographs: 1960–68, circ., 1972; Fendrick Gallery, Washington, D.C., 1972; Houston/MFA, 1972; Hofstra U., 1972; Lo Spazio, Rome, 1974; Modern Art Agency, Naples, 1974; Galerie Folker Skulima, Berlin, 1974; Galerie Mikro, Berlin, 1974; Museum of Modern Art, Oxford, England, 1974; Arts Council of Great Britain, Drawings, 1975; Janie C. Lee Gallery, Houston, 1976, 79; Brooke Alexander, NYC, 1977; Margo Leavin Gallery, Los Angeles, 1978; Galerie Nancy Gillespie, Paris, 1978; Galerie Valeur, Nagoya, 1978, 79; Baltimore/MA, 1978; John Berggruen Gallery, San Francisco, 1978; Basel, circ., 1979; Tucson Museum of Art, 1979. **Retrospective:** Jewish Museum, 1964; Whitechapel Art Gallery, London, 1964; Pasadena/AM, 1965; WMAA, circ., 1977. **Group:** Jewish Museum, The New York School, Second Generation, 1957; A.F.A., Collage in America, circ., 1957–58; Houston/MFA, Collage International, 1958; XXIX & XXXII Venice Biennials, 1958, 64; Carnegie, 1958, 61, 64, 67; Houston/MFA, Out of the Ordinary, 1959; Daniel Cordier, Paris, Exposition Internationale de Surrealisme, 1959; Columbus, Contemporary American Painting, 1960; A.F.A., School of New York—Some Younger American Painters, 1960; Martha Jackson Gallery, New Media—New Forms, I & II, 1960, 61; WMAA, Annuals, 1960, 61, 62, 64, 65; SRGM, Abstract Expressionists and Imagists, 1961; Dallas/MFA, 1961–62; SRGM/USIA, American Vanguard, circ., Europe, 1961–62; MOMA, Abstract Watercolors and Drawings: USA, circ., Europe, 1961–62; MOMA, Lettering by Hand, 1962; Seattle World's Fair, 1962; Berne, 4 Americans, 1962; Chicago/AI,   1962;   Stockholm/National; Amsterdam/Stedelijk; Salon du Mai, Paris, 1962, 64; SRGM, Six Painters and the Object, circ., 1963; WGMA, The

Popular Image, 1963; Musée Cantonal des Beaux-Arts, Lausanne, I Salon International de Galeries Pilotes, 1963; ICA, London, The Popular Image, 1963; Buffalo/Albright, Mixed Media and Pop Art, 1963; El Retiro Parquet, Madrid, Arte de America y Espana, 1963; Jewish Museum, Black and White, 1963; Hartford/Wadsworth, Black, White, and Gray, 1964; Tate, Dunn International, 1964; Tate, Painting and Sculpture of a Decade, 1954–64; SRGM, 1964; Documenta III & IV, Kassel, 1964, 68; Palais des Beaux-Arts, Brussels, 1965; MOMA, Art in the Mirror, 1966; Jewish Museum, 1966; Expo '67, Montreal, 1967; IX Sao Paulo Biennial, 1967; Gallery of Modern Art, Ljubljana, Yugoslavia, VII International Exhibition of Prints, 1967; MOMA, Dada, Surrealism and Their Heritage, 1968; Vancouver, 1969; Cincinnati/Contemporary, Monumental Art, 1970; Dublin/Municipal, International Quadriennial (ROSC), 1971; Chicago/Contemporary, White on White, 1971–72; ICA, U. of Pennsylvania, Grids, 1972; WMAA Biennial, 1973; New York Cultural Center, 3D into 2D, 1973; Seattle/AM, American Art—Third Quarter Century, 1973; Parcheggio di Villa Borghese, Rome, Contemporanea, 1973; Art Museum of South Texas, Corpus Christi, Eight Artists, 1974; Chicago/AI, Idea and Image in Recent Art, 1974; WMAA, American Pop Art, 1974; Walker, Eight Artists, 1974; NCFA, Sculpture, American Directions 1945–1975, 1975; MOMA, Drawing Now, 1976; Chicago/AI, 1976; A.F.A., American Master Drawings and Watercolors, 1976; Cambridge, Jubilation, 1977; Minnesota/MA, American Drawing, 1927–1977, circ., 1977; Amsterdam/Stedelijk, At Second Sight, 1978; WMAA, Art About Art, circ., 1978; Buffalo/Albright, American Painting of the 1970's, circ., 1978; Corcoran Biennial, 1979. **Collections:** Amsterdam/Stedelijk; Basel; Buffalo/Albright; Cologne; Dallas/MFA; Des Moines; Hartford/Wadsworth; Hirshhorn; MOMA; Ohara Art Museum; SFMA; Seibu Museum of Art, Tokyo; Stockholm/National; Tate; Victoria and Albert Museum; WMAA. **Bibliography:** Alloway 1; Battcock, ed.; Becker and Vostell; Bihalji-Merin; Calas, N. and E.; *Contemporanea;* **Crichton**; Davis, D.; De Vries, ed.; Dienst 1; Downes, ed.; Finch; Friedman, ed.; Gablik; Honnef; Hunter, ed.; Janis and Blesh 1; Honisch and Jensen, eds.; **Kozloff 2**, 3; Johnson, Ellen H.; Licht, F.; Lippard 5; Lynton; *Metro;* Krauss 2; *Poets & Painters;* Rickey; Rodman 3; Rose, B., 1, 4; Rubin 1; Russell and Gablik; Sandler; Seitz 3; **Steinberg, L.**; Tomkins; Tomkins 2; Tomkins and Time-Life Books; Warhol and Hackett; Weller.

JOHNSON, BUFFIE. b. February 20, 1912, NYC. **Studied:** ASL; Atelier 17, Paris, with S. W. Hayter (engraving); UCLA, MA. Traveled extensively, Europe, Mexico, USA. **Taught:** Parsons School of Design, 1946–50; US State Department lecturer; UCLA; Aegina Art Center, Greece, 1973. **Member:** Artists Equity. **Commissions:** Astor Theater, NYC, 1959 (murals). **Awards:** Le Salon International de la Femme, Nice, Second Prize, 1970; Yaddo Fellowship, 1974. **Address:** 102 Greene Street, NYC 10012. **One-man Exhibitions:** (first) Jake Zeitlin Gallery, Los Angeles, 1937; Galerie Rotge, Paris, 1939; Wakefield Gallery, NYC, 1939; Vose Gallery, Boston, 1942; Caresse Crosby, Washington, D.C., 1944; "67" Gallery, NYC, 1945; Ringling, 1948; Galleria del Cavallino, Venice, 1948; Hanover Gallery, 1949; Galerie Colette Allendy, Paris, 1949; Betty Parsons Gallery, 1950; Choate School, Wallingford, Conn., 1951; Galleries Bing, Paris, 1956, 60; Bodley Gallery, NYC, 1960; Thibaut Gallery, NYC, 1961; Granville Gallery, NYC, 1964; Galeria Antonio Souza, Mexico City, 1964; Max Hutchinson Gallery, 1973; Palm Beach Gallery, Palm Beach, Fla., 1975; New School for Social Research; Andre Zarre Gallery, NYC; Stamford Museum. **Group:** Carnegie, 1941; Art of This Century, NYC, 1943;

Salon des Realites Nouvelles, Paris, 1949, 50; Baltimore/MA; Walker; Brooklyn Museum, 1950, 54; WMAA; U. of Illinois, 1955; Kunsthaus, Hamburg, American Women Artists, 1972; New York Cultural Center, Women Choose Women, 1973; WMAA Biennial; Cranbrook, Waves, 1974. **Collections:** Baltimore/MA; Bezalel Museum; Boston/MFA; Brooklyn Museum; Calcutta; Ciba-Geigy Corp.; Cincinnati/AM; City Investing Corp; Cornell U.; U. of Illinois; International Nickel Co.; Layton School of Art; U. of Michigan; NCFA; NYU; Newark Museum; U. of New Mexico; The Ohio State U.; Purchase/SUNY; RISD; Santa Barbara/MA; SRGM; U. of Texas; Utica; Valley Bank of Springfield; WMAA; Walker; Yale U. **Bibliography:** Archives.

JOHNSON, LESTER. b. January 27, 1919, Minneapolis, Minn. **Studied:** Minneapolis Institute School (with Alexander Masley, Glen Mitchell), St. Paul School of Art (with Cameron Booth), Chicago Art Institute School, 1942–47. Traveled Europe. **Taught:** St. Bernard School, NYC, 1955–61; The Ohio State U., 1963; U. of Wisconsin, 1964; School of Visual Arts, NYC, 1964; Yale U., 1964– ; American Center, Paris, summer, 1966; Director of Studies, Graduate Painting, Yale U., 1969–74. **Awards:** Alfred Pillsbury Scholarship; St. Paul Gallery Scholarship; Midwestern Artists Competition, First Prize, 1942; Guggenheim Foundation Fellowship, 1973; Brandeis U., Creative Arts Award, Painting, 1978. **Address:** % Dealer. **Dealer:** Gimpel & Weitzenhoffer Ltd., NYC. **One-man Exhibitions:** (first) Artists' Gallery, NYC, 1951; Korman Gallery, NYC, 1954; The Zabriskie Gallery, 1955, 57, 58, 59, 61; Sun Gallery, Provincetown, 1956–59; City Gallery, NYC, 1959; HCE Gallery, Provincetown, 1960–62; Minneapolis/Institute, 1961; B.C. Holland Gallery, 1962; Dayton/AI, 1962; Fort Worth; The Ohio State U.; Martha Jackson Gallery, NYC, 1962, 63, 66, 69, 71, 73, 74, 75;

Donald Morris Gallery, Detroit, 1965, 74; 78; Smithsonian, 1968; Alpha Gallery, 1972; Gallery Moos, Toronto, 1973; Richard Gray Gallery, 1973; Ruth S. Schaffner Gallery, Santa Barbara, 1973, 74; Smith-Andersen Gallery, Palo Alto, 1974; Peter M. David Gallery, Minneapolis, 1974, 78; Livingstone-Learmonth Gallery, NYC, 1975; U. of Connecticut, Storrs, 1975; Alpha Gallery, Boston, 1976; Gimpel & Weitzenhoffer Ltd., NYC, 1977, 80; Gallery Moos Ltd., Toronto, 1977; Ruth S. Schaffner Gallery, Los Angeles, 1978; Louisiana State U., 1979; Gimpel Fils, London, 1979; Gimpel-Hanover, Zurich, 1980; Galerie Andre Emmerich, Zurich, 1980. **Group:** PAFA; Minneapolis/Institute; Jewish Museum, The New York School, Second Generation, 1957; Minneapolis/Institute, American Painting, 1945–57; 1957; Baltimore/MA, Critics Choice, 1958; WMAA, 1958; 68, Annual, 1967; ICA, Boston, 100 Works on Paper, circ., Europe, 1959; A.F.A., The Figure, circ., 1960; ICA, Boston, Future Classics, 1960; A.F.A., Graphics '60, 1960; Carnegie, 1961, 68; MOMA, Recent Amer-

Lester Johnson   *Street Scene*   1979

ican Painting and Sculpture, circ., USA and Canada, 1961–62; Chicago/AI, Recent Trends in Painting, USA, 1962; MOMA, Recent Painting USA, The Figure, circ., 1962–62; Lehigh U., 1967; MOMA, The 1960's, 1967; Dublin/Municipal, I International Quadrennial (ROSC), 1967; U. of Kentucky, 1968; Madrid/Nacional, II Biennial, 1969; Star Turtle Gallery, NYC, The Tenants of Sam Wapnowitz, 1969; Philadelphia Art Alliance, 1969; Smithsonian, Neue Figuration USA, circ., 1969; Brooklyn Museum Print Biennial, 1970; Carnegie, 1970; U. of North Carolina, Works on Paper, 1971; SRGM, 10 Independents, 1972; Chicago/AI, 70th American Exhibition, 1972; Minnesota/MA, 1973; WMAA, 1973; NAD, 1974; Indianapolis, 1976; Provincetown Art Association, Provincetown Artists, 1977; Chicago/AI, 100 Years—100 Artists, 1979; Oklahoma, Masters of the Portrait, 1979. **Collections:** U. of Arizona; Baltimore/MA; Buffalo/Albright; California College of Arts and Crafts; Chase Manhattan Bank; Ciba-Geigy Corp.; Dayton/AI, Goldring International; Hirshhorn; Hartford/Wadsworth; MOMA; NCFA; U. of Nebraska; New School for Social Research; Norfolk/Chrysler; Northwestern U.; Ohio State U.; Philip Morris Collection; Phoenix; Purchase/SUNY; SRGM; Smithsonian; Stony Brook/SUNY; Tulsa/Philbrook; U.S. Steel Corp.; Walker; U. of Wisconsin; Yale U. **Bibliography:** Sandler 1.

JOHNSON, RAY. b. October 16, 1927, Detroit, Mich. **Studied:** ASL; Black Mountain College (with Josef Albers, Robert Motherwell, Mary Callery, Ossip Zadkine), 1945–48. **Member:** American Abstract Artists, 1949–52. Operates the New York Correspondence School. **Awards:** NIAL Grant, $2,000, 1966; National Endowment for the Arts, 1976, 77; CAPS, 1977. **Address:** 44 West Seventh Street, Locust Valley, NY 11560. **Dealer:** Brooks Jackson Gallery Iolas, NYC. **One-man Exhibitions:** (first) The

Willard Gallery, 1965, also 1966, 67; Richard Feigen Gallery, Chicago, 1966, NYC, 1968, 70, 71; Wooster Community Art Center, Danbury, Conn., 1968; Kunstmarkt, Cologne, 1968; U. of Virginia, 1968; U. of British Columbia (two-man), 1969; Boylston Print Center Gallery, Cambridge, Mass.; U. of Sacramento, 1969; WMAA, New York Correspondence School, 1970; Betty Parsons Gallery, 1972; Angela Flowers Gallery, London, 1972; Jacob's Ladder Gallery, Washington, D.C., 1972; Chicago/AI, Correspondence Show, 1972; Marion Locks Gallery, Philadelphia, 1973; Gertrude Kasle Gallery, 1975; Massimo Valsecchi Gallery, Milan, 1975; Brooks Jackson Gallery Iolas, NYC, 1978; Sid Deutsch Gallery, NYC, 1976. **Retrospective:** Raleigh/NCMA, 1976. **Group:** American Abstract Artists, 1949–52; MOMA, Art in the Mirror, 1966; Chicago/Contemporary, Pictures to be Read/Poetry to be Seen, 1967; Finch College, NYC; A.F.A., circ., 1967; Hayward Gallery, London, Pop Art, 1969; U. of British Columbia, Concrete Poetry, 1969; Fort Worth, Drawings, 1969; Dallas/MFA, Poets of the Cities, 1974. **Collections:** Chicago/AI; Dulin Gallery; Houston/MFA; Lincoln, Mass./De Cordova; MOMA. **Bibliography:** Alloway 4; Becker and Vostell; *Correspondence;* Hansen; *Happening & Fluxus;* Ruhe; Russell and Gablik. Archives.

JOHNSTON, YNEZ. b. May 12, 1920, Berkeley, Calif. **Studied:** U. of California, Berkeley, BA, 1946, MA. Traveled Europe, USA, India, England, Italy, Japan. **Taught:** Colorado Springs Fine Arts Center, summers, 1945, 55; U. of California, Berkeley, 1950–51; Otis Art Institute. **Commissions:** International Graphic Arts Society, 1958, 60. **Awards:** Guggenheim Foundation Fellowship, 1952; MMA; 1952; L.C. Tiffany Grant, 1955; SFMA, James D. Phelan Award, 1958; Tamarind Fellowship, 1966; National Endowment for the Arts, grant, 1976. **Address:** 569 Crane Boulevard,

Los Angeles, CA 90065. **Dealers:** Jodi Scully Gallery; Van Straaten Gallery; Graphics Gallery; Mekler Gallery, Los Angeles; Worthington Gallery, Inc., Chicago. **One-man Exhibitions:** SFMA, 1943; U. of Redlands, 1947; American Contemporary Gallery, Hollywood, 1948; Fraymont Gallery, Los Angeles, 1952; Chicago/AI, 1952 (two-man); Santa Barbara/MA, 1952, 57; Paul Kantor Gallery, Beverly Hills, Calif., 1952, 53, 57, 58, 59, 64; Pasadena/AM, 1954; Colorado Springs/FA, 1955; California Palace, 1956; Ohana Gallery, London, 1958; California State U., Long Beach, 1967; Moore Galleries, Inc., San Francisco, 1968; Benjamin Galleries, Chicago, 1969; Jodi Scully Gallery, 1971, 72, 74; Tokyo-Shoten Gallery, NYC, 1976; Elizabeth Weiner Gallery, NYC, 1977; Mitsukoshi Gallery, Tokyo, 1977; Cornell U., 1978; Mekler Gallery, Los Angeles, 1978; Ericson Gallery, NYC, 1979; Worthington Galleries, Inc., Chicago, 1979. **Retrospective:** Mount San Antonio College, 1974. **Group:** WMAA, 1951–55; U. of Illinois, 1951–54; Carnegie, 1955; SFMA; Los Angeles/County MA; MOMA, New Talent; Ohio U., Ultimate Concerns, 1968; Palazzo Strozzi, Florence, Italy, I Biennale Internazionale della Grafica, 1968; California State U., Los Angeles, Small Images, 1969; California Institute of Technology, Pasadena, Four Printmakers, 1969; U. of Kentucky, Graphics '71, 1971; International Exhibitions Foundation, Washington, D.C., Tamarind; A Renaissance of Lithography, circ., 1971–72; Scripps College, California Women Artists, 1972; SFMA, Painting and Sculpture in California: The Modern Era, 1976; SFMA, World Print, 1977; College of St. Rose, Albany, N.Y., Drawing Invitational, 1980. **Collections:** Albion College; California State U., Los Angeles; Cedars-Sinai Medical Center, Los Angeles; Cornell U.; Hartford/Wadsworth; Hirshhorn; U. of Illinois; La Jolla; Los Angeles/County MA; MMA; MOMA; Michigan State U.; U. of Michigan; Milwaukee; Montclair/AM; Oakland; PMA; Pasadena/AM;

RISD; St. Louis/City; San Diego; Santa Barbara/MA; Schaeffer School of Design; Tulsa/Philbrook; Tusculum College; WMAA. **Bibliography:** Pousette-Dart, ed.

JONES, HOWARD W. b. June 20, 1922, Ilion, N.Y. **Studied:** Syracuse U., BFA cum laude, 1948; Columbia U.; Cranbrook. USAAF, World War II. Traveled Europe, Near and Middle East, North Africa. **Taught:** Tulane U., 1951–54; Florida State U., 1954–56; Washington U. (St. Louis), 1957–80; Yale U., 1967. Subject of TV film *Artist in America: Howard Jones.* **Commissions:** WMAA, 1968; Kansas City/Nelson, 1968. **Awards:** *Art in America* (magazine), New Talent, 1966; Graham Foundation Fellowship, 1966–67; Syracuse U., Roswell S. Hill Prize; Syracuse U., four-year scholarship; National Endowment for the Arts, grant, 1977. **Address:** 12 North Newstead, St. Louis, MO 63108. **One-man Exhibitions:** Utica; Mitchell Gallery, Woodstock, N.Y.; Florida State U.; Fairmont Gallery, St. Louis, 1961; H. Balaban Carp Gallery, St. Louis, 1963; Kansas City/Nelson, 1965; Royal Marks Gallery, 1966; The Howard Wise Gallery, 1968, 70; Electric Gallery, Toronto, 1971; St. Louis/City, 1973; Kansas City/Nelson, 1973; Hartford/Wadsworth, 1974; Forbes Magazine Foundation, NYC, 1976. **Group:** Kansas City/Nelson, Sound, Light, Silence, 1966; ICA, Boston, 1966; Worcester/AM, 1967; Flint/Institute, 1967; U. of Illinois, 1967; Walker and Milwaukee, Light Motion Space, 1967; ICA, London, circ., 1968; Milwaukee, Directions I:Options, circ., 1968; WMAA, Light: Object and Image, 1968; Kansas City/Nelson, The Magic Theatre, 1968; La Jolla, 1969; Jewish Museum, Superlimited, 1969; Hayward Gallery, London, Kinetics, 1970; Princeton U., American Art since 1960, 1970; Rockefeller U., Kinetic Art, 1970; PMA, Multiples, 1971; Trenton/State, Responsive Environment, 1972; Memphis/Brooks, Recent Media—Ten Years,

1977; Huntsville Museum of Art, Alabama, Art of the Space Era, 1978. **Collections:** Buffalo/Albright; Jewish Museum; Kansas City/Nelson, Memphis/Brooks; Milwaukee; NCFA: Princeton U.; Ridgefield/Aldrich; St. Louis/City; Walker; Washington U. (St. Louis). **Bibliography:** Atkinson.

JONES, JOHN PAUL. b. November 18, 1924, Indianola, Iowa. **Studied:** State U. of Iowa, 1949, BFA, 1951, MFA. Traveled Europe; resided Great Britain, 1960–61. **Taught:** U. of Oklahoma, 1951–52; State of Iowa, 1952–53; UCLA, 1953–63; U. of California, Irvine 1969– . **Awards:** L. C. Tiffany Grant, 1951; Guggenheim Foundation Fellowship, 1960; and more than 40 others. **Address:** 22370 Third Avenue, South Laguna, CA 92677. **Dealer:** Makler Gallery, Los Angeles. **One-man Exhibitions:** Iowa Wesleyan College, 1951; Des Moines, 1951; Fort Dodge/Blanden, 1951; San Antonio/McNay, 1951; U. of Oklahoma, 1952; Los Angeles/County MA, 1954 (two-man); Kalamazoo/Institute, 1955; Oakland/AM, 1956; Felix Landau Gallery, 1956, 58, 62, 64, 67, 70; Laguna Blanca School, Santa Barbara, 1958; Santa Barbara/MA, 1958; Pasadena/AM, 1959; Taft College, 1959; Galleria Cadario, 1961; Arizona State U., 1962; U. of Minnesota, 1963; U. of Nebraska, 1963; Terry Dintenfass, Inc., 1963, 65; Louisville/Speed, 1964; San Jose State College, 1965; Container Corp. of America, 1965; Brook Street Gallery, London, 1965; The Landau-Alan Gallery, NYC, 1967, 69; La Jolla, 1970; Graphics Gallery, 1973; Jodi Scully Gallery, 1973, 75; Charles Campbell Gallery, 1974; U. of California, Riverside, 1975. **Retrospectives:** Brooklyn Museum, 1963; Los Angeles/County MA, 1965. **Group:** Youngstown/Butler; U. of Illinois; State U. of Iowa; MOMA; WMAA; Oakland/AM; Santa Barbara/MA; SFMA; Pasadena/AM; Library of Congress; Brooklyn Museum; U. of Minnesota. **Collections:** Achenbach Foundation; Ball State U.; Bibliotheque

Nationale; Bradley U.; Brooklyn Museum; U. of Calgary; California State Fair; UCLA; Coos Bay; Dallas/MFA; Des Moines; Fort Dodge/Blanden; U. of Illinois; Iowa State Fair; Iowa Wesleyan College; State U. of Iowa; Kalamazoo/Institute; Kansas City/Nelson; Kansas State College; Karachi; Kentucky Southern College; La Jolla; Library of Congress; Los Angeles/County MA; Lytton Savings and Loan Association; MOMA; Michigan State U.; Minnesota/MA; NYPL; National Gallery; U. of Nebraska; Oakland/AM; Omaha/Joslyn; Otis Art Institute; Palomar College; Pasadena/AM; SFMA; San Diego; Santa Barbara/MA; Seattle/AM; Texas Western College; Tulane U.; Utica; Victoria and Albert Museum; Walker; Youngstown/Butler.

JUDD, DON. b. June 3, 1928, Excelsior Springs, Mo. **Studied:** College of William and Mary, 1948–49; Columbia U., BS, 1949–53, MFA; ASL, with Johnson, Stewart Klonis, Robert Beverly Hale, Louis Bouche, Will Barnet. Traveled western Europe, southwestern USA. **Taught:** Allen Stevenson School, 1957–61; Hunter College, 1966; Yale U., 1967. **Awards:** Swedish Institute Grant, 1965; U.S. Government Grant, 1967; Guggenheim Foundation Fellowship, 1968. **Address:** 101 Spring Street, NYC 10012; Box 218, Marsa, TX 79843. **Dealers:** Leo Castelli Inc.; Ileana Sonnabend Gallery, Paris; Galerie Rudolf Zwirner. **One-man Exhibitions:** (first) Green Gallery, NYC, 1964; Leo Castelli Inc., 1966, 67; WMAA, 1968; Ileana Sonnabend Gallery, Paris, 1969; Galerie Rudolf Zwirner, 1969; Eindhoven, 1970; Joseph Helman Gallery, St. Louis, 1970; Essen, 1970; Hannover/Kunstverein, 1970; Whitechapel Art Gallery, London, 1970; Locksley-Shea Gallery, 1970, 73; Janie C. Lee Gallery: Dallas, 1970, Houston, 1976; Galerie Heiner Friedrich, Munich, 1971, 78; Ronald Greenberg Gallery, St. Louis, 1972; Galerie Rolf Ricke, 1972; Leo Castelli Inc., NYC, 1973, 76, 78, 79; Galerie

Daniel Templon, Paris, 1973, 75; Gian Enzo Sperone and Galerie Konrad Fischer, Rome, 1973; Gian Enzo Sperone, Turin, 1973; Galerie Annemarie Verna, Zurich, 1973, 79; Lisson Gallery, London, 1974, 75; Portland (Ore.) Center for the Visual Arts, 1974; Basel, circ., 1976; Sable-Castelli Gallery Ltd., Toronto, 1976; Heiner Friedrich Gallery, NYC, 1977, 78; Corpus Christi, 1977; Cincinnati/Contemporary, 1977; Heiner Friedrich, Cologne, 1977, 79; Moderne Galerie, Bottrop (Switzerland), 1977; ACE Gallery, Venice, Calif., 1977; Berlin/National, 1978; Foyer MGB, Zurich, 1978; Vancouver, 1978; Kroller Muller, Otterlo, 1978; Young-Hoffman Gallery, Chicago, 1978; Eindhoven, 1979; Akron/AI, 1979; Thomas Segal Gallery, Boston, 1979. **Retrospective:** WMAA; Ottawa/National, 1975. **Group:** VIII Sao Paulo Biennial, 1965; ICA, U. of Pennsylvania, 1965; Stockholm/National, 1965; Jewish Museum, Primary Structures, 1966; WMAA, Contemporary American Sculpture, Selection I, 1966; Walker, 1966; WMAA Sculpture Annual, 1966, 68; Los Angeles/County MA, American Sculpture of the Sixties, 1967; Detroit/Institute, Color, Image and Form, 1967; WGMA, A New Aesthetic, 1967; SRGM, Sculpture International, 1967; Walker, 1969; Vancouver, 1969; Expo '70, Osaka, 1970; Indianapolis, 1970; Princeton U., American Art since 1960, 1970; Brooklyn Museum, Attitudes, 1970; Cincinnati/Contemporary, Monumental Art, 1970; WMAA, 1970, 73; SRGM, Guggenheim International, 1971; Dub-lin/Municipal, International Quadriennial (ROSC), 1971; High Museum, The Modern Image, 1972; Rijksmuseum Kroller-Muller, Diagrams and Drawings, 1972; New York Cultural Center, 3D into 2D, 1973; Musée Galliera, Paris, Festival d'Automne, 1973; Parcheggio di Villa Borghese, Rome, Contemporanea, 1974; Art Museum of South Texas, Corpus Christi, Eight Artists, 1974; Cologne/Kunstverein, Kunst uber Kunst, 1974; Otterlo, Functions of Drawing, 1975; NCFA, Sculpture: American Direction, 1945–1975, 1975; MOMA, Drawing Now, 1976; MOMA, Oxford, Eng. (four-man), 1976; WMAA, 200 Years of American Sculpture, 1976; Dallas/MFA, American Art since 1945, 1976; Venice Biennial, 1976; Cambridge U., Jubilation, 1977; U. of Chicago, Ideas in Sculpture, 1965–1977, 1977; Kansas City/AI, Project Drawings, 1978; WMAA, 20th Century American Masters of the 60s and 70s, 1978; ICA, Boston, The Reductive Object, 1979. **Collections:** Chicago/AI; Detroit/Institute; Los Angeles/County MA; MOMA; Pasadena/AM; St. Louis/City; WMAA; Walker. **Bibliography:** Alloway 4; *Art Now 74*; Battcock ed.; *Black and White Are Colors*; Calas, N. and E.; *Contemporanea*; Davis, D.; De Vries, ed.; Friedman, M. 2; Friedman and van der Marck; Gablik; Goossen 1; Honnef; Honisch and Jensen, eds.; Hunter, ed.; Johnson, Ellen H.; Kozloff 3; Krauss 2; Lippard 3, 4, 5; Lucie-Smith; MacAgy 2; *Report*; Rickey; Rose, B., 4; Sandler 1; **Smith., B.,** 1975; Trier 1; Tuchman 1. Archives.

K

KABAK, ROBERT. b. February 15,
1930, NYC. **Studied:** Brooklyn College,
with Burgoyne Diller, Mark Rothko, Ad
Reinhardt, Alfred Russell, Robert
Wolff, 1952, BA; Yale U., with Josef
Albers, Abraham Rattner, Ad Rein-
hardt, 1954, MFA. Traveled France,
Great Britain, Netherlands, USA.
Taught: Greenport (N.Y.) Public
Schools, 1953–54, P.S. 108, Queens
(N.Y.), 1954–56; High School of Music
and Art, NYC, 1956–60; Brooklyn Col-
lege, 1960–62; U. of California,
Berkeley, 1962–66; Northern Illinois U.,
1968–73; U. of Missouri, 1973–
Awards: MacDowell Colony Fellow-
ship, 1956, 57, 59, 60, 61, 62, 67–68;
Huntington Hartford Foundation, 1960,
61, 63; Yaddo Fellowship, 1961; U. of
California Institute for Creative Works
in the Arts, 1965–66. **Address:** 306 Hitt
Street, Columbia, MO 65201. **One-man
Exhibitions:** The Salpeter Gallery,
1958; Nonagon Gallery, NYC, 1960; An-
geleski Gallery, NYC, 1960, 61; Osgood
Gallery, NYC, 1962; Gump's Gallery,
1963; SFMA (two-man), 1964; U. of
California, 1966; Oakland/AM—Kaiser
Center, 1966; Betty Parsons Gallery,
1967; Allan Stone Gallery, 1968; Rogue
Gallery, Medford, Ore., 1968; Lower
Columbia Junior College, 1968; Western
Washington State College, 1968; Che-
ney Cowles Memorial Museum,
Spokane, 1969; Oregon State U., 1969;
Wisconsin State U., 1970; Northern Illinois U., 1970, 71, 74; Idaho State U.,
1970; Linfield College, 1970; U. of South
Dakota, 1970; Northern Arizona U.,
1971; Gallery of Modern Art, Taos,
1971; Artium Orbis, Santa Fe, 1972; U.
of Missouri, 1974, 75, 77, 80; Stephens
College, 1976; Columbia Art League,

Mo., 1976; Springfield Art Association,
Ill., 1978. **Group:** MOMA, New Talent;
WMAA Annuals, 1956, 58; U. of Illi-
nois, 1959; California Palace, 1964; State
U. of Iowa; U. of Nebraska; Southern
Illinois U.; Carnegie, 1967; Santa Fe,
NM, 1977. **Collections:** MOMA; Santa
Fe, N.M.

KACERE, JOHN. b. June 23, 1920,
Walker, Iowa. **Studied:** Mizen Academy of Art, Chicago, 1938–42; State U.
of Iowa, BFA, 1946–49, MFA, 1950–51.
Taught: State U. of Iowa, 1949–50
(graduate assistant to Mauricio Lasansky); U. of Manitoba, 1950–53; U. of
Florida, 1953–65; Cooper Union; Parsons School of Design, NYC; U. of New
Mexico. **Address:** 152 Wooster Street,
NYC 10013. **Dealer:** OK Harris Works
of Art. **One-man Exhibitions:** The Little Art Gallery, Cedar Rapids, Iowa,
1942; U. of Florida, 1953, 57; Korman
Gallery, NYC, 1954; Mirell Gallery,
Miami, Fla., 1955; Cedar Rapids/AA,
1955; The Zabriskie Gallery, 1956; Louisiana State U., 1957; Allan Stone Gallery, 1963; OK Harris Works of Art,
1971, 73, 75, 78; Galerie de Gestlo,
Hamburg, 1972, 73. **Group:** Walker,
circ., USA, Canada, South America,
1949–51; MOMA; Chicago/AI; PMA;
Omaha/Joslyn; Dallas/MFA; Ringling;
Jacksonville/AM; U. of Georgia; Corcoran, 1963; U. of Illinois, 1965; John
Michael Kohler Arts Center, Sheboygan, The Human Image, 1970; Chi-
cago/Contemporary, Radical Realism,
1971; Cleveland/MA, 32 Realists, 1972;
MOMA, The Realist Revival, 1972;
Stuttgart/WK, Amerikanischer Fotorealismus, circ., 1972; Lincoln, Mass./

De Cordova, The Super-Realist Vision, 1973; Tokyo Biennial, 1974; Chicago/AI, 1974; Wichita State U., Photo-Realism, 1975; Xerox Art Exhibition, Rochester, N.Y., Unordinary Realities, 1975; WMAA, downtown branch, Nothing but Nudes, 1977. **Collections:** Amsterdam/Stedelijk; Brandeis U.; Hartford/ Wadsworth; Mt. Holyoke College; Yale U. **Bibliography:** *Amerikanischer Fotorealismus;* Honisch and Jensen, eds.; Hunter, ed.; Sager.

KAHN, WOLF. b. October 4, 1927, Stuttgart, Germany. To Great Britain, 1939; to USA, 1940. **Studied:** Hofmann School, 1947–49; The U. of Chicago, 1950–51, BA. Traveled Europe, Mexico, USA. **Taught:** U. of California, Berkeley, 1960; Cooper Union, 1961– ; Haystack School, Deer Isle, Me., 1961, 62; Columbia U. 1978; RISD, 1978–79. **Member:** Associate, NAD. **Commissions:** Jewish Theological Seminary, NYC (portraits). **Awards:** Ford Foundation, **P.P.**, 1962; Fulbright Fellowship, 1962, 64; J.S. Guggenheim Fellowship, 1966–67; NAD, Ranger Fund, **P.P.**, 1977; AAAL, Childe Hassam Fund, **P.P.**, 1978, AAAL, Award, 1979. **Address:** 813 Broadway, NYC 10003. **Dealers:** Grace Borgenicht Gallery Inc.; Meredith Long Gallery. **One-man Exhibitions:** (first) Hansa Gallery, NYC, 1953, also 1954; Grace Borgenicht Gallery, Inc., 1956, 58, 60, 61, 62, 65, 67, 69, 71, 73, 74, 75, 77, 79; U. of California, 1960; U. of Michigan, 1961; Ellison Gallery, Fort Worth, 1961; RISD, 1961; 79; Kansas City/Nelson 1962; Michigan State U., 1963; Stewart Richard Gallery, San Antonio, 1964; Obelisk Gallery, 1964; Nashville, 1964; Sabarsky Gallery, Los Angeles, 1966; Marlboro College, 1967; Princeton Gallery of Fine Art, 1970, 72, 74, 75; Meredith Long Gallery, Houston, 1971, 73, 74, 76, 77, 78, 80; Harcus Krakow Rosen Sonnabend, 1972; U. of Nebraska, 1973; Norfolk/ Chrysler, 1973; Rudolph Galleries, Coral Gables, 1974; David Barnett Gallery, Milwaukee, 1978; L. Kornbluth

Gallery, Fairlawn, N.J., 1978; Harcus Krakow Gallery, Boston, 1976. **Group:** The Stable Gallery Annuals, 1954, 55; WMAA Annuals, 1958, 60, 61; Utica, 1959; ART: USA 59, NYC, 1959; WMAA, Young America, 1960; International Biennial Exhibition of Paintings, Tokyo; SFMA, 1961; PAFA, 1961, 65; American Art Gallery, Copenhagen, 1963; MOMA, Hans Hofmann and His Students, circ., 1963–64; Omaha/Joslyn, A Sense of Place, 1973; IIE, 20 American Fulbright Artists, 1975; US Department of the Interior, America 1976. **Collections:** Brandeis U; Brooklyn Museum; U. of California; Chase Manhattan Bank; Corcoran; Los Angeles County/ MA; MMA; Dallas/MFA; Fort Worth; Houston/MFA; ICA, Boston; U. of Illinois; Jewish Museum; Lincoln Life Insurance Co.; Springfield, Mass./MFA; MOMA; U. of Massachusetts; Michigan State U.; U. of Nebraska; U. of Nevada; St. Louis/City; Union Carbide Corp; VMFA; WMAA. **Bibliography:** Blesh 1; Downes, ed. Archives.

KAISH, LUISE. b. September 8, 1925, Atlanta, Ga. **Studied:** Syracuse U., with Ivan Mestrovic, BFA, MFA; Escuela de Pintura y Escultura, Mexico City, with Alfredo Zalce, J.G. Galvan. Traveled Europe, Scandinavia, Italy, Israel, Middle East. **Taught:** Columbia U., 1974–75; Dartmouth College, 1974; U. of Washington, Seattle, 1979. **Member:** Sculptors Guild; Trustee, American Academy in Rome, 1973–; Trustee, The Augustus Saint Gaudens Memorial, National Park Service, 1978– ; executive board, The Sculptors Guild, 1974– . **Commissions:** Temple B'rith Kodesh, Rochester, N.Y.; Container Corp. of America; Syracuse U.; Amoco Building, NYC; Jewish Museum; Temple Beth Shalom, Washington, Del.; Temple Israel, Westport, Conn.; Holy Trinity Mission Seminary, Silver Spring, Md.; Beth El Synagogue Center, New Rochelle, N.Y.; Temple B'nai Abraham, Essex County, N.J.; U.A.H.C., Jerusalem, Israel. **Awards:**

Guggenheim Foundation Fellowship; L.C. Tiffany Grant; Audubon Artists, Medal; Ball State Teachers College, **P.P.**; Joe and Emily Lowe Foundation Award; National Association of Women Artists; U. of Rochester; Syracuse/Everson; American Academy, Rome, Fellowship, 1970–71. **Address:** 610 West End Avenue, NYC 10024. **Dealer:** Staempfli Gallery. **One-man Exhibitions:** U. of Rochester, 1954; Sculpture Center, NYC, 1955, 58; Staempfli Gallery, NYC, 1968, 1981; St. Paul Gallery, 1969; Dartmouth College (two-man), 1974. **Retrospective:** Jewish Museum, 1973. **Group:** MMA, National Sculpture Exhibition, 1951; WMAA, 1955, 62, 64, 66; MOMA, Recent Sculpture USA, 1959; U. of Nebraska; Ball State Teachers College; U. of Notre Dame; Ohio U.; NAD; Sculptors Guild; Buffalo/Albright; AAAL; Newark Museum, Women Artists of America, 1966; U. of Illinois, 1968; New School for Social Research, Drawings by Painters and Sculptors, 1967; U. of Nebraska, American Sculpture, 1970; Minnesota/MA, Drawings, USA, 1970; Finch College, NYC, Artists at Work, 1970; USIS, Rome, 1973; Minnesota/MA, Drawings USA, 1976. **Collections:** Export Khleb, Moscow; General Mills Corp., Minneapolis; High Museum; Jewish Museum; U. of Miami; Minnesota/MA; U. of Rochester; Syracuse U.; WMAA.

KAMIHIRA, BEN. b. March 16, 1925, Yakima, Wash. **Studied:** Art Institute of Pittsburgh; PAFA, 1948–52. US Army, 1944–47. **Taught:** The Pennsylvania State U.; Philadelphia Museum School; PAFA, 1953– . **Awards:** PAFA, Cresson Fellowship, 1951; PAFA, J. Henry Schiedt Scholarship, 1952; NAD, Hallgarten Prize, 1952; L.C. Tiffany Grant, 1952, 58; Guggenheim Foundation Fellowship, 1955, 56; PAFA, Walter Lippincott Prize, 1958; NAD, Benjamin Altman Prize, 1958, 62; Corcoran, First William A. Clark Prize, 1961; NAD, Gold Nedal, 1975. **Address:** % Peale House, 1811 Chestnut, Philadelphia,

PA 19103. **One-man Exhibitions:** Dubin Gallery, Philadelphia, 1952; Philadelphia Art Alliance, 1954; PAFA, 1956; Janet Nessler Gallery, NYC, 1951; Durlacher Brothers, NYC, 1964; The Forum Gallery, NYC, 1966, 73, 76; Maxwell Gallery, San Francisco, 1969. **Group:** NAD, 1952, 54, 56, 58, 61; Youngstown/Butler, 1953, 1958–61; PAFA, 1954, 58, 60; WMAA, 1958; Corcoran, 1961; PAFA, Seven on the Figure, 1979. **Collections:** Colorado Springs/FA; Dallas/MFA; NAD; PAFA; Ringling; WMAA. **Bibliography:** Goodrich and Baur 1.

KAMROWSKI, GEROME. b. January 29, 1914, Warren, Minn. **Studied:** St. Paul School of Art, with L. Turner, Cameron Booth; ASL; Hofmann School. **Taught:** U. of Michigan, 1946– . Federal A.P.: mural painting in Minnesota and New York. **Awards:** Guggenheim Foundation Fellowship; Detroit/Institute, 1949, 54, 55, 61, Merit Prize, 1967; Cranbrook, Horace H. Rackham Research Grant, 1957. **Address:** 1501 Beechwood Drive, Ann Arbor, MI 48103. **Dealer:** Monique Knowlton Gallery. **One-man Exhibitions:** Mortimer Brandt, NYC, 1946; Betty Parsons Gallery, 1948; Alexander Iolas Gallery, Galerie Creuze, Paris, 1950, 58; Hugo Gallery, NYC, 1951; U. of Michigan, 1952, 59, 61; The Saginaw Museum, 1954; Jackson Art Association; Cranbrook, 1947; Gallery Mayer, NYC, 1961; S.W. Wind Gallery, Ann Arbor; Eastern Michigan U. (Two-man); Monique Knowlton Gallery, NYC, 1978. **Group:** Chicago/AI, 1945, 46; Buffalo/Albright, 1946; Galerie Maeght, 6 American Painters, 1947; WMAA Annuals, 1947, 48, 51, 53; Detroit/Institute, 1948, 50, 52, 54, 58; U. of Illinois, 1950; Sidney Janis Gallery, Surrealist and Abstract Art; MOMA; SRGM; U. of Michigan (four-man); 12 Canadian and American Painters, NYC; Hayward Gallery, London, Dada and Surrealism Revisited, 1978; Rutgers U., Surrealism and American Art, 1931–1947, 1947; U. of New Mexico, American Abstract Artists, 1977; MMA, Hans Hofmann as a Teacher, 1979. **Collections:** Detroit/Institute; Flint/Institute; Simon Frazer U.; Knoll Associates, Inc.; MMA; MOMA; Minnesota/MA; U. of New Mexico; U. of North Carolina; Phillips; WMAA. **Bibliography:** Baur 7; Breton 3; Calas; Janis, S.; Ritchie 1.

KAMYS, WALTER. b. June 8, 1917, Chicago, Ill. **Studied:** Chicago Art Institute School, 1943, with Hubert Ropp, Boris Anisfeld, privately in Mexico with Gordon Onslow-Ford, 1944. Traveled Mexico, Europe. **Taught:** The Putney School, Vermont, 1945; G. W. V. Smith Art Museum, Springfield, Mass., 1947–60; U. of Massachusetts, 1960– . Director, Art Acquisition Program, U. of Massachusetts Collection, 1962–74. **Awards:** Prix de Rome, 1942; Chicago/AI, Anna Louise Raymond Fellowship, 1942–43; Chicago/AI, Paul Trebilcock **P.P.**, 1943; Chicago/AI, James Nelson Raymond Traveling Fellowship, 1943–44; Boston Arts Festival, Second Prize, 1955; State College at Westfield, **P.P.**, 1968. **Address:** North Main Street, Sunderland, MA 01375. **One-man Exhibitions:** (first) Cliff Dwellers Club, Chicago, 1944; Dartmouth College, 1946; Margaret Brown Gallery, Boston, 1949; The Little Gallery, Springfield, Mass., 1951; Mortimer Levitt Gallery, NYC, 1954; Muriel Latow Gallery, Springfield, Mass., 1954; The Bertha Schaefer Gallery, 1955, 57, 61; Deerfield (Mass.) Academy, 1956, A Painter with a Camera (abstract photos), 1960; Concordia College, 1957; Springfield, Mass./MFA, 1948, 59; New Vision Center, London, 1960; Univision Gallery, London, 1960; U. of Massachusetts, 1961; Stanhope Gallery, Boston, 1963; Ward-Nasse Gallery, Boston, 1968; East Hampton Gallery, N.Y., 1970; Pisces Gallery, Wellfleet, Mass., 1976; Danco Gallery, Northampton, Mass., 1978. **Group:** Chicago/AI; Salon des Realities Nouvelles, Paris; PAFA; Carnegie; USIA, 20th Century American Graphics, circ.; Corcoran; ICA, Boston, Youn-

ger New England Graphic Artists, 1954; MOMA, Recent Drawings, 1956; ICA, Boston, View, 1960; Northeastern U., 1965; Silvermine Guild, 1967; Smithsonian, The Art of Organic Forms, 1968; U. of Connecticut, New England Artists, 1971; G.W.V. Smith Museum, Springfield, Mass., 1973. **Collections:** Albion College; Harvard U.; U. of Massachusetts; Mount Holyoke College; NYU; Smith College; U. of Vermont; WDAY; Westfield; Wright State U.; Yale U. **Bibliography:** Janis and Blesh 1.

KANEMITSU, MATSUMI. b. May 28, 1922, Ogden, Utah. **Studied:** Atelier Fernand Leger, Paris (painting); ASL, with Yasuo Kuniyoshi, Harry Sternberg, C.P. Austin, Byron Browne, privately with Karl Metzler in Baltimore (sculpture). US Army, 1941–46. Traveled Europe, USA, the Orient. **Taught:** Chouinard Art Institute, 1965–67; 1969–72; U. of California, Berkeley, 1966, 1970–71; Honolulu Academy School, 1967–68; Otis Art Institute, 1971; U. of California, Santa Barbara, 1972–73; California Institute of the Arts, Valencia, 1971–72. **Awards:** Ford Foundation Grant for Tamarind, 1961; Longview Foundation Grant, 1962, 64; Ford Foundation/A.F.A. Artist-in-Residence, 1964. **Address:** 854 South Berendo Street, Los Angeles, CA 90005. **Dealer:** Janus Gallery. **One-man Exhibitions:** (first) Fort Riley, Kans., 1942; Gallery 77, New Haven, 1953; Western Maryland College, 1954; Baltimore/MA, 1954; Zoe Dusanne Gallery, 1955; The New Gallery, NYC, 1957; Widdifield Gallery, NYC, 1959; Dwan Gallery, 1960, 61, 63; Stephen Radich Gallery, 1961, 62; Southern Illinois U., 1961; i Gallery, La Jolla, 1963; Akron/AI, 1964; Occidental College, 1966; U. of California, 1966; Honolulu Academy, 1967; Paul Gallery, 1967; Chouinard Art Institute, 1968; Serisawa Gallery, 1970; Michael Smith Gallery, Los Angeles, 1972; Pacific Culture Asia Museum, Pasadena, 1973; Jodi Scully Gallery, 1974. **Group:** Baltimore/MA, 1948–52; Corcoran, 1950; Chicago/AI, 1952; Academy of Fine Arts, Berlin, 1954; MOMA, 1956; WMAA, 1956; Dallas/MFA, 1960; WMAA Annual, 1962; MOMA, Art in Embassies, circ. internationally, 1963 64; MOMA, Americans 1963, circ., 1963–64. **Collections:** Akron/AI; U. of Arizona; Baltimore/MA; Baltimore/Walters; Chicago/AI; Cincinnati/AM; Corcoran; Dillard U., Fort Worth; Hall of Justice; Hiroshima State Museum; Honolulu Academy; Housatonic Community College; Kansas City/Nelson; La Jolla; Los Angeles/County MA; MOMA; NCFA; Nagoya City Hall; National Museum of Wales; U. of New Mexico; Norfolk/Chrysler; Osaka/Municipal; SFMA; Santa Barbara/MA; Tokyo/Modern; Tougaloo College; Turin/Civico; UCLA; Worcester/AM.

KANOVITZ, HOWARD. b. February 9, 1929, Fall River, Mass. **Studied:** Providence College, 1949, BS; RISD, 1949–51; ASL, Woodstock, 1951; with Yasuo Kuniyoshi; New School for Social Research, 1949–52; U. of Southern California, 1958; NYU, 1960–61. Traveled Europe, North Africa, 1956–58. **Taught:** Brooklyn College, 1961–64; Pratt Institute, 1964–66. **Address:** Box 69, Amagansett, NY 11930. **Dealer:** Alex Rosenberg Gallery, NYC. **One-man Exhibitions:** The Stable Gallery, NYC, 1962; Fall River (Mass.) Association, 1964; Jewish Museum, 1966; Waddell Gallery, 1969, 71; Everyman Gallery, NYC, 1970; M.E. Thelen Gallery, Cologne, 1970, 73; Benson Gallery, Bridgehampton, N.Y., 1970, 71, 77; Galleri Ostergren, Malmo, 1971; Hedendaagse Kunst, Utrecht, 1973; Duisburg, 1974; Stefanotty Gallery, NYC, 1975; Galerie Jollembeck, Cologne, 1977; Alex Rosenberg Gallery, NYC, 1978; Guild Hall, East Hampton, N.Y., 1978; Hamburg/Kunstverein, 1979; Akademie der Kunst, Berlin, 1979; Hannover/K-G, 1979. **Group:** Chicago/AI, 1961; U. of Illinois, 1963; WMAA, 1965, 67, 72; Riverside Museum, NYC, Paintings from the Photo, 1969; Sweden/Goteborgs, Warmwind, 1970; WMAA, 22 Realists, 1970; VMFA, American Painting, 1970; Chicago/Contemporary, Radical Realism, 1971; NIAL, 1972; Stuttgart/WK, Amerikanischer Fotorealismus, circ., 1972; Kunsthalle, Recklinghausen, Mit Kamera, Pinsel und Spritzpistole, 1973; Documenta 6, Kassel, 1977; Guild Hall, East Hampton, Aspects of Realism, 1977. **Collections:** Aachen/NG; Cologne; Duisburg; F.T.D. Association; Guild Hall, East Hampton, N.Y.; Helsinki; Indianapolis; Rotterdam; Sweden/Goteborgs; Utrecht; WMAA. **Bibliography:** *Amerikanischer Fotorealismus;* Honisch and Jensen, eds.; **Howard Kanovitz**; *Kunst um 1970;* Sager.

KANTOR, MORRIS. b. April 15, 1896, Minsk, Russia; **d.** January 30, 1974. **Studied:** Independent School of Art, with Homer Boss. **Taught:** ASL, 1934–73; U. of Michigan, 1958; Michigan State U., 1960; U. of Colorado, 1962; U. of Illinois, 1963; U. of Minnesota, Duluth, 1963; U. of New Mexico, 1964. **Member:** Federation of Modern Painters and Sculptors. Federal A.P.: Supervisor in Rockland County, N.Y. (about 6 months). **Awards:** Chicago/AI, The Mr. & Mrs. Frank G. Logan Medal, 1931; Corcoran, Third Prize, 1939; PAFA, Joseph E. Temple Gold Medal, 1940; U. of Illinois, **P.P.**, 1951; Riverside Museum, **P.P.**, 1960; National Council on the Arts, 1968. **One-man Exhibitions:** (first) Rehn Galleries, 1930, also 1932, 35, 38, 40, 43, 45, 47, 49, 53, 59; Chicago/AI, 1932; U. of Michigan, 1958; The Bertha Schaefer Gallery, 1959, 62, 65, 67; Comara Gallery, 1962; U. of Illinois, 1963; U. of Minnesota, Duluth, 1963; The Bertha Schaefer Gallery, 1971; The Zabriskie Gallery, 1971. **Retrospective:** Davenport/Municipal, 1965. **Group:** Society of Independent Artists, annually since 1920; MMA; WMAA; MOMA; Brooklyn Museum; PAFA; Newark Museum; Chicago/AI; Corcoran; XXIV Venice

Biennial, 1948; III International Biennial Exhibition of Prints, Tokyo, 1962; Smithsonian, 1966; U. of New Mexico, 1967. **Collections:** U. of Arizona; Brandeis U.; Chicago/AI; Davenport/Municipal; Des Moines; Detroit/Institute; Fort Wayne/AM; U. of Illinois; Knox College; MMA; MOMA; U. of Michigan, U. of Minnesota; NCFA; U. of Nebraska; Newark Museum; PAFA; Phillips; Santa Barbara/MA; Utica; WMAA; Wesleyan U. (Conn.); Wilmington; Worcester/AM. **Bibliography:** *Avant-Garde Painting and Sculpture;* Baur 7; Brown, Cahill and Barr, eds.; Cheney; Flanagan; Goodrich and Baur 1; Huyghe; *Index of 20th Century Artists;* Janis, S.; Jewell 2; Kootz 1; Mellquist; Pagano; Pearson 1; Phillips 1; Poore; Pousette-Dart, ed.; Wheeler; Wight 2. Archives.

KAPROW, ALLAN. b. August 23, 1927, Atlantic City, N.J. **Studied:** NYU, 1945–49, BA; Hofmann School, NYC, 1947–48; Columbia U., with Meyer Schapiro, 1950–52, MA (art history); privately with John Cage in NYC, 1956–58. Traveled Europe, USA. **Taught:** Rutgers U., 1953–61; Pratt Institute, 1960–61; Stony Brook/SUNY, 1961–69; California Institute of the Arts, Los Angeles, 1969– . A co-founder of Hansa Gallery, NYC, 1952, and Reuben Gallery, NYC, 1959. Designed sets and costumes for Eileen Passloff Dance Co., 1958. Initiated the first Environments and Happenings, 1958. **Awards:** Katherine White Foundation Grant, 1951; Rutgers U., Research Fund Grant, 1957; Copley Foundation Grant, 1962; Guggenheim Foundation Fellowship, 1967. **Address:** 1225 Linda Rose Avenue, Los Angeles, CA 90041. **One-man Exhibitions:** (first) Hansa Gallery, NYC, 1953, also 1955, 57; Rutgers U., 1953, 55; Urban Gallery, NYC, 1955, 56; Sun Gallery, Provincetown, 1957; John Gibson Gallery, NYC, 1969; Galerie Rene Block, Berlin, 1970; Galleria Bertesca, Milan, 1973; Stefanotty Gallery, NYC, 1974; U. of Northern Iowa, 1979. **En-**vironments: Hansa Gallery, NYC, 1958; Judson Gallery, NYC, 1960; Martha Jackson Gallery, 1961; U. of Michigan, 1961; Rijksmuseum, Amsterdam, and Stockholm/National, 1961; Smolin Gallery, NYC, and Stony Brook/SUNY, 1962; Smolin Gallery, NYC, 1964. **Happenings:** Douglass College, 1958; Reuben Gallery, NYC, 1959, 61; Judson Memorial Church, NYC, 1960; U. of Michigan, 1961; Maidman Playhouse, NYC, 1962; Walker, 1962; Theatre des Nations, Paris, 1963; Edinburgh, Scotland, 1963; Southern Illinois U., 1964; Miami, Fla., 1964; U. of California, Berkeley, 1964; Cornell U., 1964; Florida State U., 1965; Judson Hall, NYC, 1965; ICA, Boston, 1966; Central Park, NYC, 1966; Westchester Art Society, White Plains, N.Y., 1966; Stony Brook/SUNY, 1967; Aspen Design Conference, 1970; Merriewold West Gallery, Far Hills, N.J., 1975; and many others. **Retrospective:** Pasadena/AM, 1967. **Group:** Boston Arts Festival, 1957; A.F.A., College in America, circ., 1957–58; Cornell U., 1958; Carnegie, 1958; A.F.A., New Talent, circ., 1958; Rijksmuseum, Amsterdam, and Stockholm/National, 1960; MOMA, Hans Hofmann and His Sutdents, circ., 1963–64; Jewish Museum, Work, 1969, Software, 1970; Cologne/Kunstverein, Happening & Fluxus, circ., 1970. **Bibliography:** Alloway 4; Battcock, ed.; Becker and Vostell; *Contemporanea;* Davis, D.; Downes, ed.; Hansen; *Happening & Fluxus;* Honisch and Jensen, eds.; Hunter, ed.; Janis & Blesh 1; Johnson, Ellen H.; **Kaprow;** Kirby; Kozloff 3; Lippard 5; Lippard, ed.; *Metro;* Rubin 1; Sandler; Sontag.

KARFIOL, BERNARD. b. May 6, 1886, Budapest, Hungary; **d.** 1952. **Studied:** Academie Julian, Paris, 1901, with Jean Paul Laurens; Academie des Beaux-Arts, Paris; Pratt Institute, 1899; NAD, 1900. Traveled Mexico, Europe, West Indies. **Awards:** Pan-American Exhibition, Los Angeles, 1925; Carnegie, 1927, 29; Corcoran, First William A. Clark

Prize and Corcoran Gold Medal, 1928; Fort Dodge/Blanden, **P.P.**, 1940; VMFA, **P.P.**, 1942. **One-man Exhibitions:** (first) Joseph Brummer Gallery, NYC, 1924, also 1925, 27; The Downtown Gallery, 1931, 33, 35, 41, 43, 46, 50, 56; Baltimore/MA, 1939; Vanbark Studios, Studio City, Calif., 1946; Grover Cronin Gallery, Waltham, Mass., 1957; The Forum Gallery, NYC, 1967, 78. **Group:** Grand Salon, Paris, 1930; Salon d'Automne, Paris, 1904; The Armory Show, 1913; MOMA, Paintings by 19 Living Americans, 1929; Carnegie; Corcoran; Baltimore/MA, Six Americans 1939. **Collections:** AAAL; Andover/Phillips; Baltimore/MA; Brandeis U.; Britannica; Brooklyn Museum; California Palace; Carnegie; Corcoran; Dartmouth College; Detroit/Institute; Fisk U.; Fort Dodge/Blanden; Los Angeles/County MA; MMA; MOMA; Newark Museum; New Britain; New London; Ogunquit; Phillips; Southampton/Parrish; Upjohn Co.; VMFA; WMAA; Wellesley College; Wichita/AM. **Bibliography:** Bethers; Blesh 1; Brown; Cahill and Barr, eds.; Cheney; Goodrich and Baur 1; Hall; Halpert; Huyghe; *Index of 20th Century Artists*; Jewell 2; **Karfiol**; Kootz 1, 2; McCurdy, ed.; Mellquist; Neuhaus; Pagano; Phillips 2; Pousette-Dart, ed.; Richardson, E.P.; Ringel, ed.; **Slusser**; Wight 2. Archives.

KASTEN, KARL. b. March 5, 1916, San Francisco, Calif. **Studied:** U. of California, with Worth Ryder, John Haley, Erie Loran; State U. of Iowa, with Mauricio Lasansky; Hofmann School; San Francisco Art Institute (AB, MA). Traveled Europe, Turkey, Morocco. **Taught:** San Francisco Art Institute, 1941; U. of Michigan, 1946–47; San Francisco State College, 1947–50; U. of California, 1950– . **Member:** California Society of Printmakers. **Commissions:** North American Title Co., Berkeley, Calif. (Mural). **Awards:** U. of California Institute for Creative Work in the Arts, 1964–65; Tamarind Fellowship, 1968.

Address: 1884 San Lorenzo Avenue, Berkeley, CA 94707. **Dealers:** Arlene Lind Gallery. **One-man Exhibitions:** (first) U. of Michigan, 1946; SFMA; Galerie Breteau, Paris; Rennes; California Palace; The Lanyon Gallery; Hollis Gallery, San Francisco; St. Mary's College (Ind.); Oakland/AM; Lanai Gallery; Chico State College; Bolles Gallery; 1965, 68, 71, 73; RAC, 1968; The Catholic U. of America, 1968; Dohan Gallery, Sherman Oaks, Calif., 1969; Sacramento/Crocker 1969; Achenbach Foundation, 1975; Turkish-American Gallery, Ankara, 1975; Arlene Lind Gallery, 1975; Achenbach Gallery, 1975; U. of Alaska, 1976. **Retrospective:** Walnut Creek Civic Arts Gallery, 1973; Valley Art Center, 1978. **Group:** de Young; SFMA; WMAA; MMA; Chicago/AI; Detroit/Institute; Seattle/AM; Pasadena/AM; Oakland/AM; I & III Sao Paulo Biennials, 1951, 55; U. of Illinois, 50 Contemporary American Printmakers, 1956, Contemporary American Painting and Sculpture, 1969; Pomona College, California Drawing, 1957. Art Center, Berkeley, 1967; Los Angeles Printmakers Society, 1968; Moore College of Art, Philadelphia, American Drawings, 1968; U. of the Pacific, 1969; U. of Illinois, 1969. **Collections:** Achenbach Foundation; Auckland; U. of California; de Young; College of Idaho; Ithaca College; Los Angeles/County MA; MOMA; Mills College; NYPL; Oakland/AM; U. of Oklahoma; U. of the Pacific; Pasadena/AM; Rennes; SFMA; San Francisco State College; US State Department; Victoria and Albert Museum. **Bibliography:** Archives.

KATZ, ALEX. b. July 24, 1927, NYC. **Studied:** Cooper Union; Skowhegan School, 1959; Yale U., 1960–61; Pratt Institute, 1963–66; School of Visual Arts, NYC, 1965, 66; New York Studio School, 1968–69. Stage sets and costumes for Paul Taylor Dance Company, Festival of Two Worlds, Spoleto, 1960, 64; Kenneth Koch's *George Washington*

Crossing the Delaware, 1962; Artists Festival Theater, Southampton, *Little Eyolf*, by Henrik Ibsen, 1968. **Commissions:** Mural, Federal Courthouse Annex, NYC. Designed sets for Paul Taylor Dance Co., *Polaris*, sets and costumes, and set for *Diggity*, 1979; Kenneth Koch's *Red Robin*, 1977–78. **Awards:** Guggenheim Foundation Fellowship, 1972. **Address:** 435 West Broadway, NYC 10013. **Dealer:** Marlborough Gallery, Inc., NYC; Robert Miller Gallery, Inc., NYC. **One-man Exhibitions:** Roko Gallery, 1954, 57; The Pennsylvania State U., 1957; Sun Gallery, Provincetown, 1958; Tanager Gallery, NYC, 1959, 62; The Stable Gallery, NYC, 1960; Martha Jackson Gallery, 1962; Fischbach Gallery, 1962–68, 70, 71; Thibaudt Gallery, NYC, 1963; Tanager Gallery, NYC (two- and three-man shows), 1953, 57, 60; David Stuart Gallery, 1966; Bertha Eccles Art Center, Ogden, Utah, 1968; Phyllis Kind Gallery, Chicago, 1969, 71; Galerie Dieter Brusberg, Hanover, 1971; M.D. Thelen Gallery, 1971; Reed College, 1972; Sloan O'Sickey Gallery, Cleveland, 1972; Carlton Gallery, NYC, 1973; Assa Galleria, Helsinki, 1973; Marlborough Gallery, Inc., NYC, 1973; Colgate U., 1974; Wesleyan U. (Conn.), 1974; Marlborough Godard Ltd., Toronto and Montreal, 1974; Marlborough Fine Art Ltd., London, 1975; Galerie Arensen, Copenhagen, 1975; American Foundation for the Arts, Miami, 1976; Marlborough Godard Ltd., Toronto, 1976, 78; Marlborough Gallery, Inc., NYC, 1976, 78, 80; Marlborough Gallerie AG, Zurich, 1977; Galerie Roger d'Amecourt, Paris, 1977; Fresco Arts Center, Calif., circ., 1977–78; Brandeis U., 1978; Beaver College, 1978; Benjamin Mangel Gallery, Bela Cynwyd, Pa., 1978–79; Susan Hilberry Gallery, Birmingham, Mich., 1978; Hokin Gallery, Chicago, 1978; Brooke Alexander, NYC, 1979; Robert Miller Gallery, Inc., NYC, 1980. **Retrospectives:** U. of Utah, circ., 1971; WMAA, circ., 1974. **Group:** New York Art Alliance, Younger Artists, 1959; PAFA, 1960; WMAA,

Young America, 1960; Annual, 1967–68; Houston-MFA, 1961; Chicago/AI, 1961, 62, 64; Colby College, Maine and Its Artists, 1963; Swarthmore College, Two Generations of American Art, 1964; MOMA, 1964–65, American Collages, 1965, The Inflated Image, circ., 1968; RISD, Recent Still Life, 1966; Milwaukee, 1966; Bennington College, 1967; U. of California, San Diego, The Impure Image, 1969; Tulsa/Philbrook, The American Sense of Reality, 1969; Milwaukee, Aspects of a New Realism, 1969; Walker, Figures/Environments, circ., 1970–71; Sweden/Goteborgs, Warmwind, 1970; Corcoran Biennial, 1971; PAFA, Contemporary Realism, 1971; SFMA, Color/Constructivism/Realism in Contemporary Graphics, 1971–72; WMAA Annuals 1972, 73; Boston U., The American Landscape, 1972; WMAA, American Drawings: 1963–1973, 1973; Cleveland/MA, 1974; Lincoln, Mass./De Cordova, Candid Painting: American Genre 1950–1975, 1975; US Department of the Interior, America 1976, 1976; Tulane U., Drawing Today in New York, 1977; Philadelphia College of Art, Artists' Sets and Costumes, 1977. **Collections:** Aachen/NG; Allentown/AM; Atlantic-Richfield Corp., Los Angeles; Berlin; Boston/MFA; Bowdoin College; Brandeis U.; Chase Manhattan Bank; Chicago/AI; Ciba-Geigy Corp.; Cincinnati/AM; Cleveland; Colby College; Commerce Bank of St. Louis; Dartmouth College; Delaware; Detroit/Institute; Hartford/Wadsworth; Harvard U.; Madison Art Center; MMA; MOMA; Miami-Dade; Milwaukee; NCFA; NYU; U. of North Carolina; Oberlin College; Rice U.; RISD; Scranton/Everhart; J. Henry Schroeder Banking Corp.; U. of Southern California; Syracuse U.; Trenton/State; US State Department; WMAA; Wake Forest U. **Bibliography:** Alloway 4; *America 1976;* Arthur 1; Arthur 2; Downes, ed.; *Figures/Environments;* Honisch and Jensen, eds.; Hunter, ed.; *Kunst um 1970;* Lippard 5; O'Hara 1; *Poets & Painters;* Sandler 1; Sager. Archives.

KATZMAN, HERBERT. b. January 8, 1923, Chicago, Ill. **Studied:** Chicago Art Institute School, 1940–46. Traveled Great Britain; resided Paris, Florence. **Taught:** Rockland Foundation, 1952–53; Pratt Institute; School of Visual Arts, NYC, 1959– . **Awards:** Chicago/AI, Traveling Fellowship, 1946; Chicago/AI, Campana Prize, 1951; PAFA, J. Henry Schiedt Memorial Prize, 1954; Fulbright Fellowship, 1956; AAAL Grant, 1958; National Council on the Arts, 1967; Guggenheim Foundation Fellowship, 1968. **Address:** 463 West Street, NYC 10014. **Dealer:** Terry Dintenfass, Inc. **One-man Exhibitions:** (first) The Alan Gallery, NYC, 1954, also 1957, 59; Terry Dintenfass, Inc., NYC, 1962, 64, 66, 68, 71, 72, 75, 78; U. of Illinois; Brooklyn Museum. **Group:** Chicago/AI, 1951; MOMA, Fifteen Americans, circ., 1952; U. of Illinois; PAFA, 1952, Annuals, 1967, 69; Carnegie, 1953, 55; WMAA, The New Decade, 1954–55. XXVIII Venice Biennial, 1956; WMAA, Forty Artists under Forty, circ., 1962; Gallery of Modern Art, NYC, 1967–68; New School for Social Research, 1968; Skidmore College, Contemporary Drawings, 1975; U. of North Carolina, Art on Paper, 1977. **Collections:** Chicago/AI; Hirshhorn; MOMA; U. of Massachusetts; Minnesota/MA; NCFA; Sacramento/Crocker; St. Lawrence U.; WMAA; Wright State U. **Bibliography:** Nordness, ed.; Pousette-Dart, ed.

KAUFFMAN, CRAIG. b. March 31, 1932, Eagle Rock, Calif. **Studied:** U. of Southern California, 1950–52; UCLA, BA, MA, 1952–56. Traveled Europe, 1956–57; resided Paris, 1960–62. **Taught:** U. of California, 1967–. **Awards:** National Endowment for the Arts, grant, 1968; Chicago/AI, Prize, 1970; **Address:** 160 La Brea, Laguna Beach, Ca 92651. **Dealer:** Blum Helman Gallery, Inc., NYC. **One-man Exhibitions:** (first) Felix Landau Gallery, 1953; Dilexi Gallery, San Francisco, 1958, 60; Ferus Gallery, Los Angeles, 1958, 63, 65, 67; The Pace Gallery, 1967, 69, 70,

Craig Kauffman   *Tell Tale Heart, 3rd Version* 1980

73; Ferus/Pace Gallery, Los Angeles, 1967; Irving Blum Gallery, Los Angeles, 1969, 72; Pasadena/AM, 1970; U. of California, Irvine, 1970; Darthea Speyer Gallery, 1973; Mizuno Gallery, 1975; Robert Elkon Gallery, NYC, 1976; Cynthia Comsky Gallery, Los Angeles, 1976; Arco Center for Visual Arts, Los Angeles, 1978; Blum Helman Gallery, Inc., 1979. **Group:** SFMA Annual, 1952, 54, 59–61; UCLA, California Painters under 35, 1959; U. of Illinois, 1961, 67; Seattle/AM, 1966; Detroit/Institute, Color, Image and Form, 1967; MOMA, The 1960's, 1967; WGMA, A New Aesthetic, 1967; V. Paris Biennial, 1967; CSCS, Los Angeles, 1968; Des Moines, Painting Out from the Wall, 1968; Vancouver, 1968; Pasadena/AM, West Coast: 1945–1969, 1969; Jewish Museum, Using Walls, 1970; Govett-Brewster, The State of California Art, 1971; Corcoran Biennial, 1973; Chicago/AI, 71st American Exhibition, 1974; WMAA (downtown), Illuminations and Reflections, 1974; U. of Illinois, 1974;

ICA, Los Angeles, Current Concerns, 1975; Newport Harbor, The Last Time I Saw Ferus, 1976; Indianapolis, 1976; SFMA, 75 Years of California Art, 1976; SFMA, Painting and Sculpture in California: The Modern Era, 1977; Laguna Beach Museum of Art, Southern California 100, 1977; WMAA Biennial, 1979. **Collections:** Arco Corp.; U. of Arizona; Australia; Buffalo/Albright; Chicago/AI; Fort Worth; Laguna Beach/ AM; Long Beach/MA; Los Angeles/ County MA; Milwaukee; MOMA; Pasadena/AM; Philip Morris Collection; Newport Harbor; Ridgefield/Aldrich; Santa Barbara/MA; Seagram Collection; SFMA; Tate; U. of Sydney, Australia; WMAA; Walker. **Bibliography:** Davis, D.; Friedman, M. 2; *The State of California Painting.*

KEARL, STANLEY BRANDON. b. December 23, 1913, Waterbury, Conn. **Studied:** Yale U., 1941, BFA, 1942, MFA; State U. of Iowa, 1948, Ph.D. Traveled the world extensively; resided Rome, nine years. **Taught:** U. of Minnesota, Duluth, 1947–48; Pratt Institute, 1967; YMHA, Scarsdale, 1974–75. Federal A.P.: Easel painting. **Awards:** Fulbright Exchange Professor to Rome U., Italy, 1949–50; Institute of Contemporary Arts, Florence, Italy, 1952; Connecticut Academy Sculpture Prize, 1958. **Address:** 344 Sprain Road, Scarsdale, NY 10583. **Dealer:** Ingber Art Gallery, NYC. **One-man Exhibitions:** (first) L'Obelisco, Rome, 1950; Galerie d'Art Moderne, Basel, 1951; Samlaren Gallery, Stockholm, 1951; Marbach Galerie, Berne, 1952; Galerie 16, Zurich, 1952; Beaux Arts Gallery, London, 1956; Galleria Selecta, Rome, 1957; Obelisk Gallery, Washington, D.C., 1958; Wakefield Gallery, NYC, 1961; D'Arcy Gallery, NYC, 1962; Hudson River Museum, Yonkers, N.Y., 1964; Grand Central Moderns, NYC, 1965; 68; IIE, NYC, 1967; Benson Gallery, Bridgehampton, N.Y., 1976. **Group:** XXVI Venice Biennial, 1952; PAFA, 1959; MOMA, 1961; WMAA Annual, 1962; Hudson River

Museum Yonkers, N.Y., 1963; Institute of International Education; The Graham Gallery, 1969; Stamford Museum, 1974. **Collections:** State U. of Iowa; Marbach Galerie; U. of Minnesota; Northland College; Rome/Nazionale; Stockholm/ National; Sweden/Goteborgs. **Bibliography:** Seuphor 3.

KEARNS, JAMES. b. August 7, 1924, Scranton, Pa. **Studied:** Chicago Art Institute School; De Paul U.; The U. of Chicago, 1946–50 (BFA). **Taught:** School of Visual Arts, NYC, 1959– ; Skowhegan School, summer, 1961–64; Fairleigh Dickinson U., 1962–63. Illustrated *Can These Bones Live?* by Edward Dahlberg (New Directions, 1960), and *The Heart of Beethoven,* by Selman Rodman (Shorewood Press, 1962). Awards: NIAL Grant in Art, 1959; Montclair/ AM, First Prize for Painting, 1961. **Address:** 452 Rockaway Road, Dover, NJ 07801. **Dealers:** Grippi Gallery; David Gallery. **One-man Exhibitions:** (first) Grippi Gallery, 1956, also 1957, 60, 62, 68; Fairleigh Dickinson U., 1962; Scranton/Everhart, 1963; Lee Nordness Gallery, NYC, 1964; Bloomfield College, 1967; David Gallery, 1969, 71; Bloomfield College, 1972; Free Public Library, Fair Lawn, N.J., 1972; Sculpture Center, NYC, 1973; River Run Gallery, Edgartown, Mass., 1975, 77; Somerset Art Association, Bernardsville, N.J., 1975; Cramer Gallery, Glen Rock, N.J., 1976; Caldwell College, N.Y., 1976; Spook Farm Gallery, Far Hills, N.J., 1977. **Group:** A.F.A., Drawings, 1959; WMAA Annuals, 1959–61; A.F.A., New Talent, circ., 1960; A.F.A., Private Worlds, 1960; Newark Museum, Survey of American Sculpture, 1962; PAFA Annual; New York World's Fair, 1964–65; Monmouth Museum, Three Centuries of Art in New Jersey, 1969; San Diego, National Invitational Print Show, 1969; SAGA Annual, 1971; Schenectady Museum, Sculpture, 1976; NYC Audubon Artists, 1977. **Collections:** Caldwell College; Colby College; Hirshhorn; MMA; MOMA; Montclair/AM; NCFA;

Newark Museum; Scranton/Everhart; Topeka Public Library; Trenton/State; WMAA. **Bibliography:** Gerdts; Nordness, ed.; Rodman 1, 3.

KELLY, ELLSWORTH. b. May 31, 1923, Newburgh, N.Y. **Studied:** Boston Museum School; Academie des Beaux-Arts, Paris. US Army, 1943–46. Traveled France, 1948–54. **Taught:** Norfolk House Center, Boston, 1946; American School, Paris, 1950–51. **Commissions:** Transportation Building, Philadelphia, 1957 (sculpture); Eastmore House, NYC (mural); New York State Pavilion, New York World's Fair, 1964–65 (sculpture); UNESCO, Paris, 1969 (mural); Central Trust Co., Cincinnati, 1979; Lincoln Park, Chicago, 1979. Designed sets and costumes for Paul Taylor Dance Co. **Member:** NIAL. **Awards:** Brandeis U., 1962; Carnegie, 1962, 64; International Biennial Exhibition of Paintings, Tokyo; Chicago/AI; Flora Mayer Witkowsky Prize, 1964; Chicago/AI, Painting Prize, 1974. **Address:** Box 170B R.D., Chatham, NY 12037. **Dealers:** Leo Castelli Inc., NYC; Blum Helman Gallery, NYC. **One-man Exhibitions:** (first) Galerie Arnaud, 1951; Betty Parsons Gallery, 1956, 57, 59, 61, 63; Galerie Maeght, 1958, 64; A. Tooth & Sons, London, 1962; WGMA, 1964; ICA, Boston, 1964; Ferus Gallery, Los Angeles, 1965; Sidney Janis Gallery, 1965, 67, 71; Irving Blum Gallery, Los Angeles, 1967, 68, 73; Galerie Denise Rene/Hans Mayer, Dusseldorf, 1972; Buffalo/Albright, 1972; Leo Castelli Inc., NYC, 1973, 75 (2), 77 (2); Ronald Greenberg Gallery, St. Louis, 1973; ACE Gallery, Venice, Calif., 1975; Blum Helman Gallery, NYC, 1975, 77, 79; Janie C. Lee Gallery, Houston, 1976; Margo Leavin Gallery, Los Angeles, 1977; MOMA, 1978; MMA, 1979; Amsterdam/Stedelijk, circ., 1979–80. **Retrospectives:** MOMA, 1973; Walker, 1974; Detroit/Institute, 1974. **Group:** Salon des Realites Nouvelles, Paris, 1950, 51; Galerie Maeght, Tendence, 1951, 62; Brussels World's Fair, 1958; Carnegie,

1958, 62, 64, 66, 67; MOMA, Sixteen Americans, circ., 1959; SRGM, Abstract Expressionists and Imagists, 1961; VI Sao Paulo Biennial, 1961; Chicago/AI, 1961, 62, 64, 66; Seattle World's Fair, 1962; Jewish Museum, Toward a New Abstraction, 1963; Los Angeles/County MA, Post Painterly Abstraction, 1964; Tate, Gulbenkian International, 1964; SRGM, American Drawings, 1964; Tate, Dunn International, 1964; MOMA, The Responsive Eye, 1965; Amsterdam/Stedelijk, New Shapes of Color, 1966; SRGM, Systemic Painting, 1966; Jewish Museum, Primary Structures, 1966; XXXIII Venice Biennial, 1966; Brandeis U., 1966; WMAA, Sculpture Annuals, 1966, 68, Annual, 1967; Tokyo/Modern, 1966–67; Detroit/Institute, Color, Image and Form, 1967; Expo '67, Montreal, 1967; Los Angeles/County MA, American Sculpture of the Sixties, 1967; SRGM, 1967; MOMA, The Art of the Real, 1968; Buffalo/Albright, Plus by Minus, 1968; Documenta IV, Kassel, 1968; Pasadena/AM, Serial Imagery, 1968; WMAA, Contemporary American Sculpture, 1968–69; WMAA Annuals, 1969, 73; MMA, New York Painting and Sculpture, 1940–1970, 1969–70; Chicago/Contemporary (four-man), 1970; WMAA, The Structure of Color, 1971; MOMA, Technics and Creativity; Gemini G.E.L., 1971; ICA, U. of Pennsylvania, Grids, 1972; Kunstmuseum, Lucerne, 1973; Musée Galliera, Paris, Festival d'Automne, 1973; Parcheggio di Villa Borghese, Rome, Contemporanea, 1974; Rijksmuseum/Kroller-Muller, Functions of Drawing, 1975; NCFA, Sculpture: American Directions 1945–1975, 1975; MOMA, Drawing Now, 1976; SRGM, 20th Century American Drawings, 1976; Chicago/AI Annual, 1976; WMAA, 200 Years of American Sculpture, 1976; A.F.A., American Master Drawing and Watercolors, 1976; Paris/Beaubourg, Paris–New York, 1977; Cambridge, Jubilation, 1977; Minnesota/MA, American Drawings 1927–1977, 1977; Venice, Biennial, 1978; Buffalo/Albright, American Painting of the 1970's, 1978;

WMAA Biennial, 1979; Corcoran Biennial, 1979; California State U., Northridge, Americans in Paris, the 50s, 1979. **Collections:** Amsterdam/Stedelijk; Brandeis U.; Buffalo/Albright; Canberra/National; Carnegie; Chicago/AI; Cincinnati/AM; Cleveland/MA; Cologne; Corcoran; Dartmouth College; Detroit/Institute; Dusseldorf/KN-W; Eindhoven; Fort Worth; Foundation Maeght; Grenoble; Harvard U., Hirshhorn; Los Angeles/County MA; MMA; MOMA; Milwaukee; Munster/ WK; Omaha/Joslyn; Pasadena/AM; RISD; Rijksmuseum Kroller-Muller; St. Louis/City; SFMA; SRGM; Tate; Toronto; WGMA; WMAA; Walker; Worcester/AM; Yale U. **Bibliography:** Alloway 3; Battcock, ed.; *Black and White Are Colors;* Calas, N. and E.; *Contemporanea;* **Coplans 1,** 3; Davies; Davis, D.; Friedman, M. 2; Gaunt; **Goossen** 1, **2;** Honisch and Jensen, eds.; Hunter, ed.; Kozloff 3; *Kunst um 1970;* Lippard 5; MacAgy 2; Nordness, ed.; *Report;* Rickey; Rose, B., 1; Sandler 1; Seuphor; Tuchman 1; Weller.

KELLY, JAMES. b. 1913, Philadelphia, Pa. **Studied:** Philadelphia Museum School, 1937; PAFA, 1938; Barnes Foundation, 1941; California School of Fine Arts, 1951–54. US Air Force, 1941–45. **Taught:** U. of California, Berkeley, 1957. **Member:** Artists Equity. **Awards:** Ford Foundation Grant for Tamarind, 1963. **Address:** 463 West Street, NYC 10014. **One-man Exhibitions:** (first) California Palace, 1954; SFMA, 1956; The Stryke Gallery NYC, 1963; East Hampton Gallery, N.Y., 1965, 69; Albright College, Reading, Pa., 1966; Long Island U., 1968; Westbeth Gallery, NYC, 1971, 72. **Group:** PAFA, 1951; SFMA Annuals, 1955–58; U. of Minnesota, California Painters, 1956; Minneapolis/Institute, American Painting, 1945–57, 1957; Santa Barbara/MA, II Pacific Coast Biennial, 1957; A.F.A., West Coast Artists, circ., 1959–60; Los Angeles/County MA, Late Fifties at the Ferus, 1968; Oakland/AM, A Period of

Exploration, 1973; Newport Harbor, The Last Time I Saw Ferus, 1976; SFMA, California Painting: The Modern Era, 1976. **Collections:** Amon Carter Museum; Chase Manhattan Bank, NYC; Chicago/AI; Fort Worth; La Jolla; Los Angeles/County MA; MOMA; U. of Massachusetts; Oakland/AM; Pasadena/AM; Sacramento/Crocker; SFMA; UCLA; Westinghouse. **Bibliography:** McChesney.

KELLY, LÉON (Léon Kelly y Corrons). **b.** October 21, 1901, Philadelphia. **Studied:** Philadelphia Museum School; PAFA; privately with Arthur B. Carles, Jr., and Earl Horter. Traveled Europe, North Africa, USA; resided Paris, 1924–30. Federal A.P.; Supervisor of Artists in Philadelphia; mural and easel painting. **Taught:** Brooklyn Museum School. **Commissions:** Portraits. Awards: PAFA, Cresson Fellowship, 1924; William and Noma Copley Foundation Grant, 1959. **Address:** 268 Pompano Drive, Loveladies, NJ 08008. **Dealer:** Washburn Gallery, NYC. **One-man Exhibitions:** (first) Little Gallery of Contemporary Art, Philadelphia, 1925, also 1932; Galerie du Printemps, Paris, 1926; Contemporary Arts Gallery, NYC, 1933; Julien Levy Galleries, NYC., 1942, 44, 45; Philadelphia Art Alliance, 1943; Hugo Gallery, NYC, 1950; Galleria Amici di Francia, Milan, 1954; Hewitt Gallery, NYC, 1956; Alexandre Iolas Gallery, NYC, 1959, 61; The Zabriskie Gallery, 1963. **Retrospective:** Philadelphia Art Alliance, 1928; International Gallery, Baltimore, 1965. **Group:** European International 1927: A Century of Progress, Chicago, 1933–34; WMAA Annuals; Carnegie; U. of Nebraska; PMA; Chicago/AI; Corcoran; Newark Museum, 1968. **Collections:** Allentown/AM; Andover/Phillips; Chicago/AI; Clearwater/Gulf Coast; Hartford/Wadsworth; La France Art Institute; MMA; MOMA; Museo Nacional de Historia; National Arts Foundation; U. of Nebraska; Newark Museum; PAFA; PMA; The Pennsylvania State

U.; Steuben Glass; Tel Aviv; Utica; WMAA. **Bibliography:** *Avant-Garde Painting and Sculpture in America;* Gerdts; Janis, S. Archives.

KENT, ROCKWELL. b. June 21, 1882, Tarrytown Heights, N.Y.; **d.** March 13, 1971, Plattsburg, N.Y. **Studied:** Columbia U., 1906–10, with William M. Chase, Robert Henri, Kenneth Hayes Miller, Abbott Thayer, Traveled Canada, USA, Europe, Latin America, Greenland. **Member:** NIAL; Hon. Member, Academy of Fine Arts of the USSR. **Commissions** (murals): US Post Office, Washington, D.C.; Federal Building, Washington, D.C. **One-man Exhibitions:** Clausen Galleries, NYC, 1908, 19; Wildenstein & Co., NYC, 1925, 42; Macbeth Gallery, NYC, 1934; Richard Larcada Gallery, 1966, 69, 72; Bowdoin College, 1969. **Retrospective:** Wildenstein & Co., NYC, 1924; Syracuse/Everson, 1937; Bowdoin College, 1969. **Group:** NAD, 1905; Academy of Fine Arts, Berlin, 1910; Century Association, 1940; Cleveland/MA; WMAA. **Collections:** American Car and Foundry Co.; Andover/Phillips; Baltimore/MA; Boston/MFA; British Museum; Brooklyn Museum; Chicago/AI; Cleveland/MA; Columbus; Corcoran; Detroit/Institute; Harvard U.; Honolulu Academy; Houston/MFA; Indianapolis/Herron; Library of Congress; MMA; NYPL; Newark Museum; Phillips; Victoria and Albert Museum; WMAA; Yale U. **Bibliography:** American Artists Congress, Inc.; American Artists Group Inc. 1, 3; **Armitage**; Baur 7; Biddle 4; Birchman; Blesh 1; Brown; Cahill and Barr, eds.; Cheney; Cummings 1; Finklestein; Goodrich and Baur 1; Hall; Hartmann; *Index of 20th Century Artists;* Jackman; **Jones, D.B.**; Kent, N.; **Kent, R. 1, 2, 3; Kent R., ed.**; Lee and Burchwood; Mather 1; Mellquist; Narodny; Neuhaus; Pagano; Pearson 1; Phillips 1, 2; Reese; Richardson, E.P.; Ringel, ed.; Ritchie 1; Rose, B., 1; Smith, S.C.K.; Zigrosser 1. Archives.

KEPES, GYORGY. b. October 4, 1906, Selyp, Hungary. **Studied:** Academy of Fine Arts, Budapest, 1924–28. **Taught:** New Bauhaus, Chicago, 1937–43; a foundling collaborator, with Lazlo Moholy-Nagy and Robert Wolff, of the Institute of Design, Chicago, 1938–42; MIT, 1946– . Codirector, Rockefeller Foundation Research Project: Perceptual Form of Cities. **Commissions** (murals): Harvard U. Graduate Center; KLM Royal Dutch Airlines, NYC; Travelers Insurance Companies, Los Angeles; Sheraton Hotels, Dallas and Chicago; Children's Library, Fitchburg, Mass.; American Housing Exhibit, Paris, 1946. **Awards:** American Institute of Graphic Art, 1944, 49; U. of Illinois. **P.P.**, 1954; Guggenheim Foundation Fellowship, 1960–61; Art Directors Club, Chicago, 1963. **Address:** 90 Larchwood Drive, Cambridge, MA 02138. **Dealer:** Saidenberg Gallery. **One-man Exhibitions:** Katherine Kuh Gallery, Chicago, 1939; Chicago/AI, 1944, 54; Outline Gallery, Pittsburgh, 1945; Royal Academy, Copenhagen, 1950; Margaret Brown Gallery, Boston, 1951, 55; San Diego, 1952; Amsterdam/Stedelijk, 1952; Long Beach/MA, 1952; U. of California, Berkeley, 1952; SFMA, 1952, 54; Currier, 1953; Cranbrook, 1954; ICA, Boston, 1954; Syracuse/Everson, 1957; Houston/MFA, 1958; Dallas/MFA, 1958; L'Obelisco, Rome, 1958; Ivrea Gallery, Florence, Italy, 1958; The Howard Wise Gallery, Cleveland, 1959; Baltimore/MA, 1959; Saidenberg Gallery, 1960, 66, 68; Lincoln, Mass./De Cordova, 1969; NCFA, 1970; Saidenberg Gallery, NYC, 1970, 72, 80; Alpha Gallery, 1970, 72, 74; Museum of Science and Hayden Planetarium, Boston, 1973; Dartmouth College, 1977; Prakapas Gallery, NYC, 1977. **Retrospective:** MIT, 1978. **Group:** MOMA, 1947, 52; Chicago/AI, 1951, 53, 57; U. of Illinois, 1952, 53; SFMA; Cranbrook; Dallas/MFA; Andover/Phillips; San Diego, WMAA; Denver/AM, 1953; Carnegie, 1955. **Collections:** Andover/Phillips, Boston/MFA; Buffalo/Albright; Chase Manhattan Bank; Cranbrook;

Dallas/MFA; Des Moines; Houston/ MFA; U. of Illinois; Indianapolis/Herron; Lincoln, Mass./De Cordova; MIT; MOMA; SFMA; San Diego; VMFA; WMAA. **Bibliography: Alfieri**; Davis, D.; Janis and Blesh 1; Janis, S.; **Kepes 1, 2; Kepes, ed.**; Kuh 1; Nordness, ed.; Pearson 1; Rickey. Archives.

KEYSER, ROBERT. b. July 27, 1924, Philadelphia, Pa. **Studied:** U. of Pennsylvania; Atelier Fernand Leger, Paris, 1949–51. US Navy, World War II (three years). Traveled Europe, North Africa (two years). **Taught:** Philadelphia Museum School, 1963; Temple U., Rome, 1975–77. **Address:** Box 328 R.D. #4, Quakertown, PA, 18951. **Dealer:** Marion Locks, Philadelphia. **One-man Exhibitions:** (first) Galerie Huit, Paris, 1951; Hendler Gallery, Philadelphia, 1952; Parma Gallery, NYC, 1954, 56, 58; P. Rosenberg and Co., 1959, 60, 62, 66, 71, 75, 79; Gimpel Fils, 1962; Gallery Marc, Washington, D.C., 1972; Marion Locks Gallery, Philadelphia, 1974, 1979; Temple U., Rome, 1977. **Group:** PAFA Annual; WMAA Annual; A.F.A., Collage in America, circ., 1957–58; Joachim Gallery, Chicago, 1960; U. of Illinois, 1961; Salon du Mai, Paris; Salon d' Automne, Paris; Salon des Realites Nouvelles, Paris; Corcoran, 1975; PMA, 300 Years of American Art, 1976; PAFA, Contemporary Drawing: Philadelphia I, 1978. **Collections:** AT&T; Brandeis U.; New London; PMA; Phillips; Utica; Vassar College.

KIENBUSCH, WILLIAM. b. April 13, 1914, NYC; **d.** March 23, 1980, NYC. **Studied:** Princeton U., 1936, BA, PBK (fine-arts major); ASL, 1936–37; Colorado Springs Fine Arts Center, with Henry Poor; Academie Colarossi, Paris; privately with Anton Refregier and Stuart Davis in New York. US Army, World War II. **Taught:** Brooklyn Museum School, 1948–1979. **Awards:** Brooklyn Society of Artists Annual, First Prize, 1952; MMA, Drawing Prize,

1952; Columbia, S.C./MA, First **P.P.**, Watercolors, 1957; Guggenheim Foundation Fellowship, 1958; Ford Foundation, **P.P.**, 1961; Boston Arts Festival, First Prize for Watercolor, 1961; NIAL, Childe Hassam Fund, 1970. **One-man Exhibitions:** Kraushaar Galeries, 1949, 52, 56, 59, 63, 65, 69, 72, 78; U. of Maine, 1956; Cornell U., 1958; Princeton U., 1962; Fort Worth, 1964 (two-man). **Retrospective:** Carnegie, 1954 (two-man, with Dioda). **Group:** Buffalo/Albright; Chicago/AI; MMA, 1952; Brooklyn Museum, 1953, 59; WMAA, The New Decade, 1954–55; Carnegie, 1955; WMAA, 1955; Walker, MOMA, Twelve Americans, circ., 1956; Brussels World's Fair, 1958; PAFA Annuals, 1962, 65, 67; New York World's Fair, 1964–65; WMAA, Art of the U.S. 1670–1966, 1966. **Collections:** Atlanta U.; Boston/MFA; Bowdoin College; Brooklyn Museum; Buffalo/Albright; Carnegie; Colorado Springs/FA; Columbia, S.C./MA; Commerce Trust Co.; Currier; Dartmouth College; U. of Delaware; Des Moines; Detroit/Institute; Fort Worth; Hartford/Wadsworth; Houston/MFA; Kansas City/Nelson; Lehigh U.; MMA; MOMA; U. of Maine; U. of Michigan; U. of Minnesota; Montclair/AM; NCFA; U. of Nebraska; Newark Museum; New Britain; Norfolk/Chrysler; PAFA; PMA; Portland, Me./MA; U. of Rochester; Toledo/MA; Toronto; Utica; VMFA; WMAA; Wichita/AM; Williams College. **Bibliography:** Baur 5; Eliot; Goodrich and Baur 1; McCurdy, ed.; Nordness, ed.; Pousette-Dart, ed.; Ritchie 1; Seitz 3. Archives.

KIENHOLZ, EDWARD. b. 1927, Fairfield, Wash. **Studied:** Eastern Washington College of Education. Founded the Now Gallery, Los Angeles, 1956, and later the Ferus Gallery, Los Angeles. **Address:** Hope, Idaho 83836. **One-man Exhibitions:** (first) Cafe Galleria, Los Angeles, 1955; Syndell Studios, Los Angeles, 1956; Exodus Gallery, San Pedro, Calif.; Ferus Gallery, Los Angeles (three-man), 1958, (two-man), 1959, 60, 62; Pasadena/AM, 1961; Alexander Iolas Gallery, 1963; Dwan Gallery, Los Angeles, 1963–65; Dwan Gallery, NYC, 1967 (2); WGMA, 1967; Gallery 699, Los Angeles, 1968; Eugenia Butler, 1969; Stockholm/National, 1970; Dusseldorf/ Kunsthalle, 1970; CNAC, 1970; Zurich, 1971; ICA, London, 1971; Wide White Space Gallery, Antwerp, 1972; Galerie Onnasch, Cologne, 1973; Galleria Bocchi, Milan, 1974; Humlebaek/Louisiana, 1976. **Group:** MOMA, The Art of Assemblage, circ., 1961; WMAA, Fifty California Artists, 1962; Los Angeles/ County MA, Sculpture of the Sixties, 1967; MOMA, The Machine, 1968; MOMA, Dada, Surrealism and Their Heritage, 1968; WMAA, Human Concern/Personal Torment, 1969; Documenta IV & V, Kassel, 1968, 72; XXXVIII, Venice Bienniale, 1976; WMAA, 200 Years of American Sculpture, 1976; WMAA Biennial 1981. **Collections:** Aachen/NG; Amsterdam/ Stedelijk; Los Angeles/County MA; MOMA; Tokyo/Modern; WMAA. **Bibliography:** Battcock, ed.; Calas, N. and E.; Davis, D.; Hulten; **Edward Kienholz; Edward Kienholz:11 + 11 Tableaux**; Kozloff 3; Lippard 5; Lippard, ed.: Rose, B., 1; Rubin 1; Russell and Gablik; Tuchman 1, 2; *When Attitudes Become Form.*

KIESLER, FREDERICK, J. b. 1896, Vienna, Austria; **d.** December 27, 1965, NYC. To USA, 1926; became a citizen. Scenic Director, Julliard School of Music, NYC, 1933–57. Registered Architect; designed and built the Art of This Century Gallery, NYC (1940); the Galerie Maeght, Paris (1947); the World House Galleries, NYC (1957); and the Kamer Gallery, NYC (1959). **One-man Exhibitions:** MOMA, 1951 (sculpture); MOMA, Endless House, 1960, also 1966; U. of Houston, Architectural Plans, 1960; Leo Castelli Inc., 1961, 62; SRGM, Environmental Sculpture, 1964; The Howard Wise Gallery, NYC, 1969; Andre Emmerich Gallery,

NYC, 1979, 80. **Retrospective:** Galerie Nachst Skt. Stephan, Vienna, 1975. **Group:** WMAA; A.F.A., Universal Theater, circ., 1961–64. **Collections:** MOMA. **Bibliography:** Arp; Barr 1; Blesh 1; Breton 3; Calas; *Frederick Kiesler*; Janis and Blesh 1; Janis, S.; *Metro*; Rose, B., 1; Rubin 1; Seuphor 3; Tuchman 1. Archives.

KING, WILLIAM DICKEY. b. February 25, 1925, Jacksonville, Fla. **Studied:** U. of Florida, 1942–44; Cooper Union 1945–48, with Milton Hebald, John Hovannes; Brooklyn Museum School, 1948–49, with Hebald; Central School of Arts and Crafts, London, 1952. Traveled Italy, Greece. **Taught:** Brooklyn Museum School, 1953–60; U. of California, Berkeley, 1965–66; ASL, 1968–69; U. of Pennsylvania, 1972–73; SUNY 1974–75. **Commissions:** (murals) SS *United States*, 1952; Bankers Trust Company, NYC, 1960; Miami-Dade, 1972; Potsdam/SUNY, 1973–74; Detroit Medical Center, 1979; Madison Art and Civic Center, Wisconsin, 1979. **Awards:** Cooper Union, Sculpture Prize, 1948, Augustus Saint-Gaudens Medal, 1964; Fulbright Fellowship (Italy), 1949; Margaret Tiffany Blake Competition, First Prize, 1951; Moorehead Patterson Award (sculpture/to AMF Company), 1960; CAPS, 1974. **Address:** 42 East 12th Street, NYC 10003. **Dealer:** Terry Dintenfass, Inc. **One-man Exhibitions:** The Alan Gallery, NYC, 1954, 55, 61; Terry Dintenfass, Inc., 1962, 64–71, 1973, 74, 76, 80; The Gallery, Norwalk, Ohio, 1963; Donald F. Morris Gallery, Detroit, 1964; Washington Federal Savings & Loan Association of Miami Beach, Fla., 1965; Felix Landau Gallery, 1966; Berkeley Gallery, San Francisco, 1966; Feigen-Palmer Gallery, Los Angeles, 1966; U. of Miami, 1967; Guild Hall, 1969; Galerie Ann, Houston, 1970; The Berenson Gallery, 1970; SFMA, 1970, circ., 74; Alpha Gallery, 1971; U. of Nebraska, 1972; U. of Connecticut, 1973; Aronson Gallery, Atlanta, 1973; Moravian College, 1974; San Antonio/

McNay, circ., 1973; Davis Stuart Galleries, Los Angeles, 1974; U. of Connecticut, 1979. **Retrospective:** SFMA, circ., 1970, 74. **Group:** City of Philadelphia, Sculpture International, 1949; MOMA, New Talent; Brooklyn Museum, 1949, 50, 54, 55, 57, 58; WMAA Annuals, 1950–56, 1958–60, 1962–64, 1966, 68; U. of Illinois, 1954, 56, 62, 63, 65; New Sculpture Group, NYC, 1957–60; Carnegie, 1958; MOMA, Recent Sculpture USA, 1959; Newark Museum, Survey of American Sculpture, 1962; SRGM, The Joseph H. Hirshhorn Collection, 1962; Museum of Contemporary Crafts, 1966; Drexel Institute, 1966; Indianapolis/Herron, 1968; AAAL, 1970, 74; New School for Social Research, Humor, Satire, Irony, 1972; Harvard U., Recent Figure Sculpture, 1972; Art Gallery of Budapest, II International Biennial of Small Sculpture, 1973; San Diego, Sculpture in the Street, 1973; Cranbrook, WAVES, An Artist Selects, 1974; Newport, R.I., Monuments, 1974; AAAL, 1974; Minnesota/MA, Drawings/USA, 1975. **Collections:** Allentown/AM; American Export Isbrandtsen Lines, Inc.; Andover/Phillips; U. of Arkansas; Bankers Trust Company; Brandeis U.; U. of California; Creekwood; Cornell U.; Dartmouth College; First National Bank of Chicago; Guild Hall; U. of Massachusetts; Miami-Dade; U. of North Carolina; Syracuse U. **Bibliography:** Downes, ed.; Lippard 5; *Monumenta: Recent Figure Sculpture;* Seuphor 3. Archives.

KIPNISS, ROBERT. b. February 1, 1931, NYC. **Studied:** Wittenberg College, 1948–50; State U. of Iowa, 1950–54, BA (English literature), MFA (painting and art history); ASL, with Alice Murphy. US Army, 1956–58. **Member:** Board of Directors of Audubon Artists. **Awards:** SAGA, 1979; Audubon Artists, 1976, 78; NAD, 1976; Hon. Ph.D., Wittenberg U., 1979. **Address:** 5 Hillside Place, Tarrytown, NY

10591. **Dealers:** Hirschl & Adler Galleries, NYC; Merrill Chase Galleries, Chicago; Associated American Artists, NYC. **One-man Exhibitions:** (first) Creative Gallery, NYC, 1951; The Salpeter Gallery, NYC, 1953; The Contemporaries, NYC, 1959, 60, 66, 67; Alan Auslander Gallery, NYC, 1963; Gallery Vendome, Pittsburgh, 1964; U. of Louisville, 1965; FAR Gallery, 1968, 70, 72, 75; Merrill Chase Galleries, 1972, 74, 76, 77, 78, 79, 80; Centro de Arte Actual, Pereira, Colombia, 1975; Kalamazoo/Institute, 1975; Galerie Sandiego, Bogota, Colombia, 1975, 77; Xochipili Gallery, Rochester, Mich., 1977; Quadrum Gallery, Marblehead, Mass., 1977, 78; River Gallery, Irvington-on-Hudson, N.Y., 1977, 78, 80; A. B. Closson Co., Cincinnati, 1979; Wittenberg U., 1979; Canton Art Institute, Ohio, 1979; Museo de Arte Contemporanco, Cali, Colombia, 1975, 1980; Hirschl & Adler Galleries, NYC, 1977, 80. **Retrospective:** Museo de Arte Contemporaneo, Cali, Colombia, S.A., 1975; AAA, Ten Years of Lithography, 1977. **Group:** Youngstown/Butler, 1951; Columbus, 1958; A.F.A., New Talent, circ., 1961; U. of Minnesota, Duluth; A.F.A., circ., 1963–65; Indianapolis/Herron, 1964; Utah State Institute of Fine Arts, Salt Lake City, 1964; Cornell U., 1964; Cranbrook, 1964; Corcoran, 1966, 67; Buffalo/Albright, 1966, 67; MOMA, 1966, 67; Massillon Museum, 1967; NAD, 1974; NYPL, 1974; NAD, 1974, 76, 77; SAGA, 1979; AAIAL, 1978; Museo de Arte Contemporanea, III Biennal Graficas, 1976. **Collections:** AT&T; Atlantic Richfield Co.; Ball State U.; Buffalo/Albright; Canton Art Institute; Chase Manhattan Bank, NYC; Chicago/AI; Cleveland/MA; Continental Grain Company, NYC; Detroit/Institute; Esmark, Chicago; Flint/Institute; Glen Alden Corp., NYC; IBM, Chicago; U. of Iowa; Irving Trust Co.; Los Angeles/County MA; Library of Congress; Miami U.; Minnesota/MA; NCFA; Notre Dame U.; NYPL; Ohio U.; RISD; Singer Company, Inc., NYC; WMAA; Wittenberg U.; Yale U.

KIPP, LYMAN. b. December 24, 1929, Dobbs Ferry, N.Y. **Studied:** Pratt Institute, 1950–54; Cranbrook, 1952–53. Traveled Europe, India, Morocco. **Taught:** Bennington College, 1960–63; Hunter College, 1964–67; Herbert H. Lehman College, Bronx, N.Y., 1968–75; Dartmouth College, 1969; Hunter College 1975–. **Member:** American Association of University Professors; Artists Equity. **Commissions:** Lambert Corp., Dallas; General Services Administration, Federal Office Building and Post Office, Van Nuys, Calif.; Lake Placid, N.Y. **Awards:** Guggenheim Foundation Fellowship, 1965; Fulbright Fellowship, 1965. **Address:** % Noble, 334 West 22nd Street, NYC 10011. **Dealer:** Construct, Chicago; Max Hutchinson Gallery, NYC. **One-man Exhibitions:** Cranbrook, 1954; Betty Parsons Gallery, 1954, 56, 58, 60, 62, 64, 65, 68; Arizona State College, 1957; Myrtle Todes Gallery, Glencoe, Ill, 1957, 60; Bennington College, 1961; Dartmouth College, 1965; Buffalo/Albright, 1967; Katonah (N.Y.) Art Gallery, 1968; Obelisk Gallery, 1969; A.M. Sachs Gallery, 1970; Chapman Kelley Gallery, Dallas, 1971; Adam Gallery, NYC, 1972; City U. of New York Graduate Center, 1972; Richard Gray Gallery, 1973; Galerie Denis Rene, NYC (two man), 1974; Bridge Gallery, White Plains, N.Y., 1975; Greenway Plaza, Houston, 1975; Laguna Gloria Museum, Austin, Texas, 1976; The Art Center, Waco, Texas, 1976; Nielson Memorial Museum, Amarillo, Texas, 1977; U. of Alabama, 1977; Max Hutchinson Gallery, NYC, 1977; Sculpture Now, Inc., NYC, 1978; Construct, Chicago, 1978, 80; William Patterson College (three-man), 1979; Calvin College, Grand Rapids, Mich., 1979. **Group:** RISD, Four Young Americans, 1955; WMAA Annuals, 1956, 60, 62, 66, 68; Pensacola, Freedom of Inspiration, 1958; Claude Bernard, Paris, 1960; U. of Illinois, 1961; Carnegie, 1961, 62; Chicago/AI, 1961, 62; Sao Paulo, 1963; Drawing Society, National Exhibition, 1965; Jewish Museum, Primary Structures, 1966; Musée Cantonal des Beaux-Arts, Lausanne, II Salon International de Galeries Pilotes, 1966; Los Angeles/County MA, American Sculpture of the Sixties, 1967; Ridgefield/Aldrich, 1968; MOMA, The Art of the Real, 1968; U. of Nebraska, American Sculpture, 1970; San Diego, Art Is for People, 1973; Grand Rapids, Sculpture off the Pedestal, 1973; Newport, R.I., Monumenta, 1974; Akron/AI, Project: New Urban Monuments, circ., 1977–79. **Collections:** Buffalo/Albright; U. of California; Cranbrook; Dartmouth College; Fort Worth; High Museum; U. of Kentucky; MIT; U. of Michigan; New York Bank for Savings; South Mall, Albany; State College at Salem; Storm King Art Center; WMAA. **Bibliography:** Battcock, ed.; Goossen 1; MacAgy 2; *Monumenta*; Seuphor 3; Tuchman 1.

KIRSCHENBAUM, JULES. b. March 25, 1930, NYC. **Studied:** Brooklyn Museum School, 1948–50. **Awards:** Joe and Emily Lowe Foundation Award, 1950; PAFA, Dana Watercolor Medal, 1952; NAD, Hallgarten Prize, 1953; NAD, Isaac N. Maynard Prize, 1954; NAD, S. J. Wallace Truman Prize, 1955; Fulbright Fellowship (Italy), 1956; PAFA, Hon. Men., 1957; AAAL, Childe Hassam Award, 1957; Youngstown/Butler, First Prize, 1957; NAD, First Prize, Figure Painting, 1960. **Address:** 2829 Forest Drive, Des Moines, IA 50312. **Dealer:** The Forum Gallery. **One-man Exhibitions:** The Salpeter Gallery, NYC, 1955, 56; Des Moines, 1964; The Forum Gallery, NYC, 1969, 1977. **Group:** MMA, 1952; MOMA; PAFA, 1952, 53, 54, 57; WMAA, 1953–57; Brooklyn Museum; NYU; Chicago/AI, 1957; U. of Illinois, 1957; Youngstown/Butler, 1957; Corcoran; Festival of Two Worlds, Spoleto, 1958; Santa Barbara/MA; Pasadena/AM; Houston/MFA; Dallas/MFA. **Collections:** U. of Nebraska; WMAA; Youngstown/Butler.

KLINE, FRANZ. b. May 23, 1910, Wilkes-Barre, Pa.; **d.** May 13, 1962, NYC. **Studied:** Girard College; Boston

Franz Kline *Untitled* 1960

U., 1931–35; Heatherley School of Fine Art, London, 1937–38. **Taught:** Black Mountain College, 1952; Pratt Institute, 1953; Philadelphia Museum School, 1954. **Awards:** NAD, S. J. Wallace Truman Prize, 1944; Chicago/AI, 1957; XXX Venice Biennial, 1960. **One-man Exhibitions:** (first) Charles Egan Gallery, 1950, also 1951, 54; Margaret Brown Gallery, Boston, 1952; Institute of Design, Chicago, 1954; Allan Frumkin Gallery, Chicago, 1954; Sidney Janis Gallery, 1956, 58, 60, 61, 63; La Tartaruga, Rome, 1958; Galleria d'Arte del Naviglio, Milan, 1958; XXX Venice Biennial, 1960; Arts Club of Chicago, 1961; Collectors Gallery, NYC, 1961; New Arts Gallery, Atlanta, 1961; Galerie Lawrence, Paris, 1962; Dwan Gallery, 1962 (two-man, with Philip Guston); Kunsthalle, Basel, 1964 (two-man, with Alfred Jensen); Marlborough-Gerson Gallery, Inc., 1967; Marlborough Fine Art Ltd., London, 1972; David McKee Gallery, NYC, 1975; Binghampton/SUNY, 1977; Phillips, 1979. **Retrospectives:** WGMA, 1962; Whitechapel Art Gallery, London, 1964; WMAA, 1968. **Group:** NAD, 1942–45; Galerie de France, Paris, 1952; 10th Inter-American Conference, Caracas, 1954; WMAA, The New Decade, 1954–55; MOMA, Twelve Americans, circ., 1956; Tate, 1956; XXVIII & XXX Venice Biennials, 1956, 60; Sao Paulo, 1957; MOMA, The New American Painting, circ., Europe, 1958–59; Baltimore/MA, 1960/SRGM, 1961; Hartford/Wadsworth, 1962; WMAA, 1966, 69; U. of St. Thomas (Tex.), 1967; MOMA, The New American Painting and Sculpture, 1969. **Collections:** Baltimore/MA; Buffalo/Albright; Carnegie; Cleveland; Houston/MFA; International Minerals & Chemicals Corp.; Kansas City/Nelson; Kunsthalle, Basel; MMA;

MOMA; Norfolk/Chrysler; PMA; Raleigh/NCMA; Rockefeller Institute; SRGM; Tate; Toronto; Utica; WMAA. **Bibliography:** Ashton 5; Baur 5; Bihalji-Merin; *Black and White Are Colors*; Blesh 1; **Breeskin 1**; Calas, N. and E.; **Dawson**; Eliot; Elsen 2; Flanagan; Gaunt; Goodrich and Baur 1; **Gordon 1**; Greenberg 1; Haftman; Henning; Hess, T.B., 1; Honisch and Jensen, eds.; Hunter 1, 6; Hunter, ed.; Janis and Blesh 1; Johnson, Ellen H.; Kuh 2, 3; Langui; Lynton; McCoubrey 1; McCurdy, ed.; Mendelowitz; Neumeyer; Nordness, ed.; O'Hara 1, 3; Ponente; Pousette-Dart, ed.; Read 2; Rodman 1, 3; Rose, B., 1, 4; Sandler; Sandler 1; Seuphor 1; Tomkins and Time-Life Books; Tomkins 2; Tuchman, ed.; Weller. Archives.

KNATHS, KARL. b. October 21, 1891, Eau Claire, Wis.; **d.** March 9, 1971, Provincetown, Mass. **Studied:** Chicago Art Institute School. **Taught:** The Phillips Gallery School; Bennington College. **Member:** Audubon Artists. Federal A.P. (murals); Falmouth (Mass.) High School; US Post Office, Rehoboth Beach, Del.; Provincetown (Mass.) Town Hall. **Awards:** Chicago/AI, Norman Wait Harris Prize, 1928; Boston Tercentenary Art Exhibit, Gold Medal; Carnegie, First Prize, 1946; Carnegie International, Third Hon. Men., 1950; Chicago Art Institute School, Hon. DFA, 1951; elected to NIAL, 1955; Brandeis U., Creative Arts Award, 1961; NAD Annual, Andrew Carnegie Prize, 1962. **One-man Exhibitions:** (first) The Phillips Gallery and The Daniel Gallery, NYC. (concurrently); P. Rosenberg and Co., NYC, 1946–69, 1974–75. **Retrospective:** Provincetown Art Association, 1974. **Group:** WMAA; Corcoran; Chicago/AI; Carnegie; U. of Illinois; PAFA; MMA. **Collections:** Boston/MFA; Brooklyn Museum; Buffalo/Albright; California Palace; Chicago/AI; Corcoran; Currier; Dayton/AI; Des Moines; Ford Foundation; Hartford/Wadsworth; U. of Illinois; Indianapolis/Herron; Los Angeles/County MA;

MMA; MOMA; Mary Washington College; U. of Nebraska; PAFA; PMA; Phillips; U. of Rochester; Rockefeller Institute; St. Louis/City; Santa Barbara/MA; Stanford U.; Toledo/MA; Utica; WMAA; Walker; West Palm Beach/Norton; Wilmington; Woodward Foundation; Worcester/AM. **Bibliography:** American Abstract Artists, ed.; Baur 5, 7; Bazin; Bethers; Blanchard; Blesh 1; Cheney; Eliot; Frost; **Goodrich and Baur** 1, **2**; Hess, T.B., 1; Janis, S.; Jewell 2; Kootz 2; Leepa; McCurdy, ed.; Mellquist; **Mocsanyi**; Morris; Nordness, ed.; Pearson 1; Phillips 1, 2; Pousette-Dart, ed.; Read 2; Richardson, E.P.; Ringel, ed.; Ritchie 1; Wight 2. Archives.

KNIPSCHILD, ROBERT. b. August 17, 1927, Freeport, Ill. **Studied:** U. of Wisconsin, with Alfred Sessler, 1947–50, BA, 1950, MFA, 1951; Cranbrook, with Zoltan Sepeshy. Traveled USA, Canada, Mexico. US Army, 1945–47. **Taught:** Baltimore/MA, 1951–52; American U., 1952; U. of Connecticut, 1954–56; U. of Wisconsin, 1956–60; U. of Iowa, 1960–66; U. of Cincinnati, 1966–. **Address:** 3245 Bishop Street, Cincinnati, OH 45220. **Dealer:** Yares Gallery, Scottsdale. **One-man Exhibitions:** Cranbrook, 1951; Baltimore/MA, 1952–53, 55; American U., 1952; The Alan Gallery, NYC, 1953–55, 57, 58, 61; U. of Iowa, 1960; U. of Wisconsin, 1960–65; Lubetkin Gallery, Des Moines, 1962; Sneed-Hillman Gallery, 1962, 64, 67, 68, 75; Skidmore College, 1969; Louisiana State U., 1970; U. of Massachusetts, Madison College, 1972; U. of Cincinnati, 1974; Western Michigan U., 1975; Birmingham Gallery, Inc., Birmingham, Mich., 1975; Miami U., 1976; Findlay College, Ohio, 1976; Virginia Beach Art Center, 1976; Piedmont Gallery, Augusta, 1977, 78, 79; Yares Gallery, Scottsdale, Ariz., 1978; Ohio Wesleyan U., 1978; Western Kentucky, U. 1978. **Retrospectives:** U. of Cincinnati, 1974; Western Michigan U., 1975. **Group:** MMA, American

Painting Today, 1950; PAFA Biennial, 1951, 53; WMAA Annual, 1952; Youngstown/Butler Biennial, 1954; Corcoran; Carnegie. **Collections:** Baltimore/MA; Brandeis U.; Cedar Rapids/AA; U. of Cincinnati; Corcoran; Cranbrook; Davenport/Municipal; Grinnell College; Hirshhorn; Hope College; Illinois Wesleyan U.; Library of Congress; Madison College; U. of Michigan; Milwaukee Journal; U. of Minnesota; Murray State U.; PAFA; Phillips; Skidmore College; Springfield, Ill./State; Stephens College; Tucson Museum of Art; Upjohn Co.; U. of Wisconsin; Wisconsin State U. **Bibliography:** Archives.

KOCH, GERD. b. January 30, 1929, Detroit, Mich. **Studied:** Wayne State U., with David Mitchell, David Smith, L. J. Nobili, 1951, BFA; UCLA Graduate School, with Sam Amato, 1957; U. of California, Santa Barbara, MFA, 1967. Traveled Europe, USA extensively. **Taught:** Palos Verdes Community Arts Association, 1953– ; Ventura College, 1959–60, 1967– ; U. of California, Extension Division, 1966– . **Awards:** California Watercolor Society, M. Grumbacher **P.P.**, 1956, 60; Los Angeles/County MA, First **P.P.**, 1959; Palos Verdes Invitational, 1960; Bay Printmakers Society, Oakland, Adell Hyde Morrison Memorial Medal, 1960; California Watercolor Society, Lytton **P.P.**, 1962; California State Fair, **P.P.**, 1963; and others. **Address:** 444 Aliso, Ventura, CA 93001. **One-man Exhibitions:** (first) Ojai Music Festival, 1956; Pasadena/AM, 1958; Santa Monica (Calif.) Art Gallery, 1958; Esther Robles Gallery, 1959, 61, 63, 65; Santa Barbara/MA, 1960; Long Beach/MA, 1961; La Jolla, 1962; Esther Baer Gallery, 1964, 65, 67; Ojai Art Center, 1965, 69; Comara Gallery. **Group:** Los Angeles Art Association, 7 Artists, 1955; California Watercolor Society, 1955–60, 62, 63, 1965–68; Los Angeles/County MA, 1957, 1959–61; SMFA, 1957, 62, 63, New Paintings, 1964; Pasadena/AM, A Decade in the Contemporary Gallery, 1959; Tucson Art Center,

1960; Oakland/AM, 1960; La Jolla, 1961, 62; San Diego, 1961, 62; California State Fair, 1961–64, 67; Occidental College, Art and Anti-Art, 1964; U. of North Carolina, 1966; Youngstown/Butler, 1966; California Palace, 1967; California Art Festival, 1968. **Collections:** CSCS, Long Beach; California State Fair; La Jolla; Long Beach/MA; Los Angeles/County MA; Lytton Savings and Loan Association; Palos Verdes; Pasadena/AM; Santa Barbara/MA; VMFA.

KOCH, JOHN. b. August 18, 1909, Toledo, Ohio; **d.** April 19, 1978, NYC. Self-taught in art. Traveled France, Great Britain; resided Paris, 1929–33. **Taught:** ASL, 1944–45; Chairman of the School Committee, NAD. **Member:** NAD; Century Association; Lotus Club; Audubon Artists; NIAL. **Awards:** Salon de Printemps, Paris, Hon. Men., 1929; Carnegie, First Hon. Men., 1943; NAD, 1952; NAD, Benjamin Altman. Prize, 1959; NAD, 137th Annual, Saltus Gold Medal for Merit; Youngstown/Butler, Dr. John J. McDonough Award, 1962; Lotus Club, 1964. **One-man Exhibitions:** (first) Bonestell Gallery, Detroit, 1927; Curt Valentine Gallery, NYC, 1935; Kraushaar Galleries, NYC, 1939, 41, 43, 46, 49, 51, 54, 58, 61, 65, 69, 72, 80; Kansas City/Nelson, 1940; J. L. Hudson Art Gallery, 1941; Whyte Gallery, Washington, D.C., 1944; Philadelphia Art Alliance, 1945; Portraits, Inc., NYC; Syracuse/Everson, 1951; Cowie Galleries, Los Angeles, 1951; 460 Park Avenue Gallery, NYC, 1951; Colgate U., 1977; The Pennsylvania State U., 1977. **Retrospective:** Suffolk Museum, Stony Brook, N.Y., 1951; Museum of the City of New York, 1963; Pittsfield/Berkshire, 1963; VMFA, 1962; Louisville/Speed, 1971; Akron/AI, 1971; Columbia (S.C.), 1978. **Group:** Salon de Printemps, Paris, 1929; Salon des Tuileries, Paris, 1929; NAD, 1939– . **Collections:** ASL; Bennington College; Boston/MFA; Brooklyn Museum; California Palace, Canajoharie; Chicago/AI; Des Moines; Detroit/Institute; U. of

Georgia; Kansas City/Nelson; Lehigh U.; MMA; MOMA; NAD; Newark Museum; New Britain; Norfolk; Omaha/ Joslyn; U. of Rochester; Southampton/ Parrish; Springfield, Mass./MFA; Storm King Art Center; Toledo/MA; VMFA; Youngstown/Butler. **Bibliography:** Celebrate Ohio; **Eliot; Koch, J.;** Soyer, R. 1. Archives.

KOENIG, JOHN FRANKLIN. b. October 24, 1924, Seattle, Wash. **Studied:** U. of California, Berkeley; Washington State College; U. of Washington, 1948, BA (Romance Languages); U. of Biarritz; Sorbonne, MA. US Army, 1943–45. Traveled Europe and the Orient extensively. General Secretary, *Cimaise* (art magazine), Paris, 1953–58. Resided Paris, 1948–79. Was codirector of Galerie Arnaud, Paris. **Taught:** School of Applied Arts, Istanbul, 1976. **Commissions:** Hopital St. Antoine, Paris, 1964. **Awards:** Paris/Moderne, (Third) Prix des Peintres Etrangers, 1959; I Paris Biennial, 1959; Prix des Critiques d'Art de la Presse Parisienne. **Address:** 736 Belmont Place E., Seattle, WA 98102. **Dealers:** Galerie Erval, Paris; The John Pence Gallery, San Francisco; Galleria Lorenzelli, Bergamo. **One-man Exhibitions:** Librairie Selection, Paris, 1948; Galerie Arnaud, 1952 (collages), 1953, 55, 57, 59–61, 1963, 66, 68, 72, 74, 75; La Citadella d'Arte Internazionale e d'Avanguardia, Ascona, Switzerland, 1955, 57; Galleria del Cavallino, Venice, 1957; Brussels/Beaux-Arts, 1957; Grange (Gallery), Lyon, 1958; Zoe Dusanne Gallery, Seattle, 1958, 60; Tokyo Gallery, 1960, 62; Seattle/AM, 1960, 61, 70, 71; Gordon Woodside Gallery, Seattle and San Francisco, 1962, 65, 67; The Willard Gallery, 1963, 65; Musée de Verviers, 1963; San Antonio/McNay, 1963; Le Lutrin, Lyon, 1965, 66; Montreal/Contemporain, 1966, 73; Holst Halvorsen Konsthandel, Oslo, 1966, 69; Quebec, 1966; Portland, Ore./AM, 1966; Tacoma, 1967; Musée Vivenel, Compiegne, 1969; Galleria Lorenzelli, Bergamo, 1970; Galerie

Gilles Corbeil, Montreal, 1970, 71; Jongeward Gallery, Seattle, 1971; Galleria San Fedele, Milan, 1972; Foster-White Gallery, 1973, 74, 77; American Cultural Center, Istanbul, 1975; i.e. Graphics, Copenhagen, 1975; American Cultural Center, Katmandu, 1975; Galerie Kutter, Annenberg, 1976; Triveni Gallery, New Delhi, 1976; American Cultural Center, Madras, circ., 1976; American U., Calcutta, 1977; Galerie Influx, Marseilles, 1977; Fuji Television Gallery, Tokyo, 1977; Ocha-no-mizu Gallery, Tokyo, 1977; The John Pence Gallery, San Francisco, 1978. **Retrospective:** Musée Vivenel, Compiegne, 1969; Seattle/AM, 1970; Galerie Arnaud, Paris, 1974; Tacoma, 1980. **Group:** International Congress of Museums, Marseilles, 1953; ICA, London, Collages and Objects, 1954; Palais des Beaux-Arts, Brussels, 1954; Amsterdam/Stedelijk, 1956; Palais des Beaux-Arts, Charleroi, Belgium, L'Art de XXIeme Siecle, 1958; ICA, Boston, 100 Works on Paper, circ., Europe, 1959; Salon des Realites Nouvelles, Paris, Artistes Americains en France, circ., France, 1960; Tate, Ecole de Paris, 1962; Havana/Nacional; Carnegie, 1964; USA: Nouvelle Peinture, circ., French museums, 1965; Musée de Lyon, USA: Groupe 68, 1968; Musée Municipal, Brest, 21 Peintres Americains, 1968; Salon des Realities Nouvelles, 1973; Menton Biennale de Tapisserie, 1975. **Collections:** Bibliotheque Nationale; CNAC; Grenoble; Houston/MFA; MMA; Montreal/Contemporain; Montreal/MFA; Musée de Verviers; NYPL; National Museum of Western Art, Tokyo; Ottawa/National; Paris/Moderne; Reykjavik; St.-Etienne; Salzburg; San Antonio/McNay; Seattle/AM; Seattle Public Library; Tacoma; Tokyo/Modern; Seafirst Mortgage Corporation; Venice/Contemporaneo. **Bibliography:** Ragon 1; Read 4; **Restany 1,** 2. Archives.

KOHN, GABRIEL. b. 1910, Philadelphia, Pa., **d.** May 21, 1975, Los

Angeles, Calif. **Studied:** Cooper Union, 1929; Beaux-Arts Institute of Design, NYC, 1930–34; Zadkine School of Sculpture, Paris, 1946. **Awards:** Augustus Saint-Gaudens Medal from Cooper Union, 1925; Beaux-Arts Institute of Design NYC, 14 awards in sculpture, 1929–32, and a Silver Medal, 1932; Nicholas Roerich Society, First Prize, 1932; Cranbrook, George A. Booth Scholarship, 1952; ICA, London/ Tate, International Unknown Political Prisoner Competition, 1953; Ford Foundation Grant, 1960; Guggenheim Foundation Fellowship, 1967; Mark Rothko Foundation Grant, 1971. **One-man Exhibitions:** Atelier Mannucci, Rome, 1948; Galleria Zodiaco, Rome, 1950; Cranbrook, 1953; Tanager Gallery, NYC, 1958; Leo Castelli Inc., 1959; Otto Gerson Gallery, NYC, 1963; Ringling, 1964; La Jolla, 1963; David Stuart Gallery, 1963–66, 1972; The Zabriskie Gallery, NYC, 1972–77. **Retrospective:** Newport Harbor, circ., 1971; Corcoran, 1977. **Group:** Pershing Hall, Paris, American Veterans in Paris, 1948; Salon de la Jeune Sculpture, Paris, 1950; Los Angeles/County MA, 1950; Salon d'Art Libre, Paris, 1951; MMA, National Sculpture Exhibition, 1951; PAFA, 1953; WMAA Annuals, 1953, 60, 62; II Sculpture Biennial, Antwerp, 1953; MOMA, New Talent; MOMA, Recent Sculpture USA, 1959; Sao Paulo, 1959; Claude Bernard, Paris, Aspects of American Sculpture, 1960; New School for Social Research, Mechanism and Organism, 1961; Seattle World's Fair, 1962; MOMA, Americans 1963, circ. 1963–64; Ringling, 1964. **Collections:** Buffalo/Albright; Cranbrook; Hirshhorn; MOMA; Pasadena/AM; Ringling; WMAA. **Bibliography:** Downes ed.; Goodrich and Baur 1; Hunter, ed.; Read 3; Rose, B., 1; Sandler 1; Seuphor 3; Tuchman 1.

KOHN, MISCH. b. March 26, 1916, Kokomo, Ind. **Studied:** John Herron Art Institute, 1939; in Mexico, 1943–44, with Jose Clemente Orozco, Mendez, Diego Rivera. **Taught:** Institute of Design, Chicago; Illinois Institute of Technology, 1949–75; Indiana U.; California State U., Hayward, 1972–80. **Awards:** PAFA, Alice McFadden Eyre Medal, 1949; Seattle/AM, **P.P.**, 1950; Brooklyn Museum, **P.P.**, 1950, 51; The Print Club, Philadelphia, 1950, 51, 55, 56, 58; Chicago/AI, 1951, 52, 58; PAFA, Pennell Memorial Medal, 1952; Guggenheim Foundation Fellowship, 1952, 54; Indianapolis/Herron, 1952, 56; NAD, 1955; Salon du Mai, Paris, 1960; Gallery of Modern Art, Ljubljana, Yugoslavia, IV International Exhibition of Prints, 1961; Tamarind Fellowship, 1961; Ford Foundation Grant. **Address:** 1860 Grove Way, Castro Valley, CA 94546. **One-man Exhibitions:** Philadelphia Art Alliance; Chicago/AI; St. Amands Gallery, Sarasota, Fla., 1969; Weyhe Gallery, 1970; Los Angeles/ County MA; Kansas City/Nelson. **Retrospective:** A.F.A./Ford Foundation, 1961. **Group:** PAFA, 1949, 52, 56; Brooklyn Museum, 1949–57; Boston/ MFA; Seattle/AM; Chicago/AI, 1949–58; The Print Club, Philadelphia, 1949–58; Salon du Mai, Paris, 1952, 53. **Collections:** Brooklyn Museum; Chicago/AI; Library of Congress; MOMA; NYPL; National Gallery; PMA; Rio de Janeiro; Stockholm/National. **Bibliography:** Hayter 1; Peterdi.

KONZAL, JOSEPH. b. November 5, 1905, Milwaukee, Wis. **Studied:** ASL, with Max Weber, Walt Kuhn, Robert Laurent, 1926–30; Layton School of Art, 1927; Beaux-Arts Institute of Design, NYC, 1928–30. **Taught:** Brooklyn Museum School, 1949–71; Adelphi U., 1954–71; Newark (N.J.) Public School for Fine and Industrial Art, 1960–67; Queens College, 1966–69; Kent State U., 1971–76; Federal A.P.: Supervised Federal Art Project Gallery; architectural sculpture project. **Awards:** Brooklyn Museum Biennial, 2 First Prizes; Guggenheim Foundation Fellowship, 1966. **Address:** 360 West 21st Street, NYC 10011. **Dealer:** Andre Zarre Gallery, NYC. **One-man Exhibitions:**

(first) Eighth Street Playhouse, NYC, 1938; Contemporary Arts Gallery, NYC, 1950, 52, 55; The Bertha Schaefer Gallery, 1960, 63, 65, 67, 71; Canton Art Institute, 1974, 75; Andre Zarre Gallery, NYC, 1978, 80. **Retrospectives:** Adelphi U., 1965; Kent State U., 1971. **Group:** Chicago/AI, 1938; MOMA, Subway Art, 1938; New York World's Fair, 1939; Sculptors Guild Annuals, 1941–71; WMAA Annuals, 1948, 61, 62, 64, 66, 68; Riverside Museum, NYC, 14 Sculptors, 1958; MOMA, Recent Sculpture USA, 1959; Newark Museum, 1961, 64; Carnegie International, 1962; WMAA, Geometric Abstraction in America, circ., 1962; New York World's Fair, 1964–65; Federation of Modern Painters and Sculptors Annuals, 1964–71; Cleveland/MA, 1972; Canton Art Institute, 1973; Dayton/AI, 1974. **Collections:** American Sugar Co.; American Can Corp.; Canton Art Institute; Garcia Corp.; Kent State U.; R. H. Macy & Co.; New School for Social Research; San Antonio/McNay; Storm King Art Center; Tate; Trenton/State; Union Carbide Corp.; WMAA. **Bibliography:** Archives.

KOPMAN, BENJAMIN. b. December 25, 1897, Vitebsk, Russia; **d.** December 4, 1965, Teaneck, N. J. To USA, 1903; citizen, 1913. **Studied:** NAD. Illustrated *Crime and Punishment* (Random House, 1956). **Member:** Artists Equity. Federal A.P.: Paintings, lithographs. **Awards:** PAFA, Gold Medal for Landscape, 1947, 53; MMA, Fourth Prize for Etching. **One-man Exhibitions:** (first) Scott Thurber Gallery, Chicago; Macbeth Gallery, NYC, 1912; ACA Gallery; J. B. Neumann Gallery, NYC; The Milch Gallery; John Heller Gallery, NYC; Newhouse Gallery, NYC; The Forum Gallery; Phillips; Klutznick Hall, Washington, D.C., 1964. **Group:** NAD; PAFA; Carnegie; Corcoran; Phillips; Youngstown/Butler; Ringling; MMA; MOMA; La Napoule Art Foundation, Paris. **Collections:** Atlanta U.; Brooklyn Museum; Carnegie; Colgate

U.; Kansas City/Nelson; MMA; U. of Michigan; New Paltz/SUNY; PAFA; PMA; Syracuse U.; Tel Aviv; WMAA; Worcester/AM. **Bibliography:** Baur 7; Brown; Cheney; **Ignatoff**; Kootz 1; Mellquist; Poore; Reese; Ringel, ed.

KOPPELMAN, CHAIM. b. 1920, Brooklyn, N.Y. **Studied:** Brooklyn College, 1938; Educational Alliance, NYC, 1938; American Artists School, NYC, 1939, with Eugene Morley, Carl Holty; New School for Social Research, with Amedee Ozenfant; Art College of Western England; Bristol, 1944; Ecole Regionale de Beaux-Arts, Reims, 1945; ASL, 1946, with Will Barnet, Jose de Creeft; privately with Amedee Ozenfant, 1946–49 (and served concurrently as his assistant). US Air Force, 1942–45. **Taught:** NYU; Brooklyn College; New Paltz/SUNY; School of Visual Arts, 1959– ; Aesthetic Realism Foundation, NYC, 1971– . **Member:** Society for Aesthetic Realism; NAD, Associate, 1979. **Commissions:** International Graphic Arts Society, 1958; A.A.A. Gallery, NYC, 1959, 61, 64. **Awards:** L.C. Tiffany Grant, 1956, 59; PAFA, Hon. Men., 1959; Audubon Artists, Medal for Graphics, 1960; Library of Congress, Pennell **P.P.**; SAGA, List Prize ($1,000), 1967; IBM Gallery of Arts and Sciences, NYC, III International Miniature Print Exhibition, 1968; Brooklyn Museum, Print Biennial, 1968; CAPS, 1976. **Address:** 498 Broome Street, NYC 10012. **Dealers:** The Terrain Gallery; A.A.A. Gallery, NYC. **One-man Exhibitions:** (first) Outline Gallery, Pittsburgh, 1943; "67" Gallery, NYC, 1945; The Terrain Gallery, 1956, 69 (two-man, with wife, Dorothy), 1974; Philadelphia Art Alliance, 1959; Kornbluth Gallery, Paterson, N.J., 1964; Hinckley and Brohel Galleries, Washington, D.C. 1967; A.A.A. Gallery, NYC, 1973; AFS Gallery, Binghamton, N.Y., 1973; U. of Maine, 1974; Warwick (Eng.) Gallery (two-man), 1975. **Retrospective:** AAA, NYC, Prints, 1973; The Terrain Gallery, NYC, Drawings, 1974. **Group:** Boston/

MFA; Los Angeles/County MA; Chicago/AI; Walker; Baltimore/MA; Detroit/Institute; Brooklyn Museum Print Biennial; WMAA Annuals, 1948, 50, 61, 63; Yale U., 1949, 60; Documenta II, Kassel, 1959; USIA, Contemporary American Prints, circ., Latin America, 1959–60; II Inter-American Paintings and Prints Biennial, Mexico City, 1960; MOMA, Recent Painting USA: The Figure, circ., 1962–63; Graphics: USA, Moscow, 1964; St. Paul Gallery, 1966; Mexico City/Nacional, 1967; IBM Gallery of Arts and Sciences, NYC, 1968; Cranbrook, 6th Biennial, National Religious Art Exhibition, 1968; Western New Mexico U., 1969; Library of Congress Print Annual, 1969; A.F.A., The Indignant Eye, 1971; Purdue U., Print Invitational, 1972; Utah State U. Print Invitational, 1972; Anchorage, Print Invitational, 1972, 74; NAD, Annuals 1978, 79, 80; The Terrain Gallery NYC, 25th Anniversary Exhibition, 1980. **Collections:** Anchorage; Boston/MFA; Brooklyn Museum; CSCS, Long Beach; Caracas; Long Beach State College; MMA; MOMA; National Gallery; Otis Art Institute; Peabody Museum; Syracuse U.; US State Department; Victoria and Albert Museum; Walker; Western New Mexico U.; Yale U. **Bibliography:** Archives.

KORTLANDER, WILLIAM CLARK. b. February 9, 1925, Grand Rapids, Mich. **Studied:** Michigan State U., BA; State U. of Iowa, MA, Ph.D. US Army, 1943–46. Traveled USA, Western Europe; resided Western Europe, 1967–68. **Taught:** State U. of Iowa, 1950–54; Lawrence U., 1954–56; U. of Texas, 1956–61; Michigan State U., 1960; Ohio U., 1961–. **Awards:** Mead Painting of the Year, 1965; Ohio U., Baker Award, 1967–68. **Address:** Angel Ridge, Route 4, Box 182, Athens, OH 45701. **Dealer:** Haber/Theodore Gallery, NYC. **One-man Exhibitions:** (first—NYC) A.M. Sachs Gallery, 1967, also 1968; The Jewish Center, Columbus, Ohio, 1964; Bryson Gallery, Columbus, 1965; Denison

U., 1965; Otterbein College, 1965; Battelle Memorial Institute, Columbus, 1966; George Bennett Gallery, Toledo, Ohio, 1966; Western Electric Co., Columbus, 1966; West Virginia State College, 1966; Zanesville/AI, 1966; Merida Gallery, Inc., 1967; Montana State College, 1969; Gallery 200, Columbus, Ohio, 1974; Springfield Art Center, Ohio, 1974; Northern Ohio U., 1974; Haber/Theodore Gallery, NYC, 1980. **Retrospective:** Springfield Art Center, 1974; Ohio U., 1976. **Group:** Dallas Museum for Contemporary Arts, 1959; Witte, 1961; Ball State U., Drawings and Sculpture Annual, 1964–65; PAFA Annual, 1965; Dayton/AI, 1965; Villanova U., 1968; U. of Wisconsin, 1968; U. of North Carolina, 1970; New School for Social Research, American Drawings of the Sixties, 1970; Roanoke Fine Arts Center, Va., 1978; Marietta College, 1980. **Collections:** Abraham and Straus, Brooklyn; Chubu Institute, Nagoya; Columbus; Huntington, W. Va.; Mead Corporation; The Ohio Co.; Ohio U.; Oppenheimer Co., NYC; Otterbein College; Wylain Corp., Fort Worth; West Virginia State College; Zanesville/AI.

KOSUTH, JOSEPH. b. January 13, 1945, Toledo, Ohio. **Studied:** Toledo Museum School of Design, with Line Bloom Draper, 1955–62; Cleveland Institute of Art, 1963–64; private study; with Roger Barr, Paris, 1964–65; School of Visual Arts, NYC, 1965–67; New School for Social Research, 1971–72. Traveled Europe, South America, Asia, the Orient, Pacific Islands. **Taught:** School of Visual Arts, NYC, 1968. Founded and directed the Museum of Normal Art, NYC, 1967. **Member:** The Editorial Board of the Art and Language Press. **Award:** Cassandra Foundation Grant, 1968. **Address:** 591 Broadway, NYC 10012. **Dealer:** Leo Castelli Inc., NYC. **One-man Exhibitions:** Museum of Normal Art, NYC, 1967; Gallery 669, Los Angeles, 1968; Bradford Junior College (two-man), 1968; Douglas Gallery,

Vancouver, 1969; Instituto Torcuato di Tella, Buenos Aires, 1969; Nova Scotia College of Art and Design, Halifax, 1969; St. Martin's School of Art, London, 1969; Art & Project, Amsterdam, 1969; Coventry (Eng.) College of Art and Design, 1969; Gian Enzo Sperone, Turin, 1969, 70; A 37 90 89, Antwerp, 1969; Pinacotheca, St. Kilda, Virginia, Australia, 1969; Leo Castelli, Inc., NYC, 1969, 71, 72 (2), 1975, 79; Toronto, 1969; Pasadena/AM, 1970; Iysk Kunstgalerie, Copenhagen, 1970; Galerie Daniel Templon, Paris, 1970; Paul Maenz Gallery, Cologne, 1971; Protetch-Rivkin, Washington, D.C., 1971; Centro de Arte y Comunicacion, Buenos Aires, 1971; Lia Rumma Studio d'Arte, Naples, 1971; Carmen Lamanna Gallery, Toronto, 1971, 72, 74, 78; Galeria Toselli, Milan, 1971; Gian Enzo Sperone and Konrad Fischer Gallery, Rome, 1972, 74; Galerie Gunter Sachs, Hamburg, 1973; Paul Maenz Gallery, Brussels, 1973; Cologne, 1979; Kunstmuseum, Lucerne, 1973; Claire S. Copley Gallery, Los Angeles, 1974; Galeria La Bertesca, Dusseldorf, 1974; Galleria Peccolo, Livorno, 1975; Galerie MTL, Brussels, 1975; Lia Rumma Studio d'Arte, Naples, 1975; Durand-Desert Gallery, Paris, 1975; U. of Chicago, 1976; International Cultural Center, Antwerp, 1976; Ghent, 1977; Eindhoven, 1978; Museum of Modern Art, Oxford, 1978; New 57 Gallery, Edinburgh, 1979; Galerie Eric Fabre, Paris, 1979; Rudiger Schottle, Munich, 1979; Galeria Samon, Genoa, 1979; Musée de Chartres, 1979; P.S. 1, Queens, 1980. **Group:** Lannis Gallery, NYC, Non-Anthropomorphic Art, 1967; U. of Rochester, New York Art, 1968; A.F.A., The Square in Painting, 1968; UCLA, Electric Art, 1969; Berne, When Attitudes Become Form, 1969; Amsterdam/Stedelijk, Op Losse Schroeven, 1969; Seattle/AM, 557,087, 1969; Dusseldorf/Kunsthalle, Prospect '69, 1969; Chicago/Contemporary, Art by Telephone, 1969; WMAA Annual, 1969; Turin/Civico, Conceptual Art, Arte Povera, Land Art, 1970; Jewish Museum, Software, 1970;

Galerie im Taxispalais, Innsbruck, Concept Art, 1970; MOMA, Information, 1971; SRGM, Guggenheim International, 1971; VII Paris Biennial, 1971; Buenos Aires/Moderno, Art Systems, 1971; Kunsthalle, Nurnberg, Biennial, 1971; Munster/WK, Das Konzept ist die Form, 1972; Kunstmuseum, Lucerne, Joseph Kosuth; Investigationen uber Kunst and 'Problemkreise' seit 1965, 1973; Chicago/AI, Idea and Image in Recent Art, 1974; Kennedy Center, Art Now, '74, 1974; Cologne/Kunstverein, Kunst uber Kunst, 1974; Indianapolis, 1974; Chicago/AI Annual, 1976; Canberra/National Illusion & Reality, circ., 1977; Berlin/Akademie der Kunst; SoHo, 1976; Museum Bochum, Words, 1979. **Collections:** MOMA; Oberlin College; Ottawa/National; SRGM; Tate; WMAA. **Bibliography:** *Art Now 74;* Celant; *Contemporanea;* Davis, D.; Honisch and Jensen, eds.; Honnef; Lippard, ed.; Meyer; Sager; *When Attitudes Become Form.*

KRASNER, LEE. b. 1911, Brooklyn, N.Y. **Studied:** Cooper Union; NAD; Hofmann School, 1938. Federal A.P.: Mural Painting. **Commissions:** 2 Broadway Building, NYC (86-ft. mural). Subject of the film *Lee Krasner: The Long View,* made by Barbara Rose. **Awards:** Cooper Union, Saint-Gaudens Medal, 1974. **m.** Jackson Pollock (1944). **Address:** 180 East 79 Street, NYC 10021; Springs, East Hampton, NY 11937. **Dealer:** The Pace Gallery, NYC. **One-man Exhibitions:** (first) Betty Parsons Gallery, 1950; The Stable Gallery, 1955; Martha Jackson Gallery, 1958; The Howard Wise Gallery, NYC, 1961, 62; Whitechapel Art Gallery, London, 1965; Arts Council Gallery, London, circ., 1966; U. of Alabama, 1967; Marlborough Gallery, Inc., NYC, 1968, 69, 73; Reese Palley Gallery, San Francisco, 1969; WMAA, 1973; Miami-Dade, 1974; Gibbes Art Gallery, Charleston, S.C., 1974; Corcoran, 1975; The Pace Gallery, NYC, 1977, 79; Susanne Hilberry Gallery, Birmingham, Mich., 1977; Janie C.

Lee Gallery, Houston, 1978. **Group:** MacMillin Gallery, NYC, French and American Painting, 1942; Howard Putzell Gallery, Hollywood, 1945; Marlborough Fine Arts Ltd., London, The New, New York Scene, 1961; PAFA, 1962; PMA; MOMA, Hans Hofmann and His Students, circ., 1963–64; SRGM, American Drawings, 1964; Gallery of Modern Art, NYC, 1965; U. of Illinois, 1969; MOMA, The New American Painting and Sculpture; The First Generation, 1969; Finch College, NYC, Projected Art, 1971; WMAA, 1973; PMA/Museum of the Philadelphia Civic Center, Focus, 1974; Cornell U., Abstract Expressionism: The Formative Years, 1978. **Collections:** Buffalo/Albright; Brooklyn Museum; Dallas/MFA; High Museum; Indianapolis; MMA; MOMA; NYU; PMA; SRGM; WMAA; Yale U. **Bibliography:** *Art: A Woman's Sensibility;* Diamonstein; Hunter 6; Janis and Blesh 1; Janis, S.; Hobbs and Levin; Nemser.

KRIESBERG, IRVING. b. March 13, 1919, Chicago, Ill. **Studied:** Chicago Art Institute School, 1941, BFA; Escuela Nacional de Artes Plasticas, Mexico City, 1941–44; NYU, 1972, MA (cinema). **Taught:** Parsons School of Design, NYC, 1955–61; Pratt Institute, 1961–72; Yale U., 1962–69; City U. of New York, 1969–72; SUNY, 1972–76; Columbia U., 1977, 78. **Awards:** Ford Foundation, **P.P.,** 1946; Fulbright Fellowship (India), 1965–66; CAPS (films), 1974; CAPS (Painting), 1974; Guggenheim Foundation Fellowship, 1977. **Address:** 210 Spring Street, NYC 10012. **Dealer:** Terry Dintenfass, Inc., NYC. **One-man Exhibitions:** Curt Valentine Gallery, NYC; Chicago/AI, 1946; MOMA, 1953; St. Louis/City, 1954; Detroit/Institute, 1954; The Graham Gallery, NYC, 1957, 59, 62; Kumar Gallery, Delhi, 1966; Yale U., 1967; Terry Dintenfass, Inc., NYC, 1978, 80; Fairweather-Hardin Gallery, Chicago, 1979; Syracuse/Everson, 1980; Brandeis U., 1980. **Retrospective:** Jew-

Lee Krasner *Gothic Landscape* 1961

ish Museum, NYC, 1962. **Group:** Chicago/AI, 1946; MOMA, New Talent; MOMA, Fifteen Americans, circ., 1952; Detroit/Institute, 1953; St. Louis/City, 1954; Milwaukee, Directions 1; Options, circ., 1968; SRGM, 1972; SRGM, Ten Independents, 1972; AALA, 1978. **Collections:** Baltimore/MA; Brandeis U.; Chase Manhattan Bank, NYC; Cincinnati/AM; Corcoran; Detroit/Institute; Mead Corporation; MOMA; The Naropa Institute, Boulder; Santa Barbara/MA; St. Louis/City; WMAA. **Bibliography:** Atkinson.

KROLL, LEON. b. December 6, 1894, NYC; **d.** October 25, 1974, NYC. **Studied:** ASL, with John Henry Twachtman; NAD; Academie Julian, Paris, with Jean Paul Laurens. Traveled France, USA. **Taught:** NAD and ASL, 1911–73; Marland Institute, 1919–21; Chicago Art Institute School, 1924–25; PAFA, 1929–30. **Member:** NAD; AAAL; NIAL. Federal A.P.: Mural Division. **Commissions** (mural)**:** US Justice Department, Washington, D.C., 1936–37; Worcester (Mass.) War Memorial Building, 1938–41; Johns Hopkins U.; US Military Cemetery, Omaha Beach, France. **Awards:** Chicago/AI, The Mr. & Mrs. Frank G. Logan Prize, 1919, 32, 35; NAD, Benjamin Altman Prize, 1923, 32, 35; Chicago/AI, Potter Palmer Gold Medal, 1924; PAFA, Joseph E. Temple Gold Medal, 1927; Carnegie, First Prize, 1936; Chevalier of the Legion of Honor; and more than 20 others. **One-man Exhibitions:** (first) NAD, 1910; Buffalo/Albright, 1929; Toronto, 1930 (three-man); Worcester/AM, 1937; Cleveland/MA, 1945; French & Co. Inc., NYC, 1947; The Milch Gallery, 1947, 59; Dannenberg Gallery, 1970. **Retrospective:** Museum of Art, Ft. Lauderdale, Fla., 1980. **Group:** The Armory Show, 1913; Chicago/AI; Cleveland/MA; St. Louis/City; U. of Nebraska; WMAA; Detroit/Institute; Baltimore/MA; MMA. **Collections:** Baltimore/MA; Britannica; Carnegie; Chicago/AI; Cleveland/MA; Corcoran; Dayton/AI; Denver/AM; Detroit/

Institute; U. of Illinois; Indianapolis/Herron; Los Angeles/County MA; MMA; MOMA; Minneapolis/Institute; Municipal U. of Omaha; U. of Nebraska; PAFA; SFMA; St. Louis/City; San Diego; WMAA; West Palm Beach/Norton; Wilmington. **Bibliography:** Baur 7; Biddle 4; Boswell 1; Brown; Bruce and Watson; Bryant, L.; Cheney; Coke 2; Eliot; Gerdts; Hall; *Index of 20th Century Artists;* Jackman; Jewell 2; Kent, N.; **Kroll 1, 2;** Mather 1; McCurdy, ed.; Mellquist; Narodny; Neuhaus; Pagano, Poore; Watson 1; *Woodstock: An American Art Colony 1902–1977.* Archives.

KRUSHENICK, NICHOLAS. b. May 31, 1929, NYC. **Studied:** ASL, 1948–50; Hofmann School, NYC, 1950–51. US Army, 1947–48. **Taught:** U. of Wisconsin, 1969; Dartmouth College, 1969; Yale U., 1969, 70; Cornell U., 1970; Ball State U., 1971; Herbert H. Lehman College, Bronx, N.Y., 1972; California State U., Long Beach, 1973; U. of Alabama, 1973; St. Cloud State College, 1973; U. of California, Berkeley, 1973–74; The Ohio State U., 1974; U. of Washington, 1974. **Commissions:** Designed production of Haydn's *Man in the Moon,* Guthrie Theater, Minneapolis, 1968. **Awards:** Longview Foundation Grant, 1962; Tamarind Fellowship, 1965; Guggenheim Foundation Fellowship, 1967. **Address:** 140 Grand Street, NYC 10013. **One-man Exhibitions:** (first) Camino Gallery, NYC, 1956; Brata Gallery, NYC, 1958, 60; The Graham Gallery, 1962, 64; Cinema I and Cinema II, NYC, 1964; Fischbach Gallery, 1965; WGMA, 1965; Galerie Muller, 1966, 67; Ileana Sonnabend Gallery, Paris, 1967; The Pace Gallery, 1967, 69, 72; Galerie Nachst Skt. Stephan, Vienna, 1967; Walker, 1968; Galerie der Spiegel, Cologne, 1968; Galerie Rene Ziegler, Zurich, 1969, 70; Dartmouth College, 1969; Harcus-Krakow Gallery, 1969; U. of Southern Florida, 1970; Galerie Beyeler, 1971; Herbert H. Lehman College, Bronx, N.Y., 1972; Hannover/K-G,

Nicholas Krushenick   *Untitled Collage*   1965

1972; Galerie Denise Rene/Hans Mayer, Dusseldorf, 1973; U. of Alabama, 1973; Jack Glenn Gallery, Corona del Mar, 1973; California State U., Long Beach, 1974; ADI Gallery, San Francisco, 1974; Portland (Ore.) Center for the Visual Arts, 1974; Reed College, 1974; Foster-White Gallery, 1975; Bucknell U., 1977; Newport Art Association, 1978; Pyramid Gallery, Washington, D.C., 1978; Hokin Gallery, Chicago, 1978; Elizabeth Weiner Gallery, NYC, 1978; Suzette Schochett Gallery, Newport, L.I., 1977. **Retrospective:** Walker, 1968. **Group:** Wagner College, 1958; Galerie Creuze, Paris, 1958; Tokyo/Modern, 1959, 66; The Howard Wise Gallery, Cleveland, 1960; Barnard College, 1962; Lincoln, Mass./De Cordova, 1962; WMAA Annuals, 1963, 65, 67; Los Angeles/County MA, Post Painterly Abstraction, 1964; MOMA, Contemporary Painters and Sculptors as Printmakers, 1964; Corcoran Biennial, 1965; MOMA, American Collages, 1965; SRGM, Systemic Painting, 1966; Amsterdam/Stedelijk, New Shapes of Color, 1966; Expo '67, Montreal, 1967; Documenta IV, Kassel, 1968; Ars 69, Helsinki, 1969; ICA, U. of Pennsylvania, The Spirit of the Comics, 1969; Humlebaek/Louisiana, Amerikanst Kunst, 1950–1960, 1969; Berlin/National, 1973; WMAA Biennial, 1973; Long Beach/MA, Mixing Masters, 1974. **Bibliography:** Alloway 3; Honisch and Jensen, eds.; Lippard 5; Rose, B., 1. Archives.

KUHN, WALT. b. October 27, 1877, Brooklyn, N.Y.; **d.** July 13, 1949, NYC. **Studied:** Academie Colarossi, Paris, 1901; Academy of Fine Arts, Munich, 1901, with H. von Zugel; Artists Sketch Class, NYC, 1905. **Taught:** New York School of Art, 1908–09. Executive Secretary, Association of American Painters and Sculptors, sponsor of The Armory Show, NYC, 1913. Founder of the Penguin Club, 1917–19. Designed sets and directed many revue skits for Broadway in the 1920s. **One-man Exhibitions:** (first) Madison Gallery, NYC, 1910, also 1911; Montross Gallery, NYC, 1914, 15, 22, 24, 25; DeZayas Gallery, NYC, 1920; Grand Central, NYC, 1927; M. Knoedler & Co., 1928; The Downtown Gallery, 1928; Marie Harriman Gallery, NYC, 1930–42; Durand-Ruel Gallery, NYC, 1944, 45, 46, 48; Colorado Springs/FA, 1947, 64; Maynard Walker Gallery, NYC, 1954, 57, 62, 66; Amon Carter Museum, 1964; Kennedy Galleries, NYC, 1967, 68, 72, 77, 80. **Retrospectives:** Phillips, 1944 (two-man); A.F.A., circ., 1951; Albany/Institute, 1958; Cincinnati/AM, 1960; Fort Worth, 1964; U. of Arizona, 1966. **Group:** WMAA; Chicago/AI; Detroit/Institute; Cincinnati/AM; MOMA. **Collections:** Buffalo/Albright; Cincinnati/AM; Colorado Springs/FA; Columbus; Currier; Denver/AM; Des Moines; Detroit/Institute; New York Cultural Center; Indianapolis/Herron; Kansas City/Nelson; MMA; MOMA; U. of Nebraska; Ogunquit; Phillips; WMAA; Wellesley College; Wichita/AM. **Bibliography: Adams 1, 2**; Baur 7; Bazin; Biddle 4; **Bird**; Blesh 1; Brown 1, 2; Bulliet 1; Cahill and Barr, eds.; Cheney; Eliot; Flanagan; Genauer; Gerdts; Goodrich and Baur 1; Hunter 6; *Index of 20th Century Artists*; Janis, S.; Jewell 2; Kootz 1; **Kuhn 1, 2**; Marter, Tarbell, and Wechsler; McCurdy, ed.; Mellquist; Mendelowitz; Newmeyer; Pagano; Phillips 2; Poore;

Robert M. Kulicke   *Triptych: A Persimmon, A Dollar Bill, and a Pear*   1981

Richardson, E. P.; Ringel, ed.; Rose, B., 1; Smith, S.C.K.; Wight 2. Archives.

KULICKE, ROBERT. b. March 9, 1924, Philadelphia, Pa. **Studied:** Temple U., Philadelphia Museum School, Atelier Fernand Leger, 1946–50. **Taught:** U. of California, 1964, 1970; Kulicke Cloisonne Workshop, NYC, 1964– . **Awards:** American Institute of Interior Designers, International Design Award, 1968. **Address:** 2231 Broadway, NYC 10024. **Dealer:** Davis & Langdale Company.   **One-man Exhibitions:** Parma Gallery, NYC, 1960; Allan Stone Gallery, 1962, 63; Multiples, 1966; The Kornblee Gallery, 1968, 69, 72; Benson Gallery, 1968, 69; Davis & Long Co., NYC, 1977, 78, 79, 80. **Group:** WGMA, 1964; Silvermine Guild, 1964; Chicago/ AI, Dayton/AI; A.F.A., 100 Years of American Realism, 1965; WMAA, 1969. **Collections:** PMA. **Bibliography:** Archives.

KUNIYOSHI, YASUO. b. September 1, 1893, Okayama, Japan; **d.** May 14, 1953, NYC. To USA, 1906. **Studied:** Los Angeles School of Art, three years; NAD; Robert Henri School, 1910; Independent School of Art, 1914–16, with Homer Boss; ASL, 1916–20, with Kenneth Hayes Miller. Traveled Europe, Japan, USA. **Taught:** ASL, 1933– 53; New School for Social Research, 1936–53; Brooklyn Museum School. **Member:** Salons of America, 1922–38 (director); Hamilton Easter Field Foundation; American Artists Congress; An American Place (president, 1939–44); Artists Equity (president, 1947–50, Hon. president until his death). Federal A.P.: Graphics Division, two years, ca. 1936. **Commissions:** Radio City Music Hall, NYC (mural). **Awards:** Carnegie, Hon. Men., 1931, Second Prize, 1939, and First Prize, 1944; Los Angeles/ County MA, Second Prize, 1934; PAFA, Joseph E. Temple Gold Medal, 1934; Guggenheim Foundation Fellowship, 1935; Golden Gate International Exposition, San Francisco, 1939, First Prize, PAFA, J. Henry Schiedt Memorial Prize, 1944; VMFA, **P.P.**, 1944; Chicago/ AI, Norman Wait Harris Bronze Medal and Prize, 1945; La Tausca Competition, Fifth Award, 1947, 48; *Look* magazine poll of "Ten Best Painters," February, 1948; MMA, Second Prize, 1950. **One-man Exhibitions:** The Daniel Gallery, NYC, 1922, also 1928, 30; Tokyo/Modern and Osaka/Municipal, 1931–32; The Downtown Gallery, 1933, 36, 39, 40, 41, 45, 48, 50, 52, 55, 61, 65; ASL, 1936; Baltimore/MA, 1939; Boston Museum School, 1950; Woodstock (N.Y.) Art Gallery, 1956; FAR Gallery, 1970; Paul Gallery, 1971; U. of Texas, 1975. **Retrospectives:** The Downtown Gallery, benefit for United China Relief, 1942; WMAA, 1948; Tokyo/Modern, 1954; Boston U., 1961; U. of Florida,

1969. **Group:** Society of Independent Artists, NYC; Penguin Club, NYC, 1917; MOMA, Paintings by 19 Living Americans, 1929; MOMA, Twentieth Century Portraits, 1942; The U. of Chicago, 1948; Portland, Me./MA, 1949; XXVI Venice Biennial, 1952; U. of Illinois; U. of Nebraska. **Collections:** AAAL; Agricultural and Mechanical College of Texas; Andover/Phillips; Arizona State College; U. of Arizona; Atlanta/AA; Auburn A.; Baltimore/MA; Britannica; Brooklyn Museum; Buffalo/Albright; Carnegie; Chicago/AI; Cincinnati/AM; Clearwater/Gulf Coast; Cleveland/MA; Columbus; Cranbrook; Dallas/MFA; Des Moines; Detroit/Institute; Hamilton Easter Field Foundation; Fort Worth; U. of Georgia; Hartford/Wadsworth; Honolulu Academy; Houston/MFA; U. of Illinois; Indiana U.; Indianapolis/Herron; Kalamazoo/Institute; Kansas City/Nelson; Library of Congress; MMA; MOMA; U. of Michigan; Milwaukee; U. of Nebraska; Newark Museum; New London; Ogunquit; PMA; Phillips; Portland, Ore./AM; Santa Barbara/MA; Sao Paulo; Tel Aviv; Tokyo/Modern; Utica; VMFA; WMAA; Walker; Washington U.; West Palm Beach/Norton; Wichita/Am; Wilmington; Youngstown/Butler. **Bibliography:** American Artists Congress, Inc.; American Artists Group, Inc. 3; Barker 1; Baur 7; Bazin; Bethers; Biddle 4; Blesh 1; Boswell 1; Brown 2; Cahill and Barr, eds.; Cheney; Coke 2; Eliot; *From Foreign Shores;* Genauer; Goodrich 8; Goodrich and Baur 1; Goodrich and Imgizumi; Haftman; Hall; Halpert; Hunter, ed.; *Index of 20th Century Artists;* Jewel 2; Kootz 1, 2; **Kuniyoshi;** McCurdy, ed.; Mellquist; Newmeyer; Pagano; Pearson 1, 2; Poore; Pousette-Dart, ed.; Reese; Richardson, E.P.; Ringel, ed.; Rose, B., 1; Wheeler; Wight 2; *Woodstock: An American Art Colony 1902–1977;* Zaidenberg, ed.; Zigrosser 1. Archives.

KUNTZ, ROGER. b. January 4, 1926, San Antonio, Tex., **d.** August, 1975, Laguna Beach, Calif. **Studied:** Pomona College, 1943–44, 1946–48, BA; Claremont Graduate School, 1948–50, MFA; in France and Italy, 1950. **Awards:** Arizona State Fair, Second Prize, 1949, and First Prize, 1950; NAD Annual, Andrew Carnegie Prize, 1952; Denver/AM, **P.P.,** 1952, 53; Los Angeles/County MA, **P.P.,** 1953, 55, and First Prize, 1954; U. of Illinois, **P.P.,** 1955; Jose Drudis Foundation **P.P.,** ($400), 1956; Guggenheim Foundation Fellowship, 1956; Los Angeles Art Festival, 1959; Chaffey College, First Award, 1960. **One-man Exhibitions:** Scripps College, 1950, 54; San Diego, 1951; Felix Landau Gallery, 1952, 54, 56, 58, 62, 64; Pasadena/AM, 1953, 63; Urban Gallery, NYC, 1955; Barone Gallery, NYC, 1957; Gump's Gallery, 1957; Sierra Madre (Calif.) Public Library, 1958; San Bernardino Valley College, 1959; Whittier (Calif.) Art Association, 1960; Mount San Antonio College, 1961. **Group:** Los Angeles/County MA, California Centennial Art Exhibition, 1949, Annuals, 1951, 53, 57; NAD, 1952, 53; Denver/AM, 1952, 53, 54, 55; PAFA, 1952, 55; Corcoran, 1953; Carnegie, 1955, 64; Sao Paulo, 1955; U. of Illinois, 1955, 57; Santa Barbara/MA, I West Coast Biennial, 1958; Long Beach/MA, Arts of Southern California II, 1958; Oakland/AM, Pop Art USA, 1963. **Collections:** Denver/AM; U. of Illinois; Los Angeles/County MA; NAD; Pasadena/AM; Scripps College.

KUPFERMAN, LAWRENCE. b. March 25, 1909, Boston, Mass. **Studied:** Boston Museum School, 1929–31; Massachusetts School of Art, Boston, 1931–35, BS.Ed. **Taught:** Massachusetts College of Art, 1941–69 (head, Department of Painting). **Member:** SAGA; NAD; Fellow of the Royal Society of Arts, London; Federal A.P.: Easel painting. **Commissions** (murals): SS *Constitution* and SS *Independence,* American Export Isbrandtsen Lines, Inc. **Awards:** U. of Illinois, $1,000 **P.P.,** 1953; Rhode Island Arts Festival, First Prize for Painting, 1961. **Address:** 38

Devon Road, Newton Centre, MA 01259. **Dealer:** Childs Gallery, Boston; Horizon Gallery, Rockport, Mass. **One-man Exhibitions:** (first) Boris Mirski Gallery, Boston, 1944, also 1945, 46, 47; Mortimer Brandt, NYC, 1946; Philadelphia Art Alliance, 1947; Mortimer Levitt Gallery, NYC, 1948, 49, 51, 53; Martha Jackson Gallery, 1955; The Swetzoff Gallery, Boston, 1956; Verna Wear Gallery, NYC, 1956; Ruth White Gallery, 1958; Gropper Gallery, Cambridge, Mass., 1958; The Pace Gallery, Boston, 1960, 61, 63; Lincoln, Mass./De Cordova, 1961; Irla Kert Gallery, Montreal, 1962; Art Unlimited, Providence, 1963; Horizon Gallery, Rockport, Me., 1969; The Point Gallery, Kittery Point, Me., 1969; Horizon West, Los Angeles, 1971; Harold Ernst Gallery, Boston, 1973. **Retrospective:** Massachusetts College of Art, 1969; Brockton/Fuller, 1974. **Group:** Chateau de Rohan, Strasbourg, France; Omaha/Joslyn; U. of Connecticut; Chicago/AI Annuals; PAFA; WMAA Annuals; Venice Biennial; U. of Illinois; Brooklyn Museum Biennials; MMA; Hartford/Wadsworth; NAD; Carnegie; Musée du Petit Palais, Paris. **Collections:** Andover/Phillips; Baltimore/MA; Boston/MFA; Boston Public Library; Bowdoin College; Brooklyn Museum; Carnegie; Hartford/Wadsworth; Harvard U.; U. of Illinois; La Jolla; Library of Congress; MMA; MOMA; U. of Massachusetts; U. of Michigan; Mills College; NYU; SFMA; Syracuse U.; WMAA; Walker; Wichita State U. **Bibliography:** Baur 7; Pousette-Dart, ed.; Reese. Archives.

KUSHNER, ROBERT. b. August 9, 1949, Pasadena, Calif. **Studied:** U. of California, San Diego, BA. Traveled Iran, Afghanistan, Europe, India. Designed sets and costumes for theatrical and dance groups. **Awards:** National Endowment for the Arts, 1977, 79. **Address:** 87-89 Leonard Street, NYC 10013. **Dealer:** Holly Solomon Gallery, NYC. **One-man Exhibitions:** (first) Holly Solomon Gallery, NYC, 1975, 77,

Robert Kushner *Biarritz* (in performance) 1975

79 (2); U. of Kentucky, 1975; Thorpe Intermedia Gallery, Sparkill, N.Y., 1977; Philadelphia College of Art, 1977; Lunn Gallery, Washington, D.C., 1978; F. H. Mayor Gallery, London, 1979, 80; Daniel Templon, Paris, 1979; Dart Gallery, Chicago, 1980. **Group:** U. of California, San Diego, Costumes for Moving Bodies, 1971; Museum of Contemporary Crafts, NYC, Vegetables and Flowers Weeks, 1973; WMAA Biennial, 1975; American Foundation for the Arts, Miami, Patterning and Decoration, 1977; U. of North Carolina, Art on Paper, 1977; P. S. 1, Long Island City, N. Y., Projects of the 70's, 1977; Cincinnati/Contemporary, Arabesque, 1978; Rice U., Pattern and Decoration, 1978; Brussels/Beaux-Arts, Patterning Painting, 1978; Dayton/AI, Patterns +, 1979; Buffalo/Albright, Patterns, 1979; Aspen Center for the Visual Arts, American Portraits of the 60's and 70's, 1979; ICA, U. of Pennsylvania, The Decorative Impulse, 1979; Mannheim, Dekor, 1980; Aachen/NG, Les nouveaux fauves—Die neuen Wilden, 1980; Venice Biennale, 1980. **Bibliography:** *Drawings: The Pluralist Decade;* Lucie-Smith.

L

LABAUDT, LUCIEN. b. May 14, 1880, Paris, France; **d.** December 13, 1943, Assam, India. Primarily self-taught. To London 1903; to USA, 1906; became a citizen. French Army, World War I; US War Department, World War II. Artists War Correspondent for *Life* magazine, 1943. **Commissions** (murals): Coit Memorial Tower, San Francisco; George Washington High School, San Francisco; Beach Chalet, San Francisco; US Post Office, Los Angeles; US Court House, Los Angeles; California State Building and Auditorium, Golden Gate International Exposition, San Francisco, 1939. **Awards:** SFMA, Anne Bremer Memorial Prize, 1927; Gump's Gallery, First Prize, 1932; Radical Group, Los Angeles, First Prize, 1937; SFMA, First Municipal **P.P.,** 1937. **One-man Exhibitions:** Beaux Arts Gallery, San Francisco; California Palace; Stanley Rose Gallery, Hollywood; Stendhal Gallery, Los Angeles; Oakland/AM; San Joaquin Pioneer Museum and Haggin Art Galleries, Stockton, Calif.; SFMA, 1940; SFMA, Memorial Exhibition, 1944; Lucien Labaudt Gallery, San Francisco, Memorial Exhibition, annually. **Group:** SFMA Annuals, 1920–43; Salon des Artistes Independants, Paris, 1921–26; Society of Independent Artists, NYC, 1922–31; Salon d'Automne, Paris, 1924–26; Paris Salon, 1928; Carnegie, 1931, 1933–37; MOMA, 1933, 34, 36; Brooklyn Museum, 1936. **Collections:** SFMA; San Francisco Municipal Art Commission. **Bibliography:** Cheney. Archives.

LACHAISE, GASTON. b. March 19, 1882, Paris, France; **d.** October, 1935, NYC. **Studied:** Ecole Bernard Palissy, Paris, 1895; Academie des Beaux-Arts, Paris, 1898–1904, with G. J. Thomas. Worked for Rene Lalique. To USA, 1906. Worked for H. H. Kitson in Boston, 1906–12. **Commissions:** Electricity Building, A Century of Progress, Chicago, 1933–34; Rockefeller Center, NYC; Fairmount Park, Philadelphia. **One-man Exhibitions:** (first) Bourgeois Gallery, NYC, 1918, also 1920; Stieglitz's Intimate Gallery, NYC, 1927; Joseph Brummer Gallery, NYC, 1928; Philadelphia Art Alliance, 1932; WMAA, 1937; Brooklyn Museum, 1938; M. Knoedler & Co. 1947; Weyhe Gallery, 1956; Margaret Brown Gallery, Boston, 1957; MOMA, circ. only, 1962; Robert Schoelkopf Gallery, 1964, 66, 69, 73; Felix Landau Gallery, 1965; Cornell U., 1974; UCLA, 1975; The Zabriskie Gallery, 1975; U. of Rochester, 1979; WMAA, 1980. **Retrospective:** MOMA, 1935; Los Angeles/County MA, 1963; SFMA, 1967. **Group:** MOMA; WMAA; Phillips; Hartford/Wadsworth; Harvard U., Three American Sculptors and the Female Nude, 1980. **Collections:** Andover/Phillips; Arizona State College; Cincinnati/AM; Cleveland/MA; Hartford/Wadsworth; Harvard U.; Los Angeles/County MA; MMA; MOMA; Museum of the City of New York; New London; PMA; Phillips; U. of Rochester; Santa Barbara/MA; Smith College; U. of Texas; WMAA. **Bibliography:** *Avant-Garde Painting and Sculpture in America 1910–25;* Baur 7; Biddle 4; Blesh 1; Brumme; Cahill and Barr, eds.; Cheney; Elsen 2; Fierens; *From Foreign Shores;* **Gallatin 4;** Goodrich and Baur 1; Hunter 6; **Kramer 3;** Lee and Burchwood; Marter, Tarbell, and Wechsler;

Gaston Lachaise *Equestrienne* 1918

McCurdy, ed.; **Nordland 1, 2**; Parkes; Ringel, ed.; Ritchie 3; Rose, B., 1, 4; Selz, Jr.; Seuphor 3; Seymour; Sutton; Archives.

LADERMAN, GABRIEL. b. October 26, 1929, Brooklyn, N.Y. **Studied:** Hans Hofmann School, 1949; privately with Willem de Kooning, 1949–50; Brooklyn College, 1948–52, BA; Atelier 17, Paris, 1949–50, 1952–53; Cornell U., 1955–57, MFA; Academy of Fine Arts, Florence, Italy, 1962–63. **Taught:** Cornell U., 1955–57; New Paltz/SUNY, 1957–59; Art Center of Northern New Jersey, 1960–64; Brooklyn College, 1961–62, 1967–68; Queens College, 1965–66, 1968–75; Pratt Institute, 1959–68, 1968–75; Yale U., 1968–69; Louisiana State U., 1966–67. **Awards:** L. C. Tiffany Award, 1969; Yaddo Fellowship, 1960, 61, 65; Fulbright Fellowship, 1962–63; Ingram Merrill Foundation Grant, 1975. **Address:** 760 West End Avenue, NYC. **Dealer:** Robert Schoelkopf Gallery. **One-man Exhibitions:** Cornell U., 1957; New Paltz/SUNY, 1958; Woodstock (N.Y.) Artists' Association, 1958, 59; Three Arts Gallery, 1959; Montclair State College (three-man), 1961; Pratt Institute, 1961; Robert Schoelkopf Gallery, 1964, 67, 69,

72, 74, 75, 76, 77; Felix Landau Gallery (four-man), 1965; Louisiana State U., 1966; Gallery 331, New Orleans, 1967; Hobart and William Smith College, 1970; U. of Rhode Island, 1970; Tyler School of Art, Philadelphia, 1971; Harwood Gallery, Springfield, Mo., 1972; Tanglewood, Mass., 1973. **Group:** Laurel Gallery, NYC, 1949; Brooklyn College, 1951, 57, 58, 60; Library of Congress, 1955, 56, 57; Philadelphia Print Club, 1955, 56, 58; Tanager Gallery, NYC, 1957, 62; Utica, 1957; SAGA, 1960; Cornell U.; Arts Festival, 1961; Boston U., Nine Realists, 1964; Columbia U., The Natural Vision, 1965; U. of North Carolina, 1966, 67; Tulsa/Philbrook, The American Sense of Reality, 1969; Milwaukee, Aspects of a New Realism, 1969; Indiana U., Six Figurative Artists, 1969; New Paltz/SUNY, 20 Representational Artists, 1969; WMAA, 22 Realists, 1970; Trenton/State, Four Views, 1970; Lincoln, Mass./De Cordova, Landscape, 1971; A.F.A., Realist Revival, 1972; Boston U., The American Landscape, 1972; AAAL, 1972; Arts Club of Chicago, American Landscape, 1973; The Pennsylvania State U., Contemporary Artists and the Figure, 1974; Boston/MFA, Trends in Contemporary Realist Painting, 1974; Museum of Fine Arts, St. Petersburg, Fla., The Figure as Form: American Painting 1930–1975, 1975; NAD, 1977. **Collections:** Chase Manhattan Bank; Cornell U.; Fidelity Bank, Philadelphia; Montclair State College; New Paltz/SUNY; Uris-Hilton Hotels. **Bibliography:** *America 1976;* Sager.

LAMIS, LEROY. b. September 27, 1925, Eddyville, Iowa. **Studied:** New Mexico Highlands U., BA, 1953; Columbia U., MA, 1956. Traveled Europe, Canada, Mexico, England. **Taught:** Cornell College, 1956–60; Indiana State U. (Terre Haute), 1961–; Dartmouth College, Artist-in-Residence, 1970. **Member:** American Abstract Artists. **Commissions:** New York State Council on the Arts, 1970. **Address:** 3101 Oak

Street, Terre Haute, IN 47803. **One-man Exhibitions:** (first) Staempfli Gallery, 1966, also 1969; Gilman Galleries, Chicago, 1967; Fort Wayne/AM, 1968; Louisville/Speed, 1969; Indianapolis/Herron, 1969; Des Moines, 1969; La Jolla, 1969; Dartmouth College; Indiana State U., 1976; Sheldon Swope Art Gallery, Terre Haute, Ind., 1979. **Group:** Buffalo/Albright, Mixed Media and Pop Art, 1963, Art Today, 1965; WMAA Sculpture Annual, 1964, 66, 68; MOMA, The Responsive Eye, 1965; Ridgefield/Aldrich, 1965–66; Riverside Museum, 1965–67; U. of Illinois, 1965–69; Flint/Institute, I Flint Invitational, 1966. **Collections:** Brooklyn Museum; Buffalo/Albright; Des Moines; Evansville; Hirshhorn; Indianapolis; Louisville/Speed; Lytton Savings and Loan Associations; Ridgefield/Aldrich; Terre Haute/Swope; WMAA; Walker.

LANDAU, JACOB. b. December 17, 1917, Philadelphia, Pa. **Studied:** Philadelphia Museum School, with Franklin Watkins, H. C. Pitz; New School for Social Research, 1947–48, 1952–53; Academie de la Grande Chaumiere, Paris, 1949–52. US Army, 1943–46. **Taught:** School of Visual Arts, NYC, 1954; Philadelphia College of Art, 1954–56; Pratt Institute, 1958– . **Member:** Philadelphia Watercolor Club; NAD; SAGA. **Commissions:** International Graphic Arts Society; A.A.A. Gallery; National Broadcasting Co.; The Limbach Co.; McGraw Hill, Inc. **Awards:** The Print Club, Philadelphia, Lessing J. Rosenwald **P.P.**, 1955, 59; L. C. Tiffany Grant, 1962; PAFA, Watercolor Prize, 1963; Tamarind Fellowship, 1965; National Council on the Arts, Sabbatical Leave Grant ($7,500), 1966; Guggenheim Foundation Fellowship, 1968; AAAL, Childe Hassam **P.P.**, 1973; Ford Foundation Grant, 1974; SAGA, **P.P.**, 1977, 79. **Address:** 2 Pine Drive, Roosevelt, NJ 08555. **Dealers:** A.A.A. Gallery, NYC; Nardin Gallery, NYC. **One-man Exhibitions:** (first) Galerie Le Bar, Paris, 1952; Philadelphia Art Alliance, 1954; Samuel S. Fleisher Art Memorial,

Philadelphia, 1959; A.A.A. Gallery, NYC, 1960, 70; U. of Maine, 1961, 71; Cober Gallery, 1961, 63; Zora Gallery, Los Angeles, 1964; Glassboro State College, 1966; Manhattanville College of the Sacred Heart, 1966; Earlham College, 1967; Instituto General Electric, Montevideo, 1967; U. of Notre Dame, 1969; U. of New Hampshire, 1970; U. of Connecticut, 1971; Galeria Pecanins, Mexico City, 1972; The Ohio State U., 1973; Imprint, San Francisco, 1973; ACA Gallery, 1976. **Group:** NAD Annual, 1953; Boston/MFA, 1955; Seattle/AM, 1957; Cober Gallery, The Insiders, 1960; Brooklyn Museum Biennials, 1960, 62; SAGA; PAFA Annuals, 1961, 63; St. Paul Gallery, Drawings, USA, 1961, 68; A.A.A. Gallery, NYC, 100 Prints of the Year, 1962; MOMA, Recent Painting USA: The Figure, circ., 1962–63; USIA, Graphic Arts—USA, circ., USSR, 1963; Library of Congress, 1963; PCA-USIA, 30 Contemporary Prints, circ., Europe, 1964; Corcoran, 1964; Otis Art Institute, 1964; New York World's Fair, 1964–65; PMA, 1965; New Jersey Tercentenary Exhibition, New Brunswick, 1965; WMAA Annual, 1966; U. of Southern California, 1967; Mexico City/Nacional, 1967; U. of Kentucky, 1968; MOMA, Tamarind: Homage to Lithography, 1969; SAGA, Fifty Years of American Printmaking, 1969; WMAA, Human Concern/Personal Torment, 1969; A.F.A., The Indignant Eye, 1971; Museo de Arte Contemporaneo, Cali, Colombia, S.A., 1971, 73; Sao Paulo, American and Brazilian Printmakers, 1972; NAD, 1974; NCFA, print annual, 1977. **Collections:** Baltimore/MA; Bibliotheque Nationale; Brooklyn Museum; U. of California; High Museum; U. of Kentucky; Library of Congress; Los Angeles/County MA; MMA; MOMA; U. of Maine; Malmo; U. of Minnesota; Montclair/AM; NYPL; Newark Museum; New Orleans/Delgado; Norfolk; Nurnberg; PAFA; PMA; Princeton U.; Rutgers U.; San Antonio/McNay; Slater; Syracuse U.; Trenton/State; Utica; VMFA; Yale U.; Youngstown/Butler.

LANDON, EDWARD. b. March 13, 1911, Hartford, Conn. **Studied:** Hartford Art School; ASL, with Jean Charlot; privately in Mexico with Carlos Merida. Traveled Europe, Scandinavia, Mexico. **Taught:** privately (serigraphy). Subject of a film, *How to Make a Serigraph,* produced by the Harmon Foundation. **Member:** Charter member and past president National Serigraph Society; Boston Printmakers; American Color Print Society; The Print Club, Philadelphia. Federal A.P.: Easel painting and murals. **Awards:** Northwest Printmakers Annual, 1944, 46, 52; Brooklyn Museum, 1947; American Color Print Society, 1947, 54, 57, 58; Boston Printmakers, 1979; San Francisco Art Association, 1949; Fulbright Fellowship (Norway), 1950, 51. **Address:** Lawrence Hill Road, Weston, VT 15161. **Dealer:** Gallery 2, Woodstock, Vt.; Gallery North Star, Grafton, Vt. **One-man Exhibitions:** (first) Boston/MFA, 1934; Smith College, 1941; Norlyst Gallery, NYC, 1945; Unge Kunstneres Samfund, Oslo, 1950; The Print Club, Philadelphia, 1953; Fine Arts Gallery, Hartford, 1954; Doris Meltzer Gallery, NYC, 1957, 58; Bennington, Vt., 1967; Sunapee, N.H., 1968; Woodstock, Vt., 1969; Southern Vt. Artists Assn., Manchester. **Group:** Brooklyn Museum; Northwest Printmakers Annuals; American Color Print Society; National Serigraph Society; MOMA; Library of Congress; MMA; Cooper Union, 1968; Lincoln, Mass./De Cordova, By the People, for the People: New England, 1947. **Collections:** Bezalel Museum; Bibliotheque Nationale; Brooklyn Museum; Buffalo/Albright; Library of Congress; Kansas City/Nelson; MMA; MOMA; NCFA; PMA; SFMA; Tel Aviv; Turku Museum, Finland; Victoria and Albert Museum; Worcester/AM. **Bibliography:** American Artists Congress, Inc.; Landon; Reese. Archives.

LANDSMAN, STANLEY. b January 23, 1930, NYC. **Studied:** U. of New Mexico (with Randall Davey, Adja

Yunkers, Agnes Martin), BFA, 1947–50, 1954–55. US Navy, 1950–54. Traveled around the world. **Taught:** Adelphi College; School of Visual Arts, NYC; Pratt Institute; Artist-in-Resident, Aspen Institute and U. of Wisconsin. **Address:** 45 Downing Street, NYC 10014. **Dealer:** Leo Castelli Inc., NYC. **One-man Exhibitions:** (first) March Gallery, NYC; Allan Stone Gallery; Richard Feigen Gallery, NYC; Richard Feigen Gallery, Los Angeles, 1965; Leo Castelli Inc., 1966; Iris Clert Gallery (two-man); Houston/Contemporary, 1970. **Group:** Kansas City/Nelson, Sound, Light, Silence, 1966; MOMA, The 1960's, 1967; Kansas City/Nelson, 1967; Ridgefield/Aldrich; New Delhi, First World Triennial, 1968; Cleveland/MA, 1968; Milwaukee, Directions I; Options, circ., 1968; WMAA, Light: Object and Image, 1968; WMAA Sculpture Annual, 1968; UCLA, Electric Art, 1969; U. of Illinois, 1969; Automation House, NYC, 1970. **Collections:** Des Moines; Kansas City/Nelson; MOMA; Milwaukee; Paris/Moderne; Ridgefield/Aldrich; WMAA; Walker. **Bibliography:** Atkinson; Davis, D. Archives.

LANGLAIS, BERNARD. b. July 23, 1921, Old Town, Me.; **d.** December 27, 1977, Portland, Me. **Studied:** The Corcoran School of Art; Skowhegan School; Brooklyn Museum School; Academie de la Grande Chaumiere; Academy of Art, Oslo. US Navy, 1942–48. **Taught:** The Pennsylvania State U., 1972; U. of Pennsylvania, 1974. **Member:** Maine State Commission on the Arts and Humanities. **Commissions:** Samoset Hotel, Rockland, Me., 1974; GSA, Federal Building, Sandpoint, Idaho. **Awards:** Fulbright Fellowship (Norway), 1954; Ford Foundation, **P.P.,** 1963; Guggenheim Foundation Fellowship, 1972; Maine State Commission on the Arts and the Humanities Award, 1972; Hon. DFA, U. of Maine; National Endowment for the Arts, grant, 1977. **One-man Exhibitions:** Roko Gallery, NYC, 1956; Area Gallery, NYC, 1959;

U. of Maine, 1960, 67, 74; Leo Castelli Inc., 1961; Allan Stone Gallery, 1962; Grippi and Waddell Gallery, NYC, 1964; Seton Hall U., 1965; Makler Gallery, 1966, 72; Portland, Me./MA, 1968; Maine Art Gallery, 1969; Marlboro (Vt.) College, 1969; Bowdoin College, 1969; Lee Ault & Co. NYC, 1971, 76; Alpha Gallery, 1972, Exeter, 1972; Governor Dummer Academy, Byfield, Mass., 1973; Frost Gully Gallery, 1974; Bates College, 1974; Colby College, 1974; Farnesworth, Rockland, Me., 1978; Ahima Gallery, Wellfleet, Mass., 1976; Hobe Sound Gallery, Fla., 1978; Manchester Institute of Arts and Sciences, Manchester, N.H., 1977; Unity College, Unity, Me., 1976. **Group:** ART:USA:58 and ART:USA:59, NYC, 1958, 59; Yale U., Best of Contemporary Painting from New York Galleries, 1960; Boston Arts Festival, 1960, 61; Martha Jackson Gallery, New Media—New Forms, I & II, 1960, 61; Chicago/AI Annuals, 1960, 61, 64; WMAA Annuals, 1960, 63; Houston/MFA, New Media, 1961; MOMA, The Art of Assemblage, circ., 1961; Carnegie, 1961; A.F.A., circ., 1961–62; Colby College, Maine and Its Artists, 1963, Drawing Exhibition, 1970. **Collections:** Chase Manhattan Bank; Chicago/AI; Chrysler Corp.; Colby College; U. of Indiana; U. of Maine; Norfolk/Chrysler; Ogunquit; Olsen Foundation Inc.; PMA; Philadelphia Zoological Gardens; The Singer Company, Inc.; J. Walter Thompson Co.; WMAA. **Bibliography:** Archives.

LANING, EDWARD. b. April 26, 1906, Petersburg, Ill. **d.** May 6, 1981, NYC. **Studied:** The U. of Chicago; ASL, with Boardman Robinson, Max Weber, John Sloan, Kenneth Hayes Miller; Academy of Fine Arts, Rome. Traveled USA, Europe, North Africa. **Taught:** Cooper Union, 1938–41; Kansas City Art Institute and School of Design, 1945–50; Pratt Institute, 1952–56; ASL, 1952–75. **Member:** NAD; ASL; National Society of Mural Painters. Federal A.P. (murals): Ellis Island; New York Public

Library; US Post Offices, Rockingham, N.C., and Bowling Green, Ky. **Commissions:** *Life* magazine (paintings); murals for Sheraton Corporation hotels in Los Angeles, Dallas, Louisville, Niagara Falls, NYC; US Department of Interior, Bureau of Reclamation, 1969; Union Station, Ogden, Utah, 1979. **Awards:** Guggenheim Foundation Fellowship, 1945; AAAL Grant; VMFA, 1945; Chicago/AI, 1945; Fulbright Fellowship, 1950. **One-man Exhibitions:** (first) Dudensing Gallery, NYC, 1932; The Midtown Galleries; Kansas/Nelson, 1945; Hewitt Gallery, NYC, 1950; The Griffin Gallery, NYC, 1963; Dannenberg Gallery, 1969; NAD, 1973. **Group:** WMAA; MMA; Chicago/AI; Cleveland/MA; VMFA; NAD; Audubon Artists. **Collections:** Kansas City/Nelson; MMA; WMAA. **Bibliography:** Boswell 1; Cheney; Hall. Archives.

LANSNER, FAY. b. June 21, 1921, Philadelphia, Pa. **Studied:** Wanamaker Institute, 1939–41; Stella Elkins Tyler School of Fine Arts, Temple U., 1945–47; Columbia U., 1947–48; ASL, 1947–48, with Vaclav Vytlacil; Hofmann School, 1948; Atelier Fernand Leger, Paris, 1950; Academie Andre Lhote, Paris, 1950. Traveled Europe extensively; resided Paris, 1950–52. **Taught:** New School for Social Research, 1974–75; coproducer, writer, editor, *The Circle of Charmion von Wiegand*, 1977, videotape, for WNET. **Address:** 317 West 80th Street, NYC 10024. **Dealers:** Arras Gallery; Marlborough Gallery, Inc., NYC. **One-man Exhibitions:** (first) Galerie Huit, Paris, 1951; Le Gerrec, Paris, 1952; Peretz Johannes Gallery, NYC, 1952; Hansa Gallery, NYC, 1955, 56, 58; Hood College, 1961; David Herbert Gallery, NYC, 1961; The Zabriskie Gallery, 1963; The Kornblee Gallery, 1963, 65; James David Gallery, Miami, 1965; Douglass College, 1975; Lehigh U., 1976; Ingber Art Gallery, NYC, 1980; Benson Gallery, Bridgehampton, N.Y., 1970, 72, 76. **Group:** Finch College, NYC, Paul

Ellen Lanyon *The Pond* 1976

Magriel Collection; Southampton/Parrish; Houston/MFA, The Emerging Figure, 1961; Louis Alexander Gallery, NYC, Recent American Drawings, 1962; Stanhope Gallery, Boston, Works on Paper; New School for Social Research, International Year of the Woman, 1975; Huntington, N.Y./Heckscher, Aspects of Change: Drawing Today, Guild Hall, East Hampton, N.Y., 1978; Tenth Street Days—The Coops of the 50s, 1978; Denver, Poets and Painters, 1979; MMA, Hans Hofmann as Teacher, 1979. **Collections:** Ciba-Geigy Corp.; Corcoran; Douglass College; Lehigh U.; MMA; NYU; Newsweek; U. of North Carolina; Purchase/SUNY. **Bibliography:** *Art: A Woman's Sensibility;* **Fay Lansner;** *Poets & Painters.*

LANYON, ELLEN. b. December 21, 1926, Chicago, Ill. **Studied:** Chicago Art Institute School; The U. of Chicago;

Roosevelt College (with Max Kahn, Kathleen Blackshear, Joseph Hirsch, 1944–48, BFA); State U. of Iowa, with Mauricio Lasansky, Eugene Ludnis, 1948–50, MFA; Courtauld Institute, 1950–51. **Taught:** Chicago/AI, 1952–54 (Junior School), 1964–65, 73; Rockford College, 1954; Saugatuck Summer School of Painting, 1961, 62, 67, 68, 69; U. of Illinois, 1966; Oxbow Summer School, 1970, 71, 72, 73; U. of Wisconsin, 1972; Stanford U., 1973; U. of California, Davis, 1973; Sacramento State U., 1973; The Pennsylvania State U., 1974; Boston U., 1975; U. of Iowa, 1975; Cooper Union, 1979–80; Parsons School of Design, NYC, 1979–80; Director Oxbow Summer School of Painting, Workshop, 1978; School of Visual Arts, 1980. **Member:** Chicago/AI Exhibition Momentum, 1948–52; CAA, Women's Caucus for Art. **Awards:** Chicago/AI, Mr. & Mrs. Frank H. Armstrong Prize,

1946, 55, 77; Denver/AM, **P.P.**, 1950; Library of Congress, Pennell **P.P.**, 1950; Fulbright Fellowship (England), 1950; Chicago/AI, Martin B. Cahn Award, 1961; Chicago/AI, Pauline Palmer Prize, 1962, 64; Dallas/MFA, 1965; Chicago/AI, Vielehr Award, 1967; Cassandra Foundation Grant, 1971; Yaddo Fellowship, 1974, 75, 76; National Endowment for the Arts, grant, 1974. **m.** Roland Ginzel. **Address:** 138 Prince Street, NYC 10012. **Dealers:** Richard Gray Gallery, Chicago; Odyssia Gallery, NYC; Fendrick Gallery, Washington, D.C. **One-man Exhibitions:** (first) Carlebach Gallery, NYC, 1949; Bordelon's, Chicago, 1952; Superior Street Gallery, Chicago, 1958; Stewart Rickard Gallery, San Antonio, 1962, 65 (two-man); Fairweather-Hardin Gallery, 1962; The Zabriskie Gallery, 1962, 64, 69, 72; Haydon Calhoun Gallery, Dallas, 1963; B.C. Holland Gallery, 1965, 68; Fort Wayne/AM, 1967; Kendall College, 1967; Richard Gray Gallery, 1970, 73, 76, 79; Wabash Transit Gallery, Chicago, 1972; Madison Art Center, 1972; NCFA, 1972; Stephens College, 1973; U. of California, Davis, 1974, 80; The Pennsylvania State U., 1974; Odyssia Gallery, Rome, 1975, 76; Documenta Gallery, Rome, 1975; Harcus Krakow Rosen Sonnabend, Boston, 1976; U. of Illinois, 1976; Oshkosh Public Museum, 1976; U. of Missouri, 1976; The Woman's Building, L.A., 1977; Lake Forest College, 1977; Fendrick Gallery, Washington, D.C., 1978; U. of Houston, 1977; Culver-Stockton College, 1978; Kentucky State U., 1978; Bradley U., 1979; Illinois Wesleyan U., 1979; Landfall Press Gallery, Chicago, 1980. **Retrospectives:** Rockford College 1970; One Illinois Center, Chicago, 1973; John Michael Kohler Arts Center, Sheboygan, 1974; Kansas State U., 1976; U. of Missouri, 1976; Northern Illinois U., 1978. **Group:** PMA, 1946, 47, 50, 54; Chicago/AI Annuals, 1946, 47, 51, 53, 55, 57, 58, 60, 61, 62, 66, 69; Chicago/AI, Exhibition Momentum, 1948, 50, 52, 54, 56; Omaha/Joslyn, 1949, 58; Library of Congress, 1950, 52; Denver/AM, 1951, 52; MMA, 1952; U.

of Illinois, 1953; MOMA, Young American Printmakers, 1953, The Downtown Gallery, Chicago Artists, 1954; Chicago/AI, Prints from The Graphic Workshop, 1955; Corcoran, 1961; MOMA, Recent Painting USA: The Figure, circ., 1962–63; Northern Illinois U., 1966; Illinois Arts Council, circ., 1967–69; Chicago/Contemporary, 1968, Chicago Imagist Art, 1972; Moore College of Art, Philadelphia, Artists' Books, 1973; Galleria Comunale d'Arte Contemporanea, Una Tendenza Americana, 1973; Sacramento State U., National Print Annual, 1974; US Department of the Interior, America 1976, circ., 1976; Illinois Arts Council, Naive Art in Illinois, 1839–1976, 1976; Purdue U., Chicago Art, 1976; San Antonio/McNay, American Artists, 76, 1976; Sacramento/Crocker, The Chicago Connection, circ., 1976; Chicago Culture Center, Masterpieces of Chicago Art, 1977; U. of Michigan, Chicago: The City & Its Artists, 1945–78, 1978; Los Angeles/County MA, Private Images: Photographs by Painters, 1977; Chicago/AI, 100 Artists, 100 Years, 1979; Chicago/AI, Chicago and Vicinity, Prizewinners Revisited, 1980. **Collections:** Albion College; AT&T; Borg-Warner International Corporation; Boston Public Library; Brandeis U.; Brooklyn Museum; Chicago/AI; Container Corp. of America; Crocker Bank, San Francisco; U. of Dallas; Denver/AM; Des Moines; F.T.D. Association; First National Bank of Chicago; Galleria Comunale d'Arte Contemporanea; IIE; Illinois Bell Telephone Company; U. of Illinois; Illinois Wesleyan U.; Kansas State U.; Library of Congress; Madison Art Center; U. of Massachusetts; NCFA; The Singer Company, Inc.; Springfield, Ill./State; Trenton/State. **Bibliography:** *Art: A Woman's Sensibility*, Arthur 2. Archives.

LASANSKY, MAURICIO. b. October 12, 1914, Buenos Aires, Argentina. **Studied:** Superior School of Fine Arts, Buenos Aires. Traveled Europe, Latin America. To USA, 1943; citizen, 1952.

Taught: Director, Free Fine Arts School, Villa Maria, Argentina, 1936; Taller Manualidad, 1939; Atelier 17, NYC; State U. of Iowa, 1954–. **Awards:** Guggenheim Foundation Fellowship (USA), 1943, renewed 1944; Seattle/AM, Seattle International, First Prize, 1944; The Print Club, Philadelphia, **P.P.,** 1945, 48; Library of Congress, Pennell **P.P.,** 1945, 48, 50, 56, 59, 62, 63; Denver/AM, **P.P.,** 1946, 47; Des Moines, **P.P.,** 1946, 49, 51, 57, 58; Iowa State Fair, First Prize, 1947; Society of American Etchers and Engravers, NYC, 1947; PAFA, Alice McFadden Eyre Medal, 1948, 57; Brooklyn Museum, **P.P.,** 1948, 58; Northwest Printmakers Annual, **P.P.,** 1948, 51, 55, 59, 61; Walker, First and Second Prizes, 1949; The Print Club, Philadelphia, Charles M. Lea Prize, 1951, 57, 62; Printmakers of Southern California, **P.P.,** 1952; Bradley U., **P.P.,** 1952; Des Moines, IV Annual, Edmundson Award, 1952; Des Moines, V Annual, Special Commendation, 1953; Des Moines, Prize in Painting, 1955; Des Moines Younkers Professional Award, 1956; I Inter-American Paintings and Prints Biennial, Mexico City, Posada Award, 1958; Silvermine Guild, **P.P.,** 1958; Walker Biennial, **P.P.,** 1958; De Pauw U., **P.P.,** 1959; Hon. DFA, Illinois Wesleyan College, 1959; Kansas City/Nelson, **P.P.,** 1960; II Inter-American Paintings and Prints Biennial, Mexico City, Special Hon. Men. with Gold Medal, 1960; PAFA, Hon. Men. and one-man exhibition, 1961; Pasadena/AM, **P.P.,** 1962; Ford Foundation, **P.P.,** 1962; Guggenheim Foundation Fellowship (Spain and France), 1963, 64; Hon. DFA, Pacific Lutheran U., 1969; Philadelphia Print Club Annual, Bertha von Moschzisker Prize, 1971; Dickinson College Arts Award, 1974. **Address:** Quail Creek Condominium, Rural Route 1, North Liberty, Iowa 52317. **One-man Exhibitions:** (first) Fort General Roca, Rio Negro, Argentina, 1935; Whyte Gallery, Washington, D.C., 1945; SFMA, 1945, 50; Chicago/AI, 1947; U. of Louisville, 1948; Walker, 1949; Houston/MFA,

1949; Milwaukee, 1949; Purdue U., 1949; Santa Barbara/MA, 1950; Northwestern U., 1950; Cornell U., 1951; Tulane U., 1952; Memphis/Brooks, 1953; Madrid/Nacional, 1954; Oakland/AM, 1958; USIA, Intaglios (one-man and his students), circ., Latin America and USA, 1959–61; PAFA Annual, 1961; Des Moines, 1967; Carleton College, 1965; PMA, circ., 1966; Dickinson College, 1972; Fort Dodge/Blanden, 1973. **Retrospectives:** State U. of Iowa, 1957; A.F.A./Ford Foundation, circ., 1960–62; Iowa State U., 1967; U. of Iowa, 1976. **Group:** Carnegie, American Prints, 1949; Sao Paulo, 1951; U. of Illinois, Graphic Art, USA, 1954; France/National, 50 Ans d'Art aux Etats-Unis, circ., Europe, 1955; Gallery of Modern Art, Ljubljana, Yugoslavia, I, II, and V International Exhibitions of Prints, 55, 57, 63, 67, 71; Michigan State U., 20 American Printmakers, 1956; Achenbach Foundation, Prints since the 14th Century, 1957; SAGA, 1957; U. of California, Berkeley, Modern Master Prints, 1958; I and II Inter-American Paintings and Prints Biennials, Mexico City, 1958, 60; ICA, Boston, 100 Works on Paper, circ., Europe, 1959; PAFA, 1959, 60; PCA, American Prints Today, circ., 1959–62; Yale U., American Prints, 1950–60, 1960; USIA, Graphic Arts—USA, circ., USSR, 1963; I & II International Print Biennials, Kracow, 1966, 68; MOMA, The Artist as His Subject, 1967; National Academy of Fine Arts, Amsterdam, American Prints, 1968; Bradford, England, British Print Biennial, 1969; XXXV Venice Biennial, 1970; San Juan, Puerto Rico, Biennial del Grabado, 1970, 72, 74; Graphische Sammlung Albertina, Graphik der Welt, 1971; WMAA, Oversized Prints, 1971. **Collections:** Albion College; American Life and Casualty Insurance Co.; Argentina/Nacional; Barcelona; Bradley U.; Brooklyn Museum; Buenos Aires/Municipal; Cedar Rapids/AA; Chicago/AI; Colorado Springs/FA; Cordoba/Municipal; Cordoba/Provincial; U. of Delaware; De Pauw U.; Des Moines; Detroit/Institute;

First National Bank, Iowa City; Flint/ Institute; U. of Georgia; Gettysburg College; IBM; Illinois State Normal U.; U. of Illinois; Indiana U.; Iowa Wesleyan College; State College of Iowa; State U. of Iowa; Kansas City/ Nelson; La Plata; Library of Congress; Louisiana State U.; Luther College; MOMA; Madrid/Nacional; U. of Maine; Melbourne/National; Mendoza; U. of Michigan; Millikin U.; U. of Minnesota; Museo Rosario; NYPL; National Gallery; U. of Nebraska; New Britain; Oakland/AM; Omaha:/Joslyn; PAFA; PMA; Pasadena/AM; Portland, Ore./AM; Rio Cuarto; SFMA; St. Louis/City; Salt Lake City Public Library; Seattle/AM; Silvermine Guild; Southwest Missouri State College; Springfield, Mo./AM; Syracuse U.; Time Inc.; USIA; U. of Utah; Walker; Washburn U. of Topeka; Washington U.; U. of Washington; Wesleyan U.; Yale U. **Bibliography:** *From Foreign Shores;* Hayter 1, 2; Marter, Tarbell, and Wechsler; **Honig;** Moser 1; Reese; Soyer, R. 1; **Zigrosser 2.**

LASSAW, IBRAM. b. May 4, 1913, Alexandria, Egypt. To USA, 1921; citizen, 1928. **Studied:** City College of New York; Clay Club, 1926–30; Beaux-Arts Institute of Design, NYC, 1930–31; Ozenfant School of Art, NYC. Traveled Europe. US Army, 1942–44. **Taught:** American U., 1950; Duke U., 1962–63; Long Island U., 1966–; U. of California, Berkeley, 1965–66; Brandeis U., 1972; Mt. Holyoke College, 1978; and privately. A founder and member of American Abstract Artists (president, 1946–49); charter member, Artist's "Club," 1949. Federal A.P.: 1933–42; Artists Equity. **Commissions:** Beth El Temple, Springfield, Mass.; Beth El Temple, Providence, R.I.; Temple of Aaron, St. Paul; Temple Anshe Chesed, Cleveland; Kneses Tifereth Israel Synagogue, Port Chester, N.Y.; House of Theology of the Franciscan Fathers, Centreville, Ohio; Washington U., 1959; New York Hilton Hotel; Yale & Towne Inc.; Rockefeller Center, NYC,

Celanese Building; Long Island Hall of Fame; Springfield, Mass./MFA. **Awards:** American Academy and Institute of Arts and Letters, 1975. **Address:** 678 Fireplace Road, Springs, East Hampton, NY 11937. **Dealer:** The Zabriskie Gallery, NYC. **One-man Exhibitions:** (first) The Kootz Gallery, NYC, 1951, also 1952, 54, 58, 60, 63, 64; Duke U., 1963; Benson Gallery, 1966; Gertrude Kasle Gallery, 1968; Carnegie-Mellon U., 1969; Vanderbilt U., 1970; Guild Hall, East Hampton, 1971; The Zabriskie Gallery, NYC, 1977; Yares Gallery, Scottsdale, 1970. **Retrospective:** MIT, 1957; Huntington, N.Y./ Heckscher, 1973. **Group:** WMAA Annuals, 1936–46; American Abstract Artists Annuals, 1937– ; Salon des Realites Nouvelles, Paris, 1950; MOMA, Abstract Painting and Sculpture in America, 1951; MOMA, Sculpture of the XXth Century, 1953; XXVII Venice Biennial, 1954; Chicago/AI, 1954; WMAA, The New Decade, 1954–55; U. of Illinois, 1955, 57, 59, 61; MOMA, Twelve Americans, circ., 1956; IV Sao Paulo Biennial, 1957; Brussels World's Fair, 1958; Documenta II, Kassel, 1959; Cleveland/MA, Paths of Abstract Art, 1960; Carnegie, 1961; Seattle World's Fair, 1962; WGMA, Sculptors of Our Time, 1963; WMAA, Between the Fairs, 1964; Musée Rodin, Paris, 1965; Indianapolis/Herron, 1965; Public Education Association, NYC, 1966; WMAA, Art of the U.S. 1670–1966, 1966; WMAA, The 1930's, 1968; MOMA, The New American Painting and Sculpture, 1969; Washburn Gallery Inc., Art of the 1940s, 1972; Duke U., 1972; Katonah (N.Y.) Art Gallery, Drawing in Space, 1972; Society of the Four Arts, Contemporary American Sculpture, 1974; NIAL, 1974; Sculpture–American Directions, 1945–75, 1976; Hirshhorn, The Golden Door, 1976; WMAA, 200 Years of American Sculpture, 1976; Rutgers U., Vanguard American Sculpture 1919–1939, 1979. **Collections:** Buffalo/ Albright; Calcutta; U. of California; Carnegie; U. of North Carolina; Chase Manhattan Bank; Cornell U.; Hartford/

Wadsworth; Harvard U.; MOMA; Metalcraft Corp.; NCFA; Newark Museum; Rio de Janeiro; Springfield, Mass./MFA; WMAA; Washington U.; Wichita/AM; Williams College; Worcester/AM. **Bibliography:** Baur 5, 7; Blesh 1, Brumme; Craven, W.; Giedion-Welcker 1; Goodrich and Baur 1; *From Foreign Shores;* **Goossen 5;** Henning; Hunter 6; Hunter, ed.; Marter, Tarbell, and Wechsler; Mendelowitz; Myers 2; Read 3; Ritchie 1, 2; Rose B., 1; Seuphor 3; Trier 1; Weller. Archives.

LAUFMAN, SIDNEY. b. October 29, 1891, Cleveland, Ohio. **Studied:** Chicago Art Institute School, with Reynolds, Buehr; ASL, with Robert Henri. Traveled Europe, resided France, 1920–33. **Taught:** ASL, 1938–50; Brandeis U., 1959–60. **Member:** NAD; Woodstock Artists Association. Federal A.P.: Easel painting. **Awards:** Chicago/AI, The Mr. & Mrs. Frank G. Logan Prize, 1932; Carnegie, Third Prize, 1934; NAD, Benjamin Altman Prize, 1937, 63, Landscape Prize, 1971; NAD, Special Landscape Prize, 1949; ASL, Diamond Jubilee, **P.P.,** 1950; PAFA, Jennie Sesnan Gold Medal, 1951; Corcoran, Hon. Men., 1951; NAD, Samuel F. B. Morse Gold Medal, 1953, 70; Youngstown/Butler, First **P.P.,** 1954; NAD Annual, Andrew Carnegie Prize, 1959; Woodstock Artists Association, Sally Jacobs Memorial Award, 1968. **Address:** 1038 S. Osprey Avenue, Sarasota, FL 35377. **Dealer:** The Forum Gallery. **One-man Exhibitions:** (first) Galerie Devambez, Paris, 1922; Marie Sterner Gallery, NYC, 1923; Gage Gallery, Cleveland, 1927; Arts Club of Chicago, 1927; The New Gallery, NYC, 1927; Galerie Granoff, Paris, 1930; de Hauke Gallery, NYC, 1931; The Milch Gallery, 1934, 44, 48, 53, 56, 58; East End Gallery, Provincetown, 1960, 61, 62, 63; The Forum Gallery, 1962; Rudolph Gallery, Coral Gables, Fla., 1964; Peabody Museum, 1963; U. of Miami, 1964; Brandeis U., 1960. **Group:** Carnegie; NAD; PAFA; Corcoran; WMAA; Chicago/AI;

Youngstown/Butler; and many others since 1922. **Collections:** AAAL; Bezalel Museum; Brandeis U.; Chicago/AI; Cleveland/MA; Colorado Springs/FA; Corcoran; Fort Lauderdale; U. of Georgia; Hagerstown/County MFA; Hirshhorn; Indianapolis/Herron; Kansas City/Nelson; Lakeview Center; MMA; MOMA; U. of Miami; Minneapolis/Institute; NCFA; Norfolk/Chrysler; U. of Oregon; Peabody College; Rochester Institute; St. Louis/City; Southampton/Parris; Tel Aviv; Toledo/MA; WMAA; Youngstown/Butler; Zanesville/AI. **Bibliography:** *Woodstock: An American Art Colony, 1902–1977.*

LAURENT, JOHN. b. November 27, 1921, Brooklyn, N.Y. **Studied:** Syracuse U.; Indiana U. (MFA); Academie de la Grande Chaumiere (with Walt Kuhn, Othon Friesz, Stephen Greene). Traveled France, Italy. **Taught:** Virginia Polytechnic Institute, 1949–53; U. of New Hampshire, 1954– ; Ogunquit School of Painting, 1952– . **Commissions:** U. of New Hampshire (mural for Student Union building). **Awards:** L.C. Tiffany Grant; Syracuse U., Traveling Fellowship; Silvermine Guild, Larry Aldrich Prize; National Council on the Arts, Sabbatical Leave Grant ($7,500), 1966. **Address:** Mill Lane Road, York, ME 03909. **Dealer:** Sunne Savage Gallery, Boston. **One-man Exhibitions:** (first) Kraushaar Galleries, 1955; Smithsonian; U. of New Hampshire, 1956, 67; Lincoln, Mass./De Cordova, 1959; Bowdoin College, 1959; Indiana U.; Currier, Ogunquit, 1967; Frost Gully Gallery, Portland, Me., 1977: St. Paul's School, Concord, Vt., 1978. **Retrospective:** Andover/Phillips, 1973. **Group:** WMAA Annual; PAFA, 1951, 54; ART:USA:58, NYC, 1958;: Boston Arts Festival; U. of Nebraska; MMA; Carnegie; Corcoran; Chicago/AI; Audubon Artists; Newark Museum. **Collections:** Andover/Phillips; Hollins College, Illinois Wesleyan U.; U. of Illinois; Indiana U.; Lehigh U.; U. of Nebraska; Syracuse U. **Bibliography:** Archives.

LAURENT, ROBERT. b. June 29, 1890, Concarneau, France; **d.** April 20, 1970, Cape Neddick, Me. **Studied:** British School, Rome, 1908–09, with Frank Burty; also with Hamilton Easter Field, Maurice Sterne, Giuseppe Doratore. US Naval Aviation, World War I. Traveled Europe, Cuba, Canada, Mexico, USA; resided France, Italy. **Taught:** ASL, fifteen years intermittently (sculpture); Vassar College, 1939–40; Goucher College, 1940–41; The Corcoran School of Art, 1940–42; Indiana U., 1942–60 (prof. emeritus, 1960–69). **Member:** Sculptors Guild; National Sculpture Society; Audubon Artists; Indiana Artists; New England Sculptors Association, Cambridge, Mass. Federal A.P.: Federal Trade Building, Washington, D.C. (relief); New York World's Fair, 1939; US Post Office, Garfield, N.J. **Commissions:** Fairmount Park, Philadelphia (sculpture); Radio City Music Hall, NYC; Indiana U. (a relief, a fountain, and several sculptures); many portrait busts. **Awards:** Chicago/AI, First Prize, and The Mr. & Mrs. Frank G. Logan Medal, 1924, 38; Fairmount Park (Philadelphia), International Sculpture Competition, 1935 (monument); Brooklyn Museum, First Prize, 1942; Audubon Artists, 1945; Indianapolis/Herron, five First Prizes; Louisville/Speed, First Prize, 1954; Artist-in-Residence, American Academy, Rome, 1954–55. **One-man Exhibitions:** (first) The Daniel Gallery, NYC, 1915; Bourgeois Gallery, NYC; Curt Valentine Gallery, NYC; Worcester/AM; Arts and Crafts Club, New Orleans; Vassar College; Corcoran; Indiana U.; Indianapolis/Herron; Kraushaar Galleries; Galleria Schneider, Rome; Art Association of Richmond, Ind.; New England Sculptors Association, Cambridge, Mass. **Retrospective:** Indiana U., Laurent; Fifty Years of Sculpture, 1961; U. of New Hampshire, 1972. **Group:** Salons of America, NYC; Society of Independent Artists, NYC; Audubon Artists; Sculptors Guild; American Society of Painters, Sculptors and Graveurs; National Sculpture Society; WMAA; MMA; Brooklyn Museum; Newark Museum; Portland, Me./ MA; Boston/MFA; Colby College; Riverside Museum; Louisville/Speed; Indianapolis/Herron; Chicago/AI; PMA; American Painting and Sculpture, Moscow, 1959. **Collections:** Barnes Foundation; Brookgreen Gardens; Brooklyn Museum; Chicago/AI; Colby College; Hartford/Wadsworth; IBM; Indiana U.; MMA; MOMA; U. of Nebraska; Newark Museum; Ogunquit; PAFA; Society of the Four Arts; Vassar College; WMAA. **Bibliography:** *Avant-Garde Painting and Sculpture;* Baur 7; Blesh 1; Brumme; Cahill and Barr, eds.; Cheney; Craven, W.; Goodrich and Baur 1; *Index of 20th Century Artists;* **Moak;** Parkes; Richardson, E.P.; Ringel, ed.; Rose, B., 1; *Sculpture of the Western Hemisphere.* Archives.

LAWRENCE, JACOB. b. September 7, 1917, Atlantic City, N.J. **Studied:** College Art Association, Harlem Workshop, 1932, with Charles Alston, Federal Art Project class, NYC, 1934–37, with Henry Bannarn; American Artists School, NYC, 1937–39, with Anton Refregier, Sol Wilson, Eugene Morley. Traveled USA, British West Indies, Africa. **Taught:** Black Mountain College, summer, 1947; Five Towns Music and Art Foundation, Cedarhurst, N.Y., 1956–60; Pratt Institute, 1956–71; Brandeis U., 1965; New School for Social Research, 1966–70; ASL, 1967–71; U. of Washington, 1971– ; California State College, Hayward, 1970–71. **Member:** NIAL. Federal A.P.: Easel painting, 1938–39; Artists Equity; NAD; American Academy and Institute of Arts and Letters. **Commissions:** *Fortune* magazine, 1947 (10 paintings); Mural for Kingdome Stadium, Seattle; Howard U. **Awards:** Scholarship to American Artists School, NYC, 1937; Lessing J. Rosenwald Fund Fellowship, 1940, 41, 42; MMA, Sixth **P.P.,** 1942; Guggenheim Foundation Fellowship, 1946; PAFA, Hon. Men., 1948; Brooklyn Museum, Hon. Men., 1948; Chicago/AI, Norman Wait Harris Silver

Medal, 1948; NIAL Grant, 1953; Chapelbrook Foundation Grant, 1954; NAACP, Springarn Medal, 1970; NAD, 1971; Hon. DFA, Pratt Institute, 1972; Hon. Ph.D., Colby College and Denni son U. **Address:** 4316 37 Avenue, N.E., Seattle WA 98105. **Dealer:** Terry Din tenfass, Inc. Francine Seders Gallery, Seattle. **One-man Exhibitions:** (first) Harlem YMCA, NYC, 1938; Baltimore/ MA, 1938; Columbia U., 1940; The Downtown Gallery, 1941, 43, 45, 47, 50, 53; Portland, Me./MA, 1943; MOMA, 1944; Institute of Modern Art, Boston, 1945; Trenton/State, 1947; The Alan Gallery, NYC, 1957, 60; Terry Dinten fass, Inc., 1963, 65, 68, 73, 78; Seattle/ AM, 1974; St. Louis/City, 1974; Bir mingham, Ala./MA, 1974; Kansas City, 1975; Norfolk/Chrysler, 1979. **Retro spectives:** A.F.A., circ., 1960; WMAA, 1974. **Group:** WMAA; Brooklyn Mu seum; Phillips; PAFA Annuals, 1966, 67; City College, 1967; Johnson C. Smith U., 1968; Dartmouth College 1968; Carnegie, 1968; MOMA, The Art ist as Adversary, 1971; Princeton U., Fragments of American Life, 1976; Lewis and Clark College, Blacks in the Arts, 1979. **Collections:** Alabama Poly technic; Andover/Phillips; U. of Ari zona; Atlanta U.; Auburn U.; Baltimore/ MA; Boston/MFA; Brandeis U.; Brooklyn Museum; Buffalo/Albright; U. of California; Container Corp. of Amer ica; Cornell U.; Detroit/Institute; George Washington Carver Junior Col lege; Harmon Foundation, Inc.; Hirshhorn; Howard U.; IBM; Johnson Publishing Co.; Karamu House; MMA; MOMA; Milwaukee; NCFA; Newark Public Library; Olympia State Capitol Museum; Omaha/Joslyn; Phillips; Port land, Me./MA; RISD; Sao Paulo; South ern Illinois U.; Spelman College; Tougaloo College; Trenton/State; The Vatican, Rome; VMFA; WMAA; Wich ita/AM; Worcester/AM. **Bibliography:** Dover; Eliot; Finkelstein; Goodrich and Baur 1; Halpert; McCurdy, ed.; New meyer; Nordness, ed.; Pearson 2; Richardson, E.P.; Shapiro, ed. Ar chives.

LAWSON, ERNEST. b. 1873, San Fran cisco, Calif.; **d.** 1939, Miami Beach, Fla. **Studied:** ASL; Cos Cob, Conn., with John Henry Twachtman, J. Alden Weir; Academie Julian, Paris, with Jean Pierre Laurens, B. Constant. Traveled Europe, USA. **Taught:** Broadmoor Art Acad emy, Colorado Springs; Kansas City Art Institute and School of Design. **Member:** NAD; NIAL; National Arts Club; Century Association. **Awards:** St. Louis Exposition, 1904, Silver Medal; PAFA, Jennie Sesnan Gold Medal, 1907; American Academy of Arts and Sciences, Gold Medal, 1907; NAD, Hall garten Prize, 1908; Panama-Pacific Ex position, San Francisco, 1915, Gold Medal; NAD, Benjamin Altman Prize, 1916, 21, 28; Corcoran, Second William A. Clark Prize, 1916; NAD, Innes Gold Medal, 1917; PAFA, Joseph E. Temple Gold Medal, 1920; Carnegie, First Prize, 1921; NAD, Saltus Gold Medal for Merit, 1930. **One-man Exhibitions:** The Milch Gallery; Ferargil Galleries, NYC; The Babcock Gallery; Hirschl & Adler Galleries, Inc., NYC, 1964; ACA Gal lery, 1967; Berry-Hill Gallery, NYC, 1970; Danenberg Gallery, 1970. **Re trospective:** Ottawa/National, 1967. **Group:** WMAA; MMA; NAD; Cor coran; Brooklyn Museum; Carnegie; PAFA. **Collections:** Barnes Founda tion; Brooklyn Museum; Carnegie; Chi cago/AI; Columbus; Corcoran; Detroit/ Institute; Kansas City/Nelson; MMA; Montclair/AM; National Gallery; New ark Museum; St. Louis/City; San Diego; Savannah/Telfair; Toronto; WMAA; Worcester/AM; Youngstown/Butler. **Bibliography:** Baur 7; Bazin; Blesh 1; Born; Brown; Cahill and Barr, eds.; Canaday; Cheney; **DuBois 3;** Eliot; Ely; Gallatin 2; Glackens; Goodrich and Baur 1; Hartmann; Hunter 6; Mc Coubrey 1; McCurdy, ed.; **O'Neal;** Perl man; Phillips 2; Richardson, E.P.; Ringel, ed.; Rose, B., 1; Sutton. Ar chives.

LEBRUN, RICO. b. December 10, 1900, Naples, Italy; **d.** May 10, 1964, Malibu, Calif. **Studied:** Academy of Fine Arts,

Naples, 1919–21. Italian army, 1917–18. To USA, 1924. Traveled USA, Europe. **Taught:** ASL, 1936–37; Chouinard Art Institute, Los Angeles, 1938–39; H. Sophie Newcomb Memorial College, 1942–43; Colorado Springs Fine Arts Center, 1945; Jepson Art Institute, Los Angeles, 1947–50; Escuela de Bellas Artes, San Miguel de Allende, Mexico, 1953; Yale-Norfolk Summer Art School, 1956; UCLA, summers, 1956, 57; Yale U., 1958–59; American Academy, Rome, 1959–60; Santa Barbara Museum School, 1962. **Commissions** (murals): Pomona College; Pennsylvania Station, NYC, 1936–38. **One-man Exhibitions:** San Diego, 1940; Faulkner Gallery, Santa Barbara, 1940, 47; de Young, 1942; Santa Barbara/MA, 1942, 47, 51, 56 (three-man, with Channing Peake and Howard Warshaw); Julien Levy Galleries, NYC, 1944; Colorado Springs/FA, 1945; Philadelphia Art Alliance, 1945, 50; Jepson Art Institute, Los Angeles, 1947, 49; A.F.A., Drawings, 1949; J. Seligmann and Co., 1950, 51; Los Angeles/County MA, 1950, 61; Frank Perls Gallery, 1958; Chicago/AI, 1955; Whyte Gallery, Washington, D.C., 1956; Pomona Gallery, 1956; Toronto, 1958; Yale U., 1958; Boston U.; Boris Mirski Gallery, Boston, 1959, 62; U. of California, Santa Barbara, 1960; Esther Baer Gallery, 1960; Princeton U., 1961; Obelisk Gallery, Washington, D.C., 1962; Cornell U., 1962; Syracuse U., 1962; Nordness Gallery, NYC, 1962, 64, 69; AAAL, 1965; Antioch College, 1966. **Retrospective:** Los Angeles/County MA, 1967. **Group:** U. of Illinois; MOMA; Chicago/AI; SFMA; Oakland/AM; Carnegie, 1945, 52, 55, 59; WMAA, 1948, 50, 52, 57, 58, 60; XXV Venice Biennial, 1950; PAFA, 1951, 52, 53, 56. **Collections:** Andover/Phillips; Boston/MFA; Britannica; Colby College; de Young; Denver/AM; Harvard U.; U. of Hawaii; U. of Illinois; Kansas City/Nelson; Los Angeles/County MA; MMA; MOMA; Mills College; U. of Nebraska; Pomona College; RISD; Santa Barbara/MA; Syracuse U.; Toronto; Utica; WMAA. **Bibliography:**

Barker 1; Baur 7; Biddle 4; Frost; Getlein, F. and D.; Goodrich and Baur 1; Mendelowitz; Miller, ed. 1; Nordness, ed.; Pearson 2; Pousette-Dart, ed.; Rodman 1, 2, 3; Sachs; **Seldis;** Weller; Wight 2. Archives.

LECHAY, JAMES. b. July 5, 1907, NYC. **Studied:** U. of Illinois, 1928, BA; privately with Myron Lechay. Traveled Canada, Europe, USA. **Taught:** State U. of Iowa, 1945– ; Stanford U., 1949; NYU, 1952; Skowhegan School, summer, 1961. Federal A.P.: Easel painting; Chinese U. of Hong Kong, 1976. **Awards:** Chicago/AI, Norman Wait Harris Medal, 1941; PAFA, Lambert **P.P.,** 1942; Society for Contemporary American Art, Presentation Prize, 1942; Chicago/AI, Hon. Men., 1942, 43; Portrait of America Prize, 1945; Iowa State Fair, First Prize, 1946, Second Prize, 1951; Denver/AM, Hon. Men., 1946; Walker, First Prize, 1947; Des Moines, Edmundson Trustee Prize, 1950, Davenport/Municipal, 1950; Des Moines, First Prize, 1952, 53; Hon. DFA, Coe College, 1961; two University Fellowships, 1962, 67; Tamarind Fellowship, 1973; AAAL, Childe Hassam Fund **P.P.,** 1974; NAD, Benjamin Altman Prize for Landscape, 1977; NAD, Ranger Fund, **P.P.,** 1979. **Address:** 1191 Hotz Avenue, Iowa City, IA 52240; summer, Box 195, Wellfleet, MA 02667. **Dealers:** Kraushaar Galleries; Cherry Stone Gallery. **One-man Exhibitions:** (first) Another Place, NYC, 1936; Artists' Gallery, NYC, 1938, 40; Ferargil Galleries, NYC, 1942, 43; Toledo/MA, 1943; Wally Findlay Galleries, Chicago, 1944; American-British Gallery, NYC, 1945; Macbeth Gallery, NYC, 1946, 47, 50; Cedar Rapids/AA, 1946; Springfield (Ill.) Art Association, 1946; Louisville (Ky.) Art Center, 1949; Des Moines, 1951, 60; U. of Iowa, 1951, 55, 59, 64, 67, 72; Fort Dodge/Blanden, 1952; Wesleyan U. (Conn.), 1953; Kraushaar Galleries, 1955, 64, 68, 70, 73, 77; Cedar Falls Art Association, 1955; Davenport/Municipal, 1956; Sioux City (Iowa) Art Center,

1958; Omaha/Joslyn, 1958; Coe College, 1959; Dubuque/AA, 1961; Rochester (Minn.) Art Center, 1962; U. of Northern Iowa, 1962; Lubetkin Gallery, Des Moines, 1963; Hollins College, 1964; Waterloo, 1970; MacNider Museum, 1971; Luther College, 1971; Cherry Stone Gallery, Wellfleet, Mass., 1975, 79; Iowa Arts Council, 1976; La Lanterna, 1974. **Retrospective:** U. of Iowa, 1972. **Group:** Toledo/MA; MMA; Corcoran; RAC; WMAA; Carnegie; Arts Club of Chicago; St. Louis/City; Worcester/AM; California Palace; U. of Illinois; Indiana U.; Phillips. **Collections:** American Life and Casualty Insurance Co.; Andover/Phillips; U. of Arizona; Brooklyn Museum; Chicago/AI; Coe College; Davenport/Municipal; Des Moines; First National Bank of Chicago; First National Bank, Iowa City; Grinnell College; Hirshhorn; Illinois Wesleyan U.; State College of Iowa; State U. of Iowa; Luther College; Memphis/Brooks; NCFA; U. of Nebraska; New Britain; U. of Northern Iowa; Omaha/Joslyn; PAFA; Potsdam/SUNY; Rensselaer Polytechnic Institute; U. of Rochester; Syracuse U.; Tulsa/Philbrook; Washburn U. of Topeka; Waterloo; Wichita/AM.

LEIBER, GERSON. b. 1921, Brooklyn, N.Y. **Studied:** Academy of Fine Arts, Budapest; ASL, with Will Barnet, Louis Bosa, Vaclav Vytlacil, Morris Kantor; Brooklyn Museum School, with Gabor Peterdi. US Armed Forces, 1943–47. Traveled Europe. **Taught:** Creative Graphic workshop, NYC (five years); Newark (N.J.) School of Fine and Industrial Art, 1959–66. **Member:** Boston Printmakers; SAGA; California Society of Printmakers; American Color Print Society; ASL; NAD; SAGA, president, 1978–80. **Awards:** L. C. Tiffany Grant (2); Audubon Artists, Joseph Mayer Award, Gold Medal of Honor, Presidents Award; Brooklyn Museum, **P.P.;** Arden Prize; Francesca Wood Award; A.A.A. Gallery, NYC, National Print Competition, Second Prize; Henry B.

Shope Prize; Hunterdon County (N.J) Art Center, **P.P.;** SAGA, $1,000 **P.P.,** 1968; American Color Print Society, Sonia Wather Award, 1968; NAD, John Taylor Arms Memorial Prize, 1971; Los Angeles Printmaking Society, **P.P. Address:** 20 East 32nd Street, NYC 10016. **Dealers:** A.A.A. Gallery, NYC. **One-man Exhibitions:** Oakland/AM, 1960; Matrix Gallery, NYC, 1960; A.A.A. Gallery, NYC, 1961–64; Roko Gallery, NYC, 1961–64, 72; East Side Gallery, NYC, 1963; Riverdale-on-the-Hudson Museum, Riverdale, N.Y., 1963; Queens College; Raleigh/NCMA, 1964. **Group:** Library of Congress; Cincinnati/AM, Cincinnati International Biennial of Contemporary Color Lithography; PCA, American Prints Today, circ., 1959–62; Brooklyn Museum; PAFA; WMAA; Oakland/AM; Lincoln, Mass./De Cordova; MMA; Cincinnati/AM; SAGA. **Collections:** Abbot Academy; Anchorage; Boston/MFA; Brooklyn Museum; Cincinnati/AM; Clairol Inc.; Cooper Union; U. of Delaware; Free Library of Philadelphia; Guild Hall; Hamilton College; Karachi; Library of Congress; Lincoln, Mass./De Cordova; Lindenwood College; MMA; U. of Maine; Malmo; Memphis/Brooks; Minneapolis/Institute; Montclair/AM; NCFA; NYPL; NYU; National Gallery; U. of Nebraska; New York Hilton Hotel; Norfolk; The Ohio State U.; PMA; Potsdam/SUNY; Rutgers U.; Seattle/AM; Topeka Public Library; USIA; US State Department; Victoria and Albert Museum; WMAA; Wilmington; Walker; Wesleyan U.; Yale U.

LEKAKIS, MICHAEL, b. March 1, 1907, NYC. Self-taught, US Army Air Corps, 1942–45. Traveled Mexico, Europe, Egypt, Greece. **Award:** Guggenheim Foundation Fellowship. **Address:** 57 West 28th Street, NYC 10001. **One-man Exhibitions:** Artists' Gallery, NYC, 1941; San Antonio/McNay, 1946; The Bertha Schaefer Gallery, 1946, 48; American U., 1949; Signa Gallery, East Hampton, N.Y., 1959; The Howard

Wise Gallery, NYC, 1961; Dayton/AI, 1968, 69; Flair Gallery, Cincinnati, 1968, 69; WMAA, 1973. **Group:** WMAA Annuals, 1948–52, 1958, 60, 62; SRGM, Sculpture and Drawings, 1958; Cleveland/MA, 1961; Boston Arts Festival, 1961; Hartford/Wadsworth, Continuity and Change, 1962; Seattle World's Fair, 1962; MOMA, Americans 1963, circ., 1963–64. **Collections:** Dayton/AI; Greece/National; Hartford/Wadsworth; U. of Kentucky; MOMA; U. of Nebraska; U. of North Carolina; PMA; Pinakothiki, Athens; Portland, Ore./ AM; SRGM; Seattle/AM; Tel Aviv; WMAA. **Bibliography:** *Sculpture and Drawings.* Archives.

LEONG, JAMES C. b. November 27, 1929, San Francisco, Calif. **Studied:** California College of Arts and Crafts, 1951–53, BFA, MFA; San Francisco State College, 1954, MA. US Army, 1952–53. Traveled Europe, USA; U. of Oslo, 1956–58. **Taught:** U. of Georgia, 1971. Prologue sequence for *Freud,* directed by John Huston, 1962. **Commissions** (murals): Chung Mei Home for Boys, El Cerrito, Calif., 1950; Ping Yuen Federal Housing Project, San Francisco, 1951; San Francisco State College, 1951. **Awards:** Fulbright Fellowship; Guggenheim Foundation Fellowship; San Francisco Art Festival, Third Prize, 1951; SFMA, 1962. **Address:** Piazza del Biscione 95, Interno 4, Rome 00186, Italy. **One-man Exhibitions:** (first) Hungry i, San Francisco, 1951; Barone Gallery, NYC, 1955, 56, 57, 60; American Gallery, Los Angeles, 1955; Holst Halvorsen Gallery, Oslo, 1956; Galerie Paletten, Oslo, 1957; Erling Haghfelt, Copenhagen, 1957; L'Obelisco, Rome, 1960, 61; Feingarten Gallery, NYC, 1962; Galleria dell'-Ariete, 1962; Royal Athena II, NYC, 1963, 67; Temple U., Rome, 1967; Cerberus Gallery, 1969; Gloria Luria Gallery, 1970; U. of Georgia, 1971; Middle Tennessee State U., 1971; The Pennsylvania State U., 1971; Kama Studio, 1975; Richard Larcada Gallery, 1975;

Galleria Galtung, Oslo, 1976; Gallery 47, Copenhagen, 1976; Gallerie Oljemark, Helsinki, 1976; Studiodue, Rome, 1976. **Group:** SFMA; de Young, WMAA, 1955; American Academy, Rome; MOMA, 1960; Internazionale di Arte Astratta, Prato, Italy, 1960; Brooklyn Museum, 1961; Carnegie, 1961; U. of Rochester, 1962; Rome National Art Quadrennial, 1967; NIAL, 1967; AFA, Inverse Illusionism, 1971–72; USIA, Rome, Four American Artists, 1972; Rome, V Quadriennial, 1977. **Collections:** Brooklyn Museum; Dallas/MFA; U. of Georgia; Harvard U.; Indianapolis; MIT; Middle Tennessee State U.; NYU; Princeton U.; Purchase/ SUNY; U. of Rochester; U. of Texas. **Bibliography:** Archives.

LESLIE, ALFRED. b. October 29, 1927, NYC. Studied with Tony Smith, William Baziotes, Hale Woodruff, John McPherson; NYU, 1956–57; Pratt Institute; ASL. US Coast Guard, 1945–46. **Taught:** Great Neck (N.Y.) Adult Education Program, 1956–57; San Francisco Art Institute, summer, 1964. Codirector-producer (with Robert Frank and Jack Kerouac) of the film *Pull My Daisy.* **Awards:** Guggenheim Foundation Fellowship, 1969; Butler Institute of American Art, First Prize, 1977. **Address:** 1641 South East Street, South Amherst, MA 01002. **Dealer:** Allan Frumkin Gallery, NYC. **One-man Exhibitions:** (first) Tibor de Nagy Gallery, 1951, also 1952, 53, 54, 57; Martha Jackson Gallery, 1959, 60; Holland-Goldowsky Gallery, Chicago, 1960; Noah Goldowsky, 1968, 69, 71; Allan Frumkin Gallery, NYC, 1975, 78; Allan Frumkin Gallery, Chicago, 1977; Youngstown State U., 1977; U. of Connecticut, 1978. **Group:** Festival of Two Worlds, Spoleto, 1958; Paris/Moderne, Young Americans, 1958; V Sao Paulo Biennial, 1959; Walker, Sixty American Painters, 1960; Carnegie, 1961; Stockholm/National, Four Americans, 1961; WMAA Annuals, 1961, 65, 67, 68, 71, 72, 73; Kunsthalle, Basel, 4 Americans, 1963;

Barry Le Va *Installation Study for Any Rectangular Space: Accumulated Vision: Boundaries Designated* (Configurations Indicated) 1977

Bennington College, Recent Figurative Art, 1967; MOMA, In Memory of My Feelings; Frank O'Hara, 1967; WMAA, 22 Realists, 1970; MIT, Contemporary Views of Man, 1971; WMAA, American Drawings: 1963–1973, 1973; St. John U., The Figure in Recent American Painting, 1974; New York Cultural Center, Three Centuries of the American Nude, 1975; St. Petersburg, Fla./MFA, The Figure as Form: American Painting 1930–1975, 1975; Venice Biennial, 1976; US Department of the Interior, America '76, circ., 1976; Youngstown/Butler, 41st Annual Midyear Show, 1977; Indianapolis, Perceptions of the Spirit in 20th Century American Art, 1977; PAFA, 8 Contemporary American Realists, 1977. **Collections:** Aachen; U. of Alabama; Amsterdam/Stedelijk; Buffalo/Albright; Chicago/AI; Cornell U.; Hirshhorn; Kunsthalle, Basel; MOMA; Milwaukee; Minneapolis/Institute; Norfolk/Chrysler; PAFA; Stockholm/National; U. of Virginia; WMAA; Walker. **Bibliography:** *America 1976*; Arthur 2; Downes, ed.; Friedman, ed.; Goodyear; Hunter 1; Hunter, ed.; Janis and Blesh 1; *Kunst um 1970*; Sager; Sandler 1. Archives.

LE VA, BARRY. b. 1941, Long Beach, Calif. **Studied:** Los Angeles Art Center School; Otis Art Institute, Los Angeles, BA, MFA, 1964–67. **Taught:** Minneapolis College of Art and Design, 1969–70; Princeton U., 1973–74. **Award:** Los Angeles County/MA, Young Talent Grant, 1968. **Address:** c/o Dealer. **Dealer:** Ileana Sonnabend Gallery, Inc., NYC. **One-man Exhibitions:** Minneapolis School of Art, 1969; Galerie Ricke, Cologne, 1970, 71, 72, 73, 76; Nigel Greenwood Gallery, London, 1971; U. of Utrecht, 1971; Bykert Gallery, NYC, 1972, 73, 74, 75; Gallery Projection, Cologne, 1972; Felix Handshin Gallery, Basel, 1973; Zwirner Gallery, Cologne, 1973; The Texas Gallery, Houston, 1974, 76, 78; Hartford (Conn.) Art School, 1974; Galleria Toselli, Milan, 1974; Daniel Weinberg Gallery, San

Francisco, 1975, 76; Claire Copley Gallery, Los Angeles, 1975, 76; Espace 5, Montreal, 1975; Montreal/Contemporain, 1975; Ileana Sonnabend Gallery, NYC, 1976, 78; Galerie Sonnabend, Paris, 1976; Wright State U., 1977. **Retrospective:** The New Museum, NYC, 1979. **Group:** California State College, Los Angeles, 2 Painters, 1 Sculptor, 1968; SFA, Conception-Perception, 1968; WMAA, Anti-Illusion, 1969; Seattle/AM, 557,087, 1969; La Jolla, Projections, 1970; MOMA, Information, 1970; WMAA Annuals, 1971, 76; Dusseldorf/Kunsthalle, Prospect, 1971; Documenta 5, Kassel, 1971; Yale U., Options and Alternatives, 1973; Cincinnati/Contemporary, Bochner, La Va, Rockburne, Tuttle, 1975; Baltimore/MA, Fourteen Artists, 1975; Leverkusen, U.S.A. Drawings III, 1975; WMAA, 200 Years of American Sculpture, 1976; Philadelphia College of Art, Line, 1976; U. of Chicago, Installations, 1977; U. of Santa Barbara, Contemporary Drawing New York, 1978; U. of North Carolina, Drawings about Drawing Today, 1979. **Collections:** Los Angeles County/MA; WMAA. **Bibliography:** *Drawings: The Pluralist Decade;* Gablik; Pincus-Witten.

LEVEE, JOHN. b. April 10, 1924, Los Angeles, Calif. **Studied:** UCLA, BA (philosophy); New School for Social Research, with Stuart Davis, Yasuo Kuniyoshi, Adja Yunkers, Abraham Rattner; Academie Julian, Paris. Traveled Europe, North Africa, Middle East; resides Paris, 1949– . **Taught:** U. of Illinois, 1965; Washington U. (St. Louis) 1967, 68; NYU, 1967–68; U. of Southern California, Los Angeles, 1971. **Awards:** Deauville Salon, 1951; California Watercolor Society, 1955, 56; I Paris Biennial, First Prize, 1959; VMFA, Virginia Artists Biennial, **P.P.,** 1966; Tamarind Fellowship, 1969; Woolmark Foundation Prize, 1974. **Address:** 119 rue Notre Dame des Champs, Paris 6, France. **Dealers:** Margo Leavin Gallery; Andre Emmerich, NYC. **One-man Exhibi-**

tions: (first) Galerie Huit, Paris, 1951; Twenster, Rotterdam, 1953; Felix Landau Gallery, 1954; Andre Emmerich Gallery, NYC, 1956, 58, 59, 62, 65, 66; Gimpel Fils Ltd., 1958, 60, 66; Galerie de France, Paris, 1958, 61, 62, 64, 69; Esther Robles Gallery, 1962, 63, 65; Haifa, 1964; Phoenix, 1964; U. of Illinois, 1965; Walker, 1965; Margo Leavin Gallery, 1970; Galerie Henri Mayer, Lausanne, 1971; Galerie Liatowitsch, Basel, 1972; American Embassy, London, 1974; Palm Springs Desert Museum, 1976, 77. **Retrospectives:** Tel Aviv, 1969; Galerie la Tortue, Paris, 1975. **Group:** Carnegie, 1955, 58; Corcoran, 1956, 58, 66; WMAA, Young America, 1957; Brooklyn Museum, Watercolor Biennials; MOMA, Younger American Painters, circ., 1957–59; Arts Club of Chicago, 1958; Smithsonian, American Painters in France, circ., USA; WMAA Annuals, 1958, 59, 65, 66; Foundation Maeght, l'Art Vivant, circ., French museums, 1966, 67; UNESCO, 1975; Comparison Salon, Paris, 1978; American Cultural Center, Paris, 1981. **Collections:** Allentown/AM; Amsterdam/Stedelijk; U. of Arizona; Baltimore/MA; Basel; CNAC; U. of California, Berkeley; Carnegie; Cincinnati/AM; Columbus; Corcoran; Dallas/MFA; Des Moines; Djakarta Museum; Grenoble; Haifa; Harvard U.; Hirshhorn; Honolulu Academy; Los Angeles/County MA; MOMA; Musée du Havre; NYPL; Oberlin College; Oklahoma; Palm Springs Desert Museum; Phoenix; SRGM; Santa Barbara/MA; Smith College; U. of Sydney; Tel Aviv; Towner Art Gallery; VMFA; WGMA; WMAA; Walker; Washington U.; Yale U. **Bibliography:** Juin; Read 2.

LEVI, JOSEPH. b. February 17, 1938, NYC. **Studied:** U. of Connecticut (with Walter Meigs), BA; Columbia U. Traveled Spain, France, Belgium, Holland, England, Mexico, Middle East. US Army, 1960–67. **Taught:** Appalachian State U., Artist-in-Residence, 1969, Fairleigh Dickinson U., 1971. Director,

Encounter, Inc. (drug rehabilitation program), NYC, 1974. **Taught:** Pennsylvania State U., 1977. **Awards:** U. of Illinois, **P.P.,** 1967. **Member:** Artists Equity. **Address:** 171 West 71st Street, NYC 10023. **Dealer:** A.M. Sachs Gallery. **One-man Exhibitions:** (first) The Stable Gallery, NYC, 1966, also 1967, 69, 70; Arts Club of Chicago, 1968; Louisville/Speed, 1968; Appalachian State U., 1969; Lambert Studios, Inc., Los Angeles, 1971; Jacobs Ladder Gallery, Washington, D.C., 1972; Images Gallery, Toledo, 1972; A.M. Sachs Gallery, NYC, 1975, 76, 78. **Group:** Houston/Contemporary, 1966; Kansas City/Nelson, Sound, Light, Silence, 1966; U. of Illinois, 1967; Walker, Light Motion Space, 1967; MOMA, The 1960's, 1967; Flint/Institute, 1967; Indianapolis/Herron, 1968; WMAA Annual, 1968; Brooklyn Museum, 1969; RISD, 1972; WMAA, Art about Art, 1978. **Collections:** Albion College; AT&T; The Bank of New York; Buffalo/Albright; Chrysler Corp.; Corcoran; Des Moines; Exxon Corp., NYC; U. of Illinois; Louisville/Speed; Minolta Corp., NYC; MOMA; U. of Maryland; Newark Museum; U. of Notre Dame; Ridgefield/Aldrich; Spelman College; Storm King Art Center.

LEVI, JULIAN, b. June 20, 1900, NYC. **Studied:** PAFA, with Henry Breckenridge, Arthur B. Carles, Jr.; and five years in France and Italy. **Taught:** ASL; PAFA, 1964–77; New School for Social Research. **Awards:** PAFA, Cresson Fellowship, 1920; Chicago/AI, The M.V. Kohnstamm Prize, 1942; Chicago/AI, Norman Wait Harris Medal, 1943; Carnegie, Hon. Men., 1945; NAD, The Adolph and Clara Obrig Prize, 1945; U. of Illinois, 1948; PAFA, Fellowship, 1954; NIAL Grant, 1955; elected to the NIAL, 1960. **Address:** 79 West 12th Street, NYC 10011; summer: 791 Fireplace Road, East Hampton, NY 11937. **Dealer:** Babcock Gallery, NYC. **One-man Exhibitions:** Crillon Galleries, Philadelphia, 1933; The Downtown Gal-

lery, 1940, 42, 45, 50, Philadelphia Art Alliance, 1953, 63; The Alan Gallery, NYC, 1955; Lee Nordness Gallery, NYC, 1961; Anna Werbe Gallery, Detroit, 1961. **Retrospective:** Boston U., 1962; New Britain; Rehn Galleries, 1974. **Group:** Detroit Institute, 1961; PAFA; NAD; U. of Illinois; WMAA; Newark Museum; Youngstown/Butler. **Collections:** U. of Arizona; Britannica; Buffalo/Albright; Chicago/AI; Cranbrook; Des Moines; Detroit/Institute; U. of Georgia; U. of Illinois; MMA; MOMA; Michigan State U.; NAD; NCFA; U. of Nebraska; Newark Museum; New Britain; PAFA; Reed College; Santa Barbara/MA; Scripps College; Springfield, Mass./MFA; Toledo/MA; WMAA; Walker/Wilmington; Youngstown/Butler. **Bibliography:** Baur 7; Blesh 1; Halpert; Hess, T.B., 1; Kootz 2; Nordness, ed.; Pagano; Passloff; Rose, B. 1; Watson, E.W., 2; Wheeler. Archives.

LEVINE, JACK. b. January 3, 1915, Boston, Mass. Studied with Denman W. Ross, Harold Zimmerman. Traveled Europe, Mexico; resided Rome, one year. **Member:** NIAL; American Academy of Arts and Sciences; Artists Equity. Federal A.P.: Easel painting. **Taught:** American Art School, NYC; PAFA; Skowhegan School; Cleveland/MA; Chicago/AI; U. of Illinois. **Awards:** Carnegie, 1946; Corcoran, 1959; PAFA, 1948; NIAL, 1946; Guggenheim Foundation Fellowship, 1946; Hon. DFA, Colby College; NAD, Benjamin Altman Prize, 1975. **m.** Ruth Gikow. **Address:** 68 Morton Street, NYC 10014. **Dealer:** Kennedy Gallery. **One-man Exhibitions:** The Downtown Gallery, NYC, 1939, 48, 52; Boris Mirski Gallery, Boston, 1950; The Alan Gallery, NYC, 1953, 57, 59, 63, 66; Chicago/AI, 1955; Philadelphia Art Alliance, 1955; Colby College, 1956; Randolph-Macon Woman's College, 1960; New Art Center, Detroit, 1962; B'nai B'rith Building, Washington, D.C., 1965; Kovler Gallery, Chicago, 1966; Athena Gallery, New Haven, 1967; Graphics, Inc.,

NYC, 1967; George Washington U., 1967; Galeria Colibri, San Juan, 1968; Lincoln, Mass./De Cordova, 1968; Galleria d'Arte il Gabbiano, Rome, 1968; Muggleton Art Gallery, Auburn, N.Y., 1968; Art Harris Art Gallery, L.A., 1970; Kennedy Gallery, NYC, 1972, 73, 75, 77; Rodman Hall Arts Center, St. Catherines, Ont., 1978. **Retrospectives:** Long Beach/MA, 1971. **Group:** MOMA, New Horizons in American Art, 1936; WMAA Annuals, 1937 to 1967; Musée du Jeu de Paume, Paris, Three Centuries of American Art, 1938; Carnegie, International Exhibition, 1938–1955; MOMA; Art in Our Time, 1939; PAFA Annuals, 1940–1968; MOMA, Thirty-Five under Thirty-Five, circ., 1940; Institute of Modern Art, Boston, Painting by 50 Oncoming Americans, 1941; MMA, Artists for Victory, 1942; WAC, 92 Artists, 1943; NAD, 1946; Tate Gallery, London, American Painting from the Eighteenth Century to the Present Day, 1946; Corcoran Biennials, 1947–1959; ICA, Boston, American Painting in Our Century, circ., 1949; U. of Illinois, 1949–1967; MMA, American Painting Today, 1950; U. of Minnesota, 40 American Painters, 1940–1950; Sao Paulo, Biennial, 1951; Youngstown/Butler, The American Jew in Art, 1955; MOMA, Modern Art in the U.S.A., circ. internationally, 1955; XXVIII Venice, Biennial, 1956; Smithsonian, Fulbright Painters, circ., 1958, U.S. Dept. of State, American Painting and Sculpture, circ. internationally, 1959; Milwaukee Art Center, ART: USA: NOW, 1962; Washington (D.C.) Gallery of American Art, US Government Art Projects: Some Distinguished Alumni, 1963; Minneapolis/Institute, Four Centuries of American Art, 1963; MMA, Three Centuries of American Paintings, 1965; Corcoran, Two Hundred Fifty Years of American Art, 1966; Cleveland/MA, Four Centuries of American Art, 1966; WMAA, Art in the United States, 1670–1966, 1966; WMAA, The 1930s; Painting and Sculpture in America, 1968; Omaha/Joslyn, The Thirties Decade: American Artists and Their Euro-pean Contemporaries, 1971; Pushkin Museum, Moscow, Representations of America, circ., 1977. **Collections:** Andover/Phillips; Boston/MFA; Brooklyn Museum; California Palace; Chicago/AI; Harvard U.; State U. of Iowa; U. of Kansas; MMA; MOMA; U. of Nebraska; U. of Oklahoma; PAFA; Phillips; Portland, Ore./AM; Utica; WMAA; Wichita/AM; Walker. **Bibliography:** Barker 1; Baur 7; Blesh 1; Cheney; Christensen; Eliot; Finkelstein; Frost; Genauer; **Getlein 2;** Getlein, F. and D; Goodrich and Baur 1; Halpert; Hunter 6; Kootz 2; McCurdy, ed.; Mendelowitz; Miller, ed., 1; Munsterberg; Newmeyer; Nordness, ed.; Pousette-Dart, ed.; Read 2; Richardson, E.P.; Rodman 1, 2, 3; Rose, B., 1: Sachs; Shapiro, ed.; Soby 5, 6; Soyer, R. 1; Wight 2. Archives.

LEVINE, LES. b. October 6, 1935, Dublin, Ireland. **Studied:** Central School of Arts and Crafts, London. To Canada, 1958; to USA, 1966. Traveled Australia, Europe, South America. Founder/President, The Museum for Mott Art, Inc., 1970. **Taught:** NYU, 1972–73; William Paterson College; Nova Scotia College of Art and Design, 1973. Artist-in-Residence, Aspen Institute, 1967, 69. Produced *Levine's Restaurant*, NYC, 1969. **Awards:** National Endowment for the Arts, 1974; CAPS, 1980; The Architectural League of New York, Grant, 1972. **Address:** 20 East 20th Street, NYC 10003. **Dealers:** Ronald Feldman Fine Arts, Inc., NYC.; Isaacs Gallery, Toronto; Jollembeck Gallery, Cologne. **One-man Exhibitions:** U. of Toronto, 1964; Blue Barn Gallery, Ottawa, 1964, 66; David Mirvish Gallery, 1965; Isaacs Gallery, 1965, 67, 70, 73; Fischbach Gallery, 1966, 67, 68, 69, 70, 72, 73; Toronto, 1966; Lofthouse Gallery, Ottawa, 1966; Walker, 1967; MOMA, 1967; York U., 1968; John Gibson Gallery, 1968; Molly Barnes Gallery, Los Angeles, 1969; ICA, Chicago, 1969; U. of Michigan, 1969; Rowan Gallery, London, 1969; Phyllis Kind Gallery,

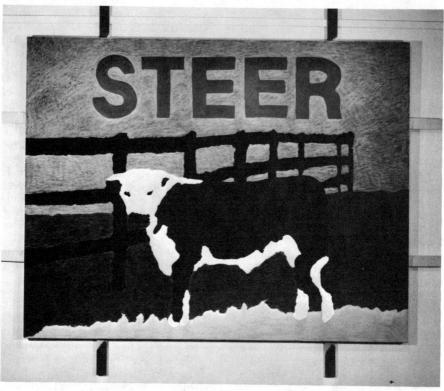

Les Levine   *Billboard Project for Outside the Department of Commerce, "Steer"*   1979

Chicago, 1969; NYU, 1969; Galerie de Gestlo, 1971, 73, 74; Finch College, NYC, 1972; Rivkin Gallery, Washington, D.C., 1972; Nova Scotia College of Art and Design, 1973; Vancouver, 1974; U. of California, San Diego, 1974; Stefanotty Gallery, NYC, 1974; The Video Distribution Inc., 1974; Gallerie Gilles Gheerbrant, Montreal, 1976; M. L. D'Arc Gallery, NYC, 1976, 77; Hartford/Wadsworth, 1976; California State U., Los Angeles, 1976; Art Gallery of New South Wales, Adelaide, Australia, 1976; National Gallery of Victoria, Melbourne, Australia, 1976; U. of Melbourne, Australia, 1976; Syracuse/Everson, 1977; Buffalo/Albright, 1977; Galerie de Gestlo, Hamburg, 1977; Isaacs Gallery, Toronto, 1977; Vehicule Art, Inc., Montreal, 1977; Galerie Arnesen, Copenhagen, 1977; International Cultural Centrum, Antwerp, 1978; Rot-terdamse Kunststichting, Rotterdam, 1978; Station Gallery, Whitby, Canada, 1978; Laurentian U., 1978; Parry Sound Public Library, Canada, 1979; Canadian Cultural Center, Paris, 1979; Northwestern Illinois U., 1979; Ronald Feldman Fine Arts, NYC, 1979; Galerie Jollembeck, Cologne, 1979; PMA, 1979; Plattsburgh/SUNY, 1979; Alberta College of Art, Calgary, 1979; Marion Goodman Gallery, NYC, 1980. **Group:** Ottawa/National, Canadian Sculpture Exhibitions, 1964, 65, 67; MOMA, The Object Transformed, 1966; ICA, Boston, Nine Canadians, 1967; Expo '67, Montreal, 1967; MOMA, Dada, Surrealism, and Today, 1967; MOMA, Canadian Prints Today, 1967; Union Carbide Corp., NYC, Canada '67, 1967; ICA, Boston, The Projected Image, 1967; Finch College, NYC, Schemata 7, 1967; U. of North Carolina, Works on Paper,

1968; Newark College of Engineering, Light as Art, 1968; Edinburgh Festival; 1968; Finch College, NYC, Destructionists, 1968; HemisFair '68, San Antonio, Tex., 1968; Brandeis U., Vision and Television, 1969; Milwaukee, A Plastic Presence, circ., 1969; Edmonton Art Gallery, Alberta, Place and Process, 1969; X Sao Paulo Biennial, 1969; ICA, U. of Pennsylvania, Between Object and Environment, 1969; Buffalo/Albright, Manufactured Art, 1969; UCLA, Electric Art, 1969; Cincinnati/Contemporary, Monumental Art, 1970; Moore College of Art, Philadelphia, Recorded Image, 1970; ICA, London, Multiple Art, 1970; Jewish Museum, Software, 1970; MOMA, Information, 1971; Montreal/Contemporain, Conceptual Decorative, 1971; Dalhousie U., Halifax, Morbus Exhibition, 1973; Walker, New Learning Spaces, 1974; Cologne, Project '74, 1974; ICA, U. of Pennsylvania, Video and Television, 1975; ICA, Philadelphia, Video and Television, 1975; XII Sao Paulo Biennial, 1975; U. of California, Berkeley, Milwaukee, From Foreign Shores, 1976, Commissioned Video Tapes, 1976; Philadelphia College of Art, Artists' Maps, 1977; Kunsthaus, Zurich, Painting and Photography in Dialogue from 1840 to Today, 1977; Documenta 6, Kassel, 1977; Smith College, Artists' Stamps, 1977; Museum of Contemporary Crafts, NYC, The Great American Foot, 1978–80; Purchase/SUNY, The Sense of Self, 1978; ICA, Boston, Wit and Wisdom, 1978. **Collections:** Art Gallery of Ontario; Art Gallery of South Australia; Corcoran; U. of Georgia, Athens; Hartford/Wadsworth; MMA; MOMA; NYPL; National Gallery of Australia; National Gallery, Victoria; Ottawa/National; PMA; Paris/Beaubourg; Sydney/AG; WMAA. **Bibliography:** Calas, N. and E.; Davis, D.; *From Foreign Shores;* Lippard, ed.; *Report.* Archives.

LEVINSON, MON. b. January 6, 1926, NYC. **Studied:** U. of Pennsylvania, 1948, BS Econ.; self-taught in art. US

Army, 1945–46. Traveled Mexico, Europe. **Taught:** Boston Museum School, 1969; C. W. Post College, 1970–72. **Commissions:** Betsy Ross Flag & Banner Co. 1963 (banner); MOMA, 1964 (greeting card); Astor Foundation Grant, 1967 (sculpture for P.S. 166, NYC); Housing and Redevelopment Board, NYC, 1967–69 (murals for demountable vest-pocket parks); Great Southwest Industrial Park, 1968 (mural); Machpelah Cemetery, Flint, Mich., 1969 (sculpture). **Awards:** Cassandra Foundation Grant, 1972; CAPS, New York State Council on the Arts, 1974; National Endowment for the Arts, 1976. **Address:** 309 West Broadway, NYC 10013. **One-man Exhibitions:** (first) The Kornblee Gallery, 1961, also 1963–66, 1968, 69, 71, 72; Cinema I and Cinema II, NYC, 1965; Franklin Siden Gallery, Detroit, 1965–67, 69; Obelisk Gallery, 1968; C. W. Post College, 1970; A Clean Well-Lighted Place, Austin, Tex., 1970; Southern Methodist U., 1971; John Weber Gallery, 1973; Gertrude Kasle Gallery, 1975; Rosa Esman Gallery, NYC, 1976 (two-man), 77; Deson-Zaks Gallery, Chicago, 1976; Suzette Schochett Gallery, Newport, R.I., 1976. **Group:** Martha Jackson Gallery, New Media—New Forms, I, 1960; MOMA, 1962, 63; Sidney Janis Gallery, 1964; Chicago/AI, 1964; A.F.A., circ.; Buffalo/Albright, 1964; RISD, 1965; Staatliche Kunsthalle, Baden-Baden, 1965; MOMA, 1967; Buffalo/Albright, Plus by Minus, 1968; Finch College, 1968; Museum of Contemporary Crafts, 1968; Flint/Institute, Made of Plastic, 1968; Grand Rapids, 1969; Jewish Museum, Superlimited, 1969; Foundation Maeght, L'Art Vivant, 1970; WMAA, 1970, 73; Lincoln, Mass./De Cordova, Refracted Images, 1973; Indianapolis, 1973; U. of Miami, Less Is More: The Influence of the Bauhaus on American Art, 1974; Renwick Gallery, Washington, D.C., The Object as Poet, 1978; NCFA, New Ways with Paper, 1978; NYU, Drawing and Collage, 1977; Albright/Buffalo, Paper about Paper, 1980. **Collections:** Brandeis U.; Caracas; Cornell U.; NYU; Princeton U.; Spelman College; Springfield, Mo./AM; Storm King Art Center: WMAA. **Bibliography:** MacAgy 2, Rickey.

LEVITAN, ISRAEL. b. June 13, 1912, Lawrence, Mass. **Studied:** Chicago Art Institute School; Ozenfant School of Art, 1948; Hofmann School, NYC, 1948–50; Zadkine School of Sculpture, Paris, 1950–51. US Navy, 1942–47. Traveled Europe, USA extensively; India. **Taught:** Cooper Union, 1955; Brooklyn Museum School, 1956–60; NYU, 1956–65, 1967; U. of California, Berkeley, 1962; Philadelphia Museum School, 1962–66; Florida Humanistic Institute, St. Petersburg, Fla.; and privately. **Commissions:** Interchurch Center, NYC. **Awards:** MacDowell Colony Fellowship, 1956; Guild Hall, First Prize, Sculpture, 1960. **Address:** 1348 High Bluff Drive, Largo, FL 33540; summer: 45 Alewive Brook Road, East Hampton, NY 11937. **One-man Exhibitions:** (first) Artists' Gallery, NYC, 1952; Weyhe Gallery, 1953; Barone Gallery, NYC, 1957, 59, 60; U. of California, Berkeley, 1962; PMA, 1963; Grand Central Moderns, NYC, 1964; The Gallery, Memphis, 1964; Benson Gallery, 1970; Artist Market Gallery, Clearwater, Fla., 1963–73; Eckerd College, St. Petersburg, Fla., 1978. **Retrospective:** U. of California, Berkeley, 1962. **Group:** WMAA Annuals, 1952–53; American Abstract Artists, 1953–57; PAFA; Paris/Moderne; SFMA; Brooklyn Museum; PMA; Claude Bernard, Paris, Aspects of American Sculpture, 1960; Clearwater/Gulf Coast, 1972. **Collections:** Guild Hall; Interchurch Center, NYC. **Bibliography:** Seuphor 3.

LEWANDOWSKI, EDMUND D. b. July 3, 1914, Milwaukee, Wis. **Studied:** Layton School of Art, 1932–35. **Taught:** Florida State U., 1949–54; Layton School of Art, 1945–49, 1954–72; Winthrop College, 1979– . **Commissions:** Commemorative Stamp, Polish Millen-

nium. **Awards:** Hallmark International Competition, 1950, 53, 57; Milwaukee, Medal, 1940. **Address:** 537 Meadowbrook Lane, Rockhill, SC 29730. **Dealer:** Fairweather-Hardin Gallery. **One-man Exhibitions:** Layton School of Art; Minnesota State Fair; Florida State U., 1950; Fairweather-Hardin Gallery, Chicago, 1973, 1978. **Group:** Chicago/AI; Carnegie; Corcoran; PAFA; Brooklyn Museum; New York World's Fair, 1939, Phillips. **Collections:** AAAL; Allen-Bradley Co. Inc.; Andover/Phillips; Beloit College; Boston/MFA; Brooklyn Museum; Chicago/AI; Dartmouth College; Flint/Institute; Florida State U.; Gimbel Bros.; Grand Rapids; Hallmark Collection; Krakow/National; Layton School of Art; MOMA; Marquette U.; U. of Oklahoma; St. Patrick's, Mensasha, Wis.; Shell Oil Co.; US Maritime Commission; Warsaw; Warsaw/National; U. of Wisconsin. **Bibliography:** Baur 7; Cheney; Halpert; Pousette-Dart, ed.; Ritchie, 1.

LEWIS, NORMAN. b. July 23, 1909, NYC; **d.** August 27, 1979, NYC. **Studied:** Columbia U., with Augusta Savage. **Taught:** Junior high school, NYC, 1935; Harlem Art Center, NYC, 1937; Thomas Jefferson School, NYC, 1944–49; Indian Hill Music School, Stockbridge, Mass., 1954; HARYOU-ACT, 1965–70; ASL, 1972–78. Traveled Europe, North Africa, Greece. Organized an art center at Bennett College under government sponsorship, 1938. Supervised a mural for Thomas Jefferson High School, St. Albans, N.Y., 1939; cofounder of Cinque Gallery, NYC. **Awards:** Carnegie, Popularity Prize, 1955; AAAL, 1970; NIAL, 1971; Mark Rothko Foundation, 1972; National Endowment for the Arts, 1972. **One-man Exhibitions:** Harlem Artists Guild, 1936; Fisk U., 1939; Baltimore/MA, 1939; The Willard Gallery, 1949, 51, 52, 54, 56. **Retrospective:** City U. of New York, 1976. **Group:** Carnegie, 1955; XXVIII Venice Biennial, 1956; U.

of Illinois; NIAL; PAFA; PMA; Library of Congress; Boston, MFA, Black Artists: New York and Boston, 1970. **Collections:** Andover/Phillips, Chicago/AI; IBM; MOMA; Manufacturers Hanover Trust Co.; Utica. **Bibliography:** Baur 5; Dover; Motherwell and Reinhardt, eds.; *Norman Lewis: A Retrospective*; Ritchie 1. Archives.

LE WITT, SOL. b. 1928, Hartford, Conn. **Studied:** Syracuse U., 1945–49, BFA. **Taught:** MOMA School, 1964–67; Cooper Union, 1967. **Commissions:** GSA, Syracuse, N.Y., 1979; Hartford (Conn.) Coliseum, 1980. DANCE, in collaboration with Lucinda Childs and Phil Glass, Brooklyn Academy of Music, 1979. **Address:** 117 Hester Street, NYC 10002. **Dealer:** John Weber Gallery; Young-Hoffman Gallery, Chicago. **One-man Exhibitions:** The Daniel Gallery, NYC, 1965; Dwan Gallery, NYC, 1966, 68, 70, 71; Dwan Gallery, Los Angeles, 1967; Galerie Bischofberger, Zurich, 1968; Galerie Heiner Friedrich, Munich, 1968; Konrad Fischer Gallery, Dusseldorf, 1968, 69, 71, 75, 77, 79; ACE Gallery, Los Angeles, 1968; Galleria l'Attico Rome, 1969, 73; Galerie Ernst Joachim, Hanover, 1969; Krefeld/Haus Lange, 1969; Wisconsin State U., 1970; Art & Project, Amsterdam, 1970, 71; Yvon Lambert, Paris, 1970, 73, 74; The Hague, 1970; Pasadena/AM, 1970; Protetch-Rivkin, Washington, D.C., 1971; Galleria Toselli, Milan, 1971; Lisson Gallery, London, 1971, 73, 74, 77, 79; John Weber Gallery, 1971, 73, 74, 77, 78, 80; Dunkelman Gallery, Toronto, 1971; MIT, 1972; Harkus-Krakow Gallery, 1972; Dayton/AI, 1972; Berne, 1972, 74; Rosa Esman Gallery, 1973, 79; Vehicule Art Inc., Montreal, 1973; Museum of Modern Art, Oxford, England, 1973; Galerie MTL, Brussels, 1973; Portland (Ore.) Center for the Visual Arts, 1973; Cusack Gallery, Houston, 1973; Max Protetch Gallery, Washington, D.C., 1974; Galerie December, Munster, 1974; Brussels/Beaux-Arts, 1974; Rijksmuseum Kroller-Muller, 1974;

Amsterdam/Stedelijk, 1974, 75; Douglas Christmas, Los Angeles, 1974; Weinberg Gallery, San Francisco, 1974; Gian Enzo Sperone, Turin, 1970, 74, 75; Vancouver, 1974; Galerie Vega, Liege, 1974; Sperone Westwater Fisher Inc., NYC, 1974; Galleria Scipione, Macerata, Italy, 1975; Young-Hoffman Gallery, Chicago, 1979; Israel Museum 1975; Basel/Kunsthalle 1975; National Gallery of Victoria, 1977; Sydney/AG, 1977; Brooklyn Museum, 1978; Art & Project, Amsterdam, 1970, 71, 72, 73, 75; Galeria Genoa, Italy, 1974, 75, 77; Yvon Lambert, Paris, 1974, 79; Annemarie Verna, Zurich, 1975; Hartford, 1976; Utah, 1977. **Retrospectives:** SFMA (drawings), circ., 1974–76; MOMA, circ., 1978. **Group:** World House Galleries, NYC, 1965; Finch College, 1966, 67; WMAA Sculpture Annual, 1967; Los Angeles/County MA; PMA, American Sculpture of the Sixties, 1967; Ridgefield/Aldrich, 1968; The Hague, Minimal Art, 1968; Documenta IV, Kassel, 1968; Prospect '68, Dusseldorf, 1968; Munich/Modern, New Art: USA, 1968; Stadtische Kunsthalle, Dusseldorf, 1969; U. of British Columbia, 1969; U. of Illinois, 1969; Berne, When Attitudes Become Form, 1969; ICA, U. of Pennsylvania, Between Object and Environment, 1969; Seattle/AM, 557,087, 1969; Chicago/Contemporary, Art by Telephone, 1969; Chicago/AI, 1970; Tokyo Biennial, 1970; Turin/Civico, Conceptual Art, Arte Povera, Land Art, 1970; MOMA, Information, 1971; SRGM, Guggenheim International, 1971; Arnhem, Sonsbeek '71, 1971; Chicago/Contemporary, White on White, 1971–72; ICA, U. of Pennsylvania, Grids, 1972; Walker, Painting: New Options, 1972; New York Cultural Center, 3D into 3D, 1973; Basel, Diagrams and Drawings, 1973; WMAA, American Drawings; 1963–1973, 1973; Hartford Art School, Drawings: Seventies, 1973; Princeton U., Line as Language, 1974; Cologne/Kunstverein, Kunst uber Kunst, 1974; Neuer Berliner Kunstverein, Berlin, Multiples, 1974; Indianapolis, 1974; Documenta 6, Kassel, 1977; Cleveland/MA, Book Art, 1978; La Jolla, Numerals, 1978; ICA, Boston, The Reductive Object, 1979; Dublin/Municipal, 1980; Hayward Gallery, London (Pier and Ocean), 1980. **Collections:** Amsterdam/Stedelijk; Basel; Buffalo/Albright; Canberra/National; CNAC; Dayton/AI; Detroit/Institute; Edinburgh/Modern; Edinburgh National; Gilman Paper Corp.; U. of Illinois; Indianapolis; Grenoble; Krefeld/Kaiser Wilhelm; Humlebaek/ Louisiana; International Quadrennial (ROSC/MA); Jerusalem/National; La Jolla; Los Angeles/County MA; U. of Mass.; MOMA; New Britain; Oberlin College; RISD; Rotterdam; Saint Louis/ City; SRGM; Stockholm/National; Storm King Art Center; Tate; Toronto; Walker; WMAA. **Bibliography:** Alloway 4; *Art Now 74*; Battcock, ed.; Calas, N. and E.; *Contemporanea*; De Vries, ed.; *Drawings: The Pluralist Decade*; Gilsok; Goossen 1; Honnef; Honisch and Jensen, eds.; Johnson, Ellen H.; Krauss 2; Lippard 2, 3, 4; Lippard, ed.; Meyer; Muller; Pincus-Witten; *Sol Le Witt*; *When Attitudes Become Form*; Tuchman 1. Archives.

LIBERMAN, ALEXANDER. b. 1912, Kiev, Russia. **Studied:** Academie Andre Lhote, Paris, 1929–31 (painting); Academie des Beaux-Arts, Paris, with August Perret (architecture). With the Louvre Museum, made *La Femme francaise*, 1936, one of the first color films on painting. US citizen, 1946. Art editor of *VU*, 1933–37. Joined *Vogue* magazine, 1941; became its art director, 1943; became art director of Condé Nast Publications, Inc., USA and Europe, 1944, and the organization's editorial director, 1962. **Address:** 173 East 70th Street, NYC 10021. **Dealer:** Andre Emmerich Gallery, NYC. **One-man Exhibitions:** MOMA, The Artist in His Studio, 1959; Betty Parsons Gallery, 1960, 62, 63, 64, 67, 69; Robert Fraser Gallery, 1964; Bennington College, 1964; Galleria dell'Ariete, 1965; Galeria d'Arte, Naples, 1965; Jewish Museum,

1966; Andre Emmerich Gallery, 1967–69, 73, 74 (two-man), 79 (two-man); Janie C. Lee Gallery, Houston, 1974; Van Straaten Gallery, Chicago, 1977; Vernissage, Rome, 1978; Greenberg Gallery, St. Louis, 1979; Landau/ Alexander Gallery, Los Angeles, 1979; Arts Gallery Limited, Baltimore, 1979. **Retrospectives:** Houston/MFA, 1970; Corcoran, 1970; Honolulu Academy, 1972; Storm King Art Center, 1977. **Group:** SRGM, Younger American Painters, 1954; A. Tooth & Sons, London, Six American Painters, 1961; MOMA, Modern American Drawings, circ., Europe, 1961–62; Chicago/AI, 1961, 62; WMAA, Geometric Abstraction in America, circ., 1962; III International Biennial Exhibition of Prints, Tokyo, 1962; WMAA Annuals, 1962, 63, 65; Corcoran, 1963; Roswell, 1963; Hartford/Wadsworth, 1964; Los Angeles/County MA, Post Painterly Abstraction, 1964; MOMA, Contemporary Painters and Sculptors as Printmakers, 1964; SRGM, American Drawings, 1964; Galerie Denise Rene, Paris, Hard Edge, 1964; New York World's Fair, 1964–65; PAFA, 1965; MOMA, The Responsive Eye, 1965; Amsterdam/Stedelijk, New Shapes of Color, 1966; WMAA Sculpture Annuals, 1966, 69; Los Angeles/ County MA, American Sculpture of the Sixties, 1967; U. of Illinois, 1967; Hemis-Fair '68, San Antonio, Tex., 1968; MOMA, The Art of the Real, 1968; PMA, 1969; MOMA, The New American Painting and Sculpture, 1969; Newport, R.I., Monumenta, 1974; MOMA, Color as Language, circ., 1975; Pomona College (Calif.), Black and White Are Colors, 1979. **Collections:** Akron/AI; Andover/Phillips; Atlantic Richfield Co., Los Angeles; Brandeis U.; Buffalo/ Albright; U. of California; Chase Manhattan Bank; Chicago/AI; Civic Center Synagogue, NYC; Corcoran; Dayton/ AI; Houston/MFA; MOMA; Memphis/ Brooks; MFA; MMA; U. of Nebraska; NCFA; Oklahoma; U. of Pennsylvania; Smith College; SRGM; Storm King Art Center; Tate; VMFA; WGMA; WMAA; Woodward Foundation; Yale U. **Bibli-**

ography: Alexander Liberman; Alloway 4; Battcock, ed.; *Black and White Are Colors;* Calas, N. and E.; Goossen 1; *Monumenta;* Rickey; Tuchman 1.

LICHTENSTEIN, ROY. b. October 27, 1923, NYC. **Studied:** The Ohio State U., 1940–43, BFA, 1946–49, MA; ASL, 1940, with Reginald Marsh. US Army, 1943–46. **Taught:** The Ohio State U., 1946–51; New York State College of Education, Oswego, 1957–60; Douglass College, 1960–63. **Member:** American Academy of Arts and Science. **Commissions:** New York State Pavilion, New York World's Fair, 1964–65 (mural). **Award:** Skowhegan Award for Graphics, 1977; Hon. DFA, California Institute of the Arts, 1977. **Address:** P.O. Box 1369, Southampton, NY 11968. **Dealer:** Leo Castelli Inc. **One-man Exhibitions:** (first) Carlebach Gallery, NYC, 1951; John Heller Gallery, NYC, 1952, 53, 54, 57; Leo Castelli Inc., NYC, 1962–65, 67, 69, 71, 72, 73, 74, 75, 77, 78, 79; Ferus Gallery, Los Angeles, 1963; Ileana Sonnabend Gallery, Paris, 1963, 65, 70; Il Punto, Turin, 1964; Galleria Apollinaire, Milan, 1965; Cleveland/MA, 1966; Contemporary Arts Center, Cincinnati, 1967; Amsterdam/Stedelijk, 1967; Berne, 1968; Irving Blum Gallery, Los Angeles, 1968, 69, 71; Hannover/KG, 1969; U. of Puerto Rico, 1970; Kansas City/Nelson, 1970; Chicago/Contemporary, 1970; Seattle/AM, 1970; Columbus, 1970; U. of California, Irvine, 1970; Houston/Contemporary, 1972; Ronald Greenberg Gallery, St. Louis, 1973; Galerie Beyeler, 1973; Galerie Mikro, Berlin, 1974; Margo Leavin Gallery, 1974, 76; Current Editions, Seattle, 1974; F.H. Mayor Gallery, London, 1974, 76, 77; CNAC, 1975; ACE Gallery, Los Angeles, Calif., 1975, 78; Albert White Gallery, Toronto, 1975; Galerie de Gestlo, Hamburg, 1976; Seattle, 1976; School of Visual Arts, NYC, 1976; California State U., Long Beach, 1977; Mannheim, 1977; Blum Helman Gallery, NYC, 1977; Washington Gallery, Indianapolis,

1978; ICA, Boston, 1978; U. of Miami, 1979; Stony Brook/SUNY, 1979. **Retrospectives:** Pasadena/AM, 1967; Tate, 1968; SRGM, 1969. **Group:** Dayton/AI, 1962; Pasadena/AM, New Paintings of Common Objects, 1962; Sidney Janis Gallery, The New Realists, 1962; Galerie Saqqarah, Gstaad, Switzerland, The Figure and the Object from 1917 to the New Vulgarians, 1962; Chicago/AI, 1963; SRGM, Six Painters and The Object, circ., 1963; WGMA, The Popular Image, 1963; ICA, London, The Popular Image, 1963; Houston/Contemporary Pop Goes the Easel, 1963; Brandeis U., New Directions in American Painting, 1963; Festival of Two Worlds, Spoleto, 1965; SRGM, Word and Image, 1965; WMAA Annuals, 1965, 68; ICA, U. of Pennsylvania, The Other Tradition, 1966; RISD, Recent Still Life, 1966; XXXIII Venice Biennial, 1966; Expo '67, Montreal, 1967; U. of St. Thomas (Tex.), 1967; Carnegie, 1967; IX Sao Paulo Biennial, 1967; Documenta IV, Kassel, 1968; Brooklyn Museum, Print Biennial, 1968; Turin/Civico, 1969; Ars 69, Helsinki, 1969; WMAA Annuals, 1970, 72, 73; Expo '70, Osaka, 1970; Foundation Maeght, L'Art Vivant, 1970; Cincinnati/Contemporary, Monumental Art, 1970; Corcoran Biennial, 1971; Buffalo/Albright, Kid Stuff, 1971; Chicago/AI, 70th American Exhibition, 1972; Indianapolis, 1972; Detroit/Institute, Art in Space, 1973; Art Museum of South Texas, Corpus Christi, Eight Artists, 1974; Chicago/AI, Idea and Image in Recent Art, 1974; WMAA, American Pop Art, 1974; MOMA, Works from Change, 1974; MOMA, Drawing Now, 1976; SRGM, 20th Century American Drawings, 1976; Cambridge U., Jubilation, 1977; Minnesota/MA, American Drawing 1927–1977, circ., 1977; Syracuse/Everson, The Cartoon Show, 1978; WMAA, Art about Art, circ., 1978; Philadelphia College of Art, Point, 1978; Dusseldorf/Kunsthalle, About the Strange Nature of Money, circ., 1978; Buffalo/Albright, American Painting of the 1970s, 1978; U. of Illinois, 1979; Aspen Center for the Visual

Arts, American Portraits of the Sixties and Seventies, 1979; Milwaukee, Emergence and Progression, circ., 1979. **Collections:** Amsterdam/Stedelijk; Brandeis U.; Buffalo/Albright; Chicago/AI; Cologne; Darmastadt/Hessisches; Dayton/AI; Des Moines; Detroit/Institute; Dusseldorf/KN-W; Hirshhorn; Indiana U.; Kansas City/Nelson; Louisiana/Humlebaek; Milwaukee; U. of Minnesota; PMA; Pasadena/AM; RISD; SRGM; Stockholm/National; Tate; Tokyo/Seibu; WMAA; Walker. **Bibliography:** Alloway 1, 4; Battcock, ed.; Becker and Vostell; **Beeren;** Bihalji-Merin; Calas, N. and E.; *Contemporanea;* **Coplans 2; Coplans, ed.;** Davis, D.; Dienst 1; Diamonstein; Downes, ed.; Finch; Honisch and Jensen, eds.; Hunter, ed.; Johnson, Ellen H.; Kozloff 3; *Kunst um 1970;* Lippard 5; Lucie-Smith; *Metro; Report;* Rose, B., 1, 4; Rubin 1; Rublowsky; Russell and Gablik; Sandler 1; Tomkins 2; Tomkins and Time-Life Books; Warhol and Hackett; Weller. Archives.

LINDNER, RICHARD. b. November 11, 1901, Hamburg, Germany; **d.** April 16, 1978, Paris. **Studied:** School of Fine and Applied Arts, Nurnberg; Academy of Fine Arts, Munich, 1924; in Berlin, 1927–28. Concert pianist, 1919–23. To Paris, 1933–39; English army, 1939–41; to USA, 1941; citizen, 1948. Traveled Europe, Mexico. **Taught:** Pratt Institute, 1951–63; Yale U., 1963. **Awards:** Copley Foundation Grant, 1957. **One-man Exhibitions:** Betty Parsons Gallery, 1954, 56, 59; Cordier and Warren, NYC, 1961; Robert Fraser Gallery, 1962; Cordier & Ekstrom, Inc., 1963–67; Claude Bernard, Paris, 1965; Galleria d'Arte Contemporanea, Turin, 1966; Il Fante di Spade, Rome, 1966; Leverkusen, 1968; Hannover/K-G, 1968; Kunstverein Museum, Berlin, 1969; Staatliche Kunsthalle, Baden-Baden, 1969; U. of California, Berkeley, 1969; Galerie Rudolph Zwirner, 1969; Spencer A. Samuels & Co., NYC, 1971; Kunstsalon Wolfsberg, Zurich, 1971;

Fischer Gallery, London, 1972; Rotterdam, 1974; Dusseldorf/Kunsthalle, 1974; Harold Reed Gallery, NYC, 1977; Galerie Maeght, Paris, 1977. **Retrospective:** Paris/Moderne, 1974; Chicago/Contemporary, 1977. **Group:** Walker, 1954; Chicago/AI, 1954, 57, 66; Brooklyn Museum, 1955; Yale U., 1955; WMAA, 1959, 60, 61, 67; MOMA, Americans 1963, circ., 1963–64; Tate, Dunn International, 1964, Gulbenkian International, 1964; Documenta III, Kassel, 1964; Brandeis U., Recent American Drawings, 1964; Corcoran, 1965; Milwaukee, 1965; Worcester/AM, 1965; International Biennial Exhibition, Tokyo; SFMA, 1966; Flint/Institute, I Flint Invitational, 1966; Detroit/Institute, Color, Image, and Form, 1967; U. of Colorado, 1967; IX Sao Paulo Biennial, 1967; ICA, London, The Obsessive Image, 1968. **Collections:** Chicago/AI; Cleveland/MA; MOMA; Tate; WMAA. **Bibliography: Ashton 4;** Battcock, ed.; **Dienst 2;** Honisch and Jensen, eds.; Hunter, ed.; Lippard 5; **Tillim.** Archives.

LIPCHITZ, JACQUES, b. August 22, 1891, Druskieniki, Lithuania; **d.** March 26, 1973, NYC. **Studied:** Academie des Beaux-Arts, Paris, 1909–11, with Jean Antonine Ingalbert, Dr. Richet; Academie Julian, Paris, with Raoul Verlet; Academie Colarossi, Paris. Became French citizen, 1924; to USA, 1941. Traveled Europe, Middle East, USA. Fire destroyed Manhattan studio, 1952. **Commissions:** Dr. Albert Barnes, 1922 (5 bas-reliefs); Vicomte Charles de Noailles, Hyeres, France, 1927 (Joy of Life); Paris World's Fair, 1937 *(Prometheus);* Brazilian Ministry of Health and Education, 1943 *(Prometheus Strangling the Vulture);*Notre Dame de Toute-Grace, Assy, Haute-Savoie, France, 1956 (baptismal font); Mrs. John D. Rockefeller III, 1950 (bas-relief); Fairmount Park Association, Philadelphia, 1958 (sculpture); Presidential Scholars Medallion (USA), 1965; U. of Minnesota, Duluth, 1964 (9-ft. statue of Sieur Duluth). **Awards:** Academie Julian, Paris. First Prize for Sculpture, 1909; Paris World's Fair, 1937, Gold Medal; Legion of Honor (France), 1946; PAFA, George D. Widener Memorial Gold Medal, 1952; Hon. DFA, Brandeis U., 1958; AAAL, Gold Medal, 1966. **One-man Exhibitions:** (first) Leonce Rosenberg Gallery, Paris, 1920; Galerie de la Renaissance, Paris, 1930; Joseph Brummer Gallery, NYC, 1935; Musée du Petit Palais, Paris World's Fair, 1937; Buchholz Gallery, NYC, 1942, 43, 46, 48, 51; Galerie Maeght, 1946; Petite Galerie Seminaire, Brussels, 1950; Portland, Ore./AM, 1950; SFMA, 1951, 63; Cincinnati/AM, 1951; Frank Perls Gallery, 1952, 57; Santa Barbara/MA, 1952; XXVI Venice Biennial, 1952; MOMA, 1954; Walker, 1954, 63; Cleveland/MA, 1954; Otto Gerson Gallery, NYC, 1957, 59, 61; Amsterdam/Stedelijk, 1958; Rijksmuseum Kroller-Muller, 1958; Brussels/Royaux, 1958; Basel, 1958; Paris/Moderne, 1959; Tate, 1959; Cornell U., 1961; Denver/AM, 1962; UCLA, 1963; Fort Worth 1963; Buffalo/Albright, 1963; Des Moines, 1964; PMA, 1964; Omaha/Joslyn, 1964; Marlborough-Gerson Gallery Inc., 1964, 66; Newark Museum, 1965; Boston U., 1965; AAAL, 1966; Dunkelman Gallery, Toronto, 1967; Marlborough Gallery Inc., NYC, 1968, 77, 79; Tel Aviv, 1971; Marlborough Godard Ltd., Toronto, 1972; Marlborough Fine Art Ltd., London, 1973; Makler Gallery, 1973. **Retrospectives:** Berlin/National, 1971; MMA, 1972. **Group:** Salon d'Automne, Paris, 1913; WMAA; MOMA; Tate; Paris/Moderne; Chicago/AI. **Collections:** Baltimore/MA; Barnes Foundation; Buffalo/Albright; Carleton College; Chicago/AI; Cleveland/MA; Cornell U.; Currier; Dartmouth College; Des Moines; Detroit/Institute; Harvard U.; Hunt Foods & Industries; Jewish Museum; Los Angeles/County MA; MOMA; Mansion House Project; U. of Minnesota; Montreal/MFA; U. of Nebraska; New Orleans/Delgado; PMA; Paris/Moderne; Phillips; Princeton

U.; Regina/MacKenzie; Rijksmuseum Kroller-Muller; Rouen; SRGM; St. Louis/City; Syracuse U.; Tate; Tel Aviv; Toronto; Utica; Zurich. **Bibliography:** Barr 1; Baur 7; Biddle 4; Biederman 1; Bihalji-Merin; Blesh 1; Canaday; Cassou; Craven, W.; Elsen 2; Fierens; George 1; Gertz; Giedion-Welcker 1, 2; Goodrich and Baur 1; Greenberg; Hayter 1, 2; Henning; Hess, T.B., 1; **Hope;** Huyghe; **Jacques Lipchitz;** Kuh 2, 3; Langui; Licht, E.; Lowry; McCurdy ed.; Mendelowitz; *Metro;* Moser 1; Myers 2; Neumeyer; **Raynal 2;** Read 1, 3; Rickey; Rodman 1; Rose, B., 1; Roseblum 1; Rothschild; Rubin 1; Sachs; Salvini; Selz, J.; Seuphor 3; Seymour; Strachan; Tomkins and Time-Life Books; Trier 1, 2; Valentine 2; **Van Bork;** Waldberg 4; Wingler, ed.; Zervos.

LIPPOLD, RICHARD. b. May 3, 1915, Milwaukee, Wisc. **Studied:** The U. of Chicago and Chicago Art Institute School, 1933–37, BFA (industrial design). Traveled Mexico, Europe, Greece, Turkey, North Africa. **Taught:** Layton School of Art, 1940–41; U. of Michigan 1941–44; Goddard College, 1945–47; Trenton Junior College (Head of Art Department), 1947–52; Queens College, 1947–48; Black Mountain College, 1948; Hunter College, 1952–68. Designer, Chicago Corporation, 1937–41. Began wire constructions, 1942. **Member:** American Academy of Arts & Letters. **Commissions:** Harvard U. Law School, 1950; MMA, 1952–56; Inland Steel Building, Chicago, 1957; Longview Bank, Longview, Tex., 1958; Four Seasons Restaurant, NYC, 1959; Festival of Two Worlds, Spoleto, 1959 (stage set); Benedictine Chapel, Portsmouth, R.I., 1960; Musée du Vin, Chateau Mouton Rothschild, Pouillac, France, 1960; J. Walter Thompson, NYC, 1960; Pan-Am Building, NYC, 1961; Philharmonic Hall, Lincoln Center for the Performing Arts, NYC, 1961; Jesse Jones Hall, Houston, Tex.; Cathedral of St. Mary, San Francisco, 1969; North Carolina National Bank, Charlotte, 1969; Fairlane, Dearborne, 1974; Christian Science Center, Boston, 1974; Hyatt Regency Hotel, Atlanta, 1975; National Air and Space Museum, Washington, D.C., 1975. **Awards:** ICA, London/Tate, International Unknown Political Prisoner Competition, Third Prize, 1953; Brandeis U., Creative Arts Award, 1953, 58; American Institute of Architects, Chicago Chapter, Honors Award, 1958; American Institute of Architects, New York Chapter, Silver Medal, 1960; Hon. PBK, NYC, 1961; Municipal Art Society of New York, Citation, 1963; elected to NIAL, 1963; Hon. DFA, Ripon College, 1968; American Institute of Architects, Fine Arts Medal, 1970; Guild for Religious Architecture, Honorary member, 1970. **Address:** P.O. Box 248, Locust Valley, NY 11560. **Dealer:** The Willard Gallery. **One-man Exhibitions:** (first) The Willard Gallery, NYC, 1947, also 1948, 50, 52, 68, 73; Arts Club of Chicago, 1953; Brandeis U., 1958; Corcoran, 1954; Utica, 1959; U. of Chicago, 1965; Boston/MFA (two-man), 1966. **Group:** MOMA, Fifteen Americans, circ., 1952; PMA, Sculpture of the Twentieth Century, 1953; ICA, London/Tate, International Unknown Political Prisoner Competition, 1953; WMAA, The New Decade, 1954–55; France/National, 50 Ans d'Art aux Etats-Unis, circ., Europe, 1955; Brooklyn Museum, Sculpture in Silver, 1955; Newark Museum, Abstract Art, 1910 to Today, 1956; WMAA, Geometric Abstraction, 1962; NCFA, Sculpture; American Directions, 1945–1975, 1975; WMAA, 200 Years of American Sculpture, 1976; Indianapolis, Perception of the Spirit in 20th Century American Art, circ., 1978; Chicago/AI, 100 Artists—100 Years, 1979. **Collections:** Andover/Phillips; Des Moines; Detroit/Institute; Harvard U.; Hartford/Wadsworth; MMA; MOMA; Memphis/Brooks; Milwaukee; Mobile Art Center and Gallery, Ala.; Musée du Vin; Newark Museum; Utica; VMFA; WMAA; Yale U. **Bibliography:** Baur 7; Blesh 1; Brumme; Craven, W.; Flanagan; Giedion-Welcker 1; Hunter 6; Licht, F.; McCurdy, ed.; Mendelowitz; *Metro*; Motherwell and Reinhardt, eds.; Neumeyer; Read 1, 3; Rickey; Ritchie 1, 3; Rose, B. 1; Seuphor 3; Trier 1; Weller. Archives.

LIPTON, SEYMOUR. b. November 6, 1903, NYC. **Studied:** City College of New York, 1922–23; Columbia U., 1923–27. **Taught:** Cooper Union, 1943–44; Newark State Teachers College, 1944–45; Yale U., 1957–59; New School for Social Research, 1940–64. **Member:** NIAL, 1975. **Commissions:** Temple Israel, Tulsa, Okla.; Temple Beth-El, Gary, Ind.; Manufacturers Hanover Trust Co., NYC; Inland Steel Building, Chicago; Reynolds Metals Co. (NYC); International Business Machines Corp. (Yorktown Heights, N.Y.); Dulles International Airport, Washington, D.C.; Golden Gateway Redevelopment Project, San Francisco; Philharmonic Hall, Lincoln Center for the Performing Arts, NYC; Milwaukee Center for the Performing Arts, 1967. **Awards:** Chicago/AI, 1957; IV Sao Paulo Biennial, Acquisition Prize, 1957; NIAL, 1958; Guggenheim Foundation Fellowship, 1960; New School for Social Research, 1960; Ford Foundation Grant, 1961; PAFA, George D. Widener Memorial Gold Medal, 1968. **Address:** 302 West 98th Street, NYC 10025. **Dealer:** Marlborough Gallery, Inc., NYC. **One-man Exhibitions:** ACA Gallery, 1938; Gallery St. Etienne, NYC, 1943; Betty Parsons Gallery, 1948, 50, 52, 54, 58, 62; Watkins Gallery, Washington, D.C., 1951; New Paltz/SUNY, 1955; Troy, N.Y., 1961; Phillips, 1964; Marlborough-Gerson Gallery, Inc., 1965; Milwaukee, 1969; U. of Wisconsin, 1969; Marlborough Gallery, Inc., NYC, 1971, 76; MIT, 1971; VMFA, 1972; Cornell U., 1973; Syracuse/Everson, 1973; Marlborough Galerie AG, Zurich, 1974. **Retrospective:** NCFA, 1979. **Group:** WMAA Annuals since 1941; IV Sao Paulo Biennial, 1957; XXIX Venice Biennial, 1958; Carnegie, 1958, 61; Brussels World's Fair, 1958; Seattle World's Fair,

1962; New York World's Fair, 1964–65; Chicago/AI Annual, 1966; Flint/Institute, 1 Flint Invitational, 1966; MOMA, Dada, Surrealism and Their Heritage, 1968; PAFA Annual 1968; Smithsonian, 1968; MOMA, The New American Painting and Sculpture. **Collections:** Baltimore/MA; Brooklyn Museum; Buffalo/Albright; Cornell U.; Davenport/Municipal; Des Moines; Detroit/Institute; Didrichsen Foundation; Franklin Institute; Hartford/Wadsworth; H. J. Heinz Co.; Hirshhorn; IBM; Inland Steel Co.; U. of Kansas; MMA; MOMA; Manufacturers Hanover Trust Co.; U. of Massachusetts; U. of Michigan; NCFA; New School for Social Research; NYU; Pepsico Museum; RISD; Reynolds Metals Co.; Santa Barbara/MA; South Mall, Albany; Purchase/SUNY; Sperry Rand Corp.; Tel Aviv; Toronto; Utica; VMFA; WGMA; WMAA; Yale U. **Bibliography:** Baur 5, 7; Biddle 4; Blesh 1; Brumme; Chaet; Craven, W.; Christensen; Elsen 1, 3; Flanagan; Goodrich and Baur 1; Henning; Hunter 6; Hunter, ed.; Krauss 2; Langui; McCurdy, ed.; Marter, Tarbell, and Wechsler, Rand; Mendelowitz; *Metro:* Myers 2; Neumeyer; Read 3; Ritchie 1, 3; Rose, B., 1; Seuphor 3; Strachan; Trier 1; Weller. Archives.

LOBDELL, FRANK. b. 1921, Kansas City, Mo. **Studied:** St. Paul School of Art, 1938–39, with Cameron Booth; California School of Fine Arts, 1947–50; US Army, 1942–46. Resided Paris, 1950–51. **Taught:** California School of Fine Arts, 1957– ; Stanford U., 1965– . **Awards:** SFMA, Artists Council Prize, 1948; SFMA, **P.P.,** 1950; SFMA, Nealie Sullivan Award, 1960; Tamarind Fellowship, 1966; A Knight of Mark Twain, 1971. **Address:** 340 Palo Alto Avenue, Palo Alto, CA 94301. **Dealer:** Smith-Anderson Gallery, Palo Alto, Calif. **One-man Exhibitions:** (first) Lucien Labaudt Gallery, San Francisco, 1949; Martha Jackson Gallery, N.Y., 1958, 60, 63, 72, 74, 77; de Young, 1959; Pas-

adena/AM, 1961; Ferus Gallery, Los Angeles, 1962; Galerie D. Benador, Geneva, 1964; Galerie Anderson-Mayer, Paris, 1965; Pasadena/AM and Stanford U., 1966; Maryhurst College, 1967; SFMA, 1969; St. Mary's College, Moraga, Calif., 1970, 71. Smith-Anderson Gallery, 1978. **Retrospective:** Pasadena/AM, 1963. **Group:** San Francisco Art Association Annual, 1950; III Sao Paulo Biennial, 1955; WMAA, Fifty California Artists, 1962–63; SRGM, American Drawings, 1964; U. of Washington, Drawings by Americans, 1967; Albany/SUNY, Giant Prints, 1967; Eindhoven, Kompas IV, 1969–70; Pasadena/AM, West Coast, 1945–69, 1969; Corcoran, 1971; WMAA Annual, 1972; U. of Illinois. **Collections:** Los Angeles/County MA; Oakland/AM; Pasadena/AM; SFMA; Stanford U. **Bibliography: Hopps.**

LOBERG, ROBERT W. b. December 1, 1927, Chicago, Ill. US Marine Corps, 1946–47. **Studied:** Glendale College, 1948, City College of San Francisco, 1948–50, AA; U. of California, Berkeley, 1950–52, BA, 1953–54, MA (painting, with Karl Kasten, Ward Lockwood, John Haley, Erie Loran, James McCray, Glenn Wessels, Worth Ryder, Felix Ruvulo, William H. Calfee, Carl Holty, Kyle Morris); Hofmann School, Provincetown, 1956, with Hans Hofmann. Traveled northern China, Japan, Europe. **Taught:** U. of California, Berkeley, 1955, 56, 58, 59, 65; California College of Arts and Crafts, 1961–62; San Francisco Art Institute, 1962–66; U. of Washington, 1967–68. **Awards:** California State Fair, Hon. Men., 1955; RAC, Prize in Graphics, 1955; Yaddo Fellowship, 1957; RAC, Prize in Watercolors, 1959; MacDowell Colony Fellowship, 1959, 60; SFMA, Anne Bremer Memorial Prize, 1961; San Francisco Art Festival, **P.P.,** in Painting, 1962; La Jolla, Prize in Painting, 1962. **Address:** 2020 Vine Street, Berkeley, CA 94709. **One-man Exhibitions:** (first) Artist's Gallery, NYC, 1959; SFMA (three-man),

1961, Staempfli Gallery, 1962; David Stuart Gallery, 1962, 64; Richard White Gallery, Seattle, 1968; California College of Arts and Crafts, 1969; Berkeley Gallery, 1969; California College of Arts and Crafts, 1969; Berkeley Craft Center, 1977; San Jose Museum 1978; Paule Anglim Gallery, San Francisco, 1979. **Retrospective:** U. of Washington, 1968. **Group:** Chicago/AI, 1948, 62; RAC; Oakland/AM; SFMA Annuals since 1955; de Young; California Palace; Carnegie, 1959; SFMA, Abstract Expressionism, in the West, circ., 1961; SFMA, Collage in San Francisco, 1962; WMAA, Fifty California Artists, 1962–63; SFMA, New Paintings, 1964. **Collections:** California College of Arts and Crafts; Chicago/AI; Oakland/AM; Portland, Ore./AM; San Francisco Municipal Art Commission; WGMA; U. of Washington.

LOEW, MICHAEL. b. May 8, 1907, NYC. **Studied:** City College of New York; ASL, 1926–29, with Richard Lahey, Boardman Robinson; Academie Scandinave, Paris, 1930, with Othon Friesz; Hofmann School, NYC, 1947–49; Atelier Fernand Leger, Paris, 1950, with F. Leger. US Navy "Seabees," Battalion Artist, Pacific theater, 1943–46. Traveled France, Germany, Italy, Africa, Mexico, Central America, Spain, England. **Taught:** Portland (Ore.) Museum School, 1956–57; U. of California, Berkeley, 1960–61, 1967; School of Visual Arts, NYC, 1958– . **Member:** American Abstract Artists; Federation of Modern Painters and Sculptors. Federal A.P.: Gustave Straubenmuller Junior High School, NYC (series of 5 murals); U. of California, Berkeley, 1960–61, 1966. **Commissions:** (murals) Hall of Man and Pharmacy Building, New York World's Fair, 1939; US Post Offices, Amherst, Ohio, and Belle Vernon, Pa. **Awards:** Sadie May Fellowship, 1929; Section of Fine Arts, National Mural Competition for Social Security Building and War Department Building, Washington, D.C., Hon.

Men., 1941, 42; Ford Foundation, **P.P.,** 1964; Chicago/AI Annual, 1964; National Endowment for the Arts, grant, 1976; Guggenheim Foundation Fellowship, 1979. **Address:** 280 Ninth Avenue, NYC 10001. **Dealer:** Marilyn Pearl Gallery, NYC. **One-man Exhibitions:** (first) Artists' Gallery, NYC, 1949; Rose Fried Gallery, 1953, 55, 57, 59; Portland, Ore./AM, 1956; Rutgers U. (two-man), 1959; T.K. Gallery, Provincetown, Mass., 1959; Holland-Goldowsky Gallery, Chicago, 1960; U. of California, Berkeley, 1960, 67; The Stable Gallery, NYC, 1961, 62, 64, 65; Landmark Gallery, Inc., NYC, 1973, 76; Marilyn Pearl Gallery, NYC, 1977, 79. **Retrospectives:** Holland-Goldowsky Gallery, Chicago, 1960; The Stable Gallery, 1962. **Group:** American Abstract Artists Annuals, 1949– ; Salon des Realites Nouvelles, Paris, 1950; WMAA, 1950, 61; MMA, 1952; Walker, The Classic Tradition, 1953; International Association of Plastic Arts, Contemporary American Painting, circ., Europe, 1956–57; A.F.A., Collage in America, circ., 1957–58; Douglass College, 1959; ART:USA:59, NYC, 1959; Federation of Modern Painters and Sculptors Annuals, 1959– ; WMAA, Geometric Abstraction in America, circ., 1962; MOMA, Hans Hofmann and His Students, circ., 1963–64; Chicago/AI, 1964; Colby College, 100 Artists of the 20th Century, 1964; PAFA, 1966; Allentown/AM, Monhegan Island Painters, 1974; Newark Museum, Geometric Abstraction and Related Works, 1978. **Collections:** Buffalo/Albright; McCrory Corp., NYC; Lehman Bros., New York; WMAA; PMA; U. of Nebraska; Hampton Institute; U. of California, Berkeley; Hirshhorn; U. of St. Lawrence, Canton, N.Y.; Calcutta; Ciba-Geigy Corp.; Wichita State U.; Union Carbide Corp. NYC; **Bibliography:** Archives.

LONGO, VINCENT. b. February 15, 1923, NYC. **Studied:** Cooper Union, with Leo Katz, Sidney Delevant, 1942–46; Brooklyn Museum School, 1950, with Max Beckmann, 1953, with

Louis Schanker. Traveled Europe. **Taught:** Brooklyn Museum School, 1955–56; Yale U. Summer School, Norfolk, Conn., 1967–68; Bennington College, 1957–67; Hunter College, 1967– . **Member:** SAGA. **Awards:** Fulbright Fellowship (Italy), 1951; Philadelphia Print Club, First Prize, 1954; Yaddo Fellowship, 1954; Guggenheim Foundation Fellowship, 1971; Cooper Union, Achievement Citation, 1973; National Endowment for the Arts, 1974. **Address:** 50 Greene Street, NYC 10013. **Dealer:** Andrew Crispo Gallery, NYC. **One-man Exhibitions:** Regional Arts Gallery, NYC, 1949; Korman Gallery, NYC, 1954; The Zabriskie Gallery, 1956; Yamada Art Gallery, Kyoto, 1959; Area Gallery, NYC, 1960; Wheaton College, 1969; Thibault Gallery, NYC, 1963; U. of Vermont, 1965; Reese Palley Gallery, NYC, 1970; Susan Caldwell Inc., 1974; Bard College, 1975; U. of Notre Dame, 1976; Andre Crispo Gallery, NYC, 1976. **Retrospectives:** Bennington College, 1970; Corcoran, 1970; Detroit/Institute, 1970. **Group:** WMAA Annuals, 1951, 71; PAFA Annual, 1953; MOMA, Young Printmakers, 1954; Brooklyn Museum, 1954, 55; Philadelphia Print Club (three-man), 1955; MOMA, Drawings USA, 1956; American Abstract Artists, 1957, 58, 59; New York Coliseum, ART:USA:59, 1959; U. of Kentucky, Graphics '60, 1960; USIA, Contemporary American Woodcut and Its Variations, 1962; PCA, American Prints Today, 1962; Brooklyn Museum, Two Decades of American Prints, 1969; WMAA, American Drawings 1963–1973, 1973. **Collections:** Bibliotheque Nationale; Brooklyn Museum; Ciba-Geigy Corp.; Corcoran; Detroit/Institute; Library of Congress; Milwaukee-Downer Institute; MMA; MOMA; National Gallery, NCFA; New London; Oakland/AM; PMA; Stockholm/National; Syracuse/Everson; U. of Vermont; Washington U.; WMAA. **Bibliography:** Archives.

LORAN, ERLE. b. October 3, 1905, Minneapolis, Minn. **Studied:** U. of Minnesota; Minneapolis Institute School, with Cameron Booth; Hofmann School, 1954. Traveled Europe extensively. **Taught:** U. of California, Berkeley. Federal A.P.: Easel painting, teaching. **Awards:** Chaloner Prize Foundation Award ($6,000), 1926; SFMA, Artists' Fund Prize, 1944; Pepsi-Cola Bronze Medal, 1949; San Francisco Art Association, **P.P.,** 1956; California Palace, H.S. Crocker Co. Award, 1963; U. of Illinois, **P.P.,** 1965; Minneapolis Institute School, Hon. MFA, 1968; and some 20 others. **Address:** 10 Kenilworth Court, Berkeley, CA 94707. **Dealer:** Allrich Gallery, San Francisco. **One-man Exhibitions:** (first) Kraushaar Galleries, 1931; SFMA, 1936, 39, 44; Artists' Gallery, NYC, 1938; Pasadena/AM, 1947; Santa Barbara/MA, 1947, 50; Dalzell Hatfield Gallery, 1949; de Young, 1949, 54, 63; Catherine Viviano Gallery, 1952, 54; Comara Gallery, 1964; The Bertha Schaefer Gallery, 1965; Arleigh Gallery, 1969. **Group:** MOMA, 1935; Oakland/AM, 1936, 46; SFMA, 1936–64; WMAA, 1937, 41, 44, 48, 51, 52; Chicago/AI, 1938, 39, 43, 44, 46, 48; Carnegie, 1941; Toledo/MA, 1943; PAFA, 1945; U. of Illinois, 1949, 52, 53, 63, 65, 69; MMA, 1951, 53; Cranbrook, 1953; Sao Paulo, 1955, 56, 61; California Palace, 1961, 62, 63; MOMA, Hans Hofmann and His Students, circ., 1963–64. **Collections:** Brigham Young U.; U. of California; Denver/AM; IBM; U. of Illinois; U. of Minnesota; SFMA; San Diego; Santa Barbara/MA; Smithsonian; US State Department; Utah State U. **Bibliography:** Bethers; Blanchard; Cheney; Flanagan; **Loran 1, 2;** Pousette-Dart, ed. Archives.

LORBER, STEPHEN. b. August 30, 1943, Brooklyn, N.Y. **Studied:** Pratt Institute, BFA, 1961–66; Brooklyn College, MFA, 1966–68; Yale, 1964. Resided Rome, 1969–70; New Mexico, 1973–74. **Taught:** Roswell, 1973–74. **Awards:** Stoeckel Fellow, Yale U., 1964; Yaddo Fellowship, 1971, 75; National Endowment for the Arts; Fellowship,

1976. **Address:** R.D. 3, Box 198, Greenwich, NY 12834. **Dealers:** A. M. Sachs Gallery; Delahunty Gallery, Dallas; Gladstone Gallery, NYC. **One-man Exhibitions:** (first) A. M. Sachs Gallery, NYC, 1974, 75, 76, 77, 78; Russell Sage College, Troy, N.Y., 1976; Delahunty Gallery, Dallas, 1975, 77, 80; Roswell, 1974. **Group:** PAFA, 1969; U. of North Carolina, Art on Paper, 1974, 76; Minnesota/MA, American Drawing, 1927–77, circ., 1977. **Collections:** Amerada Hess Corp., NYC; AT & T, NYC; Atlantic Richfield Co., Chase Manhattan Bank, NYC; IBM, NYC; 3M Corp., St. Paul; Mobil Oil Co., NYC; Prudential Insurance Co. of America, Newark; Reynolds Tobacco, Inc.; A. G. Beck Co., Inc.; Lehman Bros., NYC; E. F. Hutton, Inc., NYC; American Airlines, NYC; Owens-Corning Fiberglas Corp.; Roswell; Western New Mexico U; U. of Illinois; U. of North Carolina; Oklahoma/AC.

LOUIS, MORRIS. b. November 28, 1912, Baltimore, Md.; **d.** September 7, 1962, Washington, D.C. **Studied:** Maryland Institute, 1920–33. **One-man Exhibitions:** (first) Martha Jackson Gallery, 1957; French & Co. Inc., NYC, 1959, 60; ICA London, 1960; Bennington College, 1960; Galleria dell'-Ariete, 1960; Galerie Neufville, Paris, 1961; Galerie Schmela, 1962; Galerie Lawrence, Paris, 1962; Galerie Muller, 1962; Andre Emmerich Gallery, NYC, 1961, 62, 65, 68, 69, 72, Zurich, 1973; Ziegler Gallery, 1964; Staatliche Kunsthalle, Baden-Baden, 1965; WGMA, 1966; Seattle/AM, 1967; MOMA (three-man), 1968; Lawrence Rubin Gallery, NYC, 1970, 73, 74; David Mirvish Gallery, 1971; National Gallery, 1976; Walker, 1977; NCFA, 1979. **Retrospective:** SRGM, 1963; XXXII Venice Biennial, 1964; WGMA, 1967; Boston/MFA, circ., 1967. **Group:** The Kootz Gallery, NYC, New Talent, 1954; Rome–New York Foundation, Rome, 1960; SRGM, Abstract Expressionists and Imagists, 1961; Seattle World's Fair, 1962; WMAA, 1962; Jewish Museum, Toward a New Abstraction, 1963; Tate, Painting and Sculpture of a Decade, 1954–64, 1964; Corcoran; Los Angeles/County MA, Post Painterly Abstraction, 1964; Documenta III & IV, Kassel, 1964, 68; MOMA, The Responsive Eye, 1965; SFMA, The Colorists, 1965; WGMA, 1965–66; WMAA, Art of the U.S. 1670–1966, 1966; Chicago/AI Annual, 1966; Wurttembergischer Kunstverein, Stuttgart, 1967; Detroit/Institute, Color, Image and Form, 1967; Trenton/State, Focus on Light, 1967; MOMA, The Art of the Real, 1968; Pasadena/AM, Serial Imagery, 1968; MOMA, The New American Painting and Sculpture, 1969; WMAA, 1970; Edmonton Art Gallery, Alberta, Ten Washington Artists: 1950–1970, 1970; Auckland, 1971; Hayward Gallery, London, 1974. **Collections:** Allentown/AM; Boston/MFA; Brandeis U.; Buffalo/Albright; Harvard U.; MOMA; Phillips; SRGM; WGMA. **Bibliography:** Battcock, ed.; Calas, N. and E.; Coplans 3; Davis, D.; Fried 1, 2; Goossen 1; Headley; Honisch and Jensen, eds.; *The Great Decade*; Hunter, ed.; Kozloff 3; Rickey; Sandler; Tomkins 2; Weller. Archives.

LOZOWICK, LOUIS. b. December 10, 1892, Ludvinovka, Russia; **d.** September 9, 1973, South Orange, N.J. To USA, 1906. **Studied:** The Ohio State U., 1915–1918, BA; NAD, with Carlson, Ivan Olinsky, 1912–15. US Army, 1918–19. Traveled Europe, Russia, the Orient. **Taught:** Educational Alliance, NYC; and privately. **Member:** SAGA; Boston Printmakers. Federal A.P.: Main Post Office, NYC. (mural); printmaker. **Awards:** Brewster Prize for Lithography; PMA, International Print Competition, First Prize; Society of American Etchers and Engravers, NYC, Knobloch Prize; Brooklyn Museum, **P.P.;** U. of Rochester, 150 Years of Lithography, Second Prize; SAGA; Audubon Artists. **One-man Exhibitions:** (first) Heller Gallery, Berlin, 1923; Weyhe Gallery;

Courvoisier Gallery, San Francisco; Stendahl Gallery, Los Angeles; Casson Gallery, Boston; J. B. Neumann's New Art Circle, NYC; The Zabriskie Gallery, 1961, 71, 72; Galerie Zak, Paris; Smithsonian; Argus Gallery, Madison, N.J., 1965; Heritage Art Gallery, South Orange, N.J., 1967; WMAA, 1972; Robert Dain Gallery, NYC, 1973; Lynn Gallery, Washington, D.C., 1975; Hirschl & Adler Gallery, NYC, 1980. **Retrospectives:** Newark Public Library, 1969; Seton Hall U., South Orange, N.J., 1975; Long Beach/MA, 1975; NCFA, 1975. **Group:** Brooklyn Museum, 1926; Chicago/AI, 1929; Carnegie, 1930, 39; Corcoran, 1932; A Century of Progress, Chicago, 1933–34; WMAA Annuals, 1933, 41; New York World's Fair, 1939; MMA, 1942; MOMA, 1943; Youngstown/Butler, 1960; Gallery of Modern Art, NYC, 1965; Boston/MFA. **Collections:** Boston/MFA; Cincinnati/AM; Cleveland/MA; Honolulu Academy; Houston/MFA; Library of Congress; Los Angeles/County MA; MMA; MOMA; Montclair/AM; Moscow/Western; NYPL; Newark Museum; PMA; U. of Rochester; Syracuse/Everson; Trenton/State; Victoria and Albert Museum; WMAA. **Bibliography:** American Artists Congress, Inc.; American Artists Group Inc. 3; Baur 7; Brown 2; Gerdts; *Index of 20th Century Artists;* Cityscape 1917–39; Mellquist; Reese. Archives.

LUCCHESI, BRUNO. b. July 31, 1926, Fibbiano, Italy. To USA, 1957. **Studied:** Institute of Art, Lucca, 1953, MFA. **Taught:** Academy of Fine Arts, Florence, 1952–57; New School for Social Research, 1962– . **Commissions:** Trade Bank and Trust Co., NYC; Cornell U. **Awards:** NAD, Elizabeth N. Watrous Gold Medal, 1961; Guggenheim Foundation Fellowship, 1962; National Arts Club, NYC, Gold Medal, 1963; NAD, Samuel F. B. Morse Medal, 1965. **Address:** 14 Stuyvesant Street, NYC 10003. **Dealer:** The Forum Gallery. **One-man Exhibitions:** The Forum Gallery, NYC, 1961, 63, 66, 68, 73, 75, 76, 80. **Group:** Corcoran; NAD; PAFA; WMAA. **Collections:** Columbia, S.C./MA; Dallas/MFA; Hirshhorn; PAFA; Ringling; WMAA.

LUKIN, SVEN. b. February 14, 1934, Riga, Latvia. **Studied:** U. of Pennsylvania. **Awards:** J. S. Guggenheim Fellowship, 1966. **Address:** 807 Avenue of the Americas, NYC 10001. **One-man Exhibitions:** (first) Nexus Gallery, Boston, 1959; Betty Parsons Gallery, 1961; Martha Jackson Gallery, 1962; Dwan Gallery, Los Angeles, 1963; The Pace Gallery, Boston, 1963; The Pace Gallery, NYC, 1964, 66, 68. **Group:** Carnegie, 1961; WMAA Annual, 1962, 66, 68; Chicago/AI, 1964; SRGM, American Drawings, 1964, The Shaped Canvas, 1964; U. of Illinois, 1965; Torcuato di Tella, Buenos Aires, 1965; Amsterdam/Stedelijk, New Shapes of Color, 1966; U. of Colorado, 1967; Des Moines, Painting: Out from the Wall, 1968. **Collections:** American Republic Insurance Co.; Buffalo/Albright; Los Angeles/County MA; U. of Miami; Ridgefield/Aldrich; South Mall, Albany; U. of Texas; WMAA. **Bibliography:** Battcock, ed.; Brown 2, Hunter, ed.; Weller.

LUND, DAVID. b. October 16, 1925, NYC. **Studied:** Queens College, with Vaclav Vytlacil, Cameron Booth, 1944–48, BA (major in painting); NYU, 1948–50, with Hale Woodruff; New School for Social Research, with Yasuo Kuniyoshi. Traveled Europe, southwestern USA, Mexico. **Taught:** Cooper Union, 1955–57, 1959–69; Parsons School of Design, 1963–66, 1967– ; Queens College, 1964–66; Washington U. (St. Louis), 1966–67; Columbia U. 1969– . **Awards:** Fulbright Fellowship (Rome), 1957–58, renewed 1958–59; WMAA Annual, Ford Foundation Purchase, 1961; AAAL, Childe Hassam Fund **P.P.,** 1978. **Address:** 470 West End Avenue, NYC 10024. **Dealer:** Grace Borgenicht Gallery Inc. **One-man**

Exhibitions: (first) Grand Central Moderns, NYC, 1954; Galleria Trastevere di Topazia Alliata, Rome, 1955; Grace Borgenicht Gallery, Inc., 1960, 63, 67, 69, 76, 78; Martin Schweig Gallery, 1966. **Group:** Tanager Gallery, NYC, Invitational; The Stabe Gallery Annual, 1956; Galleria Schneider, Rome, Fulbright Artists, 1958, 59; WMAA, Fulbright Artists, 1958; Hirschl & Adler Galleries, Inc., NYC, Experiences in Art, I, 1959; WMAA, Young America, 1960; WMAA Annual, 1961; WMAA, Forty Artists under Forty, circ., 1962; PAFA, 1965, 69; School of Visual Arts, NYC, 1966; Omaha/Joslyn, A Sense of Place, 1973; City Hall, Rockport, Me., Maine Coast Artists, 1974; Oklahoma, Contemporary American Landscape Painting, 1975; IIE, 20 American Fulbright Artists, 1975; NAD, 1977. **Collections:** Baltimore/MA; Brandeis U.; Bristol-Meyers Co., NYC; Burlington Industries, NYC; Chase Manhattan Bank; Colby College; Commerce Trust Co.; Corcoran; J.C. Penney Co., NYC; Kansas City, Mo.; Fort Worth; Harcourt Brace Jovanovich Inc.; Manufacturers Hanover Trust Co.; U. of Massachusetts; Montclair/AM; McDonnell & Co. Inc.; Prudential Insurance Co. of America, Newark; The New York Times; The Pure Oil Co., NYC; South County Bank; Toronto; Union Carbide Corp. NYC; WMAA.

LUNDEBERG, HELEN. b. June 1908, Chicago, Ill. **Studied:** Privately with Lorser Feitelson, Federal A.P.: Painting, lithography, mural designer. **Address:** 8307 West 3 Street, Los Angeles, CA 90048. **One-man Exhibitions:** (first) Stanley Rose Gallery, Hollywood, 1933; Mid-20th Century Art Gallery, Los Angeles, 1947; Art Center School, Los Angeles (two-man); Lucien Labaudt Gallery, San Francisco (two-man), 1949; Pasadena/AM; Santa Barbara, 1958; Paul Rivas Gallery, Los Angeles, 1959; Long Beach/MA, 1963; Occidental College, 1965; David Stuart Gallery, 1970, 71, 77. **Retrospective:** Pasadena/AM,

1953; La Jolla, 1971; Los Angeles Municipal Art Gallery, 1979. **Group:** Brooklyn Museum, 1936; SFMA, 1936; MOMA, Fantastic Art, DADA, Surrealism, 1936; MOMA, Americans 1942, circ., 1942; Chicago/AI, Abstract and Surrealist Art, 1948; U. of Illinois, 1950–52, 55, 57, 65; Carnegie, 1952; III Sao Paulo Biennial, 1955; WMAA, Geometric Abstraction in America, circ., 1962; WMAA, Fifty California Artists, 1962–63; WMAA Annuals, 1965, 67; Sacramento/Crocker, 1968; Los Angeles Institute of Contemporary Art, 1974; MOMA, Painting and Sculpture in California: The Modern Era, 1976; San Antonio McNay, American Artists '76, 1976; Rutgers U., Surrealism and American Art: 1931–1947, 1977; Denver/AM Biennial, 1979. **Collections:** Atlantic Richfield Co.; Bank of Tulsa, Tulsa; Chaffey College; Craig Ellwood Associates; Great Western Savings and Loan Association; Hirshhorn; Honolulu Academy; La Jolla; Lansing Sound Corp.; Los Angeles/County MA; NCFA; Oakland/AM; Palm Springs Desert Museum; Pasadena/AM; SFMA; Santa Barbara/MA; Xerox Corp. **Bibliography:** Rickey. Archives.

LYE, LEN. b. July 5, 1901, Christchurch, New Zealand; **d.** May 15, 1980, Warwick, N.Y. **Studied:** Wellington Technical College; Canterbury College of Fine Arts. To London, 1926; to USA, 1946; became a citizen. Traveled Samoa, Europe, USA, around the world, 1968. **Taught:** City College of New York (film technique); NYU. International awards for experimental films. Began kinetic constructions in the 1920s. Created "direct animation" technique, working directly on film strip without camera, 1935. National Endowment for the Arts, grant, 1979. **One-man Exhibitions:** London Film Society (*Tusalava*), 1928; MOMA, Tangible Motion Sculpture, 1961; St. Luke's School, NYC, Wind Wands, 1962; The Howard Wise Gallery, 1965; Buffalo/Albright, 1965; Govett-Brewster Gallery, New

Plymouth, N.Z., 1977; Auckland Gallery, N.Z., 1980. **Group:** Seven & Five Society, London, 1928–33; a Surrealists group, London, 1937; Amsterdam/ Stedelijk, Art in Motion, circ., Europe, 1961–62; WMAA Annual, 1962; The Howard Wise Gallery, NYC, On The Move, 1963. **Collections:** Buffalo/Albright; U. of California, Berkeley; Chicago/AI; Tel Aviv; WMAA. **Film Collections:** U. of California, Berkeley; London Film Society; MOMA. **Bibliography:** Battcock, ed.; Bihalji-Merin; Calas, N. and E.; Davis, D.; Kuh 3; Read 5; *Report:* Rickey; Selz, P., 1; Tuchman 1.

LYTLE, RICHARD. b, February 14, 1935, Albany, N.Y. **Studied:** Cooper Union, with Nicholas Marsicano, Victor Candell; Yale U., with Josef Albers (whom he assisted as teaching fellow in color and drawing), James Brooks, Bernard Chaet, 1957, BFA, 1960, MFA. Traveled Europe, northeastern USA. **Taught:** Yale U., 1960–63, 1966–?; Dean, Silvermine Guild, 1963–66. **Commissions:** Fairfield U. (concrete relief mural). **Awards:** Scholarship to the Cummington School of Fine Arts, 1956; Fulbright Fellowship (Italy), 1958; New Haven Arts Festival, First Prize, 1958.

Address: Sperry Road, Woodbridge, CT 06525. **Dealer:** Marilyn Pearl Gallery, NYC. **One-man Exhibitions:** (first) Grace Borgenicht Gallery, Inc., 1961, also 1963, 64, 66, 68, 72; Silvermine Guild, 1964; Cortland/SUNY, 1969; U. of Hartford, 1970; U. of Connecticut, 1973; Lincoln, Mass./De Cordova, 1974; Marilyn Pearl Gallery, NYC, 1977, 79; Munson Gallery, New Haven, 1979; Munson Gallery, Santa Fe, 1980. **Group:** Brooklyn Museum, 1956; A.F.A., American Art, circ., Europe, 1956–59; Boston Arts Festival, 1958; MOMA, Sixteen Americans, circ., 1959; Chicago/AI Annuals, 1960, 61; Houston/MFA, The Emerging Figure, 1961; Seattle World's Fair, 1962; PAFA, 1962, 63, 64; Art: USA: Now, circ., 1962–67; WMAA, 1964; Silvermine Guild, 1964; U. of Illinois, 1967; Yale U., 1967; Ringling, Young New England Painters, 1969; Yale U., American Drawing, 1970–1973, 1973; Harvard U., Works by Students of Josef Albers, 1974; IIE, 20 American Fulbright Artists, 1975; U. of North Carolina, 1978, 80; Buffalo/Albright, Works on Paper, 1979. **Collections:** AT&T; Chase Manhattan Bank; Cincinnati/AM; Citicorp, NYC; Columbia U.; Lincoln, Mass./De Cordova; MOMA; U. of Massachusetts; NCFA; Yale U. **Bibliography:** Nordness, ed.

M

MAC CONNEL, KIM. **b.** 1946, Oklahoma City, Oklahoma. **Studied:** U. of California, San Diego, BA, honors, 1969; MFA, honors, 1972. **Awards:** California State Scholar, 1970. **Address:** c/o Dealer. **Dealer:** Holly Solomon Gallery, NYC. **One-man Exhibitions:** Holly Solomon Gallery, NYC, 1975, 77, 78, 79, 80; Metropolitan Museum and Art Center, Miami, 1975; La Jolla, 1975; Galerie Ehrensperger, Zurich, 1976; U. of California, Berkeley, 1978; Galerie Bischoisberger, 1978; F. H. Mayor Gallery, London, 1978; Dart Gallery, Chicago, 1979, 80. **Group:** U. of California, San Diego, Decorations, 1971; The Clocktower, NYC, Toys Artists Make, 1974; WMAA Biennials, 1975, 77, 79; American Foundation for the Arts, Miami, Patterning and Decoration, 1977; Philadelphia College of Art, Artists, Sets and Costumes, 1977; ICA, U. of Pennsylvania, Improbable Furniture, 1977; La Jolla, Southern California, Styles of the 60's and 70's, 1978; Rice U., Pattern and Decoration, 1978; Cincinnati/Contemporary, Arabesque, 1978; ICA, U. of Pennsylvania, The Decorative Impulse, 1979; Hirshhorn, Directions, 1979; Buffalo/Albright, Patterns, 1979; Mannheim, Dekor, 1980; Aachen/NG, Les Nouveaux Fauves—/ Die neuen Wilden, 1980. **Bibliography:** *Drawings: The Pluralist Decade;* Luie-Smith.

MacDONALD-WRIGHT, STANTON. **b.** July 8, 1890, Charlottesville, Va.; **d.** August 24, 1973, Pacific Palisades, Calif. **Studied:** Sorbonne; Academie des Beaux-Arts, Paris; Academie Colarossi, Paris; Academie Julian, Paris; ASL, with W. T. Hedges, J. Green-

Kim MacConnel *Jingle* 1980

baum. Met Morgan Russell in Paris, 1912, and with him founded the Synchromist movement in 1913. Studied the color theories of Michel Eugene Chevruel, Herman von Helmholz, and O. N. Rood. Returned to USA, 1916. Traveled Japan, 1937, 1952–53. **Taught:** U. of California, 1942–50; U. of Southern California; Scripps College, 1946; U. of Hawaii, 1949; Fulbright Exchange Professor to Japan, 1952–53; lectured on art history and Oriental aesthetics. Federal A.P.: California State Director, 1935–42, and technical advisor to seven western states. **Commissions** (murals): Santa Monica (Calif.) Public Library; Santa Monica City Hall; Santa Monica High School (mosaic). **One-man Exhibitions:** (first) Photo-Secession, NYC, 1917; Stendahl Gallery, Los Angeles, 1942 (two man); Rose Fried Gallery, 1955; Duveen-Graham Gallery, NYC, 1956; Esther Robles Gallery, 1965; UCLA, 1970; Suzuki Graphics, NYC, 1972; St. Petersburg Museum, Fall, 1977; Harmon Gallery, Naples, 1975,

78. **Retrospectives:** Los Angeles/ County MA, 1956; NCFA, 1967. **Group:** Salon d'Automne, Paris, 1910; The Synchromists, Munich and Paris, 1913; Salon des Artistes Independants, Paris, 1913–14; MMA; Brooklyn Museum; Honolulu Academy. **Collections:** Boston/MFA; Brooklyn Museum; Carnegie; Chicago/AI; Columbus; Corcoran; Denver/AM; Detroit/Institute; Grand Rapids; Los Angeles/County MA; MMA; MOMA; U. of Minnesota; Newark Museum; Omaha/Joslyn; PMA; Pasadena/AM; San Diego; Santa Barbara/MA; Toledo/MA; WMAA; Walker. **Bibliography:** *Avant-Garde Painting and Sculpture in America, 1910–25;* Baur 7; Blanchard; Blesh 1; Brown 2; Cheney; Chipp; Christensen; Craven, T., 1; Goodrich and Baur 1; Haftman; Hess, T. B., 1; Hunter 6; Huyghe; Jackman; Janis, S.; Levin 2; McCurdy, ed.; Mellquist; Neuhaus; Read 2; Richardson, E.P.; Rickey; Ringel, ed.; Ritchie 1; Rose, B., 1, 4; **Scott;** Seuphor 1, 2; Wright 1, 2. Archives.

MacIVER, LOREN. b. February 2, 1909, NYC. **Studied:** ASL, 1919–20. Traveled Europe. Lighting and decor for four Coffee Concerts, MOMA, 1941. **Member:** NIAL, 1959. Federal A.P.: 1936–39, New York. **Commissions** (murals): Moore-McCormack Lines, Inc., SS *Argentina*, 1947; American Export Lines, SS *Excalibur*, SS *Exeter*, SS *Exochorda*, SS *Excambion*, 1948. **Awards:** Corcoran, First Prize, 1957; Ford Foundation Grant, 1960. **Address:** 61 Perry Street, NYC 10014. **One-man Exhibitions:** (first) East River Gallery, NYC, 1938; Pierre Matisse Gallery, 1940, 44, 49, 56, 61, 70; Arts Club of Chicago, 1941; MOMA, circ., 1941; Baltimore/ MA, 1945; Vassar College, circ., 1950; Santa Barbara/MA, 1951; Margaret Brown Gallery, Boston, circ., 1951; Phillips, 1951; Corcoran, 1956; Fairweather-Hardin Gallery, 1959; Southern Vermont Art Center, Manchester, Vt., 1968; Paris/Moderne, 1968; Musées Classes de Nice, 1968. **Retrospectives:** WMAA, circ., 1953; Paris/Moderne,

1968. **Group:** WMAA annuals; MOMA, Fourteen Americans, circ., 1946; Corcoran. **Collections:** Andover/Phillips; Baltimore/MA; Bibliotheque Nationale; Brooklyn Museum; Chicago/AI; Corcoran; Detroit/Institute; Hartford/Wadsworth; Los Angeles/County MA; MMA; MOMA; National Gallery; Newark Museum; U. of Oklahoma; PMA; Phillips; Utica; Vassar College; WMAA; Walker; Williams College; Yale U. **Bibliography:** Barr 3; **Baur 4,** 5, 7; Bazin; Blesh 1; Eliot; Flanagan; Genauer; Goodrich and Baur 1; Hunter 6; Janis, S.; McCurdy, ed.; Mendelowitz; Miller, ed. 2; Newmeyer; Nordness, ed.; Pousette-Dart, ed.; Read 2; Richardson, E.P.; Soby 5, 6; Wight 2. Archives.

MADSEN, LOREN. b. March 29, 1943, Oakland, Calif. **Studied:** Reed College; UCLA, BA, 1966; MA, 1970. Traveled Switzerland, 1959–60, Europe, 1963–64. **Taught:** UCLA. **Commissions:** Prudential Insurance Co., Florham Park, N.J., 1974; Los Angeles Museum of Art, Calif., 1977; Prudential Insurance Co., Woodland Hills, Calif.; Cedars-Sinai Medical Center, Beverly Hills, Calif., 1977; Michael's Restaurant, Santa Monica, Calif., 1979; Newport Harbor Art Museum, Newport Beach, Calif., 1980; First Bank Atrium, Pillsbury Center, Minneapolis, Minn.; SSA Metro West (G.S.A.), Baltimore, Md.; Stamford Town Center, Stamford, Conn.; Iowa State University, Ames, Iowa, 1980–81. **Awards:** Los Angeles/County MA, New Talent, **P.P.,** 1975; National Endowment for the Arts, Fellowship, 1975 and 1980. **Address:** 428 Broome Street, NYC 10013. **Dealer:** David McKee Gallery, NYC; L. A. Louver Gallery, Los Angeles; Zolla-Lieberman Gallery, Chicago. **One-man Exhibitions:** (first) Mizuno Gallery, Los Angeles, 1973, 74; MOMA, 1975; David McKee Gallery, NYC, 1976, 77; Site, San Francisco, 1976; L. A. Louver Gallery, Los Angeles, 1976; Zolla-Lieberman, Chicago, 1978; Wright State U., 1980. **Group:** Scripps College, Young Sculptors, 1972; Long Beach/MA, Constructions, 1974; Los Angeles/County MA, Six Artists, 1974; Los Angeles Municipal Art Gallery, 24 from Los Angeles, 1974; SFAI, 8 Los Angeles Artists, 1974; Hayward Gallery, The Condition of Sculpture, 1975; Walker, Dill, Ginnever, Madsen, 1975; Omaha/Joslyn, L.A. in the Seventies, 1979; Hirshhorn, Directions, 1979; Sacramento/Crocker, Aspects of Abstract Art, 1979. **Collections:** Los Angeles/County MA; Walker; MOMA; Jerusalem/National; Paris/Beaubourg; Hirshhorn; Vancouver; Newport Harbor.

MALDARELLI, ORONZIO. b. September 9, 1892, Naples, Italy; **d.** January 4, 1963, NYC. To USA, 1900. **Studied:** Cooper Union, 1906–08; NAD, 1908, with Leon Kroll, Ivan Olinsky, Hermon McNeil; Beaux-Arts Institute of Design, NYC, 1912, with Solon Borglum, Jo Davidson, John Gregory, Elie Nadelman. **Taught:** Sarah Lawrence College, 1933–61. **Member:** NIAL; NAD; Architectural League of New York; National Sculpture Society. **Commissions:** St. Patrick's Cathedral, NYC, 1947; James Weldon Johnson Houses, NYC, 1953–55; State Insurance Fund Building, NYC, 1957–58; Hartford (Conn.) Public Library, 1957–58. **Awards:** Fairmount Park Association, Philadelphia, First Prize, Sculpture, 1930; Guggenheim Foundation Fellowship, 1931–33; Chicago/AI, The Mr. & Mrs. Frank G. Logan Medal, 1941; NIAL Grant, 1948; PAFA, George D. Widener Memorial Gold Medal, 1951; Architectural League of New York, Silver Medal of Honor, 1954, 56. **One-man Exhibitions:** NAD, 1922, 23, 58, 62, 63; California Palace, 1930; Chicago/AI, 1935, 36, 40, 42, 57; WMAA, 1936, 56, 62; U. of Minnesota, 1937; Society of Independent Artists, NYC, 1941; PAFA, 1943; Sao Paulo, 1951; MOMA, 1953; U. of Illinois, 1953, 55; Hartford/Wadsworth, 1957; P. Rosenberg and Co., 1959, Memorial Exhibition, 1963. **Collections:** Chicago/AI; Dallas; MFA; Fairmount Park Association; MMA; Newark Museum; Ogunquit; PAFA;

Sara Roby Foundation; Utica; VMFA; WMAA. **Bibliography:** Baur 7; Brumme; Cheney; Pearson 2; Ritchie 3.

MALLARY, ROBERT. b. December 2, 1917, Toledo, Ohio. **Studied:** La Escuela de las Artes del Libro, Mexico City, 1938; privately with Koloman Sokol (graphics), Mexico City and New York, 1941–42. **Taught:** Pratt Institute, 1959–67; The Pennsylvania State U., 1962; U. of California, Davis, 1963, 67; U. of Minnesota, 1965; U. of Massachusetts, 1967– . Director, ARSTECNICA, U. of Massachusetts/Amherst College. **Commissions:** Beverly Hilton Hotel, Beverly Hills, Calif., 1954–55 (mural, with Dale Owen); New York State Pavilion, New York World's Fair, 1964–65. **Awards:** Tamarind Fellowship, 1962; Guggenheim Foundation Fellowship, 1964. **Address:** P.O. Box 48, Conway, MA. 01341. **Dealer:** Allan Stone Gallery. **One-man Exhibitions:** SFMA, 1944; Sacramento/Crocker, 1944, 52; Santa Barbara/MA, 1952; Gump's Gallery, 1953; San Diego, 1953; Urban Gallery, NYC, 1954; U. of New Mexico, 1956–59; Jonson Gallery, Albuquerque, N.M., 1957–59; Santa Fe, N.M., 1958; Allan Stone Gallery, 1961, 62, 66; Yale U. (two-man), 1965; Purdue U., 1974. **Retrospective:** Potsdam/SUNY, 1969. **Group:** Salon de Grabado, Mexico City, 1942; SFMA, 1945; Los Angeles/County MA Annuals, 1951, 53, 56; Denver/AM Annual, 1955; III & VII Sao Paulo Biennials, 1955, 63; Smithsonian, California Painters, circ., USA, 1956–58; MOMA, Recent Sculpture USA, 1959; MOMA, Sixteen Americans, circ., 1959; SRGM, Guggenheim International, 1960; WMAA Annuals, 1960, 62; MOMA, The Art of Assemblage, circ., 1961; Martha Jackson Gallery, New Media—New Forms, II, 1961; Seattle World's Fair, 1962; A.F.A., Relief Sculpture, circ., 1964; Brandeis U., Recent American Drawings, 1964; ICA, London, Cybernetic Serendipity, 1968; WMAA, Human Concern/Personal Torment, 1969; Akron/AI, Celebrate Ohio, 1971. **Collections:** Brandeis

U.; Buffalo/Albright; U. of California; Houston/MFA; Kalamazoo/Institute; Los Angeles/County MA; MOMA; U. of New Mexico; U. of North Carolina; Roswell; Smith College; U. of Texas; WMAA. **Bibliography:** *Celebrate Ohio;* Davis, D.; Hunter, ed.; Janis and Blesh 1; *Report;* Seitz 3; Weller.

MALLORY, RONALD. b. June 17, 1935, Philadelphia, Pa. **Studied:** U. of Colorado, 1951; U. of Florida, B. Arch., 1952; School of Fine Arts, Rio de Janeiro (with Roberto Burle Marx), 1956; Academie Julian, Paris, 1958. Resided France, 1971; Italy 1971. Traveled Brazil, Europe, USA. **Taught:** U. of California, Berkeley, 1972. A filmmaker. **Address:** 353 West 12th Street, NYC 10014. **One-man Exhibitions:** (first) Galerie Claude Volney, 1960; Mirell Gallery, Miami, Fla., 1961; The Stable Gallery, 1966, 67; Esther Robles Gallery, 1968; Galeria Bonino Ltd., 1969, 73. **Group:** Palais des Beaux-Arts, Brussels, 1965; Houston/Contemporary, 1966; U. of Illinois, 1967, 68; Carnegie, 1967; ICA, Boston, 1967; Flint/Institute, 1967; Worcester/AM, 1967; Salon des Jeunes Peintres, Paris, 1967; HemisFair '68, San Antonio, Tex., 1968; UCLA, Electric Art, 1969; Torcuato di Tella, Buenos Aires, 1969; MOMA; WMAA. **Collections:** U. of Arizona; Buffalo/Albright; U. of California; Chase Manhattan Bank; ICA, Boston; Jerusalem/National; La Jolla; Los Angeles/County MA; MOMA; Munich/Modern; NCFA; Ridgefield/Aldrich; Santa Barbara/MA; WMAA.

MANGOLD, ROBERT. b. 1937, North Tonawanda, N.Y. **Studied:** Cleveland Institute of Art, 1956–59; Yale U., 1959, 1960–62, BFA, 1963, MFA. **Taught:** School of Visual Arts, NYC, 1963– ; Hunter College, 1964–65; Skowhegan School, 1968; Yale U. Summer School, Norfolk, Conn., 1969; Cornell U., 1970. **Address:** Bull Road, Washingtonville, N.Y. **Dealer:** John Weber Gallery, NYC. **One-man Exhibitions:** Thibaut

Gallery, NYC, 1964; Fischbach Gallery, 1965, 67, 69, 70, 71, 73; Galerie Muller, 1968; SRGM, 1971; Yvon Lambert, 1973; Galleria Toselli, Milan, 1973; Lisson Gallery, 1973; Galerie Annemarie Verna, Zurich, 1973; Galleria Marilena Bonomo, Bari, Italy, 1973; Max Protetch, Washington, D.C., 1973; Weinberg Gallery, San Francisco, 1973; John Weber Gallery, 1974; Konrad Fischer Gallery, Dusseldorf, 1974; Protetch-McIntosh Gallery, Washington, D.C., 1978; Bielefeld, Kunsthalle, 1980. **Group:** SRGM, Systemic Painting, 1966; Yale U., Twelve Yale Artists, 1966; ICA, U. of Pennsylvania, A Romantic Minimalism, 1967; Ithaca College, Selected New York Artists, 1967; Trenton/State, Focus on Light, 1967; WMAA, Artists under Forty, 1968; Buffalo/Albright, Modular Paintings, 1970; Documenta V, Kassel, 1972; WMAA, American Drawings, 1963–1973, 1973; Parcheggio di Villa Borghese, Rome, Contemporanea, 1973; Chicago/Contemporary, Five Artists: A Logic of Vision, 1974; MOMA, Color as Language, circ., 1975. **Collections:** Amsterdam/Stedelijk; Los Angeles/County MA; MOMA; McCrory Corporation; Oberlin College; RISD; Ridgefield/Aldrich; SRGM; WMAA. **Bibliography:** *Art Now 74; Contemporanea; Fundamentele Schilderkunst;* Gablik; Honisch and Jensen, eds.; Lippard 2; Murdoch 1; *Options and Alternatives;* **Waldman 4.**

MANGOLD, SYLVIA PLIMACK. b. September 18, 1938. **Studied:** Cooper Union, NYC, 1956–59; Yale U., BFA, 1961. **Taught:** School of Visual Arts, NYC, 1970–71. **Address:** Bull Road, Washingtonville, N.Y. **Dealer:** Droll/Kolbert Gallery, Inc., NYC. **One-man Exhibitions:** Fischbach Gallery, NYC, 1974, 75; Daniel Weinberg Gallery, San Francisco, 1974; Droll/Kolbert Gallery, NYC, 1978, 80; Galerie Annemarie Verna, Zurich, 1978. **Group:** Vassar College, Realism Now, 1968; U. of North Carolina, Art on Paper, 1968; Potsdam/SUNY, New Realism, 1972; WMAA Annual, 1972; Yale U., Amer-

Man Ray   *Etude pour la Fortune*   1938

ican Drawing 1970–1973, 1973; Yale U., Seven Realists, 1974; California Institute of the Arts, Valencia, Anonymous Was a Woman, 1974; Skidmore College, 20th Century Drawings, 1975; San Antonio/McNay, American Artists, '76, 1976; Akron/AI, Contemporary Images in Watercolor, 1976; Indianapolis, 1976; Documenta 6, Kassel, 1977; Buffalo/Albright, American Painting of the 1970's, 1978; Ljubljana, 13th Print Biennial, 1979; Denver, The Reality of Illusion, 1979; Walker, Eight Artists; The Elusive Image, 1979. **Bibliography:** *Art: A Woman's Sensibility; Drawings: The Pluralist Decade;* Lippard 3.

MAN RAY (Emmanuel Radinski). b. August 27, 1890, Philadelphia, Pa; **d.** November 18, 1976, Paris. **Studied:** NAD, 1908; ASL; Ferrer Center, NYC, with Robert Henri and George Bellows. Cofounder (with Marcel Duchamp and Francis Picabia) of DADA group, NYC, 1917. Co-organizer (with Katherine S. Dreier and Marcel Duchamp) of Societe Anonyme (Museum of Modern Art), 1920. Published one issue of *New York DADA* with Marcel Duchamp, 1921. To Paris, 1921, and became a member of the DADA and Surrealist groups, 1924–39. Developed the rayography technique in photography, 1921. Created abstract and surrealist films: *Le Retour de la Raison,* 1923; *Emak Bakia,* 1926; *L'Etoile de Mer,* 1928; *Les Mysteres du Chateau de Des,* 1929. Resided Hollywood, 1940–50; returned to Paris. **One-man Exhibitions:** (first) Daniel Gallery, NYC, 1915, also 1916, 19; Librairie Six, Paris, 1922; Galerie Surrealiste, Paris, 1926; Myrbor Galerie, Paris, 1929; Galerie Vanleer, Paris, 1929; Galerie Vignon, Paris, 1932; Curt Valentine Gallery, NYC, 1936; Galerie Beaune, Paris, 1939; The London Gallery, London, 1939; Frank Perls Gallery,

1941; Julien Levy Galleries, NYC, 1945; Copley Gallery, Hollywood, Calif., 1948; Paul Kantor Gallery, Beverly Hills, 1953; Galerie Furstenberg, Paris, 1954; Galerie Rive Droite, Paris, 1959; Bibliotheque Nationale, 1962; Cordier & Ekstrom, Inc., 1963, 70; Princeton U., 1963; Galleria Schwarz, 1964, 71; Los Angeles/County MA, 1966; Martha Jackson Gallery, 1968; Galerie der Spiegel, Cologne, 1968, 75; Hanover Gallery, 1969; Trenton/State, 1969; Noah Goldowsky, 1971; La Boetie, NYC, 1972; MMA, 1973; Alexandre Iolas Gallery, NYC, 1974; Galleria Il Fauno, Turin, 1974; Studio Marconi, Milan, 1975; Chicago/Contemporary, 1975. **Retrospectives:** Paris/Moderne, 1971; New York Cultural Center, 1974. **Group:** Societe Anonyme, NYC, 1920; Brooklyn Museum, 1926; Springfield, Mass./MFA, 1929; MOMA, 1936; WMAA, 1946; Yale U., 1948. **Collections:** MOMA. **Bibliography:** Ammann and Bussmann; *Avant-Garde Painting and Sculpture in America, 1910–25;* Barr 1; Baur 7; Biddle 4; Blesh 1; **Bourgeade;** Breton 1, 2, 3; Brown 2; Cassou; Christensen; Crespelle; Davis, D.; Flanagan; Gascoyne; Gerdts; Guggenheim, ed.; Haftman; Hulten; Honisch and Jensen, eds; Hunter 6; Hunter, ed.; Kozloff 3; Krauss 2; Kyrou; **Langsner; Man Ray 1, 2, 3, 4; Man Ray;** McCurdy, ed.; Marter, Tarbell, and Wechsler; Mellquist; Motherwell 1; **Penrose;** Raynal 3; Read 2, 3, 5; **Ribemont-Dessaignes;** Richter; Ritchie 1; Rose, B., 1; Rubin 1; Seitz 3; Soby 1; Tashijian; Tomkins; Tomkins and Time-Life Books; Verkauf; Waldberg 2, 3, 4; Wright 1; Zervos.

MANSHIP, PAUL. b. December 25, 1885, St. Paul, Minn.; **d.** February 1, 1966, NYC. **Studied:** St. Paul School of Art, 1892–1903; ASL, 1905; PAFA, 1906–08; American Academy, Rome, 1909–12. Traveled Europe, USA; resided Paris, 1922–26. **Taught:** PAFA, 1943–46. **Member:** (Federal) Commission of Fine Arts (president, 1937–41); National Sculpture Society (president,

Paul Manship *Atalanta* 1921

1939–42); AAAL (president, 1948–53); Century Association (president, 1950–54); Academy of St. Luca, Rome, 1952. **Commissions:** Designed coinage for Irish Free State, 1927. **Awards:** NAD, Helen Foster Barnett Prize, 1913, 17; PAFA, George D. Widener Memorial Gold Medal, 1914; Panama-Pacific Exposition, San Francisco, 1915, Gold Medal; NAD, 1920; elected to the NIAL, 1920; American Independent Artists Medal, 1921; American Institute of Architects, Gold Medal, 1921; NAD, Saltus Gold Medal for Merit, 1924; Philadelphia Art Week, Gold Medal, 1925; Philadelphia Sesquicentennial, Gold Medal, 1926; Legion of Honor, 1929; elected to the AAAL, 1932; Paris World's Fair, 1937, Diplome d'Honneur; National Sculpture Society, Medal of Honor, 1939; NIAL, Gold Medal, 1945. **One-man Exhibitions:** Architectural League of New York, 1912; A.F.A., 1914; Corcoran, 1920, 37; Leicester Gallery, London, 1921; PMA, 1926; U. of Rochester, 1927; Toronto, 1928; Averell House, NYC, 1933; Tate, 1935; Century Association, 1935;

VMFA, 1936; Arden Gallery, NYC, 1941; AAAL, 1945; Walker, 1948; St. Paul Gallery, 1967; Robert Schoelkopf Gallery, 1971, 72; Hamline U., 1972. **Retrospectives:** Smithsonian, 1958; NCFA, 1966. **Group:** Corcoran, 1920; PAFA; NAD; WMAA; MMA; and many others in America and abroad. **Collections:** American Academy, Rome; Andover/Phillips; Chicago/AI; Cochran Memorial Park; Detroit/Institute; Harvard U.; League of Nations; MMA; Minneapolis/Institute; New York Coliseum; Pratt Institute; Rockefeller Center; St. Louis/City; Smith College; West Palm Beach/Norton. **Bibliography:** Baur 7; **Beggs;** Birnbaum; Brumme; Cahill and Barr, eds.; Cortissoz 1; **Gallatin 7;** *Index of 20th Century Artists;* Jackman; Lee and Burchwood; **Leach;** Licht, F.; Mather 1; Mellquist; Mendelowitz; **Murtha;** Pach 1; Poore; Rose, B., 1; **Vitry.** Archives.

MANSO, LEO. b. April 15, 1914, NYC. **Studied:** Educational Alliance, NYC, 1929; NAD, 1930–34; New School for Social Research. Traveled Mexico, Africa, India, Nepal, Italy, Sicily, Tunisia. **Taught:** Cooper Union, 1947–70; NYU, 1950–72; Columbia U., 1950–55; NYC, 1950–1980; Provincetown Workshop, 1959 (cofounder); ASL, NYC, 1974, 1975–80; New School for Social Research, 1975. **Member:** American Abstract Artists. **Commissions:** Public Library, Lincoln, Neb. (mural), 1965. **Awards:** U. of Illinois, **P.P.,** 1951, Audubon Artists, 1952, 57; Ford Foundation, **P.P.,** 1963; AAAL, Childe Hassam Award, 1968. **Address:** 460 Riverside Drive, NYC 10027. **Dealer:** Long Point Gallery, Provincetown, Mass. **One-man Exhibitions:** (first) Norlyst Gallery, NYC, 1947; Guadalajara Institute, Mexico, 1948; Mortimer Levitt Gallery, NYC, 1950; The Babcock Gallery, 1953, 56; Columbia U., 1954; NYU, 1957; Grand Central Moderns, NYC, 1957, 60, 61, 63, 64; Philadelphia Art Alliance, 1961, 69; Tirca Karlis Gallery, 1963, 65, 67, 69, 70, 72, 73; Arts Council of Winston-Salem (N.C.), 1966; Rose Fried Gallery, 1966, 68, 70; George Washington U., 1968; Rehn Galleries, 1974; E. P. Gurewitsch Gallery, NYC, 1975, 78; Syracuse/Everson, 1976; Long Point Gallery, Provincetown, Mass. 1977, 79. **Group:** PAFA, 1947–50, 1952, 54, 61, 62, 64, 68; WMAA Annuals, 1948–66; U. of Illinois, 1950, 51, 52, 54, 57; A.F.A., circ.; U. of Nebraska Annual; American Abstract Artists Annual; Brooklyn Museum, Watercolor Biennials; ART: USA:58, NYC, 1958; MOMA, The Art of Assemblage, circ., 1961; NIAL, 1961, 68; MOMA, 1965. **Collections:** Alcoa; Boston/MFA; Brandeis U.; Brooklyn Museum; Cape Town; Charleston, W. Va.; Corcoran; U. of Illinois; MOMA; Michigan State U.; Mount Holyoke College; NYU; U. of Nebraska; Norfolk; PAFA; Portland, Ore./AM; RISD; Safad; Syracuse U.; WMAA; Wesleyan U.; West Palm Beach/Norton; Worcester/AM. **Bibliography:** Seitz 3. Archives.

MARCA-RELLI, CONRAD. b. June 5, 1913, Boston, Mass. **Studied:** Cooper Union, one year; mostly self-taught. US Army, 1941–45. Traveled Europe, USA, Mexico. **Taught:** Yale U., 1954–55, 1959–60; U. of California, Berkeley, 1958; New College, Sarasota, Fla., 1966. Federal A.P.: Easel and mural painting; also art teacher. **Member:** NIAL, 1976. **Awards:** Chicago/AI, The Mr. & Mrs. Frank G. Logan Medal, 1954; Ford Foundation, 1959; Detroit/Institute, **P.P.,** 1960; II Inter-American Paintings and Prints Biennial, Mexico City, 1960, Hon. Men.; Chicago/AI, The M.V. Kohnstamm Prize, 1963. **Address:** Box 1367, Apaquogue Road, East Hampton, NY 11937; Urbanization Can Pepsimo, Ibiza (Baleares), Spain. **Dealer:** Marlborough Gallery, Inc., NYC. **One-man Exhibitions:** (first) Niveau Gallery, NYC, 1948, also 1950; The New Gallery, NYC, 1951; The Stable Gallery, 1953–58 (4); Frank Perls Gallery, 1956; La Tartaruga, Rome, 1957, 62; The Kootz Gallery, NYC, 1959–64; Bolles Gallery, 1961; Galerie Schmela, 1961 (two-man,

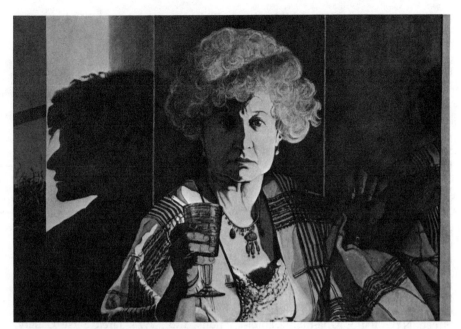

Marcia Marcus   *Double Self-Portrait III*   1979

with Robert Motherwell), 71; Lima, Peru, 1961; Joan Peterson Gallery, 1961; Galerie de France, Paris, 1962; Galerie Charles Leinhard, Zurich, 1963; Tokyo Gallery, 1963; James David Gallery, Miami, 1966, 67; Makler Gallery, 1967, 74; WMAA, 1967; Brandeis U., 1967–68; U. of Alabama, 1968; Buffalo/Albright, 1968; Alpha Gallery, 1968; Reed College, 1969; Seattle/AM, 1969; Marlborough Gallery, Inc., NYC, 1970, 75; U. of Maryland, 1970; West Palm Beach/Norton, 1970; Fort Lauderdale, 1971; U. of Miami, 1971; Galeria Carl van der Voort, Ibiza, 1972; Darthea Speyer Gallery, 1972; Galerie Numaga, Auvernier, Switzerland, 1973; Galeria Inguanzo, Madrid, 1973; Marlborough Galerie AG, Zurich, 1974; Marlborough Godard Ltd., Toronto, 1975. **Retrospective:** WMAA, 1967. **Group;** Ninth Street Exhibition, NYC, 1951; WMAA Annuals; Chicago/AI; U. of Illinois; U. of Nebraska; Carnegie; Venice Biennial; Yale U.; Corcoran; Arts Club of Chicago; Rome–New York Foundation, Rome; Boston Arts Festival; Minneapolis/Institute; PAFA; Montreal/MFA; Brussels World's Fair, 1958; Documenta II, Kassel, 1959; American Painting and Sculpture, Moscow, 1959; Sao Paulo Biennial; Seattle World's Fair, 1962; A.F.A., 1967–68; MOMA, The New American Painting and Sculpture, 1969; WMAA Annual, 1969; New School for Social Research, NYC, American Drawings of the Sixties, 1969; U. of California, Santa Barbara, Trends in Twentieth Century Art, 1970; VMFA, American Painting, 1970; NAD, Annual, 1972; AAAL, Newly Elected Members, 1976. **Collections:** U. of Alabama; Brandeis U.; Buffalo/Albright; Carnegie; Chase Manhattan Bank; Chicago/AI; Cleveland/MA; Colby College; Columbia Broadcasting System; Detroit/Institute; Hartford/Wadsworth; Harvard U.; High Museum; Hirshhorn; Houston/MFA; Indianapolis/Herron; International Minerals & Chemicals Corp.; Los Angeles/County MA; MMA; MOMA; U. of Michigan; Minneapolis/Institute; Minnesota/MA; NCFA; U. of Nebraska; PAFA; U. of Rochester; SFMA; SRGM; Seattle/AM; The Singer Company Inc.; U. of Texas; Union Carbide Corp.;

Utica; WMAA; Waitsfield/Bundy; Walker; Washington U.; Yale U. **Bibliography: Agee; Arnason 1;** Chaet; Goodrich and Baur 1; Henning; Hunter, ed.; Janis and Blesh 1; *Metro;* Nordness, ed.; Rodman 3; Rose, B., 1; Seitz 3; **Tyler, P., 2.**

MARCUS, MARCIA. b. January 11, 1928, NYC. **Studied:** NYU 1943–47, BFA; Cooper Union, 1950–52; ASL, 1954, with Edwin Dickinson. Traveled Europe. **Taught:** Purdue U.; Moore Institute of Art, Science and Industry; RISD; Cooper Union, 1970–71; Louisiana State U., 1972; NYU, 1972; Vassar College, 1973–74; Cornell U., 1975; Iowa State U., 1979–80. **Awards:** Ingram Merrill Grant, 1964; NIAL, Richard and Hinda Rosenthal Foundation Award, 1964; Ford Foundation Grant, 1966. **Address:** 80 North Moore Street, NYC 10013. **One-man Exhibitions:** (first) March Gallery, NYC, 1957; Delancey Street Museum, NYC, 1960; Cober Gallery, 1961; The Alan Gallery, NYC, 1962; RISD, 1966; The Graham Gallery, 1966; Tirca Karlis Gallery, 1966, 67; The Zabriskie Gallery, 1970; Makler Gallery, 1972; Louisiana State U., 1972; Vassar College, 1974; ACA Gallery, 1974; Syracuse/Everson, 1975; Bloomsburg College, 1976; Benson Gallery, Bridgehampton, N.Y., 1978; Terry Dintenfass Inc., NYC, 1979; Wheaton College, 1980; Cedar Rapids Art Center, 1980. **Group:** WMAA, Young America, 1960; WMAA Annual, 1963; NIAL, 1964; MOMA, Contemporary Portraits, circ.; New York Cultural Center, Women Choose Women, 1973; PMA/Museum of the Philadelphia Civic Center, Focus, 1974; Syracuse/Everson, Provincetown Painters, 1977; Indianapolis, 1978; U. of Missouri, Kansas City, The Opposite Sex: A Realistic Viewpoint, 1979; Lehigh U., The Revival of Realism, 1979. **Collections:** Canton Art Institute; Hampton Institute; Hirshhorn; NIAL; Newark Museum; Phoenix/ SUNY; Phoenix; Purdue U.; RISD; Randolph Macon Jr. College; Syracuse/Everson; Williamstown/Clark; WMAA.

Bibliography: *Art: A Woman's Sensibility.* Archives.

MARDEN, BRICE. b. October 15, 1938, Bronxville, N.Y. **Studied:** Boston U., 1958–61, BFA; Yale U. Summer School, Norfolk, Conn., 1961; Yale U., 1961–63, MFA. Traveled USA, France, Greece. **Taught:** School of Visual Arts, NYC, 1969–74. **Address:** 105 Bowery, NYC 10002. **Dealer:** The Pace Gallery, NYC. **One-man Exhibitions:** (first) Swarthmore College, 1964; Bykert Gallery, 1966, 68, 69, 70, 72, 73, 74; Yvon Lambert, 1969, 73; Francoise Lambert, Milan, 1970; Gian Enzo Sperone, Turin, 1971, 77; U. of Utah, 1971; Locksley-Shea Gallery, Minneapolis, 1972, 74; Jack Glenn Gallery, Corona del Mar, 1973; Konrad Fischer Gallery, Dusseldorf, 1972, 73, 75; John Berggruen Gallery (two-man), 1972; Cirrus Editions, Ltd., 1974; Jared Sable Gallery, Toronto, 1974; SRGM, 1975; Alessandro/Ferranti, Rome, 1975; Sperone, Westwater, Fischer, NYC, 1976; Brown, U., 1977; Jean and Karen Bernier, Athens, 1977; Max Protetch Gallery, Washington, D.C., 1977; The Pace Gallery, NYC, 1978, 80; Kunstraum, Munich, 1979; Institut fur Moderne Kunst, Nuremberg, 1980; Rice U. (three-man), 1975. **Group:** New London, Drawings by New England Artists, 1960; U. of Illinois, 1967; Ithaca College, Drawings, 1967, 1967; ICA, U. of Pennsylvania, A Romantic Minimalism, 1967; WMAA Annuals 1968, 73; Buffalo/Albright, Modular Painting, 1970; Foundation Maeght, L'Art Vivant, 1970; WMAA, The Structure of Color, 1971; U. of Utah, 1971; U. of Rochester, Aspects of Current Painting, 1971; Chicago/Contemporary, White on White, 1971–72; Indianapolis, 1972; U. of California, Berkeley, Eight New York Painters, 1972; Chicago/AI, 1972; Walker, Painting: New Options, 1972; Documenta V, Kassel, 1972; Yale U., Options and Alternatives, 1973; WMAA, American Art: Third Quarter Century, 1973; MOMA, Some Recent American Art, circ., 1973; Chicago/Contemporary,

Five Artists: A Logic of Vision, 1974; MOMA, Eight Contemporary Artists, 1974; UCLA, 14 Abstract Painters, 1975; Paris/Moderne, Tendances Actuelles de la Nouvelle Peinture Americaine, 1975; Amsterdam/Stedelijk, Fundamental Painting, 1975. **Collections:** Amsterdam/Stedelijk Buffalo/Albright; Fort Worth; Musée de Grenoble; Harvard U.; National Gallery of Canada; MOMA; SRGM; Walker; WMAA. **Bibliography:** *Contemporanea; Fundamentele Schilderkunst;* Honisch and Jensen, eds.; Licht, J.; Murdoch 1; *New in the Seventies; Options and Alternatives;* **Shearer.** Archives.

MARGO, BORIS. b. November 7, 1902, Wolotschisk, Russia. **Studied:** Polytechnic School, Odessa, 1919; Futemas, Moscow, 1924; Filonoy School, Leningrad, 1927. To USA, 1930; citizen, 1937. Traveled Western Europe, Israel, 1968; Hawaii. **Taught:** Master Institute of United Arts, Inc., 1932; American U., 1946; U. of Michigan, 1957; Chicago Art Institute School, 1957; Michigan State U., 1959; U. of Illinois, 1960; U. of Minnesota, Duluth, 1962; U. of North Carolina, 1963; Ford Foundation/A.F.A., Artist-in-Residence, 1965; Syracuse U., 1966–67; The Ohio State U., 1968; Honolulu Academy, 1973; Potsdam/SUNY, 1974; Fine Arts Work Center, Provincetown, Mass., 1974. **Member:** SAGA. Federal A.P.: Newark (N.J.) Airport (assisted Arshile Gorky on a mural). **Commissions:** Honolulu Academy (sculpture), 1973. **Awards:** Chicago/AI, Watson F. Blair Prize, 1947; Brooklyn Museum, Print Exhibitions, 1947, 53, 55, 60, 64, 68; Portland, Me./MA, **P.P.,** 1960; National Endowment for the Arts, grant, 1974. **m.** Jan Gelb. **Address:** 749 West End Avenue, NYC 10025. **Dealers:** Monique Knowlton Gallery, NYC. **One-man Exhibitions:** (first) Artists' Gallery, NYC, 1939, also 1941, 42; Norlyst Gallery, NYC, 1943; Mortimer Brandt, NYC, 1946, 47; American U., 1946, 47; J. Seligmann and Co., 1947; Brooklyn Museum, 1947; Smithsonian,

1948; Betty Parsons Gallery, 1950, 53, 55, 57, 60; World House Galleries, NYC, 1964; Honolulu Academy, 1973; Monique Knowlton Gallery, NYC, 1974. **Retrospectives:** Syracuse U., 1966; A.A.A. Gallery, NYC, 1967. **Group:** MMA, Artists for Victory, 1942; Mortimer Brandt, NYC, Abstract and Surrealist Art in the U.S., circ., western museums, 1944; NAD, 1946; Library of Congress, 1946; Carnegie, 1946, 52; WMAA Annuals, 1947–50, 1953–55; Chicago/AI, Abstract and Surrealist Art, 1948; U. of Illinois, 1950, 52; Chicago/AI, 1950, 54; I Sao Paulo Biennial, 1951; MOMA, XXVth Anniversary Exhibition, 1954; Federation of Modern Painters and Sculptors Annual, 1955; XXXV Venice Biennial, 1970; U. of Illinois, 1971. **Collections:** Albion College; Andover/Phillips; Baltimore/MA; Brooklyn Museum; Brown U.; Buffalo/Albright; Chase Manhattan Bank; Chicago/AI; Cincinnati/AM; Corcoran; Cornell U.; Currier; Dartmouth College; Evansville; U. of Georgia; U. of Illinois; Kalamazoo/Institute; Los Angeles/County MA; Louisville/Speed; MIT; MMA; MOMA; U. of Maine; U. of Michigan; U. of Minnesota; NYPL; National Gallery; New Orleans/Delgado; U. of North Carolina; The Ohio State U.; Omaha/Joslyn; PMA; Phoenix; RISD; SFMA; San Jose State College; Sao Paulo; Slater; Syracuse U.; Utica; WMAA; Yale U. **Bibliography:** Baur 5, 7; Blesh 1; Hayter 1; Janis, s.; Peterdi; Pousette-Dart, ed.; Reese; **Schmeckebier 1.** Archives.

MARIN, JOHN. b. December 3, 1870, Rutherford, N.J.; **d.** October 1, 1953, Cape Split, Me. **Studied:** Hoboken Academy; Stevens Preparatory School; Stevens Institute of Technology; PAFA, 1899–1901, with Thomas Anshutz, Henry Breckenridge; ASL, 1901–03, with Frank V. DuMond. Worked as a freelance architect. Traveled Europe, 1905–11. **Member:** AAAL, 1945. **Awards:** Philadelphia Watercolor Club, 1940; American Institute of Architects, 1948; Hon. DFA, U. of Maine, 1940;

MMA, 1952; PAFA, Joseph E. Temple Gold Medal, 1954; Hon. DFA, Yale U. **One-man Exhibitions:** (first) Photo-Secession, NYC, 1909, also 1910, 13, 15; Brooklyn Museum, 1922; Montross Gallery, NYC, 1922, 24; Stieglitz's Intimate Gallery, NYC, 1925, 28; An American Place (Gallery), NYC, 1929–35, 1937–42, 1944–50; Cleveland/MA, 1939; The Downtown Gallery, 1939, 48, 1950–54, 1963; ICA, Boston, 1947; de Young, 1949; XXV Venice Biennial, 1950; A.F.A., 1952–54; Detroit/Institute, 1954; Philadelphia Art Alliance, 1954; The Willard Gallery, 1965; La Jolla, 1966; M. Knoedler & Co., 1967; U. of Utah, 1969; PMA, 1969; Los Angeles/County MA, 1970; Marlborough Gallery Inc., NYC, 1972, 77, 78. **Retrospectives:** The Daniel Gallery, NYC, 1920; MOMA, 1936; Trenton/State, 1950; U. of Michigan, 1951; Houston/MFA, 1953; AAAL, 1954; UCLA, 1955. **Group:** Salon d'Automne, Paris, 1908; Salon des Artistes Independants, Paris, 1904; The Armory Show, 1913; WMAA; MOMA; Chicago/AI; Detroit/Institute; Cleveland/MA; Walker; Cincinnati/AM; SFMA; Toronto; Dallas/MFA; Utica; Corcoran; MMA. **Collections:** Andover/Phillips; Arizona State U.; Auburn U.; Baltimore/MA; Brooklyn Museum; Buffalo/Albright; Chicago/AI; Cleveland/MA; Colorado Springs/FA; Columbus; Cranbrook; Denver/AM; Des Moines; Detroit/Institute; Fisk U.; U. of Georgia; Hagerstown/County MFA; Hartford/Wadsworth; Harvard U.; Houston/MFA; IBM; Indiana U.; Indianapolis/Herron; Lane Foundation; MMA; MOMA; U. of Maine; The Miller Co.; National Gallery; U. of Nebraska; Newark Museum; New Britain; Ogunquit; Omaha/Joslyn; PAFA; Phillips; U. of Rochester; Roswell; SFMA; St. Louis/City; San Antonio/McNay; San Diego; Santa Barbara/MA; Springfield, Mo./AM; Utica; WMAA; Walker; Wellesley College; West Palm Beach/Norton; Wichita/AM; Wilmington; Yale U.; Youngstown/Butler.   **Bibliography:** American Artists Group Inc. 3; *Avant-Garde Painting and Sculpture in America,*
1910–25; Baldinger; Becker 1; Barr 3; Baur 5, 7; Bazin; Beekman; Benson; Bethers; Biddle 4; Blesh 1; Born; Brown 1, 2; Bryant, L.; Cahill and Barr, eds.; Canaday; Cassou; Cheney; Chipp; Christensen; *Cityscape 1919–39;* Coke 2; Craven, T., 1; Downes, ed.; *8 American Masters of Watercolor;* Eliot; Elsen 2; Flanagan; Flexner; Flockhart; *Forerunners;* Frank, ed.; Frost; Gallatin 1; Gaunt; Gerdts; Goldwater and Treves, eds.; Goodrich 1; Goodrich and Baur 1; Haas; Haftman; Hartmann; **Helm; Helm and Wight;** Hess, T. B., 1; Hunter 6; Huyghe; *Index of 20th Century Artists;* Janis, S.; Jewell 2; Johnson, Ellen H; Kootz 1, 2; Kuh 1, 3; Lane; Langui, Lee and Burchwood; Leepa; Mather 1; **McBride;** McCoubrey 1; McCurdy, ed.; Mellquist; Mendelowitz; Munsterberg; Neuhaus; Newmeyer; **Norman; Norman, ed.;** Pach 1; Pearson 2; Phillips 1, 2; Pousette-Dart, ed.; Raynal 3, 4; Read 2; Richardson, E.P.; Ritchie 1; Rodman 2; Rose, B., 1, 4; Rosenblum 1; Rubin 1; Sachs; **Seligmann, ed.;** Soby 5, 6; Sutton; Tashijan; Tomkins and Time-Life Books; Valentine 2; Wight 2; Wright 1; Zigrosser 1. Archives.

MARISOL (Escobar). b. May 22, 1930, Paris, France. **Studied:** ASL, 1950, with Yasuo Kuniyoshi; Hofmann School, 1951–54; Academie des Beaux-Arts, Paris, 1949; New School for Social Research, 1951–54. Traveled Venezuela, USA, Europe. Designed sets for Martha Graham and Louis Falco dance companies. **Awards:** Academy of Achievement, San Diego; Hon. DFA, Moore College of Art. **Taught:** State U. of Montana. **Member:** AAAL. **Address:** 427 Washington Street, NYC 10013. **Dealer:** Sidney Janis Gallery, NYC. **One-man Exhibitions:** (first) Leo Castelli Inc., NYC, 1957; The Stable Gallery, NYC, 1962, 64; Arts Club of Chicago, 1965; Sidney Janis Gallery, NYC, 1966, 67, 73, 75, 81; Hanover Gallery, 1967; XXIV Venice Biennial, 1968; Moore College of Art, Philadelphia, 1970; Worcester/AM, 1971;

New York Cultural Center, 1973; Ohio U., 1974; Estudio Actual, Caracas, 1974; Makler Gallery, Philadelphia, 1975; Houston/Contemporary, 1977. **Group:** Festival of Two Worlds, Spoleto, 1958; Dallas/MFA, Humor in Art, 1958; Chicago/AI, Pan American Art, 1959; Carnegie, 1959, 64, 67; U. of Illinois, 1961; MOMA, The Art of Assemblage, circ., 1961; A.F.A., Wit and Whimsy in 20th Century Art, circ., 1962–63; WMAA Annuals, 1962, 64, 66; MOMA, Americans 1963, circ., 1963–64; Chicago/AI, 1963, 66, 68; Tate, Painting and Sculpture of a Decade, 1954–64, 1964; The Hague, New Realism, 1964; WMAA, Art of the U.S. 1620–1966, 1966; II Internationale der Zeichnung, Darmstadt, 1967; Los Angeles/County MA, American Sculpture of the Sixties, 1967; Houston Festival of Arts, 1967; ICA, London, 1968; MOMA, circ., 1968–70; Finch College, NYC, The Dominant Woman, 1968; Chicago/AI, 1969; Hayward Gallery, London, Pop Art, 1969; Carnegie, 1970; Foundation Maeght, 1970; Skidmore College, Contemporary Women Artists, 1970; Potsdam/SUNY, Contemporary Women Artists, 1972; Baltimore/MA, Drawing Exhibition, 1973; Art Students League, 100th Anniversary, NYC, 1975; New York Cultural Center, The Nude in America, 1975; Hirshhorn, The Golden Door, 1976; Williamstown/Clark, The Dada/Surrealist Heritage, 1976; Bronx Museum, The Year of the Woman, 1976; San Antonio/McNay, Women Artists, 1976, 1977; Brooklyn Museum, Contemporary Women, 1977; U. of Missouri, The Opposite Sex, 1979. **Collections:** Arts Club of Chicago; Brandeis U.; Buffalo/Albright; Chicago/Contemporary; Cologne; Hakone Open Air Museum, Japan; Memphis/Brooks; MOMA; Ringling. **Bibliography:** Bihalji-Merin; Calas, N. and E.; Craven, W.; *From Foreign Shores*; Hunter, ed.; Lippard 5; **Medina;** Nemser; Seitz 3; Seuphor 3; Trier 1; Tuchman 1; Weller. Archives.

MARKMAN, RONALD. b. May 29, 1931, Bronx, N.Y. **Studied:** Yale U.,

BFA, 1957, MFA, 1959. **Taught:** U. of Florida, 1959; Chicago/AI, 1960–64; Indiana U., 1964– . **Awards:** Fulbright Fellowship, 1962. **Address:** 719 South Jordan, Bloomington, IN 47401. **Dealer:** Terry Dintenfass, Inc. **One-man Exhibitions:** Terry Dintenfass, Inc., 1965, 66, 68, 71, 72, 76, 79; Reed College, 1966; U. of Manitoba, 1972; Curwen Gallery, London (two-man), 1971; The Gallery, Bloomington, Inc., 1972, 79; Queens College, N.Y., 1972; Indianapolis, 1974; Indianapolis/Herron, 1976; Tyler School of Art, Philadelphia, 1976; Franklin College, 1980; J. Walter Thompson, NYC, 1977. **Group:** Boston Arts Festival, 1959, 60; WMAA, Young America, 1960; Chicago/AI, 1964; Ball State U., 1966; PAFA Annual, 1967; Anderson (Ind.) Fine Arts Center, 1967; Brooklyn Museum, Print Biennial; Indianapolis/Herron, 1968, 69; New School for Social Research, Humor, Satire, and Irony, 1972; Indianapolis, 1972, 74; Harvard U., Work by Students of Josef Albers, 1974. **Collections:** U. of Alberta; U. of Arkansas; Brooklyn Museum; Chicago/AI; Cincinnati/AM; Library of Congress; Cornell U.; Hirshhorn; Indiana U.; U. of Manitoba; MMA; MOMA; Worcester/AM.

MARSH, REGINALD. b. March 14, 1898, Paris, France; **d.** July 3, 1954, Dorset, Vt. **Studied:** The Lawrenceville School, 1915–16; Yale U., 1916–20, AB; ASL, 1919, 1920–24, 1927–28, with John Sloan, Kenneth Hayes Miller, George Bridgeman, George Luks. Traveled Europe extensively. Artist War Correspondent for *Life* magazine, 1943. **Taught:** ASL; Moore Institute of Art, Science and Industry, Philadelphia, 1953–54. **Commissions:** US Post Office, Washington, D.C., 1937; US Customs House, NYC, 1937. **Awards:** Chicago/AI, The M. V. Kohnstamm Prize, 1931; Wanamaker Prize, 1934; NAD, The Thomas B. Clarke Prize, Limited Editions Club, 1938; Chicago/AI, Watson F. Blair Prize, 1940; PAFA, Dana Watercolor Medal, 1941; NAD, 1943; Corcoran, First William A. Clark

Prize, 1945; Salmagundi Club, NYC, T. J. Watson Prize, 1945; NIAL, 1946; NIAL, Gold Medal for Graphics, 1954. **One-man Exhibitions:** (first) Whitney Studio Club, NYC, 1924, also 1928; Curt Valentine Gallery, NYC, 1927; Weyhe Gallery, 1928; Marie Sterner Gallery, NYC, 1929; Rehn Galleries, 1930–34, 36, 38, 40, 41, 43, 44, 46, 48, 50, 53, 62, 64, 65, 70, 73; Yale U., 1937; Andover/ Phillips, 1937; McDonald Gallery, NYC, 1939; Carnegie, 1946; Print Club of Cleveland, 1948 (two-man); Philadelphia Art Alliance, 1950; Martha Jackson Gallery, 1953; Steeplechase Park, Coney Island, NYC, 1953; Moravian College, 1954; Kennedy Gallery, 1964; Danenberg Gallery, 1969, 71; U. of Arizona, 1969; City Center Gallery, NYC, 1969. **Retrospectives:** Gallery of Modern Art, NYC, 1964; Newport Harbor, 1972. **Group:** WMAA; MMA; MOMA; Corcoran; Carnegie. **Collections:** Andover/Phillips; Boston/MFA; Chicago/ AI; Hartford/Wadsworth; MMA; U. of Nebraska; PAFA; Springfield, Mass./ MFA; WMAA. **Bibliography:** American Artists Group Inc. 1, 3; Baigell 1; Barker 1; Baur 7; Bazin; Boswell 1; Brown 2; Bruce and Watson; Cahill and Barr, eds.; Canaday; Cheney; Christensen; *Cityscape 1919–39*; Craven, T., 2; Eliot; Flanagan; Flexner; Gerdts; **Goodrich** 1, **11;** Goodrich and Baur 1; Hall; Hunter 6; Kent, N.; Kuh 1; McCoubrey 1; McCurdy, ed.; **Marsh;** Mellquist; Mendelowitz; Moser 1; Newmeyer; Nordmark; Pagano; Pearson 1; Reese; Richardson, E.P.; Ringel, ed.; Rose, B., 1, 4; **Sasowsky;** Soyer, R. 1; Sutton; Wight 2. Archives.

MARSICANO, NICHOLAS. b. October 1, 1914, Shenandoah, Pa. **Studied:** PAFA and Barnes Foundation, 1931–34; abroad, 1933–36. Traveled Europe, North Africa, Mexico, USA. **Taught:** Cooper Union, 1948– ; U. of Michigan, summer, 1950; Yale U., summers, 1951–54; Brooklyn Museum School, · 1951–58; Pratt Institute, 1957–60; Cornell U., summer, 1959; Silvermine College of Fine Arts, 1965–69; Davenport/ Municipal, summer, 1972; Purchase/ SUNY, 1974– . **Awards:** PAFA, Cresson Fellowship, and Barnes Foundation Scholarship, 1933–36; V. Hallmark International Competition, Second Prize, 1960; Guggenheim Foundation Fellowship, 1974. **Address:** 42 West 15th Street, NYC 10011. **Dealer:** Gruenebaum Gallery, NYC. **One-man Exhibitions:** The Salpeter Gallery, NYC, 1948; The Bertha Schaefer Gallery, 1957, 59, 60, 61; San Joaquin Pioneer Museum and Haggin Art Galleries, Stockton, Calif., 1959; Stewart Richard Gallery, San Antonio, 1959; The Howard Wise Gallery, NYC, 1963; Des Moines, 1963, 64; Huntington, W. Va., 1967; A. M. Sachs Gallery, 1971, 72, 73; Davenport/ Municipal, 1972; Landmark Gallery, NYC, 1976; Utica, 1979; Gruenebaum Gallery, NYC, 1980. **Group:** U. of Nebraska, 1954, 58, 60; Walker, Vanguard, 1955; II Inter-American Paintings and Prints Biennial, Mexico City, 1960; A.F.A., The Figure, circ., 1960; WMAA Annuals, 1960–62; Chicago/AI, 1961, 64; Dallas/MFA, 1961, 62; MOMA, Abstract American Drawings and Watercolors, circ., Latin America, 1961–63; PAFA, 1962–64; MOMA, Recent Painting USA; The Figure, circ., 1962–63; U. of Kentucky, 1963; U. of Texas, 1968; MOMA, The New American Painting and Sculpture, 1969. **Collections:** Amarillo; Baltimore/MA; Chicago/AI; Ciba-Geigy Corp.; Dallas/MFA; Davenport/Municipal; Des Moines; Hallmark Collection; Housatonic Community College; Huntington, W. Va.; ICA, Boston; MIT; MOMA; U. of Massachusetts; NYU; U. of North Carolina; Ridgefield/Aldrich; SFMA; U. of Texas. **Bibliography:** Archives.

MARTIN, AGNES. b. March, 1912, Maklin, Canada. To USA, 1932. **Studied:** Columbia U. Teachers College, 1941–42, 1951–52, with Arthur Young; Columbia U., MFA; Western Washington College; U. of New Mexico. Traveled the world and has resided in many locations in the U.S. **Awards:** National Endowment for the Arts Grant, $5,000, 1966. Did not paint 1967–74. Hon. DFA, New Mexico State U.; Skowhegan Medal for Painting, 1978. **Address:** Cuba, NM 87013. **Dealer:** The Pace Gallery. **One-man Exhibitions:** Betty Parsons Gallery, 1958, 59, 61; Robert Elkon Gallery, NYC, 1961, 63, 66, 70, 72, 76; Nicholas Wilder Gallery, 1966, 67, 73; Visual Arts Gallery, NYC, 1971; Kunstraum, Munich, 1973; Pasadena/ AM, 1973; ICA, U. of Pennsylvania, 1973; MOMA, 1973; The Pace Gallery, 1975, 76, 77, 78, 79, 80; F.H. Mayor Gallery, London, 1978; Galerie Rudolf Zwirner, Cologne, 1978; Harcus-Krakow Gallery, Boston, 1978; Margo Leavin Gallery, Los Angeles, 1979; Santa Fe, N.M., 1979. **Retrospective:** Hayward Gallery, London, circ., 1977. **Group:** Carnegie, 1960; WMAA, Geometric Abstraction, 1962; Hartford/ Wadsworth, Black, White, and Grey, 1964; SRGM, American Drawings, 1964, Systemic Painting, 1966; MOMA, The Responsive Eye, 1965; ICA, U. of Pennsylvania, A Romantic Minimalism, 1967; WMAA Annual, 1967; Detroit/ Institute, Color, Image and Form, 1967; Corcoran, 1967; PMA, The Pure and Clear, 1968; Chicago/Contemporary, White on White, 1971–72; ICA, U. of Pennsylvania, Grids, 1972; Documenta V, Kassel, 1972; WMAA (downtown), Nine Artists/Coenties Slip, 1974; Amsterdam/Stedelijk, Fundamental Painting, 1975; U. of Massachusetts, Critical Perspectives in American Art, 1976; Venice Biennial, 1976; MOMA, Drawing Now, 1976; WMAA Biennial, 1977; Cleveland/MA, Four Contemporary Painters, 1978; Buffalo/Albright, American Painting of the 1970's; 1978; ICA, Boston, The Reductive Object, 1979. **Collections:** Aachen/NG; Amsterdam/Stedelijk; Albright/Buffalo; Canberra/National; Hartford/Wadsworth; High Museum; Hirshhorn; Los Angeles/County MA; MOMA; NYU; Ontario; Pasadena/AM; Ridgefield/Aldrich; RISD; SRGM; Tate; Walker; WMAA; Worcester/AM; Yale U. **Bibli-**ography: *Fundamentele Schilderkunst; Lippard 3; Options and Alternatives.*

MARTIN, FLETCHER. b. April 29, 1904, Palisade, Colo.; **d.** May 30, 1979, Guanajuato, Mexico. Self-taught in art. **Taught:** State U. of Iowa, 1940; Kansas City Art Institute and School of Design, 1941–42; ASL, 1948–67; U. of Florida, 1949–52; Mills College, 1951; U. of Minnesota, 1954; San Antonio Art Institute, 1957; Los Angeles/County MA, 1958–59; Washington State U., 1960–61. Artist War Correspondent for *Life* magazine, 1943. Federal A.P.: Mural painting, 1936–37. Traveled USA, Mexico, Europe, North Africa, Australia. **Member:** Woodstock Artists Association; NAD. **Commissions:** US Bureau of Reclamation, 1971–73; National Aeronautics & Space Administration, 1975. **Awards:** PAFA, Walter Lippincott Prize, 1947; NAD, Benjamin Altman Prize, 1949; Ford Foundation/ A.F.A., Artist-in-Residence Grant, 1964. **One-man Exhibitions:** San Diego, 1934; Jake Zeitlin Gallery, Los Angeles, 1939; The Midtown Galleries, 1940, 43; A.A.A. Gallery, NYC, 1948; John Heller Gallery, NYC, 1955, 57. **Retrospectives:** U. of Minnesota, 1954; Roberson Center for the Arts & Sciences, Binghamton, N.Y., 1968. **Group:** MOMA, Americans 1942, circ., 1942; U. of Minnesota; Venice Biennial. **Collections:** Abbott Laboratories; Albany/Institute; Andover/Phillips; Brandeis U.; Britannica; Carleton College; Clearwater/Gulf Coast; Cranbrook; Davenport/ Municipal; Denver/AM; Houston/MFA; Huntington, W. Va.; IBM; State U. of Iowa; Kansas City/Nelson; Library of Congress; Los Angeles County Fair Association; Los Angeles/ County MA; MMA; MOMA; U. of Maine; U. of Miami; U. of Minnesota; PAFA; Roswell; SFMA; WMAA; Witte; Youngstown/Butler. **Bibliography:** American Artists Group Inc. 2; Baur 7; **Ebersole;** Kent, N.; Miller, ed. 1; Zaidenberg, ed. Archives.

MARTIN, FRED. b. June 13, 1927, San Francisco, Calif. **Studied:** U. of California (with James McCray, Glenn Wessels), BA, 1949, MA, 1954; California School of Fine Arts (with David Park, Clyfford Still, Mark Rothko), 1949–50. **Taught:** Oakland/AM, 1954–56; San Francisco Art Institute, 1958– ; Director, 1965– . **Awards:** National Council on the Arts Fellowship, 1971. **Address:** 232 Monte Vista, Oakland, CA 94611. **Dealer:** Quay Gallery, San Francisco. **One-man Exhibitions:** (first) Contemporary Gallery, Sausalito, Calif., 1949; Lucien Labaudt Gallery, San Francisco, 1950; Zoe Dusanne Gallery, Seattle, 1952; de Young, 1954, 64; 6 Gallery, San Francisco, 1955; Oakland/AM, 1958; SFMA, 1958; Spasta Gallery, San Francisco, 1959; Dilexi Gallery, San Francisco, 1961, 66, 68; Cain Gallery, Aspen, Colo., 1962; Minami Gallery, 1963; The Lanyon Gallery, 1964; Royal Marks Gallery, 1965, 66, 68, 70; RAC, 1969; Berkeley Gallery, San Francisco, 1970, 71; SFAI, 1972; SFMA, 1973; Quay Gallery, San Francisco, 1979. **Group:** de Young; California Palace; SFMA, Bay Area 1945–1962, 1968; WMAA Annual, 1969, Extraordinary Realities, 1973. **Collections:** Achenbach Foundation; Oakland/AM; Pasadena/AM; RAC; SFMA; WMAA. **Bibliography:** *Art as a Muscular Principle.* Archives.

MARTIN, KNOX. b. 1923, Barranquilla, Colombia. **Studied:** ASL. US Navy, three years. **Taught:** Yale U., 1965–71; ASL, 1972, 1974–76; U. of Minnesota, 1972. **Address:** 128 Fort Washington Avenue, NYC. **Dealer:** Jack Gallery, NYC. **One-man Exhibitions:** Charles Egan Gallery, 1954, 61; Avant Garde Gallery, NYC, 1956; Holland-Goldowsky Gallery, Chicago, 1958; Rose Fried Gallery, 1963; Fischbach Gallery, 1964, 66; Galeria Bonino Ltd., 1972, 74; Ingber Art Gallery, 1974; IKI Dusseldorf, 1974; National Arts Club, NYC, 1975; Gallery G., Wichita, 1975; Jack Gallery, NYC, 1978; Jankovsky Gallery, NYC, 1975; Ingber Gallery,

NYC, 1976. **Group:** WGMA, 1963; Chicago/AI, 1963; Baltimore/MA, 1963; Buffalo/Albright, 1963; WMAA, 1972; Bradford, England, British Print Biennial, 1974. **Collections:** Austin; U. of California, Berkeley; Corcoran; U. of Illinois; MOMA; NYU; WMAA.

MARTINELLI, EZIO. b. November 27, 1913, West Hoboken, N.J. **Studied:** Academy of Fine Arts, Bologna, Italy, 1931; NAD, 1932–36, with Leon Kroll, Gifford Beal, Robert Aitken (sculpture), Ivan Olinsky. Traveled France, Italy. **Taught:** Pennsylvania School of Industrial Art, Philadelphia, 1946–49; Philadelphia Museum School, 1946–49; Sarah Lawrence College, 1947–75; Parsons School of Design, 1953– ; American Academy, Rome, Artist-in-Residence, 1964–65 (appointed trustee, 1966). Painted only until 1952; began sculpture in 1938. Federal A.P.: Teacher, NYC; easel painter and unit supervisor, 1937–41. **Commissions:** United Nations General Assembly Building, NYC (30-ft. sculpture); Joint Industries Board, 1964 (bronze); Revere Aluminum Co., 1966 (aluminum). **Awards:** L. C. Tiffany Grant, 1936, 64; Guggenheim Foundation Fellowship, 1958, 62; NAD, President's Award; Ford Foundation, **P.P.,** 1963; appointed to the Jury of Selection, John Simon Guggenheim Memorial Foundation, 1963; Ford Foundation/A.F.A., Artist-in-Residence, Sarasota, 1964; NIAL, 1966. **Address:** 11 Jane Street, Saugerties, NY 12477. **One-man Exhibitions:** Philip Ragan Gallery, Philadelphia, 1943; The Willard Gallery, 1946, 47, 52, 55, 64, 66; Seattle/AM; U. of Minnesota; Chicago/AI; Benson Gallery, 1968. **Group:** Art of This Century, 1942–44; PAFA, 1944, 58, 64, 67; Brooklyn Museum, 1947; Chicago/AI, Abstract and Surrealist Art, 1948; WMAA Annuals, 1948, 61, 62, 66; Chicago/AI, Drawings, 1952; Contemporary American Drawings, circ., France, 1954; Walker, Expressionism, 1900–1955, 1956; A.F.A., Major Work in Minor Scale, circ., 1957;

USIA, Eight American Artists, circ., Europe and Asia, 1957–58; VMFA, American Sculpture Today, 1958; Carnegie, 1959; NIAL, 1959, 66; WMAA, Business Buys American Art, 1960; Claude Bernard, Paris, Aspects of American Sculpture, 1960; Newark Museum, Survey of American Sculpture, 1962; Gallery of Modern Art, NYC, 1965; Lincoln, Mass./De Cordova, 1965; U. of St. Thomas (Tex.) 1966. **Collections:** Brooklyn Museum; Chicago/AI; U. of Illinois; Memphis/Brooks; Newark Museum; PMA; SRGM; Seattle/AM; United Nations; WMAA; U. of Wisconsin. **Bibliography:** Moser 1; Seuphor 3. Archives.

MARYAN. b. January 1, 1927, Poland; **d.** June 1977, NYC. **Studied:** Bezalel Art School; l'Ecole National Superieure des Beaux-Arts, Paris, 1951–53. Traveled Israel, Europe, USA; resided Paris, 1950–62. **Awards:** Prix des Critiques d'Art a Paris, 1959. **One-man Exhibitions:** (first) Jerusalem, Israel, 1949; Galerie Breteau, Paris, 1952; Galerie Le Miroir, Brussels, 1954; Tourcoing, 1956; Galerie Rive Gauche, Paris (two-man), 1957; Galerie de France, Paris, 1958, 60, 65; Galerie Kunstnernes Kunsthandel, Copenhagen, 1959; Andre Emmerich Gallery, 1960; Allan Frumkin Gallery, NYC, 1963–66, 68, 69, Chicago, 1963–66, 70; Galleria Juana Mordo, 1964; David Stuart Gallery, 1964; Galerie D. Benador, Geneva, 1966; Galerie Van der Loo, Munich, 1966; Galerie Nova Spectra; The Hague, 1966, 71; Claude Bernard, Paris, 1966, 70; Galeria Sen., Madrid, 1970; Galerie Nord, Lille, 1970; Eindhoven, 1970; Galerie Nicholas, Amsterdam, 1971, 73; Galeria d-Arte la Bussola, Turin, 1971; Galerie Espace, Amsterdam, 1973, 74; Galerie Ariel, Paris, 1977. **Retrospective:** Galerie de France, Paris, 1974. **Group:** Salon des Surindependants, Paris, 1952, 53; Salon du Mai, Paris, 1953–65; Festival de l'Art d'Avant-Garde, Marseilles, 1956; Paris Biennial, Musée de Nantes, 1958; Festival de Bayreuth,

1958; Walker, 1958, 59; XXX Venice Biennial, 1960; Carnegie, 1961, 64, 67; SFMA, Directions—Painting U.S.A., 1963; Torcuato di Tella, Buenos Aires, 1963; Ghent, The Human Figure since Picasso, 1964; The Hague, New Realism, 1964; Chicago/AI, 1964; Paris/Moderne, 1965; PAFA Annual, 1965; Foundation Maeght, 1967; U. of Colorado, 1967; MOMA, 1969; SRGM, 10 Independents, 1972. **Collections:** Carnegie; Chicago/AI; LeHavre/Municipal; MOMA; Museum des 20. Jahrhunderts; Paris/Moderne; Tourcoing.

MASON, ALICE TRUMBULL. b. November 16, 1904, Litchfield, Conn.; **d.** June 28, 1971, NYC. **Studied:** British School, Rome, 1972; NAD, 1923; privately with C. W. Hawthorne, 1924, and Arshile Gorky, 1926. Traveled Italy and around the world, 1920. **Member:** American Abstract Artists; Federation of Modern Painters and Sculptors; SAGA; American Color Print Society. **Awards:** The Print Club, Philadelphia, Charles M. Lea Prize, 1945; Longview Foundation Grant, 1963. **One-man Exhibitions:** (first) Museum of Living Art, NYC, 1948; Hansa Gallery, NYC, 1958; The XXth Century Gallery, NYC, 1967; Washburn Gallery, Inc., NYC, 1974, 77, 80. **Retrospectives:** Nassau Community College, Garden City, N.Y., 1967; WMAA, circ., 1974. **Group:** Federation of Modern Painters and Sculptors Annuals; A.A.A. Gallery, NYC, Annuals: PMA, "8 x 8," 1945; Brooklyn Museum, 1949. **Collections:** Brooklyn Museum; Free Library of Philadelphia; ICA, Washington, D.C.; Library of Congress; MMA; NYPL; PMA; The Pennsylvania State U.; WMAA. **Bibliography:** Moser 1; Reese. Archives.

MATULKA, JAN. b. November 7, 1890, Vlachovo Brezi, Bohemia; **d.** June 22, 1972, Queens, N.Y. To USA, 1907. **Studied:** NAD, with G.W. Maynard, 1908–17. ASL, 1924–25. Traveled Eu-

Jan Matulka   *Bohemian Landscape*   1920–21

rope, USA. **Taught:** ASL, 1929–31. Federal A.P.: Mural for a hospital in Brooklyn, N.Y. **Awards:** Pulitzer Scholarship for Painting. **One-man Exhibitions:** (first) The Artists' Gallery, NYC, 1925; Whitney Studio Club, NYC, 1926, 29; Art Center, NYC, 1926; Modern Gallery, NYC, 1927, also 1930; Rehn Galleries, 1928, 29, 31, 32, 33, 35, 56; The Zabriskie Gallery, 1965; SRGM; Columbia U., 72; ACA Gallery, NYC, 1944; Robert Schoelkopf Gallery, NYC, 1970, 72, 79; Bartholet Gallery, NYC, 1969, 79. **Retrospective:** NCFA, 1979. **Group:** WMAA, 1944; MMA; Chicago/AI; Carnegie, 1944; U. of New Mexico, 1967; Galleries of the Societe Anonyme, NYC, Second Exhibition of Modern Art, 1920; Brooklyn Museum, 1923; Salon des Independants, Paris, 1924; AIGA, Annual, 1925, 26; PAFA, Annual, 1930, 31, 32, 33; Carnegie Annual, 1930, 33; WMAA, First Annual, 1931, 33, 36, 41, 44; WMAA, Abstract Painting in America, 1935; Delaware Art Museum, Avant-Garde Painting and Sculpture in America 1910–25, 1975; NCFA, America as Art, 1976; Houston/MFA, Modern American Painting 1910–40, 1977; WMAA, Synchromism and American Color Abstraction 1910–1925, 1978. **Collections:** ASL; Boston/MFA; Brooklyn Museum; Chicago/AI; Cincinnati/AM; Des Moines; Detroit/Institute; Hartford/Wadsworth; Hirshhorn; MMA; MOMA; Nashville; NCFA; U. of Nebraska; Newark Public Library; U. of New Mexico; U. of North Carolina; NYPL; PAFA; Portland (Ore.)/AM; Prague/National; Seattle/AM; SFMA; St. Louis/City; SRGM; Syracuse/Everson; WMAA; Yale U. **Bibliography:** *Avant-Garde Painting & Sculpture in America, 1910–25*; Blesh 1; Hunter; Hunter 6; Janis, S.; Rose, B., 1; Jan Matulka. Archives.

MAYHEW, RICHARD. b. April 3, 1924, Amityville, N.Y. **Studied:** Brooklyn Museum School, with Edwin Dickinson, Reuben Tam. **Taught:** ASL, to 1969; Smith College, 1969–70; Pratt Institute; Hunter College, 1971–75; The Pennsylvania State U., 1977–79. **Member:** NAD. **Awards:** John Hay Whitney Fellowship, 1958; Ingram Merrill Foundation Grant, 1960; L.C. Tiffany Grant, 1963; NAD, **P.P.,** 1964; NIAL Grant, 1966; NAD, Benjamin Altman Prize, 1970. **Address:** 102 Visual Art Building, University Park, PA 16802. **Dealer:** The Midtown Galleries. **One-man Exhibitions:** The Morris Gallery, NYC, 1957; Washington Irving Gallery, NYC, 1958; Robert Isaacson Gallery, NYC, 1959, 61, 62; Durlacher Brothers, NYC, 1963, 66; The Contemporaries, NYC, 1967; The Midtown Galleries, 1969, 71, 73, 74. **Group:** NAD, 1955, 59; Brooklyn Society of Artists Annual, 1956; ART: USA: 58, NYC, 1958; Chicago/AI, 1961; Youngstown/Butler, 1961; Carnegie, 1961; Brooklyn Museum, 1961; WMAA Annuals; U. of Illinois, 1963. **Collections:** Brooklyn Museum; MMA; NAD; WMAA.

MAZUR, MICHAEL B. b. November 2, 1935, NYC. **Studied:** Amherst College, 1954–58, BA; Academy of Fine Arts, Florence, Italy, 1956–57; Yale U., with Gabor Peterdi, Rico Lebrun, Josef Albers, Jon Schueler, Bernard Chaet, Nicholas Carone, 1959–61, BFA, MFA; privately with Leonard Baskin (printmaking), 1956–58. **Taught:** Yale U., 1960–61, 1972; RISD, 1961–64; Yale U. Summer School, Norfolk, Conn., 1963; Brandeis U., 1965, 1972– ; Queens College, 1973; Brown U., 1974; U. of California, Santa Barbara, 1974, 75. **Commissions:** US Department of the Interior. **Awards:** Memphis/Brooks, **P.P.,** 1961, 62; Boston Printmakers, **P.P.,** 1962; L.C. Tiffany Grant, 1962; Guggenheim Foundation Fellowship, 1964; NIAL, 1964; Library of Congress, Pennell **P.P.;** SAGA, Second Prize; Tamarind Fellowship, 1968; NAD, 1974; Philadelphia Print Club, **P.P. Address:** 5 Walnut Avenue, Cambridge, MA 02140. **Dealers:** Robert Miller Gallery, Inc., NYC; Harcus-Krakow Gallery, Boston. **One-man Exhibitions:** (first)

Michael Mazur *In the Wood—Afterwards* 1980

The Kornblee Gallery, 1961, also 1962, 63, 65; The Gallery, Northampton, Mass., 1963; Boris Mirski Gallery, Boston, 1964; Silvermine Guild, 1964; Alpha Gallery, 1966, 68, 74; Juniata College, 1966; A.A.A. Gallery, NYC, 1968; Finch College, NYC, 1971; U. of Connecticut, 1972; Exeter, 1972; Kutztown State College, 1973; Cortland/SUNY (two-man), 1973; The Ohio State U., 1975; Colgate U., 1973; Terry Dintenfass, Inc., NYC, 1974, 76; Robert Miller Gallery, Inc., NYC, 1978, 80; Harcus Krakow Gallery, Boston, 1978, 80. **Retrospectives:** Brandeis U., 1969; Colgate U., 1973. **Group:** USIA, 10 American Printmakers, circ., Europe; MOMA, 60 Modern Drawings, 1963, also 1965; Library of Congress; Seattle/AM; Kansas City/Nelson; Smith College; The Print Club, Philadelphia; Boston Arts Festival; WMAA Annual, 1967; PAFA, 1967, 69; ICA, Boston, Boston Now; Boston/MFA, Prints of the Sixties; Salon du Mai, Paris, 1969; Museo de Arte Contemporaneo, Cali., Colombia, S.A., I & II Biennials Graficas; XXXV Venice Biennial, 1970; Pratt Graphics Center, NYC, Monotypes, 1972; Library of Congress, 1972, 73, 74; Cleveland/MA, 32 Realists, 1972; Omaha/Joslyn, A Sense of Place, 1973; MOMA, American Prints: 1913–1963, 1974–75; Smithsonian, New American Monotypes, circ., 1978–80; Brussels/

Beaux Arts, La Nouvelle Subjectivite, 1979; MMA, The Painterly Print, 1980. **Collections:** Andover/Phillips; Boston/MFA; Boston Public Library; Brandeis U.; Brooklyn Museum; Chicago/AI; Cincinnati/AM; Colgate U.; Cortland/SUNY; Delaware Art Museum; Fredonia/SUNY; Harvard U.; Kalamazoo/Institute; Library of Congress; MOMA; U. of Maine; U. of Massachusetts; Memphis/Brooks; Minneapolis/Institute; Montreal/MFA; The Ohio State U.; PMA; The Pennsylvania State U.; Portland, Ore./AM; Smith College; Toledo/MA; USIA; WMAA; Wellesley College; Westminster Foundation; Yale U. **Bibliography:** *America 1976;* Arthur 2.

McCHESNEY, ROBERT P. b. January 16, 1913, Marshall, Mo. **Studied:** Washington U., with Fred Conway; Otis Art Institute, Los Angeles. Resided Mexico, one year. Traveled around the world, Mexico, Cuba. **Taught:** California School of Fine Arts, 1949–51; Santa Rosa Junior College, 1957–58. Federal A.P.: Federal Building, Golden Gate International Exposition, San Francisco, 1939 (mural). **Member:** San Francisco Art Institute, board of trustees. **Commissions:** SS *Monterey* (wall decoration); San Francisco Social Service Building (mural), 1978. **Awards:** San Francisco Municipal Art Commission, **P.P.,** 1950, 69; WMAA Annual, **P.P.,** 1955; SFMA, First Prize, 1960; San Francisco Art Festival, Prize, 1979. **Address:** 2955 Sonoma Mountain Road, Petaluma, CA 94952. **One-man Exhibitions:** (first) Raymond and Raymond, Inc., San Francisco, 1944; Pat Wall Gallery, Monterey, 1946; Lucien Labaudt Gallery, San Francisco, 1947, 51; Marquis Gallery, Los Angeles, 1949; SFMA, 1949, 53, 57, 64; Daliel Gallery, Berkeley, 1950; Gump's Gallery, 1952, 53, 55; Myrtle Todes Gallery, Glencoe, Ill., 1958; Bolles Gallery, NYC, 1960; San Francisco, 1960, 61; Parsons Gallery, Los Angeles, 1960, 61; Marshall Art Gallery, Marshall, Calif., 1964; Twentieth Century West Gallery, NYC, 1965; Triangle Art Gallery, 1966; San Francisco Theological Seminary, San Anselmo, Calif., 1966, 69; California State College, Sonoma, 1970; Both-Up Gallery, Berkeley, Calif., 1973, 74; Santa Rosa City Hall, Calif., 1974; California State U., Hawyward, 1977; Capricorn Asunder Gallery, San Francisco, 1974; Lincoln Arts Center, Santa Rosa, 1978. **Retrospective:** Capricorn Asunder Gallery, San Francisco, 1974. **Group:** SFMA, 1945, 50, 53, 60; Phillips, 1947; de Young, 1947, 51, 53, 59, 60, 61; Chicago/AI Annuals, 1947, 54, 60, 61; Los Angeles/County MA, 1949; Sao Paulo, 1955; WMAA Annual, 1955; Corcoran, 1957; California Palace, 1962, 64; Oakland/AM, 1972; Reed College, 1973; UCLA Extension Gallery, 1975. **Collections:** Chicago/AI; Oakland/AM; SFMA; San Francisco Municipal Art Commission; WMAA. **Bibliography:** McChesney. Archives.

McCLELLAN, DOUGLAS EUGENE. b. October 10, 1921, Pasadena, Calif. **Studied:** Art Center School, Los Angeles; Colorado Springs Fine Arts Center, with Boardman Robinson, Jean Charlot; Claremont Graduate School, MFA. **Taught:** Chaffey College, 1950–59; Otis Art Institute, Los Angeles, 1959–61; Scripps College; U. of California, Santa Cruz. **Awards:** Los Angeles/County MA, **P.P.,** 1950, 53; National Orange Show, 1954. **Address:** c/o Art Department, U. of California, Santa Cruz, CA 95064. **One-man Exhibitions:** Felix Landau Gallery, 1953, 55, 57, 59; Pasadena/AM, 1954; U. of California, Riverside, 1955. **Group:** Library of Congress, 1948; SFMA, 1949, 52; Los Angeles/County MA, 1949, 50, 52, 54, 55; Los Angeles County Fair, 1949, 53; MMA, 1950; PAFA, 1953; Corcoran, 1953; Santa Barbara/MA, I Pacific Coast Biennial, 1955; Carnegie, 1955, 57; WMAA, 1957. **Collections:** Los Angeles/County MA; Los Angeles County Fair Association; Pasadena/AM.

McCRACKEN, JOHN. b. December 9, 1934, Berkeley, Calif. **Studied:** California College of Arts and Crafts, 1962, BFA, and 1962–65. **Taught:** U. of California, Irvine and Los Angeles, 1965–68; School of Visual Arts, NYC, 1968–69; Hunter College, NYC, 1971; U. of Nevada. **Address:** c/o Dealer. **Dealer:** Robert Elkon Gallery, NYC. **One-man Exhibitions:** Nicholas Wilder Gallery, 1965, 67, 68; Robert Elkon Gallery, 1966, 67, 68, 72, 73; Ileana Sonnabend Gallery, Paris, 1969, Toronto, 1969, NYC, 1970; ACE Gallery, Vancouver, 1970; Pomona College, 1971; U. of Nevada, 1974. **Group:** Barnsdall Park Municipal Art Gallery, Los Angeles, Los Angeles Sculpture, 1965; Jewish Museum, Primary Structure Sculptures, 1966; WMAA, 1966, 68, 70; Seattle/AM, Ten from Los Angeles, 1966; Los Angeles/County MA, Sculpture of the Sixties, circ., 1967; WGMA, A New Aesthetic, 1967; Paris/Moderne, 1967; Milwaukee, Directions 1: Options, circ., 1968; MOMA, The Art of the Real, 1968; ICA, U. of Pennsylvania, Between Object and Environment, 1969; Eindhoven, Kompas IV, 1969–70; Chicago/AI, 1970; Chicago/Contemporary, Permutations: Light & Color, 1970; MOMA, Ways of Looking, 1971; Documenta V, Kassel, 1972. **Collections:** Chicago/AI; Los Angeles/County MA; MOMA; Milwaukee; Pasadena/AM; SRGM; Toronto; WMAA. **Bibliography:** *Report; USA West Coast.*

McFEE, HENRY LEE. b. April 14, 1886, St. Louis, Mo.; **d.** 1953, Claremont, Calif. **Studied:** Washington U. School of Fine Arts; ASL, Woodstock, N.Y., 1908, with Birge Harrison; Stevenson Art Center, Philadelphia. **Awards:** Carnegie, Hon. Men., 1923; Corcoran, Fourth William A. Clark Prize, 1928; Carnegie, First Hon. Men., 1930; VMFA, **P.P.,** 1935; PAFA, Joseph E. Temple Gold Medal, 1937; Los Angeles County Fair, **P.P.,** 1940, 49; Guggenheim Foundation Fellowship, 1941; NIAL, 1945; elected an associate of the NAD, 1949. **One-man Exhibitions:** Rehn Galleries, 1927, 29, 33, 36, 50; Pasadena/AM, 1950. **Retrospective:** Scripps College, 1950. **Group:** Panama-Pacific Exposition, San Francisco, 1915; Detroit/Institute; Cleveland/MA; Anderson Galleries, NYC, Forum Exhibition, 1916; Carnegie, 1923–49; Corcoran, 1921, 26, 1928–44; PAFA; Chicago/AI; St. Louis/City; U. of New Mexico, Cubism: Its Impact in the USA, 1967. **Collections:** Brooklyn Museum; Buffalo/Albright; Carnegie; Cleveland/MA; Columbus; Corcoran; Detroit/Institute; Los Angeles County Fair Association; MMA; PMA; Phillips; St. Louis/City; Scripps College; Taft Museum; VMFA; WMAA. **Bibliography:** Barker 2; Baur 7; Brown; Brown 2; Cahill and Barr, eds.; Cheney; Hall; Hunter 6; Huyghe; *Index of 20th Century Artists;* Janis, S.; Kent, N.; Mellquist; Mendelowitz; **Millier 1;** Pearson 2; Poore; Pousette-Dart, ed.; Richardson, E.P.; Smith, S.C.K.; Watson, E.W., 2; *Woodstock: An American Art Colony 1902–1977;* Wright 1.

McGARREL, JAMES. b. February 22, 1930, Indianapolis, Ind. Resides Italy, 1971– . **Studied:** Indiana U., with Alton Pickens, Leo Steppat, AB; UCLA, with John Paul Jones, Gordon Nunes, MA; Skowhegan School; Academy of Fine Arts, Stuttgart. Traveled USA, Europe; resided Paris, 1964–65. **Taught:** Reed College, 1956–59; Indiana U., 1959– ; Skowhegan School, summers, 1964, 68. Foreign correspondent member of the Academie des Beaux-Arts de l'Institut de France, 1970. **Member:** CAA, board of directors, 1969–73; National Advisory Board, Tamarind Institute, 1977–. **Awards:** Fulbright Fellowship, 1955; Tamarind Fellow, 1962; NIAL, Grant, 1963; Ford Foundation, **P.P.,** 1963, 64; J.S. Guggenheim Fellowship, 1964; National Council on the Arts, Sabbatical Grant to Artists Who Teach. **Address:** 5699 East Lampkins Ridge Road, Bloomington, IN 47401; Polgeto, 06019 Umbertide, Italy. **Dealer:** Allan

James McGarrell   *Double Double Portrait,*
Gail 1968

Frumkin Gallery, NYC and Chicago;
Galleria II Fante Di Spade, Milan;
Galerie Claude Bernard, Paris. **One-
man Exhibitions:** (first) Frank Perls
Gallery, 1955, also 1957, 58, 62, 64;
Portland, Ore./AM, 1959, 62; Indiana
U., 1960, 63; Allan Frumkin Gallery,
Chicago, 1960, 62, 65, 67, 71, 74; Salt
Lake Art Center, Salt Lake City, 1962;
Gallery 288, St. Louis, 1963; U. of Flor-
ida, 1964; Galleria Galatea, Turin, 1965,
66, 68; Pittsfield/Berkshire, 1966; Tragos
Gallery, Boston, 1967; Galleria II Fante
de Spada, Rome, 1967, 71, 72, 74, 76;
Claude Bernard, Paris, 1967, 68, 74;
Galleria dei Lanzi, Milan, 1970, 72;
Utah, 1972; Allan Frumkin Gallery,
NYC, 73, 77, 80; Bedford House Gal-
lery, London, 1973; Clark-Benton Gal-
lery, Santa Fe, 1977. **Group:** WMAA
Annuals, 1957, 59, 60, 67; MOMA, New
Images of Man, 1959; U. of Illinois,
1959, 61, 63; Carnegie, 1959, 64; III
International Biennial Exhibition of
Prints, Tokyo, 1962; WMAA, Fifty Cal-
ifornia Artists, 1962–63; Chicago/AI An-
nual, 1963; Tate, Dunn International,
1964; Documenta III, Kassel, 1964;
PAFA, 1964; U. of Kentucky, 1966,

Graphics 1968, 1968; XXXIV Venice
Biennial, 1968; SFMA, 1968; Smithso-
nian, 1969; Indiana U., American
Scene: 1900–1970, 1970; Le Centre
Cultural Americain, Paris (four-man),
1971; Kansas City/AI, Narrative Paint-
ing, 1972; Dayton/AI, Eight American
Painters, 1972; Galleria Communale
d'Arte Contemporanea, Una Tendenza
Americana, 1973; MOMA, American
Prints 1913–1963, 1974–75; Boston U.,
Drawings by American Realists, 1977;
WMAA, Art about Art, 1978; Venice
Biennale, 1980. **Collections:** Baltimore/
MA; Boston/MFA; Brooklyn Museum;
Chicago/AI; Hamburg; Hirshhorn; Indi-
ana U.; Kansas City/AI; Kansas City/
Nelson; MOMA; U. of Massachusetts;
National Gallery; U. of Nebraska; U. of
Oregon; PAFA; Paris/Beaubourg; Paris/
Moderne; Portland, Ore./AM; Reed
College; SFMA; Santa Barbara/MA; U.
of Texas; Utah; WMAA; U. of Wichita.
Bibliography: Arthur 2; Geske;
Honisch and Jensen, eds.

McLAUGHLIN, JOHN. b. May 21,
1898, Sharon, Mass.; **d.** March 1976,
Dana Point, Calif. **Studied:** Roxbury
Latin School; Andover/Phillips; self-
taught in art. US Army Intelligence,
1941–45. Traveled the Orient, resided
Japan for many years beginning 1935.
Began to paint 1938. **Awards:** Tamarind
Fellowship, 1963; Corcoran Biennial,
Bronze Medal, 1967; National Council
on the Arts, Visual Arts Award, 1967.
One-man Exhibitions: Felix Landau
Gallery, 1953, 58, 62, 63, 66; U. of
California, Riverside, 1958; Long Beach/
MA, 1960; K. Kazimir Gallery, Chicago,
1964; Occidental College, 1968; The
Landau-Alan Gallery, NYC, 1968; U. of
California, Irvine, 1971; Nicholas Wil-
der Gallery, 1972; Andre Emmerich
Gallery, NYC, 1972, 74; Corcoran and
Corcoran, Coral Gables, 1973; Felicity
Samuel Gallery, London, 1975. **Retro-
spectives:** Pasadena/AM, 1956, 63;
Corcoran, 1968; WMAA, 1974; La Jolla,
1973. **Group:** Los Angeles/County MA
Annuals, 1949, 50, 54–60; California

State Fair, 1950; Los Angeles/County MA, Contemporary Painting in the United States, 1951; Sao Paulo, 1955; SFMA, Art in the Twentieth Century, 1955; Corcoran, 1955; Long Beach/MA, Fifteen Americans, circ., 1956; Walker, 1956; Houston/MFA, The Sphere of Mondrian, 1957; VMFA, American Painting, 1958; U. of Nebraska, 1958; Denver/AM, 1958; Los Angeles/County MA, Four Abstract Classicists, circ., 1959–61; ICA, London, 1960; A.F.A., Purist Painting, circ., 1960–61; SFMA, Fifty California Artists, circ., 1962; WMAA, Geometric Abstraction in America, circ., 1962; Chicago/AI, 1964; MOMA, The Responsive Eye, 1965; Corcoran, 1967; Pasadena/AM, West Coast: 1945–1969, 1969; Hayward Gallery, London, 11 Los Angeles Artists, 1971; MOMA, Color as Language, circ., 1975; Los Angeles/County MA, Los Angeles Hard Edge, 1977; Los Angeles/County MA, California: Five Footnotes to Modern Art History, 1977; Lincoln, Mass./De Cordova, Born in Boston, 1979; Claremont Colleges, Black and White Are Colors, 1979. **Collections:** Amherst College; Andover/Phillips; Bowdoin College; U. of California; Corcoran; Hartford/Wadsworth; Long Beach/MA; Los Angeles/County MA; MIT; MMA; MOMA; NCFA; U. of New Mexico; Oakland/AM; Pasadena/AM; Santa Barbara/MA; Stanford U. **Bibliography:** *Black and White Are Colors;* **John McLaughlin;** *7 Decades; The State of California Painting;* Weller. Archives.

McLEAN, RICHARD. b. April 12, 1934, Hoquiam, Wash. **Studied:** California College of Arts and Crafts, 1958, BFA; Mills College, 1962, MFA; Oakland/AM, 1962. **Taught:** San Francisco State College, 1963– ; California College of Arts and Crafts, 1963–65. **Address:** 5840 Heron Bridge, Oakland, CA 94718. **Dealer:** OK Harris Works of Art. **One-man Exhibitions:** Lucien Labaudt Gallery, San Francisco, 1957; RAC, 1963; Berkeley Gallery, San Francisco, 1964,

66, 68; Valparaiso U. (Ind.), 1965; U. of Omaha, 1967; OK Harris Works of Art (two-man), 1971, 73, 75, 78; Galerie de Gestlo, Hamburg, 1976; John Berggruen Gallery, San Francisco, 1976. **Group:** SFAI Annuals, 1961, 62, East Bay Realists, circ., 1966; Hayward Gallery, London, Four Painters, 1967; U. of Arizona, 80 Contemporaries in the West, 1967; U. of California, Davis, People Painters, 1970; WMAA, 22 Realists, 1970; Expo '70, Osaka, 1970; Chicago/Contemporary, Radical Realism, 1971; Documenta V. Kassel, 1972; Buffalo/Albright, Working in California, 1972; Stuttgart/WK, Amerikanischer Fotorealismus, cir., 1972; Cleveland/MA, 32 Realists, 1972; New York Cultural Center, Realism Now, 1972; Lunds Konsthall, Sweden, Amerikansk Realism, 1973; Los Angeles Municipal Art Gallery, Separate Realities, 1973; CNAC, Hyperrealistes Americains/Realistes Europeens, 1974; Hartford/Wadsworth, New/Photo Realism, 1974; Tokyo Biennial, 1974; Wichita State U., The New Realism, Rip-Off or Reality? 1975; Reed College, American Realism, 1975; Purchase/SUNY, Photo-Realist Watercolors, 1976; SFMA, Painting and Sculpture in California; The Modern Era, 1976; Stratford, Ontario, Aspects of Realism, 1976; California State U., Chicago, A comparative Study of 19th Century California Painting and Contemporary California Realism, 1977; Canberra/National, Illusion and Reality, 1977. **Collections:** Aachen/NG; A.V. Gunuchian, Inc.; Reed College; VMFA; WMAA. **Bibliography:** *Amerikanischer Fotorealismus; Kunst un 1970;* Sager; *The State of California Painting.*

McNEIL, GEORGE. b. February 22, 1908, NYC. **Studied:** Pratt Institute, 1927–29; ASL, 1930–33; Hofmann School, 1933–36; Columbia U., BS, MA, Ed.D. US Navy, 1943–46. Traveled Cuba, Europe, North Africa, the Orient. **Taught:** Pratt Institute, 1946– ; U. of Wyoming, 1946–48; U. of California,

Berkeley, 1955–56; Syracuse U., 1974; Columbia U., 1975. Federal A.P.: Designed abstract murals, 1935–40. **Awards:** Ford Foundation, **P.P.**, 1963; National Council on the Arts, 1966; Guggenheim Foundation Fellowship, 1969. **Address:** 195 Waverly Avenue, Brooklyn, NY 11205. **One-man Exhibitions:** (first) Lyceum Gallery, Havana, 1941; Black Mountain College, 1947; U. of Wyoming, 1948; U. of New Mexico, 1948; U. of Colorado, 1948; Charles Egan Gallery, Boston, 1953; Hendler Gallery, Philadelphia, 1954; Poindexter Gallery, 1957, 59; The Howard Wise Gallery, NYC, 1960, 62, 64, 67; Nova Gallery, Boston, 1961; Colby Junior College, 1965; U. of Texas, 1966; Great Jones Gallery, NYC, 1966; Des Moines, 1969; Pratt Institute, Manhattan Center, NYC, 1973; U. of California, Santa Cruz, 1974; Northern Arizona U., 1975; Landmark Gallery, NYC, 1975; Aaron Berman Gallery, NYC, 1977; Terry Dintenfass, Inc., NYC, 1979. **Group:** American Abstract Artists, 1936; MOMA, New Horizons in American Art, 1936; New York World's Fair, 1939; Chicago/AI, Abstact and Surrealist Art, 1948; MOMA, Abstract Painting and Sculpture in America, 1951; WMAA Annuals, 1953, 57, 61; Carnegie, 1953, 55, 58; Walker, 60 American Painters, 1960; Cleveland/MA, Some Contemporary American Artists, 1961; SRGM, Abstract Expressionists and Imagists, 1961; USIA, American Painting, circ., Latin America, 1961; PAFA, 1962; Hartford/Wadsworth, 1962; Chicago/AI, 1963; MOMA, Hans Hofmann and His Students, circ., 1963–64; WMAA, The 1930's, 1968; MOMA, The New American Painting and Sculpture, 1969; U. of New Mexico, American Abstract Artists, 1977. **Collections:** Alcoa; Brooklyn Museum; Ciba-Geigy Corp.; Havana/Nacional; U. of Michigan; MOMA; NYU; Newark Museum; U. of New Mexico; U. of North Carolina; Oklahoma; U. of Texas; WGMA; WMAA; Waitsfield/Bundy; Walker. **Bibliography:** Passloff; Pousette-Dart, ed.; Ritchie 1; Sandler. Archives.

MEEKER, DEAN JACKSON. b. May 18, 1920, Orchard, Colo. **Studied:** Chicago Art Institute School, BFA, MFA; Northwestern U.; U. of Wisconsin. **Taught:** U. of Wisconsin, 1946– . **Awards:** Milwaukee, Medal of Honor, 1952, 56; Guggenheim Foundation Fellowship, 1959. **Address:** c/o Art Department, U. of Wisconsin, Madison, WI 33706. **Dealer:** Jane Haslem Fine Arts, Washington, D.C. **One-man Exhibitions:** Milwaukee, 1950; Lawrence College, 1953; U. of North Dakota, 1954; U. of Wisconsin, 1955; Chicago/AI, 1956; U. of New Mexico, 1956; Los Angeles/County MA, 1957; La Gravure, Paris, 1959; Maxwell Galleries, Ltd., San Francisco, 1968; Haslem Fine Arts, Inc., 1969; Jacques Baruch Gallery, 1974. **Group:** PAFA, 1946–53; Brooklyn Museum, 1951–55; Chicago/AI, 1952; SFMA, 1952–54; Walker, 1952–54; Chicago/AI, Exhibition Momentum, 1952–54; Milwaukee; Connecticut College; U. of Missouri; Lawrence College; Library of Congress, 1952, 54, 55; MMA, 1953; Seattle/AM, 1953–1955; The Hague, 1954; Boston/MFA, 1954–56; MOMA, 1955; Los Angeles/County MA, 1959. **Collections:** Beloit College; Bibliotheque Nationale; Boston/MFA; Brooklyn College; Carleton College; Cornell U.; Dallas/MFA; Denison U.; Denver/AM; Kansas City/Nelson; Library of Congress; Lincoln, Mass./De Cordova; MOMA; Milwaukee; U. of Oklahoma; PAFA; The Print Club, Philadelphia; SFMA; Seattle/AM; USIA; Victoria and Albert Museum; U. of Wisconsin. **Bibliography:** Hayter 1.

MEHRING, HOWARD. b. February 19, 1931, Washington, D.C. **Studied:** Wilson College, BS. Ed., 1953; The Catholic U. of America, MFA, 1955. Traveled Spain, Portugal, Italy, France, England, 1962–66, 1968. **Awards:** Corcoran, First Prize, 1965. **Address:** c/o Dealer. **Dealer:** A.M. Sachs Gallery. **One-man Exhibitions:** (first) Sculptors Studio, Washington, D.C., 1957; Origo

Gallery, Washington D.C., 1959; Jefferson Place Gallery, 1961, 62; Adams Morgan Gallery, Washington, D.C., 1963; A.M. Sachs Gallery, 1965, 66, 68, 70; Galerie Haselem, Munich, 1970. **Group:** Carnegie, 1961; Los Angeles/County MA, Post Painterly Abstraction, 1964; WGMA, circ., 1965–66; Corcoran, 1966; NCFA, 1966; SRGM, Systemic Painting, 1966; SRGM, Seven Decades, 1967; MOMA, The 1960's, 1967; WMAA Annual, 1967; Ringling, Washington Painters, 1969; Edmonton Art Gallery, Alberta, Ten Washington Artists, 1950–1970, 1970. **Collections:** Brandeis U.; Chase Manhattan Bank; Corcoran; Hartford/Wadsworth; Los Angeles/County MA; MOMA; NCFA; The New York Bank for Savings; Phillips; SRGM; Seagram Collection; U. of Texas; WGMA; WMAA; Woodward Foundation. **Bibliography:** Alloway 3.

MEIGS, WALTER. b. September 21, 1918, NYC. **Studied:** Ecole des Beaux-Arts, Fontainebleau, Diplome, 1939; Syracuse U., BFA, 1941; State U. of Iowa, MFA, 1949; and with R. Lotterman. US Army, more than three years, World War II. Traveled France, Greece; resided Greece, 1961–64, Spain, 1965– . **Taught:** U. of Nebraska, 1949–53; U. of Connecticut, 1953–61. **Awards:** Walker, 1951; Silvermine Guild, 1954; Slater, First Prize, 1955, 56; Boston Arts Festival, Grand Prize, 1956; and some 20 others. **Address:** c/o Dealer. **Dealer:** Harmon Gallery, Naples, Fla. **One-man Exhibitions:** (first) The Downtown Gallery; U. of Nebraska, 1952; The Alan Gallery, NYC, 1954; Wesleyan U., 1956; New London, 1956; Boris Mirski Gallery, Boston, 1957; Lee Nordness Gallery, NYC, 1958, 64, 67; Lincoln, Mass./De Cordova, 1959; Frank Oehlschlaeger Gallery, Sarasota, Fla., 1965; Harmon Gallery, Naples, Fla., 1966. **Group:** Walker Biennial, 1951; Omaha/Joslyn, 1952; Boston Arts Festival; Berkshire Art Festival; Youngstown/Butler, 1957; Carnegie; WMAA Annuals; U. of Illinois. **Collections:** Amherst College;

Birmingham, Ala./MA; Denver/AM; Fort Worth; Hartford/Wadsworth; Lincoln, Mass./De Cordova; The Pennsylvania State U.; Springfield, Mo./AM; USIA; Utica; Youngstown/Butler. **Bibliography:** Nordness, ed. Archives.

MENKES, SIGMUND. b. May 7, 1896, Lwow, Poland. **Studied:** In Europe. **Member:** NAD; Federation of Modern Painters and Sculptors. **Awards:** Corcoran, 1941, First Prize, Gold Medal, 1947; PAFA, Medal, 1945; NIAL, 1955; ART:USA:58, NYC, 1958; Audubon Artists, Gold Medal of Honor, 1965, Silver Anniversary Medal, 1967; Polish Institute of Arts and Sciences, Award for Collective Work, 1968. **Address:** 5075 Fieldstone Road, Riverdale, N.Y. **One-man Exhibitions:** Mrs. Cornelius J. Sullivan Gallery, NYC; Le Portique, Paris, 1928; A.A.A. Gallery, NYC, 1936–54; Durand-Ruel Gallery, NYC, 1941. **Group:** Carnegie; Chicago/AI; Corcoran; PAFA; U. of Nebraska; Cleveland/MA; American U.; State U. of Iowa; Cranbrook; MMA; WMAA; Toronto. **Collections:** Abbott Laboratories; Belgrade/National; Britannica; Brooklyn Museum; Cranbrook; Davenport/Municipal; Denver/AM; Greece/National; Hirshhorn; Jerusalem/National; MMA; U. of Miami; Montclair/AM; Musée du Jeu de Paume; NIAL; PAFA; Tel Aviv; WMAA; Walker; Warsaw/National; Wichita/AM. **Bibliography:** Genauer; Pousette-Dart, ed.; Zaidenberg, ed.

MESIBOV, HUGH. b. December 29, 1916, Philadelphia, Pa. **Studied:** Graphic Sketch Club, Philadelphia; PAFA; Barnes Foundation. Traveled Europe, Mediterranean, Israel, USA. **Taught:** Lenox Hill Neighborhood Association, NYC, 1949–57; Wiltwyck School for Boys, Esopus, N.Y., 1957–66; Rockland Community College, Suffern, N.Y., 1966. **Member:** PAFA Fellowship Association; Philadelphia Watercolor Club. Federal A.P.: Graphics, drawings, watercolors, oils, mural design. **Commissions:** US Post Office, Hubbard, Ohio (mural). **Awards:** The Print Club, Philadelphia, 1941, 46; Hallmark International Competition, 1952; PAFA, 1952, 58; Philadelphia Watercolor Club, Thornton Oakley Memorial Prize, 1968, 76. **Address:** 377 Saddle River Road, Monsey, NY 10952. **One-man Exhibitions:** (first) Carlen Gallery, Philadelphia, 1940; Philadelphia Art Alliance, 1945; Chinese Gallery, NYC, 1947; Bookshop Gallery, Aspen, Colo., 1951, 53; The Morris Gallery, NYC, 1954; Pied Piper Gallery, Aspen, Colo., 1954; Artists' Gallery, NYC, 1956, 58; Sunken Meadow Gallery, Kings Park, N.Y., 1958; Gallery Mayer, NYC, 1959; Elizabeth Nelson Gallery, Chicago, 1962; Rockland Community College, 1964–68, 69, 72; Mansfield State College, 1968; High Point Galleries, Lenox, Mass., 1968; Tappan Zee Theater, Nyack, N.Y., 1967, 68, 69; St. Thomas Aquinas College, Sparkhill, N.Y., 1971; Finkelstein Memorial Library, Spring Valley, N.Y., 1978; Hopper House Gallery, Nyack, N.Y., 1979. **Group:** New York World's Fair, 1939; Carnegie, 1939; Philadelphia Art Alliance, 1940, 41, 45; Harrisburg, Pa.; PAFA, 1943, 1952–55, 57; Library of Congress, 1951; Brooklyn Museum, 1951, 1953–55; WMAA, 1956–59; Corcoran, 1959; MOMA, 1961; Philadelphia Art Alliance, 1967; AAAL, 1967. **Collections:** Albion College; Barnes Foundation; Canadian Society of Graphic Art; Carnegie; Free Library of Philadelphia; MMA; NYU; New York Hilton Hotel; U. of Oregon; PAFA; PMA; WMAA; U. of Wyoming.

MESTROVIC, IVAN. b. August 15, 1883, Vrpolje, Croatia; **d.** January 17, 1962, Notre Dame, Ind. **Studied:** Privately with Otto Koenig in Vienna, 1899; Academy of Fine Arts, Vienna, 1900–04, with E. Hellmer, H. Bitterlich, Otto Wagner. Member of Yugoslav Provisional National Assembly, 1919. Traveled Italy, France, Austria, USA. To USA, 1947; citizen, 1954. **Taught:** Syracuse U., 1947–55; U. of Notre Dame, 1956–62. **Member:** AAAL, 1953. **Commissions:** Grant Park, Chicago, 1925; Unknown Soldier Memorial, Belgrade, 1934; equestrian figure of King Carl, 1938–39; Vatican commissions, 1942. **Awards:** Hon. Member, Academy of Fine Arts, Vienna, 1952; AAAL, Award of Merit Medal, 1953; American Institute of Architects, Fine Arts Medal, 1955; Hon. DFA, Colgate U., Ohio Wesleyan U., Syracuse U., Marquette U., U. of Notre Dame, and Columbia U. **One-man Exhibitions:** Vienna Secession, 1909; Mestrovic Museum, 1910; Musée du Jeu de Paume, 1933; MMA, 1947; Musée Rodin, Paris, 1969. **Group:** Vienna Secession, 1903, 04; Salon d'Automne, Paris, 1905; International Exhibition, Rome, 1911; Victoria and Albert Museum, 1915; Musée du Petit Palais, Paris, 1919. **Collections:** Belgrade/National; Brooklyn Museum; Buffalo/Albright; Chicago/AI; Detroit/Institute; Mestrovic Gallery; Mestrovic Museum; U. of Minnesota; Montreal/MFA; Prague/National; St. Anthony's College; San Diego; Syracuse U.; Tate; Toronto; Victoria and Albert Museum. **Bibliography:** Bulliet 1; Cheney; Christensen; **Keckemet;** Lee and Burchwood; Licht, F.; Mendelowitz; Pach 1; Ramsden 2; Salvini; Selz, J.; Taft.

METCALF, JAMES. b. March 11, 1925. NYC. **Studied:** Dayton Art Institute School; PAFA, 1944–46; Central School of Arts and Crafts, London, 1950–53. US Army, 1943–44. Traveled Europe, USA; resided Paris. **Commissions:** War Memorial for Middletown, Ohio, 1949. **Awards:** Copley Foundation Grant, 1957; Clark Foundation Grant. **Address:** Springfield Pike, Yellow Springs, OH 45387. **One-man Exhibitions:** Galerias Augusta, Barcelona, 1955; Galerie Furstenberg, Paris, 1959; Alexander Iolas Gallery, 1961; Galerie J. Paris, 1962; Galerie Europe, Paris, 1963; Albert Loeb Gallery, NYC, 1964. **Group:** Dayton/AI, 1946; Cincinnati/

AM, 1947; a gallery in Springfield, Ohio, 1947, 48; Goldsmith's Hall, London, 1952; III Biennial of Spanish-American Art, Barcelona, 1955; V Sao Paulo Biennial, 1959; Exposition Internationale de la Sculpture, Paris, 1962; Actualite de la Sculpture, Paris, 1963; Documenta III, Kassel, 1964. **Collections:** U. of Arizona; Museum des 20. Jahrhunderts; New York Hilton Hotel; Yale U. **Bibliography: Hunter 4;** Read 3; Seuphor 3.

MILLER, KENNETH HAYES. b. March 11, 1878, Oneida, N.Y.; **d.** January 1, 1952, NYC. **Studied:** ASL, with H.S. Mowbray, Kenyon Cox, F.L. Mora, Frank V. DuMond. Traveled Europe. **Taught:** New York School of Art, 1899–1911; ASL, 1911–35, 1937–43, 1945–52. **Member:** NAD; Artists Equity; NIAL. **Awards:** Chicago/AI, Ada S. Garrett Prize, 1945; NAD, Gold Medal, 1943; NIAL, 1947. **One-man Exhibitions:** Montross Gallery, NYC, 1922, 23, 25, 28; Rehn Galleries, 1929, 35; Utica, 1953; ASL, 1953; The Zabriskie Gallery, NYC, 1970, 71, 79; AAA, NYC, 1979. **Group:** Chicago/AI; The Armory Show, 1913; Buffalo/Albright; RISD, PAFA; Musée de Luxembourg; Paris; Brooklyn Museum; Carnegie; Corcoran; NAD; WMAA. **Collections:** Andover/Phillips; Bibliotheque Nationale; Chicago/AI; Cleveland/MA; Columbus; Hartford/Wadsworth; Library of Congress; Los Angeles/County MA; MMA; MOMA; NYPL; PAFA; Phillips; San Diego; Utica; VMFA; WMAA; Youngstown/Butler. **Bibliography:** Brown 2.

MILLER, RICHARD. b. March 15, 1930, Fairmount, W. Va. **Studied:** PAFA, with Franklin Watkins, 1948; American U., with William H. Calfee, BA, 1949–53; Columbia U., with John Heliker, MA, 1956. Traveled Europe and USA extensively. **Taught:** Kansas City/AI, 1968–69; Scarsdale Studio School, 1970–75; Rye Art Center, 1976–80; privately. Professional actor-

singer. **Commissions:** General Motors Building, NYC. **Awards:** Gertrude V. Whitney Scholarship, 1948, 56; Fulbright Fellowship (Paris), 1953. **Address:** 222 West 83rd Street, NYC 10024. **Dealers:** E. P. Gurewitsch Gallery, NYC; Barbara Fiedler, Washington, D.C. **One-man Exhibitions:** (first) Washington D.C., Public Library, 1945; Trans-Lux Gallery, Washington, D.C., 1948; Watkins Gallery, Washington, D.C., 1951; Bader Gallery, Washington, D.C., 1954, 61; Baltimore/MA, 1955; The Graham Gallery, 1960, 62, 63, 65; Jefferson Place Gallery, 1966; Drew U., 1967; Jewish Community Center, Kansas City, Mo., 1969; Albrecht Gallery, St. Joseph, Mo., 1969; Long Island U., 1973; Rye (N.Y.) Library Gallery, 1980. **Group:** WMAA Annual; PAFA Annual; WMAA, Fulbright Artists, 1958; Salon National, Paris; Pan-American Union, Washington, D.C.; U. of Nebraska; San Antonio/McNay, 1960; Carnegie, 1961; Corcoran, 1961; Finch College; V International Biennial Exhibition of Prints, Tokyo, 1966. **Collections:** U. of Arizona; Columbia U.; Hirshhorn; Phillips; U. of Rochester; St. Joseph/Albrecht.

MILLER, RICHARD McDERMOTT. b. April 30, 1922, New Philadelphia, Ohio. **Studied:** Cleveland Institute of Art, 1940–42, 1949–52. US Army, 1942–46. Traveled Mexico, Europe, China. **Taught:** Queens College, City University of New York, 1967. **Members:** Sculptors Guild; NAD Alliance of Figurative Artists. **Awards:** May Page Scholarship, Cleveland Institute of Art, 1951; Youngstown/Butler, **P.P.,** 1970; NAD, Elizabeth N. Watrous Gold Medal, 1974; AAIAL, 1978. **Address:** 61 Grove Street, NYC 10014. **Dealer:** Washburn Gallery, NYC. **One-man Exhibitions:** Peridot Gallery, 1964, 66, 67, 69; Holland Gallery, 1965; Feingarten, 1966; Duke U., 1967; Raleigh/NCMA, 1967; Cleveland/MA 1968; Alwin Gallery, London, 1968; Columbia, S.C./MA, 1969; Duke U. (two-man), 1971; Washburn Gallery, Inc., 1971, 74, 75,

77; Joe deMers Gallery, Hilton Head, S.C., 1971; Queens College, N.Y., 1978. **Group:** WMAA, Sculpture Annual, 1964; NIAL, 1965; New Paltz/SUNY, 20 Representational Artists, 1969; Baltimore/MA, The Part Is the Whole, 1969; Youngstown/Butler, Sculpture Annual, 1970, 71; U. of Nebraska, American Sculpture, 1970, 73; St. Cloud State College, New Realism, '70, 1970; WMAA Biennial, 1971; The Pennsylvania State U., Living American Artists and the Figure, 1974; New York Cultural Center, Three Centuries of the American Nude, 1975; Sculptors Guild Annual, NYC, 1977. **Collections:** Ashland Oil Inc., NYC; Canton Art Institute; Columbia, S.C./MA; Hirshhorn; U. of Houston; Massillon Museum; U. of Nebraska; U. of North Carolina; Union National Bank & Trust Co., Kansas City, Mo.; WMAA; Youngstown/Butler.

MILLMAN, EDWARD. b. January 1, 1907, Chicago, Ill.; **d.** February 11, 1964, Woodstock, N.Y. **Studied:** Chicago Art Institute School, 1923–28, with Leon Kroll; privately with Diego Rivera in Mexico City, 1934–35 (fresco painting). **Taught:** Florida Gulf Coast Art Center, Inc., 1951; Indiana U., 1951–52; Washington U., 1952; U. of Arkansas, 1953; Cornell U., 1954; ASL, 1954–56, summer, 1950; Layton School of Art, 1955; U. of Buffalo, 1955, summer, 1956; Munson-William-Proctor Institute, Utica, N.Y., 1955–56; Rensselaer Polytechnic Institute, 1956–64. **Commissions** (murals): US Post Offices in Moline, Ill., 1935, Decatur, Ill., 1936, and St. Louis, Mo. (with Mitchell Siporin), 1939–41; Chicago City Hall. **Awards:** Guggenheim Foundation Fellowship, 1945; Ohio U., First Prize, 1952. **One-man Exhibitions:** The Downtown Gallery, 1942; A.A.A. Gallery, NYC, 1948; U. of Kansas City, 1949; Louisiana State U., 1949; Florida State U., 1949; Clearwater/Gulf Coast, 1950; Indiana U., 1951; U. of Arkansas,

1953; Tulsa/Philbrook, 1953; The Alan Gallery, NYC, 1954; Cornell U., 1954; Layton School of Art, 1955; Buffalo/Albright, 1955; Utica, 1956; Chicago/AI, 1956, 62; Lee Nordness Gallery, NYC, 1959, 61; Galleria d'Arte Annunciata Milan, 1960; Rensselaer Polytechnic Institute, 1961; Ulster Community College, Stone Ridge, N.Y. (two-man), 1972. **Group:** WMAA Annuals; Chicago/AI; Brooklyn Museum; and many others. **Collections:** Abbott Laboratories; Brandeis U.; Brooklyn Museum; Chicago/AI; Clearwater/Gulf Coast; Jewish Museum; MOMA; PAFA; U. of Pennsylvania; St. Louis/City; US Navy; Utica; WMAA; Washington U.; Youngstown/Butler. **Bibliography:** Bruce and Watson; Nordness, ed.; Pousette-Dart, ed.; *Woodstock: An American Art Colony 1902–1977*; Zaidenberg, ed. Archives.

MITCHELL, FRED. b. November 24, 1923, Meridian, Miss. **Studied:** Carnegie Institute of Technology, 1942–43; Cranbrook Academy of Art, 1946–48, BFA, MFA; Academy of Fine Arts, Rome. **Taught:** Cranbrook Academy of Art, 1955–59; Positano (Italy) Art Workshop, 1956; NYU, 1961– ; Cornell U., 1969; Binghamton/SUNY, 1976– ; Utica, 1977. A cofounder of the Tanager Gallery, NYC. **Commissions:** Mississippi State College for Women (cast concrete screen). **Awards:** Scholarship to Carnegie Institute of Technology; Traveling Fellowship (Italy), 1948–51; Ford Foundation Artist-in-Residence, Columbia, S.C./MA. **Address:** 92 Hester Street, NYC 10002. **One-man Exhibitions:** (first) Municipal Gallery Jackson, Miss., 1942; Tanager Gallery, NYC, 1953; Positano (Italy) Art Workshop, 1956; The Howard Wise Gallery, Cleveland, 1957, 59; The Howard Wise Gallery, NYC, 1960, 63; i Gallery, La Jolla, 1964; Kasha Heman, Chicago, 1964; Columbia, S.C./MA, 1965; Wooster Community Center, Danbury, Conn., 1966; Cornell U. (three-man), 1969; Roko Gallery, 1973. **Group:** SRGM, Younger American Painters, 1954; Dallas/MFA, 1954; Walker, Vanguard, 1955; Cranbrook. 1958; Carnegie, 1961. **Collections:** Columbus; Cranbrook. **Bibliography:** Archives.

MITCHELL, JOAN. b. 1926, Chicago, Ill. **Studied:** Smith College, 1942–44; Columbia U.; Chicago Art Institute School, 1944–47, BFA; NYU, 1950, MFA. Resides in France. **Address:** La Tour, Avenue Claude Monet, Vetheuil, 95510, France. **Dealer:** Fourcade Inc. **One-man Exhibitions:** U. of Illinois, 1946 (two-man, with Richard Bowman); St. Paul Gallery, 1950; The New Gallery, NYC, 1952; The Stable Gallery, 1953, 54, 55, 57, 58, 61, 65; Galerie Neufville, Paris, 1960; B. C. Holland Gallery, 1961; Dwan Gallery; Southern Illinois U.; Jacques Dubourg, Paris, 1962; Galerie Lawrence, Paris, 1962; Klipstein & Kornfeld, Berne, 1962; MIT, 1962; Galerie Fournier, Paris, 1967, 69, 71; Martha Jackson Gallery, 1968, 71, 72; Syracuse/Everson, 1972; Ruth S. Schaffner Gallery, Santa Barbara, 1974; Arts Club of Chicago, 1974; Galerie Jean Fournier, Paris, 1976, 78; Xavier Fourcade, Inc., NYC, 1976, 77, 80; Ruth S. Schaffner Gallery, Los Angeles, 1978; Webb & Parsons, Bedford Village, N.Y., 1978; Paule Anglim Gallery, San Francisco, 1979; Richard Hines Gallery, Seattle, 1980. **Retrospective:** WMAA, 1974. **Group:** U. of Illinois, 1950, 67; WMAA, 1950, 65–66, Annuals, 1967, 73; Chicago/AI; Walker, Vanguard, 1955; Corcoran; Arts Club of Chicago; U. of North Carolina; Minneapolis/Institute; PAFA, 1966; MOMA, Two Decades of American Painting, circ., Japan, India, Australia, 1967; U. of Illinois, 1967; Jewish Museum, 1967; Montclair/AM, The Recent Years, 1969; Carnegie, 1970; VMFA, 1970; MOMA, Younger Abstract Expressionists of the Fifties, 1971; Carnegie, Fresh Air School, circ., 1972; New York Cultural Center, Women Choose Women, 1973;

Joan Mitchell *No Daisies* 1980

WMAA, American Drawings, 1963–1973, 1973; Indianapolis, 1974; Corcoran, 1975; San Antonio/McNay, American Artist 76, 1976; Albright College, Reading, Pa., Perspective 78, 1978; Buffalo/Albright, American Painting of the 1970s, 1978. **Collections:** Basel; Buffalo/Albright; Chase Manhattan Bank; Chicago/AI; MOMA; Phillips; Rockefeller Institute; The Singer Company, Inc.; Union Carbide Corp.; WMAA; Walker. **Bibliography:** Baur 5; Blesh 1; Downes, ed.; Friedman, ed.; Hunter 1; Hunter, ed.; Johnson, Ellen H.; **Joan Mitchell;** McCoubrey 1; *Metro;* Nordness, ed.; O'Hara 1; Plous; Read 2; Sandler 1; Seuphor 1.

MITCHELL, WALLACE. b. October 9, 1911, Detroit, Mich.; **d.** 1977, Detroit, Mich. **Studied:** Northwestern U., BA; Cranbrook Academy of Art, with Zoltan Sepeshy; Columbia U., MA. **Taught:** Cranbrook Academy of Art, 1936–76. **Awards:** Springfield, Ill./State, Old Northwest Territory Exhibition; Detroit/Institute, 1945. **One-man Exhibitions:** Detroit Artists Market, 1938;

Cranbrook, 1947, 53; The Bertha Schaefer Gallery, 1950, 57, 58; U. of Minnesota, 1954. **Retrospective:** Cranbrook, 1970. **Group:** Chicago/AI, 1938–41; Detroit/Institute; Buffalo/Albright, 1939; U. of Nebraska; Springfield, Ill./State, Old Northwest Territory Exhibition. **Collections:** Cranbrook; Detroit/Institute.

MOHOLY-NAGY, LAZLO. b. July 20, 1895, Bacsbarsod, Hungary; **d.** November 24, 1946, Chicago, Ill. **Studied:** U. of Budapest, 1913–14, LL.B. **Taught:** Staatliches Bauhaus, Berlin, 1922; a founding collaborator with Gyorgy Kepes and Robert Wolff of the Institute of Design, Chicago, 1938–42; director of the New Bauhaus, Chicago. Designed for State Opera and the Piscator Theatre, Berlin, 1928. Traveled Europe extensively. To England, 1935, where he produced three volumes of photo documents and a film, *Life of the Lobster*. To USA, 1937. **One-man Exhibitions:** Amsterdam/Stedelijk; Brno, Czechoslovakia; Hamburg; Mannheim; Cologne; Budapest/National; Stockholm/National; A.F.A.; The London Gallery, London, 1937; Houston/Contemporary, 1948; Harvard U., 1950; Rose Fried Gallery, 1950; Colorado Springs/FA, 1950; Zurich, 1953; Kunst Kabinett Klihm, 1956, 59, 62, 66, 71; Kleeman Gallery, NYC, 1957; New London Gallery, London, 1961; Dusseldorf, 1961; Eindhoven, 1967, 72; Brandeis U., 1968; The Howard Wise Gallery, NYC, 1970; Galerie Rudolf Zwirner, 1971; Bauhaus-Archiv, Berlin, 1972; Ileana Sonnabend Gallery, NYC, 1973. **Retrospectives:** SRGM, 1947; Chicago/AI, 1969; Chicago/Contemporary, circ., 1969; Stuttgart/WK, 1974. **Group:** WMAA; SRGM; Yale U.; Harvard U.; MOMA, The Machine as Seen at the End of the Mechanical Age, 1968, and others. **Collections:** Chicago/AI; Dayton/AI; Detroit/Institute; Jacksonville/AM; Los Angeles/County MA; MOMA; SFMA; SRGM. **Bibliography:** Barr 1; Battcock, ed.; Bihalji-Merin; Blanchard; Calas, N. and E.; Cassou; Craven, W.; Davis, D.; Frost; Giedion-Welcker 2; Goodrich and Baur 1; Hulten; Huyghe; Janis and Blesh 1; Janis S.; **Kostelanetz;** Langui; Licht, F.; MacAgy 2; **Moholy-Nagy, L. 1, 2; Moholy-Nagy, S. 1, 2;** Morris; Motherwell 1; Ramsden 1; Read 3; Roters; Selz, J.; Seuphor 3; Tomkins; Trier 1; Valentine 2; **Weitemeir;** Weller; Wingler, ed. Archives.

MOLLER, HANS. b. March 20, 1905, Wuppertal-Barmen, Germany. **Studied:** Art School, Barmen, 1919–27; Academy of Fine Arts, Berlin, 1927–28; To USA, 1928. **Taught:** Cooper Union, 1944–56. **Member:** Federation of Modern Painters and Sculptors. **Commissions:** William Douglas McAdams, Inc., NYC (mural); Percival Goodman, Architect; tapestry design for synagogue ark curtains; A.F.A./Stained Glass Industry (stained-glass window); Christ Church, Washington, D.C. (stained-glass windows), 1968. **Awards:** Art Directors Club, NYC, Distinctive Merit Award, 1944, 55, 56; Corcoran, Hon. Men., 1949; American Institute of Graphic Art, Certificate of Excellence, 1949 (2), 51; National Religious Art Exhibition, Detroit, First Prize, 1964; Audubon Artists Annual, Salmagundi Club Award, 1967; NAD, Edwin Palmer Memorial Prize, 1968, 1980; NAD, Samuel F.B. Morse Gold Medal, 1969; Audubon Artists, Murray Kupferman Prize, 1973; NAD, Andrew Carnegie Prize, 1974; AAAL, Childe Hassam Fund, 1976; Youngstown/Butler, 1st Prize, 1978. **Address:** 2207 Allen Street, Allentown, PA 18104; summer: Monhegan, ME 04852. **Dealer:** The Midtown Galleries. **One-man Exhibitions:** (first) Bonestell Gallery, NYC, 1942, also 1943; Arts Club of Chicago, 1945; U. of Michigan, 1945; Kleeman Gallery, NYC, 1945, 47, 49, 50; Pen and Palette Gallery, St. Louis, 1949; Macon, Ga. 1949; Atlanta/AA, 1950; Grace Borgenicht Gallery, Inc., 1951;

53, 54, 56; Fine Arts Associates, NYC, 1957, 60; Albert Landry, NYC, 1962; The Midtown Galleries, NYC, 1964, 67, 70, 73, 76, 79; Philadelphia Art Alliance, 1968; Allentown/AM, 1969; Norfolk, 1970; Muhlenberg College, 1977. **Retrospectives:** The Olsen Foundation Inc., Leetes Island, Conn., Hans Moller, 1926–56, circ., 1956–64; Lehigh U., 1977. **Group:** MMA; Brooklyn Museum; PAFA; Chicago/AI; The Print Club, Philadelphia; Des Moines; Detroit/Institute; Corcoran; U. of Illinois; Walker; Buffalo/Albright; SFMA; Colby College, 100 Artists of the 20th Century, 1964; WMAA Annual, 1965 and others; NAD Annuals, 1965, 67, 68, 69; Federation of Modern Painters and Sculptors, 1966, 67; NIAL, 1969. **Collections:** Allentown/AM; Bennington College; Brooklyn Museum; Container Corp. of America; Detroit/Institute; U. of Georgia; IBM; MOMA; Melbourne/National; Meta-Mold Aluminum Co.; NYPL; Norfolk; PAFA; Phillips; Princeton U.; Sacred Heart Seminary; Society of the Four Arts; Spelman College; U. of Texas; USIA; U.S. Rubber Co.; WMAA; Walker; Washington U.; Wuppertal; Yellowstone Art Center; Youngstown/Butler. **Bibliography:** Baur 5; Genauer.

MOORE, JOHN. b. 1941, St. Louis, Missouri. **Studied:** Washington U., 1962–66; Yale U., 1966–68. **Taught:** Tyler School of Art, Philadelphia, 1968–. **Awards:** National Endowment for the Arts, grant, 1966; John F. Milliken Foreign Travel Fellowship, 1968; Schless Memorial Prize, Yale U., 1968; AAAL, Hassam Award, 1973. **Commission:** Poster for Lincoln Center for the Performing Arts, 1977. **Address:** c/o Dealer. **Dealer:** Fischbach Gallery, NYC. **One-man Exhibitions:** Princeton U., 1970; Fischbach Gallery, NYC, 1973, 75, 78, 80; PAFA, 1973; David Gallery, Pittsfield, N.Y., 1974; Vick Gallery, Philadelphia, 1974; Alpha Gallery, Boston, 1974; Dart Gallery, Chicago,

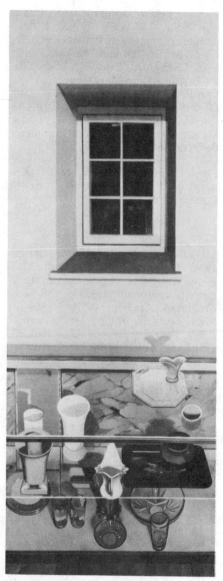

John Moore *Downtown* 1980

1977; Vick, Klaus, Rosen Gallery, Philadelphia, 1977; U. of Missouri, 1978; Marion Locks Gallery, Philadelphia, 1979; College of William and Mary, 1981. **Group:** U. of Rhode Island, From Life, 1971; Potsdam/SUNY, New Realism, 1971; U. of Illinois, 1974; Queens Museum, New Images in American

Painting, 1974; Minnesota/MA, Drawings U.S.A., '75, 1975; Akron/AI, Contemporary Images in Watercolor, 1976; U. of North Carolina, Art on Paper, 1976; Chicago/AI, Drawings of the 70s, 1977; William and Mary College, American Realism, 1978; Kent State U., Still Life, 1980. **Collections:** American Can Corp.; Arizona State U.; AT&T; Chase Manhattan Bank, NYC; Commerce Bank of Kansas City; Dartmouth College; First National Bank, Houston; IBM Corp.; Lehman Brothers, NYC; Minnesota/MA; PAFA; PMA; RISD; Smith College.

MORIN, THOMAS. b. September 22, 1934, Malone, N.Y. **Studied:** Massachusetts School of Art, with Lawrence Kupferman, 1952–56, BS. Ed.; Cranbrook Academy of Art, 1956–57, MFA; Academy of Fine Arts, Florence, Italy, 1960–61; Brown U., 1962–63. Traveled Europe. **Taught:** Cranbrook Academy of Art, 1957–58; Silvermine Guild, 1958–60; RISD, 1961– . **Member:** American Foundrymen's Society. **Commissions:** Brown U. (40 x 8-ft. cast aluminum relief). **Awards:** Fulbright Fellowship, 1960; Silvermine Guild, First Prize, 1960; Rhode Island Arts Festival, First Prize. **Address:** 62 Waterman Street, Providence, RI 02906. **One-man Exhibitions:** (first) Margaret Brown Gallery, Boston, 1954; Gallery Four, Detroit, 1957; Kanegis Gallery, Boston, 1958, 60; Silvermine Guild, 1960; The Kornblee Gallery, 1961, 64; Lincoln, Mass./De Cordova, 1963; Providence (R.I.) Art Club, 1963; Trinity Square Playhouse, Providence, R.I., 1966; South County Art Association, Kingston, R.I., 1966; U. of New Hampshire, 1968; Oneonta/SUNY, 1968. **Group:** Boston Arts Festival, 1953, 54, 55, 58, 59, 60, 62; PAFA, 1958, 64; Detroit/Institute Annuals, 1958, 64; ICA, Boston, View, 1960; WMAA Annual, 1961; Houston/MFA, Ways and Means, 1961; Audubon Artists Annual, 1962; Hartford/Wadsworth, Eleven New England Sculptors, 1963; Silvermine Guild, 1963; Lincoln, Mass./De Cordova, 1964. **Collections:** Brown U.; VMFA.

MORLEY, MALCOLM. b. 1931, London, England. **Studied:** Camberwell School of Arts and Crafts, London, 1953; Royal College of Art, London, 1957; Yale U., MFA. **Address:** 2 Spring Street, NYC 10012. **Dealer:** Xavier Fourcade, Inc. **One-man Exhibitions:** The Kornblee Gallery, 1967, 69; Stefanotty Gallery, NYC, 1973; Galerie Gerald Piltzer, Paris, 1973; Stefanotty Gallery, NYC, 1974; The Clocktower, NYC, 1976, 79; Galerie Jurka, Amsterdam, 1977; Nancy Hoffman Gallery, NYC, 1979; Susanne Hilberry Gallery, Birmingham, Mich., 1979; Hartford/Wadsworth, 1980; Xavier Fourcade, Inc., 1981. **Group:** SRGM, The Photographic Image, 1966; IX Sao Paulo Biennial, 1967; Vassar College, Realism Now, 1968; Akron/AI, Directions 2; Aspects of a New Realism, 1969; Riverside Museum, NYC, Paintings from the Photo, 1969; WMAA, 22 Realists, 1970; Princeton U., American Art since 1960, 1970; Documenta V, Kassel, 1972; Wurttemburgischer Kunstverein, Amerikanischer Fotorealismus, 1972; Serpentine Gallery, London, Photo-Realism, 1973; Akademie der Kunste, Berlin, SoHo, 1976; Royal Academy of Arts, London, British Painting 1952–1977, 1977; Documenta 6, Kassel, 1977; Zurich, Painting in the Age of Photography, 1977; Canberra/National, Illusion of Reality, 1977; Oklahoma, Cityscape, 78, 1978. **Collections:** Aachen/NG; Cologne/NG; Detroit/Institute; Fordham U.; Hartford/Wadsworth; Hirshhorn; Humlebaek/Louisiana; MMA; MOMA; The Ohio State U.; Paris/Moderne; Victoria and Albert Museum; Utrecht. **Bibliography:** Alloway 4; *Amerikanischer Fotorealismus*; Honisch and Jensen, eds.; Johnson, Ellen H.; *Kunst um 1970*; Lucie-Smith; Sager.

MORRIS, CARL. b. May 12, 1911, Yorba Linda, Calif. **studied:** Fullerton Junior College, 1930–31; Chicago Art Institute School; Kunstgewerbeschule, Vienna, 1933–34; Academy of Fine Arts, Vienna, 1933–34. Traveled Italy. **Taught:** ASL, 1937–38; privately 1940–41; U. of Colorado, summer, 1957. Federal A.P.: Director at Spokane, Wash., 1938–39. **Commissions** (murals): US Post Office, Eugene, Ore., 1941–42; Hall of Religion, Oregon Centennial Exposition, Portland, 1959. **Awards:** Austro-American Scholarship, 1935; Institute of International Education Fellowship (Paris), 1935–36; Werkbund Scholarship, 1939, Seattle/AM, Hon. Men.,1939, 46, 47; Seattle/AM, Second Prize, 1943; Denver/AM, **P.P.,** 1946; Seattle/AM, Margaret E. Fuller Award, 1946; SFMA, Anne Bremer Memorial Prize, 1946; Pepsi-Cola Bronze Medal, 1948; SFMA, James D. Phelan Award, 1950; U. of Illinois, **P.P.,** 1958. **Address:** 919 N.W. Skyline Boulevard, Portland, OR 97229. **Dealers:** Kraushaar Galleries; Triangle Art Gallery; Gordon Woodside Gallery; Fountain Gallery. **One-man Exhibitions:** (first) Fondation des Etats-Unis, Paris, 1935; Paul Elder Gallery, San Francisco, 1937; Seattle/AM, 1940; Portland, Ore./AM, 1946, 52, 55; California Palace, 1947; U. of Oregon, 1947; Opportunity Gallery, NYC, 1948; Santa Barbara/MA, 1956; Zivile Gallery, Los Angeles, 1956; Mills College, 1956; Rotunda Gallery, San Francisco, 1956; Kraushaar Galleries, 1956, 57, 58, 61, 64, 67, 73; Reed College, 1959, 69 (two-man, with Hilda Morris), 1972; U. of Colorado, 1957; Fountain Gallery, 1963, 64, 65, 69, 71, 75; Feingarten Gallery, San Francisco, 1965; Triangle Art Gallery, 1966, 68, 70, 73; Gordon Woodside Gallery, 1966, 69, 73. **Retrospective:** A.F.A./Ford Foundation, circ., 1960. **Group:** Chicago/AI; Carnegie; Corcoran; MMA; WMAA; SRGM; Younger American Painters, 1954; III Sao Paulo Biennial, 1955; Colorado Springs/FA, 1965; Denver/AM, 1965; Art in the USA, 1965; Tamarind Lithography Workshop, 1967; PAFA,

1969; SFMA, Tamarind, 1969; MOMA, Tamarind: Homage to Lithography, 1969; Minnesota/MA, Drawings USA, 1971; NCFA, Art of the Pacific Northwest, 1974; NAD, 1974; Seattle/AM, Northwest Traditions, 1978. **Collections:** Allentown/AM; Buffalo/Albright; California Palace; Chicago/AI; Colorado Springs/FA; U. of Colorado; Columbus; Corcoran; Dayton/AI; Denver/AM; Eastern Oregon College; Hartford/Wadsworth; Houston/MFA; Hirshhorn; U. of Illinois; Kansas City/Nelson; MMA; Mead Corporation; Michigan State U.; Mills College; Minnesota/MA; NCFA; Norfolk/Chrysler; U. of Oregon; City of Portland, Ore.; Portland, Ore./AM; Portland State College; Reed College; U. of Rochester; SFMA; SRGM; Santa Barbara/MA; Sao Paulo; Seattle/AM; Southern Oregon College; Stanford U.; U. of Texas; Toronto; Utica; WMAA; Walker; Wichita. **Bibliography:** *Art of the Pacific Northwest;* Monte and Tucker; Nordness, ed.; *Northwest Traditions;* Pousette-Dart, ed.; Read 2.

MORRIS, GEORGE L.K. b. November 14, 1905, NYC; **d.** June 26, 1975, Stockbridge, Mass. **Studied:** Groton School, 1924; Yale U., 1928, BA; ASL, with John Sloan, Kenneth Hayes Miller; Academie Moderne, Paris, with F. Leger, Amedee Ozenfant. Traveled around the world and spent much time in Paris. **Taught:** ASL, 1943–44; St. John's College, Annapolis, Md., 1950–61. Editor: Yale Literary Magazine, 1928; *The Miscellany,* 1929–31; *Plastique,* Paris, 1937–39; *Partisan Review,* 1937–43. **Member:** American Abstract Artists (a founder, 1936, and president, 1948–50); Federation of Modern Painters and Sculptors; NAD, Saltus Gold Medal, 1973. **Commissions:** Lenox (Mass.) Elementary School (mosaic). **Awards:** Pepsi-Cola, 1948; Pittsfield/Berkshire, Berkshire Hills Award, 1963; PAFA, Joseph E. Temple Gold Medal, 1965. **One-man Exhibitions:** (first) Valentine Dudensing Gallery, 1933; Pittsfield/Berkshire, 1933; Museum of Living Art, NYC,

1935; Passedoit Gallery, NYC, 1938; The Downtown Gallery, 1943, 44, 50, 64, 67; Galerie Colette Allendy, Paris, 1946; The Alan Gallery, NYC, 1955; Montclair/AM, 1971; Jacksonville/Cummer, 1973; Chattanooga/AA, 1973; Charleston/Carolina, 1973; Hirschl & Adler Galleries, 1974, 79. **Retrospectives:** ICA, Washington, D.C., 1958; Sharon (Conn.) Creative Arts Foundation; Century Association; Corcoran; Pittsfield/Berkshire; Hirschl & Adler Galleries, 1971. **Group:** WMAA; American Abstract Artists, annually; Salon des Realites Nouvelles, Paris; MOMA; SRGM; Chicago/AI; SFMA; Rome/Nazionale. **Collections:** Brandeis U.; Brooklyn Museum; Chattanooga/AA; Corcoran; Dallas/MFA; Darmstadt/Kunsthalle; U. of Georgia; High Museum; Honolulu Academy; U. of Illinois; MMA; Madison Square Garden; U. of Michigan; Montclair/AM; U. of Oklahoma; PAFA; PMA; Phillips; Pittsfield/Berkshire; Portland, Ore./AM; Raleigh/NCMA; Syracuse U.; Utica; WMAA; Wichita/AM; Yale U. **Bibliography:** American Abstract Artists, ed.; Arp; Baur 7; Biederman 1; Blanchard; Blesh 1; Cheney; Flanagan; Frost; Kootz 2; Marter, Tarbell, and Wechsler; McCurdy, ed.; **Morris;** Newmeyer; Pagano; Pearson 2; Pousette-Dart, ed.; Read 2; Ritchie 1; Rose, B., 1, 4; Seuphor 1, 3; "What Abstract Art Means to Me." Archives.

MORRIS, KYLE R. b. January 17, 1918, Des Moines, Iowa; **d.** August 17, 1979, Southampton, N.Y. **Studied:** Northwestern U., 1935–39, BA, 1940; Chicago Art Institute School, 1935–39; Cranbrook Academy of Art, 1947, MFA. US Army Air Force, 1942–45. Traveled Europe. **Taught:** Stephens College, 1940–41; U. of Texas, 1941–42, 1945–46; U. of Minnesota, 1947–51; U. of California, Berkeley, 1952–54; Cooper Union, 1958. Art Consultant to Sandak, Inc. Editor and Publisher, *Contemporary Slides* (magazine), 1954–59. Organized the Vanguard, 1955, exhibition for The Walker Art Center. **Commission:** Kel-

logg Citizens National Bank (mural), 1975. **Awards:** Walker, **P.P.,** 1948; SFMA, Oil Painting Award, 1953; II Inter-American Paintings and Prints Biennial, Mexico City, 1960, Hon. Men.; Ford Foundation, **P.P.,** 1963. **One-man Exhibitions:** (first) Pepsi-Cola Opportunity Art Gallery, NYC, 1945; Walker, 1952; Des Moines, 1955; The Stable Gallery, 1955; The Kootz Gallery, NYC, 1959, 60, 61, 63, 64; Galleria d'Arte del Naviglio, Milan, 1960; James David Gallery, Miami and Sarasota, 1966, 67; Landmark Gallery Inc., NYC, 1974. **Group:** WMAA Annuals from 1952; SRGM, Younger American Painters, 1954; Chicago/AI, 1954; U. of Nebraska, 1954; U. of Illinois, 1954, 56, 61, 63; Corcoran, 1956, 58, 61, 63; Minneapolis/Institute, 1957; WMAA, Nature in Abstraction, 1958; Brussels World's Fair, 1958; VMFA, 1958; Rome-New York Foundation, Rome, 1958; PAFA, 1959, Annual, 1964; Detroit/Institute, 1959; Carnegie, 1961; SRGM, SRGM, Abstract Expressionists and Imagists, 1961; Brandeis U., New Directions in American Painting, 1963; Boston/MFA 1966; Arts Club of Chicago, Liberman, Morris, Tworkov, 1975. **Collections:** Buffalo/Albright; Chase Manhattan Bank; Ciba-Geigy Corp.; Continental Grain Company; Des Moines; Detroit/Institute; Ellerby Associates; U. of Illinois; Newark Museum; Reynolds Metals Co.; SRGM; The Singer Company Inc.; Toledo/MA; Union Carbide Corp.; WMAA; Walker; Washington U. **Bibliography:** Baur 5; Sandler 1.

MORRIS, ROBERT. b. February 9, 1931, Kansas City, Mo. **Studied:** Kansas City Junior College; Kansas City Art Institute, 1948–50; U. of Kansas City; San Francisco Art Institute; Reed College, 1953–55; Hunter College, MA, 1966. US Army Engineers. Traveled USA, Orient, Europe. **Taught:** Hunter College, 1967– . **Commissions:** National Planning Commission, Ottawa, Earth Project. **Awards:** National Council on the Arts, **P.P.;** Chicago/AI, 1966; SRGM, 1967; Torcuato di Tella, Buenos Aires, 1967; Guggenheim Foundation Fellowship, 1969; Skowhegan Medal of Progress and Environment, 1978. **Address:** 109 No. Mountain Road, Gardiner, NY 12525. **Dealer:** Leo Castelli Inc. **One-man Exhibitions:** (first) Dilexi Gallery, San Francisco, 1957, also 1958; Green Gallery, NYC, 1963, 64, 65; Galerie Schmela, 1964; Dwan Gallery, Los Angeles, 1966; Leo Castelli Inc., 1967, 68, 69, 70, 72, 74; 76 (two-man); 79; Eindhoven, 1968; Ileana Sonnabend Gallery, Paris, 1968, 71, 73, 77, NYC, 1974, 76, 79; Corcoran, 1969, 77; Gian Enzo Sperone, Turin, 1969; Irving Blum Gallery, Los Angeles, 1969, 70; Tate, 1971; Konrad Fischer Gallery, Dusseldorf, 1973; Max Protetch Gallery, Washington, D.C., 1973; Galleria Forma, Genoa, 1973; Modern Art Agency, Naples, 1973; ICA, U. of Pennsylvania, 1974; Galerie Art in Progress, Munich, 1974; Belknap Park, Grand Rapids, 1974; Alessandro Ferranti Gallery, Rome, 1975; Humlebaek/Louisiana, 1977; Williams College, 1977; Portland (Ore.) Center for the Visual Arts, 1977; Amsterdam/Stedelijk, 1977; Galerie Art in Progress, Dusseldorf, 1977; Swarthmore College, 1978; Beaver College, 1978; Ferrara/Moderna, 1978; Wright State U., 1979. **Retrospective:** WMAA, 1970; Detroit/Institute, 1970. **Group:** Hartford/Wadsworth, Black, White and Gray, 1964; WMAA, Young America, 1965; ICA, U. of Pennsylvania, The Other Tradition, 1966; Jewish Museum, Primary Structures, 1966; WMAA, Contemporary American Sculpture, Selection I, 1966; Chicago/AI, 1966; Walker, 1966; WMAA Sculpture Annuals, 1966, 68, 70; Detroit/Institute, Color, Image and Form, 1967; Los Angeles/County MA and PMA, American Sculpture of the Sixties, 1967; MOMA, The 1960's, 1967; Torcuato di Tella, Buenos Aires, 1967; Eindhoven, 1967; SRGM, Guggenheim International, 1967, 71; Buffalo/Albright, 1968; The Hague, Minimal Art, 1968; Foundation Maeght, 1968; MOMA, The Art of

the Real, 1968; PMA, 1968; ICA, U. of Pennsylvania, 1969; Berne, When Attitudes Become Form, 1969; Walker, 14 Sculptors: The Industrial Edge, 1969; Indianapolis, 1969; WMAA, Anti-Illusion: Procedures/Materials, 1969; Hayward Gallery, London, Pop Art, 1969; MOMA, Spaces, 1969; MMA, New York Painting and Sculpture, 1940–1970, 1969–70; New School for Social Research, American Drawings of the Sixties, 1970; Boston U., American Artists of the Nineteen Sixties, 1970; Cornell U., Earth Art, 1970; Cincinnati/Contemporary, Monumental Art, 1970; ICA, U. of Pennsylvania, Against Order: Chance and Art, 1970; MOMA, Information, 1971; Kunsthalle, Nurnberg, Artist-Theory-Work, 1971; Buffalo/Albright, Kid Stuff, 1971; Dusseldorf/Kunsthalle, Prospect '71, 1971; Dublin/Municipal, International Quadriennial (ROSC), 1971; Chicago/Contemporary, Six Sculptors, 1971; Los Angeles/County MA, Art & Technology, 1971; Rijksmuseum Kroller-Muller, Diagrams and Drawings, 1972; New York Cultural Center, 3D into 2D, 1973; Parcheggio di Villa Borghese, Rome, Contemporanea, 1974; Princeton U., Line as Language, 1974; MIT, Interventions in Landscapes, 1974; Cologne/Kunstverein, Kunst uber Kunst, 1974; CNAC, Art/Voir, 1974; Dusseldorf/Kunsthalle, Surrealist-Bildrealitat: 1924–1974, 1974; Ackland, Light/Sculpture, 1975; Leverkusen, Drawings 3; American Drawings, 1975; MOMA, Drawings Now, 1976; ICA, U. of Pennsylvania, Improbable Furniture, 1977; Chicago/AI, Drawings of the 70's, 1977; U. of Chicago, Ideas in Sculpture, 1977; Kansas City/AI, Project Drawings, 1978; Ontario, Structures for Behaviour, 1978; WMAA, Art about Art, 1978. **Collections:** Dallas/MFA; Detroit/Institute; Hartford/Wadsworth; Melbourne/National; Milwaukee; National Gallery of Victoria, Melbourne; Oberlin College; Ottawa/National; Pasadena/AM; Stockholm/National; Tate; WMAA; Walker. **Bibliography:** *Art Now 74*; Alloway 4; Battcock, ed.; Calas, N. and E.; Celant;

Contemporanea; Davis, D.; *Drawings: The Pluralist Decade;* De Vries, ed.; Friedman, M. 2; Friedman and van der Marck; Gablik; Goossen 1; *Happening & Fluxus;* Honisch and Jensen, eds.; Honnef; Hunter, ed.; Johnson, Ellen H.; Krauss 2; Kozloff 3; *Kunst um 1970;* Lippard 3, 4, 5; Lippard, ed.; Lucie-Smith; Meyer; Muller; *Report;* Russell and Gablik; Trier 1; Sandler 1; Trier 1; Tuchman 1; *When Attitudes Become Form.* Archives.

MOTHERWELL, ROBERT. b. January 24, 1915, Aberdeen, Wash. **Studied:** Stanford U., 1932–37, AB (philosophy); California School of Fine Arts, ca. 1935; Harvard U., 1937–38; U. of Grenoble, summer, 1938; Columbia U., 1940–41; primarily self-taught in art. Traveled extensively, USA, Europe, Mexico. **Taught:** Hunter College, 1951–57; Columbia U., 1964–65; lectures extensively in American universities and museums. Series of paintings *Elegy to Spanish Republic* began 1947. Cofounder of a school, "Subject of the Artist," with William Baziotes, Barnett Newman, and Mark Rothko, NYC, 1948. Art Director, *Partisan Review,* 1962–65. Director, *Documents of Modern Art,* NYC, and *Documents of 20th Century Art.* **Commissions:** John F. Kennedy Federal Office Building, Boston, 1966; Stanford U., 1975; U. of Iowa; National Gallery, mural, 1978. **Awards:** IV Guggenheim International, 1964 ($2,500); Grande Medaille de Vermeil de la Ville de Paris, 1978; PAFA, Gold Medal of Honor, 1979. **Address:** 909 North Street, Greenwich, CT 06830. **Dealer:** Knoedler Contemporary Art. **One-man Exhibitions:** (first) Art of This Century, NYC, 1944; Arts Club of Chicago, 1946; The Kootz Gallery, NYC, 1946, 47, 49, 52; SFMA, 1946, 67; New London, 1953; Sidney Janis Gallery, 1957, 59, 61, 62; Bennington College, 1959; John Berggruen Gallery, Paris, 1961, San Francisco, 1973; Sao Paulo, 1961; Pasadena/AM, 1962; Galleria Odyssia, Rome, 1962; Galerie der Spiegel, Cologne,

1962; Smith College, 1963; MIT, 1963; Galerie Schmela (two-man, with Conrad Marca-Relli); Duke U., 1965; Walker, 1965, 72, 74; College of St. Benedict, 1965; U. of Utah, 1966; Witte, 1966; U. of South Florida, 1966; Baltimore/MA, 1966; Indiana U., 1966; Amsterdam/Stedelijk, 1966; Whitechapel Art Gallery, London, 1966; Essen, 1966; Turin/Civico, 1966; WMAA, 1968; VMFA, 1969; Toledo/MA, 1969; Marlborough-Gerson Gallery Inc., 1969; David Mirvish Gallery, 1970, 73; Gallerie im Erker, St. Gallen, Switzerland, 1971; Kunstverein, Freiburg, 1971; Dayton's Gallery 12, Minneapolis, 1972; Lawrence Rubin Gallery, NYC, 1972, 73; MMA, 1972; U. of Iowa, 1972; Fendrick Gallery, 1972; Houston/MFA, 1972; Gertrude Kasle Gallery, 1972; Cleveland/MA, 1973; Princeton U., 1973; Current Editions, Seattle, 1973; Hartford/Wadsworth, 1973; Knoedler Contemporary Art, 1974, 75; Brooke Alexander, 1974, 76, 79; Otis Art Institute, 1974; Museum of Modern Art, Mexico City, 1975; Knoedler Contemporary Art, 1976, 78, 80; Janie C. Lee Gallery, Houston, 1976, 79; Watson/De Nagy, Houston, 1977, 79; Galerie Andre Emmerich, Zurich, 1977; Diane Gilson Gallery, Seattle, Seattle, 1977, 79; Graphics 1 & Graphics 2, Boston, 1977; Hanson-Cowles Gallery, Minneapolis, 1977; Knoedler Gallery, London, 1978; Douglas Drake Gallery, Kansas City, Mo., 1978; Alice Simsar Gallery, Ann Arbor, 1978; U. of Connecticut, 1979; Ehrlich Gallery, NYC, 1979; Wichita State U., 1979; Galerie Veith Turske, Cologne, 1979; 2RC, Rome, 1979; U. of Missouri, 1979; Galerie Ponce, Mexico City, 1979; Gump's Gallery, San Francisco, 1979; Peter M. David Gallery, Minneapolis, 1979; West Coast Gallery, Newport Beach, 1979; Centre Cultural de la Caixa de Pensions, Barcelona, 1980. **Retrospectives:** Dusseldorf/Kunsthalle, circ., 1976, prints, circ., 1977; Phillips, 1965; MOMA, 1965–66. **Group:** Venice Biennial, Sao Paulo Biennial; WMAA Annuals; Brussels World's Fair, 1958; American Painting

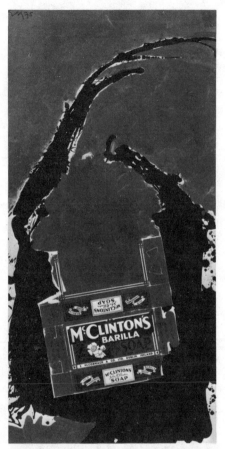

Robert Motherwell *Dublin Collage* 1975

and Sculpture, Moscow, 1959; Documenta II & III, Kassel, 1959, 64; Tate, Dunn International, 1964; Tate, Gulbenkian International, 1964; U. of Illinois, 1967; Winnipeg Art Gallery, 1967; Chicago/AI Annuals; Boston Arts Festival; ICA, Boston, 1968; Carnegie, 1968, and others; MOMA, The New American Painting and Sculpture, 1969; Edmonton Art Gallery, Alberta, Masters of the Sixties, 1972; VMFA, Twelve American Painters, 1974; Corcoran Biennial, 1975; Minnesota/MA, American Drawings, 1927–1977, circ., 1977; National Gallery, American Art at Mid-Century, 1978; Cornell U., Abstract Expressionism: The Formative Years,

1978; Montclair College, American Masters, 1979; Claremont College, Black and White Are Colors, 1979. **Collections:** Amsterdam/Stedelijk; Andover/Phillips; Baltimore/MA; Bennington College; Brooklyn Museum; Brown U.; Buffalo/Albright; Chicago/AI; Cleveland/MA; Dallas/MFA; Dayton/AI; Fort Dodge/Blanden; Harvard U.; Houston/MFA; U. of Illinois; Kultusministerium Baden-Wurttemberg; Los Angeles/County MA; MMA; MOMA; U. of Minnesota; NYU; U. of Nebraska; Pasadena/AM; Phillips; Provincetown/Chrysler; Raleigh/NCMA; Rio de Janeiro; SFMA; Smith College; Smithsonian; Society of the Four Arts; South Mall, Albany; Tel Aviv; Toronto; WMAA; Walker; Washington U.; U. of Washington; Yale U. **Bibliography:** Alloway 4; Ashton 3, 5; Baur 7; Biederman 1; Bihalji-Merin; *Black and White Are Colors;* Blanchard; Blesh 1; Carmean, Rathbone, and Hess; Chipp; Downes, ed.; Eliot; Finkelstein; Flanagan; Goodrich and Baur 1; *The Great Decade;* Greenberg 1; Haftman; Henning; Hess, T.B., 1; Hunter 1, 6; Honisch and Jensen, eds.; Hunter, ed.; Janis and Blesh 1; Janis, S.; Kozloff 3; McCoubrey 1; McCurdy, ed.; Mendelowitz; *Metro;* Miller, ed. 2; **Motherwell 1, 2; Motherwell, ed.; Motherwell and Reinhardt, eds.;** Nordness, ed.; O'Hara; Paalen; Plous; Ponente; Pousette-Dart, ed.; Read 2; Ritchie 1; Rose, B., 1, 4; Rubin 1; Sandler 1; Seitz 1, 3; Seuphor 1; Soby 5; Terentio; Tomkins 2; Tuchman, ed.; Weller; "What Abstract Art Means to Me." Archives.

MOY, SEONG. b. October 20, 1921, Canton, China. To USA, 1931. **Studied:** Federal Art Project School, with Ben Swanson; St. Paul School of Art, 1936–40, with Cameron Booth; ASL, with Vaclav Vytlacil; Hofmann School, 1941–42, with Hans Hofmann; Atelier 17, NYC, 1948–50. US Air Force, 1943–46. **Taught:** U. of Minnesota,

1951; Indiana U., 1953; Smith College, 1954; Vassar College, 1955; Cooper Union, 1957– ; Columbia U., 1959– ; ASL, 1963– ; Moy Summer School, Provincetown; City College of New York, 1970– . Federal A.P.: Assistant in graphic shop. **Member:** Artists Equity; SAGA; Audubon Society. **Commissions:** International Graphic Arts Society (3 editions); New York Hilton Hotel; Fourth National Bank and Trust, Wichita (2 murals). **Awards:** Minneapolis/Institute, First Prize, 1939; The Print Club, Philadelphia, First Prize, 1948; John Hay Whitney Fellowship, 1950; Brooklyn Museum, **P.P.,** 1953; Guggenheim Foundation Fellowship, 1955. **Address:** 100 La Salle Street, NYC 10027; studio; 2231 Broadway, NYC 10024. **One-man Exhibitions:** (first) Carmel (Calif.) Art Association, 1943; Ashby Gallery, NYC, 1947; Carlebach Gallery, NYC, 1949; Springfield, Ill./State, 1949; Hacker Gallery, NYC, 1950; Dubin Gallery, Philadelphia, 1950; U. of Minnesota, 1951; The New Gallery, NYC, 1951, 52, 54; Boris Mirski Gallery, Boston, 1955; The Contemporaries, NYC, 1955; The Howard Wise Gallery, Cleveland, 1958; Grand Central Moderns, NYC, 1959; Yamada Gallery, Kyoto, 1959; The Miller Gallery, Cincinnati, 1974. **Group:** MMA, 1950; U. of Illinois, 1951, 53, 54; Carnegie, 1955; U. of Minnesota; Brooklyn Museum; Chicago/AI; MOMA; PAFA; Library of Congress; New York World's Fair, 1964–65. **Collections:** Abbott Laboratories; Andover/Phillips; Bibliotheque Nationale; Boston/MFA; Brooklyn Museum; Indiana U.; Library of Congress; MMA; MOMA; Memphis/Brooks; U. of Minnesota; NYPL; PAFA; PMA; Smith College; Smithsonian; Tel Aviv; Victoria and Albert Museum; WMAA; Walker; Worcester/AM. **Bibliography:** Archives.

MOYER, ROY. b. August 20, 1921, Allentown, Pa. **Studied:** Columbia U., BA, MA; U. of Oslo; self-taught in art. Traveled extensively; resided in Europe (mainly Greece), four years. **Taught:** U. of Salonica, Greece, 1948–51; U. of Toronto, 1953–55. Director, American Federation of Arts, 1963–72; Now at UNICEF. **Awards:** Audubon Artists, Jane Peterson Award, 1969, 72; Youngstown/Butler, First Prize for Painting, 1973; NAD, Emil and Dines Carlsen Award, 1977. **Address:** 440 Riverside Drive, NYC 10027. **Dealers:** Sneed-Hillman Gallery, Rockford, Ill. Carl Battaglia Gallery, NYC. **One-man Exhibitions:** (first) Salonica, Greece, 1949; The Contemporaries, NYC, 1958, 59, 61, 62, 65; The Midtown Galleries, 1967; Rockford/Burpee 1969; Sneed-Hillman Gallery, 1969; Rolly-Michaux, NYC, 1974, Boston, 1975; Kendall Gallery, Wellfleet Mass., 1975. **Retrospective:** Sneed-Hillman Gallery, Rockford, Ill., 1979. **Group:** U. of Illinois, 1959; WMAA Annual, 1960; Washington U., 1967; Colorado Springs/FA, 1967; Louisville/Speed, 1967; Akron/AI, 1968; U. of Georgia, 1968; and others. **Collections:** Brandeis U.; Sara Roby Foundation; U. of Rochester; Rockford/Burpee; Wichita/AM; Youngstown/Butler.

MULLER, JAN. b. December 27, 1922, Hamburg, Germany; **d.** January 29, 1958, NYC. Traveled Czechoslavakia, Switzerland, Holland, southern France, 1933–41. To USA, 1941. **Studied:** Hofmann School, 1945–50. Cofounder of Hansa Gallery, NYC, 1952. **One-man Exhibitions:** (first) Hansa Gallery, NYC, 1953, also 1954, 55, 56, 57, 58; Sun Gallery, Provincetown 1955, 56; U. of Minnesota, 1960; The Zabriskie Gallery, 1961; Noah Goldowsky, 1970, 71, 72; Gruenebaum Gallery, NYC, 1976, 77; Rosa Esman Gallery, NYC, 1980. **Retrospective:** Hansa Gallery, NYC, 1959; SRGM, 1962. **Group:** 813 Broadway (Gallery) NYC, 1952; Chicago/AI, 1953; U. of Minnesota, 1955; The Stable Gallery Annual, 1956; Jewish Museum, The New York School, Second Generation, 1957; WMAA, Young America, 1957; Carnegie, 1958; Festival of Two Worlds, Spoleto, 1958; ICA, Boston,

1958, 59; MOMA, New Images of Man, 1959; A.F.A., The Figure circ., 1960. **Collections:** Charlotte/Mint; MOMA; Newark Museum. **Bibliography: Messer;** Sandler 1.

MULLICAN, LEE. b. December 2, 1919, Chickasha, Okla. **Studied:** Abilene Christian College, 1937; U. of Oklahoma, 1939; Kansas City Art Institute and School of Design, 1941, with Fletcher Martin. Corps of Army Engineers, 1942–46. Traveled Europe, South America. **Taught:** UCLA, 1962–75; U. of Chile, Artist-in-Residence Exchange Program, 1968. **Awards:** Guggenheim Foundation Fellowship, 1959; U. of California, Creative Arts Grant, 1964; Tamarind Fellowship, 1964–65. **Address:** 370 Mesa Road, Santa Monica, Calif. **Dealer:** Paule Anglim Gallery, San Francisco. **One-man Exhibitions:** SFMA, 1949; The Swetzoff Gallery, Boston, 1950; The Willard Gallery, 1950, 52, 53, 59, 61, 67; Dynation Exhibition, San Francisco, 1951; Oklahoma, 1951, 67; Paul Kantor Gallery, Beverly Hills, Calif., 1952, 53, 56; The Rose Rabow Gallery, San Francisco, 1955, 74; Santa Barbara/MA, 1958; Silvan Simone Gallery, 1965–67; Santiago, Chile, 1968; UCLA, 1969; Jodi Scully Gallery, 1973; Contemporary Art Gallery, Santa Fe, 1973; Paule Anglim Gallery, San Francisco, 1979. **Group:** Corcoran, 1948; Denver/AM Annuals, 1950, 55, 56, 57; Chicago/AI, 1951, 54; Carnegie, 1951, 64, 66; WMAA Annuals, 1952, 56; U. of Nebraska, 1953; U. of Illinois, 1953, 55, 57; MMA, 1954; Sao Paulo, 1955; Santa Barbara/MA, 1957; MOMA, 1957; PAFA, 1958, 67; Rome-New York Foundation, Rome, 1960; Pasadena/AM, 1961; Newport Harbor, The Artist Collects, 1975; Los Angeles/County MA, 5 Footnotes to Art History, 1977. **Collections:** U. of California; Colorado Springs/FA; Denver/AM; Detroit/Institute; Los Angeles/County MA; MOMA; New Orleans/Delgado; Oklahoma; Pasadena/AM; Phillips; SFMA; San Francisco Municipal Art Commis-

sion; Santa Barbara/MA; Santiago, Chile; Syracuse U.; Tulsa/Philbrook; Wichita State U. **Bibliography:** Pousette-Dart, ed.; Richardson, E.P.

MURCH, WALTER TANDY. b. August 17, 1907, Toronto, Canada; **d.** December 11, 1967, NYC. **Studied:** Ontario College of Art, 1924–27, with Arthur Lismer, L. Harris; ASL, 1929–30, with Kenneth Hayes Miller, William Von Schlegell; Grand Central School, NYC, 1930, with Arshile Gorsky; and privately, with Gorky, 1931–32. US citizen, 1948. Traveled Mexico, Canada, France. **Taught:** Pratt Institute, 1952–61; NYU, 1961; Boston U., 1961–67; Columbia U., 1964. **Commissions:** *Scientific American; Fortune* magazine. **Awards:** U. of Illinois, **P.P.,** 1949; NIAL, Grant, 1961; Ford Foundation, **P.P.** (2). **One-man Exhibitions:** (first) Wakefield Gallery, NYC, 1941; Mortimer Brandt, NYC, 1946; Betty Parsons Gallery, 1947, 49, 51, 54, 57, 59, 62, 66, 70, 71; St. Louis Art Center, 1949; Allan Frumkin Gallery, Chicago, 1953; Worth Avenue Gallery, Palm Beach, Fla., 1955; Choate School, Wallingford, Conn., 1959; Hampton Gallery, Huntington, W. Va., 1964; Lehigh U., 1966; Galerie Jan Krugier, Geneva, 1976. **Retrospective:** RISD, 1966. **Group:** Andover/Phillips, 1945; Corcoran, 1945, 56, 52–55, 58, 61, 64; Chicago/AI, 1945, 46, 53, 54, 55, 57, 59, 60, 63, 64; WMAA Annuals, 1945–64; Worcester/AM, 1947; U. of Illinois, 1951, 52, 54, 61, 63; Contemporary American Painting, Tokyo, 1952; Detroit/Institute, 1952, 57; MMA, Edward Root Collection, 1953; PMA, 1954; Indianapolis/Herron, 1954; WMAA, The New Decade, 1954–55; Walker, 1955; A.F.A., World at Work, 1955; ICA, London, American Painting; XXVIII Venice Biennial, 1956; Minneapolis/Institute, American Painting, 1945–57, 1957; ART: USA: 59, NYC, 1959; A.F.A., Private Worlds, 1960; Milwaukee, American Painting, 1760–1960, 1960; NIAL, 1961; New School for Social Research, The Creative Process, 1961;

Carnegie, 1964; U. of Rochester, In Focus, 1964; New York World's Fair, 1964–65; Detroit/Institute, 40 Key Artists of the Mid-20th Century, 1965; WMAA, A Decade of American Drawings, 1965; RISD, Recent Still Life, 1966. **Collections:** Andover/Phillips; Barnes Foundation; Brooklyn Museum; Buffalo/Albright; Carnegie; Chase Manhattan Bank; Corcoran; First National City Bank; Hallmark Collection; Hartford/Wadsworth; IBM; U. of Illinois; Jay Mfg. Co.; Kalamazoo/Institute; Lane Foundation; MMA; MOMA; NCFA; Newark Museum; Omaha/Joslyn; PAFA; Scientific American Inc.; Toledo/MA; Union Carbide Corp.; Upjohn Co.; Utica; WGMA; WMAA; Westmoreland County/MA. **Bibliography:** Baur 7; Cummings 3; Flanagan; *From Foreign Shores:* Goodrich and Baur 1; Nordness, ed.; Pousette-Dart, ed.; **Robbins;** Soby 5. Archives.

MURPHY, CATHERINE. b. January 22, 1946, Cambridge, Mass. **Studied:** Pratt Institute, BFA, 1967; Skowhegan School of Painting and Sculpture, with Elmer Büschoff, 1966. **Address:** % Dealer. **Dealer:** Xavier Fourcade, Inc., NYC. **One-man Exhibitions:** Piper Gallery, Mass., 1972; First Street Gallery, NYC, 1972; Fourcade Droll, Inc., NYC, 1975; Phillips, 1976; Xavier Fourcade, Inc., NYC, 1979. **Group:** WMAA Annuals, 1972, 73; Sheldon Memorial Art Gallery, Poughkeepsie, A Sense of Place, 1973; Storm King Art Center, Painting and Sculpture, 1973—The Emerging Real, 1973; Museum of the Philadelphia Civic Center, Woman's Work, 1974; U. of North Carolina, Art on Paper, 1974; PMA, In Her Own Image, 1974; Lincoln, Mass./De Cordova, Candid Painting; American Genre 1950–1975, 1975; Albright College, Perspective 78, 1978. **Collections:** Chase Manhattan Bank, NYC; Hirshhorn; Newark Museum; U. of North Carolina; Phillips; Security Pacific National Bank, Los Angeles; Trenton/State; WMAA. **Bibliography:** Arthur 2.

MURRAY, Elizabeth. b. 1940, Chicago, Ill. **Studied:** Chicago Art Institute School, BFA, 1962; Miles College, Oakland, MFA, 1964. **Taught:** Bard College, 1974–75, 76–77; Princeton U., 1977. **Address:** % Dealer. **Dealer:** Paula Cooper Gallery, NYC. **One-man Exhibitions:** Jacobs Ladder Gallery, Washington, D.C. (two-man), 1974; Paula Cooper Gallery, NYC (two-man) 1975, 76, 78; Jared Sable Gallery, Toronto, 1975; Ohio State U., 1978; Phyllis Kind Gallery, Chicago, 1978. **Group:** WMAA Annuals, 1972, 73, 77, 79; WMAA, Contemporary American Drawings, 1973; California State U., Los Angeles, New Work/New York, 1976; SRGM, Nine Artists; Theodoron Awards, 1977; RISD, Space Window, 1977; Syracuse U., Critics' Choice, 1977; New Museum, NYC, Early Work by Five Contemporary Artists, 1977; Chicago/Contemporary, Ten Years, 1977; ICA, U. of Pennsylvania, Eight Abstract Painters, 1978; Tampa Bay Art Center, Two Decades of Abstraction, 1978; Hayward Gallery, London, New Painting, New York, 1979; U. of North Carolina, Art on Paper, 1979. **Collections:** WMAA.

MURRAY, ROBERT. b. March 2, 1936, Vancouver (B.C.), Canada. **Studied:** School of Art, U. of Saskatchewan (with Arthur McKay, Roy Kiyooka, Kenneth Lochhead, R. Simmons), 1956–58; Emma Lake Artist's Workshops, U. of Saskatchewan, with Will Barnet, 1957, Barnett Newman, 1959, John Ferren, 1960, Clement Greenberg, 1962, Jack Shadbolt. Traveled Western Hemisphere, Royal Canadian Air Force (auxiliary). **Taught:** U. of Saskatchewan; Hunter College; Yale U.; U. of Oklahoma; School of Visual Arts, NYC. **Commissions:** Saskatoon City Hall, 1959–60; Long Beach State College, 1965; Expo '67, Montreal, 1967; Vancouver International Airport, 1967; Juneau Court Office Building, Juneau, Alaska, 1978. **Awards:** Canada Arts Council Scholarship, 1960, Grant, 1969; National Council on the Arts, 1968; National Endowment for the Arts, grant, 1969; Sao Paulo Biennial, Second Prize, 1969. **Address:** 66 Greene Street, NYC 10013. **Dealers:** Hamilton Gallery of Contemporary Art, NYC; Klonaridis, Inc., Toronto. **One-man Exhibitions:** (first in US) Betty Parsons Gallery, 1965, also 1966, 68; Jewish Museum, 1967; David Mirvish Gallery, 1967, 68, 70, 72, 74, 75; Vancouver (two-man), 1969 and 1970; Battery Park, NYC; Dag Hammarskjold Plaza, NYC, 1971; Paula Cooper Gallery, 1974; Janie C. Lee Gallery, Houston, 1977; Hamilton Gallery of Contemporary Art, NYC, 1977, 79, 80; Rice U., 1978; Klonaridis, Inc., Toronto, 1979. **Group:** Ottawa/National, Outdoor Sculpture Exhibition, 1962; Hart House, U. of Toronto, 1964; Finch College, NYC, Artists Select, 1964; U. of Toronto Sculpture Annuals, 1964, 67; WMAA Sculpture Annuals, 1964, 66, 68, 70, 73; WMAA, Young America, 1965; Toronto, 1965; Musée Cantonal des Beaux-Arts, Lausanne, II Salon International de Galeries Pilotes, 1966; Los Angeles/County MA, American Sculpture of the Sixties, circ., 1967; Expo '67, Montreal, 1967; ICA, Boston, Nine Canadians, 1967; SRGM, Guggenheim International, 1967; WMAA, 1967; Paris/Moderne, Canada; Art d'Aujourd'hui, 1968; Walker, 14 Sculptors; The Industrial Edge, 1969; X Sao Paulo Biennial, 1969; Grand Rapids, 1969; Cincinnati/Contemporary, Monumental Art, 1970; Chicago/Contemporary, 49th Parallel; New Canadian Art, 1971; Middelheim Park, Antwerp, XI Sculpture Biennial, 1971; Grand Rapids, Sculpture off the Pedestal, 1973; Newport, R.I., Monumenta, 1974; Akron/AI, Project; New Urban Monuments, 1977. **Collections:** U. of Alberta; Allied Chemical Building, Houston; City of Saskatoon; Columbus; Dayton/AI; Fredonia/SUNY; Hirshhorn; Honeywell, Inc., Minneapolis; Long Beach State College; Melbourne/National; MMA; Montreal/MFA; New Brunswick Museum; Ottawa/National; St. John, N.B.; Seagram Collection; Storm King Art Center; Swarthmore College; U. of Sydney; Syracuse/Everson; Toronto; Vancouver; WMAA; Walker; Wayne State U. **Bibliography:** Davies; Friedman, M., *Monumenta*; Tuchman 1.

N

NADELMAN, ELIE. b. February 20, 1882, Warsaw, Poland; **d.** December 28, 1946, NYC. **Studied:** Art Academy, Warsaw, 1901; Academie Colarossi, Paris, 1904; privately with Konstantin Lazczka, 1902. Imperial Russian Army, 1900. Traveled Russia, Europe, U.S.A. To USA, 1914. **Awards:** Sztuka Prize, 1902. **One-man Exhibitions:** (first) Galerie Drouant, Paris, 1909, also 1913; Photo-Secession, NYC, 1915; Scott and Fowles Gallery, NYC, 1917, 25; M. Knoedler & Co., NYC, 1919, 27; Galerie Bernheim Jeune, Paris, 1920, 27; Arts Club of Chicago; MOMA, 1948; The Zabriskie Gallery, 1967, 1980; Stanford U., 1968. **Retrospective:** WMAA, 1975. **Group:** Salon des Artistes Independants, Paris, 1905–08; Salon d'Automne, Paris, 1905–08; Non-Jury Salon, Berlin, 1913; The Armory Show, 1913; Photo-Secession, NYC, 1915; Carnegie, 1938; WMAA; MOMA; MMA. **Collections:** MOMA; Newark Museum; Utica; WMAA. **Bibliography:** *Avant-Garde Painting and Sculpture in America 1910–25;* **Baur 7; Biddle 4;** Birnbaum; Blesh 1; Brumme; Cherry; Craven, W.; *From Foreign Shores;* Goodrich and Baur 1; Hunter 6; Huyghe; *Index of 20th Century Artists;* **Kirstein 1, 2, 4;** Licht, F.; Marter, Tarbell, and Webster; McCurdy, ed.; Mendelowitz; Motherwell 1; **Murrell 2;** Richardson, E.P.; Ringel, ed.; Rose, B. 1; Selz, J.; Strachan.

NAKIAN, REUBEN. b. August 10, 1897, College Point, N.Y. **Studied:** Robert Henri School, with Homer Boss, A. S. Baylinson; ASL, 1912; apprenticed to Paul Manship, 1917–20, and Gaston Lachaise. Traveled Italy, France. **Taught:** Newark Fine Arts and Industrial Arts College; Pratt Institute, 1949. **Commissions:** NYU, 1960 (sculpture). **Awards:** Guggenheim Foundation Fellowship, 1930; Ford Foundation Grant, 1959 ($10,000); Sao Paulo, 1960; RISD, Athena Award, 1979. **Address:** 30 Windmill Circle, Stamford, Conn. **Dealer:** Marlborough Gallery, NYC. **One-man Exhibitions:** (first) The Downtown Gallery, 1933, also 1935; Charles Egan Gallery, NYC, 1949, 50, 52, 63, 64, 65, 68, 70; Stewart-Marean Gallery, NYC, 1958; Sao Paulo, 1961; Los Angeles/County MA, 1962; WGMA, 1963; Felix Landau Gallery, 1967; U. of Bridgeport, 1972; New York Studio School, Paris, 1974; The Graham Gallery, 1974; Gruenebaum Gallery, NYC, 1979. **Retrospective:** MOMA, 1966. **Group:** Salons of America, NYC, 1922; Whitney Studio Club, NYC; WMAA; Chicago/AI; PAFA; XXXIV Venice Biennial, 1968; MOMA, The New American Painting and Sculpture, 1969. **Collections:** MOMA; NYU. **Bibliography:** Cahill and Barr, eds.; Cheney; Craven, W.; Downes, ed.; Geske; Hunter, ed.; **O'Hara 1, 5;** *New in the Seventies;* Rose, B., 1; Tuchman 1.

NATKIN, ROBERT. b. November 7, 1930, Chicago, Ill. **Studied:** Chicago/AI School, 1952. Designed backdrop for Paul Sanasardo Dance Co., NYC, 1974. **Address:** 24 Mark Twain Lane, West Redding, CT 06896. **Dealer:** Gimpel & Weitzenhoffer, Ltd., NYC. **One-man Exhibition:** Wells Street Gallery, Chicago, 1957, 58; Poindexter Gallery, 1959, 61, 63, 65, 67, 68; Ferus Gallery, Los Angeles, 1960; Fairweather-Hardin

Robert Natkin *Apollo Series* 1980

Gallery, Chicago, 1963, 64, 66, 68, 73, 75; Gertrude Kasle Gallery, Detroit, 1966, 68, 74, 75; Meredith Long Gallery, 1968; Andre Emmerich Gallery, NYC, 1970, 73, 74, 76, 78; Zurich, 1974; The Pennsylvania State U. (two-man), 1973; Jack Glenn Gallery, Corona del Mar, 1973; Makler Gallery, Philadelphia, 1974, 75; Holburne of Menstrie Museum and Festival, Bath, England, 1974; William Sawyer Gallery, San Francisco, 1974, 75; Galerie Merian Edition, Krefeld, 1974; II Cerhio, Milan, 1974; Galleria Venezia, Venice, 1974; Chicago/AI, 1975; Hokin Gallery, Chicago, 1975, 79; Hokin Gallery, Palm Beach, 1975; Linda Farris Gallery, Seattle, 1975; Douglas Drake Gallery, Kansas City, 1976, 78; Andre Emmerich Gallery, Zurich, 1977; Gimpel Fils, London, 1977, 80; Hoshour Gallery, Albuquerque, 1978; Galerie Pudelko, Bonn; Thomas Segal Gallery, Boston, 1979; Gimpel & Weitzenhoffer, Ltd., 1979, 80;

Galerie Brusberg, Hannover, 1979; Tortue Gallery, Santa Monica, 1979; ABCD Gallery, Paris, 1979. **Retrospective:** SFMA, 1969; Kansas City Art Institute, 1976; Moore College of Art, Philadelphia, 1976; Manus Presse Gmbh; Stuttgart, 1980. **Group:** Chicago/AI, Exhibition Momentum, 1950, 56, 57, also 1955, 57, 59, 62; WMAA, Young America, 1960; Carnegie, 1961; ICA, Boston, 1961; WGMA, Lyricism in Abstract Art, 1962; International Mitsubishi, Tokyo and other Japanese cities, 1963; WMAA Annuals, 1966, 68; Galerie Paul Facchetti, 1968; SFMA, 1969; WMAA Annual, 1969; SRGM, 1970, 74; Festival of Two Worlds, Spoleto, 1972. **Collections:** Akron/AI; Brandeis U.; Brooklyn Museum; Carnegie; Duke U.; Hartford/ Wadsworth; Hirshhorn; Houston/MFA; ICA, Boston; U. of Illinois; Los Angeles/ County MA; MOMA; NYU; The Pennsylvania State U.; RISD; SFMA; SRGM; WMAA; Worcester/AM.

Bruce Nauman   *Smoke Rings: 2 Concentric Tunnels Skewed, Non Communicating*   1980

NAUMAN, BRUCE. b. December 6, 1941, Fort Worth, Ind. **Studied:** U. of Wisconsin, BS, 1960–64, with Italo Scanga; U. of California, Davis, 1965, MA. **Taught:** U. of California, Irvine, 1970. **Awards:** National Endowment for the Arts, grant, 1968; Aspen Institute, 1970. **Address:** 4630 Rising Hill Road, Altadena, CA 91001. **Dealer:** Leo Castelli, Inc., NYC. **One-man Exhibitions:** Nicholas Wilder Gallery, 1966, 69, 70, 77; Leo Castelli, Inc., NYC, 1968, 69, 71, 73, 75, 76, 78, 80; Konrad Fischer Gallery, Dusseldorf, 1968, 70, 71, 74, 75, 78; Sacramento State College, 1968; Ileana Sonnabend Gallery, Paris, 1969, 72, 76; Gian Enzo Sperone, Turin, 1970; ACE Gallery, Vancouver, 1971, 76, 78; Joseph Helman Gallery, St. Louis, 1971; Francoise Lambert, Milan, 1971; U. of California, Irvine, 1973; Eindhoven, 1973; Galerie Art in Progress, Munich, 1974; Wide White Space Gallery, Antwerp, 1974; Cirrus Editions, Ltd., 1974; Buffalo/Albright, 1975; U. of Nevada, 1976; Sperone Westwater Fischer, Inc., NYC, 1976; Minneapolis, 1978; INK, Zurich, 1978; Galerie Schmela, Dusseldorf, 1979; Deson-Zaks Gallery, Chicago, 1979; Portland (Ore.) Center for the Visual Arts, 1979; Hester van Royen Gallery, London, 1979. **Retrospec-** **tives:** Dusseldorf/Kunsthalle, 1973; Los Angeles/County MA, 1973. **Group:** SFMA, New Directions, 1966; Los Angeles/County MA, American Sculpture of the Sixties, circ., 1967; Documenta IV, Kassel, 1968; Oberlin College, Three Young Americans, 1968; A.F.A., Soft Sculpture, 1968; Corcoran, 1969; Berne, When Attitudes Become Form, 1969; WMAA, Anti-Illusion; Procedures/Materials, 1969; SRGM, 1969; Chicago/Contemporary, Holograms and Lasers, 1970; ICA, U. of Pennsylvania, Against Order: Chance and Art, 1970; WMAA, 1970; Dusseldorf/Kunsthalle, Prospect '71, 1971; MOMA, Information, 1971; Hayward Gallery, London, 11 Los Angeles Artists, 1971; Rijksmuseum Kroller-Muller, Diagrams and Drawings, 1972; Hamburg/Kunstverein, USA: West Coast, circ., 1972; New York Cultural Center, 3D into 2D, 1973; Seattle/AM, American Art—Third Quarter Century, 1973; Parcheggio di Villa Borghese, Rome, Contemporanea, 1974; Chicago/AI, Idea and Image in Recent Art, 1974; Indianapolis, 1974; CNAC, Art/Voir, 1974; MOMA, Drawing Now, 1975; Chicago/AI, 1976; WMAA, 200 Years of American Sculpture, 1976; Detroit/Institute, American Artists: A New Decade, 1976; U. of

Chicago, Ideas on Paper 1970–76, 1976; WMAA Biennial, 1977; The U. of Chicago, Ideas in Sculpture, 1965–1977, 1977; Williamstown/Clark, The Dada/Surrealist Heritage, 1977; SFMA, Painting and Sculpture in California: The Modern Era, 1976; Madison Art Center, Works on Paper by American Artists, 1977; Amsterdam/Stedelijk, Made by Sculptors, 1978; Krefeld/Haus Lange, The Broadening of the Concept of Reality in the Art of the Sixties and Seventies, 1979; Aspen Center for the Visual Arts, American Portraits of the 60s and 70s, 1979; Franklin Institute, New Spaces: The Holographer's Vision, 1979; U. of Hartford, Conn., Southern California Drawings, 1980. **Collections:** Aachen/Kunstverein; Amsterdam/Stedelijk; Buffalo/Albright; Canberra/National; Chicago/AI; Cologne; Harvard U.; Krefeld/Hans Lange; MOMA; Southwestern College, Chula Vista; SRGM; St. Louis/City; WMAA. **Bibliography:** *Art Now 74*; Celant; *Contemporanea*; Davis, D.; Honisch and Jensen, eds.; Hunter, ed., 2; Johnson, Ellen H.; Krauss 2; *Kunst um 1970*; Lippard, ed.; Lippard 3; Livingston and Tucker; Meyer; Muller; Pincus-Witten; *Report*; *USA West Coast*; *When Attitudes Become Form*.

NEAL, REGINALD. b. May 20, 1909, Leicester, England. **Studied:** Yale U., 1929–30; Bradley U., BA, 1932; State U. of Iowa, summer, 1936; The U. of Chicago, MA (art history), 1939; Colorado Springs Fine Arts Center, summer, 1941. **Taught:** Millikin U., 1940–46; Escuela de Bellas Artes, San Miguel de Allende, Mexico, summer, 1944; U. of Mississippi, 1951–57; The Contemporaries Graphic Center, NYC, summer, 1956; New Paltz/SUNY, 1957–58; Southern Illinois U., 1958–59, 1966, 67; Douglass College, Rutgers, 1959–77; Yale U., 1966. **Commissions:** A.A.A. Gallery, NYC (two editions of lithographs). **Awards:** Film Council of America, Golden Reel Award, 1956 (American Film Festival, Chicago), for a 30-min.

color film, *Color Lithography—An Art Medium*. **Address:** Circle Drive, RD 1, Lebanon, NJ 08833. **Dealers:** Princeton Gallery of Fine Arts, Princeton, N.J.; Haslem Fine Arts, Inc., Washington, D.C. **One-man Exhibitions:** Decatur, 1944; Davenport/Municipal, 1945, 51; South Bend (Ind.) Art Center 1950; A.A.A. Gallery, Chicago, 1950; U. of Mississippi, 1951, 55; The Salpeter Gallery, NYC, 1953; New Paltz/SUNY, 1953; Pratt-Contemporaries, NYC, 1960; Allan Stone Gallery, 1962; Primus-Stuart Gallery, Los Angeles, 1962; Rutgers U., 1965; A.M. Sachs Gallery, 1968; Rutgers U. 1965, 79; Haslem Fine Arts, Inc., Washington, D.C., 1973; Princeton Gallery of Fine Arts, Princeton, N.J., 1973. **Retrospectives:** Somerset (N.J.) Art Association, 1975; Rutgers U., 1975. **Group:** MMA; Cincinnati/AM, 1954, 56, 58; Brooklyn Museum; Library of Congress; Houston/MFA, 1956; Oakland/AM; Riverside Museum; Gallery of Modern Art, Ljubljana, Yugoslavia, III & IV International Exhibitions of Prints, 1959, 61; Albany/Institute, 1965; U. of North Carolina, 1965; Trenton State, 1965, 67, 68, 71, 72; Newark Museum, 1966, 68, 69, 72, 77. **Collections:** Allentown/AM; American Republic Insurance Co.; Atlanta/AA; Cincinnati/AM; Davenport/Municipal; Decatur; Des Moines; Grenchen; Hartford/Wadsworth; Library of Congress; MOMA; U. of Massachusetts; Memphis/Brooks; National Gallery; Philip Morris Collection; Newark Museum; Princeton U.; Queens U.; U. of Rochester; Rutgers U.; Southern Illinois U.; Trenton/State; WGMA. **Bibliography:** Bijalji-Merin; Reese.

NEPOTE, ALEXANDER. b. November 6, 1913, Valley Home, Calif. **Studied:** California College of Arts and Crafts, BA; Mills College; U. of California, MA. Traveled Europe. **Taught:** California College of Arts and Crafts, 1945–50; San Francisco State College, 1950–77. **Awards:** SFMA, James D. Phelan Award, 1941, 42; Oakland/AM, 1947,

48, **P.P.**, 1955, Silver Medal, 1957; San Francisco Art Festival, 1951, 53, 59, 60; San Mateo County Fair, 1954, 57; Pasadena/AM, **P.P.**, 1957; California State Fair, 1957, 58; California Palace, 1958; California Watercolor Society, First Award, 1965; Northern California Artists, First Award, 1965; Rio Hondo College Invitational, First Award, 1968; San Mateo Art Fiesta, First Award, 1969. **Address:** 410 Taylor Boulevard, Millbrae, CA 94030. **Dealer:** Suzanne Brown Gallery, Scottsdale, Ariz. **One-man Exhibitions:** Quay Gallery, 1966; Kramer Gallery, San Francisco, 1968; Richard White Gallery, Seattle, 1968; Emerson Art Gallery, Sacramento, 1969; St. Mary's College, Moraga, Calif., 1969; College of Idaho, 1970; Suzanne Brown Gallery, Scottsdale, Ariz., 1978, 80; Fresno Arts Center, Fresno, Calif., 1980. **Retrospective:** Redwood City Municipal Gallery, 1974. **Group:** United Nations Conference Exhibition, San Francisco, 1945; California Palace, 1947, 48, 52, 59, 60, 61; Grand Central, NYC, 1948; WMAA, 1951; U. of Illinois, 1951, 52; A.F.A.; MMA, 1952; Sao Paulo, 1955; SFMA, 1955; a gallery in Provincetown, Mass., 1958; ART: USA:58, NYC, 1958; VMFA, American Painting, 1962; Expo '70, Osaka, 1970; Auckland, Art of the Pacific Basin, 1971; National Watercolor Society Annuals, 1973, 74. **Collections:** California Palace; Chico State College; Denver/AM; Los Angeles/County MA; MMA; U. of Michigan; Mills College; Oakland/AM; Pasadena/AM; Rio Hondo College; SFMA; Sacramento/Crocker; San Francisco Municipal Art Commission; Southern Idaho College; Utah State U.; Walnut Creek Municipal Collection.

NERI, MANUEL. b. 1930, Sanger, Calif. **Studied:** San Francisco City College, 1949–50; U. of California, Berkeley, 1951–52; California School of Arts and Crafts, Oakland, 1952–57; California School of Fine Arts, San Francisco, 1957–59, with Elmer Bischoff. **Taught:** California School of Fine Arts, San Francisco, 1959–64; U. of California, Davis, 1964– . **Awards:** Oakland/AM, first award in sculpture, 1953; Oakland/AM, **P.P.** in painting, 1957; Nellie Sullivan Award, 1959; National Art Foundation award, 1965; Guggenheim Foundation Fellowship, 1979; National Endowment for the Arts grant, 1980. **Address:** % Dealer. **Dealer:** Gallery Paule Anglim, San Francisco; Charles Cowles Gallery, NYC. **One-man Exhibitions:** Six Gallery, San Francisco, 1957; Spatsa Gallery, San Francisco, 1959; Dilexi Gallery, San Francisco, 1960, New Mission Gallery, San Francisco, 1963; Berkeley Gallery, Berkeley, 1964; Quay Gallery, San Francisco, 1966, 68, 71, 75; Louisiana State U., 1969; St. Mary's College, Moraga, Calif., 1970; SFMA, 1971; Sacramento State College, 1972; Davis Art Center, Calif., 1972; San Jose State U., 1974; Braunstein Quay Gallery, NYC, 1976; 60 Langton St., San Francisco, 1976; Oakland/AM, 1976; Sacramento/Crocker, 1977; Gallery Paule Anglim, San Francisco, 1979; Whitman College, 1980; Richmond (Calif.) Art Center, 1980; Grossmont College, 1980. **Group:** Oakland/AM Annuals, 1955, 57; SFMA, four-man show, 1959; California Palace, San Francisco, The Nude, 1962; Stanford U., Some Points of View, 1962; Oakland/AM, Sculpture Today, 1963; Stanford U., Current Painting and Sculpture of the Bay Area, 1964; U. of California, Irvine, Abstract Expressionist Ceramics, 1966; U. of California, Berkeley, Funk Art, 1967; SFMA, On Looking Back: Bay Area 1945–1962, 1969; WMAA Annual, 1970; U. of California, Berkeley, The Eighties, 1970; SFAI, two-man show, 1970; U. of Nevada, two-man show, 1971; Sacramento/Crocker, Sacramento Sampler I, 1972; SFMA, A Third World Painting and Sculpture Exhibition, 1974; De Anza College, Survey of Sculptural Directions in the Bay Area, 1975; Sydney/AG, Biennial, 1976; SFMA, California Painting and Sculpture: The Modern Era, 1976; Santa Barbara/MA, The

Handmade Paper Object, 1976; Syracuse/Everson, A Century of Ceramics in the U.S. 1878–1978, 1978; San Diego, Sculpture in California 1975–1980; SFMA, 20 American Artists, 1980. **Collections:** U. of Colorado; The Mexican Museum, San Francisco; Oakland/AM; Sacramento/Crocker; SFMA. **Bibliography:** Archives.

NESBITT, LOWELL. b. October 4, 1933, Baltimore, Md. **Studied:** Temple U., BFA, 1950–55; Royal College of Art, London, 1955–56. US Army, 1957–58. Traveled Europe. **Taught:** Baltimore/MA; Towson State Teachers College; Morgan State College; School of Visual Arts, NYC. **Commissions:** National Aeronautics & Space Administration. **Address:** 389 West 12th Street, NYC 10014. **Dealer:** Andrew Crispo Gallery, NYC. **One-man Exhibitions:** (first) Baltimore/MA 1958, also 1959–69; Bader Gallery, Washington, DC, 1963; Corcoran, 1964; Rolf Nelson Gallery, Los Angeles, 1966; Henri Gallery 1965–67, 1969; The Howard Wise Gallery, NYC, 1965, 66; Gertrude Kasle Gallery, 1966–69, 1970, 72, 74; Jefferson Gallery, 1967; Temple U., 1967; Galleria Sperone, Turin, 1967 (two-man, with Joseph Raffael); The Stable Gallery, NYC, 1968, 69; U. of Richmond; M. E. Thelen Gallery, Cologne, 1969, 70, 72; Gimpel Fils, 1970, 74; Gimpel & Weitzenhoffer Ltd., 1971, 73; Pyramid Art Galleries, 1971, 75; Hansen-Fuller Gallery, 1972; Gimpel & Hanover, 1972; Gallerie Fabian Carlsson, Goteborg, 1972; Corcoran and Corcoran, Coral Gables, 1972; Gallerie Ostergren, Malmo, 1972; Kunstverein, Freiburg, 1972; Galerie Arnesen, Copenhagen, 1972, 74; Galerie Aronowitsch, Stockholm, 1972; Marion Locks Gallery, Philadelphia, 1973, Galerie Craven, Paris, 1973; Corcoran, 1973; Stefanotty Gallery, NYC, 1973, 74; Fendrick Gallery, 1974; Brooke Alexander, 1974; Walton Gallery, San Francisco, 1974; H.M., Brussels, 1974, 76; Museo de Bellas Artes, San Juan, 1974; U. of Rochester, 1975; City Center, NYC, 1975; Hokin Gallery, Palm Beach, 1976; Hokin Gallery, Chicago 1976; Gump's Gallery, San Francisco, 1977; Andrew Crispo Gallery, 1977, 78, 79; Wichita/Ulrich, 1977; Janus Gallerie, Venice; Cleveland, 1977; Arte/Contacto, Caracas, 1977, 80; Strong's Gallerie, Cleveland, 1978; Kent State.; B.R. Kornblatt Gallery, Baltimore, 1978; The Art Contact, Miami, 1978; San Antonio/McNay, 1980; Ridgefield/Aldrich, 1980. **Group:** Pan-American Union, Washington, D.C., circ., Latin America, 1964–66; New York World's Fair, 1964–65; Ridgefield/Aldrich, 1965; Flint/Institute, Realism Revisited, 1966; U. of Illinois, 1967; Milan, 1967; Los Angeles/County MA, 1967; International Biennial of Paintings, Tokyo, 1967; IX Sao Paulo Biennial, 1967; ICA, London, 1968; WMAA Annual, 1967; Milwaukee, Aspects of a New Realism, 1969; Sweden/Goteborgs, Warmwind, 1970; Cologne, Target Moon, 1971; Brooklyn Museum, Print Exhibition, 1972; Galerie des 4 Mouvements, Paris, Hyperrealistes Americans, 1972; Bibliotheque Nationale, L'Estampe Contemporaine, 1973; Tokyo Biennial, 1974; Paris/Moderne, 1974; West Palm Beach/Norton, Imagist Realism, 1975; U. of Redlands, Handcolored Prints, circ., 1975; US Department of the Interior, America 1976, circ., 1976; Brooklyn Museum, Thirty Years of American Printmaking, 1977; Museum of Contemporary Crafts, NYC, The Great American Foot, 1978–80. **Collections:** Aachen/NG; Amerada Hess Corp; AT&T; Baltimore/MA; The Bank of New York; Bibliotheque Nationale; CNAC; Chase Manhattan Bank; Chicago/AI; Cleveland/MA; Corcoran; Dallas/MFA; Detroit/Institute; F.T.D. Association; Ford Motor Company; Fort Worth; General Mills, Minneapolis; Goucher College; International Monetary Fund; La Jolla; Library of Congress; Milwaukee; MIT; MOMA; U. of Maryland; NCFA; National Art Gallery; Newark; Oberlin College; J. C. Penney Corp.; Phillips; PMA; Ponce; Prudential Insurance Co. of America; U. of Rochester;

Saginaw; Temple U.; U. of Virginia; Wellington, N.F.; Wells, Rich, Greene, Inc., NYC; Worcester/AM; Yale U. **Bibliography:** *America 1976;* Arthur 1; Arthur 2; Davis, D.; Honisch and Jensen, eds.; *Kunst um 1970;* Sager.

NEUMAN, ROBERT S. b. September 9, 1926, Kellogg, Ida. **Studied:** California School of Fine Arts; Mills College, with Max Beckmann; U. of Idaho; Academy of Fine Arts, Stuttgart, with Willi Baumeister. Traveled Europe, USA. **Taught:** California College of Arts and Crafts, 1951–53; California School of Fine Arts, 1952–53; SUNY, 1954–56; Massachusetts College of Art, 1957–62; Brown U., 1962–63; Harvard U., 1963–72; Keene (N.H.) State College, 1972– . **Awards:** Fulbright Fellowship, 1953; Guggenheim Foundation Fellowship, 1956–57; Boston Arts Festival, Grand Prize, 1961; Brown U., Howard Foundation Grant for Painting, 1967. **Address:** 9 Pembroke Street, Weston, MA 02193. **Dealer:** Allan Stone Gallery; Sunne Savage Gallery, Boston. **One-man Exhibitions:** Gump's Gallery, 1952; Felix Landau Gallery, 1954; La Escondida, Taos, N.M., 1956; Sala Vayreda, Barcelona, 1956; Galleria del Cavallino, Venice, 1957, 60; The Swetzoff Gallery, Boston, 1957, 58; Allan Stone Gallery, Harrison, N.Y., 1959; Gres Gallery, Washington, D.C., 1959; The Pace Gallery, Boston, 1960, 62; Lincoln, Mass./De Cordova, 1963; Allan Stone Gallery, NYC, 1966, 72; Ward-Nasse Gallery, Boston, 1966, 67; Exeter, 1967; Waitsfield/Bundy, 1968; Michael Walls Gallery, 1968; Bristol (R.I.) Museum of Art, 1968 (two-man, with Hugh Townley); U. of Idaho, 1969; Brockton (Mass.) Art Center, 1971; Keene State College, 1972; BAAK Gallery, Cambridge, Mass., 1976; Sunne Savage Gallery, Boston, 1979. **Group:** California Palace, 1951; SFMA, 1951–53; Denver/AM, 1952; MMA, 1952; WMAA, 1952, 58; U. of Illinois, 1952, 61; PAFA, 1953; Colorado Springs/FA, 1953; Kyoto, Japan, 1956; ICA, Boston, 1958–60; Carnegie, 1961; Seattle World's Fair, 1962; M. Knoedler & Co., Art across America, circ., 1965–67; New School for Social Research, 1966; State U. of Iowa, 1968; Lincoln, Mass./De Cordova, New England Drawings, 1974; Silvermine, Annual, 1976; Worcester/AM, Recent Acquisitions, 1977. **Collections:** American Broadcasting Co.; Andover/Phillips; Boston/MFA; Boston U.; Brandeis U.; Carnegie; Commercial Union Assurance Co., Boston; ICA, Boston; Lincoln, Mass./De Cordova; MOMA; U. of Massachusetts; SFMA; Worcester/AM; Yale U.

NEVELSON, LOUISE. b. 1900, Kiev, Russia. To USA, 1905. **Studied:** ASL, 1929–30, with Kenneth Hayes Miller; Hofmann School, Munich, 1931; assistant to Diego Rivera in Mexico City, 1932–33. Legion Memorial Square, in the Wall Street area of Manhattan, was renamed Louise Nevelson Plaza, 1978. *Shadows and Flags,* seven large metal sculptures, are installed there. Traveled Europe, Central and South America. **Taught:** Educational Alliance, NYC; Great Neck (N.Y.) Adult Education Program; New York School for the Deaf. **Member:** Artists Equity (President); Sculpture Guild (Vice-President); Federation of Modern Painters and Sculptors (Vice-President). Federal A.P.: Easel painting; AAAL, 1979. **Awards:** ART: USA:59, NYC, Grand Prize, 1959; Chicago/AI, The Mr. & Mrs. Frank G. Logan Prize, 1960; Tamarind Fellowship, 1963; MacDowell Colony Medal, 1969; Hamline U., Honorary Doctor of Humanities; Brandeis U., Creative Arts Award, 1971; Hobart and William Smith College, Honorary Doctor of Humane Letters, 1971; Hon. DFA, Smith College, 1973; President's Medal of the Municipal Art Society of New York. **Commissions:** Princeton U., 1969; Temple Beth-El, Great Neck, N.Y., 1970; Temple Israel, Boston, 1973; City of Scottsdale, 1973; City of Binghamton, N.Y., 1973; Federal Courthouse, Philadelphia, 1975; MIT; St. Peter's Lutheran

Church, NYC; World Trade Center, NYC; City of Jackson, Mich.; Embarcadero Center Plaza, San Francisco; Pepsico Co., Purchase, N.Y.; Bendix Corp., Southfield, Mich.; Federated Department Stores, Cincinnati, Ohio. **Address:** 29 Spring Street, NYC 10012. **Dealer:** The Pace Gallery. **One-man Exhibitions:** (first) Karl Nierendorf Gallery, NYC, 1941, also 1943, 44, 46; Norlyst Gallery, NYC, 1941, 43; Lotte Jacobi Gallery, NYC, 1950; Grand Central Moderns, NYC, 1951, 54, 56, 57, 58; Esther Stuttman Gallery, NYC, 1958; Martha Jackson Gallery, 1959, 61, 70; Daniel Cordier, Paris, 1960; David Herbert Gallery, NYC, 1960; Devorah Sherman Gallery, 1960; The Pace Gallery, Boston, 1960, 64, NYC, 1965, 66, 69, 72, 74, 76, 78, 80; Sidney Janis Gallery, 1963; Hanover Gallery, 1963; Gimpel & Hanover Galerie, Zurich, 1964; Berne, 1964; Galleria d'Arte Contemporanea, Turin, 1964; David Mirvish Gallery, 1965; Galerie Schmela, 1965; Ferus/Pace Gallery, Los Angeles, 1966; Arts Club of Chicago, 1968; Turin/Civico, 1969; Harcus-Krakow Gallery, 1969; Galerie Jeanne Bucher, Paris, 1969; Pace Gallery, Columbus, 1969, 74; Houston/ MFA, 1969; Rijksmuseum Kroller-Muller, 1969; U. of Texas, 1970; WMAA, 1970; Makler Gallery, 1971, 74, 76, 78; Dunkelman Gallery, Toronto, 1972; Parker Street 470 Gallery, Boston, 1972; Studio Marconi, Milan, 1973; Stockholm/National, 1973; Brussels/ Beaux-Arts, 1974; Paris/Moderne, 1974; Berlin/National, 1974; Minami Gallery, 1975; Galleria d'Arte Spagnoli, Florence, Italy, 1975; Harcus Krakow Rosen Sonnabend, Boston, 1975; Purchase/SUNY, 1977; The Pace Gallery, Columbus, 1978; Richard Gray Gallery, Chicago, 1978; Linda Farris Gallery, Seattle, 1978; Rockland, Maine, 1979; West Palm Beach/Norton, 1979; Jacksonville/AM, 1979; Wildenstein & Co., NYC, 1980; Scottsdale Center for the Arts, 1980; Phoenix/AM, 1980; Seattle/ AM, 1980; Winnipeg Art Gallery, Ontario, Canada, 1980; U. of Iowa, 1980; Dayton/AI, 1980. **Retrospectives:**

WMAA, 1966; Walker, circ., 1973; WMAA, 1980. **Group:** Sezession Gallery (Europe), 1933–38; Contemporary Arts Gallery, NYC; Jacobsen Gallery, NYC; Society of Independent Artists, NYC; Brooklyn Museum; ACA Gallery; Federal Art Project Gallery, NYC, 1933–38; PAFA, 1944; VMFA, 1957; Riverside Museum, Directions in Sculpture, 1957; A.F.A., Art and the Found Object, circ., 1959; Jeanne Bucher, Paris (three-man), 1958; MOMA, Sixteen Americans, circ., 1959; ART:USA:59, NYC, 1959; Rome–New York Foundation, Rome, Ciphers, 1960; Utica, Art Across America, 1960; A.F.A., Unique Impressions, 1960; XXXI Venice Biennial, 1962; WMAA Annuals, 1947, 57, 61, 64, 66, 69; Federation of Modern Painters and Sculptors Annuals, 1955, 56, 57, 59; A.F.A., Contemporary Trends, circ., 1955–56; American Abstract Artists Annuals, 1956, 57, 59, 60; Documenta III, Kassel, 1964; MOMA, Contemporary Painters and Sculptors as Printmakers, 1964; Dallas/MFA, 1965; WMAA, Art of the U.S. 1670–1966, 1966; Chicago/AI, 1966, 67; Los Angeles/County MA, American Sculpture of the Sixties, 1967; SRGM, 1967; Jewish Museum, 1968; WMAA, 1969, 73; MOMA, Tamarind; Homage to Lithography, 1969; Princeton U., American Art since 1960, 1970; Expo '70, Osaka, 1970; Carnegie, 1970; Society of the Four Arts, Calder/Nevelson/ David Smith, 1971; Seattle/AM, American Art—Third Quarter Century, 1973; National Gallery, American Art—Third Quarter Century, 1973; National Gallery, American Art at Mid-Century, 1973; Newport, R.I., Monumenta, 1974; WMAA, The 20th Century: 35 Artists, 1974. **Collections:** Arts Club of Chicago; Birmingham, Ala./MA; Brandeis U.; Buffalo/Albright; Brooklyn Museum; Carnegie; Chicago/AI; Fairmount Park Association; Grenoble; Hirshhorn; Hospital Corp. of America; Houston/ MFA; Indiana U.; Jerusalem/National; Jewish Museum; Julliard; MMA; MOMA; NYU; U. of Nebraska; Newark Museum; Paris/Moderne; Pasadena/

AM; Princeton U.; Queens College; Rijksmuseum Kroller-Muller; Sara Roby Foundation; Rockland/Farnsworth; Rotterdam; SRGM; St. Louis/City; South Mall, Albany; Tate; WMAA. **Bibliography:** Baur 5; Calas, N. and E.; Craven; W.; Diamonstein; Davies; **Friedman, M., 3;** *From Foreign Shores;* **Glimcher;** Goodrich and Baur 1; **Gordon 4;** Honisch and Jensen, eds.; Hunter, ed.; *Louise Nevelson: Atmosphere and Environments;* Janis and Blesh 1; Licht, F.; Marter, Tarbell, and Wechsler; *Metro; Monumenta;* Nemser; Moser 1; Neumeyer; Rickey; Rose, B., 1; Seitz 3; Selz, J.; Seuphor 3; Strachan; Trier 1; Tuchman 1. Archives.

NEVELSON, MIKE. b. February 23, 1922, NYC. **Studied:** NYU; self-taught in art. Traveled Europe, Mediterranean, Africa, Central and South America. **Taught:** Wooster Community Art Center, Danbury, Conn., 1965–68; Brookfield (Conn.) Craft Center, 1968; U. of New Mexico, 1969–70. **Member:** Artists Equity. **Awards:** Silvermine Guild, 1966. **Address:** 3 Milltown Road, New Fairfield, CT 06810. **One-man Exhibitions:** Roko Gallery, 1945; Rockland/Farnsworth, 1953; U. of Maine, 1953; Haystack Mountain School of Crafts, 1956; Carl Seimbab Gallery, 1959; Staempfli Gallery, 1961; The Amel Gallery, NYC, 1964; Wooster Community Art Center, Danbury, 1966; Dartmouth College, 1966; Grand Central Moderns, NYC, 1967; Expo '67, Montreal, 1967; Sachs New York, Inc., NYC, 1969; A.A.A. Gallery, NYC (two-man), 1970; Christ-Janer Gallery, New Canaan, Conn. (two-man), 1975. **Group:** Portland, Me./MA, 1956; Boston Arts Festival, 1959; Norfolk Art Festival, Va., 1959; Carnegie, 1961; Houston/Contemporary, 1961; U. of Illinois, 1961; WMAA, 1962, 64; Hartford/Wadsworth, 1963; Silvermine Guild, 1964, 68, 69; Lincoln, Mass./De Cordova, 1964; Four Seasons Restaurant, Pop Exhibition, 1965; U. of Connecticut, 1965; Brooklyn Museum, 1972; Potsdam/

SUNY, 1973; Norske Internasjonale Grafikk Biennale, Fredrikstad, Norway, 1974. **Collections:** Colby College; Hartford/Wadsworth; Housatonic Community College; Slater, Stratford College; WMAA; Youngstown/Butler. **Bibliography:** Archives.

NEWMAN, BARNETT. b. January 29, 1905, NYC; **d.** July 4, 1970, NYC. **Studied:** Cornell U., 1922–26; City College of New York, BA, 1927; ASL, with Duncan Smith, John Sloan, William Von Schlegell. Traveled USA, Canada, Europe. **Taught:** U. of Saskatchewan, 1959; U. of Pennsylvania, 1962–64. Cofounder of a school, "Subject of the Artist," with William Baziotes, Robert Motherwell, and Mark Rothko, NYC, 1948. **One-man Exhibitions:** (first) Betty Parsons Gallery, 1950, also 1951; Bennington College, 1958; French & Co., Inc., NYC, 1959; Allan Stone Gallery (two-man), 1962; SRGM, 1966; M. Knoedler & Co., 1969; Irving Blum Gallery, Los Angeles, 1970; Kammerkunsthalle, Berlin, 1970; U. of Washington, 1971. **Retrospectives:** Pasadena/AM, 1970; MOMA, 1971; Tate, 1972; Baltimore/MA, 1979. **Group:** Chicago/AI, Abstract and Surrealist Art, 1948; Minneapolis/Institute, American Painting, 1945–57, 1957; MOMA, The New American Painting, circ., Europe, 1958–59; Documenta II, Kassel, 1959; Kimura Gallery, Tokyo, 1959; SRGM, Abstract Expressionists and Imagists, 1961; SRGM/USIA, American Vanguard, circ., Europe, 1961–62; Seattle World's Fair, 1962; WMAA Annual, 1963; Brandeis U., New Directions in American Painting, 1963; Jewish Museum, Black and White, 1963; Tate, Dunn International, 1964; Chicago/AI Annual, 1964; SRGM, Guggenheim International, 1964; Kunsthalle, Basel, International Painting since 1950, 1964; MOMA, The New American Painting and Sculpture, 1969. **Collections:** Amsterdam/Stedelijk; Basel; Kunsthalle, Basel; MOMA; Stockholm/National. **Bibliography:** Alloway 4; Battcock, ed.; Calas,

N. and E.; Carmean, Rathbone, and Hess; Chipp; De Vries, ed.; *The Great Decade*; Goossen 1; Greenberg 1; Haftman; **Hess, T. B., 2, 3;** Hobbs and Levin; Honisch and Jensen, eds.; Hunter, ed.; Hunter 1; Johnson, Ellen H.; Kozloff 3; Lippard 5; *Metro; Monumenta*; Motherwell and Reinhardt, eds.; Richardson 1; Rickey; Rose, B., 1, 4; Rosenblum 2; Rubin 1; Sandler; Sandler 1; Schneider; Seuphor 1; Tomkins 2; Tuckman, ed.

NILSSON, GLADYS. b. 1940, Chicago. **Studied:** Chicago Art Institute School, 1962. **Commissions:** ART Park, Lewiston, N.Y., 1979. **Awards:** Chicago/AI, Logan Medal, 1967; Chicago/AI, Bartels Prize, 1978; National Endowment for the Arts, Grant, 1974. **m.** Jim Nutt. **Address:** 1035 Greenwood, Wilmette, IL 60091. **Dealer:** Candy Store Gallery, Folsom, Calif.; Phyllis Kind Gallery, Chicago and NYC. **One-man Exhibitions:** SFAI, 1969; Candy Store Gallery, Folsom, Calif., 1971, 72, 73; WMAA, 1973; U. of Wisconsin, Madison, 1977; Phyllis Kind Gallery, Chicago, 1970, 73, 74, 77, 78; Phyllis Kind Gallery, NYC, 1975, 79; Portland (Ore.) Center for Visual Arts, 1979; Wake Forest U., 1979. **Group:** Hyde Park Art Center, Chicago. The Hairy Who, 1966, 67, 68; Chicago/Contemporary, Don Baum Sez, "Chicago Needs Famous Artists," 1969; ICA, U. of Philadelphia, Spirit of the Comics, 1969; WMAA, Human Concern/Personal Torment, 1970; SFMA, Poetic Fantasy, 1971; Chicago/Contemporary, Chicago Imagist Art, 1972; Ottawa/Ontario, What They're Up to in Chicago, 1972; Sao Paulo, XII Biennial; Madison Art Center, Contemporary Figurative Painting in the Midwest, 1977; Sacramento/Crocker, The Chicago Connection, 1977; Chicago/AI, 100 Artists—100 Years, 1979; U. of North Carolina, Some Recent Art from Chicago, 1980. **Collections:** Chicago/AI; MOMA; Museum des 20. Jahrhunderts, Vienna; New Orleans Museum; Phoenix; U. of Rochester; WMAA.

NIVOLA, CONSTANTINO. b. July 5, 1911, Orani, Sardinia. **Studied:** Istituto Superiore d'Arte, Monza, Italy, with Marino Marini, Marcello Nizzoli, 1930–36, MA, Art Director for Olivetti Company, 1936–39. Traveled Europe, USA. To USA, 1939. Art Director, *Interiors* magazine, 1941–45. **Taught:** Director, Design Workshop of Harvard U. Graduate School, 1953–57; Columbia U., 1961–63; Harvard U., 1970–73; International U. of Art, Florence, Italy, 1971; Dartmouth College, 1978; U. of California, Berkeley, 1978–79. **Member:** Artists Equity; Architectural League of New York; NIAL. **Commissions:** Milan Triennial, 1933 (mural, with S.R. Francello); Italian Pavilion, Paris World's Fair, 1937; Olivetti Showroom, NYC, 1953–54 (mural); Four Chaplains Memorial Fountain, Falls Church, Va., 1955; 1025 Fifth Avenue, NYC, 1955 (gardens); William E. Grady Vocational High School, Brooklyn, N.Y., 1957; Mutual Insurance Co. of Hartford, Hartford, Conn., 1957 (facade); P.S. 46, Brooklyn, N.Y., 1959 (murals and sculptures for playground); McCormick Place, Exposition Hall, Chicago, 1960 (facade); Motorola Building, Chicago, 1960 (murals); Saarinen Dormitories, Yale U., 1962 (35 sculptures); designed a memorial plaza in Nuoro, Italy, 1966; P.S. 320, Brooklyn, N.Y., 1967 (sculpture); Mexico City/Nacional, 19th Olympiad, 1968 (sculpture). **Awards:** Philadelphia Decorators Club Award, 1959; Carborundum Major Abrasive Marketing Award, 1962; Municipal Art Society of New York, Certificate of Merit, 1962; Architectural League of New York, Silver Medal of Honor in Sculpture, 1962; Regional Exhibition of Figurative Art, Cagliari, Italy, Gold Medal; Federation of Graphic Arts, Diploma; Park Association of New York, NYC, Certificate of Commendation, 1965; American Institute of Architects, Fine Arts Medal, 1968. **Address:** 410 Stone Road, Springs, East Hampton, NY 11937. **One-man Exhibitions:** (first) Sassari Gallery, Sardinia, 1927 (paintings); Betty Parsons Gallery, 1940 (two-man, with Saul Steinberg); (first one-man in USA) Tibor de Nagy Gallery, 1950; The Peridot Gallery, 1954, 57; Harvard U., 1956; The Bertha Schaefer Gallery, 1958; Architectural League of New York, 1958; Galleria Il Milione, Milan, 1959; Arts Club of Chicago, 1959; A.F.A., circ., 1960; Galleria dell' Ariete, 1962; The Byron Gallery, 1964–67; Andrew-Morris Gallery, NYC; Marlborough Galleria d'Arte, Rome, 1973; The Willard Gallery, 1973; Cagliari U., Italy, 1973; ICA, Boston, 1974; Gallery Paule Anglim, San Francisco, 1978. **Group:** Brooklyn Museum, 1947; American Abstract Artists, 1947; Rome National Art Quadriennial, 1950, 73; Riverside Museum, NYC, 1955; WMAA, 1957, Carnegie, 1958; Museum of Contemporary Crafts, 1962; National Gold Medal Exhibition of the Building Arts, NYC, 1962; A.F.A., American Drawing, circ., 1964. MOMA. **Collections:** Hirshhorn; MOMA; PMA; WMAA. **Bibliography:** Giedion-Welcker 1; Licht, F.; *Metro;* Seuphor 3; Trier 1.

Isamu Noguchi   *Noh Musicians*   1958–74

NOGUCHI, ISAMU. b. November 17, 1904, Los Angeles, Calif. Resided Japan, ages 2–14. **Studied:** Columbia U., 1923–25 (premedical); apprenticed briefly to Gutzon Borglum; Leonardo da Vinci Art School, NYC; East Side Art School, NYC; apprenticed to Constantin Brancusi, Paris, 1927–29. Traveled Mexico, USSR, the Orient, Europe, Israel, USA. Designed numerous stage sets for Martha Graham Dance Co. **Member:** National Sculpture Society. **Commissions:** Connecticut General Life Insurance Co. (gardens and sculpture); First National Bank of Fort Worth, Tex. (piazza and sculpture); John Hancock Building (fountain and sculpture); Chase Manhattan Bank, NYC (garden); Associated Press, NYC (relief), 1938; Yale U. Library of Precious Books; Keyo U., Japan (2 gardens); UNESCO, Paris (garden); International Business Machines, Armonk, N.Y.; Billy Rose Garden, Jerusalem; De-troit Civic Center Memorial Fountain, 1974; Pepsico, Purchase, N.Y., 1974; Horace E. Dodge & Son Memorial Fountain, and Philip A. Hart Plaza, Detroit, Mich., 1973–79; stepped garden for Sogetsu School of Flower Arrangement, Tokyo, 1977–78. **Awards:** Guggenheim Foundation Fellowship, 1927; Bollingen Foundation Fellowship, 1950; Chicago/AI, The Mr. & Mrs. Frank G. Logan Medal; Hon. DFA, New School for Social Research, 1974. **Address:** 33–38 Tenth Street, Long Island City, NY 11106. **Dealer:** The Pace Gallery, NYC. **One-man Exhibitions:** (first) Eugene Schoen Gallery, NYC, 1929; Marie Sterner Gallery, NYC, 1930; Harvard Society for Contemporary Art, 1930; Arts Club of Chicago, 1930; Buffalo/Albright, 1930; Reinhardt Galleries, NYC, 1932; Demotte Gallery, NYC, 1932; Mellon Galleries, Philadelphia, 1933; Marie

Harriman Gallery, NYC, 1934; Sidney Burney Gallery, London, 1934; Western Association of Art Museum Directors, circ., 1934; Honolulu Academy, 1934, 39; John Becker (Gallery), NYC, 1939, 42; SFMA, 1942; Charles Egan Gallery, 1948; Daniel Cordier, Paris; Cordier & Ekstrom, Inc., 1963, 65, 67–69, 70; Gimpel & Hanover, 1968, 72; Gimpel Fils, 1968, 72; Minami Gallery, 1973; The Pace Gallery, NYC, 1975, 80; MOMA, 1977; Walker, circ., 1978–79; Andre Emmerich Gallery, NYC, 1980; WMAA, 1980. **Retrospective:** WMAA, 1968. **Group:** MOMA, Fantastic Art, Dada, Surrealism, 1936; Musée du Jeu de Paume, Trois Siecles d'Art aux Etats-Unis, 1938; MOMA, Art in Our Time, 1939; MOMA, 14 Americans, 1946; MOMA, Abstract Painting and Sculpture in America, 1951; WMAA, Nature and Abstraction, 1958; Documenta II & III, Kassel, 1959, 64; WMAA, American Art of Our Century, 1961; Seattle World's Fair, 1962; Los Angeles/County MA, American Sculpture of the Sixties, circ., 1967; WMAA, 1970; Carnegie, 1970; Venice Biennial, 1972; SRGM, Masters of Modern Sculpture, 1974; WMAA, 200 Years of American Sculpture, 1976. **Collections:** Art Gallery of Ontario, Toronto; Brooklyn Museum; Buffalo/Albright; Chicago/AI; Cleveland/MA; Des Moines; Hartford/Wadsworth; Hirshhorn; Honolulu Academy; Jerusalem/National; Kamakura; Los Angeles/County MA; MMA; MOMA; U. of Nebraska; New School for Social Research; Princeton U.; Rijksmuseum Kroller-Muller; SFMA; SRGM; Society of Four Arts; Tate; Toledo/MA; Toronto; WMAA; Walker; West Palm Beach/Norton. **Bibliography:** Baur 5, 7; Biddle 4; Blesh 1; Breton 3; Brumme; Cahill and Barr, eds.; Calas; Cheney; Craven, W.; Cummings 1; Downes, ed.; Flanagan; Giedion-Welcker 1; Goodrich and Baur 1; **Gordon 2;** Hunter 6; *Index of 20th Century Artists;* **Isamu Noguchi; Isamu 2;** Krauss 2; Kuh 2; Licht, F.; McCurdy, ed.; Marter, Tarbell, and Wechsler; Mendelowitz; *Metro;* Miller, ed. 2; Neu-

meyer; **Noguchi;** Read 3; Ritchie 1, 3; Rose, B., 1; Rubin 1; Seuphor 3; Seymour; Strachan; **Takiguchi;** Trier 1; Tuchman 1. Archives.

NOLAND, KENNETH. b. April 10, 1924, Asheville, N.C. **Studied:** Black Mountain College, 1946, with Ilya Bolotowsky; Zadkine School of Sculpture, Paris, 1948–49. US Air Force, 1942–46. **Taught:** The Catholic U. of America; ICA, Washington, D.C.; Emma Lake Artist's Workshops, U. of Saskatchewan; Bennington College. **Awards:** Corcoran, 1967. **Member:** AAAL. **Address:** % Dealer. **Dealer:** Andre Emmerich Gallery, NYC and Zurich. **One-man Exhibitions:** (first) Galerie Creuze, Paris, 1949; French & Co. Inc., NYC, 1959; Galleria dell'Ariete, 1960; Galerie Lawrence, Paris, 1961; Bennington College, 1961; Andre Emmerich Gallery, NYC, 1961–64, 1966, 67, 71, 73, 75, 77, 80; Galerie Charles Leinhard, Zurich, 1962; Galerie Schmela, 1962; 64; Kasmin Ltd., 1963, 65, 68; David Mirvish Gallery, 1965, 74, 76; Harvard U., Three American Painters (with Jules Olitski, Frank Stella), circ., Pasadena, 1965; St. John, N.B., 1966 (three-man, with Helen Frankenthaler, Jules Olitski); MMA, 1968 (three-man, with Morris Louis, Anthony Caro); Lawrence Rubin Gallery, 1969; Dayton's Gallery 12, Minneapolis, 1969 (three-man, with Anthony Caro, Frank Stella); Galerie Mikro, Berlin, 1972; Waddington Galleries, London, 1973; Jack Glenn Gallery, Corona del Mar, 1974; Janie C. Lee Gallery, Houston, 1974; Rutland Gallery, London, 1974; School of Visual Arts, NYC, 1975; Watson/De Nagy, Houston, 1975; Leo Castelli Inc., NYC, 1976, 79, 80; Galerie Wentzel, Hamburg, 1977; Thomas Segal Gallery, Boston, 1977, 79; Waddington Galleries, London, 1973, 78; Medici II Gallery, Bay Harbor Islands, Fla., 1978; Waddington Gallery, Montreal, 1979; Waddington Gallery, Toronto, 1979; Katonah (N.Y.) Art Gallery, Katona, 1979; Hokin Gallery, Palm

Beach, 1979; Waddington Galleries, London, 1979. **Retrospectives:** The Jewish Museum, 1964; SRGM, circ., 1977. **Group:** The Kootz Gallery, NYC, New Talent, 1954; Corcoran, 1958, 63, 67; SRGM, Abstract Expressionists and Imagists, 1961; Seattle World's Fair, 1962; WMAA, Geometric Abstraction in America, circ., 1962; Jewish Museum, Toward a New Abstraction, 1963; XXXII Venice Biennial, 1964; Los Angeles/County, MA, New Abstraction, 1964; Tate, Gulbenkian International, 1964; Carnegie, 1964–65, 67; Detroit/Institute, Color, Image and Form, 1967; Expo '67, Montreal, 1967; Dublin/Municipal, I International Quadrennial (ROSC), 1967; International Biennial Exhibition of Paintings, Tokyo; Documenta IV, Kassel, 1968; MOMA, The Art of the Real, 1968; Pasadena/AM, Serial Imagery, 1968; Washington U., The Development of Modernist Painting, 1969; U. of California, Irvine, New York: The Second Breakthrough, 1959–1964, 1969; MMA, New York Painting and Sculpture: 1940–1970, 1969–70; Buffalo/Albright, Color and Field: 1890–1970, 1970; WMAA, The Structure of Color, 1971; Carnegie, 1971; Boston/MFA, Abstract Painting in the '70s, 1972; Houston/MFA, The Great Decade of American Abstraction: Modernist Art 1960–1970, 1974; Corcoran Biennial, 1975; MIT, Paper Forms: Handmade Paper Projects, 1977; Chicago/Contemporary, A View of a Decade, 1977; Indianapolis, 1976; Syracuse/Everson, A Century of Ceramics in the United States, 1878–1978, 1979; Montreal/Contemporain, Artistes Americains Contemporains, 1978; Buffalo/Albright, American Painting of the 1970s, 1978; U. of Illinois, 1978; Tokyo/Modern, Print Biennial, 1979; Brockton (Mass.)/Art Center, Aspects of the '70s,: Painterly Abstraction, 1980; Grand Palais, Paris, L'Amerique aux Independants, 1980. **Collections:** Buffalo/Albright; Adelaide; Hirshhorn; St. Louis/City; Harvard U.; Baltimore/MA; WMAA; Canberra/National; Brandeis U.; Honolulu Academy; Detroit/Institute; Co-lumbus; MOMA; Chicago/AI. **Bibliography:** Alloway 3, 4; Battcock, ed.; Bihalji-Merin; Calas, N. and E.; *Contemporanea*; Coplans 3; Cummings 1; De Vries, ed.; Gablik; *The Great Decade*; Goossen 1; Honisch and Jensen, eds.; Hunter, ed.; Kozloff 3; Lippard 5; Lynton; *Metro*; Rickey; Rose, B., 1; Sandler 1; Tomkins 2; Waldman 4; Weller. Archives.

NORDFELDT, B.J.O. b. 1897; **d.** 1955. **Studied:** Chicago Art Institute School; Academie Julian, Paris. Traveled France, Italy, Sweden, 1908–09. **Taught:** Minneapolis Institute School, 1933. **Awards:** Milan Triennial, Silver Medal, 1906; Panama-Pacific Exposition, San Francisco, 1915, Silver Medal; Philadelphia Sesquicentennial, 1926, Bronze Medal; Chicago/AI, The Mr. & Mrs. Frank G. Logan Medal, 1926; Brooklyn Society of Etchers, First Prize, 1927; Chicago Society of Etchers, First Prize, 1928; Denver/AM, First Yetter Prize, 1937; Worcester/AM, **P.P.,** 1947; Corcoran, Bronze Medal, 1949. **One-man Exhibitions:** Scott Thurber Gallery, Chicago, 1912, 13; The Daniel Gallery, NYC, 1914, 17; Montross Gallery, NYC, 1923; Lilienfeld Gallery, NYC, 1937–43; Hudson D. Walker Gallery, NYC, 1940; Passedoit Gallery, NYC, 1944–55; Minneapolis/Institute; U. of Minnesota; Arts Club of Chicago; Wichita/AM; SFMA; The Zabriskie Gallery, 1962, 63, 65, 74. **Retrospective:** U. of Minnesota, 1972. **Group:** MMA, 1956; Carnegie; Corcoran; WMAA; Brussels World's Fair, 1958; A.F.A., Expressionists in American Painting. **Collections:** Atlanta U.; Corcoran; Des Moines; U. of Illinois; MMA; Minneapolis/Institute; U. of Minnesota; U. of Oregon; U. of Rochester; Santa Fe, N.M.; U. of Texas; Toledo/MA; Walker; Wichita/AM; Worcester/AM. **Bibliography:** Cheney; **Coke** 1, 2; Hartmann. Archives.

NOVROS, DAVID. b. August 8, 1941, Los Angeles, Calif. **Address:** 433 Broome Street, NYC 10013. **Dealer:**

David Novros   Untitled   1975

Sperone Westwater Fischer, Inc. **One-man Exhibitions:** Dwan Gallery, Los Angeles, 1966, NYC, 1967; Galerie Muller, Stuttgart, 1967; Bykert Gallery, 1968, 69, 73, 74; Mizuno Gallery, 1969, 70; The Texas Gallery, 1973, 75; Weinberg Gallery, San Francisco, 1973; Rosa Esman Gallery, 1973; Sperone Westwater Fischer Inc., NYC, 1976, 78. **Group:** SRGM, Systemic Painting, 1966; Kansas City/Nelson, Sound, Light, Silence, 1966; ICA, U. of Pennsylvania, A Romantic Minimalism, 1967; A.F.A., Rejective Art, 1967; WMAA, 1967, 69, 73; Washington U., The Development of Modernist Painting, 1969; Buffalo/Al-bright, Modular Painting, 1970; WMAA, The Structure of Color, 1971; Corcoran Biennial, 1971; Chicago/Contemporary, White on White, 1971–72; Chicago/AI, 1972; Chicago/Contemporary, Five Artists: A Logic of Vision, 1974. **Bibliography:** Murdock 1; *New in the Seventies.*

NOWACK, WAYNE K. b. May 7, 1923, Des Moines, Iowa. **Studied:** Drake U., 1943–45; State U. of Iowa, with Maurico Lasansky, James Lechay, Stuart Edie, 1945–57, BA, PBK, 1948, MA (art history), 1950, MFA (painting). Traveled

Mexico. **Awards:** Des Moines, First Prize, 1950; Danforth Foundation Grant, 1962; National Endowment for the Arts Grant, 1973. **Address:** RD 1, Spencer, NY 14883. **Dealer:** Allan Stone Gallery. **One-man Exhibitions:** (first) Des Moines, 1950, also 1957; Union College (N.Y.), 1957; Albany/Institute, 1961; Schenectady Museum Association, 1961; Allan Stone Gallery, 1967, 70, 74. **Group:** Omaha/Joslyn Annuals, 1947, 50; Denver/AM, 1948; Library of Congress Print Annual, 1948; Des Moines, 1948, 50–53; Silvermine Guild, 1954; Utica, 1961; Skidmore College, 1961; Brandeis U., Recent American Drawings, 1964; New School for Social Research, Albert List Collection, 1965; WMAA, Human Concern/Personal Torment, 1969; Minnesota/MA, American Drawings 1927–1977, 1977. **Collections:** Des Moines; Drake U.; Fort Worth; Hirshhorn; State U. of Iowa; Skidmore College; Union College (N.Y.); Williams College.

NUTT, JIM. b. 1938, Pittsfield, Mass. **Studied:** Chicago Art Institute School, 1965. **m.** Gladys Nilsson. **Address:** 1035 Greenwood, Wilmette, IL 60091. **Dealer:** Phyllis Kind Gallery, Chicago, NYC. **One-man Exhibitions:** Candy Store Gallery, Folsom, Calif., 1971, 72, 73; Chicago/Contemporary, 1974; Walker, 1974; SFAI, 1975; Portland (Ore.) Center for Visual Arts, 1975; Phyllis Kind Gallery, Chicago, 1970, 72, 75, 77, 79; Phyllis Kind Gallery, NYC, 1976, 77. **Retrospective:** Rotterdam, Kunstichting, 1980. **Group:** Hyde Park Art Center, Chicago, The Hairy Who, 1966, 67, 68; School of Visual Arts, NYC, The Hairy Who, 1969; Chicago/Contemporary, Don Baum Sez, "Chi-

Jim Nutt   *I Am Here to Show You*   1978–79

cago Needs Famous Artists," 1969; ICA, U. of Pennsylvania, Spirit of the Comics, 1969; WMAA, Human Concern/Personal Torment, 1970; SFAI, Surplus Slop from the Windy City, 1970; Chicago/Contemporary, Chicago Imagist Art, 1972; Sacramento/Crocker, Sacramento Sampler, 1972; Venice Biennial, 1972; WMAA, American Drawings, 1963–73, 1973; Sao Paulo Biennial, 1974; Chicago/AI, Annual, 1976; U. of Illinois, 1974; WMAA Biennials, 1973, 77; U. of Texas, Austin, New in the Seventies, 1977; Chicago/AI, Drawings of the 70s, 1977; Chicago/Contemporary, View of a Decade, 1977. **Collections:** Chicago/AI; Chicago/Contemporary; MMA; Museum des 20. Jahrhunderts, Vienna; New Orleans; U. of North Carolina; WMAA. **Bibliography:** *The Chicago Connection; New in the Seventies.*

O'HANLON, RICHARD. b. October 7, 1906, Long Beach, Calif. **Studied:** California College of Arts and Crafts, 1926–27; California School of Fine Arts, 1930–33. Traveled the Orient and around the world. **Taught:** U. of California, 1947–74. **Commissions:** Oakland/AM, 1974; U. of California, Berkeley, 1975, 79. **Awards:** SFAI, Anne Bremer Traveling Scholarship; SFMA, Edgar Walter Memorial Prize, 1940; CSFA, Albert M. Bender Fellowship, 1940; Marin Society Annual First Prize; SFMA, First Prize, 1950. **Address:** 616 Throckmorton Avenue, Mill Valley, CA 94941. **One-man Exhibitions:** The Willard Gallery, 1953; U. of Rochester; U. of Kentucky; Carnegie, 1967; Santa Barbara/MA, 1969. **Retrospective:** SFMA, 1961. **Group:** SFMA; Baltimore/MA. **Collections:** Andover/Phillips; Baltimore/MA; U. of California, Berkeley and Davis; City of Mill Valley; Denver/AM; SFMA; Smith College; Steuben Glass; WMAA; Walker; Worcester/AM.

OHASHI, YUTAKA. B. August 19, 1923, Hiroshima, Japan. **Studied:** Academy of Arts, Tokyo, 1941–46, BFA; Boston Museum School, 1950–55, with David Aronson, Karl Zerbe. Japanese Army, 1943–45. Traveled Europe, the Orient, USA. **Taught:** Boston Museum School, 1958; Cornell U., 1961, 67, 69. **Member:** Japan Artists Association. **Commissions:** Sony Corp. of America. **Awards:** Boston/MFA, James William Paige Fellowship (Europe), 1955–57; Traveling Scholarship (Japan), 1967–68; Guggenheim Foundation Fellowship (Japan) 1959. **Address:** 5 Great Jones Street, NYC 10012; 5,17-44, 3 Chome, Nishi-Azabu, Minato-Ku, Tokyo, Japan. **Dealer:** Art Asia Gallery, Boston. **One-man Exhibitions:** (first) Margaret Brown Gallery, Boston, 1955; The Alan Gallery, NYC, 1957, 60, 63, 65; The Swetzoff Gallery, Boston, 1958, 60, 63, 64, 66, 67; Dennenchof Studio, Tokyo, 1960; Cornell U., 1961; Nordness Galleries, 1969, 73; Galeria Santiago, San Juan, 1971; Boston Athenaeum, 1975; Franell Gallery, Tokyo, 1978; Art Asia Gallery, Boston 1980. **Group:** Rome–New York Foundation, Rome; SRGM; Chicago/AI; U. of Illinois; Carnegie; ICA, Boston, Contemporary Painters of Japanese Origin in America, 1958, also 1962; VMFA; Utica; Tokyo/Modern; Southern Illinois U.; Montclair/AM, 1970. **Collections:** Andover/Phillips; Boston/MFA; Buffalo/Albright; Cornell U.; Lincoln, Mass./De Cordova; Lincoln Center; Newport Harbor; SRGM; U. of Texas; Tokyo/Modern; U. of Wyoming; Yale U.

OHLSON, DOUG. b. November 18, 1936, Cherokee, Iowa. **Studied:** U. of Minnesota, 1959–61, BA. US Marine Corps, 1955–58. **Taught:** Hunter College, 1964– . **Awards:** Guggenheim Foundation Fellowship, 1969; CAPS Grant, 1974; National Endowment for the Arts, grant, 1976. **Member:** Board of Governors, Skowhegan School. **Address:** 35 Bond Street, NYC 10012. **Dealer:** Susan Caldwell Inc. **One-man Exhibitions:** Fischbach Gallery, 1964, 66, 67, 68, 69, 70, 72; Susan Caldwell Inc., 1974, 76, 77, 79; Portland (Ore.) Center for the Visual Arts, 1977. **Group:** Detroit/Institute, Color, Image and Form, 1967; MOMA, The Art of the Real, 1968; WMAA, The Structure of Color, 1971; Corcoran, 1975; UCLA, Fourteen Abstract Painters, 1975; NYU, Project Rebuild, 1976; Old Westbury/SUNY, Transitions I, 1979. **Collections:** AT&T; Brooklyn Museum; Coudert Brothers, NYC; Corcoran; Dallas/MFA; U. of Iowa; Isham, Lincoln & Beale, Chicago; Minneapolis/Institute; U. of North Carolina; Utah; Security Pacific National Bank. **Bibliography:** Murdock 1.

OKADA, KENZO. b. September 28, 1902, Yokohama, Japan. **Studied:** Meijigakuin Middle School; Tokyo U. of Arts, three semesters; in Paris, 1924–27. **Taught:** Nippon Art College, 1940–42; Musashino Art Institute, 1947–50; Tama College of Fine Arts, Tokyo, 1949–50. To USA, 1950; citizen, 1960. **Member:** Nikakai (Group), Japan, 1938– . **Awards:** Nikakai (Group), Japan 1936; Showa Shorei, 1938; Yomiuri Press, 1947; Chicago/AI, 1954, 57; Carnegie, 1955; Columbia, S.C./MA, First Prize, 1957; XXIX Venice Biennial, 1958; Tate, Dunn International Prize, 1964; Mainichi Art Award, 1966; AAAL, Marjorie Peabody Waite Award, 1977. **Address:** 101 West 12th Street, NYC 10011. **Dealer:** Betty Parsons Gallery. **One-man Exhibitions:** Nichido Gallery, Tokyo, 1929–35; Hokuso Gallery, 1948, 50; US Army Education Center, Tokyo, 1949, 50; US Army Education Center, Yokohama, 1950; Betty Parsons Gallery, 1953, 55, 56, 59, 62–64, 67, 69, 71, 73, 76, 78; Corcoran, 1955; Sao Paulo, 1955; Fairweather-Hardin Gallery, 1956; Myrtle Todes Gallery, Glencoe, Ill., 1957; Venice/Contemporaneo, 1958; Ferus Gallery, Los Angeles, 1959; MIT, 1963; Buffalo/Albright, 1965; Columbus Gallery, 1979; U. of Texas, 1979; Indianapolis, 1979; Phillips, 1979. **Retrospective:** Traveling Exhibition, 1966–67, circ., Tokyo, Kyoto, Honolulu, San Francisco, and Austin, Tex. **Group:** Salon d'Automne, Paris, 1924–27; Nikakai (Group), Japan, 1938– ;

WMAA; Chicago/AI; U. of Illinois; III Sao Paulo Biennial, 1955; Corcoran; MOMA; XXIX Venice Biennial, 1958; Tate, Dunn International, 1964. **Collections:** Baltimore/MA; Boston/MFA; Brooklyn Museum; Buffalo/Albright; Carnegie; Chase Manhattan Bank; Chicago/AI; U. of Colorado; Columbia, S.C./MA; Equitable Life Assurance Society; Hartford/Wadsworth; Honolulu Academy; Lincoln Center; MMA; MOMA; Memphis/Brooks; Phillips; Portland, Ore./AM; Reynolds Metals Co.; Rockefeller Institute; SFMA; SRGM; St. Lawrence U.; St. Louis/City; Santa Barbara/MA; Tokyo/Modern; Tougaloo College; Utica; WMAA; Yale U. **Bibliography:** Baur 5; Hunter, ed.; Goodrich and Baur 1; Nordness, ed.; Ponente; Read 2; Rodman 1.

OKAMURA, ARTHUR. b. February 24, 1932, Long Beach, Calif. **Studied:** Chicago Art Institute School, with Paul Wieghardt, 1950–54; The U. of Chicago, 1951, 53, 57; Yale U., 1954. US Army, 1954. Traveled France, Spain, North Africa, Japan; resided Mallorca for a year. **Taught:** Central YMCA College, Chicago, 1956–57; Evanston (Ill.) Art Center, 1956–57; Northshore Art League, Winnetka, Ill., 1957; Academy of Art, San Francisco, 1957; Chicago Art Institute School, 1957; California School of Fine Arts, 1958; California College of Arts and Crafts, 1958–59, 1966-69; Saugatuck Summer School of Painting, 1959, 62; U. of Utah, 1964. **Awards:** The U. of Chicago, Religious Arts, 1953; four-year scholarship to the Chicago Art Institute School; Edward L. Ryerson Traveling Fellowship, 1954; Chicago/AI, Martin B. Cahn Award, 1957; U. of Illinois, **P.P.,** 1960; WMAA, Neysa McMein **P.P.,** 1960; NIAL, **P.P.;** SFMA, Schwabacher-Frey Award, 1960. **Address:** P.O. Box 21, Ocean Parkway, Bolinas, CA 94924. **Dealers:** Ruth Braunstein Gallery, San Francisco; Charles Feingarten Gallery, Los Angeles. **One-man Exhibitions:** (first) Frank Ryan Gallery, Chicago, 1953; La

Boutique, Chicago, 1953, 54; Feingarten Gallery, Chicago, NYC, San Francisco, and Los Angeles, 1956–64, 69, 71, 73, 75, 77, 80; Santa Barbara/MA, 1958; Oakland/AM, 1959; California Palace, 1961; Dallas/MFA, 1962; La Jolla, 1963; U. of Utah, 1964; Hansen Gallery, San Francisco, 1964, 65, 66, 68, 71, 74; M. Knoedler & Co., 1965; College of the Holy Names, Oakland, Calif., 1966; SFMA, 1968; California College of Arts and Crafts, 1972; Southern Idaho College, 1972; Kent State U., 1973; Honolulu Academy, 1973; Hansen-Fuller Gallery, San Francisco, 1974; Walnut Creek Art Center (two-man), 1975. **Group:** Chicago/AI Annuals, 1951–54; U. of Illinois, 1955, 59; Ravinia Festival, Highland Park, Ill., 1956, 64; Los Angeles/County MA, Contemporary Americans, 1957; SFMA, Art in Asia and the West, 1957; PAFA, 1954; de Young, Fresh Paint, 1958; U. of Nebraska, 1958; Denver/AM, 1958; USIA, Drawings from California, circ. Europe, 1958–59; A.F.A., New Talent, circ., 1959; Dallas/MFA, 1959; California Palace, 1959, Painters behind Painters, 1967; WMAA, 1960; Forty Artists under Forty, circ., 1962, Annuals, 1962, 63, 64; Friends of the Whitney, 1964; SFMA, Sculpture and Drawings, 1961, 1966; Sacramento/Crocker, 1966; Carnegie, 1967; Expo '70, Osaka, 1970; Scripps College, Lyric View, 1973. **Collections:** Achenbach Foundation; Borg-Warner International Corporation; California College of Arts and Crafts; California Palace; Chicago/AI; The U. of Chicago; Cincinnati/AM; Container Corp. of America; Corcoran; Hirshhorn; Illinois Bell Telephone Company; Illinois State Normal U.; U. of Illinois; Kalamazoo/Institute; Miles Laboratories Inc.; NCFA; NIAL; Oakland/AM; Phoenix; SFMA; Santa Barbara/MA; Southern Idaho College; Stanford U.; Steel Service Institute; WMAA. **Bibliography:** Nordness, ed.

O'KEEFFE, GEORGIA. b. November 15, 1887, Sun Prairie, Wisc. **Studied:** Chatham Episcopal Institute (Va.),

1901; Chicago Art Institute School, 1904–05, with John Vanderpoel; ASL, 1907–08, with William M. Chase; Columbia U., 1916, with Arthur Dow, Alan Bement. Traveled Europe, Mexico, USA, Peru, Japan. **Taught:** U. of Virginia; Supervisor of Art in public schools, Amarillo, Tex., 1912–16; Columbia College (S.C.); West Texas Normal College. **Awards:** Hon. DFA, College of William and Mary, 1939; Hon. Litt.D., U. of Wisconsin, 1942; elected to the NIAL, 1947, AAAL, 1962; Brandeis U., Creative Arts Award, 1963; Hon. DFA, Randolph-Macon Woman's College, 1966; NIAL, gold medal, 1970; Hon. DHL, Columbia U., 1971; Hon. DFA, Brown U., 1971; Bryn Mawr College, M. Carey Thomas Prize, 1971; Hon. DFA, Minneapolis College of Art & Design, 1972; Edward MacDowell Medal, 1972; Skowhegan School of Painting and Sculpture, medal for Painting and gold medal, 1973; Hon. DFA, Harvard U., 1973; Governors' Award (New Mexico), 1974; Presidential Medal of Freedom, 1977; Hon. D. of Visual Arts, College of Santa Fe, 1977. **m.** Alfred Stieglitz (1924). **Address:** Abiquiu, NM 87510. **Dealer:** Juan Hamilton. **One-man Exhibitions:** (first) "291," NYC, 1917, also 1926; Anderson Galleries, NYC, 1924; Stieglitz's Intimate Gallery, NYC, 1927, 29; An American Place (Gallery), NYC, 1931, 32, 35–42, 44–46, 50; U. of Minnesota, 1937; The Downtown Gallery, 1937, 52, 55, 58, 61; College of William and Mary, 1938; La Escondida, Taos, N.M. 1951; Dallas/MFA, 1953; Mayo Hill, Delray Beach, Fla., 1953; Gibbs Art Gallery, Charleston, S.C., 1955; Pomona College, 1958; Milton College, 1965; U. of New Mexico, 1966; SFMA, 1971; Bryn Mawr College, 1971. **Retrospective:** Anderson Galleries, NYC, 1923; Chicago/AI, 1943; MOMA, 1946; Dallas/MFA, 1953; Worcester/AM, 1960; Amon Carter Museum, 1966; WMAA, 1970. **Group:** "291," NYC, 1916; MOMA, Paintings by 19 Living Americans, 1929; U. of Minnesota, 5 Painters, 1937; U. of Illinois, 1955, 57, 59, 69; Pomona College, Stieglitz Circle, 1958; MMA, 14 ` American Masters, 1958. **Collections:** Amon Carter Museum; Andover/Phillips; Arizona State College; U. of Arizona; Auburn U.; Baltimore/MA; Brooklyn Museum; Bryn Mawr College; Buffalo/Albright; Chicago/AI; Cleveland/MA; Colorado Springs/FA; Currier; Dallas/MFA; Detroit/Institute; Fisk U.; Fort Worth; U. of Georgia; IBM; Indianapolis/Herron; MMA; MOMA; The Miller Co.; Milwaukee; U. of Minnesota; NCFA; National Gallery; U. of Nebraska; Newark Museum; U. of Oklahoma; Omaha/Joslyn; PMA; Phillips; Randolph-Macon Woman's College; Reed College; U. of Rochester; Roswell; SFMA; St. Louis/City; Santa Barbara/MA; Shelburne; Smith College; Springfield, Mass./MFA; Tate; Texas Technological College; Toledo/MA; Utica; Valparaiso U. (Ind.); WMAA; Walker; Wellesley College; Westminster Academy; West Palm Beach/Norton; Wichita/AM; Wilmington. **Bibliography:** *Avant-Garde Painting and Sculpture in America, 1910-1925;* Barker 1; Baur 5, 7; Bazin; Bethers; Biddle 4; Blanchard; Blesh 1; Boswell 1; Brown 2; Bulliet 1; Cahill and Barr, eds.; Cheney; Christensen; Coke 2; Craven, T., 1; Downes, ed.; Flanagan; Frank, ed.; Frost; *Forerunners;* Goodrich and Baur 1; Goossen 1; Haftman; Hall; Hunter 6; Huyghe; *Index of 20th Century Artists;* Janis, S.; Jewell 2; Kootz 1; Kozloff 3; Kuh 1, 2, 3; Lane; Lee and Burchwood; Johnson, Ellen H.; Levin 2; Lippard 3; Mather 1; McCoubrey 1; McCurdy, ed.; Mellquist; Mendelowitz; Neuhaus; Newmeyer; Nordness, ed.; Pearson 1; Phillips 1, 2; Poore; Pousette-Dart, ed.; **Rich 1, 2;** Richardson, E.P.; Ringel, ed.; Ritchie 1; Rose, B., 1, 4; Rosenblum 2; Smith, S.C.K.; Soby 6; Sutton; Weller. Archives.

OLDENBURG, CLAES THURE. b. January 28, 1929, Stockholm, Sweden. **Studied:** Yale U., 1950, BA; Chicago Art Institute School, 1952–55, with Paul Wieghardt. Traveled USA, Europe,

Claes Oldenburg *Batcolumn* 1977

Japan. Apprentice reporter, City News Bureau, Chicago, 1950–52. Films: *Colossal Keepsake No. 1,* 1969; *Sort of a Commercial for an Icebag,* 1969; *The Great Ice Cream Robbery,* 1970; *Birth of the Flag, Part One and Two,* 1965–74; *Ray Gun Theater,* 1962–75. **Member:** NIAL; AAIAL. **Commissions:** Oberlin College, 1970; Southern Methodist U., 1970; St. Louis/City, 1971; Rijksmuseum Kroller-Muller, 1971; Morse College, Yale U., 1974; Walker, 1974; South Mall, Albany, 1975; Hirshhorn, 1975; GSA, Social Security Administration, Chicago, 1975–77; City of Munster, 1976–77; Oberlin College, 1975–80; U. of Nevada, 1978–80; Salinas Community Center, Salinas, Calif., 1978–80; Civic Center, Des Moines, Iowa, 1978–79; Rotterdam, 1977–80. **Awards:** Brandeis U., Creative Arts Award; Skowhegan School Medal; Fellow of Morse College, Yale U.; Honorary Degrees: Oberlin College, 1973; Minneapolis College of Art and Design, 1974; Moore College of Art, Philadelphia, 1974. **Address:** 556 Broome Street, NYC 10013. **Dealer:** Leo

Castelli, Inc., NYC. **One-man Exhibitions:** (first) Judson Gallery, NYC, 1959 (sculpture, drawings, poems); Judson Gallery, NYC (two-man, with Jim Dine), 1959; Reuben Gallery, NYC, 1960; Green Gallery, NYC, 1962; Dwan Gallery, 1963; Sidney Janis Gallery, 1964–67, 69, 70; The Pace Gallery, Boston, 1964; Ileana Sonnabend Gallery, Paris, 1964; Stockholm/National; 1966; Robert Fraser Gallery, 1966; U. of Illinois, 1967; Toronto, 1967 (three-man, with Jim Dine, George Segal); Chicago/Contemporary, 1967; Irving Blum Gallery, 1968; Richard Feigen Gallery, Chicago, 1969; UCLA, 1970, 77; Margo Leavin Gallery, 1971, 75; Kansas City/Nelson, 1972; Fort Worth, 1972; Des Moines, 1972; PMA, 1972; Chicago/AI, 1973; Minami Gallery, 1973; Leo Castelli, Inc., NYC, 1974, 80; Yale U., 1974; Lo Spazio, Rome, 1974; Kunsthalle, Tubingen, circ., 1975; Margo Leavin Gallery, Los Angeles, 1975, 76, 78; F. H. Mayor Gallery, London, 1975; Walker, circ., 1975; Krefeld/Haus Lange, 1975; Petersburg Press, NYC, 1975; Jered Sable Gallery, Toronto, 1976; Multiples, Inc., NYC, 1976; John Berggruen Gallery, San Francisco, 1976; Hannover K-G, 1976; Leo Castelli, Inc., NYC, 1976, 80; Amsterdam/Stedelijk, 1977; Richard Gray Gallery, Chicago, 1977; Akron/AI, 1977; Chicago/Contemporary, circ., 1977, **Environments:** Judson Gallery, NYC, Ray Gun Street, 1960; Ray Gun Mfg. Co., The Store, 1961; Sidney Janis Gallery, Bedroom Ensemble, 1964. **Happenings:** Judson Gallery, NYC, Snapshots from the City, 1960; Reuben Gallery, NYC, Ironworks and Fotodeath, 1961; Dallas/MFA, Injun, 1962; Ray Gun Mfg. Co., Ray Gun Theater, 1962; The U. of Chicago, Gayety, 1963; WGMA, Stars, 1963; Los Angeles/County MA, Autobodys, 1963; Al Roon's Health Club, NYC, Washes, 1965; Film Maker's Cinematheque, NYC, Moviehouse, 1965; Stockholm/National, Massage 1966; Esquire Magazine, The Typewriter, 1969. **Retrospective:** MOMA, 1969; Pasadena/AM, 1971; Walker, circ., 1975; Kunsthalle,

Tubingen, circ., 1975. **Group:** Buffalo/Albright, Mixed Media and Pop Art, 1963; Oberlin College, 3 Young Painters, 1963; Chicago/AI, 1962, 63; Brandeis U., New Directions in American Painting, 1963; Cincinnati/AM, An American Viewpoint, 1963; Dallas/MFA; Tate, Dunn International, 1964; ICA, London, The Popular Image, 1963; Martha Jackson Gallery, New Media—New Forms, I & II, 1960, 61; Stockholm/National, American Pop Art, 1964; MOMA, Americans 1963, circ., 1963–64; Oakland/AM, Pop Art USA, 1963; Hartford/Wadsworth, Continuity and Change, 1962; WGMA, The Popular Image, 1963; Philadelphia YM-YWHA Arts Council, Art, A New Vocabulary, 1962; Sidney Janis Gallery, The New Realists, 1962; XXXII Venice Biennial, 1964; Akademie der Kunst, Berlin, Neue Realism und Pop Art, 1965; WMAA, A Decade of American Drawings, 1965; Musée Rodin, Paris, Sculpture of the 20th Century, 1965; WMAA Annuals, 1965, 68, 69; RISD, Recent Still Life, 1966; Walker, Eight Sculptors, 1966; Los Angeles/County MA, American Sculpture of the Sixties, 1967; IX Sao Paulo Biennial, 1967; SRGM, 1967; Carnegie, 1967; Expo '67, Montreal, US Pavilion, 1967; Moore College of Art, American Drawing, 1968; ICA, London, The Obsessive Image, 1968; Documenta IV, Kassel, 1968; Hayward Gallery, London, Pop Art, 1969; Berne, When Attitudes Become Form, 1969; MMA, 1969; MOMA, Technics and Creativity; Gemini GEL., 1971; Los Angeles/County MA, Art & Technology, 1971; Arnhem, Sonsbeek '71, 1971; Expo '70, Osaka, 1970; Foundation Maeght, 1970; Documenta V, Kassel, 1972; Seattle/AM, American Art—Third Quarter Century, 1973; WMAA, American Pop Art, 1974; Newport, R.I., Monumenta, 1974; Moore College of Art, Philadelphia, North, East, West, South and Middle, 1975; U. of Massachusetts, Artists and Fabricators, 1975; NCFA, Sculpture: American Directions, 1945–57, 1975; MOMA, Drawing Now, circ., 1976; SRGM, 20th

Century American Drawings, 1976; Chicago/AI Annual, 1976; Akron/AI, Contemporary Images in Watercolor, 1976; WMAA, 200 Years of American Sculpture, 1976; Indianapolis, 1976; U. of Chicago, Ideas in Sculpture, 1976; Indianapolis, 1976; U. of Chicago, Ideas in Sculpture, 1965–1977, 1977; ICA, Philadelphia, Improbable Furniture, 1977; Cambridge, Jubilation, 1977; Minnesota/MA, American Drawing 1927–1977, circ., 1977; Flint/Institute, Art and the Automobile, 1978; WMAA, Art about Art, 1978; Nassau County Museum, Syosset, Monuments and Monoliths: A Metamorphosis, 1978; WMAA (downtown), Auto-Icons, 1979. **Collections:** Amsterdam/Stedelijk; Baltimore Museum; Basel; Brandeis U.; Brussels/Beaux-Arts; Buffalo/Albright; Chicago/AI; Cologne; Des Moines; Fort Worth; Houston/MFA; U. of Illinois; Kansas City/Nelson; London/Victoria and Albert; Los Angeles/County MA; MOMA; Milwaukee; Norfolk/Chrysler; Oberlin College; Paris/Beaubourg; Pasadena/AM; Rijksmuseum Kroller-Muller; SFAI; St. Louis/City; Southern Methodist U.; Stockholm/National; Tate; Toronto; Vancouver; WMAA; Walker. **Bibliography: Adriani, Koepplin, and Rose;** Alloway 4;Alloway 1; Battcock, ed.; Becker and Vostell; Bihalji-Merin; Callas, W.; Davies; Davis, D.; De Vries, ed.; Dienst 1; Finch; Friedman and van der Marck; *From Foreign Shores;* Hansen; *Happening & Fluxus;* **Haskell 2;** Honisch and Jensen, eds.; Hunter, ed.; Janis and Blesh 1; Johnson, Ellen H.; Kaprow; Kirby; Kozloff 3; Krauss 2; Lippard 3; Lippard 5; Lippard, ed.; Lucie-Smith; *Metro; Monumenta;* **Oldenburg 1, 2, 3;** *Oldenburg; Report;* **Rose, B., 1, 2, 4;** Rubin 1; Rublowsky; Russell and Gablik; Sandler 1; *Six Themes;* Strachan; Sontag; Tomkins and Time-Life Books; Tomkins 2; Trier 1; Tuchman 1; Van Briggen and Oldenburg; Warhol and Haskell; Weller; *When Attitudes Become Form.* Archives.

OLITSKI, JULES. b. March 27, 1922, Snovsk, USSR. **Studied:** NAD, with Sidney Dickinson, 1939–42; Beaux-Arts Institute of Design, NYC, 1940–47; Zadkine School of Sculpture, Paris, 1949; Academie de la Grande Chaumiere, 1949–50; NYU, BA, 1952; MA (Art Education), 1954; and privately with Chaim Gross. Traveled USA, Europe, Mexico. **Taught:** New Paltz/SUNY, 1954–55; C. W. Post College of Long Island U., Chairman of Fine Arts, 1956–63; Bennington College, 1963–67. Curator, NYU Art Education Gallery, 1955–56. **Awards:** Carnegie Second Prize, 1961; Ford Foundation, **P.P.,** 1964; Corcoran, 1967. **Address:** 827 Broadway, NYC 10003; summer: RD #1, Lovejoy Sands Road, Meredith, NH 03253. **Dealer:** Knoedler Contemporary Art; Andre Emmerich Gallery, NYC. **One-man Exhibitions:** (first) Galerie Huit, Paris, 1950; Alexandre Iolas Gallery, 1958; French & Co. Inc., NYC, 1959–61; Poindexter Gallery, 1961–65, 1968; Bennington College, 1962; Galleria Santa Croce, Florence, Italy, 1963; Galleria Trastevere, Rome, 1963; Galleria Toninelli, Milan, 1963; Richard Gray Gallery, 1964; David Mirvish Gallery, Toronto, 1964–75, 78; Kasmin Ltd., 1964–66, 1968–70, 1972; Galerie Lawrence, Paris, 1964; Harvard U. (three-man with Kenneth Noland, Frank Stella), 1965; St. John, N.B., 1966; Nicholas Wilder Gallery, 1966, 73; Andre Emmerich Gallery, NYC, 1966–68, 77; Zurich, 1973; ICA, U. of Pennsylvania, 1968; MIT, 1968; MMA, 1969; Lawrence Rubin Gallery, NYC, 1969–73; Knoedler Contemporary Art, 1973, 75, 76, 77, 79; Galerie Wentzel, Hamburg, 1975, 77; Dart Gallery, Inc., Chicago, 1975; Watson/DeNagy, Houston, 1976; Boston/MFA, 1977; Hirshhorn, 1977; Amerika Haus, Berlin, 1977; David Mirvish Gallery, Toronto, 1978; Knoedler Gallery, London, 1978; Edmonton Art Gallery, Edmonton, 1979. **Retrospectives:** Corcoran, circ., 1967; Boston/MFA, circ., 1973. **Group:** Carnegie, 1961, 64; WMAA Annuals, 1962, 68, 69, 70, 72; WGMA, The Formalists, 1963; Festival of Two Worlds, Spoleto, 1963; SFMA, Directions: American Painting, 1963; MOMA, Recent

Acquisitions, 1963; Worcester/AM, 1963; IV International Art Biennial, San Marino, 1963; Chicago/AI Annuals, 1964, 69; ICA, U. of Pennsylvania, The Atmosphere of 1964, 1964; Los Angeles/County MA, Post Painterly Abstraction, 1964; SRGM, American Drawings, 1964; Chicago/AI, 67th American Exhibition, 1967; Kunsthalle, Basel, Ausstellung Signale, 1965; XXXIII Venice Biennial, 1966; Corcoran, 1967; Detroit/Institute, Color, Image and Form, 1967; Tokyo Biennial, 1967; Trenton/State, Focus on Light, 1967; Jewish Museum, Large Scale American Paintings, 1967; Honolulu Academy, 1967; Documenta IV, Kassel, 1968; MMA, New York Painting and Sculpture: 1940–1970, 1969–70; Pasadena/AM, Painting in New York: 1944 to 1969, 1969; Chicago/AI, 69th American Exhibition, 1969; Buffalo/Albright, Color and Field, 1890–1970, 1970; ICA, U. of Pennsylvania, Two Generations of Color Painting, 1970; Boston U., American Artists of the 1960s, 1970; Youngstown/Butler Annual, 1970; WMAA, The Structure of Color, 1971; Boston/MFA, Abstract Painting in the '70s, 1972; Dusseldorf/Kunsthalle, Prospect '73, 1973; Montreal/Contemporain, 11 Artistes Americains, 1973; Houston/MFA, The Great Decade of American Abstraction: Modernist Art 1960–1970, 1974; Indianapolis, 1974; Monumenta, Newport, R.I., 1974, Biennial, 1975; Caracas, El Lenguaje del Color, 1975; Syracuse/Everson, New Works in Clay, Contemporary Painting and Sculpture, 1976; Indianapolis, 1976; Chicago/AI, Drawings of the 70's, 1977; U. of Nebraska, Expressionism in the Seventies, 1978; Buffalo/Albright, American Painting of the 1970s, circ., 1979; Boston/MFA, Monumental Abstractions, 1979. **Collections:** Boston/MFA; Buffalo/Albright; Cleveland/MA; Chicago/AI; Corcoran; Dallas/MFA; Dayton/AI; Detroit/Institute; Edmonton Art Gallery; Harvard U.; Hirshhorn; U. of Illinois; Jerusalem/National; Milwaukee; MIT; MOMA; NGA; Norfolk/Chrysler; Pasadena/AM; Princeton U.; Regina/MacKenzie; U. of Saskatchewan; Seattle National Bank; WMAA. **Bibliography:** Alloway 4; Battcock, ed.; Calas, N. and E.; De Vries, ed.; *From Foreign Shores; The Great Decade;* Honisch and Jensen, eds; Hunter, ed.; Kozloff 3; Krauss; Moffett; *Monumenta;* Report; Rose, B., 4; Sandler 1.

OLIVEIRA, NATHAN. b. December 19, 1928, Oakland, Calif. **Studied:** Mills College, California College of Arts and Crafts (MFA, 1952). US Army, 1953–55. Traveled Europe. **Taught:** San Francisco Art Institute; California College of Arts and Crafts, 1955–56; U. of Illinois, 1961–62; UCLA, 1963–64; Cornell U., 1964; Stanford U., 1964–79; U. of Colorado, 1965; U. of Hawaii, 1971; Cranbrook, 1972; Baltimore Art Institute, 1972; Indianapolis/Herron, 1972; Kent State U., 1973. **Awards:** L.C. Tiffany Grant, 1957; Guggenheim Foundation Fellowship, 1958; Chicago/AI, Norman Wait Harris Bronze Medal, 1960; El Retiro Parquet, Madrid, Arte de America y Espana, Special Prize, 1963; Tamarind Fellowship, 1964; National Endowment for the Arts, 1974. **Address:** 785 Santa Marin Avenue, Stanford, CA 94305. **Dealer:** Charles Cowles Gallery, NYC. **One-man Exhibitions:** (first) The Alan Gallery, NYC, 1958, also 1959, 60, 63, 65; Paul Kantor Gallery, Beverly Hills, Calif., 1959, 60, 62, 63; U. of Illinois, 1961; Walker, 1961; Felix Landau Gallery, 1965, 68; The Landau-Alan Gallery, NYC, 1967; Gump's Gallery, 1968; Galerie Bleue, Stockholm, 1968; Stanford U., 1968; SFMA, 1969; Martha Jackson Gallery, 1969; Wisconsin State U., Oshkosh, 1970; Terry Dintenfass, Inc., 1971; Michael Smith Gallery, Los Angeles, 1971; Smith Anderson Gallery, Palo Alto, 1971, 74, 76; Charles Campbell Gallery, 1972, 75, 77, 79; Jack Glenn Gallery, Corona del Mar, 1973; Fullerton Junior College, 1973; U. of California, Santa Cruz, 1976; Galerie Veith Turske, Cologne, 1978, 79; Harvard U., 1978; Dorsky Gallery, NYC, 1978; John Berggruen Gallery, San Francisco, 1977, 79; Wichita State U., 1976; U. of Connecticut, 1976. **Retrospectives:** UCLA, circ., 1963; Oakland/AM, circ., 1973; California State U., Long Beach, 1980. **Group:** Chicago/AI; Carnegie; Denver/ AM; SFMA; Corcoran Annual; I Inter-American Paints and Prints Biennial, Mexico City, 1958; WMAA Annuals, 1958–61; I Paris Biennial, 1959; MOMA, New Images of Man, 1959; SRGM, 1961; U. of Illinois, 1961, 63, 67, 69; Seattle World's Fair, 1962; MOMA, Recent Painting USA: The Figure, circ., 1962–63; WMAA, 1967, 68. **Collections:** Brooklyn Museum; U. of California; Chicago/AI; Cleveland/MA; Dallas/ MFA; Hirshhorn; Illinois Wesleyan U.; Lytton Savings and Loan Association; MOMA; U. of Michigan; NCFA; Oakland/AM; PMA; Ridgefield/Aldrich; SFMA; SRGM; Stanford U.; UCLA; Walker; Youngstown/Butler. **Bibliography:** *New in the Seventies;* Nordness, ed.; Weller; **Wight 4.** Archives.

ONSLOW-FORD, GORDON. b. December 26, 1912, Wendover, England. **Studied:** Dragon School, Oxford, England; Royal Naval College, Dartmouth and Greenwich; self-taught in art; frequent visits to the studio of Fernand Leger. Traveled Europe, the Orient, and most of the world; resided in Paris, 1936–39, and Mexico, 1941–47. **Taught:** Series of lectures, New School for Social Research, 1940–41; California College of Arts and Crafts, 1956–58. **Address:** Inverness, CA 94937. **Dealer:** Gerard Schreiner, NYC. **One-man Exhibitions:** N.S.F.S.R., NYC, 1940; Karl Nierendorf Gallery, NYC, 1946; SFMA (three-man, with Wolfgang Paalen, Lee Mullican), 1950; SFMA (two-man, with Richard Bowman), 1959; The Rose Rabow Gallery, San Francisco, 1956, 64, 72. **Retrospectives:** SFMA; de Young; Victoria (B.C.), 1971; Oakland/AM, 1977. **Group:** SFMA, 1948, 60; de Young, 1962. **Collections:** Boston/MFA; U. of California; de Young; Harvard U.; Honolulu Academy; MOMA; Oakland/ AM; SFMA; SRGM; Tate; WMAA. **Bibliography:** *Black and White Are Colors;* Breton 2; **Onslow-Ford;** Paalen; Ragon 1; Rubin 1; Weller. Archives.

OPPENHEIM, DENNIS. b. September 6, 1938. Mason City, Wash. **Studied:** Stanford U., BA, MA; California College of Arts and Crafts, with Norman Kantor. Traveled Europe, 1969–75. **Taught:** Yale U.; Chicago/AI; Stony Brook/SUNY. **Awards:** Guggenheim Foundation Fellowship, 1972; National Endowment for the Arts, 1974. **Address:** 54 Franklin Street, NYC 10013. **Dealer:** Ileana Sonnabend Gallery, NYC. **One-man Exhibitions:** John Gibson Gallery, 1968, 69, 70, 74, 77; Yvon Lambert, 1969, 71, 75; MOMA, 1969; Reese Palley Gallery, San Francisco, 1970; Gallery 20, Amsterdam 1971; Harcus-Krakow Gallery, 1971; Francoise Lambert, Milan, 1971, 75; Gallery D. Brussels, 1972, 73, 74; Galleria l'Attico, Rome, 1972; Tate, 1972; Mathias Fels & Cie, Paris, 1972; Nova Scotia College of Art and Design, Halifax, 1972; Ileana Sonnabend Gallery, NYC, 1972, 73, Paris, 1973; M.O.C.A., San Francisco, 1973; F.H. Mayor Gallery, London, 1973; Galleria Forma, Genoa, 1973, 74; Rivkin Gallery, Washington, D.C., 1973; Paolo Barrozzi, Milan, 1974; Amsterdam/Stedelijk, 1974; Galleria A. Castelli, Milan, 1975; School of Visual Arts, NYC, 1979; Multiples, NYC, 1977, 78; Deson Gallery, Chicago, 1978; d'Arc Gallery, NYC, 1976, 77; Robert Self Gallery, Newcastle upon Tyne, 1976. **Retrospectives:** Brussels/Beaux-Arts, 1975; Rotterdam, 1975. **Group:** WMAA Annuals, 1968, 70; Seattle/AM, 557, 087, 1969; Berne, When Attitudes Become Form 1969; Amsterdam/Stedelijk, Op Losse Schroeven, 1969; MOMA, New Media; New Methods, circ., 1969; ICA, U. of Pennsylvania, Against Order: Chance and Art, 1970; Turin/ Civico, Conceptual Art, Arte Povera, Land Art, 1970; New York Cultural Center, Conceptual Art and Conceptual Aspects, 1970; Finch College, NYC, Artist/Videotape/Performance, 1971; VII Paris Biennial, 1971; Dusseldorf/Kunsthalle, Prospect '71, 1971; Documenta V, Kassel, 1972; WMAA, American Drawings, 1963–73, 1973; Cologne, Project '74, 1974; MIT, Interventions in Landscape, 1974; Venice, Biennale, 1975. **Collections:** Amsterdam/Stedelijk; MOMA; Oakland/AM; Tate; Toronto; Turin/Civico. **Bibliography:** Alloway 4; *Art Now 74;* Celant; *Contemporanea;* Honisch and Jensen, eds.; Honnef; Hunter, ed.; Johnson, Ellen H.; Lippard, ed.; Lippard 3; Lucie-Smith; Meyer.

OPPER, JOHN. b. October 29, 1908, Chicago, Ill. **Studied:** Cleveland Institute of Art, 1926–28; Chicago Art Institute School, 1928–29; Western Reserve U., BS, 1931; Hofmann School, 1936; Columbia U., MA, 1942, Ed.D., 1952. Traveled Europe. **Taught:** U. of Wyoming, 1945–49; U. of North Carolina, 1952–57; Columbia U.; NYU, 1957–74. **Member:** American Abstract Artists, since 1936. Federal A.P.: Easel painting. **Awards:** Guggenheim Foundation Fellowship, 1969–70; National Endowment for the Arts, 1974. **Address:** Box 347, Amagansett, NY 11930. **Dealer:** Grace Borgenicht Gallery, Inc. **One-man Exhibitions:** (first) Artists' Gallery, NYC, 1938, also 1940; SFMA, 1939; San Diego, 1939; Charles Egan Gallery, 1955; The Stable Gallery, 1959, 60, 61, 62; Drew U., 1966; Grace Borgenicht Gallery, Inc., 1966, 68, 69, 71, 73, 75, 77, 79; Benson Gallery, 1967, 74; Guild Hall, 1973. **Retrospective:** Drew U. 1976; Montclair/AM, 1978. **Group:** Carnegie; MOMA; MMA; Brooklyn Museum; Chicago/AI; Baltimore/MA; Santa Barbara/MA, 1964. **Collections:** Amstar Corp., NYC; Atlantic Richfield Oil Co., NYC; Chase Manhattan Bank; First National City Bank, NYC; Harcourt Brace Jovanovich Inc., High Museum; Inmont Corp, NYC; Marine Midland Bank, Buffalo, N.Y.; MOMA; Montclair/AM; NYU; U. of North Carolina; Prudential Insurance Co. of America, Newark; U. of Texas; Union Carbide Corp. **Bibliography:** Archives.

ORTMAN, GEORGE. b. October 17, 1926, Oakland, Calif. **Studied:** Califor-

nia College of Arts and Crafts, 1947–48; Atelier 17, NYC, 1949, with S.W. Hayter; Academie Andre Lhote, Paris, 1950; Hofmann School, 1950–51. Traveled Europe, North America. **Taught:** School of Visual Arts, NYC, 1960–65; NYU, 1963–65; Fairleigh Dickinson College, summer, 1964; Princeton U., 1966–69; Honolulu Academy, 1969–70; Cranbrook, 1970– . **Awards:** Birmingham, Ala./MA 1966; Trenton/State, 1967; Guggenheim Foundation Fellowship; Ford Foundation Grant. **m.** Constance Whidden. **Address:** 45 Academy Way, Bloomfield Hills, MI 48013; summer: Box 192, Castine, ME 04421. **One-man Exhibitions:** (first) Tanager Gallery, NYC, 1953; Wittenborn Gallery, NYC, 1956; The Stable Gallery, 1957, 60; The Swetzoff Gallery, Boston, 1961, 62; The Howard Wise Gallery, NYC, 1962, 63, 64, 67, 69; Fairleigh Dickinson U., 1962; David Mirvish Gallery, 1964; Container Corp. of America, 1965; Walker, 1965; Milwaukee, 1966; Dallas/MFA, 1966; Akron/AI, 1966; Portland, Me./MA, 1966; Harcus-Krakow Gallery, 1966; David Stuart Gallery, 1966; The U. of Chicago, 1967; Galeria Van der Voort, 1967–69; Princeton U., 1967; Temple U., 1968; Middlebury College, 1969; Reed College, 1970; Cranbrook, 1970; J.L. Hudson Art Gallery, Detroit, 1971; Indianapolis, 1971; Western Michigan U., 1972; Gimpel & Weitzenhoffer, Ltd., 1972; Gertrude Kasle Gallery, Detroit, 1976. **Retrospective:** Fairleigh Dickinson U., 1963; Walker, 1965; Princeton U., 1967. **Group:** Salon du Mai, Paris, 1950; SFMA Annual, 1952; Martha Jackson Gallery, New Media—New Forms I, 1960; Claude Bernard, Paris, 1960; WMAA, Young America, 1960; Carnegie, 1960, 64, 67, 70; Chicago/AI Annuals, 1961, 62; WMAA, Geometric Abstraction in America, circ., 1962; Seattle World's Fair, 1962; MOMA, Hans Hofmann and His Students, circ., 1963–64; Amsterdam/Stedelijk, 1963; Jewish Museum, Toward a New Abstraction, 1963; SFMA, Directions—Painting U.S.A., 1963; WMAA Annuals 1962–67; A.F.A., Contemporary Wall

Sculpture, circ., 1963–64; A.F.A., Decade of New Talent, circ., 1964; International Biennial Exhibition of Paintings, Tokyo; WMAA, A Decade of American Drawings, 1965; U. of Illinois, 1965; WMAA, Art of the U.S. 1670–1966, 1966; Finch College, NYC, Holograms, 1971. **Collections:** Allentown/AM; American Republic; U. of California; Christian Theological Seminary; Des Moines; Lincoln, Mass./De Cordova; MOMA; Manufacturers Hanover Trust Co.; U. of Massachusetts; Milwaukee; NYPL; NYU; Omaha/Joslyn; P.S. 144, NYC; Portland, Me./MA; St. George's Episcopal Church, Princeton, N.J.; WMAA; Walker; Worcester/AM. **Bibliography:** Calas, N. and E.; Honisch and Jensen, eds.; Janis and Blesh 1; Moser 1; Sandler 1; Weller. Archives.

OSSORIO, ALFONSO. b. August 2, 1916, Manila, Philippine Islands. **Studied:** in England, 1924; Harvard U., BA, 1938; RISD, 1938–39. To USA, 1929. US Army, 1943–46. **Address:** P.O. Box 70, Wainscott, NY 11975. **One-man Exhibitions:** (first) Wakefield Gallery, NYC, 1941, also 1943; Mortimer Brandt, NYC, 1945; Galerie Paul Facchetti, 1951; Betty Parsons Gallery, 1951, 53, 56, 58, 59, 61; Galerie Stadler, Paris, 1960, 61; Cordier & Ekstrom, Inc., 1961, 64, 65, 67, 68, 69, 72. **Group:** WMAA Annuals, 1953– ; The Downtown Gallery, 1954; The Stable Gallery Annuals, 1955, 56; Rome–New York Foundation, Rome, 1957–59; Galerie Beyeler, Basel; Turin Art Festival, 1959; Martha Jackson Gallery, New Media—New Forms; Osaka (Japan) Art Festival; Gutai Sky Festival, Osaka, Carnegie; MOMA; The Art of Assemblage, circ., 1961; SRGM/USIA, American Vanguard, circ., Europe, 1961–62; Musée Cantonal des Beaux-Arts, Lausanne, I Salon International de Galeries Pilotes, 1963; St.-Etienne, 1964; Documenta III, Kassel, 1964; Intuitiones y Realizaciones Formales, Buenos Aires, 1964; U. of Illinois, 1965; Chicago/AI, 1966; WMAA, Art of the U.S. 1670–1966, 1966; MOMA, The

1960s, 1967; Munich/Modern, New Art: USA, 1968; MOMA, Dada, Surrealism and Their Heritage, 1968; MOMA, The New American Painting and Sculpture, 1969. **Collections:** Brandeis U.; Cuenca; Hartford/Wadsworth; International Institute for Aesthetic Research; MMA; Manila; NYU; PMA; WMAA; Yale U. **Bibliography:** Calas, N. and E.; **Friedman, B.H., 1;** *From Foreign Shores;* Hunter, ed.; Seitz 3; **Tapie** 1, **2.** Archives.

OSVER, ARTHUR. b. July 26, 1912, Chicago, Ill. **Studied:** Northwestern U., 1930–31; Chicago Art Institute School, with Boris Anisfeld. Traveled Europe; resided in France and Italy for several years. **Taught:** Brooklyn Museum School, 1947; Columbia U., 1950–51; U. of Florida, 1954; Cooper Union, 1955, 58; Yale U., 1956–57; American Academy, Rome, 1957–58; Washington U., 1960– . **Member:** Artists Equity; Audubon Artists. Federal A.P.: teaching, painting. **Commissions:** *Fortune* magazine, 1960 (cover). **Awards:** Chicago/AI, James Nelson Raymond Traveling Fellowship ($2,000), 1936; VMFA, John Barton Payne Medal; Pepsi-Cola $500 Award, 1947; PAFA, Joseph E. Temple Gold Medal, 1947; Guggenheim Foundation Fellowship, 1948; renewed 1949; U. of Illinois, **P.P.,** 1949; Prix de Rome, 1952; renewed 1953; Audubon Artists, Emily Lowe Prize, 1961; Art Directors Club, Chicago, Medal, 1961; PAFA, J. Henry Schiedt Memorial Prize, 1966; National Council on the Arts, Sabbatical Leave Grant ($7,500), 1966; AAAL, **P.P.,** 1974. **Address:** 465 Foote Avenue, St. Louis, MO 63119. **Dealer:** Fairweather-Hardin Gallery. **One-man Exhibitions:** (first) Mortimer Brandt, NYC, 1943; Grand Central Moderns, NYC, 1947, 49, 51, 57; Hamline U., 1950; U. of Florida, 1951, 55; Fairweather-Garnett Gallery, Evanston, 1955; Fairweather-Hardin Gallery, 1955, 57, 62, 64, 66; U. of Chattanooga, 1958; Syracuse U., 1959; Philadelphia Art Alliance, 1959; Milton

College, 1964; Maryville College (Mo.), 1966; Martin Schweig Gallery, 1966; Coe College, 1966; Iowa State U., 1968; Webster College, 1968; Iowa State U., 1968; **Retrospective:** St. Louis Artists' Guild, 1964; **Group:** Chicago/AI; PAFA: MMA: PMA: WMAA: MOMA: Carnegie; Corcoran; Phillips; Detroit/Institute; Brooklyn Museum; VMFA; Des Moines; Walker; Venice Biennial; Tokyo/Modern. **Collections:** Abbott Laboratories; Cincinnati/AM; Colorado Springs/FA; Davenport/Municipal; Des Moines; U of Georgia; Houston/MFA; IBM; U. of Illinois; Inland Steel Co.; S. C. Johnson & Son, Inc.; MMA; OMMA; U. of Michigan; Montclair/AM/ U of Nebraska; New Orleans/Delgado; PAFA; PMA; Peabody Museum; Phillips; Rio de Janeiro; U. of Rochester; St. Louis/City; Syracuse/Everson; Toledo/MA; WMAA; Walker; Washington U.; Wilmington. **Bibliography:** Bethers;; Nordness, ed.

OTT, JERRY. b. 1947, Albert Lee, Minn. **Studied:** Mank c/o State College;

U. of Minnesota. **Address:** c/o dealer. **Dealer:** Louis K. Meisel Gallery, NYC. **One-man Exhibitions:** Mankota State College, 1967; One Hundred and Eighteen Gallery, Minneapolis, 1973; Louis K. Meisel Gallery, NYC, 1973, 75, 79; Smith Fine Art, Monte Carlo, Monaco, 1974; Morgan Gallery, Shawnee Mission, Kansas, 1977, 79; Hanson-Cowles Gallery, Minneapolis, 1978; St. Cloud State U., 1978. **Group:** Minnesota/MA, Drawings USA, 1971; Recklinghausen, Mit Camera, Penzil und Spritzpistol, 1973; Indianapolis, 1974; Tokyo, Biennale, 1974; New York Cultural Center, Three Centuries of the American Nude, 1975; Christchurch, New Zealand, Photo Realism, American Paintings and Prints, circ., 1975; Potsdam/SUNY, The Presence and Absence of Realism, 1976; Madison Art Center, Figurative Painting in the Midwest, 1977; U. of Kansas, Artists Look at Art, 1978; Minneapolis/Institute, Five Realist Painters, 1979. **Collections:** Federal Reserve Bank, Minneapolis; U. of Georgia; U. of Kansas; Minneapolis/Institute; Tokyo/Contemporary; Walker.

P

PACE, STEPHEN. b. 1918, Charleston, Mo. **Studied:** Evansville Museum School, 1937–41, with Robert Lahr; Escuela de Bellas Artes, San Miguel de Allende, Mexico, 1945–46; ASL, 1948–49, with Cameron Booth, Morris Kantor; Academie de la Grande Chaumiere, 1950; Academy of Fine Arts, Florence, Italy, 1951; Hofmann School, 1951. US Army, 1943–46. Traveled Mexico, Europe, Canada, USA. **Taught:** Washington U., 1959; Pratt Institute, 1962–69; U. of California, Berkeley, 1968; Bard College, 1969–71; Des Moines, 1970; Kansas City/AI, 1973; Syracuse U., 1975. **Awards:** Dolia Laurian Fund Award, 1954; Hallmark International Competition, 1961; CAPS Grant, 1974. **Address:** 2812 Connecticut Avenue NW, Washington, DC 20008. **Dealer:** A. M. Sachs Gallery. **One-man Exhibitions:** (first) Evansville, 1946; Hendler Gallery, Philadelphia, 1953; Artists' Gallery, NYC, 1954; Poindexter Gallery, 1956, 57; HCE Gallery, Provincetown, Mass., 1956–59, 62–66; Washington U., 1959; Dilexi Gallery, San Francisco, 1960; Holland-Goldowsky Gallery, Chicago, 1960; The Howard Wise Gallery, Cleveland, 1960, NYC, 1960, 61, 63, 64; Dwan Gallery, 1961; MIT, 1961; Ridley Gallery, Evansville, Inc., 1966; U. of California, 1968; The Graham Gallery, 1969; Walker, 1962; Columbus, 1962; Kalamazoo/Institute, 1962; Des Moines, 1970; U. of Texas, 1970; Kansas City/AI, 1973; A. M. Sachs Gallery, 1974, 76, 78, 79; Drew U., 1975; Robert Polo Gallery, Washington, D.C., 1976; New Harmony, New Harmony, Ind., 1977; Spook Farm Gallery, Far Hills, N.J., 1978; Barbara Fiedler, Washington, D.C., 1980; Chas-

tenet Fine Arts Gallery, London, 1980. **Retrospective:** Bard College, 1975; American U., 1976. **Group:** Brooklyn Museum, 1953, 55; WMAA Annuals, 1953, 54, 56, 57, 58, 61; PAFA, 1954; Carnegie, 1955; Walker, Vanguard, 1955; International Biennial Exhibition of Paintings, Tokyo; Walker, 60 American Painters, 1960; Cleveland/MA, Paths of Abstract Art, 1960; Hallmark Art Award, 1960 Brandeis U. (two-man), circ., 1961; USIA, American Paintings, circ., Latin America, 1961; Corcoran, 1963; MOMA, Hans Hofmann and His Students, circ., 1963–64; U. of Texas, Recent American Painting, 1964; MOMA, circ., Europe, Asia, Australia, 1964–66; Chicago/AI, 1966; AAA, Childe Hassam Purchase Exhibition, 1977; U. of North Carolina, Art on Paper, 1978–79; Syracuse/Everson, Provincetown Painting, 1890s–1970s, 1977; MMA, Hans Hofmann as Teacher, 1979. **Collections:** Boston/MFA; U. of California; Chase Manhattan Bank; Ciba-Geigy Corp.; Des Moines; Evansville; MMA; Norfolk; Norfolk/Chrysler; U. of North Carolina; Phillips; Prudential Insurance Co. of America; Southern Illinois U.; U. of Texas; Utica; WMAA; Waitsfield/Bundy; Walker. **Bibliography:** Archives.

PACHNER, WILLIAM. b. April 7, 1915, Brtnice u Jihlavy, Moravia, Czechoslovakia. **Studied:** Kunstgewerbeschule, Vienna, 1930–33. Staff artist, Melantrich Publishing Co., Prague, 1933–35. To USA, 1939. Art Director, *Esquire* magazine, 1940–43. **Taught:** Florida Gulf-Coast Art Center, Inc.,

1953–57; Tampa Art Institute, Inc., 1957; director of own school, 1957–69. **Awards:** NIAL Grant, 1949; Mead Painting of the Year, $1,000 Prize, 1958; New Orleans/Delgado, First Prize, 1958; Youngstown/Butler, First Prize, 1959; Guggenheim Foundation Fellowship, 1960. **Address:** 962 Ohayo Mountain Road, Woodstock, NY 12498; 2901 San Carlos, Tampa, FL 33609. **One-man Exhibitions:** Barry Stephens Gallery, NYC, 1945; Weyhe Gallery, 1948; A.A.A. Gallery, NYC, 1949; Ganso Gallery, NYC, 1951, 55; Ringling, 1954; The Krasner Gallery, 1959, 60, 61, 68, 69; J. Camp Gallery, NYC, 1974. **Retrospective:** A.F.A./Ford Foundation, circ., 1959. **Group:** Carnegie, 1948; WMAA, 1948–51, 58, 60; Corcoran, 1949, 51; PAFA, 1950, 59; ART: USA: 58, NYC, 1958; U. of Nebraska; U. of Michigan; Detroit/Institute, 1959; New York World's Fair, 1965; New York Cultural Center, 1968. **Collections:** Ain Harod; Brandeis U.; Fort Worth; Hirshhorn; State College of Iowa; Milwaukee; Norfolk/Chrysler; Ringling; WMAA; White; Youngstown/Butler.   **Bibliography:** Zaidenberg, ed.

PADOVANO, ANTHONY. b. July 19, 1933, NYC. **Studied:** Brooklyn Museum School; Pratt Institute, with Alexander Kostellow; Columbia U., with Oronzio Maldarelli, 1957, BFA; Carnegie Institute of Technology. Traveled Italy, Switzerland; resided Rome, two years. **Taught:** U. of Connecticut, 1962–64; Columbia U., 1964–70; Queens College, 1971–73; Sarah Lawrence College, 1974–79; Westchester County Center, 1973–75; 1974–79; Columbia Greene Community College, 1976–79; Kingsborough Community College, 1978–79. **Member:** Silvermine Guild; American Association of University Professors; Sculptors Guild (vice-president). **Commissions:** World Trade Center, NYC, 1971; U. of Northern Iowa, 1972. **Awards:** Prix de Rome, 1960–62; III International Exhibition of Figurative Art, Rome, First Prize, 1962;

Silvermine Guild, Olivetti Prize for Sculpture, 1963, 64; Guggenheim Foundation Fellowship, 1964; Ford Foundation, **P.P.,** 1964; AAAL, 1976. **Address:** RD #1, General P.O., Putnam Valley, NY 10579. **Dealer:** The Graham Gallery. **One-man Exhibitions:** Lincoln, Mass./ De Cordova, 1954 (drawings); Geejon Gallery, NYC, 1957; Sculptors Studio, Washington, D.C., 1958; Galleria George Lester, Rome, 1962; Ruth White Gallery, 1962; U. of Connecticut, 1962; 63; Richard Feigen Gallery, NYC, 1964; The Bertha Schaefer Gallery, 1968, 70; The Graham Gallery, N.Y., 1972, 75, 78; IFA Gallery, Washington, D.C., 1975, 76; Alwin Gallery, London, 1978. **Group:** Carnegie, 1952; Portland, Me./ MA, 1959; American Academy, Rome, 1960, 61, 62; Palazzo dell'Esposizione, Rome, 1961, 62; WMAA Annual, 1962; Baltimore/MA, 1963; Waitsfield/Bundy, Bundy Sculpture Competition, 1963; Lincoln, Mass./De Cordova, New England Sculpture, 1964, 66, 68, 72, 75, 76; Finch College, 1964; HemisFair '68, San Antonio, Tex., 1968. **Collections:** American Academy, Rome; U. of Delaware; First National City Bank, Chicago; U. of Illinois; Indianapolis/ Herron; NCFA; U. of Nebraska; U. of Northern Iowa; Port Authority of New York & New Jersey; Ridgefield/Aldrich; St. Lawrence U.; Silvermine Guild; Trenton/State; Wichita/AM; WMAA; Worcester/AM.

PALMER, WILLIAM C. b. January 20, 1906, Des Moines, Iowa. **Studied:** ASL, 1924–26, with Boardman Robinson, Henry Schnakenberg, A. Tucker, Thomas Hart Benton, Kenneth Hayes Miller, and privately with Miller, 1928–29; Ecole des Beaux-Arts, Fontainebleau, with M. Baudoin. US Army, 1943–45. **Taught:** ASL, 1936–40; Hamilton College, 1941–47; Munson-Williams-Proctor Institute, Utica, N.Y., 1941–73. Federal A.P.: Mural painter and supervisor, 1933–39; murals for: Queens General Hospital, Jamaica, N.Y., 1934–36; US Post Office Department Building, Washington, D.C., 1936; US Post Offices at Monticello, Iowa, 1935, and Arlington, Mass., 1938. **Commissions** (murals): First National City Bank, Socony Building, NYC; Homestead Savings and Loan Association, Utica, N.Y., 1957. **Awards:** Paris Salon Medal, 1937; NAD, 1946, elected National Academician, 1965; Audubon Artists, 1947; AAAL Grant, 1953; NAD, Andrew Carnegie Prize, 1980. **Address:** Butternut Hill, Chestnut Street, Clinton, NY 13323. **Dealer:** The Midtown Galleries. **One-man Exhibitions:** (first) The Midtown Galleries, 1932, also 1937, 40, 44, 50, 52, 54, 57, 59, 62, 67, 68, 69, 74, 77; Des Moines, 1948, 49, 79; Cazenovia Junior College, 1949; Utica, 1956; Syracuse U.; Skidmore College; Kansas City/Nelson; Colgate U.; St. Lawrence U.; Jacksonville/Cummer, 1972. **Retrospective:** Utica, 1971. **Group:** Corcoran; VMFA; Carnegie, 1936; Brooklyn Museum; Chicago/AI; Toledo/MA; WMAA; New York World's Fair, 1939; MOMA; Kansas City/Nelson; Audubon Artists. **Collections:** AAAL; Allentown/AM; Andover/Phillips; Atlanta U.; Baltimore/MA; Britannica; Columbia S.C./MA; Columbus; Columbus, Ga.; Continental Grain Company; Cranbrook; Dallas/MFA; Des Moines; MMA; Phoenix; U. of Rochester; St. Lawrence U.; Syracuse U.; Transamerica Corp.; Trenton/State; Upjohn Co.; Utica; WMAA; The White House, Washington, D.C. **Bibliography:** Boswell 1; Bruce and Watson; Palmer; Watson, E.W., 2. Archives.

PAONE, PETER. b. October 2, 1936, Philadelphia, Pa. **Studied:** Barnes Foundation, 1953–54; Philadelphia Museum School, 1953, BA. Traveled Europe; resided London, two years. **Taught:** Pratt Institute, 1956–66, 1970–72; Philadelphia Museum School, 1958–59; Samuel S. Fleisher Art Memorial, Philadelphia, 1958–65; Positano (Italy) Art Workshop, 1961; U. of New Mexico, 1974; PAFA, 1979–80. **Member:** SAGA. **Awards:** PMA, **P.P.,** 1959; Library of Congress; Pennell **P.P.,** 1962; L.C. Tiffany Grants, 1962, 64; The Print Club, Philadelphia, **P.P.,** 1963; Syracuse U., **P.P.,** 1964. **Address:** 1027 Westview Street, Philadelphia, PA 19119. **Dealer:** Robinson Galleries; Hooks Epstein, Houston; Robert Lapelle, Philadelphia. **One-man Exhibitions:** (first) Dubin Gallery, Philadelphia, 1957; The Print Club, Philadelphia, 1958, 61, 62; Gallery Ten, New Hope, Pa., 1959; Grippi Gallery, NYC, 1959–62; Fort Worth, 1964; The Forum Gallery, 1965; Jessop Gallery, London, 1967; Benson Gallery, 1967; David Gallery, 1968; Roswell, 1977; Amarillo Art Center; Art Center, Waco; Hooks Epstein Gallery, Houston, 1978. **Group:** PMA, 1959, 62; Brooklyn Museum, 1962, and Print Biennials; Escuela Nacional de Artes Plasticas, Mexico City, 1963; III Paris Biennial, 1963; Dallas/MFA, Four Young Artists, 1964; Syracuse/Everson, American Printmakers, 1964; New York World's Fair, 1964–65; Otis Art Institute. **Collections:** British Museum; Fort Worth; Free Library of Philadelphia; General Mills Inc.; Library of Congress; MOMA; U. of Massachusetts; National Gallery; PAFA; PMA; Princeton U.; The Print Club, Philadelphia; Carl Sandburg Memorial Library; Syracuse U.; Trenton/State; U. of Utah; Victoria and Albert Museum; Youngstown/Butler. **Bibliography:** Rodman 3.

PARIS, HOWARD P. b. August 16, 1925, Edgemere, N.Y.; **d.** 1979, Oakland, Calif. **Studied:** Atelier 17, NYC, 1949; Creative Workshop, NYC, 1951–52; Academy of Fine Arts, Munich, 1953–56. Traveled Europe. **Taught:** U. of California, Berkeley. **Awards:** L. C. Tiffany Grant, 1949; Guggenheim Foundation Fellowship, 1953; Fulbright Fellowship (Germany), 1953; U. of California, Creative Arts Award and Institute Fellowship, 1967–68. **One-man Exhibitions:** (first) Argent Gallery, NYC, 1951; Philadelphia Art Alliance, 1951; Village Art

Center, NYC, 1952; Wittenborn Gallery, NYC, 1952; Galerie Moderne, NYC, 1953; Esther Stuttman Gallery, NYC, 1960; Tulane U., 1960; Pratt Graphic Art Center, 1960; Silvan Simone Gallery, 1960; U. of California, Berkeley, 1961; Paul Kantor Gallery, Beverly Hills, Calif., 1961; Bolles Gallery, 1962 (two-man, with Angelo Ippolito); Humboldt State College, 1963; Hansen Gallery, San Francisco, 1965, 67; Mills College, 1967; Reed College, 1967; Sally Judd Gallery, Portland, Ore., 1968; Michael Smith Gallery, Los Angeles, 1972; Smith-Andersen Gallery, San Francisco, 1975, 76, 77; Stephen Wirts Gallery, San Francisco, 1979. **Group:** MMA; Boston/MFA; Vienna Sezession; The Hague; Amerika Haus, Munich; California Palace; Baltimore/MA; Smithsonian; New Orleans/Delgado; Pasadena/AM; Brooklyn Museum, 1948, 49, 50, 52, 54; PAFA, 1949, 50, 52, 54; Galerie Kunst der Gegenwart, Salzburg, 1952; MOMA, 1953; PMA, 1953–56, 1959, 64; SFMA, 1953, 1960–65, Annual, 1963; III Biennial of Spanish-American Art, Barcelona, 1955; Ottawa/National, 1956; WMAA, 1956, Sculpture Annual, 1964; Salon de la Jeune Sculpture, Paris, 1958; Stanford U., Some Points of View for '62, 1961; Museum of Contemporary Crafts, 1963, 66; U. of California, circ., 1963–64; France/National, 1964; San Francisco Art Institute, 1964; New School for Social Research, 1964; La Jolla, 1965; The Pennsylvania State U., 1965; Newport Harbor Art Museum, Balboa, Calif., 1965; M. Knoedler & Co., Art across America, circ., 1965–67; Los Angeles/County MA, 1966. **Collections:** California Palace; U. of California; Chicago/AI; U. of Delaware; Goddard College; La Jolla; Library of Congress; MOMA; Memphis/Brooks; NYPL; U. of North Dakota; Oakland/AM; Ottawa/National; PMA; SFMA; WMAA; U. of Wisconsin. **Bibliography:** Selz, P. 2; Tuchman 1.

PARK, DAVID. b. March 17, 1911, Boston, Mass.; **d.** September 20, 1960, Berkeley, Calif. **Studied:** Otis Art Institute, Los Angeles, 1928; assistant to Ralph Stackpole, 1929. **Taught:** Various private schools, San Francisco, 1931–36; Winsor School, Boston, 1936–41; California School of Fine Arts, 1943–52; U. of California, Berkeley, 1955–60. Designed sets and costumes for the U. of California, Berkeley, production of the opera *The Sorrows of Orpheus,* by Darius Milhaud, 1958. Federal A.P.: Mural painting, San Francisco. **Awards:** SFMA, 1935, 51, 53, 55, 57; Oakland/AM, Gold Medal, 1957; PAFA, Walter Lippincott Prize, 1960. **One-man Exhibitions:** SFMA, 1935, 40; Delphic Studios, NYC, 1936; New Gallery, Boston, 1939; Albany/Institute (two-man, with Dorothy Dehner), ca. 1944; California Palace, 1946; Paul Kantor Gallery, Beverly Hills, Calif., 1954; RAC, 1955; U. of California, College of Architecture, 1956; Oakland/AM, 1957; de Young, 1959; Staempfli Gallery, 1959, 61, 63, 65; U. of California, Berkeley, circ., 1964; Santa Barbara/MA, 1968; Maxwell Galleries, Ltd., San Francisco, 1970. **Retrospective:** Oakland/AM, 1977. **Group:** PAFA, 1950; U. of Illinois, 1952, 57, 59, 61; III Sao Paulo Biennial, 1955; ART:-USA:58 and ART:USA:59, NYC, 1958, 59; WMAA Annual, 1959; Indiana U., New Imagery in American Painting, 1959; A.F.A., The Figure, circ., 1960; Chicago/AI; Corcoran; SRGM/USIA, American Vanguard, circ., Europe, 1961–62; J.L. Hudson Art Gallery, Detroit, Four California Painters, 1966. **Collections:** U. of California, Berkeley; ICA, Boston; U. of Illinois; Indian Head Mills, Inc.; Oakland/AM; SFMA; WMAA. **Bibliography:** Goodrich and Baur 1; Sandler 1. Archives.

PARKER, RAYMOND. b. August 22, 1922, Beresford, S.D. **Studied:** U. of Iowa, 1946, BA, 1948, MFA. **Taught:** Hunter College, 1955– ; U. of Southern California, summer, 1959; State U. of Iowa; U. of Minnesota; Columbia U., 1970–71. **Awards:** Ford Foundation, **P.P.,** 1963; Ford Foundation/A.F.A. Artist-in-Residence Grant, 1965; Na-

Ray Parker   Untitled 102   1980

tional Council on the Arts, 1967; Guggenheim Foundation Fellowship, 1967. **Address:** 52 Carmine Street, NYC. **Dealer:** Betty Cuningham, NYC. **One-man Exhibitions:** Walker, 1950; Memphis/Brooks, 1953; Paul Kantor Gallery, Beverly Hills, Calif., 1953, 56; Louisville/Speed, 1954; Union College (N.Y.), 1955; Widdifield Gallery, NYC, 1957, 59; U. of Southern California, 1959; Dwan Gallery, 1960, 62; Galerie Lawrence, Paris, 1960; The Kootz Gallery, NYC, 1960–64; Galleria dell'Ariete, 1961; SRGM, 1961; Bennington College, 1961; Des Moines, 1962 (three-man); Gertrude Kasle Gallery, 1966, 70; U. of New Mexico, 1967; Galerie Muller, 1967; Simone Sterne Gallery, New Orleans (two-man), 1968; Molly Barnes Gallery, Los Angeles, 1968, 70; Quay Gallery, 1970, 72, 74; Fischbach Gallery, 1971, 73, 74; Arts Club of Chicago, 1971; Miami-Dade, 1971; Michael Berger Gallery, Pittsburgh, 1974; Portland (Ore.) Center for the Visual Arts, 1974; Benson Gallery, 1974; Berenson Gallery, Miami, 1974; American U., 1975; Susan Caldwell Gallery, NYC, 1976, 77; U. of Maryland, 1977; U. of Texas, Austin, 1977; The Billiard Room Gallery, Cambridge, Mass., 1979; Betty Cuningham, NYC, 1979; Phillips, 1979. **Retrospectives:** Dayton/AI, 1965; WGMA, 1966; SFMA, 1967; School of Visual

Arts, NYC, 1971. **Group:** Minnesota State Historical Society, St. Paul, Centennial Minnesota; Walker Biennials, 1949, 51; MOMA, New Talent; MMA, American Paintings Today, 1950; WMAA Annuals, 1950, 52, 58, 67, 79, 72, 73; Oberlin College, 1951; Walker, Vanguard, 1955; Tokyo/Modern, 1957; Walker, 60 American Painters, 1960; II Inter-American Paintings and Prints Biennial, Mexico City, 1960; SRGM, Abstract Expressionists and Imagists, 1961; U. of Illinois, 1961, 62; Seattle World's Fair, 1962; Corcoran, 1963; Jewish Museum, Toward a New Abstraction, 1963; Hartford/Wadsworth, Black, White, and Gray, 1964; Chicago/AI, 1964; Los Angeles/County MA, Post Painterly Abstraction, 1964; Tate, Painting and Sculpture of a Decade, 1954–64, 1964; XXXII Venice Biennial, 1964; Cambridge, 1964, 65; MOMA, The Art of the Real, 1968; MOMA, Younger Abstract Expressionists of the Fifties, 1971; U. of Texas, Color Forum, 1972. **Collections:** AAAL; Akron/AI, Allentown/AM; Brandeis U.; Buffalo/Albright; Chicago/AI; Ciba-Geigy Corp.; Cleveland/MA; Commerce Bank of Kansas City; Dayton/AI; Des Moines; Fort Worth; Hartford/Wadsworth; International Minerals & Chemicals Corp.; State U. of Iowa; Los Angeles/County/MA; MIT; MMA; MOMA;

Miami-Dade; Minneapolis/Institute; Minnesota State Historical Society; U. of New Mexico; New Orleans/Delgado; PMA; Portland, Ore./AM; Phillips; Princeton U.; Ridgefield/Aldrich; SFMA; SRGM; Tate; U. of Texas; Vassar College; WMAA; Walker. **Bibliography:** Friedman, ed.; Goossen 1; McChesney; *New in the Seventies; Metro;* Rickey; Sandler; Weller.

PARKER, ROBERT ANDREW. b. May 14, 1927, Norfolk, Va. **Studied:** Chicago Art Institute School, with Paul Wieghardt, Rudolph Pen, Max Kahn, 1948–52, B.A. Ed.; Atelier 17, NYC, 1952–53, with Peter Grippe. US Army Air Force, 1945–46. Traveled Europe, Africa, Central and South America. **Taught:** New York School for the Deaf, 1952–55; School of Visual Arts, NYC, 1959–63. **Member:** American Federation of Musicians. Worked on film *The Days of Wilfred Owen,* with Richard Burton. **Commissions:** Illustrated 8 Poems by Marianne Moore (MOMA, 1962); sets for the MOMA production of *The Mighty Casey,* opera by William Schuman; New York World's Fair, 1964–65. **Awards:** Chicago/AI, 1952; Skowhegan School, 1952; Chicago/AI, Maurice L. Rothschild Scholarship, 1962; NIAL, Richard and Hinda Rosenthal Foundation Award, 1962; Tamarind Fellowship, 1967; Guggenheim Foundation Fellowship, 1969. **Address:** Kent Cliffs Road, Carmel, NY 10512. **Dealer:** Terry Dintenfass, Inc. **One-man Exhibitions:** (first) The Little Gallery, Chicago, 1949; Roko Gallery, NYC, 1953, 54, 57, 58, 59; Palmer House Galleries, Chicago, 1957; Nexus Gallery, Boston, 1957; Katonah (N.Y.) Library, 1957, 63; Felix Landau Gallery, 1961; St. Paul Gallery, 1961; Nashville, 1961; World House Galleries, NYC, 1961, 62, 64; Raymond Burr Gallery, Los Angeles, 1962; Obelisk Gallery, Washington, D.C., 1963; J. L. Hudson Art Gallery, Detroit, 1963, 69; Terry Dintenfass, Inc., 1966, 67, 69, 70, 71, 72, 78, 79; The Schuman Gallery, Rochester, N.Y., 1967; Lehigh U., 1969;

U. of Connecticut, 1971; Achim Moeller Ltd., London, 1973; Martin Sumers Graphics, NYC, 1978; Bethel (Conn.) Art Gallery, 1978. **Group:** MMA, American Watercolors, Drawings and Prints, 1952; MOMA, Young American Printmakers, 1953; WMAA Annuals, 1955, 56, 59; A.F.A., New Talent, circ., 1956; La Napoule, France, 5 Masters of Line, 1957; WMAA, Young America, 1957; USIA, Contemporary Graphic Art in the USA, circ., Europe and Asia, 1957–59; WMAA, Forty Americans under Forty, circ., 1962; Brooklyn Museum, 1963, 1968–69; MOMA, 1966; PAFA Annuals, 1966, 67; Indianapolis/Herron, 1967, 68; Brooklyn Museum Print Biennials, 1968, 69; U. of North Carolina, 1969, 71; New School for Social Research, Humor, Satire, and Irony, 1972; NAD Annual, 1977; Indiana U., Contemporary Pastel and Watercolors, 1977; Potsdam/SUNY, Off the Beaten Path, 1977; NAD, Ward Ranger Annual Exhibition, 1979. **Collections:** Amerada Hess Corp.; U. of Arkansas; Brooklyn Museum; Dublin/Municipal; Hirshhorn; Kalamazoo/Institute; Los Angeles/County MA; MOMA; U. of Massachusetts; U. of Michigan; Minnesota/MA; Montclair/AM; The Morgan Library; NAD; Nashville; Newark Museum; Pasadena/AM; Phoenix; NAD; Nashville; Newark Museum; Pasadena/AM; Phoenix; Raleigh/NCMA; Smith College; Tacoma; WMAA.

PASCHKE, ED. b. 1939, Chicago. **Studied:** Chicago Art Institute School, BFA, MA. **Taught:** Meramac College, St. Louis, 1970–71; Chicago Art Institute School, 1973; Barat College, Lake Forest, 1971– . **Address:** 707 N. Clark, Chicago, Ill. **Dealer:** Phyllis Kind Gallery, NYC, Chicago. **One-man Exhibitions:** Deson Zaks Gallery, Chicago, 1970, 72, 73, 75; Richard DeMarco Gallery, Edinburgh, 1973; Cincinnati/Contemporary, 1974; Hundred Acres Gallery, NYC, 1971, 74; Pyramid Gallery, Washington, D.C., 1975; Marion Locks Gallery, Philadelphia, 1976; Galerie

Ed Paschke   *Fumare Blanco*   1979

Darthea Speyer, Paris, 1974, 76, 78; Phyllis Kind Gallery, Chicago, 1977; Phyllis Kind Gallery, NYC, 1978, 79. **Group:** Chicago/Contemporary, Don Baum Sez, "Chicago Needs Famous Artists," 1969; Chicago/AI, Chicago and Vicinity, 1962, 67, 73; Chicago/Contemporary, Chicago Imagist Art, 1972; Ottawa/Ontario, What They're Up to in Chicago, 1972; WMAA Biennial, 1973; Chicago Art Institute School, Former Famous Alumni, 1976; Sacramento/Crocker, The Chicago Connection, 1977; U. of Texas, New in the Seventies, 1977. **Collections:** Brooklyn Museum; Baltimore/MA; Chicago/AI; Chicago/Contemporary; Museum des 20. Jahrhunderts, Vienna; Paris/Moderne; Phoenix. **Bibliography:** *The Chicago Connection; New in the Seventies.*

PATTISON, ABBOTT. b. May 15, 1916, Chicago, Ill. **Studied:** Yale U., 1937, BA, 1939, BFA. US Navy, four years. Resided China, Japan, France, Italy. **Taught:** Chicago Art Institute School, 1946–50; Northshore Art League, Winnetka, Ill., 1947–62; U. of Georgia, 1954–55; Skowhegan School, summers, 1955, 56. **Member:** Arts Club of Chicago; Sculptors Guild. **Commissions:** National Bar Association; Mayo Clinic, Rochester, Minn.; Stanford U. Medical Center; Inland Steel Co.; Union Tank Co.; U. of Chicago; Central National Bank, Cleveland; Illinois State Capitol, Springfield. **Awards:** Yale U. Traveling Fellowship; MMA, $1,500 Prize; Chicago/AI(5); Waitsfield/Bundy, Bundy Sculpture Competition, Second Prize; and some dozen others. **Address:** 334 Woodland Avenue, Winnetka, IL 60093; Lincolnville, ME 04849. **Dealer:** Fairweather-Hardin Gallery. **One-man Exhibitions:** (first) Chicago/AI, 1946; Sculpture Center, NYC; Santa Barbara/MA; La Jolla; U. of Georgia; U. of Florida; U. of Pittsburgh; U. of Wisconsin; Lee Nordness Gallery, NYC; Feingarten Gallery, Chicago; Fairweather-Hardin Gallery, Chicago, 1975, 78. **Group:** MMA; WMAA; PMA;

Cleveland/MA; Detroit/Institute; Los Angeles/County MA; Oakland/AM; Santa Barbara/MA; Chicago/AI. **Collections:** Andover/Phillips; Brandeis U.; Buckingham Palace; California Palace; Chicago/AI; Corcoran; Davenport/Municipal; Evansville; Fort Wayne; U. of Georgia; Jerusalem/National; La Jolla; Minnesota/MA; U. of Minnesota; Mount Holyoke College; Norfolk/Chrysler; Northwestern U.; U. of Notre Dame; Palm Springs Desert Museum; Phoenix; Portland, Me./MA; SFMA; St. Louis/City; Syracuse U.; WMAA; Wells College; Wichita/AM. **Bibliography:** *Northwest Traditions.* Archives.

PEAKE, CHANNING. b. October 24, 1910, Marshall, Colo. **Studied:** California College of Arts and Crafts, 1928; Santa Barbara School of Art, 1929–31; ASL, 1935–36, with Rico Lebrun. Traveled Europe, Mexico, Guatemala. A founder of the Santa Barbara (Calif.) Museum of Art. Operates a large ranch in Limpoc, California; first president, American Quarter Horse Association. **Commissions** (murals): Busch-Reisinger Museum, Harvard U., 1936 (assistant to Louis Rubenstein); Pennsylvania Station, NYC, 1936–38 (assistant to Rico Lebrun); Santa Barbara (Calif.) Public Library, 1958 (with Howard Warshaw). **Address:** Box 662, Santa Ynez, CA 93460. **Dealer:** Maxwell Galleries, Ltd., San Francisco. **One-man Exhibitions:** Frank Perls Gallery, 1952; Santa Barbara/MA, 1953, 56 (three-man, with Rico Lebrun and Howard Warshaw); de Young (three-man), 1953; J. Seligmann and Co. (two-man, with Howard Warshaw), 1957; Galerie Zak, Paris, 1961; The Willard Gallery, 1963; Portland, Ore./AM, 1964; Galleria Toninelli, Rome, 1969; Esther Baer Gallery, 1970; Mary Moore Gallery, La Jolla, 1971, 72; Santa Barbara/MA, 1975; Chelsea Galleries, Venice, Calif., 1976; Bradley Gallery, Santa Barbara, 1978; Syracuse/Everson, 1978. **Group:** PAFA; U. of Illinois, 1953, 55; Colorado Springs/FA; Los Angeles/County MA; Santa Bar-

bara/MA, 1974. **Collections:** Los Angeles/County MA; MIT; Portland (Ore.)/AM; Santa Barbara/MA; Syracuse/Everson.

PEARLSTEIN, PHILIP. b. May 24, 1924, Pittsburgh, Pa. **Studied:** Carnegie Institute of Technology, with Sam Rosenberg, Robert Lepper, Balcomb Greene; NYU, BA, MFA. **Taught:** Pratt Institute, 1959–63; Brooklyn College, 1963– . **Member:** Tanager Gallery, NYC. **Awards:** Fulbright Fellowship (Italy), 1958; National Council on the Arts Grant, 1969; AAAL, **P.P.**, 1973. **Address:** 163 West 88 Street, NYC 10024. **Dealer:** Allan Frumkin Gallery, NYC and Chicago. **One-man Exhibitions:** (first) Tanager Gallery, NYC, 1955, also 1959; The Periodot Gallery, 1956, 57, 59; Allan Frumkin Gallery, Chicago, 1960, 65, 69, 73, 75, NYC, 1961–67, 1969, 72, 74, 76, 78; Kansas City/Nelson, 1962; Reed College, 1965; Ceeje Galleries, Los Angeles, 1965, 66; Bradford Junior College, 1967; Carnegie, 1968; U. of South Florida, 1969; Chatham College, Pittsburgh, 1970; Graphics I & Graphics II, Boston, 1971; M.E. Thelen Gallery, Cologne, 1972; Galleri Ostergren, Malmo, 1972; Galerie Kornfeld, Zurich, 1972; Staatliche Museen-Kupferstichkabinett, Berlin, 1972; Donald Morris Gallery, 1972; Parker Street 470 Gallery, Boston, 1973; Galerie La Tortue, Paris, 1973; Finch College, NYC, circ., 1974; Gimpel Fils, 1975; Purchase/SUNY, 1975; Friedland Gallery, Toronto, 1975; John Berger Gallery, Pittsburgh, 1975; Fendrick Gallery, Washington, D.C., 1976; Donald Morris Gallery, Detroit, 1976; Harcus-Krakow Gallery, Boston, 1978; Gimpel Fils, London, 1979; Jollembeck, Cologne, 1979; Plattsburgh/SUNY, 1979; Carnegie Mellon U., 1979; Reed College, 1979. **Retrospective:** U. of Georgia, 1970; Springfield, Mass./MFA, 1978. **Group:** The Kootz Gallery, NYC, New Talent, 1954; The Stable Gallery Annuals, 1955–57; Carnegie, 1955, 66; 73; U. of Nebraska, 1956, 57; Walker, Expressionism, 1900–1955, 1956, also 1958; Chicago/AI, 1959, 62; Kansas City/Nelson, 1962; U. of Colorado, 1962, 67; SFMA, Directions—Painting U.S.A., 1963, also 1968; Boston U., 1964; U. of Illinois, 1965, 67, 69; U. of Texas, 1966; Corcoran, 1967; Harvard U., 1967; Trenton/State, Focus on Light, 1967; Torcuato di Tella, Buenos Aires; Vassar College, 1968; Smithsonian, circ., Latin America, 1968–70; Milwaukee, Aspects of a New Realism, 1969; WMAA, 22 Realists, 1970; MIT, Leslie, Pearlstein, Thiebaud, 1971; Indianapolis, 1972; A.F.A., Realist Revival, 1972; WMAA, American Drawings, 1963–1973, 1973; Yale U., American Drawing: 1970–1973, 1973; Hofstra U., The Male Nude, 1973; Ars 74, Helsinki, 1974; VMFA, Twelve American Painters, 1974; Westminster College, The Figure in Recent American Painting, 1974; Cleveland/MA, Aspects of the Figure, 1974; Yale U., Seven Realists, 1973; Corcoran Biennial, 1975; Lincoln, Mass./De Cordova, Candid Painting; American Genre 1950–1975, 1975; PAFA, Eight Contemporary Realists, 1977; Darmstadt/Kunsthalle, Realism and Reality, 1975, U. of Colorado, Six Painters of the Figure, 1979; US Dept. of the Interior, America 1976, circ., 1976; WMAA Biennial, 1979. **Collections:** Chicago/AI; Colgate U.; Colorado Springs/FA; Corcoran; Des Moines; Hirshhorn; U. of Indiana; Louisville/Speed; MOMA; Milwaukee; NYU; U. of Nebraska; Newark Museum; U. of North Carolina; Reed College; Rensselaer Polytechnic Institute; Syracuse U.; Vassar College; WMAA. **Bibliography:** *America 1976*; Arthur 1, 2; Cummings 1; Goodyear; Honisch and Jensen, eds.; *Kunst um 1970*; Nochlin; Rubin 1; Sandler 1; Sager; Weller. Archives.

PEARSON, HENRY CHARLES. b. October 8, 1914, Kinston, N.C. **Studied:** U. of North Carolina; Yale U., BA, MFA; ASL, 1953–55, with Reginald Marsh, Will Barnet, Robert Hale. US Army and Air Force, 1942–53. Traveled USA, the Orient. **Taught:** Boston Museum School; New School for Social Research; U. of Minnesota, Duluth; Ball State U.; PAFA; and privately. **Member:** American Abstract Artists; Century Association. **Awards:** Raleigh/NCMA, 1957; Tamarind Fellowship, 1964; Corcoran, **P.P.,** 1965; PAFA, J. Henry Schiedt Memorial Prize, 1968; North Carolina Governor's Arts Medal, 1969. **Address:** 58 West 58th Street, NYC 10019; 1601 Cambridge Drive, Kinston, NC 28501. **Dealer:** Marilyn Pearl Gallery, NYC. **One-man Exhibitions:** (first) Workshop Gallery, NYC, 1958; Stephen Radich Gallery, NYC, 1961, 62, 66, 69; Ball State U.; 1965; U. of Minnesota, 1965; Parsons-Truman Gallery, NYC, 1975, 77; Marilyn Pearl Gallery, NYC, 1980. **Retrospective:** Raleigh/NCMA, 1969. **Group:** Scranton/Everhart, Contemporary Americans, 1956; PAFA, 1956, 64; American Abstract Artists Annuals, 1958–64; A.F.A., Purist Painting, circ., 1960–61; A.F.A., Drawings from the WMAA Annual 1960, circ., 1961–62; WMAA, Geometric Abstraction in America, circ., 1962; MOMA, Contemporary Painters and Sculptors as Printmakers, 1964, The Responsive Eye, 1965, also 1969; Corcoran Biennial, 1965; Chicago/AI, 1965; Gallery of Modern Art, NYC, 1965; WMAA Annuals, 1965, 66, 68; Brooklyn Museum, Print Biennial; Grolier Club, 1966; Gallery of Modern Art, Ljubljana, Yugoslavia, VII International Exhibition of Prints, 1967; Utica, 1968; WMAA, Twentieth-Century Drawings from the Whitney Museum of American Art, circ., 1979–81. **Collections:** Ackland; Allentown/AM; Buffalo/Albright; Burlington Mills Collection; Chase Manhattan Bank; Chicago/AI; Ciba-Geigy Corp.; Cincinnati/AM; Columbia Broadcasting System; Corcoran; Housatonic Community College; Kansas City/Nelson; MMA; MOMA; Malmo; U. of Massachusetts; Minneapolis/Institute; U. of Minnesota; NYPL; U. of Nebraska; U. of North Carolina; Oslo/National, Raleigh/NCMA; St. Louis/City; The Singer Company, Inc.; Southern Illinois

U.; SRGM; Trinity College, Dublin; U.S. Steel Corp.; Union Carbide Corp.; WMAA; Wells College. **Bibliography:** Archives.

PEIRCE, WALDO. b. December 17, 1884, Bangor, Me.; **d.** March 8, 1970, Newburyport, Mass. **Studied:** Phillips Academy; Harvard U., 1908, A.B.; Academie Julian, Paris, 1911. Traveled Europe, North Africa, Spain. **Commissions** (murals): US Post Offices, Westbrooke, Me., Troy, N.Y., and Peabody, Mass.; Field Service Building, NYC, 1961. **Awards:** Pomona College, 1939; Pepsi-Cola, 1944; Carnegie, First Hon. Men., 1944. **One-man Exhibitions:** (first) Wildenstein & Co., NYC, 1926, 41 (two-man); The Midtown Galleries, 1939, 41, 44, 45, 49, 60, 68, 72. **Retrospective:** Rockland/Farnsworth, 1950. **Group:** Salon du Mai, Paris, 1912, 13, 14; Salon d' Automne, Paris, 1922. **Collections:** Andover/Phillips; Arizona State U.; U. of Arizona; Augusta, Me./State; Bangor Public Library; Britannica; Brooklyn Museum; Carnegie; Colby College; Columbus; Harvard U.; MMA; U. of Maine; U. of Nebraska; PAFA; Pepsi-Cola Co.; Rockland/Farnsworth; Upjohn Co.; WMAA; Youngstown/Butler. **Bibliography:** American Artists Group Inc. 3; Baur 7; Bazin; Bethers; Boswell 1; Eliot; **Hale;** Hall; Mellquist; **Peirce;** *7 Decades;* **Varga.** Archives.

PENNEY, JAMES. b. September 6, 1910, St. Joseph, Mo. **Studied:** U. of Kansas, with Albert Bloch, Karl Mattern, R. J. Eastwood, 1931, BFA; ASL, 1931–34, with George Grosz, Charles Locke, William Von Schlegell, Thomas Hart Benton, John Sloan. Traveled USA, Mexico, Europe, Canada. **Taught:** U. of Kansas, 1938–39; Hunter College, 1941–42; Bennett College (N.Y.), 1945–46; Bennington College, 1946–47; School for Art Studies, NYC, 1947; Munson-Williams-Proctor Institute, Utica, N.Y., 1948–55; Hamilton College, 1948–76; Kansas State U., summer, 1955; Vassar College, 1955–56; California College of Arts and Crafts, summer, 1960; **Member:** ASL; National Society of Mural Painters; Audubon Artists; NAD. Federal A.P. (murals): Greenpoint Hospital, Brooklyn, N.Y. (with Moses Soyer); Flushing (N.Y.) High School, P.S. 231, NYC; Far Rockaway (N.Y.) High School; New York World's Fair, 1939. **Commissions** (murals): Section of Fine Arts, Washington, D.C., 1939; Bristol Center, Hamilton College, 1959; Nebraska State Capitol, 1962–63(3); US Post Offices, Union, Mo., and Palmyra, Mo.; Omaha National Bank Centennial, 1966. **Awards:** Kansas City/Nelson, Medal, 1931; Section of Fine Arts, 1939, 40, 41; Pepsi-Cola, Award and Medal, 1948; Western New York Printmakers Annual, First Prize, 1950; Kansas State U., **P.P.,** 1951, 53, 57; AAAL, Childe Hassam Award, 1953; Utica, **P.P.,** 1955, 57; Yaddo Fellowship, 1956, 61; Our Town Competition, 1958; Audubon Artists Award, 1967; Audubon Artists Annual, Sterne Award, 1977. **Address:** 101 Campus Road, Clinton, NY 13323. **Dealer:** Kraushaar Galleries. **One-man Exhibitions:** U. of Kansas, 1934, 37; Eighth Street Playhouse, NYC, 1936; Mulvane Art Museum, 1937; Hudson D. Walker Gallery, NYC, 1939; Bennington College, 1946; Kraushaar Galleries, 1950, 54, 57, 61, 65, 69, 74; Utica, 1951, 74; Colgate U., 1952, 54; Wells College, 1953; Union College (N.Y.), 1955; Kansas State College, 1955; Wichita/AM, 1955; Vassar College, 1956; Syracuse U., 1957; Cazenovia Junior College, 1962; Kirkland Art Center, Clinton, N.Y., 1964; Omaha/Joslyn, 1966; Root Art Center, Hamilton College, 1967, 71, 76; Upstairs Gallery, Ithaca, N.Y., 1967–68; Cooperstown (N.Y.) Art Association, 1969. **Retrospectives:** Utica, 1955; Hamilton College, 1962; Utica College, 1972. **Group:** Carnegie; Brooklyn Museum; PAFA; American Watercolor Society; New York World's Fair, 1939; Pepsi-Cola; Audubon Artists; U. of Illinois; Chicago/AI; WMAA Annuals; California

Palace; Kansas City/Nelson; Cleveland/
MA; National Gallery; Newark Mu-
seum; Walker; Fort Worth; Colby Col-
lege; Toledo/MA; Atlanta/AA; NIAL;
New York State Fair, Syracuse, 1966;
NAD, 1973, 74, 75; Syracuse U., Art in
Crisis, 1974; AAAL, 1973. **Collections:**
Clearwater/Gulf Coast; Columbus; Con-
tinental Grain Company; Des Moines;
Exeter; Fort Worth; Hamilton College;
Hirshhorn; Howard U.; Kansas City/
Nelson; Kansas State College; Lehigh
U.; Lincoln Life Insurance Co.; Lincoln-
Rochester Trust Co.; U. of Minnesota;
Montreal/MFA; Mount Holyoke Col-
lege; NAD; NCFA; U. of Nebraska;
New Britain; Ohio Oil Co., NYC;
Omaha/Joslyn; St. Joseph/Albrecht;
Springfield, Mass./MFA; Syracuse U.;
Upjohn Co.; Utica; Wichita/AM. **Bibli-
ography:** Baur 5.

PEPPER, BEVERLY. b. December 20,
1924, Brooklyn. **Studied:** Pratt Institute, 1939–41, BA; Art Students
League, 1946; Academie de la Grande
Chaumiere, Paris; Atelier Andre l'Hote,
1948, and Atelier Fernand Leger.
Painted from 1949–60, then began
sculpture. Advertising art director,
1942–48. Traveled Europe, North Africa, Israel, Orient; since 1949 has lived
in Italy. **Commissions:** Festival di Due
Mondi, Spoleto, 1962; U.S. Plywood
Building, NYC, 1963; Weizmann Institute, Rehovoth, Israel, 1964; Southland Mall, Memphis, 1966; Government
Center, Boston, 1971; North Park Shopping Mall, Dallas, 1971; Albany (N.Y.)
Mall, 1973; Federal Reserve Bank, Philadelphia, 1974; San Diego Federal Building, 1975; AT&T, Long Lines Building,
Bedminster, N.J., 1974; Dartmouth College, 1975; The Carborundum Co.,
Niagara Falls, 1978; City Hall, Toledo,
Ohio, 1979; Physiocontrol Co., Seattle,
1979; City of Niagara Falls, 1979; Todi,
Italy, 1979; Toledo (O.) Civic Center,
1979; Buffalo (N.Y.) Convention Center, 1979. **Address:** Torre Gentile di
Todi, Perugia 06059, Italy. **Dealer:** Andre Emmerich Gallery, NYC. **One-man**

Beverly Pepper   *Ternana Wedge*   1980

Exhibitions: (first) Galleria dello Zodiaco, Rome, 1952; Barone, NYC, 1954, 56,
68; Obelisk Gallery, Washington, D.C.,
1955; Galleria d'Arte l'Obelisco, Rome,
1959; Galleria Pogliani, Rome, 1961;
Thibaut Gallery, NYC, 1961; Marlborough Galleria d'Arte, Rome, 1965,
68, 72; McCormick Place-on-the-Lake,
Chicago, 1966; Galleria d'Arte La Bussola, Turin, 1968; Paola Barozzi, Venice,
1968; Marlborough Gallery, NYC, 1969;
Chicago/Contemporary, 1969; MIT,
1969; Buffalo/Albright, 1969; Syracuse/
Everson, 1970; Piazza della Rotonda,
Milan, 1970; Studio Marconi, Milan,
1971; Galerie Hella Nebelung, Dusseldorf, 1971; Piazza Margana, Rome,
1971; Parker Street 470 Gallery, Boston,
1971; Qui Arte Contemporanea, Rome,
1972; Tyler School, Temple U.; Rome,
1973; Hammarskjold Plaza, NYC, 1975;
Andre Emmerich Gallery, NYC, 1975,
77, 79; SFMA, 1976; Seattle/AM, 1977;
Indianapolis, 1977, 78; Dartmouth College, 1977; Princeton U., 1978; Hofstra
U., 1979; Thomas Segal Gallery,
Boston, 1980; Andre Emmerich Gallery,

Zurich, 1980; Nina Freudenheim Gallery, Buffalo, 1980. **Group:** Rome–New York Foundation, Rome, The Quest and the Quarry, 1961; Buffalo/Albright, Plus by Minus, 1968; Indianapolis, 1970; Venice, Biennale, 1972; Philadelphia Civic Center, Women's Work: American Art, 1974, 1974; Quadrieniale, 1977; Documenta 6, Kassel, 1977; GSA, Washington, D.C., Drawings for Outdoor Sculpture: 1946–1977, 1978. **Collections:** Harvard U.; MIT; Buffalo/Albright; Fidelity Union Life Insurance Co., Dallas; Jacksonville/AM; Florence (Italy) Modern; Walker; Instituto Italiano di Cultura, Stockholm; Syracuse/Everson; Turin/Civico; Graphische Sammlung Albertina; Hirshhorn; Worcester/AM; Parkersburg Art Center, W. Va.; Dartmouth College; AT&T; Milwaukee; Indianapolis; Mount Holyoke College; U. of Rochester.

PEREIRA, I. RICE. b. August 5, 1901, Boston, Mass.; **d.** January 11, 1971, Marbella, Spain. **Studied:** ASL, with Richard Lahey, Jan Matulka. Traveled Europe, North Africa, resided London, Paris. **Taught:** Pratt Institute. Federal A.P.: Easel painting, teaching. **Awards:** Pepsi-Cola, 1943. **One-man Exhibitions:** ACA Gallery, 1933, also 1934, 35, 46, 49; Howard U., 1938; East River Gallery, NYC, 1939; Julien Levy Galleries, NYC, 1939; Art of This Century, NYC, 1944; Arts Club of Chicago, 1945; SFMA, 1947; Barnett Aden Gallery, Washington, D.C., 1948; Andover/Phillips, 1949; Santa Barbara/MA, 1950; Portland, Ore./AM, 1950; de Young, 1950; Syracuse U., 1951; Baltimore/MA, 1951; Ball State Teachers College, 1951; Durlacher Brothers, NYC, 1951; Phillips, 1952; Dayton/AI, 1952; Adele Lawson Gallery, Chicago, 1954; Hofstra College, 1954; U. of Michigan, 1954; Philadelphia Art Alliance, 1955; Corcoran, 1956; Adele Lawson Gallery, NYC, 1956; Lee Nordness Gallery, NYC, 1958, 59, 61; Rome–New York Foundation, Rome, 1960; A.A.A. Gallery, Washington, D.C., 1961; The

Amel Gallery, NYC, 1961; Galerie Internationale, NYC, 1964; Agra Gallery, 1965; Distelheim Gallery, 1965; Wilmington College (N.C.), 1968; U. of North Carolina, 1968; Charlotte/Mint, 1968; Andre Zarre Gallery, NYC, 1974, 78, 79; Andrew Crispo Gallery, NYC, 1976; Andre Zarre Gallery, NYC, 1978, 79. **Retrospective:** WMAA, circ., 1953. **Group:** Venice Biennial; Tate; ICA, London; MOMA, Fourteen Americans, circ., 1946; Darmstadt/Kunsthalle; Lille; Internationale Kunstausstellung, Berlin, 1951; Chicago/AI Annuals; PAFA; Carnegie; I Sao Paulo Biennial, 1951; USIA, 20th Century Highlights, circ., 1957–58; WMAA, 1966–68; Corcoran, 1969. **Collections:** Allentown/AM; Andover/Phillips; Arizona State College; U. of Arizona; Atlanta U.; Ball State U.; Baltimore/MA; Boston/MFA; Boston U.; Brandeis U.; The Catholic U. of America; Chicago/AI; Connecticut College; Dallas/MFA; Detroit/Institute; Goucher College; Hartford/Wadsworth; Harvard U.; Howard U.; State U. of Iowa; Kansas City/Nelson; MMA; MOMA; The Miller Co.; U. of Minnesota; NCFA; Newark Museum; New London; New Orleans/Delgado; New Paltz/SUNY; Norfolk; Phillips; Phoenix; SFMA; SRGM; Smith College; Syracuse U.; Toledo/MA; Utica; Vassar College; WMAA; Walker; Worcester/AM; Youngstown/Butler. **Bibliography:** Baur 4, 5, 7; Bazin; Flanagan; Genauer; Goodrich and Baur 1; Janis, S.; Kootz 2; Mendelowitz; Miller, ed. 2; Nordness, ed.; Pearson 2; Pousette-Dart, ed.; Read 2; Richardson, E.P.; Ritchie 1; Soby 5, 6; Wight 2. Archives.

PERLIN, BERNARD. b. November 21, 1918, Richmond, Va. **Studied:** New York School of Design, 1934–36; NAD, 1936–37, with Leon Kroll; ASL, 1936–37, with Isabel Bishop, William Palmer, Harry Sternberg. Traveled Europe, Mediterranean, the Orient; resided Italy, 1948–54. **Taught:** Brooklyn Museum School, 1947–48; Wooster Community Art Center, Danbury,

Conn., 1967–69. **Commissions:** US Treasury Department; US Post Office Department, 1940. **Awards:** Kosciuszko Foundation, 1938; Chaloner Prize Foundation Award, 1948; Fulbright Fellowship, 1950; Guggenheim Foundation Fellowship, 1954, 59; NIAL, 1964. **Address:** 56 Shadow Lake Road, Ridgefield, CT 06877. **One-man Exhibitions:** M. Knoedler & Co., 1948; Catherine Viviano Gallery, 1955, 58, 63, 66, 70; Wooster School, Danbury, Conn., 1968. **Retrospective:** U. of Bridgeport, 1969. **Group:** Chicago/AI Annuals, 1948, 54, 59; Carnegie, 1949, 52; MMA, 1950; Palazzo di Venezia, Rome, 1950; ICA, London, 1950; WMAA Annuals, 1951, 55; Corcoran, 1953, 59; WMAA, The New Decade, 1954–55; U. of Illinois, 1955, 59; XXVIII Venice Biennial, 1956; Brussels World's Fair, 1958; Cincinnati/ AM, 1958; Detroit/Institute, 1960; PAFA, 1960. **Collections:** California Palace; Chicago/AI; Denver/AM; Detroit/Institute; Kansas City/Nelson; MOMA; NCFA; Princeton U.; Springfield, Mass./MFA; Tate; WMAA. **Bibliography:** Baur 7; Eliot; Goodrich and Baur 1; McCurdy, ed.; Mendelowitz; Pousette-Dart, ed.; Rodman 1, 2. Archives.

PETERDI, GABOR. b. September 17, 1915, Budapest, Hungary. **Studied:** Academy of Fine Arts, Budapest, 1929; Academie Julian, Paris, 1931; Academie Scandinave, Paris, 1932; Academy of Fine Arts, Rome, 1930; Atelier 17, Paris, 1935. **Taught:** Brooklyn Museum School, 1948–53; Yale U., 1954– ; Hunter College, 1960– . **Member:** Silvermine Guild. **Awards:** Prix de Rome, 1930; Paris World's Fair, 1937, Gold Medal (jointly with Lurcat); Brooklyn Museum, 1950, 52, 60; American Color Print Society, 1951; Oakland/AM, 1957, 60; PAFA, Gold Medal, 1957; Boston Printmakers, 1959; Seattle/AM, **P.P.**, 1960; Pasadena/AM, **P.P.**, 1960; Bay Printmakers Society, Oakland, Adell Hyde Morrison Memorial Medal, 1960; Ford Foundation Grant, 1960; PAFA,

Pennell Memorial Medal, 1961; IV International Biennial Exhibition of Prints, Tokyo, Museum of Western Art Prize, 1964; Guggenheim Foundation Fellowship, 1964–65. **Address:** 108 Highland Avenye, Rowayton, CT 06853. **Dealers:** Grace Borgenicht Gallery Inc.; Haslen Fine Arts, Inc.; Jacques Baruch Gallery; Nielsen Gallery. **One-man Exhibitions:** (first) Ernst Museum, Budapest, 1930, also 1934; Bratislava, Czechoslovakia, 1930; Prague/National, 1930; Rome/ Nazionale, 1930; Jeanne Bucher, Paris, 1936; Julien Levy Galleries, NYC, 1939; Norlyst Gallery, NYC, 1943, 44; Laurel Gallery, NYC, 1948, 49; Philadelphia Art Alliance, 1950, 55; Smithsonian, 1951; Silvermine Guild, 1952; Grace Borgenicht Gallery, Inc., 1952, 55, 59, 61, 66, 74, 79; Kanegis Gallery, 1956, 57, 59, 61; St. George's Gallery, London, 1958; The Howard Wise Gallery, Cleveland, 1959; Boston/MFA, 1959; Achenbach Foundation, 1960; Lincoln, Mass./ De Cordova, 1964; Corcoran, 1964; Michigan State U., 1964; Yale U., 1964; Atlanta/AA, 1965; Ridgefield/Aldrich, 1965. **Group:** Salon des Surindependants, Paris, 1936, 38; Library of Congress, 1943, 47; The Print Club, Philadelphia, 1948; Brooklyn Museum, 1948, 49, 64; WMAA, 1949; MOMA, 1949; Yale U., 1949; Corcoran, 1949; PAFA, 1949, 61; Silvermine Guild; NYPL; Chicago/AI; Achenbach Foundation; U. of Nebraska; Minneapolis/Institute; Oakland/AM; U. of Illinois. **Collections:** Abilene Christian College; Achenbach Foundation; Albion College; Andover/Phillips; Baltimore/MA; Beloit College; Berea College; Boston/ MFA; Brandeis U.; Brooklyn Museum; Brown U.; Budapest/National; Buffalo/ Albright; Chicago/AI; Clearwater/Gulf Coast; Cleveland/MA; Columbia, S.C./ MA; Corcoran; Cranbrook; Currier; Dartmouth College; U. of Georgia; Hartford/Wadsworth; Honolulu Academy; Illinois Wesleyan U.; U. of Illinois; Indiana U.; MMA; MOMA; Memphis/ Brooks; Michigan State U.; U. of Michigan; Minneapolis/Institute; NYPL; U. of Nebraska; Northwestern U.; Oakland/

AM; U. of Oklahoma; Oregon State U.; PAFA; PMA; Pasadena/AM; Prague/National; Princeton U.; RISD; Rome/Nazionale; Rutgers U.; Sao Paulo; Seattle/AM; Smith College; Smithsonian; Texas Wesleyan College; Vassar College; WMAA; Walker. **Bibliography:** Baur 5; Chaet; Goodrich and Baur 1; Hayter 1; **Johnson 1; Peterdi.** Archives.

PETERSEN, ROLAND CONRAD. b. March 31, 1926. Endelave, Horsens, Denmark. **Studied:** With Glenn Wessels, Chiura Obata, Erle Loran, John Haley, Worth Ryder, James McCray, U. of the Pacific and U. of California, AB, 1949, MA, 1950; Hofmann School, 1950–51; Atelier 17, Paris, 1950, and with S. W. Hayter, Paris, 1963, 70; California School of Fine Arts, 1954. Traveled Europe, 1950–51, 1963–64, 1970–71. **Taught:** Washington State U.; 1952–56; U. of California, 1956–. **Awards:** Sigmund Martin Heller Traveling Fellowship, 1950; SFMA, Anne Bremer Memorial Prize, 1950; Oakland/AM, First Prize, Gold Medal, 1953; California State Fair. **P.P.**, 1957, 60; Guggenheim Foundation Fellowship, 1963; U. of the Pacific, **P.P.**, 1969; Fulbright Fellowship, 1970; U. of California Regents Fellow, 1977. **Address:** 858 Linden Lane, Davis, CA. 95616. **Dealer:** Staempfli Gallery. **One-man Exhibitions:** (first) Oakland/AM, 1954; Spokane Art Center of Washington State U., 1954, 55, 57; Boise (Idaho) Art Association, 1954; Esther Robles Gallery, 1961; City Library, Sacramento, Calif., 1961; California Palace, 1961; Gump's Gallery, 1962; Staempfli Gallery, 1963, 65, 67; Sacramento/Crocker, 1966; Adele Bednarz Gallery, 1966, 69, 72, 73, 75, 76; Chico State College, 1966; de Young, 1968; Western Association of Art Museum Directors, circ., 1968–69; Phoenix, 1972; Santa Barbara/MA, 1973; Whitman College, 1974; Solano Community College, Solano, 1975; U. of California, Davis, 1976; American River College, 1976; College of Siskiyous, 1977; Artists Cooperative Gallery, Sacramento, 1977; California State College, Stanislaus, 1978; Shasta College, Redding, 1978. **Retrospectives:** Chico State College (15-year, 1950–65), 1966; de Young (5-year, 1963–68), 1968; U. of California, Davis, 1978; Washington State U., Pullman, 1976. **Group:** Pasadena/AM, Pacific Profile, 1961; Poindexter Gallery, 1961; U. of Illinois, 1961, 63, 69; Santa Barbara/MA, 1962; Carnegie, 1964; Chicago/AI Annual, 1965; VMFA, American Painting, 1966; New School for Social Research, Humanist Tradition, 1968; Oakland/AM, California Landscape, 1975; U. of Wisconsin, Madison, Atelier 17, 1977. **Collections:** Achenbach Foundation; CSCS; U. of California, Davis; Chase Manhattan Bank; De Beers Collection; de Young; Illinois Wesleyan U.; La Jolla; Long Beach/MA; MOMA; U. of Miami; Musée Municipal, Brest; NCFA; U. of North Carolina; Oakland/AM; Oakland Public Library; Ohio U.; PMA; U. of the Pacific; Phoenix; Sacramento/Crocker; San Diego; Santa Barbara/MA; Shasta College; Spokane Coliseum; VMFA; WMAA; Washington State U. **Bibliography:** Hager 1.

PETLIN, IRVING. b. December 17, 1934, Chicago, Ill. **Studied:** Chicago/AI; 1952–56, BFA; Yale U., 1959, MFA, with Josef Albers. US Army, 1957–59. Traveled USA; resided France, 1959–63. **Taught:** UCLA, 1963–66; RISD, 1978; Cooper Union, NYC, 1977–80. **Awards:** Ryerson Fellowship, 1956; Copley Foundation Grant, 1961; Guggenheim Foundation Fellowship, 1971. **Address:** 257 West 11th Street, NYC 10014. **Dealers:** Marlborough Gallery, NYC; Rebecca Cooper Gallery; Galerie Nina Dausset, Paris. **One-man Exhibitions:** (first) Dilexi Gallery, San Francisco, 1958; Cliffdweller Gallery, Chicago, 1956; Galerie du Dragon, Paris, 1960, 62, 63, 64, 68; Galatea, Turin, 1962; Hanover Gallery, London, 1964; Palais des Beaux-Arts, Paris, 1965; Rolf Nelson Gallery, Los Angeles, 1966; Odyssia Gallery, NYC, 1967, 68, 69, 70, 79; Galleria Odyssia, Rome, 1969, 71, 76; Galleria il Fante di Spade, Rome, 1968; Galleria Bergamini, Turin, 1974; Documenta, Turin, 1974; Rebecca Cooper Gallery, Washington, D.C., 1976; Galleria Bergamini, Milan, 1977; Purchase/SUNY, 1978; Arts Club, Chicago, 1978; Gallerie Nina Dausset, Paris, 1980. **Retrospective:** Brussels/Beaux-Arts, 1965. **Group:** Chicago/AI, 1953, 56, 72; Paris/Moderne, 1961–66; WMAA, 1973; Chicago/Contemporary, Chicago Imagist Art, 1972. **Collections:** Amsterdam/Stedelijk; Chicago/AI; Chicago/Contemporary; Des Moines; MOMA; Paris/Moderne; Recklinghausen. **Bibliography:** Schulze.

PETTET, WILLIAM. b. October 10, 1942, Whittier, Calif. **Studied:** California Institute of the Arts, Valencia; Chouinard Art Institute, 1965, BFA. Traveled Canada, Europe, Mexico. **Taught:** Skowhegan School, 1972; Empire State College, N.Y., 1977. **Awards:** Tamarind Fellowship, 1970. **Address:** 14 Beach 213th St., Breezy Point, NY 11697. **Dealer:** S. & G. Mathews Gallery, San Antonio, Tex. **One-man Exhibitions:** (first) Nicholas Wilder Gallery, 1966, 68, 70; Robert Elkon Gallery, 1968, 69; David Whitney Gallery, NYC, 1970, 71; Dunkelman Gallery, Toronto, 1971, 73; The Willard Gallery, 1973, 74, 75; S. & G. Mathews Gallery, San Antonio, 1978, 79. **Group:** Trenton/State, Focus on Light, 1967; WMAA Annuals, 1967, 69, 73; Corcoran, 1969; Washington U., Here and Now, 1969; Ridgefield/Aldrich, Lyrical Abstraction, 1970; ICA, U. of Pennsylvania, Two Generations of Color Painting, 1970; Santa Barbara/MA, Spray, 1971; WMAA, Lyrical Abstraction, 1971; Hamburg/Kunstverein, USA: West Coast, circ., 1972; WMAA, 35 American Artists, 1974; MOMA, 60s and 70s, 1974; U. of Texas, Austin, New in the Seventies,

1977. **Collections:** Hirshhorn; MOMA; WMAA. **Bibliography:** *New in the Seventies; USA West Coast.*

PFRIEM, BERNARD. b. September 7, 1916, Cleveland, Ohio. **Studied:** John Huntington Polytechnical Institute, 1934–36; Cleveland Institute of Art, 1936–40. US Air Force, 1942–46. Traveled Europe, Mediterranean; resided Mexico, 1940–42, Paris, 1952–63. **Taught:** Cleveland Institute of Art School, 1938–40; Peoples Art Center (MOMA), 1946–51; Cooper Union, 1963–71; Sarah Lawrence College, 1969–76. US Army Air Force, 1942–46. Assistant to Jose Clemente Orozco on frescoes, Jiquilpan (Michoacan), Mexico, and to Julio Castellanos on murals, Mexico City, Chief Designer, US Government exhibitions and pavilions in Europe, 1953–56. **Awards:** Agnes Gund and Mary S. Ranney Traveling Fellowship, 1940; Copley Foundation Grant, 1959. **Member:** Century Association; Chelsea Arts Club, London. Designer for Tibor deNagy Marionette Co., 1946–50. **Address:** 115 Spring Street, NYC 10012. **Dealer:** Staempfli Gallery, NYC; Brooks Jackson Iolas Gallery, NYC. **One-man Exhibitions:** (first) Hugo Gallery, NYC, 1951; US Cultural Center, Paris, 1954; Galerie du Dragon, 1960; Alexandre Iolas Gallery, NYC, 1961, 63; Obelisk Gallery, Washington, D.C., 1963; International Gallery, Baltimore, 1965; Wooster Community Art Center, Danbury, 1965; Richard Feigen Gallery, Chicago, 1966; Sarah Lawrence College, 1969; U. of Arkansas, 1970; Midtown Gallery, Atlanta, 1971. **Retrospective:** Cleveland Institute of Art, 1963. **Group:** Cleveland/MA, 1939–41; Youngstown/Butler, 1941; Columbus, 1942; Carnegie, 1942; Hugo Gallery, NYC, 1948, 49, 50; WMAA Annual, 1951; Smithsonian, circ., American Drawings, circ., 1965; WMAA, A Decade of American Drawings, 1955–1965, 1965; American Drawing Society, 1970; Cleveland Institute of Art, 1973; The Pennsylvania State U., 1974. **Collec-**

tions: U. of Arkansas; Brooklyn Museum; Chase Manhattan Bank; Chicago/AI; Columbia Banking, Savings and Loan Association; Corcoran; MMA; MOMA; Minnesota/MA; Utah; Worcester/AM. **Bibliography: Waldberg 1, 2.**

PINEDA, MARIANNA. b. May 10, 1925, Evanston, Ill. **Studied:** Cranbrook, with Carl Milles, 1942; Bennington College, 1942–43; U. of California, Berkeley, with Raymond Puccinelli, 1943–45; Columbia U., with Oronzio Maldarelli, 1945–46; with George Stanley, Los Angeles (sculpture); with Ossip Zadkine, Paris, 1949–50; Scholar, Radcliffe Institute for Independent Study, 1962–64. Resided Paris, 1949–51, Florence, 1954–57, Rome, 1966. **Taught:** Newton College, Mass., 1972–75; Boston U., 1974–78; Boston College, 1975–77. **Member:** Artists Equity; Sculptors Guild; Boston Visual Artists Union. **Commissions:** Boston Conservatory of Music, Jan Veen Memorial Medal; State Capitol, Honolulu, 1980. **Awards:** Buffalo/Albright, 1948; Walker, **P.P.,** 1951; Boston Arts Festival, 1957, 60; San Francisco Art Association, First Prize for Sculpture, 1955; Chicago/AI, 1957. **m.** Harold Tovish. **Address:** 380 Marlborough Street, Boston, MA 02115. **One-man Exhibitions:** (first) Slaughter Gallery, San Francisco, 1951; Walker, 1952; The Swetzoff Gallery, Boston, 1953, 64; Lincoln, Mass./De Cordova, 1954; Premier Gallery, Minneapolis, 1963; Alpha Gallery, 1972; Bumpus Gallery, Duxbury, 1974. **Group:** Buffalo/Albright, 1948; WMAA, 1953, 54, 57, 59; MMA, 1957; U. of Illinois, 1957; Chicago/AI, 1957, 60; Boston Arts Festival, 1957, 58, 60; Carnegie, 1958; MOMA, 1959; Waitsfield/Bundy, 1963; New York World's Fair, 1964–65; Lincoln, Mass./De Cordova, Sculpture in the Park, 1972; The Pennsylvania State U., Contemporary Artists and the Figure, 1974; Lincoln, Mass./De Cordova, New England Women, 1975; Los Angeles/County MA, Women Artists 1550–1950, 1976;

Brockton/Fuller, Artists in Boston, 1978. **Retrospectives:** Honolulu Academy, 1970; Newton College, 1972. **Collections:** Andover/Phillips; Boston/MFA; Boston Public Library; Bowdoin College; Dartmouth College; Hartford/Wadsworth; Harvard U.; U. of Massachusetts; Mount Holyoke College; Radcliffe College; State of Hawaii; Utica; Walker; Williams College.

PITTMAN, HOBSON L. b. January 14, 1900, Tarboro, N.C.; **d. May 5, 1972, Bryn Mawr, Pa. Studied:** Rouse Art School, Tarboro, 1912–16; Penn State College, 1921–22; Carnegie Institute of Technology, 1924; Columbia U., 1925–26 (with Molly Rouse, Albert Heckman, Doris Rosenthal, Harold Dickson). Traveled Europe, North Africa, USA, Mexico, Canada, South America, Far East; summered in Woodstock, N.Y., 1920–30. **Taught:** Friends Central School, Philadelphia, 1931–58; PAFA; The Pennsylvania State U., Philadelphia Museum School. **Member:** Philadelphia Watercolor Club; International Institute of Arts and Letters; NAD; Fellowship of the PAFA; past member, Artists Equity. **Commissions:** *Holiday* magazine (cover); De Beers Diamonds (painting); Radio Corporation of America (2 paintings for music advertisements). **Awards:** Golden Gate International Exposition, San Francisco, 1939, Hon. Men.; PAFA, J. Henry Schiedt Memorial Prize, 1943; PAFA, Dawson Memorial Medal, 1944; California Palace, American Exhibition, Second Prize, 1947; Corcoran, William A. Clark Prize, 1947; Carnegie, Third Prize, 1949; Youngstown/Butler, First Prize, 1950; Corcoran, Second William A. Clark Prize, 1953; Guggenheim Foundation Fellowship, 1956; PAFA, Distinguished Artist of Pennsylvania, 1960; State of North Carolina Medal in Fine Arts, 1968. **One-man Exhibitions:** (first) Edward Side Gallery, Philadelphia, 1928; Hudson D. Walker Gallery, NYC, 1938; Biltmore Galleries, Los Angeles, 1940, 46; Philadelphia Art Alliance, 1941; The Pennsylvania State U., 1945, 60; San Antonio/McNay; PAFA, 1946, 60, 64; The Milch Gallery, 1947, 54; Raleigh/NCMA, 1950; Sheppard Memorial Gallery, Greenville, N.C., 1957; Winston-Salem (N.C.) Gallery of Fine Arts, 1968; The Babcock Gallery, 1970. **Retrospectives:** Youngstown/Butler, 1942; Raleigh/NCMA, 1963. **Group:** Carnegie; PAFA; Corcoran; Venice Biennial; Chicago/AI; WMAA; MMA; PMA; Golden Gate International Exposition, San Francisco, 1939; New York World's Fair, 1939; Tate, American Painting, 1946; Raleigh/NCMA; Youngstown/Butler. **Collections:** Abbott Laboratories; Andover/Phillips; Britannica; Brooklyn Museum; Carnegie; Cleveland/MA; Corcoran; Cranbrook; Eaton Paper Co.; Florence, S.C., Museum; IBM; Indianapolis/Herron; MMA; MOMA; Memphis/Brooks; Montclair/AM; NIAL; U. of Nebraska; North Carolina/State; Oklahoma; PAFA; PMA; The Pennsylvania State U.; Phillips; Phoenix; Raleigh/NCMA; St. Albans School, Washington, D.C.; San Antonio/McNay; Santa Barbara/MA; Toledo/MA; Twentieth Century–Fox Film Corp.; VMFA; WMAA; Wilmington; Youngstown/Butler. **Bibliography:** American Artists Congress, Inc.; Baur 7; Genauer; Hall; **Pittman**; Watson, E.W., 2.

PLAGENS, PETER. b. March, 1, 1941, Dayton, Ohio. **Studied:** Syracuse U., MFA, 1964; U. of Southern California, MFA, magna cum laude, 1962. **Taught:** California State College, Northridge, 1969–79; U. of California, 1979; contributing editor, *Artforum*, 1966–76; chairman, board of directors, ICA, Los Angeles, 1977–79. **Awards:** Guggenheim Foundation Fellowship, 1972; National Endowment for the Arts, Grant in Criticism, 1973; National Endowment for the Arts, Grant, Painting, 1977. **Address:** % Dealer. **Dealer:** Nancy Hoffman Gallery, NYC; John Berggruen Gallery, San Francisco; Galerie Farideh Cadot, Paris. **One-man Exhibitions:** Riko Mizuno, Los Angeles, 1971; Reese Palley Gallery, NYC, 1971; Reese Palley Gallery, San Francisco, 1972; SFAI, 1972; U. of Oklahoma, 1973; Texas Gallery, Houston, 1973, 75; Leslie Collins Art Works, Dallas, 1973; John Berggruen Gallery, San Francisco, 1974, 77; California State U., San Jose, 1974; Betty Gold Gallery, Los Angeles, 1974; Dootson-Calderhead, Seattle, 1975; Nancy Hoffman Gallery, NYC, 1975, 76, 77; Galerie Doyle, Paris, 1975; Hirshhorn, 1976; Baum/Silverman Gallery, Los Angeles, 1977; Marianne Deson Gallery, Chicago, 1978; ICA, Los Angeles, 1979. **Group:** Oakland/AM, Contemporary American Drawings and Prints, 1969; LA/County MA, 24 Young Los Angeles Artists, 1971; Oakland/AM, Off the Stretcher, 1972; Scripps College, Painting: Color, Form, Surface, 1974; Utrecht, Young Americans, 1975; Potsdam/SUNY, New Directions in Abstraction, 1975; Fort Wayne, Hue and Far Cry of Color, 1976; Youngstown/Butler, 1976; SFMA, Painting and Sculpture in California: The Modern Era, 1977; ICA, Los Angeles, 100+, 1977; ICA, Los Angeles, Unstretched, 1977. **Collections:** Baltimore/MA; Buffalo/Albright; Continental Grain Corp., NYC; Dechert, Price and Rhodes, Philadelphia; Harris Bank, Chicago; Miami-Dade Community College; Newark Museum; U. of North Carolina; Owens-Corning Fiberglas Corp.; Prudential Insurance Co. of America; Toledo.

POLLACK, REGINALD. b. July 29, 1924, Middle Village, N.Y. **Studied:** ASL, with Wallace Harrison, Moses Soyer, Boardman Robinson. US Navy, 1941–45. Resided France, 1948–59, 1960–61. Traveled France, Italy, Caribbean Islands. **Taught:** Yale U., 1962–63; Cooper Union, 1963–64. **Member:** board, WPA, Washington, D.C., 1975–79. **Commissions:** Seagram Corporation; Container Corp. of America; New York State Telephone System; original film using his painting on the theme of riots, segregation, and war, commissioned by Zubin Mehta for the Los Angeles Philharmonic Orchestra; Washington Cathedral, 1974. **Awards:** Prix Neumann, Paris, 1952; Prix Othon Friesz, Paris, Menton, 1954, 57; Paris/Moderne, Prix de Peintres Etrangers, Second Prize, 1958; Ingram Merrill Foundation Grant, 1964, 70, 71. **Address:** 205 River Bend Road, Great Falls, VA 22066. **One-man Exhibitions:** (first) Charles Fourth Gallery, NYC, 1948; The Peridot Gallery, 1949, 52, 55, 56, 57, 59, 61, 63, 65, 67, 69; Galerie Saint-Placide, Paris, 1952; Dwan Gallery, 1960; Goldwach Gallery, Chicago, 1964–66; Felix Landau Gallery, 1964, 66; Original Graphics Ltd., Los Angeles, 1968; Olson-Resnick Gallery, Los Angeles, 1968; Jefferson Gallery, Los Angeles, 1969; Gallery Z, Beverly Hills, 1973, 75; Jack Rasmussen Gallery, Washington, D.C. 1978, 80. **Retrospective:** WPA, Washington, D.C., 1977. **Group:** WMAA, 1953, 55, 56, 58, 63; U. of Nebraska, 1957; Chicago/AI; Carnegie; NIAL; PAFA, 1962, 66; Salon du Mai, Paris; U. of Illinois, 1964; Salon des Artistes Independants, Paris, 1952, 53, 54; Corcoran, 1963; Newark Museum, 1964; New School for Social Research, 1964; Lytton Art Center, Los Angeles, 1967; Long Beach/MA, circ.; Smithsonian, circ., 1968–69. **Collections:** Bezalel Museum; Brooklyn Museum; Collection de l'Etat; U. of Glasgow; Haifa; MOMA; U. of Nebraska; Newark Museum; New York Hilton Hotel; Rockefeller Institute; Southern Illinois U.; Tel Aviv; WMAA; Worcester/AM; Yale U. **Bibliography:** Tomkins. Archives.

POLLOCK, JACKSON. b. January 28, 1912, Cody, Wyo.; **d.** August 11, 1956, Southampton, N.Y. **Studied:** ASL, 1929–31, with Thomas Hart Benton. Federal A.P.: Easel painting, 1938–42. **m.** Lee Krasner (1944). Subject and narrator of a 1951 film, *Jackson Pollock,* produced by Hans Namuth and Paul Falkenberg. **One-man Exhibitions:** (first) Art of This Century, NYC, 1943,

also 1946, 47; Arts Club of Chicago, 1945, 51; Museo Civico Correr, Venice; Galleria d'Arte del Naviglio, Milan, 1950; Galerie Paul Facchetti, 1952; Sidney Janis Gallery, 1952, 54, 55, 57; Zurich, 1953; IV Sao Paulo Biennial, 1957; Marlborough Galleria d'Arte, Rome, 1962; Marlborough-Gerson Gallery, Inc., NYC, 1964, 69; Marlborough Fine Art Ltd., London, 1965; WMAA, 1970; Berry-Hill Galleries, NYC, 1977; Yale U., 1978; American Cultural Center, Paris, 1979; Paris/Moderne, 1979. **Retrospective:** MOMA, 1956, 67, 80. **Group:** XXIV, XXV, and XXVIII Venice Biennials, 1948, 50, 56; I Sao Paulo Biennial, 1951; MOMA, Fifteen Americans, circ., 1952; Galerie de France, Paris, American Vanguard, 1952; MOMA, 12 Modern American Painters and Sculptors, circ., Europe, 1953–55; WMAA, The New Decade, 1954–55; SRGM, 75 Paintings from The Solomon R. Guggenheim Museum, circ., Europe, 1957; PAFA; Chicago/AI; Brooklyn Museum; Buffalo/Albright; MOMA, The New American Painting and Sculpture, 1969. **Collections:** Andover/Phillips; Baltimore/MA; Brooklyn Museum; Buffalo/Albright; Canberra/National; Carnegie; Chicago/AI; Dallas/MFA; Dusseldorf/KN-W; Hartford/Wadsworth; State U. of Iowa; Los Angeles/County MA; MMA; MOMA; Ohara Art Museum; Omaha/Joslyn; Ottawa/National; Rio de Janeiro; SFMA; SRGM; Stuttgart; Utica; WMAA; Washington U.; West Palm Beach/Norton; Yale U. **Bibliography:** Alloway 4; Ashton 5; Barr 3; Battcock, ed.; Baur 5, 7; Bazin; Beekman; Biddle 4; Bihalji-Merin; *Black and White Are Colors;* Blesh 1; Brion 1; Carmean, Rathbone, and Hess; Calas, N. and E.; Canaday; Chipp; Christensen; Davis, D.; De Vries, ed.; Downes, ed.; Eliot; Elsen 2; Finch; Flanagan; **Friedman, B. H., 2**; Gablik; Gaunt; Goodrich and Baur 1; Goossen 1; Greenberg 1; Greengood; Haftman; Henning; Hess, T. B., 1; Hobbs and Levin; Honisch & Jensen, eds.; Hunter 1, 6; Hunter, ed.; Janis and Blesh 1; Janis, S.; Johnson, Ellen

H.; **Kligman**; Kozloff 3; Krauss 2; Kuh 3; Langui; Leepa; Lippard 3; Lowry; Lynton; McCoubrey 1; McCurdy, ed.; Mendelowitz; Moser 1; Motherwell, ed.; Neumeyer; O'Doherty; **O'Hara** 1, **4**; Paalen; Ponente; Pousette-Dart, ed.; Ragon, 1, 2; Read 2, 3, 6; Restany 2; Richardson, E.P.; Rickey; Ritchie 1; **Robertson 2**; Rodman 1, 2, 3; Rose, B., 1, 4; **Rose, Bernice**; Rosenblum 2; Rubin 1; Sandler 1; Seuphor 1; Soby 5; Tapie 1; Tomkins 2; Tomkins and Time-Life Books; Tuchman, ed.; Weller. Archives.

PONCE DE LEON, MICHAEL. b. July 4, 1922, Miami, Fla. **Studied:** NAD; ASL, with Cameron Booth, Vaclav Vytlacil, Will Barnet, Harry Sternberg; PAFA; Brooklyn Museum, with Ben Shahn, Gabor Peterdi, John Ferren; U. of Mexico City, BA. US Air Force, three years. Traveled Mexico, Norway, and Europe extensively. **Taught:** Vassar College; Cooper Union; Pratt Graphic Art Center; Hunter College; in India and Pakistan, 1967–68; NYU, 1977; Pratt Institute, 1978; ASL, 1978. **Member:** SAGA. **Commissions:** US Post Office Department (design for fine-arts commemorative stamp). **Awards:** L.C. Tiffany Grant, 1953, 55; Bradley U., **P.P.**, 1954; Dallas/MFA, **P.P.**, 1954; SAGA, Gold Medal, 1954; U. of Nebraska; Oakland/AM, Gold Medal; Fulbright Fellowship, 1956, 57; The Print Club, Philadelphia, 1958; Audubon Artists, Gold Medal of Honor; Guggenheim Foundation Fellowship, 1967. **Address:** 463 West Street, NYC 10014. **One-man Exhibitions:** (first) Galeria Proteo, Mexico City, 1954; Oslo/National; Oakland/AM; Corcoran, 1967; Cynthia Comsky Gallery, 1970. **Retrospective:** Pioneer-Moss Gallery, NYC, 1975. **Group:** MMA; MOMA; Brooklyn Museum; Walker; Victoria and Albert Museum; PAFA; SAGA; Portland, Me./MA; Audubon Artists; Denver/AM; Bradley U.; Chicago/AI; I Inter-American Paintings and Prints Biennial, Mexico City, 1958; NAD; Boston/MFA; U. of Illinois. **Collections:** Achenbach Foundation, Brooklyn Museum; Cincinnati/AM; Columbia, S.C./MA; Dallas/MFA; U. of Florida; U. of Illinois; Indiana U.; Jacksonville/AM; Library of Congress; MOMA; Melbourne/National; Mexico City/Nacional; NYPL; NYU; National Gallery; U. of Nebraska; Oslo/National; PAFA; PMA; SFMA; US State Department; United Nations; Victoria and Albert Museum; Walker. **Bibliography:** Archives.

POND, CLAYTON. b. June 10, 1941, Bayside, N.Y. **Studied:** Hiram College, 1959–61; Carnegie Tech, BFA, 1964; Pratt Institute, MFA, 1964–66. Traveled Europe, Africa, Japan. **Taught:** Junior High School, Palm Beach, Fla., 1964; C. W. Post College, 1966–68; School of Visual Arts, NYC, 1968–70; U. of Wisconsin, Madison, 1972. **Member:** Boston Printmakers; The Print Club, Philadelphia. **Commissions:** New York State Council on the Arts, 1967. **Awards:** Bradley U., Print Annual, **P.P.**, 1966; Kalamazoo/Institute, **P.P.**, 1966; Arden Prize, 1966; US State Department Grant, 1967; Albion College, **P.P.**, 1968; Boston Printmakers, **P.P.**, 1968; Dulin Gallery Fifth National Print and Drawing Exhibition, **P.P.**, 1969. **Address:** 130 Greene Street, NYC 10012; Turnbridge, VT 05077. **One-man Exhibitions:** (first) Pratt Institute, 1966; Dartmouth College, 1966; C.W. Post College (two-man), 1966; Gordon Craig Gallery, Miami, Fla., 1968; WGMA, 1968; Princeton U. (2-man), 1968; Martha Jackson Gallery, 1968, 72, 73, 75; Port Washington (N.Y.) Public Library, 1968, 72; Kalamazoo/Institute, 1969; The Print Club, Philadelphia, 1969; Nassau Community College, Garden City, N.Y., 1969; Upstairs Gallery, Ithaca, 1970; Gallery 2, Woodstock, Vt., 1970; Van Staaten Gallery, 1971, 73; Images Gallery, Toledo, 1971; Lincoln, Mass./De Cordova, 1972; Madison Art Center, 1972; Arts & Crafts Center of Pittsburgh, 1972; Langman Gallery, Jenkintown, Pa., 1973; Graphics I &

Graphics II, Boston, 1973, 75; Montgomery Museum, 1973; U. of Florida, Gainsville, 1973; U. of Nebraska, 1974; Phoenix, 1974; Yumi Gallery, Tokyo, 1975; Roanoke Art Center, 1976; Martha Jackson Gallery, NYC, 1977, Editions Limited Gallery, Indianapolis, 1977; Graphic Eye Gallery, Port Washington, N.Y., 1977. **Group:** San Francisco Art Institute Annual, 1965; Brooklyn Museum, Print Biennial; NAD, 1966; Pratt Institute, 1966; Pacific Print Invitational, 1966–67; WMAA Sculpture Annual, 1966; Boston/MFA, 1967–69; Gallery of Modern Art, Ljubljana, Yugoslavia, VII International Exhibition of Prints, 1967; Seattle Civic Center, 1968; Library of Congress Print Annual, 1969; Boston/MFA, Boston Printmakers, 1969; Expo '70, Osaka, 1970; Paris/Moderne, International Exhibition of Colored Prints, 1970; USIA, Vienna, New American Prints, circ., 1971; City Museum and Art Gallery, Hong Kong, Graphics Now! USA, 1972; NCFA, XXIII Library of Congress Exhibition, 1973. **Collections:** AT&T; Albany/SUNY; Albion College; American Republic Insurance Co.; The Bank of New York; Bezalel Museum; Boston/MFA; Bradley U.; Buffalo/Albright; U. of California; Amon Carter Museum; Chase Manhattan Bank; Chicago/AI; Colgate U.; College of St. Benedict; Columbus, Ga.; Dartmouth College; Dulin Gallery; First National Bank of Chicago; Fort Worth; Grunwald Foundation; Indiana U.; Indianapolis/Herron; Kalamazoo/Institute; Library of Congress; Los Angeles/County MA; MOMA; Manufacturers Hanover Trust Co.; Minneapolis/Institute; NCFA; PMA; Pasadena/AM; Potsdam/SUNY; Princeton U.; Quaker Oats Co.; U. of Tennessee; Toledo/MA; US State Department; *Washington Post;* Western Michigan U.; U. of Wisconsin.

POONS, LARRY. b. October 1, 1937, Tokyo, Japan. **Studied:** New England Conservatory of Music, 1955–57; Boston Museum School, 1958. **Address:** 831 Broadway, NYC 10013. **Dealer:** Andre Emmerich Gallery, NYC. **One-man Exhibitions:** (first) Green Gallery, NYC, 1963, also 1964, 65; Leo Castelli, Inc., 1967, 68, 69; Kasmin Ltd., 1968, 71; Lawrence Rubin Gallery, NYC, 1969, 70, 72; David Mirvish Gallery, 1970, 76; ACE Gallery, Los Angeles, 1975, 77; Galerie Andre Emmerich, Zurich, 1975; Knoedler Contemporary Art, NYC, 1975, 76, 77; Daniel Templon, Paris, 1976; Watson/De Nagy, Houston, 1977; Galerie 99, Bay Harbor Islands, Fla,. 1978; Andre Emmerich Gallery, NYC, 1979. **Group:** WGMA, 1963; Sidney Janis Gallery, The Classic Spirit, 1964; SRGM, American Drawings, 1964, Systemic Painting, 1966; MOMA, The Responsive Eye, 1965; Smithsonian, 1965; VIII Sao Paulo Biennial, 1965; WMAA Annuals, 1965, 67, also Young America, 1965; Chicago/AI, 1966; Corcoran, 1967; Carnegie, 1967; Documenta IV, Kassel, 1968; WMAA Annnual, 1969; MMA, New York Painting and Sculpture, 1940–1970, 1969; Washington U., The Development of Modernist Painting; Jackson Pollock to the Present, 1969; Pasadena/AM, Painting in New York: 1944–1969, 1969; Buffalo/Albright, Color and Field, 1890–1970, 1970; WMAA, The Structure of Color, 1971; Buffalo/Albright, Six Painters, 1971; Boston/MFA, Abstract Painting in the '70s, 1972; Kansas City/Nelson, Color Field Painting to Post Color Field Abstraction, 1972; Houston/MFA, The Great Decade of American Abstraction: Modernist Art, 1960–1970, 1974; U. of Miami (Fla.), Less Is More: The Influence of the Bauhaus on American Art, 1974; Caracas, El Lenguaje del Color, 1974; Corcoran Biennial, 1975; Syracuse/Everson, New Works in Clay by Contemporary Painters and Sculptors, 1976; Everson/Syracuse, A Century of Ceramics in the U.S., 1878–1978, 1979. **Collections:** Boston/MFA; Buffalo/Albright; Cleveland/MA; Eindhoven; Milwaukee; MOMA; Oberlin College; Tate; WMAA. **Bibliography:** Alloway 3; Battcock, ed.; Calas, N. and E.; Goossen 1; *The Great Decade;* Hansen; Hunter, ed.;

Johnson, Ellen H.; Kozloff 3; Lippard 2, 5; MacAgy 2; Rickey; Rose, B., 1; Wood.

POOR, HENRY VARNUM. b. September 30, 1888, Chapman, Kans.; **d.** December 8, 1970, New City, N.Y. **Studied:** Stanford U., AB, PBK, 1910; U. of London, Slade School, 1910, with Walter Sickert; Academie Julian, Paris, 1911, with Jean Paul Laurens. US Army, 1918. **Taught:** Stanford U.; Mark Hopkins Art School, 1917; Colorado Springs Fine Arts Center, 1937; Skowhegan School. Active 1920–30 only as a potter; there are no paintings from this period. **Commissions** (murals): Justice Department, Washington, D.C., 1935; Interior Department, Washington, D.C., 1937; Penn State College, 1940; Deerfield (Mass.) Academy; Mt. Sinai Hospital, NYC. **Awards:** Chicago/AI, Norman Wait Harris Silver Medal, 1932; Carnegie, Third Prize, 1933; Syracuse/Everson, First Prize, 1937; Architectural League of New York, Gold Medal of Honor, 1938. **One-man Exhibitions:** (first) H. Kevorkian, NYC, 1920; Montross Gallery, NYC, 1921–31; Rehn Galleries, 1933–70. **Group:** WMAA; Carnegie; Chicago/AI; U. of Illinois. **Collections:** Andover/Phillips; Brooklyn Museum; Cleveland/MA; Columbus; U. of Kansas; MMA; U. of Nebraska; Newark Museum; SFMA; San Diego; WMAA; Wichita/AM. **Bibliography:** Baur 7; Biddle 4; **Boswell 1, 2;** Bruce and Watson; Cahill and Barr, eds.; Cheney; Genauer; Goodrich and Baur 1; Hall; Kent, N.; Mellquist; Nordmark; **Poor 1, 2;** Richardson, E.P.; Soyer, R. 1. Archives.

PORTER, DAVID. b. May 18, 1912, Chicago Art Institute School, briefly. Traveled USA, Mexico, Italy, France, Switzerland. **Taught:** Privately, 1952–57; Ogunquit, 1964; Dartmouth College, 1964; Cooper Union, 1968. Coauthor of the Broadway play *Mrs. Patterson*. Operated the David Porter Gallery, Washington, D.C., 1942–46. Publisher, *Cosmopolitan* magazine, 1954–55; Guild Hall, East Hampton, 1974–79. **Awards:** Guild Hall, Hon. Men., 1951; Provincetown Arts Festival, First Prize, 1958; Sassoferrato (Italy) International, Second Gold Medal, 1960, and First Prize, Gold Medal of President Gronchi, 1961; Guild Hall, First Prize, 1964; NIAL, Grant, 1970. **Address:** Box 711, Wainscott, NY 11975. **One-man Exhibitions:** (first) Hugo Gallery, NYC, 1952; Deerfield (Mass.) Academy, 1953; Galerie Hervé, NYC, 1955; The New Gallery, NYC, 1957; Obelisk Gallery, Washington, D.C., 1958; Tirca Karlis Gallery, 1959; Galleria L'Incontro, Rome, 1960; Modern Art Gallery, Palermo, Sicily, 1960; Ann Ross Gallery, White Plains, N. Y., 1961, 62; Southampton/Parrish, 1962; Alan Auslander Gallery, NYC, 1962; Ferrill Galleries, Santa Fe, N. M., 1963; Royal Athena II, NYC, 1964; Mickelson's Gallery, Washington, D. C., 1964, 68; Dartmouth College, 1964; NYPL, 1966; American Institute of Architects, N. Y. Chapter, 1969; Guild Hall, East Hampton, 1970. **Group:** Ninth Street Exhibition, NYC, 1951; WMAA Annual, 1951; Guild Hall, 1951, 54, 55, 56, 58, 64; Chicago/AI, 1952; U. of Illinois, 1952, 53; Carnegie, 1958; Corcoran, 1959; Dayton/AI, Modern Americans, 1959; Lincoln, Mass./De Cordova, 1965; Huntington, N. Y./Heckscher, Artists of Suffolk County, Part III; Figurative Traditions, 1971. **Collections:** American Airlines; Brown U.; Chase Manhattan Bank, NYC; Dartmouth College; Dayton/AI; Guild Hall; Hempstead Bank; Miami/Modern; NYU; Norfolk; Norfolk/Chrysler; Southampton/Parrish; Union Carbide Corp.; WMAA. **Bibliography:** Janis and Blesh 1. Archives.

PORTER, FAIRFIELD. b. June 10, 1907, Winnetka, Ill.; **d.** September, 1975, Southampton, N. Y. **Studied:** Harvard U.; ASL, with Boardman Robinson, Thomas Hart Benton. Traveled Europe, USSR, Scandinavia, USA, Canada. **Taught:** Long Island U.,

Southampton College, 1965–66; Queens College, 1968; Amherst College, 1969–70; School of Visual Arts, NYC, 1974–75. Editorial associate, *Art News* magazine, 1951–58; art critic, *The Nation* magazine, 1959–60. **Awards:** Longview Foundation (for art criticism), 1959; Purdue U., **P.P.**, 1966; NAD, **P.P. One-man Exhibitions:** (first) Community House, Winnetka, Ill., 1939; Tibor de Nagy Gallery, 1951–70; RISD, 1959; U. of Alabama, 1963; Reed College, 1965; Trinity College (Conn.), 1966; Kent State U., 1967; Swarthmore College, 1967; Hirschl & Adler Galleries, 1972, 74, 76, 79; Southampton/Parrish, 1971, 76; Maryland Institute, 1973. **Retrospectives:** Cleveland/MA, 1966; Huntington, N.Y./Heckscher, circ., 1974. **Group:** Dayton/AI, 1961; MOMA, 1961; Yale U., 1961–62; WMAA Annuals, 1961–66; PAFA, 1962; NIAL, 1962; U. of Nebraska, 1963; Colby College, Maine and Its Artists, 1963; Chicago/AI; Venice Biennial; New York World's Fair, 1964–65; Gallery of Modern Art, NYC, 1965; Purdue U., 1966; Akron/AI, 1967; Flint/Institute, 1967. **Collections:** Boston/MFA; Brooklyn Museum; Chase Manhattan Bank; Cleveland/MA; Corcoran; Dayton/AI; Hartford/Wadsworth; Hirshhorn; MMA; MOMA; U. of Nebraska; U. of North Carolina; Purdue U.; Santa Fe, N. M.; Toledo, MA; WMAA; Woodward Foundation. **Bibliography:** *America 1976*; Arthur 1; Cummings 1; Downes, ed.; Geske; McCoubrey 1; **Porter**; Sandler 1. Archives.

PORTER, KATHERINE. b. 1941, Iowa. **Studied:** Colorado College, BA, 1959–1963; Boston U., 1962. **Address:** % Dealer. **Dealer:** David McKee, Inc., NYC. **One-man Exhibitions:** Parker 470 Gallery, Boston 1971, 72; U. of Rhode Island, 1971; Henri Gallery, Washington, D.C., 1972; Worcester, 1973; MIT, 1974; David McKee, Inc., NYC, 1975, 78, 79; Harcus-Krakow Gallery, Boston, 1976; Alpha Gallery, Boston (two-man), 1979; San Francisco/ Achenbach, 1980. **Group:** WMAA An-

nuals, 1969, 73; MIT, Six Artists, 1970; ICA, Boston, Drawings Re-examined, 1970; ICA, U. of Pennsylvania, Six Visions, 1973; SRGM, Theodoron Awards, 1977; Brandeis U., From Women's Eyes, 1977; Otis Art Institute, Los Angeles, New York: A Selection from the Last 10 Years, 1979; Winter Olympics, Lake Placid, NY, 1980. **Collections:** Andover; Carnegie; Chase Manhattan Bank, NYC; Currier; Denver/AM; Harvard U.; Prudential Insurance Co. of America, Newark; San Francisco/Achenbach; SRGM; WMAA; Worcester/AM. **Bibliography:** Lucie-Smith.

PORTER, LILIANA. b. October 6, 1941, Buenos Aires, Argentina. **Studied:** National School of Fine Arts, Buenos Aires, 1954–57; Universidad Iberoamericana, Mexico City, 1958–60; School of Fine Arts, Buenos Aires, 1961–63. Traveled Mexico, Europe, South America. **Taught:** New York Graphic Workshop, 1965–70; Old Westbury/SUNY, 1974–76. **Member:** Artists

Liliana Porter *Still Life* (detail) 1979

Equity. **Awards:** Salon de Otono, Buenos Aires, first prize, 1962; Salon Artes Plasticas Hebraica Argentina, first prize, 1962; San Juan, first prize, 1st Latin American Biennial of Prints, 1970; Museum of Fine Arts, Buenos Aires, first prize, 1978; Guggenheim Foundation Fellowship, 1980. **Address:** 48 Beach Street, NYC 10013. **Dealer:** Barbara Toll Fine Arts, NYC. **One-man Exhibitions:** (first) Galeria Proteo, Mexico City, 1959; Galeria Municipal de Veracruz, Mexico, 1960; Galeria Galatea, Buenos Aires, 1961; Galeria Nice, Buenos Aires, 1962; Galeria Plasticas de Mexico, Mexico City, 1963; Prints International, Toronto, 1963; Galeria Lirolay, Buenos Aires, 1963, 66; Van Bovenkamp Gallery, NYC, 1964; Galeria Amigos del Arte, Montevideo, 1966; Caracas, 1969; A.A.A. Gallery, NYC, 1969; Santiago de Chile/MFA, 1969; Instituto Torcuato Di Tella, Buenos Aires, 1969; Galleria Diagramma, Milan, 1972; Hundred Acres Gallery, (two-man), 1973, 75, 77; MOMA, 1973; Galleria Conz, Venice, 1973; Galeria Colibri, San Juan, 1974; Galeria Conkright, Caracas, 1974; Galerie Stamps, Basel, 1974; Bogota/MOMA, 1974; Galeria Belarca, Bogota, 1975; Galleria della Villa Schifanoia, Florence, 1976; Cali/MOMA, 1978; Galeria Artemultiple, Buenos Aires, 1977, 78; Barbara Toll Fine Arts, NYC, 1979, 1980. **Retrospective:** School of Architecture, Caracas, 1969; Galerie Arte Nuevo, Buenos Aires, Center for InterAmerican Relations, NYC, 1980. **Group:** Jewish Museum, NYC, 100 Contemporary Prints, 1965; Ljubljana Biennials, 1965, 73, 75, 77, 79; NYU, Art in Editions, 1968; Krakow, print biennials, 1968, 70, 74; ICA, London, Printmaking in America, 1969; San Juan, print biennials, 1970, 72; MOMA, Information, 1970; Paris/Bibliotheque Nationale, L'Estampe Contemporaine, 1973; U. of California, Berkeley, Books Made by Artists, 1973; Segovia, print biennial, 1974; Bradford (England) print biennials, 1974, 76, 79; Canberra/National, Illusion and Reality, 1977; Wil-

liam Paterson College, Works on the Wall, 1979; Syracuse/Everson, Roots-Visions, 1979. **Collections:** Cali/Moderna; Caracas; Chase Manhattan Bank, NYC; Columbia U.; MOMA; Musée del Grabado, Buenos Aires; Museo Universitario, Mexico City; NYPL; Paris/Bibliotheque Nationale; PMA; Santiago; R.C.A. Corp., NYC.

POSEN, STEPHEN. b. September 27, 1939, St. Louis, Mo. **Studied:** Washington U., 1962, BFA; Yale U., 1964, MFA. US Army, 1957. Traveled Europe. **Taught:** Cooper Union. **Awards:** Fulbright Fellowship, 1964–66; Milliken Traveling Scholarship, 1964; CAPS, 1973. **Address:** 115 Spring Street, NYC 10012. **Dealer:** Robert Miller Gallery Inc., NYC. **One-man Exhibitions:** OK Harris Works of Art, 1971, 74; Robert Miller Gallery, Inc., NYC, 1978. **Group:** Chicago/Contemporary, Radical Realism, 1971; Eindhoven, Relativerend Realisme, 1972; WMAA Annual, 1972; Documenta V, Kassel, 1972; Cleveland/MA, 32 Realists, 1972; Yale U., 7 Realists, 1973; Chicago/AI, New Realism, 1973; Lunds Konsthall, Sweden, Amerikansk Realism, 1974; Tokyo Biennial, 1974; Chicago/AI, 71st American Exhibition, 1974; Potsdam/SUNY, New Realism Revisited, 1974; Taft Museum, Tromp L'Oeil, 1975, Canberra/National, Illusion and Reality, circ., 1977–78; PAFA, Eight Contemporary American Realists, 1977. **Collections:** Chase Manhattan Bank; PAFA; RAC. **Bibliography:** Arthur 1, 2; Goodyear; Hunter, ed.; Lucie-Smith; Sager.

POUSETTE-DART, NATHANIEL. b. September 7, 1886, St. Paul, Minn.; **d.** October 17, 1965, Valhalla, N.Y. **Studied:** ASL; W.M. Chase School, NYC, 1918; with Robert Henri; PAFA, 1920–24, with Thomas Anshutz. Traveled Europe, southern USA. **Taught:** Minnesota College; College of Saint Catherine; various art schools in NYC. **Member:** Federation of Modern Painters and Sculptors (president); Art Directors Club, NYC (an organizer and past president); American Society for Aesthetics; Architectural League of New York; Fellowship of The Pennsylvania Academy of the Fine Arts. **Awards:** PAFA, Cresson Fellowship (2); Westchester (N.Y.) Art Society, First Prize, 1963; Nantucket, First Prize, 1963. **One-man Exhibitions:** (first) Stevens Art Gallery, St. Paul, 1910; American-British Art Center, NYC, 1934; Kenneth Taylor Gallery, Nantucket, 1959; Sunken Meadow Gallery, King Park, N.Y., 1961. **Retrospective:** Anderson Galleries, NYC, 1926. **Bibliography:** Blesh 1; **Pousette-Dart; Pousette-Dart, ed.**

POUSETTE-DART, RICHARD. b. June 8, 1916, St. Paul, Minn. **Studied:** Bard College, 1936. Traveled France. **Taught:** New School for Social Research, 1959–61; School of Visual Arts, NYC, 1965; Columbia U., 1968–69; Sarah Lawrence College, 1970–74. **Awards:** Guggenheim Foundation Fellowship, 1951; Ford Foundation Grant, 1959; Corcoran Biennial, Silver Medal, 1965; Honorary Doctor of Humane Letters, Bard College, 1965; National Endowment for the Arts Grant, 1967. **Address:** 286 Haverstraw Road, Suffern, NY 10901. **Dealer:** Andrew Crispo Gallery. **One-man Exhibitions:** (first) Artists Gallery, NYC, 1941; The Willard Gallery, 1943, 45, 56; Art of This Century, NYC, 1947; Betty Parsons Gallery, 1948–51, 1953, 55, 58, 59, 61, 64, 67; Katonah (N.Y.) Art Gallery, 1967; Washington U., 1969; Obelisk Gallery, 1969; Andrew Crispo Gallery, 1974, 76, 78; MOMA, circ., 1969–70; Allentown/AM, 1975; Wichita State U., 1975; Arts Club of Chicago, 1978. **Retrospectives:** WMAA, 1963, 74. **Group:** Chicago/AI, Abstract and Surrealist Art, 1948; WMAA Annuals, 1949, 51, 53, 1955–59, 1961, 72, 73; MOMA, Abstract Painting and Sculpture in America, 1951; U. of Illinois, 1951–53; Buffalo/Albright, Expressionism in American Painting, 1952; WMAA, The New Decade,

1954–55; WMAA, Nature in Abstraction, 1958; I Inter-American Painting and Prints Biennial, Mexico City, 1958; Carnegie, 1958, 61; Documenta II, Kassel, 1959; SRGM, Abstract Expressionists and Imagists, 1961; MOMA, The Art of Assemblage, circ., 1961; Hartford/Wadsworth, Continuity and Change, 1962; MOMA, The New American Painting and Sculpture, 1969; National Gallery, American Art at Mid-Century, 1973; Philadelphia College of Art, Private Notations: Artists' Sketchbooks, 1976; Bronx Museum of the Arts, The Magic Circle, 1977; Indianapolis, Perceptions of the Spirit in 20th Century American Art, circ., 1977; Cornell U., Abstract Expressionists: Formative Years, 1978. **Collections:** Andover/Phillips; Buffalo/Albright; Chase Manhattan Bank; Ciba-Geigy Corp., Ardsley; Corcoran; Cornell U.; Equitable Life Assurance Society; MMA; MOMA; U. of Nebraska; NCFA; Newark Museum; North Central Bronx Hospital; PMA; Pasadena/AM; Ringling; The Singer Company, Inc.; SRGM; Union Carbide Corp.; Upjohn Co.; WMAA; Wichita State U. **Bibliography:** Baur 5; Blesh 1; Goodrich and Baur 1; Janis and Blesh 1; Motherwell and Reinhardt, eds.; Nordness, ed.; Pousette-Dart, ed.; Ragon 2; Ritchie 1; Seitz 3; Tuchman, ed. Archives.

POZZATTI, RUDY. b. January 14, 1926, Telluride, Colo. **Studied:** U. of Colorado, with Wendell Black, Ben Shahn, Max Beckmann, 1948, BFA, 1950, MFA. US Army, 1943–46. Traveled Europe, USSR, Mexico, South America; resided Italy. **Taught:** U. of Colorado, 1948–50, summers, 1951, 54; U. of Nebraska, 1950–56; Cooper Union, summer, 1955; Indiana U., 1956–60; Yale-Norfolk Summer Art School, 1957; The Ohio State U., summer, 1959; Florence, Italy, Print Workshop, summer, 1967; Honolulu Academy, 1971; Instituto d'Arte, Massa, Italy, 1974. **Member:** SAGA; Board of Directors, College Art Association,

1974–78. Subject of *Artists in America,* half-hour TV color film, N.E.T., 1971; Academia Italia della Arte e del Lavoro. **Commissions:** International Graphic Arts Society (3 editions); Print Club of Cleveland; New York Hilton Hotel. **Awards:** U. of Illinois, Graphic Art Exhibition, First Prize, 1949; Walker, **P.P.**, 1951; Youngstown/Butler, **P.P.**, 1951, 52; St. Louis/City, Vladimir Golschmann Prize, 1952; Fulbright Fellowship (Italy), 1952–53; St. Louis/City, Henry V. Putzell Prize, 1955; The Print Club, Philadelphia, Mildred Boericke Award, 1955, also 1969; PAFA, Alice McFadden Eyre Medal, 1957; Library of Congress, Pennell **P.P.**, 1958; Boston Printmakers, Paul J. Sachs Award 1958, 61; PAFA, **P.P.**, 1959 (2); AAAL, **P.P.**, 1960; SAGA, 100 Prints of the Year, First Prize, 1963; Guggenheim Foundation Fellowship, 1963–64; Ford Foundation Grant; US State Department Cultural Exchange Grant, 1965; Flint/Institute, 1965; American Color Print Society, **P.P.**, 1968; III Annual 500 Mile Race Art Exhibit, Indianapolis, First Prize, ($1,000), 1968; U. of Colorado, George Norlin Silver Medal for Distinguished Achievements in Chosen Profession, 1972; Honorary Doctor of Humane Letters, U. of Colorado, 1973; and many others; Carl Zigrosser Memorial Award, American Color Print Society, 1979. **Address:** 117 South Meadowbrook, Bloomington, IN 47401. **Dealer:** Haslem Fine Arts, Inc. **One-man Exhibitions:** (first) Chicago/AI, 1953; Philadelphia Art Alliance, 1953; Martha Jackson Gallery, 1954; Cleveland/MA, 1955; Kansas City/Nelson, 1955; U. of Maine, 1956; U. of Nebraska, 1956; Gump's Gallery, 1956, 60; Weyhe Gallery, 1957; Clarke College, 1957; Carleton College, 1957; U. of Minnesota, 1958; Louisville/Speed, 1958; Ohio U., 1960; Walker, 1960; J. Seligmann and Co., 1961; U. of Louisville, 1963; Jane Haslem Gallery, Durham, N.C., 1963; Kalamazoo/Institute, 1967; Merida Gallery, Inc., 1967; Daberkow Gallery, Frankfort, 1969; Karlsruhe, 1969; Honolulu Academy,

1971; Louisville/Speed, 1973; Institute of Fine Arts, Salvadore, Brazil, 1974; Institute of Fine Arts, Sao Paulo, 1974; I.B.E.U., Rio de Janeiro, 1974; US Embassy, Ankara (two-man), 1975; Terre Haute/Swope, 1979; Cushing Gallery, Dallas, 1977; Roswell, 1980. **Retrospective:** U. of Nebraska, 1971. **Group:** The Print Club, Philadelphia, 1954; U. of Oklahoma, 1956; WMAA, Fulbright Artists, 1958; U. of Michigan, 1959; The Pennsylvania State U., 10 American Printmakers, 1959; WMAA, Young America, 1960; Syracuse U., 1962; PCA, American Prints Today, circ., 1962; U. of Kentucky, Graphics IV, 1962; IBM Gallery of Arts and Sciences, NYC, 30 American Printmakers, circ., 1974. **Collections:** Achenbach Foundation; Albion College; Allegheny College; Alverthorpe Gallery; Anchorage; Ashland Oil Inc.; Ball State U.; Baltimore/MA; Bibliotheque Nationale; Boston/MFA; Bradley U.; Brooklyn Museum; U. of California, Berkeley; Cleveland/MA; U. of Colorado; Concordia Teachers College (Neb.); Davidson, N.C.; Dayton/AI; U. of Delaware; De Pauw U.; Duke U.; Eastern Michigan U.; Hamline U.; Harvard U.; Indiana U.; Indianapolis/Herron; State College of Iowa; Jacksonville/AM; Kansas City/Nelson; Kansas State College; Kemper Insurance Co.; La Jolla; Library of Congress; Los Angeles/County MA; Louisville/Speed; U. of Louisville; MMA; MOMA; U. of Maine; Malmo; Marshall U.; U. of Michigan; National Gallery; Nebraska State Teachers College; U. of Nebraska; Newark Museum; Oakland/AM; Oberlin College; The Ohio State U.; Oklahoma City U.; U. of Oklahoma; Omaha/Joslyn; PAFA; PMA; U. of Puerto Rico; SFMA; St. Cloud State College; St. Lawrence U.; St. Louis/City; St. Mary's College (Ind.); San Jose State College; Seattle/AM; Sioux City Art Center; Springfield, Mo./AM; Syracuse U.; Texas Western College, Toronto; Texas Tech U.; US State Department; Utica; Victoria and Albert Museum; Walker; Washburn U. of Topeka; Wichita/AM; College of William and Mary; U. of

Wisconsin; Yale U.; Youngstown/ Butler; Youngstown U. **Bibliography:** Chaet; **Print Club of Cleveland.**

PRESTOPINO, GREGORIO. b. June 21, 1907, NYC. **Studied:** NAD, with C. W. Hawthorne. Traveled Europe, southwestern USA, Mexico. **Taught:** Veterans Art Center, MOMA, 1946–48; Brooklyn Museum School, 1946–59; New School for Social Research, 1949–56, 57, 65; American Academy, Rome, 1968–69. Federal A.P.: Easel painting. **Awards:** PAFA, Joseph E. Temple Gold Medal, 1946; Pepsi-Cola, Third Prize, 1946; Youngstown/Butler, First Prize, 1958; Cannes Film Festival, First Prize (for the art film *Harlem Wednesday*), 1958; NIAL Grant, 1961; NAD, Benjamin Altman Prize, 1972; Emily Goldsmith Award, NAD, 1977. **Address:** 20 Farm Lane, Roosevelt, NJ 08555. **Dealer:** Terry Dintenfass, Inc. **One-man Exhibitions:** (first) ACA Gallery, 1943, also 1946, 48, 50, 51, 53, 54, 57; Lee Nordness Gallery, NYC, 1959, 60, 61, 62, 64; Rex Evans Gallery, 1961; White; Terry Dintenfass, Inc., 1966, 68, 71, 74; Virginia Union U., 1967. **Retrospective:** Michigan State U. **Group:** WMAA annuals; MOMA; Corcoran; New York World's Fair, 1939; Golden Gate International Exposition, San Francisco, 1939; Chicago/AI; Venice Biennial; USIA; PAFA Annual, 1967; and others. **Collections:** U. of Alabama; Andover/Phillips; Brandeis U.; Chicago/AI; Currier; U. of Hawaii; IBM; U. of Illinois; MOMA; Martha Washington U.; Mary Washington College; Montclair/AM; NCFA; U. of Nebraska; U. of Notre Dame; U. of Oklahoma; Phillips; U. of Rochester; Southern Methodist U.; U. of Texas; Trenton/ State; WMAA; Walker; Youngstown/ Butler. **Bibliography:** Genauer; Nordness, ed.; Pousette-Dart, ed. Archives.

PRICE, CLAYTON S. b. May 24, 1874, Bedford, Iowa; **d.** May 1, 1950, Portland, Ore. **Studied:** Washington U.

School of Fine Arts, 1905–06. Traveled Canada, western USA. PWA, 1933–34. Federal A.P.: Easel painting, intermittently 1935–40. **Awards:** Seattle/AM, Katherine Baker Memorial Award, 1929; Portland, Ore./AM, **P.P.**, 1950; Hon. MA, Reed College, 1948. **One-man Exhibitions:** (first) Beaux Arts Gallery, San Francisco, 1925; Berkeley (Calif.) League of Fine Art, 1927; Oregon Society of Artists, Portland, 1929; Valentine Dudensing Gallery, NYC, 1945; Reed College, 1948; Portland, Ore./AM, 1949; The Willard Gallery, 1949. **Retrospective:** Portland, Ore./AM, Price Paintings, 1900–42, 1942; Portland Ore./AM, Memorial Exhibition, circ., 1951. **Group:** Detroit/ Institute, 1944; MOMA, Fourteen Americans, circ., 1946. **Collections:** Andover/Phillips; Beach Public School; Detroit/Institute; Los Angeles/County MA; MMA; U. of Oregon; Pendleton High School; Portland, Ore./AM; Reed College; Seattle/AM; US Treasury Department; Utica. **Bibliography:** *Art of the Pacific Northwest;* Baur 7; Blesh 1; Janis, S.; Miller, ed. 2; *Northwest Traditions;* Richardson, E.P.

PRICE, KENNETH. b. 1935, Los Angeles, Calif. **Studied:** U. of California; Otis Art Institute; Chouinard Art Institute; U. of Southern California, BFA, 1956; Alfred/SUNY, MFA, 1958. **Awards:** Tamarind Fellowship, 1968. **Address:** Taos, NM 87571. **Dealer:** The Willard Gallery. **One-man Exhibitions:** U. of California, 1956; Ferus Gallery, Los Angeles, 1960, 61, 64; Los Angeles/ County MA (two-man), 1966, 78; Kasmin Ltd., 1968, 70; WMAA, 1969; Mizuno Gallery, 1969, 71; David Whitney Gallery, NYC, 1971; Galerie Hans R. Neuendorf, Cologne, 1971, Hamburg, 1971; D.M. Gallery, London, 1972; Nicholas Wilder Gallery, 1973; Felicity Samuel Gallery, London, 1974; The Willard Gallery, 1974, 79; Ronald Greenberg Gallery, St. Louis, 1976; James Corcoran Galleries, Los Angeles, 1976; Los Angeles/County MA, 1978;

Gallery of Contemporary Arts, Taos, 1978; The Texas Gallery, Houston, 1979; Hansen Fuller Goldeen Gallery, San Francisco, 1979. **Group:** SFMA, Fifty California Artists, circ., 1962; Pasadena/AM, New American Sculpture, 1964; Seattle/AM, Ten from Los Angeles, 1966; U. of California, Irvine, Abstract Expressionist Ceramics, 1966; Los Angeles/County MA, American Sculpture of the Sixties, 1967; MOMA, Tamarind; Homage to Lithography, 1969; Fort Worth Drawings, 1969; Pasadena/AM, West Coast: 1945–69, 1969; Eindhoven, Kompas IV, 1969–70; WMAA Biennial, 1970; Brooklyn Museum, Print Annual, 1980; Hayward Gallery, London, Eleven Los Angeles Artists, 1971; MOMA, Technics and Creativity: Gemini: G.E.L. 1971; Cologne/Kunstverein, USA, West Coast, 1972; Rotterdam (three-man exhibition), 1972; NCFA, Sculpture: American Directions, 1945–1975, 1975; WMAA, 200 Years of American Sculpture, 1976; Brooklyn Museum, 30 Years of American Printmaking, 1976; Syracuse/Everson, New Works in Clay by Contemporary Painters and Sculptors, 1976; Syracuse/Everson, A Century of Ceramics in the U.S., 1878–1978, 1979; WMAA Biennial, 1979. **Collections:** Chicago/AI; Eindhoven; Denver; Hirshhorn; Los Angeles/County MA; MOMA; Pasadena/AM; Art Museum of South Texas; SFMA; Victoria and Albert; WMAA. **Bibliography:** Selz, P., 2; *The State of California Painting; USA West Coast.*

QUAYTMAN, HARVEY. b. April 20, 1937, Far Rockaway, N.Y. **Studied:** Syracuse U., 1955–57; Skowhegan School, 1957; Boston Museum School, with Jan Cox, 1957–60; Tufts U., 1957–60, BFA; Royal College of Art, London, 1961–62. **Taught:** Tufts U., 1959; Boston Museum School, 1960, 1962–63; Middlebury College, 1961; Newton Creative Arts Center, 1961, 63, 64; Roxbury (Mass.) Latin School, 1962–63; Harvard U., 1961, 64, 65; School of Visual Arts, NYC, 1969–71; Cooper Union, 1972–77; Syracuse U., 1977; Parsons School of Design, 1978. **Awards:** New York Board of Regents Scholarship, 1955–57; Boston/MFA; James William Paige Traveling Fellowship, 1960; CAPS, 1973. **Address:** 231 Bowery, NYC 10002. **Dealer:** David McKee Gallery. **One-man Exhibitions:** A.I.A. Gallery, London, 1962; Ward-Nasse Gallery, Boston, 1964; Royal Marks Gallery, 1966; Ohio State U., 1967; Houston/Contemporary, 1967, 73; Paula Cooper Gallery, 1967, 71; U. of Rochester, 1972; Galerie Onnasch, Cologne, 1971; Galerie Mikro, Berlin, 1971; Galleri Ostergren, Malmo, 1973; Henri 2, Washington, D.C., 1973; Cunningham-Ward Gallery, 1974; David McKee Gallery, 1975; 77, 78; Nielsen Gallery, Boston, 1976, 78; Charles Casat Gallery, La Jolla, 1977. **Group:** ICA, Boston, Painting without a Brush, 1965; U. of Illinois, 1967; WMAA Annuals, 1969, 71, 73; Indianapolis, 1970; Jewish Museum, Beautiful Painting & Sculpture, 1970; Foundation Maeght, 1970; WMAA, The Structure of Color, 1971; UCLA, Fourteen Abstract Painters, 1975; ICA, Boston, Contemporary Painters, 1975; High Museum, The New Image, 1975; Rice U., Drawing Today in New York, 1976; U. of Texas, Austin, New Painting in New York, 1977; Rutgers U., Contemporary American Abstractionists, 1979; Buffalo/Albright, Constructivism and the Geometric Tradition, 1979. **Collections:** Carnegie; Chase Manhattan Bank; Corcoran; Cornell U.; Dartmouth College; Emory U.; Harvard U.; Houston/MFA; Jerusalem/National; Kent State U.; U. of Massachusetts; MIT; McCrory Corp., NYC; Middlebury College; U. of Minnesota, Duluth; NYU; Oberlin College; Pasadena/AM; Port Authority of New York & New Jersey; Prudential Insurance Co. of America; Purchase/SUNY; Rutgers U.; U. of Sydney; Tate; Trenton/State; VMFA; Wellington/National Gallery; WMAA; Worchester/AM; Wright State U. **Bibliography:** *New in the Seventies.*

QUIRT, WALTER. b. November 24, 1902, Iron River, Mich.; d. March 19, 1968, Minneapolis, Minn. **Studied:** Layton School of Art, 1921–23. Traveled Mexico, Canada. **Taught:** Layton School of Art, 1924–29; U. of Minnesota, 1945–47, 1952–67. Federal A.P.: Easel painting, 1936–37. **Commissions:** Bellevue Hospital, NYC, 1939 (mural). **Awards:** Detroit/Institute, Cranbrook Prize, 1946. **One-man Exhibitions:** (first) Julien Levy Galleries, NYC, 1936, also 1939; The Pinacotheca, NYC, 1942; A.A.A. Gallery, NYC, 1943; Durlacher Brothers, NYC, 1944, 45; U. of Minnesota, 1949, 59, 68; The New Gallery, NYC, 1951; Duveen-Graham Gallery, NYC, 1957; The Greer Gallery, NYC, 1963; Wichita/AM, 1964; Paul Kramer Gallery, St. Paul, 1966; Gallery Dresdner, Toronto, 1967. **Retrospective:** A.F.A./Ford Foundation, circ., 1960; U. of Minnesota, Minneapolis, 1980. **Group:** MOMA; WMAA; California Palace; St. Louis/City; Hartford/Wadsworth; Walker; Minneapolis/Institute; Newark Museum; U. of Illinois. **Collections:** Andover/Phillips; Hartford/Wadsworth; U. of Illinois; State U. of Iowa; La Jolla; MOMA; U. of Minnesota; Newark Museum; WMAA; Walker; Washington U. **Bibliography:** Baur 7; Biddle 4; Coates; Janis, S.; Kootz 2; *Walter Quirt: A Retrospective.* Archives.

QUISGARD, LIZ WHITNEY. b. October 23, 1929, Philadelphia, Pa. **Studied:** Johns Hopkins U.; U. of Baltimore; Maryland Institute, 1947–49, MFA, 1966; privately with Morris Louis, 1957–60. Traveled Europe, North America. **Taught:** Baltimore Hebrew Congregation, 1962–; Maryland Institute, 1965–; Goucher College, 1966–68; U. of Maryland, 1970–71. Art critic, *Baltimore Sun*, 1968–70. Set designer for theater productions at Goucher College, Center Stage, and Theater Hopkins, 1966–; Villa Julia College, Stevenson, Md.; Beth El Congregation, Baltimore. **Commission:** William Fell School, Baltimore, mural. **Awards:** Baltimore/MA, Second Prize, 1958; Maryland Institute, Fellow of the Rinehart School of Sculpture, 1964–65; National Scholastic Art Awards Scholarship; E. M. Reed Scholarship; Maryland Arts Council, Grant, 1979. **Address:** 321 Rossiter Avenue, Baltimore, MD 21212. **One-man Exhibitions:** (first) Ef Gallery, Baltimore, 1954; Main Gallery, Maryland Institute, 1955; Martick's Gallery, Baltimore, 1956, 58; Johns Hopkins U., 1958; Jefferson Place Gallery, 1961; Key Gallery, NYC, 1961; Andre Emmerich Gallery, NYC, 1962; Arts and Science Center, Nashua, N. J., 1975; Gannon College, Erie, Pa., 1978; Mechanics Gallery, Baltimore, 1978; Fells Point Gallery, Baltimore, 1980. **Group:** Peale Museum, Baltimore, 1947, 50; Baltimore/MA, 1951, 52, 53, 58; Youngstown/Butler, 1956; Corcoran, 1957, 64; PAFA Annual, 1964. **Collections:** U. of Arizona; U. of Baltimore; Hampton School; Johns Hopkins U.

R

RABKIN, LEO. b. July 21, 1919, Cincinnati, Ohio. **Studied:** U. of Cincinnati, BA, B. Ed.; Art Academy of Cincinnati; NYU, with Robert Iglehart, Hale Woodruff, Tony Smith, William Baziotes, MA. Traveled Mexico, Europe, Guatemala. **Taught:** NYC public school system. **Member:** American Abstract Artists (past president). **Awards:** MOMA, Larry Aldrich **P.P.**, 1959; Ford Foundation, **P.P.**, 1961; Silvermine Guild, Watercolor Award, 1961, 64. **Address:** 218 West 20th Street, NYC 10011. **One-man Exhibitions:** (first) Stairway Gallery, NYC, 1954; Muriel Latow Gallery, NYC, 1961; Gotham Gallery, New Hope, Pa., 1961; Louis Alexander Gallery. NYC, 1962, 63; Gertrude Kasle Gallery, 1965; Richard Feigen Gallery, 1965, 67; Drew U., 1966; Benson Gallery, 1970; Fairleigh Dickinson U., 1971; Allentown/AM, 1977; Truman Gallery, NYC, 1978, 79; Parsons-Dreyfuss Gallery, NYC, 1980. **Retrospective:** Storm King Art Center, 1970. **Group:** Brooklyn Museum, Watercolor Biennial; Hirschl & Adler Galleries, Inc., NYC, Experiences in Art, I & II, 1959, 60; MOMA, New Talent; WMAA Annual, 1959; Martha Jackson Gallery, New Media—New Forms, I & II, 1960, 61; MOMA, Abstract American Drawings and Watercolors, circ., Latin America, 1961–63; A.F.A., Affinities, circ., 1962; SRGM, 1962, 65; American Abstract Artists Annuals, 1963, 64, 66, 68, 70; WMAA, 1959, 60, 61, 64, 66, 68, 69; Eindhoven, 1966; Walker, Light Motion Space, 1967; Smithsonian, 1967; Trenton/State, Focus on Light, 1967; Brooklyn Museum Print Exhibitions; Finch College, NYC, Destructionists, 1968; Milwaukee, A Plastic Presence,

circ., 1969; Honolulu Academy, 1971; Sculptors Guild, 1972, 74; Brooklyn Museum, Print Exhibition, 1972; Drew U., Reality in Art, 1978; Betty Parsons Gallery, NYC, American Abstract Artists, 1979; Albright College, Small Is Beautiful, 1979. **Collections:** U. of California, Berkeley; Chase Manhattan Bank; Ciba-Geigy Corp.; MOMA; NYU; Purchase/SUNY; Raleigh/NCMA; Randolph-Macon College; SRGM; Savings Bank Association of New York State; The Singer Company, Inc.; Smithsonian; Storm King Art Center; WMAA; Woodward Foundation. **Bibliography:** Archives.

RACZ, ANDRE. b. November 21, 1916, Cluj, Rumania. **Studied:** U. of Bucharest, 1935, BA; Atelier 17, NYC, 1943–45; New School for Social Research, 1943–45. To USA, 1939; citizen, 1948. Traveled Europe, Latin America, Mexico. **Taught:** U. of Chile, 1957; Columbia U., 1951– ; U. of Kentucky, 1960. **Member:** American Association of University Professors; SAGA. **Awards:** SAGA, Mrs. A. W. Erickson Prize, 1953; Noyes Memorial Prize, 1955; Guggenheim Foundation Fellowship, 1956; Fulbright Research Scholar (Chile), 1957; U. of Kentucky, **P.P.**, 1959; Ford Foundation, **P.P.**, 1962. **Address:** P.O. Box 43, Demarest, NJ 07627. **One-man Exhibitions:** (first) New School for Social Research, 1942; A.F.A., circ., 1948–51; and exhibits in NYC nearly every year. **Retrospective:** NYPL, 1954; Museo de Bellas Artes, Santiago, Chile, 1957; U. of Kentucky, 1960. **Group:** MOMA; WMAA Annuals; Brooklyn Museum; Corcoran; Library of Congress; MOMA, 50 Years of American Art, circ., Europe, 1955; I Inter-American Paintings and Prints Biennial, Mexico City, 1958; I International Religious Art Biennial, Salzburg, 1958; MOMA, American Prints, 1913–1963, 1974–75; Rutgers U., Surrealism and American Art, 1977; U. of Wisconsin, Atelier 17, 1977. **Collections:** Paris/Bibliotheque Nationale; Brooklyn Museum; Columbia U.; Cordoba/Provincial; George Washington U.; U. of Kentucky; Library of Congress; MMA; MOMA; Melbourne/National; U. of Minnesota; NYPL; National Gallery; Oslo/National; PMA; SFMA; Salzburg; Smith College; Smithsonian; WMAA; Youngstown/ Butler. **Bibliography:** Baur 7; Hayter 2; Janis, S.; Moser 1.

RAFFAEL, JOSEPH. b. February 22, 1933, Brooklyn, N.Y. **Studied:** Cooper Union, 1951–54, with Sidney Delevante, Leo Manso; Yale U., with Josef Albers, James Brooks, BFA. Traveled Europe, Hawaiian Islands; resided Rome and Florence, 1958–60. **Taught:** U. of California, Davis, 1966, Berkeley, summer, 1969; School of Visual Arts, NYC, 1967–69; California State U., Sacramento, 1969–74. **Awards:** Yale-Norfolk Summer Art School Fellowship, 1954, 55; Fulbright Fellowship, 1958; L.C. Tiffany Grant, 1961; Tokyo Biennial, First Prize, Figurative Painting, 1974. **Address:** 3 Tamarack Drive, San Geronimo, CA 94963. **Dealer:** Nancy Hoffman Gallery; John Berggruen, San Francisco; Fendrick Gallery, Washington, D.C. **One-man Exhibitions:** (first) Kanegis Gallery, 1958; Numero Galleria d'Arte, Florence, Italy, 1959; D'Arcy Gallery, NYC, 1962, 63; The Stable Gallery, 1965, 66, 68; Galleria Sperone, Turin, 1967 (two-man, with Lowell Nesbitt); Berkeley Gallery, San Francisco, 1968; Sacramento State U., 1969; U. of California, Berkeley, 1969, 73; Wichita/AM, 1970; Reese Palley Gallery, San Francisco, 1970, 72; U. of California, San Diego, 1971; Nancy

Hoffman Gallery, NYC, 1972, 73, 74, 76, 79; Chicago/Contemporary, 1973; Worcester/AM (three-man), 1974; de Young, 1975; Barbara Okum Gallery, St. Louis, 1974; U. of Saskatchewan, 1975; U. of Nevada, Las Vegas, 1975; Quay Gallery, San Francisco, 1976; Roy Boyd Gallery, Chicago, 1977; Arco Center for Visual Arts, Los Angeles, 1977; Museum of Fine Arts, St. Petersburg, Fla., 1977; Fendrick Gallery, Washington, D.C., 1978; Valparaiso U., 1971; John Berggruen Gallery, San Francisco, 1978. **Retrospective:** SFMA, circ., 1978–79. **Group:** Brooklyn Museum; Chicago/AI, 1965; Corcoran, 1966; MOMA, Art in the Mirror, 1966, and others; ICA, U. of Pennsylvania, The Other Tradition, 1966; IX Sao Paulo Biennial, 1967; Los Angeles/County MA, 1967; U. of Illinois, 1967; U. of Miami, 1968; ICA, London, The Obsessive Image, 1968; Indianapolis/Herron, 1969; WMAA, Human Concern/Personal Torment, 1969; VMFA, American Painting, 1970; Darmstadt Biennial, 1970; U. of Miami, Phases of New Realism, 1972; Chicago/AI, 1972, 74; WMAA Annual, 1973; Cincinnati/Contemporary, Options, 70/ 30, 1973; Los Angeles Municipal Art Gallery, Separate Realities, 1973; Hartford/ Wadsworth, New/Photo Realism, 1974; Indianapolis, 1974; U. of Illinois, 1974; Oklahoma, Contemporary American Landscape, 1974; Rutgers U., A Response to the Environment, 1975; Akron/AI, Contemporary Images in Watercolor, 1976; SFMA, California Painting and Sculpture: The Modern Era, 1976; Fort Wayne/AM, Hue and Far Cry of Color, 1976; PAFA, 8 Contemporary American Realists, 1977; U. of Missouri; St. Louis, West Coast Art 1970–76, 1977; Chicago/AI, Drawings of the '70's, 1977; Huntsville Museum of Art, Ala., The Modern Era: Bay Area Update, 1977; US Department of the Interior, America 1976, 1976; Sydney, Australia, Gallery Directors Council, Illusions and Reality, 1976; Indianapolis, Perceptions of the Spirit in 20th Century American Art, 1977; Creighton U.,

A Century of Master Drawings, 1978; Smithsonian, New American Monotypes, circ., 1978–80. **Collections:** Brooklyn Museum; U. of California, Berkeley; Chicago/AI; Chicago/Contemporary; U. of Connecticut; Des Moines; U. of Florida; Hagerstown/County MFA; Hirshhorn; U. of Illinois; Jacksonville/AM; Long Beach/MA; Los Angeles/County MA; MMA; U. of Massachusetts; NCFA; U. of New Mexico; Oakland/AM; Omaha/Joslyn; PMA; SFMA; Sacramento/Crocker; St. Petersburg, Fla.; Santa Barbara/MA; Syracuse/Everson; Toledo/MA; Utah; VMAA; WMAA; Walker. **Bibliography:** *America 1976;* Arthur 1, 2; Goodyear; Lucie-Smith; *Three Realists.*

RAMBERG, CHRISTINA. b. 1946, Fort Campbell, Ky. **Studied:** Chicago Art Institute School, 1968, BA; 1973, MFA. **Address:** % Dealer. **Dealer:** Phyllis Kind Gallery, NYC & Chicago. **One-man Ehibitions:** Phyllis Kind Gallery, Chicago, 1974; Phyllis Kind Gallery, NYC, 1977. **Group:** Hyde Park Art Center, Chicago, False Image, 1968, 69; Chicago/Contemporary, Don Baum Sez, "Chicago Needs Famous Artists," 1969; ICA, U. of Pennsylvania, Spirit of the Comics, 1969; Chicago/Contemporary, Chicago Imagist Art, 1972; Ottawa/Ontario, What They're Up to in Chicago, 1972; WMAA Biennials, 1972, 79; Sao Paulo, Biennale, 1973; Chicago Art Institute School, Former Famous Alumni, 1976; Sacramento/Crocker, The Chicago Connection, 1976. **Collections:** Ball State U., Baltimore/MA; Baxter Laboratories, Chicago; Chicago/AI; Chicago/Contemporary; Elmhurst College; Museum des 20. Jahrhunderts, Vienna; South Bend Art Center; WMAA. **Bibliography:** *The Chicago Connection.*

RAMOS, MEL. b. July 24, 1935, Sacramento, Calif. **Studied:** San Jose State College, 1954–55; Sacramento State College, AB, MA, 1955–58. Traveled En-

Christina Rambert *Sedimentary Disturbance* 1980

gland, Spain, France, Italy, 1964, Hawaii, 1967, Africa. **Taught:** Mira Loma High School, Sacramento, Calif., 1960–66; California State College at Hayward, 1966–; Arizona State U., 1967. **Awards:** SFMA, **P.P.**, 1948; Oakland/AM, **P.P.**, 1959. **Address:** 5941 Ocean View Drive, Oakland, CA 94618; Moragrega 38, Horta de San Juan (Tarragone), Spain. **Dealers:** Louis K. Meisel Gallery; David Stuart Gallery; Galerie Rolf Ricke. **One-man Exhibitions:** (first) The Bianchini Gallery, NYC, 1964, also 1965; David Stuart Gallery, Los Angeles, 1965, 67, 68, 74; Galerie Rolf Ricke, Kassel, 1966; Galerie Tobies-Silex, Cologne, 1967; Berkeley Gallery (two-man), 1967; SFMA, 1967; Galleries Reese Palley, 1969; Galerie Bischofberger, Zurich, 1971; Utah, 1972; Louis K. Meisel Gallery, NYC, 1974, 76; Krefeld/Haus Lange, 1975; U. of Nevada, 1978; Galleria Cadaques, Spain, 1979; Morgan Gallery, Shawnee Mission, Mo., 1977; California State U., Chico, 1979. **Retrospective:** Krefeld/Kaiser Wilhelm, 1975; Oakland/MA, 1977. **Group:** California Palace, 1959,

60, 61, Painters behind Painters, 1967; Houston/Contemporary, Pop Goes the Easel, 1963; Oakland/AM, Pop Art USA, 1963; Los Angeles/County MA, 1963; Buffalo/Albright, Mixed Media and Pop Art, 1963; ICA, London, The Popular Image, 1963; II American Art Biennial, Cordoba, Argentina, 1964; Akademie der Kunst, Berlin, 1965; Palais des Beaux-Arts, Brussels, 1965; Hamburg, 1965; Milwaukee, 1965; La Jolla, 1966; Portland, Ore./AM, 1968; WMAA, Human Concern/Personal Torment, 1969; Omaha/Joslyn, Looking West, 1970; WMAA, American Pop Art, 1974; U. of Illinois, 1974; New York Cultural Center, Three Centuries of the American Nude, 1975; SFMA, California Painting and Sculpture: The Modern Era, 1976; WMAA, Art about Art, 1978; Berlin/National, Aspekte der 60er Jahre, 1978. **Collections:** Aachen; Krefeld/Kaiser Wilhelm; Norfolk/ Chrysler; Oakland/AM; SFMA; U.S. Pro Action, Inc., Reno. **Bibliography:** Alloway 1; Honisch and Jensen, eds.; *Kunst um 1970;* Lippard 5; Lucie-Smith; *Mel Ramos: Watercolors;* Sager.

RANDELL, RICHARD, K. b. 1929, Minneapolis, Minn. **Taught:** Assistant to John Rood, Minneapolis, 1954–57; Hamline U., 1954–61; Macalaster College, 1961; U. of Minnesota, 1961–65; Sacramento State College, 1966. **Awards:** Walker Biennial, **P.P.**, 1956, 62, 66; Minneapolis/Institute, First Prize and **P.P.**, 1957, Hon. Mention, 1959; St. Paul Gallery, **P.P.**, 1961. **Address:** % Dealer. **Dealer:** Smith-Anderson Gallery, Palo Alto, Calif. **One-man Exhibitions:** Walker, 1959, 64; Minneapolis/Institute, 1964; Royal Marks Gallery, 1965, 66, 68, 69, 71. **Group:** Minneapolis/Institute, 1956, 57, 59, 61, 63; Walker Biennial, 1956, 58, 62, 66; PAFA Annual, 1959; Detroit/Institute, 1959; Chicago/AI Annual, 1961; St. Paul Gallery, 1961; Museum of Contemporary Crafts, 1963; M. Knoedler & Co., Art across America, circ., 1965–67; New York World's Fair, 1964–65; The Ohio State

U., 1966; U. of Illinois, 1967; Los Angeles/County MA, American Sculpture of the Sixties, 1967; Southern Illinois U., 1967; Indianapolis/Herron, 1967. **Collections:** Minneapolis/Institute; Minnesota/MA; U. of Minnesota; Walker. **Bibliography:** Friedman, M., 2; Tuchman 1.

RATTNER, ABRAHAM. b. July 8, 1895, Poughkeepsie, N.Y.; **d.** February 14, 1978, New York. **Studied:** George Washington U.; The Corcoran School of Art; PAFA, 1916–17; Academie des Beaux-Arts, Paris; Academie Julian, Paris; Academie Ranson, Paris; Academie de la Grande Chaumiere, 1920. US Army, 1917–19. Traveled Europe, USA; resided New York and Paris. **Taught:** New School for Social Research, 1947–55; Yale U., 1949; Brooklyn Museum School, 1950–51; American Academy, Rome, 1951; U. of Illinois, 1952–54; ASL, 1954; PAFA, 1954; Sag Harbor Summer Art Center, 1956; Michigan State U., 1956–58. **Commissions:** St. Francis Monastery, Chicago, 1956; Fairmount Temple, Cleveland, 1957; Loop Synagogue, Chicago, 1958; Duluth (Minn.) Synagogue; De Waters Art Center, Flint, Mich., 1958; US Navy Department, Washington, D.C. **Awards:** PAFA, Cresson Fellowship, 1919; PAFA, Joseph E. Temple Gold Medal, 1945; Pepsi-Cola, Second Prize, 1946; La Tausca Competition, First Prize, 1947; Carnegie, Hon. Men., 1949; U. of Illinois. **P.P.**, 1950; Corcoran, First Prize, 1953; NIAL, 1958. **One-man Exhibitions:** (first) Galerie Bonjean, Paris, 1935; Julien Levy Galleries, NYC, 1936–41; Courvoisier Gallery, San Francisco, 1940; Arts Club of Chicago, 1940; P. Rosenberg and Co., 1943, 44, 46, 48, 50, 52, 56; Stendahl Gallery, Los Angeles, 1943; Santa Barbara/MA, 1943; Philadelphia Art Alliance, 1945; Arts and Crafts Club, New Orleans, 1952; Chicago/AI,1955; Renaissance Society, 1957; The Downtown Gallery, 1957, 58, 60, 66; Corcoran, 1958; North Shore Congregation Israel, Chicago, 1958; WMAA, 1959 (four-

Abraham Rattner   *Portrait of Don Quixote*
1950

man); Galerie Internationale, NYC, 1961; The Contemporaries, NYC, 1967; Kennedy Gallery, 1969, 70, 72, 74, 75, 78, 79; New School for Social Research, 1970; NCFA, 1976. **Retrospectives:** Baltimore/MA, 1946; Vassar College, 1948; U. of Illinois, 1952; A.F.A., circ., 1960. **Group:** PAFA; Corcoran; Chicago/AI; U. of Illinois; Carnegie; MMA; WMAA; Buffalo/Albright; Baltimore/MA; Detroit/Institute; Des Moines; New School for Social Research. **Collections:** Arizona State College; Ball State U.; Buffalo/Albright; CIT Corporation; Chicago/AI; Cornell U.; Dartmouth College; Des Moines; Detroit/Institute; Fort Worth; Hartford/Wadsworth; U. of Illinois; Jewish Museum; Johnson College; MMA; Manufacturers Hanover Trust Co.; Marquette U.; Michigan State U.; Musée du Jeu de Paume; U. of Nebraska; Newark Museum; New School for Social Research; U. of Oklahoma; PAFA; PMA; Phillips; St. Louis/City; Santa Barbara/MA; Vassar College; WMAA; Walker; Washington U.; Williams College; Yale U.; Youngstown/Butler. **Bibliography:** Baur 5, 7; Biddle 4; Eliot; Frost; Gen-

auer; Getlein 2; **Goodrich and Baur** 1, **2**; Hayter 1, 2; Janis, S.; Kootz 2; Leepa; Mendelowitz; Moser 1; Newtown 1; Nordness ed.; Pagano; Pearson 2; Pousette-Dart, ed.; Read 2; Richardson, E.P.; Weller, Wight 2. Archives.

RAUSCHENBERG, ROBERT. b. October 22, 1925, Port Arthur, Tex. **Studied:** Kansas City Art Institute and School of Design, 1946–47; Academie Julian, Paris, 1947; Black Mountain College, 1948–49, with Josef Albers; ASL, 1949–50, with Vaclav Vytlacil, Morris Kantor. US Navy. Traveled Italy, North Africa, 1952–53. **Taught:** Black Mountain College, 1952. Designs stage sets and costumes for the Merce Cunningham Dance Co. (since 1955); technical director since early 1960s. **Awards:** Gallery of Modern Art, Ljubljana, Yugoslavia, V International Exhibition of Prints, First Prize, 1963; XXXII Venice Biennial, First Prize, 1964; Corcoran, First Prize, 1965; New York City Mayor's Award of Honor in Arts and Culture, 1977; RISD, President's Fellow Award, 1978. **Address:** 381 Lafayette Street, NYC 10003. **Dealer:** Leo Castelli, Inc. **One-man Exhibitions:** Betty Parsons Gallery, 1951; The Stable Gallery, 1953; Gallerie d'Arte Contemporanea, Florence, Italy, 1953; Charles Egan Gallery, 1955; Leo Castelli, Inc., NYC, 1958–61, 63, 65, 67–69, 70, 71, 73, 74, 75, 77, 79; La Tartaruga, Rome, 1959; Galerie 22, Dusseldorf, 1959; Daniel Cordier, Paris, 1961; Galleria dell'Ariete, 1961; Dwan Gallery, 1962; L'Obelisco, Rome, 1963; Ileana Sonnabend Gallery, Paris, 1963, 64, 71, 72, 73, 75, 77, NYC, 1974, 77, 79; Galleria Civica d'Arte Moderna, Turin, 1964; Amerika Haus, Berlin, 1965; Contemporary Arts Society, Houston, 1965; Walker, 1965; Stockholm/National, 1965; MOMA, 1966, 68; Douglas Gallery, Vancouver, 1967, 69; Amsterdam/Stedelijk, 1968; Peale House, Philadelphia, 1968; Cologne/Kunstverein, 1968; Paris/Moderne, 1968; Fort Worth,

Robert Rauschenberg   *Jackpot Derby (Spread)*
1979

1969; Newport Harbor, 1969; Phoenix, 1970; Seattle/AM, 1970; ICA, U. of Pennsylvania, 1970, 71, 75; Automation House, NYC, 1970; New York Cultural Center, 1970; Minneapolis/Institute, 1970; Hannover/Kunstverein, 1970; Chicago/Contemporary, 1970; Fort Worth, 1970; Galerie Rene Ziegler, Zurich, 1970; Visual Arts Gallery, NYC, 1970; Chicago/AI, 1971; Centro C., Caracas, 1971; Galerie Buren, Stockholm, 1972; F. H. Mayor Gallery, London, 1973, 78; ACE Gallery, Venice, Calif., 1973, 74, 77, 79; Jack Glenn Gallery, San Diego, 1973; Galerie Mikro, Berlin, 1974; Jerusalem National, 1974; Modern Art Agency, Naples, 1974; Galerie Sonnabend, Geneva, 1974; Jared Sable Gallery, Toronto, 1974; Margo Leavin Gallery, Los Angeles, 1975, 76; Galerie de Gestlo, Hamburg, 1975; ACE Gallery, Vancouver, 1973, 75; Galerie Tanit, Munich, 1975, 79; Museo d'Arte Radema, Venice, 1975; Greenberg Gallery, St. Louis, 1976; H.M., Brussels, 1976; Alberta College, 1976; Robinson Galleries, Houston, 1977; Galerie Rudolf Zwirner, Cologne, 1977; Linda Farris Gallery, Seattle, 1977; Janie C. Lee Gallery, Houston, 1977; Vancouver Art Gallery, 1978; Richard Gray Gallery, Chicago, 1979; Richard Hines Gallery, Seattle, 1979; Portland (Ore.) Center for the Visual Arts, 1979; Kunsthalle, Tubingen, 1979; Musée d'Art, Toulon, France, 1979; Tucson/MA, 1979; Palm Springs Desert Museum, 1979; Galerie Mathilde, Amsterdam, 1979; Ohio State U., 1980; West Coast Gallery, Newport Beach, 1980. **Retrospective:** Jewish Museum, 1963; Whitechapel Art Gallery, London, 1964; NCFA, circ., 1976. **Group:** The Stable Gallery Annuals, 1951–56; Jewish Museum, The New York School, Second Generation, 1957; A.F.A., Collage in America, circ., 1957–58; Houston/MFA, Collage International, 1958; Carnegie, 1958, 61, 64, 67; A.F.A., Art and Found Object, circ., 1959; I Paris Biennial, 1959; Daniel Cordier, Paris, Exposition Internationale de Surrealisme, 1959; MOMA, Sixteen Americans, circ., 1959; V & IX Sao Paulo Biennials, 1959, 67; Documenta II & IV, Kassel, 1959, 68; A.F.A., School of New York—Some Younger American Painters, 1960; Martha Jackson Gallery, New Media—New Forms, I & II, 1960, 61; Des Moines, Six Decades of American Painting, 1961; MOMA, The Art of Assemblage, circ., 1961; SRGM, Abstract Expressionists and Imagists, 1961; Galerie Rive Droite, Paris, Le Nouveau Realisme, 1961; MOMA, Abstract Watercolors and Drawings: USA, circ., Latin America and Europe, 1961–62; SRGM/USIA, American Vanguard, circ., Europe, 1961–62; Stockholm/National, 4 Americans, circ., 1962; Salon du Mai, Paris, 1962; Seattle World's Fair, 1962; III International Biennial Exhibition of Prints, Tokyo, 1962; Art: USA: Now, circ., 1962–67; SRGM, Six Painters and the Object, circ., 1963; WGMA, The Popular Image, 1963; Musée Cantonal des Beaux-Arts, Lausanne, I Salon International de Galeries Pilotes, 1963; ICA, London, The Popular Image, 1963; El Retiro Parquet, Madrid, Arte de America y Espana, 1963; Gallery of Modern Art, Ljubljana, Yugoslavia, V International Exhibition of Prints, 1963; Brandeis U., New Directions in American Painting, 1963; Jewish Museum, Black and White, 1963; Corcoran, 1963, 65; Chicago/AI, 1963, 66; Tate, Dunn International, 1964; Hartford/Wadsworth, Black, White, and Gray, 1964; New York State Pavilion, New York World's Fair, 1964–65; SRGM, 1964, 65; Kunstverein in Hamburg, 1965; U. of Texas, 1965; Cincinnati/Contemporary, 1965; Kansas City/ Nelson, Sound, Light, Silence, 1966; Flint/Institute, I Flint Invitational, 1966; Expo '67, Montreal, 1967; MOMA, The 1960's, 1967; Eindhoven, 1967; Foundation Maeght, L'Art Vivant, circ., French museums, 1968; MOMA, Dada, Surrealism and Their Heritage, 1968; Milwaukee, Directions I: Options, circ., 1968; Jewish Museum, 1968; Vancouver, 1968; U. of California, Irvine, 1968; Arts Council of Great Britain, 1968; MMA, New York Painting and Sculpture: 1940–1970, 1969–70; Expo '70, Osaka, 1970; Los Angeles/County MA, Art & Technology, 1971; WMAA, 1973; Parcheggio di Villa Borghese, Rome, Contemporanea, 1974; Chicago/ AI, Idea and Image in Recent Art, 1974; WMAA, American Pop Art, 1974; MOMA, Drawing Now, 1976; WMAA, 200 Years of American Sculpture, 1976; WMAA, New York on Paper, 1977; Williamstown/Clark, The Dada/Surrealist Heritage, 1977; Cambridge, Jubilation, 1977; Minnesota/MA, American Drawings, 1927–1977, 1977; NCFA, New Ways with Paper, 1978; WMAA, Art about Art, 1978; MOMA, Artists and Writers, 1978; Buffalo/Albright, American Painting of the 1970s, circ., 1978; Corcoran Biennial, 1979. **Collections:** Amsterdam/Stedelijk; Baltimore/ MA; Buffalo/Albright; Chicago; Cologne; Cornell U.; Dusseldorf; Goucher College; Hartford/Wadsworth; Hirshhorn; Minneapolis/Institute; NCFA; Aachen/NG; PMA; Pasadena/AM; The Singer Company, Inc.; Stockholm/National; Tate; WMAA. **Bibliography:** Alloway 4; *Art Now 74;* Ashton 5; Atkinson; Battcock, ed.; Becker and Vostell; Bihalji-Merin; Callas, N. and E.; *Contemporanea;* Davis, D.; De Vries, ed.; Diamonstein; Dienst 1; Downes, ed.;

Elsen 2; Finch; Friedman, ed.; Gablick; *Happening & Fluxus;* Honisch and Jensen, eds.; Hulten; Hunter, ed.; Janis and Blesh 1; Johnson, Ellen H.; Kaprow; Kozloff 3; Kramer 2; *Kunst um 1970;* Licht, F.; Lippard 5; Lynton; *Metro;* Newmeyer; Nordness, ed.; O'Doherty; *Poets & Painters;* Read 3; *Report;* Rickey; Robert Rauschenberg; Rodman 3; Rose B., 1, 4; Rubin 1; Russell and Gablik; Sager; Sandler 1; Sontag; Tomkins and Time-Life Books; Tuchman 1; Warhol and Hackett; Weller.

REDER, BERNARD. b. June 29, 1897, Czernowitz, Bukovina, Austria; **d.** September 7, 1963, NYC. Austrian Army, 1914–18. **Studied:** Academy of Fine Arts, Prague, 1919, with Peter Bromse, Jan Stursa. Traveled Cuba, USA, Europe extensively. To USA, 1943; citizen, 1948. **Awards:** International architectural competition to house the monument to Christopher Columbus in Santo Domingo, 1927; Ford Foundation Grant, Program in Humanities and the Arts ($10,000), 1960. **One-man Exhibitions:** (first) The Rudolphinium, Prague, 1928 (watercolors); Manes Gallery, Prague, 1935; Galerie de Berri, Paris, 1940; Lyceum Gallery, Havana, 1942; U. of Ravenna, 1942; Weyhe Gallery, 1943; Philadelphia Art Alliance, 1950; Bezalel Museum, 1950; The Print Club, Philadelphia, 1950; Tel Aviv, 1950, 63; Grace Borgenicht Gallery, Inc., 1951, 52, 53; Dominion Gallery, Montreal, 1953; Chicago/AI, 1953; Galleria d'Arte Moderna L'Indiano, Florence, Italy, 1956, 57; The Contemporaries, NYC, 1956; Palazzo Torrigiani, Florence, Italy, 1957; World House Galleries, NYC, 1951, 61. **Retrospective:** WMAA, 1961. **Group:** WMAA, European Artists in America, 1945; Chicago/AI; PMA, 1949; MOMA, 1949, 51; U. of Illinois, 1953. **Collections:** Baltimore/MA; Brooklyn Museum; Chicago/AI; Harvard U.; Jewish Museum; MMA; MOMA; NYPL; National Gallery; PMA; Sao Paulo. **Bibliography: Bernard Reder**; Goodrich and Baur 1; Licht, F. Archives.

REICHEK, JESSE. b. August 16, 1916, Brooklyn, N.Y. **Studied:** Institute of Design, Chicago, 1941–42; Academie Julian, Paris (diploma), 1947–51. US Army Engineers, 1942–46. Traveled Europe, India, the Orient; resided Paris, India. **Taught:** U. of Michigan, 1946–47; Illinois Institute of Technology, 1951–53; U. of California, Berkeley, 1953– ; American Academy, Rome, 1971. **Awards:** Graham Foundation Grant, 1962; Tamarind Fellowship, 1966. **Address:** 5925 Red Hill Road, Petaluma, CA 94952. **Dealers:** Betty Parsons Gallery. **One-man Exhibitions:** (first) Galerie des Cahiers d'Art, 1951, also 1959; U. of California, 1954; Betty Parsons Gallery, 1958–60, 63, 65, 67, 68, 70; Wittenborn Gallery, NYC, 1962; Molton Gallery, London, 1962; Bennington College, 1963; American Cultural Center, Florence, Italy, 1964; U. of New Mexico, 1966; Axiom Gallery, London, 1968; Yoseido Gallery, Tokyo, 1968; Galeria Van der Voort, 1969; Los Angeles/County MA, 1971. **Retrospective:** U. of Southern California, 1967. **Group:** Brooklyn Museum, 1959; MOMA, 1962; Buffalo/Albright, 1965; Cincinnati/AM, 1966; Arts Club of Chicago, 1966; Cranbrook, 1967; Finch College, 1967; Caracas, 1969; Foundation Maeght, 1971. **Collections:** Bibliotheque Nationale; U. of California; Amon Carter Museum; Chicago/AI; Grunwald Foundation; La Jolla; Los Angeles/County MA; MOMA; U. of New Mexico; Pasadena/AM; San Diego; Victoria and Albert. **Bibliography:** *Report.*

REINHARDT, AD. b. December 24, 1913, Buffalo, N.Y.; **d.** August 30, 1967, NYC. **Studied:** Columbia U., with Meyer Schapiro, 1931–35, BA, 1936–37; NAD, 1936–37, with Francis Criss, Carl Holty; NYU, Institute of Fine Arts, 1945–51, with Alfred Salmony. US Navy photographer, 1944–45. Traveled Europe and Asia extensively. **Taught:** Brooklyn College, 1947–67; California School of Fine Arts, 1950; U. of Wyoming, 1951; Yale U., 1952–53; Syracuse U., 1957; Hunter College, 1959–67. Worked for *PM* (newspaper), NYC, 1944–47. Articles in *Art International, Art News, College Art Journal, It Is* (magazines). **Member:** American Abstract Artists, 1937–47; Asia Society; Chinese Art Society. Federal A.P.: Easel painting, 1936–39. **One-man Exhibitions:** (first) Columbia U., 1943; Artists Gallery, NYC, 1944; Mortimer Brandt, NYC, 1945; Brooklyn Museum School, 1946; Betty Parsons Gallery, 1946–53, 55, 56, 59, 60; Syracuse U., 1957; Leverkusen, 1961; Dwan Gallery, 1961, 63; Iris Clert Gallery, 1963; ICA, London, 1964; Marlborough Gallery Inc., NYC, 1970, 74, 77, 80; Irving Blum Gallery, Los Angeles, 1970; Richard Feigen Gallery, 1970; Dusseldorf/Kunsthalle, 1972; Eindhoven, 1973; Marlborough Galerie AG, Zurich, 1974; The Pace Gallery, NYC, 1976; Truman Gallery, 1976; WMAA, 1980. **Retrospective:** Jewish Museum, 1967. **Group:** New York World's Fair, 1939; American Abstract Artists Annuals; MOMA, Abstract Painting and Sculpture in America, 1951; WMAA, The New Decade, 1954–55, and others; Brussels World's Fair, 1958; SRGM, Abstract Expressionists and Imagists, 1961; Seattle World's Fair, 1962; MOMA, Americans 1963, circ., 1963–64; Tate, 1964; WMAA, The 1930's, 1968; MOMA, The New American Painting and Sculpture, 1969. **Collections:** Baltimore/MA; Buffalo/Albright; Dayton/AI; Leverkusen; Los Angeles/County MA; MOMA; U. of Nebraska; Oslo/National; PMA; SFMA; Toledo/MA; WMAA; Yale U. **Bibliography:** Alloway 4; Battcock, ed.; Blesh 1; Calas, N. and E.; *Contemporanea;* Coplans 3; De Vries, ed.; Downes, ed.; Goossen 1; Hess, T.B., 1; Hobbs and Levin; Honisch and Jensen, eds.; Janis and Blesh 1; Janis, S.; Lippard 1, 3; MacAgy 2; McChesney; **Motherwell and Reinhardt, eds.**; Rickey; Ritchie 1;

Ad Reinhardt Untitled *(New York World's Fair)* 1939

Rodman 1; Rose, B., 1, 4; Rose, ed.; Sandler; Sandler 1; Tomkins 2; Tuchman, ed.; Weller. Archives.

REINHARDT, SIEGFRIED GERHARD. b. July 31, 1925, Eydkuhnen, Germany. To USA, 1928; citizen, 1936. **Studied:** Washington U., AB. **Taught:** Washington U., 1955–70. **Commissions:** (murals) St. Louis Airport; Fabick Tractor Co. US Army, 1944–46. **Awards:** Scholarship, John Herron Art Institute, 1943; 20th Century Book Club Award, 1945; St. Louis Artists' Guild, 1951, 53, 54, 55, 57, 58; St. Louis/City, 1951, 53, 55, 56; Cincinnati/AM, 1958; International Novara, Trieste, 1961; Hon. DFA, London Institute for Applied Research, 1973; Doctor of Humanities, Occidental U., 1977; DFA and Humanities, Concordia Seminary, 1977. **Address:** 635 Craig Woods Drive, Kirkwood 22, MO 63122. **Dealer:** The Midtown Galleries. **One-man Exhibitions:** Eleanor Smith Gallery, St. Louis, 1942, 43, 47; Southern Illinois U., 1951, 52, 69; St. Louis Artists' Guild, 1951, 58; Stevens-Gross Gallery, Chicago, 1952; Art Mart, Clayton, Mo., 1953; Texas Western College, 1954; Illinois State Normal U., Normal, Ill., 1954; Martin Schweig Gallery, 1956; Hewitt Gallery, NYC, 1957; The Midtown Galleries, 1961, 66; St. Louis Artists Guild, 1958, 65; Chase Park Plaza Hotel, St. Louis, 1967; U. of Miami, 1968; Tulsa/Philbrook, 1969; Southern Illinois, The School of the Ozarks, 1969; Jack O'Grady Galleries, Chicago, 1977. **Group:** St. Louis/City 1943, 45, 47, 49, 51, 53, 58, 61; Chicago/AI, 1947, 54; Washington U., 1950; MMA, 1950; Los Angeles/County MA, 1951, 55; WMAA, 1951–55, 1960; Walker, 1954; Dallas/MFA, 1954; Beloit College, 1954; A.F.A. (stained glass), circ.; Cincinnati/AM, 1955, 58, 61; ICA, Boston, 1958; PAFA, 1958, ART:USA: 58, NYC, 1958; Kansas State College, 1958; USIA, circ., Europe, 1959; Boston/

MFA, 1960, 61; Columbus, 1961; Trieste, 1961; NAD, 1977. **Collections:** AAAL; Abbott Laboratories; Beloit College; Cincinnati/AM; Concordia Teachers College (Neb.); Jacksonville/Cummer; Kansas City/Nelson; Newark Museum; RISD; St. Louis/City; Southern Illinois U.; WMAA. **Bibliography:** Nordness, ed.; Pousette-Dart, ed.

REMINGTON, DEBORAH. b. June 25, 1930, Haddonfield, N. J. **Studied:** California School of Fine Arts, 1949–52; San Francisco Art Institute, BFA, 1955. Traveled Asia, 1955–58, Europe, 1967–68. **Taught:** San Franciso Art Institute, 1958–65, 66, 68; U. of California, Davis, 1962; San Francisco State College, 1965; Cooper Union, 1970–. **Awards:** Tamarind Fellowship, 1973; National Endowment for the Arts, fellowship, 1979. **Address:** 309 West Broadway, NYC 10013. **One-man Exhibitions:** SFMA, 1964; Dilexi Gallery, San Francisco, 1962, 63, 65; Bykert Gallery, 1967, 69, 72, 74; Darthea Speyer Gallery, 1968, 71, 73; Obelisk Gallery, 1971; Pyramid Art Galleries, Washington, D.C., 1973, 76; Michael Berger Gallery, Pittsburgh, 1974, 79; Brooke Alexander, 1974; Zolla-Lieberman, Chicago, 1976; Hamilton Gallery of Contemporary Art, NYC, 1977; Portland (Ore.) Center for the Visual Arts, 1977; U. of Missouri, Kansas, 1977; Miami Dade Community College, 1978; Bonfoey Gallery, Cleveland, 1980. **Group:** WMAA Annuals, 1965, 67, Recent Acquisitions, 1966; Musée Cantonal des Beaux-Arts, Lausanne, II Salon International de Galeries Pilotes, 1966; U. of Illinois Biennial, 1967; Smithsonian, The Art of Organic Forms, 1968; Foundation Maeght, l'Art Vivant, circ., French museums, 1968; U. of North Carolina, Works on Paper, 1968; Foundation Maeght, 1970; VMFA, American Painting, 1970; Oakland/AM, A Period of Exploration, 1973; PMA/Museum of the Philadelphia Center, Focus, 1974; Chicago/AI, 71st American Exhibition, 1974; Toledo/MA, Image, Color and Form, 1975; ICA, Boston, Painting Endures, 1975; San Antonio/McNay, American Artists, '76: A Celebration, 1976; SFMA, Painting and Sculpture in California: The Modern Era, 1976; North Texas State U., Three Artists, Three Viewpoints, 1976; Chicago/AI, Drawings of the '70s, 1977; U. of Texas, Austin, New in the Seventies, 1977. **Collections:** Achenbach Foundation; Andover/Phillips; Auckland; CNAC; CSCS; California Palace; U. of California, Berkeley; Crown Zellerbach Foundation Indianapolis; U. of New Mexico; Phoenix; Rotterdam; SFMA; Toledo/MA; WMAA. **Bibliography:** *Art: A Woman's Sensibility;* McChesney; *New in the Seventies.* Archives.

RENOUF, EDDA. b. June 17, 1943, Mexico City. **Studied:** Putney School, 1957–61; Sarah Lawrence College, BA, 1961–65; Columbia U, MFA, 1968–71; Institut d'art et d'archeologie, Paris, 1963–64; Academie Julian, Paris, 1963–64; Atelier Geitlinger, Munich, 1966–67; ASL, 1967–68; Akademie der Bildenden Kunste, Munich, 1969–70. Traveled Mexico, Iran, Turkey; resided in Paris, 1963–64, 71–75; Munich, 1966–67, 69–70. **Taught:** Sarah Lawrence College, Paris, 1974. **Address:** 20 West 30th Street, NYC 10001. **Dealer:** Blum Helman Gallery, NYC; Yvon Lambert, Paris. **One-man Exhibition:** (first) Yvon Lambert, Paris, 1972, 74, 75, 78; Francoise Lambert, Milan, 1973, 75, 76, 78; Konrad Fischer Gallery, Dusseldorf, 1974, 79; Galerie MTL, Brussels, 1974, 77; Galleria Marilena Bonomo, Bari, 1975; Rolf Preisig Gallery, Basel, 1976; Allesandro Ferranti, Rome, 1976; Julian Pretto and Co., New York, 1976; Weinberg Gallery, San Francisco, 1977, 79; Kathryn Markel Fine Arts, Inc., New York, 1977; Hartford/Wadsworth, 1978; Blum Helman Gallery, NYC, 1978, 79, 80; Ugo Ferranti, Rome, 1978; Graeme Murray Gallery, Edinburgh, 1978; Margo Leavin Gallery, Los Angeles, 1978; Young-Hoffman Gallery, Chicago, 1978;

Ronald Greenberg Gallery, St. Louis, 1980. **Group:** VIII Paris Biennale, 1973; Dusseldorf, Prospekt, 1973; Rome, Contemporanea, 1973; Amsterdam/ Stedelijk, Fundametal Painting, 1975; Paris/Moderne, Tendances actuelles de la nouvelle peinture americaine, 1975; MOMA, Extraordinary Women, 1977; U. of California, Santa Barbara, Contemporary Drawing/New York, 1978; WMAA Biennial, 1979. **Collections:** MOMA; WMAA; PMA; Chicago/AI; Grenoble; Paris/Beaubourg; Dallas/ MFA; St. Louis/City; MMA; McCrory Corp. **Bibliography:** *Fundamentele Schilderkunst.*

RESIKA, PAUL. b. August 15, 1928, NYC. **Studied:** Privately in NYC with Sol Wilson, 1940–44, and Hans Hofmann, 1945–47. Traveled France, Italy. **Taught:** U. of Oregon, 1965; ASL, 1968–69; Cooper Union, 1966–77; Dartmouth College, 1972; Skowhegan School, 1973; U. of Pennsylvania, 1974; Purchase/SUNY, 1977. **Awards:** Bordighera, Americans in Europe, **P.P.**, 1952; L. C. Tiffany Grant, 1959; NAD, Ranger Fund **P.P.**, 1961; Ingram Merrill Grant, 1969; AAAL, Childe Hassam Fund **P.P.**, 1970; AAAL, 1977. **Address:** 114 East 84th Street, NYC 10028. **Dealer:** Graham Gallery, NYC. **One-man Exhibitions:** (first) George Dix Gallery, NYC, 1948; The Peridot Gallery, 1964, 65, 67–69, 1970; Washburn Gallery, Inc., 1971–73; Dartmouth College, 1972; Swain School of Design, New Bedford, Mass., 1974; Carlton Gallery, NYC, 1975; Graham Gallery, 1976. **Group:** American Painters in Venice, 1952; Hartford/Wadsworth, Figures, 1964; Swarthmore College, 1968; Rijksakademie Amsterdam, 1968; State University of New York, 1969; AAAL, 1969, 70, 71, 75; A.F.A., Realism and Surrealism in American Art, 1971; NAD, 1972; Omaha/Joslyn, A Sense of Place, 1973; Queens Museum, New Images, 1974; AAAL, Childe Hassam Fund Exhibition, 1976; Parsons School of Design, NYC, In Praise of Space, 1976; NAD

Annual, 1977. **Collections:** Bordighera; Chase Manhattan Bank; Colby College; Dartmouth College; Goddart Art Center; Hirshhorn; Indianapolis/Herron; Lenox School; Memorial Sloan-Kettering Cancer Center, NYC; NAD; U. of Nebraska.

RESNICK, MILTON. b. January 8, 1917, Bratslov, Russia. **Studied:** Pratt Institute, 1935; American Artists School, 1936–37. US Army, 1940–45. Resided Paris, 1946–48. **Taught:** Pratt Institute, 1954–55; U. of California, Berkeley, 1955–56. Federal A.P.: Teacher. **Address:** 80 Forsyth Street, NYC 10002. **Dealer:** Max Hutchinson Gallery, NYC. **One-man Exhibitions:** (first) Poindexter Gallery, 1955, also, 1957, 59; de Young, 1955; Ellison Gallery, Fort Worth, 1959; Holland-Goldowsky Gallery, Chicago, 1959; The Howard Wise Gallery, Cleveland, 1960; The Howard Wise Gallery, NYC, 1960, 61, 64; Feiner Gallery, NYC, 1964; Anderson Gallery, Edgartown, Mass., 1969; Fort Worth, 1971; Max Hutchinson Gallery, NYC, 1972, 77. **Group:** WMAA Annuals, 1957, 59, 61, 63; Carnegie, 1958; Walker, 60 American Painters, 1960; SRGM, Abstract Expressionists and Imagists, 1961; USIA, Contemporary American Prints, circ., Latin America, 1961–62; Chicago/AI Annual, 1962; PAFA Annual, 1962; Seattle World's Fair, 1962; SFMA, Directions— Painting U.S.A., 1963; MOMA, The New American Painting and Sculpture, 1969; U. of California, Santa Barbara, 5 American Painters, 1974. **Collections:** Akron/AI; U. of California, Berkeley; Canberra/National; Ciba-Geigy Corp.; Cleveland/MA; Dartmouth College; Hartford/Wadsworth; Honolulu Academy; Milwaukee; MOMA; National Gallery; North Carolina; NYU; Reed College; Roswell; Skidmore, Owings & Merrill, NYC; WMAA; Waitsfield/ Bundy. **Bibliography:** *From Foreign Shores;* Goodrich and Baur 1; Hunter 1; Nordness, ed.; Passloff; Plous; Sandler 1. Archives.

REYNAL, JEANNE. b. April 1, 1903, White Plains, N.Y. Privately educated; apprenticed to Atelier Boris Anrep, Paris, 1930–38. Traveled the world extensively. **Commissions:** Ford Foundation, 1959; Our Lady of Florida Monastery, 1962. **Awards:** SFMA, Emanuel Walter Bequest and Purchase Award, 1945. **Address:** 240 West 11th Street, NYC 10014. **Dealer:** Betty Parsons Gallery. **One-man Exhibitions:** (first) SFMA, 1942, also 1943–46; Arts Club of Chicago, 1943; Baltimore/MA, 1943; Betty Parsons Gallery, 1971; Bodley Gallery, NYC, 1976. **Group:** SFMA, 1944, 45; WMAA Annuals, 1950–56; Seattle World's Fair, 1962; MOMA; Hartford/Wadsworth, 1962. **Collections:** Andover/Phillips; Ciba-Geigy Corp.; Denver/AM; Ford Foundation; MOMA; Mills College of Education; NYU; SFMA; WMAA. **Bibliography:** *Art: A Woman's Sensibility;* **Ashton 1;** Breton 3; Calas; Janis and Blesh 1; Ritchie 1. Archives.

RICE, DAN. b. June, 1926, Long Beach, Calif. **Studied:** UCLA, 1943; U. of California, Berkeley, 1946; Black Mountain College, with Franz Kline, Robert Motherwell, Ben Shahn, Jack Tworkov. US Navy, 1943–46. **Taught:** ASL, 1968– . **Address:** Rocklanding Road, Haddam Neck, East Hampton, CT 06424. **One-man Exhibitions:** Catherine Viviano Gallery, 1960, 62, 63, 66, 70. **Group:** U. of Virginia; Buffalo/Albright; Mary Washington College. **Collections:** Dillard U.; Princeton U.

RICHARDSON, SAM. b. July 19, 1934, Oakland, Calif. **Studied:** California College of Arts and Crafts, 1956, BA, 1960, MFA. **Taught:** Oakland City College, 1959–60; San Jose State College, 1963– . Art Director, Museum of Contemporary Crafts, 1960–63. **Address:** 4121 Sequoyah Road, Oakland, CA 94605. **Dealer:** Hansen-Fuller Gallery. **One-man Exhibitions:** Hansen Gallery, San Francisco, 1961, 66, 68, 69; Hum-boldt (Calif.) State College, 1967; Esther Robles Gallery, 1968; California State U., Fullerton, 1968; U. of Nebraska, 1968; Martha Jackson Gallery, 1969, 70, 73, 74, 75; Hansen-Fuller Gallery, 1971, 74, 75; Akron/AI, 1972; Contemporary Arts Center, Cincinnati, 1972; Mills College, 1973; Cranbrook, 1973; St. Mary's College, Moraga, Calif., 1975; Rutgers U., 1975; Dallas/MFA, 1976; Richard Gray Gallery, Chicago, 1976; Oakland/AM, 1976. **Group:** California Palace, Winter Invitational, 1961; SFMA, 1965, 66; California Palace, Painters behind Painters, 1967; U. of Illinois, 1967, 69; Sacramento/Crocker, West Coast '68, 1968; Museum of Contemporary Crafts, Plastic as Plastic, 1968; WMAA, 1968; ICA, U. of Pennsylvania, Plastics and New Art, 1969; MOMA, New Media; New Methods, circ., 1969; Occidental College, Los Angeles, Four Directions, 1969; WMAA, Contemporary American Sculpture, 1968–69; Milwaukee, A Plastic Presence, circ., 1969; SFAI, Centennial Exhibition, 1971; Chicago/Contemporary, White on White, 1971–72; Stanford U., Sculpture '72, 1972; Vassar College, New American Landscapes, 1972; Museum of Contemporary Crafts, Creative Casting, 1973; Rutgers U., Response to the Environment, 1975. **Collections:** Fort Worth; Milwaukee; U. of Nebraska; U. of Sydney; WMAA; U. of Wisconsin.

RICHENBURG, ROBERT B. b. July 14, 1917, Boston, Mass. **Studied:** Boston Museum School; George Washington U.; Boston U.; The Corcoran School of Art; Ozenfant School of Art, NYC; Hofmann School; ASL, with Reginald Marsh, George Grosz. US Army, 1942–45. **Taught:** Schrivenham American U.; Brooklyn-Queens Central YMCA, 1947–51; City College of New York, 1947–52; Pratt Institute, 1951–64; Cooper Union, 1954–55; NYU, 1960–61; Cornell U., 1964–67; Hunter College, 1967–70; Ithaca College, 1970. **Awards:** Boston Museum School, Scholarship; *Art in America* (magazine), New Talent.

Address: 512 Cayuga Heights Road, Ithaca, NY 14850. **One-man Exhibitions:** (first) Hendler Gallery, Philadelphia, 1954; Artists' Gallery, NYC, 1957; Artists' Gallery, Provincetown, 1958; Hansa Gallery, NYC, 1958; Tibor de Nagy Gallery, 1959–64; Dwan Gallery, 1960; RISD, 1960 (four-man); Santa Barbara/MA, 1961; Dayton/AI, 1962; Cornell U., 1964. **Retrospectives:** Colgate U., 1970; Ithaca College, 1971. **Group:** SRGM, 1949; Eighth Street Exhibition, NYC; Ninth Street Exhibition, NYC; MOMA, The Art of Assemblage, circ., 1961; SRGM, Abstract Expressioniss and Imagists, 1961; Baltimore/MA, 1961; WMAA Annuals, 1961, 64, 68, Sculpture Annuals, 1966–69; Dayton/AI, 1962; Kansas City/Nelson, 1962; U. of Illinois, 1963; Corcoran, 1963; MOMA, Hans Hofmann and His Students, circ., 1963–64; U. of Nebraska; A.F.A., New Talent, circ., 1964, also 1968–69; Seattle/AM, 1965; Hamilton College, 1965; A.F.A., The Square in Painting, 1968; WMAA Annual, 1968. **Collections:** Allentown/AM; U. of California; Hirshhorn; Ithaca College; MOMA; Norfolk; Norfolk/Chrysler; PMA; Pasadena/AM; Ridgefield/Aldrich; U. of Texas; WMAA; College of William and Mary. **Bibliography:** Seitz 3.

RICKEY, GEORGE. b. June 6, 1907, South Bend, Ind. To Scotland, 1913. **Studied:** Trinity College, Glenalmond, Scotland, 1921–26; Balliol College, Oxford, 1926–29, BA, 1941, MA with honors; Ruskin School of Drawing and of Fine Art, Oxford, 1928–29; Academie Andre Lhote and Academie Moderne, Paris, 1929–30; NYU, 1945–46; State U. of Iowa, 1947, with Maurico Lasansky; Institute of Design, Chicago, 1948–49. Traveled Europe and Mexico extensively; resided Paris, 1933–34. US Army Air Corps, 1941–45. **Taught:** Groton School, 1930–33 (history department); Knox College, 1940–41; Muhlenberg College, 1941, 1946–48; U. of Washington, 1948; Indiana U., 1949–55; Tulane U., 1955–62; U. of California, Santa Barbara, 1960; Rensselaer Polytechnic Institute, 1961–65. Editorial department, *Newsweek* magazine, 1936. Director, The Kalamazoo Institute of Arts, 1939–40. Shifted emphasis from painting to sculpture, 1950. **Member:** NIAL. **Commissions** (murals): Olivet College, 1938–39; US Post Office, Selinsgrove, Pa., 1938; Knox College, 1940–41; (sculpture), Belle Boas Memorial Library, Baltimore Museum, 1955; Union Carbide Corp., Toronto, 1960; The Joseph H. Hirshhorn Collection, NYC, 1962; Hamburger Kunsthalle, 1963; Westland Center, Detroit, 1964; Keene Teachers College, 1964; Lytton Savings and Loan Association, Oakland, Calif., 1964; The Singer Company, Inc., 1964; Hood College, 1964; Berlin/National; Rijksmuseum Kroller-Muller; Oakland/AM; Siemens Research Center, Erlangen, Germany; Henkel GMBH, Germany; NCFA; Nordpark, Dusseldorf, 1965; State Employment Building, Albany, 1966; Omaha National Bank, 1967; Berlin/National, 1969; High Museum, 1969; The Free University, Berlin, 1969; Neue Heimat Bayern, Munich, 1969; U. of Glasgow, 1971; U. of Heidelberg, 1972; Fort Worth City Hall, 1974; US Federal Courthouse, Honolulu, 1975; Universitatsbauamt, Ulm, 1977; Ruhr U., 1978; K & B Plaza, New Orleans, 1978; Peoria Airport, 1978; Pasadena/AM, 1978; Central Trust Co., Cincinnati, 1979; Oliver Tyrone Corp., Cleveland, 1980; Jackson Hospital, Miami, 1980. **Awards:** Guggenheim Foundation Fellowship, 1960, 61; Hon. DFA, Knox College, 1970; American Institute of Architects, Fine Arts Honor Award, 1972; Hon. DFA, Williams College, 1972; Skowhegan School, Medal for Sculpture, 1973; Union College, 1973; Hon. DFA, Indiana U., 1974; Hon. Degree, Kalamazoo College, 1977; Hon. Doctor of Letters, York U., 1978; Brandeis U., Creative Arts Award, 1979. **Address:** RD #2, East Chatham, N.Y. **One-man Exhibitions:** (first) Caz-Delbo Gallery, NYC, 1933; Denver/AM, 1935, 43, 45, 48; Indianapolis/Herron,

1953 (first sculpture shown); The Little Gallery, Louisville, 1954; Kraushaar Galleries, 1955, 59, 61; New Orleans/Delgado, 1956; Amerika Haus, Hamburg, 1957; Orleans Gallery, New Orleans, 1960; Santa Barbara/MA, 1960; U. of Oklahoma, 1961; Phoenix, 1961; Primus-Stuart Gallery, Los Angeles, 1962; Galerie Springer, Berlin, 1962; Grand Rapids, 1962; Hyde Park Art Center, Chicago, 1963; Williams College, 1963; U. of Rochester, 1963; Dartmouth College, 1963; ICA, Boston, 1964; David Stuart Gallery, 1964; Kalamazoo/Institute, 1964 (two-man, with Ulfert Wilke); Staempfli Gallery, 1964, 67, 71, 75; Skidmore College, 1965; Walker, 1967; Haus am Waldsee, Berlin, circ., 1969; Kunsthalle, Nurnberg, 1969; Trenton/State, 1969; Whatcom, 1970; U. of Washington, 1970; Indiana U. (three-man), 1970; U. of Iowa, 1972; Hannover/K-G, 1973; Berlin/National, 1973; Galerie Buchholz, Munich, 1974; Galerie Espace, Amsterdam, 1974; Gimpel & Hanover, Zurich, 1975, 78; Gimpel Fils, 1975; Fordham U., 1975; Bielefeld, 1976; Frankfurt am Main, 1977; Gallery Kasahara, Osaka, 1978; Amerika Haus, Berlin, 1979; Ministry of Cultural Affairs, Montreal, 1980. **Retrospectives:** Corcoran, 1966; SRGM, 1979; UCLA, circ., 1971. **Group:** Salon des Artistes Independents, Paris, 1930; MMA, National Sculpture Exhibition, 1951; WMAA, 1952, 53, 66, 68–69, Annual, 1964; PAFA, 1953, 54; Chicago/AI, Exhibition Momentum, 1954, 55; U. of Nebraska, 1955; U. of Minnesota, 1955; MOMA, Recent Sculpture, USA, 1959; Santa Barbara/MA, 1960; Amsterdam/Stedelijk, Art in Motion, circ., Europe, 1961–62; Battersea Park, London, International Sculpture Exhibition, 1963; Documenta III & IV, Kassel, 1964, 68; Berne, 1965; Palais des Beaux-Arts, Brussels, 1965; Staatliche Kunsthalle, Baden-Baden, 1965; St. Louis Bicentennial Sculpture Exhibition, 1965; Park Sonsbeek, Holland, 1966; Los Angeles/County MA, 1967; Carnegie, 1967; XXXIV Venice Biennial, 1968; Denver/AM, Report on the Sixties, 1969; Hayward Gallery, London, Kinetics, 1970; U. of Nebraska, American Sculpture, 1970; Katonah (N.Y.) Art Gallery, Drawing in Space, 1972; Newport, R.I., Monumenta, 1974; Documenta IV, Kassel, 1968; Antwerp Biennial, 1971; Hayward Gallery, London, Pier and Ocean, 1980. **Collections:** Allentown/AM; Andover/Phillips; Atlanta/AA; Ball State U.; Baltimore/MA; Bethlehem Steel Corp.; Bochum/Museum Bochum; Boston/MFA; Buffalo/Albright; Cincinnati/AM; Columbus; Corcoran; Dallas/MFA; Dartmouth College; Denver/AM; Detroit/Institute; Flint/Institute; U. of Glasgow; Hamburg; High Museum; Hirshhorn; Honolulu Academy; Humlebaek/Louisiana; Indiana U.; U. of Iowa; Jackson Hospital, Miami; Kalamazoo/Institute; Kansas City/Nelson; Long Beach/MA; MOMA; Max Planck Institute, Freiburg; Memphis/Brooks; Minnesota/MA; Raleigh/NCMA; NCFA; Newark Museum; U. of North Carolina; Oakland/MA; Princeton U.; Ruhr U.; Santa Barbara/MA; The Singer Company, Inc., NYC; SRGM; Storm King Art Center; Syntex Research Center, Palo Alto; Tate, Toronto; Trenton/State; Ulm U.; Union Carbide Corp.; WMAA; Walker; Yale U.; York U. **Bibliography:** Battcock, ed.; Calas, N. and E.; Chipp; Craven, W.; Davis, D.; **George Rickey**; MacAgy 2; *Monumenta*; Read 3; **Rickey**; Rodman 1; Selz, P., 1; Trier 1; Tuchman 1. Archives.

RIVERS, LARRY. b. August 17, 1923, Bronx, NY. US Army Air Corps, 1942–43. **Studied:** Julliard School of Music, NYC, 1944–45; Hofmann School; NYU, 1947–48. Traveled Europe, USA, USSR, Africa. Active as a professional jazz musician. Began sculpture 1953. Appeared on "$64,000 Question" (CBS–TV) as an art expert and ran his winnings to $32,000 on "$64,000 Challenge," 1957–58. **Commissions:** Outdoor billboard for First New York Film Festival, 1963. **Awards:** Corcoran, Third Prize, 1954. **Address:** 92 Little Plains Road, Southhampton, NY 11968.

Dealer: Marlborough Gallery, Inc.; Robert Miller Gallery, NYC. **One-man Exhibitions:** (first) Jane Street Gallery, NYC, 1949; Tibor de Nagy Gallery, 1951–54, 1957–60, 1962; The Stable Gallery, 1954 (sculpture); Martha Jackson Gallery, 1960 (sculpture); Dwan Gallery, 1960; Galerie Rive Droite, 1962; Gimpel Fils, London, 1962, 64, 76; Marlborough Gallery, Inc., 1970, 71, 73, 75, 77; Brandeis U.; Chicago/AI, circ., 1970; Quay Gallery, 1972; Tower Gallery, Southampton, 1973; Olympia Galleries, Glenside, Pa., 1975; Robert Miller Gallery, NYC, 1977; Hokin Gallery, Chicago, 1977; ACA Gallery, NYC, 1977. **Group:** WMAA Annuals, 1954, 58, 60, 61, 63, 66; MOMA, Twelve Americans, circ., 1956; Sao Paulo, 1957; Carnegie, 1958, 61; WMAA, Business Buys American Art, 1960; II Inter-American Paintings and Prints Biennial, Mexico City. 1960; Seattle World's Fair, 1962; PAFA, 1963; WMAA, Between the Fairs, 1964; WMAA, Art of the U.S. 1670–1966, 1966; Flint/Institute, I Flint Invitational, 1966; Indianapolis/Herron, 1966; SFMA, 1966; MOMA, Two Decades of American Painting, circ., Japan, India, Australia, 1967; U. of Illinois, 1967; Documenta IV, Kassel, 1968. **Collections:** Baltimore/MA; Brandeis U.; Brooklyn Museum; Buffalo/Albright; Chicago/AI; Container Corp. of America; Corcoran; Fort Wayne/AM; Hirshhorn; Kansas City/AI; Kansas City/Nelson; MMA; MOMA; Minneapolis/Institute; National Gallery; New England Merchants National Bank, Boston; New Paltz/SUNY; Norfolk/Chrysler; U. of North Carolina; RISD; Raleigh/NCMA; Seagram Collection; Southampton/Parrish; Stockholm/SFK; Tate; Utica; Victoria and Albert Museum; WMAA. **Bibliography:** Alloway 1; Calas, N. and E.; Dienst 1; Diamonstein; Friedman, ed.; Gaunt; Honisch and Jensen, eds.; **Hunter 5**; Hunter, ed.; Lippard 5; McCurdy ed.; *Metro;* Nordness, ed.; O'Hara 1; *Poets & Painters;* Rodman 1; Russell and Gablik; Sandler 1; Soby 6; Tomkins 2; Warhol and Hackett; Weller. Archives.

ROBINSON, BOARDMAN. b. September 6, 1876, Somerset (Nova Scotia), Canada; **d.** September 6, 1952. Colorado Springs, Colo. To USA, 1894. **Studied:** Academie Colarossi, Academie des Beaux-Arts, and Academie Julian, Paris, 1898–1900; Boston Normal Art School, 1894–97, with E. W. Hamilton. Traveled the world extensively. **Taught:** ASL, 1919–22, 1924–26; Fountain Valley School, Colorado Springs, 1930–44; Colorado Springs Fine Arts Center, 1937–39; Michigan State College, 1945. Illustrated many editions of classics, as well as popular books. Drew cartoons for the *Morning Telegraph,* 1907–10, and the *New York Tribune* (four years). **Commissions:** (murals) Kaufmann Department Store, Pittsburgh, 1928–29; Colorado Springs/FA, 1936; Justice Department Building, Washington, D.C., 1937 (18); US Post Office, Englewood, Colo., 1940. **One-man Exhibitions:** Thumb Box Gallery, NYC, 1916; M. Knoedler & Co., 1919; Weyhe Gallery, 1924; ASL, 1929; Delphic Studios, NYC, 1930; Hudson D. Walker Gallery, NYC, 1940; Chicago/AI, 1942; Forum Gallery, NYC, 1979; NCFA, 1979. **Retrospective:** Colorado Springs/FA, 1943; Dallas/MFA, 1946; Kraushaar Galleries, 1946. **Group:** WMAA; Chicago/AI; Colorado Springs/FA; Cleveland/MA; Los Angeles/County MA; MMA; NAD. **Collections:** AAAL; U. of Arizona; Chicago/AI; Cleveland/MA; Colorado Springs/FA; Cranbrook; Dallas/MFA; Denver/AM; U. of Georgia; Harvard U.; IBM; Los Angeles/County MA; MMA; Minneapolis/Institute; NYPL; NYU; U. of Nebraska; Newark Museum; New Britain; PMA; U. of Vermont; WMAA; Wichita/AM. **Bibliography:** Baur 7, **Biddle 2, 4**; Brown; Bruce and Watson; Cahill and Barr, eds.; Cheney; **Christ-Janer**; Gallatin 2; Genauer; *Index of 20th Century Artists;* Mather 1; Mellquist; Poore; Richardson, E.P.; Rose, B., 1.

ROBUS, HUGO. b. May 10, 1885, Cleveland, Ohio; **d.** January 14, 1964, NYC. **Studied:** Cleveland Institute of

Art, 1904–08; NAD, 1910–11; Academie de la Grande Chaumiere, 1912–14, with Antoine Bourdelle. **Taught:** Myra Carr Art School, ca. 1915–17; Columbia U., summers, 1942, 43, 46, 48, 50, 52, 53, 55, 56; Munson-Williams-Proctor Institute, Utica, N.Y., 1948; Hunter College, 1950–58; Brooklyn Museum School, 1955–56. Changed from painting to sculpture, 1920. Federal A.P.: 1937–39. **Awards:** MMA, Artists for Victory, Second Prize, 1942; PAFA, George D. Widener, Memorial Gold Medal, 1950; PAFA, Alfred G. B. Steel Memorial Prize, 1953; NIAL, Citation and Grant, 1957. **One-man Exhibitions:** (first) Grand Central, NYC, 1946, also 1948; Utica, 1948; Corcoran, 1958; The Forum Gallery, 1963, 66, 74, 79; NCFA, 1979. **Retrospective:** A.F.A./ Ford Foundation, 1961. **Group:** WMAA; PAFA; MMA; Corcoran. **Collections:** Cleveland/MA; Corcoran; Fairleigh Dickinson U.; IBM; MMA; MOMA; Utica; WMAA. **Bibliography:** *Avant-Garde Painting and Sculpture in America 1910–25;* Baur 7; Brumme; Craven, W.; Goodrich and Baur 1; Mendelowitz; Marter, Tarbell, and Wechsler; Pearson 2. Archives.

ROCKLIN, RAYMOND. b. August 18, 1922, Moodus, Conn. **Studied:** MOMA School, 1940; Cooper Union, 1951, with Milton Hebald, John Hovannes, Warren Wheelock; Educational Alliance, NYC, with Abbo Ostrowsky; Temple U., 1942; Cooper Union, BFA, 1977. Traveled Europe, USA. **Taught:** American U., 1956; U. of California, Berkeley, 1959–60; Scarsdale Studio Workshop, 1960– ; Ball State Teachers College, 1964; YMHA, Essex County, N. J., 1971–74. **Member:** Sculptors Guild. **Awards:** Fulbright Fellowship (Italy), 1952; Yaddo Fellowship, 1956. **Address:** 232B Watch Hill Road, Peekskill, NY 10566. **One-man Exhibitions:** (first) Tanager Gallery, NYC, 1956; American U., 1956; Oakland/AM, 1956; U. of California, Berkeley, 1959; Pomona College, 1960; Santa Barbara/

MA, 1960; Dilexi Gallery, San Francisco, 1960; The Bertha Schaefer Gallery, 1960 (two-man); Ball State Teachers College, 1964; Briarcliff College, 1973. **Group:** WMAA, Young America; WMAA, New Talent, 1957; U. of Illinois, 1959; WMAA Annual, 1960; Claude Bernard, Paris, 1960; American Abstract Artists Annuals; U. of Nebraska, 1960. **Collections:** Norfolk/ Chrysler; Skowhegan School; Temple Israel, St. Louis; WMAA. **Bibliography:** Seuphor 3.

ROESCH, KURT. b. September 12, 1905, near Berlin, Germany. **Studied:** Jaeckel School, Berlin, 1924; Academy of Fine Arts, Berlin, 1925–26, with Karl Hofer, and 1928–29, with Hofer and Meid. To USA, 1933. Traveled Europe, USA; resided Paris, Berlin, NYC. **Taught:** New School for Social Research, 1934–36; Sarah Lawrence College, 1934–72; Skowhegan School. **Member:** Artists Equity. **Commissions:** Designed stage sets for Jean Erdman Dance Co. **Awards:** Prize of the League of German Artists, 1931; Medal of the Academy of Fine Arts, Berlin, 1932; MMA, Artists for Victory, Sixth Prize, 1942; First New Hampshire Art Association Annual, J. W. Hill Co. Award, 1937; Century Association Medal, 1969. **Address:** Richards Lane, New Canaan, CT 06840. **One-man Exhibitions:** Berlin Sezession, 1928; Gallery A. Flechtheim, Berlin, 1930; New School for Social Research, 1934; U. of Minnesota, 1936; Buchholz Gallery, NYC, 1939, 41, 43, 45, 46; Curt Valentine Gallery, NYC, 1949, 53; Rose Fried Gallery, NYC, 1958; Katonah Art Gallery, Katonah, N.Y., 1970. **Retrospective:** Currier Gallery, Manchester, N. J., 1955. **Group:** U. of Illinois; Carnegie; Documenta, Kassel; PMA; New Hampshire Art Association Annuals, 1947, 48, 49; MMA; WMAA, 1964. **Collections:** Brandeis U.; Buffalo/Albright; Colby College; Currier; Fort Worth; MMA; MOMA; U. of Minnesota;

NYPL; U. of Nebraska; RAC; Sarah Lawrence College; VMFA. **Bibliography:** Janis, S.; Pousette-Dart, ed.

ROGALSKI, WALTER. b. April 10, 1923, Glen Cove, N.Y. **Studied:** Brooklyn Museum School, 1947–51, with Xavier Gonzalez, Arthur Osver, C. Seide, Gabor Peterdi. US Marine Corps, 1941–42. **Taught:** Pratt Graphic Art Center; Brooklyn Museum School; Pratt Institute. **Member:** SAGA. **Awards:** Brooklyn Museum, **P.P.**, 1951, 52; New Britain, **P.P.**; Northwest Printmakers Annual, **P.P.**; Dallas/MFA, **P.P.**, 1953. **Address:** Pratt Institute, Dept. of Printing, Brooklyn, NY 11205. **One-man Exhibitions:** Korman Gallery, NYC, 1954, 55; Cleveland/MA, 1954. **Group:** U. of Minnesota, 1950; Brooklyn Museum, 1951, 52, 54, 60; Library of Congress, 1951; MOMA, New Talent; Seattle/AM, 1952; Dallas/MFA, 1953; The Print Club of Philadelphia, 1958, 60; Riverside Museum, 1959; The Terrain Gallery, 1961; SAGA, 1961; A.A.A. Gallery, NYC, 1961; Merrick (Long Island) Art Gallery, 1961. **Collections:** Brooklyn Museum; Cleveland/MA; Dallas/MFA; Harvard U.; MOMA; NYPL; New Britain; Seattle/AM; Yale U. **Bibliography: Rogalski.**

ROHM, ROBERT. b. February 6, 1934, Cincinnati, Ohio. **Studied:** Pratt Institute, B. Industrial Design, 1956; Cranbrook Academy of Art (with Bethold Schweitz), MFA, 1960. Traveled USA, England; resided Mexico, 1964; traveled around the world, 1980. **Taught:** Columbus College of Art and Design, 1956–59; Pratt Institute, 1960–65; U. of Rhode Island, 1965–; Stourbridge (Eng.) College of Art, 1974. **Member:** Sculptors Guild. **Awards:** PAFA, Hon. Men., 1959; Columbus, Sculpture Prize, 1957, 59; Guggenheim Foundation Fellowship, 1964; U. of Rhode Island Research Grant-in-Aid, 1965, 66, 69; Cassandra Foundation, 1966; Rhode Island State Council on the

Arts Grant, 1973; National Endowment for the Arts, 1974. **Address:** 26 Lake Street, Wakefield, RI 02879. **Dealers:** OK Harris Works of Art. **One-man Exhibitions:** Columbus (two-man), 1958; Aspen, (Colo.) Art Gallery, 1963; Royal Marks Gallery, 1964; U. of Rhode Island, 1966, 72; U. of Maine (two-man), 1969; Nova Scotia College of Art and Design, Halifax, 1969; Massachusetts College of Art, Boston, 1970; Parker Street 470 Gallery, Boston, 1970, 72; OK Harris Works of Art, NYC, 1970, 72, 73, 76, 77, 80; U. of Rochester, 1971; Hobart and William Smith College, 1973; Boston/MFA (two-man), 1974; Suzette Schochett Gallery, Newport, R.I., 1978; Worcester/AM, 1979. **Group:** PAFA, 1961; Silvermine Guild, 1962; Aspen (Colo.) Art Gallery, 1963; Waitsfield/Bundy, Bundy Sculpture Competition, 1963; WMAA Annual, 1963, 64; Tufts U., 1968; The Pennsylvania State U., 1968; WMAA, 1969; Lincoln, Mass./ De Cordova, 1969; Trenton/State, Soft Art, 1969; WMAA, Anti-Illusion: Procedures/Materials, 1969; Seattle/AM, 557,087, 1969; Indianapolis, 1970; MIT, Six Artists, 1970: ICA, Boston, Art on Paper, 1970; WMAA Annuals, 1970, 73; New Delhi, Second World Triennial, 1971; Harvard U., Recent Abstract Art, 1971; U. of Rochester, N.Y., Drawings and Prints—New York, 1977. **Collections:** Brandeis U.; Columbus; Federal Reserve Bank, NYC; Fontana-Hollywood Corp.; MOMA; Oberlin College; The Pennsylvania State U.; St. Lawrence U.; Sarah Lawrence College; VMFA; Waitsfield/Bundy; Worcester/AM; WMAA; Zurich. **Bibliography:** Monte and Tucker.

RONALD, WILLIAM. b. August 13, 1926, Stratford (Ont.), Canada. **Studied:** Ontario College of Art, 1951, with Jock Macdonald. US citizen, 1963. **Commissions:** National Arts Center, Ottawa, 1969 (mural). Host of Canadian television programs, "The Umbrella," 1966–67; "Theme and Variations," 1968; "As It Happens," 1969; "Free for All,"

1972–74. Founding Member: Painters Eleven; Royal Canadian Academy. **Awards:** Hallmark International Competition, 1952; Canada Foundation Scholarship, 1954; SRGM, Award for Canadian Painting, 1956; The Canadian Council Award, 1977. **Address:** Summer: Box 902, Wellfleet, MA 02667; 392 Brunswick Avenue, Toronto 4 (Ont.) Canada M5R224. **Dealer:** Jerrold Morris Gallery, Toronto. **One-man Exhibitions:** (first) Hart House, U. of Toronto, 1954; Greenwich Gallery, Toronto, 1957; The Kootz Gallery, NYC, 1957–61, 1963; Laing Galleries, Toronto, 1960; Douglass College, 1960; Isaacs Gallery, 1961, 63; Princeton U., 1963; David Mirvish Gallery, 1964, 65; Dunkelman Gallery, Toronto, 1970; Tom Thomson Memorial Gallery, Owen Sound, Ont., 1971; Brandon U., Manitoba, 1972; Robert McLaughlin Gallery, Oshawa, Ont., 1975; Jerrold Morris Gallery, Toronto, 1975, 77, 78, 79; Montreal/Contemporain, 1975; Rodman Hall Arts Centre, St. Catherines, Ont., 1975; Beaverbrook Art Gallery, Fredericton, N.B., 1975; Confederation Centre Art Gallery & Museum, Charlottetown, P.E.I., 1975; Edmonton Art Gallery, Alberta, 1975; Burnaby Art Gallery, 1976; Art Gallery of Windsor, 1976; Gustafssen Gallery, Brampton, Ont., 1976; Brampton Public Library and Art Gallery, Bramalea, Ont., 1976; Dominion Corinth Galleries, Ottawa, 1978. **Retrospective:** Robert McLaughlin Gallery, Oshawa, circ., 1975. **Group:** Smithsonian, 1956; Toronto Gallery, Toronto, Four Young Canadians, 1956; Carnegie, 1958, 61; Brussels World's Fair, 1958; V Sao Paulo Biennial, 1959; WMAA Annual, 1959; U. of Illinois, 1961, 63; Corcoran, 1962. **Collections:** Baltimore/MA; Brandeis U.; Briarcliff College; U. of British Columbia; Brooklyn Museum; Buffalo/Albright; Burnaby Art Gallery, B.C.; The Canada Council; Canadian Industries Ltd.; Carnegie; Chicago/AI; Columbus; U. of Connecticut; Corcoran; Hartford/Wadsworth; Hirshhorn; Hudson River Museum; International Minerals & Chemicals Corp.;

MOMA; Montral/MFA; Notre Dame U.; NYU; Newark Museum; U. of North Carolina; U. of Oklahoma; Ottawa/National; Pasadena/AM; U. of Pennsylvania; Phoenix; Princeton U.; Purchase/SUNY; Queens U.; RISD; Ridgefield/Aldrich; U. of Rochester; Springfield, Mass./MFA; SRGM; Syracuse U.; U. of Texas; The Toronto Dominion Bank, Toronto; Toronto; Trenton/State; U. of Virginia; WGMA; WMAA; Walker; Williams College; Windsor; York U. **Bibliography:** Archives.

ROOD, JOHN. b. February 22, 1906, Athens, Ohio; **d.** March 1974, Minneapolis, Minn. Self-taught in art. Traveled the world extensively. **Taught:** Ohio U., 1945; U. of Minnesota, 1944–68. Published a literary magazine, *Manuscript,* 1933–36. **Member:** Artists Equity (president, 1959–63). **Commissions:** Minneapolis Public Library; Wellesley College; St. Marks Cathedral, Minneapolis; Hamline U. **One-man Exhibitions:** (first) Passedoit Gallery, NYC, 1937, also 1940–45; Colgate U., 1941; Durand-Ruel Gallery, NYC, 1944; Newark Museum, 1944; Minneapolis/Institute, 1945; U. of Minnesota, 1945, 46; Ward Eggleston Gallery, NYC, 1946, 47 (paintings); A.A.A. Gallery, Chicago, 1949; Galleria del Fiori, Milan, 1956; L'Obelisco, Rome, 1956; Weintraub Gallery, 1969. **Retrospective:** U. of Minnesota, 1974. **Group:** WMAA; U. of Minnesota; Walker; Corcoran; Cranbrook. **Collections:** Andover/Phillips; Corcoran; Cranbrook; Minneapolis/Institute; U. of Minnesota; Ohio U.; Walker. **Bibliography:** Brumme; **Rood;** Seuphor 3.

ROSATI, JAMES. b. 1912, Washington, Pa. Violinist with the Pittsburgh Symphony for two years. **Taught:** Cooper Union; Pratt Institute; Yale U., 1960–73; U. of Pennsylvania, 1977–79; Dartmouth College, 1960–73; Federal A.P.: Sculptor. **Commissions:** St.

John's Abbey, Collegeville, Minn. (sculpture). **Awards:** Brandeis U., Creative Arts Award, 1960; Chicago/AI, The Mr. & Mrs. Frank G. Logan Medal and Prize, 1962; Carborundum Major Abrasive Marketing Award, 1963; Guggenheim Foundation Fellowship, 1964; National Council on the Arts Grant, 1968; Design in Steel Award, American Iron and Steel Institute, 1973. **Address:** 252 West 14th Street NYC 10011. **Dealer:** Marlborough Gallery, Inc., NYC. **One-man Exhibitions:** (first) The Peridot Gallery, 1954; Otto Gerson Gallery, NYC, 1959, 62; Dartmouth College, 1963; Colgate U., 1968; Brandeis U., 1969; Buffalo/Albright, 1970; Yale U., 1970; Marlborough Gallery Inc., NYC, 1970, 77. **Group:** Ninth Street Exhibition, NYC, 1951; WMAA Annuals, 1952, 53, 54, 60, 62, 66; Carnegie, 1958, 61, 64; Claude Bernard, Paris, 1960; A.F.A., Contemporary Sculpture, 1960; International Outdoor Sculpture Exhibitions, Otterlo, Holland, 1961; Chicago/AI, 1961, 62; Seattle World's Fair, 1962; WMAA, First Five Years, 1962; Festival of Two Worlds, Spoleto, 1962; Battersea Park, London, International Sculpture Exhibition, 1963; New York World's Fair, 1964–65; Flint/Institute, 1 Flint Invitational, 1966; Colby College, 1967; Museum of Contemporary Crafts, circ., 1967–68; HemisFair, San Antonio, 1968; Grand Rapids, Sculpture of the 60s, 1969; Foundation Maeght, l'Art Vivant Aux Etats Unis, 1979; U. of Nebraska, American Sculpture, 1970; Baltimore/MA, The Partial Figure in Modern Sculpture, 1970; Antwerp, Biennial Middleheim, 1971; Newport, R.I., Monumenta, 1974; U. of Massachusetts, Artist and Fabricator, 1975; Stamford Museum, The American Salon des Refuses, 1976. **Collections:** Atlantic Richfield Oil Co., Los Angeles; Bank of Oklahoma, Tulsa; Buffalo/Albright; Brandeis U.; Carnegie; Ciba-Geigy Corp.; Colby College; Dartmouth College; Davenport/Municipal; Drake U.; Edmonton Art Gallery; Hirshhorn; Honolulu Academy; The Hubert Humphrey Building, Washington,

D.C.; MOMA; National Gallery; Spencer Museum of Art/Lawrence, Kans.; NYU; Newark Museum; Park Hilton Hotel, Seattle; Prudential Insurance Co. of America; Rockefeller University; WMAA; World Trade Center; Yale U. **Bibliography:** Davies; *Monumenta;* Read 3; Selz, J.; Seuphor 3.

ROSENQUIST, JAMES. b. November 29, 1933, Grand Forks, N.D. **Studied:** U. of Minnesota, with Cameron Booth; ASL; U. of Minnesota, AA, 1954. **Commission:** State Capitol, Tallahassee, 1978 (Mural). **Awards:** Torcuato di Tella, Buenos Aires, International Prize, 1965. **Address:** Box 4, ˙Aripeka, FL 33502; 162 Chambers Street, NYC 10007. **Dealer:** Leo Castelli, Inc. **One-man Exhibitions:** (first) Green Gallery, NYC, 1962, also 1964; Dwan Gallery, 1964; Ileana Sonnabend Gallery, Paris, 1964, 65, 68; Galleria d'Arte Contemporaneo, Turin, 1965; Leo Castelli, Inc., 1965, 66, 69, 70, 73, 75, 77, 81; Stockholm/National, 1966; Amsterdam/Stedelijk, 1966, 73; Berne, 1966; Humlebaek/Louisiana, 1966; Staatliche Kunsthalle, Baden-Baden, 1966; Ottawa/National, 1968; Galleria Sperone,

James Reuquist *untitled* 1980

Turin, 1968; MMA, 1968; Galerie Rolf Ricke, 1970; Cologne, 1972; Margo Leavin Gallery, 1972, 74; Chicago/Contemporary, 1972; Courtney Sales Gallery, Dallas, 1973; Jack Glenn Gallery, Corona del Mar, 1973; Portland (Ore.) Center for the Visual Arts, 1973; Max Protetch Gallery, Washington, D.C., 1974; Jared Sable Gallery, Toronto, 1974; Galerie Michael Pabst, Vienna, 1974; Gallery A, Sydney, Australia, 1976; The Berenson Gallery, Bay Harbor Islands, Miami Beach, Fla., 1976; Corcoran & Greenberg Inc., Coral Gables, Fla., 1976; F.H. Mayor Gallery, London, 1976, 78; Paule Anglim Associates, San Francisco, 1976; Ronald Greenberg Gallery, St. Louis, 1976; Sable-Castelli Gallery, Ltd., Toronto, 1977; National Gallery of Victoria, Melbourne, Australia, 1977; Institute of Modern Art, Brisbane, 1977; Ringling, 1979; The Plains Art Museum, Moorhead, Minn., 1979; Multiples, NYC, 1978. **Group:** Hartford/Wadsworth, 1962; Dallas/MFA, 1962; WGMA, The Popular Image, 1962; Chicago/AI, 1962, 66; SRGM, Six Painters and the Object, 1963; Buffalo/Albright, Mixed Media and Pop Art, 1963; ICA, U. of Pennsylvania, The Atmosphere of '64, 1964; Salon du mai, Paris, 1964; Tate, Dunn International, 1964; Amsterdam/Stedelijk, American Pop Art, 1964; New York State Pavilion, New York World's Fair, 1964–65; Worcester/AM, 1965; Palais des Beaux-Arts, Brussels, 1965; Torcuato di Tella, Buenos Aires, 1965; Hamburger Kunstkabinett, 1965; MOMA, Around the Automobile, 1965; Kansas City/Nelson, Sound, Light, Silence, 1966; Flint/Institute, 1 Flint Invitational, 1966; Expo '67, Montreal, 1967; IX Sao Paulo Biennial, 1967; MOMA, The 1960's, 1967; Eindhoven, 1967; Palazzo Grassi, Venice, 1967; WMAA Annual 1967; Documenta IV, Kassel, 1968; Vancouver, 1969; U. of California, Irvine, New York: The Second Breakthrough 1959–1964, 1969; Hayward Gallery, London, Pop Art, 1969; MMA, Prints by Four New York Painters, 1969, New York Painting and Sculpture:

1940–1970, 1969–70; VMFA, American Painting, 1970; Foundation Maeght, 1970; Indiana U., American Scene: 1900–1970, 1970; Buffalo/Albright, Kid Stuff, 1971; Los Angeles/County MA, Art & Technology, 1971; Musee Galleria, Paris, Festival d'Automne, 1973; Yale U., American Art—Third Quarter Century, 1973; WMAA, American Pop Art, 1974; MOMA; Works from Change, 1974; MMA, Contemporary American Prints, 1976; Williamstown/Clark, The Dada/Surrealist Heritage, 1977; Cambridge, Jubilation, 1977; Venice Biennial, 1978; Flint/Institute, Art and the Automobile, 1978; Buffalo/Albright, American Painting of the 1970s, circ., 1978; Scripps College, Black and White Are Colors: Paintings of the 1950s–1970s, 1979. **Collections:** Aachen; Brandeis U.; Buffalo/Albright; Chicago/Contemporary; Dallas/MFA; Hirshhorn; MOMA; Norfolk/Chrysler; Oberlin College; Ottawa/National; Paris/Beaubourg; Pasadena/AM; Stockholm/National; Purchase/SUNY; Toronto; Tate; WMAA. **Bibliography:** Alloway 1; Becker and Vostell; Bihalji-Merin; *Black and White Are Colors;* Honisch and Jensen, eds.; Hulten; Hunter, ed.; Johnson, Ellen H.; Kozloff 3; Lippard 2; *Metro; Report;* Pincus-Witten; Rose, B., 1; Rublowsky; Russell and Gablik; Sandler 1; Tomkins 2; Tomkins and Time-Life Books; Warhol and Hackett; Weller.

ROSENTHAL, BERNARD (TONY). b. August 9, 1914, Highland Park, Ill. **Studied:** U. of Michigan, 1936, BA; Chicago Art Institute School; Cranbrook Academy of Art, with Carl Milles. Corps of Army Engineers, 1942–46. Traveled Mexico, Europe, USA, France. **Taught:** California School of Art, 1947–48; UCLA, 1953. Federal A.P.: U.S. Post Office, Nakomis, Ill. (relief). **Commissions:** Elgin Watch Building, New York World's Fair, 1939; Museum of Science and Industry, Chicago, 1941; General Petroleum Building, Los Angeles, 1949; 260 Beverly

Drive, Beverly Hills, 1950 (bronze reliefs, 3 storeys high); Bullock's Westwood, Los Angeles, 1951; RKO Studios, Hollywood, 1952; UCLA Elementary School, 1952; J. W. Robinson Department Store, Beverly Hills, 1952; Capri Theatre, San Diego, 1954; 1000 Lake Shore Drive, Chicago, 1954 (30-ft. relief); Beverly Hilton Hotel, Beverly Hills, 1955; Temple Emanuel, Beverly Hills, 1955; Century City (Alcoa Development), 1963; U. of Michigan, 1968; CSCS, Fullerton, 1969; NYC Department of Parks for Astor Place, 1967; City of New York, Police Headquarters, 1971; to design and execute a sculpture park in NYC, 1980; Temple Beth-El, Birmingham, Michigan, 1973; Cranbrook, 1980. **Awards:** SFMA, Sculpture Award, 1950; Los Angeles/County MA, **P.P.**, 1950; Los Angeles All-City Show, Sculpture Prize, 1951; Audubon Artists, Sculpture Award, 1953; PAFA, Hon. Men., 1954; Los Angeles/County MA, Sculpture Award, 1957; American Institute of Architects, Southern California Chapter, Honor Award, 1959; Ford Foundation, **P.P.**, 1963; Tamarind Fellowship, 1964; U. of Michigan, Outstanding Achievement Award, 1967; Carborundum Major Abrasive Marketing Award, 1969; American Iron and Steel Instrument, Design in Steel Award, 1975. **Address:** 173 East 73rd Street, NYC 10021. **Dealer:** Knoedler Contemporary Art. **One-man Exhibitions:** (first) Pat Wall Gallery, Monterey, 1947; A.A.A. Gallery, Chicago, 1947; Scripps College, 1948; SFMA, 1950; A.A.A. Gallery, NYC, 1950; Santa Barbara/MA, 1952; Long Beach/MA, 1952; Catherine Viviano Gallery, 1954, 58, 59; Carnegie, 1959; The Kootz Gallery, NYC, 1961, 63, 66; M. Knoedler & Co. 1968, 77; Gertrude Kasle Gallery, 1973; Hammarskjold Sculpture Plaza, NYC, 1977; Federal Plaza, NYC, 1977; Cranbrook, 1980. **Group:** MMA; MOMA; Sao Paulo Biennial; Brussels, World's Fair, 1958; Chicago/AI; PAFA; Sculptors Guild; Audubon Artists; Walker; ICA, Boston; Yale U.; WMAA, 1964, 66, 68; Buffalo/

Albright, 1965; Boston/MFA, 1966; Sculpture in Environment, New York Citywide Exhibition, 1967; HemisFair '68, San Antonio, Tex., 1968; Grand Rapids, 1969; Grand Rapids, Sculpture of the 60s, 1969; Cincinnati/Contemporary, Monumental Art, 1970; Indianapolis, Seven Outside, 1971; U. of Illinois, 1971; Newport, R.I., Monumenta, 1974; Stamford Museum, The American Salon des Refuses, 1976; P.S. 1, NYC, A Great Big Drawing Show, 1979. **Collections:** Antwerp/Middelheim; Arizona State College; Astor Place, NYC; Baltimore/MA; Buffalo/Albright; Calcutta; Carborundum Company; Connecticut College; U. of Illinois; Indianapolis; Indianapolis/Herron; Jerusalem/National; Lincoln, Mass./De Cordova; Long Beach/MA; Los Angeles/County MA; Lytton Savings and Loan Association; MOMA; U. of Michigan; Milwaukee; NCFA; NYU; New School; Newark Museum; Norfolk/Chrysler; Princeton U.; Ridgefield/Aldrich; SRGM; San Diego; Santa Barbara/MA; South Mall, Albany; Springfield, Ill./State; Stony Brook/SUNY; UCLA; Yale U.; WMAA; Xerox Corp. **Bibliography:** Hunter 8; *Monumenta*; Read 3; Rodman 2; Trier 1. Archives.

ROSS, CHARLES. b. December 17, 1937, Philadelphia, Pa. **Studied:** U. of California, AB, 1960, MA, 1962. **Taught:** U. of California, 1962, 65; Cornell U., 1964; U. of Kentucky, Artist-in-Residence, 1965; School of Visual Arts, NYC, 1967, 70–71; Herbert H. Lehman College, Bronx, N. Y., 1968; U. of Utah, 1972–74; MIT, 1977. Codirector and collaborator, Dancers Workshop Company, San Francisco, 1964–66. Films: *Sunlight Dispersion*, 16 mm, 1972: *Arisaig, July 10, 1972*, 16 mm, 1972. **Commissions:** Temple of Porat Yeshivat Joseph, Jerusalem, 1972; GSA, Federal Building, Lincoln, Neb., 1975; U. of Pennsylvania, 1977; Prestonwood Town Center, Dallas, 1978; Dietrich Foundation, Phila., 1978; Lincoln Court Building, Denver, 1980. **Awards:** U. of California, James D. Phelan Traveling

Scholarship, 1962; National Endowment for the Arts, grant, 1976. **Address:** 383 West Broadway, NYC 10012. **Dealer:** Susan Caldwell, Inc., NYC; Fine Arts Services, Los Angeles. **One-man Exhibitions:** (first) Dilexi Gallery, San Francisco, 1961, also 1965, 66, 68; RAC, 1962; Cornell U., 1964; U. of Kentucky, 1965; Dwan Gallery, 1968, 69, 71; Dayton's Gallery 12, Minneapolis, 1968; John Weber Gallery, 1972, 79; The Clocktower, NYC, 1974; Utah, 1975; La Jolla, 1976; Chicago/Contemporary, 1977; John Weber Gallery and Susan Caldwell Inc., 1977; MIT, 1977; John Weber Gallery, NYC, 1979. **Group:** Dance theater; Judson Dance Theater, NYC, A Collaborative Event (with the Judson Dancers), 1963; Musée Cantonal des Beaux-Arts, Lausanne, II Salon International de Galeries Pilotes, 1966; Paris Biennial; Architectural League of New York, 1967; A.F.A., 1967; Finch College, 1967; Ridgefield/Aldrich, 1967; Kansas City/Nelson, The Magic Theatre, 1968; Newark Museum, 1968; Milwaukee, Directions I: Options, circ., 1968; Prospect '68, Dusseldorf, 1968; ICA, U. of Pennsylvania, WMAA Sculpture Annual, 1969; Toronto, New Alchemy: Elements, Systems, Forces, 1969; Dusseldorf/Kunsthalle, Prospect '69, '71, 1969, 71; Finch College, NYC, Projected Art, 1971; U. of Wisconsin, Earth, Air, Fire, Water, 1974; Indianapolis, 1974; Leverkusen, Drawings 3: American Drawings, 1975; U. of Colorado, Locate, Order, Measure, 1975; Philadelphia College of Art, Time, 1977; Museum of Natural History, NYC, Maps: Their Science and Their Art, 1977; Hirshhorn; Probing the Earth, 1977; Worcester, Two Decades of American Printmakers, 1957–1977, 1978; Taft Museum, Galaxies, 1978. **Collections:** U. of California, Berkeley; Indianapolis; Kansas City/Nelson; WMAA. **Bibliography:** Atkinson.

ROSSI, BARBARA. b. 1940, Chicago. **Studied:** Chicago Art Institute School, 1968–70. **Address:** % Dealer. **Dealer:** Phyllis Kind Gallery, Chicago and NYC. **One-man Exhibitions:** Phyllis Kind Gallery, NYC, 1975, 76, 78; Phyllis Kind Gallery, Chicago, 1980. **Group:** Chicago/Contemporary, Don Baum Sez, "Chicago Needs Famous Artists," 1969; ICA, U. of Pennsylvania, Spirit of the Comics, 1969; Chicago/Contemporary, Chicago Imagist Art, 1972; Ottawa/Ontario, What They're Up to in Chicago, 1972; WMAA, American Drawings, 1963–1973, 1973; Sao Paulo, Biennial, 1973; WMAA Biennial, 1975; Chicago Art Institute School, Former Famous Alumni, 1976; Sacramento/Crocker, The Chicago Connection, 1977; U. of Texas, New in the Seventies, 1977; Hirshhorn, Directions, 1979. **Collections:** Baltimore/MA; Chicago/AI; Chicago/Contemporary; Mid-America Club, Chicago; Museum des 20. Jahrhunderts, Vienna. **Bibliography:** *The Chicago Connection; New in the Seventies.*

ROSZAK, THEODORE. b. May 1, 1907, Pozman, Poland. **d.** Sept. 2, 1981, New York City. **Studied:** Columbia U., 1925–26; Chicago Art Institute School, 1922–29, with John W. Norton, Boris Anisfeld; NAD, 1925–26, with C. W. Hawthorne. Traveled Latin America, Europe extensively. **Taught:** Chicago Art Institute School, 1927–29; Design Laboratory, NYC, 1938–40; Sarah Lawrence College, 1940–56; Columbia U., 1970–72; lectured at many museums and universities. Began abstract constructions, 1936, free-form sculpture, 1946. **Member:** Commission of Fine Arts, Washington, D.C. (appointed for 1963–67); Advisory Committee on the Arts, US State Department (appointed for 1963–67); National Council on Art and Government. Federal A.P.: Easel painting. **Member:** New York City Art Commission, 1969–75; NIAL. **Commissions:** Yale & Towne, Inc.; MIT (spire and bell tower); Reynolds Metals Co. (aluminum sculpture memorial); American Embassy, London; Maremont Building, Chicago; New York World's

Theodore Roszak Untitled 1959

Fair, 1964–65; New Public Health Laboratory, NYC (outdoor sculpture), 1968; Lafayette Square, Washington, D.C.; Court of Claims, NYC. **Awards:** World's Fair, Poland, 1929, Silver Medal; Chicago/AI, Joseph N. Eisendrath Prize, 1934; Chicago/AI, The Mr. & Mrs. Frank G. Logan Medal, 1947, 51; I Sao Paulo Biennial, 1951; ICA, London/Tate, International Unknown Political Prisoner Competition, 1953; PAFA, George D. Widener Memorial Gold Medal, 1958; Chicago/AI, Campana Prize, 1961; Ball State Teachers College, Griner Award, 1962; elected to the NIAL; Century Association, Medal for Sculpture. **One-man Exhibitions:** (first) Allerton Galleries, Chicago, 1928; Nicholas Roerich Museum, 1935; Albany/Institute, 1936; Artists' Gallery, NYC, 1941; Julien Levy Galleries, NYC, 1941; Pierre Matisse Gallery, 1957, 62, 74, 76; ICA, Boston, circ., 1959; XXX Venice Biennial, 1960; Century Association, 1971; Harold Ernst Gallery, 1973; Arts Club of Chicago, 1977; Fairweather-Hardin Gallery, Chicago, 1977;

Zabriskie Gallery, NYC, 1978; MIT, 1979. **Retrospective:** WMAA, circ., 1956. **Group:** Chicago/AI Annuals, 1931, 32, 35, 37, 38, 41; WMAA Annuals, 1932–38, 1941, 57, 58, 59, 62, 1964–68; A Century of Progress, Chicago, 1933–34; MOMA, Fourteen Americans, circ., 1946; PAFA, 1946, 64; A.F.A., Tradition and Experiment in Modern Sculpture, circ., 1950–51; Documenta I & II, Kassel, 1955, 59; Brussels World's Fair, 1958; Carnegie, 1958; NIAL, 1958, 59; Tate, 1959; American Painting and Sculpture, Moscow, 1959; Seattle World's Fair, 1962; Silvermine Guild, 1962; Museum des 20. Jahrhunderts, 1962; MOMA, 1963; Cleveland/MA, 1964; MOMA, The New American Painting and Sculpture, 1969. **Collections:** Akron/AI; U. of Arizona; Baltimore/MA; Chicago/AI; Cleveland/MA; U. of Colorado; Hirshhorn; Houston/MFA; U. of Illinois; Industrial Museum, Barcelona; U. of Iowa; MIT; MOMA; U. of Michigan; Newark/Museum; U. of North Carolina; PAFA; SRGM; Purchase/SUNY; St. Joseph/Albrecht; Sao Paulo; Smithsonian; Tate; Trenton/State; WMAA; Walker; West Palm Beach/Norton; Wichita/Ulrich; U. of Wisconsin; Worcester/AM; Yale U. **Bibliography: Arnason 5**; Baur 7; Blesh 1; Brumme; Chipp; Craven, W.; *From Foreign Shores*; Gertz; Giedion-Welcker 1; Goodrich and Baur 1; Hunter 6; Kepes 2; Kuh 1, 3; Langui; Licht, F.; Marter, Tarbell, and Wechsler; McCurdy, ed.; Mendelowitz; *Metro*; Miller, ed., 2; Myers 2; Neumeyer; Read 3; Ritchie 1, 3; Rodman 3; Seuphor 3; Seymour; Trier 1; Weller. Archives.

ROTH, FRANK. b. February 22, 1936, Boston, Mass. **Studied:** Cooper Union, 1954; Hofmann School, 1955. Traveled Europe, Mexico. **Taught:** School of Visual Arts, NYC, 1963–79; State U. of Iowa, 1964; U. of California, Berkeley, 1968, Irvine, 1971–73. **Awards:** Chaloner Prize Foundation Award, 1961; Guggenheim Foundation Fellowship, 1964; Ford Foundation Artist-in-Residence, 1966; IV International Young Artists Exhibit, America-Japan, Tokyo, Minister of Foreign Affairs Award, 1967; National Endowment for the Arts, Grant, 1977. **Address:** 135 Wooster Street, NYC 10012; 120 Acabonac Road, East Hampton, NY 11973. **One-man Exhibitions:** (first) Artists' Gallery, NYC, 1958; Grace Borgenicht Gallery, Inc., 1960, 1962–65; The American Gallery, NYC, 1962; Galerie Anderson-Mayer, Paris, 1964; American Embassy, London, 1965; Hamilton Galleries, London, 1965, 67; U. of Utah, 1967; Martha Jackson Gallery, 1967, 68, 70, 71; Molly Barnes Gallery, Los Angeles, 1968; Galerie Paul Facchetti, 1968; Obelisk Gallery, 1969; Gimpel & Weitzenhoffer Ltd., 1974; OK Harris Works of Art, NYC, 1975. **Group:** Buffalo/Albright, 1958; WMAA Annuals, 1958; WMAA, Young America, 1960; Walker, 60 American Painters, 1960; Corcoran, 1962; Flint/Institute, 1963; Tate, 1965; U. of Illinois, 1965; M. Knoedler & Co., Art across America, circ., 1965–67; IV International Young Artists Exhibit, America-Japan, Tokyo, 1967; RISD, 1967; Kent State U., 1968; A.F.A., 1968; Moore College of Art, Science, and Industry, 1969; Philadelphia Art Alliance, 1969; VMFA, American Painting, 1970; Foundation Maeght, 1970; Indianapolis, 1970; Amherst College, Color Painting, 1972; Lehigh U., Contemporary American Painting, 1972. **Collections:** American Republic Insurance Co,; Baltimore/MA; Bellevue Hospital; Buffalo/Albright; Chase Manhattan Bank; Colonial Bank & Trust Co.; Cornell U.; Des Moines; Hirshhorn; Leicester Education Committee; MOMA; Manufacturers Hanover Trust Co.; McDonald & Company; Mead Corporation; Michigan State U.; NYU; U. of Oklahoma; Pasadena/AM; Prudential Insurance Co. of America; RISD; Ringling; Santa Barbara/MA; Schiedam/Stedelijk; Tate; U. of Utah; WMAA; Walker. **Bibliography:** Gerdts.

ROTHKO, MARK. b. September 25, 1903, Dvinska, Russia; **d.** February 25, 1970, NYC. To USA, 1913. **Studied:** Yale U., 1921–23; ASL, 1925, with Max Weber. Traveled Europe, USA. **Taught:** Center Academy, Brooklyn, N.Y., 1929–52; California School of Fine Arts, summers, 1947, 49; Brooklyn College, 1951–54; U. of Colorado, 1955; Tulane U., 1956. A cofounder of the Expressionist group The Ten, 1935. Cofounder of a school, "Subject of the Artist," with William Baziotes, Robert Motherwell, and Barnett Newman, NYC, 1948. Federal A.P.: 1936–37. **Awards:** Hon. DFA, Yale U., 1969. **One-man Exhibitions:** (first) Contemporary Arts Gallery, NYC, 1933; Portland, Ore./AM, 1933; Art of This Century, NYC, 1945; Santa Barbara/MA, 1946; Betty Parsons Gallery, 1946–51; RISD, 1954; Chicago/AI, 1954; Sidney Janis Gallery, 1955, 58; Houston/MFA, 1957; XXIX Venice Biennial, 1958; Phillips, 1960; MOMA, 1961; Whitechapel Art Gallery, London, 1961; Amsterdam/Stedelijk, 1961; Palais des Beaux-Arts, Brussels, 1962; Kunsthalle, Basel, 1962; Paris/Moderne, 1962, 72; Marlborough Fine Art Ltd., London, 1964, 70; Marlborough Gallery, Inc., NYC, 1970, Zurich, 1971; Berlin/National, 1971; Newport Harbor, 1974; The Pace Gallery, NYC, 1978; Mantova (Italy), 1977. **Retrospective:** SRGM, 1978. **Group:** PAFA, 1940; WMAA, 1945–50; XXIV Venice Biennial, 1948; MOMA, Abstract Painting and Sculpture in America, 1951; MOMA, Fifteen Americans, circ., 1952; 10th Inter-American Conference, Caracas, 1954; 3rd International Contemporary Art Exhibition, New Delhi, 1957; Carnegie, 1958, 61; MOMA, The New American Painting, circ., Europe, 1958–59; Documenta II, Kassel, 1959; Federation of Modern Painters and Sculptors Annuals; Walker, 60 American Painters, 1960; Cleveland/MA, 1966; MOMA, The New American Painting and Sculpture, 1969; MMA, New York Painting and Sculpture; 1940–1970, 1969–70; Venice Biennial, 1974; SRGM, 20th Century American Drawing: Three Avant-Garde Generations, 1976. **Collections:** U. of Arizona; Baltimore/MA; Brooklyn Museum; Buffalo/Albright; Chicago/AI; Dusseldorf/KN-W; Kansas City/Nelson;

MOMA; Paris/Moderne; Phillips; Rio de Janeiro; SFMA; Tate; Utica; Vassar College; WMAA. **Bibliography:** Alloway 4; Ashton 3, 5; Barker 1; Barr 3; Battcock, ed.; Baur 7; Bihalji-Merin; Blesh 1; Calas, N. and E.; Carmean, Rathbone, and Hess; Chipp; Downes, ed.; Eliot; Elsen 2; *From Foreign Shores;* Goodrich and Baur 1; Goossen 1; *The Great Decade;* Greenberg 1; Haftman; Henning; Hess, T.B., 1; Hobbs and Levin; Honisch and Jensen, eds.; Hunter 1, 6; Hunter, ed.; Janis and Blesh 1; Janis, S.; Johnson, Ellen H.; Kozloff 3; Lucie-Smith; Lynton; McChesney; McCoubrey 1; McCurdy, ed.; *Metro;* Motherwell, ed.; O'Doherty; Ponente; Read 2; Restany 2; Richardson, E.P.; Rickey; Ritchie 1; Rodman 1, Rose, B., 1, 4; Rosenblum 2; Rubin 1; Sandler; Sandler 1; Seitz 1; **Selz, P., 4**; Seuphor 1; Soby 5; Tomkins 2; Tuchman, ed.; Waldman 5; Weller. Archives.

ROTTERDAM, PAUL Z. (Werner Paul Zwietnig-Rotterdam) **b.** February 12, 1939, Neustadt, near Vienna. **Studied:** Academy of Fine and Applied Arts, Vienna, 1959–60; U. of Vienna. Resided Paris, Rome, Vienna, 1961; to USA, 1968; to NYC, 1973. **Taught:** Harvard U., 1968; Cooper Union, NYC, 1974. **Awards:** Premio internazionale d'art grafica, Livorno, 1965; Ancona, prize, prints, 1968. **Address:** 115 West Broadway, NYC 10013. **Dealer:** Susan Caldwell Inc., NYC; Nielsen Gallery, Boston; Galerie Maeght, Paris. **One-man Exhibitions:** (first) Numero Gallery, Florence, 1961; Lincoln, Mass./De Cordova, 1970; Kunstverein, Freiburg, 1971; Graz/Johanneum, 1971; Nielsen Gallery, Boston, 1973, 76; Susan Caldwell Inc., NYC, 1975, 76, 78; Musée l'Abbaye, St. Croix, Les Sables d'Olonne, France, 1976; Galerie Parallele, Geneva, 1976; Galerie Maeght, Paris, 1979; Nice/Municipa, 1976; Annely Juda Fine Art, London, 1978; Galerie Charles Kriwin, Brussels, 1980. **Group:** Vienna/Stadt, Oesterreichische Kunst seit 1960. 1963; Biennial, Tokyo/Modern, 1965; Biennial of Young Art-

Paul Rotterdam   *Substance #328   1979*

ists, Paris, 1965; WMAA Biennial, 1975; Hirshhorn, The Golden Door: Immigrant Artists of America, 1876–1976, 1976; Tulane U., Drawing Today in New York, 1976. **Collections:** Graphische Sammlung Albertina; Birmingham Museum of Art, Birmingham, Mich.; Busch-Reisinger Museum; SRGM; Graz Johanneum; Museum der Stadt Leoben, Austria; MOMA; U. of Sydney; Vassar College.

RUBEN, RICHARDS. b. November 29, 1925, Los Angeles, Calif. **Studied:** Chouinard Art Institute, 1944–46; Bradley U., BFA, 1951. US Army, 1942–44. **Taught:** Arts and Crafts Center, Pittsburgh, 1949; Chouinard Art Institute, 1954–61; Pomona College, 1958–59; Pasadena Museum School; UCLA, 1958–62; Cooper Union, 1962–64; Otis Art Institute; NYU, 1963– . **Awards:** International Arts Festival, Newport, R.I., First Prize, 1951; Bradley U., **P.P.,** 1952; Brooklyn Museum, First Prize, 1953, 54; SFMA, Anne Bremer Memorial Prize, 1954; L.C. Tiffany Grant, 1954. **Address:** 85 Mercer Street, NYC 10012. **One-man Exhibitions:** Felix Landau Gallery, 1952, 54; Pasadena/AM, 1954, 55, 61; Oakland/AM, 1957; Paul Kantor Gallery, Beverly Hills, Calif., 1958; Grand Central Moderns, NYC, 1958; Ferus Gallery, Los Angeles, 1960, 61, 63; California Palace, 1961; Poindexter Gallery, 1962, 64, 69; SFMA, 1970; Ericson Gallery, NYC, 1979; Purchase/SUNY, 1977, Cornell U., 1976; Peter Rose Gallery, NYC, 1977. **Group:** Los Angeles/County MA, 1948, 53, 55, 57; Bradley U., 1952; U. of Illinois, 1952, 56; Dallas/MFA, 1953; Corcoran, 1953; PAFA, 1954; SRGM, Younger American Painters, 1954; Sao Paulo, 1955; Carnegie, 1955; Santa Barbara/MA, 1955, 58; Brooklyn Museum, 1957, 59; I Paris Biennial, 1959; WMAA, Fifty California Artists, 1962–63; El Retiro Parquet, Madrid, Arte de America y Espana, 1963; WMAA, 1964. **Collections:** Boston/MFA; Bradley U.; Brooklyn Museum; Los Angeles/County MA; Oakland/AM; Pasadena/AM; Raleigh/NCMA; W. & J. Sloane, Inc.; U. of Southern California; Stanford U.

RUDA, EDWIN. b. May 15, 1922, NYC. **Studied:** ASL, 1940–41; Cornell U., 1947, BS; New School for Social Research, 1948; Columbia U., 1949, MA; School of Painting and Sculpture, Mexico City, 1949–51; U. of Illinois, 1956, MFA. Traveled Mexico, Europe, Southwest Pacific, Australia. US Naval Reserve, 1943–46. **Taught:** School of Visual Arts, NYC; Pratt Institute; U. of Texas; Syracuse U., 1978; Ohio State U., 1978; Tyler School of Art, Philadelphia, 1979. **Awards:** CAPS, 1978. **Address:** 44 Walker Street, NYC 10013. **One-man Exhibitions:** (first) Globe Gallery, NYC, 1961; Feiner Gallery, NYC, 1963; Park Place Gallery, NYC, 1966–67; Paula Cooper Gallery, 1969, 71, 73, 75; Gallery A, Sydney, 1973; Tyler School of Art, Philadelphia, 1974, 79; Max Hutchinson Gallery, NYC, 1978–79; Ohio State U., 1978. **Group:** New York World's Fair, 1965; SRGM, Systemic Painting, 1966; U. of Illinois, 1967, 74; ICA, U. of Pennsylvania, Art in the City, 1967; Newark Museum, Cool Art,

1968; Fort Worth Art Museum, Drawings, 1969; WMAA Annuals, 1969, 73; Indianapolis, 1970, 72; Chicago/AI, 1970; ICA, U. of Pennsylvania, Two Generations of Color Painting, 1970; U. of Texas, Color Forum, 1972; Cincinnati/Contemporary, Options, 73/70, 1973; WMAA Biennial, 1973; U. of Illinois, 1974; Buffalo/Albright, SoHo Scenes, 1975; Baltimore/MA, Drawing Exhibition, 1976. **Collections:** Allentown/AM; Canberra/National; Chase Manhattan Bank; U. of Connecticut; Cornell U.; Great Southwest Industrial Park; Greenville; Indianapolis; U. of North Carolina; South Mall, Albany.

RUSCHA, EDWARD. b. December 16, 1937, Omaha, Neb. **Studied:** Chouinard Art Institute (with Richards Ruben). Traveled Europe. **Taught:** U. of Arizona; U. of North Dakota; UCLA; Vancouver (B.C.) School of Art; SFAI. **Films:** *Premium,* 16 mm, 1970; *Miracle,* 16mm, 1974. **Awards:** National Council on the Arts, 1967; Guggenheim Foundation Fellowship, 1971; Ljubljana Biennial, **P.P.,** 1977. **Address:** 1024¾ N. Western Avenue, Hollywood, CA 90029. **Dealer:** Leo Castelli Inc., NYC. **One-man Exhibitions:** (first) Ferus Gallery, Los Angeles, 1963, also 1964, 65; Alexandre Iolas Gallery, NYC, 1967, 70; Irving Blum Gallery, Los Angeles, 1968, 69; Galerie Rudolf Zwirner, 1968; Pavilion Art Gallery, Newport Beach, Calif. (two-man), 1968; Galerie Heiner Friedrich, Munich, 1970; Nigel Greenwood Ltd., London, 1970; Contract Graphics Associates, Houston, 1971; Janie C. Lee Gallery, Dallas, 1972; Corcoran and Corcoran, Coral Gables, 1972; Minneapolis/Institute, 1972; D.M. Gallery, London, 1972; Leo Castelli, Inc., NYC, 1973, 74, 78; John Berggruen Gallery, 1973; Projections: Ursula Wevers Gallery, Cologne, 1973; Ronald Greenberg Gallery, St. Louis, 1973; ACE Gallery, Los Angeles, 1973, 75, 77; Colgate U., 1973; Yvon Lambert, 1973; Francoise Lambert, Milan, 1973; The

Texas Gallery, 1974; Galerie Rolf Ricke, Cologne, 1975, 78; Jared Sable Gallery, Toronto, 1975; U. of North Dakota, Grand Forks, 1975; Arts Council of Great Britain, circ, 1975; Northern Kentucky State College, Highland Heights, 1975; ACE Gallery, Vancouver, 1976, 78; ICA, Los Angeles, 1976; Hartford/ Wadsworth, 1976; Amsterdam/ Stedelijk, 1976; Dootson Calderhead Gallery, Seattle, 1976; ICA, London, 1976; Sable-Castelli Gallery, Toronto, 1976; U. of Lethbridge, Alberta, 1977; U. of Calgary, 1977; Fort Worth, 1977; Galerie MTL, Brussels, 1978; Rudiger Schottle, Munich, 1978; U. of Redlands, 1978; Auckland, 1978; Getler/Pall, NYC, 1978; Richard Hines Gallery, Seattle, 1979; The Texas Gallery, Houston, 1979; inK, Zurich, 1979; Portland (Ore.) Center for the Visual Arts, 1980. **Retrospective:** Buffalo/Albright, 1976. **Group:** Oklahoma, 1960; Pasadena/ AM, New Paintings of Common Objects, 1962; Oakland/AM, Pop Art USA, 1963; SRGM, American Drawings, 1964; M. Knoedler & Co., Art across America, circ., 1965–67; SRGM, 1965; Seattle/ AM, 1966; IX Sao Paulo Biennial, 1967; V Paris Biennial, 1967; WMAA Annual, 1967; Hayward Gallery, London, Pop Art, 1969; XXXV Venice Biennial, 1970; Hayward Gallery, London, Eleven Los Angeles Artists, 1971; Akron/AI, Four Artists, 1972; Amerika Haus, Berlin, 1973; Yale U., American Drawings: 1970–1973, 1973; Oakland/AM, Cirrus Editions, 1974; WMAA, American Pop Art, 1974; VMFA, Works on Paper, 1974; Malmo, New Media I, 1975; Moore College of Art, Philadelphia, North, East, West, South, and Middle, 1975; Newport Harbor, The Last Time I Saw Ferus, 1976; SFMW, Painting and Sculpture in California: The Modern Era, 1976; The Image and the Myth, Beverly Hills, L.A. Art 2001, 1976; Brooklyn Museum, Twenty Years of American Printmaking, 1976; ICA, Los Angeles, 100+, Current Directions in Southern California Art, 1977; Laguna Gloria Art Museum, Austin, Texas; Joe Goode, Edward Ruscha, Drawings,

1977; Philadelphia College of Art, Time, 1977; Williamstown/Clark, The Dada/ Surrealist Heritage, 1977; MOMA, Bookworks, 1977; Minnesota/AM, American Drawing 1927–1977, circ., 1977; X Biennial de Paris, 1977; Honolulu Academy, California: 3 by 8 Twice, 1978; SFMA, Aesthetics of Graffiti, 1978; MOMA, Mirrors and Windows, 1978; U. of North Carolina, Drawings about Drawing Today, 1979; Buffalo/ Albright; American Painting of the 1970s, circ., 1978–79; Museum Bochum, Words, circ., 1979. **Collections:** Amsterdam/Stedelijk; Auckland; Chicago/AI; Fort Worth; Hirshhorn; Los Angeles/County MA; MOMA; U. of Massachusetts; Mead Paper Co.; Minneapolis/Institute; Pasadena/AM; Pomona College; Reynolda House, Winston-Salem; U. of Rochester; Art Museum of Southern Texas, Corpus Christi; WMAA; Yale U. **Bibliography:** Alloway 1; *Contemporanea;* Finch; Honisch and Jensen, eds.; Hunter, ed.; Lippard 5; Lippard, ed.; Meyer; *The State of California Painting: USA West Coast.*

RUSSELL, MORGAN. b. January 25, 1886, NYC; **d.** 1953, Broomall, Pa. **Studied:** Privately with Robert Henri; ASL (with James E. Fraser). Traveled Europe; resided Paris, 1906–1946. Developed Synchromism, with Stanton Macdonald-Wright, in Paris, 1912. **One-man Exhibitions:** Galerie Bernheim-Jeune, Paris, 1013; Neue Kunstsalon, Munich, 1913; Carrol Gallery, NYC, 1914; Galerie la Licorne, Paris, 1923; Rose Fried Gallery, 1953; Walker, 1954; Washburn Gallery, NYC, 1978, 80. **Group:** Salon d'Automne, Paris, 1910; Salon des Artistes Independants, Paris, 1913; The Armory Show, 1913; Anderson Galleries, NYC, Forum Exhibition, 1916; Dallas/Contemporary, 1960; WMAA, 1963; M. Knoedler & Co., 1965; Marlborough-Gerson Gallery Inc., 1967; U. of New Mexico, Cubism: Its Impact in the USA, 1967; Cornell U., Synchromism and American Color Abstraction, 1978. **Collections:** Evansville; Los Angeles/County MA; MOMA; NYU; Utica; WMAA. **Bibliography:** *Avant Garde Painting & Sculpture in America 1910–25*; Baur 7; Blesh 1; Brown; Brown 2; Canaday; Haftman; Hunter 6; Levin 2; Richardson, E.P.; Rickey; Rose, B., 1; Seuphor 1; Wright 2; Archives.

RUVOLO, FELIX. b. April 28, 1912, NYC. Throughout his youth, family resided in Italy, where he first attended art school (Catania). **Studied:** Chicago Art Institute School. Traveled Europe, Mexico, Canada, USA. **Taught:** Chicago Art Institute School, 1945–47; Mills College, summer, 1948; U. of California, Berkeley, 1950– ; U. of Southern California, 1963. Federal A.P.: Easel painting. **Commissions:** Merchandise Mart, Chicago (murals). **Awards:** SFMA, Anne Bremer Memorial Prize, 1942; Chicago/AI, **P.P.**, 1942, 46, 47; California Palace, Gold Medal, 1946; Milwaukee, Kearney Memorial Prize, 1946; Pepsi-Cola, 1947, 48; Hallmark International Competition, 1949; U. of Illinois, **P.P.**, 1949; SFMA, **P.P.**, 1950; U. of California Institute for Creative Work in the Arts, Travel Fellowship, 1964; and some two dozen others. **Address:** 78 Strathmoor Drive, Berkeley, CA 94705. **One-man Exhibitions:** (first) Durand-Ruel Gallery, NYC, 1946; Mills College, 1947; de Young, 1947, 58; Grand Central Moderns, NYC, 1948; Catherine Viviano Gallery, 1949, 50, 52, 54; Poindexter Gallery, 1957, 58; U. of Southern California, 1963; Galleria Van der Voort, 1970; Jason Avers Gallery, San Francisco, 1971. **Group:** U. of Illinois, 1947, 61; MOMA, Abstract Painting and Sculpture in America, 1951; Buffalo/Albright, Expressionism in American Painting, 1952; Walker, 60 American Painters, 1960; Chicago/AI Annuals; MMA; Corcoran; PAFA; WMAA. **Collections:** Auckland; U. of California; Chicago/AI; Denison U.; Denver/AM; Des Moines; U. of Illinois; Mills College; SFMA; U. of Southern

California; Tulsa/Philbrook; Walter. **Bibliography:** Genauer; Pousette-Dart, ed.; Ritchie 1.

RYMAN, ROBERT. b. May 30, 1930, Nashville, Tenn. **Studied:** Tennessee Polytechnic Institute, 1948–49; George Peabody College, 1949–50. US Army, 1950–52. **Member:** American Abstract Artists. **Awards:** Guggenheim Foundation Grant, 1973. **Address:** 17 West 16th Street, NYC 10003. **Dealers:** Sidney Janis Gallery. **One-man Exhibitions:** Paul Bianchini Gallery, NYC, 1967; Konrad Fischer Gallery, Dusseldorf, 1968, 69, 73; Galerie Heiner Friedrich, Munich, 1968, 69, 73; Fischbach Gallery, 1969, 70, 71; Francoise Lambert, Milan, 1969; Yvon Lambert, 1969; ACE Gallery, Los Angeles, 1969; Current Editions, Seattle, 1971, 72; Dwan Gallery, NYC, 1971; Galerie Heiner Friedrich, Cologne, 1971, 72; John Weber Gallery, NYC, 1972, 73, 74; 75; Galerie Annemarie Verna, Zurich, 1972; Galleria del Cortile, Rome, 1972; Lisson Gallery, 1972; Galleria San Fedele, Milan, 1973; Art & Project, Amsterdam, 1973; Brussels/Beaux-Arts, 1975; Basel, 1975; P.S. #1, L.I.C., 1977; Gian Enzo Sperone, Rome, 1977; Galerie Annemarie Verna, Zurich, 1977; Whitechapel Art Gallery, London, 1977; Galerie Charles Kriwin, Brussels, 1977; inK, Zurich, 1978; Sidney Janis Gallery, NYC, 1979. **Retrospective:** SRGM, 1972. **Group:** New York World's Fair, 1964–65; American Abstract Artists, 1965; SRGM, Systemic Painting, 1966; A.F.A., Rejective Art, 1967; ICA, U. of Pennsylvania, A Romantic Minimalism, 1967; A.F.A., The Square in Painting, 1968; Washington U., Here and Now, 1969; Berne, When Attitudes Become Form, 1969; WMAA, Anti-Illusion: Procedures/Materials, 1969; Seattle/AM, 557,087, 1969; Dusseldorf/Kunsthalle, Prospect '69, 1969; Fort Worth Art Museum, Drawings, 1969; Amsterdam/Stedelijk, Op Losse Schroeven, 1969; Buffalo/Albright, Modular Painting, 1970; Cincinnati/Contemporary, Monu-

Robert Ryman   *Sentinel*   1980

mental Art, 1970; New Delhi, Second
World Triennial, 1971; SRGM, Guggenheim International, 1971; Chicago/
Contemporary, White on White,
1971–72; Chicago/AI, 1972; Documenta

V, Kassel, 1972; Seattle/AM, American
Art: Third Quarter Century, 1973;
MOMA, U. of California, Santa Bar-
bara, 1975; UCLA, Fourteen Abstract
Painters, 1975; Amsterdam/Stedelijk;
Fundamental Painting, 1975; MOMA,
Drawing Now, 1976; Detroit/Institute,
American Artists, A New Decade, 1976;
WMAA, Biennial, 1977; Documenta 6,
Kassel; Sarah Lawrence College, Ferra,
Lichtenstein, Nevelson, Ryman, 1977;
Worcester/AM, Two Decades of Amer-
ican Printmaking, 1957–1977; Chicago/
AI, 1979; AAAL, Childe Hassam Fund
Exhibition, 1979. **Collections:** Amster-
dam/Stedelijk; Dayton/AI; Hartford/
Wadsworth; MOMA; Milwaukee; Min-
neapolis/Institute; WMAA. **Bibliogra-
phy:** *Contemporanea;* Lippard, ed.; Di-
amonstein; *Fundamentele Schilderkunst;*
Gablik; Honisch and Jensen, eds.; Lip-
pard 3; Lippard, ed.; Murdock 1; *Robert
Ryman; When Attitudes Become Form.*
Archives.

SAGE, KAY. b. June 25, 1898, Albany, N.Y.; **d.** January 7, 1963, Woodbury, Conn. Self-taught. Resided Italy, 1900–14, 1919–37, Paris 1937–39. **m.** Yves Tanguy. **One-man Exhibitions:** (first) Galleria Il Milione, Milan, 1936; Pierre Matisse Gallery, 1940; SFMA, 1941; Julien Levy Galleries, NYC, 1944, 47; Catherine Viviano Gallery, 1950, 52, 56, 58; L'Obelisco, Rome, 1953; Galerie Nina Dausset, Paris, 1953; Hartford/ Wadsworth, 1954 (two-man); Mattatuck Historical Society Museum, Waterbury, Conn., 1965; Cornell U., 1977. **Retrospective:** Catherine Viviano Gallery, 1960. **Group:** Salon des Surindependants, Paris, 1938; International Surrealist Exhibition, NYC, 1942; Chicago/ AI, 1945, 47, 51; Carnegie, 1946–50; WMAA, 1946–55; Toledo/MA, 1947, 49; California Palace, 1949, 50; U. of Illinois, 1949, 51; Brussels World's Fair, 1958. **Collections:** California Palace; Chicago/AI; MMA; MOMA; SFMA; WMAA; Wesleyan U. **Bibliography:** Breton 3; Goodrich and Baur 1; Krieger; Pearson 2; Seitz 3; Tomkins and Time-Life Books; Waldberg 3. Archives.

SALEMME, ATTILIO. b. October 18, 1911, Boston, Mass.; **d.** January 24, 1955, NYC. Self-taught. US Marine Corps, 1927–28. Traveled USA. **Commissions** (murals): Moore-McCormack Lines, Inc., 1949; 200 East 66th Street, NYC 1950. **Awards:** Chicago/AI, Flora Mayer Witkowsky Prize, 1949; MMA, **P.P.,** 1950; William and Norma Copley Foundation Grant, 1954. **One-man Exhibitions:** (first) "67" Gallery, NYC, 1945; Carlebach Gallery, NYC, 1947; Passedoit Gallery, NYC, 1948; Saiden-

berg Gallery, 1950; Grace Borgenicht Gallery, Inc., 1953; Duveen-Graham Gallery, NYC, 1955; ICA, Boston, 1958; Walker, 1958; Catherine Viviano Gallery, 1960; Staempfli Gallery, 1963; Terry Dintenfass, Inc., 1974. **Retrospectives:** WMAA, 1960; NCFA, 1978. **Group:** Carnegie; WMAA Annuals; Chicago/AI Annuals; U. of Illinois, 1955. **Collections:** Brooklyn Museum; MMA; MOMA; WMAA. **Bibliography:** Goodrich and Baur 1; Kent, N.; McCurdy, ed.; Newmeyer; Pousette-Dart, ed. Archives.

SAMARAS, LUCAS. b. September 14, 1936, Kastoria, Macedonia, Greece. To USA, 1948; citizen, 1955. **Studied:** Rutgers U., 1955–59, BA; Columbia U. Graduate School, 1959–62. **Taught:** Yale U., 1969; Brooklyn College, 1971–72. **Commissions:** GSA, for Hale Boggs Federal Courthouse, New Orleans, 1976. Traveled Europe, Near East, Japan. Completed film, *Self*, 22 ½ minutes, with Kim Levin, 1969. **Awards:** Woodrow Wilson Fellow, Columbia U. **Address:** 52 West 71st Street, NYC 10023. **Dealer:** The Pace Gallery, NYC. **One-man Exhibitions:** Rutgers U., 1955, 58; Reuben Gallery, NYC, 1959; Green Gallery, NYC, 1961, 64; Dwan Gallery, Los Angeles, 1964; The Pace Gallery, NYC, 1966, 68, 70, 71, 72, 74, 75, 76, 78, 80; Hannover/ Kunstverein, 1970; MOMA, 1975; Makler Gallery, Philadelphia, 1975; California State U., Long Beach, 1975; U. of North Dakota, 1976; Wright State U., 1976; ICA, Boston, 1976; Seattle, 1976; Alberta College, Calgary, 1976; Margo Leavin Gallery, Los Angeles, 1976;

Lucas Samaras   *Reconstruction #71*   1980

Zabriskie Gallery, Paris, 1977; Walker, 1977; F.H. Mayor Gallery, London, 1978; Akron/AI, 1978; Richard Gray Gallery, Chicago, 1979. **Retrospectives:** Chicago/Contemporary, 1971; WMAA, 1972. **Group:** Martha Jackson Gallery, New Media—New Forms, II, 1961; MOMA, The Art of Assemblage, circ., 1961; MOMA, Lettering by Hand, 1962; Corcoran, 1963; Brandeis U., Recent American Drawings, 1964; WMAA Annuals, 1964, 68, 70, Young America, 1965; SRGM, 1965; RISD, 1965, Recent Still Life, 1966; WMAA, Contemporary American Sculpture, Selection I, 1966; MOMA, 1966; Walker, 1966; Los Angeles/County MA, American Sculpture of the Sixties, 1967; Chicago/AI, 1967, 74; ICA, London, The Obsessive Image, 1968; MOMA, Dada, Surrealism and Their Heritage, 1968; Documenta IV & V, Kassel, 1968, 72; Monumenta, Newport, R.I., 1974; Chicago/Century, Bodyworks, 1975; WMAA, 200 Years of American Sculpture, 1976; Documenta 6, Kassel, 1977; Williamstown/Clark, The Dada/Surrealist, Heritage, 1977; ICA, Philadelphia, The Decorative Impulse, 1979. **Collections:** Buffalo/Albright; Canberra/National; Chicago/AI; Chicago/Contemporary; Dallas/MFA; Fort Worth; Hartford/Wadsworth; Harvard U.; Hirshhorn; Indiana U.; Los Angeles/County MA; Miami-Dade; Minneapolis/Institute; MMA; MOMA; New Orleans/Museum; PMA; Phoenix; Princeton U.; Prudential Insurance Co. of America; Ridgefield/Aldrich; RISD; SFMA; Seattle; SRGM; St. Louis/City; U. of St. Thomas (Tex.); WMAA; Walker. **Bibliography: Alloway 2,** 4; Battcock, ed.; Cummings 1; Diamonstein; Davies; *Drawings: The Pluralist Decade;* Finch; Friedman and van der Marck; *From Foreign Shores;* Hansen; *Happening & Fluxus;* Hunter, ed.; Kozloff 3; Lippard 5; *Monumenta;* Pincus-Witten; Rickey; **Samaras;** Seitz 3; Tuchman 1. Archives.

SANDBACK, FRED. b. 1943, Bronxville, N.Y. **Studied:** Williston Academy, 1957–61; Theodor Heuss Gymnasium, Heilbronn, 1961–62; Yale U., 1962–66; Yale School of Art and Architecture, 1966–69. **Awards:** CAPS Grant, 1972. **Address:** 561 Broadway, NYC 10012. **Dealer:** John Weber Gallery. **One-man Exhibitions:** (first) Konrad Fischer Gallery, Dusseldorf, 1968; Galerie Heiner Friedrich, Munich, 1968, 70, 72, 73, 74, 75, 76, 78; Dwan Gallery, NYC, 1969, 70; ACE Gallery, Los Angeles, 1969; Francoise Lambert, Milan, 1970; Yvon Lambert, 1970; Galerie Reckermann, Cologne, 1970, 72; Galerie Annemarie Verna, Zurich, 1971, 72; John Weber Gallery, 1972, 74, 76; Galerie Diogenes, Berlin, 1972; Galerie Nachst St. Stephen, Vienna, 1973; Galerie im Taxispalais, Innsbruck, 1973; Berne, 1973; Galleria Martano Due Torino, 1974; Galeria Milano, Milan, 1974; Galeria Piano Primo, Rome, 1974; Leverkusen, 1974; Galerie Heiner Friedrich, Cologne, 1974; Essen, 1974; Kunstraum, Munich, 1975; Darmstadt/Hessisches, 1975; Galerie d & c Mueller-Roth, Stuttgart, 1975; Galerie Dorothea Loehr, Frankfurt, 1975; Galerie Klein, Bonn, 1975; Brooke Alexander, Inc., NYC, 1976; Galerie Annemarie Verna, Zurich, 1976; Galleria Primo Piano, Rome, 1976; Galleria Durand-Dessert, Paris, 1976; Lisson Gallery, London, 1977; Hester Van Royen Gallery,

London, 1977; Heiner Friedrich Gallery, NYC, 1978; P.S. 1, Long Island City, 1978; MOMA, 1978. **Group:** WMAA, 1968; Dusseldorf/Kunsthalle, Prospect '68, 1968; MOMA, New Media: New Methods, circ., 1969; Berne, When Attitudes Become Form, 1969; ICA, U. of Pennsylvania, Between Object and Environment, 1969; Arnhem, Sonsbeek '71, 1971; Neuer Berliner Kunstverein, Berlin, Multiples, 1974; MOMA, Drawing Now, 1976; Leverkusen, Drawings 3, 1975; Sydney, Biennale, 1976; Chicago/AI, Americans, 1979. **Collections:** Krefeld/Kaiser Wilhelm; MOMA; RISD; WMAA. **Bibliography:** Honisch and Jensen, eds.

SANDER, LUDWIG. b. July 18, 1906, NYC; **d.** July 31, 1975, NYC. **Studied:** NYU, BA; Hofmann School, Munich, two semesters. Traveled Europe, 1927, 1931–32. US Army, World War II. **Taught:** Colorado College, summers, 1951, 52, 53; Bard College, 1956–58. **Member:** NIAL. **Awards:** Hallmark International Competition; Longview Foundation Grant; National Council on the Arts; Guggenheim Foundation Fellowship, 1968; AAAL, Childe Hassam Fund Purchase, 1973. **One-man Exhibitions:** (first) Morton Gallery, NYC, 1930; Hacker Gallery, NYC, 1952; Leo Castelli, Inc., 1959, 61; The Kootz Gallery, NYC, 1962, 64, 65; A. M. Sachs Gallery, 1967, 69; Lawrence Rubin Gallery, NYC, 1970, 72, 73; Waddington Galleries, London, 1972; Knoedler Contemporary Art, 1974, 75, 77, 79; The Berenson Gallery, Bay Harbor Islands, Miami, 1975; Rosa Esman Gallery, NYC, 1977. **Group:** Ninth Street Exhibition, NYC, 1951; SRGM, Abstract Expressionists and Imagists, 1961; Chicago/AI Annuals, 1961, 62; MOMA, Recent American Painting and Sculpture, circ., USA and Canada, 1961–62; WMAA, Geometric Abstraction in America, circ., 1962; Seattle World's Fair, 1962; Los Angeles/County MA, Post Painterly Abstraction, 1964; XXXII Venice Biennial, 1964; Toledo/MA,

Ludwig Sander   Untitled   1970

Form of Color, 1970; WMAA, 1973; SRGM, American Painters through Two Decades, 1973; U. of Miami, Less Is More; The Influence of the Bauhaus on American Art, 1974; Corcoran, 1975. **Collections:** American Republic Insurance Co.; Baltimore/MA; Brandeis U.; Buffalo/Albright; Chase Manhattan Bank; Chicago/AI; Ciba-Geigy Corp; Columbia Broadcasting System; Corcoran; Fort Worth; International Minerals & Chemicals Corp.; MIT; MMA; Ridgefield/Aldrich; SFMA; SRGM; U. of Texas; Union Carbide Corp.; Uris Building Corp.; WMAA; Walker. **Bibliography:** MacAgy 2; Weller. Archives.

SANDOL, MAYNARD. b. 1930, Newark, N.J. **Studied:** Newark State Teachers College, 1952. Traveled Europe. **Taught:** Hackettstown (N.J.) High School, 1964– ; Fairleigh Dickinson U., 1965–68. **Address:** Bunn Street, Box 364, R.R. 2, Clifton, NJ 07830. **One-man Exhibitions:** Suttman-Riley Gallery, NYC, 1958; Artists' Gallery, NYC, 1959; Castellane, NYC, 1960, 63; Castellane, Provincetown, 1962, 63; Athena Gallery, New Haven, 1963; Chapman Kelly

Gallery, 1964; The Peridot Gallery, 1967, 68; Washburn Gallery Inc., 1971. **Group:** Newark Museum; Hartford/Wadsworth; MOMA; Corcoran; New York World's Fair, 1964–65; Trenton/State. **Collections:** Brandeis U.; Hartford/Wadsworth; Hirshhorn; Newark Museum; Princeton U. **Bibliography:** Gerdts.

SARET, ALAN. b. December 25, 1944, NYC. **Studied:** Cornell U., 1961–66, B. Arch; Hunter College, 1967–68. Traveled Europe, Mexico, North Africa; resided in India, 1971–73. **Taught:** U. of California, Irvine, 1979. **Awards:** Guggenheim Foundation Fellowship, 1969; National Endowment for the Arts, grant, 1975; CAPS, award, 1976. **Address:** 54 Leonard Street, NYC 10013. **Dealer:** Charles Cowles Gallery, NYC; Weinberg Gallery, San Francisco. **One-man Exhibitions:** Bykert Gallery, 1968, 70; The Clocktower, NYC, 1973; Seattle/AM, 1977, and/or, Seattle, 1977; U. of California, Berkeley, 1978; SITE, San Francisco, 1979; Weinberg Gallery, San

Francisco, 1979; Charles Cowles Gallery, NYC, 1980. **Group:** WMAA, 1968; Oberlin College, 1968; U. of North Carolina, 1969; Amsterdam/Stedelijk, Op Losse Schroeven, 1969; Berne, When Attitudes Become Form, 1969; MOMA, New Media; New Methods, circ., 1969; New Delhi, Second World Triennial, 1971; Akademie der Kunst, Berlin, SoHo, 1976; U. of Georgia, Open to New Ideas, 1977; Venice Biennial, 1980; ICA, Boston, Drawing/Structures, 1980; Wave Hill, NYC, Temporary Structures, 1980. **Collections:** Art Museum of South Texas; Chicago/Contemporary; Dallas/MFA; Detroit/Institute; U. of Georgia; Los Angeles/County MA; MOMA; SFMA; Society of the Four Arts; Toronto; WMAA. **Bibliography:** *Drawings: The Pluralist Decade;* Johnson, Ellen H.; *When Attitudes Become Form.*

SARKISIAN, PAUL. b. 1928, Chicago, Ill. **Studied:** Chicago Art Institute School, 1945–48; Otis Art Institute, Los Angeles, 1953–54; Mexico City College, 1955–56. **Taught:** Pasadena/AM,

Paul Sarkisian   Untitled #3   1980

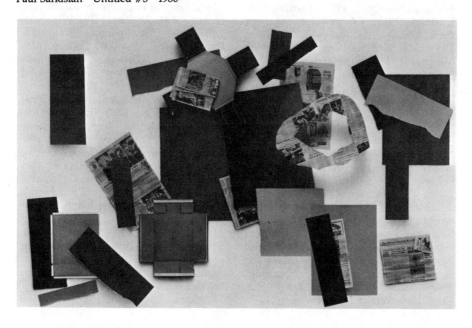

1965–69; U. of Southern California, Los Angeles, 1969; U. of California, Berkeley, 1970; U. of Oregon, 1971; U. of Southern Florida, 1972. **Address:** Cerrillos, NM 87010. **Dealer:** Nancy Hoffman Gallery, NYC. **One-man Exhibitions:** Nova Gallery, Boston, 1958; Aura Gallery, Pasadena, 1962; La Jolla, 1963; Pasadena/AM, 1968; Corcoran, 1970; Michael Walls Gallery, San Francisco, 1970; Santa Barbara/MA, 1970; Chicago/Contemporary, 1972; Michael Walls Gallery, Los Angeles, 1973; Houston/Contemporary, 1977; Nancy Hoffman Gallery, NYC, 1978; Arts Club, Chicago, 1979. **Group:** Pasadena/AM, Annual, 1960; Pasadena/AM, 100 California Artists, 1963; Los Angeles/County MA, Late Fifties at the Ferus, 1968; WMAA Annual, 1969; Los Angeles Municipal Art Gallery, Separate Realities, 1973; Expo '74, Spokane, 1974; Chicago/AI, 71st American Exhibition, 1974; Corcoran Biennial, 1975; Indianapolis, 1976; SFMA, Painting and Sculpture in California: The Modern Era, 1976; Chicago/AI, Visions, 1976; Jacksonville/AM, New Realism, 1977; Zurich, Painting in the Age of Photography, 1977; Canberra/National, Illusions of Reality, 1977; Denver/AM, Biennial, 1979. **Collections:** Aachen; Albuquerque; Corcoran; Des Moines; U. of Georgia; Hirshhorn; Indianapolis; Milwaukee; Minneapolis/Institute; U. of New Mexico; Oakland/AM; Pasadena/AM; Roswell; Santa Barbara/MA; Santa Fe. **Bibliography:** Arthur 1.

SATO, TADASHI. b. February 6, 1923, Maui, Hawaii. **Studied:** Honolulu Academy School; Brooklyn Museum School; Pratt Institute, with Stuart Davis, John Ferren, Ralston Crawford. Traveled USA, Japan, and around the world. **Member:** Hawaii Painters and Sculptors League; Lahaina Art Society (Hawaii); Honolulu Academy; Hui Noeau Association (Hawaii). **Awards:** Brooklyn Museum School Scholarship, 1948; Dallas/MFA, Hon. Men., 1953; John Hay Whitney Fellowship, 1954;

Honolulu Community Foundation Scholarship, 1955; Albert Kapp Award, 1958. **Address:** P.O. Box 476, Lahaina, Honolulu, HI 96761. **One-man Exhibitions:** Gima's Art Gallery, Honolulu, 1950; Library of Hawaii, Honolulu, 1950; 442nd Infantry Memorial Hall, Honolulu, 1950, 52; Gallery 75; NYC, 1955; The Gallery, Honolulu, 1956; The Willard Gallery, 1958, 59, 61; McRoberts & Tunnard Gallery, London, 1961. **Retrospective:** The Willard Gallery, 1969. **Group:** U. of Nebraska, 1954; SRGM, 1954; SFMA, 1957; Silvermine Guild, 1958. **Collections:** U. of Arizona; Ball State U.; Buffalo/Albright; Fort Worth; Honolulu Academy; Omaha/Joslyn; SRGM; WMAA. **Bibliography:** Read 4.

SAUL, PETER. b. August 16, 1934, San Francisco, Calif. **Studied:** Stanford U.; California School of Fine Arts, 1950–52; Washington U., with Fred Conway, 1952–56, BFA. Traveled Europe. Resided Holland, 1956–58; Paris, 1958–62; Rome, 1962–64. **Awards:** *Art in America* (magazine), New Talent, 1962; William and Noma Copley Foundation Grant, 1962; National Endowment for the Arts, Grant, 1980. **Address:** 393 Whippoorwill Road, Chappaqua, NY 10514. **Dealer:** Allan Frumkin Gallery, NYC and Chicago. **One-man Exhibitions:** Allan Frumkin Gallery, Chicago, 1961, 63, 64, 66, 69, 72, NYC, 1962–64, 66, 68, 69, 71, 73, 75, 77; Galerie Breteau, Paris, 1962, 63, 64, 67; La Tartaruga, Rome, 1963; Rolf Nelson Gallery, Los Angeles, 1963; Notizie Gallery, Turin, 1964; Galerie Anne Abels, Cologne, 1965; Contemporary Gallery, Kansas City, 1967; Palos Verdes Estates, Calif., 1967; Wanamaker Gallery, Philadelphia, 1967; San Francisco Art Institute, 1968; Reed College, 1968; California College of Arts and Crafts, 1968; Darthea Speyer Gallery, 1969, 72; Musée d'Art et d'Industrie, Paris, 1971; California State U., Sacramento, 1973. **Group:** Salon des Jeunes Peintres, Paris, 1959, 60; Dayton/AI, International Selection,

1961; U. of Colorado, 1962; Chicago/AI, 1962, 63, 64; SFMA, Directions—Painting U.S.A., 1963; U. of Michigan, 1963, 65; Musée Cantonal des Beaux-Arts, Lausanne, I Salon International de Galeries Pilotes, 1963; Abbey Saint-Pierre, Ghent, Forum, 1963; Brandeis U., Recent American Drawings, 1964; The Hague, New Realism, 1964; Des Moines, 1965; Indianapolis/Herron, 1966; U. of Kentucky, 1966; Carnegie, 1967; MOMA, circ., 1968; U. of Oklahoma, 1968; U. of Illinois, 1969; WMAA, Human Concern/Personal Torment, 1969; Corcoran, 1971; Chicago/AI, 1972; Paris/Beaubourg, Paris–New York, 1977; WMAA, Art about Art, 1978. **Collections:** U. of California, Berkeley; Chicago/AI; U. of Illinois; MOMA; U. of Massachusetts; Oberlin College; WMAA. **Bibliography:** Lucie-Smith.

SAUNDERS, RAYMOND. b. October 28, 1934, Homestead, Pa. **Studied:** U. of Pennsylvania, 1954–57; Barnes Foundation, 1953–55; PAFA, 1953–57; Carnegie Institute of Technology, 1959–60, BFA; California College of Arts and Crafts, 1960–61, MFA. Traveled Mexico, Europe, USA. **Taught:** RISD; California State U., Hayward, 1968–. **Awards:** PAFA, Cresson Fellowship, 1956; AAAL Grant, 1963; Eakins Prize; Ford Foundation, **P.P.**, 1964; Prix de Rome, 1964, 65; Guggenheim Foundation Fellowship, 1976; National Endowment for the Arts, grant, 1977. **Address:** 6007 Rock Ridge Boulevard, Oakland, CA 94618. **Dealer:** Terry Dintenfass, Inc. **One-man Exhibitions:** (first) Pittsburgh Playhouse Gallery, 1953, also 1955; Terry Dintenfass, Inc., 1962, 64, 66–69, 71, 73, 75; Dartmouth College, 1969; Simpson College, Indianola, Iowa, 1969; Lehigh U., 1970; Miami-Dade, 1971; Spelman College, 1972; RISD, 1972; Carleton College, 1974; Peale House, Philadelphia (two-man), 1974; U. of California, Berkeley, 1975; U. of California, La Jolla, 1979; Baum/Silverman Gallery, Los Angeles,

1979; Stephen Wirtz Gallery, San Francisco, 1970; Los Angeles Municipal Art Gallery, 1980; Santa Clara/Triton, 1980. **Group:** PAFA Annuals, 1962–67; SFMA Annuals; New School for Social Research; WMAA, 1971, Annuals, 72, 73; NAD; UCLA, The Negro in American Art, 1966; A.F.A., 1966, 67; Dartmouth College, 1968; 30 Contemporary Black Artists, circ., 1968–69; Westmoreland County/MA, 1969; Boston/MFA, Black Artists: New York and Boston, 1970; Oakland/AM, Oakland Artists, 1974; VMFA, 1974; Cranbrook, Drawings by Contemporary American Artists, 1975; Skidmore College, Contemporary Drawings, 1975; Afro-American Art Pavilion, Expo 74, Spokane, 1974; Oakland/AM, 1979. **Collections:** Allentown/AM; Andover/Phillips; California College of Arts and Crafts; U. of California, Berkeley; Dartmouth College; Fisk U.; Howard U.; Miami-Dade Community College; MOMA; NIAL; Oakland/AM; PAFA; St. Louis/City; U. of Texas; Tougaloo College; WMAA; U. of Wisconsin.

SAVELLI, ANGELO. b. October 30, 1911, Pizzo Catanzaro, Italy. **Studied:** Liceo Artistico, Rome, 1930–32; Academy of Fine Arts, Rome, with Ferruccio Ferrazzi, Diploma di Decorazione, 1932–36. To USA, 1954. Traveled Europe, USA. A cofounder of The Art Club, Rome, with Gino Severini, Enrico Pramolini, Fazzini, and others, 1944. **Taught:** Collegio Nazionale, Rome, 1939–40; Liceo Artistico, Rome, 1940–43, 1948–54; Scarsdale Art Workshop, 1957–61; New School for Social Research, 1959–64; Positano (Italy) Art Workshop, 1960–62; U. of Pennsylvania, 1960–69, 76; Columbia U., 1966; Hunter College, 1968; U. of Minnesota, 1974; Cornell U., 1974; PAFA, 1975; U. of Arkansas, 1975; U. of Texas, Arlington, 1978, 79. **Member:** Artists Equity. **Commissions:** Sora, Italy (church facade, fresco); F.A.U., Rome (mural); Italian Line (paintings for SS *Leonardo da Vinci* and SS *Michelangelo*);

Lincoln Plaza, Syracuse, N.Y.; Audubon Art Center, New Haven, Conn. **Awards:** Fellowship from the Italian Ministry of Education, 1948; Bergamo, First Prize, 1941, 42; Battistoni, First Prize, 1958; XXXII Venice Biennial, 1964, Grand Prize for Graphics; Potsdam/SUNY, **P.P.**, 1965; Vancouver, **P.P.**, 1968; Tiffany Grant, 1976; Guggenheim Foundation Fellowship. **Address:** 22 Cornelia Street, NYC 10014. **Dealer:** Max Hutchinson Gallery. **One-man Exhibitions:** (first) Galleria Roma, Rome, 1941; La Spiga, Milan, 1942; Galleria Ritrove, Rome, 1943; Galleria San Marco, Rome, 1944, 51; Galleria Cronache, Bologna, Italy, 1946; Oblo Capri, 1946; Galleria d'Arte del Naviglio, Milan, 1947, 54, 61; Galleria Sandri, Venice, 1947; Centre d'Art Italien, Paris, 1952; Numero Galleria d'Arte, Florence, Italy, 1953; The Contemporaries, NYC, 1955; D'Amecourt Gallery, Washington, D.C., 1956; Leo Castelli, Inc., 1958; Galleria del Cavallino, Venice, 1958; Galleria Selecta, Rome, 1959; U. of Minnesota, 1960, 74; Peter H. Deitsch Gallery, 1962; D'Arcy Gallery, NYC, 1963; Philadelphia Art Alliance, 1963; XXXII Venice Biennial, 1964; Eastern Illinois U., 1964; Wellfleet Art Gallery, 1964; Contemporary Prints and Drawings, Chicago, 1966; Henri Gallery, 1969; Peale House, Philadelphia, 1969; Syracuse/Everson, 1972; Stout State U., Menomonie, Wisc., 1973; U. of Minnesota, Duluth, 1973; The Pennsylvania State U., 1975, 76; Max Hutchinson Gallery, NYC, 1978; Sculpture Now, NYC, 1978; Parsons-Dreyfus Gallery, NYC, 1978. **Retrospective:** Catanzaro, Italy, 1954. **Group:** Rome National Art Quadrennial, 1943–; Venice Biennial, 1948–; Rose Fried Gallery, International Collage Exhibition, 1956; Hartford/Wadsworth, Graphics, 1956; A.F.A., Collage in America, circ., 1957–58; Library of Congress, 1959; Brooklyn Museum, 1962, 63; Gallery of Modern Art, Ljubljana, Yugoslavia; A.F.A., Moods of Light, circ., 1963–64; Sidney Janis Gallery, 1964; WMAA Annuals, 1966,

67; PAFA Annual, 1963; Brooklyn Museum, 1968; Corcoran Biennial, 1969; Salon du Mai, Paris, 1969; Madrid/Nacional, II Biennial, 1969; Corcoran, 1969; Chicago/Contemporary,   White on White, 1971–72; Festival of Two Worlds, Charleston, N.C., 1978; Italian Cultural Institute, NYC, 1979. **Collections:** Brooklyn Museum; Chase Manhattan Bank; Cincinnati/AM; Corcoran; Eliat; Helsinki; High Museum; Kalamazoo/Institute; Library of Congress; MOMA; U. of Minnesota; National Gallery; NCFA; NYPL; Norfolk/Chrysler; PMA; U. of Pennsylvania; Phoenix; Rome/Nazionale;   Syracuse/Everson; Turin/Civico; Vancouver; Victoria and Albert Museum.

SCARPITTA, SALVATORE. b. 1919, NYC. To Italy to study, 1936; returned to NYC, 1959. Traveled Italy, Switzerland. **Taught:** Maryland Institute, 1965–. **Address:** 307 East 84th Street, NYC 10028. **Dealer:** Leo Castelli Inc. **One-man Exhibitions:** Gaetano Chiurazzi, Rome, 1949; Galleria II Pincio, Rome, 1951; La Tartaruga, Rome, 1955, 57, 58, 76; Galleria d'Arte del Naviglio, Milan, 1956, 58; Leo Castelli Inc., 1959, 60, 63, 65, 75, 80; Leo Castelli Warehouse, 1969; Dwan Gallery, NYC, 1961; Galerie Schmela, 1963; Galleria dell'Ariete,   1963;   Brussels/Royaux, 1964; Galleria Notizie, Turin, 1972; Galerie Jacques Benador, Geneva, 1973; L'Uomo e l'Arte, Milan, 1974; Robinson Galleries, Houston, 1978; Portland (Ore.) Center for the Visual Arts, 1978. **Retrospective:** Houston/Contemporary, 1977. **Group:** Galleria Roma, Rome, 1944; Rome National Art Quadrennial, 1948; XXVI, XXVIII, and XXIX Venice Biennials, 1952, 56, 58; Columbus, 1960; Martha Jackson Gallery, New Media—New Forms I & II, 1960, 61; Houston/MFA, Ways and Means, 1961; Corcoran, 1963; Musée Cantonal des Beaux-Arts, Lausanne, I Salon International de Galeries Pilotes, 1963; Maryland Institute, 1964; Chicago/AI, 1964; U. of Illinois, 1965; ICA, U. of Pennsylvania, Highway, 1970; Hofstra U., Art around the Automobile, 1971; Rome, III Quadrennial, 1972; The Fine Arts Building, NYC, Personal Mythologies, 1976; Vassar College, Contemporary Primitivism, 1976; Queens Museum, Private Myths, 1978; The New Museum, NYC, Sustained Vision, 1979. **Collections:** Amsterdam/Stedelijk; Buffalo/Albright; Los Angeles/County MA; MOMA; Tel Aviv. **Bibliography:** Janis and Blesh 1; *Metro;* Weller. Archives.

SCHANKER, LOUIS. b. July 20, 1903, NYC; **d.** May 7, 1981, NYC. **Studied:** Educational Alliance, NYC; Cooper Union; ASL. Traveled Europe, Africa, USA. **Taught:** New School for Social Research, 1940–60; Bard College, 1949–64; U. of Colorado, 1953; U. of Minnesota, 1959. Federal A.P.: 1940–41. **Member:** Sculptors Guild; Federation of Modern Painters and Sculptors. **One-man Exhibitions:** (first) Contemporary Arts Gallery, NYC, 1933; Kleemann Gallery, NYC; New School for Social Research, 1938; Artists' Gallery, NYC, 1939; Brooklyn Museum, 1943; The Willard Gallery, 1944, 45, 56, 48, 50; Mortimer Brandt, NYC, 1945; Hacker Gallery, NYC, 1950; Grace Borgenicht Gallery, Inc., 1952, 55; Dorsky Gallery; The New Bertha Schaefer Gallery, 1973. **Retrospective:** Walker, 1959. **Group:** WMAA; Brooklyn Museum; MMA; Utica; Chicago/AI; U. of Michigan. **Collections:** Brooklyn Museum; Chicago/AI; Hirshhorn; MMA; U. of Michigan; NYPL; Newark Museum; PMA; Phillips; Toledo/MA; Utica, Wesleyan U. **Bibliography:** American Artists Congress, Inc.; Baur 7; Cheney; Hayter 1; Pousette-Dart, ed. Archives.

SCHAPIRO, MIRIAM. b. 1923, Toronto, Canada. **Studied:** State U. of Iowa, 1945, BA; 1946, MA; 1949. **Taught:** State U. of Iowa, 1946–49; Scarsdale School of Art, 1965–66; Connecticut College for Women, 1966; Parsons School of Design, NYC, 1966–67;

U. of California, 1967–69; California Institute of the Arts, Valencia, 1971–75; Nova Scotia College of Art and Design, Halifax, 1974; Bryn Mawr College, 1977; Tyler School of Art, Philadelphia, 1977–78; Amherst College, 1978. **Awards:** Tamarind Fellowship, 1963; National Endowment for the Arts, grant, 1976. **Member:** Board of Directors, College Art Association and Los Angeles Institute of Contemporary Art; ICA, Los Angeles, founding member, 1974–75; CAAA, board of directors, 1974–78; Women's Caucus for Art, Advisory Board 1974– ; Heresies Collective, founding member, 1976–; Feminist Art Institute, founding member, 1977; **m.** Paul Brach. **Address:** 393 W. Broadway, NYC 10012; Montauk Highway, East Hampton, NY 11037. **Dealers:** Lerner Heller Gallery, NYC; Barbara Gladstone Gallery, NYC. **One-man Exhibitions:** U. of Missouri, 1950; Illinois Wesleyan U., 1951; Andre Emmerich Gallery, NYC, 1958, 61, 63, 67, 69, 71, 73, 76, 77; Skidmore College, 1964; Franklin Siden Gallery, Detroit, 1965; Vassar College, 1973; Cynthia Comsky Gallery, 1974, 75; Douglass College Library, 1975; Benson Gallery, 1975; Mills College, 1975; College of St. Catherine, St. Paul, Minn., 1976; U. of Wisconsin, La Crosse, 1976; A.R.C. Gallery, Chicago, 1976; Douglas Drake Gallery, Kansas City, Kansas, 1976; Douglass College, New Brunswick, N.J., 1976; Oberlin College, 1977; State U. of Oregon, Corvallis, 1977; Reed College, 1978; Lerner Heller Gallery, NYC, 1979; Gladstone/Villani Gallery, NYC, 1979. **Retrospectives:** New London, 1966; Newport Harbor and La Jolla, Paul Brach and Miriam Schapiro, 1969; U. of California, San Diego, 1975. **Group:** MOMA, New Talent; U. of Nottingham (England), Abstract Impressionists, 1958; International Biennial Exhibition of Paintings, Tokyo; Carnegie, 1959; WMAA, 1959; MOMA, Abstract American Drawings and Watercolors, circ., Latin America, 1961–63; Jewish Museum, Toward a New Abstraction, 1963; SFMA, Directions—Painting

U.S.A., 1963; Walker; Denver/AM; Brooklyn Museum; Chicago/AI; Brandeis U., New Directions in American Painting, 1963; PAFA 1963, 64; Dayton/ AI, 1967; Fort Worth Art Museum, Drawings, 1969; Jewish Museum, Superlimited: Books, Boxes, and Things, 1969; Long Beach/MA, Invisible/Visible, Twenty-one Artists, 1972; Scripps College, California Women Artists, 1972; Womanhouse, Los Angeles, 1972; U. of North Dakota, 14 Women, 1973; Womanspace, Los Angeles, Female Sexuality/Female Identity, 1973; PMA/ Museum of the Philadelphia Civic Center, Focus, 1974; Newport Harbor, The Audacious Years, 1974; Cerritos College Art Gallery, Norwalk, Calif., 16 Los Angeles Women Artists, 1974; Bronx Museum of Art, The Year of the Woman, 1975; San Antonio/McNay, American Artists, '76, 1976; Guild Hall, Artists of East Hampton, 1850–1975, 1976; West Palm Beach/Norton, Hi Mom, What's New?, 1977; The American Foundation for the Arts, Miami, Patterning and Decoration, 1977; Brussels/Beaux Arts, Pattern and Decoration, 1979. **Collections:** Albion College; Amstar Corp.; Avco Corp.; Bank of America; Best Products Co., Ashland, Va.; Hirshhorn; Illinois Wesleyan U.; IBM, Atlanta; U. of Iowa; La Jolla; Levin Townsend Computer Corp.; MOMA; Mills College; Minneapolis/Institute; Mulvane; NYU; Newport Harbor; Oberlin College; St. Louis/City; Security Pacific Bank; Stanford U.; Stephens College; Tougaloo College; United Nations; Williams College; WMA; Worcester/AM. **Bibliography:** *Art: A Woman's Sensibility*; Lippard 3; Lucie-Smith; **Miriam Schapiro.**

SCHLEMOWITZ, ABRAM. b. July 19, 1911, NYC. **Studied:** Beaux-Arts Institute of Design, NYC, 1928–33; ASL, 1934; NAD, 1935–39. **Taught:** Contemporary Art Center, YMHA, NYC, 1936–39; Pratt Institute, 1962–63; U. of California, Berkeley, 1963–64; U. of Kentucky, 1965; U. of Wisconsin, Madi-

son, 1965–67; City U. of New York, 1969–76; NYU, 1978–79; Sculpture Center, NYC, 1980; Organizing chairman of the New Sculpture Group, 1957–58. **Awards:** Guggenheim Foundation Fellowship, 1963. **Address:** 139 West 22nd Street, NYC 10011. **One-man Exhibitions:** The Howard Wise Gallery, NYC, 1961, 62, 67; City U. of New York, Kingsborough College, Brooklyn, 1977. **Group:** Betty Parsons Gallery, American Abstract Artists, 1959; Claude Bernard, Paris, 1960; The Stable Gallery, Sculpture Annuals, 1960, 61; Museum of Contemporary Crafts, Collaboration: Artist and Architect, 1962; Riverside Museum, 12 New York Sculptors, 1962; New School for Social Research, Humanists of the 60's, 1963; MOMA, Art in Embassies, circ. internationally, 1963–64; Tyler School, Temple U., Rome, Artists of 3 Continents, 1968; Landmark Gallery, NYC, 118 Artists, 1975, 76. **Collections:** U. of California, Berkeley; City U. of New York, Kingsborough College; Norfolk/Chrysler.

SCHMIDT, JULIUS. b. 1932, Stamford, Conn. **Studied:** Oklahoma A. and M. College, 1950–51; Cranbrook Academy of Art, 1952, BFA, 1955, MFA; Zadkine School of Sculpture, Paris, 1953; Academy of Fine Arts, Florence, Italy. Traveled Europe, USA, Mexico, Mediterranean. **Taught:** Silvermine Guild School of Art, summers, 1953, 54; Cleveland Institute of Art, 1957; Kansas City/AI, 1954–59; RISD, 1959–60; U. of California, Berkeley, 1961–62; Cranbrook, 1962–70; U. of Iowa, 1970– . **Awards:** Mid-American Biennial, First Prize and **P.P.;** Guggenheim Foundation Fellowship, 1963. **Address:** U. of Iowa, Art Department, Iowa City, IA 52242. **One-man Exhibitions:** Silvermine Guild, 1953; Kansas City/AI, 1956, 1965–66; Santa Barbara/MA, 1961; Otto Gerson Gallery, NYC, 1961, 63; Franklin Siden Gallery, Detroit, 1964; Gertrude Kasle Gallery, 1965, 67, 72, 74; U. of Arkansas, 1966; Talladega College, 1966; Marlborough-Gerson Gallery Inc.,

1966, 71; Rockford (Ill.) College Museum of Art, 1974; Terre Haute/Swope, 1980. **Retrospective:** U. of Iowa, 1974. **Group:** Detroit/Institute, 1958; PAFA, 1958, Annual, 1964; MOMA, Sixteen Americans, circ., 1959; Claude Bernard, Paris, Aspects of American Sculpture, 1960; Chicago/AI, 1960; WMAA Annuals, 1960–63; Carnegie, 1961; Dayton/AI, 1961; Boston Arts Festival, 1961; MOMA, American Painting and Sculpture, circ., 1961; New School for Social Research, Mechanism and Organism, 1961, also 1966; SFMA, 1962; SRGM, The Joseph H. Hirshhorn Collection, 1962; Battersea Park, London, International Sculpture Exhibition, 1963; Sao Paulo, 1963; Walker, Ten American Sculptors, 1964; Flint/Institute, 1965; WMAA, Contemporary American Sculpture, Selection I, 1966; U. of Illinois, 1967; PMA, American Sculpture of the Sixties, 1967; U. of California, 1968; U. of Wisconsin, 1975. **Collections:** American Republic Insurance Co.; Brenton Bank; Buffalo/Albright; Buffalo/SUNY; Chase Manhattan Bank; Chicago/AI; Cranbrook; Davenport/Municipal; Detroit/Institute; U. of Illinois; U. of Iowa; Kalamazoo/Institute; Kansas City/Nelson; MOMA; U. of Massachusetts; U. of Michigan; U. of Nebraska; Oswego/SUNY; Princeton U.; Santa Barbara/MA; WMAA; Walker; Washington U. **Bibliography:** Read 3.

SCHNAKENBERG, HENRY. b. September 14, 1892, New Brighton (Staten Island), N.Y.; **d.** October 15, 1970, Newton, Conn. **Studied:** ASL, 1914, with Kenneth Hayes Miller. US Army, 1917–19, with Kenneth Hayes Miller. US Army, 1917–19. Traveled Mexico, Europe. **Taught:** ASL. **Commissions** (murals): US Post Offices, West New York, N.J., and Amsterdam, N.Y. **Awards:** Hon. DFA, U. of Vermont; elected to the NIAL, 1952. **One-man Exhibitions:** (first) Whitney Studio Club, NYC, 1921; Alfredo Valente Gallery, NYC, 1926; Hartford/Wadsworth (two-man), 1955; Kraushaar Galleries,

1929, 35, 37, 40, 41, 42, 46, 48, 50 54, 56, 60, 63, 69. **Group:** MMA; WMAA; U. of Nebraska; Chicago/AI; Brooklyn Museum; Newark Museum. **Collections:** ASL; Andover/Phillips; Brooklyn Museum; California Palace; Chicago/AI; Dallas/MFA; Dartmouth College; Hartford (Conn.) State Library; Hartford/Wadsworth; MMA; Minneapolis/Institute; Montclair/AM; U. of Nebraska; Newark Museum; New Britain; PAFA; Princeton U.; SFMA; Scripps College; Springfield, Mass./MFA; U.S. Military Academy; U. of Vermont; WMAA; Wichita/AM; Yale U. **Bibliography:** *America 1976*; Baur 7; Cheney; **Goodrich 6**; Goodrich and Baur 1; Hall; *Index of 20th Century Artists*; Kent, N.; Mellquist; Pearson 1; Richardson, E.P. Archives.

SCHRAG, KARL. b. December 7, 1912, Karlsruhe, Germany. **Studied:** Humanistisches Gymnasium, Karlsruhe, 1930; Ecole des Beaux-Arts, Geneva, 1931; Atelier Lucien Simon, Paris; Academie Ranson, Paris, with Roger Bissiere; Academie de la Grande Chaumiere, 1931–35; ASL, with Harry Sternberg; Atelier 17, NYC, with S.W. Hayter. To USA, 1938; citizen, 1944. Traveled Europe, Mexico. **Taught:** Brooklyn College, 1953; Cooper Union 1954–68; Director of Atelier 17, NYC, 1950. **Member:** Artists Equity; SAGA; ASL. **Awards:** Brooklyn Museum Biennals, **P.P.,** 1947, 50; SAGA, **P.P.,** 1954; The Print Club, Philadelphia, Charles M. Lea Prize, 1954; American Color Print Society, 1958, Florence Tonner Prize, 1960, Sonia Wather Award, 1964; Ford Foundation Fellowship for work at Tamarind Lithography Workshop; Syracuse State Fair, Nelson Rockefeller Award, 1963; AAAL, 1966; Albion College, **P.P.,** 1968; AAAL, Childe Hassam Fund **P.P.,** 1969, 73; Ball State U., Drawings Prize, 1970; Davidson College, **P.P.,** 1974; SAGA, award, 1971; SAGA, James R. Marsh Memorial Award, 1977. **Address:** 127 East 95th Street, NYC 10028. **Dealer:** Kraushaar

Galleries; A.A.A. Gallery. **One-man Exhibitions:** (first) Galerie Arenberg, Brussels, 1938; Smithsonian, 1945; Kraushaar Galleries, 1947, 50, 52, 56, 59, 62, 64, 66, 68, 71, 75, 77, 79; U. of Alabama, 1949; Philadelphia Art Alliance, 1952; U. of Maine, 1953; State U. of New York, Oneonta, 1958; Gesellschaft der Freunde junger Kunst, Baden-Baden, Germany, 1958; Storm King Art Center, 1967; NCFA, 1972. **Retrospectives:** A.F.A./Ford Foundation, circ., 1960–62; A.A.A. Gallery, 1972, 80; NCFA, 1972. **Group:** SAGA; PAFA; The Print Club, Philadelphia; Brooklyn Museum; Graphische Sammlung Albertina; SFMA, 1941, 45, 46; WMAA, 1943, 55, 57; Carnegie, 1944, 47; Musee du Petit Palais, Paris, 1949; Chicago/AI; Instituto Nacional de Bellas Artes, Mexico City, 1958; U. of Nebraska, 1973; MOMA, 1975; MOMA, American Prints 1913–1963, circ. internationally, 1976; MMA, Contemporary American Prints from the Singer Collection, 1976; Brooklyn Museum, 30 Years of American Printmaking, 1976. **Collections:** Achenbach Foundation; U. of Alabama; Atlanta U.; Bibliotheque Nationale; Boston/MFA; Bradley U.; Brandeis U.; Brooklyn Museum; Chicago/AI; Cleveland/MA; Commerce Trust Co., Kansas City, Mo.; Dartmouth College; Detroit/Institute; Hartford/Wadsworth; Hirshhorn; U. of Illinois; Karlsruhe; Lehigh U.; Library of Congress; Lincoln Life Insurance Co.; Los Angeles/County MA; MMA; MOMA; U. of Maine; U. of Nebraska; NYPL; National Gallery; Newark Museum; Oakland/AM; Omaha/Joslyn; PMA; The Pennsylvania State U.; RISD; Smithsonian; Springfield, Mass./MFA; SRGM, Syracuse/Everson; Syracuse U.; U.S. Rubber Co.; Utica; Victoria and Albert Museum; WMAA; Yale U.; Youngstown/Butler. **Bibliography: Gordon 3**; Hayter 1, 2; Moser; Reese. Archives.

SCHUCKER, CHARLES. b. January 19, 1908, Gap, Pa. **Studied:** Maryland Institute, 1928–34. **Taught:** NYU,

1947–54; Pratt Institute, 1956– ; CCNY, 1955–56. **Member:** Yaddo Board of Directors. Federal A.P.: Easel painting in Chicago, 1938–42. **Awards:** Henry Walters Traveling Fellowship; Guggenheim Foundation Fellowship, 1953; Audubon Artists, Prize for Oil Painting; AAAL, Childe Hassam Fund, **P.P.**, 1952. **Address:** 33 Middagh Street, Brooklyn, NY 11201. **One-man Exhibitions:** (first) Renaissance Society, Chicago; Albert Roullier Gallery, Chicago; Chicago/AI; The Chicago Artists Room; Macbeth Gallery, NYC, 1946, 49, 53; Passedoit Gallery, NYC, 1955, 58; Katonah (N.Y.) Art Gallery, 1955, 73, 78; The Howard Wise Gallery, NYC, 1963; Lincoln Center, 1968; WMAA, 1971; Max Hutchinson Gallery, 1972, 74, 75; Aaron Gallery, Washington, D.C., 1978; Gallery Camino Real, Boca Raton, Fla., 1980. **Group:** MOMA, Painting and Sculpture from 16 American Cities, 1933; Carnegie, 1949; Walker, Contemporary American Painting, 1950; MMA, American Paintings Today, 1950; PAFA, 1951, 52, 53; California Palace Annual, 1952; WMAA Annuals, 1952–57, 1960, 61, 63; Chicago/AI, 1954; SFMA, Art in the Twentieth Century, 1955; WMAA, Nature in Abstraction, 1958; Corcoran; Brooklyn Museum; Riverside Museum, NYC; Amherst College, Color Painting, 1972; Cincinnati/Contemporary, Options, $^{7}/_{30}$, 1973; WMAA, 1973; Katonah (N.Y.) Art Gallery, 1973; Potsdam/SUNY, Abstraction Alive & Well, 1975. **Collections:** AAAL; Brooklyn Museum; Harcourt Brace Jovanovich Inc.; Newark Museum; New Britain; WMAA. **Bibliography:** Baur 5; Goodrich and Baur 1. Archives.

SCHUELER, JON. b. September, 12, 1916, Milwaukee, Wisc. **Studied:** U. of Wisconsin, 1934–38, BA (economics), 1939–40, MA (English literature); Bread Loaf School of English, Middlebury, Vt., 1941; California School of Fine Arts, 1948–51, with David Park, Elmer Bischoff, Richard Diebenkorn, Hassel

Smith, Clyfford Still, Clay Spohn. US Air Force, 1941–43. Traveled Europe, Great Britain, USA extensively. **Taught:** U. of San Francisco, 1947–49 (English literature); Yale U., 1960–62, and summer school, 1960, 61; Maryland Institute, 1963. **Commissions:** New York Hilton Hotel, 1962 (lithograph). **Address:** 40 West 22nd Street, NYC, 10010. **One-man Exhibitions:** (first) Metart Gallery, San Francisco, 1950; The Stable Gallery, NYC, 1954, 62, 64; Leo Castelli Inc., 1957, 59; B.C. Holland Gallery, 1960; Hirschl & Adler Galleries, Inc., NYC, 1960; Cornell U., 1962; Columbia U. School of Architecture, 1962; Maryland Institute, 1962, 64; Richard Demarco Gallery, Edinburgh, 1973; Edinburgh College of Art, 1973; WMAA, 1975; Cleveland/MA (three-man), 1975; Landmark Gallery, NYC, 1977; House Gallery, London, 1978. **Group:** Walker, 1955; WMAA Annuals, 1956, 59, 61, 63; Corcoran, 1958, 62; A.F.A., School of New York—Some Younger American Painters, 1960; Walker, 60 American Painters, 1960; WMAA, 50 Years of American Art, 1964. **Collections:** New York Hilton Hotel; Union Carbide Corp.; WMAA. **Bibliography:** Baur 5; Friedman, ed.; Goodrich and Baur 1; McChesney.

SCHWABACHER, ETHEL. b. May 20, 1903, NYC. **Studied:** ASL, 1927–28, with Robert Laurent, Max Weber; and privately with Arshile Gorky, 1934–36. Resided Europe, 1928–34. **Address:** 1192 Park Avenue, NYC 10028. **One-man Exhibitions:** (first) Passedoit Gallery, NYC, 1935, also 1947; Betty Parsons Gallery, 1953, 56, 57, 60, 62, 64; Greenross Gallery, NYC, 1964; Buffalo/SUNY, 1972; Bodley Gallery, NYC, 1976. **Group:** WMAA Annuals, 1947, 49, 51, 52, 54, 56, 57, 59, 61, 63; A.F.A., 1953; Brooklyn Museum, 1956, 60; Corcoran, 1958; WMAA, Nature in Abstraction, 1958; Walker, 1960; Mexico City/Nacional, 1960; Carnegie, 1961; Buffalo/Albright, 1962, Abstract Expressionism: First and Second Generations,

1972. **Collections:** Buffalo/Albright; Cathedral of St. John the Divine, NYC; Rockefeller Institute; WMAA. **Bibliography:** Baur 5; Goodrich and Baur 1; **Schwabacher.** Archives.

SCHWARTZ, MANFRED. b. November 11, 1909, Lodz, Poland; **d.** November 7, 1970, NYC. **Studied:** ASL, with George Bridgeman, John Sloan. Traveled Europe, Algeria. **Taught:** NYU; Skowhegan School; Brooklyn Museum School; Pratt Institute; New School for Social Research; 1964–70. **Member:** Federation of Modern Painters and Sculptors. **Awards:** Silvermine Guild, Silvermine Prize ($500), 1965, Silvermine Marine Award, 1967; PAFA, Jennie Sesnan Gold Medal, 1968. **One-man Exhibitions:** (first) Lilienfeld Gallery, NYC, 1940; Durand-Ruel Gallery, NYC, 1947, 48, 49; Otto Gerson Gallery, NYC, 1955, 57; Albert Landry, NYC, 1962, 63; Brooklyn Museum, Drawings and Pastels, 1959; New School for Social Research, 1967; WMAA, 1971; RISD, 1974; Knoedler Contemporary Art, 1974, 78. **Retrospective:** Brooklyn Museum, Manfred Schwartz; 20-Year Retrospective, 1961. **Group:** Cincinnati/AM; Brooklyn Museum; MMA; MOMA; U. of Minnesota; Newark Museum; New School for Social Research; PMA; U. of Rochester; SRGM; WMAA. **Bibliography:** Genauer. Archives.

SEERY, JOHN. b. October 29, 1941, Cincinnati, Ohio. **Studied:** Miami U., 1959–63; Cincinnati Art Academy, 1963; Ohio State U., 1963–64. Traveled Europe, Australia, Pacific Islands. **Taught:** Hunter College, 1973. **Address:** % Dealer. **Dealer:** Andre Emmerich Gallery, NYC. **One-man Exhibitions:** Andre Emmerich Gallery, NYC, 1970, 72, 74, 77; Richard Gray Gallery, Chicago, 1971, 72, 75, 78; New Gallery, Cleveland, 1971; Ohio State U., 1972; Gallery A, Sydney, 1974; Madison Art Center (two-man), 1974; Galerie Andre Emmerich, Zurich, 1975; Reed College,

George Segal   *Three Bathers with Birch Tree*   1980

1977; Berenson Gallery, Bay Harbor Islands, Miami, Fla., 1979. **Group:** ICA,
U. of Pennsylvania, Two Generations
of Color Painting, 1970; Cincinnati/Con-
temporary, Young American Artists,
1970; Spoleto, Festival of Two Worlds,
1972; Glassboro State College, Paintings
on Paper, 1972; U. of North Carolina,
Six Painters of the 70s, 1973; WMAA
Annual, 1973; Milwaukee, Art Works,
1976; Syracuse U., The Critics' Choice,
1977; Indianapolis, 1978. **Collections:**
Baltimore/MA; Boston/MFA; Canberra/
National; Chicago/AI; Fort Lauderdale;
Houston/Contemporary; ICA, Boston;
Louisville/Speed; Madison Art Center;
RISD; Toledo/MA. **Bibliography:** *Poets
& Painters.*

SEGAL, GEORGE. b. November 26,
1924, NYC. **Studied:** NYU, 1950, BS;
Rutgers U., 1963, MFA. **Taught:** New
Jersey high schools, 1957–63. **Awards:**
Walter K. Gutman Foundation Grant,
1962; Chicaco/AI, First Prize, 1966;
Hon. Ph.D., Rutgers U., 1970. **Ad-
dress:** RFD #4, Box 323, North
Brunswick, NJ 08902. **Dealer:** Sidney
Janis Gallery. **One-man Exhibitions:**
(first) Hansa Gallery, NYC, 1956, also
1957, 58, 59; Rutgers U., 1958; Green
Gallery, NYC, 1960, 62, 64; Ileana Son-
nabend Gallery, Paris, 1963; Galerie
Schmela, 1963; Sidney Janis Gallery,
1965, 67, 68, 70, 71, 73, 74, 77, 78, 80;
Toronto (three-man, with Jim Dine,
Claes Oldenburg); Chicago/Contempo-

rary, 1968; Darthea Speyer Gallery, 1969, 71; Galerie der Spiegel, Cologne, 1970; Galerie Onnasch, Cologne, 1971; Zurich, circ., 1971, 73; Trenton/State (two-man), 1971; U. of Wisconsin, Milwaukee, 1973; Andre Emmerich Gallery, Zurich, 1975; Dartmouth College, 1975; ICA, U. of Pennsylvania, 1976; Nina Freudenheim Gallery, Buffalo, 1976; Newport (R.I.) Art Association, 1976; Suzette Schochett Gallery, Newport, R.I., 1976; Santa Barbara/MA, 1976; Greenwich (Conn.) Arts Council, 1977; Ohio U., 1978. **Retrospectives:** California State U., Long Beach, circ., 1977–78; Walker, circ., 1978–79. **Group:** Boston Arts Festival, 1956; Jewish Museum, The New York School, Second Generation, 1957, Recent American Sculpture, 1964, also 1966; WMAA Annuals, 1960, 64, 68; A.F.A., The Figure, circ., 1960, also 1968; Sidney Janis Gallery, The New Realists, 1962; VII & IX Sao Paulo Biennials, 1963, 67; Stockholm/National, American Pop Art, 1964; Corcoran Biennial, 1965; Cordier & Ekstrom, Inc., 1965; Palais des Beaux-Arts, Brussels, 1965; WMAA, A Decade of American Drawings, 1965; SRGM, 1965, 67; RISD, Recent Still Life, 1966; Chicago/AI, 1966, 74; Walker, 1966; Los Angeles/County MA, American Sculpture of the Sixties, 1967; MOMA, The 1960's, 1967; Carnegie, 1967; II Internationale der Zeichnung, Darmstadt, 1967; Trenton/State, Focus on Light, 1967; Gelsenkirchen, 1967; Documenta IV, Kassel, 1968; St. Paul Gallery, 1968; ICA, London, The Obsessive Image, 1968; Fort Worth Art Museum, Drawings, 1969; Grand Rapids, Sculpture of the 60s, 1969; Boston U., American Artists of the Nineteen Sixties, 1970; Expo '70, Osaka, 1970; Indianapolis, 1970; Carnegie, 1970; WMAA, 1970; Walker, Figures/Environments, circ., 1970–71; Chicago/AI, Contemporary Drawings, 1971; Chicago/Contemporary, White on White, 1971–72; Utica, 1972; Harvard U., Recent Figure Sculpture, 1972; Cleveland/MA, Contemporary American Artists, 1974; Chicago/Contemporary, 1974, 76; Darmstadt,

Kunsthalle, Realism and Reality, 1975; New York Cultural Center, Three Centuries of the American Nude, 1975; NCFA, Sculpture: American Directions 1945–75, 1975; Philadelphia College of Art, Artists' Sketchbooks, 1976; Documenta, Kassel, 1977; WMAA, Art about Art, 1978. **Collections:** Aachen/NG; Akron/AI; Amsterdam/Stedelijk; Birmingham, Ala./MA; CNAC; Charlotte/Mint; Chicago/AI; Carnegie; Cleveland/MA; von der Heydt/Cologne; Dartmouth College; Detroit/Institute; Hartford/Wadsworth; Helsinki; Indiana U.; Krefeld/Kaiser Wilhelm; MOMA; Milwaukee; Munich/SG; NCFA; Newark Museum; U. of North Carolina; Omaha/Joslyn; Ottawa/National; PAFA; PMA; Rotterdam; SFMA; St. Louis/City; Schwebber Electronics; SRGM; Stockholm/National; Stuttgart; Toronto; Trenton/State; Vancouver; WMAA; Walker, Zurich; Wuppertal. **Bibliography:** Alloway 4; Battcock, ed.; Becker and Vostell; Bihalji-Merin; Calas, N. and E.; *Contemporanea*; Craven, W.; Diamonstein; Dienst 1; *Figures/Environments*; Finch; Friedman and van der Marck; Gerdts; Hansen; Honisch and Jensen, eds.; Hunter, ed.; Johnson, Ellen H.; Kaprow; Kozloff 3; *Kunst um 1970*; Licht, F.; Lippart 5; *Recent Figure Sculpture*; Sandler 1; Trier 1; Tuchman 1; Weller. Archives.

SELEY, JASON. b. May 20, 1919, Newark, N.J. **Studied:** Cornell U., 1936–40; BA; ASL, with Ossip Zadkine, 1943–45; Academie des Beaux-Arts, Paris, 1950. Traveled Europe, Haiti, Israel, Canada, Russia. **Taught:** Le Centre d'Art, Port-au-Prince, Haiti, 1946–49; Hofstra U., 1953–65; NYU, 1963–67; Dartmouth College, 1968; Cornell U., 1968– ; Deutscher Akademischer Austauschdienst, Berlin, 1970–71. **Commissions:** Haitian Government, 1949; Episcopal Cathedral, Port-au-Prince, Haiti, 1952. **Awards:** US State Department Grant, 1947–49; Fulbright Fellowship (France), 1949; Silvermine Guild, First Prize for Sculpture, 1962. **Address:** 209 Hudson

Street, Ithaca, NY 14850. **Dealer:** Louis K. Meisel Gallery. **One-man Exhibitions:** (first) Le Centre d'Art, Port-au-Prince, Haiti, 1946, also 1947, 48, 49; American-British Art Center, NYC, 1947, 48; A.A.A. Gallery, NYC, 1955; Hofstra College, 1957; Barone Gallery, NYC, 1960; The Kornblee Gallery, 1962, 64, 67, 69; Dartmouth College, 1968; U. of Vermont, 1968; Dunkelman Gallery, Toronto, 1968; Wesleyan U. (Conn.), 1969; Amerika Haus, Berlin, 1971; Colgate U., 1974; Louis K. Meisel Gallery, 1974, 78; Elmira College, 1976; Upstairs Gallery, Ithaca, 1976; Syracuse/Everson, 1977; Gallery Place, Corning, N.Y., 1977. **Retrospective:** Cornell U., 1965, 80. **Group:** WMAA Sculpture Annals, 1952, 53, 62, 64, 66, 68–69; Newark Museum, 1958, 61, 64; MOMA, Recent Sculpture USA, 1959; MOMA, The Art of Assemblage, circ., 1961; SRGM, The Joseph H. Hirshhorn Collection, 1962; Festival of Two Worlds, Spoleto, 1962; Battersea Park, London, International Sculpture Exhibition, 1963; MOMA, Americans 1963, circ., 1963–64; Documenta III, Kassel, 1964; MOMA, Around the Automobile, 1965; WMAA, Contemporary American Sculpture, Selection I, 1966; MOMA, The 1960's, 1967; WMAA, 1967; Toronto International Sculpture Symposium, 1967; Kirkland College, Three-man show, 1972; Flint/Institute, Art and the Automobile, 1978. **Collections:** U. of California; Casper College; Chase Manhattan Bank; Cornell U.; Cortland/SUNY; Dartmough College; Fredonia/SUNY; Hirshhorn; MOMA; Newark Museum; U. of North Carolina; Ottawa/National; Ridgefield/Aldrich; St. Lawrence U.; South Mall, Albany; Syracuse/Everson; Toronto; Trenton/State; WMAA. **Bibliography:** Craven, W.; Read 3; *Jason Seley;* Seitz 3.

SELIGER, CHARLES. b. June 3, 1926, NYC. Self-taught in art. Traveled Switzerland, France. **Taught:** Mt. Vernon (N.Y.) Art Center, 1950–51. **Address:** 10 Lenox Avenue, Mount Ver-

non, NY 10552. **Dealer:** Andrew Crispo Gallery. **One-man Exhibitions:** (first) Art of This Century, NYC, 1945, also 1946; Carlebach Gallery, NYC, 1948, 49; de Young, 1949; Art Center School, Los Angeles, 1949; Willard Gallery, NYC, 1951, 53, 55, 57, 61, 62, 65, 66, 67, 78; Otto Seligman Gallery, 1955, 58, 65, 66; Haydon Calhoun Gallery, Dallas, 1962; Nassau Community College, Garden City, N.Y., 1966; Andrew Crispo Gallery, NYC, 1974, 76, 78, 79; Les Copains Art Ltd., Buffalo, N.Y., 1976; Makler Gallery, Philadelphia, 1979. **Retrospective:** Wooster Community Art Center, Danbury, Conn., 1969. **Group:** VMFA, 1946; Chicago/AI, Abstract and Surrealist Art, 1948; XXIV Venice Biennial, 1948; WMAA Annuals, 1948, 49, 51, 52, 53, 54, 55, 56, 57, 58, 60; Guggenheim Collection; Brooklyn Museum, 1949; Cornell U., Young Painters, 1951; MOMA, Abstract Painting and Sculpture in America, 1951; Chicago/AI, 1952; USIA, American Painting, circ., Europe, 1956; Utica, 1957; Rome–New York Foundation, Rome, 1960; Norfolk; St. Paul Gallery, 1966; AAAL, 1966, 68; The Willard Gallery, 1967; Smithsonian, The Art of Organic Forms, 1968; Skidmore College, Watercolors: Historical and Contemporary, 1976. **Collections:** Andover/Phillips; Baltimore/MA; Brandeis U.; Chicago/AI; The Hague; Hartford/Wadsworth; Hirshhorn; Iowa State U.; Jerusalem/National; Karlsruhe; MMA; MOMA; Newark Museum; Seattle/AM; Southern Illinois U.; SRGM; Tel Aviv; US State Department; Utica; Vancouver; Vassar College; WMAA. **Bibliography:** Baur 7; Read 2, 4; Richardson, E.P.; Ritchie 1. Archives.

SELIGMANN, KURT. b. July 20, 1900, Basel, Switzerland; **d.** January 2, 1962, NYC. **Studied:** Ecole des Beaux-Arts, Geneva, 1920; Academy of Fine Arts, Florence, Italy, 1927. To USA, 1939; became a citizen. **Taught:** Brooklyn Museum School. Designed sets for modern dance and ballet groups. Authority on magic. **One-man Exhibi-**

tions: Jeanne Bucher, Paris, 1932, 35; Zwemmer Gallery, London, 1933; Mitzowko-Shi, Tokyo, 1935; Wakefield Gallery, NYC; Karl Nierendorf Gallery, NYC, 1939, 41; New School for Social Research, 1940; Mexico City/Nacional, 1943; Durlacher Brothers, NYC, 1944, 46, 48, 50, 53; Arts Club of Chicago, 1946; Alexander Iolas Gallery, 1953; Walker, 1958; Fine Arts Associates, NYC, 1960; Ruth White Gallery, 1960, 61, 68; D'Arcy Gallery, NYC, 1964; Berne, 1967; Galerie Jacques Benador, Geneva, 1974; John Bernard Myers Gallery, NYC, 1974; Springfield, Mass./ MFA, 1974; La Boetie, Inc., NYC, 1973, 76. **Retrospective:** La Boetie, NYC, 1973. **Group:** WMAA; MOMA; Chicago/AI; Detroit/Institute; U. of Illinois; MMA; NYPL; PAFA; Buffalo/Albright, Drawings and Watercolors, 1968. **Collections:** Aubusson; Bibliotheque Nationale; Brooklyn Museum; Buffalo/ Albright; Chicago/AI; College des Musées Nationaux de France; U. of Illinois; Kunstkredit; Lodz; MMA; MOMA; Mexico City/Nacional; NYPL; PAFA; Smith College; WMAA. **Bibliography:** *Abstraction Création 1931–1936*; Blesh 1; Breton 2; Dorner; Flanagan; Frost; Goodrich and Baur 1; Huyghe; Jakovski; Janis and Blesh 1; Janis, S.; Kuh 1; Pearson 1; Pousette-Dart, ed.; Richardson, E.P.; Rubin 1; Sachs; **Seligmann;** Tomkins and Time-Life Books; Waldberg, 4. Archives.

SENNHAUSER, JOHN. b. December 10, 1907, Rorschach, Switzerland; **d.** January 7, 1978, Escondido, Calif. **Studied:** Technical Institute, Treviso, Italy; Academy of Fine Arts, Venice; Cooper Union. Traveled Europe, USA. **Taught:** Leonardo da Vinci Art School, NYC, 1936–39; Contemporary School of Art, NYC, 1939–42. **Member:** American Abstract Artists; Federation of Modern Painters and Sculptors; International Institute of Arts and Letters. **Commissions:** Murals for banks and private buildings in NYC and other cities. **Awards:** WMAA, **P.P.,** 1951; Tulsa/

Philbrook, **P.P.**, 1951; Mark Rothko Foundation Grant, 1971, 72. **One-man Exhibitions:** (first) Leonardo da Vinci Art School Gallery, NYC, 1936; Contemporary Arts Gallery, NYC, 1939; Theodore A. Kohn Gallery, NYC, 1942; Artists' Gallery, NYC, 1947, 50, 52; Brown U., 1954; U. of Maine, 1955; Black Mountain College, 1956; The Zabriskie Gallery, 1956, 57; Knapik Gallery, NYC, 1961; The Salpeter Gallery, NYC, 1964; Meierhans Art Galleries, Perkasie, Pa., 1963, 68; Lenox (Mass.) Library, 1972; San Diego Public Library, 1979. **Group:** Brunswick U.; Bennington College; Worcester/AM; Walker; Dallas/MFA; NAD; PAFA; Chicago/AI; Museum of Non-Objective Art, NYC; Corcoran; U. of Illinois; Brooklyn Museum; Baltimore/MA; Salon des Realites Nouvelles, Paris; A.F.A., Collage in America, 1958; A.F.A., Geometrical Abstraction of the 1930s, 1972. **Collections:** American Museum of Immigration; Calcutta; U. of Georgia; St. Lawrence U.; SRGM; Tulsa/Philbrook; Utica; Wichita State U.; WMAA. **Bibliography:** Pousette-Dart, ed. Archives.

SERISAWA, SUEO. b. April 10, 1910, Yokohama, Japan. **Studied:** Otis Art Institute, Los Angeles, 1932–33, with George Barker; Chicago Art Institute School, 1943. Traveled Europe, Mexico, Far East, Japan. **Taught:** Kann Art Institute, West Hollywood, 1948–50; Scripps College, 1950–51; Claremont Graduate School, 1950–51; U. of Southern California, summer, 1974–75; and privately. **Member:** President, California Watercolor Society, 1950. **Awards:** California State Fair, 1940, 49; PAFA, Medal, 1947; Pepsi-Cola, 1948. **Address:** 3033 Warren Lane, Costa Mesa, CA 92626. **Dealer:** I. Serisawa, Los Angeles. **One-man Exhibitions:** Tone-Price Gallery, West Hollywood, 1940; Los Angeles/County MA, 1941; Dayton/ AI, 1945; Dalzell Hatfield Gallery, 1948; Pasadena/AM, 1951; Occidental College, 1952; Felix Landau Gallery, 1959,

62. **Retrospective:** Occidental College, Laguna Beach, (Calif.) Art Gallery. **Group:** MMA, 1950; Los Angeles/ County MA; California Palace; SFMA; U. of Illinois; Chicago/AI; San Diego; Santa Barbara/MA, I & II Pacific Coast Biennials, 1955, 57; PAFA; WMAA Annuals; Corcoran; Sao Paulo Biennial; International Biennial Exhibitions of Paintings, Tokyo; U. of Nebraska; Carnegie; Walker. **Collections:** Arizona State College; California State Fair; Eilat; Los Angeles/County MA; Lytton Savings and Loan Association; MMA; MOMA; Pasadena/AM; San Diego; Santa Barbara.

SERRA, RICHARD. b. November 2, 1938, San Francisco, Calif. **Studied:** U. of California, Berkeley and Santa Barbara, 1957–61, BA, MA; Yale U., 1961–64; BA and MA. Traveled Italy. **Commissions:** Western Washington U., Bellingham, 1978. **Awards:** Fulbright Fellowship, 1965–66; Skowhegan School Medal, 1975. **Address:** 319 Greenwich Street, NYC 10013. **Dealer:** Leo Castelli, Inc. **One-man Exhibitions:** Galleria la Salita, Rome, 1966; Galerie Rolf Ricke, 1968, 73; Galerie Lambert, Milan, 1969; Leo Castelli, Inc., NYC, 1970, 72, 74; ACE Gallery, Los Angeles, 1970, 72, 74; U. of California, San Diego, 1970; Pasadena/AM, 1970; School of Visual Arts, NYC, 1974; ACE Gallery, Los Angeles, 1976; Portland (Ore.) Center for the Visual Arts, 1974; Galerie de Gestlo, Hamburg, 1975; ACE Gallery, Venice, Calif., 1976, 78; Galerie Daniel Templon, Paris, 1977; Galerie, Bochum-Weitmar, West Germany, 1977; Amsterdam/Stedelijk, circ., 1977; Blum Helman Gallery, NYC, 1976, 78; Oxford, England, MOMA, 1978; Richard Hines Gallery, Seattle, 1979; U. of California, Berkeley, 1979; KOH Gallery, Tokyo, 1979; Galerie Schmela, Dusseldorf, 1979. **Group:** Yale U., Drawings, 1966; Ithaca College, Drawings 1967, 1967; A.F.A., Soft Sculpture, 1968; WMAA, 1968, 70, 73; MOMA, New Media: New Methods, circ., 1969;

Seattle/AM, 557,087, 1969; Trenton/ State, Soft Art, 1969; Berne, When Attitudes Become Form, 1969; WMAA, Anti-Illusion: Procedures/Materials, 1969; SRGM, Nine Young Artists, 1969; Chicago/Contemporary, Art by Telephone, 1969; U. of California, Irvine, Five Sculptors, 1969; Hannover/ Kunstverein, Identifications, 1970; SRGM, Guggenheim International, 1971; Dusseldorf/Kunsthalle, Prospect '71, 1971; Los Angeles/County MA, Art & Technology, 1971; Arnhem, Sonsbeek '71, 1971; Documenta V, Kassel, 1972; Rijksmuseum Kroller-Muller, Diagrams and Drawings, 1972; Festival of Two Worlds, Spoleto, 1972; New York Cultural Center, 3D into 2D, 1973; Yale U., Options and Alternatives, 1973; Detroit/Institute, Art in Space, 1973; Yale U., American Drawings, 1970–1973, 1973; Parcheggio di Villa Borghese, Rome, Contemporanea, 1974; Princeton U., Line as Language, 1974; MIT, Interventions in Landscapes, 1974; CNAC, Art/Voir, 1974; Oakland/AM, Public Sculpture; Urban Environment, 1974; Baltimore/MA, Artists, 1975; Hayward Gallery, London, The Condition of Sculpture, 1975; WMAA, Projected Video, 1975; NCFA, Sculpture: American Directions, 1945–1975, 1975; MOMA, Drawing Now, 1976; WMAA, 200 Years of American Sculpture, 1976; Philadelphia College of Art, Private Notation: Artists' Sketchbooks II, 1976; Akademie der Kunst, Berlin, SoHo, 1976; Documenta 6, Kassel, 1977; WMAA Biennial, 1977; U. of Chicago, Ideas in Sculpture, 1977; Worcester/ AM, Between Sculpture and Painting, 1978; Amsterdam/Stedelijk, Made by Sculptors, 1978; Krefeld/Haus Lange, The Broadening of the Concept of Reality in the Art of the 60s and 70s, 1979; P.S. 1, Long Island City, Great Big Drawing Show, 1979. **Collections:** Amsterdam/Stedelijk; Canberra/National; Cologne; Krefeld/Haus Lange; Kyoto; La Jolla; Melbourne/National; MMA; MOMA; Oberlin College; Ontario; Ottawa/National; Pasadena/AM; Ridgefield/Aldrich; Rijksmuseum

Kroller-Muller; SRGM; Stockholm/National; Tate; WMAA; Yale University. **Bibliography:** *Art Now 75;* Celant; *Contemporanea;* Gablik; Honisch and Jensen, eds.; Johnson, Ellan H.; Krauss 2; *Kunst um 1970;* Lippard, 3; Lippard, ed.; Muller; *Options and Alternatives;* Pincus-Witten; *Report; When Attitudes Become Form.*

SHAPIRO, JOEL. b. September 27, 1941, New York City. **Studied:** NYU, 1964, BA; 1969, MA; with the Peace Corps in India, 1965–66. **Taught:** Princeton U., 1974–76; School of Visual Arts, 1977–. **Awards:** National Endowment for the Arts, grant, 1975. **Address:** 284 Lafayette Street, NYC 10012. **Dealer:** Paula Cooper Gallery. **One-man Exhibitions:** (first) Paula Cooper Gallery, 1970, 72, 74, 75, 76, 77, 79; The Clocktower, NYC, 1973; Galerie Salvatore, Ala, Milan, 1974; Garage Gallery, London (two-man), 1975; Walter Kelly Gallery, Chicago, 1975; Chicago/ Contemporary, 1976; Max Protetch Gallery, Washington, D.C., 1977; Buffalo/ Albright, 1977; Susanne Hilberry Gallery, Detroit, 1977; Galerie Nancy Gillespie–Elisabeth de Laage, Paris, 1977, 79; Gallerie Aronowitsch, Stockholm, 1977; Greenberg Gallery, St. Louis, 1978; Galerie M. Bochum, West Germany, 1978; Akron/AI, 1979; Ohio State U., 1979; Whitechapel Art Gallery, London, 1980. **Group:** WMAA, Anti-Illusion: Procedure/Material, 1969; MOMA, Paperworks, 1970; WMAA Annuals, 1970, 77, 79; WMAA, American Drawings, 1963–1973, 1973; Chicago/AI, 1974; U. of Massachusetts, Critical Perspectives in American Art, 1976; Venice Biennial, 1976; Akademie der Kunst, Berlin, SoHo, 1976; ICA, U. of Pennsylvania, Improbable Furniture, 1977; Documenta 6, Kassel, 1977; Walker, Scale and Environment, 1977; U. of Chicago, 33 Ideas in Sculpture, 1977; Vassar College, five-man show, 1978; Amsterdam/Stedelijk, Made by Sculptors, 1978; U. of North Carolina, Drawings about Drawings Today, 1979.

Joel Shapiro Untitled 1980

Collections: Amsterdam/Stedelijk; Art Museum of South Texas, Corpus Christi; Buffalo/Albright; Canberra/National; Colgate U.; Dallas/MFA; Detroit/ Institute; Des Moines; Fort Worth; Friuli, Italy/MOMA; MMA; Harvard U.; Jerusalem/National; La Jolla; McCrory Corporation, NYC; U. of North Carolina; Ohio State U.; R.S.M. Co., Cincinnati; Walker; Whitney Communications, NYC; WMAA; Zurich. **Bibliography:** *Drawings: The Pluralist Decade;* Lucie-Smith.

SHAHN, BEN. b. September 12, 1898, Kovno, Lithuania; **d.** May 14, 1969, NYC. To USA, 1906. **Studied:** NYU; City College of New York, 1919–22 (biology); NAD, 1922; ASL. Traveled Europe, Japan, North Africa, USA. Photographer and designer for Farm Security Administration, 1935–38. Designed posters for Office of War Information, 1942, and for CIO, 1944–46. Designed sets for *Ballets: USA* and for the Festival of Two Worlds, Spoleto, 1958. **Commissions:** Community Building, Roosevelt, N.J., 1938–39; US Post Offices, Bronx, N.Y., 1938–39 (with Bernarda Bryson), and Jamaica, N.Y., 1939; Social Security Building,

Washington, D.C., 1940–42; William E. Grady Vocational High School, Brooklyn, N.Y., 1957 (mosaic). **Awards:** PAFA, Pennell Memorial Medal, 1939, 53, Alice McFadden Eyre Medal, 1952, Joseph E. Temple Gold Medal, 1956; *Look* magazine poll of "Ten Best Painters," 1948; II Sao Paulo Biennial, 1953; XXVII Venice Biennial, 1954; Harvard U., Medal, 1956; American Institute of Graphic Art, Medal, 1958; North Shore, Long Island, N.Y., Art Festival Annual Award, 1959. **One-man Exhibitions:** The Downtown Gallery, 1930, 32, 33, 44, 49, 51, 52, 55, 57, 59, 61; Julien Levy Galleries, NYC, 1940; MOMA, 1947; Arts Council of Great Britain, circ., 1947; Albright Art School, 1950; Perls Galleries, 1950; Arts Club of Chicago, 1951; Santa Barbara/MA, circ., 1952, also 1967; Houston/MFA, 1954; Detroit/Institute (three-man), 1954; Chicago/AI, 1954; XXVII Venice Biennial, 1954; Southern Illinois U., 1954; American Institute of Graphic Art, 1957; St. Mary's College (Ind.), 1958; Bucknell U., 1958; Katonah (N.Y.) Art Gallery, 1959; Leicester Gallery, London, 1959, 64; U. of Louisville, 1960; U. of Utah, 1960; Library of the New Haven (Conn.) Jewish Community Center, 1961; Institute of Modern Art, Boston, Documentary, 1957; Amsterdam/Stedelijk, 1961; Rome/Nazionale, 1962; MOMA, Ben Shahn, circ., Europe, 1962; Randolph-Macon Woman's College, 1966; PMA, 1967; Orlando, 1968; Kennedy Gallery, 1968–69, 1970, 71, 73; Nantenshi Gallery, Tokyo, 1970; Syracuse U., 1977; Nardin Gallery, NYC, 1979. **Retrospectives:** MOMA, 1947; ICA, Boston, 1948; Osaka Municipal, 1970; National Museum of Western Art, Tokyo, 1970; Jewish Museum, NYC, 1976; Fort Worth, 1977. **Group:** Corcoran; Carnegie; WMAA; Chicago/AI; U. of Nebraska; Brooklyn Museum; MOMA; Buffalo/Albright. **Collections:** Abbott Laboratories; Andover/Phillips; Arizona State College; U. of Arizona; Auburn U.; Baltimore/MA; Brandeis U.; Brooklyn Museum; Buffalo/Albright; California Palace; Carnegie; Chicago/

AI; Container Corp. of America; Cranbrook; Dartmouth College; Des Moines; Detroit/Institute; Fort Wayne/AM; U. of Georgia; Grand Rapids; Hartford/Wadsworth; Harvard U.; U. of Illinois; Indiana U.; Inland Steel Co.; Jewish Museum; MMA; MOMA; Mary Washington College; U. of Michigan; Museum of the City of New York; U. of Nebraska; Newark Museum; U. of Oklahoma; Omaha/Joslyn; PAFA; Phillips; Sara Roby Foundation; St. Louis/City; Santa Barbara/MA; Smith College; Springfield, Mo./AM; Syracuse U.; Terry Art Institute; VMFA; WMAA; Walker; Wellesley College; Wesleyan U.; Wichita/AM; Youngstown/Butler. **Bibliography:** Baigell 1; Barr 3; Baur 7; Bazin; Biddle 4; Bihalji-Merin; Blesh 1; **Bush 1**; Brown 2; Canaday; Christensen; *Cityscape 1919–39*; Eliot; Finkelstein; Flanagan; Flexner; *From Foreign Shores*; Gaunt; Gerdts; Goodrich and Baur 1; Greengood; Haftman; Honisch and Jensen, eds.; Hunter 6; Kepes 2; Kuh 1, 2; Langui; Lee and Burchwood; McCurdy, ed.; Mendelowitz; *Metro*; **Morse**; Munsterberg; Newmeyer; Newton 1; Nordness, ed.; Pearson 1, 2; Pousette-Dart, ed.; Read 2; Richardson, E.P.; Rodman 1, 2, 3; Sachs; **Shahn 1, 2; Shahan, B.B.;** Shapiro; **Soby 2, 3, 4, 5;** Sutton; Weller; Wight 2. Archives.

SHAW, CHARLES. b. May 1, 1892, NYC; **d.** April 2, 1974, NYC. **Studied:** Yale U., Ph.D.; Columbia U. School of Architecture; ASL, with Thomas Hart Benton; and privately with George Luks. US Army, World War I. Traveled Europe extensively, Scandinavia, West Indies. Author of children's books, poetry, and articles for *Vanity Fair, The Bookman, Smart Set,* and other magazines. **Member:** American Abstract Artists; Federation of Modern Painters and Sculptors; Fellow of the International Institute of Arts and Letters. **Commissions:** *Vanity Fair* (magazine) (covers); Shell-Mex Ltd. (poster). **Awards:** Nantucket, First and Second Prizes; Century Association, Hon. Men., 1964. **One-man Exhibitions:** (first) Curt Valentine Gallery, NYC, 1934, also 1938; Museum of Living Art, NYC, 1935; SRGM, 1940; Passedoit Gallery, NYC, 1945, 46, 50, 51, 54, 1956–59; Nantucket, 1954–68; Albert Landry, NYC, 1960, 61; Art Association of Newport (R.I.), 1960, 62; U. of Louisville, 1963; Southampton East Gallery, Southampton, N.Y., 1963, 64; The Bertha Schaefer Gallery, 1963, 64, 66, 68, 71; Faure Gallery, La Jolla, 1964; Century Association, 1967, 75; Washburn Gallery, NYC, 1976, 79. **Group:** WMAA Annuals; Chicago/AI; Carnegie; Walker; SFMA; U. of Illinois; Corcoran; American Abstract Artists, annually, 1936–68; Federation of Modern Painters and Sculptors, annually, 1940–68; PMA, "8×8," 1945; MOMA, Abstract Painting and Sculpture in America, 1951; International Association of Plastic Arts, Contemporary American Paintings, circ., Europe, 1956–57; WMAA, Geometric Abstraction in America, circ., 1962; PAFA, 1966; U. of Colorado, 1966. **Collections:** Atlanta U.; Baltimore/MA; Boston/MFA; Brandeis U.; Brooklyn Museum; California Palace; Chase Manhattan Bank; Chicago/AI; Cincinnati/AM; Cleveland/MA; Corcoran; Dayton/AI; Denver/MA; Detroit/Institute; Fort Worth; U. of Georgia; Hartford/Wadsworth; Los Angeles/County MA; U. of Louisville; MMA; MOMA; NYU; Nantucket; Newark Museum; Norfolk/Chrysler; U. of North Carolina; PMA; Paris/Moderne; Phillips; Pittsfield/Berkshire; RISD; Raleigh/NCMA; Rockefeller Institute; SFMA; SRGM; WMAA; Walker; Wichita/AM; Williams College; Yale U. **Bibliography:** Baur 7; Cheney; Kootz 2; Marter, Tarbell, and Wechsler; Pousette-Dart, ed.; Ritchie 1. Archives.

SHEELER, CHARLES. b. July 16, 1883, Philadelphia, Pa.; **d.** May 7, 1965, Dobbs Ferry, N.Y. **Studied:** Pennsylvania School of Industrial Art, Philadelphia, 1900–03; PAFA, 1903–06, with William M. Chase. Traveled Europe, USA. **Taught:** Phillips Academy, 1946; Currier Gallery School, 1948. Collaborated with Paul Strand on the film *Mannhattana.* **Commissions:** Ford Motor Co., photographed the Ford Plant, 1927. **Awards:** Chicago/AI, Norman Wait Harris Medal, 1945; PAFA, Alumni Award, 1957; Hallmark International Competition, 1958 ($1,000); AAAL, Award of Merit Medal, 1962. **One-man Exhibitions:** (first) Modern Gallery, NYC, 1918 (photographs); De-Zayas Gallery, NYC, 1920 (paintings); The Daniel Gallery, NYC, 1922; Whitney Studio Club, NYC, 1924; J. B. Neumann Gallery, NYC (two-man), 1926; Art Center, NYC, 1926; The Downtown Gallery, 1931, 38, 40, 41, 43, 46, 49, 51, 56, 58, 65, 66; Arts Club of Chicago, 1932; Harvard U. (three-man), 1934; Society of Arts and Crafts, Detroit, 1935; Cincinnati/AM (four-man), 1941; Dayton/AI, 1944; Andover/Phillips, 1946; Currier, 1948; Houston/MFA (two-man), 1951; Walker, 1952; Detroit/Institute (three-man), 1954; Katonah (N.Y.) Art Gallery, 1960; State U. of Iowa, 1963; NCFA, 1968; Terry Dintenfass, Inc., 1974, 80; WMAA, 1980. **Retrospective:** MOMA, 1939; UCLA, circ., 1954; MIT, 1959; Allentown/AM, 1961; Cedar Rapids/AA, 1967; NCFA, 1968. **Group:** NAD, 1906; PAFA, 1907, 1908–10; The Armory Show, 1913; Anderson Galleries, NYC, Forum Exhibition, 1916; Society of Independent Artists, NYC, 1917; Brooklyn Museum, 1923, 25; Cincinnati/AM, 1924, 1927–31, 34, 35, 39; Whitney Studio Club Annuals, NYC, 1925, 27, 30; Cleveland/MA, 1926, 1927–29, 31, 32, 34; Royal Academy, London, 1930; St. Louis/City, 1931–34, 41, 42, 44, 45; Carnegie, 1931, 33, 35, 37, 40, 41, 43, 45, 48, 52; WMAA, 1932, 34, 36, 42; XVII & XXVIII Venice Biennials, 1934, 56; Chicago/AI, 1935, 37, 38, 41, 46, 48, 59, 51, 54. **Collections:** Albany/Institute; Andover/Phillips; Arizona State College; Boston/MFA; Britannica; Brooklyn Museum; Buffalo/Albright; California Palace; Chicago/AI; Cleveland/MA; Colonial Williamsburg; Columbus; Currier; Detroit/Institute; General Motors Corp.; Harvard U.; Kansas City/Nelson; MMA; MOMA; The Miller Co.; Mount Holyoke College; U. of Nebraska; Newark Museum; New Britain; PAFA; PMA; Phillips; RISD; Sara Roby Foundation; Santa Barbara/MA; Smith College; Springfield, Mass./MFA; Tel Aviv; Toledo/MA; Utica; VMFA; WMAA; Walker; Wesleyan U.; West Palm Beach/Norton; Wichita/AM; Williams College; Worcester/AM; Yale U.; Youngstown/Butler. **Bibliography:** *Avant-Garde Painting and Sculpture in America, 1910–25;* Barker 1; Barr 3; Baur 7; Bazin; Beam; Biddle 4; Blesh 1; Born; Boswell 1; Brown 2; Bulliet 1; Cahill and Barr, eds.; **Charles Sheeler;** Cheney; Christensen; *Cityscape, 1919–39;* **Dochterman;** Dorner; Eliot; Flanagan; Flexner; *Forerunners;* Frank, ed.; Frost; Goldwater and Treves, eds.; Goodrich and Baur 1; Haftman; Hall; Halpert; **Hirsch;** Hunter 7; Huyghe; *Index of 20th Century Artists;* Janis and Blesh 1; Janis, S.; Jewell 2; Kootz 1, 2; Kouvenhoven; Kuh 1; Levin 2; Mather 1; McCoubrey 1; McCurdy, ed.; Mellquist; Mendelowitz; Nauhaus; Newmeyer; Nordness, ed.; Pagano; Phillips 1, 2; Poore; Pousette-Dart, ed.; Rose, B., 1, 4; Rosenblum 1; **Rourke;** Sachs; Sager; Soby 5; Tashijan; Wight 2; **Williams, W. C.** Archives.

SHEETS, MILLARD. b. June 24, 1907, Pomona, Calif. **Studied:** Chouinard Art Institute, Los Angeles, 1925–29, with F.T. Chamberlain, Clarence Hinkle. Traveled Europe, Central America, Mexico, USA, Pacific, China, Russia, the Orient. **Taught:** Chouinard Art Institute, 1928–35; Scripps College, 1932–54, 1955–72; Director, Los Angeles County Art Institute, 1953–60. **Member:** California Watercolor Society; NAD; American Watercolor Society; Society of Motion Picture Art Directors; Bohemian Club. President, Millard Sheets Designs, Inc.; architectural designer; Federal A.P.: Assistant Director with Merle Armitage, S. MacDonald-

Wright. **Commissions** (murals): Pomona (Calif.) First Federal Savings and Loan Association; Our Lady of the Assumption Church, Ventura, Calif. (interior and exterior); over 100 murals and mosaics including San Jose Airport Terminal, 1977. **Awards:** Witte, Edgar B. Davis Prize; California Watercolor Society, 1927; Arizona State Fair, 1928, 29, 30; California State Fair, 1930, 32 (first prize), 33, 38; Los Angeles/County MA, First Prize, 1932, and 1945; Chicago/AI, 1938; Hon. LLD, U. of Notre Dame. **Address:** Barking Rocks, Gualala, CA 95445. **Dealer:** Kennedy Galleries, NYC. **One-man Exhibitions:** (first) Los Angeles, Calif. 1929; Los Angeles/County MA; California Palace; San Diego; Fort Worth, 1931, 34; Milwaukee; Baltimore/MA; Buffalo/Albright; Albany/Institute; Witte, 1931, 34; New Orleans/Delgado; Memphis/Brooks; Springfield, Mass./MFA; U. of Oklahoma; U. of Rochester; A. Tooth & Sons, London, 1964; Dalzell-Hatfield Gallery, Los Angeles, 1975; Kennedy Galleries, NYC, 1978, 80. **Retrospective:** Scripps College, 1976. **Group:** Chicago/AI, 1931–35; NAD Annuals, 1932–35; A Century of Progress, Chicago, 1933–34; Denver/AM, 1935; Sao Paulo, 1955; WMAA; Carnegie; Oakland/AM; Buffalo/Albright; Kansas City/Nelson; U. of Nebraska. **Collections:** Albany/Institute; Britannica; Brooklyn Museum; Carnegie; Cleveland/MA; Chicago/AI; Dayton-AI; de Young; Fort Worth; High Museum; Houston/MFA; Los Angeles/County MA; Los Angeles Public Library; MMA; MOMA; Montclair/AM; Montpelier; Muskegon/Hackley; U. of Oklahoma; RISD; SFMA; San Diego; Seattle/AM; WMAA; Witte. **Bibliography:** Cheney; Hall; **Miller 2;** Pagano. Archives.

SHIELDS, ALAN. b. February 4, 1944, Lost Springs, Kansas. **Studied:** Kansas State U.; U. of Maine. **Award:** Guggenheim Foundation Fellowship, 1973. **Address:** P.O. Box 1554, Shelter Island, NY 11964. **Dealer:** Paula Cooper Gal-

Alan Shields *Mt. St. Helena* 1980

lery. **One-man Exhibitions:** Paula Cooper Gallery, 1969, 70, 72, 74, 76, 78; Janie C. Lee Gallery, Dallas, 1970, 71; New Gallery, Cleveland, 1971; Ileana Sonnabend Gallery, Paris, 1971; Galleria dell'Ariete, 1972; Hansen-Fuller Gallery, 1973; U. of Rhode Island, 1973; Madison Art Center, 1973; Galerie Aronowitsch, Stockholm, 1973; Richard Gray Gallery, 1974, 76; Phoenix Gallery, San Francisco, 1974; Barbara Okun Gallery, St. Louis, 1974, 77, 78; The Texas Gallery, 1974; U. of Kansas, 1975; E.G. Gallery, Kansas City, 1975; Dootson Calderhead Gallery, Seattle, 1975; Galerie Daniel Templon, Paris, 1975, 78; St. Etienne, 1976; Portland (Ore.) Center for the Visual Arts, 1976; Paula Cooper Gallery, Los Angeles, 1976; Rio de Janeiro, 1976; Galerie Simone Stern, New Orleans, 1976; Moore College of Art, Philadelphia, 1977; Nina Freudenheim Gallery, Buffalo, 1977; Strasbourg/Moderne, 1977; Galerie Munro, Hamburg, 1978; P.S. 1, Long Island City, 1978; Galeria Luisa Strina, Sao Paulo, 1978; Thomas Segal Gallery, Boston, 1979; Gimpel & Hanover Gallery, Zurich, 1979; Andre Emmerich Gallery, Zurich, 1979; Williams College, 1979. **Retrospectives:** Chicago/Contemporary, 1973; Houston/Contemporary, 1973. **Group:** Trenton/State, Soft Art, 1969; WMAA, 1969, 72; Indianapolis, 1970; Chicago/AI, 1970, 72, 73; ICA, U. of Pennsylvania, Two Generations of Color Painting, 1970; U. of North Carolina, 1970; Corcoran, Depth and Presence, 1971; U. of Rochester, Aspects of Current Painting, 1971; SRGM, Contemporary Prints and Drawings, 1971; ICA, U. of Pennsylvania, Grids, 1972; U. of California, Berkeley, Eight New York Painters, 1972; Documenta V, Kassel, 1972; Detroit/Institute, 12 Statements, 1972; New York Cultural Center, Soft as Art, 1973; Seattle/AM, American Art: Third Quarter Century, 1973; VIII Paris Biennial, 1973; Indianapolis, 1974; MOMA, Printed, Folded, Cut and Torn, 1974; Corcoran Biennial, 1975; Toledo/MA, Image, Color and Form, 1975; Tyler School of Art, Philadelphia, Drawings,

1975; Akron/AI, Contemporary Images in Watercolor, 1976; Venice Biennial, 1976; Brooklyn Museum, 30 Years of American Printmaking, 1976; Chicago/AI, Drawings of the 70s, 1977; Ljubljana Biennial, 1977; Minnesota/MA, American Drawing 1927–1977, circ. 1977; The American Foundation for the Arts, Miami, Patterning and Decoration, 1970; WMAA, Recent Drawings by Younger Artists, 1978; Tampa Bay Art Center, Two Decades of Abstraction, 1978; Buffalo/Albright, American Painting in the 70s, 1978; Georgia State U., two-man, 1979; U. of North Carolina, Drawings about Drawings, 1979; U. of North Carolina, Art on Paper, 1979; ICA, U. of Pennsylvania, Masks, Tents, Vessels, Talismans, 1979. **Collections:** Akron/AI; Boston/MFA; Chase Manhattan Bank; Chicago/AI; Cleveland/MA; Commerce Bank, Kansas City; Dallas/MFA; First City National Bank, Houston; First National City Bank, NYC; Harvard U.; High Museum, Atlanta; Hirshhorn; MOMA; McCrory Corporation; Milwaukee; National Gallery; Oberlin College; U. of Pennsylvania; PMA; Prudential Insurance Co. of America, Newark; Ridgefield/Aldrich; RSM Co., Cincinnati; Rutgers U.; SRGM; Strasbourg/Moderne; Vassar College; Walker; Westinghouse Corp., Pittsburgh; WMAA. **Bibliography:** *Art Now 74.*

SHINN, EVERETT. b. November 6, 1876, Woodstown, N.J.; **d.** January 2, 1953, NYC. **Studied:** PAFA. Wrote and produced a number of melodramas in NYC. **Member:** The Eight. **Commissions** (murals): Trenton (N.J.) City Hall; Spring Garden Institute, Philadelphia. **Awards:** Chicago/AI, Watson F. Blair Prize, 1939; elected to the NIAL, 1951. **One-man Exhibitions:** M. Knoedler & Co. 1903, 69; 56th Street Gallery, NYC, 1930; Metropolitan Gallery, NYC, 1931; Morton Gallery, NYC, 1935; One-Ten Gallery, NYC, 1939; Ferargil Galleries, NYC, 1943; James Vigeveno Gallery, Los Angeles, 1945, 47,

48; American-British Art Center, NYC, 1945, 56, 49; The Graham Gallery, 1952, 58, 65; Davis Gallery, 1959; U. of Pennsylvania, 1959; Trenton/State, 1971. **Retrospective:** Trenton/State, 1973. **Group:** Macbeth Gallery, NYC, The Eight, 1908; The Armory Show, 1913; Brooklyn Museum, The Eight, 1943; PMA, 1945; Syracuse/Everson, The Eight 1958; U. of Pittsburgh, 1959. **Collections:** Boston/MFA; Brooklyn Museum; Buffalo/Albright; Chicago/AI; Detroit/Institute; MMA; New Britain; Phillips; WMAA. **Bibliography:** Baur 7, Biddle 4, Blesh 1; Brown; Brown 2; Canaday; Cheney; Eliot; Flanagan; Flexner; Gallatin 8; Gerdts; Glackens; Goodrich and Baur 1; Hartmann; Hunter 6; Kent, N.; McCoubrey 1; McCurdy, ed.; Mellquist; Mendelowitz; Neuhaus; Pagano; Perlman; Richardson, E.P.; Rose, B., 1; Sutton. Archives.

SIMON, SIDNEY. b. June 21, 1917, Pittsburgh, Pa. **Studied:** Carnegie Institute of Technology; PAFA; U. of Pennsylvania, with George Harding, BFA; Barnes Foundation. US Army artist, 1943–46. Traveled Austria, Italy, Morocco. **Taught:** Skowhegan School, 1946–58 (vice-president and director), 1975; Cooper Union, 1947–48; Brooklyn Museum School, 1950–52, 1954–56; Parsons School of Design, 1962–63; Salzburg Center for American Studies, 1971; ASL, 1973– ; Castle Hill Art Center, 1973–74; U. of Pennsylvania, 1980. **Member:** Artists Equity (national director, treasurer, vice-president, 1946–60); Century Association; Architectural League of New York; vice-president, Sculptors Guild; New York City Art Commission, 1975–79; NAD. Federal A.P.: US Post Office, Fleminsburgh, Ky. (mural). **Commissions:** Fort Belvoir, Va., 1942 (3 murals); Temple Beth Abraham, Tarrytown, N.Y.; Walt Whitman Junior High School, Yonkers, N.Y.; stage set for NYC production of *Ulysses in Nighttown*, by James Joyce, 1959; Federation of Jewish Philanthropies; *The Family*, sculpture group for the film *David and Lisa*, 1962 (with Robert Cook and Dorothy Greenbaum); Protestant Council of New York (Family of Man Medal, presented to President John F. Kennedy, 1963); *The Circus*, sculpture for Woodland House, Hartford, Conn., 1963; Our Lady of the Angels Seminary, Glenmont, N.Y., 1965; Downstate Medical Center, Brooklyn, N.Y. 1967; Prospect Park Playground, 1968; 747 Third Avenue Building, NYC, 1973. **Awards:** PAFA, Cresson Fellowship; Edwin Austin Abbey Fellowship, 1940; Prix de Rome, Hon. Men., 1940; Chicago/AI, Posner Painting Prize; PAFA, Fellowship, 1960; Chautauqua Institute, Babcock Memorial Award, 1963; Century Association, Gold Medal for Sculpture, 1969; AAAL, Award, 1976; National Arts Club, Silver Medal, 1978; NAD, Gold Medal, 1980. **Address:** 95 Bedford Street, NYC 10014. **One-man Exhibitions:** (first) PAFA, 1946; Niveau Gallery, NYC, 1949; Grand Central Moderns, NYC, 1951, 53; Rockland Foundation, 1955; Motel on the Mountain, 1959; Market Fair, Nyack, N.Y., 1960; Grippi Gallery, NYC, 1963 and others; Pittsburgh Plan for Art; Yale U., 1966; Wellfleet Art Gallery, 1966–67, 69, 71, 73; New School for Social Research, 1969; The Graham Gallery, 1970; Longpoint Gallery, Provincetown, Mass., 1977, 79; Sculpture Center, NYC, 1979. **Retrospective:** Sarah Lawrence College, 1971. **Group:** NAD Annuals, 1944–60; PAFA, 1948–53, 1962; MMA, American Painters under 35, 1950; WMAA, 1950, 52–55, 59, 62, 63; International Biennial Exhibition of Paintings, Tokyo; Brooklyn Museum, 1953; U. of Nebraska Annuals, 1954, 55; Corcoran, 1955; MOMA, The Art of Assemblage, circ., 1961; A.F.A., Educational Alliance Retrospective, 1963. **Collections:** ASL; Century Association; Chautauqua Institute; Colby College; Cornell U.; MMA; U. of North Carolina; The Pentagon; Sports Museum; Smith College; US State Department; Williams College. **Bibliography:** Seitz 3. Archives.

SIMONDS, CHARLES. b. November 14, 1945, New York City. **Studied:** U. of California, Berkeley, 1963–67, BA; Rutgers U., 1967–69; MFA. **Taught:** Newark State College, 1969–71. **Member:** Lower East Side Coalition for Human Housing. **Awards:** National Endowment for the Arts, grant, 1974; New York State Council on the Arts, grant, 1974. Also active as a filmmaker. **Address:** 138 Prince Street, New York, NY 10012. **One-man Exhibitions:** Paris, CNAC, 1975; Galleria Saman, Genoa, 1975; MOMA, 1976. **Group:** Biennale de Paris, 1973, 75; WMAA Biennials, 1975, 77; Vassar College, Primitive Presence in the 70s, 1975; Chicago/AI, Small Scale, 1975. **Collections:** MIT; MOMA; Oberlin College; Paris/Beaubourg; Paris/CNAC. **Bibliography:** Lucie-Smith.

SIMPSON, DAVID. b. January 20, 1928, Pasadena, Calif. **Studied:** California School of Fine Arts, with Leonard Edmondson, Clyfford Still, 1956, BFA; San Francisco State College, 1958, MA. US Navy, 1945–46. Traveled Mexico, 1953, Western Europe, 1969. **Taught:** American River Junior College, 1959–61; Contra Costa College, 1961–65; U. of California, Berkeley, 1965– . **Address:** 565 Vistamont Avenue, Berkeley, CA 94708. **Dealers:** Modernism Gallery, San Francisco; Janus Gallery, Venice, Calif. **One-man Exhibitions:** (first) San Francisco Art Association, 1958; David Cole Gallery, Sausalito, Calif., 1959; Santa Barbara/MA, 1960; Esther Robles Gallery, 1960; de Young, 1961; Joachim Gallery, Chicago, 1961; Robert Elkon Gallery, 1961, 63, 64; David Stuart Gallery, 1963, 64, 66, 68; Henri Gallery, 1968; Galeria Van der Voort, 1969; Hank Baum Gallery, San Francisco, 1972, 73, Los Angeles, 1972; Cheney Cowles Memorial Museum, Spokane, 1962; St. Mary's College, Moraga, Calif., 1974; Modernism Gallery, San Francisco, 1979, 80; Los Angeles State U., 1980. **Retrospectives:** SFMA, 1967; Oakland, 1978. **Group:**

Carnegie, 1961, 62, 67; Portland (Ore.)/ AM, 1968; U. of Illinois, 1963, 69; Los Angeles/County MA, Post Painterly Abstraction, 1964; Chicago/AI; Walker; PAFA, 1967; U. of Illinois, 1969; Spokane World's Fair, 1974; SFMA, California, Painting and Sculpture: The Modern Era, 1976. **Collections:** Baltimore/MA; Central Research Corp.; Columbia Broadcasting System; Crown Zellerbach Foundation; First National Bank of Seattle; Golden Gateway Center; La Jolla; MOMA; NCFA; Oakland/ AM; PMA; Phoenix; SFMA; Seattle/AM; Stanford U.; Storm King Art Center.

SINTON, NELL. b. June 4, 1910, San Francisco, Calif. **Studied:** California School of Fine Arts, with Maurice Sterne, Spencer Mackay, Ralph Stackpole. Traveled Europe, India, the Orient, Africa, South America, Middle East, USA, Mexico. **Taught:** SFAI, 1970, 71; San Francisco Student League, 1973–75; Institute for Creative and Artistic Development, Oakland, 1974, 75. **Member:** San Francisco City Art Commission; Artists Committee, San Francisco Art Institute (Trustee). **Address:** 1020 Francisco Street, San Francisco, CA 94109. **Dealer:** Braunstein Gallery, San Francisco. **One-man Exhibitions:** (first) California Palace, 1949; Santa Barbara/MA, 1950; SFMA (two-man), 1957; Bolles Gallery, San Francisco and New York, 1962; SFMA (four-man), 1962; Quay Gallery, 1969, 71, 74; SFMA, 1970; Jacqueline Anhalt Gallery, 1972; U. of California, San Francisco, 1975; Louisiana State U., 1976; Oakland/AM, 1977; Temple Emanu-El, San Francisco, 1977; Braunstein-Quay Gallery, NYC, 1977, 78; U. of Illinois, 1978; Mills College, 1979; Braunstein Gallery, San Francisco, 1980. **Retrospective:** Mills College, 1981. **Group:** MMA, 1952; ART:USA:58, NYC, 1958; Vancouver, 1958; Denver/AM, 1958, 60; SFMA; de Young; California Palace; Oakland/AM, Scripps College, 1961; Los Angeles/ County MA, 1961; A.F.A.; Stanford U.; U. of Nevada, 1969; Claremont College,

1973; SFAI, 1974; SFMA, California Painting and Sculpture: The Modern Era, 1976. **Collections:** AT&T; U. of California, Berkeley; Chase Manhattan Bank; Lytton Savings and Loan Association; Oakland/AM; SFMA. **Bibliography:** Archives.

SIPORIN, MITCHELL. b. May 5, 1910, NYC; **d.** June 11, 1976, Newton, Mass. **Studied:** Crane Junior College; Chicago Art Institute School; privately with Todros Geller; American Academy, Rome, 1949–50. US Army, 1942–45. Traveled Mexico, Latin America, Africa, Europe. **Taught:** Boston Museum School, 1949; Columbia U., 1951; Brandeis U., 1957–76; American Academy, Rome, Artist-in-Residence, 1966–67. **Member:** Brandeis U. Creative Arts Award Commission; Fellow, American Academy, Rome. Federal A.P.: Mural painting. **Commissions:** Bloom Township High School, Chicago, 1938 (mural); US Post Offices, Decatur, Ill., 1940, and St. Louis, Mo. (with Edward Millman), 1940–42 (mural); Berlin Chapel, Brandeis U. (ark curtain). **Awards:** Chicago/AI, Bertha Aberle Florsheim Prize, 1942; Guggenheim Foundation Fellowship, 1945, 46; PAFA, Pennell Memorial Medal, 1946; Chicago/AI, The Mr. & Mrs. Frank G. Logan Medal, 1947; State U. of Iowa, First **P.P.**, 1947; Prix de Rome, 1949; Hallmark International Competition, Second Prize, 1949; Boston Arts Festival, Second Prize, 1954; and Third Prize, 1955; AAAL, 1955; Youngstown/ Butler, First Prize for Watercolors, 1961; Fulbright Fellowship (Italy), 1966–67. **One-man Exhibitions:** The Downtown Gallery, 1940, 42, 46, 47, 57; Springfield, Mass./MFA; Chicago/AI, 1947; Philadelphia Art Alliance, 1949; Boris Mirski Gallery, Boston, 1952; Jewish Community Center, Cleveland, 1953; The Alan Gallery, NYC, 1954; Lincoln Mass./De Cordova, 1955; U. of Vermont, 1956; Park Gallery, Detroit, 1960; Lee Nordness Gallery, NYC, 1960; U. of Oklahoma, 1980. **Retrospective:** Lincoln, Mass./De Cordova, 1954; Brandeis U., 1976. **Group:** A Century of Progress, 1933–34; MOMA, New Horizons in American Art, 1936; New York World's Fair, 1939; Golden Gate International Exposition, San Francisco, 1939; MOMA/USIA, Pintura Contemporanea Norteamericana, circ., Latin America, 1941; MOMA, Americans 1942, circ., 1942; Chicago/AI, 1942–46; WMAA, 1942–57; Carnegie, 1944–49; Paris/Moderne, 1946; ICA, Boston, American Painting in Our Century, circ., 1949; Contemporary American Drawings, circ. France, 1956; Art: USA: Now, circ., 1962–67; NCFA, After the Crash, 1980. **Collections:** Andover/Phillips; U. of Arizona; Auburn U.; Brandeis U.; Britannica; Chicago/AI; Cranbrook; U. of Georgia; Harvard U.; U. of Illinois; State U. of Iowa; MMA; MOMA; NCFA; NYPL; U. of Nebraska; Newark Museum; U. of New Mexico; PMA; Smith College; WMAA; Wichita/AM; Woodstock Art Association; Worcester/AM; Youngstown/Butler. **Bibliography:** Baur 7; Goodrich and Baur 1; Halpert; Miller, ed. 1; Nordness, ed.; Pagano; Pousette-Dart, ed.; Wight 2. Archives.

SLOAN, JOHN. b. August 2, 1871, Loch Haven, Pa.; **d.** September 7, 1951, Hanover, N.H. **Studied:** Spring Garden Institute, Philadelphia; PAFA, 1892, with Thomas Anshutz. **Taught:** ASL, 1914–26, 1935–37; Archipenko School of Art, 1932–33; George Luks School, 1934. Art Editor of *The Masses* (magazine), 1912–16. Organized a group called The Eight. **Member:** Society of Independent Artists, NYC (President, 1918–42); NIAL. **Awards:** Carnegie, Hon. Men., 1905; Panama-Pacific Exposition, San Francisco, 1915, Medal; Philadelphia, Sesquicentennial, 1926, Medal; PAFA; Carol H. Beck Gold Medal, 1931; MMA, 1942 ($500); NIAL, Gold Medal, 1950. **One-man Exhibitions:** (first) Whitney Studio Club, NYC, 1916; Hudson Guild, NYC, 1916; Kraushaar Galleries, 1917, 26, 27, 30, 37, 39, 43, 48, 52, 60, 66; Corcoran,

1933; Montross Gallery, NYC, 1934; WMAA, 1936, 52; Carnegie, 1939; Currier, 1940; The U. of Chicago, 1942; PMA, 1948; Santa Fe, N.M., 1951; Wilmington, 1961; Bowdoin College, 1962; Kennedy Gallery, 1964 (two-man); U. of Connecticut, 1971; Harbor Gallery, Cold Spring, N.Y., 1972; WMAA, 1980; Salander-O'Reilly Galleries, Inc., NYC, 1980. **Retrospectives:** Wanamaker Gallery, Philadelphia, 1940; Dartmouth College, 1946; Andover/Phillips, 1946; National Gallery, 1971. **Group:** Macbeth Gallery, NYC, The Eight, 1908; The Armory Show, 1913; MMA; Brooklyn Museum, The Eight, 1943; PMA; Syracuse/Everson, The Eight, 1958; Chicago/AI; Detroit/Institute; PAFA; Carnegie; Corcoran; WMAA, The 1930's, 1968, and others. **Collections:** Barnes Foundation; Boston/MFA; Brooklyn Museum; Carnegie; Chicago/AI; Cincinnati/AM; Cleveland/MA; Corcoran; Detroit/Institute; Hartford/Wadsworth; IBM; MMA; NYPL; Newark Public Library; PMA; The Pennsylvania State U.; Phillips; U. of Rochester; San Diego; Santa Fe, N.M.; WMAA; Walker. **Bibliography:** Baur 7; Bazin; Beam; Blesh 1; Boswell 1; Brooks; Brown; Brown 2; Bryant, L.; Cahill and Barr, eds.; Canaday; Cheney; *Cityscape 1919–39*; Coke 2; Craven, T., 1, 2; Downes, ed.; Du Bois 4; Eliot; Ely; Finkelstein; Flanagan; Flexner; **Gallatin 2, 5**; Gerdts; Glackens; **Goodrich 7**; Goodrich and Baur 1; Greengood; Haftman; Hall; Hartmann; Hunter 6; Huyghe; *Index of 20th Century Artists*; Jackman; Jewell 2; Kent, N.; Kouvenhoven; Mather 1; McCoubrey 1; McCurdy, ed.; Mendelowitz; Newmeyer; Pach 1, 3; Pagano; Pearson 1; Perlman; Phillips 2; Poore; Pousette-Dart, ed.; Reese; Richardson, E.P.; Ringel, ed.; Rose, B., 1, 4; Sachs; **St. John; St. John, ed.; Sloan, H.F.; Sloan, ed.; Sloan, J., 1, 2, 3, 4, 5**; Smith, S.C.K.; Sutton; Wight 2. Archives.

SMITH, DAVID. b. 1906, Decatur, Ind.; **d.** May 24, 1965, Bennington, Vt.

David Smith   Untitled   1946

Studied: Ohio U., 1924: ASL, 1926–30, with John Sloan, Jan Matulka. Traveled Europe, USSR, 1935; resided Voltri and Spoleto, Italy, 1962. **Taught:** Sarah Lawrence College, 1948; U. of Arkansas, 1953; Indiana U., 1954; U. of Mississippi, 1955. Created a series of 15 bronze "Medals of Dishonor," 1937–40. **Awards:** Guggenheim Foundation Fellowship, 1950, 51; Brandeis U., Creative Arts Award, 1964. **One-man Exhibitions:** East River Gallery, NYC, 1938; Skidmore College, 1939, 43, 46; Neumann-Willard Gallery, NYC, 1940; The Willard Gallery, NYC, 1940, 43, 46, 47, 50, 51, 54, 55, 56; Kalamazoo/Institute, 1941; Walker, 1943, 43, 52; Buchholz Gallery, NYC, 1946; Cooling Gallery, London, 1946; Utica, 1947; Kleemann Gallery, NYC, 1952; Tulsa/Philbrook, 1953; The Kootz Gallery, NYC, 1953; Cincinnati/AM, 1954; MOMA, 1957; Fine Arts Associates, NYC, 1957; Otto Gerson Gallery, NYC, 1957, 61; French & Co., Inc., NYC, 1959, 60; MOMA,

circ. only, 1960; Everett Ellin Gallery, Los Angeles, 1960; ICA, U. of Pennsylvania, 1964; Marlborough-Gerson Gallery Inc., 1964, 67, 68; Harvard U., 1966; Storm King Art Center, 1971; Glens Falls, N.Y., 1974; Dart Gallery, Chicago, 1975; Storm King Art Center, 1976; Knoedler Contemporary Art, NYC, 1974, 76, 77, 78, 80; Galerie Wentzel, Hamburg, 1979; Caracas, 1979; Hyde Collection, 1974; Hirshhorn, 1979; M. Knoedler Ltd., London, 1980. **Retrospectives:** Tate, 1966; SRGM, 1968; WMAA, circ., 1979. **Group:** XXIX Venice Biennial, 1958; Sao Paulo, 1959; Documenta II & III, Kassel, 1959, 64; WMAA; Chicago/AI; Carnegie; MOMA, The New American Painting and Sculpture, 1969, and others; Houston/MFA, The Great Decade of American Abstraction, 1974; Edmonton Art Gallery, Sculpture in Steel, 1974; U. of California, Santa Barbara, Sculptors in the 1950s, Alberta, 1976; Syracuse/Everson, New Works in Clay, 1976;

Norfolk/Chrysler, 300 Years of American Art, 1976; WMAA, 200 Years of American Sculpture, 1976; Brown U., Graham, Gorky, Smith, and Davis, 1977; Minnesota/MA, American Drawing, 1927–1977, 1977; National Gallery, American Art at Mid-Century: The Subjects of the Artists, 1978; Rutgers U., Vanguard American Sculpture, 1919–1939, 1979. **Bibliography:** Alloway 4; Battcock, ed.; Baur 5, 7; Blesh 1; Brumme; Calas, N. and E.; Carmean, Rathbone, and Hess; Chipp; **Cone 1**; Craven, W.; Cummings 2; Davis, D.; Downes, ed.; Fry; Gertz; Giedion-Welcker 1; Goodrich and Baur 1; Goossen 1; *Graham, Gorky, Smith & Davis in the Thirties; The Great Decade;* Greenberg 1; Henning; Honisch and Jensen, eds.; Hunter 6; Hunter, ed.; Janis and Blesh 1; Kozloff 3; **Kramer 1**; Krauss 2; Kuh 1, 2, 3; Licht, F.; Lynton; Marten, Tarbell, and Wechsler; **McCoy**; McCurdy, ed.; Mendelowitz; *Metro; Monumenta;* Moser 1; Motherwell, ed.; Motherwell and Reinhardt, eds.; Myers 2; **O'Hara** 1, 2; Passloff; Read 3; Rickey; Ritchie 1, 3; Rodman 1, 3; Rose, B. 1, 4; Rubin 1; Sandler 1; Seitz 3; Selz, J.; Seuphor 3; Seymour; **Smith, D.**; Strachan; Trier 1; Tuchman 1. Archives.

SMITH, HASSEL W., Jr. b. April 24, 1915, Sturgis, Mich. **Studied:** Northwestern U., BS; California School of Fine Arts, with Maurice Sterne. Traveled Europe, USA, Mexico. **Taught:** California School of Fine Arts, 1945, 47, 48, 52; San Francisco State College, 1946; U. of Oregon, 1947–48; Presidio Hill School, San Francisco, 1952–55; U. of California, Berkeley, 1963–65, 77–80; UCLA, 1965–66; Bristol (Eng.) Polytechnic, 1966– ; SFAI, 1978, 79, 80. **Awards:** Abraham Rosenberg Foundation Fellowship, 1941. **Address:** 19 Ashgrove Road, Bristol 6, England. **Dealer:** Gallery Paule Anglim, San Francisco. **One-man Exhibitions:** (first) California Palace, 1947, also 1952; California School of Fine Arts, 1956; New Arts Gallery, Houston, 1960, 62; Ferus Gallery, Los Angeles, 1960; Gimpel Fils Ltd., 1961; Pasadena/AM, 1961; Andre Emmerich Gallery, NYC, 1961, 62, 63; Dilexi Gallery, San Francisco, 1962; U. of Minnesota, 1962; Galleria dell'Ariete, 1962; David Stuart Gallery, 1963, 68, 73; U. of California, Berkeley, 1964; Santa Barbara/MA, 1969; Suzanne Saxe Gallery, San Francisco, 1970, 73; City Art Gallery, Bristol, 1972; ARCO Center for Visual Art, Los Angeles, 1978; Tortue Gallery, Santa Monica, 1980; Gallery Paule Anglim, 1977, 78, 79. **Retrospective:** San Francisco State College, 1964; SFMA, 1976. **Group:** California Palace; Pasadena/AM; WMAA Annuals; Los Angeles/County MA; Oakland/AM; SFMA; U. of California, Berkeley; Oakland/AM, A Period of Exploration, 1973; SFMA, 200 Years of California Painting, 1976. **Collections:** Buffalo/Albright; Corcoran; Dallas/MFA; Hirshhorn; Houston/MFA; Los Angeles/County MA; New Paltz/SUNY; Oakland/AM; Pasadena/AM; Phillips; SFMA; St. Louis/City; Tate; WMAA; Washington U. **Bibliography:** McChesney.

SMITH, KIMBER. b. 1922, Boston; **d.** April 21, 1981, East Hampton, N.Y. **Studied:** ASL. Resided Paris, 1954–65. **Taught:** Dayton/AI, 1965–68. **One-man Exhibitions:** New Gallery, NYC, 1951, 54; Peridot Gallery, NYC, 1954, 60; Kornfeld and Lipstein Gallery, Berne, 1959; Galerie Lawrence, Paris 1962, 63; Galerie Handschin, Basel, 1961, 74; Kunstverein, Dusseldorf, 1962; Galerie Ziegler, Zurich, 1963, 73, 75, 77, 79; Dayton/AI, 1965, 67; Galerie Hite, Basel, 1965; U. of Kentucky, 1972; Andre Emmerich Gallery, NYC, 1973; Susan Caldwell Gallery, NYC, 1973, 77; Robert Elkon Gallery, NYC, 1979. **Group:** Carnegie, International, 1958; Amsterdam/Stedelijk, Collection Sandberg, 1961; Salon de Mai, Paris, 1964. **Collections:** Amsterdam/Stedelijk; Dayton/AI; Geneva/Moderne; Musée de Reims; Zurich. **Bibliography:** Honisch and Jensen, eds.

SMITH, LEON P. b. May 20, 1906, Chickasha, Okla. **Studied:** East Central State College, AB; Columbia U., MA. Traveled Mexico, Europe, Canada, USA, Venezuela. **Taught:** Oklahoma public schools, 1933–39; Georgia University System, Teachers College, 1939–41; State Supervisor, Delaware, 1941–43; Rollins College, 1949–51; Mills College of Education, 1951–58; Artist-in-Residence, Brandeis U., 1968, and U. of California, Davis, 1972. **Awards:** Guggenheim Foundation Fellowship, 1944; Longview Foundation Grant, 1959; National Council on the Arts; Tamarind Fellowship; AAIAI, **P.P.**, 1979. **Address:** 31 Union Square West, NYC 10003. **One-man Exhibitions:** (first) Uptown Gallery, MYC, 1940; Savannah/Telfair, 1941; Rose Fried Gallery, 1942, 46, 49; Santa Fe, N.M., 1943; Charles Egan Gallery, 1945; Betty Parsons Gallery, 1957, 59; The Stable Gallery, 1960, 62; Caracas, 1962; Galerie Muller, 1964; Galerie Chalette, 1967, 68, 69, 70; Brandeis U., 1968; SFMA, 1968; Fort Worth Art Museum, 1968; Galerie Denise Rene, Paris, 1973, 75; Pelham-von Stoffler Gallery, Houston, 1977, 78; Old Westbury/SUNY, 1978; Susan Caldwell Inc., NYC 1979; ACE Gallery, Vancouver, 1979; ACE Gallery, Venice, Calif., 1979; Paule Anglim Associates, San Francisco, 1979. **Group:** WMAA, 1959; Helmhaus Gallery, Zurich, Konkrete Kunst, 1960; SRGM, Abstract Expressionists and Imagists, 1961; WMAA Annual, 1962; WMAA, Geometric Abstraction in America, circ., 1962; Chicago/AI, 1962; Dallas/MFA, "1961," 1962; Corcoran, 1963; Brandeis U., New Directions in American Painting, 1963; MOMA, American Collages, 1965; MOMA, The Responsive Eye, 1965; SFMA, Colorists 1950–1965, 1965; SRGM, Systemic Painting, 1966; Carnegie, 1967, 70; Buffalo/Albright, Plus by Minus, 1968; Chicago/Contemporary, Post-Mondrian Abstraction in America, 1973; Carnegie, Celebration, 1974–75; Paris/Moderne, Paris–New York, 1977; Claremont College, Black and White Are Colors, 1979; Yale U.,

Mondrian and Neoplasticism in America, 1979. **Collections:** Aachen; Birmingham, Ala./MA; Brandeis U.; Buffalo/Albright; Carnegie; Cleveland/MA; Detroit/Institute; First National Bank of Chicago; Fort Worth; Indianapolis; Los Angeles/County MA; Milwaukee; MMA; MOMA; Oklahoma State Art Collection; RISD; SRGM; Springfield, Mass./MFA; U. of Sydney; WMAA. **Bibliography:** Alloway 3; *Black and White Are Colors*; American Artists Group Inc. 2; Battcock, ed.; Calas, N. and E.; *Kunst um 1970*; MacAgy 2; Rickey; Sandler 1; Seuphor 1.

SMITH, TONY. b. 1912, South Orange, N.J.; **d.** December 26, 1980, NYC. **Studied:** ASL, 1933–36; New Bauhaus, Chicago, 1937–38. Worked on new buildings designed by Frank Lloyd Wright, 1938–39. **Taught:** NYU, 1946–50; Cooper Union, 1950–53; Pratt Institute, 1950–53, 1957–58; Bennington College, 1958–61; Hunter College, 1962–74. **Awards:** Longview Foundation Grant, 1966; National Council on the Arts, 1966; Guggenheim Foundation Fellowship, 1968; College Art Association, Distinguished Teaching of Art Award, 1974; Brandeis U., Creative Arts Award for Sculpture, 1974. **One-man Exhibitions:** Hartford/Wadsworth, 1966; ICA, U. of Pennsylvania, 1966; Walker, 1967; Galerie Muller, Stuttgart, 1967; Bryant Park, NYC, 1967; Galerie Rene Ziegler, 1968; Yvon Lambert, 1968; Donald Morris Gallery, Detroit, 1968; MOMA, circ., 1968; U. of Hawaii, 1969; Newark Museum, 1970; Montclair/AM, 1970; Princeton U., 1979; Trenton/State, 1970; Knoedler Contemporary Art, 1970; MOMA, 1970; U. of Maryland, 1974. **Group:** Hartford/Wadsworth, Black, White, and Grey, 1964; Jewish Museum, Primary Structure Sculptures, 1966; WMAA, 1966, 71, 73; Detroit/Institute, Color, Image and Form, 1967; Chicago/AI, A Generation of Innovation, 1967; Los Angeles/County MA,

American Sculpture of the Sixties, circ., 1967; Carnegie, 1967; Corcoran, Scale as Content, 1967; SRGM; Guggenheim International, 1967; A.F.A., Rejective Art, 1967; Finch College, NYC, Schemata 7, 1967; Documenta IV, Kassel, 1968; Buffalo/Albright, Plus by Minus, 1968; HemisFair '68, San Antonio, Tex., 1968; MMA, New York Painting and Sculpture; 1940–1970, 1969–70; Akademie der Kunst, Berlin, Minimal Art, 1969; Expo '70, Osaka, 1970; Cincinnati/Contemporary, Monumental Art, 1970; U. of Nebraska, American Sculpture, 1970; Los Angeles/County MA, Art & Technology, 1971; Foundation Maeght, 1971; Arnhem, Sonsbeek, '71, 1971; Indianapolis, 1974. **Collections:** Corcoran; Detroit/Institute; Hartford/Wadsworth; MOMA; Mutual Life Insurance Building, Chicago; U. of Pennsylvania; Princeton U.; Rice U.; Rijksmuseum Kroller-Muller; Trenton/State; Walker. **Bibliography:** Calas, N. and E.; *Monumenta; Report; Tony Smith.* Archives.

SMITHSON, ROBERT. b. January 2, 1938, Passaic, N.J.; **d.** July 20, 1973, Tecovas Lake, Tex. **Studied:** ASL, 1953, with John Groth; Brooklyn Museum School, 1956. US Army Reserve Forces, Special Services. Traveled USA, Mexico, London, Rome. **One-man Exhibitions:** (first) Artists' Gallery, NYC, 1959; Galleria George Lester, Rome, 1961; Dwan Gallery, NYC, 1966–69, 70; Konrad Fischer Gallery, Dusseldorf, 1968–69; Galleria l'Attico, Rome, 1969; ACE Gallery, Los Angeles and Vancouver, 1970; New York Cultural Center, circ., 1974; Kunstmuseum, Lucerne, circ., 1975; John Weber Gallery, NYC, 1976; Portland (Ore.) Center for Visual Arts, 1977; U. of Massachusetts, 1976. **Retrospective:** Cornell U., 1980. **Group:** ICA, U. of Pennsylvania, Current Art, 1965; Jewish Museum, Primary Structure Sculptures, 1966; Finch College, NYC, 1966, 67; WMAA, 1966, 69, 70, Annual, 1969; Los Angeles/County MA, American Sculpture of the

Sixties, 1967; Trenton/State, Focus on Light, 1967; The Hague, Minimal Art, 1968; MOMA, The Art of the Real, 1968; Buffalo/Albright, Plus by Minus, 1968; Dusseldorf/Kunsthalle, Prospect '68, '69, 1968, 69; Milwaukee, Directions 1: Options, circ., 1968; Amsterdam/Stedelijk, Op Losse Schroeven, 1969; Berne, When Attitudes Become Form, 1969; ICA, U. of Pennsylvania, Between Object and Environment, 1969; Chicago/Contemporary, Art by Telephone, 1969; Seattle/AM, 557,087, 1969; ICA, U. of Pennsylvania, Against Order: Chance and Art, 1970; Chicago/AI, 69th and 70th American Exhibitions, 1969, 72; MOMA, Information, 1971; Documenta V, Kassel, 1972; Rijksmuseum Kroller-Muller, Diagrams and Drawings, 1972; New York Cultural Center, 3D into 2D, 1973; MIT, Interventions in Landscape, 1974; Neuer Berliner Kunstverein, Berlin, Multiples, 1974; Rutgers U., Response to the Environment, 1975. **Collections:** Kingsborough Community College; MOMA; Milwaukee; WMAA. **Bibliography:** Alloway 4; Atkinson; Battcock, ed.; Calas, N. and E.; Celant; Cummings 1; De Vries, ed.; *Drawings: The Pluralist Decade;* Gablik; Goossen 1; Holt ed.; Honisch and Jensen, eds.; Johnson, Ellen H.; Krauss 2; *Kunst um 1970;* Lippard 3, 4; Lippard, ed.; MacAgy 2; Muller; *Report;* Tuchman 1; *When Attitudes Become Form.* Archives.

SMYTH, DAVID. b. December 2, 1943, Washington, D.C. **Studied:** Skowhegan School, 1964; The Corcoran School of Art, 1962–64; Chicago Art Institute School, 1964, 67, BFA; 1967–69, MFA. **Taught:** Chicago Academy of Fine Art, 1968–69; Indiana U., 1969–70; School of Visual Arts, NYC, 1974–77; Yale U., 1975; Ithaca College, 1977–79. **Awards:** George D. Brown traveling fellowship, Chicago/AI, 1967; Richard Rice Jenkins Memorial Prize, Chicago/AI, 1968. **Address:** % Dealer. **Dealer:** Ronald Feldman Fine Arts, Inc., NYC. **One-man Exhibitions:** Allan Frumkin Gallery, Chicago, 1968; WMAA, 1972; Ronald Feldman Fine Arts, NYC, 1973, 74, 75, 77, 79; Berry College, 1975; Barbara Fendrick Gallery, Washington, D.C., 1976; Marianne Deson Gallery, Chicago, 1976; Tortue Gallery, Santa Monica, 1977; Isy Brachot, Brussels, 1977; Ithaca College, 1978; Droscher Gallery, Hamburg, 1978. **Group:** Chicago/AI, Print and Drawing Biennial, 1966, 68; Chicago/AI, Artists under Thirty, 1968; U. of Illinois, 1969; Brooklyn Museum, Prints, 1974; Chicago Art Institute School, Alumni Painting and Sculpture, 1976; Chicago/AI, Drawings of the Seventies, 1977; Indianapolis, 1978, Chicago/AI, 100 Artists—100 Years, 1979; Pratt Institute, NYC, First Person Singular, 1980. **Collections:** Blue Cross–Blue Shield; WMAA.

SNELGROVE, WALTER. b. March 22, 1924, Seattle, Wash. **Studied:** U. of Washington; U. of California, Berkeley, with James McCray, M. O'Hagan, BA, MA; California School of Fine Arts, with Hassel Smith, Antonio Sotamayor, James Weeks. US Navy, 1943–47. Traveled Europe; resided Florence, Italy. **Taught:** U. of California, 1951–53. **Awards:** U. of California, James D. Phelan Traveling Scholarship, 1951; SFMA, M. Grumbacher Award, 1959; Oakland/AM, First Prize, 1962. **Address:** % Dealer. **Dealer:** Gump's Gallery, San Francisco. **One-man Exhibitions:** (first) Oakland/AM, 1959; California Palace; Santa Barbara/MA; Gump's Gallery; Colorado Springs/FA. **Retrospective:** Foothill College, 1967. **Group:** de Young; SFMA; RAC; Oakland/AM, Contemporary Bay Area Figurative Painting, 1957; Los Angeles/County MA; WMAA, Fifty California Artists, 1962–63; VMFA; U. of Illinois, 1963; Carnegie, 1964; Denver/AM, 1964; U. of Washington; Des Moines. **Collections:** A.F.A.; California Palace; Colorado Springs/FA; Oakland/AM; Stanford U.; WMAA.

SNELSON, KENNETH. b. June 29, 1927, Pendleton, Ore. **Studied:** U. of Oregon (with Jack Wilkinson); Black Mountain College (with Josef Albers, Buckminster Fuller, Willem de Kooning); Academie Montmartre, Paris (with Fernand Leger). US Naval Reserve, 1945–46. Traveled Europe, Near East, Far East. **Taught:** Cooper Union; Pratt Institute; School of Visual Arts, NYC; Southern Illinois U.; Yale U. **Commission:** Reynolds Metals Co., Sculpture Award, 1974. **Awards:** Milan Triennial, Silver Medal, 1964; New York City Council on the Arts Award, 1971; DAAD Fellowship, Berlin, 1975; National Endowment for the Arts, 1975. **Address:** 140 Sullivan Street, NYC 10012. **One-man Exhibitions:** (first) Pratt Institute, 1963; New York World's Fair, 1964–65; Dwan Gallery, NYC, 1966, 68; Dwan Gallery, Los Angeles, 1967; Bryant Park, NYC, 1968; Fort Worth, 1969; Rijksmuseum Kroller-Muller, 1969; Stadtische Kunsthalle, Dusseldorf, 1969; Hannover/Kunstverein, 1971; John Weber Gallery, 1972; Galeria van der Voort, Ibiza, 1972; Waterside Place, NYC, 1974; Galerie Buchholz, Munich, 1975; Berlin/National, 1977; Duisburg, 1977; Gallery de Gestlo, Hamburg, 1977; Maryland Academy of Science, Baltimore, 1978; Sonnabend Gallery, NYC, 1978. **Group:** MOMA, 1959, 62; Milan Triennial, 1964; WMAA Sculpture Annual, 1966–69; Los Angeles/County MA, American Sculpture of the Sixties, 1967; CSCS, Los Angeles, 1967; Chicago/AI, 1967; Buffalo/Albright, Plus by Minus, 1968; Dusseldorf/Kuntshalle, Prospect '68, 1968; PMA, 1968; Grant Park, Chicago, Sculpture in the Park, 1974; AAAL, 1977; NYU, Panoramic Photography, 1977. **Collections:** Amsterdam/Stedelijk; City of Baltimore; Bundeswehr; Carnegie; Chattanooga/Hunter; Chicago/AI; Duisburg; City of Hamburg; City of Hannover; Hirshhorn; City of Iowa; Japan Iron and Steel Federation, Osaka; Milwaukee; MOMA; Rijksmuseum Kroller-Muller; City of San Diego; Storm King Art

Center; WMAA. **Bibliography:** Mac-Agay 2; Tuchman 1.

SOLOMON, HYDE. b. May 3, 1911, NYC. **Studied:** Columbia U., with Meyer Shapiro; American Artists School, NYC, 1938; Pratt Institute; ASL, 1943, with Ossip Zadkine. Traveled Europe. **Taught:** Princeton U., 1959–62; Goddard College, summers, 1954, 55. **Member:** American Abstract Artists. **Awards:** MacDowell Colony Fellowship, 1949, 50, 51, 52; Yaddo Fellowship, 1951, 56, 57, 58, 59, 62, 63, 64; AAAL, **P.P.**, 1971; Mark Rothko Foundation, 1973; Wurlitzer Foundation Grant, 1974; Rothko Foundation Grant, 1973; Gottlieb Foundation Grant, 1978. **Address:** P.O. Box 2538, Taos, NM 87571. **Dealers:** Stables Gallery, Taos; Ledoux Gallery, Taos. **One-man Exhibitions:** (first) Vendome Galleries, NYC, 1941; Jane Street Gallery, NYC, 1945, 48; The Peridot Gallery, 1954, 55, 56; Poindexter Gallery, 1956, 58, 60, 63, 65, 67, 69, 70, 71, 73; Princeton U., 1959; Rutgers U., 1961; Skidmore College, 1962; Ledoux Gallery, Taos, 1979; Stables Gallery, Taos, 1980. **Group:** MOMA; Walker; Brooklyn Museum; Newark Museum; Yale U.; Hartford/Wadsworth; PMA; The Kootz Gallery, NYC, New Talent, 1950; WMAA, Nature in Abstraction, 1958; Annual, 1965, and others; Carnegie, 1964, 67; VMFA, American Painting, 1966; New School for Social Research, Humanist Tradition, 1968; Allentown/AM, Monhegan Island Painters, 1974; NAD, 1977, 78. **Collections:** Brandeis U.; U. of California, Berkeley; Chase Manhattan Bank; Ciba-Geigy Corp.; Ford Foundation; Hartford/Wadsworth; Mitsui Bank of Japan; Newark Museum; Reader's Digest; Utica; WMAA; Walker; Westinghouse. **Bibliography:** Archives.

SOLOMON, SYD. b. July 12, 1917, Uniontown, Pa. **Studied:** Chicago Art Institute School, 1934; Academie des Beaux-Arts, Paris, 1945. **Taught:** Art Institute of Pittsburgh, 1947; Ringling School of Art, 1948–50; Famous Artists Schools, Inc., 1954–67; Sarasota School of Art, 1950, 55; Fine Arts Institute of New College, Sarasota, Fla., 1964–65, 1967–69; U. of Illinois, 1968; Robertson Center for the Arts and Sciences, Binghamton, N.Y., 1969; Tampa Bay Art Center, 1972; U. of California, 1976; Boca Raton Center for Art, 1977; Fort Lauderdale, 1978; US Corps of Engineers, World War II. **Commissions** (murals): St. Petersburg Times Building; Far Horizons Hotel, St. Petersburg, Fla. **Awards:** Hallmark International Competition, 1952; Youngstown/Butler, First **P.P.**, 1957; Audubon Artists, Gold Medal of Honor, 1957; American Institute of Architects, Medal of Honor, 1959; Ringling, First Prize, 1962; Silvermine Guild, 1962; Ford Foundation, **P.P.**, 1964; Florida State Fair, First Prize; AAIAL, Hassam and Speicher Fund, **P.P.**, 1979. **Address:** 9210 Blind Pass Road, Sarasota, FL 33581. **Dealer:** Adley Gallery, Sarasota; Carone Gallery, Fort Lauderdale. **One-man Exhibitions:** Farnham Castle, England; Clearwater (Fla.) Museum of Art, 1951; U. of Miami, 1953; U. of Florida, 1954; A.A.A. Gallery, NYC, 1955; Clearwater/Gulf Coast, 1956, 74, 75; Saidenberg Gallery, 1959–62, 1964, 67, 70; Safrai Gallery, Jerusalem, 1960; Tel Aviv, 1960; U. of Tennessee, 1961; Sarasota (Fla.) Art Association, 1961; James David Gallery, Ltd., Miami Beach, 1963, 64; Jacksonville U., 1968; The Berenson Gallery, 1969, 71, 74; Midtown Gallery, Atlanta, 1971; Contemporary Gallery, St. Petersburg, 1971; Trend House Gallery, Tampa, 1972, 74, 76; Hokin Gallery, Palm Beach, 1973; Ridge Art Association, Winter Haven, Fla., 1973; Brevard College, Cocoa, Fla, 1974; Benson Gallery, Bridgehampton, N.Y., 1975; Brookhaven National Laboratory, L.I., N.Y., 1975; Carone Gallery, Ft. Lauderdale, 1976, 78; Tampa Bay Art Center, 1976; U. of West Florida, 1977; LeMoyne Art Foundation, 1977; Boca Raton Center for the Arts, 1977; Harmon Gallery, Naples, Fla., 1977;

Adley Gallery, Sarasota, 1978, 79, 80; The Art and Culture Center of Hollywood, Fla., 1978; St. Petersburg, Fla., 1979; Genesis Galleries, Ltd., NYC, 1979; McDowell Gallery, Toronto, 1979. **Retrospective:** Ringling, 1974. **Group:** New Orleans/Delgado, 1951, 57; MMA, 1952; Hallmark Art Award, 1952; U. of Florida, 1953; Dallas/MFA, 1954; Youngstown/Butler, 1954, 56–57; NAD, 1955, 57, 59; Houston/MFA, 1955; Ringling, Fifty Florida Painters, 1955; Carnegie, 1956; Corcoran, 1959; WMAA Annual, 1959; AAAL, 1959; Art: USA: 59, NYC, 1959; Corcoran, 1959; Chicago/AI, 1961; U. of Illinois, 1965; Colorado Springs/FA, 1966; SRGM, 1966; Pan American Union, Washington, D.C., Florida Seventeen, 1968; AAIAL, 1979. **Collections:** Adelphi U.; Atlanta/AA; Baltimore/MA; Birmingham, Ala./MA; Brandeis U.; Cincinnati/AM; Clearwater/Gulf Coast; First National Bank, Tampa; Florida Southern College; Friends of Art; Georgia Institute of Technology; Gulf Life Insurance Co.; Hartford/Wadsworth; High Museum; Hirshhorn; International Minerals & Chemicals Corp.; Jacksonville U.; Louisiana State U.; Mead Corporation; U. of Miami; New Orleans/Delgado; New Orleans Museum; Norfolk/Chrysler; PMA; Ringling; SRGM; U. of South Florida; Tupperware Museum; WMAA; West Palm Beach/Norton; Witte; Youngstown/Butler. **Bibliography:** Pousette-Dart, ed.; *Syd Solomon.*

SONENBERG, JACK. b. December 28, 1925, Toronto, Canada. **Studied:** NYU; Washington U., BFA, 1951, with Paul Burlin; Farnham School of Art, England, 1945–56; Ontario College of Art, 1942. **Taught:** School of Visual Arts, NYC, 1962–74; Pratt Institute, 1967–80; Brooklyn College, 1972; U. of New Mexico, 1970. **Commissions:** International Graphic Arts Society; New York Hilton Hotel. **Awards:** L. C. Tiffany Grant (printmaking), 1962; Silvermine Guild, First Prize, 1962; St. Paul Gallery, Drawing USA, **P.P.**; Bradley U.,

Print Annual, **P.P.**; Ford Foundation/A.F.A., Artist-in-Residence, 1966; Guggenheim Foundation Fellowship, 1973; CAPS, New York State Council of the Arts, 1973, 76. **Address:** 217 East 23rd Street, NYC 10010. **One-man Exhibitions:** (first) Washington Irving Gallery, NYC, 1958; Carl Siembab Gallery, Boston, 1959; Roko Gallery, NYC, 1961; Feingarten Gallery, Los Angeles, 1962, NYC, 1963; Des Moines, 1964; The Byron Gallery, 1965, 68; Hampton Institute, 1966; Grand Rapids, 1968; U. of Iowa, 1969; Flint/Institute, 1973; Fischbach Gallery, 1973; 55 Mercer Street, NYC, 1980. **Group:** Brooklyn Museum, Print Biennials; Chicago/AI; Silvermine Guild; SRGM; Des Moines; WMAA, American Prints Today, 1959, Annual, 1968; Youngstown/Butler, 1961; U. of Illinois, 1963; New York World's Fair, 1964–65; Finch College, 1965; PAFA, 1969; WMAA, 1973; MOMA, Printed, Folded, Cut and Torn, 1974; Kent State U., Blossom Festival, 1978; NCFA, New Ways with Paper, 1978. **Collections:** Bradley U.; Brandeis U.; Grand Rapids; Hampton Institute; MMA; MOMA; Minnesota/MA; NYPL; PMA; Purchase/SUNY; SRGM; Syracuse U.; WMAA; Washington U.

SONFIST, ALAN. b. May 26, 1946, New York City. **Studied:** ASL, 1963; Pratt Institute, 1965, 66; Western Illinois U., 1964–67, BA; Hunter College, 1969; Ohio State U., 1968. **Taught:** Lombard (Ill.) H.S., 1967; Ohio State U., 1968; MIT, 1967–76; Philadelphia College of Art, 1975–76. **Commissions:** Airco Industries, Mountainville, N.J.; Chase Manhattan Bank, NYC; Ponderosa Inc., Dayton; Best Products, Inc., Richmond, Va.; Brooklyn Planning Board, NYC; Sunforest Medical Center, Toledo. **Awards:** National Endowment for the Arts, grant, 1975, 78; Citibank Foundation grant; Gilman Foundation grant; CAPS, 1977; Graham Foundation grant, 1972. **Address:** 833 Broadway, NYC 10003. **Dealer:** Leo Castelli Gallery,

NYC; Multiples Gallery, NYC. **One-man Exhibitions:** Reese Palley Gallery, NYC, 1970; Harcus-Krakow Gallery, Boston, 1971; Deson Zaks Gallery, Chicago, 1971; Finch College, NYC, 1971; ICA, London, 1972; Automation House, NYC, 1972; Akron/AI, 1972; Paley & Lowe Gallery, NYC, 1977; Solway Gallery, Cincinnati, 1974, 77; Galerie Thelen, Cologne, 1974; Stefanotty Gallery, NYC, 1975; Cornell U., 1975; Adiene Gallery, NYC, 1975; Galeria Massimo Valsecchi, Milan, 1976; Galleria Cavellino, Venice, 1976; Purchase/SUNY, 1978; Leo Castelli Gallery, NYC, 1978. **Group:** Indianapolis, 1972; Cologne, Projects 74, 1974; Venice, Biennale, 1976; Paris, Biennale, 1975; Aachen, 1975; Boston/MFA, 1977; Kassel, Documenta, 1977. **Collections:** Boston/MFA; Chase Manhattan Bank; Cologne; Cornell U.; First National Bank, Chicago; General Telephone Co., NYC; MOMA; U. of North Carolina; Oberlin College; Syracuse/Everson. **Bibliography:** Lucie-Smith.

SONNIER, KEITH. b. 1941, Mamou, La. **Studied:** U. of Southwestern Louisiana, 1959–63, BA; Rutgers U., 1965–66, MFA. Resided France, 1963–64. **Awards:** Tokyo Print Biennial, First Prize, 1974; Guggenheim Foundation Fellowship, 1974. **Address:** 33 Rector Street, NYC 10006. **Dealer:** Leo Castelli, Inc., NYC. **One-man Exhibitions:** Douglass College, New Brunswick, N.J., 1966; Galerie Rolf Ricke, 1968, 71, 72, 75, 78; Leo Castelli, Inc., NYC, 1970, 72, 74, 75, 76, 78, 79; ACE Gallery, Los Angeles, 1970, 75, 77; Eindhoven, 1970; MOMA, 1971; Seder/Creigh Gallery, Coronado, 1974, 76; Rosamund Felsen Gallery, Los Angeles, 1978; The Clocktower, NYC, 1978; Krefeld, 1979; Galerie Michele Lachowsky, Brussels, 1979; Eric Fabre Gallery, Paris, 1979. **Group:** A.F.A., Soft Sculpture, 1968; American Abstract Artists, 1968; Trenton/State, Soft Art, 1969; Washington U., Here and Now, 1969; Berne, When Attitudes Become Form, 1969; WMAA, Anti-Illusion: Procedures/Materials, 1969; Chicago/AI, 1970; ICA, U. of Pennsylvania, Against Order: Chance and Art, 1970; WMAA, 1970; MOMA, Information, 1971; Dusseldorf/Kunsthalle, Prospect '71, 1971; New Delhi, Second World Triennial, 1971; Humlebaek/Louisiana, American Art, 1950–1970, 1971; Venice Biennial, 1972; Festival of Two Worlds, Spoleto, 1972; Yale U., Options and Alternatives, 1973; New York Cultural Center, 3D into 2D, 1973; Parcheggio di Villa Borghese, Rome, Contemporanea, 1974; WMAA, 1973; Seattle/AM, American Art—Third Quarter Century, 1973; CNAC, Art/Voir, 1974; WMAA, Projected Video, 1975; NCFA, Sculpture; American Directions 1945–1975, 1975; WMAA, 200 Years of American Sculpture, 1976; Fort Worth, American Artists: A New Decade, 1976; New Orleans Museum, Five From Louisiana, 1977; Rutgers U., Twelve From Rutgers, 1977; Aspen Center for the Visual Arts, American Portraits of the Sixties and Seventies, 1970. **Collections:** Aachen; Canberra/National; Cologne; Harvard U.; MOMA; U. of North Carolina; Stockholm/National; WMAA. **Bibliography:** *Art Now 74; Celant; Contemporanea; Davis, D.; Kunst um 1970; Lippard, ed.; Muller; Options and Alternatives; Honisch and Jensen, eds.; Pincus-Witten; When Attitudes Become Form.* Archives.

SOYER, MOSES. b. December 25, 1899, Tombov, Russia; **d.** September 2, 1974, NYC. To USA, 1913; citizen, 1925. **Studied:** Cooper Union; NAD; Educational Alliance, NYC; Ferrer School, San Francisco, with Robert Henri, George Bellows. Traveled Europe, Russia. **Taught:** Contemporary School of Art, NYC; New School for Social Research; Educational Alliance, NYC; and elsewhere. **Member:** NAD; Artists Equity; Audubon Artists; NIAL. Federal A.P.; US Post Office, Philadelphia, Pa.; Greenpoint Hospital, Brooklyn, N.Y. (mural, with James Penney); 10 portable murals for libraries. **Awards:** AAAL, Childe Hassam Award (2); NAD, Annual, Andrew Carnegie Prize. **One-man Exhibitions:** (first) J. B. Neumann's New Art Circle, NYC, 1928; Kleeman Gallery, NYC, 1935; Macbeth Gallery, NYC, 1940; 41, 43; Boyer Gallery, NYC; ACA Gallery, 1944, 47, 70, 72, 77; Guild Hall, 1972. **Retrospective:** U. of North Carolina, 1972. **Group:** MMA; WMAA; Brooklyn Museum; Detroit/Institute;   Youngstown/Butler; NAD. **Collections:** AAAL; Birmingham, Ala./MA; Brooklyn Museum; Detroit/Institute; Hartford/Wadsworth; U. of Kansas; Library of Congress; MMA; MOMA; NAD; Newark Museum; PMA; Phillips; Toledo/MA; WMAA; Youngstown/Butler. **Bibliography:** Brown 2; Cheney; Finkelstein; Mendelowitz; **Smith, B.; Soyer, M.; Soyer, R., 1; Wheeler; Willard.** Archives.

Raphael Soyer   *Paul Resika and Warren Brandt*   1977

SOYER, RAPHAEL. b. December 25, 1899, Tombov, Russia. To USA, 1912. **Studied:** Cooper Union; NAD, 1919–21; ASL, with Guy DuBois. **Taught:** ASL; American Art School, NYC; New School for Social Research; NAD, 1965–67. **Member:** NIAL; NAD. Federal A.P.: Easel painting. **Commissions:** US Post Office, Kingsessing, **Awards:** Carnegie, Hon. Men. (3); Chicago/AI, The M. V. Kohnstamm Prize, 1932; Chicago/AI, Norman Wait Harris Gold Medal, 1932; PAFA, Carol H. Beck Gold Medal, 1934; Chicago/AI, Norman Wait Harris Bronze Medal, 1940; PAFA, Joseph E. Temple Gold Medal, 1943; PAFA, Walter Lippincott Prize, 1946; Corcoran, William A. Black Prize and Corcoran Gold Medal, 1951; ART:USA:59, NYC, $1,000 Prize, 1959. **Address:** 88 Central Park West, NYC 10023. **Dealer:** The Forum Gallery. **One-man Exhibitions:** The Daniel Gallery, NYC, 1929; L'Elan Gallery, NYC, 1932; Curt Valentine Gallery, NYC, 1933, 34, 35, 57, 38; Frank K.M. Rehn Gallery, NYC, 1939; Treasury Section, Fine Arts Division, 1939; A.A.A. Gallery, NYC, 1940, 41, 48, 53, 55; Weyhe Gallery, 1944; Philadelphia Art Alliance, 1949; ACA Gallery, 1960; Alfredo Valente Gallery, NYC, 1961; Bernard Crystal Gallery, NYC, 1962; The Forum Gallery, 1964, 66, 67, 72, 77; The Margo Feiden Galleries, NYC, 1972; Galerie Albert Loeb, Paris, 1980. **Retrospective:** WMAA, circ., 1967. **Group:** Salons of America, NYC, 1926; WMAA Annuals, 1932– ; PAFA, 1934, 43, 46; Corcoran, 1937, 51; VMFA, 1938; Chicago/AI, 1940; Brooklyn Museum, 1941; Carnegie, 1944; Phillips, 1944; Dallas/MFA, 1945; California Palace, 1945; MOMA, 1946; NAD, 1951, 52; A.F.A., 1967; NAD, American Portrait Drawings, 1980; Trenton/State, American Art of the 1930's, 1979; Akademie der Kunst, Berlin, American Art: 1920–1940, 1980. **Collections:** Andover/Phillips; U. of Arizona; Boston/MFA; Brooklyn Museum; Buffalo/Albright; Columbus; Corcoran; Detroit/Institute; Hartford/Wadsworth; MMA; MOMA; Montclair/AM; U. of Nebraska; Newark Museum; Norfolk/Chrysler; Oslo/National; Phillips; WMAA. **Bibliography:** American Artists Congress, Inc.; American Artists Group Inc. 3; Bazin; Biddle

4; Boswell 1; Brown 2; Cheney; Finkel-stein; **Foster;** *From Foreign Shores;* **Goodrich 10**; Goodrich and Baur 1; **Gutman**; Hall; Kent, N.; Mellquist; Mendelowitz; Nordness, ed.; Pagano; Reese; **Soyer, R., 1, 2, 3**; Wheeler; Zigrosser 1. Archives.

SPEICHER, EUGENE. b. April 5, 1883, Buffalo, N.Y.; **d.** 1962. **Studied:** Buffalo Fine Arts Academy, 1902–06; ASL, 1907–08, with Frank V. DuMond, William M. Chase; Robert Henri School, 1909, with Robert Henri. Traveled Europe extensively. **Member:** NIAL; NAD; National Arts Club. **Awards:** ASL, Kelley Prize, 1907; NAD, Thomas R. Proctor Prize, 1911; Salmagundi Club, Jose S. Isadora Prize, 1913; NAD, Hallgarten Prize, 1914, 15; Panama-Pacific Exposition, San Francisco, 1915, Silver Medal; PAFA, Carol H. Beck Gold Medal, 1920; Carnegie, Third Prize, 1921, Second Prize, 1923; Chicago/AI, Potter Palmer Gold Medal, 1926; Corcoran, Second William A. Clark Prize, 1928; Corcoran, First Prize; VMFA, **P.P.**; Hon. DFA, Syracuse U., 1945. **One-man Exhibitions:** Montross Gallery, NYC, 1918; M. Knoedler & Co., 1920; Carnegie, 1924; Boston Arts Club, 1925; Rehn Galleries, 1925, 29, 34, 41, 43; Des Moines, 1926; Denver/AM, 1948; Wildenstein & Co., NYC, 1954; AAAL, Memorial Exhibition, 1963; ACA Gallery, 1965. **Retrospective:** Buffalo/Albright, 1950. **Group:** WMAA; PAFA; Carnegie; Century Association, Robert Henri and Five Pupils, 1946; MOMA; Chicago/AI. **Collections:** ASL; Andover/Phillips; Boston/MFA; Britannica; Brooklyn Museum; Buffalo/Albright; Cincinnati/AM; Cleveland/MA; Corcoran; Decatur; Des Moines; Detroit/Institute; Galveston; Harvard U.; IBM; Indianapolis/Herron; Kansas City/Nelson; Los Angeles/County MA; MMA; MOMA; Minneapolis/Institute; Phillips; RISD; St. Louis/City; Toledo/MA; VMFA; WMAA; West Palm Beach/Norton; Worcester/AM; Yale U. **Bibliography:** Baur 7; Bazin; Biddle 4; Blesh

1; Boswell 1; Brown; Bryant, L.; Burchfield 3; Cahill and Barr, eds.; Cheney; Elliot; Goodrich and Baur 1; Hall; *Index of 20th Century Artists;* Jackson; Jewell 2; Kent N.; **Mather 1, 2**; McCurdy, ed.; Mellquist; Mendelowitz; Narodny; Neuhaus; Pagano; Phillip 2; Poore; Richardson, E.P.; Sachs; Smith, S.C.K.; **Speicher**; Watson, E.W. 1; *Woodstock: An American Art Colony, 1902–1977;* Zaidenberg, ed. Archives.

SPENCER, NILES. b. May 16, 1893, Pawtucket, R.I.; **d.** May 15, 1952, Dingman's Ferry, Pa. **Studied:** RISD, 1913–15; Ferrer School, NYC (with Robert Henri, George Bellows), 1915; ASL (with Kenneth Hayes Miller), 1915. Traveled Europe, 1921–22, 1928–29. **Taught:** RISD, 1915. **Awards:** Carnegie, Hon. Mention, 1930; MMA, **P.P.**, 1942. **One-man Exhibitions:** (first) The Daniel Gallery, NYC, 1925, also 1928; The Downtown Gallery, 1947, 52; Washburn Gallery Inc., 1972. **Retrospective:** Downtown Gallery, 1947, 52; MOMA, 1954; U. of Kentucky, 1965. **Group:** Whitney Studio Club, NYC, from 1923; MOMA, Paintings by 19 Living Americans, 1929; Cincinnati/AM, A New Realism, 1941; Providence (R.I.) Art Club; Carnegie; MMA, Artists for Victory, 1942; Walker, The Precisionist View, 1960; WMAA, 1966; U. of New Mexico, Cubism: Its Impact in the USA, 1967. **Collections:** Andover/Phillips; Arizona State College; U. of Arizona; Buffalo/Albright; Columbus; Cornell U.; Illinois Wesleyan U.; MMA; MOMA; U. of Michigan; U. of Nebraska; Newark Museum; Phillips; RISD; SFMA; San Francisco Art Institute; Santa Barbara/MA; WMAA; Walker; Wichita/AM; Youngstown/Butler. **Bibliography:** Baur 7; Brown 2; Hunter 6; *Cityscape 1919–39; Index of 20th Century Artists;* Kootz 1, 2; Pousette-Dart, ed. Archives.

SPOHN, CLAY E. b. November 24, 1898, San Francisco, Calif.; **d.** December 19, 1977, New York City. **Studied:** California College of Arts and Crafts, 1910–12, 1916, 20; Augusta Military Academy (Va.), 1917–18; U. of California, Berkeley, 1919–22; privately with Armin Hansen, 1921; San Francisco Art Institute, 1921, 27; ASL, 1922–24, with Guy Du Bois, George Luks, Boardman Robinson, Kenneth Hayes Miller, Kimon Nicolaides; Academie Moderne, Paris, 1926, with Othon Friesz. Traveled Europe, USA, Mexico, Canada. **Taught:** San Francisco Art Institute, 1945–50; Mount Holyoke College, 1958; School of Visual Arts, NYC, 1964–69; and privately. Federal A.P. (murals, 1935–41): Shriner Hospital, San Francisco; Volunteer Fire Department, Carmel, Calif.; Contra Costa County (Calif.) Community Center. **One-man Exhibitions:** (first) Art League Gallery, San Francisco, 1929, also 1931; SFMA, 1942; Rotunda Gallery, San Francisco, 1946; Stables Gallery, Taos, N.M., 1957. **Retrospective:** Oakland/AM, 1974. **Group:** San Francisco Art Association, intermittently 1929–38; de Young, ca. 1937–38; SFMA, Art of Our Time, 1945; California Palace, 1945, 48, 50; American Abstract Artists Annual, 1949; Denver/AM, 1952; U. of Illinois, 1953. **Collections:** SFMA. **Bibliography:** McChesney. Archives.

SPRINCHORN, CARL. b. May 13, 1887, Broby, Sweden; **d.** September 1971. To USA, 1903. **Studied:** New York School of Art, 1903–10, with William M. Chase, Robert Henri; Academie Colarossi, Paris, 1914–15. Traveled France, Scandinavia, Caribbean, USA. **Taught:** Art League of Los Angeles, 1912–14. Manager, Robert Henri School, 1907–10. Director, The New Gallery, NYC, 1922–25. **One-man Exhibitions:** (first) George S. Hallman Gallery, NYC, 1916; M. Knoedler & Co., NYC, 1917; Marie Sterner Gallery, NYC, 1922–32; Frank K.M. Rehn Gallery, NYC, 1927; Ainslie Gallery, NYC, Philadelphia, Detroit, 1930; Mrs. Cornelius J. Sullivan Gallery, NYC, 1933–37; Mac-

beth Gallery, NYC, 1941–53; American Swedish Historical Museum; Worcester/AM; Arts Club of Chicago. **Group:** The Armory Show, 1913; Independent Artists, NYC; PAFA; Corcoran; Brooklyn Museum; Phillips; PMA; WMAA, 1963; Colby College. **Collections:** American Swedish Historical Museum; Atlanta/AA; Boston/MFA; Brooklyn Museum; Dayton/AI; Harvard U.; MMA; U. of Maine; Museum of the City of New York; New Britain; PMA; Phillips; RISD; Virginia State College. **Bibliography:** Blesh 1; *Carl Sprinchorn;* Rose, B., 1.

SPRUANCE, BENTON. b. June 25, 1904, Philadelphia, Pa.; **d.** December 6, 1967, Philadelphia, Pa. **Studied:** U. of Pennsylvania, 1924; PAFA, 1925–29. **Taught:** Beaver College, 1933–67; Philadelphia College of Art, Director, Department of Printmaking, 1934–65. **Member:** NAD; SAGA; The Print Club, Philadelphia; Philadelphia Art Alliance. **Commissions:** Municipal Court Building, Philadelphia (mural). **Awards:** PAFA, Cresson Fellowship, 1928, Pennell Memorial Medal, 1937, 66, Alice McFadden Eyre Medal, 1944, First Prize, 1948; Audubon Artists, First Prize, 1948; National Color Print Society, First Prize, 1948; Library of Congress, First Pennell **P.P.**, 1948; Guggenheim Foundation Fellowship, 1951; Hon. Member, American Institute of Architects, 1967. **One-man Exhibitions:** Rehn Galleries, 1949; Carnegie, 1949; Philadelphia Art Alliance, 1951; Mount Holyoke College, 1951; Beaver College, 1964; Muhlenberg College, 1964; The Print Club, Philadelphia, 1964. **Retrospective:** Philadelphia College of Art, 1967; PAFA, 1968. **Group:** PAFA; Library of Congress; NYPL; PMA; WMAA; Carnegie. **Collections:** Carnegie; Library of Congress; NYPL; National Gallery; PAFA; PMA. **Bibliography:** American Artists Group Inc. 3; Bethers; Cheney; Hall; Reese; Zigrosser 1.

SPRUCE, EVERETT. b. December 25, 1908, Conway, Ark. **Studied:** Dallas Art Institute, 1925–29, with O. H. Travis, T.M. Stell, Jr. **Taught:** Dallas Museum School, 1936–40 (Assistant Director and Instructor); U. of Texas, 1940–75. **Awards:** Scholarship, Dallas Art Institute; Dallas/MFA, First Prize, 1935, 55; Pepsi-Cola, 1946; Houston/MFA, First Prize, 1946; Carnegie, Hon. Men., 1946; La Tausca Competition, 1947; PAFA, J. Henry Schiedt Memorial Prize, 1947; Corcoran, Hon. Men., 1949; Texas State Fair, D.D. Feldman Award, 1955. **Address:** 15 Peak Road, Austin, TX 78746. **One-man Exhibitions:** Dallas/MFA, 1932, 58; Joseph Sartor Gallery, Dallas, 1934; Delphic Studios, NYC, 1936; Hudson D Walker Gallery, NYC, 1938; Witte, 1943; Mortimer Brandt, NYC, 1943; Santa Barbara/MA, 1945; Mortimer Levitt Gallery, NYC, 1945, 46, 48, 50, 51; Arts Club, Washington, D.C., 1948; San Antonio/McNay, 1959; U. of Texas, Austin, 1979. **Retrospective:** A.F.A., 1959. **Group:** Dallas/MFA, 1932, 35, 38, 40; Corcoran, 1939, 41, 43, 45, 51; MOMA, 1942; Denver/AM, 1946; Pepsi/Cola, 1946; Carnegie, 1948, 49, 51; U. of Illinois, 1948, 50, 51, 52; Bordighera, 1955; U. of Texas, Austin, 1979. **Collections:** U. of Alabama; Austin; Baltimore/MA; California Palace; Colorado Springs/FA; Dallas/MFA; Des Moines; de Young; Illinois Wesleyan U.; Kansas City/Nelson; MMA; MOMA; NYPL; U. of Nebraska; Newark Museum; New Orleans/Delgado; North Texas State U.; Ohio Wesleyan U.; PAFA; Phillips; Rio de Janeiro; Southern Methodist U.; Tulane U.; WMAA; Walker; Wichita/AM; Witte. **Bibliography:** Baur 7; Goodrich and Baur 1; Hall; Miller, ed. 1; Pearson 1; Pousette-Dart, ed.

SQUIER, JACK. b. February 27, 1927, Dixon, Ill. **Studied:** Oberlin College; Indiana U., with Robert Laurent, Leo Steppat, 1950, BS; Cornell U., with John Hartell, 1952, MFA. Traveled Central and South America, Europe, Middle East, the Orient, Russia. **Taught:** Cornell U., 1952– . **Address:** 221 Berkshire Road, Ithaca, NY 14850. **One-man Exhibitions:** (first) The Alan Gallery, NYC, 1956, also 1959, 62, 64, 66, 68; Cornell U., 1959, 64, 68; Lima, Peru, 1963. **Group:** WMAA; MOMA; Houston-MFA; Andover/Phillips; Boston/MFA; Brussels World's Fair, 1958; U. of Illinois; Chicago/AI; Boston Arts Festival; Carnegie; Claude Bernard, Paris; Buffalo/Albright. **Collections:** Cornell U.; Hirshhorn; Ithaca College; Lima, Peru; MOMA; St. Lawrence U.; Potsdam/SUNY; Stanford U.; Syracuse/Everson; WMAA. **Bibliography:** Weller.

STAMOS, THEODOROS. b. December 31, 1922, NYC. **Studied:** American Artists School, NYC, with Simon Kennedy, Joseph Konzal. Traveled Europe, Near East, Greece. **Taught:** Black Mountain College; Cummington School of Fine Arts; ASL, 1958–75; Brandeis U. **Commissions:** Moore McCormack Lines Inc., SS *Argentina* (mural). **Awards:** L.C. Tiffany Grant, 1951; NIAL, 1956; Brandeis U., Creative Arts Award 1959; National Arts Foundation, 1967. **Address:** Plateia Hrwon, Paralia 6, Lefkada, Greece; 37 West 83rd Street, NYC 10024. **Dealer:** Louis K. Meisel Gallery, NYC. **One-man Exhibitions:** (first) Wakefield Gallery, NYC, 1940; Mortimer Brandt, NYC, 1945; Betty Parsons Gallery, 1947, 56; Phillips, 1950, 54; Philadelphia Art Alliance, 1957; Andre Emmerich Gallery, NYC, 1958, 59, 60, 63, 66, 68; San Antonio/McNay, 1960; Gimpel Fils Ltd., 1960; Galleria d'Arte del Naviglio, Milan, 1961; Brandeis U., 1967; Waddington Fine Arts Ltd., Montreal, 1968; Marlborough Gallery, Inc., NYC, 1970; Omaha/Joslyn, 1973; Athens Gallery, 1974; Louis K. Meisel Gallery, NYC, 1977, 79, 81; Galerie Le Portail, Heidelberg, 1977; Morgan Art Gallery, Shawnee Mission, 1977; Union College, 1978; Hokin Gallery, Palm Beach, 1978; Wichita State U., 1979; Utica, 1980. **Retrospective:**

Corcoran, 1959; New Paltz/SUNY, 1980. **Group:** Carnegie, 1955, 58, 61, 64; International Biennial Exhibition of Paintings, Tokyo; MOMA, The New American Painting, circ., Europe, 1958–59; WMAA, Nature in Abstraction, 1958, Annual, 1963; Venice Biennial; Documenta II, Kassel, 1959; SRGM, Abstract Expressionists and Imagists, 1961; MMA, 1965; WMAA, Art of the U.S. 1670–1966, 1966; Corcoran Biennial, 1967; MOMA, Dada, Surrealism and Their Heritage, 1968; MOMA, The New American Painting and Sculpture, 1969; Cornell U., Abstract Expressionism, The Formative Years, 1978. **Collections:** Andover/Phillips; U. of Arizona; Baltimore/MA; Brandeis U.; Buffalo/Albright; California Palace; Case Institute; Chase Manhattan Bank; Chicago/AI; Ciba-Geigy Corp.; Colorado Springs/FA; Corcoran; Cornell U.; Des Moines; Detroit/Institute; Hartford/Wadsworth; Hirshhorn; U. of Illinois; State U. of Iowa; La Jolla; MIT; MMA; MOMA; Memphis/Brooks; Michigan State U.; U. of Michigan; NYU; U. of Nebraska; U. of North Carolina; Phillips; Phoenix; Rio de Janeiro; SFMA; San Antonio/McNay; Smith College; Tel Aviv; Toronto; Trenton/State; Utica; Vassar College; WGMA; WMAA; Walker; Wellesley College; Yale U.; Youngstown/Butler. **Bibliography:** Alloway 4; Barker 1; Baur 5, 7; Biddle 4; Blesh 1; Eliot; Goodrich and Baur 1; Haftman; Hobbs and Levin; Janis and Blesh 1; McCurdy, ed.; Mendelowitz; Nordness, ed.; **Pomeroy**; Pousette-Dart, ed.; Read 2; Richardson, E.P.; Ritchie 1; Rubin 1; Sandler; Seuphor 1; Soby 5. Archives.

STANCZAK, JULIAN. b. November 5, 1928, Borownica, Poland. To USA, 1950; citizen, 1956. **Studied:** Borough Polytechnic, London, 1949–50; Cleveland Institute of Art, BFA, 1950–54; Yale U. (with Josef Albers, Conrad Marca Relli), MFA, 1954–56. Traveled Poland, Russia, Persia, India, East Africa, England, Western Europe. **Taught:** Art Academy of Cincinnati, 1957–64; Cleve-

land Institute of Art, 1964– ; Dartmouth College, Artist-in-Residence, 1968. **Member:** American Abstract Artists. **Commissions:** First National Bank, Dayton, Ohio, 1972; National City Bank, Dayton, Ohio, 1973; Cleveland Area Arts Council, 1974; Ohio Building Authority, Columbus, 1974; Rotweil, West Germany (flag design), 1974; Ohio Arts Council, 1975; Cleveland Public Library, 1979. **Awards:** Ohio State Council on the Arts Award, 1972. **Address:** 6229 Cabrini Lane, Seven Hills, OH 44131. **One-man Exhibitions:** (first) Dayton/AI, 1964; Martha Jackson Gallery, 1964, 65, 68, 71, 72, 73, 75, 79; Miami U., 1965; U. of Wisconsin, 1965; Feingarten Gallery, 1966; Kent State U., 1968; Dartmouth College, 1968; Makler Gallery, Philadelphia, 1969; London Arts, Detroit, 1969, 72, London, 1971; Akron/AI, 1970; Women's City Club, Cleveland, 1970; The Packard Gallery, Akron, 1970; Images Gallery, Toledo, 1971, 72; Carl Solway Gallery, Cincinnati, 1972; Corcoran, 1972; Cincinnati/AM, 1972; New Gallery, Cleveland, 1972, 76; Haslem Fine Arts, Inc., 1972; Phoenix Gallery, San Francisco, 1974; Canton Art Institute, 1974; Pollock Gallery, Toronto, 1975; Lakeland College, 1975; Alice Simsar Inc., Ann Arbor, 1975; Marjorie Kauffman Graphics, Los Angeles, 1976; Kingpitcher Gallery, Pittsburgh, 1976; Ohio State U., 1976; The Miller Gallery, Cincinnati, 1978; A.S.A. Gallery, Oak Ridge, 1978; Kauffman Fine Arts, Houston, 1978; International Monetary Fund, Washington, D.C., 1978; Youngstown/Butler, 1980. **Retrospective:** Cleveland Institute of Art, 1971; Lakeland College, Sheboygan, Wis., 1975. **Group:** MOMA, The Responsive Eye, 1965; Buffalo/Albright, 1965, Plus by Minus, 1968; Riverside Museum; Detroit/Institute; U. of Illinois, 1965, 69; WMAA Annual, 1967; Carnegie, 1967; Indianapolis/Herron, 1969; U. of Illinois, 1969, 74; Flint/Institute International, 1969; Carnegie, 1970; NCFA, Black and White, 1970–72; Amherst College, Color Painting, 1972; Mansfield Art Center, Stanczak-

Anuszkiewicz, 1973; Minnesota/MA, Drawings USA, 1973; U. of Miami, Less Is More: The Influence of the Bauhaus on American Art, 1974; Akron, Forms of Color, 1975; Indianapolis, 1976; Brooklyn, Thirty Years of American Printmaking, 1976. **Collections:** Akron/AI; American Republic Insurance Co.; Baltimore/MA; Buffalo/Albright; Canton Art Institute; Cincinnati/AM; Cleveland/MA; Corcoran; Dartmouth College; Dayton/AI; Houston/Contemporary; Indianapolis/Herron; U. of Miami; Miami-Dade; Milwaukee; National Gallery; Oklahoma; PAFA; Ridgefield/Aldrich; SFMA; Trade Bank and Trust Company, NYC; Youngstown/Butler. **Bibliography:** MacAgy 2; Weller. Archives.

STANKIEWICZ, RICHARD P. b. October 18, 1922, Philadelphia, Pa. **Studied:** Hofmann School, 1948–49, with Hans Hofmann; Atelier Fernand Leger, Paris, 1950–51; Zadkine School of Sculpture, Paris, 1950–51. **Taught:** Albany/SUNY, 1967– . Traveled Europe, Australia, USA. An organizer of Hansa Gallery, NYC, 1952. US Navy, 1941–47. **Member:** International Institute of Arts and Letters; NIAL; Century Association. **Awards:** Brandeis U.; National Academy of Arts and Sciences; Ford Foundation Grant. **Address:** Star Route, Huntington, MA 01050. **Dealer:** The Zabriskie Gallery. **One-man Exhibitions:** (first) Hansa Gallery, NYC, 1953, also 1954–58; The Stable Gallery, 1959–63; Galerie Neufville, Paris, 1960; The Pace Gallery, Boston, 1961; Walker, 1963 (two-man, with Robert Indiana); Daniel Cordier, Paris, 1964; Tampa/AI, 1965; Frank Watters Gallery, 1969; Melbourne/National, 1969; The Zabriskie Gallery, 1972, 73, 75, 77. **Retrospective:** Albany/SUNY, 1979. **Group:** PAFA, 1954; WMAA, 1956, 60, 62, Young America, 1957; Houston/MFA, Irons in the Fire, 1957; XXIX Venice Biennial, 1958; Carnegie, 1958, 61; A.F.A., Recent Sculpture, USA, 1959; MOMA, Sixteen Americans, circ., 1959; Claude Bernard, Paris, Aspects of

American Sculpture, 1960; Amsterdam/Stedelijk, 1961; Chicago/AI, 1961, 62; VI Sao Paulo Biennial, 1961; MOMA, The Art of Assemblage, circ., 1961; Stockholm/National, 4 Americans, circ., 1962; Seattle World's Fair, 1962; SRGM, The Joseph H. Hirshhorn Collection, 1962; WMAA, Forty Artists under Forty, circ., 1962; Amsterdam/Stedelijk, Four Americans, 1962; MOMA, Hans Hofmann and His Students, circ., 1963–64; Battersea Park, London, International Sculpture Exhibition, 1963; Jewish Museum, Recent American Sculptors, 1964; MOMA, The Machine, 1968. **Collections:** Akron/AI; Buffalo/Albright; Chicago/AI; Dayton/AI; Fredonia/SUNY; Hirshhorn; MOMA; Newark Museum; Paris/Beaubourg; PMA; Smith College; SRGM; Stockholm/National; Storm King Art Center; Springfield, Mass./MFA; Tel Aviv; WMAA; Walker. **Bibliography:** Blesh 1; Chipp; Craven, W.; Downer, ed.; Friedman, ed.; Goodrich and Baur 1; Hulten; Hunter, ed.; Janis and Blesh 1; Kuh 3; Licht, F.; Lowry; *Metro*; Read 3; Sandler 1; Seitz 3; Seuphor 3; Weller. Archives.

STANLEY, ROBERT. b. January 3, 1932, Yonkers, N.Y. **Studied:** Oglethorpe U. (with Marion O'Donnell, Wendell Brown), BA, 1953; ASL, 1953; Brooklyn Museum School (with Yonia Fain, William King), 1954–56. Traveled USA, Holland, Germany, Caribbean. **Taught:** School of Visual Arts, NYC, 1970–72; Louisiana State U., 1976; Syracuse U., 1978; Princeton U., 1979–80. **Awards:** Cassandra Foundation, 1969. **Address:** 3 Crosby Street, NYC 10013. **Dealer:** Elizabeth Weiner Gallery, NYC. **One-man Exhibitions:** (first) The Bianchini Gallery, NYC, 1965, also 1966; Orez International Gallery, The Hague, 1966; Cincinnati/Contemporary, 1966; Galerie Rolf Ricke, Kassel, 1966, 67; Galerie Kuckels, Bochum, Germany, 1967; Kleine Galerie, Frankfurt, 1968; Gegenverkehr, Aachen, 1969; On First, NYC, 1969; Warren Benedek Gallery, NYC, 1972; New York

Cultural Center, 1974; Louisiana State U., 1976; P.S. 1, Long Island City (two-man), 1977; Hal Bromm Gallery, NYC, 1978; Elizabeth Weiner Gallery, NYC, 1978; St. Thomas Aquinas College, 1978. **Group:** Van Bovenkamp Gallery, NYC, 1965; Chicago/AI, 1965–69; Indianapolis/Herron, 1967; WMAA Annual, 1967; Documenta IV, Kassel, 1968; ICA, London, The Obsessive Image, 1968; Milwaukee, Aspects of a New Realism, 1969; David Stuart Gallery, 1969; Chicago/AI, 1969; Cincinnati/Contemporary, Monumental Art, 1970; WMAA, 1972, 73; Eindhoven, Relativerend Realisme, 1972; U. of North Carolina, 1973; New York Cultural Center, Three Centuries of the American Nude, 1975; P.S. 1, Long Island City, Another Aspect of Pop, 1978. **Collections:** American Republic Insurance Co.; Cincinnati/Contemporary; Cologne; Donaldson, Lufkin, & Jenrette, Inc.; Harvard U.; Housatonic Community College; MMA; McCrory Corporation; Milwaukee; Norfolk/Chrysler; Time Inc.; WMAA; Washington U. (St. Louis); Westport Art Education Society. **Bibliography:** Honisch and Jensen, eds.; Lippard 5.

STASIK, ANDREW. b. March 16, 1932, New Brunswick, N.J. **Studied:** NYU; Columbia U., BA; State U. of Iowa; Ohio U., MFA. **Taught:** New School for Social Research; Ohio U.; Ball State Teachers College; Pratt Graphic Art Center; Pratt Institute; Yale U.; U. of Calgary, Editorial Staff, *Artist's Proof* magazine. Director, Pratt Graphics Center, NYC. **Awards:** Cleveland/MA, First Prize in Lithography, 1958; Bay Printmakers Society, Oakland, **P.P.**, 1958; Cleveland/MA, First Prize in Serigraphy, 1958; Pasadena/AM, **P.P.**, 1958; Gallery of Modern Art, Ljubljana, Yugoslavia, III International Exhibition of Prints, 1959, Le Prix Internationale de 100,000 dn; Achenbach Foundation, Open Award for All Media, 1961; The Print Club, Philadelphia, Collins Prize; L.C. Tiffany Grant, 1966; Audubon Artists Medal, 1969; Silver-

mine Guild, **P.P.**, 1974; Texas Tech U., **P.P.**, Colorprint USA, 1974. **Address:** Pratt Graphics, 160 Lexington Avenue, NYC 10016. **One-man Exhibitions:** Ohio U., 1956; Avant Garde, NYC, 1958; Ball State Teachers College, 1959; Ross Widen Gallery, Cleveland, 1960; Miami/Modern, 1960; Samuel S. Fleisher Art Memorial, Philadelphia, 1961; Yoseido Gallery, Tokyo, 1961; Castagno Gallery, NYC, 1966; Gallery of Graphic Arts, NYC, 1967; Pollock Gallery, Toronto, 1968; Museu de Arte, Rio Grande do Sul, Brazil, 1968; Union of Plastic Gallery, Krakow, 1968; Centar Gallery, Zagreb, 1968; Galeria Colibri, San Juan, Puerto Rico, 1968; U. of Calgary, 1969; Mala Gallery, Ljubljana, Yugoslavia, 1969; Bader Gallery, Washington, D.C. (two-man), 1969; Secession Gallery, Vienna, 1970; Spectrum Gallery, NYC, 1971; A.A.A. Gallery, 1971; Graphics Gallery, 1971; Molloy College, Rockville Centre, N.Y., 1971; Jacques Baruch Gallery, 1973; Montclair State College (two-man), 1974. **Group:** Cincinnati/AM Biennials, 1956, 58, 60, 62, 68; PCA, American Prints Today, circ., 1959–62; Gallery of Modern Art, Ljubljana, Yugoslavia, III, IV, VI, VII & VIII International Exhibition of Prints, 1959, 61, 65, 67, 69; A.F.A., Prints of the World, 1962; The Print Club, Philadelphia, 1962; Library of Congress; MOMA, Prize-Winning American Prints, circ. Canada; Krakow Print Biennials, 1968, 70, 72; U. of Washington, 1969; International Print Biennials, Ljubljana, Yugoslavia, 1969, 71, 73; U. of Washington, Prints/Multiples, 1970; IV American Biennial, Santiago, 1970. **Collections:** Amsterdam/Stedelijk; Ball State U.; Budapest/National; California Palace; Cincinnati/AM; Library of Congress; MMA; MOMA; NCFA; NYPL; NYU; National Gallery; U. of Nebraska; Oakland/AM; PMA; Pasadena/AM; Rockefeller Brothers Fund; Warsaw/National.

STEFANELLI, JOSEPH. b. March 20, 1921, Philadelphia, Pa. **Studied:** Philadelphia Museum School, 1938–40;

PAFA, 1941–42; ASL, 1946–48; Hofmann School, 1948–49. Traveled Europe, Middle East. **Taught:** U. of California, Berkeley, 1960, 63; Princeton U., 1963–66; Columbia U., 1966– ; New School for Social Research, 1966– . Artist for *Yank* magazine, 1942–46 (field drawings made during World War II are in the permanent collection of the War Archives Building, Washington, D.C.). **Awards:** Fulbright Fellowship (Rome), 1958–59; New York State Council on the Arts Grant, 1971. **Address:** 463 West Street, NYC 10014. **One-man Exhibitions:** Artists' Gallery, NYC, 1950, 54; The New Gallery, NYC, 1952; Hendler Gallery, Philadelphia, 1953; Ganymede Gallery, NYC, 1956; Poindexter Gallery, 1957, 58, 60; Hacker Gallery, NYC, 1962; Thibaut Gallery, NYC, 1963; Princeton U., 1964; U. of Arkansas, 1965; Westbeth Gallery, NYC, 1971; New School for Social Research, 1972; The New Bertha Schaefer Gallery, 1973, 74; Terry Dintenfass Gallery, NYC, 1974; Andre Zarre, 1977. **Group:** Ninth Street Exhibition, NYC, 1951; PAFA; WMAA; Corcoran; Carnegie; U. of Illinois; Buffalo/Albright; Walker; Chicago/AI; MOMA. **Collections:** Baltimore/MA; U. of California, Berkeley; Chase Manhattan Bank; Chicago/AI; Cornell U.; U. of Massachusetts; U. of Montana; NYU; Norfolk; Norfolk/Chrysler; Sarah Lawrence College; Union Carbide Corp.; WMAA; Walker. **Bibliography:** Sandler 1.

STEG, J. L. b. February 6, 1922, Alexandria, Va. **Studied:** Rochester Institute of Technology; State U. of Iowa, BFA, MFA. Traveled Europe, Mexico, Spain. **Taught:** Cornell U., 1949–51; Tulane U., 1951– . **Member:** SAGA. **Awards:** Carnegie Exchange Fellowship (Italy); VIII Lugano Drawing and Print Show, 1,000 Franc Award; Brooklyn Museum, P.P.; Seattle/AM, **P.P.**; Dallas/MFA, **P.P.**; Birmingham, Ala./MA, **P.P.**; U. of Minnesota, **P.P.**; Syracuse State Fair, **P.P.**; The Print Club, Philadelphia, **P.P.**; Minnesota/MA, **P.P.**, 1980. **Address:**

7919 Spruce Street, New Orleans, LA 70118. **Dealer:** A.A.A. Gallery, NYC; Gallery 1640. **One-man Exhibitions:** (first) Weyhe Gallery, 1945; Utica, 1951; Philadelphia Art Alliance, 1957; Davenport/Municipal, 1958; Dallas/MFA; Orleans Gallery, New Orleans; A.A.A. Gallery, NYC; U. of South Florida; Baton Rouge; Studio-Craft Gallery, Miami; Bienville Gallery, 1970; The Ohio State U., 1971; Tulane U., 1972, 74; USIS, Ankara, 1975; Newcomb College, 1975; Circle Gallery Ltd., NYC, 1976, 78; USIA, Cultural Center, Ankara, Turkey, 1977; U. of Mississippi, Oxford, 1978. **Retrospective:** New Orleans Museum, circ., 1978. **Group:** ART:USA, NYC; New York World's Fair, 1964–65; Oakland/AM; USIA; Philadelphia Art Alliance, 50th Anniversary, 1968; U. of Pittsburgh; Oneonta/SUNY, 1969; Smithsonian Exhibition, American Drawings II, circ., 1965; Trenton State, National Drawings, 1979. **Collections:** Albion College; Bezalel Museum; Bowling Green State U.; Brooklyn Museum; Carnegie; Cleveland/MA; Colgate U.; Dallas/MFA; U. of Delaware; George Washington U.; Georgia State U.; Harvard U.; IBM; Library of Congress; MOMA; Malmo; U. of Minnesota; NYPL; U. of Nebraska; New Orleans/Delgado; The Ohio State U.; Oklahoma; Oslo/National; PMA; Princeton Print Club; The Print Club, Philadelphia; Print Club of Rochester; Randolph-Macon College; Remington-Rand Corp.; Roanoke; Sao Paulo; San Antonio/McNay; Seattle/AM; Smithsonian; Southern Illinois U.; USIA; US State Department; Utica; Worcester/AM.

STEIN, RONALD. b. September 15, 1930, NYC. **Studied:** Cooper Union, with Will Barnet; Yale U., with Josef Albers, BFA; Rutgers U., MFA. Traveled Europe, North Africa. **Taught:** Worcester Museum School, 1959–60; Rutgers U., 1960–61. **Member:** The Players Club, NYC. **Commissions:** Uris Building Corp. (80-ft. mosaic mural for Number Two Broadway, NYC). **Awards:** Yale U. Traveling Fellowship. **Address:** 836 Fireplace Road, East Hampton, NY 11937. **Dealer:** Marlborough Gallery, Inc., NYC. **One-man Exhibitions:** (first) Boris Mirski Gallery, Boston, 1956; Gallery Mayer, NYC, 1960, 61; Irving Galleries, Inc., Milwaukee, 1961; Cheekwood, 1961; Tibor de Nagy Gallery, 1964; Eleanor Rigelhaupt Gallery, Boston, 1966; Marlborough Fine Art Ltd., 1967; Phyllis Kind Gallery, Chicago, 1969; Irving Galleries, Milwaukee, 1971. **Group:** Chicago/AI, 1956, 57; Lincoln, Mass./De Cordova, 1958; Carnegie, 1959; Corcoran, 1961; Pan-Pacific Exhibition, circ., Japan, 1961; MOMA; ICA, Boston, 1961; New York World's Fair, 1964–65. **Collections:** A.F.A.; Buffalo/Albright; Carnegie; Cheekwood; De Beers Collection; Guild Hall; Guild Plastics Co.; Hartford/Wadsworth; Loch Haven Art Center; New York Hilton Hotel; North Shore State Bank; Ringling; SRGM; Uris Buildings Corp.; Wellesley College.

STEINBERG, SAUL. b. June 15, 1914, Ramnicul-Sarat, Rumania. **Studied:** U. of Milan, 1932–40. To USA, 1942; citizen, 1943. US Navy, 1943–46. **Commissions:** Terrace Plaza Hotel, Cincinnati, 1948 (mural). **Address:** Amagansett, NY 11930. **Dealer:** Sidney Janis Gallery; Betty Parsons Gallery, NYC; Galerie Maeght, Paris. **One-man Exhibitions:** Betty Parsons Gallery, 1940 (two-man with Constantino Nivola), 1966, 69, 73, 76; Wakefield Gallery, NYC, 1943; Sao Paulo, 1952; Frank Perls Gallery, 1952; Galerie Blanche, Stockholm, 1953; Amsterdam/Stedelijk, 1953; Arts Club of Chicago, 1953; A.F.A., circ., 1953–55; Galerie Maeght, 1953, 66, 73, 74, 77, Zurich, 1971, 73, 77; Hannover/K-G, 1954; Basel, 1954; ICA, London, 1957; ICA, Boston, 1974; Sidney Janis Gallery, 1966, 69, 73, 76; Rotterdam, 1967; Obelisk Gallery, 1967; Irving Galleries, Inc., Milwaukee, 1968; J. L. Hudson Art Gallery, Detroit, 1969;

Kiko Gallery, Houston, 1970; Felix Landau Gallery, 1971; Richard Gray Gallery, Chicago, 1971; Galleria Galatea, Milan, 1973; NCFA, 1973; Kolnischer Kunstverein, circ., 1974. **Retrospectives:** Cologne/Kunstverein, circ., 1974–75; WMAA, circ., 1978. **Group:** MOMA, Fourteen Americans, circ., 1946; Chicago/AI, 1949; L'Obelisco, Rome, 1951; ICA, London, 1952; Brussels World's Fair, 1958; Salon du Mai, Paris, 1966; Carnegie, 1970; Foundation Maeght, L'Art Vivant, 1970; Chicago/AI, 1971; Bibliotheque Nationale, Paris, Les Dessins d'humor, 1971; Recklinghausen, Zeitgenossische Karikaturen Zeitgenossen, 1972; Yale U., American Drawing, 1970–1973, 1973; Akron/AI, Contemporary Images in Watercolor, 1976; Documenta 6, Kassel, 1977; Renwick Gallery, Washington, D.C., The Object as Poet, 1977; Minneapolis/MA, American Drawings 1927–1977, 1977. **Collections:** Buffalo/Albright; Detroit/Institute; Harvard U.; MMA; MOMA; Utica; Victoria and Albert Museum. **Bibliography: Baudson; Baur 7; Biddle 4; Kepes 2;** *From Foreign Shores;* Kepes 2; *Metro;* Miller, ed. 2; Richardson, E.P.; Rodman 1; Rosenberg 3; Sachs; Schneider; **Steinberg, S., 1, 2, 3.** Archives.

STEINER, MICHAEL. b. 1945, NYC. **Studied:** ASL, with Stephen Green. **Awards:** Guggenheim Foundation Fellowship, 1971. **Address:** 704 Broadway, NYC 10003. **Dealer:** Andre Emmerich Gallery, NYC. **One-man Exhibitions:** (first) Fischbach Gallery, 1964; Dwan Gallery, NYC, 1966, 68; U. of Saskatchewan, Regina, 1970; Marlborough Gallery, Inc., NYC, 1970, 72, 74; Mackler Gallery, 1970; David Mirvish Gallery, 1970, Toronto 1976, 78; U. of Toronto, 1971; Noah Goldowsky/Richard Bellamy, NYC, 1972; Boston/MFA, 1974; Andre Emmerich Gallery, NYC, 1976, 78, 79, 80; Galerie Wentzel, Hamburg, 1976, 79; Bielefeld/Kunsthalle, 1977; Watson/deNagy, Houston, 1977; Galerie Andre Emmerich, Zurich, 1977; Harcus-Krakow Gallery, Boston, 1977, 79; Galerie Gerard Piltzer, Paris, 1978; Kunst-und-Museumsverein, Wuppertal, 1978; America House, Berlin, 1979; Amerika Haus, Hannover, 1979; Gallery Ninety-Nine, Bay Harbor Islands, Fla., 1980. **Group:** Ridgefield/Aldrich, 1968; The Hague, 1968; Wellesley College, 1970; Toledo/MA, The Form of Color, 1970; WMAA, 1970, 72; Akron/AI, 20th Century Sculpture, 1971; Edmonton Art Gallery, Alberta, Masters of the Sixties, 1972; Montreal/Contemporain, 11 Artists Americains, 1973; NIAL, 1975; Syracuse/Everson, New Works in Clay, 1976; Wuppertal, Skulpturen und Gemalde aus New York, 1978; Syracuse/Everson, A Century of Ceramics in the United States, 1878–1978, 1979.

STELLA, FRANK. b. May, 1936, Malden, Mass. **Studied:** Phillips Academy, with Patrick Morgan; Princeton U., with William Seitz, Stephen Greene. Awards: International Biennial Exhibition of Paintings, Tokyo, First Prize, 1967. **Taught:** Dartmouth College, 1963; Brandeis U., 1969. **Address:** 17 Jones Street, NYC 10013. **One-man Exhibitions:** Leo Castelli Inc., 1960, 62, 64, 66, 67, 69, 70, 73, 75, 79 and two-man, 1962; Galerie Lawrence, Paris, 1961, 64; Ferus Gallery, Los Angeles, 1963, 65; Kasmin Ltd., 1964, 66, 68, 71; Harvard U., Three American Painters (three-man, with Kenneth Noland, Jules Olitski), circ., Pasadena, 1965; Pasadena/AM, 1966, 71; David Mirvish Gallery, 1966, 68, 71; Seattle/AM, 1967; Galerie Bischofberger, Zurich, 1967; Douglas Gallery, Vancouver, 1967; WGMA, 1968; Irving Blum Gallery, Los Angeles, 1968, 69, 70, 72; Bennington College, 1968; U. of Puerto Rico, 1969; Brandeis U., 1969; MOMA, 1970; Lawrence Rubin Gallery, NYC, 1970, 71; Galerie Rene Ziegler, 1970; Hayward Gallery, London, 1970; Amsterdam/Stedelijk, 1970; Joseph Helman Gallery, St. Louis, 1970; Toronto, 1971; Hansen-Fuller Gallery, 1971; John Berggruen Gallery, 1971; Knoedler Contemporary Art, 1973; Portland (Ore.) Center for the Visual Arts, 1974; U. of Washington, Seattle, 1974; ACE Gallery, Vancouver, 1974, Venice, Calif., 1975; Galerie Daniel Templon, Paris, 1975; Janie C. Lee Gallery, Houston, 1975; Galerie Andre Emmerich, Zurich, 1976; Basel, 1976; Sears Bank, Chicago, 1976; Knoedler Contemporary Art, NYC, 1976; David Mirvish Gallery, Toronto, 1976; B. R. Kornblatt Gallery, Baltimore, 1976; Galerie M., Bochum, 1977; Baltimore/MA, 1977; Bielefeld, 1977; Museum of Modern Art, Oxford, 1977; Linda Farris Gallery, Seattle, 1977; Knoedler Ltd., London, 1977; School of Visual Arts, NYC, 1978; MOMA, 1979; Brandeis U., 1979; Galerie Valeur, Nagoya, 1979; Galerie 99, Bay Harbor Islands, Fla., 1980. **Retrospective:** Fort Worth, circ., 1978. **Group:** Oberlin College, 3 Young Painters, 1959; MOMA, Sixteen Americans, circ., 1959; SRGM, Abstract Expressionists and Imagists, 1961; Houston/MFA, Ways and Means, 1961; A.F.A., Explorers of Space, circ., 1961–62; Seattle World's Fair, 1962; WMAA, Geometric Abstraction in America, circ., 1962; Chicago/AI, 1963, 65; Corcoran, 1963; Biennial, 1967; WGMA, The Formalists, 1963; Jewish Museum, Toward a New Abstraction, 1963; Musee Cantonal des Beaux-Arts, Lausanne, 1 Salon International de Galeries Pilotes, 1963; Brandeis U., New Directions in American Painting, 1963; Jewish Museum, Black and White, 1963; Hartford/Wadsworth, Black, White and Gray, 1964; Los Angeles/County MA, Post Painterly Abstraction, 1964; XXXII Venice Biennial, 1964; WMAA Annuals, 1964, 67; MOMA, The Responsive Eye, 1965; VII Sao Paulo Biennial, 1965; SRGM, Systemic Painting, 1966; Kansas City/Nelson, Sound, Light, Silence, 1966; Amsterdam/Stedelijk, New Shapes of Color, 1966; Expo '67, Montreal, 1967; International Quadriennial (ROSC), 1971; High Museum, The Modern Image, 1972; Kansas City/Nelson, Color Field Painting to Post Color Field Abstraction,

1972; Houston/MFA, The Great Decade of American Abstraction: Modernist Art 1960–1970, 1974; U. of Miami, Less Is More: The Influence of the Bauhaus on American Art, 1974; VMFA, Twelve American Painters, 1974; High Museum, The New Image, 1975; SRGM, 20th Century American Drawing, 1976; Cambridge U., Jubilation, 1977; Museum of the American Foundation for the Arts, Miami, Pattern & Decorative Painting, 1977; NCFA, New Ways with Paper, 1977; Flint/Institute, Art and the Automobile, 1976; Worcester/AM, Between Sculpture & Painting, 1978; WMAA, Art about Art, 1978; Buffalo/Albright, American Painting of the 1970s, 1978; Pomona College, Black and White Are Colors, 1979; ICA, Boston, The Reductive Object, 1979; P.S. 1, Long Island City, A Great Big Drawing Show, 1979; WMAA Biennial, 1979; School of Visual Arts, NYC, Shaped Paintings, 1979; Lincoln/De Cordova, Born in Boston, 1979. **Collections:** Amsterdam/Stedelijk; Baltimore/MA; Basel; Brooklyn Museum; Buffalo/Albright; Chicago/AI; Cologne; Des Moines; Detroit/Institute; Fort Worth; Los Angeles/County MA; MOMA; NCFA; Nagoya Museum, Japan; PMA; Pasadena/AM; SFMA; Tate; WMAA; Walker. **Bibliography:** Alloway 3, 4; Battcock, ed.; Bihalji-Merin; *Black and White Are Colors*; Calas, N. and E.; *Contemporanea*; Coplans 2; De Vries, ed.; *Drawings: The Pluralist Decade*; Gablik; Gooseen 3; *The Great Decade*; Honisch and Jensen, eds.; Hunter, ed.; Johnson, Ellen H.; Krauss 2; Kozloff 3; Lippard 5; Lucie-Smith; MacAgy 2; Rickey; Rose, B., 1, 4; **Rubin 2**; Sandler 1; *7 Decades*; Tomkins 2; Warhol and Hackett.

STELLA, JOSEPH. b. June 13, 1877, Muro Lucano, Italy; **d.** November 5, 1946, NYC. To USA, 1896; citizen, 1923. **Studied** medicine and pharmacology, 1896; ASL, 1897; New York School of Art, 1898–1900, with William M. Chase. Traveled Europe, USA. **Member:** Societe Anonyme. **Awards:** One-year scholarship to New York School of Art, 1899. **One-man Exhibitions:** (first) Carnegie, 1910; Italian National Club, NYC, 1913; Bourgeois Gallery, NYC, 1920; Societe Anonyme, NYC; Dudensing Gallery, NYC, 1924; The New Gallery, NYC, 1926; Des Moines Art Association, 1926; Curt Valentine Gallery, NYC, 1926, 28, 31, 35; Angiporto Galleria, Naples, 1929; Galerie Sloden, Paris, 1930; Washington Place, Paris, 1932; Cooperative Gallery, Newark 1937; A.A.A. Gallery, NYC, 1941; M. Knoedler & Co., NYC, 1942; ACA Gallery, 1943; The Zabriskie Gallery, 1958, 59, 60, 61; MOMA, circ., 1960 (drawings); Robert Schoelkopf Gallery, NYC, 1963, 64, 66, 70, 77, 79; U. of Maryland, 1968; Rutgers U., 1970. **Retrospective:** Newark Museum, 1939; WMAA, 1963. **Collections:** Indiana State College; Iowa State Education Association; MMA; MOMA; U. of Nebraska; Newark Museum; WMAA; Walker; Yale U. **Bibliography:** *Arthur Dove: The Years of Collage; Avant-Garde Painting and Sculpture in America, 1910–25*; **Baur 3,** 5, 7; Bethers; Biddle 4; Blanchard; Blesh 1; Brown 2; Cahill and Barr, eds.; Christensen; Dreier 2; Eliot; Elsen 2; Flanagan; *Forerunners; From Foreign Shores*; Frost; Gerdts; Goodrich and Baur 1; Haftman; Hess, T.B., 1; Hulten; Hunter 6; Janis and Blesh 1; Janis, S.; Kozloff 3; Kuh 1; Levin 2; McCoubrey 1; McCurdy, ed.; Mellquist; Mendelowitz; Poore; Richardson, E.P.; Ritchie 1; Rose, B., 1, 4; Rosenblum 1; Rubin 1; Seitz 3; Soby 5; Tashijian; Tomkins and Time-Life Books. Archives.

STEPHAN, GARY. b. December 24, 1942, Brooklyn, N.Y. **Studied:** Parsons School of Design, NYC, 1960–61; ASL, 1961; Pratt Institute, 1961–64; San Francisco Art Institute, 1964–67, MFA. Traveled France, Italy. **Taught:** School of Visual Arts, NYC, 1973. **Address:** 530 Canal Street, NYC 10013. **Dealer:** Mary Boone Gallery, NYC. **One-man Exhibitions:** (first) David Whitney Gallery,

Joseph Stella   *Boy with Bagpipe*   1910–12

NYC, 1969, 70, 71; Quay Gallery, San Francisco, 1971; Galleri Hans R. Neuendorf, Cologne, 1972; Galleri Hans R. Neuendorf, Hamburg, 1972; The Texas Gallery, Houston 1973, 75, 76, 78; Galleri Ostergren, Malmo, 1973; Galleri Fabian Carlson, Goteborg, 1973; Weinberg Gallery, San Francisco, 1973, 75, 77; Alfred/SUNY, 1974; Bykert Gallery, NYC, 1974, 75, 76; Mary Boone Gallery, NYC, 1978, 79, 80; Arnold Gallery, Atlanta, 1978; Margo Leavin Gallery, Los Angeles, 1979. **Group:** WMAA Biennials, 1969, 71, 73; Pratt Institute, NYC, Recent Abstract Paintings, 1973; P.S. 1, Long Island City, The Altered Photograph/20 Walls, 20 Curators, 1979; NYU, American Painting: The Eighties, 1979.

STERNBERG, HARRY. b. July 19, 1904, NYC. **Studied:** ASL; and privately with Harry Wickey. Traveled Mexico, Canada, Great Britain. **Taught:** ASL, 1933–68; New School for Social Research, 1942–45, 1950–51; Brigham Young U., 1958; U. of Southern California, 1959–69; Palomar College, 1974.

Directed and produced a film, *The Many Worlds of Art*, 1960. Federal A.P. (murals): US Post Offices, Sellersville, Pa., and Chester, Pa. (1935–37); advisor on graphic project. **Commission:** Mural, Escondido, Calif. Community Clinic, 1979. **Awards:** Fifty Prints of the Year, 1930; Fine Prints of the Year, 1932, 33, 34; Guggenheim Foundation Fellowship, 1936; 100 Prints of the Year, 1938; The Print Club, Philadelphia, 1942; Audubon Artists, 1955; AAAL, **P.P.**, 1972. **Address:** 1606 Conway Drive, Escondido, CA 92027. **One-man Exhibitions:** Keppel & Co., NYC, 1937; Weyhe Gallery, 1941; ACA Gallery, 1947, 50, 56, 58, 61, 62, 64, 66, 68, 70, 72, 74; U. of Minnesota, 1957; Garelick's Gallery, Detroit, 1958; Brigham Young U., 1958; Idyllwild Art School, 1958; Gallery Eight, Santa Barbara, 1961; Salt Lake Art Center, Salt Lake City, 1961; Art and Design Gallery, Nonsall, Calif., 1976. **Group:** WMAA; Chicago/AI; Walker; U. of Minnesota; de Young; Brooklyn Museum; MOMA; 100th Anniversary Exhibition of ASL, NYC, 1976. **Collections:** ASL; Andover/Phillips; Auckland; Bibliotheque Nationale; Brooklyn Museum; City College, NYC; Cleveland/MA, de Young; Harvard U.; Library of Congress; MMA; MOMA; U. of Minnesota; NYPL; Phillips; U. of Southern California; Syracuse U.; Tel Aviv; Victoria and Albert Museum; WMAA; Walker. **Bibliography:** American Artists Congress, Inc.; American Artists Group Inc. 3; Hayter 1; *Index of 20th Century Artists*; Mellquist; Reese; **Smith, A.; Sternberg, 1, 2;** Zigrosser 1. Archives.

STERNE, HEDDA. b. August 4, 1916, Bucharest, Rumania. Citizen, 1944. **Studied:** U. of Bucharest; Kunsthistorisches Institut der Universitat Vienna; and at academies in Paris. To USA, 1941, Traveled Europe extensively, Mexico, Latin America, Africa, S. America. **Taught:** Carbondale College, 1964. **Awards:** Chicago/AI, Second Prize, 1957; Fulbright Fellowship,

1963; AAAL, Childe Hassam Fund, **P.P.**, 1971. **Address:** 179 East 71st Street, NYC 10021. **Dealer:** Betty Parsons Gallery. **One-man Exhibitions:** (first) Wakefield Gallery, NYC, 1943; Mortimer Brandt, NYC, 1945; Betty Parsons Gallery, 1947, 48, 50, 53, 54, 57, 58, 61, 63, 68, 70, 74, 75; Sao Paulo, 1953; L'Obelisco, Rome, 1953, 61; Arts Club of Chicago, 1955; Vassar College, 1956; Saidenberg Gallery, 1956; Rizzoli Gallery, NYC, 1968; U. of Rochester, 1973; Upstairs Gallery, East Hampton, 1973; Lee Ault & Co., 1975; Fairweather-Hardin Gallery, Chicago, 1976. **Retrospective:** Montclair/AM, 1977. **Group:** Art of This Century, NYC, 1943, 44; WMAA, The New Decade, 1954–55; Chicago/AI, 1954, 55, 57, 60; MOMA, 1955; RISD, 1955; Stanford U., 1955, 56; U. of Illinois, 1955, 60; Corcoran, 1955, 56, 58, 63; Carnegie, 1955, 58, 61, 64; XXVIII Venice Biennial, 1956; Smithsonian, 1956; VMFA, American Painting, 1958; PAFA, 1958 and Annuals; State U. of Iowa, 1958, 59; Rome–New York Foundation, Rome, 1959, 61; II Inter-American Paintings and Prints Biennial, Mexico City, 1960; WMAA Annuals; U. of Colorado, 1960; Finch College, NYC, Artists at Work, 1971; Minnesota/MA, Drawings USA, 1971. **Collections:** Buffalo/Albright; Carnegie; Chase Manhattan Bank; Chicago/AI; Detroit/Institute; Ford Foundation; U. of Illinois; Inland Steel Co.; MMA; MOMA; Minnesota/MA; Montclair/AM; U. of Nebraska; PAFA; Rockefeller Institute; St. Joseph/Albrecht; Toledo/MA; US State Department; United Nations; VMFA; WMAA. **Bibliography:** Motherwell and Reinhardt, eds.; Pousette-Dart, ed.; Read 4. Archives.

STERNE, MAURICE. b. 1878, Libau, on the Baltic; **d.** 1957, NYC. To USA, 1889. **Studied:** Cooper Union, 1892; NAD, 1894–99, with Thomas Eakins. Traveled Europe, India, Burma, Java, Egypt. **Member:** National Fine Arts Commission, 1945–51. **Commissions:** Justice Department, Washington, D.C.

(mural); Fairmount Park, Philadelphia (monument); Rogers-Kennedy Memorial, Worcester, Mass., 1926. **Awards:** Mooney Traveling Scholarship, 1904; Chicago/AI, The Mr. & Mrs. Frank G. Logan Prize, 1928; Corcoran, William A. Clark Prize and Corcoran Gold Medal, 1930; Carnegie, Hon. Men., 1930; Golden Gate International Exposition, San Francisco, 1939; NAD Annual, Andrew Carnegie Prize, 1959. **One-man Exhibitions:** Paul Cassirer Gallery, Berlin, 1910; Berlin Photograph Co., NYC, 1910, 15; Chicago/AI, 1917; Bourgeois Gallery, NYC, 1917, 22; Boston Arts Club, 1919; Scott and Fowles Gallery, NYC, 1926; Reinhardt Galleries, NYC, 1928, 30; SFMA, 1936, 38; Honolulu Academy, 1939; The Milch Gallery, 1962. **Retrospective:** MOMA, 1933; Phillips, 1952; Hirschl & Adler Galleries, Inc., NYC, 1962. **Group:** Rome National Art Quadrennial, 1925; Chicago/AI; Corcoran; WMAA; SFMA; Brooklyn Museum; Newark Museum. **Collections:** Carnegie; Chicago/AI; Cleveland/MA; Cologne; Corcoran; Detroit/Institute; MMA; Phillips; RISD; San Diego; Yale U. **Bibliography:** Baur 7; Biddle 4; Birnbaum; Blesh 1; Brown; Cahill and Barr, eds.; Cheney; Coke 2; Eliot; Genauer; Goodrich and Baur 1; Hall; *Index of 20th Century Artists;* Jackman; Jewell 2; **Kallem;** Kent, N.; Kootz 1; Mather 1; Mayerson, ed.; McCurdy, ed.; Mendelowtiz; Neuhaus; Parkes; Phillips 2; Richardson, E.P.; Ringel, ed.; Rose, B., 1; Sachs. Archives.

STEVENSON, HAROLD. b. March 11, 1929, Idabel, Okla. **Studied:** U. of Oklahoma; U. of Mexico; ASL. Traveled Europe, Mexico, USA; resided Paris ten years. Subject of the Andy Warhol film *Harold,* 1964. **Taught:** Austin College, Artist-in-Residence. **Address:** 302 Southeast Adams, Idabel, OK 74745. **Dealer:** Brooks Jackson Iolas Gallery, NYC. **One-man Exhibitions:** (first) Alexandre Iolas Gallery, NYC, 1956, also 1958, 65, 72, 73, 74; Galerie la Cour d'Ingres, Paris, 1960; Iris Clert Gallery, 1962, 63, 68; Robert Fraser Gallery, 1962; Richard Feigen Gallery, Chicago, Los Angeles, and NYC, 1964; Galerie Svensk-Franska, Stockholm, 1965; American Embassy, Paris, 1969; Knoedler & Co., Paris, 1970; Galeria Blu, Milan, 1971; La Medusa Gallery, Rome, 1970, 73; Alexandre Iolas Gallery, Paris, 1973; Galerie Zoumbulaskis, Athens, 1973; Brooks Jackson Iolas Gallery, NYC, 1976. **Group:** Salon du Mai, Paris, 1962; WMAA Annual, 1964; Musée de la Haye, Amsterdam, 1964; Palais des Beaux-Arts, Brussels, 1965; Galerie Svensk-Franska, Stockholm, 1965; ICA, London, The Obsessive Image, 1968; Dusseldorf/Kunsthalle, Prospect '68, 1968; HemisFair '68, San Antonio, Tex., 1968; Musée du Louvre, Paris, Comparaisons, 1969; CNAC, L'Image en Question, 1971; Paris, Salon d-Automne, 1971. **Bibliography:** Lippard 5. Archives.

STILL, CLYFFORD. b. November 30, 1904, Grandin, N.D.; **d.** June 23, 1980, Baltimore, Md. **Studied:** Spokane U., 1933, BA; Washington State College, MA. **Taught:** Yaddo, 1934, 35; Washington State College, 1935–45; College of William and Mary, 1944; California School of Fine Arts 1946–50; "Subject of the Artist," NYC, 1947–48; Hunter College, 1952; Brooklyn Museum School, 1952; U. of Pennsylvania, 1963. Encouraged California students to form a group, which became the Metart Gallery. **Awards:** Skowhegan School, Medal for Painting, 1975; AAAL, award of merit medal for painting, 1972; Hon. DFA, North Dakota U., 1972; Hon. DFA, SFAI, 1976. **One-man Exhibitions:** (first) SFMA, 1943; Art of This Century, NYC, 1946; Metart Gallery, San Francisco, 1950; ICA, U. of Pennsylvania, 1964; Marlborough-Gerson Gallery Inc., 1969, 71; Buffalo/Albright, 1980. **Retrospective:** Buffalo/Albright, 1959; MMA, 1979. **Group:** MOMA, Fifteen Americans, circ., 1952; MOMA, The New American Painting, circ. Eu-

rope, 1958–59; Documenta II, Kassel, 1959; MOMA, The New American Painting and Sculpture, 1969; Corcoran Biennial, 1971; Carnegie, International, 1978. **Collections:** Baltimore/MA; Buffalo/Albright; MOMA; Phillips; SFMA; WMAA. **Bibliography:** Alloway 4; Ashton 5; Battcock, ed.; Blesh 1; Chipp; **Clyfford Still;** Downes, ed.; Finkelstein; Flanagan; Gaunt; Goosen 1; *The Great Decade;* Greenberg 1; Haftman; Hess, T.B., 1; Hobbs and Levin; Honisch and Jensen, eds.; Hunter 1, 6; Hunter, ed.; O'Neill, ed.; McChesney; McCurdy, ed.; *Metro;* Ponente; Read 2; Richardson, E.P.; Rickey; Rose, B., 1; Rosenblum 2; Rubin 1; Sandler 1; Seuphor 1; Tomkins 2; Tuchman, ed. Archives.

STONE, SYLVIA. b. June 18, 1928, Toronto, Canada. **Studied:** ASL, 1950–52, with Vaclav Vytlacil and Morris Kantor. Traveled Europe, Central America, Morocco. **Taught:** Brooklyn College, 1968–. **Commissions:** Xerox Corp., NYC, 1969; Sunrise Mall, Massapequa, N.Y., 1972; GSA, Federal Court House, Ft. Lauderdale, 1979. **Awards:** CAPS, 1971; National Endowment for the Arts, grant; City University of New York, research grant, 1977. **m.** Al Held. **Address:** 435 W. Broadway, NYC 10012. **Dealer:** Andre Emmerich Gallery, NYC. **One-man Exhibitions:** Brata Gallery, NYC (two-man), 1959; Tibor de Nagy, NYC, 1967, 68, 69; Andre Emmerich Gallery, NYC, 1972, 75, 78, 79; Bennington College, 1978. **Group:** Newark Museum, Cool Art, 1968; Walker, 14 Sculptors: The Industrial Edge, 1969; WMAA, 1969, 71, 73; ICA, U. of Pennsylvania, Plastics and New Art, 1969; Milwaukee, A Plastic Presence, circ., 1969; WMAA Biennials, 1970, 73; U. of North Carolina, Works on Paper, 1971; Indianapolis, 1974; Hayward, London, The Condition of Sculpture, 1975; WMAA, 200 Years of American Sculpture, 1976; Albright College, Perspective 1976, 1976. **Collections:** Buffalo/Albright; Hartford/

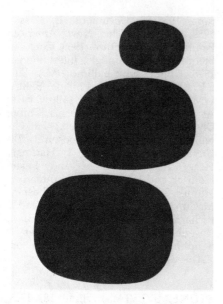

Myron Stout   Untitled   1957–63

Wadsworth; The New Museum, NYC; University of North Carolina; Omni Corp., NYC; Ridgefield/Aldrich; WMAA; Walker. **Bibliography:** Friedman, M., 2.

STOUT, MYRON. b. December 5, 1908, Denton, Tex. **Studied:** North Texas State U., 1930, BS; Columbia U., with C. J. Martin, MA; Academia San Carlos, Mexico City, 1933; Hofmann School. US Army and Air Force, 1943–45. Traveled France, Italy, Mexico, Greece, Turkey. **Taught:** Fine Arts Work Center, Provincetown, Mass., Artist-in-Residence, 1968. **Awards:** National Council on the Arts, 1966; J. S. Guggenheim Fellowship, 1969. **Address:** 4 Brewster Street, Provincetown, MA 02657; 716 Ector, Denton, TX 76201. **Dealer:** Richard Bellamy, NYC. **One-man Exhibitions:** (first) The Stable Gallery, NYC, 1954, Hansa Gallery, NYC, 1957, 58, (three-man); Houston/Contemporary, 1977. **Retrospective:** WMAA, 1980. **Group:** WMAA Annual, 1958; Carnegie, 1959; ICA, Boston, 100 Works on Paper, circ., Europe, 1959;

ICA, Boston, Paintings, USA, 1959; A.F.A., New Talent, circ., 1960; WMAA, Geometric Abstraction in America, circ., 1962; Jewish Museum, 1964; SRGM, American Drawings, 1964; Corcoran Biennial; Buffalo/Albright, Plus by Minus, 1968; WMAA, American Drawings: 1963–1973, 1973. **Collections:** Brooklyn Museum; Carnegie; Hirshhorn; MOMA; McCrory Corp., NYC; NYU; National Gallery, Washington, D.C.; SRGM; WMAA; Woodward Foundation. **Bibliography:** MacAgy 2.; Sandler 1; Schwartz.

STROUD, PETER ANTHONY. b. May 23, 1921, London, England. **Studied:** London University; Central School of Arts and Crafts, London, 1950, BFA, 1952, BA. Ed., 1953, MFA. British Army, 1939–45. Traveled Europe, Near East. **Taught:** Maidstone College of Art, 1962–63; Bennington College, 1963–64, 1966–68; Hunter College, 1965–66; Maryland Institute, 1968; Rutgers U., 1968– . **Commissions:** Royal Festival Hall, London, "Groupe Espace" Project, 1958; International Union of Architects, London (mural), 1961; State School, Leverkusen, Germany (mural), 1963; Manufacturers Hanover Trust Co., NYC (mural), 1969; Watertown (N.Y.) State Office Building, 1970. **Address:** 311 Church Street, NYC 10013. **One-man Exhibitions:** ICA, London, 1961; Bennington College, 1964; U. of Vermont, 1966; Marlborough-Gerson Gallery Inc., 1966; Nicholas Wilder Gallery, 1967; Axiom Gallery, London, 1968; Galerie Muller, 1969; Gertrude Kasle Gallery, 1969; Rutgers U., 1969; Max Hutchinson Gallery, 1970, 72; 73; Bernard Jacobson Gallery, London, 1971; Hoya Gallery, London, 1974; Annely Juda Fine Art, London, 1977; Union College, N. J., 1978. **Group:** Groupe Espace, London and Paris, 1957; New Vision Centre, London, Form and Experiment, 1957; Drian Gallery, London, Construction Great Britain: 1950–60, 1960; Carnegie, 1961, 64; Leverkusen, Construction

1962, 1962; Kunsthalle, Basel, Seven Young British Painters, 1963; MOMA, The Responsive Eye, 1965; Jewish Museum, European Painters Today, 1968; Museum of Modern Art, Oxford, Painters of the Sixties, 1969; Melbourne/ National, Form and Structure, 1970; U. of California, Santa Barbara, Constructivist Tendencies, circ., 1970; Ulster Museum, From Sickert to Conceptual Art, 1971; Finch College, NYC, The Constructivist Tradition, 1972. **Collections:** Detroit/Institute; Leverkusen; Los Angeles/County MA; Newark Museum; Pasadena/AM; SRGM; San Diego; Tate; Trenton/State; U. of Vermont; Whitworth.

STUEMPFIG, WALTER. b. 1914, Germantown, Pa.; **d.** November 30, 1970, Ocean City, N.J. **Studied:** PAFA, 1931–35. **Taught:** PAFA, 1946–70. **Member:** NIAL. **Awards:** PAFA, Cresson Fellowship, 1933. **One-man Exhibitions:** Philadelphia Art Alliance, 1942; Durlacher Brothers, NYC, 1943–62; de Young, 1946; Artists' Gallery, Philadelphia, 1947; Woodmere Art Gallery, Philadelphia, 1953; U. of Miami, 1960; MIT, 1960; Art Association of Newport (R.I.), 1961; Maynard Walker Gallery, NYC, 1962; Richard Larcada Gallery, 1965, 70; PAFA, 1970. **Group:** PAFA; PMA. **Collections:** Chicago/AI; Corcoran; Harvard U.; MMA; MOMA; PMA; WMAA. **Bibliography:** Bazin; Eliot; Hunter 6; Mendelowitz; Nordness, ed.; Soby 5; Wight 2.

SUGARMAN, GEORGE. b. May 11, 1912, NYC. **Studied:** Zadkine School of Sculpture, Paris, 1955–56. Traveled Mexico, USA, Europe; resided Paris, 1951–55. **Taught:** Hunter College, 1960– ; Yale U., 1967–68. **Commissions:** Geigy Chemical Corp. (wall structure); Xerox Data Systems, El Segundo, Calif.; First National Bank of St. Paul, Minn.; Albert M. Greenfield School, Philadelphia; City of Leverkusen, West Germany; South Mall, Albany; Brussels World Trade Center; Garmatz Federal Building, Baltimore; International Building, Miami, Fla., Airport, 1977; Federal Court House and Office Building, Baltimore, 1976–78; Detroit General Hospital, 1980. **Awards:** Longview Foundation Grant, 1960, 61, 63; Carnegie, Second Prize, 1961; Ford Foundation, 1965; National Council on the Arts, 1966. **Address:** 21 Bond Street, NYC 10012. **Dealer:** Robert Miller Gallery, NYC. **One-man Exhibitions:** Union Dime Savings, NYC, 1958; Widdifield Gallery, NYC, 1960; Stephen Radich Gallery, 1961, 64, 65, 66; Philadelphia Art Alliance, 1965; Dayton's Gallery 12, Minneapolis, 1966; Fischbach Gallery, 1966–69; Galerie Schmela, 1967; Ziegler Gallery, 1967; Kunsthalle, Basel, 1969; Krefeld/Kaiser Wilhelm, 1969; One Hundred and Eighteen: An Art Gallery, Minneapolis, 1971; Dag Hammarskjold Plaza, NYC, 1974; The Zabriskie Gallery, 1974; Robert Miller Gallery, NYC, 1978, 79, 80; Galerie Liatowitach, Basel, 1979. **Retrospective:** Kunsthalle, Basel, circ., Amsterdam, West Germany, 1969. **Group:** A.F.A., Sculpture in Wood, circ., 1941–42; Salon de la Jeune Sculpture, Paris, 1952, 54; Salon des Realites Nouvelles, Paris, 1954; Silvermine Guild, 1958; Claude Bernard, Paris, 1960; Carnegie, 1961; Seattle World's Fair, 1962; Hartford/ Wadsworth, 1962; A.F.A., Sculpture for the Home, circ., 1962; Chicago/AI, 1962, 66; VII Sao Paulo Biennial, 1963; Walker, Ten American Sculptors, 1964; Jewish Museum, Recent American Sculpture, 1964; ICA, U. of Pennsylvania, 1964; New York World's Fair, 1964–65; NYU, 1965; Flint/Institute, 1965; WMAA, Art of the U.S., 1670–1966, 1966; Los Angeles/County MA, American Sculpture of the Sixties, 1967; WMAA Sculpture Annuals, 1967, 69; Foundation Maeght, L'Art Vivant, circ., French museums, 1968; XXXIV Venice Biennial, 1968; MOMA, 1969; Foundation Maeght, L'Art Vivant, 1970; U. of Nebraska, American Sculpture, 1970; WMAA, 1970, 73; Cincinnati/Contemporary, Monumental Art,

George Sugarman *The Big Ride* 1979

1970; Middelheim Park, Antwerp, XI Sculpture Biennial, 1971; MIT, Outdoor Sculpture, 1972; WMAA, American Drawings: 1963–1973, 1973; Newport, R. I., Monumenta, 1974; NCFA, Sculpture: American Directions, 1945–1975, 1975; WMAA, 200 Years of American Sculpture, 1976; ICA, U. of Pennsylvania, The Decorative Impulse, circ., 1979. **Collections:** Basel; Buffalo/Albright; Chicago/AI; Ciba-Geigy Corp.; Kalamazoo/Institute; Krefeld/Haus Lange; MMA; MIT; MOMA; Museum Schloss Marberg; NCFA; NYU; St. Louis/City; The Singer Company, Inc.; Torrington Mfg. Corp.; Walker; Wuppertal. **Bibliography:** Battcock, ed.; Calas, N. and E.; Davies; Janis and Blesh 1; *Monumenta*; Rickey; Sandler 1; Tuchman 1. Archives.

SUMMERS, CAROL. b. December 26, 1925, Kingston, N.Y. **Studied:** Bard College, with Stefan Hirsch, Louis Schanker, 1951, BA. US Marine Corps, 1944–48. Traveled the Orient, Italy, France, Czechoslovakia, Central America, India, Nepal. **Taught:** Hunter College, 1963–64; Brooklyn Museum School; School of Visual Arts, NYC; Pratt Graphics Center, NYC; Columbia U.; Haystack Mountain School of Crafts; U. of Pennsylvania; SFAI, 1973. **Awards:** Italian Government Travel Grant, 1955; L. C. Tiffany Grant, 1955, 61; J. S. Guggenheim Fellowship, 1959; Fulbright Fellowship (Italy), 1961. **Address:** 133 Prospect Court, Santa Cruz, CA 95065. **Dealers:** A.A.A. Gallery, NYC; ADI Gallery, San Francisco. **One-man Exhibitions:** (first) The Contemporaries, NYC, 1954, also 1961; MOMA, circ., 1964–66; A.A.A. Gallery, NYC, 1967, 80; Bard College, 1968; ADI Gallery, San Francisco, 1980. **Retrospective:** SFMA, 1967; Brooklyn Museum, 1977. **Group:** Major national print exhibitions. **Collections:** Baltimore/MA; Bibliotheque Nationale; Boston/MFA; Bradley U.; Brooklyn Museum; Chicago/AI; Cincinnati/AM; Cornell U.; Free Library of Philadelphia; U. of Kentucky; Library of Congress; Los Angeles/County MA; Lugano; MMA; MOMA; Milwaukee-Downer College; U. of Minnesota; NYPL; National Gallery; U. of Nebraska; New Britain; Ohio U.; PMA; Seattle/AM; U. of Tennessee; U. of Utah; Victoria and Albert Museum; Walker. **Bibliography:** *Carol Summers. Woodcuts 1950–1967.* Archives.

SUTTMAN, PAUL. b. July 16, 1933, Enid, Okla. **Studied:** Adelphi College, with Robert Cronbach; U. of New Mexico, with Adja Yunkers, Robert Mallory, 1956, BFA; Cranbrook, with Tex Schwetz, Maija Groten, 1958, MFA; with Giacomo Manzu, 1960. Traveled Europe, Latin America; resided Mexido, Italy. **Taught:** U. of Michigan, 1958–62; Dartmouth College, 1973. **Commissions:** Roswell (N.M.) Museum and Art Center (bronze relief for facade); National Educational Television, 1961 ("The Bronze Man," a film illustrating casting techniques); Hughes, Hatcher & Suffrin Building, Detroit, 1964; U. of Michigan, 1967. **Awards:** Cranbrook, Horace H. Rackham Research Grant (Florence, Italy), 1960; Fulbright Fellowship (Paris), 1963; Prix de Rome, 1965, 66, 67; Ingram Merrill Foundation Grant, 1972. **Address:** % Dealer. **Dealers:** Terry Dintenfass, Inc.; Richard Gray Gallery; Donald Morris Gallery. **One-man Exhibitions:** Roswell, 1959; Park Gallery, Detroit, 1959, 62; Donald Morris Gallery, 1959, 62, 65, 67, 69; U. of Michigan, 1962; Terry Dintenfass, Inc., 1962, 64, 65, 67, 69, 71, 73; Felix Landau Gallery, 1970; Robinson Galleries, 1971; Galleria Nuovo Carpine, Sardinia, 1972; Dartmouth College, 1973. **Group:** Youngstown/Butler; Detroit/Institute; U. of Michigan; Santa Barbara/MA; de

Young; U. of New Mexico; American Academy, Rome, 1966–68; Musee Rodin, Paris, International Sculpture, 1968; Indianapolis/Herron, 1969; PAFA Annual, 1969; USIS, Rome, 1969, 70, 72; Colorado Springs Fine Arts Center, Ten Take Ten, 1977. **Collections:** Detroit/Institute; First National Bank of Chicago; Kalamazoo/Institute; Layton School of Art; MOMA; Macomb County Community College; U. of Michigan; Roswell. **Bibliography:** Walker. Archives.

SUZUKI, JAMES HIROSHI. b. September 19, 1933, Yokohama, Japan. **Studied:** Privately with Yoshio Markino; Portland (Me.) School of Fine and Applied Art, 1952; The Corcoran School of Art, 1953–54. To USA, 1952. Traveled USA. Japan. **Taught:** U. of California, Berkeley, 1962–63; U. of Kentucky, 1966–68. **Awards:** Corcoran, Eugene Weiss Scholarship, 1954; John Hay Whitney Fellowship, 1958; Silvermine Guild, Larry Aldrich Prize, 1959. **Address:** 2021 E. 29th Street, Oakland, CA 94606. **Dealer:** Braunstein Quay Gallery, San Francisco. **One-man Exhibitions:** (first) The Graham Gallery, 1957, also 1958, 59, 61, 62; U. of California, Berkeley, 1963; Nihonbashi Gallery, Tokyo, 1963; Seido (Gallery), Kyoto, 1963; Comara Gallery, 1970; Palos Verdes, 1970; Quay Gallery, 1973; Braunstein Quay Gallery, 1976, 78; Sacramento State U., 1978. **Group:** Corcoran, 1956, 58, 60; WMAA; Baltimore/MA; ICA, Boston, Contemporary Painters of Japanese Origin in America; Cincinnati/AM; Des Moines; A.F.A., Cross-Currents, circ., 1957–58; Syracuse/Everson, 1958; Silvermine Guild, 1959; Hartford/Wadsworth, 1959; Houston/MFA, Waning Moon and Rising Sun, 1959; U. of Nebraska, 1960; SFMA, 1963, 64; Tokyo/Modern, 1964; SFMA, Aesthetics of Graffiti, 1978. **Collections:** Corcoran; Hartford/Wadsworth; Kamakura; McDonnell & Co. Inc.; Rockefeller Institute; Tokyo/Modern; Toledo/MA.

SWAIN, ROBERT. b. December 7, 1940, Austin, Texas. **Studied:** American U., Washington, D.C., BA, 1964. Traveled Central America, Europe. **Taught:** Hunter College, 1968. **Awards:** Guggenheim Foundation Fellowship, 1969; National Endowment for the Arts, grant, 1976. **Address:** 57 Leonard Street, NYC 10013. **Dealer:** Susan Caldwell Inc., NYC. **One-man Exhibitions:** (first) The Thenen Gallery, NYC, 1965; Fischbach Gallery, NYC, 1968, 69; Syracuse/Everson, 1974; Susan Caldwell Inc., NYC, 1974, 75, 78; The Texas Gallery, Houston, 1975; Columbus, 1975; Lockwood-Matthews Mansion Museum, Norwalk, Conn., 1978; Darien, Conn., Library, 1978; Nina Freudenheim Gallery, Buffalo, 1978; Toni Birckhead Gallery, Cincinnati, 1980. **Group:** MOMA, The Art of the Real, circ., 1968; Corcoran Biennial, 1968; U. of North Carolina, Art on Paper, 1968; WMAA, The Structure of Color, 1971; Indianapolis, 1974; MOMA, Color as Language, circ., 1974; UCLA, Fourteen Abstract Painters, 1975. **Collections:** Buffalo/Albright; Columbus; Corcoran; Detroit/Institute; Syracuse/Everson; VMFA; Walker; American Republic Insurance Co.; Chase Manhattan Bank; Ciba-Geigy Corp.; Ardsley; Ball State U.; McCrory Corp., NYC; Amerada Hess Corp., NYC; Prudential Insurance Co. of America; Travenol Laboratories, Deerfield, Ill.; The Harris Bank, Chicago; Mobil Oil Co., NYC; Trina Inc., NYC; Lehman Brothers, NYC.

TAKAI, TEIJI. b. February 5, 1911, Osaka, Japan. **Studied:** Shinano Bashi Art School, Osaka, 1929. Traveled north and central China, Europe. **Taught:** Kodo Art School, Tokyo; Winthrop College, Rock Hill, S.C., 1972–74. **Member:** "Nika" (Japanese Modern Art Group), 1939 (accepted for exhibition 1931); Kodo Art Group, 1947. To USA, 1954. **Awards:** Niki Prize, 1938; Okada Prize, 1941; Japanese Government Prize, 1943; Fukushima Prize, 1963. **Address:** % Dealer. **Dealer:** Poindexter Gallery, NYC. **One-man Exhibitions:** Takahimaya Gallery, Tokyo; Diamaru, Osaka; 1949–54; Collectors Gallery, NYC, 1956; Poindexter Gallery, 1959, 61, 63, 65, 68, 72. **Retrospective:** Takashimaya Gallery, Tokyo, 1967. **Group:** ICA, Boston, 1958; WMAA Annuals, 1960, 62; Corcoran, 1960, 62; Carnegie, 1961, 64; Columbia, S.C./MA, 1963; IV, V, & VI International Biennial Exhibitions of Prints, Tokyo, 1964, 66, 68. **Collections:** Columbia, S.C./MA; Corcoran; Friends of Art; Tokyo/Modern; WMAA.

TAKAL, PETER. b. December 8, 1905, Bucharest, Rumania. **Studied:** Paris, Berlin. To USA, 1939; citizen, 1944. Traveled Europe, Africa, North and South America, Mexico. **Taught:** Beloit College, 1965; Central College, Iowa, 1968. **Member:** Artists Equity; Color Print Society, SAGA. **Commissions** (graphic art): International Graphic Arts Society, 1956, 59, 63; Print Club of Cleveland, 1956, 57; The Contemporaries, NYC, 1957; A.A.A. Gallery, NYC, 1958. **Awards:** The Print Club, Philadelphia, Max Katzman Award, 1957; Silvermine Guild, Nancy A. Fuller Award, 1959; Yaddo Fellowship, 1961; Pasadena/AM Annual, **P.P.,** 1962; Tamarind Fellowship, 1963–64; Ford Foundation/A.F.A., Artist-in-Residence, 1965. **Address:** Saylorsburg, PA 18353; 116 East 68th Street, NYC 10021; 40 rue du Mole, CH 1201, Geneva, Switzerland. **Dealers:** Weyhe Gallery; A.A.A. Gallery, NYC; Gallerie Benador, Geneva. **One-man Exhibitions:** (first) Gallery Gurlitt, Berlin, 1932; Galerie Zak, Paris, 1933; Galerie Jeanne Castel, Paris, 1935, 37; Galerie Derche, Casablanca, 1937; Katharine Kuh Gallery, Chicago, 1937, 39, 41; Galerie Charpentier, Paris, 1939; Chauvin Gallery, Algiers, 1939; Carstairs Gallery, NYC, 1940; Santa Barbara/MA, 1941, 57; de Young, 1942; Karl Nierendorf Gallery, NYC, 1942; Artists' Gallery, NYC, 1954; Duveen/Graham Gallery, NYC, 1955, 58, 1957–58 (circ., American museums and colleges); Wittenborn Gallery, NYC, 1956; Pasadena/AM, 1956; Minneapolis/Institute, 1957; Los Angeles/County MA, 1957; Dallas/MFA, 1957; La Jolla, 1957; Carnegie College of Art, 1957; Mills College, 1957; The Print Club of Philadelphia, 1958; Kansas City/Nelson, 1958; Cleveland/MA, 1959; Memphis/Brooks, 1959; Galeria de Arte Mexicano, Mexico City, 1959; Smithsonian, circ., USA, 1959–60; Cushing Galleries, Dallas, 1959–60, 1966; The Contemporaries, NYC, 1959, 60, 62, 66; Palazzo Strozzi, Florence, Italy, 1960; Sabersky Gallery, Los Angeles, 1961; Kestner-Museum, circ., Germany, 1961–62; Philadelphia Art Alliance, 1962; Mary Harriman Gallery, Inc., Boston, 1964; Weyhe Gallery, 1964, 65, 68, 72; Beloit College, 1965; Scranton/

Everhart, 1967; Central College, 1968; Carnegie/Mellon U., 1969; Hunt Botanical Library, Pittsburgh, 1969; Galerie Benador, Geneva, 1977. **Retrospective:** Galerie du Grand-Mezel, Geneva, 1970. **Group:** Salon d'Automne, Paris, 1933–35; A.F.A.; PAFA, 1953, 59, 60, 63, 65, 67, 69; Brooklyn Museum, Print Biennials, 1955–64; WMAA Annuals, 1955–60, 1962–64; Library of Congress Print Annuals, 1955, 58, 59, 60, 62; MOMA, Recent Drawings USA, 1956; The Print Club, Philadelphia, 1956–58, 1961–63; Boston Printmakers, 1956–59, 1962, 63, 64; ICA, Boston, 100 Works on Paper, circ., Europe, 1959; PCA, American Prints Today, circ., 1959–62; Gallery of Modern Art, Ljubljana, Yugoslavia, IV International Exhibition of Prints, 1961; MOMA, circ., Europe and Far East, 1961 (drawings); St. Paul Gallery, Drawings, USA, 1963; SAGA Annual, 1963, 65; Minnesota/MA, 1963; 1966–68, 1971–73; The Japan Print Association, Tokyo, 1967; WMAA, 1968, 69; MOMA, Tamarind: Homage to Lithography, 1969; SAGA, 1979. **Collections:** Achenbach Foundation; Alboin College; Andover/Phillips; Baltimore/MA; Beloit College; Berlin/National; Bibliotheque Nationale; Brandeis U.; Bremen; Brooklyn Museum; U. of California, Berkeley; Carnegie; Chicago/AI; Cincinnati/AM; Cleveland/MA; Copenhagen; Dallas/MFA; Darmstadt/Hessisches; de Young; Exeter; Fort Worth; Graphische Sammlung der E.T.H.; Grenoble; Hamburg; Indianapolis/Herron; Karlsruhe; Kassel; Kestner-Museum; Kupferstichkabinett; La Jolla; Library of Congress; Lincoln, Mass./De Cordova; Los Angeles/County MA; MMA; MOMA; U. of Maine; Mills College; U. of Minnesota; Minnesota/MA; Montreal/MFA; NYPL; NYU; National Gallery; Omaha/Joslyn; Oran; PAFA; PMA; Paris/Moderne; Paris/Outre-Mer; Pasadena/MA; RISD; Recklinghausen; Saarlandmuseum; Stockholm/National; Stuttgart; Stuttgart/WK; U. of Texas; Topeka Public Library; UCLA; USIA; US State Department; Uffizi Gallery; Victoria and Albert Museum; WMAA; Walker; U. of Wisconsin; Wuppertal; Yale U. **Bibliography:** Kent, N.

TALBOT, WILLIAM H. M. b. January 10, 1918, Boston, Mass.; **d.** November 16, 1980. **Studied:** PAFA, 1936–38, 1940–41, with Walker Hancock; privately with George Demitrios, Boston, 1938–39; Academie des Beaux-Arts, Paris, 1945–46, with Marcel Gaumont. US Army, 1941–46. Traveled USA extensively, Mexico, Canada, Europe (esp. Greece), Egypt, Sudan. **Taught:** Birch Wathen School, 1947–48; Visiting Lecturer, U. of Michigan, 1949; St. Lawrence U. **Member:** President, Sculptors Guild, 1965–68; Federation of Modern Painters and Sculptors to 1970; Architectural League of New York; Century Association. **Commissions:** Bryn Mawr College, 1948; Fitchburg (Mass.) Youth Library, 1950; National Council of State Garden Clubs, St. Louis, Mo., 1957–59; Johnson Rehabilitation Center, Barnes Hospital, St. Louis, Mo., 1964. **Awards:** PAFA, Cresson Fellowship, 1941; Prix de Rome, 1941; Connecticut Academy of Fine Arts, Howard Penrose Prize, 1950; NIAL, 1975. **One-man Exhibitions:** (first) Carroll-Knight Gallery, St. Louise, 1949; Andrew-Morris Gallery, NYC, 1963; Earlham College, 1964; Martin Schweig Gallery, 1965, 69; St. Lawrence U., 1966; Hartford (Conn.) Jewish Community Center, 1967; Mattatuck Historical Society Museum, Waterbury, Conn., 1967; Rehn Galleries, 1968, 71; Arts Club of Chicago, 1972. **Group:** Federation of Modern Painters and Sculptors Annuals; Fairmount Park Association, Philadelphia, Sculpture International; Boston Arts Festival; WMAA; PMA; St. Louis/City; Dallas/MFA; Lincoln, Mass./De Cordova; Andover/Phillips; U. of Michigan, 1949; New York World's Fair, 1964–65; PAFA, 1966, and Annuals; Hartford/Wadsworth, 1966; Stamford (Conn.) Museum and Nature Center, 1968; Sculptors Guild, 1968, 69, and Annuals; NIAL, 1975. **Collections:** Bryn Mawr

College; The Cambridge School; Earlham College; Fitchburg (Mass.) Public Library; Missouri Botanical Gardens, St. Louis; Rumsey Hall School; St. Lawrence U.; WMAA; Washington U.

TAM, REUBEN. b. January 17, 1916, Kapaa, Hawaai. **Studied:** U. of Hawaii, 1933–37, with Huc Luquiens and Henry Rempel, BA; graduate study, 1937–38; California School of Fine Arts, 1940; Columbia U.; New School for Social Research, NYC, 1943–45, with Erwin Edman, Meyer Schapiro, Maurice Wertheimer, Rudolf Arnheim; ASL, 1941; Hans Hoffmann, 1941. **Taught:** Brooklyn Museum School, 1948– ; Oregon State U., 1966; Queens College, 1973. **Awards:** Guggenheim Foundation Fellowship, 1948; Golden Gate International Exposition, San Francisco, 1939, First Prize; U. of Illinois, **P.P.;** Honolulu Academy, First Prize, 1939, 40; Brooklyn Museum, First Prize, 1952, 58; NAD, Landscape Prize, 1974; NAD, first prize, 1974, 77; AAIAL, award, 1978. **Address:** 549 West 123rd Street, NYC 10027; summer: Monhegan Island, Me. **Dealer:** Coe Kerr Gallery. **One-man Exhibitions:** (first) California Palace, 1940; Sacramento/Crocker, 1941; Honolulu Academy, 1941, 67; The Downtown Gallery, 1945, 46, 49, 52; U. of Illinois, 1949, 51, 53, 55, 59; Philadelphia Art Alliance, 1954; The Alan Gallery, NYC, 1955, 57, 59, 61, 64; Portland, Ore./AM, 1966; Oregon State U., 1966; The Landau-Alan Gallery, NYC, 1967; Coe Kerr Gallery, NYC, 1971, 75, 79; Wichita Art Association, 1971; Molloy College, Rockville Centre, N.Y., 1973; Joe de Mers Gallery, Hilton Head, 1974, 76; U. of Nebraska, 1976; Savannah, Telfair, 1976; Palm Beach Galleries, 1978; El Paso Museum, 1978. **Group:** Carnegie; Brooklyn Museum, Watercolor Biennials; PAFA; Corcoran; Chicago/AI Annuals; VMFA; Walker; WMAA Annuals; WMAA, Artists of Maine; MMA, American Paintings Today, 1950; MMA, American Painting, 1953; MOMA, Recent Drawings USA,

1956; U. of Illinois, 1961, 65, 69; Smithsonian, 1969; Omaha/Joslyn, A Sense of Place, 1973; AAAL, 1973; U. of Iowa, 1974; NAD, 1974, 75; NAD, 1975, 76, 77, 78, 79, 80; ICA, Boston, Bicentennial Exhibit, 1976. **Collections:** AAAL; Andover/Phillips; Berea College; Bowdoin College; Brooklyn Museum; Colby College; Corcoran; Dallas/MFA; Des Moines; Endicott, N. Y.; Fort Worth; U.of Georgia; Hawaii State Foundation; Hirshhorn; IBM; U. of Illinois; MMA; MOMA; U. of Maine; U. of Michigan; Montclair/AM; NCFA; NYPL; U. of Nebraska; Newark Museum; U. of North Carolina; The Pennsylvania State U.; Tel Aviv; Temple U.; Utica; WMAA; Wichita/AM; Youngstown/Butler.

TANGUY, YVES. b. January 5, 1900, Paris, France; **d.** January 15, 1955, Woodbury, Conn. French Army, 1920–22. Traveled Africa, USA. To USA, 1939; citizen, 1948. **m.** Kay Sage. **One-man Exhibitions:** (first) Galerie Surrealiste, Paris, 1928; Galerie des Cahiers d'Art, Paris, 1935, 47; Stanley Rose Gallery, Hollywood, 1935; Julien Levy Galleries, NYC, 1936; Howard Putzell Gallery, Hollywood 1936; Palais des Beaux-Arts, Brussels (three-man), 1937; Bucher-Myrbor Galerie, Paris, 1938; Guggenheim Jeune Gallery, London, 1938; Hartford/Wadsworth, 1939; Pierre Matisse Gallery, 1939, 42, 43, 45, 46, 50, 63; Arts Club of Chicago, 1940; "G" Place Gallery, Washington, D.C., 1943; SFMA, 1946; Musée du Luxembourg, Paris, 1947; Galerie Maeght, 1947; Copley Gallery, Hollywood, 1948; Galerie Nin Dausset, Paris, 1949; ICA, Washington, D.C., 1952; Kunsthalle, Basel, 1952; L'Obelisco, Rome, 1953; Hartford/Wadsworth, 1954 (two-man); MIT (two-man); Bodley Gallery, NYC, 1960; Petit Galerie, Paris, 1961; Galatea Galleria d'Arte, Turin, 1971; Acquavella Gallery, NYC, 1974. **Retrospective:** MOMA, 1955. **Group:** Chicago/AI; Hartford/Wadsworth; WMAA; MOMA; Fantastic

Art, DADA, Surrealism, 1936; Palais des Beaux-Arts, Brussels, 6 Surrealist Painters, 1967. **Collections:** Buffalo/ Albright; Chicago/AI; Hartford/ Wadsworth; U. of Illinois; MMA; MOMA; PMA; WMAA; Washington U. **Bibliography:** Battcock, ed.; Baur 7; Blanchard; Blesh 1; **Breton** 1, 2, 3, **4;** Canaday; Christensen; Flanagan; Ford; Gascoyne; Genauer; Goodrich and Baur 1; Guggenheim, ed.; Haftman; Hunter 6; Hunter, ed.; Janis, S.; Kozloff 3; Kuh 1; Langui; McCurdy, ed.; Mendelowitz; Pearson 2; Pousette-Dart, ed.; Ramsden 1; Raynal 3; Read 5; Richardson, E.P.; Rosenblum 2; Rubin 1; Sachs; Seitz 3; **Soby** 1, **8; Tanguy;** Tomkins and Time-Life Books; Waldberg 3, 4; Zervos.

TANIA (Schreiber). b. January 11, 1924, Warsaw, Poland. **Studied:** McGill U., 1941–42; Columbia U., 1942–44, MA; ASL, 1948–51, with Yasuo Kuniyoshi, Morris Kantor, Vaclav Vytlacil, Harry Sternberg. Traveled Europe extensively, Canada, USA, Caribbean. **Taught:** NYU, 1963–70; Montclair State College, 1967; Southampton College, 1968–69; PAFA, 1974–75; Purchase/SUNY, 1975–76; U. of Alabama, 1976. **Commissions:** Civic Center Synagogue, NYC, 1966; mural for City Walls Inc.; Dresdner Bank, NYC, 1972; Albright College, 1972. **Address:** 362 West Broadway, NYC 10013. **One-man Exhibitions:** (first) Albert Landry, NYC, 1959, also 1961, 62; The Bertha Schaefer Gallery, 1963, 64, 66; The New Bertha Schaefer Gallery, NYC, 1966; NYU, 1966; Benson Gallery, Bridgehampton, 1967, 69, 76; U. of Alabama, 1976. **Retrospective:** Jack Gallery, NYC, 1978. **Group:** NYU, 3 Artists; U. of Illinois; U. of Virginia, Color and Space; WGMA, The Formalists, 1963; Oakland/AM; World House Galleries, NYC, International, 1964; Albion College, Pop and Op, 1965; New York Cultural Center, Women Choose Women, 1973; Guild Hall, East Hampton, members exhibition, 1980. **Collections:** AT&T; Albright College; Bran-

deis U.; Chase Manhattan Bank, NYC; Lincoln Hospital, Bronx; MMA; Morgan State College; Morrisania Hospital, Bronx; NYU; Price Waterhouse and Co., NYC; Stony Brook/SUNY.

TAUBES, FREDERIC. b. April 15, 1900, Lwow, Poland. **Studied:** Academy of Fine Arts, Munich, 1918–20, with Franz von Stuck, Max Doerner; Bauhaus, Weimar, 1920–21, with Josef Itten; and in Berlin and Italy. Traveled Europe extensively, USA, Africa, Near East, Far East. To USA, 1930. **Taught:** Mills College, 1938; U. of Hawaii, 1939; U. of Illinois, 1940–41; Cooper Union, 1943; U. of Wisconsin, 1943; U. of Oklahoma; London U.; Oxford; Royal College of Art; contributing editor, *American Artist* magazine, 1943–62; columnist and American editor, *Artist* magazine; U. of Alberta. **Member:** Fellow, Royal Society of Arts; International Society of Arts and Letters; formulator of Taubes varnishes and Copal painting media, manufactured by Permanent Pigments Co. **Address:** The Studio, Haverstraw, NY 10927. **One-man Exhibitions:** (first) Vienna/Stadt, 1921; The Midtown Galleries; San Diego; Los Angeles/County MA; SFMA; Sacramento/Crocker; Honolulu Academy; U. of Nebraska; Kansas City/Nelson; Mills College; Seattle/AM. **Group:** PAFA, 1935–44; Chicago/AI, 1935–46; Carnegie, 1936–46; Corcoran, 1936–46; VMFA, 1938–46; Memphis/Brooks. **Collections:** American Locomotive Co.; Atlanta/AA; Britannica; de Young; IBM; Indiana U.; Kansas City/Nelson; MMA; Mills College; SFMA; San Diego; Santa Barbara/MA; Standard Oil Co.; Stony Brook/SUNY. **Bibliography:** Allen, C.C., ed.; Boswell 1; **Boswell, ed.;** Kent, N.; **Taubes 1, 2, 3, 4, 5, 6, 7, 8, 9, 10, 11, 12, 13;** Watson, E. W., 2.

TCHELITCHEW, PAVEL. b. September 21, 1898, District of Kaluga, near Moscow, Russia; **d.** July 31, 1957, Grotta Ferrata, Italy. **Studied:** U. of

Moscow; Kiev Academy, 1918–20. Traveled Europe, USA, North Africa, USSR. To USA, 1934; citizen, 1952. Designed sets and costumes for ballets by Balanchine, Massine, and others. **One-man Exhibitions:** (first) Claridge Gallery, London, 1928; A. Tooth & Sons, London, 1933, 35, 38; Julien Levy Galleries, NYC, 1934, 37, 38; Arts Club of Chicago, 1935, 38; Durlacher Brothers, NYC, 1942, 45, 51; Hanover Gallery, 1949; Institute of Modern Art, Buenos Aires, 1949; Detroit/Institute, 1952; Galerie Rive Gauche, Paris, 1954, 56; Galleria d'Arte del Naviglio, Milan, 1955; Catherine Viviano Gallery, 1964, 67; Galerie Lucie Weile, Paris, 1966; MOMA, 1972; Alpine Club London, 1972, 74, 76. **Retrospective:** Durlacher Brothers, NYC, 1948; Gallery of Modern Art, NYC, 1964. **Group:** Many national and international exhibitions. **Collections:** Hartford/Wadsworth; Kansas City/Nelson; MMA; MOMA; U. of Michigan; Santa Barbara/MA; Tretyakov Art Gallery, Yale U. **Bibliography:** Bazin; Canaday; Flanagan; Ford; Frost; Holme 1; Huyghe; **Kirstein 3; Kirstein, ed.;** Kuh 1; McCurdy, ed.; Mendelowitz; Pousette-Dart, ed.; Richardson, E.P.; **Soby 1, 7; Tyler, P., 1;** Wight 2.

THEK, PAUL. b. November 2, 1933, Brooklyn, N.Y. **Studied:** Cooper Union, ASL, Pratt Institute, 1951–54. Traveled Europe; resided Rome, 1967–75. **Commissions:** Nederlands Dans Theater, sets and costumes for the ballet *Arena*, by Glen Tetley, 1969. **Awards:** Fulbright Fellowship, 1967. **Address:** % Dealer. **Dealer:** Brooks Jackson Gallery Iolas, N.Y. **One-man Exhibitions:** Mirell Gallery, Miami, Fla., 1957; Galleria 88, Rome, 1963; The Pace Gallery, NYC, 1966; The Stable Gallery, 1964, 67, 69, 70; M. E. Thelen Gallery, Cologne, 1968, 72; Loernerscuit Gallery, Amsterdam, 1968, 69; Amsterdam/Stedelijk, 1969; Stockholm/National, 1969, 71; Galerie 20, Amster-

Paul Thek   *Uncle Tom's Cabin*   1975

dam (two-man), 1969; Alexandre Ïolas Gallery, NYC, 1975; Loernerscuit Gallery, Amsterdam (two-man), 1969; Lucerne, 1973; Gallerie Stahli, Lucerne, 1973; Duisburg, 1973; Galerie Alexandre Iolas, Paris, 1976; Il Fante di Spade, Rome, 1977; Brooks Jackson Gallery Iolas, N. Y. 1977, 80. **Group:** Carnegie, 1967; ICA, London, The Obsessive Image, 1968; Documenta 4, Kassel, 1968; Walker, 1968; Cologne, 1969; MOMA, Art in the Mirror, 1966; ICA, U. of Pennsylvania, The Other Tradition, 1966; Carnegie, 1967; ICA, U. of

Pennsylvania, The Obsessive Image, 1968; Indianapolis, 1968; WMAA, Human Concern/Personal Torment, 1969; Walker, Figures/Environments, circ., 1970–71; La Jolla, Continuing Art, 1971; Documenta 5, Kassel, 1972; Venice Biennials, 1976, 80; ICA, U. of Pennsylvania, Processions, 1977. **Collections:** CNAC; Cologne. **Bibliography:** *Figures/Environments;* Lucie-Smith.

THIEBAUD, WAYNE. b. November 15, 1920, Mesa, Ariz. **Studied:** San Jose State College; Sacramento State College, BA, MA. US Army Air Force, 1942–45. Traveled Europe, Mexico, USA. **Taught:** Sacramento City College, 1951–60; Sacramento State College, 1954–55; California School of Fine Arts, 1958; U. of California, Davis, 1960– ; Cornell U., summer, 1967. Produced 11 educational motion pictures; 22-minute color film produced by Carr Films, 1971, covers 9 years of work. **Commissions:** California State Fair, 1950, 52, 55; Sacramento (Calif.) Municipal Utility Building, 1959 (mosaic mural). **Awards:** California State Fair, Art Film Festival, First Prize, 1956; Film Council of America, Golden Reel Award, 1956 (American Film Festival, Chicago); Columbia Records Award, 1959 ($6,000); Scholastic Art Awards for the films *Space* and *Design,* 1961; Creative Research Foundation, $1,000 Grant, 1961. **Address:** 1617 7th Ave., Sacramento, CA 95817. **Dealers:** Allan Stone Gallery; John Berggruen, San Francisco. **One-man Exhibitions:** (first) Sacramento/Crocker, 1951, 69; Artists Co-op Gallery, Sacramento, 1957, 58; SFMA, 1961, 78; de Young, 1962; Allan Stone Gallery, 1962–67; 77, 78, 79, 80; Galleria Schwarz; Stanford U., 1965; Albright Museum, Kansas City, Mo., 1966; Pasadena/AM; WMAA, 1971; John Berggruen, San Francisco, 1980, Denver, 1975; U. of California, Santa Cruz, 1976; U. of California, Davis, 1977; Diablo Valley College, 1977. **Retrospective:** Walker, 1979; Phoenix, 1976. **Group:** SFMA Annual; Chicago/

AI Annual; WMAA Annual; Los Angeles/County MA; California Palace; Denver/AM; ICA, London; Pasadena/AM, New Paintings of Common Objects, 1962; Houston-Contemporary, Pop Goes the Easel, 1963; IX Sao Paulo Biennial, 1967; Documenta V, Kassel, 1972; and print exhibitions abroad. **Collections:** Achenbach Foundation; American Broadcasting Co.; Brandeis U.; Bryn Mawr College; Buffalo/Albright; California State Library; Chicago/AI; Corcoran; Dallas/MFA; Hartford/Wadsworth; Harvard U.; Houston/MFA; Immaculate Heart College; Kansas City/Nelson; Library of Congress; MMA; MOMA; U. of Miami; Milwaukee; U. of Nebraska; Newark Museum; Oakland/AM; PMA; RISD; SFMA; Sacramento/Crocker; Sacramento State College; San Jose State College; Shasta College; Southern Illinois U.; Stanford U.; Time Inc.; Utah; WGMA; WMAA. **Bibliography:** Alloway 4; *America 1976;* Arthur 1, 2; Hunter, ed.; Lippard 5; *New in the Seventies;* Sager; *The State of California Painting;* Weller.

THOMAS, ROBERT C. b. April 19, 1924, Wichita, Kans. **Studied:** Zadkine School of Sculpture, Paris, 1948–49; U. of California, Santa Barbara, 1950, BA; California College of Arts and Crafts, 1952, MFA; and privately with David Green, Pasadena, 1946–47. US Air Force, 1943–46. Traveled Spain, France, Italy; resided Paris, 1960–61, Florence, Italy, 1972–73. **Taught:** U. of California, Santa Barbara, 1954– . **Commissions:** I. Magnin, Century City, Calif.; U. of California, Santa Barbara; Whatcom. **Awards:** Los Angeles Art Festival, Bronze Medal, 1949; Walnut Creek (Calif.) Pageant, Third Prize for Sculpture, 1951; San Francisco Art Association Annual, Bank of America Award, 1952; RAC, First Prize, 1952; San Francisco Art Association, American Trust Co. Award, 1953; RAC, First Prize, Sculpture, 1953; California State Fair, Second Prize and Silver Medal, 1954;

Santa Barbara/MA, III Pacific Coast Biennial, **P.P.,** 1959; U. of California Institute for Work in the Creative Arts, 1967–68; and others. **Address:** 38 San Mateo Avenue, Goleta, CA 93017. **Dealer:** Bradley Galleries, Santa Barbara. **One-man Exhibitions:** (first) U. of California, Santa Barbara, 1949; Coit Lane Gallery, Santa Barbara, 1950; Paul Desch Gallery, Santa Barbara, 1952; Santa Barbara/MA, 1955, 1959 (two-man), 1963 (three-man); Esther Robles Gallery, 1959, 60, 61, 63, 66; La Jolla, 1960; Esther Bear Gallery, 1961; Adele Bednarz Gallery, 1970, 71, 72, 74, 76; Peppers Art Center, Redlands, Calif. (two-man), 1976; Bradley Galleries, Santa Barbara, 1978; Opus 5 Gallery (two-man); Solano Beach, 1980. **Retrospective:** U. of California, Santa Barbara, 1966. **Group:** Salon des Artistes Independants, Paris, 1949; Salon du Mai, Paris, 1949; City of Los Angeles Annual, 1949; Los Angeles/County MA, 1950, 55, 56; RAC, 1951, 53; SFMA, 1952, 53, 56, 57; California State Fair, 1954, 57, 58, 59, 60, 62; Oakland/AM, 1954, 55, 56, 58; Denver/AM, 1959, 62; La Jolla, 1962; Ball State Teachers College, 1962, 63. **Collections:** Hirshhorn; Santa Barbara/MA.

THOMPSON, BOB. b. June 26, 1937, Louisville, Ky.; **d.** May 30, 1966, Rome, Italy. **Studied:** Boston Museum School, 1955; U. of Louisville, 1955–58. Traveled Europe, North Africa; resided Paris, Ibiza, NYC, Rome. **Awards:** Walter K. Gutman Foundation Grant, 1961; John Hay Whitney Fellowship, 1962–63. **One-man Exhibitions:** Delancey Street Museum, NYC, 1960; Superior Street Gallery, Chicago, 1961; Martha Jackson Gallery, 1963, 65, 68; El Cosario Gallery, Ibiza, Spain, 1963; The Drawing Shop, NYC, 1963–64; Richard Gray Gallery, 1964, 65; Paula Johnson Gallery, NYC, 1964; Donald Morris Gallery, 1965, 70; East End Gallery, Provincetown, 1965; Louisville/Speed, 1971; U. of Massachusetts, 1974; PAFA, 1976. **Retrospective:** New School for Social Research, 1969; Studio Museum in Harlem, NYC, 1978. **Group:** Martha Jackson Gallery, 1964; Dayton/AI, International Selection, 1964; Yale U., 1964; New School for Social Research, 1965; Gallery 12 St. Marks, NYC, 1967; Star Turtle Gallery, NYC, The Tenants of Sam Wapnowitz, 1969; Brooklyn Museum, Eight Afro-American Artists, 1971. **Collections:** A.F.A.; American Republic Insurance Co.; Buffalo/Albright; Charlotte/Mint; Dayton/AI; Jay Dorf, Inc.; Miles College.

TING, WALASSE. b. October 13, 1929, Shanghai, China. To USA; citizen, 1970. Resided Paris, 1950–60. **Awards:** Guggenheim Foundation Fellowship, 1970. **Address:** 463 West Street, NYC 10014. **Dealer:** Lefebre Gallery, NYC. **One-man Exhibitions:** Hong Kong,

Walasse Ting   Untitled   1979

1952; Paul Facchetti Gallery, Paris, 1954; Martha Jackson Gallery, NYC, 1959, 60; Lefebre Gallery, NYC, 1963, 66, 67, 68, 69, 70, 71, 72, 80; Gallerie Birch, Copenhagen, 1963, 70, 75; Galerie de France, Paris, 1968; Galerie Adrien Maeght, Paris, 1974, 77. **Group:** Salon de Mai, Paris, 1964, 65, 66, 67, 68; Carnegie, International, 1961, 64, 67, 70. **Collections:** Amsterdam/Stedelijk; Chicago/AI; Detroit/Institute; SRGM; MOMA; Rockefeller U.; Buffalo/Albright; Norfolk/Chrysler.

TOBEY, MARK. b. December 11, 1890, Centerville, Wisc.; **d.** April 24, 1976, Basel, Switzerland. **Studied:** Chicago Art Institute School, 1908, with Frank Zimmerer, Prof. Reynolds. Traveled Europe, Mexico, USA, the Orient, extensively. **Taught:** Cornish School, Seattle, intermittently 1923–29; Dartington Hall, Devonshire, England, 1931–38. Federal A.P.: Easel painting, 1938. **Awards:** Seattle/AM, Katherine Baker Memorial Award, 1940; MMA, Artists for Victory, $500 Prize, 1942; Portrait of America, Fourth Prize, 1945; NIAL, 1956; Guggenheim International, $1,000 Award, 1956; American Institute of Architects, Fine Arts Medal, 1957; XXIX Venice Biennial, 1958, First Prize of the Commune of Venice; *Art in America* magazine, 1958 ($1,000); elected to American Academy of Arts and Sciences, 1960 (fails to accept election); Skowhegan School, Painting Award, 1971. **One-man Exhibitions:** (first) M. Knoedler & Co., NYC, 1917; Arts Club of Chicago, 1928, 40; Romany Marie's Cafe Gallery, NYC, 1929; Cornish School, Seattle, 1930; Contemporary Arts Gallery, NYC, 1931; Paul Elder Gallery, San Francisco, 1934; Beaux Arts Gallery, London, 1934; Stanley Rose Gallery, Hollywood, 1935; Seattle/ AM, 1942; The Willard Gallery, 1944, 45, 47, 49, 50, 51, 53, 54, 57, 71, 74; Margaret Brown Gallery, Boston, 1949, 54, 56; Portland, Ore./AM, 1950 (three-man); California Palace, circ., 1951; The U. of Chicago, 1952; Zoe Dusanne Gal-

lery, Seattle, 1952; Otto Seligman Gallery, 1954, 57, 62; Chicago/AI, 1955; Gump's Gallery, 1955; Jeanne Bucher, Paris, 1955, 59, 68, 77; Paul Kantor Gallery, Beverly Hills, Calif., 1955; ICA, London, 1955; Victoria (B.C.), 1957; Galerie Stadler, Paris, 1958; St. Albans School, Washington, D.C., 1959; Frederic Hobbs Fine Art Center, San Francisco, 1960; Mannheim, 1960; Galerie Beyeler, Basel, 1961, 70, 71; Royal Marks Gallery, 1961; Seattle World's Fair, 1962; Phillips, 1962; Hanover Gallery, 1968; Bon Marche, Seattle, 1969; PAFA, 1969; Baukunst Galerie, Cologne, 1971; WMAA, 1971; Galleria dell'Ariete, 1971; Tacoma, 1972; Cincinnati/AM, 1972; Galerie Biedermann, Munich, 1973; NCFA, 1974; Krefeld/ Haus Lange, 1975; Foster White Gallery, Seattle, 1980; Alex Rosenberg Gallery, NYC, 1979; Haslem Fine Arts, Inc., Washington, D.C., 1979; Elaine Granz Gallery, San Francisco, 1976; George Belcher Gallery, San Francisco, 1978. **Retrospectives:** Seattle/AM, circ., 1959, 70; Musee des Arts Decoratifs, 1961; MOMA, 1962; Kunstverein, Dusseldorf, 1966; Berne, 1966; Hannover/K-G, 1966; Amsterdam/Stedelijk, 1966; Dallas/MFA, 1968. **Group:** MOMA, Paintings by 19 Living Americans, 1929; New York World's Fair, 1939; Chicago/AI, 1940, 45, 47, 48, 51; MMA, 1942, 44, 45; MOMA, Romantic Painting in America, 1943; Brooklyn Museum, 1945, 51; Seattle/AM, 1945, 50, 51, 52, 53, 55, 56, 58; WMAA, 1945, 46, 47, 49, 62; Tate, 1946; MOMA, Fourteen Americans, circ., 1946; Utica, circ., 1947; XXIV, XXVIII & XXIX Venice Biennials, 1948, 56, 58; U. of Illinois, 1949, 50, 51, 55, 59; SFMA, 1949; Walker, Contemporary American Painting, 1950; MMA, American Paintings Today, 1950; MOMA, Abstract Painting and Sculpture in America, 1951; Ueno Art Gallery, Tokyo, 1951; U. of Minnesota, 40 American Painters, 1940–50, 1951; I & III Sao Paulo Biennials, 1951, 55; Carnegie, 1952, 55, 58, 61; International Biennial Exhibition of Paintings, Tokyo; Pavillion, Vendome, Aix-en-

Provence, 1954; France/National, 50 ans d'art aux Etats-Unis, circ., Europe, 1955; Darmstadt/Kunsthalle, circ., 1956; III International Contemporary Art Exhibition, New Delhi, 1957; USIA, Eight American Artists, circ., Europe and Asia, 1957–58; WMAA, Nature in Abstraction, 1958; Brussels World's Fair, 1958; American Painting and Sculpture, Moscow, 1959; Documenta II, Kassel, 1959; Walker, 60 American Painters, 1960; Seattle World's Fair, 1962; National Gallery, American Art at Mid-Century, 1973; NCFA, Art of the Pacific Northwest, 1974. **Collections:** Andover/Phillips; Baltimore/MA; Boston/ MFA; Brooklyn Museum; Buffalo/Albright; Carnegie; Chicago/AI; Detroit/ Institute; Hartford/Wadsworth; MMA; MOMA; Milwaukee; Phillips; Portland; Ore./AM; SFMA; St. Louis/City; Seattle/ AM; Utica; WMAA; West Palm Beach/ Norton. **Bibliography: Alvard;** *Art of the Pacific Northwest;* Ashton 5; Baur 5, 7; Beekman; Biddle 4; Bihalji-Merin; Blesh 1; Eliot; Gaunt; Goodrich and Baur 1; Haftman; Henning; Hess, T.B., 1; Honisch and Jensen, eds.; Hulten; Hunter 1, 6; Hunter, ed.; Janis, S.; Kuh 2, 3; Langui; Leepa; Lynton; McCurdy, ed.; *Mark Tobey;* Mendelowitz; *Metro;* Miller, ed. 2; Neumeyer; Nordness ed.; *Northwest Traditions;* Ponente; Pousette-Dart, ed.; Ragon 1, 2; Read 2; Restany 2; Richardson, E.P.; Rickey, Ritchie 1; **Roberts;** Rodman 1, 3; Rose, B., 1; **Seitz** 1, **5;** Seuphor 1; Soby 5; Tapie 1; **Thomas; Tobey;** Weller. Archives.

TODD, MICHAEL. b. June 20, 1935, Omaha, Neb. **Studied:** U. of Notre Dame, 1957, BFA, magna cum laude; UCLA, 1959, MA. **Taught:** UCLA, 1959–61, San Diego, 1968– ; Bennington College, 1966–68. **Awards:** Woodrow Wilson Fellowship, 1957–59; Fulbright Fellowship (Paris), 1961–63; National Endowment for the Arts, 1974. **Address:** % Dealer. **Dealer:** Betty Cuningham, NYC. **One-man Exhibitions:** Hanover Gallery, 1964; The Pace Gallery, NYC, 1964; Henri Gallery, 1965,

68; Gertrude Kasle Gallery, 1968; Salk Institute, La Jolla, 1969; Reese Palley Gallery, NYC, 1971; California State U., Fullerton, 1972; U. of Notre Dame, 1972; Palo Alto Square, 1973, 74; The Zabriskie Gallery, 1974, 76; Seder/ Creigh Galley, Coronado, Calif., 1975; Hammarskjold Plaza, NYC, 1976; Nicholas Wilder Gallery, Los Angeles, 1976; Charles Casat Gallery, La Jolla, 1978; Oakland/AM, 1978; Paule Anglim Gallery, San Francisco, 1978; Tortue Gallery, Los Angeles, 1978; Diane Brown Gallery, Washington, D.C., 1978; Arco Center for Visual Arts, Los Angeles, 1979; Betty Cuningham, NYC, 1979. **Group:** American Cultural Center, Paris, 1962; WMAA, 1965, 67, 68, 70; WMAA, Young America, 1965; Jewish Museum, Primary Structure Sculptures, 1966; Los Angeles/County MA, American Sculpture of the Sixties, circ., 1967; Corcoran, 1968; Maeght Foundation, 1970; San Diego, 1974; SFMA, California Painting and Sculpture: The Modern Era, 1976. **Collections:** California State U.; Hirshhorn; La Jolla; Los Angeles/County MA; U. of Notre Dame; Oakland/AM; Palomar College; Pasadena/AM; Southwestern Community College; Storm King Art Center; WMAA.

TOMLIN, BRADLEY WALKER. b. August 19, 1899, Syracuse, N.Y.; **d.** May 11, 1953, NYC. **Studied:** Studio of Hugo Gari Wagner, 1913; Syracuse U., 1917–21; Academie Colarossi, Paris, and Academie de la Grande Chaumiere, 1923. Traveled Europe. **Taught:** Buckley School, 1932–33; Sarah Lawrence College, 1932–41; Dalton Schools, NYC, 1933–34. **Member:** Federation of Modern Painters and Sculptors; Whitney Studio Club, NYC; Woodstock Artists Association. **Awards:** Scholarship to Wagner Studio, 1913; Syracuse U., Hiram Gee Fellowship; Scholarship to L. C. Tiffany Foundation, Oyster Bay, N.Y.; Carnegie, Hon. Men., 1946; U. of Illinois, **P.P.,** 1949. **One-man Exhibitions:** Skaneateles and Cazenovia,

N.Y., 1922; Anderson Galleries, NYC, 1923; Montross Gallery, NYC, 1926, 27; Frank K. M. Rehn Gallery, NYC, 1931, 44; Betty Parsons Gallery, 1950, 53; Phillips, 1955; Buffalo/Albright, 1975. **Retrospective:** WMAA, circ., 1957; Hofstra U., 1975. **Group:** U. of Illinois, 1949, 51; MOMA, Abstract Painting and Sculpture in America, 1951; U. of Minnesota, 1951; MOMA, Fifteen Americans, circ., 1952; MMA, 1953; WMAA, The New Decade, 1954–55; France/National, 1955; MOMA, The New American Painting and Sculpture, 1969. **Collections:** Andover/Phillips; Cranbrook; U. of Illinois; MMA; Phillips; Utica; WMAA. **Bibliography:** Baur 7; Blesh 1; Flanagan; Goodrich and Baur 1; Haftman; Hess, T. B., 1; Hobby and Levin; Hunter 1, 6; Hunter, ed.; McCoubrey 1; McCurdy, ed.; Mendelowitz; Motherwell and Reinhardt, eds.; Pagano; Ponente; Pousette-Dart, ed.; Read 2; Ritchie 1; Rose, B., 1; Sandler; Seuphor 1; Tuchman, ed.; Weller; *Woodstock: An American Art Colony, 1902–1977.* Archives.

TOOKER, GEORGE. b. August 5, 1920, NYC. **Studied:** Phillips Academy, 1936–38; Harvard U., AB, 1942; ASL, with Reginald Marsh, Paul Cadmus, Kenneth Hayes Miller, Harry Sternberg. US Marine Corps, 1942–43. Traveled France, Italy, Great Britain. **Taught:** ASL, 1965–68. **Member:** NAD. **Awards:** NIAL Grant, 1960. **Address:** Hartland, Vt. **Dealer:** Rehn Galleries. **One-man Exhibitions:** (first) Hewitt Gallery, NYC, 1951, also 1955; Robert Isaacson Gallery, NYC, 1960, 62; Durlacher Brothers, NYC, 1964, 67; Dartmouth College, 1960, 62, 67. **Retrospective:** WMAA, 1974. **Group:** WMAA; MOMA; MMA, 1950, 52; Chicago/AI, 1951; Corcoran, 1951; ICA, London; PAFA, 1952; XXVIII Venice Biennial, 1956; Carnegie, 1958; Festival of Two Worlds, Spoleto, 1958. **Collections:** Dartmouth College; MMA; MOMA; NCFA; Sara Roby Foundation; WMAA; Walker. **Bibliography:** Garver; Goodrich and Baur 1; Mendelowitz; Newmeyer; Nordness, ed.; Pousette-Dart, ed.; Rodman 1; Weller. Archives.

TOVISH, HAROLD. b. July 31, 1921, NYC. **Studied:** WPA Art Project, with Andrew Berger; Columbia U., 1940–43, with Oronzio Maldarelli; Zadkine School of Sculpture, Paris, 1949–50; Academie de la Grande Chaumiere, 1950–51. Traveled France, Italy, Japan, Indonesia, Nepal, Iran, Turkey. **Taught:** New York State College of Ceramics, 1947–49; U. of Minnesota; 1951–54; Boston Museum School, 1957–66; U. of Hawaii, 1969–70; Boston U., 1971– . **Member:** Artists Equity; Boston Visual Artists Union. **Awards:** Minneapolis/Institute, First Prize, Sculpture, 1954; Boston Arts Festival, First Prize for Drawing, 1958, First Prize for Sculpture, 1959; NIAL Grant, 1971. **m.** Marianna Pineda. **Address:** 380 Marlborough Street, Boston, MA 02115. **Dealer:** Terry Dintenfass, Inc., NYC; Alpha Gallery, Boston. **One-man Exhibitions:** (first) Walker, 1953; The Swetzoff Gallery, Boston, 1957, 60, 65; Fairweather-Hardin Gallery, 1960; Terry Dintenfass, Inc., 1965, 73, 80; Andover/Phillips, 1965; Alpha Gallery, 1968, 73; Boston U., 1980. **Retrospective:** Wheaton College, 1967; SRGM, 1968. **Group:** MMA, Artists for Victory, 1942; Toledo/MA, Sculpture Today, 1947; Walker, 1951; SFMA, 1952; Minneapolis/Institute, 1952, 54; WMAA, 1952, 54, 57, 60, 64, 67; Denver/AM, 1955; Carnegie, 1958; Chicago/AI, 1959; MOMA, Recent Sculpture USA, 1959; Venice Biennial; SRGM, The Joseph H. Hirshhorn Collection, 1962; Lincoln, Mass./De Cordova, 1964; U. of Illinois, 1964, 67, 68, 69; PAFA Annual, 1967; HemisFair '68, San Antonio, Tex., 1968. **Collections:** Andover/Phillips; Boston/ MFA; Boston Public Library; Chicago/ AI; MOMA; Minneapolis/Institute; U. of Minnesota; PMA; SRGM; WMAA; Walker; Worcester/AM. **Bibliography:** Weller.

TOWNLEY, HUGH. b. February 6, 1923, West Lafayette, Ind. **Studied:** U. of Wisconsin, 1946–48; privately with Ossip Zadkine, Paris, 1948–49; Central School of Arts and Crafts, London, 1949–50, with Victor Passmore. Traveled France, Great Britain, Holland, Brazil, Peru. **Taught:** Layton School of Art, 1951–56; Beloit College, 1956–57; Boston U., 1957–61; U. of California, Berkeley, 1961, Santa Barbara, 1968; Harvard U., 1967; Brown U., 1961– . **Member:** Artists Equity, Boston, 1961. **Commissions:** YMCA, Milwaukee, 1956; Sobin Chemical Co., Boston, 1963. **Awards:** SFMA Annual, 1952; Chicago/AI, Exhibition Momentum, 1952, 53; MIT, Summer Fellowship, 1956; ICA, Boston, Selections, 1961; Berkshire Art Association Annual, 1961, 63; Hon. MFA, Brown U., 1962; Rhode Island Arts Festival, 1962, 63; Silvermine Guild, 1963; Yaddo Fellowship, 1964; Kalamazoo Art Center, Lithographic Workshop, Fellowship, 1964; NIAL, 1967; Tamarind Fellowship, 1969; Rhode Island, Governor's Arts Award, 1972. **Address:** 131 Hope Street, Bristol, RI 02809. **One-man Exhibitions:** Studio 40, The Hague, 1950 (two-man); Gallerie Apollinaire, London, 1951; U. of Wisconsin, 1955, 68; Beloit College, 1956 (two-man); Milwaukee, 1957; Arts Council of Winston-Salem (N.C.), 1958; The Swetzoff Gallery, Boston, 1958, 59; Connecticut College, 1960; The Pace Gallery, Boston, 1960, 64, NYC, 1964; U. of Connecticut, 1964; Valparaiso U. (Ind.), 1965; Mitchem Gallery, Milwaukee, 1965; U. of New Hampshire, 1965; Temple U., 1966; Eleanor Rigelhaupt Gallery, Boston, 1966; Exeter, 1966; Yale U., 1966; Bristol (R.I.) Museum of Art, 1968 (two-man, with Robert S. Neuman); Michael Walls Gallery, 1968 (two-man); Lincoln, Mass./De Cordova, 1969; Graphics Gallery, 1969; Bradley Galleries, Milwaukee, 1970; Brockton/Fuller (two-man), 1971; Brown U., 1972; Tyler School, Philadelphia, 1972; U. of Oregon, 1976; Suzette Schochett Gallery, Newport, R.I., 1977; Western Car-

olina U., 1978; Worcester/AM, 1980. **Group:** USIA, Americans in Paris, circ., Europe, 1949; SFMA Annual, 1952; MOMA, New Talent; Chicago/AI, Exhibition Momentum, 1952, 53, 56, 57, also 1964; Walker, 1956; WMAA, Young America, 1957, Annual, 1962; Carnegie, 1958; Boston Arts Festival, 1958, 61, 64; Silvermine Guild, 1959, 60, 62, 63, 64, 66; ICA, Boston, View, 1960, Selections, 1961; U. of Illinois, 1961, 63; Hartford/Wadsworth, Eleven New England Sculptors, 1963; Lincoln, Mass./De Cordova, 1964; M. Knoedler & Co., Art across America, circ., 1965–67; Andover/Phillips, 1966; Birmingham, Mich., Art Museum, 1966; U. of North Carolina, 1966; Flint/Institute, I Flint Invitational, 1966; NIAL, 1967; Oakland/AM, 1969; Utica, 1970; Newport, R.I., Monumenta, 1974; Portland, Ore./AM, 1976. **Collections:** Andover/Phillips; Boston/MFA; Brandeis U.; Brown U.; Chicago/AI; Colby College; First National Bank of Boston; First National Bank, St. Paul; Harvard U.; Kalamazoo/Institute; Lincoln, Mass./De Cordova; Los Angeles/County MA; MOMA; Mead Corporation; Milwaukee; Princeton U.; U. of Rhode Island; RISD; SFMA; Utica, WMAA; Williams College; Wrexham Foundation. **Bibliography:** *Monumenta.*

TREIMAN, JOYCE. b. May 29, 1922, Evanston, Ill. **Studied:** Stephens College, 1941, AA; State U. of Iowa, with Philip Guston, Lester Longman, 1943, BFA. Traveled Europe, Mediterranean, Middle East. **Taught:** U. of Illinois, 1958–60; San Fernando Valley State College, 1968; UCLA, 1969–70; Art Center School, Los Angeles, 1968; California State U., Long Beach, 1977. **Awards:** Graduate Fellowship to State U. of Iowa, 1943; L. C. Tiffany Grant, 1947; Denver/AM, **P.P.,** 1948; Springfield, Ill./State; Chicago/AI, Mr. & Mrs. Frank H. Armstrong Prize, 1949; Chicago/AI, The Mr. & Mrs. Frank G. Logan Prize, 1951; Chicago/AI, Pauline Palmer Prize, 1953; Tupperware Art Fund, 1955; Chicago/

AI, Martin B. Cahn Award, 1949, 60; Ford Foundation, **P.P.**, 1960; Pasadena/AM, 1962; La Jolla, 1962; Tamarind Fellowship, 1962; Ford Foundation/A.F.A. Artist-in-Residence, 1963; Los Angeles, All-City Show, **P.P.**, 1964, Sculpture Prize, 1966; Los Angeles Times, Woman of the Year for Art, 1965. **Address:** 712 Amalfi Drive, Pacific Palisades, CA 90272. **Dealers:** The Forum Gallery; Fairweather-Hardin Gallery; Tortue Gallery, Los Angeles. **One-man Exhibitions:** (first) Paul Theobald Gallery, Chicago, 1942; John Snowden Gallery, Chicago, 1945; Chicago/AI: The Chicago Artists Room, 1947; Fairweather-Garnett Gallery, Evanston, Ill., 1950; Hewitt Gallery, NYC, 1950; Palmer House Galleries, Chicago, 1952; Elizabeth Nelson Gallery, Chicago, 1953; Feingarten Gallery, Chicago, 1955; Cliff Dwellers Club, Chicago, 1955; Fairweather-Hardin Gallery, 1955, 58, 62, 64, 73; The Willard Gallery, 1960; Felix Landau Gallery, 1961, 64; The Forum Gallery, NYC, 1963, 66, 71, 75; Adele Bednarz Gallery, Los Angeles, 1969, 71, 74, 76; Palos Verdes Art Center, circ., 1976; Tortue Gallery, Santa Monica, 1978, 79. **Retrospective:** La Jolla, 1972; Municipal Art Gallery, Los Angeles, 1978. **Group:** Denver/AM, 1943, 48, 55, 58, 60, 64; Chicago/AI Annuals, 1945–59, Directions in American Painting, 1946, 51, 54, 56, 59, 60, also 1964, 68; MMA, American Painters under 35, 1950; U. of Illinois, 1950, 51, 52, 56, 61, 63; WMAA Annuals, 1951, 52, 53, 58, Young America, 1957; Library of Congress, 1954; Carnegie, 1955, 57; Corcoran, 1957; U. of Nebraska, 1957; PAFA, 1958; MOMA, Recent Painting USA: The Figure, circ., 1962–63; WMAA, Fifty California Artists, 1962–63; Ravinia Festival, Highland Park, Ill.; U. of Illinois, 1965, 67, 69, 71, 74; NAD, 1972, 73; AAAL, 1974; Chicago/AI, Visions, 1976; ICA, Los Angeles, Current Directions in Southern California Art, 1978; Smithsonian, New American Monotypes, circ., 1978–80. **Collections:** Abbott Laboratories; Ball State U.; U. of California,

Santa Cruz; Chicago/AI; Denver/AM; Loan Association, Los Angeles; Illinois State U.; U. of Illinois; International Minerals & Chemicals Corp.; State U. of Iowa; Long Beach/MA; Los Angeles/County MA; MOMA; Oberlin College; U. of Oregon; Orlando; Pasadena/AM; San Fernando Valley State U.; Springfield, Ill./State; Santa Barbara/MA; Tupperware Museum; UCLA; Utah State U.; WMAA. **Bibliography:** Pousette-Dart, ed. Archives.

TROVA, ERNEST. b. February 19, 1927, St. Louis, Mo. Self-taught in art. **Address:** 6 Layton Terrace, St. Louis, MO 63124. **Dealer:** The Pace Gallery. **One-man Exhibitions:** Image Gallery, St. Louis, 1959, 61; H. Balaban Carp Gallery, St. Louis, 1963; The Pace Gallery, Boston, 1963, NYC, 1963, 65, 67, 69, 70, 71, 73, 75, 76, 80; Hanover Gallery, 1964, 66, 68, 70; Famous-Barr Co., St. Louis Bicentennial, 1964; MIT; Container Corp. of America, Chicago and NYC, 1965; The Pace Gallery, Columbus, 1966, 70, 75, 76; J. L. Hudson Art Gallery, Detroit, 1967; Harcus-Krakow Gallery, 1968; Dunkelman Gallery, Toronto, 1969; Gimpel & Hanover, 1970; Galerie der Spiegel, Cologne, 1970; Rene Block Gallery Ltd., 1970; Galerie Dieter Brusberg, Hanover, 1970; Fundacion Eugenio Mendoza, Caracas, 1971; Jerusalem/National, 1971; Makler Gallery, 1972; Galerie Charles Kriwin, Brussels, 1972; Elizabeth Stein Gallery, St. Louis, 1973; Phoenix, 1974; Hokin Gallery, Palm Beach, 1975; Hanover Gallery, London, 1979; Kingpitcher Gallery, Pittsburgh, 1975; Lakeview Center for the Arts & Sciences, Peoria, 1975; Hokin Gallery, Chicago, 1978; Medici/Berenson Gallery, Miami, 1979; Arte/Contacto, Caracas, 1979. **Group:** Oakland/AM, Pop Art USA, 1963; Chicago/AI Annual, 1964, 67; SRGM, American Drawings, 1964; Dallas/MFA, 1965; SRGM, 1965–66; Walker, 1966; SFMA, 1966; WMAA, Art of the U.S. 1670–1966, 1966; WMAA Sculpture Annual, 1966, 68; VMFA, American Painting, 1966; U. of Illinois, 1967; SRGM, Sculpture International, 1967; MOMA, Dada, Surrealism and Their Heritage, 1968; Documenta IV, Kassel, 1968; WMAA, Human Concern/Personal Torment, 1969; ICA, U. of Pennsylvania, Highway, 1970; Cincinnati/Contemporary, Monumental Art, 1970; Museo de Arte Contemporaneo, Cali, Colombia, S.A., Bienal Graficas, 1973; V International Poster Biennial, Warsaw, 1974; Hirshhorn, Inaugural Exhibition, 1974. **Collections:** Brandeis U.; Buffalo/Albright; Baltimore/MA; Des Moines; High Museum; Houston/MFA; Indiana U.; Indianapolis; Kansas City/Nelson; Los Angeles/County MA; MMA; MOMA; NYU; New Orleans Museum; Phoenix; RISD; Ridgefield/Aldrich; Raleigh/NCMA; Society of the Four Arts; Springfield, Mass./MFA; SRGM; St. Louis/City; Syracuse/Everson; Tate; VMFA; WMAA; Walker; Wichita State U.; Worcester/AM; Yale U. **Bibliography:** Finch; Friedman and van der Marck; Lippard 5; Rubin 1; Trier 1; Tuchman 1; Weller. Archives.

TRUITT, ANNE. b. March 16, 1921, Baltimore, Md. **Studied:** Bryn Mawr College, 1943, BA; ICA, Washington, D.C., 1948–49; Dallas/MFA, 1950. **Awards:** Guggenheim Foundation Fellowship, 1971; National Endowment for the Arts, 1972; National Endowment for the Arts, commission for sculpture, 1978; National Endowment for the Arts, grant, 1977; Yaddo Fellowship, 1974, 75, 78. **Address:** % Dealer. **Dealers:** Andre Emmerich Gallery, NYC; Pyramid Art Galleries Ltd. **One-man Exhibitions:** Andre Emmerich Gallery, NYC, 1963, 65, 69, 75, 80; Minami Gallery, 1964, 67; Baltimore/MA, 1969, 74; Pyramid Art Galleries Ltd., 1971, 73, 75, 77; WMAA, 1973; Corcoran, 1974; Bayley Museum, Charlottesville, 1975; U. of Virginia, 1976; Osuna Gallery, Washington, D.C., 1979. **Group:** Pan American Union, Washington, D.C., Artists of the United States in Latin America, 1955; Hartford/Wadsworth,

Black, White, and Grey, 1964; ICA, U. of Pennsylvania, 7 Sculptors, 1965; Jewish Museum, Primary Structure Sculptures, 1966; Los Angeles/County MA, American Sculpture of the Sixties, circ., 1967; HemisFair '68, San Antonio, Tex., 1968; WMAA, 1968, 70, 72; Chicago/Contemporary, Five Artists: A Logic of Vision, 1974; Corcoran Biennial, 1975; NCFA, Sculpture: American Directions, 1945–75, 1975; WMAA, 200 Years of American Sculpture, 1976; AAIAL, 1979; Brooklyn Museum, American Drawings in Black and White: 1970–1979, 1980. **Collections:** U. of Arizona; Charlotte/Mint; Corcoran; Hirshhorn; Houston/MFA; MMA; NCFA; National Gallery; New Orleans Museum; St. Louis/City; Vassar College; WMAA; Walker.

TSUTAKAWA, GEORGE. b. February 22, 1910, Seattle, Wash. **Studied:** U. of Washington, 1937, BA, MFA, 1950. US Army, 1942–46. Traveled Europe, Japan, Southeast Asia, Near East, Orient, India, Egypt. **Taught:** U. of Washington, 1946–80. **Commissions:** Seattle Public Library; Renton Center, Renton, Wash.; Lloyd Center, Portland, Ore.; St. Marks Cathedral, Seattle; Century 21, Seattle World's Fair, 1962 (US Commemorative Medal); Northgate Shopping Center, Seattle; J.W. Robinson Department Store, Anaheim, Calif.; Pacific First Federal Savings and Loan Association, Tacoma, Wash.; Bon Marche Dept. Store, Tacoma, Wash.; Fresno (Calif.) Civic Mall; Commerce Tower, Kansas City, Mo. (sunken garden); University YMCA, Seattle; Lake City Library, Seattle; U. of Washington (Phi Mu fountain); Washington Cathedral, Washington, D.C.; UCLA School of Public Health; Jefferson Plaza, Indianapolis, 1971; Safeco Plaza, Seattle, 1973; The Pennsylvania State U., 1974; Expo '74, Spokane, US Commemorative Medal, 1974; Northwest Medical Center, Bellingham, 1976; City Hall Plaza, Aberdeen, Washington, 1977; North Kitsap H.S., Silverdale, Washington, 1979. **Film:** *Three Northwest Artists: Roethke, Anderson, Tsutakawa,* 1976, 45 min. **Awards:** Washington State, Governor's Award of Commendation, 1967. **Address:** 3116 South Irving Street, Seattle, WA 98144. **Dealer:** Foster-White Gallery, Seattle. **One-man Exhibitions:** (first) Studio Gallery, Seattle, 1947; U. of Washington, 1950, 54; Press Club, Spokane, Wash., 1953; Zoe Dusanne Gallery, Seattle, 1953, 58; U. of Puget Sound, 1955, 64; Tacoma; Seattle/AM, 1957; Foster-White Gallery, Seattle, 1977, 78. **Retrospective:** Whitman College (with Morris Graves), 1978. **Group:** Seattle/AM Annuals, 1933– ; Oakland/AM, 1951; Spokane Art Center of Washington State U., 1954–57; III Sao Paulo Biennial, 1955; Vancouver, 1955, 57; SFMA, 1955, 58, 60; Portland, Ore./AM, 1955, 60; Yoseido Gallery, Tokyo, 1956; Santa Barbara/MA, 1959, 60, 61; San Diego, 1960; Los Angeles/County MA, 1960; Denver/AM, 1960, 64; Amerika Haus, East Berlin, International Arts Festival, 1965, 66; Expo '70, Osaka, 1970; NCFA, Art of the Pacific Northwest, 1974; U. of Oregon, Annual, 1968; U. of Washington, Art of the Thirties, 1972; AAIAL, 1978; Seattle, Northwest Traditions, 1978. **Collections:** Bellevue, Wash.; Denver/MA; Memphis/Brooks; Santa Barbara/MA; Seattle/AM; U. of Washington. **Bibliography:** *Art of the Pacific Northwest; Northwest Traditions.*

TUM SUDEN, RICHARD. b. December 9, 1936, Shanghai. **Studied:** Cooper Union, 1956–57; Wagner College, 1958, BA cum laude; NYU, 1961; Hunter College, 1962, MFA, with R. Motherwell, R. Kippold, W. Baziotes; Haystack Mountain School of Crafts, 1963; Brooklyn Museum School, 1965; Parsons School of Design. **Taught:** Cornell U., 1964; Hunter College, 1964, 72; Hull College of Art, England, 1964; New York Institute of Technology, 1967; U. of California, Davis, 1968; C. W. Post College, 1970–72; New School for Social Research, 1972, 73; ASL, 1973; U. of

Minnesota, 1974; Parsons School of Design, NYC, 1974– . Traveled Canada, Great Britain. **Awards:** Brooklyn Museum Sculpture Prize, 1959; Yaddo Fellowship, 1964; CAPS, 1976. **Address:** % Parsons School of Design. **One-man Exhibitions:** Hilda Carmel Gallery, NYC, 1961; Tibor de Nagy Gallery, NYC, 1963, 64, 67, 68; Cornell U., 1964; French & Co., Inc., NYC, 1971; Nancy Hoffman Gallery, 1973, 74; New School for Social Research, NYC, 1975; Cole & Co., NYC, 1976. **Group:** Chicago/AI, 1965. **Collections:** Chase Manhattan Bank; MOMA; NYU; Rybak.

TUTTLE, RICHARD. b. 1941, Rahway, N.J. **Studied:** Trinity College, Hartford, Conn., 1963; Cooper Union, 1963–64. **Address:** 734 11th Avenue, NYC 10019. **Dealer:** Betty Parsons Gallery. **One-man Exhibitions:** Betty Parsons Gallery, 1965, 67, 68, 70, 72, 74, 78; Galeria Schmela, 1968; Nicholas Wilder Gallery, 1969; Buffalo/Albright, 1970; Galerie Rudolph Zwirner, 1970, 72; Dallas/MFA, 1971; Galerie Lambert, Paris, 1972, 74, 76, 78; Galerie Schlesa, Dusseldorf, 1972; MOMA, 1972; Konrad Fischer Gallery, Dusseldorf, 1973; Kunstraum, Munich, 1973; Weinberg Gallery, San Francisco, 1973; Galerie Annemarie Verna, Zurich, 1973, 79; The Clocktower, NYC, 1973; Galleria Toselli, Milan, 1974; Galleria Marilena Bonomo, Bari, 1974, 79; Cusack Gallery, Houston, 1974, 75; Nigel Greenwood, Inc., Ltd., London, 1974; Parsons-Truman Gallery, NYC, 1975; d'Alessandro Ferranti, Rome, 1975; Hartford/Wadsworth, 1975; Otis Art Institute, Los Angeles, 1976; Brooke Alexander, Inc., NYC, 1976, 79; Northwest Artists Workshop, Portland, Ore., 1976; Fine Arts Building Gallery, NYC, 1976; U. of Western Ontario, 1976; Graeme Murray Gallery, Edinburgh, 1976; Ohio State U., 1977; Ugo Ferranti, Rome, 1977, 78, 79; Kunsthalle, Basel, 1977; Kunstraum, Munich, 1977; Galerie Heiner Friedrich, Munich, 1977; Young-Hoffman Gallery, Chicago, 1978; Brown

U., 1978; Daniel Weinberg Gallery, San Francisco, 1978; Francoise Lambert, Milan, 1978; Ghent/Moderne, 1978; Galerie Schmela, Dusseldorf, 1978; Amsterdam/Stedelijk, 1979; Truman Gallery, NYC, 1979; U. of California, Santa Barbara, 1979; Centre d'Arts Plastiques Contemporains, Bordeaux, 1979; Krefeld, 1980; Centre d'Art Contemporain, Geneva, 1980; California Institute of Technology, Pasadena, 1980. **Retrospective:** WMAA, 1975. **Group:** American Abstract Artists, 1968; Des Moines, Painting, Out from the Wall, 1968; Detroit/Institute, Other Ideas, 1969; Berne, When Attitudes Become Form, 1969; WMAA, Anti-Illusion: Procedures/Materials, 1969; Corcoran, 1969; Bennington College, Paintings without Supports, 1971; Utica, 1972; Documenta V, Kassel, 1972; Stockholm/National, Young American Artists, 1973; MOMA, Printed, Folded, Cut and Torn, 1974; Baltimore/MA, 14 Artists, 1975; Princeton U., Line as Language; Six Artists Draw, 1974; A.F.A., Recent Drawings, 1977; Cincinnati/Contemporary, Bochner, Le Va, Rockburne, Tuttle, 1975; U. of North Carolina, Works on Paper, 1975; MOMA, Drawing Now, 1976; Amherst College, Critical Perspectives in American Art, 1976; Venice Biennial, 1976; Documenta, Kassel, 1977; Yale U., Long, Hewitt, Tuttle, 1977. **Collections:** Amsterdam/Stedelijk; Cologne; Corcoran; Krefeld/Kaiser Wilhelm; MOMA; National Gallery of Canada; Ottawa/National; St. Louis/City; WMAA; Zurich. **Bibliography:** Art Now 74; Contemporanea; Honisch and Jensen, eds.; List of Drawing Material of Richard Tuttle; Options and Alternatives; Pincus-Witten; When Attitudes Become Form.

TWARDOWICZ, STANLEY. b. July 8, 1917, Detroit, Mich. **Studied:** Skowhegan School, 1946–47, with Henry Poor. Traveled Mexico, Europe, Canada. **Taught:** The Ohio State U., 1946–51; Hofstra U., 1954–. **Awards:** Guggenheim Foundation Fellowship, 1956. **Address:** 57 Main Street, North-

port, NY 11768; 133 Crooked Hill Road, Huntington, NY 11743. **One-man Exhibitions:** (first) Contemporary Arts Gallery, NYC, 1949, also 1951, 53, 56; The Peridot Gallery, 1958–61, 1963–65, 67, 68, 70; Dwan Gallery, 1959, 61; Columbus, 1963. **Retrospective:** Huntington, N.Y./Heckscher, 1974. **Group:** PAFA, 1950; SRGM, 1954; Chicago/AI, 1954, 55; WMAA, 1954, 55, 57, 64; Carnegie, 1955; Sao Paulo, 1960; U. of Nebraska, 1960; MOMA, The New American Painting and Sculpture, 1969. **Collections:** Columbus; Fisk U.; Harvard U.; Hirshhorn; Huntington, N.Y./Heckscher; Los Angeles/County MA; MOMA; U. of Massachusetts; Milwaukee; NYU; Newark Museum; U. of North Carolina; St. Joseph/Albrecht; Vassar College; Youngstown/Butler.

TWOMBLY, CY. b. 1929, Lexington, Va. **Studied:** Boston Museum School; ASL; Black Mountain College, with Franz Kline, Robert Motherwell. Resided Rome, 1957– . **Address:** 149 via Monserrato, Rome, Italy. **Dealer:** Leo Castelli, Inc. **One-man Exhibitions:** The Kootz Gallery, NYC, 1951; The

Cy Twombly *Roma* 1963

Stable Gallery, 1953, 55, 57; Galleria del Cavallino, Venice, 1958; Gallerie d'Arte del Naviglio, Milan, 1958, 60; La Tartaruga, Rome, 1958, 60, 63; Galerie 22, Dusseldorf, 1960; Leo Castelli, Inc., 1960, 64, 66, 67, 68, 72, 74, 76; Galerie J. Paris, 1961; Galerie Rudolf Zwirner, Essen, 1961, Cologne, 1963, 69; Notizie Gallery, Turin, 1962; Galleria del Leone, Venice, 1962; Brussels/Royaux, 1962, 65; Galerie Anne Abels, Cologne, 1963; Galerie Jacques Benador, Geneva, 1963, 75; Galerie Bonnier, Lausanne, 1963; Galerie Handschin, Basel, 1964; Galerie Friedrich & Dahlem, Munich, 1964; Amsterdam/Stedelijk, 1966; Milwaukee, 1968; Nicholas Wilder Gallery, 1969; Galerie Hans R. Neuendorf, Cologne, 1970; Stockholm/SFK, 1970; Galerie Bonnier, Geneva, 1970; Gian Enzo Sperone, Turin, 1971, 73; Yvon Lambert, 1971, 77; Galleria dell'Ariete, 1971; Galerie Mollenhoff, Cologne, 1971; Dunkelman Gallery, Toronto, 1972; Janie C. Lee Gallery, Houston, 1972; F. H. Mayor Gallery, London, 1973; Berne, 1973; Galerie Oppenheim, Brussels, 1973, 74; Galerie Heiner Friedrich, Munich, 1974; Modern Art Agency, Naples, 1975; Galerie Art in Progress, Munich, 1975; ICA, U. of Pennsylvania, 1975; SFMA, 1975; Galleria Bertesca, Genoa, 1975; Galerie Art in Progress, Dusseldorf, 1976, Paris/ Moderne, 1976; Galerie Jacques Brosser, Paris, 1976; Gian Enzo Sperone, Rome, 1976; School of Visual Arts, NYC, 1977; Galerie Klewan, Munich, 1978; Heiner Friedrich, Inc., NYC, 1978; Lucio Amelio Gallery, Naples, 1979; Galleriet, Lund, 1979; Galerie Karsten Greve, Cologne, 1979. **Retrospective:** WMAA, 1979. **Group:** Gutai 9, Osaka, 1958; Festival of Two Worlds, Spoleto, 1961; Premio Lissone, 1961; Premio Marzotto, 1962; Amsterdam/Stedelijk, Art and Writing, 1963; Salon du Mai, Paris, 1963; L'Aquila, Aspetti dell'Arte Contemporanea, 1963; SRGM, 1964; MOMA, 1966; NYU, 1967; WMAA Annual, 1967; Indianapolis/Herron, 1969; WMAA Biennials, 1969, 73; Indianapolis, 1969; Dublin/Municipal

(ROSC), 1971; WMAA, The Structure of Color, 1971; Dusseldorf/Kunsthalle, Surrealität-Bildrealitat, 1924–1974, 1974; MOMA, Drawing Now, 1976; SRGM, Twentieth Century American Drawings, 1976. **Collections:** Cologne; Darmstadt/Hessisches; First National City Bank, Houston; MOMA; Milwaukee; RISD; Rome/Nazionale; WMAA. **Bibliography:** Calas, N. and E.; *Contemporanea*; Downes, ed.; Honisch and Jensen, eds.; *Kunst um 1970*; *Metro*; Restany 2; Tomkins 2.

TWORKOV, JACK. b. August 15, 1900, Biala, Poland. To USA, 1913; citizen, 1928. **Studied:** Columbia U., 1920–23; NAD, 1923–25, with Ivan Olinsky, C. W. Hawthorne; privately with Ross Moffett, 1924–25; ASL, 1925–26, with Guy Du Bois, Boardman Robinson. **Taught:** Fieldston School, NYC, 1931; Queens College, 1948–55; American U., 1948–51; Black Mountain College, summer, 1952; Pratt Institute, 1955–58; Yale U., 1963–69; American Academy, Rome, 1972; Dartmouth College, 1973; Columbia U., 1973; Royal College of Art, London, 1974. Federal A.P.: Easel painting, 1935–41. **Member:** Century Association. **Awards:** Corcoran, William Al Clark Prize and Corcoran Gold Medal, 1963; Guggenheim Foundation Fellowship, 1970; Hon. DFA, Maryland Institute, 1971; Honorary Doctor of Humane Letters, Columbia U., 1972; Skowhegan School Painting Award, 1973; Hon. DFA, RISD, 1979. **Address:** 161 West 22nd Street, NYC 10011; 30 Commercial Street, Provincetown, MA 02657. **Dealer:** Nancy Hoffman Gallery. **One-man Exhibitions:** (first) ACA Gallery, 1940; Charles Egan Gallery, 1947, 49, 52, 54; Baltimore/MA, 1948; U. of Mississippi, 1954; Walker, 1957; The Stable Gallery, 1957, 58, 59; B. C. Holland Gallery, 1960, 63; Leo Castelli, Inc., 1961, 63; Tulane U., 1961; Yale U., 1963; Gertrude Kasle Gallery, 1966, 67, 69, 71, 73; WMAA, 1971; Toledo/MA, 1971; Dartmouth College, 1973; Portland

(Ore.) Center for the Visual Arts, 1974; Reed College, 1974; Denver/AM, 1974; Jack Glenn Gallery, Corona del Mar, 1974, 76; Harcus Krakow Rosen Sonnabend, 1974; Nancy Hoffman Gallery, 1974, 75, 77; Ohio State U., 1975; Youngstown State U., 1975; Cincinnati/Contemporary, 1975; New Gallery, Cleveland, 1975; Washburn U., 1976; Jack Glenn Gallery, 1976; John Berggruen Gallery, San Francisco, 1976; Dobrick Gallery, Chicago, 1977; U. of California, Santa Barbara, 1977; Baum-Silverman Gallery, Los Angeles, 1979. **Retrospectives:** WMAA, 1964; Third Eye Center, Glasgow, circ., 1979. **Group:** PAFA, 1929; MOMA, The New American Painting, circ., Europe, 1958–59; Documenta II, Kassel, 1959; Walker, 60 American Painters, 1960; Carnegie, 1961; SRGM, Abstract Expressionists and Imagists, 1961; U. of Illinois, 1961; SRGM/USIA, American Vanguard, circ., Europe, 1961–62; MOMA, Abstract American Drawings and Watercolors, circ., Latin America, 1961–63; Seattle World's Fair, 1962; ART:USA:Now, circ., 1962–67; WMAA Annual, 1963; Corcoran, 1963; MOMA, The New American Painting and Sculpture, 1969; VMFA, 12 American Painters, 1974; Santa Barbara/MA, Five Americans, 1974; Indianapolis, 1974; U. of Illinois, 1974; ASL, 100 Years, NYC, 1975; Fort Wayne, Hue and Far Cry of Color, 1976; Hirshhorn, The Golden Door: Artist Immigrants of America, 1876–1976, 1976; Milwaukee, From Foreign Shores, 1976; Rice U., Drawing Today in New York, circ., 1977; Chicago/AI, Drawings of the 70's, 1977; Montclair/AM, Drawing the Line, 1978; Philadelphia College of Art, Seventies Painting, 1978; Creighton U., A Century of Master Drawings, 1978; Pomona College, Black and White Are Colors, 1979. **Collections:** AAAL; Allentown/AM; Amerada-Hess Corp., NYC; American U.; Baltimore/Albright; U. of California, Santa Barbara; Chase Manhattan Bank, NYC; Cleveland/MA; Dartmouth College; Denison U.; Detroit/Institute; Hartford/Wadsworth; Honolulu Academy; Indianapolis; Kent State U.; MMA; MOMA; McCrory Corp., NYC; NCFA; New Paltz/SUNY; Owens-Corning Fiberglas Corp.; Phillips; Prudential Insurance Co. of America, Newark; RISD; Rockefeller Institute; SRGM; Santa Barbara/MA; Storm King Art Center; Toledo/MA; U. of Texas, Austin; Union Carbide Corp.; WGMA; WMAA; Walker; U. of Wisconsin; Yale U. **Bibliography:** *Black and White Are Colors;* Downes, ed.; *From Foreign Shores;* Goodrich and Baur 1; Hess, T.B., 1; Hunter 1, 6; Hunter, ed.; *Metro;* Nordness, ed.; Plous; Pousette-Dart, ed.; Read 2; Rodman 3; Rose, B., 1; Sandler 1; Tomkins 2. Archives.

U

URRY, STEVEN. b. September 5, 1939, Chicago, Ill. **Studied:** U. of Chicago, 1957–59. Chicago/AI, 1957–59; California College of Arts and Crafts, 1960–61; SFAI, 1962–63. **Taught:** Chicago/AI, 1968; Cranbrook, 1970; U. of Kentucky, 1971, 72; Carnegie-Mellon U., 1975. **Commissions:** Loyola U., 1969; Popeil Bros., Inc., 1971; Shire National Corp., 1975; Carnegie-Mellon U., 1975; R. Lavin & Sons, 1976; Nebraska Bicentennial Interstate 80 Sculpture, 1976. **Awards:** U. of Illinois, **P.P.,** 1966; National Endowment for the Arts Award, 1966; Chicago/AI, Linde Prize, 1967; Chicago/AI, Emilie L. Wild Prize, 1967. **Address:** 64 Wooster Street, NYC 10012. **Dealer:** The Zabriskie Gallery. **One-man Exhibitions:** Kendall College, Evanston, Ill., 1966; Dell Gallery, Chicago, 1966; The U. of Chicago, 1967, 68; Royal Marks Gallery, 1967; De Paul U., Chicago, 1968; Chicago/AI, 1969; The Zabriskie Gallery, NYC, 1969, 72, 76; Phyllis Kind Gallery, Chicago, 1972, 74; Hakeley Art Museum, Muskegon, Mich., 1977; Grand Rapids, 1977. **Group:** SFAI, 1962; Illinois Institute of Technology, Chicago, 1965; U. of Illinois, 1966, 74; Chicago/AI, 1967, 70; U. of Nebraska, 1970; Grand Rapids, Off the Pedestal, 1974; Stamford, Conn., American Salon des Refuses, 1976. **Collections:** Chicago/AI; Carnegie; Envair Corp.; Hakeley Art Museum, Muskegon, Mich.; U. of Illinois; K-Mart Corp.; Kendall College; NCFA; Loyola U.; Palm Springs Desert Museum; Playboy Enterprises, Inc.; Standard Oil Co.; U. of Wisconsin.

V

VALENTINE, DeWAIN. b. August 27, 1936, Fort Collins, Colorado. **Studied:** U. of Colorado, BFA, 1958; MFA, 1960; Yale U. Summer School, Norfolk, Conn. 1958. **Taught:** U. of Colorado, 1958–61, 64–65; U. of California, Los Angeles, 1965–67. **Award:** Guggenheim Foundation Fellowship, 1980. **Address:** 69 Market Street, Venice, CA 90291. **One-man Exhibitions:** U. of Colorado, 1958, 60; The Gallery, Denver, 1964; Douglas Gallery, Vancouver, 1968; ACE Gallery, Los Angeles, 1968; U. of California, Santa Barbara, 1968; U. of Washington, Seattle, 1969; U. of British Columbia, 1969; Galerie Bischofberger, Zurich, 1969; Pasadena/AM, 1970; Galerie Denise Rene, NYC, 1973; Walter Kelly Gallery, Chicago, 1973; San Jose/Museum of Art, 1974; Edward Thorp Gallery, Santa Barbara, 1974; Betty Gold, Los Angeles, 1974; La Jolla, 1975; Long Beach/MA, 1975; California State U., Northridge, 1975; Santa Barbara/MA, 1977; Los Angeles/MA, 1979; U. of California, Irvine, 1979. **Group:** WMAA Annuals, 1966, 68, 70; Los Angeles/County MA, American Sculpture of the Sixties, 1967; Portland, Ore./AM, West Coast Now, 1968; HemisFair, '68, San Antonio, Tex., 1968; Museum of Contemporary Crafts, NYC, Plastic as Plastic, 1968; Jewish Museum, NYC, A Plastic Presence, 1969; Seattle/AM, American Art, Third Quarter Century, 1973; Chicago/AI, 1974; ICA, Los Angeles, One Hundred Plus, 1977; U. of Hartford, Conn., Southern California Drawings, 1980; U. of California, Irvine, Structural Imagery, 1980, San Diego, Sculpture in California, 1975–1980, 1980. **Collections:** Atlantic Richfield Co., Washington, D.C.; Avco Finance Corp.; Bradley U.; Chicago/AI; Colorado State U.; U. of Colorado; Denver/AM; Fourth Financial Corp., Wichita; Omaha/Joslyn; La Jolla; Los Angeles Times; Los Angeles/County MA; Milwaukee; U. of New Mexico; Newport Beach; Palm Springs Desert Museum; Pasadena/AM; Ridgefield/Aldrich; Roswell; San Diego; Stanford U.; Vancouver; WMAA; Xerox Corp., Rochester, N.Y.

VAN BUREN, RICHARD. b. 1937, Syracuse, N.Y. **Studied:** San Francisco State College; U. of Mexico; Mexico City College. **Taught:** NYU; School of Visual Arts. **Address:** 155 Wooster Street, NYC 10012. **Dealer:** Paula Cooper Gallery. **One-man Exhibitions:** New Mission Gallery, San Francisco, 1961; SFMA, 1962; Dilexi Gallery, San Francisco, 1964; Bykert Gallery, 1967, 68, 69; Bennington College, 1970; Ithaca College (three-man), 1970; Janie C. Lee Gallery, Dallas (two-man), 1971; Paula Cooper Gallery, 1972, 75, 77; Greene Street, NYC, 1973; The Texas Gallery, 1974; Rice U., 1974; City U. of New York, 1975. **Group:** SFMA, Bay Area Artists, 1964; Jewish Museum, Primary Structure Sculptures, 1966; ICA, U. of Pennsylvania, A Romantic Minimalism, 1967; U. of Illinois, 1967; Ridgefield/Aldrich, Cool Art: 1967, 1968; WMAA, 1968, 70; Milwaukee, A Plastic Presence, circ., 1969; Finch College, NYC, Art in Process, 1969; Chicago/AI, 1969, 72; Foundation Maeght, 1970; Akron/AI, Watercolors and Drawings by Young Americans, 1970; Walker, Works for New Spaces, 1971; Milwaukee, Directions 3: Eight Artists, 1971; Buffalo/

Albright, Kid Stuff, 1971; Harvard U., New American Graphic Art, 1973; Cincinnati/Contemporary, Options 73/70, 1973; Indianapolis, 1974; VMFA, Works on Paper, 1974. **Collections:** MOMA; Walker. **Bibliography:** *Art Now 74.*

VANDER SLUIS, GEORGE. b. December 18, 1915, Cleveland, Ohio. **Studied:** Cleveland Institute of Art, 1934–39; Colorado Springs Fine Arts Center, 1939–40, with Boardman Robinson. US Army, 1942–45. Traveled Europe, USA. **Taught:** Colorado Springs Fine Arts Center, 1940–42, 1945–47; Syracuse U., 1957. Federal A.P.: Mural Painting, 1939. Designed 9¢ and 11¢ US postage stamps in 1971. **Commissions:** US Post Office, Rifle, Colo., 1941, and Riverton, Wyo., 1942; Syracuse U., 1955; J. C. George Company, Syracuse, N.Y., 1947. **Awards:** Fulbright Fellowship (Italy), 1951–52; New York State Council on the Arts, 1966. **Address:** 4132 Onondaga Boulevard, Camillus, NY 13031. **One-man Exhibitions:** (first) Salt Lake Art Center, Salt Lake City, Utah, 1942; Columbia U., 1943; Colorado Springs/FA, 1945; Southern Methodist U., 1946; U. of Nebraska, 1947; Hood College, 1948; Galleria d'Arte Contemporanea, Florence, Italy, 1952; Syracuse U., 1955, 74; Syracuse/Everson, 1956, 61, 71, 77; Alfred U., 1957; Colgate U., 1957; U. of Rochester, 1959, 69; J. Seligmann & Co., 1959; Cleveland Institute of Art, 1962; Royal Marks Gallery, 1962, 63, 64; Utica, 1963; The Krasner Gallery, 1968, 69, 71; Lubin House, NYC, 1978; Hanover Gallery, Syracuse, 1979. **Group:** Cleveland/MA, The May Show, 1937, 38, 40, 41; Smithsonian, American Watercolors, 1941; Chicago/AI Annual, 1941; San Francisco Art Association Annuals, 1941, 42; MMA, Artists for Victory, 1942; Pepsi-Cola Co., Paintings of the Year, 1946, 47; Corcoran, 1947, 57; Utica Annuals, 1948–70; PAFA, 1953; WMAA, 1954; WMAA, Fulbright Artists, 1958; U. of Illinois, 1961; The White House, Washington, D.C., 1966–69;

Museum of Contemporary Crafts, The Door, 1968; New York State Fair, Enviro-Vision, circ., 1972. **Collections:** Arnot; Brookings Institute; Cleveland/MA; Colgate U.; Colorado Springs/FA; General Electric Corp.; Hamline U.; Kalamazoo/Institute; Kansas City/Nelson; New Britain; U. of Rochester; St. Lawrence U.; Southern Methodist U.; Syracuse/Everson; Syracuse U.; Utica.

VASILIEFF, NICHOLAS. b. November 3, 1892, Moscow, Russia; **d.** October 13, 1970, Lanesboro, Mass. **Studied:** Academy of Fine Arts, Moscow, with Leonid Pasternack. Traveled Turkey, France, Germany. **Taught:** Academy of Fine Arts, Moscow, 1918–19; and privately. To USA, 1921. **Commissions:** (murals) a nightclub in Constantinople, Turkey, 1921; Club Troika, Washington, D.C., 1932; a nightclub in Baltimore, Md., 1934. **Awards:** Academy of Fine Arts, Moscow, Gold Medal; La Tausca Competition, 1948 ($3,000); U. of Illinois, **P.P.,** 1954. **One-man Exhibitions:** (first) Artists' Gallery, NYC, 1938; John Heller Gallery, NYC; The Bertha Schaefer Gallery; The Amel Gallery, NYC. **Group:** PAFA; Yale U.; Corcoran; WMAA; Buffalo/Albright; Carnegie; NIAL; Brooklyn Museum, 1926; Bordighera, 1955; Art: USA:Now, circ., 1962–67; U. of Illinois, 1963. **Collections:** Albany/Institute; Ball State U.; Brooklyn Museum; Colby College; Corcoran; U. of Florida; Hartford/Wadsworth; U. of Illinois; Kansas City/Nelson; U. of Minnesota, Duluth; Mount Holyoke College; NYU; U. of Nebraska; New Orleans/Delgado; PAFA; PMA; Phoenix; Pittsfield/Berkshire; Rutgers U.; Santa Barbara/MA; Tel Aviv; WMAA; Yale U.; Youngstown/Butler. **Bibliography:** Nordness, ed.

VENEZIA, MICHAEL. b. July 23, 1935, Brooklyn, N.Y. **Studied:** Buffalo/SUNY, BS, 1963, with Peter Busa; U. of Michigan, MFA, 1968; ASL, 1954. Traveled England. **Taught:** U. of Michigan, Ann Arbor, 1967–68; U. of Rochester, 1968; Guildford College, Surrey, 1967–68; London College of Printing, 1967–68. Designed sets and projections for *Brechtsongs*, London, 1966. **Award:** CAPS, 1974; L. C. Tiffany Grant, 1980. **Address:** 20 North Moore Street, NYC 10013. **Dealer:** Sperone Westwater Fischer, Inc., NYC. **One-man Exhibitions:** (first) Bykert Gallery, NYC, 1942, 73; Heiner Friedrich Gallery, NYC, 1976; Nina Freudenheim, Buffalo, 1976; Sperone Westwater Fischer, Inc., NYC, 1977, 79. **Retrospective:** Detroit/Institute, 1980. **Group:** MOMA, Works on Paper, 1974; U. of North Carolina, Drawing about Drawing Today, 1979; U. of Rochester, Contemporary Drawings on Watercolors, 1980. **Collections:** Best Products, Richmond, Va.; U. of Michigan; MOMA; National Gallery of Canada, Ottawa; Potsdam/SUNY; U. of Rochester; Whitney Communications, NYC.

VICENTE, ESTEBAN. b. January 20, 1904, Segovia, Spain. **Studied:** Real Academia de Bellas Artes de San Fernando, Madrid, BA. Resided Paris, 1927–32. To USA, 1936. **Taught:** U. of California, Los Angeles and Berkeley, 1954–55; Queens College; Black Mountain College; High Field School, Falmouth, Mass.; NYU; Yale U.; and in Puerto Rico; Princeton U., Artist-in-Residence, 1965, 69, 70, 71; New York Studio School, Paris, 1965–79; Honolulu Academy, 1969; American U., 1973; Columbia U., 1974. **Awards:** Ford Foundation, 1961, 62; Tamarind Fellowship, 1962; AAAL, 1971. **Address:** Main Street, Bridgehampton, NY 11932; 1 West 67th Street, NYC 10023. **Dealer:** Gruenebaum Gallery, NYC. **One-man Exhibitions:** Kleemann Gallery, NYC, 1937; The Peridot Gallery, 1950, 51; Allan Frumkin Gallery, Chicago, 1953; Charles Egan Gallery, 1955; Rose Fried Gallery, 1957, 58; Leo Castelli, Inc., 1958; U. of Minnesota, 1959; Holland-Goldowsky Gallery, Chicago, 1960; An-

dre Emmerich Gallery, NYC, 1960, 62, 64, 65, 69, 72, 75; Primus-Stuart Gallery, Los Angeles, 1961; New Arts Gallery, Houston, 1962; B.C. Holland Gallery, 1963; Dayton/AI, 1963; St. John's Gallery, Annapolis, Md., 1963; Des Moines, 1967; Princeton U., 1967, 71; Cranbrook, 1968; Honolulu Academy, 1969; Benson Gallery, 1969, 72; Guild Hall, 1970; J.L. Hudson Art Gallery, Detroit, 1972; Gruenebaum Gallery, NYC, 1979, 81; Yares Gallery, 1979; Hoshour Gallery, 1979; Light Gallery, Southampton, N.Y., 1979; Fischbach Gallery, NYC, 1977. **Group:** International Biennial Exchange of Paintings, Tokyo; Corcoran; The Kootz Gallery, NYC, New Talent, 1950; Ninth Street Exhibition, NYC, 1951; Carnegie, 1958, 59, 61; WMAA Annuals, 1958, 59, 61, 62, 65, 67, 70; ICA, Boston, 100 Works on Paper, circ., Europe, 1959; Columbus, Contemporary American Paintings, 1960; Walker, 60 American Painters, 1960; Chicago/AI, 1960, 66; MOMA, The Art of Assemblage, circ., 1961; SRGM, Abstract Expressionists and Imagists, 1961; SRGM/USIA, American Vanguard, circ., Europe, 1961–62; Seattle World's Fair, 1962; Hartford/Wadsworth, Continuity and Change, 1962; Sao Paulo, 1963; New York World's Fair, 1964–65; Black Mountain College, 1966; MOMA, The New American Painting and Sculpture, 1969. **Collections:** Baltimore/MA; Brandeis U.; U. of California, Berkeley; Chase Manhattan Bank; Chicago/AI; Ciba-Geigy Corp.; Dallas/MFA; Dartmouth College; Hartford/Wadsworth; Honolulu Academy; Iowa State U.; Kansas City/Nelson; Los Angeles/County MA; MMA; MOMA; NCFA; NYU; Newark Museum; U. of North Carolina; Princeton U.; Reynolds Metals Co.; U. of Rochester; SFMA; Shuttleworth Carton Co.; The Singer Company, Inc.; Tate; Trenton/State; Union Carbide Corp.; Vanderbilt U.; WGMA; WMAA; Worcester/AM; Yale U. **Bibliography:** Hess, T.B., 1; Hunter 6; Janis and Blesh 1; Sandler 1; Seitz 3. Archives.

VOLLMER, RUTH. b. Munich, Germany. To USA, 1935; citizen, 1943. Traveled Europe, Middle East, Mediterranean. **Taught:** Fieldston School, NYC, 1956–61. **Member:** American Abstract Artists; Sculptors Guild. **Commissions:** Uris Building Corp. (mural for 575 Madison Avenue, NYC); MOMA exhibits; Committee for Economic Development (anniversary award sculpture), 1967. **Address:** 25 Central Park West, NYC 10023. **Dealer:** Betty Parsons Gallery. **One-man Exhibitions:** Betty Parsons Gallery, 1960, 63, 66, 66, 68, 70, 73, 77, 79; Drew U. (two-man), 1966; Syracuse/Everson, 1974; Adler Gallery, Los Angeles, 1978. **Retrospective:** Purchase/SUNY, 1975. **Group:** Brussels World's Fair, 1958; PAFA; U. of Colorado, 1961; American Abstract Artists Annuals, 1963–68; Sculptors Guild, 1964–68; Musée Cantonal des Beaux-Arts, Lausanne, II Salon International de Galeries Pilotes, 1966; U. of Connecticut, Sculpture in the Spring, 1970; Skidmore College, Contemporary Women Artists, 1970; USIA, New American Sculpture, circ., 1971; Williams College, Women Artists, 1973; P.S. 1, Long Island City, Indoor-Outdoor Sculpture, 1978. **Collections:** Brandeis U.; MOMA; NCFA; NYU; Syracuse/Everson; WGMA; WMAA. **Bibliography:** Archives.

VON SCHLEGELL, DAVID. b. May 25, 1920, St. Louis, Mo. **Studied:** U. of Michigan, 1940–42; ASL, with William Von Schlegell (his father) and Yasuo Kuniyoshi, 1945–48. US Air Force, 1943–44. **Taught:** Privately, 1950-55; U. of California, 1968; School of Visual Arts, NYC, 1969–70; Yale U., 1971– . **Commissions:** Sculpture, Miami Lakes, Fla., 1974; State Park, Duluth, Minn., 1974; GSA, 1975; City of Baltimore, 1977; NASA, at Clark U., 1978; Arabian Royal Navy Headquarters Bldg., Saudi Arabia, 1978; Indiana U., 1979; Yeatmen's Cove Sculpture Project, Cincinnati, 1979; Tulsa International Airport, 1980. **Awards:** Rhode Island Arts Festival, First Prize, 1962; Carnegie, **P.P.,** 1967; National Council on the Arts, $5,000 Award, 1968; Guggenheim Foundation Fellowship, 1974; Skowhegan School Medal for Sculpture, 1978. **Address:** 190 Dromara Road, Guilford, CT 06437. **Dealer:** The Pace Gallery, NYC. **One-man Exhibitions:** (first) The Swetzoff Gallery, Boston, 1955, also 1961; Poindexter Gallery, 1960; Stanhope Gallery, Boston, 1964; U. of New Hampshire, 1964; NYU (three-man), 1966; Ogunquit, 1965; Royal Marks Gallery, 1966–67; Ward-Nasse Gallery, Boston, 1968; Obelisk Gallery, 1968; Reese Palley Gallery, NYC, 1970, 71; The Pace Gallery, NYC, 1974–77; ICA, Boston, 1976. **Retrospective:** Brandeis U., 1968. **Group:** WMAA Annuals, 1960–68; ICA, Boston, 1963; Hartford/Wadsworth, 1963; WMAA, Contemporary American Sculpture, Selection I, 1966; Jewish Museum, Primary Structures, 1966; Los Angeles/County MA, American Sculpture of the Sixties, 1967; Carnegie, 1967; Walker, Works on New Space, 1971; Middelheim Park, Antwerp, XI Sculpture Biennial, 1971; U. of Washington, 1971. **Collections:** Andover/Phillips; U. of California, Santa Barbara; Carnegie; Cornell U.; Hirshhorn; Lannan Foundation; Lincoln, Mass./De Cordova; MIT; U. of Massachusetts; Ogunquit; Ridgefield/Aldrich; RISD; South Mall, Albany; Storm King Art Center; WMAA; Yale U. **Bibliography:** Calas, N. and E.; Davies; Tuchman 1.

VON WEIGAND, CHARMION. b. March 4, 1900, Chicago, Ill. **Studied:** Barnard College; Columbia U.; NYU; self-taught in art. Traveled Europe, Mexico. **Member:** American Abstract Artists (president, 1952–53). **Awards:** Cranbrook, Religious Art Exhibition, First Prize, 1969. **Address:** 333 East 34 Street, NYC 10016. **Dealer:** Marilyn Pearl Gallery, NYC. **One-man Exhibitions:** Rose Fried Gallery, 1942, 48, 56; Saidenberg Gallery, 1952; John Heller, NYC, 1956; Zoe Dusanne Gallery, Seat-

Charmion von Wiegand   Untitled, 107' 59
1959

tle, 1958; La Cittadella d'Arte Internazionale e d'Avanguardia, Ascona, Switzerland, 1959; The Howard Wise Gallery, NYC, 1961; U. of Texas, 1969; Birmingham, Ala./MA, 1970; Galleria Fiamma Vigo, Rome and Venice, 1973; Annely Juda Fine Art, London, 1974; Noah Goldowsky Gallery, NYC, 1975; Andre Zarre Gallery, NYC, 1975; Marilyn Pearl Gallery, NYC, 1978, 81. **Group:** Art of This Century, NYC, The Women, 1945; American Abstract Artists Annuals; Helmhaus Gallery, Zurich, Konkrete Kunst, 1950; MMA, 1951; Walker, The Classic Tradition, 1953; WMAA, 1955, 57; Houston/MFA, The Sphere of Mondrian, 1957; Galerie Chalette, Construction and Geometry in Painting, circ., 1960; WMAA, Geometric Abstraction in America, circ., 1962; Amsterdam/Stedelijk, Art and Writing, 1963. **Collections:** Carnegie; Ciba-Geigy Corp.; Cincinnati/AM; Cleveland/MA; Container Corp. of America; Cornell U.; Hirshhorn; MOMA; McCrory Corporation; NYU; Newark Museum; New York Hospital; U. of Notre Dame; Seattle/AM; Springfield, Mass./MFA; U. of Texas; WMAA. **Bibliography:** Janis and Blesh 1; MacAgy 2; Rickey; Seitz 3; Seuphor 1. Archives.

VON WICHT, JOHN. b. February 3, 1888, Holstein, Germany; **d.** January 22, 1970, Brooklyn, N.Y. **Studied:** Private art school of the Grand Duke of Hesse, 1909–10, BA; School of Fine and Applied Arts, Berlin, 1912. Traveled Europe. To USA, 1923; citizen, 1936. **Taught:** ASL, 1951–52; John Herron Art Institute, 1953. **Member:** American Abstract Artists; Audubon Artists; Federation of Modern Painters and Sculptors; International Institute of Arts and Letters; SAGA. Federal A.P.: Mural painting. **Commissions:** Pan American Airways Terminal, Miami, Fla.; McGill U.; New York World's Fair, 1939; Pennsylvania Railroad Station, Trenton, N.J. **Awards:** Brooklyn Museum, First Prize, 1948, 49, **P.P.,** 1951, 64; SAGA, Mrs. A.W. Erickson Prize, 1953; The Print Club, Philadelphia, William H. Walker Memorial Prize, 1957; Audubon Artists, Gold Medal of Honor, 1958; Ford Foundation, **P.P.,** 1960; SAGA, **P.P.,** 1967–68. **One-man Exhibitions:** (first in USA) Architects Building, NYC, 1936; 608 Fifth Avenue, NYC, 1939; Artists' Gallery, NYC, 1944; Kleemann Gallery, NYC, 1946, 47; UCLA, 1947; Passedoit Gallery, NYC, 1950, 51, 52, 54, 56, 57, 58; Indianapolis/Herron, 1953; Esther Robles Gallery, 1959; Pasadena/AM, 1959; Liege, 1959; The Bertha Schaefer Gallery, 1960, 61, 62, 64, 66; Galerie Neufville, Paris, 1962; Grippi Gallery, 1966. **Retrospective:** Santa Barbara/MA, 1959. **Group:** California Palace, 1964; Brooklyn Museum; Audubon Artists; MMA; WMAA Annuals; Federation of Modern Painters and Sculptors; Corcoran; PAFA; SRGM; Carnegie; NAD; Chicago/AI. **Collections:** Baltimore/MA; Boston/MFA; Brandeis U.; Brooklyn Museum; Chase Manhattan Bank; Cincinnati/AM; Jewish Museum; S.C. Johnson & Son, Inc.; Library of Congress; Liege; Lincoln, Mass./De Cordova; MMA; MOMA; Madrid/Nacional; NCFA; PMA; Paris/Moderne; Norfolk/Chrysler; Stockholm/National; Union Carbide Corp.; WMAA; Yale U. **Bibliography:** Baur 7; Nordness, ed.; Pousette-Dart, ed. Archives.

VOULKOS, PETER. b. January 29, 1924, Bozeman, Mont. **Studied:** Montana State College, BS; California College of Arts and Crafts, MFA. Traveled Italy, 1967. **Taught:** Archie Bray Foundation, Helena, Mont.; Black Mountain College; Los Angeles County Art Institute; Montana State U.; U. of California, Berkeley, 1959– ; Greenwich House Pottery, NYC; Teachers College, Columbia U. *Voulkos and Company*, 16mm film produced by Clyde Smith, 1972. **Awards:** RAC, First Prize; National Decorative Art Show, Wichita, Kans., First Prize; Portland, Ore./AM, Northwest Craft Show, First Prize; Pacific Coast Ceramic Show, First Prize; Denver/AM, **P.P.;** Cranbrook, **P.P.;** Smithsonian, **P.P.;** Los Angeles/County Fair, **P.P.;** Pasadena/AM, **P.P.;** Ford Foundation, **P.P.;** International Ceramic Exhibition, Ostend, Belgium, Silver Medal, 1959; International Ceramic Exhibition, Cannes, France, Gold Medal; I Paris Biennial 1959; Rodin Museum Prize in Sculpture; SFMA, Ford Foundation, **P.P.;** L.H.D. (Hon.), Montana State U., 1968. **Address:** 1306 3rd Street, Berkeley, CA 94710. **Dealer:** Braunstein Quay Gallery, San Francisco. **One-man Exhibitions:** Gump's Gallery; U. of Florida; Historical Society of Montana; Felix Landau Gallery; Chicago/AI; Bonniers, Inc., NYC.; Fresno State College; Scripps College; U. of Southern California; Pasadena/AM; David Stuart Gallery, 1967; Los Angeles/County MA; Hansen Gallery, San Francisco; Quay Gallery, 1968, 74, SFMA, 1972; Kansas City, 1975; Detroit/Institute, 1976; Exhibit A, Chicago, 1979; Braunstein Quay Gallery, San Francisco, 1975, 78. **Retrospective:** SFMA, circ., 1978. **Group:** MMA; Scripps College; Syracuse/Everson, National Ceramic Exhibition; U. of Tennessee; Brussels World's Fair, 1958; de Young; Seattle World's Fair, 1962; Stanford U.; Denver/AM; Smithsonian; Los Angeles/County MA; Battersea Park, London, International Sculpture Exhibition, 1963; Los Angeles State College, 1964; U. of California, Irvine, 1966; WMAA, 1970; WMAA, 200 Years of American Sculpture, 1976; Houston/Contemporary, 1978. **Collections:** Baltimore/MA; Archie Bray Foundation; City of Fresno; Cranbrook; Denver/AM; U. of Florida; Fresno State College; U. of Illinois; State U. of Iowa; Iowa State Teachers College; Japanese Craft Museum; La Jolla; Los Angeles County Fair Association; Los Angeles/County MA; MOMA; Montana State College; Museum of Contemporary Crafts; Oakland/AM; Pasadena/AM; Portland, Ore./AM; SFMA; Santa Barbara/MA; Smithsonian; Syracuse/Everson; Tokyo Folk Art Museum; WMAA; Wichita/AM; U. of Wisconsin. **Bibliography:** Read 3; *Report*; Selz, P., 2; Trier 1; Tuchman 1.

VYTLACIL, VACLAV. b. November 1, 1892, NYC. **Studied:** Chicago Art Institute School, 1908–12; ASL, 1912–14; Hofmann School, Munich, 1922–26. Traveled extensively; resided Europe 16 years. **Taught:** Minneapolis Institute School, 1918–22; U. of California, Berkeley, summers, 1927–28; ASL, 1928–69; California College of Arts and Crafts, summers, 1936, 37; Colorado Springs Fine Arts Center, summers, 1947, 48, 49; Chicago Art Institute School, 1954; U. of Georgia, 1968. **Member:** Federation of Modern Painters and Sculptors; American Abstract Artists. Federal A.P.: Organized an art school in Harlem, NYC. **Awards:** Chicago/AI, William R. French Memorial Gold Medal. **Address:** Sparkill, N.Y. **One-man Exhibitions:** (first) Feigl Gallery, NYC, 1942; Phillips; U. of Rochester; Baltimore/MA; Minneapolis Institute School; The Krasner Gallery; Southern Vermont Art Center, Manchester; U. of Notre Dame, 1975; Martin Diamond Gallery, NYC, 1979. **Retrospective:** Montclair/AM, 1975. **Group:** American Abstract Artists Annuals; Federation of Modern Painters and Sculptors Annuals; Chicago/AI; Carnegie; PAFA;

WMAA; Corcoran; MMA. **Collections:** ASL; Colorado Springs/FA; Dalton School; U. of Georgia; Hartford/ Wadsworth; MMA; Montclair/AM; PAFA; Phillips; U. of Rochester; WMAA. **Bibliography:** Baur 7; Blesh 1; Cheney; Janis, S.; Marter, Tarbell, and Wechsler; Pousette-Dart, ed. Archives.

WALD, SYLVIA. b. October 30, 1914, Philadelphia, Pa. **Studied:** Moore Institute of Art, Science and Industry, Philadelphia, 1931–35. Traveled Europe, Central America, Greece, Spain, India, Nepal, Kashmir. Federal A.P.: Teacher. **Awards:** MOMA, **P.P.,** 1941; Library of Congress, Pennell **P.P.,** 1944; National Serigraph Society, NYC, First Prize, 1948; Brooklyn Museum, **P.P.,** 1951, 54; Pratt Institute, International Miniature Competition, 1967; The Print Club, Philadelphia, 1969. **Address:** 417 Lafayette St., NYC 10003. **One-man Exhibitions:** (first) ACA Gallery, 1939; Kent State College, 1945; U. of Louisville, 1945, 49; National Serigraph Society, NYC, 1946; Grand Central Moderns, NYC, 1957; Devorah Sherman Gallery, 1960; Briarcliff (N.Y.) Public Library, 1966; New School for Social Research, 1967; Book Gallery, White Plains, N.Y., 1968; Benson Gallery, Bridgehampton, N.Y., 1977; Amerika Haus, Munich, 1979; Knoll International, Munich, 1979. **Group:** WMAA; National Sculpture Society, 1940; City of Philadelphia, Sculpture International, 1940; Chicago/AI, Directions in American Painting, 1941; Brooklyn Museum, Print Biennials, MOMA, 1941, 53, 56; Library of Congress, 1943, 52, 58; WMAA Annuals, 1948, 55; PAFA Annuals, 1950, 53, 54, 57; International Print Exhibition, Salzburg and Vienna, 1952; II Sao Paulo Biennial, 1953; Smithsonian, Curators' Choice— 1942–52, circ., USA, 1954; MOMA, 50 Years of American Art, circ., Europe, 1955; Brooklyn Museum, 10 Years of American Prints, 1947–56, 1956; Bordighera, 1957; PCA, American Prints Today, circ., 1959–62; New York

Cultural Center, Women Choose Women, 1973; MOMA, American Prints: 1913–1963, 1974–75. **Collections:** Aetna Oil Co.; American Association of University Women; Ball State U.; Bibliotheque Nationale; Brandeis U.; Brooklyn Museum; Howard U.; State U. of Iowa; Library of Congress; Louisville/Speed; U. of Louisville; MOMA; NYPL; National Gallery; U. of Nebraska; Ohio U.; U. of Oklahoma; PMA; Princeton U.; Raleigh/NCMA; SRGM; Toronto; Utica; Victoria and Albert Museum; WMAA; Walker; Worcester/AM. **Bibligraphy:** Peterdi.

WALDMAN, PAUL. b. August 1, 1936, Erie, Pa. **Studied:** Brooklyn Museum School; Pratt Institute. **Taught:** New York Community College, 1963–64; Brooklyn Museum School, 1963–67; The Ohio State U., 1966; U. of California, Davis, 1966; School of Visual Arts, NYC, 1966– . **Awards:** Ford Foundation, Artist-in-Residence, 1965. **Address:** 38 West 26th Street, NYC 10010. **Dealer:** Leo Castelli, Inc., NYC. **One-man Exhibitions:** (first) Allan Stone Gallery, 1963, 65; St. Joseph/Albrecht, 1966; Leo Castelli, Inc., NYC, 1973, 75, 78; Blum Helman Gallery Inc., NYC, 1978. **Group:** Barnard College, Young Americans, 1962; Louis Alexander Gallery, NYC, Recent American Drawings, 1962; WGMA, 1963, 64; Brandeis U., Recent American Drawings, 1964, Hartford/Wadsworth, Figures, 1964; U. of Colorado, Survey of World Painting and Sculpture, 1964; Brooklyn Museum, Print Biennials; Finch College, 1966, 67 (circ.), 68; Smithsonian, circ., Germany, 1967; WMAA Annual, 1967;

Finch College, NYC, The Dominant Female, 1968; Hirshhorn, Inaugural Exhibition, 1974; Philadelphia College of Art, Private Notation, Artists' Sketchbooks, 1976. **Collections:** Achenbach Foundation; Brandeis U.; Brooklyn Museum; U. of California; Colby College; Colgate U.; Cornell U.; Darmouth College; Denver/AM; Des Moines; Fairleigh Dickinson U.; Harvard U.; Hirshhorn; John Hopkins U.; Houston/MFA; J. Turner Jones, Inc.; Kansas City/Nelson; La Jolla; Los Angeles/County MA; MIT; MOMA; U. of Massachusetts; Mount Holyoke College; NYU; Newark Museum; Oberlin College; Pasadena/AM; RISD; U. of Rochester; Russell Sage College; Rutgers U.; The Singer Company, Inc.; Smithsonian; SRGM; Stony Brook/SUNY; Storm King Art Center; Toledo/MA; Washington U.; Yale U.

WALKOWITZ, ABRAHAM. b. March 28, 1878, Tyumen, Russia; **d.** January 18, 1965. **Studied:** NAD; Academie Julian, Paris, with Jean Paul Laurens. Traveled Europe extensively. **Taught:** Educational Alliance, NYC. **Awards:** AAAL, Marjorie Peabody Waite Award, 1962. **One-man Exhibitions:** "291," NYC, 1912; The Downtown Gallery, 1930; Park Gallery, NYC, 1937; Brooklyn Museum, 1939; Newark Museum, 1941; NYPL, 1942; Schacht Gallery, NYC, 1944; Chinese Gallery, NYC, 1946; Charles Egan Gallery, 1947; Jewish Museum, 1949; Hartford/Wadsworth, 1950; ACA Gallery, 1955; The Zabriskie Gallery, 1959, 64, 66, 68, 69, 70, 73, 74; Danenberg Gallery, 1971. **Retrospective:** Utah, 1974. **Group:** NAD, 1904; WMAA; The Armory Show, 1913; Anderson Galleries, NYC, Forum Exhibition, 1916. **Collections:** Andover/Phillips; Boston/MFA; Brooklyn Museum; Columbus; Kalamazoo/Institute; Library of Congress; MMA; MOMA; Newark Museum; Phillips; WMAA. **Bibliography:** *Avant-Garde Painting and Sculpture in America 1910-25;* Baur 7; Biddle 4; Blesh 1;

Brown 2; Cahill and Barr, eds.; Cheney; Frank, ed.; Goodrich and Baur 1; Haftman; Hartmann; Hunter 5; Janis, S.; Levin 2; McCoubrey 1; McCurdy, ed.; Mellquist; Richardson, E.P.; Rose, B., 4; **Walkowitz 1, 2;** Wright 1. Archives.

WARHOL, ANDY. b. August 6, 1928; McKeesport, Pa. **Studied:** Carnegie, BFA, 1945–49. Illustrator for *Glamour* magazine, 1949–1950; commercial artist, 1950–57; produced and directed films with Paul Morrissey. **Award:** Art Directors Club Medal, 1957. Publisher of Andy Warhol's *Interview*. **Address:** c/o Dealer. **Dealer:** Leo Castelli, Inc. **One-man Exhibitions:** Ferus Gallery, Los Angeles, 1962, 63; The Stable Gallery, 1962, 64; Ileana Sonnabend Gallery, Paris, 1964, 65, 67, 74; Leo Castelli, Inc., NYC, 1964, 66, 77; Morris International Gallery, Toronto, 1965; Galleria Sperone, Turin, 1965; Galleria Rubbers, Buenos Aires, 1965; ICA, U. of Pennsylvania, 1965; Eva de Buren Gallery, Stockholm, 1965; ICA, Boston, 1966; Galerie Hans R. Neuendorf, Hamburg, 1966; Galerie Rudolf Zwirner, 1967; Stockholm/National, 1968; Rowan Gallery, London, 1968; Leo Castelli, Inc./David Whitney Gallery, 1969; Chicago/Contemporary, 1970; Eindhoven, 1970; Paris/Moderne, 1970; Tate, 1971;

Andy Warhol *Marilyn* 1968

WMAA, 1971; Gotham Book Mart, NYC, 1971; Modern Art Agency, Naples, 1972; Walker, 1972; New Gallery, Cleveland, 1973; Musée Galliera, Paris, 1973; Jared Sable Gallery, Toronto, 1974; F. H. Mayor Gallery, London, 1974, 76; Margo Leavin Gallery, 1975; Hugo Gallery, NYC, 1952; Bodley Gallery, NYC, 1956, 57, 58, 59, 62; Baltimore/MA, 1975; Greenberg Gallery, St. Louis, 1975; Max Protetch Gallery, Washington, D.C., 1975; Dusseldorf/Kunsthalle, 1976; Freeman-Anacker, New Orleans, 1976; Arno Schefler Gallery, NYC, 1976; Coe Kerr Gallery, NYC (two-man), 1976, 77; Pyramid Art Galleries, Ltd., Washington, D.C., 1977; Sable-Castelli Gallery, Ltd., Toronto, 1977; ACE, Los Angeles, 1977; ACE, Venice, Calif., 1977, 78; Seattle/AM, 1977; Optica, Montreal, 1977; Galerie Heiner Friedrich, Cologne, 1977; Musée d'art et d'histoire, Geneva, 1978; Texas Gallery, Houston, 1978; SMU, 1978; ICA, London, 1978; Humlebaek/Louisiana, 1978; Heiner Friedrich, Inc., NYC, 1979; Massimo Valsecchi Gallery, Milan, 1979; ACE Gallery, Vancouver, 1979; Hartford/Wadsworth, 1979. **Retrospective:** Stuttgart, Kunstverein, circ., 1976; Zurich, 1978; WMAA, 1979. **Group:** SRGM, Six Painters and the Object, circ., 1963; WGMA, The Popular Image, 1963; Kansas City/Nelson, 1963; Oakland/AM, Pop Art USA, 1963; ICA, London, The Popular Image, 1963; Stockholm/National, American Pop Art, 1964; Salon du Mai, Paris, 1964; U. of Rochester, 1964; Worcester/AM, 1965; Palais des Beaux-Arts, Brussels, 1965; Hamburger Kunstkabinett, 1965; SRGM, 1966; RISD, Recent Still Life, 1966; Flint/Institute, I Flint Invitational, 1966; Expo '67, Montreal, 1967; Detroit/Institute, Color, Image and Form, 1967; IX Sao Paulo Biennial, 1967; MOMA, The 1960's, 1967; Carnegie, 1967; Eindhoven, 1967; Palazzo Grassi, Venice, 1967; WMAA Annual, 1968; Jewish Museum, 1968; Documenta IV, Kassel, 1968; Milwaukee, Directions I: Options, circ., 1968; Finch College, NYC, 1968; Jewish Museum, Superlimited: Books, Boxes and Things, 1969; Ars 69, Helsinki, 1969; Indianapolis, 1969; U. of California, Irvine, New York: The Second Breakthrough, 1959–1964, 1969; Hayward Gallery, London, Pop Art, 1969; MMA, New York Painting and Sculpture, 1940–1970, 1969; Denver/AM, Report on the Sixties, 1969; Pasadena/AM, Painting in New York: 1944–1969, 1969; WMAA, 1969, 73; Expo '70, Osaka, 1970; Indianapolis, 1970; Kunsthalle, Nurnberg, The Thing as Object, 1970; Cincinnati/Contemporary, Monumental Art, 1970; Buffalo/Albright, Kid Stuff, 1971; Dusseldorf/Kunsthalle, Prospect, '71, 1971; ICA, U. of Pennsylvania, Grids, 1972; High Museum, The Modern Image, 1972; Detroit/Institute, Art in Space, 1973; Parcheggio di Villa Borghese, Rome, Contemporanea, 1974; Seattle/AM, American Art—Third Quarter Century, 1974; Chicago/AI, Idea and Image in Recent Art, 1974, WMAA, American Pop Art, 1974; Lincoln Center, NYC, The Florists Transworld Delivery Collection, 1974; MOMA, Drawings Now, 1976; High Museum, The New Image, 1976; SRGM, 20th Century American Drawing, 1976; Dallas/MFA, American Art Since 1945, 1976; Venice Biennial, 1976; Cambridge U., Jubilation, 1977; Minnesota/MA, American Drawing 1927–1977, 1977; WMAA, Art about Art, 1978; Buffalo/Albright, American Painting of the 1970s, circ., 1978; Pomona College, Black and White Are Colors, 1979; Milwaukee, Emergence and Progression, circ., 1979. **Collections:** Brandeis U.; Buffalo/Albright; Canberra/National; Chicago/AI; Cologne; Des Moines; Detroit/Institute; Hirshhorn; Kansas City/Nelson; Los Angeles/County MA; MOMA; MMA; Pasadena/AM; Stockholm/National; Tate; Toronto; WGMA; WMAA; Walker. **Bibliography:** Alloway 1, 4; *Art Now 74*; Battcock, ed.; Becker and Vostell; *Black and White Are Colors*; Honisch and Jensen, eds.; Calas, N. and E.; *Contemporanea*; Coplans 3; **Coplans, Mekas, and Tomkins; Crone;** Davis, D.; Dienst 1; Finch; Green;

Hunter, ed.; Johnson, Ellen H.; **Koch, S.;** Kosloff 3; *Kunst um 1970;* Lippard 5; Lucie-Smith; *Report;* Rose, B., 1; Rublowsky; Russell and Gablik; Sandler 1; Sager, Tomkins and Time-Life Books; Tomkins 2; **Warhol; Warhol et al, eds.;** Whitney, ed., Weller.

WARSHAW, HOWARD. b. August 14, 1920, NYC.; **d.** 1977, Carpenteria, Calif. **Studied:** ASL, 1938–42, with Homer Boss, Howard Trafton. Traveled Europe, Japan. **Taught:** Jepson Art Institute, Los Angeles, 1948–52; State U. of Iowa, 1950–51; U. of California, Santa Barbara, 1955–77. **Commissions** (murals): Wyle Laboratory, El Segundo, Calif., 1955; Santa Barbara, (Calif.) Public Library, 1958 (with Channing Peake); U. of California, Santa Barbara, Dining Commons, 1960; Bowdoin College; U. of California, Los Angeles, San Diego, Riverside, Santa Barbara. **One-man Exhibitions:** The Little Gallery, Beverly Hills, 1944; Gallery of International Art, Los Angeles, 1945; Julien Levy Galleries, NYC, 1946, 1948 (two-man, with Arshile Gorky); Frank Perls Gallery, 1949, 52, 54; Santa Barbara/MA (three-man, with Rico Lebrun and Channing Peake), 1956; J. Seligmann and Co., 1957 (two-man, with Channing Peake), 1958; Felix Landau Gallery, 1957, 59; Pasadena/AM; de Young; Los Angeles/County MA; Richard Larcada Gallery, NYC, 1976. **Group:** U. of Illinois, 1951, 58; U. of Nebraska, 1958; Carnegie; WMAA; Sao Paulo; Paris/Moderne; MMA; PAFA. **Collections:** Carnegie; City of Oakland; Los Angeles/County MA; PAFA; Santa Barbara/MA; U. of Southern California; UCLA. **Bibliography:** Archives.

WASHINGTON, JAMES W., JR. b. November 10, 1909, Gloster, Miss. Studied painting privately with Mark Tobey in Seattle. Changed from painting to sculpture in 1956. Traveled Mexico, Europe, Middle East. Federal A.P.: Teacher (Vicksburg, Miss.). **Taught:** Baptist Academy, Vicksburg, Miss., 1938; Western Washington College, 1968; Director, Baptists Training Union, Mt. Zion Baptist Church, Seattle, 1947–51. **Member:** Sculptors Institute. **Commissions:** Island Park School, Mercer Island, Seattle, Wash. (sculpture); First National Bank of Seattle, 1968; World Trade Center, Seattle. **Awards:** SFMA, **P.P.,** 1956; Oakland/AM, **P.P.,** 1957; Seattle World's Fair, 1962, Second Prize; Hon. DFA, Graduate Theological Union, 1975. **Address:** 1816 26th Avenue, Seattle, WA 98122. **Dealer:** Foster-White Gallery. **One-man Exhibitions:** Feingarten Gallery, Los Angeles, 1958; Haydon Calhoun Gallery, Dallas, 1960, 61; Nordness Galleries, 1962; Gordon Woodside Gallery, 1963, 64, 65; Richard White Gallery, Seattle, 1968; St. Mary's College (Ind.), 1969; Foster-White Gallery, Seattle, 1972, 74, 76, 78; (first) US Army Base, Auburn, Wash., 1954; San Diego, American Baptist Sculpture, 1977. **Group:** Santa Barbara/MA, 1959; Otis Art Institute, 1963; Seattle World's Fair, 1962; Expo '70, Osaka, 1970; Seattle Urban League, 1978. **Collections:** Oakland/AM; SFMA; Seattle/AM. **Bibliography:** *Art of the Pacific Northwest;* Dover.

WATKINS, FRANKLIN C. b. December 30, 1894, NYC; **d.** December 3, 1972, Italy. **Studied:** U. of Virginia, 1911–12, U. of Pennsylvania, 1912–13; PAFA, 1913–14, 1916–17, 1918. US Navy, 1917–18. Traveled Europe, North Africa. **Taught:** Stella Elkins Tyler School of Fine Arts, Temple U., 1935; PAFA, 1935–72; American Academy, Rome, 1953–54. Designed sets and costumes for a ballet, *Transcendence,* 1934. **Awards:** PAFA, Cresson Fellowship, 1917, 18; Art Club of Philadelphia, 1925; Carnegie, First Prize, 1931; Paris World's Fair, 1937, Bronze Medal; Chicago/AI, 1938; Golden Gate International Exposition, San Francisco, 1939; Corcoran, Gold Medal, 1939; PAFA, Carol H. Beck Gold Medal, 1941, Gold

Medal, 1949; Hon. DFA, Franklin and Marshall College, 1954; Philadelphia Art Alliance, Medal of Achievement, 1957. **One-man Exhibitions:** (first) Rehn Galleries, 1934, also 1937, 42, 48; Smith College, 1940; PMA (two-man), 1946; Detroit/Institute, 1954; PAFA, 1972. **Retrospectives:** MOMA, 1950; PMA, 1964. **Group:** Corcoran; PAFA; Carnegie; Chicago/AI; WMAA. **Collections:** Baltimore/MA; The Budd Co.; Buffalo/Albright; Corcoran; Courtauld Institute; Detroit/Institute; Harvard U.; Kansas City/Nelson; MMA; MOMA; Marquette U.; Newark Museum; PMA; U. of Pennsylvania; Phillips; Randolph-Macon Woman's College; Santa Barbara/MA; Smith College; WMAA; Wichita/AM. **Bibliography:** Baur 7; Cahill and Barr, eds.; **Clifford;** Flexner; Goodrich and Baur 1; Pousette-Dart, ed.; Richardson, E.P.; Wheeler; Wight 2. Archives.

WATTS, ROBERT M. b. June 14, 1923, Burlington, Iowa. **Studied:** U. of Louisville, 1944, B. Mech. Eng.; Columbia U., 1951, AM; ASL, with Bernard Klonis, John McPherson, Ethel Katz, Morris Kantor, William Zorach. US Naval Reserve, 1941–46. Traveled Mexico, Europe, Caribbean. **Taught:** Institute of Applied Arts and Sciences, Brooklyn, 1951–52; Rutgers U., 1952–53; Douglass College, 1953– . Changed from painting to sculpture, 1956; changed to light-sound-motion sculpture, 1957; first Events and Happenings, 1958. Designed costumes for James Waring Dance Co. Films: *Cascade,* 1962, *G.W. & Sons,* 1963; *89 Movies,* 1965; *Alice,* 1958. **Awards:** Rutgers U. Research Fund Grant, 1961, 62, 63; Carnegie Corporation Grant, 1965. **Address:** R.D. 3, Bangor, PA 18013. **One-man Exhibitions:** Douglass College Art Gallery, 1953, 57; U. of Alabama, 1957; Delacorte Gallery, NYC, 1958 (welded sculpture); Grand Central Moderns, NYC, 1960, 61; Smolin Gallery, NYC, 1960 (Magic Kazoo), 1963; The Kornblee Gallery, 1963; Galerie Rolf Ricke, 1966,

67; Galleria Christian Stein, Turin, 1967; SFAI, 1969; Apple Gallery, NYC, 1971; Galleria Bertesca, Milan, 1973; Galerie Baecker, 1973; Multipla, 1974, 75. **Group Exhibitions, Events, Happenings:** Newark Museum, New Jersey Artists, 1955; Montclair/AM, New Jersey State Annual, 1955, 56; American Abstract Artists, 1957; Martha Jackson Gallery, New Media—New Forms, II, 1961; Amsterdam/Stedelijk, Art in Motion, circ., Europe, 1961–62; MOMA, The Art of Assemblage, circ., 1961; Fluxus International Festival, NYC, 1962–63; WGMA, The Popular Image, 1963; Smolin Gallery, NYC, Yam Festival, A Series of Events, 1963 III Paris Biennial, Two Inches (event), 1963; Buffalo/Albright, Mixed Media and Pop Art, 1963; Dwan Gallery, Boxes, 1964; Douglass College, 1964; MOMA, The Machine, 1968; MOMA, Photography into Sculpture, 1970; Cologne/Kunstverein, Happening & Fluxus, 1970; MOMA, Information 1971; Documenta V, Kassel, 1972; Akademie der Kunst, Berlin, SoHo, 1976. **Bibliography:** Atkinson; *Contemporanea;* Gerdts; *Happening & Fluxus;* Hulten; Kozloff 3; *Kunst um 1970;* Lippard 5; *Report;* Ruhe; Seitz 3.

WAYNE, JUNE. b. March 7, 1918, Chicago, Ill. Self-taught in art. Traveled Europe extensively. Federal A.P.: Easel painting. **Member:** Artists Equity; Society of Washington Printmakers; The Print Club, Philadelphia; SAGA, Founder and director of Tamarind Lithography Workshop, Inc. (1959–75), funded by the Program in Humanities and the Arts of the Ford Foundation. Visiting Committee of the School of Visual and Environmental Studies, Harvard U., 1972–76. **Awards:** Los Angeles County Fair, **P.P.,** 1950; Los Angeles/County MA, **P.P.,** 1951; Library of Congress, Pennell **P.P.,** 1953; The Print Club, Philadelphia, **P.P.,** 1958; Pasadena/AM, **P.P.,** 1958, 59; SAGA, Edna Pennypacker Stauffer Memorial Prize, 1963; and others; Academy of Motion

Pictures Arts and Sciences Nomination, documentary category, 1974; *The Golden Eagle* (film); AEA/AFEA, Recognition Award, 1978. Advisor: Board of Directors, California Confederation of the Arts, 1975– . **Address:** 1108 North Tamarind Avenue, Los Angeles, Calif. **Dealers:** La Demeure; Prints on Prince Street; Peter Plone Associates; Van Doren Gallery. **One-man Exhibitions:** (first) Boulevard Gallery, Chicago, 1935; Mexico City/Nacional, 1936; SFMA, 1950; Santa Barbara/MA, 1950, 53, 58; Pasadena/AM, 1952; Chicago/AI, 1952; The Contemporaries, NYC, 1953; de Young, 1956; California Palace; Achenbach Foundation, 1958; Los Angeles/County MA, 1959; Long Beach/MA, 1959; Philadelphia Art Alliance, 1959; U. of New Mexico, 1968; U. of Iowa, 1970; Grunwald Graphic Arts Foundation, Los Angeles, 1971; Gimpel & Weitzenhoffer, 1972; Los Angeles Municipal Art, 1973; Van Doren Gallery, San Francisco, 1974, 76; Muchenthaler Cultural Center, Fullerton, Calif., 1974; La Demeure, Paris, 1975, 76; Artemisia, Chicago, 1975; U. of Wisconsin, Oshkosh, 1975; U. of Southern Colorado, 1976; Adams State College, 1976; French American Institute, Rennes, 1976; Brest, Musée Municipal, 1977; Rubicon Gallery, Los Altos, 1977; Cypress College, 1977; Les Premontres, Nancy, France, 1977; Palm Springs Desert Museum, 1977; Claremont College, 1978; Arizona State U., 1979; Corvallis Art Center, 1979; American Library, Brussels, 1978; Foundation Pescatore, Luxembourg, 1979; Maison de la Culture Andre Malraux, Reims, 1979; Musee de Chartres, 1979; Lyons, Musee, 1979. **Retrospectives:** FAR Gallery, 1969; Cincinnati/AM, 1969. **Group:** Library of Congress; Brooklyn Museum; Seattle/AM; PAFA; U. of Illinois; Los Angeles/County MA; MMA; SAGA Annuals; MOMA, circ. (graphics); MOMA, Young American Printmakers, 1953; California State Fair; San Diego; Denver/AM; WMAA Annuals; Sao Paulo, 1955; Smithsonian; Achenbach Foundation; PCA, American Prints To-day, circ., 1959–62; Paris/Moderne; The Japan Print Association, Tokyo, 1961; Smithsonian, 1964; CSCS, Fullerton, 1964; SFAI, 1965; Cincinnati/AM, 1968; and many others. **Collections:** Achenbach Foundation; Bibliotheque Nationale; Bibliotheque Royale de Belgique; UCLA; U. of California, Santa Barbara; Chicago/AI; Cincinnati/AM; Columbia, S.C./MA; De Pauw U.; Fort Worth; Grunwald Foundation; Iowa State U.; La Jolla; Lehigh U.; Library of Congress; Long Beach/MA; Los Angeles/County MA; MOMA; U. of Minnesota; NYPL; National Gallery; Newberry Library; U. of New Mexico; Northwestern U.; Oberlin College; PMA; Pasadena/AM; The Print Club, Philadelphia; San Diego; San Jose State College; Santa Barbara/MA; Smithsonian; Walker. **Bibliography:** *Art: A Woman's Sensibility*; Rodman 1, 3. Archives.

WEBER, HUGO. b. May 4, 1918, Basel, Switzerland; **d.** 1971. **Studied:** U. of Basel, 1942–46; Kunstgewerbeschule, Basel; Atelier Suter, Basel; Atelier Gimond, Paris, 1939; and with Aristede Maillol, Jean Arp, Alberto Giacometti, 1939–45. Swiss Army, 1939–41. Traveled USA, Canada, Europe; resided Paris. **Taught:** Institute of Design, Chicago, 1946–55; Oslo, Norway, 1955; The Pennsylvania State U.; NYU, 1963–70. Produced two films, *Vision in Flux*, 1951, and *Process Documentation by the Painter*, 1954. **Member:** Abstract and Concrete Artists Alliance, 1947–53. **Commissions:** Container Corp. of America (bronze bust of Lincoln). **One-man Exhibitions:** (first) Colorado Springs/FA, 1951; Chicago/AI, 1951; Galerie 16, Zurich, 1952; Institute of Design, Chicago, 1952; Galerie Parnass, Wuppertal, 1952; Allan Frumkin Gallery, Chicago, 1953, 55; Betty Parsons Gallery, 1953, 55, 59; American U., Beirut, Lebanon, 1954; B.C. Holland Gallery, 1961; Gres Gallery, Chicago, 1962; The Howard Wise Gallery, NYC, 1962–63; Galerie Hutter, Basel, 1963;

Finch College, NYC, 1974; Landmark Gallery, Inc., NYC, 1974. **Group:** Kunsthalle, Basel, 1945, 56; Toledo/MA, Sculpture Today, 1947; Chicago/AI Annuals, 1947, 49; Salon des Realities Nouvelles, Paris, 1948, 58, 59; Chicago/ AI, Directions in American Painting, 1951; SRGM, Younger American Painters, 1954; Salon des Comparaisons, Paris, 1956; Galerie Creuze, Paris, 50 Years of Abstract Painting, 1957; Galerie Arnaud, L'Art Moral, 1957; Palais des Beaux-Arts, Charleroi, Belgium, L'Arte de Siecle, 1958; Zurich, 16 Basel Maler, 1960; Salon du Mai, Paris, 1961; Dayton/AI, International Selection, 1963. **Collections:** Chicago/AI; Cincinnati/AM. **Bibliography:** *Avant-Garde Painting and Sculpture.* Archives.

WEBER, IDELLE. b. March 12, 1932, Chicago, Ill. **Studied:** Scripps College; UCLA, BA; Chouinard Art Institute, with Millard Sheets; Otis Art Institute; with Else Palmer Paynes and Theodore Lukits in Los Angeles; ASL, with Theodore Stamos; Brooklyn Museum, with Reuben Tam. Traveled England, Southern France, Italy, Spain, Greece. **Taught:** UCLA, 1955; NYU, 1976–80. **Member:** Women's Caucus for Art; trustee of the Museum of Holography. **Address:** 429 West Broadway, NYC 10012. **Dealer:** OK Harris Works of Art, NYC. **One-man Exhibitions:** (first) Bertha Schaefer Gallery, NYC, 1963, 64; Hundred Acres Gallery Ltd., NYC, 1973, 75, 77; Chatham College, 1979; OK Harris Works of Art, NYC 1979. **Group:** SRGM, American Drawings, 1964; Worcester/AM, New Realism, 1965; Hartford/Wadsworth, New/Photo Realism, 1974; Wichita State U., The New Realism; Rip-Off or Reality?, 1975; San Antonio/McNay, American Artists, 76: A Celebration, 1976; Smithsonian, America as Art, 1976; St. Petersburg, Fla., Photo Realism, 1978; U. of Connecticut, Photo Realism, 1979. **Collections:** Buffalo/Albright; NCFA; NYPL; Rochester U.; San Antonio/McNay; VMFA; Worcester.

WEBER, MAX. b. April 18, 1881, Byalestok, Russia; **d.** October, 1961, Great Neck, N.Y. To USA, 1891. **Studied:** Pratt Institute, 1898–1900, with Arthur Dow; Academie Julian, Paris, 1905–06, with Jean Paul Laurens; Academie de la Grande Chaumiere; Academie Colarossi, Paris, 1906–07. Traveled Europe extensively. **Taught:** Lynchburg, Va. public schools, 1901–03; U. of Virginia (summer); State Normal School, Duluth, Minn., 1903–05; helped organize a class under Henri Matisse, Paris, 1907–08; White School of Photography, NYC, 1914–18; ASL, 1920–21, 1925–27; U. of Minnesota, 1931. **Member:** Society of Independent Artists, NYC (Director, 1918–19); American Artists Congress (National Chairman, 1937, Hon. National Chairman, 1938-40). **Awards:** Chicago/AI, Potter Palmer Gold Medal, 1928; PAFA, Joseph E. Temple Gold Medal, 1941; Corcoran, Third William A. Clark Prize, 1941; Chicago/AI, Ada S. Garrett Prize, 1941; Pepsi-Cola, Second Prize, 1945, 1946, ($500), 1947 ($750); Carnegie, Fourth Prize, 1946; La Tausca Competition, First Prize, 1946. **One-man Exhibitions:** (first) Haas Gallery, NYC, 1909; Photo-Secession, NYC, 1911; Murray Hill Gallery, NYC, 1912; Ehrich Galleries, NYC, 1915; Jones Gallery, Baltimore, 1915; Montross Gallery, NYC, 1915, 23; J. B. Neumann Gallery, NYC, 1924, 25, 27, 30, 35, 37; The Downtown Gallery, 1928, 57, 58; Dayton/AI, 1938; A.A.A. Gallery, NYC, 1941, 70; Baltimore/MA, 1942; P. Rosenberg and Co., 1942, 43, 45, 46, 47; Carnegie, 1943; Santa Barbara/MA, 1947; WMAA, 1949; Walker, 1949; California Palace, 1949; Jewish Museum, 1956; Weyhe Gallery, 1956; Brandeis U., 1957; Pomona College, Stieglitz Circle, 1958; Pratt Institute, 1959; B'nai B'rith Gallery, Washington, D.C., 1961; U. of California, Santa Barbara, 1968; Danenberg Gallery, 1969, 70, 71, 72; Graham Gallery, 1970; Pratt Manhattan Center, NYC, 1971; Long Beach/MA, 1971; Alpha Gallery, 1974; Medici II Gallery, Bay Harbor Island, Fla. 1974; The

Max Weber   *Apollo in Matisse's Studio*   1908

Forum Gallery, 1975, 79, 81. **Retrospective:** Danenberg Gallery, 1969; Newark Museum, 1913, 59; Galerie Bernheim-Jeune, Paris, 1924; MOMA, 1930; P. Rosenberg and Co., 1944; A.F.A., circ., 1953; AAAL, Memorial, 1962. **Group:** MOMA, Paintings by 19 Living Americans, 1929; Corcoran; Chicago/AI; MOMA; WMAA; Akademie der Kunst, Berlin, American Art 1920–1940, 1980. **Collections:** Andover/Phillips; Arizona State College; Baltimore/MA; Bezalel Museum; Brandeis U.; Britannica; Brooklyn Museum; Buffalo/Albright; California Palace; Carnegie; Chicago/AI; Cleveland/MA; Columbus; Cranbrook; Dartmouth College; Des Moines; Detroit/Institute; Fort Worth; Hartford/Wadsworth; Harvard U.; Howard U.; State U. of Iowa; Jewish Theological Seminary; Kansas City/Nelson; La Jolla; Los Angeles/County MA; MMA; MOMA; U. of Nebraska; Newark Museum; U. of North Carolina; PMA; Phillips; Sara Roby Foundation; San Antonio/McNay; San Diego; Santa Barbara/MA; Seattle/AM; Tel Aviv; Utica; Vassar College; WMAA; Walker;

West Palm Beach/Norton; Wichita/AM; Youngstown/Butler.   **Bibliography:** American Artists Congress, Inc.; *Arthur Dove: The Years of Collage;* Ashton 5; *Avant-Garde Painting & Sculpture in America 1910–25;* Barker 1; Baur 7; Bazin; Biddle 4; Blesh; Brown 2; Bulliet 1; **Cahill;** Cahill and Barr, ed.; Cassou; Cheney; Christensen; Eliot; Flanagan; Flexner; Frost; *From Foreign Shores;* Genauer; **Goodrich 9;** Goodrich and Baur 1; Haftman; Hartmann; Hess, T.B., 1; Hunter 6; *Index of of 20th Century Artists;* Janis, S.; Kootz 1, 2; Lee and Burchwood; Levin 2; McCoubrey 1; McCurdy, ed.; Marter, Tarbell, and Wechsler; Mellquist; Mendelowitz; Munsterberg; Newmeyer; Pagano; Pearson 1, 2; Phillips 1, 2; Poore; Pousette-Dart, ed.; Read 2; Richardson, E.P.; Ringel, ed.; Ritchie 1; Rose, B., 1; Rosenblum 1; Sachs, Smith, S.C.K.; Soby 5; Story; Sutton; **Weber 1, 2;** Wight 2. Archives.

WEEKS, JAMES. b. December 1, 1922, Oakland, Calif. **Studied:** San Francisco Art Institute, 1940–42, with David Park; Nebraska State Teachers College, 1943; Hartwell School of Design, 1946–47; Escuela de Pintura y Escultura, Mexico City, 1951. US Army Air Force, 1942–45. **Taught:** San Francisco Art Institute, 1947–50, 1958, 64; Hartwell School of Design, 1948–50; California College of Arts and Crafts, 1958–59; UCLA, 1967–70; Tanglewood Summer Art Program, 1970–72; Brandeis U., 1973; Boston U., 1970– . **Commission:** US Department of the Interior, Bicentennial Program, 1975. **Awards:** Abraham Rosenberg Foundation Fellowship, 1952; Howard U., 1961; California Palace, 1961, 62; National Endowment for the Arts, grant, 1978. **Address:** 11 Notre Dame Road, Bedford, MA 01730. **Dealers:** Sunne Savage Gallery, Boston; Charles Campbell, San Francisco. **One-man Exhibitions:** (first) Lucien Labaudt Gallery, San Francisco, 1951; California Palace, 1953; Gallery 6, San Francisco, 1955; The East-West Gallery,

San Francisco, 1958; Poindexter Gallery, NYC, 1960, 61, 63, 74; Felix Landau Gallery, 1963, 65, 66, 67, 70; Sunne Savage Gallery, Boston, 1976, 80; Charles Campbell, San Francisco, 1977. **Retrospective:** SFMA, 1965; Boston U., 1971; Brandeis U., circ., 1978. **Group:** Los Angeles/County MA, 1957; Birmingham, Ala./MA, Figure Painting, 1961; Corcoran Biennial, 1961; California Palace, 1961, 62; Houston/MFA, 1961, 62; Yale U., 1962; St. Louis Artists' Guild, 1962; State U. of Iowa, Five Decades of the Figure, 1962; Chicago/AI, 1963; La Jolla, 1963; Skowhegan School, 1969; Carnegie, 1966; U. of Illinois, 1968; Scripps College, Figurative Painting, 1968; Expo '70, Osaka, 1970; Oakland/AM, A Period of Exploration, 1973; US Department of the Interior, America 1976, circ., 1976, Brown U., Recent Landscape Painting, 1979. **Collections:** A.F.A.; Boston/MFA; Boston Public Library; Brandeis U.; Corcoran; First National Bank of Seattle; Howard U.; Lytton Savings and Loan Association; New England Mutual Life Insurance Co., Boston; Norfolk/Chrysler; Oakland; Ringling; SFMA; US Department of the Interior. **Bibliography:** *America 1976*; Arthur 2; McChesney.

WEINBERG, ELBERT. b. May 27, 1928, Hartford, Conn. **Studied:** Hartford Art School, 1946–48 (certificate), with Henry Kreis; RISD, 1948–51, BFA with Waldemar Raemisch and Gilbert Franklin; Yale U., with Waldemar Raemisch 1953-55, MFA. **Taught:** RISD, Yale U.; Cooper Union; Union College. **Commissions:** Atlanta, Ga. (copper eagle for a facade); Alavath Achim Synagogue, Atlanta, Ga.; 405 Park Avenue, NYC (terra cotta mural); Jewish Museum, 1959 (sculpture for the garden); Brandeis U.; Colgate U.; Jewish Community Center, White Plains, N.Y.; Washington, (D.C.) Hebrew Congregation; Jewish Theological Seminary. **Awards:** Prix de Rome, 1951–53; ICA, London/Tate, International Unknown Political Prisoner Competition, Hon. Men. 1953; *Progressive Architecture*

magazine, 1954; Yale U., Silver Medal for Achievement in the Arts, 1959; Guggenheim Foundation Fellowship, 1960. **Address:** c/o Dealer. **Dealer:** Grace Borgenicht Gallery, Inc. **One-man Exhibitions:** Providence (R.I.) Art Club, 1951, 54; Grace Borgenicht Gallery, Inc., NYC, 1957–66, 1969, 70, 75; Menges Museum, Berkeley, 1974. **Group:** WMAA, 1935, 36, 57, Annuals, 1957, 58, 60, 64, 65; Andover/Phillips, 1954; Silvermine Guild, 1954; Jewish Museum, 1954; ICA, Boston, 1957; Hartford/Wadsworth, Connecticut Artists, 1957; AAAL, 1958; A.F.A./USIA, Religious Art, circ., Europe, 1958–59; U. of Nebraska, 1958, 59, 61; Carnegie, 1958, 61; MOMA, Recent Sculpture USA, 1959; Chicago/AI, 1959, 61; Utica, 1960; Boston Arts Festival, 1961; PAFA 1961; Smithsonian, 1961. **Collections:** Andover/Phillips; Brandeis U.; Colgate U.; Dartmouth College; 405 Park Avenue, NYC; Harcourt Brace Jovanovich, NYC; Hartford/Wadsworth; Jewish Museum; MOMA; RISD; Storm King Art Center; WMAA; Yale U. **Bibliography:** Chaet; Rodman 3.

WELLIVER, NEIL. b. July 22, 1929, Millville, Pa. **Studied:** Philadelphia Museum School, 1948–52, BFA; Yale U., with Josef Albers, James Brooks, Burgoyne Diller, Conrad Marca-Relli, 1953–54, MFA. Traveled Southeast Asia, Europe. **Taught:** Cooper Union, 1953–57; Yale U., 1955–65; Swarthmore College, 1966; U. of Pennsylvania, 1966–77. **Commissions:** Painted murals for the architect Paul Randolph. **Awards:** NAD, Samuel F. B. Morse Fellowship, 1962. **Address:** RD 2, Lincolnville, ME 04849. **Dealer:** Fischbach Gallery. **One-man Exhibitions:** (first) Alexandra Grotto, Philadelphia, 1954; Boris Mirski Gallery, Boston, 1949; The Stable Gallery, 1962–65; Swarthmore College, 1966; Tibor de Nagy Gallery, NYC, 1968–69, 1970; McLeaf Gallery, Philadelphia, 1969; John Bernard Myers Gallery, NYC, 1970, 71; Parker Street 470 Gallery, Boston, 1970; U. of Rhode Island, 1974; Fischbach Gallery, NYC,

1974, 76, 79, 80; Bates College, 1976; Munson Gallery, New Haven, 1977; Brooke Alexander, NYC, 1978. **Group:** PAFA Annual, 1962; A.F.A., Wit and Whimsy in 20th Century Art, circ., 1962–63; Baltimore/MA, 1963; Swarthmore College, Two Generations of American Art, 1964; WMAA Annuals; U. of Illinois, 1964; Vassar College, 1968; PAFA, 1968; A.F.A., Painterly Realism, 1970; NIAL, 1971; 1971; Boston U., The American Landscape, 1972; U. of North Carolina, Works on Paper, 1972; WMAA Annuals, 1972, 73; U. of Nebraska, 1973; Queens Museum, New Images, 1974; Oklahoma, Contemporary American Landscape Painting, 1974; Tokyo, 1st Biennial of Figurative Painting, 1975; Lincoln, Mass./De Cordova, Candid Painting: American Genre 1950–1975, 1975; US Department of the Interior, America 1976, circ., 1976; U. of Missouri, American Painterly Realists, 1977; PAFA, 8 Contemporary American Realists, 1977; Youngstown/Butler, Annual, 1977; William and Mary College, American Realism, 1978. **Collections:** Amerada-Hess Corp., NYC; AT&T; Baltimore/MA; Bank of New York; Boston/MFA; Brandeis U.; Cameron Iron Works, Houston; Chase Manhattan Bank; Colby College; Commerce Bank of Kansas City; Des Moines; Federal Reserve Bank, Boston; Hirshhorn; Houston/MFA; IBM; J. Henry Schroeder Banking Corp., NYC; Lehman Brothers, NYC; Madison Art Center; MMA; MOMA; New England Life Insurance Co., Boston; NYU; U. of North Carolina; PAFA; Prudential Insurance Corp. of America, Newark; Philadelphia Free Library; Smith College; Springfield, Mo./AM; Security Pacific Corp.; Los Angeles/County MA; SFMA; Trenton State; Utah; Vassar College; Westinghouse Electric Corp., Pittsburgh; WMAA; Youngstown/Butler. **Bibliography:** *America 1976*; Arthur 2; Goodyear.

WELLS, LYNTON. b. October 21, 1940, Baltimore, Md. **Studied:** RISD, 1962, BFA; Cranbrook, 1965, MFA. Resided Rome, 1961–62. **Taught:** Yale U., 1974; School of Visual Arts, NYC, 1976– . **Awards:** CAPS, 1975, 77; National Endowment for the Arts, grant, 1976. **Address:** 307 West Broadway, NYC 10013. **Dealer:** Holly Solomon Gallery, NYC; Sable-Castelli Gallery Ltd., Toronto. **One-man Exhibitions:** (first) Cranbrook, 1969, 72; Newark College of Engineering, 1969; Syracuse/Everson, 1971; Cunningham-Ward Gallery, NYC, 1973, 74; Jared Sable Gallery, Toronto, 1974, 75, 76; Andre Emmerich Gallery, NYC, 1975, 77; Claire S. Copley Gallery, Los Angeles, 1976; Galerie Andre Emmerich, Zurich, 1976; Sable-Castelli Gallery Ltd. Toronto, 1977, 78, 79, 80; Nina Freudenheim Gallery, Buffalo, 1977; Grapestake Gallery, San Francisco, 1977; Droll/Kolbert Gallery, NYC, 1978; U. of Wisconsin, Eau Claire, 1979; Tortue Gallery, Los Angeles, 1979; Holly Solomon Gallery, NYC, 1980. **Retrospective:** Princeton U., 1979. **Group:** MOMA, Photography into Sculpture, 1970; Walker, Figures/Environments, 1970–71; Vassar College, New American Abstract Painting, 1972; WMAA Biennial, 1973; Cincinnati/Contemporary, Options 73/30, 1973; Rutgers U., Photographic Process as Medium, 1976; Cornell U., Photo/Synthesis, 1976; C.W. Post College, An Exploration of Photography, 1836–1976, 1976; Indianapolis, 1976; Santa Barbara/MA, Attitudes: Photography in the 1970s, 1979; Florida International U., Other Media, 1980. **Collections:** Arnot; Cornell U.; Dallas/MFA; Indianapolis; MOMA; U. of New Mexico; Princeton U.; U. of Sydney; Vassar College; U. of Virginia; VMFA; Walker.

WESLEY, JOHN. B. November 25, 1928, Los Angeles, Calif. Traveled USA, Europe. **Taught:** School of Visual Arts, NYC, 1970–73. **Address:** 52 Barrow Street, NYC 10014. **Dealer:** Robert Elkon Gallery. **One-man Exhibitions:** Robert Elkon Gallery, 1963, 64, 65, 67, 69, 71, 72, 73, 74, 76, 78, 79, 80; Galerie Rudolf Zwirner, 1973; Carl Solway Gallery, Cincinnati, 1974; U. of Rochester,

1974. **Group:** Washington (D.C.) Gallery of Modern Art, Popular Image, 1965; Brussels/Beaux-Arts, Nouveau Realisme, 1967; A.F.A., The Figure International, 1967–68; WMAA, 1968, 69; Indianapolis, 1969; Documenta V, Kassel, 1972: Indianapolis, 1976; Long Island City, Another Aspect of Pop Art, 1978; WMAA, Art about Art, 1978. **Collections:** Brandeis U.; Chase Manhattan Bank, Minneapolis; Buffalo/Albright; Hirshhorn; MOMA; U. of Rochester; U. of Texas. **Bibliography:** Honisch and Jensen, eds.

WESSELMANN, TOM. b. February 23, 1931, Cincinnati, Ohio. **Studied:** Hiram College, 1949–51; U. of Cincinnati, BA (psychology), 1951–52; Art Academy of Cincinnati, 1954–56; Cooper Union, with Nicholas Marsicano, 1956–59. **Address:** 115 East 9th Street, NYC 10002. **Dealers:** Sidney Janis Gallery. **One-man Exhibitions:** (first) Tanager Gallery, NYC, 1961; Green Gallery, NYC, 1962, 64, 65; Ileana Sonnabend Gallery, Paris, 1966; Sidney Janis Gallery, NYC, 1966, 68, 70, 72, 74, 76, 79; Galleria Sperone, Turin, 1967; Dayton's Gallery 12, Minneapolis, circ., 1968; Newport Harbor, circ., 1970; Jack Glenn Gallery, Corona del Mar, 1971; Rosa Esman Gallery, 1972; Galerie Aronowitsch, Stockholm, 1972; Multiples Inc., Los Angeles, 1973; California State U., Long Beach, circ., 1974; Galerie des 4 Mouvements, Paris, 1974; Boston, 1978. **Group:** Sidney Janis Gallery, The New Realists, 1962; MOMA, Recent Painting USA: The Figure, circ., 1962–63; Dwan Gallery, 1962, 64; Ileana Sonnabend Gallery, Paris, 1963; Buffalo/Albright, Mixed Media and Pop Art, 1963; WGMA and ICA, London, The Popular Image, 1963; Amsterdam/Stedelijk, American Pop Art, 1964; Stockholm/National, 1964; Chicago/AI, 1964; Carnegie, 1964, 67; Milwaukee, 1965; Palais des Beaux-Arts, Brussels, 1965; WMAA, Young America, 1965; WMAA, Annuals, 1965, 68, 72, 73; MOMA, Art in the Mirror, 1966;

Toronto, 1966; WMAA, Art of the U.S. 1670–1966, 1966; RISD, Recent Still Life, 1966; IX Sao Paulo Biennial, 1967; Expo '67, Montreal, 1967; Trenton/State, Focus on Light, 1967; Documenta IV, Kassel, 1968; WMAA, Artists under 40, 1968; Vancouver, circ., 1969; Cincinnati/Contemporary, Monumental Art, 1970; Mathildenhole, Darmstadt, III Internationale der Zeichnung, 1970; ICA, U. of Pennsylvania, Highway, 1970; Roko Gallery, Homage to Tanager: 1952–62, 1971; Dublin/Municipal, International Quadriennial (ROSC), 1971; Hofstra U., Art around the Automobile, 1971; Chicago/AI, 1972, 74; WMAA, American Drawings, 1963–1973, 1973; Turin/Civico, La Fotografia e l'Arte, 1973; New School for Social Research, Erotic Art, 1973; Yale U., American Drawing: 1970–1973, 1973; WMAA, American Pop Art, 1974; Corcoran Biennial, 1975; New York Cultural Center, Three Centuries of the American Nude, 1975; Philadelphia College of Art, Private Notations: Artists' Sketchbooks II 1976; de Young, The Great American Foot Show, 1976; Sydney/AG; Illusions of Reality, 1976; Williamstown/Clark, The Dada/Surrealist Heritage, 1977; WMAA, Art about Art, 1978. **Collections:** Aachen/Suermondt; Brandeis U.; Buffalo/Albright; Cincinnati/AM; Cologne; Dallas/MFA; Darmstadt/Hessisches; Hirshhorn; U. of Kansas; Kansas City, Mo./Atkins; Krefeld/K-W; MOMA; Minneapolis/Institute; U. of Nebraska; Oslo; PMA; Princeton U.; Rice U.; U. of Texas; Walker; Washington U.; WMAA; Worcester/AM. **Bibliography:** Alloway 1, 4; Battcock, ed.; Bihalji-Merin; *Black and White Are Colors*; Calas, N. and E.; *Celebrate Ohio*; Davis, D.; Dienst 1; Honisch and Jensen, eds.; Hunter, ed.; *Kunst um 1970*; Lippard 5; Rose, B., 1; Rublowsky; Russell and Gablik; Sager; Weller.

WESTERMANN, H.C. b. December 11, 1922, Los Angeles, Calif. **Studied:** Chicago Art Institute School, 1947–54, with Paul Wieghardt. US Marine

H. C. Westermann   *The Sweetest Flower*   1978

Corps, World War II. Traveled the Orient. **Member:** Artists Equity. **Awards:** Chicago/AI, Campana Prize, 1964; National Council on the Arts, 1967; Tamarind Fellowship, 1968; Sao Paulo Biennial Prize, 1973; Chicago/AI, The Mr. & Mrs. Frank G. Logan Medal, 1974. **Address:** Box 28, Brookfield Center, CT 06805. **Dealer:** Xavier Fourcade, Inc., NYC. **One-man Exhibitions:** Allan Frumkin Gallery, Chicago, 1957, also 1962, 67, 71, NYC, 1961, 63, 65, 67, 68, 70, 71, 73, 74, 76; Dilexi Gallery, Los Angeles, 1962, San Francisco, 1963; Kansas City/Nelson, 1966; U. of California, Berkeley, 1971; Moore College of Art, Philadelphia, 1972; Galerie Rudolf Zwirner, 1972; Galerie Hans R. Neuendorf, Hamburg, 1973; Galerie Thomas Borgmann, Cologne, 1973; James Corcoran Galleries, Los Angeles, 1974; National College of Education, Wilmette, 1954; Rockford College, 1956. **Retrospectives:** Los Angeles/County MA, 1968; Chicago/Contemporary, 1969; WMAA, circ., 1978. **Group:** Houston/ MFA; Hartford/Wadsworth; A.F.A.; MOMA, New Images of Man, 1959; MOMA, The Art of Assemblage, circ., 1961; U. of Illinois, 1961; Tate, Gulbenkian International, 1964; The Hague, New Realism, 1964; Chicago/ AI, 1964, 67, and Exhibition Momentum; WMAA, 1964, 68; Worcester/AM, 1965; RISD, 1965; Walker, 1966; The Ohio State U., 1966; Los Angeles/ County MA, 1967; Carnegie, 1967; Documenta IV, Kassel, 1968; ICA, U. of Pennsylvania, The Spirit of the Comics, 1969; WMAA, Human Concern/Personal Torment, 1969; La Jolla, Continuing Art, 1971; SRGM, 10 Independents, 1972; Chicago/Contemporary, Chicago Imagist Art, 1972; New York Cultural Center, 3D into 2D, 1973; WMAA, American Drawings: 1963–73, 1973; Sao Paulo Biennials, 1973, 74, 79; Chicago/AI, 1974; NCFA, Made in Chicago, 1974; Portland, Ore./Art, Masterworks in Wood: The Twentieth Century, 1975; NCFA, Sculpture: American Directions 1945–1975; WMAA, 200 Years of American Sculpture, 1976; U. of Massachusetts, Critical Perspectives in American Art, 1976; Venice Biennial, 1976; Chicago Art Institute School, Visions, 1976; WMAA Biennials, 1977, 79; School of Visual Arts, NYC, The Intimate Gesture, 1979. **Collections:** Chicago/AI; Des Moines; Hartford/Wadsworth; Indiana U.; Los Angeles/County MA; Pasadena/AM; WMAA; Walker; Wichita/AM. **Bibliography:** Atkinson; Friedman and van der Marck; Haskell 3; Janis and Blesh 1; **Kozloff 1;** Lippard 5; Read 3; Rose, B., 1; Schulze; Seitz 3; Tuchman 1; Weller.

WHITMAN, ROBERT. b. 1935, NYC. **Studied:** Rutgers U., 1957; Columbia U. **Address:** c/o Dealer. **Dealer:** Dia Art Foundation, Inc., 393 West Broadway, NYC 10012. **One-man Exhibitions:** (first) Hansa Gallery, NYC, 1959; Reuben Gallery, NYC, 1959; The Pace Gallery, 1967; Chicago/Contemporary, 1968; Jewish Museum, 1968; MOMA, 1973; Bykert Gallery, 1974; Galleria l'Attico, Rome, 1974. **Happenings:** Since 1960, more than 15 theater pieces, incl. *Prune Flat, The American Moon, The Night Time Sky.* **Cinema Pieces:** *Cinema, Shower,* and others. **Group:** Reuben Gallery, NYC, 1959; Martha Jackson Gallery, New Media—New Forms, I & II 1960, 61, also 1962; Nine Great Jones Street, NYC (two-man, with Walter de Maria), 1963; SRGM, 1965; Finch College, 1967; Walker, 1968; Newark College of Engineering, 1968; Walker, 6 Artists—6 Exhibitions, 1968; Newark College of Engineering, Light as Art, 1968; Kansas City/Nelson, Magic Theater, 1968; Expo '70, Osaka, 1970; Los Angeles/County MA, Art & Technology, 1971; MOMA, **Projects:** Robert Whitman, 1973. **Collections:** Chicago/Contemporary; Jewish Museum. **Bibliography:** *Art Now 74;* Becker and Vostell; *Contemporanea;* Davis, D.; *Figures/Environments;* Hansen; *Happening &*

Fluxus; Hunter, ed.; Kaprow; Kirby; Lippard 5; *Report;* Sontag; Tomkins 2.

WIEGHARDT, PAUL. b. August 26, 1897, Germany; **d.** December 9, 1969, Evanston, Ill. **Studied:** School of Fine Arts, Cologne; Bauhaus, Weimar, with Paul Klee; Academy of Fine Arts, Dresden. **Taught:** Chicago Art Institute School, 1946–68; Illinois Institute of Technology, 1950–68. **One-man Exhibitions:** Pittsfield/Berkshire, 1941; Harvard U.; St. Paul Gallery; Phillips; M. Knoedler & Co., NYC; Springfield; Mass./MFA; Chicago/AI; Illinois Institute of Technology; Syracuse U.; Milwaukee; Hagen; U. of Arizona; 1920 Art Center, Chicago. **Group:** Salon d'Automne, Paris; Salon des Tuileries, Paris; Salon des Artistes Independants, Paris; Exposition Nationale, Paris; Chicago/AI; PAFA; Library of Congress; Stanford U.; U. of Illinois. **Collections:** Barnes Foundation; Buffalo/Albright; Phillips; Pittsfield/Berkshire; Smith College.

WILDE, JOHN. b. December 12, 1919, Milwaukee, Wisc. **Studied:** U. of Wisconsin, 1947, MA. **Taught:** U. of Wisconsin, 1948– , Alfred Sessler Distinguished Professor of Art. **Address:** RFD #1, Evansville, WI 53536. **Dealers:** Frank Oehlschlaeger Gallery, Chicago; Bradley Galleries, Milwaukee; Haslem Fine Arts, Inc., Washington, D.C. **One-man Exhibitions:** (first) U. of Wisconsin, 1942; David Porter Gallery, Washington, D.C., 1944; Kalamazoo/Institute, 1945; Layton School of Art, 1947; Milwaukee, 1948, 59; Pennsylvania College for Women, 1949; Hewitt Gallery, NYC, 1950, 53, 55; Bresler Galleries Inc., Milwaukee, 1949, 51, 53, 55, 58, 61, 63; Newman Brown, Chicago, 1953; Robert Isaacson Gallery, NYC, 1959, 61; Columbia, S.C./MA, 1960; Lane Gallery, Los Angeles, 1960; U. of Wisconsin, Milwaukee, 1960; Durlacher Brothers, NYC, 1963; The Banfer Gallery, 1968; Northern Illinois U., 1969; Veldman Galleries, 1971, 73; Nordness Galleries, 1971; Frank Oehlschlaeger Gallery, Chicago, 1974; Bradley Galleries, Milwaukee, 1979; Haslem Fine Arts, Inc., Washington, D.C. 1980. **Retrospective:** Milwaukee, 1967. **Group:** Chicago/AI, 1940, 41, 42, 51, 52, 54, Abstract and Surrealist Art, 1948; PAFA, 1941, 46, 50, 52, 53, 58, 59, 60, 62; Walker, 1947, 49, 51, 62; Reality and Fantasy, 1954; U. of Illinois, 1948, 52, 55, 57, 58, 61, 63; A.F.A., American Watercolors, 1949; MMA, 1950, 52, Americans under 35, 1954; WMAA, 1950, 52, 53, 55, 56, 58, 60, 62, 70; Corcoran, 1953; Youngstown/Butler, 1953, 55, 57, 60; Denver/AM, 1955, 56; Hallmark Art Award, 1955, 58; MOMA, Recent Drawings USA, 1956; Carnegie, 1958; Detroit/Institute, 1959; ART:-USA:Now, circ., 1962–67; NAD, 1968; St. Joseph/Albrecht, Drawing—America; 1973, 1973; A.F.A., American Master Drawings and Watercolors, 1976; San Diego American Drawings Invitational, 1977; U. of Nebraska, Things Seen, 1978; WMAA, 20th Century Drawings from the Permanent Collection, 1975; NPG, Distinguished American Portrait Drawings, 1980. **Collections:** Carnegie; Chicago/AI; De Beers Collection; Detroit/Institute; Hartford/Wadsworth; Kalamazoo/Institute; Marquette U.; Milwaukee; Milwaukee Journal; Minnesota/MA; NCFA; U. of Nebraska; Neenah/Bergstrom; U. of North Carolina; PAFA; Sara Roby Foundation; St. Joseph/Albrecht; Santa Barbara/MA; Stony Brook; SUNY; U. of Vermont; U. of Wisconsin; WMAA; Walker; Washington Federal Bank, Miami; U. of Wisconsin; Worcester/AM; Yale U.; Youngstown/Butler. **Bibliography:** Nordness, ed. Archives.

WILEY, WILLIAM T. b. October 21, 1937, Bedford, Ind. **Studied:** California School of Fine Arts, 1956–60, BFA. **Taught:** U. of California, Davis, 1962–ca. 1968. **Awards:** CSFA, Painting Award, 1959, Fletcher Award, 1960;

William T. Wiley *Vague-A-Bond* 1975

SFMA, First Prize, 1960; Oakland/AM, cash award, 1961; Chicago/AI, First Prize and Guest of Honor Award, 1961; Los Angeles/County MA, sculpture prize, 1962; San Francisco/MA, Nealie Sullivan Award, 1968; Chicago/AI, William H. Bartels Prize, 1976. **Address:** Box 654, Woodacre, CA 94973. **Dealer:** Allan Frumkin Gallery, NYC; Hansen Gallery, San Francisco. **One-man Exhibitions:** RAC, 1960; Staempfli Gallery, 1960, 62, 64; The Lanyon Gallery, 1965; Allan Frumkin Gallery, NYC, 1968, 70, 73, 76, Chicago 1969, 74, 79; Hansen-Fuller Gallery, San Francisco, 1969, 71, 72, 75, 78; SFAI, 1969; Eugenia Butler, 1969; Studio Marconi, Milan, 1971; James Manolides Gallery, Seattle, 1972; Margo Leavin Gallery, 1972; Eindhoven, 1973; U. of Utah, 1974; U. of Texas, Austin (three-man), 1975; MOMA, 1976; Galerie Paul Fachetti, Paris, 1977; Landfall Press Gallery, Chicago, 1978; Delahunty Gallery, Dallas, 1978. **Retrospective:** U. of California; Walker, circ., 1979. **Group:** SFMA, 1959, 60; RAC, 1959, 60; San Francisco Art Festival, 1960; WMAA, Young America, 1960; Chicago/AI, 1961; U. of Illinois, 1961; U. of Nebraska, 1961; California Palace, 1961; WMAA, Fifty California Artists, 1962; Los Angeles/

County MA, American Sculpture of the Sixties, 1967; U. of California, Berkeley, Funk, 1967; WMAA Annual, 1967; Moore College of Art, Philadelphia, Beyond Literalism, 1968; Tampa Bay Art Center, Forty California Sculptors, 1968; Chicago/Contemporary, Violence in Recent American Art, 1968; Indianapolis, 1969; Berne, When Attitudes Become Form, 1969; MOMA, New Media; New Methods, circ., 1969; Eindhoven, Kompas IV, 1969–70; Foundation Maeght, 1970; Omaha/Joslyn, Looking West, 1970; SFAI, Centennial Exhibition I, 1970; Sacramento/Crocker, Sacramento Sampler I, 1972; Documenta V, Kassel, 1972; Venice Biennial, 1972; Ringling, After Surrealism, 1972; WMAA, 1973; WMAA, Extraordinary Realities, 1973; U. of Illinois, 1974; WMAA, Annual, 1974; Dusseldorf, Kunsthalle, Surrealitat-Bildrealitat: Words and Images, 1975; WMAA, 200 Years of American Sculpture, 1976; SFMA, Painting and Sculpture in California, 1976; Minnesota/MA, American Drawings, 1927–1977, 1977; U. of Texas, Austin, New in the Seventies, 1977; San Diego, American Drawing Invitational, 1977; The Hague, Recent Art from San Francisco, 1977; Houston/Contemporary, American Narrative/Story Art, 1977; ICA, Boston, Narration, 1978; Buffalo/Albright, American Painting of the 1970s, 1978; Rijeka, 6th International, Drawings, 1978; Denver/AM, Biennial, 1979. **Collections:** U. of California, Berkeley; Brooklyn Museum; Chicago/AI; Dallas/MFA; Denver/AM; Des Moines; Eindhoven; Fort Worth; U. of Illinois; Illinois Bell Telephone Company; U. of Kansas; Los Angeles/County/MA; U. of Massachusetts; MOMA; Minneapolis/Institute; Oakland/AM; SFMA; WMAA. **Bibliography:** *Art Now 74;* Lippard, ed.; *Report;* Richardson, B., 2; Selz, P. 2; *The State of California Painting;* Tuchman 1; *When Attitudes Become Form; Drawings: The Pluralist Decade; New in the Seventies.*

WILFRED, THOMAS (Richard Edgar Løvstrøm). b. June 18, 1889, Naestved,

Denmark; **d.** August 15, 1968, West Nyack, N.Y. **Studied:** Sorbonne. Traveled Europe, USA. **Awards:** Hon. Ph.D., Philadelphia College of Art, 1968. **Group:** MOMA, Fifteen Americans, circ., 1952; Stockholm/National, Art in Motion, 1961; Eindhoven, Kunst-Licht-Kunst, 1966; Walker and Milwaukee, Light Motion Space, 1967; Trenton/State, Focus on Light, 1967; The Howard Wise Gallery, Lights in Orbit, 1967; and Festival of Lights, 1968; Worcester/AM, Light and Motion, 1968. **Collections:** Clairol, Inc.; Cleveland/MA; Honolulu Academy; MMA; MOMA; Omaha/Joslyn. **Bibliography:** Davis, D.; Rickey; Rubin 1.

WILKE, ULFERT S. b. July 14, 1907, Bad Toelz, Germany. **Studied:** Arts and Crafts School, Brunswick, 1924–25; privately with Willy Jaeckel, 1923; Academie de la Grande Chaumiere, 1927–28; Academie Ranson, Paris, 1927–28; Harvard U. Graduate School, 1940–41; State U. of Iowa, 1946–47, MA. Traveled Europe extensively, Japan. US citizen, 1943. US Army, 1942–45. **Taught:** Kalamazoo College, 1940–42; Springfield (Ill.) Art Association, 1946–47; State U. of Iowa, 1947–48; U. of Louisville, 1948–55, 1958–59, 1961–62; U. of Georgia, 1955, 56; Rutgers U., 1962–67. Director, Museum of Art, State U. of Iowa, 1968–75. **Commissions:** Mural for Prudential Insurance Company Building, Merillville, Ind., 1978; Rockwell International, Cedar Rapids, Iowa, 1980; Deere & Co., Moline, Ill., 1973. **Awards:** Albrecht Durer Prize, 1928; New Orleans/Delgado, First Prize, 1928; US Army Arts Contest, Gold Medal, 1945; Louisville Art Center Annual Exhibition, First Prize, Painting, 1951; Georgia Museum of Art, **P.P.,** 1956; Guggenheim Foundation Fellowship, 1959, 60; AAIAL, prize 1978. **Address:** R.R. #3, Solon, IA 52333; winters: Box 409, Anahola, Kauai, HI 96703. **One-man Exhibitions:** (first) a gallery in Germany, 1927; Brunswick Castle, 1929; Anton Ullrich

Museum, Brunswick, 1933; Westermann Gallery, NYC, 1939; Harvard U., 1940; Denver/AM, 1943; Springfield (Ill.) Art Association, 1946; Decatur, 1947; Kalamazoo/Institute, 1947; Muhlenberg College, 1947; Memphis Academy of Arts, 1948; U. of Louisville, 1948; Santa Barbara/MA, 1949; Sweet Briar College, 1949; U. of Nebraska, 1949; The Little Gallery, Louisville, 1950, 53; Kunstverein Hannover, 1952; Kraushaar Galleries, 1958, 60; Tulane U., 1958; Yamada Gallery, Kyoto, 1958; de Young, 1959; Dallas/MFA, 1960; American Academy, Rome, 1960; Primus-Stuart Gallery, Los Angeles, 1961; Rutgers U., 1963; Kalamazoo/Institute, 1964 (two-man, with George Rickey); The Howard Wise Gallery, 1965 (three-man); Design Center of Berea, Cleveland, 1970; Des Moines, 1970; SFMA, 1971; Omaha/Joslyn, 1971; Columbus, 1971; Percival Galleries, Des Moines, 1972, 78; Jodi Scully Gallery, Los Angeles, 75, 1972; Poindexter Gallery, 1973; Waterloo, 1974; MacNider Museum, 1974; Makler Gallery, Los Angeles, 1978; James Willis Gallery, San Francisco, 1978; U. of Iowa, 1975; E.F. Gurewitsch Gallery, NYC (two-man), 1976. **Group:** Academy of Fine Arts, Berlin, 1929, 31; *Life* magazine, War Art, circ., USA, 1942; Chicago/AI, 1943–47; MMA, 1952; SRGM, Younger American Painters, 1954; Brooklyn Museum, 1955, 56, 57, 58, 61; Smithsonian, Italy Rediscovered, circ., USA, 1955–56; MOMA, Lettering by Hand, 1962; M. Knoedler & Co. Art across America, circ., 1965-67; International Biennial Exhibition of Paintings, Tokyo. **Collections:** Aetna Oil Co.; Brandeis U.; Brunswick; Buffalo/Albright; Carnegie; Chase Manhattan Bank; Citizens Fidelity Bank; Louisville; Columbia U.; Cooper Union; Dayton/AI; Decatur; U. of Georgia; Hartford/Wadsworth; Honolulu Academy; U. of Illinois; State U. of Iowa; Kultusministerium; Louisville State U.; Mills College; Minneapolis/Institute; NYU; U. of Notre Dame; Nurnberg; Omaha-Joslyn; PMA; Phoenix; Pratt Institute; SFMA; Seagram Collection; Stanford U. **Bibliography:** Lippard 3; **Seldis and Wilke; Wilke.** Archives.

WILLENBECHER, JOHN. b. May 5, 1936, Macungie, Pa. **Studied:** Brown U. (with William Jordy, George Downing), BA, 1958; NYU (with Craig Hugh Smyth), 1958–61. Traveled Europe. **Taught:** Philadelphia College of Art, 1972–73; Designed decor for Andre de Groat and Dancers, Brushes of Conduct, 1979; presented outdoor sculpture performance, Artpark, 1978. **Awards:** MacDowell Colony Grant, 1974; National Endowment for the Arts, grant, 1977; MacDowell Colony Fellowship, 1974, 80. **Address:** 145 West Broadway, NYC 10013. **Dealer:** Hamilton Gallery of Contemporary Art, NYC; Dart Gallery, Chicago. **One-man Exhibitions:** (first) Feigen-Herbert Gallery, NYC, 1963; Feigen-Palmer Gallery, Los Angeles, 1964; Richard Feigen Gallery, Chicago, 1964, 68, NYC, 1965, 67; A.M. Sachs Gallery, 1973, 75; Syracuse/Everson, 1975; Brown U., 1975; Arts Club of Chicago, 1976; Hamilton Gallery of Contemporary Art, NYC, 1977 (two-man), 1979; Wright State U. 1977; U. of Massachusetts, 1977; Dartmouth College, 1977; U. of Rhode Island, 1978. **Retrospective:** Purchase/SUNY, 1979. **Group:** Buffalo/Albright, Mixed Media and Pop Art, 1963; ICA, U. of Pennsylvania, Current Art, 1965; RISD, 1965; WMAA, Young America, 1965; Eindhoven, Kunst-Licht-Kunst, 1966; U. of Illinois, 1967; WMAA Annual, 1968; Brooklyn Museum Print Exhibition, 1970; Indianapolis, 1970; Finch College, NYC, Projected Art, 1971; Rice U., Gray is the Color, 1974; U. of North Carolina, Works on Paper, 1974; AAAL, 1974; Purchase/SUNY, Images of Power, Sources of Energy, 1975; U. of California, Santa Barbara, Contemporary Tableau/Construction, 1977; Taft/Museum, Galaxies, 1978; Queens Museum, Private Myths: Unearthings of Contemporary Art, 1978. **Collections:** Alberta College of Art; AT&T, NYC; Austin;

Brown U.; Boise-Cascade Corp.; Buf-falo/Albright; Champion Paper, Inc.; Chase Manhattan Bank; Chicago/AI; Cornell U.; Hirshhorn; U. of Massachusetts; MMA; Paris/Beaubourg; PMA; U. of Pennsylvania; Purchase/SUNY: RISD; Ridgefield/Aldrich; SRGM; Syracuse/Everson; U. of Texas; 3M Company; WMAA. **Bibliography:** *John Willenbecher.*

WILLIAMS, HIRAM. b. February 11, 1917, Indianapolis, Ind. **Studied:** ASL, 1939, with Jean Charlot, Robert Brackman; The Pennsylvania State U., with Hobson Pittman, Victor Lowenfeld, 1949–50, BS, 1951, MA. Ed. US Army, 1941–45. Traveled Europe. **Taught:** Harrington (Del.) public schools, 1949–51; U. of Southern California, 1952–53; U. of Texas, 1954–60; U. of South Carolina, summer, 1957; UCLA, summer, 1959; U. of Florida, 1960– . **Awards:** Texas State Fair, D.D. Feldman Award, 1956, 58, 59; U. of Texas Research Grant, 1958; Guggenheim Foundation Fellowship, 1963; Longview (Tex.) Art Museum, **P.P.,** 1966. **Address:** 2804 N.W. 30 Terrace, Gainesville, FL 32605. **Dealer:** Harmon Gallery, Sarasota. **One-man Exhibitions:** (first) Muncy (Pa.) Library, 1940; Witte, 1957; Nye Gallery, Dallas, 1958, 61, 64; Laguna Gloria Gallery, Austin, Tex., 1959; Texas Fine Arts Association, 1959; Felix Landau Gallery, 1959; Cushman Gallery, Houston, 1960; Lee Nordness Gallery, 1961, 63, 68; Chapman Kelly Gallery, 1965 (two-man, with Hobson Pittman); Longview (Tex.) Art Museum, 1966 (two-man); U. of Wisconsin, 1966; Kovler Gallery, 1966; Florida State U., 1967; U. of Florida, 1967; U. of Missouri, 1967; U. of Colorado, 1967; Northern Illinois U., 1967; U. of Wichita, 1967; Troy State College, 1967; Palm Beach (Fla.) Junior College, 1969. **Group:** PMA, 1951; Austin, 1955, 57; MOMA, 1960, Recent Painting USA: The Figure, circ., 1962–63; PAFA, 1960, 63; WMAA Annual, 1960, also 1965, 66; Houston/MFA, The Emerging Figure, 1961; Corcoran, 1961; Biennial, 1965;

SFMA, 1963; Carnegie, 1964; U. of Illinois; M. Knoedler & Co., Art Across America, circ., 1965–67; Florida State U., 1966; NIAL, 1966; Huntington, N.Y./Heckscher, 1969. **Collections:** Ball State U.; Corcoran; Dallas/MFA; MOMA; Milwaukee; NCFA; PAFA; The Pennsylvania State U.; Ringling; U. of Texas; WMAA; Wilmington. **Bibliography:** Nordness, ed.; **Williams, H.** Archives.

WILLIAMS, NEIL. b. August 19, 1934, Bluff, Utah. **Studied:** California School of Fine Arts, 1959, BFA. Traveled Europe, Southwest USA. **Taught:** School of Visual Arts, NYC, 1974– ; Syracuse U., 1977; Metro State College, Denver, 1975. **Awards:** National Council on the Arts Award, 1966; Guggenheim Foundation Fellowship, 1968. **Address:** Box 114, Sagaponack, NY 11962. **One-man Exhibitions:** City Lights Book Store, San Francisco, 1959; Green Gallery, NYC, 1964; Dwan Gallery, Los Angeles, 1966; LoGiudice Gallery, NYC, 1971; Walter Kelly Gallery, 1973; Metro State College, Denver, 1975. **Group:** San Francisco Art Association, 1958; RAC, 1959; SRGM, 1964, also Systemic Painting, 1966; WMAA, Young America, 1965; Oberlin College, 1965; Amsterdam/Stedelijk, New Shapes of Color, 1966; Southern Illinois U., 1967; Southern Illinois U., Decade Seven, 1967; Carnegie, 1967; WMAA, 1967, 72; Des Moines, Painting, Out from the Wall, 1968; Vassar College, Current Minimal Paintings, 1969; WMAA Biennial, 1972. **Collections:** MIT; RAC; WMAA. **Bibliography:** Alloway 3; Johnson, Ellen H.

WILLIAMS, WILLIAM T. b. July 17, 1942, Cross Creek, N.C. **Studied:** City U. of New York; New York City Community College, AAS, 1960–62; Skowhegan School of Painting and Sculpture, 1965; Pratt Institute, BFA, 1962–66; Yale U. MFA, 1966–68. **Taught:** Pratt Institute, Brooklyn, 1970; School of Visual Arts, NYC, 1970;

Brooklyn College, 1971– . **Awards:** National Endowment for the Arts, grant, 1965, 70; CAPS, 1975; Director pro tem., Skowhegan School of Painting and Sculpture, 1979. **Address:** 654 Broadway, NYC 10012. **One-man Exhibitions:** Reese Palley Gallery, NYC, 1971; Fisk U., 1975; Carlton Gallery, NYC, 1976; Illinois State U., 1976; Miami Dade Community College, 1977; U. of Wisconsin, Menomonie, 1979; U. of Wisconsin, Madison, 1980. **Group:** Studio Museum, NYC, X to the Fourth Power, 1969; WMAA Biennial, 1969; Foundation Maeght, St. Paul de Vence, L'Art vivant aux Etats-Unis, 1970; WMAA, Structure of Color, 1971; Rice U., The Deluxe Show, 1971; U. of Utah, Drawings by New York Artists, circ., 1972; Hartford/Wadsworth, Extensions, 1974; Fisk U., Amistad II: Afro American Art, 1975; National Museum, Lagos, Second World Black and African Festival of Art and Sculpture, 1977; Studio Museum, NYC, Another Generation, 1979; P.S.1, Long Island City, Afro-American Abstraction, 1980. **Collections:** Chase Manhattan Bank, NYC; Colby College; Cornell U.; Fisk U.; Hartford/Wadsworth; MOMA; Morgan State U.; Schomberg Center for Research in Black Culture, NYC; Syracuse/Everson; WMAA; Yale U.

WILMARTH, CHRISTOPHER. b. June 11, 1943, Sonoma, Calif. **Studied:** Cooper Union, 1960–62, 1964, 65, BFA. Traveled Europe, Peru, Romania. **Taught:** Cooper Union 1969– ; Yale U.; 1971–72; Columbia U., 1976–78. **Awards:** National Endowment for the Arts, 1968; Guggenheim Foundation Fellowship, 1970; Chicago/AI, Norman Wait Harris Award, 1972; Brown U., Howard Foundation Fellowship, 1972; National Endowment for the Arts, grant 1977, 80. **Address:** P.O. Box 203, Canal Street Station, NYC 10013. **One-man Exhibitions:** (first) The Graham Gallery, 1968; Paula Cooper Gallery, 1971, 72; Galleria dell'Ariete, 1973; Janie C. Lee Gallery, Dallas and Houston, 1974; Weinberg Gallery, San Francisco, 1974; Rosa Esman Gallery, 1974; Hart-

Christopher Wilmarth   *Gnomon's Parade (Parting)* 1980

ford/Wadsworth, 1974, 77; St. Louis/City, 1975; Galerie Aronowitsch, Stockholm, 1975; Daniel Weinberg Gallery, San Francisco, 1978; Studio for the First Amendment, NYC, 1978; NYU, 1978; Seattle/AM 1979; Andre Emmerich Gallery, NYC, 1978. **Group:** WMAA, 1966, 68, 70, 73; Park Place Gallery, NYC, 1966; Foundation Maeght, 1970; Chicago/AI, 1972; MOMA, 1972, 74; MMA, 1974; Hayward Gallery, London, 1975; WMAA 20 Years of American Sculpture, 1976; PMA, Eight Artists, 1978; WMAA Biennial, 1979. **Collections:** Buffalo/Albright; Chicago/AI; Dallas/MFA; Denver/AM; Des Moines; Harvard U.; St. Louis City; MMA; MOMA; PMA; Princeton U.; RISD; Seattle/AM; SFMA; Walker; Wichita/AM; Woodward Foundation; Yale U.

WILSON, JANE. b. April 29, 1924, Seymour, Iowa. **Studied:** State U. of Iowa, with Stuart Edie, James Lechay,

Mauricio Lasansky, 1945, BA, PBK, 1947, MA (painting). Traveled Mexico, USA extensively, Europe. **Taught:** State U. of Iowa, 1947–49; Parsons School of Design, NYC, 1971– ; Columbia U., 1975– ; Cooper Union, 1977–78; U. of Iowa, 1974; Pratt Institute, 1967–69; and privately. **Member:** NAD. **Awards:** Ingram Merrill Foundation Grant, 1963; L.C. Tiffany Grant, 1967; NAD, Ranger Fund, **P.P.,** 1977; **Address:** 317 West 83rd Street, NYC 10024. **Dealer:** Fischbach Gallery, NYC. **One-man Exhibitions:** St. John's College, Annapolis, Md., 1951; Hansa Gallery, NYC, 1953, 55, 57; Esther Stuttman Gallery, NYC, 1958, 59; Tibor de Nagy Gallery, 1960–66; Gump's Gallery, 1963; Esther Baer Gallery, 1963, 64; The Graham Gallery, NYC, 1968, 69, 71, 73, 75; Fischbach Gallery, NYC, 1978; Port Washington Public Library, 1979; Sordoni Art Gallery, Wilkes Barre, 1979; Bowling Green, U., 1971; Benson Gallery, East Hampton, N.Y. 1974; Westark Community College, 1976. **Group:** Chicago/AI, 1946; The Stable Gallery Annuals, 1951, 52; MOMA, New Talent, circ., 1957–59; WMAA Annual, 1962; A.F.A., circ., 1963; MIT; Corcoran; New York World's Fair, 1964–65; Huntington, N.Y./Heckscher, The New Landscape, 1970; New York Cultural Center, The Realist Revival, 1972; Queens Museum, New Images, 1974; William and Mary College, American Realists, 1978. **Collections:** Carnegie Corp., NYC; Chase Manhattan Bank; Cincinnati/AM; The Commerce Bank of Kansas City; Corcoran; Hartford/Wadsworth; Hirshhorn; Indianapolis/Herron; Kalamazoo/Institute; MOMA; National Bank of Commerce, Dallas; Rockefeller Institute; The Singer Company, Inc.; Oneonta/SUNY; PAFA; Parker Pen Co., NYC; Uris Buildings Corp.; Vassar College; WMAA.

WINES, JAMES. b. June 27, 1932, Oak Park, Ill. **Studied:** Syracuse U., with Ivan Mestrovic, 1950–55, BA. Traveled Europe, USA; resided Rome, 1956–62. **Taught:** School of Visual Arts, NYC,

1965–71; NYU, 1965– ; Cornell U., 1969; Buffalo/SUNY, 1970; N. Jersey School of Architecture, Newark, 1975– ; President, SITE, Inc., 1969– . **Commissions:** Hoffmann-LaRoche Pharmaceutical Co. (3 large sculptures for New Jersey offices); Towson State College, 1968. **Awards:** Pulitzer Fellowship, 1953; Prix de Rome, 1956; Guggenheim Foundation Fellowship, 1962; Ford Foundation Grant, 1964; Syracuse/Everson, First award, 1972; Iron and Steel Institute of America, Award, 1971; National Endowment for the Arts, 1973, 75; Graham Foundation, Grant, 1974. **Address:** 60 Greene Street, NYC 10012. **Dealer:** Ronald Feldman Gallery, NYC. **One-man Exhibitions:** National Academy of Istanbul, Turkey, 1956; Baltimore/MA, 1958; Silvan Simone Gallery, 1958, 59, 61; Alphonse Chave, Vence, France, 1960 Galleria Trastevere di Topazia Alliata, Rome, 1960, 61; Otto Gerson Gallery, NYC, 1960, 62; Syracuse U., 1962; Walker, 1964; Colgate U., 1966. **Group:** Syracuse/Everson, 1951–54, 1963; Baltimore/MA, 1952, 53, 54; Uffizi Loggia, Florence, Italy, 1957; Los Angeles/County MA, 1958; Sacramento Arts Festival, 1958; WMAA Annuals, 1958, 60, 62; MOMA, Recent Sculpture USA, 1959; Chicago/AI, 1959, 63; U. of Illinois, 1959, 63, 65, 69; Museum des 20. Jahrhunderts; Amsterdam/Stedelijk; Carnegie, 1961; VII Sao Paulo Biennial, 1963; Flint/Institute, I Flint Invitational, 1966. **Collections:** Amsterdam/Stedelijk; Buffalo/Albright; Chicago/AI; Cleveland/MA; Colgate U.; Columbia Broadcasting System; Currier; Hoffmann-La Roche Inc.; Indianapolis/Herron; Kansas City/Nelson; Los Angeles/County MA; U. of Massachusetts; Museum des 20. Jahrhunderts; NYU; South Mall, Albany; Syracuse/Everson; Tate; Towson State College; Treadwell Corp.; Utica; WMAA; Walker; U. of Wisconsin. **Bibliography:** Goodrich and Baur 1; Read 3. Archives.

WIRSUM, KARL. b. September 27, 1939, Chicago, Ill. **Studied:** Chicago Art

Institute School, 1961, BFA, 1966. **Address:** 1936 W. Bradley, Chicago, IL 60613. **Dealer:** Phyllis Kind Gallery, Chicago and NYC. **One-man Exhibitions:** Dell Gallery, Chicago, 1967; St. Xavier College, 1970; Wabash Transit Gallery, Chicago, 1971; Phyllis Kind Gallery, Chicago, 1974, 76, 78; Phyllis Kind Gallery, NYC, 1977, 79. **Group:** Hyde Park Art Center, Chicago, The Hairy Who, 1966, 67, 68; WMAA Biennial, 1968; Chicago/Contemporary, Paintings to Be Read, Poetry to Be Seen, 1968; Chicago/Contemporary, Don Baum Sez, "Chicago Needs Famous Artists," 1969; ICA, U. of Pennsylvania, Spirit of the Comics, 1969; WMAA, Human Concern/Personal Torment, 1970; Chicago/Contemporary, Chicago Imagist Art, 1972; Ottawa/Ontario, What They're Up to in Chicago, 1972; Sao Paulo, XII Biennial, 1973; Chicago/AI, Former Famous Alumni, 1976; Sacramento/Crocker, The Chicago Connection, 1977; U. of North Carolina, Some Recent Art from Chicago, 1980. **Collections:** WMAA, Chicago/AI; Museum des 20. Jahrhunderts, Vienna; Kalamazoo/Institute; AT&T; Ball State U. **Bibliography:** *The Chicago Connection.*

WITKIN, ISAAC. b. May 10, 1936, Johannesburg, South Africa. **Studied:** St. Martin's School, London, 1957–60, with Anthony Caro; assistant to Henry Moore, 1962–63. **Taught:** Maidstone College of Art, Kent, England, 1963; St. Martin's School of Art, 1963–65; Ravensbourne School of Art, 1964–65; Bennington College, 1965; Parsons School of Design, NYC, 1975– . To England, 1956; USA citizen, 1975. **Address:** 1 Fifth Avenue, NYC 10003. **Dealer:** Hamilton Gallery of Contemporary Art, NYC. **One-man Exhibitions:** Rowan Gallery, London, 1963; Robert Elkon Gallery, NYC, 1965, 67, 69, 71, 73; Waddington Gallery, London, 1966, 68; Bridgeport U., 1970; Marlborough Gallery, NYC, 1975, 76, 78; Keene/Thorne, 1977; Tanglewood Music Festival, 1977; Hamilton Gallery of Con-

temporary Art, NYC, 1979. **Retrospective:** Bennington College, 1971. **Group:** Whitechapel Art Gallery, London, The New Generation, 1965; Smith College, Inside Outside, 1965; Jewish Museum, NYC, Primary Structures, 1965; Paris/Biennale, 1965; Sonsbeek, Holland, Open Air Sculpture, 1966; Amsterdam/Stedelijk, Nine English Sculptors; Hayward Gallery, London, Sculpture of the 60's, 1970; Storm King Art Center, Indoor Sculpture, Outdoors, 1973; Hayward Gallery, London, Condition of Sculpture, 1975; Hirshhorn, The Golden Door, 1976; AAAL, 1977; Indianapolis, 1978. **Collections:** American Republic Insurance Co.; Chase Manhattan Bank; Columbus; Federal Reserve Bank, Washington, D.C.; Hirshhorn; U. of Illinois; Milwaukee; MIT; Storm King Art Center; U. of Sydney; Vassar College; Worcester/AM.

WOELFFER, EMERSON. b. July 27, 1914, Chicago, Ill. **Studied:** Chicago/AI School, with Francis Chapin, Boris Anisfeld, 1935–37, BA. US Air Force, 1939–42. Traveled USA, Mexico and Europe extensively. **Taught:** New Bauhaus, Chicago, 1941–49; Black Mountain College, 1949; Chouinard Art Institute, 1959; Colorado Springs Fine Arts Center; Southern Illinois U., 1962; California Institute of the Arts, Valencia, 1969–73; Honolulu Academy, 1970; Otis Art Institute, 1974– ; Parsons School of Design, Paris, summer, 1980. Federal A.P.: Easel painting and project assistant. **Awards:** SFMA, Hon. Men., 1948; Chicago/AI, Pauline Palmer Prize, 1948; Tamarind Fellowship, 1961, 70; US State Department Grant (Turkey), 1965; Guggenheim Foundation Fellowship, 1967–68; PAFA, Raymond A. Speiser Memorial Prize, 1968; Los Angeles All-City show, **P.P.,** 1968. **Address:** 475 Dustin Drive, Los Angeles, CA 90065. **Dealer:** Gruenebaum Gallery, NYC. **One-man Exhibitions:** Bennington College, 1938; 740 Gallery, Chicago, 1946; Black Mountain College, 1949; Chicago/AI, 1951; Margaret

Brown Gallery, Boston, 1951; Artists Gallery, NYC, 1951, 54; Paul Kantor Gallery, Beverly Hills, Calif., 1956, 60; Poindexter Gallery, 1959, 61, 75; Primus-Stuart Gallery, Los Angeles, 1961; La Jolla, 1962; Quay Gallery, 1968; David Stuart Gallery, 1969; Jodi Scully Gallery, 1972, 73; Phillips, 1974; Gruenebaum Gallery, NYC, 1979. **Retrospective:** Pasadena/AM, 1962. **Group:** WMAA, 1947, 49, Six American Painters; Salon des Realites Nouvelles, Paris, 1948; ICA, Boston, 1950; MIT, Four Americans, 1952; Corcoran, 1952; Carnegie, 1952, 54, 55, 58; Houston/MFA; 1957; SRGM, 1962; WMAA, Fifty California Artists, 1962–63; Los Angeles/ County MA, Post Painterly Abstraction, 1964; PAFA, 1968; Chicago/AI, 100 Artists—100 Years, 1979. **Collections:** Avco Corp.; ARCO (Atlantic Richfield Corp.), Los Angeles; California State U., Los Angeles; U. of California, Berkeley; Amón Carter Museum; Chicago/AI; Colorado Springs/FA; Dresdener Bank; Fort Worth; Honolulu Academy; U. of Illinois; U. of Iowa; La Jolla; Los Angeles/County MA; MOMA; New Orleans/Delgado; Pasadena/ AM; Raleigh/NCMA; UCLA; WGMA; WMAA. **Bibliography:** Archives.

Philip Wofford *Dancer* 1980

Harbor Islands, 1976; Max Hutchinson Gallery, Houston, 1978; Osuna Gallery, Washington, D.C., 1979; Nancy Hoffman Gallery, NYC, 1979. **Group:** SFMA, 1958; Oakland/AM, 1958; Yale U., Young New York Painters, 1964; WMAA, 1969, 72, 73; WMAA, Lyrical Abstraction, 1971; Corcoran, The Way of Color, 1973; U. of Illinois, 1974; U. of Vermont, Landscape Images, 1976. **Collections:** Brooklyn Museum; Canberra/ National; Corcoran; Corning Fiberglas Corp.; Northside Parklane National Bank, St. Louis; Ridgefield/Aldrich.

WOFFORD, PHILIP. b. August 14, 1935, Van Buren, Ark. **Studied:** U. of Arkansas, 1957, BA; U. of California, 1958. **Taught:** NYU, 1964–68; Bennington College, 1969– . **Awards:** Oakland Museum Bronze Medal, 1958; Woodrow Wilson Foundation Fellowship, 1957; National Endowment for the Arts, grant, 1974; CAPS, 1977. **Address:** RD #2, Hoosick Falls, NY 12090. **Dealer:** Nancy Hoffman Gallery, NYC. **One-man Exhibitions:** Green Gallery, NYC, 1962; Allan Stone Gallery, 1964; David Whitney Gallery, NYC, 1970, 71; Andre Emmerich Gallery, NYC, 1972, 74, 76; Little Rock/MFA, 1973; Corcoran, 1972; Yale U., 1973; Pyramid Gallery, Washington, D.C., 1974; Windham College, 1974; Bennington College, 1975; Berenson Gallery, Bay

WOLFF, ROBERT JAY. b. July 27, 1905, Chicago, Ill.; **d.** December 29, 1977, New Preston, Conn. **Studied:** Yale U., 1923–26; Academie des Beaux-Arts, Paris, with Henri Bouchard; and privately with Georges Mouveau in Paris. US Army and Air Force, 1942–45; US Naval Reserve. Traveled Europe extensively, 1921–31; resided Paris, 1929–31. **Taught:** A founding collaborator, with Lazlo Moholy-Nagy and Gyorgy Kepes, of the Institute of Design, Chicago, 1938–42; Brooklyn College, 1946–71; U. of Wisconsin, 1955; MIT, 1961; Harvard U., 1961. **Member:** American Abstract Artists, 1937–50. Federal A.P.: Illinois State Supervisor of Painting, 1937. **Awards:** Chicago/AI, Robert Jenkins Prize, 1933. **One-man**

Exhibitions: Chicago/AI, 1934 (first sculpture shown); Reinhardt Galleries, NYC, 1935 (sculpture); Quest Gallery, Chicago, 1936 (first paintings shown); Karl Nierendorf Gallery, NYC, 1937; Katherine Kuh Gallery, Chicago, 1938, 39; SFMA, 1940; MOMA, Elements of Design, circ., 1947; Kleemann Gallery, NYC, 1947, 48; SRGM, 1952; Saidenberg Gallery, 1953, 54; Grace Borgenicht Gallery, Inc., 1956, 58; Washburn Gallery, NYC, 1980; MIT, 1961. **Group:** American Abstract Artists Annuals, 1937–50; Corcoran; WMAA; PAFA; U. of Illinois; U. of Nebraska; SFMA; MIT. **Collections:** Brooklyn College; Brooklyn Museum; Chicago/AI; First National Bank of Chicago; Hartford/Wadsworth; Kenyon College; RISD; SRGM; Tate; Towin Corp., Torrington, Conn. **Bibliography:** Baur 7; Cheney; Janis, S. Archives.

WOLFSON, SIDNEY. b. June 18, 1914, Brooklyn, N.Y.; **d.** March 9, 1973. **Studied:** Pratt Institute, with George Bridgeman, Denman W. Ross, Oronzio Maldarelli, Ogden Pleissner. US Air Force, four years. Traveled Caribbean, Latin America, Far East. **Taught:** Creative Arts Academy, NYC, Artist-in-Residence, summer, 1968; Dutchess Community College, Poughkeepsie, N.Y., 1971. **One-man Exhibitions:** (first) Three Arts Gallery, Poughkeepsie, 1952, also 1965; Salisbury (Conn.) Public Library, Pittsfield/Berkshire; Betty Parsons Section Eleven (Gallery), NYC, 1959, 61; World House Galleries, NYC, 1964; Bennett College, 1966; The Contemporaries, NYC, 1967. **Retrospective:** Bennington College, 1962; Vassar College, 1972. **Group:** ART:USA:NYC; Helmhaus Gallery, Zurich, Konkrete Kunst, 1960; A. Tooth & Sons, London, Six American Painters, 1961; WMAA, Geometric Abstraction in America, circ., 1962; Carnegie; U. of St. Thomas (Tex.), Art Has Many Facets; Syracuse U., Modern Classicism. **Collections:** Colgate U.; Columbia U.; Hartford/Wadsworth; Stony Brook/SUNY; Vassar College; WMAA.

WONNER, PAUL JOHN. b. April 24, 1920, Tucson, Ariz. **Studied:** California College of Arts and Crafts, 1937–41, BA; ASL, 1947; U. of California, Berkeley, 1950–53, MA, 1955, MLS. US Army, 1941–45. Traveled Europe. **Taught:** U. of California, Berkeley, 1952–53, Los Angeles, 1962–63; Otis Art Institute, 1965–68. **Address:** 468 Jersey Street, San Francisco, CA 94994. **Dealer:** John Berggruen Gallery. **One-man Exhibitions:** (first) de Young, 1955; San Francisco Art Association, 1956; Felix Landau Gallery, 1959, 60, 62, 63, 64, 68, 71; Santa Barbara/MA, 1960, California Palace, 1961; Poindexter Gallery, 1962, 64, 71; Esther Baer Gallery, 1964 (two-man, with William T. Brown); San Antonio/McNay, 1965; Waddington Gallery, London, 1965; The Landau-Alan Gallery, NYC, 1967; Charles Campbell Gallery, 1972; Jodi Scully Gallery, 1973; John Berggruen Gallery, San Francisco, 1978. **Group:** SRGM, Younger American Painters, 1954; III Sao Paulo Biennial, 1955; Walker, Vanguard, 1955; Oakland/AM, Contemporary Bay Area Figure Painting, 1957; Festival of Two Worlds, Spoleto, 1958; Carnegie, 1958, 64; ART:USA:59; NYC, 1959; WMAA Annuals, 1959, 67; U. of Illinois, 1961, 63; Chicago/AI Annuals, 1961, 64; VMFA, American Painting, 1962; MOMA, Recent Painting USA: The Figure, circ., 1962–63; Denver/AM, 1964. **Collections:** Lytton Savings and Loan Association; NCFA; U. of Nebraska; U. of North Carolina; Oakland/AM; Reader's Digest; SFMA; SRGM. **Bibliography:** Nordness, ed.; *The State of California Painting.*

WOOD, GRANT. b. February 13, 1891, Anamosa, Iowa; **d.** February 12, 1942, Iowa City, Iowa. **Studied:** State U. of Iowa; Minneapolis School of Design; Academie Julian, Paris. US Army, 1918–19. Traveled Germany, France.

Taught: Rosedale, Iowa, 1911–12; Jackson, Iowa, 1919–23; Chicago Art Institute School, 1916; State U. of Iowa, 1934–42. **Member:** NAD; National Society of Mural Painters. Federal A.P.: Director, Iowa Division, 1934. **Commissions:** Cedar Rapids (Iowa) Memorial Building, 1926–28 (stained glass window). **Awards:** Iowa State Fair, First Prize, 1929, 30, 31, 32; Carnegie, 1934; Hon. Ph.D., U. of Wisconsin; Hon. MA, Wesleyan U.; Hon. DFA, Lawrence College; Hon. DFA, Northwestern U. **One-man Exhibitions:** Ferargil Galleries, NYC, 1935; Lakeside Press Gallery, Chicago, 1935; Hudson D. Walker Gallery, NYC, 1936. **Retrospective:** U. of Kansas, 1959; Davenport/Municipal, 1966; Cedar Rapids/AA, 1969. **Group:** Chicago/AI, 1930; Carnegie, 1934; Iowa State Fair; WMAA. **Collections:** Abbott Laboratories; Cedar Rapids/AA; Chicago/AI; Dubuque/AA; MMA; U. of Nebraska; Omaha/Joslyn; Terre Haute/Swope; WMAA. **Bibliography:** Baigell 1; Barr 3; Baur 7; Bazin; Beam; Beaton 1; Biddle 4; Blanchard; Blesh 1; Boswell 1; Brown; Canaday; Cheney; Christensen; Craven, T. 1; Eliot; Finkelstein; Flanagan; **Garwood;** Gaunt; Goodrich and Baur 1; Haftman; Hall; Hunter 6; *Index of 20th Century Artists;* Kent, R., ed.; Kootz 2; Kouvenhoven; Lee and Burchwood; McCurdy, ed.; Mellquist; Mendelowitz; Newmeyer; Pagano; Pearson 1; Reese; Richardson, E.P.; **Rinard and Pyle;** Rose, B., 1; Wight 2. Archives.

WYETH, ANDREW. b. July 21, 1917, Chadds Ford, Pa. **Studied:** with N. C. Wyeth. **Member:** NAD; Audubon Artists; NIAL; AAAL. **Awards:** AAAL, Medal of Merit, 1947; Hon. DFA, Harvard U., 1955; Hon. DFA, Colby College, 1955; Hon. DFA, Dickinson College, 1958; Hon. DFA, Swarthmore College, 1958; Freedom Medal, 1963; Hon. DFA, Princeton U.; Hon. DFA, Tufts U.; Hon. DFA, Franklin and Marshall College; Hon. DFA, Northeastern U.; Hon. DFA, Amherst College; Hon. DFA, Bowdoin College; Hon. DFA, U. of Pennsylvania; Hon. DFA, U. of Delaware; Hon. DFA, La Salle U. **Address:** Chadds Ford, PA 19317; Cushing, Me. **Dealer:** Coe Kerr Gallery. **One-man Exhibitions:** Currier, 1951; Doll and Richards, Boston, 1938, 40, 42, 44, 46; Macbeth Gallery, NYC, 1938, 39, 48; Rockland/Farnsworth, 1951, 63; de Young, 1956, 73; Santa Barbara/MA, 1956; Wilmington, 1957; M. Knoedler & Co., NYC, 1958; MIT, 1960; Buffalo/Albright, 1962; Pierpont Morgan Library, 1963; Corcoran, 1963; Harvard U., 1963; Southampton/Parrish, 1966; PAFA, 1966; WMAA, 1966; Chicago/AI, 1966; Baltimore/MA, 1966; Brandywine Museum, Chadds Ford, Pa., 1971. **Retrospective:** Tokyo/Modern, circ., 1974; MMA, 1976. **Group:** Houston/MFA; MOMA; PMA; Wilmington; PAFA, 1938, 39, 41–45, 49–52, 58, 63; WMAA, 1946, 48, 51, 52, 53, 56, 57, 59, 63, 64; Carnegie, 1947–50, 52, 55, 58, 61, 64; U. of Illinois, 1948, 49, 63, 65, 69; A.F.A., 1954; Brussels World's Fair, 1958; Tate, 1963. **Collections:** Andover/Phillips; Boston/MFA; California Palace; Chicago/AI; Colby College; Currier; Dallas/MFA; Hartford/Wadsworth; Houston/MFA; MOMA; McDonnell & Co. Inc.; Montclair/AM; National Gallery; U. of Nebraska; New London; Omaha/Joslyn; Oslo/National; PMA; Rockford/Farnsworth; Utica; Wilmington; Winston-Salem; Public Library. **Bibliography:** *Andrew Wyeth* (two titles); Barker 1; Baur 7; Canaday; *8 American Masters of Watercolor;* Eliot; Flanagan; Gaunt; Hoving; Hunter 6; McCurdy, ed.; Mendelowitz; Nordness, ed.; O'Doherty; **Pitz;** Pousette-Dart, ed.; Richardson, E.P.; Rodman 1, 3; Rose, B., 1; Sachs; Watson, E.W., 1.

X

XCERON, JEAN. **b.** February 24, 1890, Isari, Greece; **d.** March 29, 1967, NYC. To USA, 1904. **Studied:** The Corcoran School of Art, 1910–16, with George Lohr, Abraham Rattner. Resided Paris, 1927-37. Art reviewer for American newspapers from Paris, 1930–34. **Member:** American Abstract Artists; Federation of Modern Painters and Sculptors. Federal A.P.: Christian Science Chapel, Rikers Island, NYC, 1941–42 (murals). **Commissions:** U. of Georgia, 1947. **Awards:** U. of Illinois, **P.P.,** 1951. **One-man Exhibitions:** (first) Galerie de France, Paris, 1931 (sponsored by Cahiers d'Art); Galerie Percier, Paris, 1933; Galerie Pierre, Paris, 1934; Garland Gallery, NYC, 1935; Karl Nierendorf Gallery, NYC, 1938; Bennington College, 1944; Sidney Janis Gallery, 1950; Rose Fried Gallery, 1955, 57, 60, 61, 62, 63, 64; The Peridot Gallery, NYC, 1971; Andre Zarre Gallery, NYC, 1975, 77, 80. **Retrospectives:** Jean Xceron, circ. seven museums in the Southwest and West Coast, 1948–49; SRGM, 1952. **Group:** Independent Artists, NYC, 1921–24; Salon des Surindependents, Paris, 1931–35; New York World's Fair, 1939; Golden Gate International Exposition, San Francisco, 1939; SRGM, 1939–52, 1954, 55, 56, 58, 62; American Abstract Artists, 1941–44, 1951–57; Carnegie, 1942, 43, 44, 44, 46, 47, 48, 49, 50; Federation of Modern Painters and Sculptors, 1945, 46, 48, 49, 50, 51, 53, 54, 55, 56; California Palace; WMAA Annuals, 1946, 49, 52, 56; Salon des Realites Nouvelles, Paris, annually,

Jean Xceron   *U Form No. 553 A*   1962

1947–52; U. of Illinois, 1948, 49, 50, 52, 55, 57; Houston/MFA, The Sphere of Mondrian, 1957; MOMA, circ., Latin America, 1963–64. **Collections:** Andover/Phillips; Brandeis U.; Carnegie U. of Georgia; U. of Illinois; Karlsruhe; MOMA; NYU; U. of New Mexico; Phillips; Pittsfield/Berkshire; SRGM; Smith College; WMAA; Washington U.; Wellesley College. **Bibliography:** Bethers; Blanchard; Hess, T. B., 1; Hunter, ed.; Janis and Blesh 1; Kootz 2; Pousette-Dart, ed.; Rickey; Rose B., 1. Archives.

Y

YEKTAI, MANOUCHER. b. December 22, 1922, Teheran, Iran. **Studied:** with Amedee Ozenfant and Robert Hale, 1945; Academie des Beaux-Arts, Paris, 1946, with Andre Lhote. **Address:** 225 West 86th Street, NYC 10024. **One-man Exhibitions:** Grace Borgenicht Gallery, Inc., 1952–54; A.A.A. Gallery, NYC, 1956; Poindexter Gallery, 1957, 59, 60, 62; Galerie Anderson-Mayer, Paris, 1963; Galerie Semiha Huber, Zurich, 1963; Picadilly Gallery, 1963, 66, 72, 73; Felix Landau Gallery, 1963; Gertrude Kasle Gallery, 1965, 66, 67, 68, 70; Feingarten Gallery, Chicago; Robert Elkon Gallery; Gump's Gallery; Benson Gallery. **Group:** Salon des Comparaisons, Paris; Walker, 60 American Painters, 1960; Carnegie, 1961; USIA, Paris, 1961; MOMA, Recent Painting, USA: The Figure, circ., 1962–63; Chicago/AI, Directions in American Painting, 1963; Paris/Moderne, 1963. **Collections:** Baltimore/MA; Charleston/Carolina; MOMA; Syracuse/Everson; Union Carbide Corp.

YOSHIDA, RAY. b. October 3, 1930, Kapaa, Kauai, Hawaii. **Studied:** U. of Hawaii, BA, 1951; Chicago Art Institute School, BAE, 1953; Syracuse U., MFA, 1958. US Army, 1954–56. Traveled Europe, Mexico, the Orient, South America. **Taught:** Syracuse U., 1956–57; Rochester Institute of Technology, 1957–58; Rockford College, 1959–61; Washington U., 1965; Chicago Art Institute School, 1965–80. **Awards:** Frank G. Locan Medal, 1971. **Address:** 1944 N. Wood Street, Chicago, IL 60622. **Dealer:** Phyllis Kind Gallery, NYC, Chicago. **One-man Exhibitions:** Phyllis Kind Gallery, Chicago, 1975, 77, 81; Syracuse U., 1957; **Group:** Chicago/Contemporary, Don Baum Sez "Chicago Needs Famous Artists," 1969; ICA, U. of Pennsylvania, Spirit of the Comics, 1969; SFAI, Surplus Slop from the Windy City, 1970; Chicago/Contemporary, Imagist Art, 1972; Ottawa/National, What They're Up to in Chicago, 1972; Sao Paulo, Biennial, 1974; NCFA, Made in Chicago, 1974; Chicago/AI, Famous Alumni, 1976; Sacramento/Crocker, The Chicago Connection, circ., 1976. **Collections:** AT&T NYC; Ball State U.; Chicago/AI; Chicago/Contemporary; Museum des 20. Jahrhunderts, Vienna; South Bend Art Center; Syracuse/Everson. **Bibliography:** *The Chicago Connection.*

YOUNGERMAN, JACK. b. March 25, 1926, Webster Groves, Mo. **Studied:** U. of North Carolina (US Navy Training Program), 1944–46; U. of Missouri, 1947, BA; Academie des Beaux-Arts, Paris, 1947–48. Traveled Europe, Near East; resided Europe, 1947–54. Designed stage sets for *Histoire de Vasco,* produced by Jean-Louis Barrault, Paris, 1956, and *Deathwatch,* by Jean Genet, NYC, 1958. **Commissions:** Federal Court Building, Portland, Ore., 1975; PPG Industries/Howard Heinz Foundation, 1977. **Awards:** *Art in America* Magazine, New Talent, 1959; National Endowment for the Arts, grant, 1972; Guggenheim Foundation Fellowship, 1976. **Address:** 130 West 4th Street, NYC 10012. **One-man Exhibitions:** Galerie Arnaud, 1951; Gres Gallery, Washington, D.C., 1957 (two-man); Betty Parsons Gallery, 1957, 60, 61, 64,

Jack Youngerman *Tabriz* 1981

65, 67, 68; Galleria dell'Ariete, 1962; Galerie Lawrence, Paris, 1962, 65; Everett Ellin Gallery, Los Angeles, 1963; Worcester/AM, 1965; MIT, 1966; Galerie Maeght, 1966; Phillips, 1968; The Pace Gallery, NYC, 1971, 72, 73, 75, J. L. Hudson Art Gallery, Detroit, 1971; The Berenson Gallery, 1972; Portland (Ore.) Center for the Visual Arts, 1972; Seattle/AM, 1972; Arts Club of Chicago, 1973; Galerie Denise Rene, Paris, 1973; Fendrick Gallery, 1974; Kingpitcher Gallery, Pittsburgh, 1974; Fendrick Gallery, Washington, D.C., 1974; Southampton/Parrish, 1976; Tampa Bay Museum, 1977; Truman Gallery, NYC, 1978. **Group:** Galerie Maeght, Les Mains Eblories, 1950; Galerie Denise Rene, Paris, 1952; Carnegie, 1958, 61, 67, 71; MOMA, Sixteen Americans, circ., 1959; Corcoran, 1959, 62; Kimura Gallery, Tokyo, American Painters, 1960; SRGM, Abstract Expressionists and Imagists, 1961; Chicago/AI, 1961, 62; MOMA, Recent American Painting and Sculpture, circ., USA and Canada, 1961–62; Seattle World's Fair, 1962; International Biennial Exhibition of Paintings, Tokyo; SRGM, American Drawings, 1964; WMAA, A Decade of American Drawings, 1965; SRGM, Systemic Painting, 1966; Rotterdam, 1966; WMAA Annual, 1967; Utica, American Prints Today, 1968; Indianapolis, 1969; Jewish Museum, Superlimited; Books, Boxes, and Things, 1969; Foundation Maeght, L'Art Vivant, 1970; Carnegie, International, 1971; U. of North Carolina, Art on Paper, 1973; U. of Texas, Austin, Abstract Expressionists and Imagists, 1976; Montgomery, Ala., Art Inc., 1979; Museo de Arte Moderno, Bogota, 25 Anos Despues, 1970; California State U., Northbridge, Americans in Paris; the 50s, 1979. **Collections:** Buffalo/Albright; U. of California, Berkeley;

Carnegie; Chase Manhattan Bank; Chicago/AI; Corcoran; Equitable Life Assurance Society; Hartford/Wadsworth; Hirshhorn; Milwaukee; MOMA; NCFA; Phillips; Reynolds Metals Co.; SRGM; VMFA; WMAA; Wichita/AM; Worcester/AM; Yale U. **Bibliography:** Alloway 3; Battcock, ed.; Nordness, ed.; Rickey; Rose, B., 1; Sandler; Weller. Archives.

YRISARRY, MARIO. b. March 29, 1933, Manila, Philippines. **Studied:** Queens College, 1955, BA, with Robert Goldwater, John Ferren; Cooper Union, 1955–58, with Charles Cajori. Traveled around the world, 1951; USA, Mexico, Canada. **Taught:** School of Visual Arts, NYC, 1968–69; California Institute of the Arts, Valencia, 1970–71; Herbert H. Lehman College, Bronx, N.Y. 1974–75. **Awards:** Tamarind Fellowship, 1973. **Address:** 297 Third Avenue, NYC 10010. **Dealers:** A.M. Sachs Gallery, NYC; Leah Levy, San Francisco; Luz Gallery, Manila. **One-man Exhibitions:** Udinotti Gallery, Tempe, Ariz., 1960; Thompson Gallery, Provincetown, Mass., 1961; The Graham Gallery, 1964, 65, 67; Galerie Gunar, Dusseldorf, 1967; Obelisk Gallery, 1969; Deson-Zaks Gallery, Chicago, 1970; OK Harris Works of Art, 1969, 70, 72; Jerrold Morris Gallery, Toronto (two-man), 1970; Luz Gallery, Manila, 1975; William Patterson College, 1975. **Group:** ICA, Boston Painting without a Brush, 1965; Bennington College, 5 Painters and a Sculptor, 1967; U. of Illinois, 1967; WMAA Annuals, 1969, 70; Indianapolis, 1970; WMAA, The Structure of Color, 1971; ICA, U. of Pennsylvania, Grids, 1972; Youngstown/Butler, 1973; U. of Miami, The International Style in America, 1974; P.S.1, Pattern Painting, 1977. **Collections:** Baltimore/MA; Brandeis U.; Connecticut Community College; Crocker Bank, Los Angeles; Hotel Corp. of America; Hirshhorn; Indianapolis; Jones & Laughlin Steel Corp.; MIT; Ridgefield/Aldrich; Storm King Art Center; Wichita/AM; WMAA; Worcester/AM.

YUNKERS, ADJA. b. July 15, 1900, Riga, Latvia. **Studied:** art in Leningrad, Berlin, Paris, and London. Traveled the world extensively; resided Paris 14 years, Stockholm during World War II. Edited and published art magazines *ARS* and *Creation* in Sweden, 1942–45. To USA, 1947; became a citizen. **Taught:** New School for Social Research, 1947–54; U. of New Mexico, summers, 1948, 49; Cooper Union, 1956–67; Honolulu Academy, 1964; U. of California, Berkeley, 1966; U. of Colorado, 1967; Columbia U., 1974; Bard College, 1969–78. **Commissions:** Syracuse U., 1966; Stony Brook/SUNY, 1967. **Awards:** Guggenheim Foundation Fellowship, 1949–50; renewed 1954–55; Ford Foundation, 1959; Chicago/AI, Norman Wait Harris Medal, 1961; Tamarind Fellowship, 1961. **Address:** c/o Dealer. **Dealers:** The Zabriskie Gallery; Smith Andersen Gallery, Palo Alto. **One-man Exhibitions:** (first) Maria Kunde Gallery, Hamburg, 1921 or 1922; Galerie Per, Oslo; Tokanten (Gallery), Copenhagen, 1947–54; Kleemann Gallery, NYC; Corcoran; Smithsonian; Chicago/AI; Pasadena/AM; Colorado Springs/FA; Grace Borgenicht Gallery, Inc., 1954, 55; Galerie Paul Facchetti; Gallerie Schneider, Rome; Salon des Realites Nouvelles, Paris, 1955; Zwemmer Gallery, London, 1957–59; Los Angeles/County MA; Rose Fried Gallery; The Howard Wise Gallery, Cleveland; Andre Emmerich Gallery, NYC; Honolulu Academy, 1964–65; The Zabriskie Gallery, NYC, 1974, 75. **Retrospective:** Baltimore/MA; U. of Utah; Mexico City/Nacional, 1975. **Group:** MOMA, The New American Painting and Sculpture, 1969. **Collections:** Arts Council of Great Britain; Atlanta/AA; Baltimore/MA; Basel; Bibliotheque Nationale; Bibliotheque Royale de Belgique; Boston/MFA; Brandeis U.; Brooklyn Museum; UCLA; Carnegie; Cleveland/MA; Colorado Springs/FA; Corcoran; Florence (Italy)/Modern; Hamburg; Harvard U.; Johannesburg/Municipal; Library of Congress; Lima, Peru; Louisville/

Speed; MMA; MOMA; Memphis/ Brooks; Minneapolis/Institute; Minnesota/MA; NCFA; NYPL; National Gallery; Oslo/National; PMA; The Print Club, Philadelphia; Rijksmuseum Amsterdam; SRGM; Sao Paulo; Springfield, Mass./MFA; Stockholm/National; Trenton State; U. of Utah; Victoria and Albert Museum; WMAA; Walker; Wellesley College; Worcester/AM. **Bibliography:** Goodrich and Baur 1; *From Foreign Shores;* Nordness, ed.; Read 2. Archives.

Z

ZACHARIAS, ATHOS. b. June 17, 1927, Marlborough, Mass. **Studied:** RISD, 1952, BFA; ASL, with Yasuo Kuniyoshi, summer, 1952; Cranbrook Academy of Art, with Zoltan Sepeshy, 1953, MFA. Traveled Europe, eastern USA. **Taught:** Brown U., 1953–55; Parsons School of Design, 1963–65; Long Island U., summer, 1967; Wagner College, 1969– . **Commissions:** Fram Corporation, 1963 (painting of explorer ship *Fram*). **Awards:** Scholarship to RISD, 1950; Longview Foundation Grant, 1962; Guild Hall, First and Second Prizes; Long Island U., **P.P.,** 1968; MacDowell Colony Fellowship, 1969. **Address:** 463 West Street, NYC 10014. **One-man Exhibitions:** (first) Brown U., 1954; Great Jones Gallery, NYC, 1960; Joachim Gallery, Chicago, 1961; Gallery Mayer, NYC, 1961; Bob Keene, Southampton, N.Y., 1961–64; Louis Alexander Gallery, NYC, 1962, 63; Guild Hall, 1965; Benson Gallery, Bridgehampton, N.Y. 1967, 78; Westbeth Gallery, NYC, 1970, 71; Landmark Gallery, Inc., NYC, 1973; Glassboro State College, 1976; James Yu Gallery, NYC, 1977; Fred Dorfman Gallery, NYC, 1978; Guild Hall, East Hampton, 1980. **Group:** Boston Arts Festival, 1954; ART: USA: 59, NYC, 1959; Raleigh/NCMA, 1959; Pan-Pacific Exhibition, circ., Japan, 1961; Tenth Street Days, NYC, 1978. **Collections:** Best Products, Richmond, Va.; E.F. Hutton & Company, NYC; Kalamazoo/Institute; McCrory Corp., NYC; U. of North Carolina; Phoenix; RISD; Westinghouse.

ZAJAC, JACK. b. December 13, 1929, Youngstown, Ohio. **Studied:** Scripps College, 1949–53, with Millard Sheets, Henry McFee, Sueo Serisawa. Traveled the world extensively. Changed from painting to sculpture, 1955. **Taught:** Pomona College, 1959; Dartmouth College, 1970. **Commissions:** Reynolds Metals Co., 1968. **Awards:** California State Scholarship, 1950; Youngstown/Butler, Second Prize, 1950; Pasadena/AM, **P.P.,** 1951; Los Angeles/County MA, **P.P.,** 1953, 58; Prix de Rome, 1954, 56, 57; AAAL, 1958; Guggenheim Foundation Fellowship, 1959; Limited Editions Club, $2,500 Prize for Etching, 1959; Sarasota Art Association, Prize for Sculpture, 1959; Grace Cathedral, San Francisco, Art in Religion, First Prize, 1960; National Religious Art Exhibition, Birmingham, Mich., 1962. **Address:** c/o Dealer. **Dealers:** The Forum Gallery; Fairweather-Hardin Gallery, Chicago. **One-man Exhibitions:** (first) Pasadena/AM, 1951; Felix Landau Gallery, 1951, 53, 54, 56, 58, 60, 62, 63, 66, 68, 70; Santa Barbara/MA, 1953; Scripps College, 1955; Galleria Schneider, Rome, 1955; John Young Gallery, Honolulu, 1956; Il Segno Rome, 1957; The Downtown Gallery, 1960; Devorah Sherman Gallery, 1960; Roland, Browse and Delbanco, London, 1960; Gallery Marcus, Laguna Beach, Calif., 1961; The Landau-Alan Gallery, NYC, 1966, 68; Alpha Gallery, 1969; Fairweather-Hardin Gallery, 1970; The Forum Gallery, 1971, 74, 78; La Margherita Gallery, Rome, 1972; Galleria d'Arte l'Obelisco, 1973; Jodi Scully Gallery, 1973; San Diego, 1975; Santa Barbara/MA, 1978. **Retrospectives:** Newport Harbor, 1965; California Institute of Technology, Pasadena, 1969; Temple U., Rome, 1969; Dartmouth College, 1970. **Group:** Santa

Barbara/MA, 1959; WMAA Annual, 1959; Chicago/AI, Annual, 1959; MOMA, Recent Sculpture USA, 1959; Los Angeles/County MA, 1959, 60; Claude Bernard, Paris, Aspects of American Sculpture, 1960; Smithsonian, Drawings by Sculptors, circ., USA, 1961–63; SRGM, The Joseph H. Hirshhorn Collection, 1962; WMAA, American Painters Today, circ., 1962; VMFA, American Painting, 1962; WMAA, Fifty California Artists, 1962–63; MOMA, Recent Painting USA: The figure, circ., 1962–63; Carnegie International, 1965; U. of Illinois, 1965; Biennale de Roma, 1968; Laguna Beach Museum of Art, 1979. **Collections:** California Federal Savings and Loan Association; Gibraltar Savings & Loan Association; Hirshhorn; Home Savings and Loan Association; Kansas City/Nelson; Los Angeles/County MA; Lytton Savings and Loan Association; MOMA; Milwaukee; U. of Nebraska; PAFA; Pasadena/AM; Santa Barbara/MA; State of California; Syracuse U.; Utica; Walker. **Bibliography: Seldis and Wilke;** Weller.

ZAKANITCH, ROBERT S. b. May 24, 1935, Elizabeth, N.J. **Taught:** U. of California, San Diego, 1974; Chicago Art Institute School, 1976. **Address:** 18 Warren Street, NYC 10007. **Dealer:** Robert Miller Gallery, Inc., NYC. **One-man Exhibitions:** Henri Gallery, Alexandria, Va., 1965; Stable Gallery, NYC, 1968; Reese Palley Gallery, NYC, 1970, 71; Holly Solomon Gallery, NYC, 1977; Galerie Liatowitsch, Basel, 1978; Robert Miller Gallery, NYC, 1978, 79, 80; Galerie Rudolf Zwirner, Cologne, 1979. **Group:** WMAA Annual, 1968; U. of Illinois, 1969; U. of Rochester, Aspects of Current Painting, 1971; WMAA, Structure of Color, 1971; Indianapolis, 1972; Vassar College, New American Abstract Painting, 1972; Corcoran, Biennial, 1973; P.S. 1, Long Island City, Pattern Painting, 1977; Rice U., Pattern and Decoration, 1978; Dayton/AI, Pattern Plus, 1979; The New Museum, NYC, The 1970s, 1979; ICA, U. of Pennsylvania, The Decorative Impulse, 1979; Mannheim/Kunstverein, Dekor, 1980. **Collections:** Blue Cross–Blue Shield, Chicago; Hartford/Wadsworth; Phoe-

Robert S. Zakanitch *Savannah Nights* 1979

nix; PMA; Ridgefield/Aldrich; VMFA; WMAA. **Bibliography:** *Drawings: The Pluralist Decade.* Archives.

ZAMMITT, NORMAN. b. February 3, 1931, Toronto, Canada. US Air Force, 1951–56. US Citizen, 1956. **Studied:** Pasadena City College AA, 1950–51, 1956–57; Otis Art Institute, MFA, 1957–61. **Taught:** School of Fine Arts, Los Angeles, 1962–63; Occidental College, 1963; U. of New Mexico, 1963–64; CSCS, Fullerton, 1964–66; California Institute of the Arts, Los Angeles, 1967; U. of Southern California, 1968–69; UCLA, 1971–72. **Awards:** Pasadena City College, Ruth Estes Bissiri Memorial Scholarship, 1957; Otis Art Institute, four-year scholarship, 1957–61, 50th Anniversary Sculpture Exhibition, **P.P.,** 1968; Tamarind Fellowship; Guggenheim Foundation Fellowship, 1968; Long Beach/MA. **Address:** 233 N. Wilson Avenue, Pasadena, CA 91106. **One-man Exhibitions:** Felix Landau Gallery, 1962, 63, 69; Robert Schoelkopf Gallery, 1963; The Landau-Alan Gallery, NYC, 1967, 68; Santa Barbara/MA, 1968; Los Angeles/County MA, 1977; Corcoran, 1978. **Group:** Los Angeles/County MA, 1961, 64, American Sculpture of the Sixties, 1967; Pasadena/AM, 1962; U. of St. Thomas (Tex.), 1965; MOMA, 1965; U. of Illinois, 1967; Hansen Gallery, San Francisco, 1967; Lytton Art Center, Los Angeles, 1967. **Collections:** Library of Congress; MOMA; Ridgefield/Aldrich. **Bibliography:** Davis, D.; Tuchman 1.

ZERBE, KARL. b. September 16, 1903, Berlin, Germany; **d.** November 28, 1972, Tallahassee, Fla. **Studied:** Technische Hochschule, Friedberg, 1920; Debschitz School, Munich, with Josef Eberz, 1921–23, DFA. Traveled Europe, USA, Mexico, Canada. To USA, 1934; citizen, 1939. **Taught:** Fine Arts Guild, Cambridge, Mass., 1935–37; Boston Museum School, 1937–55; Florida State U., 1954–72. **Member:** Artists Equity (President, 1957–59). Federal A.P.:

Easel painting. **Awards:** VMFA, John Barton Payne Medal, 1942; ICA, Boston, First Prize, 1943; Chicago/AI, Watson F. Blair Prize, 1944; Chicago/AI, Norman Wait Harris Silver Medal and Prize, 1946; Carnegie, Third Prize, 1948; PAFA, J. Henry Schiedt Memorial Prize, 1949; Boston Arts Festival, First Prize, 1953; U. of Illinois, **P.P.,** 1955. **One-man Exhibitions:** (first) Gallery Gurlitt, Berlin, 1922; Marie Sterner Gallery, NYC, 1934, 35, 56, 37; Grace Horne Galleries, Boston, 1936, 38, 39, 40; Vose Gallery, Boston, 1941; Buchholz Gallery, NYC, 1941; Mount Holyoke College, 1943; Pittsfield/Berkshire, 1943, 47; The Downtown Gallery, 1943, 46, 48, 51, 52; Chicago/AI, 1945, 46; Detroit/Institute, 1946; Philadelphia Art Alliance, 1948, 49; Boris Mirski Gallery, Boston, 1948, 55, 66; Utica, 1950; The Alan Gallery, NYC, 1954; Ringling, 1958; Nordness Galleries, 1958, 59, 64, 70; WMAA, 1962 (two-man); Florida State U., 1962; St. Armands Gallery, Florida, 1963; James David Gallery, Miami, 1963; Mickelson's Gallery, Washington, D.C., 1963; Glassboro State College, 1964; U. of Tampa, 1965; Kovler Gallery, 1966. **Retrospective:** ICA, Boston, circ., 1951–52; A.F.A., circ., 1961–62. **Group:** ICA, Boston; Chicago/AI; Carnegie; PAFA; U. of Illinois; WMAA. **Collections:** Andover/Phillips; Auburn U.; Baltimore/MA; Boston/MFA; Britannica; Brooklyn Museum; Buffalo/Albright; Chicago/AI; Colby College; Cranbrook; Detroit/Institute; Fort Worth; Frankfurt am Main; U. of Georgia; Harvard U.; IBM; Illinois Wesleyan U.; U. of Illinois; Indianapolis/Herron; State U. of Iowa; Kestner-Museum; Los Angeles/County MA; MIT; MMA; MOMA; Milwaukee; U. of Minnesota; NIAL; U. of Nebraska; Newark Museum; New Britain; Oberlin College; U. of Oklahoma; PMA; Phillips; RAC; RISD; Rio de Janeiro; U. of Rochester; St. Louis/City; San Diego; Sarah Lawrence College; Smith College; Staatliche Graphische Sammlung Munchen; Syracuse U.; Tel Aviv; Utica; WMAA; Walker; Washington U.; U. of

Washington; Wichita/AM; Youngstown/Butler. **Bibliography:** Baur 7; Bethers; Chaet; Genauer; Goodrich and Baur 1; Halpert; Nordness, ed.; Pearson 2; Pousette-Dart, ed.; Richardson, E.P.; Wight 2. Archives.

ZOGBAUM, WILFRID. b. September 10, 1915, Newport, RI; **d.** January 7, 1965, NYC. **Studied:** Yale U., 1933–34; with John Sloan, NYC, 1934–35; Hoffmann School, NYC and Provincetown, 1935–37 (class monitor). US Army, 1941–46. Traveled Europe, the Orient, West Indies, USA. Began sculpture, 1954. **Taught:** U. of California, Berkeley, 1957, 1961–63; U. of Minnesota, 1958; Pratt Institute, 1960–61; Southern Illinois U., 1961. **Member:** American Welding Society; Sculptors Guild. **Awards:** S. R. Guggenheim Fellowship for Painting, 1937; U. of California Institute for Creative Work in the Arts, 1963. **One-man Exhibitions:** (first) Alexander Iolas Gallery, 1952 (paintings); The Stable Gallery, 1954, 58; Walker, 1958; Staempfli Gallery, 1960; Obelisk Gallery, Washington, D.C. 1962; Dilexi Gallery, San Francisco, 1962; U. of California, Berkeley, 1962; Grace Borgenicht Gallery Inc., 1963; Everett Ellin Gallery, Los Angeles, 1963; Hansen-Fuller Gallery, San Francisco, 1969; SFMA, 1973; Zabriskie Gallery, NYC, 1979. **Group:** American Abstract Artists, 1935–41; Oakland/AM, 1957; U. of Nebraska, 1961; Baltimore/MA, 1961; MOMA, Modern American Drawings, circ., Europe, 1961–62; Seattle World's Fair, 1962; WMAA Annuals; Chicago/AI, 1962; Carnegie, 1962; Turin/Civico, 1962. **Collections:** Brooklyn Museum; U. of California; Hirshhorn; International Institute for Aesthetic Research; New School for Social Research; SFMA; WMAA. **Bibliography:** Hunter, ed.; Tuchman 1. Archives.

ZORACH, MARGUERITE. b. September 25, 1887, Santa Rosa, Calif.; **d.** June 27, 1968, Brooklyn, N.Y. **Studied** in Paris, 1906–10. Traveled Europe, Mexico, Central America, and around the world, 1911–12. **Taught:** Provincetown, 1913–18; Columbia U., intermittently during the 1940s. **Commissions** (murals): US Post Offices, Peterborough, N.H., and Ripley, Tenn. **Awards:** Chicago/AI, The Mr. & Mrs. Frank G. Logan Medal, 1920; Golden Gate International Exposition, San Francisco, 1939, Silver Medal; Hon. Ph.D., Bates College. **m.** William Zorach. **One-man Exhibitions:** (first) The Daniel Gallery, NYC, 1915, also 1917; Montross Gallery, NYC, 1921; Joseph Brummer Gallery, NYC, 1930; The Downtown Gallery, 1935, 38; M. Knoedler & Co., NYC, 1944; Kraushaar Galleries, 1953, 57, 62, 68, 74. **Retrospective:** NCFA, 1973. **Group:** Salon d'Automne, Paris, 1910; The Armory Show, 1913; WMAA; MOMA. **Collections:** Colby College; Louisville/Speed; MMA; MOMA; Massillon Museum; Newark Museum; WMAA. **Bibliography:** *Avant-Garde Painting & Sculpture in America, 1910–25*; Biddle 4; Brown 2; Cheney; Goodrich and Baur 1; Hunter 6; Marter, Tarbell, and Wechsler; Richardson, E.P.; Ringel, ed.; **Tarbell;** Wright 1.

ZORACH, WILLIAM. b. February 28, 1887, Eurburg, Lithuania; **d.** November 15, 1966, Bath, Me. To USA, 1891. **Studied:** Cleveland Institute of Art, 1902–05; NAD, 1908–10; and in Paris, 1910–11. **Taught:** ASL, 1929–66; The Des Moines Art Center, 1954. **Member:** NIAL (vice-President, 1955–57); Sculptors Guild. **Commissions:** Radio City Music Hall, NYC, 1932; US Post Office, Benjamin Franklin Station, Washington, D.C., 1937; New York World's Fair, 1939; Mayo Clinic, Rochester, Minn., 1954; Municipal Court Building, NYC, 1958; R.S. Reynolds Memorial Award, 1960 (a sculpture). **Awards:** Chicago/AI, The Mr. & Mrs. Frank G. Logan Medal, 1931, 32; Architectural League of New York, Hon. Men., 1939;

Bates College, Citation, 1958; Hon. MA, Bowdoin College, 1958; NIAL, Gold Medal for Sculpture, 1961; PAFA, George D. Widener Memorial Gold Medal, 1962. **m.** Marguerite Zorach. **One-man Exhibitions:** Taylor Galleries, Cleveland, 1912; The Daniel Gallery, NYC, 1915, 16, 18; O'Brien's Gallery, Chicago, 1916; Dayton/AI, 1922; U. of Rochester, 1924; Kraushaar Galleries, 1924, 26, 48; Arts and Crafts Club, New Orleans, 1927; Eastman-Bolton Co., NYC, 1929; The Downtown Gallery, 1931, 32, 33, 36, 43, 44, 47, 51, 55, 67; Passedoit Gallery, NYC, 1937; Ansel Adams Gallery, San Francisco, 1941; Boston Museum School, 1941; Dallas/MFA, 1945; California Palace, 1946; San Diego, 1946; Pasadena/AM, 1946; Ten Thirty Gallery, Cleveland, 1948; Coleman Gallery, NYC, 1949; New Paltz/SUNY, 1950; Clearwater/Gulf Coast, 1952; Des Moines, 1954; San Antonio/McNay, 1956; Bowdoin College, 1958; Philadelphia Art Alliance, 1961; Coe College, 1961; Queens College, 1961; Brooklyn Museum, 1968; Danenberg Gallery, 1970; The Zabriskie Gallery, 1974. **Retrospectives:** ASL, 1950, 69; WMAA, circ., 1959. **Group:** Salon d'Automne, Paris, 1910; The Armory Show, 1913; Society of Independent Artists, NYC, 1914–16; Anderson Galleries, NYC, Forum Exhibition, 1916; PAFA, New Tendencies, 1918; A Century of Progress, Chicago, 1933–34; American Painting and Sculpture, Moscow, 1959; PAFA; MOMA; WMAA; Corcoran; Chicago/AI. **Collections:** AAAL; Andover/Phillips; Arizona State College; Baltimore/MA; Bezalel Museum; Buffalo/Albright; Chicago/AI; Cleveland/MA; Colby College; Columbia U.; Columbus; Corcoran; Dallas/MFA; Des Moines; Dubuque/AA; Fairleigh Dickinson U.; Fort Worth; IBM; Los Angeles/County MA; MMA; MOMA; U. of Nebraska; Newark Museum; New Britain; Oberlin College; Ogunquit; PMA; The Pennsylvania State U.; Phillips; Pittsfield/Berkshire; Sara Roby Foundation; Shelburne; Syracuse U.; Tel Aviv; Terre Haute/Swope; Utica; VMFA; WMAA; West Palm Beach/Norton; Wichita/AM; Wilmington. **Bibliography:** *Avant-Garde Painting & Sculpture in America, 1910–25;* Baur 7; Beam; Biddle 4; Blesh 1; Brown 2; Brumme; Bryant, L.; Cahill and Barr, eds.; Cheney; Craven, W.; Flanagan; *From Foreign Shores;* Gertz; Goodrich and Baur 1; Hall; Halpert; **Hoopes;** Hunter 6; *Index of 20th Century Artists;* Jewell 2; Lee and Burchwood; Marter, Tarbell, and Wechsler; McCurdy, ed.; Mellquist; Mendelowitz; Myers 2; Neuhaus; Parkes; Pearson 2; Phillips 2; Richardson, E.P.; Ringel, ed.; Ritchie 3; Rose, B., 1; Seuphor 3; Weller; Wheeler; **Wingert;** Wright 1; **Zorach 1, 2.** Archives.

ZOX, LARRY. b. May 31, 1936, Des Moines, Iowa. **Studied:** U. of Oklahoma, with Amelio Amero, Eugene Bavinger; Drake U., with Karl Mattern; The Des Moines Art Center, with George Grosz, Louis Bouche, Will Barnet. Traveled USA, Mexico, and Canada extensively. **Taught:** Cornell U., Artist-in-Residence, 1961; U. of North Carolina, Artist-in-Residence, 1967; School of Visual Arts, NYC, 1967–68, 1969–70; Juniata College, Artist-in-Residence, 1968; Dartmouth College, Artist-in-Residence, 1969; Yale U., 1972; Kent State U., 1974. **Awards:** Guggenheim Foundation Fellowship, 1967; National Council on the Arts Award, 1969; National Endowment for the Arts, Grant, 1969. **Address:** 238 Park Avenue South, NYC 10003. **Dealer:** Andre Emmerich Gallery, NYC. **One-man Exhibitions:** (first) The American Gallery, NYC, 1962; The Kornblee Gallery, 1964, 66, 68, 69, 70, 71; J. L. Hudson Art Gallery, Detroit, 1967; Galerie Rolf Ricke, 1968; Colgate U., 1968; Dartmouth College, 1969; Janie C. Lee Gallery, Dallas, 1970, 74, Houston, 1974; Akron/AI, 1971; Des Moines, 1971, 74; WMAA, 1973; Andre Emmerich Gallery, NYC, 1973, 75, 76.; WMAA, 1973; Galerie Daniel Templon, Paris, 1975; Medici-Berenson Gallery,

Bay Harbor Islands, 1978. **Group:** Des Moines, 1955, 56; Gallery of Modern Art, NYC, 1965; WMAA, Young America, 1965, Annuals, 1965–66, 1967–68, 1969, 70, 73; Chicago/AI, 1965; Boston/MFA, 1966; SRGM, Systemic Painting, 1966; Expo '67, Montreal, 1967; New Delhi, First World Triennial, 1968; Kent State U., 1968; Worcester/AM, The Direct Image, 1969; The Edmonton Gallery, New Abstract Sculpture, 1977. **Collections:** American Republic Insurance Co.; Columbia Broadcasting System; Cornell U.; Dallas/MFA; Dartmouth College; Des Moines; Des Moines Register & Tribune; Hirshhorn; Houston/MFA; Indianapolis; MOMA; National Bank of Des Moines; Oberlin College; South Mall, Albany; Tate; WMAA. **Bibliography:** Alloway 3; Battcock, ed.; Hunter, ed.; **Monte;** Rose, B., 1.

Bibliography

I. = Illustrated; **B.** = Bibliography; **D.** = Diagrams; **G.** = Glossary; **P.** = Plans; **C.** = Chronologies; **A.** = Appendices.
In cases of more than one entry for the same author, the numeral immediately following the author's name is keyed to the Bibliography section of the Artists' entries. A supplemental list of Books of General Interest follows the main bibliography.

Abstraction création 1931–1936. Münster: Westfälisches Landesmuseum, 1978. Foreword by Peter Berghaus. Preface by Jacques Lassaigne. Essay by Gladys C. Fabre. I.B.D.C. (German and French text.) *Documentation and major survey of this art movement.*

ADAMS, PHILIP RHYS. 1. *Painter of Vision: Walt Kuhn.* Tucson: University of Arizona Art Gallery, 1966. Foreword by William B. Steadman. I. *Major retrospective catalogue.*

_____, 2. Walt Kuhn. *Cincinnati: The Cincinnati Art Museum, 1960. I.* Monograph.

ADRIANI, GOETZ; KOEPPLIN, DIETER; and ROSE, BARBARA. *Zeichnungen von Claes Oldenburg.* Tubingen: Kunsthalle Tubingen, 1975. I.B.C. (German text.) *A major exhibition and study of the drawings.*

AGEE, WILLIAM C. *Marca-Relli.* New York: The Whitney Museum of American Art, 1967. I.B. *Retrospective catalogue.*

AGEE, WILLIAM C., and ROSE, BARBARA. *Patrick Henry Bruce: American Modernist.* New York: The Museum of Modern Art, 1979, I.C. *A catalogue raisonné. Documents the life and work of the painter.*

ALBERS, JOSEF. 1. *Day and Night.* Los Angeles: Tamarind Lithography Workshop, Inc., 1964. *Boxed folio of 10 lithographs (ed. 20).*

_____, 2. *Despite Straight Lines.* New Haven, Conn.: Yale University Press, 1961. I.B. *Captions by Albers; analysis of his graphic constructions, by François Bucher. (German edition, Trotz der Geraden. Berne: Benteli, 1961).*

_____, 3. *Homage to the Square. Ten Works by Josef Albers.* New Haven, Conn.: Ives-Sillman, 1962. Preface by Richard Lippold. *Ten color silkscreens in folio.*

_____, 4. *Interaction of Color.* New Haven, Conn., and London: Yale University Press, 1963. I. *More than 200 color studies, with commentaries.*

_____, 5. *Poems and Drawings.* New Haven, Conn.: Readymade Press, 1958. I. (German and English text.)

_____, 6. *Poems and Drawings* (2nd ed., rev. and enlarged). New York: George Wittenborn, Inc., 1961. I. (Bilingual text.)

_____, 7. *Zeichnungen—Drawings.* New York: George Wittenborn, Inc.; Berne: Spiral Press, 1956. (Text by Max Bill in German and English.) *Twelve b/w plates loose in folio.*

Albert Bloch: 1882–1961. Utica, N.Y.: Munson-William-Proctor Institute, 1974. I. *Exhibition catalogue.*

Alexander Archipenko. A Memorial Exhibition. Los Angeles: University of California, 1967. Foreword by Katherine Kuh. Archipenko Collection: Frances Archipenko. Life and Work: Frederick S. Wight. The Drawings and Prints: Donald H. Karshan. I.B. *Well-documented retrospective catalogue.*

Alexander Calder. Berlin: Akademie der Kunste, 1967. Preface by William Sandberg. I.B. (German text.) *Retrospective catalogue.*

Alexander Calder. New York: A Studio Book/Viking Press, 1971. Introduction by H. Harvard Arnason. Photographs and design by Ugo Mulas. I.B. *Photo survey of Calder, his works, and his milieu.*

Alexander Liberman: Painting and Sculpture 1950–1970. Washington, D.C.: Corcoran Gallery of Art, 1970. Introduction by James Pilgrim. I.B.C. *Retrospective catalogue.*

ALFIERI, BRUNO. *Gyorgy Kepes,* Ivrey, Italy: Centro Culturale Olivetti, 1958. I.B. *Monograph.*

Alfred Jensen. Bern: Kunsthalle Bern, 1973. I.B. (German and English text.) *Retrospective catalogue.*

Al Held. San Francisco: San Francisco Museum of Art, 1968. I.B. *One-man exhibition catalogue.*

ALLEN, CLARENCE CANNING, ed. *Are You Fed Up with Modern Art?* Tulsa, Okla.: The Rainbow Press, 1957. I. *Popular reaction against the new art.*

ALLEN, VIRGINIA. *Jim Dine Designs for "A Midsummer Night's Dream."* New York: The Museum of Modern Art, 1967. I. *Costume designs for the play.*

ALLOWAY, LAWRENCE. 1. *American Pop Art.* New York: Collier Books, 1974. I.B. *Exhibition survey of pop art.*

____, 2. *Samaras: Selected Works 1960–1966.* New York: The Pace Gallery, 1966. I.B. *Includes a statement by the artist.*

____, 3. *Systemic Painting.* New York: The Solomon R. Guggenheim Museum, 1966. I.B. *Catalogue including artists' statements.*

____, 4. *Topics in American Art since 1945.* New York: W. W. Norton & Co., Inc., 1975. I. *Collected reviews and articles written in the sixties and early seventies.*

____, 5. *William Baziotes.* New York: The Solomon R. Guggenheim Museum, 1965. I.B. *Retrospective catalogue.*

ALVARD, J. *Mark Tobey.* Paris: Musée des Arts Décoratifs, Palais du Louvre, 1961. I.B. (French and English text.) *Retrospective catalogue.*

America 1976. Washington, D.C.: The Hereward Lester Cooke Foundation, 1976. Foreword by Thomas S. Kleppe. Painting America First: Robert Rosenblum. Inclusive Painting: Neil Welliver. Pyrography: John Ashbery. On the United States Considered as a Landscape: Richard Howard. I. *US Department of the Interior commissions realist artists.*

AMERICAN ABSTRACT ARTISTS, ed. *American Abstract Artists.* New York: American Abstract Artists, 1946. I. *Documents members and activities.*

AMERICAN ARTISTS CONGRESS, INC. *America Today, a Book of 100 Prints.* New York: Equinox Cooperative Press, 1936. I.

AMERICAN ARTISTS GROUP, INC. 1. *Handbook of the American Artists Group.* New York: American Artists Group Inc., 1935. I.B. *Members and organizational information.*

____, 2. *Missouri, Heart of the Nation.* New York: American Artists Group, Inc., 1947. I.B. *Midwest art of the 1930s and 1940s.*

____, 3. *Original Etchings, Lithographs and Woodcuts by American Artists.* New York: American Artists Group, Inc., 1936. I.

Amerikanischer Fotorealismus. Stuttgart: Wurttembergischer Kunstverein, 1972. Introduction by Uwe M. Schneede. I.C. (German text.) *Survey exhibition, including artists' statements.*

AMMANN, JEAN-CHRISTOPHE, and BUSSMANN, G. *Man Ray: Inventionen und Interpretationen.* Frankfurt: Frankfurter Kunstverein, 1979. *Retrospective catalogue: various essays; includes artist's statement.*

ARCHIPENKO, ALEXANDER. 1. *Archipenko, 50 Creative Years.* New York: Tekhne, 1960. I.B. *Autobiography.*

____, 2. *Archipentura.* New York: Anderson Galleries, 1928. B. *Exhibition catalogue.*

Arman: Selected Works 1958–1974. La Jolla: La Jolla Museum of Contemporary Art, 1974. Introduction by Jan van der Marck. I.B. *Retrospective catalogue.*

ARMITAGE, MERLE. *Rockwell Kent.* New York: Alfred A. Knopf, 1932. I.B. *Monograph.*

ARNASON, H. HARVARD. 1. *Marca-*

Relli. New York: Harry N. Abrams Inc., 1962. I. *Monograph.*

____, 2. *Philip Guston.* New York: The Solomon R. Guggenheim Museum, 1962. I.B. *Exhibition catalogue.*

____, 3. *Stuart Davis.* Minneapolis: The Walker Art Center, 1957. I. *Exhibition catalogue.*

____, 4. *Stuart Davis, Memorial Exhibition.* Washington, D.C.: National Collection of Fine Arts, 1965. I.B. *Major retrospective catalogue.*

____, 5. *Theodore Roszak.* Minneapolis: The Walker Art Center, 1956. I.B. *Exhibition catalogue.*

ARP, HANS. *Onze Peintres.* Zurich: Editions Girsberger, 1949. (French and German text.) I.

Art as a Muscular Principle. South Hadley, Mass.: Mount Holyoke College, 1975. I.B. *A study of ten artists and San Francisco, 1950–1965.*

Art: A Woman's Sensibility. Valencia, Calif: California Institute of the Arts, 1975. Introduction by Deena Metzger. I. *Exhibition catalogue; includes artists' statements.*

Arthur Dove: The Years of Collage. College Park, MD.: University of Maryland Art Gallery, 1967. I.B. *Major study of the collages of Dove.*

ARTHUR JOHN. 1. *Realism/Photorealism.* Tulsa: Philbrook Art Center, 1980. Foreword by Jesse G. Wright, Jr. I.C. *An examination and defense of this school of recent painting.*

____, 2. *Realist Drawings & Watercolors: Contemporary American Works on Paper.* Boston: New York Graphic Society, 1980. I. *Brief examination of various modes of realism.*

Art Now 74: A Celebration of the American Arts. Washington, D.C.: Artrend Foundation, 1974. Foreword by Jocelyn Kress. Introduction by Henry T. Hopkins and Maurice Tuchman. I. *Catalogue of performances and exhibition objects: includes artists' statements.*

Art of the Pacific Northwest: From the 1930s to the Present. Washington, D.C.: National Collection of Fine Arts, 1974. Foreword by Adelyn D. Breeskin.

Introduction by Joshua C. Taylor. Essays by Rachel Griffin and Martha Kingsbury. I.B. *Important survey exhibition and catalogue.*

ASHTON, DORE. 1. *The Mosaics of Jeanne Reynal.* New York: George Wittenborn, Inc., 1964. I. *Monograph.*

____, 2. *Philip Guston.* New York: Grove Press, Inc., 1960. I.B. *Monograph.*

____, 3. *A Reading of Modern Art.* Cleveland and London: The Press of Case Western Reserve University, 1969. I. *Criticisms of recent modern art and literature.*

____, 4. *Richard Lindner.* New York: Harry N. Abrams Inc., 1970. I. *Monograph.*

____, 5. *The Unknown Shore.* Boston: Little, Brown and Co., 1962. I. *Collected essays mostly reprinted from Art and Architecture magazine.*

____, 6. *Yes, But . . . A Critical Study of Philip Guston.* New York: The Viking Press, 1976. I.B.C. *An evaluation of the artist's work.*

ASHTON, DORE, ed. *A Joseph Cornell Album.* New York: Viking Press, 1974. I. *Collected writings by and about Cornell.*

ATKINSON, TRACY. *Directions I: Options 1968.* Milwaukee: Milwaukee Art Center, 1968. Preface by Lawrence Alloway. I. *Catalogue of "people involved in art" with statements by artists.*

AULT, LOUISE. *Artist in Woodstock. George Ault: The Independent Years.* Philadelphia: Dorrance & Co., 1978. *A brief life of the artist.*

Avant-Garde Painting and Sculpture in America: 1910–1925. Wilmington: Delaware Art Museum, 1975. Preface and acknowledgements by William Innes Homer. Foreword by Charles T. Wyrick, Jr. I.B.C. *Useful essays by various authors on modern tendencies in American art.*

BAER, DONALD. *Russell Cowles.* Los Angeles: Dalzell Hatfield Gallery, 1946. I. *Monograph.*

BAIGELL, MATTHEW. 1. *The American Scene: American Paintings.* New York:

Praeger Publishers (American Art and Artists of the 1930s), 1974. I.B. *Superficial survey.*

____, 2. *Thomas Hart Benton.* New York: Harry N. Abrams Inc., 1974. I.B.C. *Heavily illustrated monograph.*

BALDES, ALTON PARKER. *Six Maryland Artists.* Baltimore: Balboa Publishers, 1955. I.

BALDINGER, WALLACE.S., in collaboration with Harry B. Green. *The Visual Arts.* New York: Holt, Rinehart and Winston, Inc., 1960. I.B. *Includes chapters on the visual arts.*

BALLO, FERDINANDO, ed. *Grosz.* Milan: Rosa e Balio Editori, 1956. I. (German and Italian text.) *Critical essays.*

BARKER, VIRGIL. 1. *From Realism to Reality in Recent American Painting.* Lincoln: University of Nebraska Press, 1959. I. *Essays on the rise of abstract and nonfigurative painting.*

____, 2. *Henry Lee McFee.* New York: The Whitney Museum of American Art (American Artists Series), 1931. I. *Monograph.*

BARNES, ALBERT C. *The Art in Painting.* Merion, Pa.: The Barnes Foundation Press, 1925. I. *Dr. Barnes's theories.*

BARO, GENE. *Paul Feeley,* New York: The Solomon R. Guggenheim Museum, 1968. I.B. *Retrospective catalogue.*

BARR, ALFRED, H., Jr. 1. *Cubism and Abstract Art.* New York: The Museum of Modern Art, 1936. I.B. *Essays on Cubism and its evolution.*

____, 2. *Edward Hopper.* New York: The Museum of Modern Art, 1933. I.B. *Exhibition catalogue.*

____, 3. *What Is Modern Painting?* New York: The Museum of Modern Art, 1956. I. *Popular introduction to modern art.*

BASKIN, LEONARD. *Leonard Baskin.* Brunswick, Me.: Bowdoin College, 1962. I.B. *Exhibition catalogue.*

BATES, KENNETH. *Brackman, His Art and Teaching.* Noank, Conn.: Noank Publishing Studio, 1951. I. *Monograph.*

BATTCOCK, GREGORY, ed. *Minimal Art: A Critical Anthology.* New York: E.P. Dutton, 1968. I. *Critical essays reprinted from periodicals and exhibition catalogues.*

BAUDSON, PIERRE. *Steinberg: Zeichnungen und Collagen.* Hamburg: Hamburger Kunsthalle, 1968. Foreword by Helmut R. Leppien. I.B. (German text.) *Retrospective catalogue including an interview with the artist.*

BAUR, JOHN I.H. 1. *Charles Burchfield.* New York: The Whitney Museum of American Art, 1956. I.B. *Retrospective catalogue.*

____, 2. *George Grosz.* New York: The Whitney Museum of American Art, 1954. I.B. *Retrospective catalogue.*

____, 3. *Joseph Stella.* New York: The Whitney Museum of American Art, 1963. I.B. *Retrospective catalogue.*

____, 4. *Loren MacIver—Rice Pereira.* New York: The Whitney Museum of American Art, 1953. I.B. *Exhibition catalogue.*

____, 5. *Nature in Abstraction.* New York: The Macmillan Company, for The Whitney Museum of American Art, 1958. I.B. *Nature considered as catalyst for abstraction.*

____, 6. *Philip Evergood.* New York: Frederick A. Praeger, for The Whitney Museum of American Art, 1960. I.B. *Monograph.*

____, 7. *Revolution and Tradition in Modern American Art.* Cambridge, Mass.: Harvard University Press, 1959. I. *Important essays on conservative and advance guard art.*

BAYER, HERBERT. 1. *Book of Drawings.* Chicago: Paul Theobald and Co., 1961. I.B.

____, 2. *Herbert Bayer: Painter, Designer, Architect.* New York: Reinhold Publishing Co., 1967. I.B.D.P. *Autobiographical monograph.*

BAZALGETTE, LEON. *George Grosz.* Paris: Les Ecrivains Reunis, 1927. I.B. (French text.) *Monograph.*

BAZIN, GERMAIN. *History of Modern Painting.* New York: Hyperion Press, Harper and Brothers, 1951. I.B. *Includes recent American artists of inter-*

national reputation.

BEAM, PHILIP C. *The Language of Art.* New York: The Ronald Press, 1958. I.B. *Essays on interpretation.*

BECKER, JURGEN, and VOSTELL, WOLF. *Happenings, Fluxus, Pop, Nouveau Realism.* Reinbeckbei Hamburg: Rowohlt Verlag GMBH, 1965. I. *International survey.*

BEEKMAN, AARON. *The Functional Line in Painting.* New York: Thomas Yoseloff Inc., 1957. I.

BEEREN, WIM. *Roy Lichtenstein.* Amsterdam: Stedelijk Museum, 1967. I.B. (Dutch and English text.) *Major retrospective catalogue includes interview of the artist by John Coplans.*

BEGGS, THOMAS M. *Paul Manship.* Washington, D.C.: Smithsonian Institution, 1958. I. *Exhibition catalogue.*

BENSON, E.M. *John Marin, The Man and His Work.* Washington, D.C.: American Federation of Arts, 1935. *Monograph.*

BENTON, THOMAS HART. 1. *An American in Art.* Lawrence: University of Kansas, 1969. I. *Autobiography.*

_____, 2. *An Artist in America.* New York: Robert M. McBride and Co., 1937. I. *Autobiography.*

_____, 3. *Thomas Hart Benton.* New York: American Artists Group Inc., 1945. I. *Autobiographical monograph.*

_____, 4. *Thomas Hart Benton.* Lawrence: University of Kansas, 1958. I. *Exhibition catalogue.*

BERMAN, EUGENE. *Imaginary Promenades in Italy.* New York: Pantheon Books, 1956. I. *Illustrated essays.*

Bernard Reder. Tel Aviv: The Tel Aviv Museum of Art, 1963. I.B. *Retrospective catalogue including statements by the artist.*

BETHERS, RAY. *How Paintings Happen.* New York: W.W. Norton and Co., 1951. I. *Artists at work.*

BIDDLE, GEORGE. 1. *An American Artist's Story.* Boston: Little, Brown and Co., 1939. I. *Autobiography.*

_____, 2. *Ninety-Three Drawings,* Colorado Springs: Colorado Springs Fine Arts Center, 1937. I. *Essays on Boardman Robinson's drawings.*

_____, 3. *Tahitian Journal.* St. Paul: University of Minnesota, 1968. I. *Travel book.*

_____, 4. *The Yes and No of Contemporary Art.* Cambridge, Mass.: Harvard University Press, 1957. I. *An artist comments on the contemporary scene.*

BIEDERMAN, CHARLES. 1. *Art as the Evolution of Visual Knowledge.* Red Wing, Minn.: Privately published, 1948. I.B. *History, aesthetics, and theory.*

_____, 2. *Letters on the New Art.* Red Wing, Minn.: Privately published, 1951. *Essays.*

_____, 3. *The New Cezanne.* Red Wing, Minn.: Art History, 1955. I.B. *Homage to Cezanne and theories of subsequent developments.*

BIHALJI-MERIN, OTO. *Adventures of Modern Art.* New York: Harry N. Abrams Inc., 1966. I.B. *Sets postwar Americans in the world art scene.*

BIRCHMAN, WILLIS. *Faces and Facts.* New York: Privately published, 1937. 1. *Short biographies with photographs.*

BIRD, PAUL. *Fifty paintings by Walt Kuhn.* New York: Studio Publications, 1940. 1. *Monograph.*

BIRNBAUM, MARTIN. *Introductions.* New York: Frederic Fairchild Sherman, 1919. *New talent in 1919.*

BITTNER, HUBERT. *George Grosz.* New York: A Golden Griffin Book, Arts, Inc., 1959. I. *Monograph.*

Black and White Are Colors: Paintings of the 1950s–1970s. Claremont, Calif.: Pomona College, 1979. Foreword by David W. Steadman. Essay by David S. Rubin. I. *A psychological-aesthetic investigation of the problems.*

BLANCH, ARNOLD. 1. *Arnold Blanch.* New York: American Artists Group Inc., 1945. I. *Autobiographical monograph.*

_____, 2. *Methods and Techniques for Gouache Painting.* New York: American Artists Group Inc., 1946. I.

_____, 3. *Painting for Enjoyment.* New York: Tudor Publishing Co., 1947. I.

BLANCHARD, FRANCES BRADSHAW. *Retreat from Likeness in the Theory of Painting.* New York: Columbia University Press, 1949. I.B. *From art as illustration to the object as art.*

BLESH, RUDI. 1. *Mo(ern Art, USA. Men—Rebellion—Conquest 1900–1956.* New York: Alfred A. Knopf, 1956. I. *Popular study of American art from 1900 to 1956.*

_____, 2. *Stuart Davis.* New York: Grove Press Inc., 1960. I. *Monograph.*

BORN, WOLFGANG. *American Landscape Painting, an Interpretation.* New Haven, Conn.: Yale University Press, 1948. I.

BOSWELL, PEYTON, Jr. 1. *Modern American Painting.* New York: Dodd, Mead and Co., 1939. I. *Painting in the first 40 years of the twentieth century.*

_____, 2. *Varnum Poor.* New York: Hyperion Press, Harper and Brothers, 1941. I.B. *Monograph.*

BOSWELL, PEYTON, Jr., ed. *An Appreciation of the Work of Frederic Taubes.* New York: Art Design Monographs, 1939. I. *Monograph.*

BOURDON, DAVID. *Christo.* New York: Harry N. Abrams Inc., 1971. I.B.C. *Considerable biographical data included in this critical study.*

BOURGEADE, PIERRE. *Bonsoir, Man Ray.* Paris: Pierre Belfond, 1972. *An interview, in French.*

BREEKSIN, A.D. 1. *Franz Kline.* Washington, D.C.: Washington Gallery of Modern Art, 1962. I. *Retrospective catalogue.*

_____, 2. *Ilya Bolotowsky.* New York: The Solomon R. Guggenheim Museum, 1974. I.B. *Retrospective catalogue; includes artist's statements.*

BRETON, ANDRE. 1. *Le Surrealisme et la peinture.* Paris: N.F.R., Gallimard, 1928. I. *The Surrealist movement in art.*

_____, 2. *Le Surrealisme et la peinture.* New York: Brentano's, 1945. I. *Revised and expanded edition of the above entry.*

_____3. *Le Surrealisme en 1947.* Paris: Editions Maeght, 1947.

_____, 4. *Yves Tanguy.* New York: Pierre Matisse Editions, 1946. I. (French and English text.) *Monograph.*

BRION, MARCEL. 1. *Art abstrait.* Paris: Editions Albin Michel, 1956. I.

(French text.) *Development of abstract art in the twentieth century.*

_____, 2. *Modern Painting: From Impressionism to Abstract Art.* London: Thames and Hudson, 1958. I.

BROOK, ALEXANDER. *Alexander Brook.* New York: American Artists Group Inc., 1945. I. *Autobiographical monograph.*

BROOKS, VAN WYCK. *John Sloan, a Painter's Life.* New York: E.P. Dutton, 1955. I. *Biography.*

BROWN, MILTON W. 1. *American Painting: From the Armory Show to the Depression.* Princeton, N.J.: Princeton University Press, 1955. I.B.

_____, 2. *The Modern Spirit. American Painting 1908–1935.* London: Arts Council of Great Britain, 1977. Foreword by Joanna Drew. I.B. *Major study of American art of this period seen in Britain.*

Bruce Conner Drawings: 1955–1972. San Francisco: San Francisco Museum of Art, 1974. Preface by Ian McKibbin White. Introduction by Thomas H. Garver. I. *Retrospective catalogue of drawings.*

BRUCE, EDWARD, AND WATSON, FORBES. *Art in Federal Buildings.* Washington, D.C.: Art in Federal Buildings, Inc., 1936. I.P.

BRUMME, C. LUDWIG. *Contemporary American Sculpture.* New York: Crown Publishers Inc., 1948. I.B.

BRYANT, EDWARD. *Nell Blaine.* Southampton, N.Y.: Parrish Art Museum, 1974. I.B.C. *Retrospective exhibition catalogue.*

BRYANT, LORINDA M. *American Pictures and Their Painters.* New York: John Lane Co., 1917. I.

BULLIET, C.J. 1. *Apples and Madonnas.* Chicago: Pascal Covici, Inc., 1927. I. *Critical essays on American artists.*

_____, 2. *The Significant Moderns and Their Pictures.* New York: Covici-Friede, Publishers, 1936. I.

BUNCE, LOUIS. *Louis Bunce.* Portland, Ore.: Portland Art Museum, 1955. I. *Exhibition catalogue.*

BURCHFIELD, CHARLES. 1. *Charles Burchfield.* Buffalo: Buffalo Fine Arts

Academy, Albright Art Gallery, 1944. I. *Exhibition catalogue.*

——, 2. *Charles Burchfield.* New York: American Artists Group Inc., 1945. I. *Autobiographical monograph.*

——, 3. *Eugene Speicher.* Buffalo: Albright Art Gallery, 1950. I. *Exhibition catalogue.*

BURROUGHS, ALAN. *Kenneth Hayes Miller.* New York: The Whitney Museum of American Art (American Artists Series), 1931. I.B. *Exhibition catalogue.*

BUSH, MARTIN H. 1. *Ben Shahn: The Passion of Sacco and Vanzetti.* Syracuse: Syracuse University, 1968. I.B. *A history of the development of the mural.*

——, 2. *Doris Caesar.* Syracuse, N.Y.: Syracuse University, 1970. Introduction by Marya Zaturenska. I.B. *Appreciation with some biographical data.*

BUSH, MARTIN H., and MOFFETT, KENWORTH. *Goodnough.* Wichita: Wichita Art Museum, 1973. I.B.C. Retrospective catalogue.

BYWATERS, JERRY. 1. *Andrew Dasburg.* Dallas: Dallas Museum of Fine Arts, 1957. I. *Exhibition catalogue.*

——, 2. *Andre Dasburg.* New York: American Federation of Arts, 1959. I. *Retrospective catalogue.*

CABANNE, PIERRE. *Dialogues with Marcel Duchamp.* Translated by Ron Padgett. New York: Viking Press (The Documents of 20th-Century Art), 1971. Preface by Salvador Dali. Introduction by Robert Motherwell. Appreciation by Jasper Johns. I.B.C. *Talking with Marcel, with an eye on history.*

CAGE, JOHN. *The Drawings of Morris Graves, with Comments by the Artist.* Boston: For the Drawing Society, Inc., by the New York Graphic Society Ltd., 1974. Preface by David Daniels. I.C. *Survey of drawings.*

CAHILL, HOLGER. *Max Weber.* New York: The Downtown Gallery, 1930. I. *Monograph.*

CAHILL, HOLGER, AND BARR, ALFRED, H., Jr., eds. *Art in America, a Complete Survey.* New York: Reynal and Hitchcock, 1935. I.B. *Considers architecture, fine arts, folk art, etc.*

CALAS, NICOLAS. *Bloodflames, 1947.* New York: Hugo Galleries, 1947. I. *Essays on the advance guard in New York in the 1940s.*

CALAS, NICOLAS and ELENA. *Icons and Images of the Sixties.* New York: E.P. Dutton, 1971. I. *Collected essays.*

CALDER, ALEXANDER. 1. *Calder: An autobiography with pictures.* New York: Pantheon Books, 1966. Foreword by Robert Osborn. I. *Folksy presentation of Calder's life.*

——, 2. *Three Young Rats.* New York: The Museum of Modern Art, 1946, 2nd ed. I. *A children's story.*

CALDER, ALEXANDER, and LIEDL, CHARLES. *Animal Sketching.* Pelham, N.Y.: Bridgeman Publishers, Inc., 1941, 6th ed. I.

CAMPOS, JULES. *Jose de Creeft.* New York: Erich S. Herrmann, Publisher, 1945. I. *Monograph.*

CANADAY, JOHN. *Mainstreams of Modern Art.* New York: Simon and Schuster, 1959. I. *Popular history of art.*

Carl Andre Sculpture: 1958–1974. Bern: Kunsthalle Bern, 1975. Foreword by Johannes Gachnang. Introduction by Carl Andre. I.B.C.

Carl Holty Memorial Exhibition. New York: Andrew Crispo Gallery, 1974. Introduction by Andrew J. Crispo. I.B.C. *Catalogue includes encomiums by friends.*

Carl Sprinchorn: A Memorial Exhibition. Orono, Me.: University of Maine, 1972. Foreword by Richard S. Sprague. I.C. *Exhibition catalogue.*

CARMEAN, E.A., Jr., and RATHBONE, ELIZA E., with HESS, THOMAS B. *American Art at Mid-Century: The Subjects of the Artist.* Washington, D.C.: National Gallery of Art, 1978. Foreword by J. Carter Brown. I. *A review of the major post-–World War II figures.*

Carol Summers. Woodcuts 1950–1967. San

Francisco: San Francisco Museum of Art, 1967. Preface by Anneliese Hoyer. I. *Retrospective catalogue; includes statements by the artist.*

CASSOU, JEAN. *Gateway to the 20th Century.* New York: McGraw-Hill Book Co., Inc., 1962. I. *Development of nineteenth-century art and indications of its twentieth-century ramifications.*

CELANT, GERMANO. *Arte Povera.* New York: Praeger Publishers, 1969. I. *Catalogues artists' statements and illustrations of their works: earthworks, actual art, concept art.*

Celebrate Ohio. Akron: Akron Art Institute, 1971. Foreword by Orrel Thompson. Introduction by Alfred Radloff. I.C. *Exhibition catalogue.*

CHAET, BERNARD. *Artists at Work.* Cambridge, Mass.: Webb Books Inc., 1960. I. *Interviews with artists.*

Charles Biederman: The Structurist Relief 1935–1964. Minneapolis: The Walker Art Center, 1965. Introduction by Jan van der Marck. I.B.G.C. *Retrospective catalogue.*

Charles Demuth: The Mechanical Encrusted on the Living. Santa Barbara: University of California Press, 1971. Introduction by Phyllis Plous. I.B.C. *A bad centennial retrospective catalogue.*

Charles Sheeler. Washington, D.C.: National Collection of Fine Arts, 1968. I.B. *Essays by Martin Friedman, Bartlett Hayes, Charles Millard; major retrospective catalogue.*

CHENEY, MARTHA CHANDLER. *Modern Art in America.* New York: Whittlesey House, McGraw-Hill Book Co., Inc., 1939. I.

The Chicago Connection. Sacramento: E.B. Crocker Art Gallery, 1976. Foreword by Wilma Beaty Cox. Introduction by Roger D. Clisby. I.B.C. *Survey exhibition of artists mostly born after the late 1930s.*

CHIPP, HERSCHEL B. *Theories of Modern Art.* Berkeley and Los Angeles: University of California Press, 1968. I.B. *Artists' statements.*

CHRISTENSEN, ERWIN O. *The History of Western Art.* New York: New American Library, 1959. I.

CHRIST-JANER, ALBERT. *Boardman Robinson.* Chicago: The University of Chicago Press, 1946. I.B. *Monograph.*

Cityscape 1919–39. Urban Themes in American, German, and British Art. London: Arts Council of Great Britain, 1977. Preface by Joanna Drew. Essays by Ian Jeffrey and David Mellor. I. *A study of the city and its inhabitants through the art produced therein.*

CLIFFORD, HENRY. *Franklin Watkins.* Philadelphia: The Philadelphia Museum of Art, 1964. I. *Exhibition catalogue.*

Clyfford Still. Foreword by Katherine Kuh. Buffalo: The Buffalo Fine Arts Academy, 1966. I. *Exhibition catalogue; includes statements by the artist.*

COATES, ROBERT M. *Walter Quirt.* New York: American Federation of Arts, 1959. I. *Retrospective catalogue.*

COKE, VAN DEREN. 1. *Nordfeldt, the Painter.* Albuquerque: The University of New Mexico Press, 1972. Foreword by Sheldon Cheney. I.B.C. *Exhibition catalogue.*

____, 2. *Taos and Santa Fe. The Artistic Environment. 1882–1942.* Albuquerque: University of New Mexico Press, 1963. I.

CONE, JANE HARRISON. 1. *David Smith.* Cambridge, Mass.: Fogg Art Museum, 1966. I.B. *Exhibition catalogue; includes statements by the artist.*

____, 2. *Walter Darby Bannard.* Baltimore: The Baltimore Museum of Art, 1972. Foreword by Tom Le Freudenheim. I.B. *Retrospective catalogue; includes artist's statements.*

Contemporanea. Rome: Incontri Internazionali d'Arte, 1973. Introduction by Graziella Lonardi. I.B. *(Italian and English text.) Comprehensive international avant-garde exhibition: art, cinema, theatre, photography, books, visual poetry, etc.*

COPLANS, JOHN. 1. *Ellsworth Kelly.* New York: Harry N. Abrams Inc., 1973. I.B.C. *Picturebook monograph.*

____, 2. *Roy Lichtenstein.* Pasadena: The Pasadena Art Museum, 1967. I.B. *Includes an interview with the artist.*

___, 3. *Serial Imagery*. Pasadena: The Pasadena Art Museum, 1968. I.B. *Includes statements by some artists.*

COPLANS, JOHN, ed. *Roy Lichtenstein.* New York: Praeger Publishers (Documentary Monographs in Modern Art), 1972. I.B. *Collected essays about the artist; monograph; biographical notes.*

COPLANS, JOHN, with contributions by JONAS MEKAS and CALVIN TOMKINS. *Andy Warhol.* Greenwich, Conn.: New York Graphic Society Ltd., 1970. I.B. *Monographic study; filmography.*

Correspondence, an Exhibition of the Letters of Ray Johnson. Raleigh, N.C.: North Carolina Museum of Art, 1976. Foreword by Moussa M. Domit. Introduction by William S. Wilson. I. *Mail art from the New York Correspondance School.*

CORTISSOZ, ROYAL. 1. *American Artists.* New York: Charles Scribner's Sons, 1923. *Essays on noted artists of the late nineteenth and early twentieth century.*

___, 2. *Guy Pene Du Bois.* New York: The Whitney Museum of American Art (American Artists Series), 1931. I.B. *Monograph.*

CRAVEN, THOMAS. 1. *Modern Art, The Men, The Movements, The Meaning.* New York: Simon and Schuster, 1934. I. *Essays on twentieth-century American figurative artists.*

___, 2. *The Story of Painting: From Cave Pictures to Modern Art.* New York: Simon and Schuster, 1943. I. *Popular history of art.*

___, 3. *Thomas Hart Benton.* New York: Associated American Artists, 1939. I. *Monograph.*

CRAVEN, WAYNE. *Sculpture in America.* New York: Thomas Y. Crowell Co., 1968. I.B. *Historical survey of traditional sculpture.*

CRESPELLE, J.-P. *Montparnasse vivant.* Paris, Hachette, 1962. I. *The panorama of Montparnasse life.*

CRICHTON, MICHAEL. *Jasper Johns.* New York: Harry N. Abrams Inc., Publishers, in association with The Whitney Museum of American Art, 1977. Foreword by Joseph F. Cullman, 3rd, and Tom Armstrong. I.B. *Exhibition catalogue.*

CRONE, RAINER. *Andy Warhol.* New York: Praeger Publishers, 1970. I.B. *Critical essays and catalogue of works; filmography.*

CUMMINGS, PAUL. 1. *Artists in Their Own Words.* New York: St. Martin's Press, Inc., 1979. I. *Interviews.*

___, 2. *David Smith: The Drawings.* New York: Whitney Museum of American Art, 1979. Foreword by Tom Armstrong. *Retrospective catalogue.*

___, 3. *Walter Murch.* Geneva: Galerie Jan Krugier, 1976. I.C. *Exhibition catalogue.*

CURRY, JOHN STEUART. 1. *John Steuart Curry.* New York: American Artists Group Inc., 1945. I. *Autobiographical monograph.*

___, 2. *John Steuart Curry.* Syracuse, N.Y.: Joe and Emily Lowe Art Center, Syracuse University, 1956. I. *Exhibition catalogue.*

___, 3. *John Steuart Curry.* Lawrence: University of Kansas, 1957. I. *Exhibition catalogue.*

Dan Flavin. Cologne: Kunsthalle Koln, 1973. I.B. (German and English text.) *Artist's statement.*

DAUBLER, THEODOR, and GOLL, IWAN. *Archipenko-Album.* Potsdam: Gustav Kiepenheuen Verlag, 1921. I. (German text.) *Monograph.*

DAVEY, RANDALL. *Randall Davey.* Santa Fe: Museum of New Mexico, 1957. I. *Exhibition catalogue.*

David Simpson 1957–1967. San Francisco: San Francisco Museum of Art, 1967. Preface by John Humphrey. I.B. *Retrospective catalogue; includes statements by the artist.*

DAVIDSON, MORRIS. 1. *An Approach to Modern Painting.* New York: Coward-McCann, Inc., 1948. I. *Appreciation of modern art.*

___, 2. *Understanding Modern Art.* New York: Coward-McCann, Inc., 1931. I. *Appreciation and understanding of mod-*

ern concepts in art.

DAVIES, HUGH MARLAIS. *Artist & Fabricator.* Amherst: University of Massachusetts, 1975. I. *Modern technology and commissioned sculpture; includes artists' statements.*

DAVIS, DOUGLAS. *Art and the Future.* New York: Praeger Publishers, 1973. I.B.D.G. *An effusion of the collaboration of art and science.*

DAVIS, STUART. *Stuart Davis.* New York: American Artists Group Inc., 1945. I. *Autobiographical monograph.*

DAWSON, FIELDING. *An Emotional Memoir of Franz Kline.* New York: Pantheon Books, 1967. I. *A personal memoir.*

DE CREEFT, JOSE. *Jose de Creeft.* Athens: University of Georgia Press (American Sculptors Series), 1950. I. *Autobiographical monograph.*

DEHN, ADOLF. *Watercolor Painting.* New York: Studio Publications, 1945. I.

DE KOONING, WILLEM. *De Kooning: Drawings.* New York: Walker & Co., 1967. I. *Two dozen charcoal drawings with a statement by the artist.*

DEVREE, CHARLOTTE. *Jose de Creeft.* New York: American Federation of Arts and The Ford Foundation, 1960. I. *Retrospective catalogue.*

DE VRIES, GERD, ed. *Uber Kunst/On Art.* Cologne: Verlag M. DuMont Schauberg, 1974. I.B. *(German and English text.) Artists writings on art after 1965; exhibition lists.*

D'HARNONCOURT, ANNE, and McSHINE, KYNASTON, eds. *Marcel Duchamp.* New York: The Museum of Modern Art and the Philadelphia Museum of Art, 1973. Preface by Richard E. Oldenburg and Evan H. Turner. Introduction by Anne d'Harnoncourt. I.C.B. *Retrospective exhibition catalogue.*

DIAMONSTEIN, BARBARALEE. *Inside New York's Art World.* New York: Rizzoli International Publications, Inc., 1979. I. *Transcribed from video interviews at the New School. Popular; occasional insights.*

DIENST, ROLF GUNTER. 1. *Pop-Art.* Wiesbaden: Limes Verlag, 1965. I.B. *(German text.) Pop art in Europe and the USA.*

_____, 2. *Richard Lindner.* New York: Harry N. Abrams Inc., 1970. I. *Critical study of the oeuvre.*

DOCHTERMAN, LILLIAN. *The Quest of Charles Sheeler.* Iowa City: State University of Iowa, 1963. I. *Biography.*

DORIVAL, BERNARD. *Twentieth Century Painters.* New York: Universe Books, Inc.; Paris: Editions Pierre Tisne, 1958. I.B. *Painting in Europe and America.*

DORNER, ALEXANDER. *The Way Beyond Art.* New York: New York University Press, 1958. I. *Development of art and its influence in the museums.*

DOVER, CEDRIC. *American Negro Art.* Greenwich Conn.: New York Graphic Society, 1965. I.B. *Illustrated history.*

DOWNES, RACKSTRAW, ed. *Fairfield Porter: Art in Its Own Terms.* New York: Taplinger Publishing Co., 1979. I. *Collected critical writings by the artist-writer.*

The Drawings of Charles E. Burchfield. Cleveland: Print Club of Cleveland and The Cleveland Museum of Art, 1953. I. *Exhibition catalogue. (See also Jones, ed.).*

Drawings: The Pluralist Decade. Philadelphia: Institute of Contemporary Art, University of Pennsylvania, 1980. Introduction by Janet Kardon. I.C. *39th Venice Biennale, US Pavilion, exhibition catalogue: exploratory essays by several critics.*

DREIER, KATHERINE S. 1. *Burliuk.* New York: The Societe Anonyme, Inc., 1944. I. *Monograph.*

_____, 2. *Western Art and the New Era, an Introduction to Modern Art.* New York: Brentano's, 1923. I. *Early polemic on abstract and nonfigurative art.*

DU BOIS, GUY PENE. 1. *Artists Say the Silliest Things.* New York: American Artists Group Inc., 1940. I. *Autobiography.*

_____, 2. *Edward Hopper.* New York: The

Whitney Museum of American Art (American Artists Series), 1931. I.B. *Monograph.*

____, 3. *Ernest Lawson.* New York: The Whitney Museum of American Art (American Artists Series), 1932. I.B. *Monograph.*

____, 4. *John Sloan.* New York: The Whitney Museum of American Art (American Artists Series), 1931. I.B. *Monograph.*

____, 5. *William Glackens.* New York: The Whitney Museum of American Art (American Artists Series), 1931. I.B. *Monograph.*

____, 6. *William Glackens.* New York: The Whitney Museum of American Art, 1939. *Exhibition catalogue.*

DUCHAMP, MARCEL. 1. *Marcel Duchamp.* Pasadena: The Pasadena Art Museum, 1963. I.B. *Exhibition catalogue.*

____, 2. *Marchand du Sel.* Paris: Le Terrain Vague, 1958. I.B. *Essays.*

EBERSOLE, BARBARA. *Fletcher Martin.* Gainesville: University of Florida Press, 1954. I. *Exhibition catalogue.*

Edward Kienholz. Dusseldorf: Stadtische Kunsthalle Dusseldorf, 1970. Introduction by Jurgen Harten. I.B.C. *Retrospective catalogue.*

Edward Kienholz: 11 + 11 Tableaux. Stockholm: Modern Museet, 1971. Introduction by K.G.P. Hulten. I.B. *Exhibition catalogue.*

8 American Masters of Watercolor. Los Angeles: County Museum of Art, 1968. Preface by Larry Curry. I.B. *Documented survey.*

ELIOT, ALEXANDER. *Three Hundred Years of American Painting.* New York: Time Inc., 1957. I.B. *Popular history of American art.*

ELLIOTT, JAMES. "Stuart Davis." *Bulletin of the Los Angeles County Museum of Art,* Vol. XIV, No. 3, 1962. I. *Entire issue devoted to this essay.*

ELSEN, ALBERT. 1. *Paul Jenkins.* New York: Harry N. Abrams Inc., 1973. I.B.C. *A major monograph.*

____, 2. *Purposes of Art.* New York: Holt

Rinehart and Winston, Inc., 1962. I.B. *Elucidation of the art process.*

____, 3. *Seymour Lipton.* New York: Harry N. Abrams Inc., 1969. I. *Monograph.*

ELY, CATHARINE BEACH. *The Modern Tendency in American Painting.* New York: Frederic Fairchild Sherman, 1925. I.

ETTING, EMLEN. *Drawing the Ballet.* New York: Studio Publications, 1944. I.

Eva Hesse: A Memorial Exhibition. New York: The Solomon R. Guggenheim Museum, 1972. I.B.C. *Retrospective exhibition catalogue; includes essays by Robert Pincus-Witten, Eva Hesse, Linda Shearer.*

EVANS, MYFANWY, ed. *The Painter's Object.* London: Gerald Howe Ltd., 1937. I. *Critical essays.*

FARNHAM, EMILY. *Charles Demuth: Behind a Laughing Mask.* Norman, Okla.: University of Oklahoma Press, 1971. I.B.C. *A poor book that fails profoundly.*

FARRELL, JAMES T. *The Paintings of Will Barnet.* New York: Press Eight, 1950. I. *Monograph.*

FAITH, CREEKMORE, ed. *The Lithographs of Thomas Hart Benton.* Austin and London: University of Texas Press, 1969. I. *Catalogue of the prints; includes comments by the artist.*

Fay Lansner. Swarthmore: Ava Books, 1976. Conversation with Irving H. Sandler. Introduction by Barbara Guest. I.B.C. *Illustrated essay.*

FEININGER, T. LUX. *Lyonel Feininger: At the Edge of the World.* New York: Frederick A. Praeger, 1968. I. *Essay on the development of imagery and ideas.*

FERN, ALAN. *Leonard Baskin.* Annotated by Leonard Baskin. Washington, D.C.: Smithsonian Institution Press, 1971. I.B.C. *Exhibition catalogue; filmography.*

FIERENS, PAUL. *Sculpteurs d'aujourd'hui.* Paris: Editions de Chroniques de Jour, 1933. I. (French text.)

Figures/Environments. Minneapolis: The

Walker Art Center, 1970. Introduction by Martin Friedman. I.C. *Exhibition catalogue.*

FINCH, CHRISTOPHER. *Pop Art: Object and Image.* New York: Studio Vista/Dutton Pictureback, 1968. I. *Well-illustrated popular assessment of international pop art.*

FINKELSTEIN, SIDNEY. *Realism in Art.* New York: International Publishers, 1954.

FLANAGAN, GEORGE A. *Understanding and Enjoying Modern Art.* New York: Thomas Y. Crowell Co., 1962. I.B.

FLEXNER, JAMES THOMAS. *A Short History of American Painting.* Boston: Houghton Mifflin Co., 1950. I.B. *Authoritative history of American painting.*

FLOCKHART, LOLITA L.W. *Art and Artists in New Jersey.* Somerville, N.J.: C.P. Hoagland Co., 1938. I.

FORD, CHARLES HENRI. *Poems for Painters.* New York: View Editions, 1945. I. *Poems illustrated by surrealist artists.*

Forerunners of American Abstraction. Pittsburgh: Museum of Art, Carnegie Institute, 1971. Foreword by Leon Anthony Arkus. Introduction by Herdis Bull Teilman. I.B. *Survey exhibition with biographical sketches.*

FOSTER, JOSEPH K. *Raphael Soyer, Drawings and Watercolors.* New York: Crown Publishers Inc., 1968. I. *A selection of 52 watercolors and 72 drawings.*

FRANK, WALDO, ed. *America and Alfred Stieglitz.* Garden City, N.Y.: Doubleday, Doran and Co., Inc., 1934. I. *A history of Alfred Stieglitz and his influence.*

FRASCONI, ANTONIO. *Against the Grain: The Woodcuts of Antonio Frasconi.* New York: Macmillan Publishing Co. Inc., 1974. Introduction by Nat Hentoff. Appreciation by Charles Parkhurst. I.D. *Thirty-five years of his woodcuts reviewed; includes section on his methods.*

Frederick Kiesler Architekt: 1890–1965. Vienna: Galerie Nachst St. Stephan, 1975. Introduction by Friedrich St. Florian. I.D.P. *Retrospective catalogue; includes artist's statements.*

FREUNDLICH, AUGUST L. *William Gropper: Retrospective.* Los Angeles: Ward Ritchie Press, 1968. I.B. *Retrospective catalogue including statements by the artist.*

FRIED, MICHAEL. 1. *Morris Louis.* Boston: Museum of Fine Arts, 1967. I.B. *Major retrospective catalogue including essay by Clement Greenberg.*

_____, 2. *Morris Louis.* New York: Harry N. Abrams Inc., 1970. I. *Monograph.*

FRIEDMAN, B.H. 1. *Alfonso Ossorio.* New York: Harry N. Abrams Inc., 1971. I.B.C. *Picturebook monograph.*

_____, 2. *Jackson Pollock: Energy Made Visible.* New York: McGraw-Hill Book Co., 1972. I.B. *A biographical study of the painter.*

FRIEDMAN, B.H., ed. *School of New York: Some Younger Artists.* New York: Grove Press, Inc., 1959. I. *Younger artists of promise in the 1950s.*

FRIEDMAN, MARTIN. 1. *Adolph Gottlieb.* Minneapolis: The Walker Art Center, 1963. I.B. *Exhibition catalogue.*

_____, 2. *14 Sculptors: The Industrial Edge.* Minneapolis: The Walker Art Center, 1969. I.B. *Exhibition catalogue with essays by Barbara Rose, Christopher Finch, and Martin Friedman.*

_____, 3. *Nevelson Wood Sculpture.* New York: E.P. Dutton, n.d. I.B.C. *Exhibition catalogue.*

FRIEDMAN, MARTIN, and VAN DER MARCK, JAN. *Eight Sculptors: The Ambiguous Image.* Minneapolis: The Walker Art Center, 1966. I.B.C. *Exhibition catalogue.*

Fritz Glarner. Bern: Kunsthalle Bern, 1972. Foreword by Max Bill. I.B. *Retrospective catalogue.*

From Foreign Shores. Milwaukee: Milwaukee Art Center, 1976. Introduction by I. Michael Danoff. I. *Bicentennial survey of emigrant artists from colonial times to the present.*

FROST, ROSAMOND. *Contemporary Art: The March of Art from Cezanne Until Now.* New York: Crown Publishers Inc., 1942. I.B.

FRY, EDWARD. *David Smith.* New York: The Solomon R. Guggenheim Museum, 1969. I.B. *Retrospective catalogue.*

Fundamentele Schilderkunst/Fundamental Painting. Amsterdam: Stedelijk Museum, 1975. Essay by Rini Dippel. Preface by E. de Wilde. I.B.C. *International minimalist painting.*

GABLIK, SUZI. *Progress in Art.* New York: Rizzoli International Publications Inc., 1977. I.B. *A proposed aesthetic for an abstract nonfigurative art.*

GABO, NAUM. *Of Divers Arts.* London: Faber and Faber, Ltd., 1962. I. *Critical essays.*

GALLATIN, A.E. 1. *American Watercolourists.* New York: E. P. Dutton, 1922. I.

____, 2. *Certain Contemporaries: A Set of Notes in Art Criticism.* New York: John Lane Co., 1916.

____, 3. *Gallatin Inconography.* n.p.: Privately published, 1934. I. *Genealogy through portraits.*

____, 4. *Gaston Lachaise.* New York: E. P. Dutton, 1924. I. *Critical essay.*

____, 5. *John Sloan.* New York: E.P. Dutton, 1925. I. *Critical essay.*

____, 6. *Paintings by Gallatin.* New York: Wittenborn, Schultz, Inc., 1948. I.B.

____, 7. *Paul Manship.* New York: John Lane Co., 1917. I.B. *Critical essay.*

____, 8. *Whistler, Notes and Footnotes.* New York: The Collector and Art Critic Co., 1907. I. *Critical essays.*

GARVER, THOMAS H. *George Tooker.* San Francisco: California Palace of the Legion of Honor, 1974. I.B.C. *Retrospective catalogue.*

GARWOOD, DARRELL. *Artist in Iowa.* New York: W. W. Norton and Co., 1944. *Biography.*

GASCOYNE, DAVID. *A Short Survey of Surrealism.* London: Cobden-Sanderson, 1935. I. *Essays and documentation.*

GAUNT, WILLIAM. *The Observer's Book of Modern Art from Impressionism to the Present Day.* London: Frederick Warne and Co. Ltd., 1964. I.G.

GENAUER, EMILY. *Best of Art.* Garden City, N.Y.: Doubleday and Co. Inc., 1948. I. *Painting during the 1940s.*

Gene Davis. San Francisco: San Francisco Museum of Art, 1968. Preface by Gerald Nordland. I.B. *One-man exhibition.*

George Grosz: Dessins et Aquarelles. Paris: Galerie Claude Bernard, 1966. Preface by Edouard Roditi. I. *Exhibition catalogue.*

George Rickey. Los Angeles: University of California, Los Angeles, 1971. An interview by Frederick S. Wight. I.B.D.C. *Exhibition catalogue.*

GEORGE, WALDEMAR. 1. *Les Artistes juifs et l'ecole de Paris.* Algiers: Editions du Congres Juif Mondial, 1959. I. (French text.)

____, 2. *John D. Graham.* Paris: Editions Le Triangle, n.d. I. *Critical essay.*

GERDTS, WILLIAM H., Jr. *Painting and Sculpture in New Jersey.* Princeton, N.J.: D. Van Nostrand, 1964. Foreword by Richard J. Hughes. I.B.D. *The first art history of New Jersey.*

GERSTNER, KARL. Kalte Kunst. Switzerland: Verlag Arthur Niggli, 1957. I. *(German text.) Hard-edge paintings and sculpture.*

GERTZ, ULRICH. *Contemporary Plastic Art.* Berlin: Rembrandt/Verlag, GMBH, 1955. I. (German and English text.) *Postwar painting in Europe, including American influence.*

GESKE, NORMAN A. *The Figurative Tradition in Recent American Art.* Washington, D.C.: National Collection of Fine Arts, 1968. *Catalogue for the 34th International Biennial, Venice.*

GETLEIN, FRANK. 1. *Chaim Gross.* New York: Harry N. Abrams Inc., 1974. I.B.C. *Illustrated monograph.*

____, 2. *Jack Levine.* New York: Harry N. Abrams Inc., n.d. I. *Monograph.*

____, 3. *Peter Blume.* New York: Kennedy Galleries, 1968. I. *Exhibition catalogue.*

GETLEIN, FRANK and DOROTHY. *Christianity in Art.* Milwaukee: The Bruce Publishing Co., 1959. I.B.

GIEDION-WELCKER, CAROLA. 1.

Contemporary Sculpture: An Evolution in Volume and Space. Documents of Modern Art, Vol. 12. New York: George Wittenborn, Inc., 1955. I.B.

____, 2. *Modern Plastic Art: Elements of Reality, Volume and Disintegration.* Zurich: Dr. H. Girsberger, 1937. I.B. *Twentieth-century sculpture.*

GLACKENS, IRA. *William Glackens and the Ashcan Group: The Emergence of Realism in American Art.* New York: Crown Publishers Inc., 1957. I.

GLIMCHER, ARNOLD B. *Louise Nevelson.* New York: Praeger Publishers, 1972. I.C. *Monograph.*

GOLDWATER, ROBERT, and TREVES, MARCO, eds. *Artists on Art. From the XIV to the XX Century.* New York: Pantheon Books, 1945. I.

GOMRINGER, EUGEN. *Josef Albers.* New York: George Wittenborn, Inc., 1968. I.B. *Essays on all the aspects of Albers's work, with comments by the artist.*

GOODRICH, LLOYD. 1. *American Watercolors and Winslow Homer.* New York: The Walker Art Center, for American Artists Group Inc., 1945. I.

____, 2. *The Drawings of Edwin Dickinson.* New Haven, Conn.: Yale University Press, 1963. I.

____, 3. *Edward Hopper.* New York: Penguin Books, 1949. I. *Monograph.*

____, 4. *Edward Hopper.* New York: The Whitney Museum of American Art, 1956. I.B. *Exhibition catalogue.*

____, 5. *Edwin Dickinson.* New York: The Whitney Museum of American Art, 1965. I.B. *Retrospective catalogue.*

____, 6. *H. E. Schnakenberg.* New York: The Whitney Museum of American Art (American Artists Series), 1931. I.B. *Monograph.*

____, 7. *John Sloan.* New York: The Whitney Museum of American Art, 1952. I.B. *Exhibition catalogue.*

____, 8. *Kuniyoshi.* New York: The Whitney Museum of American Art, 1948. I. *Exhibition catalogue.*

____, 9. *Max Weber.* New York: The Whitney Museum of American Art, 1949. I. *Exhibition catalogue.*

____, 10. *Raphael Soyer.* New York: The Whitney Museum of American Art, 1967. I.B. *Retrospective catalogue.*

____, 11. *Reginald Marsh.* New York: The Whitney Museum of American Art, 1955. I. *Exhibition catalogue.*

GOODRICH, LLOYD, and BAUR, JOHN I.H. 1. *American Art of Our Century.* New York: The Whitney Museum of American Art, 1961. I. *Development of American Art illustrated through the collection of the WMAA.*

____, 2. *Four American Expressionists.* New York: The Whitney Museum of American Art, 1949. I. *Exhibition catalogue: Doris Caesar, Chaim Gross, Karl Knaths, Abraham Rattner.*

GOODRICH, LLOYD, and IMGIZUMI, ATSUO. *Kuniyoshi.* Tokyo: National Museum of Modern Art, 1954. I. (Japanese and English text.) *Retrospective catalogue.*

GOODRICH, LLOYD, and MANDEL, PATRICIA FITZG. *John Heliker.* New York: The Whitney Museum of American Art, 1968. I.B. *Retrospective catalogue.*

GOODYEAR, FRANK H., Jr. *8 Contemporary Realists.* Philadelphia: Pennsylvania Academy of the Fine Arts, 1977. Preface by Richard J. Boyle. Acknowledgments by Frank H. Goodyear, Jr. I. *An exploration of realism, its definitions and uses.*

GOOSSEN, E.C. 1. *The Art of the Real USA 1948–1968.* New York: The Museum of Modern Art, 1968. I.B. *A proposal that some art is more "real" than other art.*

____, 2. *Ellsworth Kelly.* New York: The Museum of Modern Art, 1973. I.B.A. *Retrospective monograph.*

____, 3. *Helen Frankenthaler.* New York: The Whitney Museum of American Art, 1969. I.B. *Retrospective catalogue.*

____, 4. *Stuart Davis.* New York: George Braziller, Inc., 1959. I.B. *Monograph.*

____, 5. *Three American Sculptors.* New York: Grove Press Inc., 1959. I. *Monograph: Herbert Ferber, David Hare, Ibram Lassaw.*

GORDON, JOHN. 1. *Franz Kline.* New York: The Whitney Museum of American Art, 1968. I.B.C. *Retro-*

spective catalogue.

———, 2. *Isamu Noguchi.* New York: The Whitney Museum of American Art, 1968. I.B.C. *Retrospective catalogue.*

———, 3. *Karl Schrag.* New York: American Federation of Arts and The Ford Foundation, 1960. I. *Retrospective catalogue.*

———, 4. *Louise Nevelson.* New York: The Whitney Museum of American Art, 1967. I.B. *Retrospective catalogue.*

Graham, Gorky, Smith & Davis in the Thirties. Providence: Brown University, 1977. Foreword by William H. Jordy. Introduction by Ellen Lawrence. I.B.C. *Examines interplay and evolution of these artists' work in one decade.*

GRAHAM, JOHN D. *System and Dialectics of Art.* New York: Delphic Studios, 1937. *Critical essays.*

The Great Decade of American Abstraction: Modernist Art 1960 to 1970. Houston: The Museum of Fine Arts, 1974. Foreword by R. A. Carmean, Jr. Introduction by Philippe de Montebello. I.B. *Exhibition catalogue; reprints, critical essays, and essays on the conservation of color-field paintings.*

GREEN, SAMUEL ADAMS. *Andy Warhol.* Philadelphia: Institute of Contemporary Art, 1965. I. *Exhibition catalogue.*

GREENBERG, CLEMENT. 1. *Art and Culture.* Boston: Beacon Press, 1961. *Critical essays.*

———, 2. *Hofmann.* Paris: The Pocket Museum, Editions George Fall, 1961. I. *Monograph.*

GREENGOOD, LILLIAN. *Great Artists of America.* New York: Thomas Y. Crowell Co., 1963. I.B. *Popular biographical essays.*

GROSS, CHAIM. *Fantasy Drawings.* New York: Beechhurst Press (A Bittner Art Book), 1956. I. *Drawings.*

GROSSER, MAURICE. 1. *The Painter's Eye.* New York: Rinehart and Co., Inc., 1951. I. *Essays on divers topics.*

———, 2. *Painting in Public.* New York: Alfred A. Knopf, 1948. *Autobiographical.*

GROSZ, GEORGE. 1. *George Grosz.*

Berlin: Akadmie der Kunste, 1962. I. *Retrospective catalogue.*

———, 2. *George Grosz Drawings.* New York: H. Bittner and Co., 1944. I. *Drawings.*

———, 3. *Die Gezeichneten.* Berlin: Malik Verlag, 1930. I. (German text.) *Drawings.*

———, 4. *A Little Yes and a Big No. The Autobiography of George Grosz.* New York: The Dial Press, 1946. I.

———, 5. *Der Spiesser-Spiegel.* Dresden: Carl Reisser Verlag, 1925. I. (German text.) *Drawings.*

GUEST, BARBARA, and FRIEDMAN, B.H. *Goodnough.* Paris: The Pocket Museum, Editions George Fall, 1962. I. *Monograph.*

GUGGENHEIM, PEGGY, ed. *Art of This Century.* New York: Art of This Century, 1942. I. *Documents her New York gallery.*

GUTMAN, WALTER, K. *Raphael Soyer, Paintings and Drawings.* New York: Shorewood Publishing Co., Inc., 1960. I. *Monograph.*

HAAS, IRVIN. *A Treasury of Great Prints.* New York: Thomas Yoseloff Inc., 1959. I.

HAFTMAN, WERNER. *Paintings in the Twentieth Century.* New York: Frederick A. Praeger, 1960. 2 vols. I. *A major history of twentieth-century art.*

HAHN, OTTO. *Arman.* Paris: Fernand Hazan Editeur, 1972. I.B. (French text.) *Appreciation with biographical information.*

HALE, ROBERT BEVERLY. *Waldo Peirce.* New York: American Artists Group Inc., 1945. I. *Monograph.*

HALL, W.S. *Eyes on America.* New York: Studio Publications, 1939. I. *Figurative painting in America.*

HALPERT, EDITH GREGOR. *The Downtown Gallery.* New York: The Downtown Gallery, 1943. I. *Documents members of the gallery.*

HAMILTON, GEORGE H. *Josef Albers.* New Haven, Conn.: Yale University Art Gallery, 1956. I. *Exhibition catalogue.*

HAMILTON, RICHARD. *The Bride Stripped Bare by her Bachelors, Even.* New York: George Wittenborn, Inc., 1960. *Documentary essay on Marcel Duchamp.*

HANSEN, AL. *A Primer of Happenings and Time/Space Art.* New York: Something Else Press Inc., 1965. I. *People places events and Hansen in happenings and time/space.*

Happening & Fluxus. Cologne: Kolnischer Kunstverein. I.B.D.P.C. *The major documentary resource on happening, fluxus, events, non-art, 1959–1970.*

HARTLEY, MARSDEN. *Adventures in the Arts.* New York: Boni and Liveright, Inc., 1921. *Autobiography.*

HARTMANN, SADIKICHI. *A History of American Art.* Boston: L.C. Page and Co., 1932, rev. ed., 2 vols. I. *Important history of American art.*

HASKELL, BARBARA. 1. *Arthur Dove.* San Francisco: San Francisco Museum of Art, 1974. I.B.C. *Retrospective catalogue.*

____, 2. *Claes Oldenburg: Object into Monument.* Pasadena: The Pasadena Art Museum, 1971. I.B.C. *Exhibition catalogue with comments on individual pieces by the artist.*

____, 3. *H.C.W.* New York: The Whitney Museum of American Art. Introduction by Tom Armstrong. I.B.C. *Retrospective catalogue of H. C. Westermann.*

____, 4. *Marsden Hartley.* New York: The Whitney Museum of American Art in association with NYU Press, 1980. Forewords by Tom Armstrong and A. James Speyer. I.B.C. *Retrospective exhibition catalogue.*

HAYTER, S.W. 1. *About Prints.* London: Oxford University Press, 1962. I.B. *Print appreciation and techniques.*

____, 2. *New Ways of Gravure.* New York: Pantheon Books, 1949. I.D. *Printmaking techniques.*

HEADLEY, DIANE UPRIGHT. *The Drawings of Morris Louis.* Washington, D.C.: National Collection of Fine Arts, 1979. Foreword by Joshua C. Taylor. I. *Exhibition and catalogue raisonné.*

HELD, JULIUS S. *Joseph Floch.* New York: Thomas Yoseloff Inc., 1968. Foreword by Jean Cassou. I. *Monograph.*

HELM, MacKINLEY. *John Marin.* New York: Pellegrini and Cudahy, 1948. I. *Monograph.*

HELM, MacKINLEY, and WIGHT, FREDERICK S. *John Marin.* Boston: Institute of Modern Art, 1947. I. *Exhibition catalogue.*

HENNING, EDWARD. B. *Paths of Abstract Art.* Cleveland: The Cleveland Museum of Art, 1960. I. *Twentieth-century development of abstract art.*

HESS, HANS. *Lyonel Feininger.* London: Thames and Hudson, 1961. I.B. *Catalogue raisonné.*

HESS, THOMAS B. 1. *Abstract Painting: Background and American Phase.* New York: Viking Press, 1951. I. *Important documentation of abstract painting in America.*

____, 2. *Barnett Newman.* New York: Walker & Co., 1969. I.B. *Monograph.*

____, 3. *Barnett Newman.* New York: The Museum of Modern Art, 1971. I.B. *Retrospective monograph.*

____, 4. *Willem de Kooning.* New York: The Museum of Modern Art, 1968. I.B. *Retrospective monograph; includes statements by the artist.*

____, 5. *Willem de Kooning: Drawings.* Greenwich, Conn.: New York Graphic Society Ltd., 1972. I.B.C. *Essays on his drawings.*

HILDEBRANDT, HANS. *Alexander Archipenko.* Berlin: Ukrainske Slowo Publishers Ltd., 1923. I. (Ukrainian and English text.) *Monograph.*

HILL, ANTHONY, ed. *D.A.T.A.—Directions in Art, Theory and Aesthetics.* London: Faber and Faber, Ltd., 1968. I.B. *Collected statements by neoplastic and kinetic artists, including Charles Biederman.*

HIRSCH, RICHARD. *Charles Sheeler.* Allentown, Pa.: Allentown Art Museum, 1961. I. *Exhibition catalogue.*

HOBBS, ROBERT CARLETON, and LEVIN, GAIL. *Abstract Expression-*

ism: *The Formative Years.* Ithaca: Herbert F. Johnson Museum of Art, 1978. Introduction by Thomas W. Leavitt and Tom Armstrong. I. *A singular account of the evolution of this theory.*

HOFMANN, HANS. *Search for the Real.* Andover, Mass.: Addison Gallery of American Art, 1948. I. *Hofmann's theory of painting.*

HOLME, BRYAN. 1. *Master Drawing in Line.* New York: Studio Publications, 1948. I.

____, 2. *Master Drawings.* New York: Studio Publications, 1943. I.

HOLT, NANCY, ed. *The Writings of Robert Smithson: Essays with Illustrations.* New York: New York University Press, 1979. Introduction by Philip Leider. I. *Biographical note. The collected writings and interviews.*

HONIG, EDWIN. *Mauricio Lasansky— The Nazi Drawings.* Iowa City: Mauricio Lasansky Foundation, 1966. I. *Exhibition catalogue.*

HONISCH, DIETER, and JENSEN, JENS CHRISTIAN, eds. *Amerikanische Kunst von 1945 bis heute. Kunst der USA in europaischen Sammlungen.* Koln: DuMont Buchverlag, 1976. I.D. (German text.) *Collected essays in this major study on the exhibition of, collecting of, and critical efforts concerning American art. Works in public collections and lists of influential exhibitions.*

HONNEF, KLAUS. *Concept Art.* Cologne: Phaidon Verlag, 1971. I.B.D.C. (German text.) *Critical essay including artists' statements and documentation.*

HOOPES, DONELSON F. *William Zorach.* New York: Brooklyn Museum, 1968. I. *Retrospective of the paintings, drawings, and watercolors.*

HOPE, HENRY R. *The Sculpture of Jacques Lipchitz.* New York: The Museum of Modern Art, 1954. I.B. *Exhibition catalogue.*

HOPPER, EDWARD. *Edward Hopper.* New York: American Artists Group, Inc., 1945. I. *Autobiographical monograph.*

HOPPS, WALTER. *Frank Lobdell.* Pasadena: The Pasadena Art Museum, 1966. I. *Retrospective catalogue.*

HOVING, THOMAS. *Two Worlds of Andrew Wyeth: A Conversation with Andrew Wyeth.* Boston: Houghton Mifflin Co., 1978. I. *A lengthy interview.*

HOWARD, CHARLES. *Charles Howard.* San Francisco: California Palace of The Legion of Honor, 1946. I.B. *Exhibition catalogue.*

Howard Kanovitz. Duisburg: Wilhelm-Lehmbruck-Museum, 1974. I.B.C. (German and English text.) *Ten-year retrospective including artist's statements.*

HUBER, CARLO. *Cy Twombly. Bilder 1953–1972.* Bern: Kunsthalle Bern, 1973. Foreword by Carlo Huber and Michael Pelzet. I.C. (German text.) *Exhibition catalogue.*

HULTEN, K.G. PONTUS. *The Machine.* New York: The Museum of Modern Art, 1968. I.B. *Art and the mechanical age.*

HUMPHREY, JOHN. *Roy De Forest: Retrospective.* San Francisco: San Francisco Museum of Art, 1974. I.B.C. *Catalogue including artist's statements.*

HUNTER, SAM. 1. *Art since 1945.* New York: Harry N. Abrams Inc., 1958. I.B. *Comprehensive study of world art since 1945.*

____, 2. *Hans Hofmann.* New York: Harry N. Abrams Inc., 1962. I.B. *Monograph.*

____, 3. *James Brooks.* New York: The Whitney Museum of American Art, 1963. I.B. *Retrospective catalogue.*

____, 4. *James Metcalf.* Chicago: William and Noma Copley Foundation, n.d. I. *Monograph.*

____, 5. *Larry Rivers.* New York: Harry N. Abrams Inc., 1970. I. *Monograph.*

____, 6. *Modern American Painting and Sculpture.* New York: Dell Publishing Co., 1959. I. *Concise history of American art since 1900; includes biographies.*

____, 7. *Philip Guston.* New York: Jewish Museum 1966. I.B. *Major retrospective catalogue, including a dialogue with Harold Rosenberg.*

____, 8. *Rosenthal: Sculpture.* New York: M. Knoedler & Co., n.d. I. *Exhibition catalogue, including dialogue with the artist.*

HUNTER, SAM, ed. 1. *The Dada/Surrealist Heritage.* Williamstown: Sterling and Francine Clark Art Institute, 1977. I.B. *Williams College student exhibition of fine quality.*

____, 2. *New York Around the World: Painting and Sculpture.* New York: Harry N. Abrams Inc., 1966. I. *16 essays on the most modern art since 1945, updated to 1966.*

HUYGHE, RENE. *Histoire de l'art contemporain. La Peinture.* Paris: Librairie Felix Alcan, 1936. I.B. (French text.)

IGNATOFF, DAVID. *Kopman.* New York: E. Weyhe, 1930. I. *Monograph.*

Index of 20th Century Artists. New York: The College Art Association, 1933–37, 4 vols. B. *Comprehensive reference on American artists of the 1920s and 1930s.*

IRWIN, ROBERT. *Robert Irwin.* New York: The Whitney Museum of American Art, 1977. I.B.D.P. *Exhibition catalogue.*

Isabel Bishop. Tucson: University of Arizona Museum of Art, 1974. Foreword by Sheldon Reich. Introduction by Martin H. Bush. B. *Retrospective catalogue.*

Isamu Noguchi. Tokyo: Minami Gallery, 1973. I.D.C. (English and Japanese text.) *Exhibition catalogue: includes artist's statements.*

JACKMAN, RILLA EVELYN. *American Arts.* Chicago: Rand McNally and Co., 1928. I.B. *Popular essays on the arts.*

JACOBSON, J.Z., ed. *Art of Today: Chicago 1933.* Chicago: L. M. Stein, 1932. I.

JAKOVSKI, ANATOLE. *Arp, Calder, Helion, Miro, Pevsner, Seligmann.* Paris: Chez J. Povolozky, 1933. I. (French text.)

JANIS, HARRIET, and BLESH, RUDI. 1. *Collage. Personalities—Concepts—Techniques.* Philadelphia and New York: Chilton Co., 1962. I.G. *Documents development of collage in the world.*

____, 2. *de Kooning.* New York: Grove Press Inc., 1960. I. *Monograph.*

JANIS, SIDNEY. *Abstract and Surrealist Art in America.* New York: Reynal and Hitchcock, 1944. I. *Essays on the two schools of art in the 1940s.*

Jan Matulka. 1890–1972. Washington, D.C.: Smithsonian Institution Press, 1980. Foreword by Joshua C. Taylor. Acknowledgments. Introduction by Patterson Sims and Merry A. Fresta. Essays by Patterson Sims, Merry A. Fresta, Dorothy Dehner, Janet A. Flint. I.B.C. *Retrospective catalogue; includes a checklist of prints.*

Jason Seley. Ithaca: Herbert F. Johnson Museum of Art, Cornell University, 1980. Foreword by Thomas W. Leavitt. Introduction by Edward Bryant. I.B. *Retrospective catalogue.*

JENKINS, PAUL and ESTHER, eds. *Observations of Michael Tapie.* New York: George Wittenborn, Inc., 1956. I.A. *Collection of the critic's commentaries.*

Jeremy Anderson. San Francisco: San Francisco Museum of Art, 1966. Preface by Gerald Nordland. I.B. *Retrospective catalogue.*

JEWELL, EDWARD ALDEN. 1. *Alexander Brook.* New York: The Whitney Museum of American Art (American Artists Series), 1931. I.B. *Monograph.*

____, 2. *. . . America.* New York: Alfred A. Knopf, 1930. I. *Critical essays.*

____, 3. *Have We an American Art?* New York and Toronto: Longmans, Green and Co., 1939. *Critical essays.*

Joan Mitchell: My Five Years in the Country. Syracuse: Everson Museum of Art, 1972. Introduction by James Harithas. I.B.C. *Exhibition catalogue.*

John Altoon. San Francisco: San Francisco Museum of Art, 1967. Preface by Gerald Nordland. I.B. *Retrospective catalogue.*

John McLaughlin. La Jolla: La Jolla Museum of Contemporary Art, 1973. Foreword by Jay Belloli. Introduction by John McLaughlin. I.B.C. *Retrospective catalogue.*

JOHNSON, ELLEN H. *Modern Art and the Object.* New York: Harper & Row, Publishers (Icon Editions), 1976. I. Index. *Collected essays on modern art.*

JOHNSON, UNA E. 1. *Gabor Peterdi.* New York: Brooklyn Museum, 1959. I. *Exhibition catalogue.*

_____, 2. *Isabel Bishop.* New York: Brooklyn Museum, 1964. I.B. *The prints and drawings of Miss Bishop with two essays by the artists.*

_____, 3. *Paul Cadmus.* New York: Brooklyn Museum, 1968. I.B. *Catalogue of an exhibition of prints and drawings.*

John Willenbecher. Allentown: Allentown Art Museum, 1978. Foreword by Richard N. Gregg. Introduction by Jean-Louis Bourgeois. I.B. *Retrospective catalogue including artist's statements.*

JONES, DAN BURNE. *The Prints of Rockwell Kent.* Chicago: The University of Chicago Press, 1975. Foreword by Carl Zigrosser. I.B. *Catalogue raisonné.*

JONES, EDITH H., ed. *The Drawings of Charles Burchfield.* New York: Frederick A. Praeger, 1968. I. *A pictorial survey. (See also under "Drawings . . ." for Cleveland volume.)*

Jose De Rivera: Retrospective Exhibition 1930–1971. La Jolla: La Jolla Museum of Contemporary Art, 1972. Introduction by Thomas B. Tibbs. I.C. *Includes catalogue raisonné of 191 works.*

Joseph Goto. Providence: Rhode Island School of Design, 1971. Foreword by Stephen E. Ostrow. Introduction by William H. Jordy. I.C. *Exhibition catalogue.*

Joseph Hirsch. Athens, Ga.: Georgia Museum of Art, 1970. Foreword by William D. Paul, Jr. Introduction by Frank Getlein. I.C.B. *Exhibition catalogue.*

JOYNER, BROOKS. *The Drawings of Arshile Gorky.* College Park, Md.:

University of Maryland, 1969. Preface by George Levitine. Foreword by William H. Gerdts. I.B. *Major essay on the drawings.*

JUIN, HUBERT. *Seize peintres de la jeune ecole de Paris.* Paris: Le Musée de Poche, 1956. I.

KALLEM, H. M. *Maurice Sterne.* New York: The Museum of Modern Art, 1933. I.B. *Exhibition catalogue.*

KAPROW, ALLAN. *Assemblage, Environments and Happenings.* New York: Harry N. Abrams Inc., 1965. I. *Scripts. A major illustrated and documented book.*

KARFIOL, BERNARD. *Bernard Karfiol.* New York: American Artists Group Inc., 1945. I. *Autobiographical monograph.*

KARSHAN, DONALD. *Archipenko: The Sculpture and Graphic Art.* Tubingen: Ernst Wasmuth Verlag, 1974. I.B.C. *Catalogue raisonné.*

KATZ, LESLIE. *William Glackens in Retrospect.* St. Louis: The City Art Museum, 1966. I.B. *Major retrospective catalogue.*

KECKEMET, DUSKO. *Ivan Mestrovic.* Zagreb: Spektan Cpg Delo, 1970. I.B. *Poorly translated, but a major resource.*

KELDER, DIANE, ed. *Stuart Davis.* Documentary Monographs in Modern Art. New York: Praeger Publishers, 1971. I.B.C. *Collected writing of and about the artist. Monograph.*

KENT, NORMAN. *Drawings by American Artists.* New York: Watson-Guptill Publishing Co. Inc., 1947. I.

KENT, ROCKWELL. 1. *It's Me O Lord.* New York: Dodd, Mead and Co., 1955. I. *Autobiography.*

_____, 2. *Rockwell Kent.* New York: American Artists Group Inc., 1945. I. *Autobiographical monograph.*

_____, 3. *Rockwellkentiana.* New York: Harcourt, Brace and Co., 1945. I. *Autobiographical monograph.*

KENT, ROCKWELL, ed. *World Famous Paintings.* New York: Wise and Co., 1939. I. *Paintings of all ages.*

KEPES, GYORGY. 1. *Language of Vi-*

sion. Chicago: Paul Theobold and Co., 1944. I. *An aesthetic of seeing.*

———, 2. *The New Landscape in Art and Science.* Chicago: Paul Theobald and Co., 1956. I. *Convolutions of science and art.*

KEPES, GYORGY, ed. *The Visual Arts Today.* Middletown, Conn.: Wesleyan University Press, 1960. I.B. *Essays on architecture, fine arts, graphics, typography, etc.*

KIRBY, MICHAEL. *Happenings.* New York: E.P. Dutton, 1965. I. *A history with scripts of the happenings.*

KIRSTEIN, LINCOLN. 1. *Elie Nadelman.* New York: The Eakins Press, 1973. I.B. *Catalogue raisonné: monograph including artist's statements and writings.*

———, 2. *Elie Nadelman Drawings.* New York: H. Bittner and Co., 1949. I. *Drawings.*

———, 3. *Pavel Tchelitchew.* New York: Gallery of Modern Art, 1964. I.B. *Retrospective catalogue.*

———, 4. *The Sculpture of Elie Nadelman.* New York: The Museum of Modern Art, 1948. I. *Retrospective catalogue.*

KIRSTEIN, LINCOLN, ed. *Pavel Tchelitchew Drawings.* New York: H. Bittner and Co., 1947. I. *Drawings.*

KLIGMAN, RUTH. *Love Affair: A Memoir of Jackson Pollock.* New York: William Morrow & Co. Inc., 1974.

KOCH, JOHN. *John Koch in New York.* New York: Museum of the City of New York, 1963. I.B. *Retrospective catalogue.*

KOCH, STEPHEN. *Stargazer: Andy Warhol's World and His Films.* New York: Praeger Publishers, 1973. I. *Filmography.*

KOOTZ, SAMUEL M. 1. *Modern American Painters.* n.p.: Brewer and Warren Inc., 1930. I. *Survey of painting in the 1930s.*

———, 2. *New Frontiers in American Painting.* New York: Hastings House, 1943. I. *Surveys the advance guard in painting.*

KOSTELANETZ, RICHARD, ed. *Moholy-Nagy.* Documentary Monographs in Modern Art. New York:

Praeger Publishers, 1970. I.B.D.C. *Edited essays by and about the artist. Monograph.*

KOUVENHOVEN, JOHN A. *Made in America: The Arts in Modern Civilization.* Garden City, N.Y.: Doubleday and Co. Inc., 1948. I.B. *Critical essays on American culture.*

KOZLOFF, MAX. 1. *H.C. Westermann.* Los Angeles: County Museum of Art, 1968. I.B. *Retrospective catalogue.*

———, 2. *Jasper Johns.* New York: Harry N. Abrams Inc., 1967. I.B. *Well-illustrated monograph.*

———, 3. *Renderings.* New York: Simon and Schuster, 1968. I. *Collected critical essays on modern art.*

KRAMER, HILTON. 1. *David Smith.* Los Angeles: County Museum of Art, 1965. I.B. *Includes statements by the artist.*

———, 2. *Milton Avery: Paintings, 1930–1960.* New York: Thomas Yoseloff Inc., 1962. I. *Monograph.*

———, 3. *The Sculpture of Gaston Lachaise.* New York: The Eakins Press, 1967. I.B. *Well-illustrated monograph.*

KRAUSS, ROSALIND E. 1. *Jules Olitski—Recent Painting.* Philadelphia: Institute of Contemporary Art, 1968. I.B. *Exhibition catalogue.*

———, 2. *Passages in Modern Sculpture.* New York City: The Viking Press, 1977. I.B. *Observations on sculptured objects from Rodin to the late twentieth century.*

KRIEGER, REGINE TESSIER. *Kay Sage.* Ithaca: Herbert F. Johnson Museum of Art, 1977. Foreword by Thomas W. Leavitt. I.B.C. *Retrospective catalogue; quotes from the artist's writings.*

KROLL, LEON. 1. *Leon Kroll.* Cleveland: Print Club of Cleveland and The Cleveland Museum of Art, 1945. I. *Exhibition catalogue.*

———, 2. *Leon Kroll.* New York: American Artists Group Inc., 1946. I. *Autobiographical monograph.*

KUH, KATHARINE. 1. *Art Has Many Faces—The Nature of Art Presented Visually.* New York: Harper and Brothers, 1951. I.

____, 2. *The Artist's Voice: Talks with Seventeen Artists*. New York: Harper and Row, 1962. I.

____, 3. *Break-up: The Core of Modern Art*. Greenwich, Conn.: New York Graphic Society, 1965. I.

KUHN, WALT. 1. *The Story of The Armory Show*. n.p.: Privately published, 1938.

____, 2. *Walt Kuhn*. Cincinnati: The Cincinnati Art Museum, 1960. I. *Exhibition catalogue*.

KUNIYOSHI, YASUO. *Yasuo Kuniyoshi*. New York: American Artists Group Inc., 1945. I. *Autobiographical monograph*.

Kunst um 1970: Art Around 1970. Aachen: Neue Galerie der Stadt Aachen, 1972. Foreword by Wolfgang Becker, I.B. (German and English text.) *Mostly American art from the Peter Ludwig collection*.

KYROU, ADO. *Le Surrealisme au Cinema*. Paris: Le Terrain Vague, 1963. I.

LANDON, EDWARD. *Picture Framing*. New York: American Artists Group Inc., 1945. I.

LANE, JAMES W. *Masters in Modern Art*. Boston: Chapman and Grimes, 1936. I.

LANE, JOHN R. *Stuart Davis: Art and Art Theory*. Brooklyn: The Brooklyn Museum, 1978. Foreword by Michael Botwinick. I.B.C.A. *A major study of this artist's work*.

LANGSNER, JULES. *Man Ray*. Los Angeles: County Museum of Art, 1966. I.B. *Major exhibition catalogue including essays by the artist*.

LANGUI, EMILE. *Fifty Years of Modern Art*. New York: Frederick A. Praeger, 1959. I. *Critical historical survey*.

LARSON, PHILIP. *Burgoyne Diller*. Minneapolis: The Walker Art Center, 1971. I.B. *Retrospective exhibition*.

LARSON, PHILIP, and SCHJELDAHL, PETER. *De Kooning: Drawings/Sculptures*. New York: E.P. Dutton, 1974. Acknowledgements by Martin Friedman. I.B.C. *Exhibition*

catalogue.

LEACH, FREDERICK D. *Paul Howard Manship: An Intimate View*. St. Paul: Minnesota Museum of Art, 1973. Prologue by Malcolm E. Lein. I.B. *Major retrospective catalogue; quotes from the artist*.

LEBEL, ROBERT. *Marcel Duchamp*. New York: Grove Press Inc., 1959. I.B. *Monograph*.

LEE, KATHRYN DEAN and BURCHWOOD, KATHARINE TYLER. *Art Then and Now*. New York: Appleton-Century-Crofts Inc., 1949. I. *A popular history*.

LEEPA, ALLEN. *The Challenge of Modern Art*. New York: Thomas Yoseloff Inc., 1957. I. *Problems presented by abstract and nonfigurative art*.

LEVIN, GAIL. 1. *Edward Hopper, the Art and the Artist*. New York: W. W. Norton & Co. in association with The Whitney Museum of American Art, 1980. Foreword by Tom Armstrong. I.B.C. *Exhibition catalogue*.

____, 2. *Synchromism and American Color Abstraction 1910–1925*. New York: George Braziller, 1978. I.B.C.A. *Chronicles the evolution of Synchromism*.

LEVY, JULIEN. 1. *Arshile Gorky*. New York: Harry N. Abrams Inc., 1966. I.B. *Well-illustrated monograph*.

____, 2. *Eugene Berman*. New York: American Studio Books, 1947. I. *Monograph*.

LICHT, FRED. *Sculpture, 19th and 20th Centuries*. Greenwich, Conn.: New York Graphic Society, 1967. I. *Well-illustrated introduction to modern sculpture*.

LICHT, JENNIFER. *Eight Contemporary Artists*. New York: The Museum of Modern Art, 1974. I.B.D.C. *Small exhibition catalogue including artists' statements*.

LIPCHITZ, JACQUES, with ARNASON, H.H. *My Life in Sculpture*. New York: Viking Press (Documents of Twentieth Century Art), 1972. I. *Biography*.

LIPMAN, JEAN, with WOLFE, RUTH, editorial director. *Calder's Universe*.

New York: (A Studio Book) The Viking Press in cooperation with The Whitney Museum of American Art, 1976. I.B.C. *Documents with joyfulness the artist's life, work, and friends.*

LIPPARD, LUCY R. 1. *Ad Reinhardt.* New York: Jewish Museum, 1967. Preface by Sam Hunter. I.B.D. *Major retrospective catalogue.*

____, 2. *Changing: Essays in Art Criticism.* New York: E.P. Dutton, 1971. Foreword by Gregory Battcock. I. *Collected essays, written mostly in the mid 1960s.*

____, 3. *From the Center: Feminist Essays on Women's Art.* New York: E.P. Dutton, 1976. I. Biography. *Collected essays on this topic.*

____, 4. *The Graphic Work of Philip Evergood. Selected drawings and complete prints.* New York: Crown Publishers Inc., 1966. Foreword by Abram Lerner. Poem by James Michener. I. *Catalogue raisonné of prints augmented with selected drawings.*

____, 5. *Minimal Art.* The Hague: Haags Gemeentemuseum, 1968. Preface by E. Develing. I.B. (Dutch and English text.) *Important early minimal exhibition catalogue with artists' statements.*

____, 6. *Pop Art.* New York: Frederick A. Praeger, 1966. I. *Early international survey of Pop, with contributions by Lawrence Alloway, Nancy Marmer, Nicolas Calas.*

LIPPARD, LUCY R., ed. *Six Years: The Dematerialization of the Art Object from 1966 to 1972: a cross-reference book of information on some esthetic boundaries: consisting of a bibliography into which are inserted a fragmented text, art works, documents, interviews, and symposia, arranged chronologically and focused on so-called conceptual or information or idea art with mentions of such vaguely designated areas as minimal, anti-form, systems, earth or process art, occurring now in the Americas, Europe, England, Australia, and Asia (with occasional political overtones).* New York: Praeger Publishers, 1973. Annotated by Lucy R. Lippard. I.B. *See title for description.*

List of Drawing Material of Richard Tuttle and Appendices. Zurich: Gianfranco and Annemarie Verna and others, 1979. Foreword by Gianfranco Verna. I.C.A. *Catalogues 347 drawings; includes artist's statements.*

LIVINGSTON, JANE, and TUCKER, MARCIA. *Bruce Nauman: Work from 1965–1972.* Los Angeles: Los Angeles County Museum of Art, 1972. I.B.C. *Exhibition catalogue with critical essays.*

LOMBARDO, JOSEF VINCENT. *Chaim Gross.* New York: Dalton House Inc., 1949. I.B. *Monograph.*

LORAN, ERLE. 1. *Cezanne's Composition.* Berkeley: University of California Press, 1947. I.

____, 2. *Recent Gifts and Loans of Paintings by Hans Hofmann.* Berkeley: University of California Press, 1964. I.

Louise Nevelson: Atmospheres and Environments. New York: Clarkson N. Potter, Inc., Publisher, in association with The Whitney Museum of American Art, 1980. Introduction by Edward Albee. Preface and Acknowledgements by Tom Armstrong. Essays by Richard Marshall and Louise Wilson. I.B.C. *Exhibition catalogue.*

LOWRY, BATES. *The Visual Experience: An Introduction to Art.* Englewood Cliffs, N.J.: Prentice-Hall Inc.; New York: Harry N. Abrams Inc., 1961. I. *Methods for extending the visual experience.*

LUCIE-SMITH, EDWARD. *Art in the Seventies.* Ithaca: A Phaidon Book, Cornell University Press, 1980. I.B. *The 1970s, concentrating on the vanguard and the bizarre of the vanguard.*

LUNDE, KARL. *Isabel Bishop.* New York: Harry N. Abrams Inc., 1975. I.B.C. *Well-illustrated monograph.*

LYNTON, NORBERT. *The Modern World.* New York: McGraw-Hill Book Co., Inc., 1965. I.B.G. *Introduction to modernism in the arts.*

MacAGY, DOUGLAS. 1. *James Boynton.* New York: Barone Gallery, Inc., 1959. I. *Monograph.*

___, 2. *Plus by Minus: Today's Half-Century.* Buffalo: Albright-Knox Art Gallery, 1968. I.D.P. *Major survey of the development of "cool" art.*

MAN RAY. 1. *Alphabet for Adults.* Beverly Hills, Calif.: Copley Gallery, 1948. I.

___, 2. *Man Ray.* Pasadena, Calif.: Pasadena Art Institute, 1944. I. *Exhibition catalogue.*

___, 3. *Ogetti d'Affezione.* Turin: Giulio Einavdi, 1970. I. (Italian text.) *Catalogue of work.*

___, 4. *Self Portrait.* Boston: Little, Brown and Co., 1963. I. *Autobiography.*

Man Ray. Rome: Galleria Il Collezionista d'Arte Contemporanea, 1973. Introduction by Murizo Fagiolo. I.C. (Italian text.) *Retrospective catalogue.*

Mark Tobey. Basel: Editions Beyeler, 1971. Introduction by John Russell. I.C. *Exhibition catalogue including essays by John Cage, Naum Gabo, and Lyonel Feininger, and artist's statements.*

MARSH, REGINALD. *Anatomy for Artists.* New York: American Artists Group Inc., 1945. I.

MARSHALL, RICHARD. *New Image Painting.* New York: The Whitney Museum of American Art, 1978. I.B.C. *A Return to anecdotal literary figure painting; includes artists' statements.*

MARTER, JOAN M., TARBELL, ROBERTA K., and WECHSLER, JEFFREY. *Vanguard American Sculpture 1919–1939.* New Brunswick: Rutgers University Art Gallery, 1979. Introduction by Phillip Dennis Cate. I. *A major study of this tendency.*

MARTIN, HENRY. *Arman or Four and Twenty Blackbirds Baked in a Pie or Why Settle for Less When You Can Settle for More.* New York: Harry N. Abrams Inc., 1969. I.B. *A critical study of his art.*

MARTIN, J.L., NICHOLSON, B., and GABO, N., eds. *Circle.* London: Faber and Faber Ltd., 1937. I.B. *Essays on purist art.*

MATHER, FRANK JEWETT, Jr. 1. *The American Spirit in Art.* New Haven, Conn.: Yale University Press, 1927. I. *Historical survey with commentary.*

___, 2. *Eugene Speicher.* New York: The Whitney Museum of American Art (American Artists Series), 1931. I.B. *Monograph.*

Mauricio Lasansky. Iowa City: University of Iowa Museum of Art, 1976. Acknowledgements by Jan K. Muhlert. Text by Joanna Moser, J. Michael Danoff, and Jan K. Muhlert. I.B.C. *Retrospective of prints and drawings.*

MAYERSON, CHARLOTTE LEON, ed. *Shadow and Light.* New York: Harcourt Brace & World, Inc., 1964. I. *Biography of Maurice Sterne, edited from the artist's own writings.*

McBRIDE, HENRY. *John Marin.* New York: The Museum of Modern Art, 1936. I.B. *Exhibition catalogue.*

McCAUSLAND, ELIZABETH. *Marsden Hartley.* Minneapolis: University of Minnesota Press, 1952. I. *Biography.*

McCHESNEY, MARY FULLER. *A Period of Exploration: San Francisco 1945–1950.* Oakland: The Oakland Museum, 1973. Introduction by Terry N. St. John. I.A. *An excellent study and survey of five years' activity surrounding the California School of Fine Arts, San Francisco: biographies.*

McCOUBREY, JOHN W. 1. *American Tradition in Painting.* New York: George Braziller, Inc., 1963. I.B. *Postulates an American tradition.*

___, 2. *Robert Indiana.* Philadelphia: Institute of Contemporary Art, University of Pennsylvania, 1968. I.B. *Retrospective catalogue including artist's statements.*

McCOY, GARNETT, ed. *David Smith.* Documentary Monographs in Modern Art. New York: Praeger Publishers, 1973. I.B.C. *Collected writing of the artist. Monograph.*

McCURDY, CHARLES, ed. *Modern Art . . . A Pictorial Anthology.* New York: The Macmillan Company, 1958. I.B.

McSHINE, KYNASTON, ed. *Joseph Cornell.* New York: The Museum of Modern Art, 1980. I.B. *Retrospective catalogue; includes essays by Dawn*

Ades, Carter Ratcliff, P. Adams Sitney, and Lynda Roscoe Hartigan.

MEDFORD, RICHARD C. *Guy Pene Du Bois.* Hagerstown, Md.: Washington County Museum of Fine Arts, 1940. I. *Exhibition catalogue.*

MEDINA, JOSE RAMON. *Marisol.* Caracas: Ediciones Armitano, 1968. I. (Spanish text.) *Picture book of the sculpture.*

MEHRING, WALTER. *George Grosz. Thrifty Drawings and Watercolors.* New York: Erich S. Herrmann, 1944. I. *Monograph.*

MELLQUIST, JEROME. *The Emergence of an American Art.* New York: Charles Scribner's Sons, 1942.

Mel Ramos: Watercolors. Berkeley: Lancaster-Miller Publishers, 1979. Foreword by Mel Ramos. I.B.C. *Watercolors from the series "A Salute to Art History."*

MENDELOWITZ, DANIEL M. *A History of American Art.* New York: Holt, Rinehart and Winston, Inc., 1961. I.

MESSER, THOMAS M. *Jan Muller.* New York: The Solomon R. Guggenheim Museum, 1962. I. *Retrospective catalogue.*

METRO International Directory of Contemporary Art. Milan: Metro, 1964. I.B. (English and Italian text.)

MEYER, URSULA. *Conceptual Art.* New York: E.P. Dutton, 1972. *Collected exegeses of concept art.*

MILLER, DOROTHY C., ed. 1. *Americans 1942. 18 Artists from 9 States.* New York: The Museum of Modern Art, 1942. I. *Documented exhibition catalogue.*

____, 2. *14 Americans.* New York: The Museum of Modern Art, 1946. I.B. *Documented exhibition catalogue.*

____, 3. *The Sculpture of John B. Flanagan.* New York: The Museum of Modern Art, 1942. I. *Retrospective catalogue.*

MILLER, KENNETH HAYES. *Kenneth Hayes Miller.* New York: Arts Students League, 1953. I. *Exhibition catalogue.*

MILLIER, ARTHUR. 1. *Henry Lee McFee.* Claremont, Calif.: Scripps College, 1950. I. *Exhibition catalogue.*

____, 2. *Millard Sheets.* Los Angeles: Dalzell Hatfield Gallery, 1935. I. *Monograph.*

Miriam Schapiro: The Shrine, The Computer, and The Dollhouse. La Jolla: Mandeville Art Gallery, 1975. Introduction by Linda Nochlin. I.B. *Documentary exhibition catalogue including interview and essays.*

MOAK, PETER. *The Robert Laurent Memorial Exhibition.* Durham: University of New Hampshire, 1972. Foreword by Melvin J. Zabarsky. Essay by Henry Hope. I.B. *Retrospective exhibition catalogue.*

MOCSANYI, PAUL. *Karl Knaths.* Washington, D.C.: The Phillips Gallery, 1957. I.B. *Exhibition catalogue.*

MOFFETT, KENWORTH. *Jules Olitski.* Boston: Museum of Fine Arts, 1973. I.B. *Retrospective catalogue.*

MOHOLY-NAGY, LAZLO. 1. *A New Vision and Abstract of an Artist.* 4th rev. ed. New York: George Wittenborn, Inc., 1947. Preface by Walter Gropius. I.B. *A primer of modern design.*

____, 2. *Painting, Photography, Film.* Cambridge, Mass.: MIT Press, 1969. I. *English-language reprint of this famous book.*

MOHOLY-NAGY, SIBYL. 1. *Experiment in Totality.* New York: Harper and Brothers, 1950. I. *Biography: Lazlo Moholy-Nagy.*

____, 2. *Lazlo Moholy-Nagy.* Chicago: Museum of Contemporary Art, 1969. I.B. *Retrospective catalogue.*

MONTE, JAMES. *Larry Zox.* New York: The Whitney Museum of American Art, 1973. I.B.C. *Exhibition catalogue.*

MONTE, JAMES, and TUCKER, MARCIA. *Anti-illusion: Procedures/ Materials.* New York: The Whitney Museum of American Art, 1969, I.B. *Survey of the anti-illusion expression.*

Monumenta. Newport, R.I.: Monumenta Newport Inc., 1974. Introduction by Sam Hunter. I. *Catalogue of an outdoor exhibition, including interviews and statements by the artists.*

MORRIS, G.I.K. *American Abstract Art-*

ists. New York: Ram Press, 1946. I.B. *Documentation of members.*

MORSE, JOHN D., ed. *Ben Shahn.* Documentary Monographs in Modern Art. New York: Praeger Publishers, 1972. I.B.C. *Collected writings of the artist. Monograph.*

MOSER, JOANN. 1. *Atelier 17: A 50th Anniversary Retrospective Exhibition.* Madison, Wis.: Elvehjem Art Center, 1977. Foreword by Eric S. McCready. I.B. *A history of Stanley William Hayter, his teaching and art, and the artists.*

____, 2. *The Graphic Art of Emil Ganso.* Iowa City: University of Iowa Museum of Art, 1980. I.C. *A study of the prints.*

MOTHERWELL, ROBERT. 1. *The Dada Painters and Poets.* New York: Wittenborn, Schultz, Inc., 1951. Documents of Modern Art, Vol. 8. I.B. *A documented history of this group.*

____, 2. *Robert Motherwell.* Northampton, Mass.: Smith College, 1962. I. *Exhibition catalogue.*

MOTHERWELL, ROBERT, ed. *Possibilities, No. 1.* New York: Wittenborn, Schultz, Inc., 1947. I. *An occasional review concerned with all the arts.*

MOTHERWELL, ROBERT, and REINHARDT, AD, eds. *Modern Artists in America.* New York: Wittenborn, Schultz, Inc., 1951. I.B. *The European and American advance guard in the 1940s.*

MULAS, UGO, and ARNASON, H.H. *Calder.* New York: A Studio Book/Viking Press, 1971. I.B. *Picture book with comments by Calder.*

MULLER, GREGOIRE. *The New Avant-garde.* New York: Praeger Publishers, 1972. I.D. *Photographs by Gianfranco Gorgoni documenting artists and works.*

MUNSTERBERG, HUGO. *Twentieth Century Painting.* New York: Philosophical Library, 1951. I. *Critical essays.*

MURDOCK, ROBERT M. 1. *Modular Paintings.* Buffalo: Albright-Knox Art Gallery, 1970. Foreword by Gordon M. Smith. I.C. *Exhibition catalogue.*

____, 2. *Nassos Daphnis.* Buffalo: Albright-Knox Art Gallery, 1969. Foreword by Gordon M. Smith. I.B.C. *Retrospective catalogue.*

MURRELL, WILLIAM. 1. *Charles Demuth.* New York: The Whitney Museum of American Art (American Artists Series), 1931. I. *Monograph.*

____, 2. *Elie Nadelman.* Woodstock, N.Y.: William M. Fischer, 1923. I. *Monograph.*

MURTHA, EDWIN. *Paul Manship.* New York: The MacMillan Company, 1957. I. *Monograph.*

MYERS, BERNARD. 1. *Fifty Great Artists.* New York: Bantam Books, 1953. I.B. *Historical essays.*

____, 2. *Understanding the Arts.* New York: Henry Holt and Co., 1958. I. *Art appreciation.*

Nancy Graves. La Jolla: La Jolla Museum of Contemporary Art, 1973. Introduction by Jay Belloli. I.B.C. *Exhibition catalogue including artist's statements.*

Nancy Graves: Sculpture/Drawings/Films 1969–1971. Aachen: Neue Galerie im Alten Kurhaus, 1971. Introduction by Phyllis Tuchman. I.C. *Exhibition catalogue.*

NARODNY, IVAN. *American Artists.* New York: Roerich Museum Press, 1930. B. *Figurative painting before 1930.*

NELSON, JUNE KOMPASS. *Harry Bertoia, Sculptor.* Detroit: Wayne State University Press, 1970. I.B.C. *Exhibition catalogue: the essay contains some biographical data.*

NEMSER, CINDY. *Art Talk.* New York: Charles Scribner's Sons, 1975. I.B.C. *Conversations with 12 women artists.*

NESS, JUNE L., ed. *Lyonel Feininger.* New York: Praeger Publishers (Documentary Monographs in Modern Art), 1974. I.B.C. *Collected writings of and about the artist. Monograph.*

NEUHAUS, EUGENE. *The History and Ideals of American Art.* Stanford, Calif.: Stanford University Press, 1931. I.B. *Critical essays.*

NEUMEYER, ALFRED. *The Search for*

Meaning in Modern Art. Englewood Cliffs, N.J.: Prentice-Hall Inc. 1964. I. *Essays on the understanding of art.*

New in the Seventies. Austin: The University of Texas, 1977. Foreword by Donald B. Goodall. Introduction by Fred Seabolt. I.C. Some photos of artists. *Survey exhibition: figuration and abstraction.*

NEWMEYER, SARAH. *Enjoying Modern Art.* New York: Reinhold Publishing Co., 1955. I. *Popular essays on art appreciation.*

NEWTON, ERIC. 1. *The Arts of Man.* Greenwich, Conn.: New York Graphic Society, 1960. I. *Critical essays.*

____, 2. *In My View.* London: Longmans, Green and Co., 1950. *Critical essays.*

NOCHLIN, LINDA. *Philip Pearlstein.* Athens, Ga.: Georgia Museum of Art. Preface by William D. Paul, Jr. I.B.C. *Exhibition catalogue.*

NOGUCHI, ISAMU. 1. *A Sculptor's World.* New York: Harper and Row, 1968. Preface by R. Buckminster Fuller. I. *Autobiography.*

____, 2. *The Sculpture of Spaces.* New York: The Whitney Museum of American Art, 1980. Foreword by Tom Armstrong, I.C. *Exhibition catalogue concerned with sculpture, realized and unrealized projects, and theater sets.*

NORDLAND, GERALD. 1. *Gaston Lachaise.* Los Angeles: County Museum of Art, 1963. I.B. *Retrospective catalogue.*

____, 2. *Gaston Lachaise: The Man and His Work.* New York: George Braziller, Inc., 1974. I.B. *Monograph including artist's writings.*

____, 3. *Jeremy Anderson.* San Francisco: San Francisco Museum of Art, 1966. I.B. *Retrospective catalogue.*

____, 4. *Paul Jenkins: Retrospective.* Houston: Museum of Fine Arts, 1971. I.B.C. *Essay is brief sketch of the artist's life.*

NORDMARK, OLLE. *Fresco Painting.* New York: American Artists Group Inc., 1947. I.

NORDNESS, LEE, ed. *Art:USA:Now.*

Lucerne: C. J. Bucher, 1962, 2 vols. I.B. *A collection catalogue with biographies and critical essays.*

NORMAN, DOROTHY, ed. *The Selected Writings of John Marin.* New York: Pellegrini and Cudahy, 1949. I. *Letters.*

Norman Lewis: A Retrospective. New York: The Graduate School and University Center of the City University of New York, 1976. Foreword by Milton W. Brown. Text by Thomas Lawson. I.B.C.

Northwest Traditions. Seattle: Seattle Art Museum, 1978. Foreword by Willis F. Woods. Essay by Martha Kingsbury. Organized by Charles Cowles and Sarah Clark. I.B.C. *Biographies. The twentieth century, emphasizing the decades of the 1930s, '40s, '50s, '60s.*

O'DOHERTY, BRIAN. *American Masters: The Voice and the Myth.* Photographed by Hans Namuth. New York: A Ridge Press Book/Random House, n.d. I.B. *Essays incorporating extracts from interviews.*

O'HARA, FRANK. 1. *Art Chronicles: 1954–1966.* New York: George Braziller, Inc., 1975. I.B. *Collected essays.*

____, 2. *David Smith.* London: Tate Gallery, 1966. I.B. *Retrospective catalogue.*

____, 3. *Franz Kline.* London: Whitechapel Art Gallery, 1964. I. *Exhibition catalogue.*

____, 4. *Jackson Pollock.* New York: George Braziller, Inc., 1959. I.B. *Monograph.*

____, 5. *Nakian.* New York: The Museum of Modern Art, 1966. I.B. *Retrospective catalogue.*

OLDENBURG, CLAES. 1. *Log May 1974–August 1976.* Stuttgart: Edition Hansjörg Mayer, 1976. 2 vols. in slipcase. I.B.C. *Press clips and photos of the artist at work.*

____, 2. *Notes in Hand.* New York: E.P. Dutton, 1971. I.B. *Miniature version of his sketchbooks.*

____, 3. *Proposals for Monuments and Buildings.* Chicago: Follett Publishing

Co., 1969. I. *New concepts for decorating the landscape.*

———, 4. *Raw Notes.* Halifax: Nova Scotia College of Art and Design, 1973. I. *Documents and scripts for Stars, Moveyhouse, Massage, The Typewriter: annotated.*

Oldenburg: Six Themes. Minneapolis: The Walker Art Center, 1975. Introduction by Martin Friedman. I.B.C. *Exhibitions catalogue, including statements by the artist.*

OLSON, RUTH, and CHANIN, ABRAHAM. *Gabo-Pevsner.* New York: The Museum of Modern Art, 1948. I.B. *Exhibition catalogue.*

O'NEAL, BARBARA. *E. Lawson.* Ottawa: National Gallery of Canada, 1967. I.B. (French and English text.) *Retrospective catalogue.*

O'NEILL, JOHN P., ed. *Clyfford Still.* New York: The Metropolitan Museum of Art, 1979. Foreword by Philippe de Montebello. Essay by Katharine Kuh, and writings of the artist. I.B.C. *Exhibition catalogue.*

ONSLOW-FORD, GORDON. *Towards a New Subject in Painting.* San Francisco: San Francisco Museum of Art, 1948. I. *The artist's theory of painting.*

Options and Alternatives: Some Directions in Recent Art. New Haven: Yale University Art Gallery, 1973. Preface by Alan Shestack. "Toward a Definition" by Anne Coffin Hanson. "Notes on the Anatomy of an Exhibition" by Klaus Kertess. "Intellectual Cinema; A Reconsideration" by Annette Michelson. I.B.D. *Survey of new media and materials.*

Oscar Bluemner: American Colorist. Cambridge, Mass.: Fogg Art Museum, 1967. I.B. *Retrospective catalogue.*

PAALEN, WOLFGANG. *Form and Sense. Problems of Contemporary Art No. 1.* New York: Wittenborn and Co., 1945. I. *Essays in aesthetics.*

PACH, WALTER. 1. *Ananias or the False Artist.* New York: Harper and Brothers, 1928. I. *Critical essays.*

———, 2. *The Masters of Modern Art.* New York: B.W. Huebsch, Inc., 1926. I.B. *American and European art before 1926.*

———, 3. *Queer Thing, Painting.* New York: Harper and Brothers, 1938. I. *Autobiography.*

PAGANO, GRACE. *Contemporary American Painting. The Encyclopedia Britannica Collection.* New York: Duell, Sloan and Pearce, 1945. I.

PALMER, WILLIAM C. *William C. Palmer.* Utica, N.Y.: Munson-Williams-Proctor Institute, 1956. I. *Exhibition catalogue.*

PARKES, KINETON. *The Art of Carved Sculpture.* New York: Charles Scribner's Sons, 1931, 2 vols. I.B.

PASSLOFF, PATRICIA. *The 30's. Painting in New York.* New York: Poindexter Gallery, 1963. I.

PEARSON, RALPH M. 1. *Experiencing American Pictures.* New York: Harper and Brothers, 1943. I. *Appreciation of modern art.*

———, 2. *The Modern Renaissance in American Art.* New York: Harper and Brothers, 1954. I. *Development of modern art in America.*

PEIRCE, WALDO. *Waldo Peirce.* New York: American Artists Group Inc., 1945. I. *Autobiographical monograph.*

PENROSE, ROLAND. *Man Ray.* Boston: New York Graphic Society Ltd., 1975. I.B. *Appreciation and biographical sketch.*

PERLMAN, BENNARD B. *The Immortal Eight.* New York: Exposition Press, 1962.

PETERDI, GABOR. *Printmaking: Methods Old and New.* New York: The Macmillan Company, 1959. I.

PHILLIPS, DUNCAN. 1. *The Artist Sees Differently.* New York: E. Weyhe, 1931. I. *Critical essays.*

———, 2. *A Collection in the Making.* New York: E. Weyhe, 1926. I. *Development of the Phillips collection in Washington, D.C.*

PINCUS-WITTEN, ROBERT. *Postminimalism.* New York: Out of London Press, Inc., 1977. I. *Collected essays on recent American art, written between 1966 and 1976.*

PITTMAN, HOBSON. *Hobson Pittman.* Raleigh: North Carolina Museum of Art, 1963. I.B. *Retrospective catalogue.*

PITZ, HENRY C. *The Brandywine Tradition.* Boston: Houghton Mifflin Co., 1969. I.B. *Popular biographies of many recent painters, including Andrew Wyeth.*

PLOUS, PHYLLIS. *5 American Painters: Recent Work.* Santa Barbara, 1974. I.B. *Exhibition catalogue.*

Poets & Painters. Denver: Denver Art Museum, 1979. Foreword by Dianne Perry Vanderlip. Introduction by David Shapiro. I.B. *Urban artists' views accompanied by poems. Exhibition catalogue.*

POMEROY, RALPH. *Stamos.* New York: Harry N. Abrams Inc., 1974. I.B.C. *Monograph.*

PONENTE, NELLO. *Modern Painting: Contemporary Trends.* Geneva: Skira, 1960. I.B.

POOR, HENRY VARNUM. 1. *An Artist Sees Alaska.* New York: Viking Press, 1945. I.

____, 2. *A Book of Pottery, from Mud into Immortality.* Englewood Cliffs, N.J.: Prentice-Hall Inc., 1958. I.B. *Autobiographical.*

POORE, HENRY R. *Modern Art: Why, What and How?* New York: G.P. Putnam's, 1931. I. *Investigation into the reasons for modern art.*

PORTER, FAIRCHILD. *Thomas Eakins.* New York: George Braziller, Inc., 1959. I.B. *Monograph.*

POUSETTE-DART, NATHANIEL. *Paintings, Watercolors, Lithographs.* New York: Clayton Spicer Press, 1946. I.B. *Monograph.*

POUSETTE-DART, NATHANIEL, ed. *American Painting Today.* New York: Hastings House, 1956. I. *Pictorial documentation of American painting in the mid 1950s.*

PRINT CLUB OF CLEVELAND. *The Work of Rudy Pozzatti.* Cleveland: The Cleveland Museum of Art, 1955. I. *Exhibition catalogue.*

PRINT COUNCIL OF AMERICA. *Prints.* New York: Holt, Rinehart and Winston, Inc., 1962. I.

RAGON, MICHEL. 1. *L'Aventure de l'art abstrait.* Paris: Robert Laffont, 1956. I.B. (French text.) *Development of abstract art.*

____, 2. *Expression et non-figuration.* Paris: Editions de la Revue Neuf, 1951. I. (French text.) *Expressionism and the development of non-figurative art.*

RAMSDEN, E.H. 1. *An Introduction to Modern Art.* London: Oxford University Press, 1940. I.

____, 2. *Sculpture: Theme and Variations Toward a Contemporary Aesthetic.* London: Lund Humphries, 1953. I.B.

RAND, HARRY. *Seymour Lipton: Aspects of Sculpture.* Washington, D.C.: National Collection of Fine Arts, 1979. Foreword by Joshua C. Taylor. I.B. *Illustrates the working methods from drawing to maquette to sculpture.*

Raymond Duchamp-Villon/Marcel Duchamp. Paris: Musee National d'Art Moderne, 1967. I.B. (French text.) *Major exhibition of the brothers.*

RAYNAL, MAURICE. 1. *A. Archipenko.* Rome: Valori Plastici, 1923. I. (French text.) *Monograph.*

____, 2. *Jacques Lipchitz.* Paris: Édition Jeanne Bucher, 1947. I. (French text.) *Monograph.*

____, 3. *Modern Painting.* Geneva: Skira, 1953. I.B. *Survey of modern painting.*

____, 4. *Peinture moderne.* Geneva: Skira, 1953. I.B. (French text.)

READ, HERBERT. 1. *The Art of Sculpture.* Bollingen Series XXV, No. 3. New York: Pantheon Books, 1956. I. *Documented critical essays on connoisseurship of sculpture.*

____, 2. *A Concise History of Modern Painting.* New York: Frederick A. Praeger, 1959. I.B.

____, 3. *A Concise History of Modern Sculpture.* New York: Frederick A. Praeger, 1964. I.B. *Essay source book.*

____, 4. *The Quest and the Quarry.* Rome: Rome-New York Art Foundation Inc., 1961. I. *Critical essays.*

____, 5. *Surrealism.* New York: Harcourt, Brace and Co., 1939. I. *Essays on Surrealism.*

____, 6. *The Tenth Muse.* London: Routledge and Kegan Paul, 1957. I. *Critical essays.*

READ, HERBERT, and MARTIN, LESLIE. *Gabo.* London: Lund Humphries, 1957. I.B. *Monograph.*

Recent Figure Sculpture. Cambridge, Mass.: Fogg Art Museum and Harvard University, 1972. Preface by Daniel Robbins. Introduction by Jeanne L. Wasserman. I.B. *Small survey exhibition.*

REESE, ALBERT. *American Prize Prints of the 20th Century.* New York: American Artists Group Inc., 1949. I.

A Report on the Art and Technology Program of the Los Angeles County Museum: 1967–1971. Los Angeles: Los Angeles County Museum of Art, 1971. Introduction by Maurice Tuchman. Essay: Thoughts on Art and Technology, by Jane Livingston. I.D.P. *Documents an amalgam of art, science, and business.*

RESTANY, PIERRE. 1. *J. F. Koenig.* Paris: Galerie Arnaud, 1960. I. (French and English text.) *Monograph.*

_____, 2. *Lyrisme et abstraction.* Milan: Edizioni Apollinairi, 1960. *I. (French text.) Exposition of a lyrical theory in painting leading toward abstraction.*

RIBEMONT-DESSAIGNES, G. *Man Ray.* Paris: Librairie Gallimard, 1924. I. *Monograph.*

RICH, DANIEL CATTON. 1. *Georgia O'Keeffe.* Chicago: The Art Institute of Chicago, 1943. I. *Retrospective catalogue.*

_____, 2. *Georgia O'Keeffe.* Worcester, Mass.: The Worcester Art Museum, 1960. *Retrospective catalogue.*

Richard Diebenkorn: Paintings and Drawings, 1943–1976. Buffalo: Albright-Knox Art Gallery, 1976. Foreword by Robert T. Buck, Jr. Acknowledgments by Linda L. Cathcart. Essays by Robert T. Buck, Jr., Linda L. Cathcart, Gerald Nordland, and Maurice Tuchman. *Retrospective Catalogue.*

RICHARDSON, BRENDA. 1. *Barnett Newman: The Complete Drawings, 1944–1969.* Baltimore: The Baltimore Museum of Art, 1979. I.B. *Exhibition and catalogue raisonné.*

_____, 2. *Joan Brown.* Berkeley: University of California, Berkeley, 1974. I.B. *Retrospective catalogue.*

_____, 3. *William T. Wiley.* Berkeley: University of California, Berkeley, 1971. I.B. *Retrospective catalogue.*

RICHARDSON, E.P. *Painting in America, the Story of 450 Years.* New York: Thomas Y. Crowell Co., 1956. I.B. *Important history of American painting.*

RICHTER, HANS. *Dada Profile.* Zurich: Verlag Die Arche, 1961. I. (German text.) *Snapshot introductory essays on the Dadaists.*

RICKEY, GEORGE. *Constructivism: Origins and Evolution.* New York: George Braziller, Inc., 1967. I.B.D. Biographies. *History of this movement.*

RINARD, PARK, and PYLE, ARNOLD. *Grant Wood.* Chicago: Lakeside Press Galleries, 1935. I. *Exhibition catalogue.*

RINGEL, FRED J., ed. *America as Americans See It.* New York: The Literary Guild, 1932. I. *Anthology of the writings of various Americans on American culture.*

RITCHIE, ANDREW CARNDUFF. 1. *Abstract Painting and Sculpture in America.* New York: The Museum of Modern Art, 1951. I.B. *Documented exhibition catalogue.*

_____, 2. *Charles Demuth.* New York: The Museum of Modern Art, 1950. I.B. *Retrospective catalogue.*

_____, 3. *Sculpture of the Twentieth Century.* New York: The Museum of Modern Art, 1952. I.B.

ROBBINS, DANIEL. *Walter Murch.* Providence: Rhode Island School of Design, 1966. I.B. *Retrospective catalogue.*

Robert Rauschenberg. Washington, D.C.: National Collection of Fine Arts, 1976. Foreword by Joshua C. Taylor. Acknowledgments by Walter Hopps. Essay by Lawrence Alloway. I.B.C. *Retrospective exhibition and documentation of projects.*

Robert Ryman. Amsterdam: Stedelijk Museum, 1974. I.B.C. *Retrospective catalogue.*

ROBERTS, COLETTE. *Mark Tobey.* New York: Grove Press Inc., 1959. I. *Monograph.*

ROBERTSON, BRYAN. 1. *Charles Howard.* London: Whitechapel Art Gallery, 1956. I. *Retrospective catalogue.*

____, 2. *Jackson Pollock.* New York: Harry N. Abrams Inc., 1960. I.B. *Monograph.*

RODMAN, SELDEN. 1. *Conversations with Artists.* New York: Capricorn Books, 1961. I.

____, 2. *The Eye of Man.* New York: Devin-Adair, 1955. I. *Polemic devised toward figuration.*

____, 3. *The Insiders.* Baton Rouge: Louisiana State University Press, 1960. I. *A thesis for figurative artists.*

ROGALSKI, WALTER R. *Prints and Drawings by Walter R. Rogalski.* Cleveland: Print Club of Cleveland and The Cleveland Museum of Art, 1954. I. *Exhibition catalogue.*

ROOD, JOHN. *Sculpture in Wood.* Minneapolis: University of Minnesota Press, 1950. I. *Technique.*

ROSE, BARBARA. 1. *American Art since 1900, a Critical History.* New York: Frederick A. Praeger, 1967. I.B.

____, 2. *Claes Oldenburg.* New York: The Museum of Modern Art, 1969. I.B. *Retrospective catalogue.*

____, 3. *Frankenthaler.* New York: Harry N. Abrams Inc., 1971. I.B. *Monograph.*

____, 4. *Readings in American Art since 1900.* New York: Frederick A. Praeger, 1968. I.B. *Collected essays by and about artists and their work.*

ROSE, BARBARA, ed. *Art as Art: The Selected Writings of Ad Reinhardt.* Documents of Twentieth-Century Art. New York: The Viking Press, 1975. I.B. *Anthology of the painter's writings.*

ROSE, BERNICE. *Jackson Pollock: Works on Paper.* New York: The Museum of Modern Art, 1969. I. *A study of the drawings.*

ROSENBERG, HAROLD. 1. *Arshile Gorky, The Man, The Time, The Idea.* New York: Horizon Press, Inc., 1962. I.B. *Monograph.*

____, 2. *De Kooning.* New York: Harry N. Abrams Inc., 1974. I.B.C. *Monograph.*

____, 3. *Saul Steinberg.* New York: Alfred A. Knopf in association with The Whitney Museum of American Art, 1978. Foreword by Paul H. Eliker and Tom Armstrong. I.B.C. *Major retrospective catalogue.*

ROSENBLUM, ROBERT. 1. *Cubism and Twentieth Century Art.* New York: Harry N. Abrams Inc., 1961. I.B. *Chronicles Cubism and its influence.*

____, 2. *Modern Painting and the Northern Romantic Tradition: Friedrich to Rothko.* New York: Harper and Row Publishers Inc., 1975. I.B. *Essays on the dark side of romantic painting.*

ROTERS, EBERHARD. *Painters of the Bauhaus.* New York: Frederick A. Praeger, 1969. I.B. *A history of the master teachers.*

ROTHSCHILD, LEON. *Style in Art.* New York: Thomas Yoseloff Inc., 1960. I. *Critical essays.*

ROTHSCHILD, LINCOLN. *To Keep Art Alive: The Effort of Kenneth Hays Miller, American Painter.* Philadelphia: The Art Alliance Press, 1974. I.B. *Monograph.*

ROURKE, CONSTANCE. *Charles Sheeler, Artist in the American Tradition.* New York: Harcourt, Brace and Co., 1938. I. *Biography.*

RUBIN, WILLIAM S. 1. *Dada, Surrealism, and Their Heritage.* New York: The Museum of Modern Art, 1968. I.B. Chronology. *Catalogue of controversial MOMA exhibition.*

____, 2. *Frank Stella.* New York: The Museum of Modern Art, 1970. I.B.C. *A major retrospective catalogue.*

RUBLOWSKY, JOHN. *Pop Art.* New York: Basic Books, 1965. I. *Pop art, its artists, dealers, collectors, and activities.*

RUHÉ, HARRY. *Fluxus, the Most Radical and Experimental Art Movement of the Sixties.* Amsterdam: 'A,' 1979. I.B.C. *Biographies. Major document on this international manifestation.*

RUSSELL, JOHN, and GABLIK, SUZI.

Pop Art Redefined. New York: Frederick A. Praeger, 1969. I. *Includes statements by other critics.*

SACHS, PAUL J. *Modern Prints and Drawings.* New York: Alfred A. Knopf, 1954. I.B.

SAGER, PETER. *Neue Formen des Realismus.* Cologne: Verlag M. DuMont Schauberg, 1973. I.B.C. (German text.) *First international survey of various forms of new realist painting and sculpture; list of international group exhibitions; artists' statements.*

ST. JOHN, BRUCE. *John Sloan.* American Art and Artists. New York: Praeger Publishers, 1971. I.B.C. *Appreciation and life of the artist.*

ST. JOHN, BRUCE, ed. *John Sloan's New York Scene.* With an introduction by Helen Farr Sloan. New York: Harper and Row, 1964. I. *Edited from diaries, notes, and correspondence of the artist dating from 1906 to 1913.*

SALVINI, ROBERTO. *Guida all'arte moderna.* Florence: L'arco, 1949. I.B. (Italian text.)

SAMARAS, LUCAS. *Samaras Album. Autointerview Autobiography Autopolaroid.* New York: The Whitney Museum of American Art and Pace Editions Inc., 1971. I. *The complete autoexposé of Samaras.*

Sam Francis. Paintings 1947–1972. Buffalo: Albright-Knox Art Gallery, 1972. I.B.C. *A major retrospective catalogue; contains essays by Franz Meyer; Wieland Schmied; Robert T. Buck, Jr.*

SANDLER, IRVING. *The New York School: The Painters and Sculptors of the Fifites.* New York: Harper & Row, Publishers, 1978. I.B.A. *Review of the decade 1950–1960.*

_____, 2. *The Triumph of American Painting: A History of Abstract Expressionism.* New York: Praeger Publishers, 1970. I.B.C. *A history of the mid-20th-century period.*

SASOWSKY, NORMAN. *Reginald Marsh. Etchings, Engravings, Lithographs.* New York: Frederick A. Praeger, 1956. I. *Catalogue raisonné.*

SAWYER, KENNETH. *The Paintings of Paul Jenkins.* Paris: Editions Two Cities, 1961. I. *Monograph.*

SCHEYER, ERNST. *Lyonel Feininger, Caricature and Fantasy.* Detroit: Wayne State University Press, 1964. I.B. *Documentary monograph drawn from letters and notes of the artist, showing development from cartoonist to painter.*

SCHMECKEBIER, LAURENCE E. 1. *Boris Margo.* Syracuse: School of Art, Syracuse University, 1968. I.B. *Exhibition catalogue, including a catalogue raisonné of the artist's prints.*

_____, 2. *John Steuart Curry's Pageant of America.* New York: American Artists Group Inc., 1943. I. *Biography.*

SCHNEIDER, PIERRE. *Louvre Dialogues.* Translated from the French by Patricia Southgate. New York: Atheneum, 1971. I. *Interviews he made while walking through the Louvre.*

SCHULZE, FRANZ. *Fantastic Images: Chicago Art since 1945.* Chicago: Follett Publishing Co., 1972. I. *Eccentric figurative art from 1945 to 1972.*

SCHWABACHER, ETHEL K. *Arshile Gorky.* New York: The Whitney Museum of American Art, 1957. I.B. *Biography.*

SCHWARTZ, SANFORD. *Myron Stout.* New York: The Whitney Museum of American Art, 1980. Introduction by B. H. Friedman. I.B.C. *Retrospective exhibition catalogue including artist's statements.*

SCHWARZ, ARTURO. 1. *The Complete Works of Marcel Duchamp.* New York: Harry N. Abrams Inc., 1969. I.B. *Biographical, critical catalogue raisonné: the major source book.*

_____, 2. *Marcel Duchamp: Notes and Projects for the Large Glass.* New York: Harry N. Abrams Inc., 1969. I. *Facsimile reproduction of the notes for this work.*

SCOTT, DAVID W. *The Art of Stanton Macdonald-Wright.* Washington, D.C.: National Collection of Fine Arts, 1967. I.B. *Includes "A Treatise on Color" and selected writings of the artist. Retrospective catalogue.*

Sculpture and Drawings by Michael Lekakis. Dayton: Dayton Art Institute, 1968. Introduction by Priscilla Colt. I.C. *Appreciation.*

Sculpture of the Western Hemisphere. New York: International Business Machines Corp. 1942. I. *Catalogue of IBM sculpture collection.*

SEITZ, WILLIAM C. 1. *Abstract Expressionist Painting in America: An Interpretation Based on the Work and Thought of Six Key Figures.* PhD. thesis, *Princeton University, 1955. Not published; available on microfilm.*

_____, 2. *Arshile Gorky.* New York: The Museum of Modern Art, 1962. Foreword by Julien Levy. I.B. *Retrospective catalogue.*

_____, 3. *The Art of Assemblage.* New York: The Museum of Modern Art, 1961. I.B. *Documented exhibition catalogue.*

_____, 4. *Hans Hofmann.* New York: The Museum of Modern Art, 1963. I.B. *Exhibition catalogue.*

_____, 5. *Mark Tobey.* New York: The Museum of Modern Art, 1962. I.B. *Retrospective catalogue.*

SELDIS, HENRY J. *Rico Lebrun.* Los Angeles: County Museum of Art, 1967. I.B. *Retrospective catalogue with major documentation: notes on "Genesis" by Peter Selz.*

SELDIS, HENRY J., and WILKE, ULFERT. *The Sculpture of Jack Zajac.* Los Angeles: Gallard Press, 1960. I.B. *Monograph.*

SELIGMANN, HERBERT J., ed. *Letters of John Marin.* New York: An American Place, 1931.

SELIGMANN, KURT. *The Mirror of Magic.* New York: Pantheon Books, 1948. I. *This artist was an authority on magic: his art reflects its influence.*

SELZ, JEAN. *Modern Sculpture.* New York: George Braziller, Inc., 1963. I.B. *Origins of modern sculpture from 1850 to 1920.*

SELZ, PETER. 1. *Directions in Kinetic Sculpture.* Berkeley: University of California, 1966. Preface by George Rickey. I.B. *International survey exhibition catalogue including artists' statements.*

_____, 2. *Funk.* Berkeley: University of California, 1967. I.G. *Includes statements by artists.*

_____, 3. *German Expressionist Painting.* Berkeley: University of California Press, 1957. I.B. *Major work documenting the development of German Expressionism and its influence.*

_____, 4. *Mark Rothko.* New York: The Museum of Modern Art, 1961. I.B. *Retrospective catalogue.*

SEUPHOR, MICHEL. 1. *Abstract Painting. 50 Years of Accomplishment, from Kandinsky to the Present.* New York: Dell Publishing Co., 1964. I.

_____, 2. *L'Art abstrait.* Paris: Editions Maeght, 1949. I.B. *(French text.)*

_____, 3. *The Sculpture of This Century. Dictionary of Modern Sculpture.* London: A. Zwemmer, Ltd., 1959. I.B.

7 Decades. Andover, Mass.: Addison Gallery of American Art, Phillips Academy, 1969. Foreword by Bartlett H. Hayes, Jr. I.C. *Exhibition catalogue, including artists' statements.*

SEYMOUR, CHARLES, Jr. *Tradition and Experiment in Modern Sculpture.* Washington, D.C.: The American University Press, 1949. I.

SHAHN, BEN. 1. *The Biography of Painting.* New York: Paragraphic Books, 1966. I. *A testament of the artist.*

_____, 2. *The Shape of Content.* Cambridge, Mass.: Harvard University Press, 1957. I. *Critical essay.*

SHAHN, BERNARDA BRYSON. *Ben Shahn.* New York: Harry N. Abrams Inc., 1972. I.B.C. *Picture catalogue of works and biographical sketch.*

SHAPIRO, DAVID, ed. *Social Realism: Art as a Weapon.* New York: Frederick Ungar Publishing Co., 1973. I.B. *A study of the social implications of figurative art in the 1930s and 1940s.*

SHEARER, LINDA. *Brice Marden.* New York: The Solomon R. Guggenheim Museum, 1975. I.B. *A ten-year survey.*

SIEGFRIED, JOAN C. *Bruce Conner.* Philadelphia: Institute of Contemporary Art, 1967. Preface by Stephen S. Prokopoff. I. *Retrospective catalogue.*

SLOAN, HELEN FARR. *The Life and Times of John Sloan.* Wilmington, Del.: Wilmington Society of the Fine Arts, 1961. I.

SLOAN, HELEN FARR, ed. *American Art Nouveau: The Poster Period of John Sloan.* Lock Haven, Pa.: Privately published by Hammermill Paper Co., n.d. I. *New material on an unknown period of the artist's work.*

SLOAN, JOHN. 1. *The Art of John Sloan.* Brunswick, Me.: Walker Art Museum, Bowdoin College, 1962. *Exhibition catalogue.*

———, 2. *The Gist of Art.* New York: American Artists Group Inc., 1939. I. *The artist's theory of painting.*

———, 3. *John Sloan.* Andover, Mass.: Addison Gallery of American Art, Phillips Academy, 1938. I.B. *Exhibition catalogue.*

———, 4. *John Sloan.* New York: American Artists Group Inc., 1945. I. *Autobiographical monograph.*

———, 5. *John Sloan. Paintings and Prints.* Hanover, N.H.: Dartmouth College, 1946. I. *Exhibition catalogue.*

SLUSSER, JEAN PAUL. *Bernard Karfiol.* New York: The Whitney Museum of American Art (American Artists Series), 1931. I.B. *Monograph.*

SMITH, ANDRE. *Concerning the Education of a Print Collector.* New York: Harlow, Keppel and Co., 1941. I.

SMITH, BERNARD. *Moses Soyer.* New York: ACA Gallery, 1944. I. *Monograph.*

SMITH, BRYDEN. *Donald Judd.* Ottawa: National Gallery of Canada, 1975. I.B.C. *Retrospective catalogue and catalogue raisonné, 1960–1974.*

SMITH, DAVID. *David Smith.* New York: Holt, Rinehart and Winston, Inc., 1968. I. *Writings and photographs.*

SMITH, S.C. KAINES. *An Outline of Modern Painting.* London: The Medici Society, 1932. I. *Early documentation of twentieth-century art.*

SOBY, JAMES THRALL. 1. *After Picasso.* Hartford, Conn.: Edwin Valentine Mitchell; New York: Dodd, Mead and Co., 1935. I. *Critical essays.*

———, 2. *Ben Shahn.* New York: The Museum of Modern Art. West Drayton, England: Penguin Books, 1947. I. *Monograph.*

———, 3. *Ben Shahn.* New York: George Braziller Inc., 1963. I.B. *Monograph.*

———, 4. *Ben Shahn, His Graphic Work.* New York: George Braziller, Inc., 1957. I.B. *Monograph.*

———, 5. *Contemporary Painters.* New York: The Museum of Modern Art, 1948. I. *Documented exhibition catalogue.*

———, 6. *Modern Art and the New Past.* Norman: University of Oklahoma Press, 1957. *Critical essays and documentation.*

———, 7. *Tchelitchew.* New York: The Museum of Modern Art, 1942. I.B. *Exhibition catalogue.*

———, 8. *Yves Tanguy.* New York: The Museum of Modern Art, 1955. I.B. *Exhibition catalogue.*

Sol LeWitt. New York: The Museum of Modern Art, 1978. Introduction by Alicia Legg. Essays by Robert Rosenblum, Lucy R. Lippard, Bernice Rose. I.B.D. *Retrospective catalogue including artist's writings.*

SONTAG, SUSAN. *Against Interpretation.* New York: Dell Publishing Co., 1966. *Assorted collected essays.*

SOYER, MOSES. *Painting the Human Figure.* New York: Watson-Guptill Publishing Co,. Inc., 1964. I. *How-to-paint book.*

SOYER, RAPHAEL. 1. *Homage to Thomas Eakins, etc.* Rebecca L. Soyer, ed. South Brunswick, N.J.: Thomas Yoseloff, Inc., 1965. I. *Travelogue and art-world personalities.*

———, 2. *A Painter's Pilgrimage.* New York: Crown Publishers Inc., 1962. I. *A European travelogue.*

———, 3. *Raphael Soyer.* New York: American Artists Group Inc., 1946. I. *Autobiographical monograph.*

SPEICHER, EUGENE. *Eugene Speicher.* New York: American Artists Group Inc., 1945. I. *Autobiographical monograph.*

STABER, MARGIT. *Fritz Glarner.* Zurich: ABC Verlag, 1976. (English and German text.) I.B.C. *Biography.*

The monograph and catalogue raisonné.

The State of California Painting. New Plymouth, N.Z.: Govett-Brewster Art Gallery, 1972. Foreword by Robert H. Ballard. Introduction by Michael Walls. I.C. *Exhibition catalogue.*

STEINBERG, LEO. *Jasper Johns.* New York: George Wittenborn, Inc., 1964. I.B. *Monograph.*

STEINBERG, SAUL. 1. *The Art of Living.* New York: Harper and Brothers, 1945. I. *Cartoons.*

____, 2. *The Passport.* New York: Harper and Brothers, 1945. I. *Cartoons.*

____, 3. *Steinberg Dessins.* Paris: N.R.F., Gallimard, 1955. I. *Cartoons.*

STERNBERG, HARRY. 1. *Modern Methods and Materials of Etching.* New York: McGraw-Hill Book Co., Inc., 1949. I.

____, 2. *Silk Screen Color Printing.* New York: McGraw-Hill Book Co., Inc., 1942. I.

STORY, ALA. *First comprehensive retrospective exhibition in the West of Max Weber.* Santa Barbara: University of California, 1968. I.B. *Major retrospective catalogue.*

STRACHAN, W.J. *Towards Sculpture.* London: Thames and Hudson, 1976. I.B. *Biographies. From the classical tradition to Oldenburg: drawings, maquettes, and realized works.*

Stuart Edie. Iowa City: The University of Iowa Museum of Art, 1979. Foreword by Jan K. Muhlert. Introduction by Judy Cizek. I.C. *Retrospective catalogue.*

SUTTON, DENYS. *American Painting.* London: Avalon Press, 1948. I. *Mid-twentieth-century painting.*

SWEENEY, JAMES JOHNSON. 1. *Alexander Calder.* New York: The Museum of Modern Art, 1951. I.B. *Exhibition Catalogue.*

____, 2. *Jacques Villon, Raymond Duchamp-Villon, Marcel Duchamp.* New York: The Solomon R. Guggenheim Museum, 1957. I.B. *Exhibition catalogue.*

____, 3. *Sam Francis.* Houston: Museum of Fine Arts of Houston, 1967. I.

Exhibition catalogue.

____, 4. *Stuart Davis.* New York: The Museum of Modern Art, 1945. I.B. *Exhibition catalogue.*

SWEET, FREDERICK A. *Ivan Albright.* Chicago: The Art Institute of Chicago, 1964. I. *Retrospective catalogue.*

Syd Solomon. Sarasota, Fla.: John and Mable Ringling Museum of Art, 1974. Acknowledgments by Richard S. Carroll. Conversation with Solomon by Kurt Vonnegut, Jr. Introduction by Leslie Judd Ahlander. I.B. *Retrospective catalogue.*

TAFT, LORADO. *Modern Tendencies in Sculpture.* Chicago: The University of Chicago Press, 1921. I.

TAKIGUCHI, SHUZO. *Noguchi.* Tokyo: Bijutsu Shippan-Sha, 1953. I. *Monograph.*

TANGUY, YVES. *Un Recueil de Ses Ouevres/A Summary of His Work.* New York: Pierre Matisse, 1943. I.B. (French and English text.) *Catalogue raisonné.*

TAPIE, MICHEL. 1. *Un Arte autre.* Paris: Gabriel Giraud et Fils, 1952. I. (French text.) *Polemic thesis for advance-guard painting.*

____, 2. *Ossorio.* Turin: Edizioni d'Arte Fratelli Pozzo, 1961. I. (English and French text.) *Monograph.*

TARBELL, ROBERTA K. *Marguerite Zorach: The Early Years, 1908–1920.* Washington, D.C.: National Collection of Fine Arts, 1973. Foreword by Joshua C. Taylor, I.B.C. *Exhibition catalogue and detailed study of the artist's early life.*

TASHJIAN, DICKRAN. *Skyscraper Primitives.* Middletown, Conn.: Wesleyan University Press, 1975. I.B. *Observations on dadamerica.*

TAUBES, FREDERIC. 1. *Anatomy of Genius.* New York: Dodd, Mead and Co., 1948. I. *Critical essay.*

____, 2. *The Art and Techniques of Portrait Painting.* New York: Dodd, Mead and Co., 1957. I.

____, 3. *Better Frames for Your Pictures.*

New York: Studio Publications, 1952. I.

_____, 4. *Frederic Taubes*. New York: American Artists Group Inc., 1946. I.B. *Autobiographical monograph*.

_____, 5. *The Mastery of Oil Painting*. New York: Studio Publications, 1953. I. *Technique*.

_____, 6. *Modern Art, Sweet or Sour?* New York: Watson-Guptill Publishing Co. Inc., 1958. I. *Critical essays*.

_____, 7. *The Painter's Question and Answer Book*. New York: Watson-Guptill Publishing Co. Inc., 1948. I. *Technique*.

_____, 8. *Paintings and Essays on Art*. New York: Dodd, Mead and Co., 1950. I.

_____, 9. *Pen and Ink Drawing, Art and Technique*. New York: Watson-Guptill Publishing Co. Inc., 1956. I.

_____, 10. *Pictorical Composition and the Art of Drawing*. New York: Dodd, Mead and Co., 1949. I.

_____, 11. *Studio Secrets*. New York: Watson-Guptill Publishing Co. Inc., 1943. I. *Technique*.

_____, 12. *The Technique of Oil Painting*. New York: Dodd, Mead and Co., 1941. I.

_____, 13. *You Don't Know What You Like*. New York: Dodd, Mead and Co., 1947. I. *Critical essays*.

TAVOLATO, ITALO. *George Grosz*. Rome: Valori Plastici, 1924. I. (French text.) *Monograph*.

TERENZIO, STEPHANIE. *The Painter and The Printer: Robert Motherwell's Graphics, 1943–1980*. New York: The American Federation of Arts, 1980. Introduction includes a note by the artist on collaboration. I.B. *Biographical sketch. Catalogue raisonné by Dorothy C. Belknap*.

THOMAS, EDWARD B. *Mark Tobey*. Seattle: Seattle Art Museum, 1959. I. *Exhibition catalogue*.

Three Realists: Close, Estes, Raffael. Worcester, Mass.: The Worcester Art Museum, 1974. Foreword by Leon Shulman. I.B. *Exhibition catalogue*.

TILLIM, SIDNEY. *Richard Lindner*. Chicago: William and Noma Copley Foundation, n.d. I. *Monograph*.

TOBEY, MARK. *Mark Tobey*. New York: The Whitney Museum of American Art, 1951. I. *Exhibition catalogue*.

TOMKINS, CALVIN. 1. *The Bride and the Bachelors*. New York: Viking Press, 1965. I. *Essays on the avant-garde*.

_____, 2. *Off the Wall: Robert Rauschenberg and the Art World of Our Time*. Garden City: Doubleday & Co., Inc., 1980. I.C. *Extracts from "Profiles" in the New Yorker*.

TOMKINS, CALVIN, and the Editors of TIME-LIFE BOOKS. *The World of Marcel Duchamp*. New York: Time Inc., 1966. I.B.

Tony Smith: Painting and Sculpture. Baltimore: University of Maryland Art Gallery, 1974. Foreword by Eleanor Green. I. *Exhibition catalogue*.

Transparency, Reflection, Light, Space: Four Artists. Los Angeles: UCLA Art Galleries, 1971. Foreword by Frederick S. Wight. I.B.C. *Exhibition catalogue: interviews and artists' statements*.

TRIER, EDUARD. 1. *Form and Space: Sculpture in the 20th Century*. New York: Frederick A. Praeger, 1968. I.B. *Survey by concept*.

_____, 2. *Moderne Plastik von August Rodin bis Marino Marini*. Frankfurt am Main: Buchergilde Gutenberg, 1955. I.B. (German text.) *Short illustrated history of twentieth-century sculpture*.

TUCHMAN, MAURICE. 1. *American Sculpture of the Sixties*. Los Angeles: County Museum of Art, 1967. I.B.G. *Major survey exhibition catalogue includes essays by 10 critics and statements by the artists*.

_____, 2. *Edward Kienholz*. Los Angeles: County Museum of Art, 1966. I.B. *Retrospective catalogue*.

TUCHMAN, MAURICE, ed. *New York School. The First Generation: Paintings of the 1940s and 1950s*. Los Angeles: County Museum of Art, 1965. I.B. *Major exhibition catalogue with statements by artists and critics*.

TUCKER, MARCIA. *Al Held*. New York: The Whitney Museum of

American Art, 1974. I.B.C. *Retrospective catalogue.*

TYLER, KENNETH E. *Josef Albers: White Line Squares.* Los Angeles: Gemini G.E.L., 1966. I.B. *Graphics exhibition catalogue includes artist's statements.*

TYLER, PARKER. 1. *The Divine Comedy of Pavel Tchelitchew.* New York: Fleet Publishing Co., 1967. I.B. *Biography.*

____, 2. *Marca-Relli.* Paris: The Pocket Museum, Editions George Fall, 1960. I. *Monograph.*

USA West Coast. Hamburg: Kunstverein in Hamburg, 1972. Foreword by Helmut Heissenbuttel. Essay by Helene Winer. I.C. (German and English text.) *Exhibition catalogue.*

VALENTINE, W.R. 1. *Letters of John B. Flanagan.* New York: Curt Valentine, 1942.

____, 2. *Origins of Modern Sculpture.* New York: Wittenborn and Co., 1946. I.

VAN BORK, BERT. *Jacques Lipchitz: The Artist at Work.* With a critical evaluation by Dr. Alfred Werner. New York: Crown Publishers Inc., 1966. I. *Well-illustrated popular essay about the artist at work.*

VAN BRUGGEN, COOSJE, and OLDENBURG, CLAES. *Claes Oldenburg: Large-Scale Projects, 1977–1980.* New York: Rizzoli International Publications, Inc. Includes essay on his monuments by R. H. Fuchs. I.D.P. *Biographies. Documentation on ten projects.*

VARGA, MARGIT. *Waldo Peirce.* New York: Hyperion Press, Harper and Brothers, 1941. I. *Monograph.*

VERKAUF, WILLY, ed. *Dada: Monograph of a Movement.* New York: Wittenborn and Co., 1957. I.B. *Documented monograph.*

VITRY, PAUL. *Paul Manship.* Paris: Editions de la Gazette des Beaux Arts, 1927. I. *Monograph.*

WALDBERG, PATRICK. 1. *Bernard Pfriem.* Chicago: William and Noma Copley Foundation, 1961. I. (French and English text.) *Monograph.*

____, 2. *Main et merveilles.* Paris: Mercure de France, 1961. I. *Essays on Surrealism.*

____, 3. *Surrealims.* Geneva: Skira, 1962. I.B. *Documentation and essays on Surrealism.*

____, 4. *Surrealism.* New York: McGraw-Hill Co., Inc., 1965. I.B. *Chronology. A short history of Surrealism.*

WALDMAN, DIANE. 1. *Carl Andre.* New York: The Solomon R. Guggenheim Museum, 1970. I.B. *A ten-year survey of Andre's work.*

____, 2. *Chryssa: Selected Works 1955–1967.* New York: The Pace Gallery, 1968. I.B. *Well-illustrated exhibition catalogue.*

____, 3. *Joseph Cornell.* New York: The Solomon R. Guggenheim Museum, 1967. I.B. *Retrospective catalogue.*

____, 4. *Kenneth Noland: A Retrospective.* New York: The Solomon R. Guggenheim Museum, 1977. Preface and acknowledgments by Thomas M. Messer. I.B.C. *Retrospective catalogue.*

____, 5. *Mark Rothko, 1903–1970: A Retrospective.* New York: Harry N. Abrams Inc./The Solomon R. Guggenheim Museum, 1978. Acknowledgments and preface by Thomas M. Messer. Includes "The Aquamarine Sunrise: A Memory of Rothko," by Bernard Malamud. I.B.C. *Comprehensive retrospective.*

____, 6. *Robert Mangold.* New York: The Solomon R. Guggenheim Museum, 1971. I.B. *Exhibition catalogue.*

WALKOWITZ, ABRAHAM. 1. *A Demonstration of Objective, Abstract and Non-Objective Art.* Giraud, Kans.: Haldeman: Julius Press, 1945. I. *The artist's theories, illustrated.*

____, 2. *100 Drawings.* New York: B. W. Huebsch, Inc., 1925. I.

Walter Quirt: A Retrospective. Minneapolis: University Gallery, University of Minnesota. 1979. Foreword by Milton W. Brown. Essay by

Mary Towley Swanson. I.B.C. *The only study of his painting; includes reminiscences by friends.*

WARHOL, ANDY. *The Philosophy of Andy Warhol.* New York: Harcourt Brace Jovanovich, 1975. *Artist's statements.*

WARHOL, ANDY; KONIG, KASPER; HULTEN, PONTUS; and GRANTH, OLLE, eds. *Andy Warhol.* Stockholm: Moderna Museet, 1968. I. *Pictorial history of the development of the artist, his work, and friends, including comments by the artist.*

WARHOL, ANDY, and HACKETT, PAT. *POPism: The Warhol '60s.* New York: Harcourt Brace Jovanovich, 1980. I. *Gossip or history: choose!*

WATSON, ERNEST W. 1. *Color and Method in Painting.* New York: Watson-Guptill Publishing Co. Inc., 1942. I. *Studies of various artists' use of color.*

____, 2. *Twenty Painters and How They Work.* New York: Watson-Guptill Publishing Co. Inc., 1950. I.

WATSON, FORBES. *William Glackens.* New York: Duffield and Co., 1923. I. *Monograph.*

WEBER, MAX. 1. *Essays on Art.* n.p.: Privately published, 1916.

____, 2. *Max Weber.* New York: American Artists Group Inc., 1945. I. *Autobiographical monograph.*

WEITEMEIER, HANNAH. *Moholy-Nagy.* Eindhoven, Holland: Stedelijk van Abbe-Museum, 1967. I. (Dutch and English text.) *Retrospective catalogue including statements by the artist.*

WELL, HENRY W., ed. *Selected Poems by Marsden Hartley.* New York: Viking Press, 1945. I.

WELLER, ALLEN S. *The Joys and Sorrows of Recent American Art.* Urbana: University of Illinois Press, 1968. I.

"What Abstract Art Means to Me." *Bulletin of the Museum of Modern Art,* Vol. XVIII, No. 3, Spring 1951. I. *Statements by leading artists.*

WHEELER, MONROE. *Painters and Sculptors of Modern America.* New York: Thomas Y. Crowell Co., 1942. I.

When Attitudes Become Form: Works/Concepts/Processes/Situations/Information. Bern: Kunsthalle Bern, 1969. Foreword by Harold Szeemann. Introduction by John A. Murphy. I.B.C. (English, French, and German text.) *Major international exhibition of abovementioned tendencies.*

WHITNEY, DAVID, ed. *Andy Warhol: Portraits of the 70s.* New York: Random House, in Association with The Whitney Museum of American Art, 1979. Foreword by Tom Armstrong. Essay by Robert Rosenblum. I. *Exhibition catalogue and picture book of commissioned portraits.*

WIGHT, FREDERICK, S. 1. *Hans Hofmann.* New York: The Whitney Museum of American Art, 1957. I. *Exhibition catalogue.*

____, 2. *Milestones of American Painting in Our Century.* New York: Chanticleer Press, 1949. I. *Historical view of American painting.*

____, 3. *Milton Avery.* Baltimore: Baltimore Museum of Art, 1952. I. *Exhibition catalogue.*

____, 4. *Nathan Oliveira.* Los Angeles: University of California, 1963. I. *Monograph.*

WIGHT, FREDERICK S.; BAUR, JOHN I.H.; and PHILLIPS, DUNCAN. *Morris Graves.* Berkeley: University of California Press, 1956. I.B. *Exhibition catalogue.*

WIGHT, FREDERICK S., and GOODRICH, LLOYD. *Hyman Bloom.* Boston: Institute of Contemporary Art, 1944. I. *Exhibition catalogue.*

WILENSKI, R.H. *The Modern Movement in Art.* London: Faber and Faber, Ltd., 1955. I. *European and American development of modern art.*

WILKE, ULFERT. *Music to Be Seen.* Louisville, Ky.: Erewhon Press, n.d. I. (English, French, and German text.) *A collection of drawings.*

WILLARD, CHARLOTTE. *Moses Soyer.* Cleveland: World Publishing Co., 1962. I. *Monograph.*

William Baziotes: A Retrospective Exhibition. Newport Beach: Newport Harbor Art Museum, 1978. Introduction by Michael Preble, with essays by Barbara Cavaliere and Mona Hadler. I.B.C. *An important study of the artist and his works.*

WILLIAMS, HIRAM. *Notes for a Young Painter.* Englewood Cliffs, N.J.: Prentice-Hall Inc., 1963. I.

WILLIAMS, WILLIAM CARLOS. *Charles Sheeler.* New York: The Museum of Modern Art, 1939. I.B. *Exhibition catalogue.*

WINGERT, PAUL S. *The Sculpture of William Zorach.* New York: Pitman Publishing Co., 1938. I.B. *Monograph.*

WINGLER, HANS M., ed. *Graphic Work from the Bauhaus.* Greenwich, Conn.: New York Graphic Society, 1968. I.B.

WOELFFER, EMERSON. *Emerson Woelffer.* Pasadena: The Pasadena Art Museum, 1962. I. *Exhibition catalogue.*

WOOD, JAMES N. *Six Painters.* Buffalo: Albright-Knox Art Gallery, 1971. Foreword by Gordon M. Smith. I.B.C. *Exhibition catalogue.*

Woodstock: An American Art Colony 1902–1977. Poughkeepsie: Vassar College Art Gallery, 1977. Foreword by Peter Morrin. Introduction by Karal Ann Marling. I. *A history of the artists and their activities.*

WRIGHT, WILLARD HUNTING- **TON.** 1. *The Forum Exhibition of Modern American Painters.* New York: Anderson Galleries, 1916. I.B.

____, 2. *Modern Painting.* New York: Dodd, Mead and Co., 1927. I. *Essays on modern art.*

ZAIDENBERG, ARTHUR, ed. *The Art of the Artists.* New York: Crown Publishers Inc., 1951. I. *Pictorial documentation of various artists.*

ZERVOS, CHRISTIAN. *Histoire de l'art contemporain.* Paris: Editions Cahiers d'Art, 1938. I.B. *Documented history of contemporary art.*

ZERVOS, CHRISTIAN, and ADAMS, PHILIP R. *Mary Callery.* New York: Wittenborn and Co., 1961. I.B. *Monograph and catalogue raisonné.*

ZIGROSSER, CARL. 1. *The Artist in America.* New York: Alfred A. Knopf, 1942. I. *Critical essays and biographies.*

____, 2. *Mauricio Lasansky.* New York: American Federation of Arts, 1960. I. *Retrospective catalogue.*

ZORACH, WILLIAM. 1. *William Zorach.* New York: American Artists Group Inc., 1945. I. *Autobiographical monograph.*

____, 2. *Zorach Explains Sculpture, What It Is and How It Is Made.* New York: American Artists Group Inc., 1947. I.

Books of General Interest

AGEE, WILLIAM C. *The 1930's; Painting and Sculpture in America.* New York: Frederick A. Praeger, 1968. I.B. *Based on a Whitney Museum exhibition.*

America: Traum und Depression 1920–40. Berlin (West): Akademie der Kunste, 1980. I.B. Biographies (German text.) *A major survey of art, architecture, books, magazines, movies, posters, and photography in over 1,000 objects. A major study.*

AMERICAN ABSTRACT ARTISTS, ed. *The World of Abstract Art.* New York: George Wittenborn and Co., 1957. I. *Documentation of the group and its members.*

ARMSTRONG, TOM; CRAVEN, WAYNE; FEDER, NORMAN; HASKELL, BARBARA; KRAUSS, ROSALIND E.; ROBBINS, DANIEL; TUCKER, MARCIA. *200 Years of American Sculpture.* Boston: David R. Godine, Publisher, in association with The Whitney Museum of American Art, 1976. Foreword by Tom Armstrong. Introduction by David Rockefeller. I.B. *Major survey exhibition.*

ARNASON, H. HARVARD. *American Abstract Expressionists and Imagists.* New York: The Solomon R. Guggenheim Museum, 1961. B. *Documented exhibition catalogue.*

_____. *History of Modern Art.* New York: Harry N. Abrams Inc., 1968. I.B. *The world of modern art, up to date.*

ARONSON, CHIL. *Artistes americaines modernes de Paris.* Paris: Editions Le Triangle, 1932. I. (French text.)

ASHTON, DORE. *Modern American Sculpture.* New York: Harry N. Abrams Inc., 1968. I. *Well-illustrated survey book.*

_____. *The New York School: A Cultural Reckoning.* New York: Viking Press, 1973. I.B. *Sociophilosophic observations on mid-20th-century New York art and culture.*

BARR, ALFRED H., Jr., ed. *Masters of Modern Art.* New York: The Museum of Modern Art, 1955. I.B. *Major anthology of modern art.*

BATTCOCK, GREGORY, ed. *Idea Art.* New York: E.P. Dutton, 1973. I. *Reprints magazine pieces on concept art.*

_____. *The New Art, a critical anthology.* New York: E.P. Dutton, 1966. I. *Reprints of selected vital essays from periodicals and museum catalogues, with a preface by the editor.*

_____. *Super Realism.* New York: E.P. Dutton, 1975. I. *The initial critical anthology.*

_____. *Why Art.* New York: E.P. Dutton & Co., Inc., 1977. I. *General essays on the 1960s and 1970s.*

BAZIN, GERMAIN. *The History of World Sculpture.* Greenwich, Conn.: New York Graphic Society, 1968.

BELMONT, I.J. *The Modern Dilemma in Art.* New York: Harbinger House, 1944. I. *Critical evaluation of increasing abstractionism.*

BETHERS, RAY. *Art Always Changes.* New York: Hastings House, 1958. I. *Critical essays.*

BROWN, MILTON W. *The Story of the Armory Show.* New York: The Joseph H. Hirshhorn Foundation, 1963. I.B. *Documented history of the famous exhibition.*

BURNHAM, JACK. *Beyond Modern Sculpture.* New York: George Braziller, Inc., 1968. I.B. *Survey of recent modern sculpture.*

CAHILL, HOLGER. *New Horizons in American Art.* New York: The Museum of Modern Art, 1936. I. *Exhibition catalogue related to Federal Art Project.*

CALAS, NICOLAS. *Art in the Age of Risk and Other Essays.* New York: E.P. Dutton, 1968. Introduction by Gregory Battcock. I. *A collection of essays from periodicals.*

CANADAY, JOHN. *Culture Gulch: Notes on Art and Its Public in the 1960s.* New York: Farrar, Straus and Giroux, 1969. I. *Essays garnered from the* New York Times.

CHENEY, SHELDON. *A Primer of Modern Art.* New York: Boni and Liveright, 1924. I.

____. *Sculpture of the World.* New York: Viking Press, 1968. I.B. *Valuable survey of the sculpture of all time.*

____. *The Story of Modern Art.* New York: Viking Press, 1958. I. *Popular history of modern art.*

CIRLOT, JUAN-EDUARDO. *Del Expresionismo a la Abstraccion.* Barcelona: Editorial Seix Barral, S.A., 1955. I. (Spanish text.) *Development of nonfigurative art.*

CRANE, AIMEE, ed. *Portrait of America.* New York: Hyperion Press, Harper and Brothers, 1945. I. *Critical essays.*

CUMMINGS, PAUL. *American Drawings: The 20th Century.* New York: The Viking Press, 1976. I.B. *Index. Survey of 120 artists.*

DAVIDSON, MARSHALL B. *Life in America.* Boston: Houghton Mifflin Co., 1951, 2 vols. *Critical essays and documentation.*

DAVIS, DOUGLAS. *Artculture: Essays on the Post-Modern.* (Icon Editions.) New York: Harper & Row, Publishers, 1977. Introduction by Irving Sandler. I. *On politics, business, publicity, and art.*

DUFFUS, R.L. *The American Renaissance.* New York: Alfred A. Knopf, 1928. *Critical discussion of American culture.*

FAULKNER, RAY; ZIEGFELD, EDWIN; and HILL, GEROLD. *Art Today. An Introduction to the Fine and Functional Arts.* New York: Henry Holt and Co., 1941.

FELDMAN, EDMUND BURKE. *Art as Image and Idea.* Englewood Cliffs, N.J.: Prentice-Hall Inc., 1967. I.B. *The great themes of all time in art.*

GARDNER, ALBERT TEN EYCK. *History of Water Color Painting in America.* New York: Reinhold Publishing Co., 1966. I. *Popular survey of watercolor painting from the late eighteenth century to the present time.*

GELDZAHLER, HENRY. *American Painting in the 20th Century.* New York: The Metropolitan Museum of Art, 1965. I.B. *A survey based mainly on the Museum's collection.*

GOODALL, DONALD B. *Partial Bibliography of American Abstract-Expressive Painting, 1943–58.* Los Angeles: University of Southern California, Department of Fine Arts, 1958. *Periodicals and a few books.*

GOODRICH, LLOYD. *Three Centuries of American Art.* New York: Frederick A. Praeger, 1966. I. *Survey book based on a Whitney Museum exhibition.*

____. *The Whitney Studio Club and American Art: 1900–1932.* New York: The Whitney Museum of American Art, 1975. I. *Reviews the Club's history and the founding of the Museum.*

GOWANS, ALAN. *The Restless Art: A History of Painters and Painting, 1760–1960.* Philadelphia: J.B. Lippincott, 1966. I.B. *History developed by major artists and major works.*

GREGG, FREDERICK JAMES. *For and Against.* New York: Association of American Painters and Sculptors Inc., 1913. *Anthology of commentary on the Armory Show of 1913.*

GRUSKIN, ALAN D. *Painting in the USA.* Garden City, N.Y.: Doubleday and Co., 1946. I. *Survey of American painting in the 1940s.*

GUGGENHEIMER, RICHARD. *Sight and Insight, a Prediction of New Percep-*

tions in Art. New York: Harper and Brothers, 1945. *Critical discussion*.

HARSHE, ROBERT B. *A Reader's Guide to Modern Art*. San Francisco: The Wahlgreen Co., 1914. *Bibliography*.

HENNING, EDWARD B. *50 Years of Modern Art 1916–1966*. Cleveland: The Cleveland Museum of Art, 1966. I.B. *Extensive survey exhibition*.

HENRI, ADRIAN. *Total Art: Environments, Happenings, and Performance*. New York: Praeger Publishers, 1974. I.B.C.A. *International survey*.

HESS, THOMAS B., and BAKER, ELIZABETH C., eds. *Art and Sexual Politics*. New York: Collier Books, 1973. I. *Essays on women's role in the creative arts*.

HOOPES, DONELSON F. *American Watercolor Painting*. New York. Watson-Guptill Publishers, 1977. I.B. *Biographies*. *Popular introduction from the nineteenth century to the late twentieth century*.

HUNTER, SAM. *American Art of the 20th Century*. New York: Harry N. Abrams Inc., 1972 (?) I.B. *An Up-to-date survey*.

INGA-PIN, LUCIAN. *Performances: Happenings, Actions, Events, Activities, Installations*. Padova: Mastrogiacomo Editore, 1978. I.B. (*Italian text. English supplement.*) *Includes artists' statements*.

KARPEL, BERNARD, ed. *Arts in America: A Bibliography*. Washington, D.C.: Smithsonian Institution, 1979. B. 4 vols., indexed. *A massive research resource for most of the visual arts*.

KEAVENEY, SYDNEY STAN. *American Painting: A Guide to Information Sources*. Detroit: Gale Research Co., 1974.

KEPPEL, FREDERICK P., and DUFFUS, R.I. *The Arts in American Life*. New York: McGraw-Hill Book Co., Inc., 1933. *Survey of the arts and their development in America*.

KRAMER, HILTON. *The Age of the Avant-Garde: An Art Chronicle of 1956–1972*. New York: Farrar, Straus and Giroux, 1973. I. *Collected essays*.

KULTERMANN, UDO. *Art and Life*. Translated by John William Gabriel. New York: Praeger Publishers, 1971. I. *Investigations into happenings, events, environments; underground film, television, theater; intermedia, concept art*.

_____. *The New Painting*. New York: Frederick A. Praeger Publishers, 1969. I.B.C. *International critical survey of art of the 1960s*.

LIPPARD, LUCY. *955,000*. Vancouver, Canada: Vancouver Art Gallery, 1970. I.D.P. *An informative deck of 4 × 6 inch cards in a brown paper envelope*.

LOZOWICK, LOUIS. *100 Contemporary American Jewish Painters and Sculptors*. New York: YKUF Art Section, 1947. I. *Includes statements by the artists*.

LUCAS, E. LOUISE. *Art books, a basic bibliography on the fine arts*. Greenwich, Conn.: New York Graphic Society, 1968. B.

McDARRAH, FRED W. *The Artist's World in Pictures*. New York: E.P. Dutton, 1961. I. *Major pictorial documentation of the art scene in the 1950s*.

McMAHON, A. PHILIP. *The Meaning of Art*. New York: W.W. Norton and Co., 1930. B.

_____. *Preface to an American Philosophy of Art*. Chicago: The University of Chicago Press, 1945. B.

MORRIS, LLOYD R. *Incredible New York: 1850–1950*. New York: Random House, 1951. I. *Social history*.

MYERS, BERNARD S. *Modern Art in the Making*. New York: McGraw Hill Book Co., Inc., 1959. I.B. *Historical development of modern art*.

MYERS, BERNARD S., ed. *Encyclopaedia of Painting. Painters and Painting of the World from Prehistoric*

Times to the Present Day. New York: Crown Publishers Inc., 1955. I.

NAYLOR, GILLIAN. *The Bauhaus.* New York: Sutdio Vista/Dutton Picturebacks, 1968. I. *Popular introduction to the Bauhaus program.*

NEUHAUS, EUGENE. *The Appreciation of Art.* Boston: Ginn and Co., 1924. I.

____. *Painters, Pictures, and the People.* San Francisco: Philopolis Press, 1918. I.

New York–Downtown Manhattan: SoHo. Berlin: Akademie der Kunste, 1976. Werner Duttmann. (German and English text.) I. *Documents SoHo history and recent art activities and individuals.*

NORMAN, DOROTHY. *Alfred Stieglitz. Introduction to an American Seer.* New York: Duell, Sloan and Pearce, 1960. I. *Appreciation, with his famous photographs.*

O'DOHERTY, BRIAN. *Object and Idea: An Art Critic's Journal 1961–1967.* New York: Simon and Schuster, 1967. *Collection of published essays.*

OERI, GEORGINE. *Man and His Images.* New York: Viking Press, 1968. I. *A way of seeing art.*

One Hundred Prints by 100 Artists of the Art Students League of New York: 1875–1975. New York: The Art Students League, 1975. Foreword by Judith Goldman. I. *Centennial print exhibition catalogue; biographies.*

One Hundredth Anniversary Exhibition of Paintings and Sculpture by 100 Artists Associated with the Art Students League of New York. New York: The Art Students League, 1975. Foreword by Lawrence Campbell. I. *Exhibition catalogue including short history of the League; biographies and appreciations.*

PACH, WALTER. *Modern Art in America.* New York: C. W. Kraushaar Art Galleries, 1928. I. *Concise discussion of modern art and its development.*

PARK, ESTHER AILEEN. *Mural Paint-*

ers in America: A Biographical Index. Pittsburg: Kansas State Teachers College, 1949.

PARKER, R.A. *First Papers of Surrealism.* New York: Coordinating Council of French Relief Societies Inc., 1942. *Documented exhibition catalogue.*

PLAGENS, PETER. *Sunshine Muse: Contemporary Art on the West Coast.* New York: Praeger Publishers, 1974. I.B. *Survey of 20th-century West Coast art, mostly post–World War II.*

Provincetown Painters 1890–1970. Syracuse: Everson Museum of Art, 1977. Foreword by Ronald A. Kuchta. "History of the Provincetown Art Colony," by Dorothy Gees Seckler. I.B.A. *Exhibition catalogue records by means of documents and art the history of this community and its artists.*

PUMA, FERNANDO. *Modern Art Looks Ahead.* New York: The Beechhurst Press, 1947. I. *Popular essays on art.*

REID, B.L. *The Man From New York: John Quinn and His Friends.* New York: Oxford University Press, 1968. I.B. *Biography of the master patron of the early twentieth century.*

RICH, DANIEL CATTON, ed. *Essays and Criticism of Henry McBride.* New York: Athenaeum Publishers, 1975. Prefatory essay by Lincoln Kirstein. I. Index. *The collected writings of this critic.*

RICHARDSON, E.P. *A Short History of Painting in America, the Story of 450 Years.* New York: Thomas Y. Crowell Co., 1963. I. *A basic history of American painting.*

____. *Twentieth Century Painting.* Detroit: Detroit Institute of Arts, 1947, 4th ed. I.B. *Concise essays.*

RICHMAN, ROBERT, ed. *The Arts of Mid-Century.* New York: Horizon Press, Inc., 1954.

RITTERBUSH, PHILLIP C. *The Art of Organic Forms.* Washington, D.C.: Smithsonian Institution Press, 1969. I.B. *A science, art, and nature concept.*

ROBBINS, DANIEL. *The Neuberger Col-*

lection. Preface by Roy R. Neuberger. Providence: Rhode Island School of Design, 1968. I. *Documented catalogue of a major modern collection.*

ROSENBERG, HAROLD. *Artworks and Packages.* New York: Horizon Press, Inc., 1969. I. *Essays, some of which first appeared in the* New Yorker.

_____. *The De-definition of Art: Action Art to Pop to Earthworks.* New York: Horizon Press, 1972. I. *Collected essays, mostly from the* New Yorker.

_____. *Discovering the Present.* Chicago: The University of Chicago Press, 1973. *Collected essays on art, culture, and politics.*

SAYLOR, OLIVER M. *Revolution in the Arts.* New York: Brentano's, 1930. *Critical essays.*

SCHNIER, JACQUES. *Sculpture in Modern America.* Berkeley: University of California Press, 1948. I.B.

SEWCALL, JOHN IVES. *A History of Western Art.* New York: Holt, Rinehart and Winston, Inc., 1961. I.

SMITH, RALPH C. *A Biographical Index of American Artists.* Baltimore: The Williams and Wilkins Co., 1930. B.

STEBBINS, THEODORE E. Jr., with the assistance of John Caldwell and Carol Troyen. *American Master Drawings and Watercolors.* New York: Harper & Row Publishers, in association with The Drawing Society. 1976. Foreword by David Daniels. I.B. Index. *The only major survey of works on paper from the late seventeenth century to 1976.*

SWEENEY, JAMES JOHNSON. *Vision and Image.* New York: Simon and Schuster, 1968. B. *Concise commentary on our present-day culture.*

TASHJIAN, DICKRAN. *William Carlos Williams and the American Scene, 1920–1940.* New York: The Whitney Museum of American Art, 1978. I.B. *Appraisal of Dr. Williams's cultural interests and achievements and association with visual artists, utilizing literary documents and many works from the Whitney collection.*

WATSON, FORBES. *American Painting Today.* Washington, D.C.: American Federation of Arts, 1939. I. *Concerned with the period before World War II.*

WESCHER, HERTA. *Die Collage.* Cologne: M. DuMont, 1968. I.B. (German text.) *The major history of collage.*

WESTON, NEVILLE. *Kaleidoscope of Modern Art.* London: Geo. C. Harrap & Co. Ltd., 1968. I.B. *Popular introduction to international modern art.*

WICKES, GEORGE. *Americans in Paris: 1903–1939.* Paris Review Editions. Garden City, New York: Doubleday & Co., Inc., 1969. I.B. *A history of Americans in the art world abroad.*

WILMERDING, JOHN. *A History of American Marine Painting.* Salem, Mass.: The Peabody Museum, 1968. I.B. *The major work on American marine painting.*

WOLFE, TOM. *The Painted Word.* New York: Farrar, Strauss & Giroux, 1975. I. *Common opinions on high culture by a cartoonist and journalist.*

YOUNG, A.R., ed. *Art Bibliography.* New York: Teachers College of Columbia University, 1941. *A bibliography for the educator.*